www.wadsworth.com

wadsworth.com is the World Wide Web site for Wadsworth and is your direct source to dozens of online resources.

At *wadsworth.com* you can find out about supplements, demonstration software, and student resources. You can also send email to many of our authors and preview new publications and exciting new technologies.

wadsworth.com
Changing the way the world learns®

Criminology

A Contemporary Handbook

THIRD EDITION

JOSEPH F. SHELEY

California State University, Sacramento

Wadsworth
Thomson Learning™

Australia • Canada • Denmark • Japan • Mexico • New Zealand • Philippines
Puerto Rico • Singapore • Spain • United Kingdom • United States

Dedication

To the memory of James L. Smith

Criminal Justice Executive Editor: Sabra Horne
Senior Development Editor: Dan Alpert
Assistant Editor: Shannon Ryan
Editorial Assistant: Ann Tsai
Marketing Manager: Jennifer Somerville
Project Editor: Matt Stevens
Print Buyer: Karen Hunt
Permissions Editor: Susan Walters

Copy Editor: Carol Lombardi
Proofreader: Michelle Filippini
Compositor: ColorType, San Diego
Cover Designer: Norman Baugher
Cover Printer: Phoenix Color Corporation
Printer/Binder: R. R. Donnelley & Sons Co.,
    Crawfordsville

Library of Congress Cataloging-in-Publication Data

Criminology: a contemporary handbook/[edited by] Joseph F.
Sheley.—3rd ed.
        p.   cm.
    ISBN 0-534-52273-4 (casebound)
    1. Crinimology—United States. I. Sheley, Joseph F.
HV6025.C7397   1999   99-27559
364.973—dc21

 This book is printed on acid-free recycled paper.

For more information, contact:
Wadsworth/Thomson Learning
10 Davis Drive
Belmont, CA 94002-3098
USA
www.wadsworth.com

International Headquarters
Thomson Learning
290 Harbor Drive, 2nd Floor
Stamford, CT 06902-7477
USA

UK/Europe/Middle East
Thomson Learning
Berkshire House
168-173 High Holborn
London WC1V 7AA
United Kingdom

Asia
Thomson Learning
60 Albert Street #15-01
Albert Complex
Singapore 189969

Canada
Nelson/Thomson Learning
1120 Birchmount Road
Scarborough, Ontario M1K 5G4
Canada

Contents

PART THREE
Types of Crime   187

PART FOUR
Explaining Criminal Behavior   320

PART FIVE

Criminal Justice 401

PART SIX
Crime Control Issues   539

Preface

As with the first two editions of *Criminology: A Contemporary Handbook,* this revision serves as a means to transmit many criminologists' thoughts about their specialties in a relatively consistent style and format. The chapters represent the authors' ideas about the current state of the research and theory in their respective areas of expertise. The reader receives more than a summary from each. There are ideas in these chapters that no one author of a text could have provided. The present revision contains five new chapters as well as updated versions of the remaining chapters in the second edition.

I asked the authors to write within a general framework and to recognize space limitations. Beyond that, the chapters were theirs; each author was the arbiter of substance. The level of cooperation from, and the extent of consultation with, the authors exceeded every expectation. Each recognized the need for restraint and direction. *Criminology: A Contemporary Handbook* thus became a structured team effort that allowed team members to display their considerable individual talents.

Working with the authors has again taught me much about the present state of my discipline, criminology. It is important that professionals occasionally go back to school, and the authors have taken me there. In terms of a framework around which to structure the chapters, I asked the authors to step outside perceived academic concerns of their disciplines and to put themselves in the students' place. Most students enter criminology courses with very serious concerns about crime and its effect on their welfare in society. They believe they have a stake in discussions of crime by virtue of their images, fears, experiences, perceived risks, outrage, and advocated policies regarding it. Given this, *Criminology: A Contemporary Handbook* employs as its theme the notion that crime must be understood as a "social problem." Social conditions become social problems when they are defined as such by significant numbers of people. The perception may not be accurate, but the concern it generates is real. The social construction of perceptions and fears—the sources of ideas about crime and its causes, the likelihood of victimization—is itself a complex problem for study. Equally complex is how people respond to perceptions and fears. Whether at the personal or governmental level, anticrime policies carry potentially costly consequences. The decision to place bars on one's window makes entrance more difficult, but exit becomes harder as well. More prisons house more offenders but also divert funds from other important social causes. In this sense, the accuracy of the perceptions that inform such decisions obviously becomes important. The authors were asked to address this problem—to link their themes to the larger issue of challenging readers' ideas about crime and to convey to them the complexity and, more often than not, the futility of many crime control efforts. This framework links the twenty-three chapters that constitute *Criminology: A Contemporary Handbook.*

Part One includes two chapters meant to encourage readers to think about crime in terms other than "good guy–bad guy." Chapter One reviews the content and sources of public notions of contemporary crime and punishment. Chapter Two examines the role of major interest groups in determining who and what come to be labeled criminal in this society and in shaping the content of our perceptions of crime as a social problem.

Part Two explores various dimensions of criminal activity, including a critical look in Chapter Three at the statistics we use to gain a sense of crime in America. Chapters Four and Five offer detailed analyses of four correlates of criminal activity: gender, age, race, and class. Chapter Six profiles victims of crime.

Part Three explores five types of crime, some of which the public knows well, others of which the public is relatively ignorant. Chapters Seven and Eight examine violent crime and property crime, respectively, and challenge readers' stereotypes of these most feared offenses. Chapter Nine covers vice crime—about which readers will be surprised how little they know. Chapter Ten, on organized crime, and Chapter Eleven, on white collar crime, both are designed to turn readers' attention away from street crime and toward other costly criminal endeavors more intimately intertwined with conventional business pursuits.

Part Four addresses a more traditional criminological concern: explaining criminal behavior. Chapter Twelve explores potential biological links to offense behavior. Chapters Thirteen and Fourteen offer fresh looks at old causal themes—strain and subcultural theories and control and deterrence theories.

The final two parts of the book deal with crime control. Part Five studies the criminal justice system. The institution of policing is described in terms of its bare essentials in Chapter Fifteen, and the prosecution and sentencing elements of the court system are addressed in Chapter Sixteen. Correction within and without prison walls is investigated in Chapters Seventeen and Eighteen. And in Part Six, Chapters Nineteen through Twenty-three examine five contemporary, and highly controversial, crime control issues: drugs and crime, gangs and crime, gun control, incapacitating career offenders, and capital punishment.

The theme and format of *Criminology: A Contemporary Handbook* notwithstanding, the book is both comprehensive and flexible. No two instructors design their courses in precisely the same manner. Hence, I have tried to give users of this text many options. If instructors so choose, they can work through the several self-contained sections of the book in order. Or, given the number and diversity of chapters, instructors easily can adapt them to nearly any course outline. Discussion questions appearing at the end of each chapter are designed to take readers back through the important points of the chapter.

ACKNOWLEDGMENTS

Those who have contributed chapters to this book obviously deserve my thanks. As well, Wadsworth Editor Sabra Horne merits praise for keeping this project on track. Production Editor Matt Stevens and Copyeditor Carol Lombardi somehow have managed to assure that a book with so many authors nonetheless stays focused and has its parts well integrated. Special thanks to the staff of the College of Social Sciences and Interdisciplinary Studies at California State University, Sacramento, for making sure that the exchange of packages between me and the Wadsworth staff always went smoothly. Finally, very helpful reviews of the book at various stages came from the following individuals: Alexander Alvarez, Northern Arizona University; Allan Barnes, University of Alaska at Anchorage; Byron Johnson, Lamar University; P. K. Manning, Michigan State University; Harry Marsh, Indiana State University; and Roberto Hugh Potter, Morehead State University.

About the Authors

ROBERT AGNEW received the Ph.D. in sociology from the University of North Carolina. He is Professor of Sociology at Emory University. His research interests focus on the causes of delinquency. He has published widely on the topic of general strain theories of delinquency in such journals as *Criminology, Social Problems, Journal of Quantitative Criminology, Journal of Marriage and the Family,* and *Social Forces.* Additionally, he has authored or co-authored books on the same topic, including *The Causes and Control of Juvenile Delinquency.*

JAY S. ALBANESE is Professor and Chair of the Department of Criminal Justice at Virginia Commonwealth University. He received the Ph.D. in criminal justice from Rutgers University. He is past president of the Academy of Criminal Justice Sciences. Among the many books Professor Albanese has published are *Organized Crime in America* (1996) and *White Collar Crime in America* (1995). He also has authored numerous articles on organized crime and other criminal justice topics in professional journals and edited volumes.

EMILIE ALLAN received the Ph.D. in sociology from Pennsylvania State University and currently is a member of the sociology faculty at Saint Francis College of Pennsylvania. Her research focuses on crime and the labor market, social costs and benefits of incarceration, and variations in criminal behavior across age, gender, and race categories. Her publications have appeared in *American Sociological Review,*

American Journal of Sociology, and *Social Forces.*

DOREEN ANDERSON-FACILE is a Ph.D. candidate in sociology at the University of California, Riverside. In addition to her interests in criminology, she focuses her research on issues of gender and race and class inequality.

ROBERT J. BURSIK, JR. is Professor of Criminology and Criminal Justice at the University of Missouri, St. Louis, and is the current editor of the journal *Criminology.* His primary area of research is the neighborhood dynamics and network structures that make crime more or less likely in urban local communities. His most recent work has focused upon the political context of such crime rates. He has published articles in *American Journal of Sociology, Social Forces, Criminology,* and many other professional journals.

TODD CLEAR is Distinguished Professor, John Jay College of Criminal Justice. He has published widely in the area of correctional issues, and his work has been recognized through several awards, including those from the Rockefeller School of Public Policy, the American Probation and Parole Association, and the International Association of Paroling Authorities. He received the Ph.D. in criminal justice from the State University of New York at Albany.

FRANCIS T. CULLEN is Distinguished Research Professor of Criminal Justice and Sociology at the University of Cincinnati. He has served as president of the Academy of Criminal Justice Sciences and as editor of *Justice Quarterly*. He has authored numerous books, including *Combating Corporate Crime: Local Prosecutors at Work* (with Michael Benson) and *Criminological Theory: Past to Present* (with Robert Agnew). His current research interests include the measurement of sexual assault, the impact of social support on crime, and the principles of effective correctional rehabilitation.

G. DAVID CURRY is Professor of Criminology and Criminal Justice at the University of Missouri, St. Louis. His primary research interest is organized violence. He is the author of *Sunshine Patriots: Punishment and the Vietnam Offender* and *Confronting Gangs: Crime and Community* (with Scott Decker). Additionally, he has contributed numerous articles, chapters, and reports to the field of criminology.

SCOTT H. DECKER is Professor of Criminology and Criminal Justice at the University of Missouri, St. Louis. He received the Ph.D. in criminology from Florida State University. Professor Decker's primary research focus is upon criminal justice policy, gangs, violence, and the offender's perspective. He has recently co-authored *Armed Robbers in Action* and *Confronting Gangs: Crime and Community*. He is currently conducting an evaluation of gang intervention strategies at multiple urban sites.

ANTHONY R. HARRIS is a member of the Department of Sociology at the University of Massachusetts at Amherst and holds the Ph.D. in sociology from Princeton University. He has been Invited Fellow, Netherlands Institute for Advanced Studies, and Visiting Scholar, Harvard University. His research has focused on the empirical and

theoretical links between crime and the major demographic correlates of self-identity, including gender and race. His articles have appeared in *American Sociological Review, Social Science Quarterly,* and *Social Problems.*

ANDREW L. HOCHSTETLER is a Ph.D. candidate in the Department of Sociology at the University of Tennessee, Knoxville. He has published in the journal *Social Problems* and, in addition to his interests in white collar crime, continues his research into the relation of labor surplus to societal levels of punishment.

KRISTEN C. JACOBSON received the Ph.D. from the department of Human Development and Family Studies at the Pennsylvania State University. From 1996 to 1999 she worked as a research specialist in the field of behavioral genetics at the University of Arizona. She is currently a post-doctoral fellow at the Virginia Institute for Psychiatric & Behavioral Genetics in Richmond, Virginia. Her research interests include understanding the interplay of genetic and environmental influences on the development of psychopathology in adulthood and on adolescent behaviors.

ANDREW A. KARMEN received the Ph.D. in sociology from Columbia University, and is Professor of Sociology at John Jay College of Criminal Justice of the City University of New York. He is author of *Crime Victims: An Introduction to Victimology* and co-editor of *Deviants: Victims or Victimizers?* In addition, he has written articles and chapters on research taboos, news media ethics, the Rosenberg spy case, agent provocateurs, use of deadly force by police, and vigilantism.

MARVIN KROHN is Professor of Sociology at the State University of New York at Albany. He received the Ph.D. in criminology from Florida State University. His research interests include the investigation of social psychological theories of adolescent substance abuse and delinquency. He has authored or co-authored numerous books and articles, including *Delinquent Behavior* and *Theoretical Integration in the Study of Deviance and Crime.* Professor Krohn is now working on the Rochester Youth Development Study, a panel study of inner-city youth.

HENRY R. LESIEUR holds the Ph.D. in sociology from the University of Massachusetts at Amherst. Presently, he is president of the Institute on Problem Gambling. Author of *The Chase: Career of the Compulsive Gambler,* he has published in such journals as *Social Problems* and *The British Journal of Addictions* and written many papers and book chapters on problem gambling and addiction.

STEPHEN D. MASTROFSKI earned the Ph.D. at the University of North Carolina. He is Chair of the Department of Public and International Affairs at George Mason University. Among his research interests are testing theories of police behavior, understanding police reform, and measuring the performance of police organizations. His work has appeared in such outlets as *Law & Society Review, Justice Quarterly,* and *Journal of Research in Crime and Delinquency,* and he has written or edited numerous books and articles, including *Thinking About Police.*

MARTHA A. MYERS holds the Ph.D. from Indiana University and is Professor of Sociology at the University of Georgia. Her published work has appeared in such journals as *Criminology, Social Forces,* and *Law & Society Review.* Her recent work examines trends in the punishment of blacks and whites in postbellum Georgia. She has written a number of widely acclaimed books and, in 1998, published *Race, Labor, and Punishment in the New South.*

ROBERT M. O'BRIEN is Professor and Head of the Department of Sociology at the University of Oregon. He received the Ph.D. in sociology from the University of Wisconsin. He has published in the areas of criminology, measurement, and statistics and has authored *Crime and Victimization Data* and co-authored *Urban Structure and Victimization.* Much of his work in criminology has examined the relationship between macrostructural variables and crime rates. He also is particularly interested in the extent to which conclusions drawn from criminological studies depend upon the methods used to measure crime and crime rates.

ROBERT NASH PARKER holds the Ph.D. in sociology from Duke University. He is Professor of Sociology and Director of the Robert Presley Center for Crime and Justice Studies at the University of California, Riverside. His published work has appeared in such journals as *American Journal of Sociology, Social Forces,* and *Journal of Quantitative Criminology.* His current research interests focus on violent crime trends and victimization risks. He is the author of *Alcohol and Homicide: A Deadly Mix of Two American Traditions.*

DAVID C. ROWE received the Ph.D. from the University of Colorado and is Professor of Family Studies at the University of Arizona. His primary interests are in genetic and environmental influences on behaviors that occur at the onset of adolescence (sexuality and delinquency), in molecular genetics, and in evolutionary approaches to understanding behavior. He has published extensively in major professional journals and is the author of *The Limits of Family Influence: Genes, Experience, and Behavior.*

JOSEPH F. SHELEY is Dean of the College of Social Sciences and Interdisciplinary Studies at California State University, Sacramento. He received the Ph.D. in sociology from the University of Massachusetts, Amherst. He is the author of *In The Line of Fire: Youth, Guns, and Violence in Urban America,* America's *"Crime Problem,"* and numerous articles in such journals as *American Sociological Review, Social Problems, Social Forces,* and *American Journal of Public Health.* His research interests center on criminal justice and law and on control theories of deviance. At present, he is studying patterns of firearms acquisition and use by juveniles.

JAMES A.W. SHAW is a doctoral student in sociology at the University of Massachusetts, Amherst. His research interests include crime and deviance, economic sociology, and the inequalities of race, gender, and crime.

NEAL SHOVER holds the Ph.D. in sociology from the University of Illinois and is Professor of Sociology at the University of Tennessee, Knoxville. His major research interests lie in corporate crime and the social psychology of criminal careers. He has authored or co-authored four books, including *Great Pretenders: Pursuits and Careers of Persistent Thieves,* and has published numerous articles and chapters in professional books and journals.

M. DWAYNE SMITH is chair of the Department of Sociology, Anthropology, and Social Work at the University of North Carolina, Charlotte. He received the Ph.D. in sociology from Duke University. His current research

efforts are concentrated on the dynamics of homicide offending and victimization among specific populations within the United States, developing social-structural profiles of cities that demonstrate either high or low rates of violent crime, and an analysis of death penalty cases in North Carolina over a 15-year period. Editor of the journal *Homicide Studies,* he is also co-editor (with Margaret A. Zahn) of two recently published books, *Homicide: A Sourcebook of Social Research* and *Studying and Preventing Homicide: Issues and Challenges.*

SAMUEL R. STALEY is an economic development consultant, urban policy analyst, and Director of the Urban Futures Program at the Reason Public Policy Institute. He has authored or co-authored more than three dozen professional articles and reports and two books, *Drug Policy and the Decline of American Cities* and *Planning Rules and Urban Economic Performance: The Case of Hong Kong.* The former book won first place in the 1993 Sir Antony Fisher International Memorial Awards sponsored by the Atlas Economic Research Foundation.

DARRELL STEFFENSMEIER, a member of the Sociology faculty at Pennsylvania State University, received the Ph.D. in sociology from the University of Iowa. He is past president of the International Association for the Study of Organized Crime and a Fellow of the American Society of Criminology. He has published articles concerning the relationship between gender and crime and between age and crime in such journals as *American Sociological Review, American Journal of Sociology,* and *Social Forces.* On the basis of his book on trade in stolen property, *The Fence: In the Shadow of Two Worlds,* he was given the 1987 Award for Outstanding Scholarship by the Crime and Delinquency Division of the Society for the Study of Social Problems.

JODY L. SUNDT is Assistant Professor in the Center for the Study of Crime, Delinquency, and Corrections at Southern Illinois University at Carbondale. She has published in the areas of correctional policy, public attitudes toward crime control, and religion in prison. Her current research focuses on the work experiences of correctional employees.

KAREN TERRY is Assistant Professor at the John Jay College of Criminal Justice. She received the Ph.D. from the Institute of Criminology at the University of Cambridge. Currently, she is conducting research on the long-term benefits of correctional treatment programs for sex offenders.

TERI E. VAIL is a doctoral student in the Department of Sociology at Tulane University. Her research interests include criminology, deviance, and social inequality.

CHRISTY A. VISHER received the Ph.D. in sociology from Indiana University. She is Senior Research Scientist and Science Advisor to the Director at the National Institute of Justice, where she is directing the development of a new NIJ initiative in the area of child abuse and neglect interventions. Previous to coming to NIJ, Dr. Visher was a Research Associate at the National Academy of Sciences for the Panel on Research on Criminal Careers. She has published widely on many criminal justice topics, including the arrest process, jurors' decisions in sexual assault trials, factors affecting pretrial rearrest, the use of drug testing in the criminal justice system, and recidivism among violent youthful offenders.

MARK WARR received the Ph.D. in sociology from the University of Arizona and is Professor of Sociology at the University of Texas at Austin. He is known primarily for his work on public perceptions and reactions to crime, including research on fear of crime, social judgments of the seriousness of criminal offenses, and public opinion on appropriate punishments for crimes. He has also done work on the epidemiology and fear of rape, mass media crime coverage, and most recently on group delinquency. His articles have appeared in such journals as *Social Forces, Criminology,* and *Social Problems.*

MICHAEL WELCH received the Ph.D. in sociology from the University of North Texas. Presently, he is Associate Professor in the Administration of Justice program at Rutgers University. He has focused his research on correction, deviance, and social control. He has published book chapters and articles in such journals as *American Journal of Criminal Justice* and *Journal of Crime and Justice.* He is also author of *Corrections: A Critical Approach* and *Punishment in America: Social Control and the Ironies of Imprisonment.*

JAMES D. WRIGHT holds the Ph.D. in sociology from the University of Wisconsin. He is the Charles A. and Leo M. Favrot Professor of Human Relations in the Department of Sociology at Tulane University. Among his sixteen books are 3 dealing with firearms ownership and gun control issues: *Under the Gun, Armed and Considered Dangerous,* and *In the Line of Fire.* His book *Homelessness and Health* was selected for commendation by the National Press Club. He has published articles in such journals as *Science, American Sociological Review,* and *Social Problems.*

Outline

- The Study of Crime

- Sociological Interests

- Issues for Study

- Basic Concepts

- Substantive Law
  Age
  Self-Defense
  Insanity

- Procedural Law

- Contemporary Criminology

A Brief
Introduction
to Criminology

THE STUDY OF CRIME

First-time readers of a book about criminology often are surprised at how little the text contains about cops and robbers and about criminal modus operandi. Instead, in one or another fashion, the book is about the larger social contexts shaping every facet of the issue of crime—law, criminal behavior, the organization of criminal justice, correction of offenders. More formally, *criminology is the scientific study of crime as a social phenomenon* (as opposed, for example, to a legal or forensic phenomenon). That is, crime is a matter of sociological interest because it is defined within a social arena, it violates social rules, and it draws a social response. A criminal act is a social, though generally not sociable, act occurring in a social setting and implicated in a society's cultural and structural framework.

The claim to be a scientist sets the criminologist apart from others—journalists and social commentators, for example—who think and

write about crime. Criminologists employ the scientific method in their work: testable hypotheses, rigorous and replicable forms of direct observation of the empirical world, and care to the control of biases in the formation and interpretation of the outcomes of a study. The discipline seeks to establish a general, verified body of knowledge about the social aspects of crime, its definition, and responses to it.

SOCIOLOGICAL INTERESTS

Criminologists usually are sociologists, though their ranks include economists, historians, psychologists, and others. Criminal behavior is central to the most basic of sociological problems, that of order versus disorder. The sociologist is concerned with the collective aspects of human life, how one collective aspect (rapid social change, for example) influences another (suicide rate, for example). In a more social psychological vein, the sociologist seeks to know how societal conditions influence individuals so that they engage in behaviors that produce societal rates of behavior—how poverty influences individuals' perceptions of the world to the extent that they contribute to the society's crime rate or how the level of racial integration influences the extent of white citizens' pressure on police to combat crime, for instance.

These interests translate into general questions about order and disorder: What is social order? How is order created? How is it maintained and to whose benefit? What spells the difference between orderly social change and collapse into disorder?

The study of criminal behavior springs directly from these questions. Some sociologists have viewed crime as a sign of a weakened or socially disorganized society. Others have noted that, paradoxically, criminal behavior in tolerable amounts may serve to strengthen the existing social order or specific groups' hold over it. Others have studied crime as the vehicle for understanding societal members' assumptions about order, the assumptions on which those members base decisions that contribute to everyday order and disorder. Finally, some sociologists have viewed social order as the socially constructed result of competition and conflict among various groups in society. Crime thus is characterized as endangering the interests of some groups while promoting the interests of others.

ISSUES FOR STUDY

Within this framework, criminologists study these more specific issues:

1. **The creation and use of laws.** Criminology is concerned in part with the development of laws, the roles of law in a society, law as an instrument of social change, and the functions of legislation and law enforcement for various interest groups within a society.

2. **Patterns of crime.** Some criminologists study patterns of crime for a society or community at a given point in time and over various periods. This area of criminology involves the study of trends and the impact of crime on a population. It also examines the way criminal behavior is distributed among us—by gender, age, race, and so forth.

3. **Causes of crime and criminality.** Criminologists also study the conditions affecting societal crime rates and the causes of individual and group involvement in crime. This study of causes also attempts to identify distinctive types of criminal careers and their development. Traditionally, a major goal of causal analysis has been the formulation of strategies for crime prevention.

4. **The societal reaction to crime.** Criminological theory and research focus on the forces influencing a society's definitions of certain behaviors as criminal, the ways in which a society responds to individuals and their activities, the process by which individuals come to be called criminals, and individuals' reactions to society's definition of them.

5. **Criminal justice administration.** Many criminologists are interested in the criminal justice system and its organizational and bureaucratic processes, the police and the legal profession as occu-pational categories, and the criminal justice system as the primary shaper of a community's criminal population and crime rates.

6. **Custody, punishment, and rehabilitation of criminals.** A final branch of criminology is the study of society's methods of

dealing with criminals. Most research in this area is designed to evaluate the success and deterrent effects of correctional programs, from the point of view of both the public and the individual offender. Much of this research concerning prisons and other correctional agencies also is used in developing theories of bureaucracy.

BASIC CONCEPTS

Throughout this book, and certainly in the discussions it provokes, a number of terms will appear that require brief definition and conceptualization. Among these terms is **social control,** the subordination of individual interests to those of a collectivity. Stated more practically, social control involves convincing or coercing individuals to align their behavior with the **norms,** or rules, of a group. In relatively small homogeneous societies, norms are nearly universally shared, and norm violation, or **deviance,** offends the larger group to which the individual belongs. In the larger heterogeneous society, social control may also take the form of bringing the individual's behavior into line with what are nearly universally shared ideas about right and wrong; murder is an act that generally is not tolerated by the vast majority of the larger society's members. Yet, social control in the larger society also may take the form of one group's domination of an individual or another group in ways that maintain or enhance the interests of the coercive faction but are detrimental to those of the coerced faction.

Social control is accomplished primarily through **socialization,** the process by which individuals come to internalize, or form a commitment to, the values, customs, and norms of the collectivity. Collectivities apply or threaten to apply **sanctions,** or punishments, to individuals who deviate from societal or dominant group norms. The application of sanctions often has as its goal **justice** by which the collective sentiment is "set right" in knowing that a deviant has been made to suffer, at the hands of the collectivity and in terms of some generally agreed-on standard, a penalty for the norm violation. The application of a sanction is sometimes aimed at **specific deterrence** by which offending individuals are convinced not to repeat their deviant behavior. Finally, sanctions are sometimes applied or threatened to accomplish a measure of **general deterrence,** that is, to convince those who have not yet violated a norm to forgo the temptation to do so.

In all societies, socialization remains the primary mechanism by which to achieve social control; reliance on sanctions seems to increase in importance as societies grow larger and more diversified—and, thus, as the socialization process loses its uniformity of application.

In some societies, especially in larger ones, many norms are made highly explicit and come to be enforced by the state as **laws.** Laws generally proscribe behavior; they specify acts that individuals are forbidden to do. They also generally list the sanctions that accompany law violations. Pertinent to our present interests, we distinguish **civil** from **criminal** law. The former primarily concerns disputes between parties (individual versus individual, individual versus group, group versus group), one or both of whom claim to have been wronged by the other to the extent that a loss is demonstrable. A divorce action is an example of a civil law case, as is the suit brought by the residents of a neighborhood against their city for failure to enforce environmental codes. In civil law, the court is essentially a referee whose task it is to settle the dispute in the manner fairest to both parties.

Criminal law pits the individual charged with a law violation against the state. That is, though an individual may have suffered at the hands of another, criminal law treats the violation as an affront to the collectivity; by his or her actions, the offender has threatened the stability and the welfare of the people. Alleged offenders are tried in court by and on behalf of the state; those found guilty are punished by and on behalf of the state. Much stricter rules of evidence are employed in criminal courts. In criminal court proceedings, guilt must reflect the judgment that there is no reasonable doubt that the defendant violated the law in question; in civil court proceedings, a decision favoring one party over another need reflect only a "preponderance of evidence."

SUBSTANTIVE LAW

Criminal law takes two forms, one clearly recognized by most people, the other less so. The better-known form is **substantive law.** Substantive law defines acts that members of this society may not perform, for example, assault, possession of heroin, corporate price fixing. Substantive law also includes descriptions of the specific range of penalties for violation of any given statute. Violations of criminal statutes are classified as **felonies** or **misdemeanors.** The former are considered more serious and include such acts as homicide and burglary. The latter, less serious, include acts such as soliciting for prostitution and disorderly conduct.

In determining guilt or innocence, criminal law burdens the state, rather than the accused, with the obligation to demonstrate that the accused indeed violated substantive law and that he or she possessed *mens rea*—a "guilty mind"—or, in other words, intended to break the law. Practically speaking, in the vast majority of cases, proof that the individual violated the law carries with it the assumption of intent. Yet, it is possible to violate a law without intent, and the courts recognize this. Children who have not yet attained the age of reason cannot commit a crime

in the legal sense because they cannot appreciate the consequences of their own behavior; senile persons cannot commit crimes for the same reason. If one is physically coerced to violate the law or injures another in self-defense, one is not a criminal, for criminal intent is lacking. Accidents and mistakes cannot be crimes, for intent is not present (though we are responsible for the foreseeable consequences of our actions, such as accidents resulting from speeding). Finally, legal insanity can relieve one of the responsibility for a criminal act. Three of these factors—age, self-defense, and insanity—have received considerable public attention in recent years.

Age

The notion that the age of the person violating the law mitigates intent is at the heart of this country's decision to separate adult and juvenile court systems. Although different states employ different upper age limits by which to designate juveniles (generally 16 through 19 years), all consider juveniles unable to appreciate the consequences of their acts in the same manner that adults appreciate them. With rare exceptions (most states permit the prosecution of juveniles as adults for selected offenses), children who break the law are not considered criminals but, instead, persons in need of protection and treatment. Juvenile court proceedings are usually informal and conducted behind closed doors, though juveniles generally have the same rights as do adults (save the right to a jury trial). Juveniles involved in such legal proceedings cannot be identified to the press. Juvenile offenders technically are not punished but, again technically, are placed in rehabilitative situations; these include the youth's family so far as possible. When juveniles reach the age of majority, their juvenile court records are sealed and cannot be used in criminal court proceedings.

The juvenile justice system has become controversial as the public increasingly perceives juveniles as responsible for highly serious, assaultive acts. Many believe that the juvenile's awareness that he or she likely will not be punished for an act and that a new lease on legal life will begin at the age of majority translates to the relative freedom to commit acts for which adults would be punished severely. In fact, many argue that increases in crime in the past few decades are attributable in large part to government's failure to "get tough" with juveniles. Yet, although most states continue to adhere to traditional juvenile justice philosophy, using adult criminal courts to deal with especially serious juvenile offenders is increasingly common (Feiler and Sheley, 1999).

Self-Defense

To claim self-defense successfully, the defendant must show that, in terms of any reasonable person's perception of the situation, there was no avenue by which to avoid injuring another individual. If one could have avoided the danger by flight (if that could have been accomplished safely) or by calling the police, for example, then self-defense claims do not apply. Moreover, the amount of force used to defend oneself must not exceed that necessary to prevent the threatened harm. Nor can one defend property with deadly force if the situation does not also include the threat of personal harm.

With this in mind, we begin to understand the controversy often surrounding cases in which a homeowner shoots a potential prowler outside the home, through the window. The homeowner was scared and perceived the prowler as a threat. The outcome of such cases normally hinges on a jury's sense of the reasonableness of the shooting—that in a *reasonable* person's mind, there was no other avenue of avoidance of harm, that such force was necessary because the homeowner reasonably felt in danger of being the victim of a violent felony. We also begin to understand the controversy surrounding the many recent cases in which women have shot or otherwise injured abusive husbands while the husbands were sleeping. With differing degrees of success, the defendants in such cases have argued that, over long periods, they had attempted to avoid such lethal action by running away and by seeking criminal justice intervention; such planned violence became necessary only in the face of the failure of such attempts at avoidance and in the face of threats by their husbands to hunt them down should they flee.

Insanity

The same level of controversy has attached to the plea of legal insanity, especially following John Hinckley's successful use of the plea after he shot President Reagan in 1982. At issue always is the fear that criminals "fake" insanity and are set "scot-free" by gullible juries. Let us look at this complex problem.

Insanity is a legal, not a medical, concept. It means in simplest terms that a person could not avoid committing the crime in question because he or she had a mental defect. Exactly how insanity is defined in court trials varies by court system. About a third of the states utilize a formula based on the **M'Naghten Rule,** a definition of insanity established in England in 1843 during a murder trial. In essence, the M'Naghten rule states that a person is legally insane if he or she could not understand the nature and quality of the act in question or could not understand that the act was wrong at the time it was committed. Over the years, some states have added an "irresistible impulse" rule whereby criminal responsibility is negated if the person who committed the act can demonstrate that he or she was unable to control an impulse to act in a manner he or she knew was illegal. The M'Naghten rule is known as the **prosecutor's rule** because it is extremely difficult for a defendant to demonstrate insanity under its terms.

The 1940s and 1950s witnessed a growing national respect for psychiatry and with it some doubts about the fairness of M'Naghten-type formulas. These formulas cannot accommodate the person who can distinguish right from wrong and is not acting under impulse, but who is somehow emotionally compelled to violate a law. The mad bomber who cannot help himself, or a "Son of Sam" who is driven to kill for years, even though knowing that killing is wrong, serve as examples. Thus, in 1954, a judge for the U.S. Court of Appeals in the District of Columbia handed down the **Durham formula** whereby persons may be found insane if their criminal act is a product of a mental disease or defect. Knowing right from wrong and acting impulsively are not necessary elements within this formula.

Only one state actually utilizes the Durham formula now. About half the states have adopted a formula called the **Substantial Capacity Test** proposed in 1955 by the American Law Institute. Under this proposal, criminal responsibility is negated if, because of mental defect or disease, persons cannot appreciate the nature of their criminal behavior or cannot act in accord with the law. Mental defect or disease must be demonstrated independent of the criminal act. This formula is known as a **defendant's rule** because critics argue that it is too easily employed in the defendant's behalf and makes the state's case more difficult. Defendants can attempt to link their crimes to more nebulous mental problems. Prosecutors find such pleas harder to rebut "beyond a reasonable doubt." Where once psychiatrists simply could state whether, in their opinions, a defendant could distinguish right from

wrong, psychiatrists now deal in far fuzzier diagnoses of mental defect and even fuzzier links to criminal behavior. Defense attorneys may call several psychiatrists to establish insanity. Because psychiatry is a highly inexact science marked by disagreement among its practitioners, the prosecution can find an equal number of psychiatrists to contradict those employed by the defense. The jury, a group of laypersons, is left to decide which of these experts is correct.

A number of solutions have been offered to remedy the problems associated with insanity pleas. Some states have eliminated the plea altogether; others allow the jury to return a verdict of "guilty but insane." Others allow the defendant to enter a plea of "diminished capacity" (the inability fully to premeditate the offense) and be found guilty of a lesser offense. Most critics simply call for a return to the narrower M'Naghten rule. In fact, insanity is a rarely employed plea under any formula for its determination; the majority of those using it are charged with lesser offenses, and most do not use the plea successfully (Maeder, 1985). Choice of formula for the few cases using the plea must rest with one's priorities: a legal net so tight that it catches all who enter it, both guilty and not guilty, or a net so loose that some guilty escape along with those who are not guilty.

PROCEDURAL LAW

The form of criminal law less known to the public is **procedural law,** which governs actions of state officials in dealing with persons suspected or found guilty of criminal acts. This kind of law covers such phenomena as searches and arrests, the right to a fair and speedy trial, the right to counsel, admissibility of evidence, and the right to appeal. Through television crime shows, most people are familiar with at least one procedural law, the **Miranda rule,** whereby police must inform suspects of their legal rights at the time of the arrest.

There is an inherent tension between substantive and procedural law. Substantive law strives for order (the absence of crime) through control of the population. It is prevented from doing so completely by procedural law, or the rule of law, which traditionally in the United States has been placed above the enforcement of substantive law. Hence, total order is beyond reach, and perhaps the popular phrase "law and order" should read "law and a degree of disorder." We cannot presently have both total enforcement of substantive law and full protection of individual rights. Currently procedural law takes precedence and, until detection, prevention, and prosecution techniques are developed that work without violating individual rights, or until our priorities change, some apparent criminals indeed will go unpunished.

Because laws, both substantive and procedural, are essentially social definitions of, or meanings given to, certain activities, they always are changeable. What currently is not considered a right later may be defined as such. In addition, many laws are not written clearly and therefore constantly are open to changes in interpretation. Thus, rights may be affirmed totally (no restrictions), liberally affirmed (limited restrictions), conservatively affirmed (major restrictions), or abolished. Many now view crime as uncontrollable and define procedural laws as "technicalities" that give criminals the freedom to violate the law without fear of punishment. Others argue that procedural law is all that hinders the creation of a police state, a specter more dangerous than crime as we know it now.

The tension between substantive and procedural law in many ways is the stuff of contemporary criminology. For it brings to the fore matters like the importance of freedom from state dominance as well as from the predations of fellow citizens. More sociologically, this is the heart of the issue of social control in the larger society. More pragmatically, it is a point of entry for criminology's input into crime-control policy. No matter how seemingly academic the criminologist's subject for study, it likely is at least indirectly implicated in both sociological and pragmatic aspects of social control.

CONTEMPORARY CRIMINOLOGY

Apart from rough agreement concerning the basic concepts just discussed, criminologists have reached little consensus about what members of their discipline should be doing today. Indeed, there seem to be nearly as many definitions of contemporary criminology as there are criminologists. Some decry the loss of traditional theoretical orientation among criminologists—the lack of more than superficial attention to Durkheim, for example. Others argue that quantitative research fails to capture the essence of criminal and social control endeavors. How, for instance, can the study of crime and unemployment rates tell us anything about the meaning of either issue for the person violating the law? Still others view both of these matters as distractions from the applied research that criminologists "should be doing." What is the need for theory, they ask, when meaningful criminological contributions involve practical answers to today's street crime problem? Sociobiologists implore colleagues to become more interdisciplinary and to recognize the potential role of biological factors in the etiology of criminal behavior. More Marxian criminologists argue that all these issues camouflage the conflicting class interests that underpin all social problems.

This book does not try to resolve these debates (it could never do so). Nor does it seek to be all things to all readers by trying to address every possible issue. Rather, it defines contemporary criminology broadly: a criminology that tempers tradition with current dues-paying. Criminology is not just a technical discipline that addresses today's criminal justice issues and will reshape itself when tomorrow's criminal justice issues weigh on us. Neither is it what it was two or five or ten decades ago. Theoretical issues that informed the discipline early in this century (for example, criminological themes in social disorganization theory) should inform it still—but should not constitute all it does. Recent sociobiological and Marxian issues cannot be ignored; nor are they sufficiently articulated by their adherents that we can exclude all else from discussion. Contemporary criminologists should seek to make contributions to criminal justice policy issues (though we may dispute what constitutes a contribution) within some traditional criminological framework (from among many).

In what manner, then, is this book contemporary? First, it seeks a theme that integrates academic criminology with contemporary social concerns about crime. The chapters are structured so that they address the worries of the average reader—a student in a criminology or criminal justice course. Most people reading this book are neither perpetrators nor victims of serious crime. However, like most members of our society, they exhibit a great deal of fear of "street crimes," both attitudinally and behaviorally. Most make personal anticrime decisions that are conceivably problematic—to keep a gun in the house and risk an accidental shooting, for example. Equally important, fear of crime leads to demands for law and order, encouragement of legislation and criminal justice system efforts to curb crime through restraints on individual rights, and approval of tax spending for anticrime research and programs. Because all these carry potentially serious costs, we owe it to ourselves to formulate as accurate a picture of crime as possible before supporting various anticrime

measures. The authors of the chapters in this book were asked to write them in a manner that addresses the average citizen's concerns and (mis)conceptions about crime—to challenge the reader's stereotypes of victim profiles or to review the evidence that bears on the reader's beliefs about the deterrent effect of the death penalty, for example.

Second, although the book addresses the contemporary reader's concerns about crime, it provides a sense of what criminology is about more generally. It contains, for instance, a considerable amount of theory, not only in the theory chapters of Part Four, but in most other chapters as well—all aimed at showing readers that theory is not irrelevant to their fears of crime. The discussions of violent and property crimes introduce the reader to "routine activities" theory. The chapter on gender and crime relies considerably on social control theory. The themes that are covered are not traditional in all instances. The reader is introduced to the current controversy over biological explanations of criminal behavior in two chapters, for example. Nor have the authors focused solely on crimes of traditional interest, that is, street crimes. Chapters address vice crime, organized crime, and white collar crime, again with an eye to challenging the reader's taken-for-granted ideas about these activities and their importance as social problems.

Finally, as we noted, criminologists should pay their dues. This means moving beyond the academic side of criminological questions and addressing aspects of contemporary anticrime policy. As public concern about crime has grown, public patience with searches for long-range solutions to the problem of crime has worn thin. Shifting with public sentiment in recent years (and spurred in the 1970s by the availability of government and private foundation grants— money that all but disappeared in the 1980s but that has reappeared to a lesser degree in the

1990s), criminologists now are more willing to address more contemporary crime questions, with an eye to more immediate crime control strategies, than was once the case. Research of this type attempts to identify or conceptualize crime issues better, to map strategies to combat crime, and to evaluate the costs and the effects of the strategies. It assumes that criminologists can, and should, make immediate, significant contributions to the solution of crime without becoming mere technicians for hire by policy planners.

Most chapters in this book discuss policy issues—the potential for controlling violent or white collar crime, for example. Most point out the complexity of the problems we face and the attendant difficulty in combating them. The chapters on the elements of the criminal justice system (Part Five) are especially important in this regard. They make clear in short order that the system is not a simple reactive machine that needs only to be geared better to catch and punish offenders. The message in all these chapters is one of system frustration at having underconceptualized the crime problem and having failed to deliver in terms of controlling it. The five chapters that conclude the book (Part Six) exemplify good, policy-oriented research that is not simply technical work. Each takes on a major contemporary crime control issue (drugs and crime, controlling gangs, gun control, selective incapacitation, capital punishment) and dissects it in a manner that permits readers to make the informed choices they should be making—exactly the goal of this book.

DISCUSSION QUESTIONS

1. Define criminology and distinguish it from other systematic questions about crime-related topics.

2. Describe the issues on which criminologists characteristically focus their attention. With these in mind, in what ways is the study of crime sociological?

3. Discuss the concept of social control. With what mechanisms is social control generally accomplished within a society?

4. Distinguish criminal from civil law and substantive from procedural law. Include in the description of substantive law the factors that negate criminal liability for an act. In what ways are procedural and substantive law related, and what bearing does the relationship have on the public's interest in "law and order"?

5. Using the text's discussion of "self-defense," provide an example of injury done to another person that would qualify as self-defense. What is the key element of your example?

6. Discuss the various ways our courts have approached the issue of legal insanity. What are the strengths and weaknesses of each formula?

REFERENCES

Feiler, S. and J. Sheley. 1999. "Legal and Racial Elements of Public Willingness to Transfer Juvenile Offenders to Adult Court." *Journal of Criminal Justice* 27:55–64.

Maeder, T. 1985. *Crime and Madness.* New York: Harper and Row.

PART ONE

Structuring

Views of Crime

Though crime rates have been declining in recent years, public opinion polls consistently indicate that most Americans believe our society has a crime problem of very serious proportions. The majority of those expressing such sentiments have not themselves been victims of violent crimes, but nevertheless have come to consider such crimes rampant. This perception of crime as a social problem is the product of various bits of information individuals receive from others—some from relatives and friends, but most from more impersonal sources. Our commonly held beliefs about crime are based in the main on what we are told by groups trying to influence legislation, by political office seekers, by the media, and by those who publish official crime statistics.

In this sense, our notion of crime is socially constructed. No matter how many crimes actually are committed in our society, our beliefs about crime generally are fashioned by the information we receive about it. In Part One, we explore this phenomenon from two angles. First, we examine the many aspects of people's perceptions of and opinions about crime in this society. Second, we explore the many interests behind crime legislation and law enforcement, including the defining of the types of acts that come to be called "criminal."

In Chapter 1, "Public Perceptions of and Reactions to Crime," Mark Warr analyzes the public's sources of information about crime and the effects of citizens' views of crime on their lives. Warr examines many seeming contradictions regarding crime victimization and fear. He looks at citizens' sensitivity to risk and at perceived seriousness of various crimes to explain such contradictions. Warr extends his analysis by studying public conceptions of appropriate punishment for crime. He finds that desired levels of punishment are structured by more than one theory of punishment. He also finds that Americans inaccurately perceive the penalties currently assigned to various crimes and examines potential problems in linking actual punishment to public notions of what punishment should be. The latter half of Warr's chapter investigates media coverage of crime. He documents the media's distortion of the overall picture of crime in this society and the ways in which that distortion occurs. Most important, he emphasizes the link between these distortions and misperceptions and the "politics of crime."

The political discussion with which Warr concludes his chapter leads into Chapter 2, "Shaping Definitions of Crime," by Joseph F. Sheley. Sheley explores criminal status as a definitional problem through discussion of interest groups, ruling classes, and designation of acts as crimes. The vehicle that binds the elements of this discussion together is the conflict perspective. Sheley begins by introducing the more traditional consensus framework by which definitions of crime are viewed as reflections of underlying social values concerning right and wrong. He notes that the consensus model encounters problems addressing the issues of legislation and enforcement in the larger, more heterogeneous society. In shifting to a conflict model, by which definitions of crime are viewed as reflections of power groups trying to enhance their economic and other interests, the complexity and the political nature of "crime problems" in societies like ours is better appreciated. Three themes are emphasized: (1) the relativity of criminal definitions, (2) interest group control of major social institutions as a factor in determining criminal definitions, and (3) the status of law as an instrument of power. The issue ultimately pondered is the shape of the interests behind law and much of our notion of crime in this society. Are legislation and law enforcement structured by elite, powerful groups in this society or by a plurality of interest groups? What role do state agents play in defining who and what are called criminal in this society?

In conclusion, Part One suggests that our "crime problem" is no simple issue. It is not just the sum total of bad guys attacking good people and of law responding to these attacks. It also reflects a picture of life in America shaped by the efforts of various parties attempting to maintain and enhance their political, social and economic interests.

Chapter Outline

I

Public Perceptions of
and Reactions to Crime

MARK WARR
University of Texas at Austin

If you are near a television set as you begin reading this chapter, turn it on for a moment and scan the channels. As you move from news programs to dramas to "reality" programs to talk shows to feature films, do you see any common denominators? If you watch closely, one common theme should quickly become apparent. Much of what you are seeing on the screen focuses directly or indirectly on the same topic: crime. The emphasis placed on crime in television programming is remarkable (Graber, 1980; Warr, 1994), but television is merely one of the media through which people in our society are continually exposed to information about crime.

Crime, in fact, is a phenomenon that Americans routinely hear about, read about, talk about, and, particularly through the medium of television, watch. Consider the sources of information on crime that an average citizen may en-counter on any given day. During the morning drive to work, news accounts of crime are broadcast on the radio. When the television set is turned on in the evening, crime stories are likely to appear on the local and national news. Prime-time television presents a variety of crime dramas or cop shows. Bookstores devote entire sections of the store to crime fiction and frequently offer crime-related books among the bestsellers. Movies that are rented or viewed in a theater stand a good chance of having a crime-related plot, and the lyrics of popular music (especially certain genres) often concentrate on crime. Newspapers, like television, devote considerable space and time to reports of crime. The topic of crime is even likely to find its way into our daily conversations (Skogan and Maxfield, 1981).

Even though they are exposed to an abundance of communications about crime, most Americans will not become victims of serious personal crimes like murder, rape, or robbery (see Chapter 7). Consequently, most of the information that people acquire about crime is based, not on direct experience with crime (that is, as victims), but rather on indirect or vicarious information that they acquire from the mass media or through social networks. Unfortunately, such information may be far from accurate, as we will see later. Although false information may be of little consequence in some domains of life, false information about crime can be dangerous (when people fail to take necessary precautions) or tragic (when people needlessly limit their lives because of fear).

This chapter will examine public perceptions of crime and of legal punishment in the United States, as well as social reactions to crime. We begin by looking at what is perhaps the greatest consequence of crime in our society: fear.

THE FEAR OF CRIME

When we think of the consequences that crime has for individuals, we normally focus on the physical, emotional, and financial damage that victims suffer during or following the commission of a crime. Yet crime has consequences not only for victims but also for the large majority of individuals who have never themselves been victims of truly serious crime. The reason is that the mere prospect of becoming a victim can produce intense fear in people, and fear of crime is capable of shaping individuals' lifestyles and habits. Indeed, fear of crime must be understood as one of the broadest social consequences of crime, because the number of fearful individuals at any one point in time greatly exceeds the number of actual victims. To illustrate, the per-

centage of Americans who say that they frequently worry about being murdered (about 10 percent by one estimate; see Maguire and Pastore, 1997, Table 2.37) is more than 1,000 times the percentage who will actually *be* murdered in any one year.

Fear of criminal victimization is quite prevalent in the United States. According to the General Social Survey (National Opinion Research Center, 1996), a national survey conducted annually in the United States, 42 percent of Americans surveyed in 1996 answered in the affirmative when asked: "Is there anywhere right around here—that is, within a mile—where you would be afraid to walk alone at night?" In a 1993 Time/CNN/Yankelovich poll (see Warr, 1995), 55 percent of respondents answered yes to the question "Is being the victim of a crime something you personally worry about . . . ?" Notwithstanding occasional media reports of "skyrocketing" fear in the United States, the proportion of Americans who report fear of walking alone at night has changed relatively little during the past three decades, and the small changes that have occurred are consistent with national trends in the violent crime rate as measured by the National Crime Victimization Survey (Warr, 1994, 1995).

Who Is Afraid?

One of the most distinctive features of fear of victimization is that it is not uniformly distributed in the population. One of the largest differences to be found in the general population is that between men and women. Women, for example, are more than twice as likely as men to report that they would be afraid to walk alone at night near their home (Maguire and Pastore, 1997).

At first glance, this pattern might seem to reflect the actual probability of victimization. That is, women could be more afraid than men simply because they are more likely to be victims of crime. In fact, as we indicate in Chapter 6, exactly the opposite is true. Although they have the greatest fear, females are actually at substantially lower risk of victimization for most crimes than are males (see, for example, Stafford and Galle, 1984).

How, then, can we explain the greater fear of women? One major reason is that women generally exhibit greater *sensitivity to risk*. In other words, when exposed to the same risk of victimization, women are more afraid than men. Why? Apparently, women perceive crime in a way that is quite different from men. Specifically, among women, different crimes are subjectively linked in a manner that does not occur among men. For example, a substantial correlation exists between fear of burglary and fear of murder among women, suggesting that for them, murder is viewed as a likely outcome of burglary. Among men, however, the correlation is much lower, suggesting that the two crimes are not cognitively linked. In the same way, a strong correlation exists between fear of "being approached by a beggar" and fear of robbery among women, but not men. These sorts of subjective links between different types of crimes (referred to as "perceptually contemporaneous offenses") appear more frequently and more strongly among women than men. The implication is that many situations that appear relatively innocuous to men are likely to be viewed as much more dangerous by women because of the offenses they portend (Warr, 1984).

One offense that looms large for women and for which they are not at lower risk, of course, is rape. According to a study of fear of rape (Warr, 1985; see also Ferraro, 1996), (1) rape is feared more than any other crime among young women, (2) rape is viewed as approximately equal in seriousness to murder by women, (3) the highest sensitivity displayed by any age or sex group to any crime is that of young women to rape, (4) fear of rape is closely associated with a variety of other offenses for which rape is a logical (though not necessary) outcome (for example, burglary, robbery, or receiving an obscene phone call) or precursor (for example, homicide), and (5) fear of rape is strongly associated with certain lifestyle precautions (not going out alone, for example). Clearly, then, rape is at the heart of fear of crime for many women.

Setting aside gender differences, fear of crime is often thought to be strongest among the elderly. Some evidence does exist for this position, but age differences in fear occur for only some offenses and are generally not as large as sex differences in fear. Moreover, where age differences in fear do occur, fear is often strongest among middle-aged persons (i.e., those aged about 50–65) rather than among the truly elderly (Warr, 1984; Ferraro, 1995; LaGrange and Ferraro, 1989). The association between fear and age, then, is not as simple as it is sometimes portrayed.

Which Crimes Are Feared Most?

Let us turn now to another question: In any given society or population, which crimes are feared most and which least? If members of a society were subject to, say, 100 different offenses, which offense would head the list as the most feared, and how would the remaining crimes be arranged?

At first glance, the answer to the question seems obvious: The greater the perceived seriousness of a crime, the more it is feared. Hence, at the top of the list would be the most serious offenses (forms of homicide), and at the bottom, truly petty crimes. That answer, however, immediately raises a problem. As a general rule, the more serious an offense, the less frequently it occurs. Consequently, if seriousness were the only determinant of fear, individuals would fear most precisely those offenses that were least likely to happen to them. To use an analogy, this is a little like fearing injury from falling meteors more than rush-hour traffic.

To shed light on this mystery, Warr and Stafford (1983) developed a conceptual and statistical model of fear. The degree to which any crime is feared, they argued, depends on two factors: (1) the perceived seriousness of the offense and (2) the perceived risk of the offense (that is, the subjective probability that it will occur). Neither of these factors, however, is itself a sufficient condition for fear. A serious crime will not be highly feared if it is viewed as unlikely, nor will a seemingly inevitable offense be highly feared if it is not perceived to be serious. In order to provoke high fear, they contended, an offense must be viewed as both serious *and* likely to occur, meaning that fear is a multiplicative function of perceived risk and perceived seriousness. Data obtained in a survey of Seattle residents show that the multiplicative model of fear does predict the degree to which crimes are feared with high accuracy (Warr and Stafford, 1983).

Table 1.1 displays the mean fear scores (on a scale ranging from 0 to 10) of the sixteen offenses rated by respondents in the Seattle study, along with the perceived risk and perceived seriousness of the offenses (also rated on scales of 0 to 10). Observe that murder, although viewed

as the most serious offense by Seattle residents, is not highly feared because it is viewed as quite unlikely to occur. On the other hand, the most feared offense—a residential burglary that occurs when no one is home—is not even a violent crime; it is strongly feared because it is seen as moderately serious and very likely. The balance between risk and seriousness, then, determines the fear attached to any given crime. Data obtained from a survey of Dallas residents and from recent national surveys further support the hierarchy of offenses uncovered by Warr and Stafford (see Warr, 1995; Maguire and Pastore, 1997).

If perceived risk is a critical factor in producing fear, what features of the environment suggest to people that they are in danger of becoming victims of crime? In the survey of Dallas residents (Warr, 1990), respondents were provided with a set of vignettes describing situations that occur in everyday life and were asked to indicate (using a scale from 0 to 10) how afraid they would be of becoming a victim of crime in each situation. Characteristics of the situations were varied systematically in order to determine those features of the situations that were most fear-provoking. Three factors proved to be critical. To illustrate these factors, imagine yourself sitting on a bench in a crowded park during the afternoon in an area you know well. Now imagine sitting on a bench alone at night in an area where you have never been before. Why is the latter situation more frightening? One factor is novelty—novel (that is, unfamiliar) environments are more frightening to individuals than environments with which they have experience. A second factor is time—nighttime is clearly perceived to be much more dangerous than daytime. And the final factor is the presence of other people—the presence

Table 1.1   Mean Fear, Perceived Risk, and Perceived Seriousness of Sixteen Offenses Among Seattle Respondents

OFFENSE DESCRIPTIONS	FEAR		PERCEIVED RISK		PERCEIVED SERIOUSNESS	
	Mean	*Rank*	*Mean*	*Rank*	*Mean*	*Rank*
1. Having someone break into your home while you're away	5.86	1	4.50	2	7.20	8
2. Being raped*	5.62	2	2.51	11	9.33	2
3. Being hit by a drunken driver while driving your car	5.11	3	3.57	6	7.66	5
4. Having someone break into your home while you're home	4.49	4	2.72	8	7.72	4
5. Having something taken from you by force	4.05	5	2.61	9	7.48	7
6. Having strangers loiter near your home late at night	4.02	6	3.83	5	4.35	13
7. Being threatened with a knife, club, or gun	4.00	7	2.57	10	8.25	3
8. Having a group of juveniles disturb the peace near your home	3.80	8	4.25	3	4.30	14
9. Being beaten up by a stranger	3.59	9	2.12	14	7.63	6
10. Being murdered	3.39	10	1.29	15	9.66	1
11. Having your car stolen	3.35	11	2.72	8	5.77	10
12. Being cheated or conned out of your money	2.50	12	2.16	13	5.55	11
13. Being approached by people begging for money	2.19	13	6.73	1	2.15	16
14. Receiving an obscene phone call	2.07	14	3.87	4	3.18	15
15. Being sold contaminated food	1.96	15	2.24	12	5.53	12
16. Being beaten up by someone you know	1.04	16	.83	16	6.17	9

SOURCE: Warr and Stafford, 1983

*Female respondents only

of bystanders or crowds is usually reassuring, whereas being alone is frightening. The presence of others, however, is reassuring only if those others are not themselves perceived as threatening. One group consistently viewed as potentially dangerous by the general public is that of young males. Young males are particularly frightening to females, but even young males are frightened of young males. Males and females alike especially fear *groups* of young males.

One of the factors identified above—novelty—seems to account for one of the most re-current findings in research on fear of crime. That is, people tend to feel safer in their own home or neighborhood than they do away from home. To illustrate, fully 64 percent of respondents in a Dallas survey rated their city as "not very safe" or "not safe at all," but only 23 percent rated their own neighborhood that way (Warr, 1994; see also Hindelang et al., 1978). Evidently, familiarity is a strong antidote to fear.

Aside from the aforementioned factors, people seem to judge the safety of particular locations from a variety of visual cues, cues that are often referred to as *signs of incivility* (Lewis and Maxfield, 1980). These include physical signs—like litter or garbage, broken windows, graffiti, or abandoned buildings—and social cues, such as homeless people or beggars, prostitutes, and noisy young people (see Ferraro, 1995; Warr, 1994). In conjunction with local folklore, these cues act to define certain places—neighborhoods, parks, street corners, schools—as dangerous places, and a lack of them to signal safe zones.

Personal Versus Altruistic Fear

Although people commonly fear for their own safety, they also fear for the safety of others, including their children, spouses, and friends. The distinction between *personal* fear (fear for oneself) and *altruistic* fear (fear for others) is fundamentally important because the two forms of fear display quite different characteristics. Respondents in a Dallas survey (Warr, 1992) were asked about their fear for other household members. Surprisingly, husbands were more likely than wives to express altruistic fear, and the reasons are intriguing. Whereas women often expressed fear for their children, relatively few women reported fear for their husbands. Evidently, many women believe that their husbands are able to take care of themselves. Husbands, on the other hand, were somewhat less likely than wives to express fear for their children, but husbands were much more likely to express fear for their wives than vice versa. There appears, then, to be a clear and common division of labor in American families when it comes to altruistic fear. Warr also found evidence that the protection of loved ones may be as powerful a motivating force as self-protection. Males who reported altruistic fear were more than five times likelier than other males to have purchased a weapon for protection against crime.

The Consequences of Fear

We cannot leave the topic of fear without considering the social consequences of fear. Fear of crime (more specifically, personal fear) has been linked to a variety of avoidance or precautionary behaviors, including not going out at night, not going out alone, or most commonly, avoiding certain places in a city, such as downtown or public transportation (see, for example, DuBow et al., 1979; Skogan and Maxfield, 1981; Warr, 1994). As a general rule, such precautionary behaviors are much more frequent among women than men. For example, 42 percent of women in a Seattle survey reported that they avoid going out alone, but only 8 percent of men reported that precaution. And whereas 40 percent of women reported that they avoid going out at night, only 9 percent of men did so (Warr, 1985).

Fear also has an effect on transportation choices, participation in neighborhood crime watches and other crime-prevention associations, and, not surprisingly, on the use of home security precautions (DuBow et al., 1979; Skogan and Maxfield, 1981). Skogan and Maxfield (1981) report that fully 96 percent of households interviewed in San Francisco, Chicago, and Philadelphia reported at least one home security precaution. In accordance with other research (DuBow et al., 1979; Research and Forecasts, 1980), they found that the most common precautions were such simple steps as locking doors, leaving a light on, asking neighbors to watch the house, identifying persons before letting them in, or stopping mail delivery when away for extended periods. Such precautions, of course, require little financial investment or time. Yet more expensive and time-consuming precautions are not rare. Although estimates vary, roughly 25 to 40 percent of American households have invested in such measures as window bars or grates, improved locks, property engraving, alarm systems, improved lighting, or theft insurance (see, for example, DuBow et al., 1979; Research and Forecasts, 1980; Skogan and Maxfield, 1981).

Modern social commentators often assert that fear of crime has torn the social fabric of our society, making us afraid of one another as we go about our everyday business and rupturing the common trust that binds together communities. There may be truth to that argument, but it overlooks the important fact that fear of crime also brings citizens *together* through community initiatives (neighborhood watch programs, police-community associations, "take back the night" marches, and so on) that would otherwise not occur. Whether these countervailing social forces ultimately cancel each other out is difficult to say, but fear is clearly an integrative as well as a disintegrative force.

In contemplating the consequences of fear of crime, it is well to remember that, in the end, fear is a natural and beneficial emotion. It is fearless people, after all, who run through traffic, consume dangerous substances, play lethal games, or take other unnecessary risks. It is only when fear is out of proportion to objective risk that it becomes a problem for individuals or a society.

THE SERIOUSNESS OF CRIMES

Crimes come in an enormously wide variety, from homicide to forgery, shoplifting to auto theft, and terrorism to desecration of a corpse.

When we think about different types of crime, one of the most immediate and obvious differences is their *seriousness*. Although any two crimes will differ in many ways (for example, in their frequency, periodicity, and ordinary location), differences in seriousness are most readily apparent.

At first glance, seriousness appears to be an objective property of crimes, in the same way that weight and mass are objective properties of physical objects. Seriousness, however, is actually a perceptual property of crimes, meaning that it is a matter of opinion. Thus, two individuals or two cultures may disagree on the seriousness of any particular crime. Given this perceptual quality, the seriousness of crimes can be measured only by soliciting the opinions of some population, such as a city or nation. Such an investigation was conducted by Sellin and Wolfgang and described in their book *The Measurement of Delinquency* (1978). The authors measured and compared the perceived seriousness of crimes among different groups, including judges, university students, and police. Since the publication of this study, research on the perceived seriousness of crimes has continued unabated and has grown to include cross-cultural comparisons. One of the most consistent findings of this research has been that there is strong social consensus within the United States, as well as between our society and several other surveyed societies, about what constitutes serious crimes (see, for example, Rossi et al., 1974; Normandeau, 1966; Wolfgang et al., 1985). Although there is less consensus about some crimes (for example, homosexual acts) than about others, the evidence indicates that most Americans rank crimes in much the same way.

Table 1.2 presents the seriousness scores of selected crimes from a 1985 national survey of

Table 1.2 Perceived Seriousness of Selected Offenses

OFFENSE DESCRIPTIONS	PERCEIVED SERIOUSNESS
A person plants a bomb in a public building. The bomb explodes and 20 people are killed.	72.1
A man forcibly rapes a woman. As a result of physical injuries, she dies.	52.8
A person robs a victim at gunpoint. The victim struggles and is shot to death.	43.2
A man stabs his wife. As a result, she dies.	39.2
A person runs a narcotics ring.	33.8
An armed person skyjacks an airplane and holds the crew and passengers hostage until a ransom is paid.	32.7
A person intentionally sets fire to a building, causing $100,000 worth of damage.	24.9
A person robs a victim of $1,000 at gunpoint. The victim is wounded and requires hospitalization.	21.0
A person sells heroin to others for resale.	20.6
A company pays a bribe of $100,000 to a legislator to vote for a law favoring the company.	14.5
A doctor cheats on claims he makes to a federal health insurance plan for patient services.	14.1
Ten high school boys beat a male classmate with their fists. He requires hospitalization.	11.7
A person steals a locked car and sells it.	10.8
A person operates a store where he knowingly sells stolen property.	10.3
A person breaks into a department store, forces open a safe, and steals $1,000.	9.7
A person breaks into a home and steals $1,000.	9.6
Several large companies illegally fix the retail prices of their products.	9.2
A person performs an illegal abortion.	8.6
A person sells marijuana to others for resale.	8.5
A person signs someone else's name to a check and cashes it.	7.2
A person uses heroin.	6.5
A person gets customers for a prostitute.	6.4
An employee embezzles $1,000 from his employer.	6.2
A person cheats on his federal income taxes and avoids paying $10,000 in taxes.	6.1
A theater owner knowingly shows pornographic movies to a minor.	5.7
A man exposes himself in public.	4.7
A person picks a victim's pocket of $100.	4.4
A person turns in a false fire alarm.	3.8
A person breaks into a school and steals $10 worth of supplies.	3.1
A woman engages in prostitution.	2.1
A person is a customer in a place where he knows gambling occurs illegally.	1.7
A male, over 16 years of age, has sexual relations with a willing female under 16.	1.6
A person smokes marijuana.	1.4
Two persons willingly engage in a homosexual act.	1.3
A person disturbs the neighborhood with loud, noisy behavior.	1.1
A person is drunk in public.	0.8
A person under 16 years old plays hooky from school.	0.2

SOURCE: Wolfgang et al., 1985

crime seriousness in which a sample of 60,000 Americans rated the seriousness of more than 200 offenses (Wolfgang et al., 1985). The seriousness scores range from a low of 0.2 for "A person under 16 years old plays hooky from school" to a high of 72.1 for "A person plants a bomb in a public building. The bomb explodes and 20 people are killed." As a general rule, crimes against persons (homicide, rape, robbery, assault, kidnapping) receive the highest scores, followed by crimes against property (burglary, fraud), public order offenses (loitering, disturbing the peace), victimless offenses (prostitution, homosexual behavior), and various forms of petty crime. White collar offenses (such as price-fixing or bribery of a public official) receive relatively low scores, but at least one drug-related offense ("A person runs a narcotics ring") is perceived to be roughly as serious (33.8) as some forms of homicide.

When individuals rate the seriousness of a crime, what exactly are they evaluating? Are they weighing the objective *harmfulness* of the crime to the victim, or are they assessing the moral *wrongfulness* of the crime? Using survey data from residents of Dallas, Warr (1989) demonstrated that some crimes are widely perceived to be more wrong than harmful (e.g., shoplifting a pair of socks from a store), whereas other crimes are perceived to be more harmful than wrong (e.g., disturbing the peace or painting obscenities on a highway billboard). When individuals are asked to evaluate the seriousness of crimes, Warr found, it appears that they ordinarily use whichever dimension of the offense is greater in any particular case. Harmfulness and wrongfulness, to be sure, are not entirely independent of one another; crimes that are viewed as harmful are usually perceived to be wrong as well, and vice versa. Nevertheless, harmfulness and wrongfulness are distinct dimensions of seriousness that can differ substantially for some crimes.

Why is the seriousness of crimes important to study? One reason is that social judgments about the seriousness of crimes are a fundamental aspect of human cultures. Most Americans, for example, would probably feel strange living in a society where the taking of another person's property was not regarded as a serious matter.

Another reason is that the sentences imposed on offenders under our legal system are generally predicated on the seriousness of the crime for which they have been convicted. Because seriousness has become a principal criterion of sentencing in the United States, the need for careful measurement of the seriousness of crimes is obvious. Public perceptions of the seriousness of crimes are also crucial to understanding the social psychology of crime. For example, people appear to estimate the relative frequencies of different crimes on the basis of their seriousness (Warr, 1980). That is, most individuals correctly assume that murder occurs less frequently than burglary, robbery less frequently than shoplifting, and so on. Similarly, the central criterion used by Americans to judge the appropriate penalty for different crimes is the seriousness of the crime (see, for example, Hamilton and Rytina, 1980; Warr et al., 1983) and, as we noted previously, one of the factors that determines the degree to which a crime is feared is the perceived seriousness of the offense. Seriousness, then, is clearly a critical perceptual property of crimes.

PUBLIC OPINION ON PUNISHMENT

Concern over appropriate punishment for criminal offenses is a key element of public beliefs about crime. What punishments, for example, does the general public consider appropriate for any particular crime? Among other uses, data on public preferences permit an assessment of the mood of a nation or other social unit when it comes to dealing with crime. To illustrate, since reaching a low point in the 1960s, public support for the death penalty in the United States has been increasing steadily and is now at unprecedented levels (Warr, 1995). Whatever the causes of this phenomenon, Americans clearly have little tolerance for crime or criminals at the present time.

In deciding how severe a punishment ought to be for any particular crime, does the general public rely on any discernible rule or principle? The answer is yes. A number of studies (e.g., Hamilton and Rytina, 1980; Warr et al., 1983) indicate that, in deciding what punishment is appropriate for different crimes, individuals typically rely on an age-old maxim: Let the punishment fit the crime. That is, they match the severity of the punishment to the seriousness of the crime. At first glance, this might seem to indicate that the general public is guided by a desire for retribution, because a central tenet of retribution is the principle of proportionality between offense seriousness and sanction severity. Although retribution is a popular justification for punishment in the United States, it is not the only one to which Americans subscribe, and individuals may be guided by more than one theory of punishment in assigning penalties to crimes (Warr and Stafford, 1983; Warr, 1981; Vidmar and Ellsworth, 1982).

One consistent finding in the literature on public opinion about punishment concerns the form of punishment that the public desires. Simply put, Americans overwhelmingly regard imprisonment as the appropriate form of punishment for most crimes. Although the proportion who prefer prison increases with the seriousness of the crime (Blumstein and Cohen, 1980; Warr et al., 1982), imprisonment is by far the most commonly chosen penalty across crimes. For example, in their report on the National Survey of Punishment for Criminal Offenses, Jacoby and Dunn (1987: 1–2) state that "respondents overwhelmingly supported the use of imprisonment as the most appropriate punishment for criminal offenses. Over all

offense types, 71 percent of respondents said the appropriate punishment included prison. Other types of punishments (probation, a fine, or restitution) were most often combined with imprisonment, rather than being substitutes for imprisonment." Similar findings come from Warr et al. (1982) and Blumstein and Cohen (1980). It seems clear, then, that the Enlightenment conception of prison as a general or "all-purpose" form of punishment continues to hold sway among the American public.

Setting aside public preferences about criminal sanctions, consider this question: How accurate is public knowledge of existing criminal punishments? Could most Americans name the statutory punishment in their state for, say, murder or burglary? The evidence suggests that public knowledge of statutory punishments is quite limited; most individuals simply have no clear idea of what the punishments for different crimes are (Gibbs and Erickson, 1979; California Assembly, 1968; Williams et al., 1980). This is not to say that most individuals are entirely ignorant of the law; they seem to have a rough idea of which crimes receive the most severe sanctions. But even this information appears to stem not from knowledge of the law but rather from a presumption that the penalties assigned to crimes are proportional to their seriousness (Williams et al., 1980).

Public knowledge of criminal sanctions is not a minor matter. Legislatures often attempt to control crime through general deterrence, meaning that they increase or alter the penalty for an offense in order to deter persons who might contemplate the offense. But changes in criminal sanctions can scarcely have a deterrent effect if the public is unaware of them. Hence, publicizing a new sanction can be as critical as enacting it.

One possible use of public opinion data on punishment is to make criminal sanctions conform to public opinion. For example, if citizens of a state believed that armed robbery should carry a penalty of no less than ten years in prison, then the state legislature could amend the law to conform to public sentiment. Yet, as appealing as that idea might seem to be in a democratic society, it raises serious philosophical and practical problems. It can be argued, for example, that one purpose of law is precisely to protect individuals from the actions and beliefs of the general public, who may be guided more by anger and other passions than by reason, particularly when it comes to crime and punishment.

On a practical level, the use of public opinion data to determine criminal sentences is complicated by the fact that public opinion is subject to large and sometimes rapid fluctuations. Should the law be changed with each new survey? Furthermore, public opinion is not necessarily informed opinion. For example, if the general public wished to send burglars to prison for, say, a minimum of eight years, would they understand the implications of that decision for the size of the prison population? And would they be willing to pay for new prisons? Similarly, the sentencing discretion historically given to judges by legislatures reflects the belief that each case must be treated individually. Within this framework, the burglar who shows remorse, for example, should not be treated as harshly as one who shows contempt for the court and the law. These sorts of details are apt to be lost if sentencing is left to public opinion.

THE MEDIA AND CRIME

A major source of information on crime in the United States is the mass media, including television, radio, newspapers, newsmagazines, books, and movies (see Ericson et al., 1987; Graber,

1980; Conklin, 1975; Skogan and Maxfield, 1981; Warr, 1994). The depiction of crime in the mass media occurs in many formats. One of the most prominent is news coverage of crime. Even a casual viewer of the evening news (local or national) cannot fail to observe that crime stories are a staple of the news diet. In a media-saturated society such as ours, reports of particular crimes can reach a local or national audience almost instantly. Crime is routinely covered in the news not only because it occurs so frequently in our society but also because its inherent human-interest quality makes crime more "newsworthy" than many other topics.

Many critics argue that news coverage of crime, though seemingly factual and objective, actually presents a badly distorted picture of crime. Some of these criticisms date back to the days of nineteenth-century yellow journalism, although they can be applied to modern media of mass communication as well. Let us examine some of the arguments offered by critics.

"Newsworthiness" and News Distortion

Although crime statistics are sometimes reported in the news, most crime news consists of reports of particular crimes, either as they are occurring (for example, a bank robbery in progress) or shortly after they have occurred (Graber, 1980; Fishman, 1981). Because the "supply" of crimes is virtually unlimited, choices must be made about which crimes to report. As with any other kind of potential news material, the central criterion for choosing crime stories is "newsworthiness." In the case of crime, a key element of newsworthiness is seriousness: The more serious a crime, the greater the chance it will appear as a news story. The brutal homicide, for example, is more likely to be reported than the nonviolent

Table 1.3   Individual Index Offenses as Percent of Total Index Offenses Reported by Police and Media

OFFENSE	POLICE	TIMES-PICAYUNE	TV 4	TV 6	TV 8
	(%)	(%)	(%)	(%)	(%)
Homicide	.4	12	49	50	46
Robbery	12	33	31	30	32
Rape	.6	6	3	3	4
Assault	7	17	2	4	1
Burglary	23	23	3	4	6
Larceny	46	8	12	9	11
Vehicle theft	11	1	0	0	0
Total	100	100	100	100	100
Violent	20	68	85	87	83
Property	80	32	15	13	17
Total	100	100	100	100	100

SOURCE: Sheley and Ashkins, 1981

residential burglary. This standard is not in itself unreasonable, but it is at odds with a sociological reality. Recall that as a general rule, crimes occur in inverse proportion to their seriousness: The more serious the crime, the less frequently it occurs (Erickson and Gibbs, 1979). Thus, whereas thousands of homicides occur annually in the United States, *millions* of burglaries take place. By using seriousness as a criterion, the media are most likely to report precisely those crimes that are least likely to happen to individuals (Skogan and Maxfield, 1981; Sherizen, 1978; Sheley and Ashkins, 1981; Roshier, 1973).

The image of crime presented in the media is thus a reverse image of reality: The most frequent crimes are the least frequently reported, and the least frequent crimes are the most frequently reported. For example, Graber (1980) reported that murders constituted only 0.2 percent of offenses in Chicago in 1976, but they accounted for 26 percent of crime stories in the *Chicago Tribune*. Sheley and Ashkins (1981), in a study of media crime coverage in New Orleans, found much the same pattern. Table 1.3, taken from their study, lists the relative frequencies of offenses according to police data, and as they were reported in one local newspaper (the *Times-Picayune*) and on three television stations. As the table shows, no close correspondence exists between the police data and media reports, with the media, particularly television, focusing disproportionately on homicide and robbery. The bottom panel of the table reveals that, although violent crime constituted only 20 percent of offenses according to the police, it accounted for 68–87 percent of the media crime stories. An outsider who knew our world only through news coverage might have a peculiar idea of the relative frequency of different crimes. The point is not that the presentation of crime news is deliberately distorted, but rather that a standard editorial practice has an inadvertent consequence.

Aside from seriousness, another element of newsworthiness in crime stories is what Ericson et al. (1987) call "personalization." Here, a crime story becomes newsworthy because of the identity or plight of the persons involved. A crime that might not otherwise make the papers becomes news, for example, when the victim or offender is the mayor, a television celebrity, or the daughter of the chief of police. In large cities where serious crimes are commonplace, even murders and rapes will not necessarily make the news unless they involve prominent persons or public figures. Stories selected according to such criteria, however, may be highly unrepresentative of crimes in general.

Distortion in Print and Broadcast Media

Another source of distortion that may appear in media crime coverage, including both broadcast and print media, is the practice of using crime news as filler (see, for example, Graber, 1980; Gordon and Heath, 1981; Ericson et al., 1987). As we noted previously, crime news is seldom in short supply, and so, on a slow news day, column space or air time may be filled with crime stories. If crime news is routinely employed in this way, the amount of time or space devoted to crime from day to day will not accurately reflect the actual number of crimes. Crime news may also be increased in an effort to raise circulation or viewership or be heavily featured in order to

appeal to a certain kind of audience (Gordon and Heath, 1981; Dominick, 1978).

In one of the more carefully documented cases of media distortion, Fishman (1978) reported on a "crime wave" that occurred in New York City. A series of stories pertaining to crimes against the elderly first appeared in a New York newspaper. The theme was picked up in another paper and on television, adding to the number of stories on this topic. Fishman plotted the number of stories over several weeks, showing that the number of stories rose suddenly, remained high for several weeks, and then declined. Police statistics, however, did not reveal any similar pattern in the number of crimes against the elderly. What had occurred was in fact not a crime wave but rather what Fishman called a "media wave." That is, a journalistic theme—"crimes against the elderly"—had been created, and instances fitting this theme were pulled selectively from the large daily pool of crimes (see also Ericson et al., 1987).

The media can present a distorted image of crime in many other ways as well. Annual increases in the number of crimes in a city, for example, may be reported without converting the figures into rates or without reporting changes in population. To illustrate, a reported 10 percent increase in the number of crimes in a city, although a frightening statistic, would be considerably less frightening if it were noted that the population of the city had also grown by 10 percent, meaning that the probability of being victimized had in fact remained constant (Biderman et al., 1967). Similarly, a television story announcing a 20 percent increase in crime might be unnecessarily alarming if it did not also inform viewers of the *types* of crime that had actually increased. An increase in shoplifting, for example, is not the same as an increase in robbery or homicide. And the media, which frequently rely on FBI crime figures, do not always inform readers of well-known problems with those data (see Chapter 3).

Distortion in Television Programs

Quite apart from the daily presentation of crime news is the depiction of crime in television drama and printed fiction. Crime fiction has been a major element of Western literature at least since Holmes and Watson appeared in the late nineteenth century and continues today in the popular books of writers as disparate as Agatha Christie, Elmore Leonard, or Scott Turow. The market for crime fiction, however, pales in comparison to that of television crime dramas, which may draw audiences in the tens of millions on a single night. Crime and cop shows have been a staple of prime-time television fare almost since the advent of television itself, owing, no doubt, to immense public demand for such shows and to the fact that crime shows, with their emphasis on action, tension, and moral dilemma, represent ideal dramatic vehicles for writers and producers.

In television crime dramas, no official claim to objectivity is offered, although some shows are praised or advertised for their "realism." Like news coverage of crime, crime dramas on television have been subjected to withering criticism for misrepresenting the realities of crime and law enforcement. In one study, for example, investigators coded information on every prime-time crime-related program that appeared during a six-week period of the 1980–1981 television season (Lichter and Lichter, 1983). Among other things, they found that murder is by far the most commonly portrayed crime on television and that television crime, in the aggregate, is much

more violent than real-world crime. Offenders were correctly shown to be typically male, but the television offender was substantially older (usually over 30) than were real-world offenders and was frequently portrayed as either a businessman (or his flunky) or a professional criminal. Private detectives were given considerable prominence as law enforcement agents and were frequently portrayed as more effective than the police in controlling crime. And, quite unlike the real world, virtually all offenders were caught and punished. Other research has supported these findings, as well as identifying other forms of distortion that appear in crime dramas (Elias, 1986; Dominick, 1973).

The Effects of Distortion

As we have seen, there is a good deal of evidence that the image of crime presented in the media, whether in news coverage or dramatic presentations, does not closely conform to reality. Even so, some caution is necessary in interpreting this evidence. Critics of the media often seem to assume that the images of crime that appear in the media are readily accepted and adopted by the general public. This presumption rests on what is sometimes called the "hypodermic syringe" model of mass communication. According to this model, information or images that appear in the mass media are directly injected, so to speak, into the brains of the audience and become part of its members' storehouse of information or beliefs. Researchers in mass communication, however, have generally rejected this model as much too simplistic. Information or images that appear in the media, rather than simply entering the mind directly, are ordinarily filtered in many ways. In the case of television, for example, the impact of a message depends on such factors as the personality and social characteristics of the viewer, who is in the room while the television is being viewed (for example, whether it is family viewing or lone viewing), what the viewer's previous attitudes and experiences with the topic have been, and so on (see DeFleur and Ball-Rokeach, 1975; Kline and Tichenor, 1972).

To say that the media distort crime, then, is not necessarily to say that public beliefs about crime also are distorted. In order to reach any conclusions concerning the accuracy of public beliefs about crime, direct measurements of public beliefs and knowledge about crime are required. Although relatively few in number, such studies suggest that the general public does not accept crime news uncritically (Graber, 1980) and that public beliefs about crime are more accurate than commonly supposed (Warr, 1980, 1982).

In order to provide compelling evidence, studies designed to measure the impact of media messages require simultaneous measurement of both media content and the reactions of the persons exposed to that content. Such research is difficult to conduct in natural settings because of the large number of media sources and because of the problems involved in attempting to isolate—let alone control—the media messages to which individuals are exposed. One study that approaches an ideal design was conducted by Heath (1984), who questioned samples of newspaper readers in thirty-six cities, examining their fear of crime in light of characteristics of the newspapers they read. She found that individuals who read newspapers that printed a high proportion of local crime news were more afraid if the reported crimes were predominantly sensational (bizarre, violent) or random (the victim in no way provoked or pre-

cipitated the crime). However, these same factors *reduced* fear if the newspaper stories were predominantly *non-local*. Evidently, readers were reassured by the knowledge that random and sensational crimes were happening to other people in other places.

CRIME, CONTROVERSY, AND POLITICS

Criminal behavior is dangerous and sometimes dramatic behavior, and it touches on fundamental human emotions (anger, fear, protectiveness) and raises the most profound questions of justice and fairness. Consequently, one of the factors that keeps crime at the forefront of public attention is its ability to generate intense public controversy, controversy that often spills over into the political arena. Consider some of the issues surrounding crime and punishment that have sparked public debate in recent decades: gun control, prison overcrowding, the death penalty, the debate over the exclusionary rule (the rule that illegally obtained evidence cannot be used in court), the insanity defense, the legalization of drugs, police corruption or brutality, the putative leniency of American criminal courts, and a host of other issues. Controversies like these are constantly fueling American public discourse, occasionally as a result of enormous publicity over particular events, such as the O. J. Simpson trial or the police beating of Rodney King in Los Angeles. In other instances, apparent crises in the criminal justice system (for example, prison overcrowding) force an issue into the public limelight.

Although public interest in such issues often is transitory, it is important nonetheless because of its heavy influence on American politics. For example, political commercials featuring Willie Horton, who committed rape and murder while on furlough from prison, were a prominent feature of the 1988 presidential campaign; the drug problem in the United States was an important issue in the 1992 presidential election; and building new prisons was an issue in the 1996 presidential election. Crime rarely has achieved more prominence as a campaign issue than in the 1968 presidential campaign, in which Richard Nixon ran (ironically, in retrospect) on a strong "law and order" platform. At the local level, public concern about crime or a loss of confidence in the police or courts can affect the outcome of mayoral and other elections as well as political appointments (for example, police chiefs) and elections of members of the legal system (for example, judges and district attorneys). In the United States, then, crime and politics are closely intertwined. The problem with this predicament is that rational, dispassionate public policy is difficult to achieve by those with a genuine interest in doing so.

CONCLUSION

To an outsider, our society often looks like a culture obsessed with crime. Crime infuses our literature, our politics, our entertainment, our everyday conversations, and even our national identity (famous criminals like Bonnie and Clyde or Al Capone are often held up as cultural icons). Fear of crime infects our everyday lives in both subtle and profound ways. To be sure, this obsession with crime stems in part from the real threat that crime poses to us as individuals and as a nation. But there is a darker side to the phenomenon. At the same time that they express fear of crime, many Americans romanticize criminals and are fascinated by crime, so fascinated that they help to perpetuate a relentless mass media fixation with crime. In the end, perhaps we have no more or less crime in our society than we deserve.

Remember that television set that you turned on at the beginning of this chapter? Why not turn it off?

DISCUSSION QUESTIONS

1. How prevalent is fear of crime in the United States? Does fear of crime affect people equally, or do some groups display more fear than others? What accounts for such differences?

2. Describe the features of one's environment that suggest danger of becoming a crime victim. Conversely, what features suggest safety?

3. Are the members of our society in agreement concerning the seriousness of most crimes? How about concerning the punishments for crime? What types of infor-

mation are needed and what kinds are available to answer these questions?

4. Distinguish personal from altruistic crime fear. Describe the differences in various groups' levels of altruistic fear.

5. How accurate are public perceptions of the dimensions of crime in this society? To what extent are these perceptions shaped by the media? In what ways do the media distort the picture of crime?

6. Americans are fed a steady diet of crime news. In what ways does crime news spill over into the political arena?

REFERENCES

Biderman, A., L. Johnson, J. McIntyre, and A. Wier. 1967. *Report on a Pilot Study in the District of Columbia on Victimization and Attitudes Toward Law Enforcement. Field Surveys I of the President's Commission on Law Enforcement and Administration of Justice.* Washington, DC: U.S. Government Printing Office.

Blumstein, A., and J. Cohen. 1980. "Sentencing Convicted Offenders: An Analysis of the Public's View." *Law and Society Review* 14: 223–261.

California Assembly Committee on Criminal Procedure. 1968. *Deterrent Effects of Criminal Sanctions.* Sacramento: Assembly of the State of California.

Conklin, J. E. 1975. *The Impact of Crime.* New York: Macmillan.

Cromwell, P. F., J. N. Olson, and D. W. Avary. 1991. *Breaking and Entering: An Ethnographic Analysis of Burglary.* Newbury Park, CA: Sage.

DeFleur, M. L., and S. Ball-Rokeach. 1975. *Theories of Mass Communication.* New York: McKay.

Dominick, J. R. 1973. "Crime and Law Enforcement on Prime Time Television." *Public Opinion Quarterly* 37: 241–250.

———. 1978. "Crime and Law Enforcement in the Mass Media." Pp. 105–128 in *Deviance and Mass Media.* Edited by C. Winick. Beverly Hills, CA: Sage.

DuBow, F., E. McCabe, and G. Kaplan. 1979. *Reactions to Crime: A Critical Review of the Literature.* Washington, DC: U.S. Government Printing Office.

Elias, R. 1986. *The Politics of Victimization: Victims, Victimology, and Human Rights.* New York: Oxford University Press.

Erickson, M. L., and J. P. Gibbs. 1979. "Community Tolerance and Measures of Delinquency." *Journal of Research in Crime and Delinquency* 17: 55–79.

Ericson, R. V., P. M. Baranek, and J. B. L. Chan. 1987. *Visualizing Deviance: A Study of News Organization.* Toronto: University of Toronto Press.

Ferraro, K. F. 1995. *Fear of Crime: Interpreting Victimization Risk.* New York: State University of New York Press.

———. 1996. "Women's Fear of Victimization: Shadow of Sexual Assault?" *Social Forces* 75: 667–690.

Fishman, M. 1978. "Crime Waves as Ideology." *Social Problems* 25: 531–543.

Gibbs, J. P., and M. L. Erickson. 1979. "Conceptions of Criminal and Delinquent Acts." *Deviant Behavior* 1: 71–100.

Gordon, M., and L. Heath. 1981. "The News Business, Crime and Fear." Pp. 227–250 in *Reactions to Crime.* Edited by D. A. Lewis. Beverly Hills, CA: Sage.

Graber, D. A. 1980. *Crime News and the Public.* New York: Praeger.

Hamilton, V. L., and S. Rytina. 1980. "Social Consensus on Norms of Justice: Should the Punishment Fit the Crime?" *American Journal of Sociology* 85: 1117–1144.

Heath, L. 1984. "Impact of Newspaper Crime Reports on Fear of Crime: Multimethodological Investigation." *Journal of Personality and Social Psychology* 47: 263–276.

Hindelang, M. J., M. R. Gottfredson, and J. Garofalo. 1978. *Victims of Personal Crime: An Empirical Foundation for a Theory of Personal Victimization.* Cambridge, MA: Ballinger.

Jacoby, J. E., and C. S. Dunn. 1987. *National Survey on Punishment for Criminal Offenses: Executive Summary.* Paper prepared for the National Conference for Criminal Offenses, Ann Arbor, Michigan.

Kline, G., and P. Tichenor. 1972. *Current Perspectives in Mass Communication Research.* Beverly Hills, CA: Sage.

LaGrange, R. L., and K. F. Ferraro. 1989. "Assessing Age and Gender Differences in Perceived Risk and Fear of Crime." *Criminology* 27: 697–719.

Lewis, D. A., and M. G. Maxfield. 1980. "Fear in the Neighborhoods: An Investigation of the Impact of Crime." *Journal of Research in Crime and Delinquency* 17: 160–189.

Lichter, L., and S. R. Lichter. 1983. *Prime Time Crime.* Washington, DC: The Media Institute.

Maguire, K., and A. Pastore. 1997. *Sourcebook of Criminal Justice Statistics—1996.* Washington, DC: U.S. Department of Justice.

National Opinion Research Center (NORC). 1996. *General Social Survey, 1996: Codebook.* Chicago: National Opinion Research Center.

Normandeau, A. 1966. "The Measurement of Delinquency in Montreal." *Journal of Criminal Law, Criminology, and Police Science* 57: 172–177.

Research and Forecasts. 1980. *The Figgie Report on Fear of Crime, Part 1: The General Public.* Willoughby, Ohio: ATO, Inc.

Roshier, B. 1973. "The Selection of Crime News by the Press." Pp. 28–39 in *The Manufacture of News.* Edited by S. Cohen and J. Young. Beverly Hills, CA: Sage.

Rossi, P. H., E. Waite, C. E. Bose, and R. Berk. 1974. "The Seriousness of Crimes: Normative Structure and Individual Differences." *American Sociological Review* 39: 224–237.

Sellin, T., and M. Wolfgang. 1978. *The Measurement of Delinquency.* Montclair, NJ: Patterson Smith.

Sheley, J. F., and C. D. Ashkins. 1981. "Crime, Crime News, and Crime Views." *Public Opinion Quarterly* 45: 492–506.

Sherizen, S. 1978. "Social Creation of Crime News: All the News Fitted to Print." Pp. 203–224 in *Deviance and Mass Media.* Edited by C. Winick. Beverly Hills, CA: Sage.

Skogan, W. G., and M. G. Maxfield. 1981. *Coping with Crime: Individual and Neighborhood Reactions.* Beverly Hills, CA: Sage.

Stafford, M. C., and O. R. Galle. 1984. "Victimization Rates, Exposure to Risk, and Fear of Crime." *Criminology* 22: 173–185.

Vidmar, N., and P. Ellsworth. 1982. "Research on Attitudes Toward Capital Punishment." Pp. 68–84 in *The Death Penalty in America.* Edited by H. Bedeau. Oxford: Oxford University Press.

Warr, M. 1980. "The Accuracy of Public Beliefs About Crime." *Social Forces* 59: 456–470.

———. 1981. "Which Norms of Justice? A Commentary on Hamilton and Rytina." *American Journal of Sociology* 85: 433–435.

———. 1982. "The Accuracy of Public Beliefs About Crime: Further Evidence." *Criminology* 20: 185–204.

———. 1984. "Fear of Victimization: Why Are Women and the Elderly More Afraid?" *Social Science Quarterly* 65: 681–702.

———. 1984. "Public Goals of Punishment and Support for the Death Penalty." *Journal of Research in Crime and Delinquency* 21: 95–111.

———. 1985. "Fear of Rape Among Urban Women." *Social Problems* 32: 238–250.

———. 1989. "What Is the Perceived Seriousness of Crimes?" *Criminology* 27: 795–821.

———. 1990. "Dangerous Situations: Social Context and Fear of Criminal Victimization." *Social Forces* 68: 891–907.

———. 1992. "Altruistic Fear of Victimization in Households." *Social Science Quarterly* 73: 723–736.

———. 1994. "Public Perceptions and Reactions to Violent Offending and Victimization." Pp. 1–66 in *Understanding and Preventing Violence. Volume 4: Consequences and Control.* Edited by A. Reiss and J. Roth. Washington, DC: National Academy Press.

———. 1995. "Poll Trends: Public Opinion on Crime and Punishment." *Public Opinion Quarterly* 59: 296–310.

Warr, M., J. P. Gibbs, and M. L. Erickson. 1982. "Contending Theories of Criminal Law: Statutory

Penalties Versus Public Preferences." *Journal of Research in Crime and Delinquency* 19: 25–46.

Warr, M., R. F. Meier, and M. L. Erickson. 1983. "Norms, Theories of Punishment, and Publicly Preferred Penalties for Crimes." *Sociological Quarterly* 24: 75–91.

Warr, M., and M. C. Stafford. 1983. "Fear of Victimization: A Look at the Proximate Causes." *Social Forces* 61: 1033–1043.

Williams, K. R., J. P. Gibbs, and M. L. Erickson. 1980. "Public Knowledge of Statutory Penalties: The Extent and Basis of Accurate Perception." *Pacific Sociological Review* 23: 105–128.

Wolfgang, M., R. M. Figlio, P. E. Tracy, and S. I. Singer. 1985. *The National Survey of Crime Severity.* Washington, DC: U.S. Department of Justice.

Chapter Outline

- The Consensus Approach: Deviance and Social Unity
  Criticisms of the Consensus Model

- The Conflict Approach
  Criminal Definitions as Relative
  Control of Institutions
  Law As an Instrument of Power
  Control of Law Enforcement

- The Elite Dominance Approach
  Class Conflict
  Law and the Capitalists
  Instrumentalists and Structuralists

- Pluralist Theories
  Multiple Interest Groups
  State Agents
  Ideological Interests
  Symbolism
  Influencing Legal Outcomes
  Criticisms of Pluralist Theories

- Conclusion

2

Shaping Definitions
of Crime

JOSEPH F. SHELEY
California State University, Sacramento

Persistent conflict over issues like assisted suicide, abortion, pornography, and drug possession indicates a lack of consensus in this society about the morality and legality of some types of behavior. However, many criminologists are directing our attention to the seeming consensus behind other forms of behavior, those not currently the subject of debate. They ask us to consider what lies behind our apparent agreement to label certain acts (burglary, for example) and certain people "criminal."

At first blush, this challenge poses little difficulty. We call acts "crimes" when they pose a threat to society, and we label people "criminal" when we catch them committing these acts. Yet, such definitions are not as instructive as they might seem, for they leave a number of questions unanswered. For example, can we speak of society as if all members are affected similarly by crime? Can we easily say what constitutes a threat to society or groups within it? Is breaking the law the only criterion for gaining criminal status? Will it ensure this status?

Having raised such questions, this chapter will examine criminal status as a definitional problem through discussions of interest groups, ruling classes, and designations of acts and people as criminal. We will explore the possibility that the worth or quality of acts and persons is primarily a function of the meanings we give them and that these meanings are subject to change. Thus, who or what is labeled criminal at a given time may not depend on an abstract, unchanging definition but rather may reflect the social, political, and economic situation of that time (Chiricos and Delone, 1992; Lessan, 1991).

THE CONSENSUS APPROACH:
DEVIANCE AND SOCIAL UNITY

Until relatively recently, most sociological and criminological theory assumed that definitions of acts and persons as deviant or criminal reflected a value consensus within society. People were thought to hold much the same views of right and wrong because societies could not continue to function in a state of constant moral conflict. Thus, law was viewed by traditional theorists as a reflection of custom and a codification of societal values, as an institution functioning to settle disputes that arise when values and norms occasionally become cloudy, and as an expression of social control when an individual deviates too far from the normatively acceptable (see Parsons, 1962; Pound, 1943; Rich, 1978). Indeed, deviance itself and the ensuing application of the legal process were seen by some as necessary to the proper functioning of a society. Durkheim ([1895] 1958: 67; [1893] 1933: 102) provided some classic statements in this vein:

> Crime is a factor in public health, an integral part of all healthy societies.

> Crime brings together upright consciences and concentrates them. We have only to notice what happens, particularly in a small town, when some moral scandal has just been committed. They stop each other on the street, they visit each other, they seek to come together to talk of the event and to wax indignant in common. From all the similar impressions which are exchanged, for all the temper that gets itself expressed, there emerges a unique temper, more or less determinate according to the circumstances, which is everybody's without being anybody's in particular. That is the public temper.

Both Durkheim and, later, Mead (1918) were pointing up a paradox about crime. Although crime obviously is dysfunctional for a community in some ways—financial costs, personal injury, property damage, social disruption—it also may be functional in some important ways. Crime and other forms of deviance tend to remind members of a community about the interests and values they share. Community bonds are strengthened in the common outrage and indignation inspired by a deviant act. Further, deviance reassures individual members of a community of their own moral normality and righteousness.

Some authors have cautioned us not to overemphasize these positive functions of deviance to the exclusion of problems it may create. Although noting the unifying functions of punishment, Mead (1918: 91) also pointed out that punitive reactions to deviance may lead to repressive societal conditions that stifle the creativity that deviance often represents. Repressive hostility also may prevent societal self-examination and subsequent attempts at improvement. Finally, Coser (1956: 87–95) noted that, if solidarity is weak in the first place, deviance and reactions to it can further divide a community into factions.

The functions of deviance theme has prompted considerable research over the years, however. Some students of Durkheim suggest that a society actually encourages, or at least allows, a certain amount of deviance for its functional aspects. Obviously, the balance between functional and dysfunctional amounts of deviance is delicate—too much would destroy a society, yet too little would mean the loss of the societal unity derived from deviance. This unification function is considered so imperative that Durkheim ([1895] 1958: 67) once noted that if all present forms of criminal activity suddenly were eliminated, a society immediately would create new forms. Even in a society of saints, he wrote, "Faults which appear venial to the layman will create the same scandal that the ordinary offense does in ordinary consciousness."

Erikson's study (1966) of deviance in the early Puritan colonies generally supported Durkheim's conclusions. Erikson discovered three "crime waves" during the first sixty years of settlement in Massachusetts: the Antinomian controversy (a challenge to the community's religious establishment), the arrival of the Quakers from Pennsylvania, and the Salem witch hysteria. Each crime wave occurred at a time when unity in the colonies was waning, and each precipitated considerable turmoil. Erikson noted, however, that these crime waves were matters of shifts of public attention from one form of trouble to another—other problems were forgotten as each new crime problem arose. In fact, despite the crime waves, crime rates remained relatively stable over the six decades. For Erikson, this suggested a deviance "quota"—that is, the encouragement or allowance by the social system of a sufficiently functional amount of deviance to produce unity through creation of a community response to a "common enemy."

Erikson's study of the three Puritan crime waves also led him to extend Durkheim's notion of the unification functions of deviance. He argued that crime in the colonies served certain boundary definition and maintenance functions. More generally, he believed that deviance and reactions to it help set the boundaries of acceptable behavior and provide a sense of stability and direction for a fledgling society. As time passes, these boundaries tend to become somewhat vague, and new possibilities for societal growth arise. Deviance again causes the society to refocus on its character and mission, to reemphasize the common beliefs and inter-

ests of its members. Deviance thus serves to maintain the social and moral boundaries of societies (Lauderdale, 1976).

Inverarity (1976) attempted to extend Erikson's work through a study of lynchings in Louisiana between 1889 and 1896. His thesis essentially was a restatement of Erikson's: As a united group begins to lose its sense of solidarity, it seeks out and represses "enemies," thus reunifying itself. According to Inverarity, prior to the late 1800s, the South was a white-dominated, relatively closed, united society. Two general white classes existed, a wealthy planter-merchant-industrialist class and a larger, poorer, farmer-laborer class. Their relationship was fairly harmonious, even if economically inequitable. Although African-Americans at this time were considered inferior by both white classes, they were able to vote. (Laws created to exclude the African-American vote did not become widespread until the early 1900s.)

In the late 1800s, the African-American vote was controlled by the wealthy class, who utilized this control to solidify its power position. White solidarity collapsed briefly in the early 1890s, however, with the advent of the Populist revolt, an abortive attempt to capture economic and political power by some members of the lower classes. Inverarity pointed out that this disunity coincided with an increase in lynchings, primarily of African Americans but also of whites, in Louisiana parishes (counties). He posited that the lynchings were a societal mechanism to counter the lack of social unity by rallying people against their "common enemies." After the Populist movement collapsed in the 1890s, the white South reunited and lynchings declined in Louisiana. In Inverarity's opinion, the decline reflected the lessened need for a unifying mechanism—that is, a decreased necessity to search out a common threat. In short, as Erikson had suggested in his study of the early Massachusetts colonies, the societal response to deviance had functioned to strengthen a social system whose unity was threatened.

Criticisms of the Consensus Model

Erikson's Puritan colonies and, to some extent, Inverarity's Southern communities, represented small, apparently highly homogenous societies. Overall, the functions of crime thesis seems to apply far better to smaller societies than to larger, heterogeneous ones. As a society expands and becomes more differentiated, it tends to form clusters: smaller subcultures and economic groups that differ from one another in world view, social status, and economic interests. Generally, these groups compete for various scarce economic and status rewards in society. Crime and deviance within these smaller segments of a society may serve the same unification and boundary maintenance functions as did crime in smaller societies such as the Puritan colonies. More importantly, however, definitions of and reactions to crime and deviance in the larger society are tied integrally to competition and conflict *among* the smaller segments or interest groups.

Importantly, many critics of the consensus approach will not accept the notions of value consensus and functions of deviance even for the smaller society (see Chambliss, 1974; Turk, 1976). They argue that, were consensus in the small society really present, deviance would be rarer and the use of legal threats to deter deviance rarer still. They note that "societal needs" and the functioning of social phenomena like deviance to meet those needs are impossible to document; they must be accepted on faith alone. According to these critics, the argument that laws are created in the interests of a few

and then shape public values is as plausible as the belief that public values shape laws (see Michalowski, 1985). Thus, whereas the consensus position assumes that the state (specifically, legal mechanisms and processes) represents the interests of the majority, many historical studies trace a given law to the interests of a powerful minority. By contrast, no studies have tied a law directly to the expressed will of a majority independent of the influence of some interested minority.

The possibility that the consensus approach may underestimate the role of political and economic conflict within smaller societies gains legitimacy with a second look at Erikson's study of crime waves in the Puritan colonies. As Chambliss and Seidman (1982: 197–201) note, in each of the crime situations studied by Erikson, the interests of the major political figures in the community were at stake. The Antinomian controversy became a "crime problem" when the different religious views of a woman and a few of her followers began to be taken seriously enough that large numbers of people sought her counsel rather than that of established church leaders. The result? The leaders accused their rivals not only of heresy but also of trying to overthrow the government. Similarly, Quakers became a "criminal element" rather than simply a nuisance when they began gaining converts to their belief that individuals should form their own covenant with God rather than seek that covenant through the intercession of church leaders. The result? Being a Quaker became a severely punishable criminal offense. Finally, Chambliss and Seidman note, the Salem witch hunt was interwoven with a power dispute between political magistrates and leading clergy.

Similar comments pertain to Inverarity's study of lynchings in Louisiana during the Populist revolt (Pope and Ragin, 1977; Wasserman, 1977). At the very least, his findings are open to other interpretations as plausible as his consensus thesis. For example, Inverarity's (1976) data indicate that 65 percent of the lynchings were responses to alleged homicides and rapes. If a rise in such serious crime coincided with the Populist revolt, it is difficult to link the two. The lynchings may have represented a common frontier–rural response to perceived heinous crimes. If lynchings declined after the Populist failure, it is possible that crime coincidentally declined or, more likely, was deterred by the lynchings. More important is the possibility of the political use of a "crime problem" by members of either the wealthy whites, the poor whites, or both. The wealthier class, fearing success in the Populist's drive to unite African-Americans and poor whites as one working class, could easily have fomented racial unrest. More influential members of the poorer white class, whose status and economic opportunities were being eroded by the new Populism, could have countered the erosion as easily by stirring up racial hatred (Beck and Tolnay, 1990). More important, recent research ties lynching and incarceration of African Americans in Georgia at the turn of the century to changes in the supply and location of African-American male labor (Myers 1990; Soule, 1992). Rates of lynching— as a social control device—varied with level of competition between African Americans and whites in both agriculture and manufacturing. Indeed, beyond the social control aspects of the punishment of African Americans, the incarceration rate of African Americans was influenced by demands for convict labor, especially in the agrarian sector (Myers and Massey, 1991).

Finally, we note that, to date, most empirical grounding of the notion of "functions of deviance" relies on historical or field observation studies. The major exception is the work of Liska and Warner (1991), who employ data concerning crime, victimization, and social interaction among respondents in a twenty-six-city survey. They find that, in urban societies, the reaction to high crime rates increases the social isolation of citizens rather than bringing them closer together in common indignation. Ironically, in many cases the effect of the decrease in social interaction is to *lower* the crime rate. Crimes like robbery intensify fears and, therefore, constrain social activity; this in turn reduces the number of targets for robbers.

In general, then, we can find little evidence of a "solidarity effect" of crime—at least in the larger society. Few cases raised by consensus theorists are resistant to equally valid reinterpretations that focus on conflicts among interested or threatened parties. These alternative interpretations do not depend on the undocumentable notion of "societal need." Rather, they rest on potentially documentable economic and political interests of specific persons and groups and form the basis of what is known as the conflict perspective.

THE CONFLICT APPROACH

If power struggles characterize smaller societies and shape law and its enforcement to the extent that critics of the consensus model claim, it seems unlikely that the consensus model can describe accurately the sources of criminal definitions in larger societies. For this reason, an alternative approach is increasingly popular among criminologists: the conflict model. Although not all conflict models are alike, three themes cut across all models: (1) the relativity of criminal definitions, (2) the role of control of major social institutions in maintaining interests, and (3) the definition of law (legislation and enforcement) as an instrument of power.

Criminal Definitions As Relative

Basically, the conflict perspective argues that no act or individual is intrinsically moral or immoral, criminal or noncriminal. If a criminal label is attached to an act or a person, there is an underlying reason—such definitions serve some interests within society. If these labels are tied to interests, then they are subject to change as interests change. Thus, every definition of an act as immoral, deviant, or criminal (or the converse) must be viewed as tentative, always subject to redefinition.

Prime examples of the definition–redefinition process are seen in our perpetually changing attitudes, laws, and law enforcement patterns concerning "vices" (see Chapter 9 of this volume). Several states, for example, have decriminalized certain sexual acts between consenting adults (Cohn and Gallagher, 1984). At one time, possession of marijuana was legal in this country; currently, it is not—though the debate over whether it should be continues. Abortion, once illegal, has been granted a status of legality that is challenged constantly (Davis, 1986). Gambling once was illegal in Atlantic City, New Jersey; it is now legal. Prostitution is legal in certain counties in Nevada, but outlawed elsewhere in the state as well as in all other states. Being the customer of a prostitute likewise is legal in some states but not in others (Roby, 1969). For all these acts, we may wonder which definition reflects their "true" quality or nature: evil (illegal) or good (legal). In practice, we must treat current meanings as "truth," for they are the meanings employed in a court of law. From a conflict perspective, however, we soon realize that nothing is inherently sacred or sacrilegious—all definitions are subject to negotiation and change.

Some may argue that the emphasis of the conflict perspective on the relativity of moral and legal definitions is demonstrated easily with respect to vices, about which societal consensus is lacking, but may not apply so easily to acts that seem uniformly defined by most people over time. For example, cannot murder be called intrinsically wrong if nearly everyone considers it to be and has done so for a very long time?

The conflict theorist likely will counter that universal acceptance of a criminal definition, even over a long period, may be mere coincidence. Whether or not universally accepted, a criminal definition almost certainly has its origins in the protection of some power group's interests. And the definition certainly need not be permanent. Radical structural changes such as those created by a severe famine or cultural changes like those fomented in Nazi Germany in the 1930s could cause changes in the value placed on human life (Hughes, 1962). Further, the conflict theorist might argue that definitions of homicide currently are being negotiated. Continual legislative and courtroom debates over the legal status of abortion and euthanasia are, at heart, debates about the limits of acceptable life-taking versus criminal homicide. The same holds for the fight over capital punishment. Finally, history suggests that a revolutionary political assassin's status as hero or murderer depends on the success of the revolution, not on the intrinsic value of the act of assassination. In contemporary America, a crime committed by a terrorist will be punished more severely than will the same crime committed by a non-terrorist (Smith and Damphousse, 1996).

Control of Institutions

Conflict theorists argue that there are three basic means of maintaining and enhancing interests in a society: force, compromise, and domination of social institutions. Force is the least desirable, for it calls attention directly to interest preservation and basically dares others to summon enough counterforce to alter the power structure. Compromise is preferred to force because all parties involved somehow benefit; yet, compromise still carries liabilities. The granting of concessions indicates the absence of absolute power in the hands of any one interest group. It points up the weaknesses of certain parties and encourages others to organize further to exploit those weaknesses.

The strongest mechanism for gaining or holding power is domination of social institutions. Control of such institutions as the law, religion, education, government, economics, and science means control of the world views of members of society, especially regarding questions of interests and power. With respect to the problem of crime and criminals, control of legal institutions means that more-powerful groups gain legal support for their interests by outlawing behavior and attitudes that threaten them or by focusing attention away from their own wrongdoings. Control of other institutions, such as religion and education, is used to promote the interests of the more powerful by shaping the opinions of the less powerful concerning the legitimacy of the economic, political, and legal status quo. For example, we note, without arguing its validity, that the religious belief that rewards in the afterlife await those who suffer in this life serves to discourage this life's less powerful from more aggressively seeking the earthly rewards now in the hands of the more powerful. Similarly, an examination of textbooks used in most of our public and private elementary and secondary schools indicates how rarely serious questions are raised concerning the unequal distribution of wealth and power in this society. It should be noted that control of such institutions often exceeds mere instrumental use of them. Instead, the powerful, who control world views, also have their own world views shaped by these same institutions. Their efforts to shape law reflect not only their own perceptions of interests but a whole value set that labels such interests inherently right and necessary to the health of the collectivity.

Law As an Instrument of Power

Whereas consensus theorists view law as an institution expressing common societal values and controlled by the majority in society, conflict theorists view law as an instrument of control or, in Turk's (1976) words, "a weapon in social conflict." Whoever owns the law owns power. Those who own it fight to keep it; those who want it fight to get it. Indeed, Turk argues, rather than simply reducing conflict, law also produces it by virtue of its status as a resource to be won by some combatants and lost by others. This point is illustrated by the importance given to nominations of Supreme Court justices. Presidents attempt to fill court vacancies with persons sympathetic to their views, that is, with persons more likely to decide cases in a manner protecting the interests of a given president and the parties that president represents above others.

The value of law as an instrument of power should be quite evident. Most obviously, control of the legal order represents the ability to use specified agents of force to protect one's interests. Beyond this, Turk notes that decisions concerning economic power are made and enforced through law; that is, control of the legislature represents control of the process that determines in part the distribution of economic rewards through such vehicles as tax laws. Further, control of the legal process means control of the organization of governmental decisions in general, decisions concerning the structure of public education, for example. Control of the law aids in determining much of culture; law legitimizes "right" views of the world and delegitimizes "wrong" views. Finally, Turk points out that the attention commanded by the workings of law (police, trials, and so forth) serves to divert attention from more deeply rooted problems of power distribution and interest maintenance. In sum, as Quinney (1970: 13) suggests, laws that forbid particular behaviors and make others mandatory are passed by legislators who have gained office through the backing of various interest groups. The ability to have one's interests translated into public policy is a primary indicator of power.

If law is an instrument sought after and employed by powerful interest groups to enhance their position in society, and if criminal law forbids certain acts, we can reasonably define crime as acts perceived by those in power as direct or indirect threats to their interests. Conflict theorists (Chambliss and Seidman, 1982: 174, 175; Michalowski, 1985: 69, 96) note that most of our current criminal law derives directly from English common law. Jeffery (1957) argues that acts such as murder, theft, and robbery, once considered dispute problems to be settled within or between families, became crimes against the state (wrongs against society) when Henry II, king of England, attempted to centralize his power in a politically divided country by declaring them wrongs against the crown. Hall (1952) has traced theft laws in their present form to their origin in the change from a feudal economy to a capitalist, mercantile economy. As a new economic class of traders and industrialists developed, the need to protect their business interests grew. Hall (1952: 66) describes the creation of embezzlement laws:

> The patterns of conditions which gave rise to embezzlement may therefore be delineated as follows: (1) the expansion of mercantile and banking credit and the use of credit mechanisms, paper money, and securities; (2) the employment of clerks in important positions with reference to dealing with and, in particular, receiving valuables from third persons; (3) the interests of the commercial classes and their representation in parliament; (4) a change in attitude regarding the public importance of what could formerly be dismissed as merely a private breach of trust; and (5) a series of sensational cases of very serious defalcation which set the pattern into motion and produced immediate action.

The same conditions spawned laws governing the receipt of stolen property and obtaining goods under false pretenses. The conflict theorists' point is that our definitions of crime have their roots less in general beliefs about right and wrong than in perceived threats to groups with the power to legislate their interests.

Control of Law Enforcement

Law enforcement patterns as well as legislation reflect the attempts of the more powerful to protect their interests. Yeager (1987) notes the tendency of the U.S. Environmental Protection Agency to focus on smaller rather than larger firms when enforcing its regulations. Stretesky and Hogan (1998) demonstrate that racial and ethnic politics play a major role in the placement of and responses to dangerous waste disposal sites. Szasz (1984) describes industry attempts to control Office of Safety and Health Administration regulation activity—though Freitag (1983) notes that corporations generally do not dominate regulatory commissions by placing their agents on them. Likewise, Pontell et al. (1982) note the manner in which the structure of the medical profession thwarts efforts to police physicians' fraud and abuse. When sanctions are applied to Medicaid provider fraud, it is done so relatively leniently (Tillman and Pontell, 1992). In yet another political and economic arena, Smith and Jepson (1993) detail the transfer of influence over the regulation of Florida's marine resources from a once-powerful interest group (commercial fishing families) to other economic and political interests like the recreational fishing industry.

Turning to the issue of street crime, Jacobs (1979: 914) writes:

> The more there are inequalities in the distribution of economic power and economic resources, the more one can expect that the social control apparatus of the state will conform to the preferences of monied elites. In this society, the major institution responsible for the coercive maintenance of stability and order is the police.

Jacobs argues that the greater the economic differences in a community, the more likely poorer community members are to forcefully attempt to alter the inequality. Thus, economic elites utilize the police for protection and as a general stabilizer within a community. Jacobs's analysis of police strength in metropolitan areas appears to support his thesis: Law enforcement personnel are more numerous in metropolitan areas where economic inequality is most pronounced.

In the same vein, Liska et al. (1981) report that following civil disorders in the South in the 1950s, 1960s, and early 1970s, whites in cities with larger percentages of nonwhite residents and less residential segregation perceived chances of crime victimization to be greater whether or not actual crime rates changed. Hence, the more powerful whites demanded and received greater police protection. Jackson and Carroll

(1981; see Greenberg et al., 1979, for qualifying remarks) confirm this finding in their study of ninety non-Southern cities, though Jackson's (1986) subsequent work suggests that the finding pertains more to larger than to smaller cities. To the extent that African-American population and political mobilization increased in cities in the late 1960s and early 1970s, cities' expenditures on police services increased—regardless of their crime rates. The authors conclude that police expenditures are a resource that is mobilized when minority groups appear to threaten the political and economic position of more dominant groups (see also Liska and Chamblin, 1984; Chamblin, 1989). They therefore echo Silver's (1967) characterization of the police (and courts; see Feiler and Sheley, 1999) as a mechanism designed to control "dangerous classes" in a way that protects wealthier classes but does so in a manner not directly orchestrated by the wealthy. That is, police protect the wealthy while appearing to protect the poor as well—all under a "war on crime" umbrella (Jackson, 1989). Of related interest, Jacobs and O'Brien (1998) present evidence that suggests that the presence of an African-American mayor will reduce the amount of police use of lethal force against African-American citizens.

THE ELITE
DOMINANCE APPROACH

Thus far, we have reviewed characteristics common to conflict theories. However, conflict theorists hold significantly differing views concerning the distribution and use of power in our society. The clearest difference revolves around the question of who is behind legislation and law enforcement: a single dominant class or a number of relatively powerful, competing interest groups. In this section, we examine the dominant role of owner-capitalists in our society; in the next section, we focus on a number of different groups, each of which wields varying amounts of power.

Class Conflict

A number of prominent conflict theorists argue that law in this society is rooted in class conflict (see Michalowski, 1985; Jacobs and Helms, 1996; Hochstetler and Shover, 1997). Underlying this approach is the Marxian thesis of perpetual conflict between the two primary economic classes of capitalist societies: those who own or control the means of production (factories, machinery, investment capital) and those who work for these owners to turn raw materials into salable goods. Owner-capitalists strive to minimize labor and production costs in order to increase the surplus value of production (profit), which then becomes capital to be invested in other capital-producing markets. If unchecked, the capitalist instinctively and constantly works to mechanize labor, thereby reducing the costs of production, and to monopolize the production market, thereby eliminating competition and increasing the pricing potential of goods in the consumer market. This same instinct drives capitalists constantly to expand both the range of goods they produce and the markets to which they ship these goods.

To the extent that they possess a class consciousness—that is, they understand the capitalists' interests vis-à-vis their own—workers find themselves in conflict with owners. Both can lay claim to a portion of the profits from production—the owners by virtue of risked capital and the workers by virtue of their actual transformation of raw materials into usable and salable items. Because capitalists in our society have always, to varying degrees, controlled this process, it is clearly in their interest to keep workers unaware of their potential to enjoy a greater share of the surplus value of production. In terms of its sheer advantage in numbers, an aware and organized worker population could dictate the terms of profit distribution and, by moving one step further, seize the means of production from the owners.

Law and the Capitalists

Previously we mentioned the methods by which owners maintain their advantage over workers: force, compromise when necessary, and, most important, control of social institutions that shape the world view of workers, especially regarding their rights and duties within the capitalist system. Owners do not use any set combination of force, compromise, and control, however, to preserve their superior economic position. Crises within capitalism (unemployment due to increased mechanization, for example) constantly arise, forcing owners to devise new and varied solutions. The solutions in turn spawn new problems and crises (heavy government borrowing to support welfare programs designed to placate the unemployed, for example; see Devine et al., 1988). Thus, the conflict between owners and workers is dynamic, that is, characterized by constant change.

Because it would invite worker wrath during capitalism's sporadic major crises, however, capitalists seek to avoid the appearance of controlling the political economy directly. Thus, capitalists require a mechanism that appears free of direct owner influence, legitimizes the economic system, "holds things together" by defusing crises, and represses rebellion in the name of maintaining the general order. Some argue that the state itself is such a mechanism (for discussions of this thesis, see Allen, 1991; Campbell and Linberg, 1990; and Prechel, 1990). Its role is to organize and integrate economic, political, legal, and, occasionally, religious systems and processes. In this context, the legal order may be viewed as protector and enhancer of capitalist interests through tax legislation and incentives and through organization of and arbitration among various capitalist subgroups. At the same time, the state's apparent neutrality, as well as its mystical quality provided by complicated legal ritual, serves to convince workers that their general interests are maintained and protected. The legitimation given to the "law" by the workers allows capitalists to limit workers' attempts to protest or alter their situations. Thus, political and labor activism is held in check by laws governing the shapes such activism may take. Violations of these laws are addressed by the state for the "common good"—that is, because "no cause justifies illegal activity." Workers in general come to view the law as sacred and fail to appreciate the interests and forces underlying both the law and the crises it addresses.

Instrumentalists and Structuralists

Clearly, as we have noted, law is an important tool in the preservation of economic interests, a resource worth fighting to gain and to keep. Yet, some Marxian conflict theorists disagree about the extent to which the law or, more generally, the state is controlled by capitalists. One camp, known as instrumentalists, argues that a core of "monopoly capitalists"—those heading the most powerful corporate and banking interests—totally control the state, orchestrate its every action, and utilize legal processes directly to preserve their interests. This approach is rooted in the writings of such theorists as Mills (1956) and Domhoff (1967, 1978), who have demon-

strated empirically very strong economic and social ties among industrial leaders and those appointed to high-level government positions regulating business, education, financing, and media (Berkowitz and McQuaid, 1980). Quinney (1980: 84) describes the ruling class:

> The capitalist class also is divided into several factions. Two major factions are those capitalists who own major units of the economy and those whose holdings and power are less than that of the uppermost sector of the capitalist class. The upper division, the "monopoly sector," as contrasted to the "lieutenant sector," owns the largest corporations and financial institutions. . . . The other segment is largely delegated power by the monopoly sector.

So powerful are these major capitalists, in the eyes of instrumentalists, that they are able to avoid public scrutiny. Hill (1975) argues that monopoly capitalists

> use all the resources at their command to keep secret the extent of their power, their decisions, who they are, etc. . . . [They] desire to perpetuate the myth that America is a free, classless society. As long as the existence of a ruling class is hidden, the chances of rebellion against it are small. The myth that America is a "pluralistic democracy" is one of the greatest weapons in the arsenal that maintains their class rule.

And so extensive is monopoly capitalists' control of the political process, in the opinion of some instrumentalists (for example, Balkan et al., 1980: 8), that

> we can understand how even as powerful a person as President Nixon could have been forced to resign from the presidency.

In spite of continued resistance from many powerful people to label the president a criminal, a sizeable majority of power elites came to the conclusion that, given the public knowledge of the president's "questionable" activities, it would be better for the long-term maintenance of their power to replace him with someone who inspired more public confidence.

The instrumentalist's position often is criticized on several grounds. For example, it fails to consider noneconomic influences on political and legal processes. It cannot account for the outlawing of certain behaviors seemingly in the interests of capitalists, such as price-fixing. It cannot explain why, if capitalists control the law, they do not simply change it to correspond to their interests rather than sometimes violating it themselves. Finally, it fails to consider disagreements and conflict among capitalists.

To counter these criticisms, a number of Marxian theorists espouse a less "vulgar," more complex brand of ruling class theory. These theorists, called structuralists (see Chambliss and Seidman, 1982; Greenberg, 1981; Stone, 1985), argue that the state and the law reflect more than simply ruling class interests. Instead, the role the state plays in furthering and legitimating capitalism negates its strict attachment to the monopoly capitalist sector. In short, structuralists believe the state is relatively autonomous (though they dispute the degree of autonomy; see Quadagno, 1984, and Skocpol, 1980) and, as such, protects the long-term interests of capitalists, though not always their short-term interests. Thus, the state indeed often does execute the law fairly and against specific capitalists' concerns. Chambliss and Seidman (1982: 308) write:

The state and government must legitimize the existing political and economic arrange-

ments in order to provide an atmosphere in which capitalist accumulation and production can continue. . . . To serve the interests of the ruling class, the state must create [a sense of fairness] among the people. . . . [T]he state and legal order best fulfill their function as legitimizers when they appear to function as value neutral organs fairly and impartially representing the interests of everyone.

Structuralists as well as instrumentalists are open to criticism, however. For example, although they have begun to document the development of the short-term neutrality or impartiality of the state, they have yet to link short-term autonomy with the hypothesized long-term bias of the state toward capitalism. Structuralists seem as well to underemphasize legal discrimination against segments of the worker population (for example, African Americans and women). They tend often to reify the "state"—that is, believe it has a life of its own, though Chambliss and Seidman (1982: 309–316) address this problem by refining the concepts of state and autonomy. In short, whereas instrumentalists have given us a conspiratorial ruling class whose existence is difficult to prove, structuralists have given us *two* powerful interests whose relationship is equally difficult to document: capitalists and the state (Allen, 1991; Prechel, 1990).

PLURALIST THEORIES

Though essentially agreeing with Marxian theorists that legislation and law enforcement have their roots in group conflict, another cadre of conflict theorists offers a broader explanation of the legal process. Pluralist theorists argue that the legal process is not controlled by one specific interest group but emerges from or is shaped by the conflicting interests of a multiplicity of groups, all seeking something different from a given legal issue (Troyer and Markle, 1982). The object of conflict is not always economic interest; it may also reflect status concerns and moral and ideological commitments. Hence, much of what occurs in legal conflicts is symbolic rather than purely instrumental.

Pluralist theories have their roots in historical studies of the process by which issues are contested and resolved rather than in identification of specific key parties involved in conflict (a theme pursued by Marxian theorists). Although pluralists recognize the unequal distribution of wealth and power in this society and its importance in the negotiation of conflict, they do not accord it the degree of significance that Marxian theorists do (Friedman, 1972). Like Marxian theorists, pluralists consider conflict ongoing and ever-changing as new groups vie for power and as groups in power err through oversight, misdefinition of the situation, and miscalculation of policy effects. Like the Marxian approach, the pluralist approach stresses the importance of gaining and preserving power through control of the world view of groups whose explicit or implicit support is required. Pluralists also vary in the degree to which they believe the state has become an autonomous, interested party in the conflict process rather than simply a sought-after resource.

Multiple Interest Groups

Pluralists view society as composed partly of groups with varying awareness of their interests, and who organize to differing degrees to maintain and enhance these interests, and partly of groups unaware of their interests and, therefore, unorganized. Although more organized groups vary in their power to benefit themselves, none is so well organized that it enjoys total freedom

to promote its interests. Power relationships and, therefore, the positions of interest groups in the power structure continually are subject to threat of change as groups increase or decrease in awareness and organizational might. New groups constantly are becoming conscious of and organizing around their interests and are posing threats to the traditional power structure. (The women's movement is a recent clear case in point.) All powerful groups require the support of other powerful groups above and below them in the power hierarchy. Further, no group can afford to arouse direct opposition from the unorganized; failure to placate this latter group may lead to discontent, which in turn breeds awareness of interests and leads to organized threats to the status quo. This same unorganized group also provides a pool of potential support for the various organized and organizing groups.

Roby (1969) offers a detailed example of law shaped by competition among diverse interest groups. In September 1967, a law took effect in the state of New York that made prostitution and patronizing a prostitute violations—that is, acts less serious than crimes yet still illegal—punishable by a maximum of fifteen days in jail, as opposed to the maximum one-year jail term for prostitution under the previous state law. Prior to the 1967 law, patronizing a prostitute was not illegal, though prostitution itself was.

According to Roby, the new law emerged from the work of a state governor's commission appointed in 1961 to revise the state's penal code. Following the example set by other states' penal code revisions, and at the urging of a former Supreme Court justice, the commission proposed that prostitution be considered a violation, though they did not address the issue of patronizing prostitutes. However, when the proposed revision was presented at a public hearing, certain interested parties apparently caught opponents unaware and persuaded the commission to amend the proposal. An organization called the American Social Health Association argued that patronizing prostitutes should be outlawed in an effort to help prevent the spread of venereal disease. Others argued that patronizing should be outlawed for reasons of fairness—if prostitution is wrong, both parties to it are wrong. The new law, enacted in 1965 and effective as of September 1967, radically altered the legal status of prostitutes and their customers.

Before the new law took effect, however, another interest group exerted itself. Police and prosecutors argued that they would not be able to combat prostitution because customers of prostitutes would now be unwilling to testify against them in court and plainclothes officers would now face legal problems in arresting prostitutes. To force the issue, the police apparently relaxed their enforcement of prostitution laws in downtown Manhattan just before the new law was to take effect. Rumors flew concerning an "invasion" of prostitutes into the area, and this brought yet another group into the legal battle—downtown merchants and hotel owners, who claimed that businesses were being hurt by rampant street prostitution. Their political representatives began pressuring the police for more arrests. At this point, the commission that drafted the new law reentered the fray to defend it.

Just as the new law went into effect, the police flooded the courts with women charged with loitering. They argued that this was their only means to combat prostitution. This tactic brought yet other interest groups into the conflict: the New York Civil Liberties Union and the Legal Aid Society, who protested the dragnet as a violation of the arrested women's civil rights. To end the conflict, the New York City mayor appointed a new committee that accepted the police and prosecutors' proposal that prostitution be reclassified as a misdemeanor (a crime) punishable by up to a year in jail. The new proposal was presented to the appropriate state senate committee for review.

In a surprise move, the state senate committee effectively killed the proposed revision for at least a year, ostensibly because it felt a year in jail too harsh a penalty for prostitution. Yet, Roby notes that members of the senate committee had very close ties to the original commission that drafted the prostitution statute causing the conflict. One coalition—who had favored the prohibition of patronizing prostitutes—had outfought the other: Both prostitute and patron would be charged with a "violation" (an illegal act that does not attain the status of "crime.")

State Agents

No law exists in a vacuum. Every law represents the intersection of interests of many groups, some cutting across socioeconomic classes. Among interested parties, many pluralists argue, are groups (or agencies) within the state. Legislators themselves have career interests in the legislation they initiate (Hollinger and Lanza-Kaduce, 1988). The creation of laws necessitates the creation of law enforcers (regulatory bureaus, prosecutors' offices, police departments, and so on). Once formed, law enforcement agencies themselves become interest groups whose existence may be threatened by other groups' attempts to decriminalize the behaviors they police, or strengthened through their own attempts to expand the realm of activities they monitor and the procedural powers needed for monitoring. Hence, law enforcement lobbies and public relations divisions attempt to sway legislators and public opinion to preserve or strengthen laws against such activities as drug use, prostitution, and gambling (Beckett, 1994).

Ideological Interests

Pluralists note that the multiplicity of groups involved in a given legislative conflict often indicates a variety of *types* of interest in a given issue. The most obvious of these are economic concerns: Certain groups may stand to lose or to gain economically if a given law is enacted (Graham, 1972). For example, the passage of antipollution laws clearly threatens some corporate financial interests. Laws allowing attorneys to advertise and set their own fee schedules threaten the economic interests of certain established law firms, but enhance the financial interests of other law firms as well as the general public.

Ideological concerns also influence law, in that laws and the use of laws often express political and moral values (Fine, 1997). The antipollution laws mentioned may reflect the political ideologies of groups who believe corporations should be held accountable for the condition of the environment that they in part shape. Laws governing freedom to protest publicly obviously are political. The abortion issue now contested in the political arena is largely an ideological issue, not a directly economic one (Linders, 1998).

Related to the ideology question is the issue of status in the legal process. Certain groups obtain sufficient power to define in large part the character of our culture (the degree to which it is a religious or a secular culture, for example). Some are able to maintain that powerful status, whereas others lose it and new groups gain it. Thus, the passage of a given law may reflect the rising or falling sociopolitical fortunes of these various groups. The movement toward increased criminalization of "hate crimes" (offenses committed against persons because of their race or sexual orientation, for example) demonstrates the growing political clout of groups that have traditionally lacked such influence (Grattet et al., 1998; Herek and Berrill, 1992). A well-known study by Zurcher et al. (1971) of antipornography campaigns, for example, indicates that those opposing pornography are fighting for a change in lifestyle or social climate, that is, for the power to define the cultural character of their region. Their success is, therefore, a comment on the sociopolitical status of these crusaders.

Of course, in line with the pluralist's view of intersecting types of interests, it must be pointed out that the economic interests of producers and sellers of pornography also are at stake in such campaigns. Similarly, those strongly opposed to censorship have an ideological interest in the issue. Local politicians—district attorneys, legislators, and so on—may also be party to an antipornography campaign in order to better their election interests. Finally, we should note that status interests at stake in legislation need not involve large groups of people or their status within the larger society. Pfohl (1977), for example, traces modern child abuse laws to the attempt of pediatric radiologists, a low-status specialty group in medicine, to carve out their own sphere of influence within medicine. Rather than working in an area of specialization supplementary to that of the pediatrician, pediatric radiologists now can enhance their status by becoming partners with pediatricians and psychiatrists in the fight against an important illness syndrome.

Symbolism

The ideological and status interests behind some laws call attention to an important issue in most pluralist theories: symbolic interests (Calavita,

1996; Edelman, 1964; Gusfield, 1963). Often, the surface issue that is contested is less important to the parties involved than is some underlying, broader issue. Underlying issues cannot always be contested directly in legislatures and courts because they may be too vague to state in legal terms. Instead, some more specific issue, perhaps only loosely tied to the underlying conflict, often becomes symbolic of the contest, mapping out an arena where it can be fought. At times, the groups involved are concerned only with legislation. They care not whether a law can be or is enforced (though the enforcement issue eventually may become symbolic as well) but only that their view of social, moral, or economic order be given the sacred stamp of the law (Galliher and Cross, 1983; Calavita, 1996).

Galliher and Galliher (1997) provide an excellent examination of the symbolism theme in their analysis of the enactment of death-penalty legislation in Kansas. Whereas most states rewrote their capital-punishment laws quickly following a 1972 Supreme Court decision banning the death penalty as then practiced (see Chapter 23 in this text), it was not until 1994 that Kansas produced a new law, albeit a fairly restrictive one. Galliher and Galliher attribute the delay to the state's long-standing abolition history and normative ambivalence toward capital punishment.

Proponents of the death penalty, faced with relatively low homicide rates in Kansas, were able to fashion support for their position through reference to a number of brutal, high-profile homicides over a period of approximately forty years. Relatives of the victims were able to gain media attention, and support for some form of death penalty came to symbolize concern for murder victims and their families. In short, a vote against reinstatement of capital punish-

ment could be regarded as a lack of outrage, or perhaps even concern, about brutal homicides.

Opponents of the death penalty in Kansas (among them the governor and the senate president) reflected a long state history of aversion to capital punishment. Though voting for reinstatement, they nonetheless were able to attach positive symbolism to the fact that the new law was highly restrictive in scope. The law applied only to a narrow category of homicides, making it virtually certain that few executions would occur because of it. At the same time, then, opponents and proponents of a capital punishment law gained symbolic victories and, in the opinion of Galliher and Galliher, reinstatement of the death penalty served to fill an "ambivalent 'cultural space' for Kansans."

Influencing Legal Outcomes

Within the pluralist model of the creation of law, the goal of any given group seeking to maintain or enhance its interests is to influence legislators to write laws and law enforcers to administer laws as the interest group sees fit (Burstein and Bricher, 1997). Because legislators and law enforcement officials are political beings whose jobs depend on a satisfied constituency, an interest group's immediate aim is to bring constituency pressure to bear on the officeholder to the extent necessary to accomplish the desired outcome. Thus, an interest group must convince a public that is indifferent or hostile to a position to accept that position as valid and to pressure its political representatives to legitimate it. Key examples of this phenomenon are easily appreciated through the observation that only a short time ago, we had no legislation regarding domestic violence (Fagan, 1996), hate crimes (Grattet et al., 1998), and stalking (Emerson et al., 1998).

Legislatures have been influenced fairly recently to pass laws regarding these activities, even though the behaviors to which they refer have been with us for some time.

Social identity clearly plays a key role in swaying public opinion (Spector and Kitsuse, 1977; Turner, 1969). Discredited individuals and groups find it difficult to gain a sympathetic ear, whereas prominent and legitimatized persons (for example, scientific experts and religious leaders) more easily capture an audience. Those attempting to reverse a criminal stigma—that is, to alter the public's definition of a given practice, such as marijuana use or prostitution—find the task extremely difficult, for they appear to have a self-serving interest in changing the public's mind (Jenness, 1990).

Assuming equal social respectability among interested parties in a contest to influence the legal process, the decisive factor is the propaganda effort. Quality of organization and resources utilized in capturing media attention and in directing public sentiment to lawmakers and law enforcers are extremely telling variables (Cohn and Gallagher, 1984; Hollinger and Lanza-Kaduce, 1988; Tierney, 1982). Interest groups attempt to employ symbols of the problem at hand—definitions and pictures of the problem and the people implicated in it that easily capture the public imagination. Thus, stereotypes are promoted (of the drug user, the rapist, the psychopath, the pornographer, and so forth) that fit the general public conception of evil and danger. Those wishing to see more legislative attention paid to the drug problem, for example, will find greater success to the degree that they can tie that issue to the crime problem rather than to have it framed in terms of a public health phenomenon (Beckett, 1994). Edelman (1977: 14) argues that the ability to create a "personified" danger—that is, to put a face to the problem even if that face is in reality only a mask—"marshals public support for controls over a much larger number of ambiguous cases symbolically condensed into the threatening stereotype."

Vocabularies also are created that subtly (and at times not so subtly) seek to influence the public (Edelman, 1977, 1988; Spector and Kitsuse, 1977). For example, pro–abortion rights groups choose to characterize themselves as prochoice, whereas anti-abortion groups label themselves prolife. The term "domestic violence" evokes a response different from that evoked by the term "family or domestic dispute." The term "stalker" is particularly more evocative than "obsessed follower." Such tactics accomplish more than simply gaining a public forum for an issue; they transform the issue into a good versus evil contest or from a personal trouble to a social problem whereby the public can more easily take a stand (Coltrane and Hickman, 1992; Beckett, 1994).

The result of the propaganda activity by groups contesting an issue often is public indignation about the fictions that emerge from the competitive propaganda process. For the interest groups, the creation is symbolic; for the public, it is real. Gusfield (1981) offers an illustration in his study of drinking-driving laws, or laws governing driving under the influence of alcohol. So effective were the antidrunk-driver campaigns that the public now equates the image of drinking driver with that of killer. Gusfield argues that this conception is at odds with reality, at least as it is measured by the types of cases brought before the courts, most of which are treated leniently. Gentry (1988) makes the same point in her discussion of the issue of abducted children as a social problem. So skillful were interested parties in framing this issue that the public came to view the "problem" as one of over 50,000 abductions annually of children by strangers. In fact, evidence indicates that such kidnappings totaled fewer than 100 per year.

Criticisms of Pluralist Theories

The strength of the pluralist approach is essentially the weakness of the Marxian theories discussed previously. Pluralists are able to demonstrate that much of the use of legal process involves the competing interests of many parties, not simply the maneuverings of an economic elite or of the state looking out for the long-term interests of that elite. Countering the pluralists, more radical instrumentalists argue that intergroup competition for both instrumental and symbolic legal support is a mirage, that ruling elites "allow" such competition (as long as it does not threaten specific ruling elite interests) in order to promote the impression that ours is a diversified, democratic society (Calavita, 1983). Of course, this claim is, for all intents and purposes, untestable. Yet, pluralists may be open to the more modest criticism that they do not listen closely enough to the Marxian theorists' message. Thus, although they pay lip service to power differentials, to the economic clout of corporations, and to a semiautonomous state, they exclude these elements from most of their analyses.

In part, the absence of attention focused by pluralists on elites is due to the types of law creation studied by pluralists. Pornography laws, for example, reflect the activity of groups of roughly equal power and organization, and such laws tend not to threaten any specific corporate interests. But how might pluralists explain tax law structure or weak legal control of corporations responsible for oil spills on our coasts despite very organized and strong efforts to gain

such control (Molotch, 1970)? The answer lies in the pluralist penchant for defining elite involvement in the legal process as defensive, that is, as reacting only to direct economic threat. Surely, elites are sufficiently aware of their interests and sufficiently organized to pursue them that much of their activity is anticipatory and aimed at enhancement as well as at protection of interests.

Coleman (1985) also argues that the pluralist model pays insufficient attention to the outcomes of conflicts—as opposed to the process by which conflicts occur. He focuses his claim on the effects of the Sherman Antitrust Act on the petroleum industry. On the one hand, antitrust legislation would seem to epitomize the tenets of the pluralist model: an amalgam of populist forces able to constrain major corporate interests. Yet, the resources of the petroleum companies permitted them to dodge the effects of the legislation aimed at them. Companies were able to delay legal proceedings until the political climate changed; they contributed substantially to the campaigns of politicians who could influence their situations; they concealed their holdings and their activities from public and government view; and they threatened state and local economies with plant closings. In short, Coleman argues, antitrust laws have been enforced against petroleum interests rarely and poorly. Pluralism, in this instance, is a mirage.

CONCLUSION

In sum, the conflict perspective seems to address more aggressively and more convincingly the issue of the workings of the legal process than does the consensus model. Despite criticisms of elements of the instrumentalist and structuralist Marxian theories and of pluralist theories, the conflict perspective's basic argument cannot be ignored: Laws do not simply appear miraculously on our law books, and they do not reflect "society's" values. Instead, the acts and people we call criminal and our concern with crime at any given time reflect the activity of groups in this society seeking legal support for economic, ideological, and status interests. Sometimes, only a few groups are involved in the struggle for legal support; other times, many groups compete. The issue contested in a legal struggle may be explicit and instrumental, or it may be symbolic of some greater conflict. The ebb and flow of law reflects the ebb and flow of interest groups, and laws emerging from this process must be viewed as tentative and negotiable. The key issue for conflict theorists, then, concerns the political strength of the major economic interests in this society: Do they stand alone, or do they share power with other, relatively weaker groups?

DISCUSSION QUESTIONS

1. Discuss the "functions of deviance" thesis. How well does it apply to both smaller and larger societies? What are the major criticisms of the thesis?

2. Discuss the major assumptions that underlie the conflict perspective concerning the criminality of acts and individuals. How do these differ from the assumptions of the consensus approach?

3. According to the conflict perspective, how are the interests of various groups maintained and enhanced in most societies? What role does law play in this process?

4. Distinguish the instrumentalist from the structuralist camp within the elite dominance approach to understanding law and conflict.

5. Briefly describe the pluralist approach to understanding law and conflict. In what ways does it differ from the elite dominance approach? How would each view the role of state agents in shaping laws?

6. Describe the influence of ideological interests upon legislation. To what extent can ideological interests be distinguished from economic interests? Explain the role of symbolism in the process of law and conflict.

REFERENCES

Allen, M. P. 1991. "Capitalist Response to State Intervention: Political Finance in the New Deal." *American Sociological Review* 56: 679–689.

Balkan, S., R. J. Berger, and J. Schmidt. 1980. *Crime and Deviance in America: A Critical Approach*. Belmont, CA: Wadsworth.

Beck, E. M., and S. E. Tolnay. 1990. "The Killing Fields of the Deep South: The Market for Cotton and the Lynching of Blacks, 1882–1930." *American Sociological Review* 55: 526–539.

Beckett, K. 1994. "Setting the Public Agenda: 'Street Crime' and Drug Use in American Politics." *Social Problems* 41: 425–447.

Berkowitz, E., and K. McQuaid. 1980. *Creating the Welfare State: The Political Economy of Twentieth Century Reform*. New York: Praeger.

Berkowitz, L. 1968. "Impulse, Aggression, and the Gun." *Psychology Today* 2: 19–24.

Burstein, P., and M. Bricher. 1997. "Problem Definition and Public Policy: Congressional Committees Confront Work, Family, and Gender, 1945–1990." *Social Forces* 75: 135–169.

Calavita, K. 1983. "The Demise of the Occupational Safety and Health Administration: A Case Study in Symbolic Action." *Social Problems* 30: 437–448.

———. 1996. "The New Politics of Immigration: 'Balanced-Budget Conservatism' and the Symbolism of Proposition 187." *Social Problems* 43: 284–305.

Campbell, J., and L. Lindberg. 1990. "Property Rights and the Organization of Economic Activity by the State." *American Sociological Review* 55: 634–647.

Chamblin, M. 1989. "A Macro Social Analysis of Change in Police Force Size, 1972–1982." *Sociological Quarterly* 30: 615–624.

Chambliss W. J. 1974. "The State, the Law, and the Definition of Behavior as Criminal or Delinquent." In *Handbook of Criminology.* Edited by D. Glaser. Chicago: Rand McNally.

Chambliss, W. J., and R. Seidman. 1982. *Law, Order, and Power.* 2d ed. Reading, MA: Addison-Wesley.

Chiricos, T., and M. Delone. 1992. "Labor Surplus and Punishment: A Review and Assessment of Theory and Evidence." *Social Problems* 39: 421–446.

Cohn, S. F., and J. E. Gallagher. 1984. "Gay Movements and Legal Change: Some Aspects of the Dynamics of a Social Problem." *Social Problems* 32: 72–86.

Coleman, J. W. 1985. "Law and Power: The Sherman Antitrust Act and Its Enforcement in the Petroleum Industry." *Social Problems* 32: 264–274.

Coltrane, S., and N. Hickman. 1992. "The Rhetoric of Rights and Needs: Moral Discourse in the Reform of Child Custody and Child Support Laws." *Social Problems* 39: 400–420.

Coser, L. 1956. *The Functions of Social Conflict.* Glencoe, IL: Free Press.

Davis, N. 1986. "Abortion and Legal Policy." *Contemporary Crises* 10: 373–397.

Devine, J., J. Sheley, and D. Smith. 1988. "Macroeconomic and Social-Control Policy Influences on Crime Rate Changes, 1948–1985." *American Sociological Review* 53: 407–420.

Domhoff, G. 1967. *Who Rules America?* Englewood Cliffs, NJ: Prentice-Hall.

———. 1978. *The Powers That Be.* New York: Random House.

Durkheim, E. [1893] 1933. *The Division of Labor in Society.* Translated by G. Simpson. New York: Free Press.

———. [1895] 1958. *The Rules of Sociological Method.* Translated by S. A. Soloway and J. H. Mueller. Glencoe, IL: Free Press.

Edelman, M. 1964. *The Symbolic Uses of Politics.* Urbana: University of Illinois Press.

———. 1977. *Political Language.* New York: Academic Press.

———. 1988. *Constructing the Political Spectacle.* Chicago: University of Chicago Press.

Emerson, R., K. Ferris, and C. Gardner. 1998. "On Being Stalked." *Social Problems* 45: 289–314.

Erikson, K. 1966. *Wayward Puritans.* New York: Wiley.

Fagan, J. 1996. *The Criminalization of Domestic Violence: Promises and Limits.* Washington, DC: National Institute of Justice.

Feiler, S., and J. Sheley. 1999. "Legal and Racial Elements of Public Willingness to Transfer Juvenile Offenders to Adult Court." *Journal of Criminal Justice* 27: 55–64.

Fine, G. 1997. "Scandal, Social Conditions, and the Creation of Public Attention: Fatty Arbuckle and the 'Problem of Hollywood.'" *Social Problems* 44: 297–323.

Freitag, P. J. 1983. "The Myth of Corporate Capture: Regulatory Commissions in the United States." *Social Problems* 30: 480–491.

Friedman, W. 1972. *Law in a Changing Society.* Harmondsworth, England: Penguin Books.

Galliher, J. F., and J. R. Cross. 1983. *Moral Legislation Without Morality.* New Brunswick, NJ: Rutgers University Press.

Galliher, J., and J. Galliher. 1997. " 'Déjà vu All Over Again.' The Recurring Life and Death of Capital Punishment Legislation in Kansas." *Social Problems* 44: 369–385.

Gentry, C. 1988. "The Social Construction of Abducted Children as a Social Problem." *Sociological Inquiry* 58: 413–425.

Graham, J. M. 1972. "Amphetamine Politics on Capitol Hill." *Society* 9: 14–23.

Grattet, R., V. Jenness, and T. Curry. 1998. "The Homogenization and Differentiation of Hate Crime Law in the United States, 1978 to 1995." *American Sociological Review* 63: 286–307.

Greenberg, D. 1981. *Crime and Capitalism: Readings in Marxist Criminology.* Palo Alto, CA: Mayfield.

Greenberg, D., R. Kessler, and C. Logan. 1979. "A Panel Model of Crime Rates and Arrest Rates." *American Sociological Review* 44: 843–850.

Gusfield, J. R. 1963. *Symbolic Crusade.* Urbana: University of Illinois Press.

———. 1981. *The Culture of Public Problems: Drinking-Driving and the Symbolic Order.* Chicago: University of Chicago Press.

Hall, J. 1952. *Theft, Law and Society.* 2d ed. Indianapolis, IN: Bobbs-Merrill.

Herek, G., and K. Berrill. 1992. *Hate Crime: Confronting Violence Against Lesbians and Gay Men.* Newbury Park, CA: Sage.

Hill, J. 1975. *Class Analysis: United States in the 1970s.* Emeryville, CA: Class Analysis.

Hochstetler, A., and N. Shover. 1997. "Street Crime, Labor Surplus, and Criminal Punishment, 1980–1990." *Social Problems* 44: 358–368.

Hollinger, R. C., and L. Lanza-Kaduce. 1988. "The Process of Criminalization: The Case of Computer Crime Laws." *Criminology* 26: 101–126.

Hughes, E. 1962. "Good People and Dirty Work." *Social Problems* 10: 3–11.

Inverarity, J. 1976. "Populism and Lynching in Louisiana: A Test of Erikson's Theory of the Relationship Between Boundary Crises and Repressive Justice." *American Sociological Review* 41: 262–280.

Jackson, P. 1986. "Black Visibility, City Size, and Social Control." *Sociological Quarterly* 27: 185–203.

———. 1989. *Minority Group Threat, Crime and Policing.* New York: Praeger.

Jackson, P., and L. Carroll. 1981. "Race and the War on Crime." *American Sociological Review* 46: 290–305.

Jacobs, J., and R. Helms. 1996. "Toward a Political Model of Incarceration." *American Journal of Sociology* 102: 323–357.

Jacobs, J., and R. O'Brien. 1998. "Determinants of Deadly Force: A Structural Analysis of Police Violence." *American Journal of Sociology* 103: 837–862.

Jacobs, J. B. 1979. "Race Relations and the Prisoner Subculture." *Crime and Justice* 1: 1–27. Edited by N. Morris and M. Tonry. Chicago: University of Chicago Press.

Jeffery, C. R. 1957. "The Development of Crime in Early English Society." *Journal of Criminology, Law Criminology and Political Science* 47: 647–666.

Jenness, V. 1990. "From Sex as Sin to Sex as Work: COYOTE and the Reorganization of Prostitution as a Social Problem." *Social Problems* 37: 403–420.

Lauderdale, P. 1976. "Deviance and Moral Boundaries." *American Sociological Review* 41: 660–676.

Lessan, G. T. 1991. "Macro-Economic Determinants of Penal Policy: Estimating the Unemployment and Inflation Influences on Imprisonment Rate Changes in the United States, 1948–1985." *Crime, Law and Social Change* 16: 177–198.

Linders, A. 1998. "Abortion as a Social Problem: The Construction of 'Opposite' Solutions in Sweden and the United States." *Social Problems* 45: 488–509.

Liska, A., and M. B. Chamblin. 1984. "Social Structure and Crime Control Among Macrosocial Units." *American Journal of Sociology* 90: 383–395.

Liska, A., J. Laurence, and M. Benson. 1981. "Perspectives on the Legal Order: The Capacity for Social Control." *American Journal of Sociology* 87: 413–426.

Liska, A., and B. Warner. 1991. "Functions of Crime: A Paradoxical Process." *American Journal of Sociology* 96: 1441–1463.

Mead, G. H. 1918. "The Psychology of Punitive Justice." *American Journal of Sociology* 23: 577–602.

Michalowski, R. 1985. *Order, Law and Crime.* New York: Random House.

Mills, C. W. 1956. *The Power Elite.* New York: Oxford University Press.

Molotch, H. 1970. "Oil in Santa Barbara and Power in America." *Sociological Inquiry* 40: 131–144.

Myers, M. 1990. "Black Threat and Incarceration in Postbellum Georgia." *Social Forces* 69: 373–393.

Myers, M. A., and J. L. Massey. 1991. "Race, Labor and Punishment in Postbellum Georgia." *Social Problems* 38: 267–286.

Parsons, T. 1962. "The Law and Social Control." In *The Law and Sociology.* Edited by W. M. Evan. New York: Free Press.

Pfohl, S. 1977. "The Discovery of Child Abuse." *Social Problems* 24: 310–323.

Pontell, H. N., P. D. Jesilow, and G. Geis. 1982. "Policing Physicians: Practitioner Fraud and Abuse in a Government Medical Program." *Social Problems* 30: 117–125.

Pope, W., and C. Ragin. 1977. "Mechanical Solidarity, Repressive Justice, and Lynchings in Louisiana." *American Sociological Review* 42: 363–368.

Pound, R. 1943. "A Survey of Social Interests." *Harvard Law Review* 57: 1–39.

Prechel, H. 1990. "Steel and the State: Industry Politics and Business Policy Formation, 1940–1989." *American Sociological Review* 55: 648–668.

Quadagno, J. 1984. "Welfare Capitalism and the Social Security Act of 1935." *American Sociological Review* 49: 632–647.

Quinney, R. 1970. *The Social Reality of Crime.* Boston: Little, Brown.

———. 1980. *Class, State and Crime.* 2d ed. New York: Longman.

Rich, R. M. 1978. "Sociological Paradigms and the Sociology of Law." In *The Sociology of Law.* Edited by C. E. Reasons and R. M. Rich. Toronto: Butterworth.

Roby, P. A. 1969. "Politics and Criminal Law: Revision of the New York State Penal Law on Prostitution." *Social Problems* 17: 83–109.

Silver, A. 1967. "The Demand for Order in Civil Society: A Review of Some Themes in the History of Urban Crime, Police, and Riots." In *The Police.* Edited by D. Bordua. New York: Wiley.

Skocpol, T. 1980. "Political Response to Capitalist Crisis: Neo-Marxist Theories of the State and the Case of the New Deal." *Politics and Society* 10: 155–201.

Smith, B., and K. Damphousse. 1996. "Punishing Political Offenders: The Effect of Political Motive on Federal Sentencing Decisions." *Criminology* 34: 289–321.

Smith, S., and M. Jepson. 1993. "Big Fish, Little Fish: Politics and Power in the Regulation of Florida's Marine Resources." *Social Problems* 40: 39–49.

Soule, S. A. 1992. "Populism and Black Lynching in Georgia, 1890–1900." *Social Forces* 71: 431–449.

Spector, M., and J. I. Kitsuse. 1977. *Constructing Social Problems.* 2d ed. Menlo Park, CA: Benjamin/ Cummings.

Stone, A. 1985. "The Place of Law in the Marxian Structure-Superstructure Archetype." *Law & Society Review* 19: 39–67.

Stretesky, P., and M. Hogan. 1998. "Environmental Justice: An Analysis of Superfund Sites in Florida." *Social Problems* 45: 268–287.

Szasz, A. 1984. "Industrial Resistance to Occupational Safety and Health Legislation: 1971–1981." *Social Problems* 32: 103–116.

Tierney, K. 1982. "The Battered Women Movement and the Creation of the Wife Beating Problem." *Social Problems* 29: 207–220

Tillman, R., and H. Pontell. 1992. "Is Justice 'Collar-Blind'?: Punishing Medicaid Provider Fraud." *Criminology* 30: 547–574.

Troyer, R., and G. Markle. 1982. "Creating Deviant Rules: A Macroscopic Model." *Sociological Inquiry* 23: 157-169.

Turk, A. 1976. "Law as a Weapon in Social Conflict." *Social Problems* 23: 276–291.

Turner, R. 1969. "The Public Perception of Protest." *American Sociological Review* 34: 815–831.

Wasserman, I. M. 1977. "Southern Violence and the Political Process." *American Sociological Review* 42: 359–362.

Yeager, P. C. 1987. "Structural Bias in Regulatory Law Enforcement: The Case of the U.S. Environmental Protection Agency." *Social Problems* 34: 330–344.

Zurcher, L. A., R. George, R. G. Cushing, et al. 1971. "The Anti-pornography Campaign: A Symbolic Crusade." *Social Problems* 19: 217–238.

PART TWO

Dimensions of

Criminal Activity

For most people, the "reality" of crime consists in great part of news media summaries of official crime statistics. But the public really knows very little about
the statistics that inform those summaries—crimes reported; persons arrested, convicted, and imprisoned; and so forth. Further, most official crime statistics are so
problematic that other measures of crime have been developed. These include
surveys of the general population concerning the number and types of crime victimizations they have experienced and surveys of select samples of the population
regarding number and types of crimes they have committed. These measures, however, have problems as well. In Chapter 3, "Crime Facts: Victim and Offender Data,"
Robert O'Brien examines the pros and cons of each type of statistic used to tell us
something about crime. This balanced evaluation makes it clear that we can never
rely solely on one source for the information we need about crime.

Another form of information that may structure our views of crime concerns
who commits offenses. This knowledge is important, obviously, for social scientists
seeking to explain criminal activity. However, it is also important for the average citizen whose stereotypes about offenders may shape his or her everyday decisions. In
some ways, the basic correlates of criminal activity contain no real surprises: Women
commit less crime than do men; younger persons are more active criminally than
are their elders. But in Chapter 4, "Looking for Patterns: Gender, Age, and Crime,"

Darrell Steffensmeier and Emilie Allan note that the gender–age–crime link is anything but simple to explain. Only when we begin to weave together notions of culture, social constraints, and differential opportunity—that is, unequal access to the chance to commit a crime—do we understand why males are criminally more active or, more precisely, why women are not. Similar factors enter into considerations of age differences and rates of offending. In addition, the sheer power of changes in the age composition of the population over time not only influences levels of criminal behavior across age groups but also dictates to a large degree how much crime we will have to deal with as a society.

Perhaps even more difficult to understand is the interrelationship among crime, class, and race. Intuitively, we assume that the lower classes are the more criminal and that, because they are overrepresented among those classes, African Americans have higher rates of offending than do whites. In one sense, intuition serves well here, but as Anthony R. Harris and James A. W. Shaw point out in Chapter 5, "Looking for Patterns: Race, Class, and Crime," the issue is not quite that simple. Race matters above and beyond class; the question is, why? The authors are careful to examine first the possibility that bias in the criminal justice system accounts for differential rates of offending across races. They dismiss this and other common-sense explanations, not the least of which is that crime differences mirror biological variation. They look instead at some ironies of class and family composition and at subcultural differences in degree of proscription of certain offenses across races. Harris and Shaw close with a sensitive look at what too many people now believe is irrelevant to discussions of crime and other social problems: the historical recency of slavery and its cultural and psychological legacy.

Part Two concludes by shifting from profiles of offenders to profiles of victims. Ultimately, the two are very similar. In Chapter 6, "Victims of Crime: Issues and Patterns," Andrew Karmen discusses changing victimization trends in recent years and presents some findings that may surprise the average reader. In explaining differences in rates of victimization, Karmen turns to the concept of differential risk; that is, the fact that chances of being a crime victim are far from evenly distributed across our population. Population groups differ in lifestyle (exposure to crime situations) and in means to ensure protection from crime. Within groups, individuals differ along much the same lines. Does this mean that the victim is to blame for the crime? Karmen cautions against this conclusion in his examination of the poorly conceived notion of victim precipitation of crime. He closes with a discussion of a related policy question: How and to what extent should victims of crime be compensated for their losses?

Chapter Outline

◆ Uniform Crime Reports: Police Reports of Crime

Coverage

Generating UCR Crime Incidents

◆ National Crime Victimization Survey: Victim Reports

Coverage

Generating NCVS Crime Incidents

◆ Self-Report Surveys: Offender Reports

Coverage

Generating SR Crime Incidents

◆ UCR, NCVS, and SR Data: Convergence and Divergence

Convergence of Absolute Rates

Convergence of Relative Rates Across Geographic Areas

Convergence of Demographic Characteristics of Offenders

Convergence of Time Trends

◆ Conclusion

3

Crime Facts:
Victim and Offender Data*

ROBERT M. O'BRIEN
University of Oregon

Federal, state, and local governments in the United States spend tens of millions of dollars compiling and analyzing crime statistics each year, an effort involving hundreds of thousands of person hours. The uses for these data range from influencing the allocation of resources within local law enforcement agencies to testing criminological theories. Crime statistics help establish the basic "social facts" of crime: How does the crime rate vary by age, sex, race, and income levels of offenders and victims? How does it vary by the time of day, area of the city, or region of the country? How are the relationships between individuals (for example, strangers, friends, and relatives) related to the rates at which crimes are committed? These social facts form the building blocks for theories of criminal behavior and provide evi-

dence by which these theories may be evaluated. There would be no reason to speak of teenagers "aging out of crime" if the rates of street crime were the same for 17- and 44-year-olds. If southern and northeastern states had the same rates of homicide, there would be no theory of a Southern "culture of violence."

This chapter describes, evaluates, and compares the three major sources of crime data in the United States: the *Uniform Crime Reports*, the National Crime Victimization Surveys, and self-report surveys. For each of these, we briefly describe how and what sorts of data are collected and some prominent problems and uses for these data. We then compare the data from these sources to see if they give us a similar picture of crime and victimization in the United States.

*Parts of this chapter are based on *Crime and Victimization Data* (O'Brien, 1985).

UNIFORM CRIME REPORTS:
POLICE REPORTS OF CRIME

The *Uniform Crime Reports* (UCR) constitute the most widely publicized criminal statistics in the United States. When we read in a newspaper that the homicide rate in Louisiana is higher than the national average or that Detroit or Washington, D.C., or some other city's homicide rate ranks the highest of any large city in the United States, the figures are almost certainly based on UCR data.

The Uniform Crime Reporting program began collecting data in 1930 with the goal of obtaining more reliable and comparable crime statistics. Different definitions of crimes from state to state—and even between law enforcement jurisdictions within the same state—presented a major obstacle to obtaining such data. In order to make the criminal statistics more comparable, the Uniform Crime Reporting program provided uniform definitions of crimes. Law enforcement agencies in the program report crimes on the basis of procedures for classifying and scoring offenses that are contained in the *Uniform Crime Reporting Handbook* (FBI, 1985). These procedures make data on crimes more comparable from one jurisdiction to another.

Local law enforcement agencies (police departments, sheriffs' departments, and so on) tabulate data collected under the Uniform Crime Reporting program using rules specified in the crime reporting handbook. These tabulations are then sent either directly to the FBI or to a state-level UCR program. In 1996, there were forty-four state-level programs. These programs, as well as the FBI, are responsible for providing some degree of quality control for the data. Their quality checks include examining each report for arithmetic accuracy, for patterns of rates that differ from similar reporting agencies, and for trends that are unusual. Participation in the UCR program is voluntary, though many states have mandatory reporting requirements for local jurisdictions. In 1996, law enforcement agencies active in the program represented 252 million U.S. inhabitants: approximately 95 percent of the population living in the United States.

Coverage

The UCR provides a wealth of data with wide geographic coverage. Most of these data appear only in aggregate form, for example, number and rates of crimes for regions, states, metropolitan statistical areas, cities, and counties. The UCR separates crimes into two parts: Part I crimes consist of murder and non-negligent manslaughter, forcible rape, robbery, aggravated assault, burglary, larceny-theft, motor vehicle theft, and arson. Part II crimes include simple assault, forgery and counterfeiting, fraud, embezzlement, vandalism, prostitution and commercial vice, drug abuse violations, gambling, driving under the influence, disorderly conduct, vagrancy, and several other crimes. Table 3.1 contains a brief definition for each of the Part I crimes.

Crime in the United States (FBI), the public document of UCR figures, annually reports the number and rate of criminal incidents for these crimes. This publication contains several indices of crime. The total crime index represents the simple sum of all Part I crimes except arson. This index is broken down into a violent crime index (murder and non-negligent homicide, forcible rape, robbery, and aggravated assault) and a property crime index (burglary, larceny-theft, and motor vehicle theft). These crime

Table 3.1   Part I Offenses in Uniform Crime Reporting

Criminal homicide: Murder and non-negligent manslaughter: the willful (non-negligent) killing of one human being by another. Deaths caused by negligence and justifiable homicides are excluded.

Forcible rape: The carnal knowledge of a female forcibly and against her will. Included are rapes by force and attempts or assaults to rape. Statutory offenses (no force used and victim under age of consent) are excluded.

Robbery: The taking or attempting to take anything of value from the care, custody, or control of a person or persons by force or threat of force or violence or by putting the victim in fear.

Aggravated assault: An unlawful attack by one person on another for the purpose of inflicting severe or aggravated bodily injury. This type of assault is usually accompanied by the use of a weapon or by means likely to produce death or great bodily harm. Simple assaults are excluded.

Burglary-breaking or entering: The unlawful entry of a structure to commit a felony or a theft. Attempted forcible entry is included.

Larceny-theft (except motor vehicle theft): The unlawful taking, carrying, leading, or riding away of property from the possession or constructive possession of another. Attempted larcenies are included. Embezzlement, con games, forgery, worthless checks, and so forth, are excluded.

Motor vehicle theft: The theft or attempted theft of a motor vehicle. A motor vehicle is self-propelled and runs on the surface and not on rails. Specifically excluded from this category are motorboats, construction equipment, airplanes, and farming equipment.

Arson: Any willful or malicious burning or attempt to burn, with or without intent to defraud, a dwelling house, public building, motor vehicle or aircraft, personal property of another, and so on.

SOURCE: *Crime in the United States—1996* (FBI, 1997).

indices can be misleading because they weigh crimes equally regardless of their type. Thus in the crime index, an increase of 2,000 incidents in the murder and non-negligent manslaughter category would be overwhelmed by a decrease in the number of larceny thefts of 4,000. For this reason, it is usually best to examine the Part I crimes separately rather than in index form.

Table 3.2 uses data drawn from *Crime in the United States* (FBI, 1997). Here the data are aggregated at the national level. The first column, labeled "Offense," designates the crime index total, the two subindices of violent and property crimes, and each of the crimes that make up those crime indices. The next column lists the estimated number of crimes known to the police, the third column reports crime rates per 100,000 inhabitants, and the final column lists

the percent change in the crime rate between 1987 and 1996. For example, in 1996 there were 19,650 murders in the United States, a rate of 7.4 per 100,000 persons. This rate represented a 10.8 percent decrease since 1987.

In addition to crimes known to the police, which are reported for Part I crimes for the nation as a whole and for individual regions of the country, states, counties, metropolitan statistical areas, and cities, the UCR includes data such as arrests for both Part I and Part II offenses (broken down by regions, states, counties, and cities), crimes that have been "cleared" by arrests or other means, the number of law enforcement officers employed (for states, counties, and cities), and crimes that have occurred on university and college campuses. Examining a recent copy of *Crime in the United States* will give the reader a sense of the extent of UCR data coverage.

Table 3.2   Part I Crimes and Indices of Crime for the United States, 1996

OFFENSE	NUMBER	RATE PER 100,000 INHABITANTS	PERCENT CHANGE FROM 1987 TO 1996 IN RATE PER 100,000
Crime index total	13,473,580	5,078.9	−8.5
Violent crime index			
Murder	19,650	7.4	−10.8
Forcible rape	95,770	36.1	−3.5
Robbery	537,050	202.4	−4.8
Aggravated assault	1,029,810	388.2	+10.5
Subtotal violent crime	1,682,280	634.1	+4.0
Property crime index			
Burglary	2,501,500	943.0	−29.1
Larceny-theft	7,894,600	2,975.9	−3.4
Motor vehicle theft	1,395,200	525.9	−0.7
Subtotal property crime	11,791,300	4,444.8	−10.0

SOURCE: Adapted from *Crime in the United States—1996* (FBI, 1997: Table 1).

Crime in the United States also provides data in highly aggregated form with little or no information concerning crime victims and little information concerning the demographic characteristics of offenders. The general exception to this rule pertains to homicide data. For murders, the UCR provides information on the age, sex, race, and ethnic origin of victims as well as the age, sex, race, and ethnic origin of the offenders. The race and ethnic origin of victims and offenders are cross-classified, and the types of weapons (for example, firearm, knife, poison, explosives, fire, or fists) used in the offense are tabulated. The relationship between the offender and the victim (for example, wife, husband, son, daughter, boyfriend, girlfriend, neighbor, or stranger) is described. These data help policymakers and researchers because they provide a more detailed view of crime.

In the future, we can expect more data like these and even greater detail concerning criminal incidents. The FBI is moving to a National Incident-Based Reporting System (NIBRS), which we describe later. This system will provide details about criminal incidents like those currently available for homicide.

Generating UCR Crime Incidents

A key to understanding and evaluating data on crime rates is to examine how they are produced. Two major stages in the production of official crime statistics involve the reporting of crimes by citizens and the recording of crimes by law enforcement personnel.

Part I and Part II crimes usually come to the attention of the police through citizens' complaints; thus, the reporting behavior of citizens plays a major role in determining the number of crimes known to the police. Whether crimes are reported to the police depends on a number of factors: the seriousness of the crime, the relationship of the victim to the offender, embarrassment, self-incrimination, perceptions about whether the police could do anything about the crime, and fear of reprisals. Table 3.3 displays

Table 3.3   Percentage of Victimizations Reported to the Police and Type of Reasons Given for Not Reporting, 1994

	RAPE AND SEXUAL ASSAULT	PERSONAL ROBBERY	HOUSEHOLD BURGLARY	MOTOR VEHICLE THEFT
Percent reported	32	55	50	78
Reasons for *not* reporting (in %):				
Police inefficient, ineffective, or biased	8	9	6	6
Police would not want to be bothered	3*	11	10	8
Too inconvenient or time consuming	2*	5	2	5
Priviate or personal matter	18	9	5	9
Fear of reprisal	14	6	1	2*

SOURCE: Data are from *Criminal Victimization in the United States—1994* (U.S. Department of Justice, 1997: Tables 91 and 102).

*Estimate is based on about 10 or fewer sample cases.

some of the reasons for *not* reporting crimes to the police that were given by respondents in the National Crime Victimization Surveys (NCVS), which we describe in detail later in this chapter. Note that NCVS respondents claim to have reported only 32 percent of rape/sexual assault incidents to the police. Of the respondents who did not report a rape incident to the police, 18 percent said that it was a private or personal matter; 14 percent said they feared reprisal.

Once an incident comes to the attention of the police, the recording of the act in police records as a "crime known to the police" depends on factors such as the technical qualification of the incident as criminal, organizational pressures to get the crime rate up or down, police officer and offender interactions, and the professional style of particular police departments. Before incidents are recorded as crimes known to the police, they must go through a procedure to determine whether police think that a crime occurred. If incidents are unfounded or determined not to be Part I crimes, they are eliminated from the count. Some special *counting rules* outlined in the *Uniform Crime Reporting Handbook* (FBI, 1985) also affect the total. For example, only the most serious crime that occurred during a single criminal incident is counted. For this purpose, the seriousness of a crime corresponds to the order of the index offenses in Table 3.1. For example, if a person enters a house, steals a camera, then encounters and threatens the owner with a gun and steals his or her car, that person has committed a number of index crimes, but the UCR would record only the most serious—robbery. The reporting of arson serves as an exception; it is reported even if other index crimes have occurred. Another rule counts property crimes that occur in more than one dwelling unit in a multiple-unit structure (for example, a hotel or apartment building) as a single incident.

Law enforcement agencies exist in a sociopolitical environment in which their performances and needs are often evaluated on the basis of crime statistics. Their "crime count" may be interpreted as a sign of effectiveness in dealing with the crime problem or as a sign that they do not have the crime problem under control. Their requests for funding and expansion may depend on perceptions of the extent of the crime problem (Chambliss, 1984; Selke and Pepinsky, 1982). Under political pressures, law enforcement agencies may crack down on certain crimes such as gambling, prostitution, or drugs (Defleur, 1975; Sheley and Hanlon, 1978). This results in an increase in the detection, or recording, of these crimes that is not based on an increase in offending behavior. Similarly, Seidman and Couzens (1974) noted an abrupt drop in one city's reported rate of thefts that involved $50 or more following the installation of a new police chief who promised to reduce crime. Use of the $50 criterion meant that larcenies of less than $50 were not reported in the FBI crime index, and the crime rate appeared to be lower.

In addition to differences in state laws and certain differences in city and county ordinances, individual law enforcement agencies differ in degree of professionalism, style of enforcement, number of police per citizen, and so on. In a study involving eight cities, Wilson (1978) argued that there are at least three distinctive styles or strategies defining the role of patrol officers. The *watchman* style emphasizes an order maintenance function rather than the enforcement function for crimes that are not "serious." This allows patrol officers to ignore many common minor violations that are not a direct threat to public order. The *legalistic* style may induce patrol officers to handle commonplace situations as if they were matters of law enforcement rather than order maintenance. The *service* style demands that police take seriously all requests for either law enforcement or order maintenance; however, departments with this orientation are less likely to make an arrest than police with a legalistic style.

Whether an incident is recorded by the police as a crime involves discretion by individual police officers. Several criminologists have examined the factors that contribute to an incident being written up in an official report. One such study involved a research team of observers who rode with police patrols in Boston, Chicago, and Washington, D.C. In this study, Black (1970) reported that the seriousness of the alleged offense, the complainant's manifest preference for police action, the relational distance between the complainant and the offender (the greater the distance, the more likely a report will be filed), and the more deferential the complainant determined whether an official report would be made. Smith and Visher (1981) and Visher (1983) replicated many of the findings from Black's study. They found that the presence of a bystander, the preference of the complainant for formal or informal action, the demeanor of the suspect (antagonistic to police or not), whether the suspect was a stranger, whether the offense was a felony, and the complainant's race were all significantly related to whether police decided to arrest a suspect.

In sum, UCR data generally require victims who are motivated to report incidents to the police, and then these incidents must pass through the filter of police recording procedures. An alternative strategy for estimating the amount of crime is to survey the victims of crime. We turn now to this form of data.

NATIONAL CRIME VICTIMIZATION SURVEY: VICTIM REPORTS

Problems with the data presented in official reports served to motivate the creation of the National Crime Victimization Survey (prior to 1990, the NCVS was referred to as the National

Crime Survey). The NCVS was expected to provide more reliable measures of the absolute rates of serious crime and more reliable data on crime trends. In addition, the survey would supply more detailed information on a number of situational factors, such as the locations at which crimes occur (home, office, or school), the time of day at which they occur, whether a weapon was used, and how many victims were involved. Finally, the victimization surveys would collect a wealth of information on victims that was not available for most crimes recorded in the UCR: data describing their sex, race, age, educational background, marital status, whether they were injured, the amount of medical expenses incurred, and whether the property lost was insured.

The NCVS involved two separate major programs. The first of these programs conducted surveys of cities between 1972 and 1975, and the second is an ongoing national survey conducted continuously since July of 1972. The city surveys involved twenty-six large cities. Thirteen of the cities were surveyed twice and thirteen only once. Eight of the cities participated in 1972, five in 1973, and thirteen in 1974. The thirteen cities surveyed in 1972–1973 were resurveyed in 1975. The city studies used probability samples of both households and businesses, which made possible comparisons of survey-generated victimization rates for cities with city-level data on offenses reported from the UCR. The city surveys were discontinued in 1975.

The ongoing national sample, like the discontinued city sample, originally was based on both businesses and households. (Businesses were included in the national program from 1972 to 1976 and then dropped.) The household surveys began in July of 1972. They involve an ongoing panel of households (addresses), with systematic dropping and replacement of households, in which interviews are conducted at six-month intervals. The interviewer inquires about criminal incidents that may have occurred during the preceding six months. In 1994, interviews were completed with 47,600 housing units and 90,560 people age 12 or older. The United States Census Bureau, which draws the sample and conducts the interviews, has achieved a very high rate of response. (In 1994, 95 percent of the households and 92 percent of the individuals selected to participate did so.

Coverage

The classification of crimes in NCVS publications parallels closely the definitions used in the *Uniform Crime Reporting Handbook* (FBI, 1985). Two types of crime counts are made from the survey data: a count of victims of criminality and another of criminal incidents. Victim counts tally the number of people who have had crimes committed against them. Incident counts tally the number of criminal episodes. Incidents correspond to UCR crime counts; that is, only one incident is counted for a continuous sequence of criminal behavior: "If a robber enters a bar and robs the cash register receipts and a wallet from the bartender and personal property from five patrons, the UCR counts only one robbery; there was a single incident of robbery in which there were six victimizations" (Garofalo and Hindelang, 1977: 22). For crimes involving households (household burglary, household larceny, and motor vehicle theft) there is no distinction between victimizations and incidents because, in these cases, the household is considered the victim. For personal crimes, however (rape, assault, robbery, and personal larceny), the distinction between the number of incidents

Table 3.4   **Incidents and Victimizations by Type of Crime, 1994**

TYPE OF CRIME	VICTIMIZATION		INCIDENTS	
	Number (in 1,000s)	Rate per 1,000	Number (in 1,000s)	Rate per 1,000
Crimes of violence				
Rape	168	.8	165	.8
Robbery	1,299	6.1	1,210	5.7
Aggravated assault	2,478	11.6	2,120	9.9
Simple assault	6,650	31.1	6,041	28.3
Personal theft	489	2.3	484	2.3
Property crimes				
Household burglary	5,482	54.4	5,482	54.4
Theft	23,765	235.7	23,765	235.7
Motor vehicle theft	1,764	17.5	1,764	17.5

SOURCE: Data are from *Criminal Victimization in the United States*, 1994 (U.S. Department of Justice 1997: Tables 1 and 26).

and the number of persons victimized must be carefully observed.

The types of crimes included in the NCVS are more limited than those covered in the UCR. The NCVS screening questions concern only Part I crimes (with the exclusion of homicide and arson) as well as questions that elicit information on simple assaults. Table 3.4 contains NCVS estimates of the number of victimizations and the number of incidents in the United States in 1994. The number of incidents is lower than the number of victimizations for personal crimes because a single incident may involve more than one victim. For household crimes, the household is considered the victim, so the number of incidents and the number of victimizations are the same.

Several other NCVS breakdowns of victimizations are presented annually in *Criminal Victimization in the United States* (U.S. Department of Justice), for example, the percentage of victimizations involving strangers and nonstrangers; victimization rates by sex, age, race, and annual personal income; household victimizations by

race, age of head of household, and annual family income; the percentage of victimizations that were reported to the police and the reasons for not reporting; the amount of money lost to theft; and the number of days of hospitalization resulting from injuries received in victimizations.

Importantly, the FBI has begun to supply similar sorts of data on Part I and Part II offenses through the National Incident-Based Reporting System (NIBRS). The UCR currently reports most data in aggregate-level form (for example, 10,000 homicides, 4,000 completed rapes, and 3,000 attempted rapes in a particular police jurisdiction). Under the NIBRS, the incident serves as the unit of analysis. The NIBRS collects data on each incident and arrest within twenty-two crime categories. For each offense known to the police, information on the incident, the victim, the offender, and the arrestee are gathered. This system provides details about criminal incidents that now are known only regarding homicide and through the NCVS. In 1996, ten state UCR programs submitted data in NIBRS format.

The sample design of the NCVS limits its coverage. Because it samples households, it includes no data on commercial crimes, such as commercial burglaries and shoplifting. The sample is large enough to provide reliable estimates of crime rates for the United States as a whole, or even for males and females in the United States for most commonly reported crimes. However, it is not large enough to provide reliable estimates of rates for infrequently reported crimes (for example, rapes) or to estimate crime rates for states or cities.

Generating NCVS Crime Incidents

As stated regarding the UCR data, it is helpful to consider how NCVS crime rates are produced. These estimates are based on sample surveys in which respondents answer a series of questions posed by an interviewer. These interviews are social interactions in which the interviewer asks the respondents for their time and effort and offer little or nothing to respondents in return. The data that result from these interviews share many of the weaknesses of data gathered in other sample survey interviews (respondent fatigue, sampling errors, social desirability responses, forgetting about past events, and the like).

The form of the NCVS interviews has changed over time. Currently, the first interview is conducted face to face, and most follow-up interviews are conducted by phone. (Originally, an attempt was made to conduct the bulk of the interviews face to face.) One part of the interview schedule contains a series of screening questions designed to elicit information about whether a victimization of any kind has occurred. These screen questions are followed by more detailed questions concerning any inci-

dents that are reported by the respondent. Examples of some household screen questions (U.S. Department of Justice, 1997: 107) follow:

I'm going to read some examples that will give you an idea of the kinds of crimes this study covers.

As I go through them, tell me if any of these happened to you in the last 6 months, that is since ———, 19—.

Was something belonging to YOU stolen, such as—

(a) Things that you carry, like luggage, a wallet, purse, briefcase, book—

(b) Clothing, jewelry, or calculator—

(c) Bicycle or sports equipment—

The interviewer mentions several other examples of stolen items and then moves on to other household crimes and personal crimes. The screen questions were revised following extensive field-testing and introduced to half the NCVS sample in 1992–1993. The new screen questions, like the examples above, provide the interviewees with more examples of what sorts of events might qualify as incidents and give detailed cues to help the respondents recall and report incidents. The new screen questions result in more incidents being reported—this is especially the case for sexual assaults and rapes, as the interviewer now more directly asks about such events. The NCVS will provide estimates of crime trends that meld the old series (pre-1993) with the series based on 1993 and later data. This melding is made possible by having one-half of the interviews conducted using the old screen questions and one-half using the new screen questions during the 1992–1993 surveys.

These questions and others are answered by a knowledgeable adult responding for the entire household. Each household member over the age of 11 answers individual screen questions concerning personal victimizations. A knowledgeable household member may serve as a proxy interviewee for a household member in some circumstances (for example, a household member may be mentally or physically unable to be interviewed, or the parents may not want a child of 12 or 13 to be interviewed). After the screen questions, interviewers ask a series of questions designed to obtain detailed information about any incidents noted in the new screen questions.

Several of the procedures in the NCVS are based on extensive pretesting. For example, the design of the panel "bounds" all interviews after the initial one. After the first interview, the interviewer asks about incidents occurring during the six months since the last interview. This is an important design feature. An early study (Woltman and Bushery, 1975) found that unbounded interviews result in estimated victimization rates that are 30 to 40 percent higher than bounded interviews. The reference period of six months balances the forgetting of incidents that might occur if a longer reference period were used with the costs of more frequent interviews (Turner, 1972). Finally, asking all screen questions before asking details about each incident generates more reported incidents. Pretests showed that respondents required to go immediately through a long series of questions about each incident were not as likely to report a victimization.

To determine whether respondents would report crimes to NCVS interviewers that they also had reported to the police, Turner (1972) investigated 206 cases of robbery, assault, and rape appearing in police records during the past year. The victims of these reported crimes were then interviewed using a standard survey instrument that asked about criminal victimizations experienced by them during the past year. Only 63.1 percent of the incidents appearing in police records were reported in the interview. Not surprisingly, the percentage reporting these incidents to the interviewers was strongly related to the relationship of the victim and offender. When the offender was a stranger, 76.3 percent of the incidents were reported to the interviewer; when the offender was known to the victim, 56.9 percent of the incidents were reported; and when the offender was a relative, only 22.2 percent of the incidents were reported. A similar study in Baltimore (Murphy and Dodge, 1981) found a relationship between the type of crime and frequency of reporting the incidents to the NCVS interviewer: Only 37 percent of the assaults, 75 percent of the larcenies, 76 percent of the robberies, and 86 percent of the burglaries were reported.

Some of this nonreporting of crimes to interviewers can be attributed to respondent embarrassment about the incident, to the seriousness of the incident, and to other factors. Part, however, is due to memory decay or forgetting. Turner (1972) found a relationship between the number of months between the reported incident and the interview and the percentage of incidents reported to the interviewer. For those incidents occurring one to three months before the interview, 69 percent were reported to the interviewer; for those occurring four to six months before, 50 percent were reported; for those occurring seven to nine months before, 46 percent were reported; and for those occurring ten to twelve months before, only 30 percent of the victimizations were reported to the interviewer. The NCVS instituted interviews every six months rather than yearly based on this sort of evidence.

Sampling errors pose problems in all sample surveys, but they create a special problem in victimization surveys because victimization is a relatively rare phenomenon. For example, in any given year, over 90 percent of the respondents in the NCVS report no victimizations, whether attempted, minor, or major. The sampling error is greater for rare events. In any given year, for instance, 90,000 respondents are likely to report between 70 and 100 rape incidents to NCVS interviewers. If a researcher wants to study rapes involving white offenders and black victims, there are likely to be far too few incidents to make any reasonable statistical generalizations (for example, what is the typical relationship between the victim and the offender in such incidents or in what locations are such incidents most likely to occur?). Researchers often combine data from a number of years to help address this problem.

Although the NCVS provides data on the victims of crime and some information concerning the location of criminal incidents, they provide little data on offenders. For criminologists interested in the causes of criminal behavior, this is a serious shortcoming. We explore other means of obtaining such information in the following section.

SELF-REPORT SURVEYS: OFFENDER REPORTS

Self-report (SR) surveys are the third major method used to gather data on crime. They do not depend on police records or asking the victims of crimes about criminal incidents; instead,

they question the offenders themselves, or at least samples of respondents, about behavior that, were it detected, might lead to their classification as offenders.

Unlike the situation regarding the UCR and the NCVS, there is no single set of offenses investigated or single design by which SR data are gathered. Different researchers have used diverse sets of questions and sampled different populations. We focus on three well-known studies: Short and Nye (1958), because of its historical interest and its influence on the studies that followed; the National Youth Survey (NYS) (Elliott et al., 1983), because it is based on a national panel and is the most comprehensive SR study to date; and the Seattle Methods Study (Hindelang et al., 1981), because of the answers it provides concerning some of the strengths and weaknesses of SR methods.

SR studies differ on a number of dimensions. Short and Nye's original studies used questionnaires to ascertain the level of delinquency. They presented a checklist of behaviors to respondents and collected other relevant data such as the sex of the respondent, whether the respondent was from a broken home, and the socioeconomic status (SES) of the home from which the respondent came. The National Youth Survey (NYS) used face-to-face interviews. Arguments favoring the use of interviews over questionnaires can be made, and bringing empirical data to bear on this question was one of the purposes of the Seattle Methods Study.

Another dimension on which SR studies differ is sampling design. A typical design involves the sampling of a school population and of an institutionalized population or a population with known police records. For example, Short and Nye (1958) sampled high school students in three western high schools, three midwestern high schools, and a western training school. The Seattle Methods Study (Hindelang et al., 1981) sampled three separate groups in order to maximize the variance associated with delinquency and to represent the general adolescent population of Seattle. One sample was drawn from students enrolled in Seattle public schools for the 1977–1978 academic year; another from those with a record of contact with the Seattle police, but with no official juvenile court record; and the third from the population of adolescents referred to the juvenile court serving Seattle. These samples allowed comparisons of different populations but not generalizations to larger populations of cities or regions of the country. The NYS used a probability sample of households in the continental United States and was more representative of the population of the entire country.

Coverage

The SR method is the dominant method in criminology for studying the etiology of crime. It allows researchers to collect detailed information about individual offenders. This is in marked contrast to both the UCR and NCVS data. Victimization surveys provide little information about offenders, and UCR data include data on offender characteristics only for those arrested and then only for a few demographic variables. The new incident-based approach being instituted in the UCR will provide better data on offenders but will not be as detailed as that made possible by surveying offenders.

The type of information on offenders (family background, demographic characteristics, personality measures, and so on) that is included in SR studies varies from study to study, depending on the interests of the researcher. Almost all SR studies, however, include basic demographic information: the respondent's sex, age, race, and family SES. Then, depending on the researcher's interests, a series of questions focusing on other independent variables are included. For example, Short and Nye (1957) were interested in whether respondents who came from broken homes were more likely to report delinquent activities. Hirschi (1969) wanted to test social control theory and included questions on interest in school and achievement motivation. The NYS (Elliott et al., 1983) contained measures of the family structure, work status of the respondent, whether the respondent is in or out of school, perceptions of neighborhood crime and environmental problems, and religious observance.

Most recent SR studies carefully differentiate the prevalence of reported behavior from the incidence of reported behavior. "Prevalence" refers to the number of persons reporting one or more behaviors of a given type within a specified reference period, whereas "incidence" refers to the number of behaviors that occur in the reference period. Thus, "the prevalence rate is typically expressed as the proportion of persons in the population who have reported some involvement in a particular offense or set of offenses" (Elliott et al., 1983: 18). Incidence rates refer to the "average number of offenses per person, or as the number of offenses per some population base (e.g., 100, 1,000, or 100,000 persons)" (Elliott et al., 1983: 19). Incidence rates are more comparable to UCR data on crime incidents known to police. Table 3.5 presents both prevalence and incidence rates for the NYS in 1980, when the respondents were 15 to 21 years of age.

The prevalence rate indicates the percentage of respondents reporting one or more offenses in a particular category. Thus, 62 percent of the respondents claimed to have been involved in a

Table 3.5 Prevalence and Incidence Rates for 15- to 21-Year-Olds in the 1980 NYS

	PREVALENCE	INCIDENCE
	(%)	
Offense-specific scales		
Felony assault	9	.29
Minor assault	21	1.20
Robbery	2	.10
Felony theft	9	.44
Minor theft	15	1.09
Damaged property	15	.64
Hard drug use	17	5.79
Offense-category scales		
Illegal services	11	4.50
Public disorder	48	10.33
Status offense	62	18.07
Crimes against persons	24	1.60
General theft	18	1.53
Summary scales		
School delinquency	56	8.89
Home delinquency	14	.70
Index offenses	12	.62
Fraud	5	.65

SOURCE: Adapted from Elliott et al. (1983: Tables 4.29 and 4.40).

Note: Prevalence represents the percentage admitting to one or more acts in that category during the past year. The incidence rates represent the average number of reported delinquent acts per respondent during the past year.

status offense during 1980, whereas only 2 percent claimed to have been involved in a robbery. The incidence rates indicate the average number of incidents per respondent. The average number of status offenses per respondent is 18.07, whereas the average number of robberies is only .10. Involvement in delinquencies of some sort is widespread among youth; involvement in more serious crime is relatively rare.

Generating SR Crime Incidents

Because SR data are gathered using survey methods, they share many of the strengths and weaknesses of other data gathered by these methods. SR studies allow researchers to ask offenders and nonoffenders a variety of questions concerning their behaviors, perceptions, and attitudes; there is no standard set of SR offense questions. For this and other reasons, the method has great potential for studying the etiology of criminal behavior. By way of example, the seven questions employed by Short and Nye (1958) are much like those that traditionally have appeared on self-report surveys:

> Recent research has found that nearly everyone breaks rules and regulations during his or her lifetime. Some break them regularly, others less often. Below are some frequently broken rules. Check those that you have broken since the beginning of grade school.

> 1. Driven a car without a driver's license or permit? (Do not include driver training.)

> 2. Skipped school without a legitimate excuse?

> 3. Defied your parents' authority (to their face)?

> 4. Taken little things (worth less than $2) that did not belong to you?

> 5. Bought or drank beer, wine, or liquor? (Include drinking at home.)

> 6. Purposely damaged or destroyed public or private property that did not belong to you?

> 7. Had sex relations with a person of the opposite sex?

More recent studies often include questions concerning more serious crimes. The NYS (Elliott et al., 1983) asks about a wide range of delinquencies and crimes, from the trivial "lied about age" to "strong-arm robbery" and "physical threat for sex." This range of crimes is much wider than that in the original Short and Nye items. Additionally, the response categories allow for the recording of more specific frequencies for respondents who engage in a great deal of criminal behavior.

Concerning serious crimes, a problem similar to that encountered in the NCVS occurs: For rare events, a large sample is necessary to provide reliable measures. Because respondents report far fewer incidents in which they beat someone so badly that the victim required hospitalization than incidents in which they defied their parents, rates for these more serious incidents are more difficult to measure reliably.

Information concerning the geographic distribution of crime based on SR studies is even more limited than that obtained from the NCVS. The most extensive study to date is the NYS, which is based on approximately 1,500 respondents. This sample size is sufficient to generate reliable prevalence and incidence rates for the nation as a whole for most of the delinquent behaviors included in the interviews but is too small to allow detailed breakdowns by geographic area (for example, rates for states or cities).

Low response rates are typical in SR studies. In the Seattle Methods Study (discussed on pp. 69–70) by Hindelang et al. (1981), for example, only about 50 percent of students sampled agreed to participate. Importantly, the rates of participation differed for different groups of potential respondents. For example, only 48.5 percent of the African-American females drawn from official court cases in the sample were located, and only 55.7 percent of those located agreed to participate. For African-American males drawn from official court cases, 70.4 percent of the sample were located, and 66 per-

cent of those located agreed to participate (Hindelang et al., 1981: Table 22). Substantial prob-lems with response rates exist even in the well-financed surveys. The ongoing NYS (Elliott et al., 1983) originally sampled 2,360 eligible youths. Of these, 73 percent agreed to participate in 1976. By 1980, the participant group was down to 1,494, or 63 percent of the original sample of eligible youth. By 1992, when the cohort was 27 to 33 years old, only about 56 percent of the original sample participated (Maguire and Pastore, 1996).

Before Short and Nye's study (1957), many social researchers believed that the SR method would not work because people would not admit to negative behaviors. After all, the social desirability effect had been well documented in survey research; for example, people overestimate their contributions to charities and their frequency of voting in elections. It would seem unlikely, therefore, that individuals would admit to criminal or delinquent behaviors. The results surprised many social scientists; respondents admit to a great deal of delinquent behavior (see Table 3.5). This does not mean that respondents report their delinquent behaviors accurately, rather that a large number of respondents admit to some delinquent behavior. With this difference in mind, many studies have attempted to assess the validity of respondents' reported behavior.

The most rigorous approach to testing the validity of respondents' reports is to compare self-reports of official delinquency (admission of official contact) with official police and court records. Although Short and Nye did not use this validation technique, it was used in the early 1960s by Erickson and Empey (1963). Of 130 respondents who appeared in court, every one mentioned in court the offenses noted in their self-report interviews. Hardt and Peterson-Hardt

(1977) found no police record for 95 percent of their respondents reporting no record. Hindelang et al. (1981) found moderate to strong correlations between official records and each of the following: respondents' self-reported number of times picked up by the police, self-reported number of times referred to the courts by the police, and an index of self-reported official contacts for both males and females.

SR studies provide yet another picture of the volume and distribution of crime and delinquency. This picture is not based on the law enforcement perspective (police data) or on the perspective of the victims of crime, but on data from the offenders. In the next section, we compare results from these three data sources to see if they paint the same picture.

UCR, NCVS, AND SR DATA: CONVERGENCE AND DIVERGENCE

The first sections of this chapter examined three major sources of crime data. The coverage of these data sources and the methods used to produce them differ. Now we examine the data produced by these methods to see how they compare in terms of the absolute amount of crime recorded, the geographic distribution of crimes, the demographic characteristics of offenders, and trends in crime rates over time.

These comparisons are important because they indicate the extent to which the results of studies of criminal behavior depend on the data-gathering method. If the rape rate is increasing according to the UCR, but according to the NCVS it has remained stable over a period of years, we say that conclusions about crime trends based on these two data sets are method-dependent.

The comparisons also bear on the issue of the validity of the data gathered using these three techniques because such comparisons may be used to examine the convergent validity of the data. It is important to distinguish between convergence and validity. The former is an indicator of validity, because measures of the same underlying phenomenon ought to yield similar results, if the measures are valid. Thus, if both the UCR and SR methods are measuring the same phenomenon, for example, the relative rates of female and male assaults, they ought to agree with each other concerning estimates of the sex ratio for those involved in aggravated assault. If they do agree, this supports the validity of both measures; if they do not, it brings into question the validity of one or both of these measures of the ratio of male offenders to female offenders. Thus, convergence is relatively simple to establish. Validity, however, is more elusive. Before making even tentative statements about the validity of a measure, we should consider several types of evidence besides convergence—including potential data collection bias, the content of the measure, and the theoretical definitions of the phenomenon.

Note that measures may be valid for one purpose and not for another. The UCR may be invalid as a measure of the absolute amount of aggravated assault but may be a more valid indicator of the sex ratio for aggravated assault offenders. Furthermore, the measurement of some crime rates (for example, motor vehicle theft) may show more convergence than do others (for example, aggravated assault).

Convergence of Absolute Rates

Table 3.6 presents data from the NCVS and the UCR on the number of criminal incidents for the year 1994. For the NCVS, this table presents

Table 3.6   National Crime Rate Estimates for Rape, Aggravated Assault, Robbery, Burglary, and Motor Vehicle Theft Based on the *Uniform Crime Reports* and the National Crime Victimization Surveys, 1994

	NCVS		UCR	RATIO OF NCVS TO UCR	
	Number of incidents	*Number of incidents reported*	*Crimes known to the police*	*Total incidents*	*Reported incidents*
Rape	165,180	59,630	102,100	1.62	.58
Personal robbery	1,210,200	670,450	412,852	2.93	1.62
Aggravated assault	2,120,370	1,094,111	1,119,950	1.89	.98
Residential burglary	5,482,000	2,768,410	1,820,947	3.01	1.52
Motor vehicle theft	1,764,000	1,379,448	1,539,100	1.15	.90

SOURCES: NCVS data are from *Criminal Victimization in the United States—1994* (U.S. Department of Justice, 1997: Tables 1, 9, and 26). UCR data are from *Crime in the United States—1994* (FBI 1995): Table 1 for rape, aggravated assault, and motor vehicle theft; Table 23 for residential burglary and personal robbery (street-highway plus residential robbery). The data from Table 23 are corrected because they are from reporting units that represent only 86 percent of the total population.

both the total number of estimated incidents and the estimated number of incidents reported to the police. Comparing these estimates must be done cautiously. For rape, the definitions and coverage in the UCR and NCVS are quite similar, except that the NCVS allows for the victim of a rape to be a man. The NCVS shows a much larger number of rapes than the UCR: a ratio of 1.62. Thus the NCVS indicates that there are 62 percent more rapes than does the UCR. Note, however, that the number of those reporting rapes to the NCVS interviewer who say they reported the rape to the police is lower than the number of rapes "known to the police": a ratio of .58. The number of rapes reported either to the police or to the NCVS interviewer almost certainly represents a large underestimate of the frequency of rape (see O'Brien, 1991b).

The NCVS and UCR define robberies, burglaries, and motor vehicle thefts similarly, but commercial burglaries, robberies, and motor vehicle thefts are not covered in the NCVS, because commercial establishments are no longer included in the sample. The data in Table 3.6 include only estimated noncommercial burglaries and robberies from the UCR for 1994. In each case, the number of incidents recorded in the NCVS exceeds the number recorded in the UCR. However, for burglaries and robbery, the number of incidents that respondents say they reported to the police is much closer to the number recorded by police. In two cases—motor vehicle theft and rape—substantially *more* crimes appear in police records than respondents claim they reported to the police. For motor vehicle theft there is an easy answer to this contradiction: Biderman and Lynch (1992) estimate that only eight out of ten of the UCR motor vehicle thefts were thefts of household vehicles (note that theft of commercial vehicles is not covered in the NCVS). However, the seeming over-recording of rape in police records relative to the amount that victims say they reported to the police is less easily explained. For a number of reasons, the reporting of rape is especially problematic (LaFree, 1989).

Although the NYS is based on a national sample, it is difficult to compare the incident rates derived from it with the national rates from the NCVS and the UCR. A major obstacle to such comparisons is the limited age range found in the NYS (always a seven-year range). Any such comparison, however, shows that SR studies report far more crime than either the UCR or the NCVS. In 1980, for example, the rate of aggravated assault in the NYS (for youth age 15 to 21) was 1,400 per 10,000 (Jamieson and Flanagan, 1989: Table 3.104). This contrasts with rates of 90.3 and 29.9 per 10,000 for the NCVS and the UCR for the same year. Clearly, the NCVS and UCR rates would be much higher if they were based only on those aged 15 to 21, but they would not be fifteen to sixteen times higher (1,400/90.3).

Most criminologists are not optimistic about estimating the "absolute crime rate." Whether a given behavior is a crime depends in part on the perspective that one brings to the situation. Imagine, for example, the situation of an aggravated assault. The "offender" may feel that no crime was committed because the "victim" pushed first. The victim may (or may not) consider the offender's use of increased force justified given the situation and, therefore, may (or may not) consider it a crime. The police officer investigating the incident may feel that the settlement of the pushing match is better handled informally or that this "criminal incident" is a matter for arrest. In the legal system, lawyers will dispute whether the act was a crime (if the incident gets that far) and a judge's decision may be appealed. Even if the offender loses, he or she may not define the act as a crime. Thus, it is not surprising that the estimated volume of crimes occurring during a given year differs depending on whether victims or offenders are asked or whether estimates are based on official police records.

Convergence of Relative Rates Across Geographic Areas

Whether or not the UCR, NCVS, and SR studies yield similar results in terms of the absolute amount of crime, the former two could show meaningful trends when used as measures of the relative amount of crime across geographic areas, for example, metropolitan areas or states (SR studies are not comparable across areas). That is, victims may report to interviewers far more crimes than come to the attention of the police, police might record only some of the crimes that come to their attention, and so on, but these biases might be fairly constant across geographic locations. Thus, even though residential burglary is reported three times as often to NCVS interviewers than it appears as a "crime known to the police" in the UCR (see Table 3.6), the relative rate of residential burglary (between, for example, Los Angeles and Chicago) still might be ascertained using either method. This would support the use of both NCVS and UCR crime data in ecological studies of crime. Such studies investigate the relationship of crime rates to (for example) population density, age structure, income inequality, racial composition, and region. Note that crime rates may converge (or be valid) for some purposes (comparing relative rates of crime) even if they do not converge for others (estimating the absolute rate of crime).

A number of researchers have investigated the convergence of NCVS- and UCR-based crime rates for the twenty-six cities included in the NCVS city-level surveys (Booth et al., 1977; Cohen and Lichbach, 1982; Decker, 1977; Nelson, 1978, 1979; O'Brien et al., 1980). Table 3.7 contains Pearson's product moment correlations (r signifies the strength and direction of

**Table 3.7   Percentage of Variance Explained and
Zero-Order Correlations Between UCR and NCVS Crime Rates**

CRIME	ALL NCVS VICTIMS		NCVS VICTIMS WHO SAID THEY REPORTED THE VICTIMIZATION TO THE POLICE	
	%	r =	%	r =
Motor vehicle theft	82	(.91)	85	(.92)
Robbery with a weapon	65	(.81)	72	(.85)
Burglary	47	(.69)	53	(.73)
Robbery without a weapon	31	(.56)	48	(.69)
Simple assault	0	(.05)	4	(.20)
Rape	0	(.04)	0	(.07)
Aggravated assault	13	(−.36)	7	(−.26)

SOURCE: Nelson, *Alternative Measures of Crime: A Comparison of the Uniform Crime Report and the National Crime Survey in 26 American Cities* (1978: Table E).

Note: These UCR and NCVS rates are based on the population at risk. That is, NCVS rates are based on the city's residential population, whereas UCR rates are based on an estimate of the number of persons who used each city on a daily basis (see Nelson, 1978, for further details).

association) between the NCVS- and the UCR-derived crime rates for these twenty-six cities for each of seven crimes. Correlations were computed between the UCR and NCVS rates for all NCVS incidents and for only those incidents that NCVS victims said they reported to the police. Examining the columns based on all NCVS victims, the strong positive correlation (r = .91, of a possible 1.00) between NCVS and UCR motor vehicle theft rates can be interpreted as indicating that those cities with a relatively high motor vehicle theft rate according to the NCVS data also tend to have a relatively high rate according to the UCR data. The squared correlation for motor vehicle theft (multiplied by 100) indicates that the UCR and NCVS measures share 82 percent of their variance in common for this crime across these twenty-six cities.

There is surprisingly strong convergence for the rates of motor vehicle theft (r = .91) and for robbery with a weapon (r = .81). Less convergence is noted for burglary (r = .69) and rob-

bery without a weapon (r = .56), and there is essentially no agreement for simple assault and rape. We find divergence for aggravated assault. (That is, for this crime, there is a tendency for those cities with relatively high rates according to the NCVS to have relatively low rates according to the UCR.) Interestingly, the degree of convergence is greater for each of the seven crimes when correlating UCR rates and NCVS rates for crimes that victims say they reported to the police. The degree of convergence depends on the type of crime under investigation. Not surprisingly, motor vehicle theft shows the highest degree of convergence. Motor vehicle thefts must be reported to the police in order for victims to collect insurance, and typically there is little embarrassment in reporting this crime to the police or to an interviewer.

An additional question remains: What are the effects of this lack of convergence on the conclusions researchers reach when using either UCR- or NCVS-based crime rates? The answer again depends on the type of crime involved. A

Table 3.8 Zero-Order Correlations of UCR and NCVS Crime Rates with the Percentage African American and Below Poverty Line for Twenty-six Cities

	% AFRICAN AMERICAN		% BELOW POVERTY LINE	
	NCVS	*UCR*	*NCVS*	*UCR*
Assault	−.45	.47	−.42	.50
Robbery	.32	.64	.22	.49
Rape	−.26	.43	−.13	.14

SOURCE: O'Brien, R. "Metropolitan Structure and Violent Crime: Which Measure of Crime?" (1983).

Note: The crime rates were to make the results comparable to those in Blau and Blau (1982). However, the results are substantially the same whether or not this transformation is made.

number of researchers have addressed this topic (for example, Booth et al., 1977; Nelson, 1979; and O'Brien et al., 1980). A partial replication of a study by Blau and Blau (1982) using not only UCR data but also NCVS city-level crime rates found a lack of convergence in the findings based on these two different measures for the crimes of assault and rape (O'Brien, 1983). Table 3.8 presents the correlations between the crime rates for aggravated assault, robbery, and rape based on both UCR and NCVS data and the percentage of the population who are African-American and the percentage below the Social Security Administration's poverty line. Only in the case of robbery rates do the correlations based on UCR and NCVS data have the same sign (both are positive). For aggravated assault, there is a strong positive correlation with poverty and the percentage of African-Americans for the UCR measure and a strong negative correlation for the NCVS measure. Conflicting results also occur for the UCR and NCVS measures of rape. Thus, the degree of convergence between the results based on UCR and NCVS crime rates depends on the type of crime under consideration. For at least some crimes, the findings from studies investigating the structural correlates of crime rates across cities appear to be method-dependent.

Convergence of Demographic Characteristics of Offenders

Official measures such as the *Uniform Crime Reports* state that, in the United States, the rate at which males commit street crime is higher than the rate for females; the rate for African-Americans is higher than for whites; and the rate for 15- to 25-year-olds is higher than for those older than 25. However, some of the early SR studies found that the rates of delinquency were surprisingly similar for African-Americans and whites and for males and females. Later studies, however, found that UCR and SR measures converge if steps are taken to make the data comparable. The most important steps for ensuring comparability are that the crimes compared are of the same type and level of seriousness (Hindelang et al., 1979) and that the response sets employed in SR measures allow for differentiation of offenders with high frequencies of offense from those with other levels (Elliott and Ageton, 1980).

Table 3.9 presents data from the NCVS and the UCR comparing the percentage of NCVS victimizations in which the offender was perceived as African-American or white, male or female, with the percentage of arrestees who were in those categories. UCR arrest data are

Table 3.9   Characteristics of Offenders: UCR Arrestees Compared with NCVS Victims' Perceptions of Offenders, 1992–1994

		WHITE	AFRICAN AMERICAN	MALE	FEMALE
		(%)	(%)	(%)	(%)
Rape*	NCVS	66.8	33.2	98.2	1.8
	UCR	57.3	42.7	98.7	1.3
Robbery	NCVS	35.9	64.1	91.5	8.5
	UCR	37.8	62.2	91.2	8.8
Aggravated assault	NCVS	60.0	40.0	87.7	12.3
	UCR	60.0	40.0	84.3	15.7
Simple assault	NCVS	70.3	29.7	81.2	18.8
	UCR	64.8	35.2	82.1	17.9

SOURCES: *Crime in the United States—1992; 1993; 1994* (FBI 1993, 1994, 1995) and *Criminal Victimization in the United States—1992; 1993; 1994* (U.S. Department of Justice 1995, 1996, 1997). NCVS data are from Tables 43 and 45 for single offender victimizations in 1992 and Tables 38 and 40 in 1993 and 1994. For 1992 rape data are for rape and in 1993 and 1994 they are for rape/sexual assault. The latter is a broader category than UCR rape category. The UCR data are from Tables 42 and 43 for sex and race of those arrested. I computed the mean percentage of all incidents involving males and females that were committed by males and that were committed by females over the three-year period. I used the same procedure with the data for African-Americans and whites. The results reported for African-Americans and whites in this table are based on the average percent of all crimes committed by those identified as African-American or white.

*The number of rapes reported to NCVS interviewers is fewer than 100 each year. These rape rates are not highly reliable.

used rather than crimes known to the police because data by race and sex are available only for arrests. We aggregate data for 1992, 1993, and 1994, because relatively few rapes were reported to NCVS interviewers. Finally, the choice of crimes is not arbitrary. The NCVS crimes in Table 3.9 all involve contact between the victim and offender, and thus NCVS victims are more likely to be able to report the race and sex of the offender.

For all four crimes, the percentage of offenders who are male (versus female) is very similar whether UCR or NCVS data are used. The greatest difference is 3.4 percent in the case of aggravated assault. In the comparison for race, the differences are not large between the UCR and NCVS estimates of the percentages of aggravated assaults and robberies that are committed by African Americans: The differences are 0.0 and 1.9 percent, respectively. There is a 5.5 percentage point difference between the

NCVS and UCR estimates for simple assault and a 9.5 percentage point difference for rape. Whether these results indicate a bias in the criminal justice system is not clear because factors such as the differential reporting behavior of victims and the seriousness of the crimes have not been controlled. Both data sets, however, indicate that males and African Americans constitute a much greater proportion of the offenders in street crimes than one would expect, given their percentages in the population.

Further evidence on demographic differences comes from SR studies that examine the seriousness dimension when comparing the relative rates of offending for males and females and African Americans and whites. For example, in the Seattle Methods Study, Hindelang et al. (1981) found that the ratio of the percentage of males divided by the percentage of females having ever committed a theft depends on the seriousness of the theft. For whites, the sex ratio (males to females) is 1.21 for thefts under $2 and 9.6 for thefts greater than $50. The sex ratios for African Americans are in the same direction but smaller: 1.39 for thefts under $2 and 2.63 for thefts greater than $50. Elliott and Ageton (1980) found that for illegal services, public disorder, hard drug use, and status offenses, the ratio of African American to white offenders is either less than 1 or close to 1 (with no statistically significant differences). For the mean number of predatory crimes against property, however, the ratio is 2.3, and for predatory crimes against persons the ratio is 1.65 (though it is not quite statistically significant).

Convergence of Time Trends

A number of researchers have compared trends in crime rates over time based on the UCR and the NCVS. Messner (1984: 44) computed the mean percentage change in the rates of crime for the NCVS and UCR series. He concludes, "regardless of the weighting system, the average annual increase in the NVS indexes is less than 1 percent. The indexes based on the UCR data reveal much more appreciable increases in crime between 1973 and 1981—from 3.5 percent to 5 percent." Menard and Covey (1988) reported zero-order correlations between UCR and NCVS crime rates for nine categories of crimes. None of the correlations between the UCR and NCVS crimes over the nine-year time span covered in their study (1978–1981) were statistically significant, and three were negative. These results are discouraging and indicate that, whatever the UCR and NCVS rates measure, they do not seem to be measuring crime rate trends in the same way.

Building on his own work (O'Brien, 1990, 1991a) and that of Blumstein et al. (1991),

O'Brien (1996) has compared the NCVS and UCR violent crime rate trends for five types of violent crimes: NCVS rapes with UCR rapes, NCVS robbery with UCR robbery, NCVS robbery with injury with UCR robbery, NCVS aggravated assault with UCR aggravated assault, and NCVS aggravated assault with injury with UCR aggravated assault. The trends are positively correlated only for UCR robbery with NCVS robbery ($r = .17$), and this correlation is not statistically significant. The other four correlations all are negative, the largest of these being UCR aggravated assault correlated with NCVS aggravated assault ($r = -.75$).

Thus, there is no indication of convergence in these crime rate trends. This occurs because, for the years covered in O'Brien's study (1973–1992), the UCR series typically trend upward and the NCVS series are relatively flat or trend slightly downward. When these series are detrended by computing change scores for each series (that is, calculating whether the crime rate went up or down for each year and by how much), the correlation between the change scores is .36. The correlations between the change scores of the UCR and NCVS series are positive for all of the five violent crime categories considered (albeit the correlations are not strong). This means that year-to-year fluctuations in the amount of change in these crime rates, as measured by the NCVS and the UCR, show *some* convergence. The significant conclusion remains: The NCVS and UCR measures of crime trends do not converge. Using UCR data, one might well conclude that crime rates were trending upward over the 1973–1992 period and reach a different conclusion using NCVS data.

Crime rate data from the UCR, NCVS, and SR studies converge for some types of comparisons and not for others, and for some types of crimes and not for others. For serious crimes, all three data sources indicate that, in relation to their proportions in the population, males offend substantially more than do females, and African-Americans offend more than do whites. All three measures indicate a far greater rate of street crime committed by youth than by middle-aged or elderly persons. This convergence is encouraging, given early indications that the SR and official records diverged substantially with regard to the demographic characteristics of offenders. Examinations of the ecological distribution of crimes indicate that the UCR and NCVS crime rates (for twenty-six cities) are in substantial agreement with respect to relative rates of crime across large cities for motor vehicle theft and robbery with a weapon, moderate agreement for burglary and robbery without a weapon, and essentially no agreement for simple assault, rape, and aggravated assault. The comparison of the number of crimes known to the police and the number of crimes reported to NCVS interviewers shows a substantial difference for non-commercial burglaries, robberies, and rapes. Fewer than one-half of the noncommercial burglaries and robberies reported in the NCVS are recorded in the UCR. The two data sets are closest with regard to motor vehicle theft.

CONCLUSION

UCR, NCVS, and SR studies provide the majority of the data that criminologists use to describe and explain serious street crime. Therefore, it is important to have an understanding of how these data are generated, the extent of their coverage, and their strengths and weaknesses. It is also important to know the extent to which results based on these sources converge. The message from this chapter with regard to the

uses of crime data based on the three types of sources we have examined is neither wholly optimistic nor wholly pessimistic. Care is necessary when using such data, and the appropriateness of any given use depends on the type of comparison being made (absolute rates, relative rates across geographic areas, demographic characteristics of offenders, or time trends) and the types of crime being compared.

It is virtually impossible to assess the absolute rate of most crimes (for example, rape, aggravated assault, larceny, and vandalism). This is reflected in a lack of convergence among crime rates from the UCR, NCVS, and SR data sets and is consistent with many studies cited throughout this chapter on the underreporting of criminal incidents. For example, UCR crime rates depend on the direct detection of crimes by police or the reporting of crimes by citizens as well as other processes involved in the official recording of crimes. Survey-generated rates (NCVS and SR) depend on such factors as respondent recall, willingness to report, and meaningful bounding points for interviews. There are, however, some exceptions. For example, the homicide rate as measured by the UCR is probably accurate, as are statistics on commercial robberies (especially bank robberies). There is also fair agreement between the UCR and NCVS regarding estimates of motor vehicle theft.

The yearly warning in *Crime in the United States* that the UCR rates should not be compared across jurisdictions is ignored by many researchers. Although there are good reasons for this advisory, the comparison of UCR and NCVS crime rates in this chapter indicates that some comparisons across geographic areas may be legitimate. UCR arrest data and NCVS data also indicate similar patterns of involvement in crime by racial and gender categories. Caution, however, is still warranted. Convergence is more likely for some crimes (motor vehicle theft and robbery, for instance) than for others (rape and aggravated assault). Ultimately, the best protec-tion against misinterpreting any crime statistic is the reader's understanding of the processes that generate it.

DISCUSSION QUESTIONS

1. How valid and reliable are most forms of official crime statistics? By what methods did you reach your conclusion?

2. Discuss the various ways by which we come to know what frequencies and what types of crime characterize our so-ciety. In what ways are the *Uniform Crime Reports* and the National Crime Victim-ization Survey different? What are the major strengths and weaknesses of each?

3. For which types of crime can we place relatively large amounts of confidence in UCR data? For what reasons are we more confident?

4. How did the self-reported criminality (SR) survey evolve? What are the advan-tages and disadvantages of such survey data? What have we learned from these data concerning how much crime we have in society and who commits it?

5. NCVS and self-reported criminality studies both encounter a similar problem regarding the reporting of more serious crimes. What is that problem, and what is its influence on the utility of such statistics?

6. What do our various data sources tell us about differences across races and sexes regarding commission of robbery and as-sault? How much confidence can we place in these findings?

REFERENCES

Biderman, A., and J. Lynch. 1992. *Understanding Crime Incidence Statistics: Why the UCR Diverges From the NCS.* New York: Springer-Verlag.

Black, D. J. 1970. "The Production of Crime Rates." *American Sociological Review* 35: 733–748.

Blau, J. R., and P. M. Blau. 1982. "The Cost of In-equality: Metropolitan Structure and Violent Crime." *American Sociological Review* 47: 114–129.

Blumstein, A., J. Cohen, and R. Rosenfeld. 1991. "Trend and Deviation in Crime Rates: A Com-parison of UCR and NCS Data for Burglary and Robbery." *Criminology* 29: 237–263.

Booth, A., D. R. Johnson, and H. M. Choldin. 1977. "Correlates of City Crime Rates: Victimization Surveys Versus Official Statistics." *Social Problems* 25: 187–197.

Chambliss, W. J. 1984. "Crime Rates and Crime Myths." Pp. 167–177 in *Criminal Law in Action.* Edited by W. J. Chambliss. New York: John Wiley.

Cohen, J., and M. Lichbach. 1982. "Alternative Mea-sures of Crime: A Statistical Evaluation." *Socio-logical Quarterly* 23: 253–266.

Decker, S. H. 1977. "Official Crime Rates and Vic-tim Surveys: An Empirical Comparison." *Journal of Criminal Justice* 5: 47–54.

Defleur, L. B. 1975. "Biasing Influences on Drug Ar-rest Records: Implications for Deviance Re-search." *American Sociological Review* 40: 88–103.

Elliott, D., and S. Ageton. 1980. "Reconciling Race and Class Differences in Self-reported and Official Estimates of Delinquency." *American Sociological Review* 45: 95–110.

Elliott, D., S. Ageton, D. Huizinga, B. Knowles, and R. Canter. 1983. *The Prevalence and Incidence of Delinquent Behavior: 1976–1980: National Estimates of Delinquent Behavior by Sex, Race, Social Class and Other Selected Variables.* Boulder, CO: Behavioral Research Institute.

Erickson, M., and L. T. Empey. 1963. "Court Records, Undetected Delinquency and Decision-Making." *Journal of Criminal Law, Criminology, and Police Science* 54: 456–569.

Federal Bureau of Investigation. 1985. *Uniform Crime Reporting Handbook.* Washington, DC: U.S. Government Printing Office.

Federal Bureau of Investigation. 1993. *Crime in the United States—1992.* Washington, DC: U.S. Government Printing Office.

Federal Bureau of Investigation. 1994. *Crime in the United States—1993.* Washington, DC: U.S. Government Printing Office.

Federal Bureau of Investigation. 1995. *Crime in the United States—1994.* Washington, DC: U.S. Government Printing Office.

Federal Bureau of Investigation. 1997. *Crime in the United States—1996.* Washington, DC: U.S. Government Printing Office.

Garofalo, J., and M. J. Hindelang. 1977. *An Introduction to the National Crime Survey.* Washington, DC: Criminal Justice Research Center, U.S. Department of Justice.

Hardt, R. H., and S. Peterson-Hardt. 1977. "On Determining the Quality of the Delinquency Self-Report Method." *Journal of Research in Crime and Delinquency* 14: 247–261.

Hindelang, M. J., T. Hirschi, and J. Weis. 1979. "Correlates of Delinquency: The Illusion of Discrepancy Between Self-report and Official Measures." *American Sociological Review* 44: 995–1014.

——. 1981. *Measuring Delinquency.* Beverly Hills, CA: Sage.

Hirschi, T. 1969. *Causes of Delinquency.* Berkeley: University of California Press.

Jamieson, M., and T. Flanagan. 1989. *Sourcebook of Criminal Justice Statistics—1988.*

LaFree, G. 1989. *Rape and Criminal Justice: The Social Construction of Sexual Assault.* Belmont, CA: Wadsworth.

Maguire K., and A. Pastore. 1996. *Sourcebook of Criminal Justice Statistics—1995.* Washington, DC: U.S. Department of Justice.

Menard, S., and H. Covey. 1988. "UCR and NCS: Comparisons Over Space and Time." *Journal of Criminal Justice* 16: 371–384.

Messner, S. 1984. "The 'Dark Figure' and Composite Indices of Crime: Some Empirical Explorations of Alternative Data Sources." *Journal of Criminal Justice* 16: 371–384.

Murphy, L., and R. Dodge. 1981. "The Baltimore Recall Study." Pp. 16–21 in *The National Crime Survey: Working Papers. Vol. 1: Current and Historical Perspectives.* Edited by R. Lehnen and W. Skogan. Washington, DC: U.S. Government Printing Office.

Nelson, J. F. 1978. *Alternative Measures of Crime: A Comparison of the Uniform Crime Report and the National Crime Survey in 26 American Cities.* Presented at the American Society of Criminology meeting in Dallas.

——. 1979. "Implications for the Ecological Study of Crime: A Research Note." Pp. 21–28 in *Perspectives on Victimology.* Edited by W. H. Parsonage. Beverly Hills, CA: Sage.

O'Brien, R. 1983. "Metropolitan Structure and Violent Crime: Which Measure of Crime?" *American Sociological Review* 48: 434–437.

O'Brien, R. 1985. *Crime and Victimization Data.* Beverly Hills, CA: Sage.

——. 1990. "Comparison Detrended UCR and NCS Crime Rates Over Time: 1973–1986." *Journal of Criminal Justice* 18: 229–238.

——. 1991a. "Detrended UCR and NCS Crime Rates: Their Utility and Meaning." *Journal of Criminal Justice* 19: 569–574.

————. 1991b. "Sex Ratios and Rape Rates: A Power-Control Theory." *Criminology* 29: 99–114.

————. 1996. "Police Productivity and Crime Rates: 1973–1992." *Criminology* 34: 183–207.

O'Brien, R. M., D. Shichor, and D. L. Decker. 1980. "An Empirical Comparison of the Validity of UCR and NCS Crime Rates." *Sociological Quarterly* 21: 301–401.

Seidman, D., and M. Couzens. 1974. "Getting the Crime Rate Down: Political Pressure and Crime Reporting." *Law and Society Review* 8: 457–493.

Selke, W. L., and H. E. Pepinsky. 1982. "The Politics of Police Reporting in Indianapolis, 1948–1978." *Law and Human Behavior* 6: 327–342.

Sheley, J. F., and J. J. Hanlon. 1978. "Unintended Effects of Police Decisions to Actively Enforce Laws: Implications for Analysis of Crime Trends." *Contemporary Crises* 2: 265–275.

Short, J. F., and F. I. Nye. 1957. "Reported Behavior as a Criterion of Deviant Behavior." *Social Problems* 5: 207–213.

————. 1958. "Extent of Unrecorded Juvenile Delinquency: Tentative Conclusions." *Journal of Criminal Law and Criminology* 49: 296–302.

Smith, D. A., and C. A. Visher. 1981. "Street Level Justice: Situational Determinants of Police Arrest Decisions." *Social Problems* 29: 167–177.

Turner, A. G. 1972. *The San Jose Methods Test of Known Crime Victims.* National Criminal Justice Information and Statistics Service, Law Enforcement Assistance Administration. Washington, DC: U.S. Government Printing Office.

U.S. Department of Justice. 1995. *Criminal Victimization in the U.S., 1992.* Washington, DC: U.S. Government Printing Office.

U.S. Department of Justice. 1996. *Criminal Victimization in the U.S., 1993.* Washington, DC: U.S. Government Printing Office.

U.S. Department of Justice. 1997. *Criminal Victimization in the U.S., 1994.* Washington, DC: U.S. Government Printing Office.

Visher, C. A. 1983. "Gender, Police, Arrest Decisions, and Notions of Chivalry." *Criminology* 21: 5–28.

Wilson, J. Q. 1978. *Varieties of Police Behavior: The Management of Law and Order in Eight Communities.* Cambridge, MA: Harvard University Press.

Woltman, H. F., and J. M. Bushery. 1975. *A Panel Bias Study in the National Crime Survey.* Proceedings of the Social Statistics Section of the American Statistical Association.

Chapter Outline

◆ Gender and Crime

Female and Male Patterns of Offending

Explaining Female Crime

A Gendered Theory of Female Offending and the Gender Gap

Utility of Gendered Perspective

Summary

◆ Age and Crime

National Age–Crime Statistics

Explaining the Youthful Peak in Offending

Variations in the Age Curve by Crime Type

Minority Differences in the Age–Crime Curve

Cross-Cultural and Historical Differences in the Age–Crime Curve

◆ Criminal Careers

Retiring from a Life of Crime

Older Criminals

Effects of Age Structure on a Nation's Crime Rate

Effects of Cohort Size

Age-by-Gender Differences in Crime

◆ Conclusion

4

Looking for Patterns:
Gender, Age, and Crime

DARRELL STEFFENSMEIER
Pennsylvania State University

EMILIE ALLAN
St. Francis College

Two of the oldest and most widely accepted conclusions in criminology are (1) that involvement in crime diminishes with age and (2) that males are more likely than females to offend at every age. Because gender and age are far and away the two most robust predictors of criminal involvement, this chapter focuses on how these two variables affect the level and character of criminal offending.

GENDER AND CRIME

Gender is the single best predictor of crime: In all known societies and throughout all historical eras, men commit more crime than women. The prototypical criminal is a young male, and it is his behavior that most theories have tried to explain. Nevertheless, because of the universality of gender differences in crime, examining female crime and the manner in which it differs from male crime can contribute to greater understanding of both criminal behavior and gender differences.

This section has two main goals. We first summarize what is known about the levels of offending among men and women, and we examine the similarities and differences in male and female patterns of offending. Next we review efforts to explain male and female crime, with special attention to the "gender gap"—the universally lower levels of female relative to male offending rates.

Female and Male
Patterns of Offending

Many sources of information are available on gender differences in crime. We concentrate on FBI arrest statistics, the most widely used source of data on crime in contemporary America, and the one that has been available for the longest period of time. We also draw on offender information from the National Crime Victimization Survey, findings from surveys on self-reported crime, studies of criminal careers and delinquent gangs, and case studies that provide a wealth of qualitative data on the differing contexts of male and female offending.

Table 4.1 (columns 1–6) displays male and female arrest rates per 100,000 for the years 1960, 1980, and 1995, for all the offense categories in the Uniform Crime Reports except forcible rape (a male crime) and runaways/curfew (juvenile offenses). Because few crimes are committed by either those under age 10 or over the age of 65, the rates are calculated for persons ages 10 through 64—that is, for the population at risk. Table 4.1 also displays the female percentage of arrests and the profiles of male and female offenders, as we discuss below.

For both males and females, arrest rates are higher for less serious offenses. Female rates are highest for the minor property crimes like larceny and fraud and for substance abuse (DUI, drugs, and liquor law violations). In terms of trends, for both males and females, arrest rates increased in some categories, decreased in others, and did not change in still others. Overall, the pattern of change was similar for both sexes, with large increases occurring only for larceny, fraud, driving under the influence, drug violations, and assault; and with decreases in arrest rates actually occurring in the categories of public drunkenness, sex offenses, vagrancy, suspicion, and gambling. This suggests that the rates for both sexes are influenced by similar social and legal forces, independent of any condition unique to women.

The similarities in male and female offending patterns are also evident in columns 10–13, which provide profiles of male and female arrest

patterns by showing the percentage of total male and total female arrests represented by each crime category. The homicide figures of 0.2 for men in 1995 and 0.1 for women mean, respectively, that only about two-tenths of 1 percent of all male arrests were for homicide, and only one-tenth of 1 percent of all female arrests were for homicide. By comparison, a whopping 19 percent of all male arrests and 23 percent of female arrests are "other except traffic"—a residual category that includes mostly criminal mischief, harassment, public disorder, local ordinance violations, and assorted minor crimes.

For both males and females, the five most common arrest categories in 1995 are other except traffic, driving under the influence (DUI), larceny-theft, drug abuse, and other assaults. Together, these five offenses account for 63 percent of all male arrests and 62 percent of all female arrests. Note that after other except traffic, larceny arrests is the most numerous category (17 percent in 1995) for females; DUI arrests are more important for males (10 percent in 1995). As we discuss later, the offense category "other assaults" (also called simple or misdemeanor assault) includes mostly minor, even trivial, incidents of threat or physical attack against another person such as scratching, biting, throwing objects, shoving, hitting, or kicking; because of growing citizen concerns about violence and aggression in U.S. society, enhanced reporting and policing have resulted in rising rates of arrest of both males and females for other assaults in recent years.

Arrests for murder, arson, and embezzlement are relatively rare for males and females alike, and arrests for offenses such as liquor law violations (mostly underage drinking), simple assault, and disorderly conduct represent middling ranks for both sexes.

The most important gender differences in arrest profiles are the proportionately greater

Table 4.1 Male and Female Arrest Rates/100,000 (All Ages), Female Percentage of Arrests, and Male and Female Arrest Profiles

OFFENSE	MALE RATES			FEMALE RATES			FEMALE PERCENTAGE (OF ARRESTS)			OFFENDER-PROFILE PERCENTAGE* MALES		FEMALES	
	1960 (1)	1980 (2)	1995 (3)	1960 (4)	1980 (5)	1995 (6)	1960 (7)	1980 (8)	1995 (9)	1960 (10)	1995 (11)	1960 (12)	1995 (13)
Against Persons													
Homicide	8.7	15.3	16.6	1.8	2.3	1.7	17.2	12.8	9.2	0.1	0.2	0.2	0.1
Aggravated Assault	99.5	215.7	367.5	16.0	29.2	70.3	13.8	11.9	16.0	1.4	3.9	1.9	3.2
Weapons	68.2	135.3	190.5	4.1	10.2	15.6	5.7	7.0	7.6	1.0	2.0	0.5	0.7
Simple Assault	263.7	368.2	790.7	28.8	55.4	174.0	9.9	13.1	18.0	3.8	8.5	3.5	7.8
Major Property													
Robbery	64.2	123.5	132.0	3.2	9.0	12.6	4.8	6.8	8.7	0.9	1.4	0.4	0.6
Burglary	268.8	428.4	281.7	8.8	27.0	31.4	3.2	5.9	10.0	3.9	3.0	1.1	1.4
Stolen Property	21.1	96.2	114.0	1.9	11.0	17.0	8.2	10.2	12.9	0.3	1.2	0.2	0.8
Minor Property													
Larceny-Theft	390.6	728.1	810.1	77.8	300.7	381.8	16.6	29.2	32.0	5.6	8.7	9.4	17.3
Fraud	69.3	146.2	195.2	12.6	90.2	125.8	15.4	38.2	39.2	1.0	2.1	1.5	5.7
Forgery	43.0	47.8	58.8	8.1	19.8	30.8	15.9	29.4	34.4	0.6	0.6	1.0	1.4
Embezzlement	—	5.6	6.6	—	1.9	4.5	—	25.3	40.6	—	0.1	—	0.2
Malicious Mischief													
Auto Theft	122.2	125.4	140.4	4.7	11.2	19.0	3.7	8.2	11.9	1.8	1.5	0.6	0.9
Vandalism	—	202.1	217.5	—	17.7	30.6	—	8.0	12.3	—	2.3	—	1.4
Arson	—	15.3	13.5	—	2.0	2.3	—	11.3	14.5	—	0.1	—	0.1
Drinking/Drugs													
Public Drunkenness	2,499.5	946.0	499.2	207.8	72.3	62.0	7.7	7.1	11.0	35.9	5.4	25.1	2.8
DUI	340.8	1,078.5	948.4	21.2	99.1	150.8	5.9	8.4	13.7	4.9	10.2	2.6	6.8
Liquor Laws	182.7	316.3	342.8	28.0	51.8	78.0	13.3	14.1	18.5	2.6	3.7	3.4	3.5
Drug Abuse	48.5	456.2	897.5	8.2	67.6	168.8	14.5	12.9	15.8	0.7	9.6	1.0	7.6
Sex/Sex Related													
Prostitution	13.6	26.2	32.1	35.9	52.7	50.5	72.6	66.9	61.1	0.2	0.3	4.3	2.3
Sex Offenses	80.5	56.3	73.4	16.2	4.5	6.4	16.8	7.3	8.0	1.2	0.8	2.0	0.3
Disorderly Conduct	744.7	566.5	462.7	113.5	99.8	118.2	13.2	15.0	20.4	10.7	5.0	13.7	5.3
Vagrancy	251.8	27.6	18.3	22.1	8.1	3.6	8.1	21.2	16.8	3.6	0.2	2.7	0.2
Suspicion	206.9	14.3	9.1	26.4	2.2	1.6	11.3	13.2	14.8	3.0	0.1	3.2	0.1
Miscellaneous													
Against Family	88.1	44.6	76.1	8.1	4.7	18.3	8.4	9.6	19.3	1.3	0.8	1.0	0.8
Gambling	193.0	44.3	13.3	17.0	4.4	2.2	8.0	9.1	14.1	2.8	0.1	2.0	0.1
Other Except Traffic	867.4	1,382.7	2,418.9	154.0	222.3	509.4	15.1	13.9	17.4	12.5	26.0	18.6	23.0
Indices													
Violent	188.4	387.4	545.1	21.1	40.6	85.0	10.0	9.5	13.5	2.7	5.9	2.5	3.8
Property	781.6	1,286.4	1,245.8	91.3	339.5	434.5	10.5	20.8	25.9	11.2	13.4	11.1	19.6
Index	974.0	1,668.2	1,790.9	112.7	380.1	519.4	10.4	18.5	22.5	14.0	19.3	13.6	23.5
Total													
All Offenses	6,956.8	7,757.1	9,305.6	826.7	1,372.7	2,214.1	10.6	15.0	19.2	—	—	—	—

SOURCE: U.S. Department of Justice (1960–1995).

*1960 columns do not quite add up to 100% because rape (a male offense) is omitted. 1995 columns do not add up to 100% because runaways and curfew/loitering also are omitted; prior to 1964 (i.e., including 1960), the UCR lumped arrests for these two juvenile-status offenses into "other except traffic."

female involvement in minor property crimes (collectively, about 25 percent of female arrests in 1995, compared to 12 percent of male arrests), and the relatively greater involvement of males in the more serious person or property crimes (16 percent of male arrests, but only 6 percent of female arrests).

Another way of comparing female and male offending is to look at the female share of arrests: Columns 7–9 in Table 4.1 show the female percentage of arrests for three different periods: 1960, 1980, and 1995 (in all cases, the female percentage adjusts for the sex composition of the population at large). Looking first at the 1995 data, except for prostitution (the only offense category in the table for which the female arrest rate exceeds that of males), the female percentage of arrests is highest for the minor property crimes (about 35 percent) and lowest for "masculine" crimes like robbery and burglary (about 8 percent each).

Over the previous three decades, the female percentage of arrests has increased substantially for minor property crimes (from an average of 17 percent for 1960 to 27 percent for 1980 to about 35 percent for 1995). The percentages for most other crimes show slight to moderate increases (by 1–3 percent for each period). For a number of categories, the female percentage of arrests has held steady or declined slightly, including arrests for homicide, public drunkenness, drugs, and a few of the sex-related crimes. For all three periods, percentages for females have been highest for minor property and public order offenses.

Because the gender-related patterns of criminal behavior observed in official arrest data may reflect selection and processing practices of the authorities rather than actual behavior differences in male/female criminality (Chesney-Lind, 1973; Smart, 1976), it is important to compare the results with nonofficial data sources. In fact, the female and male patterns found in the Uniform Crime Reporting (UCR) data tend to be corroborated by data from a variety of other sources.

For example, female-to-male totals quite similar to those in the UCR data are found in victimization surveys like the National Crime Victimization Survey (NCVS). In NCVS interviews, victims are asked both whether their assailant was male and whether they reported the crime to the police. According to NCVS data, women offenders account for about 8 percent of robberies, 12 percent of aggravated assaults, 15 percent of simple assaults, 6 percent of burglaries, and 5 percent of all motor vehicle thefts reported by victims.

Hindelang's (1979) comparison of National Crime Survey (forerunner of the NCVS) and UCR data substantiates the low female involvement in "masculine" types of crime. Hindelang also found no clear gender differences in reporting to the police, once crime seriousness was taken into account. In other words, no evidence suggested that male chivalry—that is, males' reluctance to report crimes against them by women—reduced the number of victimizations by female offenders that were reported to the police.

The pattern of a higher female share of offending for mild forms of lawbreaking and a much lower share for serious offenses is confirmed by the numerous self-report studies in which persons (generally juveniles) have been asked to report on their own offenses (Steffensmeier and Allan, 1996). These results hold both for prevalence of offending (the percent of the male and female samples that report any offending) and especially for the frequency of offending (the number of crimes an active offender commits in a given period). Gender differences are smallest for offenses such as shop-lifting and minor drug use.

Statistics on males and females incarcerated in state and federal prisons reveal that from roughly the mid-1920s to the present, the female percentage of the total prison population varied between 3 and 6. The female percentage was about 5 in the 1920s, about 3 in the 1960s, and is about 6 today. As with male incarceration rates, female rates have risen very sharply—more than tripled—over the past two decades. Most women in prison today were convicted of homicide and assault (usually against spouse, lover, or child) and increasingly in recent years for drug offenses or for property crimes that are often drug related. A much larger percentage of female new court commitments than of male new court commitments are entering prison today for a drug offense. Also, a higher percentage of female prison inmates than male inmates was under the influence of drugs or alcohol at the time of the offense (Greenfeld and Minor-Harper, 1991).

Studies of gang participation indicate that girls have long been members of gangs (Thrasher, 1927), and some girls today continue to solve their problems of gender, race, and class through gang participation. At issue is not their presence, but the extent and form of their participation. Early studies, based on information from male gang informants, depicted female gang members as playing secondary roles as cheerleaders or camp followers, and ignored girls' occasionally violent behavior.

Recent studies, which rely more on female gang informants, indicate that girls' roles in gangs have been considerably more varied than early stereotypes would have it. Although female gang members continue to be dependent on male gangs, the girls' status is determined as much or even more so by her female peers (Campbell,

1984). Also, relative to the past, girls in gangs appear to be fighting in more arenas and even using many of the same weapons as males, and the gang context may be an important source of initiating females into patterns of violent offending. The aggressive rhetoric of some female gang members notwithstanding, their actual behavior continues to display considerable deference to male gang members, avoidance of excessive violence, and adherence to traditional gender-scripted behaviors (Campbell, 1990; Chesney-Lind and Shelden, 1992; Swart, 1991). Ganging is still a predominantly male phenomenon (roughly 85 percent). The most common form of female gang involvement has remained as auxiliaries or branches of male gangs (Miller, 1980; Swart, 1991), and females are excluded from most of the economic criminal activity (Bowker et al., 1980).

Research on criminal careers—the longitudinal sequence of crimes committed by an individual offender—has become an increasing focus of criminology. The limited research comparing male and female criminal careers is limited mainly to violent career offenders and has found substantial gender variation: (1) although violent offenses make up only a small percentage of all the offenses committed by offenders of either gender, females participate in substantially less violent crime than males during the course of their criminal careers; (2) the careers of violent females both begin and peak a little earlier than those of males; (3) females are far less likely than males to repeat their violent offenses; and (4) females are far more likely to desist from further violence (see reviews in Denno, 1994; Kruttschnitt, 1994; Weiner, 1989). In brief, long-term involvement in crime—an extensive criminal career—is extremely rare or virtually nonexistent within the female offender population.

Case studies and interviews, even with serious female offenders, indicate no strong commitment to criminal behavior (Arnold, 1989; Bottcher, 1995; Miller, 1986). This finding stands in sharp contrast to the commitment and self-identification with crime and the criminal lifestyle that is often found among male offenders (Sutherland, 1937; Prus and Sharper, 1977; Steffensmeier, 1986; Pennsylvania Crime Commission, 1991).

Case studies also show, for example, that the career paths of female teens who drift into criminality are typically a consequence of running away from sexual and physical abuse at home. The struggle to survive on the streets may then lead to other status offenses and crimes (Gilfus, 1992; Chesney-Lind, 1989), including prostitution and drug dealing (English, 1993). Especially when drug abuse is involved, other criminal involvements are likely to escalate (Anglin et al., 1987; Inciardi et al., 1993). Other researchers have chronicled how female vulnerability to male violence may drive women into illegal activities (Miller, 1986; Richie, 1995). Despite histories of victimization or economic hardship, many of these women display considerable innovation and independence in their "survival strategies" (Mann, 1984).

Finally, female involvement in professional and organized crime continues to lag far behind male involvement. Women are hugely underrepresented in traditionally male-dominated associations that engage in large-scale burglary, fencing operations, gambling enterprises, and racketeering. A 1990 report on organized crime and racketeering activities in the state of Pennsylvania during the 1980s revealed that only a handful of women were major players in large-scale gambling and racketeering, and their involvement was a direct spinoff of association with a male figure (i.e., the woman was a daughter, spouse, or sister). Moreover, the extent and character of women's involvement was comparable to their involvement during the 1960s and 1970s (Pennsylvania Crime Commission, 1991).

Drawing on these and other data, it is possible to provide a summary portrait of female crime. In terms of arrest volumes, female involvement in crime is greatest for the petty property crimes, which account for more than 20 percent of all female arrests. These are also categories where female involvement is high relative to male involvement, with women constituting a third or more of all arrests for the categories of larceny, fraud, forgery, and embezzlement. In practical terms, these offense categories comprise petty thefts and hustles such as shoplifting, theft of services, falsification of identification, passing bad checks, credit card forgery, welfare fraud, and employee pilferage. In recent decades, female arrest volumes for larceny have become so great as to have an impact upon total arrest rates.

Adult female arrests have traditionally exceeded male arrests only for the category of prostitution, and this continues to be the case. The female share of arrests has also been relatively high (about 20 percent) for sex-related public order offenses like vagrancy, disorderly conduct, and suspicion (often used as legal euphemisms for prostitution and similar offenses).

In comparison to male offenders, females are far less likely to be involved in serious offenses. Moreover, the monetary value of female thefts, property damage, drugs, or injuries is typically smaller than that for similar offenses committed by males. Female offenders, like male offenders, tend to come from disadvantaged backgrounds, but they are more likely than male offenders to have been victims of abuse.

Females are also more likely than males to be solo perpetrators, or to be part of small, relatively nonpermanent crime groups. When female offenders are involved with others, particularly in more lucrative thefts or other criminal enterprises, they typically act as accomplices to males (see Steffensmeier, 1983, for a review). One of the most significant gender differences is the overwhelming dominance of males in more organized and highly lucrative crimes, whether based in the underworld or the "upperworld."

Explaining Female Crime

Explanation of variation in female and male patterns of offending has attracted increased attention from criminologists in recent decades. Two questions are of special interest:

1. Why is there a gender gap in crime: Why is female crime always and everywhere less than male crime, particularly for serious offenses?
2. Why does the gender gap vary over time and across social settings?

Most traditional theories of crime were developed by male criminologists to explain male crime. Recent decades have seen a lively debate concerning whether such theories are equally useful in explaining female crime, or whether female crime can only be explained by gender-specific theories. Another major controversy has centered on whether and how changes in gender roles are influencing trends in female crime relative to male crime.

Some criminologists argue that the "traditional" theories are in fact male-specific theories and therefore not well suited to the explanation of female crime. However, in spite of their androcentric origins, it is possible to view traditional structural and social process theories as more or less gender neutral. These theories are as useful in understanding overall female crime as

they are in understanding overall male crime. They can also help explain why female crime rates are so much lower than male rates.

On the other hand, many of the subtle and profound differences between female and male offending patterns may be better understood by a gendered approach. To illustrate the underlying issues a bit more clearly, we start with a brief look at the so-called "traditional" theories and how they can be used to explain female crime and the gender gap in crime. This is followed by a summary of the traditional "gender equality" interpretation of space-time variations in the gender gap. Next we review recent theoretical efforts to explain female crime. We conclude by sketching the outline of a gendered approach to understanding female crime that takes a middle position between the one extreme of insisting that female crime requires special theories and the opposite extreme of claiming that the classic theories are adequate to explain all the nuances of female and male offending.

Traditional Theoretical Explanations of the Gender Gap Approaches like anomie theory and conflict theory suggest that structural factors such as poverty and inequality, particularly in the face of societal emphasis on success/profits, underlie much of conventional crime. Consistent with these approaches, both male and female criminals come disproportionately from the ranks of the poor and disadvantaged. These approaches would explain the gender gap in crime as a consequence of the lesser relevance of success/profit goals to women compared with men.

Social process approaches like differential association theory and labeling theory tend to explain conventional crime in terms of differential opportunities for the learning of criminal values and skills or in terms of self-fulfilling prophecy effects of labels imposed by social control processes. Such theories would explain the gender gap as a consequence of lower access by females to criminal learning opportunities and/or the greater consistency between male stereotypes and negative behavioral labels.

Control theory argues that weak social bonds account for much crime. Consistent with this approach, both male and female delinquents and criminals come disproportionately from dys-functional families, have lower levels of academic achievement, or exhibit other evidence of having weak stakes in conformity. The gender gap would be explained by greater female socialization toward bonding behavior.

The utility of the traditional theories is supported by evidence of considerable overlap in the causes of female and male crime. First, like males, female offenders (especially those with frequent contact with criminal justice agencies) come from social backgrounds that disportionately involve low-income, poor education, and minority status (see reviews in Chesney-Lind and Shelden, 1992; Denno, 1994; Steffensmeier and Allan, 1995). The key difference is that female offenders are more likely to have dependent children.

Second, evidence that female rates respond to the same societal forces as male rates is also found in the close parallel between female rates and male rates across time, offense categories, social groupings, or geographic areas: Female rates are high where male rates are high, and low where male rates are low (Steffensmeier and Allan, 1988; Steffensmeier et al., 1989).

Third, both aggregate and self-report studies identify structural correlates that are similar for female and male crime. Notably, areas or localities characterized by high levels of poverty, joblessness, and other indicators of structural disadvantage have high rates of female offending,

and they also have high rates of male offending (Steffensmeier and Haynie, forthcoming). Causal factors identified by traditional theories of crime such as anomie, social control, and differential association appear equally applicable to female and male offending (Steffensmeier and Allan, 1996). Measures of bonds, associations, learning, parental controls, perceptions of risk, and so forth have comparable effects across the genders.

The "Gender Equality" Hypothesis of Variations in the Gender Gap Clearly traditional theories can help understand why rates of female offending are always and everywhere lower than the rates for males. Yet the relative levels of female-to-male offending levels are not constant. The female share of arrests varies across societies and among different population subgroups, and it varies somewhat over time and by type of offense. In fact, this variability has historically been used by sociological criminologists to debunk biological theories (Steffensmeier and Clark, 1980). The traditional interpretation of these variations in the gender gap was to ascribe them to variations in gender equality, and we refer to it here as the "gender equality hypothesis."

The gender equality and crime hypothesis gained considerable vogue during the 1970s, when several criminologists suggested that increases in the female share of arrests during the 1960s to 1970s could be attributed to gains in gender equality as a result of the women's movement (Adler, 1975; Simon, 1975). This interpretation of the "dark side" of female liberation was welcomed enthusiastically by the media.

The gender equality hypothesis was perhaps important historically. Nevertheless, in many respects it was a non-theory that mainstream criminology has since passed by in favor of more plausible explanations of time-space variations in the gender gap. Chesney-Lind and Shelden

(1992: 77) are among those to point out the absurdity of "a hypothesis that assumed improving girls' and women's economic conditions would lead to an increase in female crime when almost all the existing criminological literature stresses the role played by discrimination and poverty (and unemployment or underemployment) in the creation of crime."

Alternative explanations of time-space variations in the gender gap in crime focus on time-space differences in the extent of economic insecurity and community disorganization experienced by women, the extent to which a highly formalized law enforcement apparatus and sanctioning system exists, and the availability of opportunities for "female"-type crimes. The female share of offending will be greater in those settings where economic adversity among large subgroups of women is widespread, where opportunities to commit consumer-based crimes like shoplifting and check fraud are substantial, and where record keeping and policing practices are bureaucratized (Steffensmeier, 1993).

Also, rising levels of illicit drugs appear to have more effect on female than male crime trends, even though female drug arrests have not outpaced male arrests since 1960. Drug addiction amplifies income-generating crimes of both sexes, but more so for females who face greater constraints against crime and may need greater motivational pressures before they will commit a crime—especially, a more masculine crime like robbery or burglary. Drug use is also more likely to initiate females into the underworld and to connect them to drug-dependent males who use them as crime accomplices or exploit them as "old ladies" to support their addiction or as "mules" for their drug trafficking (Covington, 1985; Miller, 1986).

Additionally, the social and institutional transformation of the inner city over the past couple of decades—in particular, toward greater detachment from mainstream social institutions (e.g., marriage, education, employment)—has created opportunities and facilitated entry of minority women into crime in ways that escalated their criminal offending as much or more than that of minority males. In turn, this escalation has swamping effects that elevate female offending levels for the population as a whole.

Recent Theoretical Developments Several macro-level approaches have taken the position that divergence rather than convergence in gender roles can help explain some of the variation in the gender gap in crime. Hartnagel and Mizannudin (1986: 12) suggest that "gender-based inequalities in the distribution of power and wealth may prove a more fruitful avenue [than gender equality] to pursue in future attempts to explain cross-national variation in female crime."

Similarly, Cloward and Piven (1979), building on the anomie theory tradition, argue that the persistence of gender segregation differentially shapes the form and frequency of male and female deviance. Specifically, limits on women's workforce opportunities in conjunction with their more extensive domestic responsibilities limit the deviant adaptations available to women. As a result, "the only models of female deviance which our society encourages or permits women to imagine, emulate and act out are essentially privatized modes of self destruction" (p. 660).

Harris (1977) makes a comparable point when he argues that societies are structured such that all behaviors are typescripted. These typescripts specify more and less acceptable forms of deviance for various categories of social actors. As a result of these typescripts, "it is unlikely or impossible for women to attempt assassination, robbery, or rape" (p. 12).

Messerschmidt (1986) uses conflict theory to further explore the relationship between social structural opportunities, behavioral expectations, and the gender gap in offending. He argues that capitalism and patriarchy structure individuals' opportunities and shape their behaviors. He contends that a capitalist-patriarchal system will channel female offending toward lower levels and toward less serious crime categories. Most serious crimes are masculine in nature and serve to reinforce male dominance in a patriarchal system via aggression. Further, in a patriarchal-capitalist system, women are more closely supervised than males and have less power in economic, religious, political, and military institutions, thereby limiting their criminal opportunities. This framework helps to explain how structural forces shape sex differences in crime rates, but it does not offer an explanation of female crime when it does occur.

Steffensmeier et al. (1989) identify a number of structural factors that can explain variations in the gender gap with greater plausibility and parsimony than the gender equality hypothesis. These factors include heightened female economic marginality, increasing the need and motive to commit crime; increased opportunities for "female" sorts of consumer-based crime such as shoplifting, bad checks, credit card misuse, and welfare fraud; and formalization of social control that increases the accuracy and vigor with which female crimes are identified and prosecuted.

Underworld sex segregation adds further structural constraints on female levels of offending, particularly in the more lucrative venues (Steffensmeier, 1983: 1025): "Compared to their male counterparts, potential female offenders are at a disadvantage in selection and recruitment into criminal groups, in the range of career paths, and access to them, opened by way of participation in these groups, and in opportunities for tutelage, increased skills, and rewards."

Recent micro-level developments may contribute even more to our ability to understand and explain female crime. Structural approaches are insensitive to individual-level differences in the influence of structural dynamics on behavioral outcomes. Micro-level theories are often better suited to explaining within-sex variations in offending.

Gender seems to act as a lens that focuses macro-level forces differently for women and men. The fact that crime is an overwhelmingly male phenomenon has led to theoretical explanations that link offending to sex roles and gender identity. Some theorists have suggested that differences in gender roles may explain the gender gap in offending. Such approaches assume that the traditional female role is incompatible with offending behavior. Thus, the degree to which women subscribe to traditional views of femininity might be expected to reduce the likelihood that they engage in crime.

However, most female (and male) offenders hold traditional gender-role definitions (Bottcher, 1995). A few studies report a relationship between non-traditional or masculine gender role attitudes and female delinquency on a given item but not on other items (Heimer, 1995; Shover et al., 1979; Simpson and Ellis, 1995). Still, the bulk of studies report that traditional rather than non-traditional views are associated with greater delinquency (see reviews in Chesney-Lind and Shelden, 1992; Pollock-Byrne, 1990; Steffensmeier and Allan, 1995).

Others have suggested that gender identity (the degree to which an individual identifies as masculine or feminine), as opposed to beliefs about traditional gender roles, should account for individual-level sex differences in offending. A masculine identity should increase the likelihood of offending and a feminine identity should decrease this likelihood. Some evidence suggests an association between gender identity and styles of pathology—masculinity is associated with delinquency among males, whereas an absence of masculinity is associated with distress and alcohol and drug problems among both females and males (Horowitz and White, 1987). However, neither the presence nor absence of femininity is related to delinquency or psychological distress.

A third approach relates offending to the accomplishment of gender as an emergent social construction. In other words, offending represents a way of "doing gender" and, more specifically, of "doing masculinity" (Messerschmidt, 1993; Simpson and Ellis, 1995). This argument suggests that crime, especially violent crime, is a means for males to validate their masculinity, because it allows them to assert and establish their dominance. Further, gendered behavior norms are such that in certain contexts, violence is socially reinforced for males, whereas it is inconsistent with femininity and socially discouraged in virtually all contexts among females. As such, violent crime as a uniquely masculine pursuit makes sense, because it is clearly inconsistent with "doing femininity."

However, to explain crime as "doing masculinity" is to make of gender a blunt instrument that leaves much female crime unexplained. Miller (1998) argues that female offenders also "do gender" when they engage in crime—even violent crimes such as robbery. Her qualitative study clarifies how gender shapes the enactment of robbery by males and females, even where their motives are the same. Males typically target other males, and their robberies involve direct

confrontation, physical violence, and guns. Females, on the other hand, most often target other females, and their violence seldom involves guns. When women do rob men, they may carry a gun, but they are more likely to soften the target with sex than with actual violence. Miller concludes that male and female robbery may be triggered by similar social and cultural factors, but that gender shapes the actual manner in which those robberies are enacted.

The implication that the processes leading to male and female offending are similar but that the content of their offending is significantly different is also evident in the theoretical framework presented by Broidy and Agnew (1997). They propose an extension of Agnew's general strain theory (1992; see Chapter 13, this volume) to explain individual-level gender differences in responses to strain and stress. For both males and females, crime results when individuals lack the legitimate coping strategies to deal effectively with strain and the negative emotions it engenders.

According to Broidy and Agnew, the similarity ends there, for the dynamics of gender shape both the types of strains males and females are exposed to and the emotional and behavioral responses available to them, thus leading to distinct outcomes. Whereas aggressive, externalizing behavioral responses are available to males in various environments, such responses are less commonly available to females (Harris, 1977; Cloward and Piven, 1979). Therefore, female responses to strain are more likely to be nonaggressive and/or self-destructive. Further, these sex differences in outcomes result not simply from sex differences in behavioral expectations but in the nature and form of stress males and females experience. Broidy and Agnew note that, whereas male stress/strain typically results in competitive interactions and environments, female strains more commonly emerge in interpersonal interactions and environments.

The biosocial approach of Caspi et al. (1993) provides still another view of how gender shapes the patterns of female and male offending. Their model highlights the relationship between biological changes associated with puberty and the social environments in which these changes occur and how this relationship affects female delinquency. They argue that early puberty is socially stressful for girls and note that the early onset of menarche "disrupts previously existing social equilibria and presents the adolescent girl with an ambiguous, novel, and uncertain event to which she must now respond" (p. 20). Girls' responses to these physical changes, they argue, are shaped by social and contextual factors, particularly in the environment of school, where peer affiliations are formed.

Caspi et al. (1993) hypothesize that early maturing girls in mixed-sex school environments will be at higher risk for delinquency than their counterparts in same-sex schools or than girls who follow normative maturation processes. Their findings support their hypotheses, indicating a link between early maturity and delinquency that is enhanced in mixed-sex school environments via association with older delinquent male peers. The implication is that early maturation is especially stressful for girls because it changes the nature of their social interaction, especially with males.

The different strains faced by females are further clarified by Chesney-Lind (1997) in her depiction of the differential impact of gender dynamics on the lives and experiences of boys and girls growing up in similar neighborhood and school environments. Specifically, gender-based socialization patterns set the stage for the sexual victimization and harassment of girls. It is this victimization that triggers girls' entry into delinquency as they try to escape abusive environments. Chesney-Lind argues that girls attempting to run away from abuse often end up in the streets with few legitimate survival options, so that they come to see crime and sexual exchange transactions as their only options for survival.

Gilfus's (1992) work supports this explanation of female crime as resulting from interpersonal victimization during both adolescence and adulthood. Gilfus describes a circular dynamic in which victimization places females at high risk for offending, which in turn puts them at risk for further victimization. This dynamic is especially problematic for minority and low-income women whose risks for both crime and victimization are already enhanced by limited access to resources (Arnold, 1995; Richie, 1995). Daly (1994) further substantiates the link between victimization and serious crime among women.

Hagan (1989; Hagan et al., 1987), through his power-control theory, integrates feminist, conflict, and control theories to explain both within- and between-sex differences in offending. Power-control theory accounts for the difference between male and female rates of delinquency by examining the interaction among family structure (patriarchal/egalitarian), class position, social control, and gender. A family's position in the class structure is hypothesized to influence socialization patterns along patriarchal or egalitarian lines. Socialization within the family generally imposes stronger controls on girls than boys, teaching girls to be risk-averse and boys to be risk-takers. This explains why boys are more likely to engage in offending, a risk-taking behavior. But the theory also suggests that this gender-based socialization and control is stronger in "patriarchal" than in "egalitarian" families, helping to explain within-sex differences in offending.

Whereas Hagan finds support for central power-control theory hypotheses, tests by other researchers have proved less supportive (Cernkovich and Giordano, 1987; Jensen and Thompson, 1990; Singer and Levine, 1988). Specifically, neither sex differences in parental control nor parental occupational categories help to account for the gender gap in delinquency.

A Gendered Theory of Female Offending and the Gender Gap

This chapter began by highlighting what we know about female crime and sex differences in offending on both the aggregate and individual level. We then explored the ability of traditional theories to account for these phenomena, noting that these theories help make sense of the general patterns noted in the data, but they cannot account for the more subtle dynamics that underlie these patterns. More recent structural and individual-level explanations of the gender gap and female offending show promise, but as yet remain fragmented and poorly integrated.

Steffensmeier and Allan (1995, 1996) provide the most ambitious attempt to build a unified theoretical framework for explaining female criminality and gender differences in crime. We take the position that a gendered theory can advance our knowledge not only of female crime but of male crime as well (although this chapter focuses on female crime). A gendered theory is quite different from gender-specific theories that propose causal patterns for female crime that are distinctly different from theories of male crime.

Rather, both female and male crime may be better understood by taking into account the ways in which the continued profound differences between the lives of women and men

shape the different patterns of female and male offending. The traditional theories shed little light on the specific ways in which gender differences in the type, frequency, and context of criminal behavior are shaped by differences in the lives of men and women.

Gender differences in crime may be better understood by taking into account gender differences in at least four key elements:

1. The organization of gender (differences in norms, moral development, social control, and affiliative tendencies, as well as reproductive, sexual, and other physical differences)

2. Access to criminal opportunity (underworld sexism, differences in access to skills, crime associates, and settings)

3. Motivation for crime (differences in taste for risk, self-control, costs-benefits, stressful events, and relational concerns)

4. The context of offending (differences in the circumstances of particular offenses, such as setting, victim–offender relationship, use of weapons)

We elaborate on each of these four areas below. Figure 4.1 provides a graphic depiction of how these elements interact to mold gender differences in crime.

The Organization of Gender We use the term "organization of gender" to refer broadly to many areas of social life that differ markedly by gender. Coupled with differences in physical and sexual characteristics, the organization of gender blunts the probability of crime on the part of women but increases that probability for men.

At least five areas of life tend not only to inhibit female crime and encourage male crime, but also to shape the patterns of female

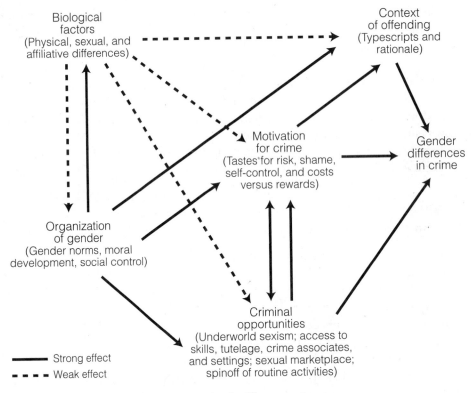

FIGURE 4.1 Gendered model of female offending and gender differences in crime.

offending that do occur: gender norms, moral development and affiliative concerns, social control, physical strength and aggression, and sexuality. These five areas overlap and mutually reinforce one another. They also condition gender differences in motivations, criminal opportunities, and contexts of offending.

Gender Norms Female criminality is inhibited by two powerful focal concerns ascribed to women: (1) role obligations and the presumption of female nurturance; (2) expectations of female beauty and sexual virtue. Such focal concerns pose constraints on female opportunities for illicit endeavors. Women, much more than men, are rewarded for building and maintaining rela-

tionships and for nurturance of family, and the constraints posed by child-rearing responsibilities are obvious. Moreover, female identity often derives from that of the males in their lives. If those males are conventional, female deviance is restrained. On the other hand, derivative identity may also push females into the roles of accomplices of husbands or boyfriends with criminal involvements.

Femininity stereotypes are the antithesis of those qualities valued in the criminal subculture (Steffensmeier, 1986), and crime is almost always more destructive of life chances for females than for males. The cleavage between what is considered feminine and what is criminal is sharp—crime is almost always stigmatizing for females—whereas the dividing line between what is considered masculine and what is criminal is often thin. Whether women actually conform to femininity stereotypes is irrelevant. Male acceptance of such stereotypes limits female access to underworld opportunities by virtue of being subjected to greater supervision by conventional parents and husbands as well as by criminal devaluation of females as potential colleagues.

Female internalization of the same stereotypes heightens fear of sexual victimization and reduces female exposure to criminal opportunity through avoidance of bars, nighttime streets, and other crime-likely locations (McCarthy and Hagan, 1992; Steffensmeier, 1983). Expectations of female sexuality also shape the deviant roles available to women, such as sexual media or service roles.

Moral Development and Affiliative Concerns Compared with men, women are more likely to refrain from crime due to concern for others. This may result from gender differences in moral development (Gilligan, 1982) and from socialization toward greater empathy, sensitivity to the needs of others, and fear of separation from loved ones. From an early age females are encouraged to cultivate interpersonal skills that will prepare them for their roles as wives and mothers (Beutel and Marini, 1995; Broidy, 1985; Rossi, 1984).

This predisposition toward an "ethic of care" restrains women from violence and other behavior that may injure others or cause emotional hurt to those they love. Such complex concerns also influence the patterns and contexts of crime when women do offend. Men, on the other hand, are more socialized toward status-seeking behavior. When they feel those efforts are blocked, they may develop an amoral ethic in which the ends justify the means. The likelihood of aggressive criminality is especially heightened among men who have been marginalized from the world of work, but such individuals may be found in the suites as well as on the streets. Their view of the world becomes one in which "people are at each other's throats increasingly in a game of life that has no moral rules" (Messerschmidt, 1986: 66).

Social Control The ability and willingness of women to commit crime is powerfully constrained by social control. Particularly during their formative years, females are more closely supervised and their misbehavior discouraged through negative sanctions. Risk-taking behavior that is rewarded among boys is censured among girls. Girls' associates are more carefully monitored, reducing the potential for influence by delinquent peers (Giordano et al., 1986), whereas attachments to conventional peers and adults are nurtured. Even as adults, women find their freedom to explore worldly temptations constricted (Collins, 1992).

Physical Strength and Aggression The weakness of women relative to men—whether real or perceived—puts them at a disadvantage in a criminal underworld that puts a premium on physical power and violence. Muscle and physical prowess are functional not only for committing crimes, but also for protection, contract enforcement, and recruitment and management of reliable associations.

Females may be perceived by themselves or by others as lacking the violent potential for successful completion of certain types of crime, or for protection of a major "score." This can help account for the less serious and less frequent nature of female crime. Female criminals sometimes deliberately restrict themselves to hustling small amounts of money in order not to attract predators. Perceived vulnerability can also help explain female offending patterns such as women's greater restriction to roles as solo players, or to dependent roles as subordinate accomplices, as in the exigencies of prostitute-pimp dependency (James, 1977).

Sexuality Reproductive-sexual differences, coupled with the traditional "double standard," contribute to higher male rates of sexual deviance and infidelity. They also reinforce the gender differences in social control described above. On the other hand, the demand for illicit sex creates opportunities for women for criminal gain through prostitution. This in turn may reduce the need for women to seek financial returns through serious property crimes, which remain a disproportionately male realm.

At the same time that male stereotypes of female sexuality open certain criminal opportunities for women, within criminal groups these same stereotypes close opportunities for women that are not organized around female attributes. The sexual tensions that may be aroused by the presence of a woman in a criminal group may force her to protect herself through sexual alignment with one man, becoming "his woman."

Despite our reference to prostitution as a criminal opportunity that women may exploit, it is of course a criminal enterprise that is controlled by men. Pimps, clients, police, businessmen who employ prostitutes: All control in various ways the working conditions of prostitutes, and virtually all are men.

Access to Criminal Opportunity All the above factors contrive to limit female access to criminal opportunity and to shape the patterns of female crime. Limits on female access to legitimate opportunities put further constraints on their criminal opportunities, because women are less likely to hold jobs—such as truck driver, dockworker, or carpenter—that would provide opportunities for theft, drug dealing, fencing, or other illegal activities. In contrast, abundant opportunities exist for women to commit and/or to be caught and arrested for petty forms of theft and fraud, for low-level drug dealing, and for sex-for-sale offenses.

Like the upperworld, the underworld has its glass ceiling. The scarcity of women in the top ranks of business and politics limits their chance for involvement in price-fixing conspiracies, financial fraud, and corruption. If anything, women face even greater occupational segregation in underworld crime groups—whether syndicates or more loosely structured organizations (Steffensmeier, 1983; Pennsylvania Crime Commission, 1991). Just as in the legitimate world, women face discrimination at every stage from selection and recruitment to opportunities for mentoring, skill development, and, especially, rewards.

Motivation The same factors that restrict criminal opportunities for women also limit the subjective willingness of women to engage in crime. Gender norms, social control, lack of strength, and moral and relational concerns all contribute to gender differences in criminal motivation: tastes for risk, likelihood of shame, level of self-control, and assessment of costs and benefits of crime.

Although motivation is different from opportunity, opportunity can amplify motivation. Being able tends to make one more willing. The opposite is also true. Female as well as male offenders tend to be drawn to those criminal activities that are easy, within their skill repertoire, a good payoff, and low risk. Women have risk-taking preferences and styles that differ from those of men (Hagan, 1989; Steffensmeier,

1980; Steffensmeier and Allan, 1995). Men will take risks in order to build status or gain competitive advantage, whereas women may take greater risks to protect loved ones or to sustain relationships. The overall level of criminal motivation is suppressed in women by their greater ability to foresee threats to life chances and by the relative unavailability of female criminal typescripts that could channel their behavior.

Context of Offending Female and male offending patterns differ profoundly in their contexts. "Context" refers to the circumstances and characteristics of a particular criminal act (Triplett and Myers, 1995), such as the setting, presence of other offenders, the relationship between offender and victim, the offender's role in initiating and committing the offense, weapon (if any), the level of injury or property loss/destruction, and purpose of the offense. Even when the same offense is charged, the "gestalt" of offending is often dramatically different for females and males (Daly, 1994; Steffensmeier, 1983, 1993). Moreover, female/male contextual differences increase with the seriousness of the offense.

Spousal murders provide a striking example of the importance of context. The proposition that wives have as great a potential for violence as husbands has had some currency among criminologists (Steinmetz and Lucca, 1988; Straus and Gelles, 1990). Although in recent years husbands have constituted only about one-fourth of spousal victims, the female share of offending has approached one-half in earlier decades. But, as Dobash et al. (1992) observe, the context of spousal violence differs dramatically for wives and husbands. Wives are far more likely to have been victims and turn to murder only when in mortal fear, after exhausting alternatives. Husbands who murder wives, however, have rarely been in fear for their lives. Rather, they are more likely to be motivated by rage at suspected infidelity, and the murder often culminates a period of prolonged abuse of their wives. Some patterns of wife-killing are almost never found when wives kill husbands: murder-suicides, family massacres, and stalking.

Another area where female prevalence often approximates that of males is in common forms of delinquency such as simple theft or assault. Here again we find important contextual differences: Girls are far less likely to use a weapon or intend serious injury (Kruttschnitt, 1994), to steal things they cannot use (Cohen, 1966), or to break into buildings or steal from building sites (Mawby, 1980). Similarly, with traditional male crimes like burglary, females are less likely to be solitary (Decker et al., 1993), more likely to be an accomplice, and less likely to share equally in the rewards (Steffensmeier and Terry, 1986). Females more often engage in burglaries that are unplanned, in residences where they have been before as maid or friend but where no one is at home (Steffensmeier, 1986, 1993).

Utility of Gendered Perspective

The real test of any approach is its ability to predict and explain female (and male) offending patterns as well as gender differences in crime. In general, the perspective correctly predicts that female participation is highest for those crimes that are most consistent with traditional gender norms and for which females have greater opportunity, and lowest for those crimes that diverge the most from traditional norms and for which females have little opportunity. The potential contributions of this gendered approach can be illustrated with examples of property, violent, and public order offending patterns.

Among property crimes, two offenses that are consistent with the traditional female roles of family shopping include shoplifting, misuse of credit cards, and bad checks, categories (larceny, fraud, forgery) for which the percent of female arrests is very high. The pink collar ghetto—the high concentration (90 percent) of women in low-level bank teller and bookkeeping positions—helps account for the high female percent of arrests for embezzlement. Embezzlement arrests are less likely to occur among higher-level accountants or auditors where women are less represented in employment (less than half). The perspective also correctly predicts gender differences in motives for embezzlement: Women tend to embezzle to protect their families or relationships, whereas men are more often trying to protect their status (Zeitz, 1981).

A gendered approach also correctly predicts the low level of female involvement in serious property crimes, whether on the streets or in the suites (Steffensmeier and Allan, 1995). Such crimes are most at odds with female stereotypes and/or present few opportunities for female participation. When women do engage in such crimes, the take is likely to be small, or they are acting as accomplices (as is the case with female burglaries, described above). Solo robberies by women typically involve small sums, such as wallet-sized thefts by prostitutes or addicts (James, 1977; see also Covington, 1985; Pettiway, 1987). As accomplices, female roles in robberies often simultaneously exploit their sexuality (e.g., as decoys) and reinforce male domination (American Correctional Association, 1983; Miller, 1986; Steffensmeier and Terry, 1986).

Lack of opportunity helps explain the negligible female involvement in serious white collar crime (Daly 1989; Steffensmeier, 1983). Female representation in high-level finance, corporate leadership, and politics is simply too limited to provide much chance for women to become involved in insider trading, price-fixing, restraint of trade, toxic waste dumping, fraudulent product production, bribery, official corruption, or large-scale governmental crimes. In lower-level occupations, even where women have the criminal opportunities, they are less likely to commit crime.

Our discussion earlier of gender differences in spousal murders provides an example of how our gendered approach can advance the understanding of female violence. Other forms of female violence are also shaped by the organization of gender. Female violence is less likely to be directed at strangers, and female murders of strangers or even casual acquaintances are rare. Victims of women are likely to be either a male intimate or a child. Furthermore, violent women are likely to commit their offenses within the home against a drunk victim, and they frequently cite self-defense or depression as their motive (Dobash et al., 1992). Women appear to require greater provocation to reach the point where they are willing to commit murder.

In the area of public order offenses, the gendered paradigm can predict with considerable accuracy those categories with a high percent of female involvement, particularly prostitution and juvenile runaways, the only categories where the rate of female arrests exceeds that of males. These are easily accounted for by gender differences in the marketability of sexual services and the patriarchal double standard. For example, customers must greatly outnumber prostitutes, yet they are less likely to be sanctioned. Similarly, concerns about sexual involvement increase the probability of arrest for female runaways, even though self-report data show that actual male runaway rates are just as high (Chesney-Lind and Shelden, 1992).

The organization of gender also shapes gender differences in substance abuse. The importance of relational concerns are reflected in the fact that women are often introduced to drugs by husbands or boyfriends (Inciardi et al., 1993; Pettiway, 1987). To the extent that females are integrated into drug subcultures or the underworld, it is more often through their male partners (Department of Health and Human Services, 1984). Because women typically are less likely to have other criminal involvements prior to addiction, the crime amplification effects are greater in terms of being driven to theft or other income-generating crimes by the need for money to purchase drugs. As the paradigm would predict, female addict crimes are likely to be nonviolent (Anglin et al., 1987).

Although we have concentrated on demonstrating the utility of a gendered paradigm in explaining female crime, it can do the same for male crime. For example, violence draws on and affirms masculinity, just as prostitution draws on and affirms femininity. For both men and women, "doing gender" can direct criminal behavior into scripted paths (although for women it more often preempts criminal involvement altogether).

As both women and men move increasingly into nontraditional roles, it will be difficult to predict the impact on levels and types of criminal involvement. Because traditional female stereotypes appear to constrain most women from crime, some have been tempted to predict that female crime rates would increase to the level of male crime rates as women's roles become more like those of men. However, entrapment in traditional roles may actually increase the likelihood of criminal involvement for some women. For example, it is wives playing traditional roles in patriarchal relationships who appear to be at greatest risk not just for victimization but also for committing spousal homicide. Similarly, emotionally dependent women

are more easily persuaded by criminal men to "do it all for love." Among Gypsies, where traditional gender roles prevail and male dominance is absolute, Gypsy women do practically all the work and earn most of the money, and the culture dictates a large female-to-male involvement in thievery (Maas, 1973).

Summary

Our knowledge about fundamental issues in the study of gender and crime has expanded greatly with the proliferation of studies over the past several decades, although significant gaps still exist. Our coverage of patterns and explanations of female offending has necessarily been selective and brief. We conclude by restating and enlarging on some key points.

Women are far less likely than men to be involved in serious crime, regardless of data source, level of involvement, or measure of participation. Female offenders tend to commit ordinary crimes—mostly minor thefts and frauds, low-level drug dealing, prostitution, and simple assaults against their mates or children. They are likely to have at least one adult conviction for theft, prostitution, or drug/alcohol involvement but return to further crime commission afterward. Some commit crime over several years and serve multiple jail or prison terms in the process. But they are not career criminals.

Often, the lives of women offenders are intertwined with those of men who are not career criminals so much as career "losers"—thieves or small-time hustlers. Along with their children, these men are the principal focus of such women's lives. The world of these men tends to be an extremely patriarchal one in which women are relegated to subordinate roles. Exploited or treated with indifference by their male partners, the women lead lives filled with misery, daily difficulties, and casual humiliations. They are routinely left to cope with the consequences of unsuccessful escapades by their men, along with the periods of incarceration these can bring.

Despite admitted progress made by the women's movement, the majority of women—offenders and non-offenders alike—continue to live lives that are limited and channeled by traditional gender norms and expectations:

The World of Work Though increasingly represented in the labor force, women continue to be concentrated in traditional "pink collar" occupations such as teaching, clerical and retail sales work, nursing, and other subordinate and helpmate roles, roles that reflect a persistence of traditional gender roles. In fact, the number of occupations that are filled largely or exclusively by women—nearly always at lower salaries than "male" occupations—has actually increased in recent years.

Gender Role Stereotypes There has been little change over the past several decades in gender-typing in children's play activities and play groups (Fagot and Leinbach, 1983; Stoneman et al., 1984; Maccoby, 1985); in the kinds of personality characteristics that both men and women associate with each sex (Leuptow and Garovich, 1992; Simmons and Blyth, 1987); in the importance placed on the physical attractiveness of women and their pressure to conform to an ideal of beauty or "femininity" (Leuptow and Garovich, 1992; Mazur, 1986); in risk-taking preferences and value orientations toward competition versus cooperation, and so forth (Beutel and Marini, 1995).

Women's Roles As Caregivers The most significant evidence, perhaps, that core elements of gender roles and relationships have changed little is the continuing dominance of women as "care takers"—for the sick, elderly parents, children, and so forth. At the group level, women today are more responsible for child rearing than 2–3 decades ago. The "degendering" of family roles—in which fathers and mothers share breadwinning and caregiving roles equally—has not gone smoothly. Men have increased their participation in child care over the last 30 years, but the amount of change has been small (Coltrane, 1995; Amato, 1996). A more significant trend is the rise in single-mother households (due to increases in divorce and non-marital birth), which has reduced the amount of time that men spend living with children over the life course (Eggebeen and Uhlenberg, 1985). Furthermore, many nonresident fathers see their children infrequently and pay no child support or less than they should (Seltzer and Bianchi, 1988). A recent review of the research in the area concludes, "Increasingly, American children are being raised with little or no assistance from fathers. These changes in behavior and family structure have led to a contradictory situation: At a time when some men are becoming more involved with children, men (as a group) are spending less time with children than ever before" (Amato, 1996: 2).

Similarly, a growing body of historical research indicates that the gender differences in quality and quantity of crime described here closely parallel those that have prevailed since at least the thirteenth century (Beattie, 1975; Hanawalt, 1979). Even where variability does exist across time, the evidence suggests that changes in the female percentage of offending (1) are limited mainly to minor property crimes or mild forms of delinquency (Steffensmeier, 1980, 1993) and (2) are due, not to more equalitarian gender roles, but to structural changes such as shifts in economic marginality of women, expanded availability of female-type crime opportunities, and greater formalization of social control (Beattie, 1995; Steffensmeier, 1993). The considerable stability in the gender gap for offending can be explained in part by historical durability of the organization of gender (Walby, 1990) and by underlying physical/sexual differences (whether actual or perceived). Human groups, for all their cultural variation, follow basic human forms.

A gendered perspective has implications both for understanding the nature of female offending and for developing female offender programs. Both theory and programmatic approaches to female offenders should include certain key elements. The first is the need to take into account how the organization of gender deters or shapes delinquency by females but encourages it by males. We use the term "organization of gender" to refer broadly to gendered norms, identities, arrangements, institutions, and relations by which human sexual dichotomy is transformed into something physically and socially different.

The second is the need to address not only gender differences in type and frequency of crime, but also differences in the context of offending. Even when men and women commit the same statutory offense, the gestalt of their offending is frequently quite different (Daly, 1994). The differing gestalt of female offending (and its link to the organization of gender) was reviewed earlier but is further reflected in this comment from an ex-female offender who now works in a drug treatment program for "serious" female offenders:

A lotta what is called "serious" crime that is committed by women is hardly that. The other day two women were referred

because they were busted for armed robbery. What happened is, they were shoplifting and had a guy as a partner. The security person spotted them and confronted them as they is [sic] leaving the store. This causes the guy partner to spray the security man with mace. They all get away but not before the security man gets the license number of the van they is driving. They all gets arrested—not for shoplifting now but for armed robbery on account of the mace.

What female robbery there is, is because a guy has them be a distraction or the watcher. Or it's a prostitute who maybe steals from a john, or it's a woman so heavy into dope that she crosses the line. I did a couple of robberies when I was heavy into drugs but it was not my thing. Selling dope, shoplifting, and prostitution were my main activities. This goes for most of the women I've known who get involved in crime on account of having to support themselves or their kids or some sponge [male] they is hooked up with (Steffensmeier and Allan, 1998: 11).

Finally, theory and programmatic approaches to female offending need to address several key ways in which women's routes to crime (especially serious crime) may differ from those of men. Building on the work of Daly (1994) and Steffensmeier (1983, 1993), such differences include (1) the more blurred boundaries between victim and victimization in women's rather than in men's case histories; (2) women's exclusion from most lucrative crime opportunities; (3) women's ability to exploit sex as an illegal moneymaking service; (4) consequences (real or anticipated) of motherhood and child care; (5) the centrality of greater relational concerns among women and the manner in which these both shape and allow women to be pulled into criminal involvements by men in their lives; (6) the frequent need of these women for protection from predatory or exploitative males.

In sum, recent theory and research on female offending have added greatly to our understanding of how the lives of delinquent girls and women continue to be powerfully influenced by gender-related conditions of life. Profound sensitivity to these conditions is the bedrock for preventive and remedial programs aimed at female offenders.

AGE AND CRIME

We turn now from the link between gender and crime to that between age and crime. Of all the factors associated with crime, the impact of age on criminal involvement is one of the strongest. The view that involvement in crime diminishes with age is one of the oldest and most widely accepted in criminology. For most forms of crime, but especially for those designated in most societies "serious" crimes (murder, rape, assault, robbery), the proportion of the population involved in crime tends to peak in adolescence or early adulthood and then decline with age. This pattern is common to most age–crime distributions across historical periods, geographic locations, and crime types. This relative consistency has led Hirschi and Gottfredson (1983) to make the controversial claim that the age–crime relationship is universal and invariant. Of course, the teenage-to-young-adult years (from early teens to about age 30) encompass a substantial segment of the life span, and as we will show, there is in fact considerable variation among offenses and across historical periods in the parameters of the age–crime curve (for example, peak age, median age, rate of de-

cline from peak age) across this fifteen- to twenty-year age span. A claim of "invariancy" in the age–crime relationship therefore overstates the case (Steffensmeier et al., 1989).

Investigators of the age–crime relationship have tended to focus on crimes against persons and property that are included in the FBI Crime Index (Hirschi and Gottfredson, 1983; Steffensmeier et al., 1989). There is general agreement that involvement in Index crimes—that is, conventional or "garden variety" offenses—is most widespread among teenage and young adult males, and that most of these persons disengage from lawbreaking after a relatively short career in crime. However, although the population-wide age–crime curves conform generally to the pattern just described, certain crimes have somewhat older peak ages and a more gradual decline in rates for older age groups—particularly for a number of crime categories not included in the Crime Index. Variations in the age–crime pattern are also found for different population groups, cultures, and historical periods.

To a large extent, variations in societal age–crime patterns reflect patterns of age-stratified inequality. Age is a potent mediator of inequality in both the legitimate and illegitimate opportunity structures of society. Just as the low-wage, dead-end jobs of the legitimate economy are disproportionately held by the young, so too are high-risk, low-yield crimes committed disproportionately by the young. At the opposite end of the opportunity scale, because it is rare to find them in positions of power and influence in business or politics, young people are unlikely to score big in the world of white collar crime or in the lucrative rackets of organized crime.

We begin our discussion of age and crime by looking at the most common societal pattern, whereby conventional crimes are dominated by casual youth offenders, and we discuss factors associated with early entrance and exit. Next we examine ways in which societal age–crime patterns vary by crime type, by race, and across cultures and over time. Then we turn to the issue of individual age–crime patterns, with a consideration of criminal career patterns of more serious offenders, factors associated with their longer persistence in crime and eventual exit, and patterns and trends in both offending and victimization among older age groups in the population. This is followed by a consideration of the impact of age structure and cohort size on societal crime rates. We conclude the chapter with a brief look at the intersection of age and sex differences in crime.

National Age–Crime Statistics

The peak age (the age group with the highest age-specific arrest rate) is younger than 25 for all crimes (except gambling) as reported in the FBI's UCR program, and rates begin to decline in the teenage years for more than half. In fact, even the median age (50 percent of all arrests occurring among younger persons) is younger than 30 for most crimes. In general, the younger age distributions (median ages in the teens or early twenties) are found for ordinary property crimes like burglary, larceny, arson, and vandalism and for liquor and drug violations. Personal crimes like aggravated assault and homicide tend to have somewhat older age distributions (median ages in the late twenties), as do some of the public order offenses, public drunkenness, driving under the influence, and certain of the property crimes that juveniles have less opportunity to commit, like embezzlement, fraud, and gambling (median ages in late twenties or thirties). Contrasts in the shape of the age distribution for different property crimes are depicted in Figure 4.2.

Although young people obviously account for a disproportionate share of arrests, official statistics may not provide a completely accurate picture of the participation in crime by different age groups. Because a relatively small proportion of crimes results in an arrest, it is possible that arrest statistics either overrepresent the young (young offenders may be easier to apprehend) or underrepresent them (law enforcement may be more lenient in the handling of youths). Other data sources can supplement our picture of the age–crime relationship.

Using data supplied by victims of crime as reported by the NCVS for the years 1973–1977, Hindelang (1981) examined the perceived age of offenders for crimes such as rape, robbery, and assault, and for certain property crimes, such as purse snatching, in which the offender was seen. Taking into account some uncertainty in victims' estimates of the age of an offender, the NCVS data paralleled the UCR arrest data fairly closely. The highest rates of offending were for those age 18–20, followed by those age 12–17. The lowest rates were for those over the age of 20.

On the other hand, according to Hindelang, although juveniles were responsible for a large proportion of the total number of crimes, they were relatively less involved than adults in serious crime, as measured by weapons use, by completion of theft, and by the size of financial loss. Nevertheless, victims were more likely to be injured by juvenile felons than by adult felons, probably because juveniles' reduced access to weapons necessitated greater use of force. Juveniles were also more likely than adults to commit their crimes in groups (thereby inflating juvenile arrest statistics); further, judging from the small monetary gains, juveniles appear to be motivated by peer pressure or sheer adventurousness more than by financial considerations.

FIGURE 4.2
1990 age curves for burglary, fraud, and gambling*

SOURCE: Adapted from Uniform Crime Reports arrest data (U.S. Dept. of Justice).

*Data averaged over 1989–1991.

†Percentage of arrests adjusted for population size of each group.

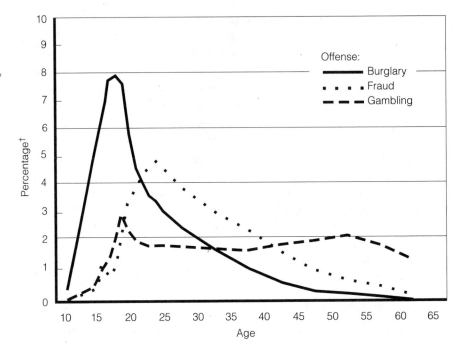

Except for crimes like purse snatching, where juveniles may select older persons as "easy targets," victims are generally from the same age group as offenders.

Self-report studies of delinquency and of adult criminality also show a general decline in rates of offending following a peak in midadolescence to young adulthood, corroborating the results reported from official data such as the UCR (Rowe and Tittle, 1977; Elliott et al., 1983).

Explaining the Youthful Peak in Offending

Rates of offending rise rapidly from preteen to teenage years, as, barred from integrating themselves into the world of adulthood, teens suddenly are faced with major sources of reinforcement for offending: money; status; power; autonomy; identity claims; strong sensate experiences stemming from sex, natural adrenaline highs, or highs from illegal substances; and peers who similarly value independence or even defiance of conventional morality. Further, their dependent status as juveniles insulates teens from many of the social and legal costs of illegitimate activities, and their stage of cognitive development limits prudence concerning the consequences of their behavior. At the same time, they possess the physical prowess required to commit crimes.

Social Factors Those adolescents most at risk are those whose occupational or "life" goals are least well developed, or whose poor social or intellectual skills place them at a disadvantage. Differences in the availability of employment help explain cross-sectional variation in juvenile arrest rates for property crimes, suggesting that jobs and petty theft constitute alternative sources of status, cash, consumer goods, and other needs of juveniles (Allan and Steffensmeier, 1989).

Involvement with drinking and kindred deviance may combine with economic and social disadvantages to facilitate the drift into delinquency. Nevertheless, a certain amount of misbehavior seems to be natural to youth; as Jolin and Gibbons (1987: 238) point out, much youthful lawbreaking is simply a stage of growing up.

As young people move into adulthood, or anticipate entering it, most find their bonds to society strengthening, with expanded access to work or further education and increased interest in establishing permanent relationships and settling down. Sampson and Laub (1990) report that job stability and strong marital attachment have important social control effects in reducing adult criminal behavior among both those with and those without official records of juvenile delinquency. Improved access to legal means of satisfying needs, along with greater maturity in setting personal goals, coincides with the more severe criminal penalties confronting those just entering adulthood. All these factors help account for the rapid drop-off in age-specific arrest rates during the transition to adulthood.

The transition also involves changes in behavioral expectations as well as in peer associations and lifestyle routines that diminish the opportunities for committing many common street offenses. Warr (1993), using panel data from the National Youth Survey, demonstrates how changes in peer associations during the late teens and the early twenties parallel the sharp decline in self-reported delinquent activity that occurs during this period of life. In fact, Warr reports that age effects on self-reported delinquency are reduced to nonsignificance once controls on peer influences are introduced.

However, for a relatively small proportion of young adults, the "American dream" of a good job and stable family life may be (or may seem to be) unattainable, and for them the rejection of illegitimate activities may be delayed. This is especially likely for those with minority status or with extensive official records of juvenile crime, for whom social bonds will have been weakened and deviant identities confirmed by repeated exposure to the justice system. Deviance amplification for those carrying a legal stigma—especially if they are also low income or from minority backgrounds—will be heightened in regions with weak labor markets, where jobs (if any) available to those with records are mainly low-wage or part-time (Allan and Steffensmeier, 1989), providing only limited alternatives to continued criminal involvement (Sullivan, 1989).

Hagan (1991: 579) reports class differences in subculture adaptations that have important implications for whether youths desist from crime and move into normal adult roles. Specifically, middle-class youths are more likely to participate in a "party" subculture than an outright "delinquent" subculture, and even though this may entail a certain amount of illegal drinking, substance abuse, sex, and the like, this party subculture serves to "socialize non-working-class males to participate in the kinds of pursuits that are later a part of male-bounded social networks." Working-class males, on the other hand, show higher rates of participation in a delinquent subculture that has "negative effects on trajectories of early adult occupational attainment," although middle-class participants in the delinquent subculture seem to be "shielded from deleterious effects."

Cognitive Development Cognitive development theory can complement our understanding of youthful lawbreaking and subsequent withdrawal from criminality. Youthful delinquency may be seen as growing out of the egocentrism, hedonism, and sense of invincibility that characterize the early phases of formal thinking during adolescence (Piaget, 1932). As analytical and cognitive skills develop, the adolescent becomes aware not only of the differences between what juveniles and adults are allowed to do (for example, drink alcohol, have sex) and to have (for example, automobiles and money) but also of the different sets of rules that adults apply to their children and to themselves. When awareness of this "double standard" and the conspicuous nature of adult freedoms is combined with youthful egocentrism, a feeling of oppression at the hands of adults is virtually inevitable, providing a convenient rationale for misbehavior and rebellion.

Subsequent cognitive development leads to a gradual decline in egocentrism, and late adolescence is marked by movement away from self-absorption to a concern for others. Individuals become more accepting of social values, more comfortable in social relations, and more concerned with the meaning of life and their place in the scheme of things (Gove, 1985). The more mature adult personality thus comes to see the casual delinquencies of youth as childish or foolish.

Biological and Physiological Factors The contribution of biological or physiological variables also has been acknowledged explicitly in sociological theorizing about the age–crime relationship (Parmelee, 1918; Reckless, 1950). In a general sense, physical abilities, such as strength, speed, prowess, stamina, aggression, and muscle, are useful for successful commission of many crimes, for protection, for enforcing contracts, and for recruiting and managing reliable associates (for a review, see Steffensmeier, 1983). Although some crimes are more physically demanding than others, persistent involvement in crime, regardless of crime type, is likely to entail a lifestyle that is physically demanding and dangerous. Thus, with age, declining physical strength and energy may make crime too dangerous or unsuccessful, especially where there are younger or stronger criminal competitors who will not be cowed (Wilson and Herrnstein, 1985).

Nonetheless, although declining physical abilities help explain the lower rates of street crime among the middle-aged and elderly in comparison to young adults, the more important issue is whether changes in physical abilities help explain the abruptness of the decline in the age curve during the late teens that occurs in many of the ordinary crimes. Gove (1985) contends that males in their late twenties experience a relatively sharp decline in physical abilities that is largely responsible for the rapid decline in what he calls "substantial risk and/or physically demanding crimes" (for example, burglary, robbery) among persons in that age group. According to Gove (1985: 138), physical variables like strength and energy peak at the same time these kinds of crime peak and "suggest that their rapid decline is a major contribution to the rapid decline in deviant behavior. If this argument is correct, it would help to explain why the age–deviance relationship seems to be universal across societies and historic time."

However, the available evidence on "fitness" or biological aging is strongly at odds with this intriguing hypothesis. Specifically, the peak age for the high-risk and physically demanding crimes is much younger than the peak age for physical abilities. Further, physically undemanding crimes like larceny-theft and drug violations have the high peaks and rapid declines predicted by Gove for riskier endeavors.

The research literature on biological aging (see especially Shock, 1984) suggests that peak functioning is typically reached between the ages of 25 and 30 for those physical variables—strength, stamina, aerobic capacity, motor control, sensory perception, and speed of movement—plausibly assumed to affect one's ability to commit crimes. Although decline sets in shortly thereafter, it is not abrupt. Rather, the decline is gradual, almost imperceptible, until the mid-fifties or so, when there begins a steady decline throughout the final period of life (Shock, 1984). Other commonly mentioned physical variables like testosterone levels peak in early adulthood but then remain at peak level until at least the age of 50. In contrast, the age curves for crimes like robbery and burglary that presuppose the need for physical abilities do not peak in the mid-twenties as Gove implies; instead, they peak in midadolescence and then decline very rapidly. In short, although biological and physiological factors may contribute toward an understanding of the rapid increase in delinquent behavior during adolescence, neither can explain the abrupt decline in the age–crime curve following the peak age.

Social Status and Roles Only in the sphere of social statuses and roles do changes of corresponding abruptness occur. If young people may be thought of as a minority, it is a minority that suddenly moves into the majority on reaching adulthood. (It is pertinent to observe that the law refers to children as "minors," whereas the age at which young people become adults is referred to as the "age of majority.") For those in late adolescence or early adulthood (roughly age 17–22, the age group showing the sharpest decline in arrest rates for Index crimes), important changes occur in at least five major spheres of life:

1. Greater access to legitimate sources of material goods and excitement: jobs, credit, alcohol, sex, and so forth

2. Age-graded norms: externally, increased expectation of maturity and responsibility; internally, anticipation of assuming adult roles, coupled with reduced subjec-

tive acceptance of deviant roles and the threat they pose to entering adult status

3. Peer associations and lifestyle: reduced orientation to same-age–same-sex peers and increased orientation toward persons of the opposite sex or persons who are older or more mature

4. Increased legal and social costs for deviant behavior

5. New patterns of illegitimate opportunities: with the assumption of adult roles, opportunities increase for crimes (for example, gambling, fraud, and employee theft) that are less risky, more lucrative, or less likely to be reflected in official statistics

Over a three- to five-year period, starting around age 17, young people make the transition from relative dependence and discredited status to relative independence and higher status, from relative uselessness to taking on most of the rights and responsibilities of adulthood, and from not being taken seriously to confronting the strong social expectation that they will "settle down." Late adolescence is a time when young people take significant charge of their lives and make choices (often stressful ones) that will to a large extent shape the rest of the life course. Leaving school, finding employment, going to college, enlisting in the military, and getting married not only increase social integration, informal social control, and social expectations oriented to the standards of conventional society but also involve a change in peer associations and lifestyle routines that diminish the opportunities for committing these offenses. With the accumulation of material goods and the taking on of social statuses that depend on favorable reactions from others, the potential costs of legal and social sanctions increase—at the same time that the legal sanctions increase substantially. In brief, the motives and opportunities for low-yield or exploratory types of crime decline with the movement (real or anticipated) out of adolescence. (The parsimony of sociological theories in explaining the age–crime relationship is detailed in Tittle, 1988; Steffensmeier et al., 1989).

To complete this maturation process successfully, the availability of adequate employment at adequate wages is crucial. When the labor market for young adults is dominated by marginal jobs with low hours, low pay, high turnover, and limited benefits and opportunities for advancement, all the other goals of a conventional life—marriage, family, community involvement—become more difficult to attain, and the proportion of the population still attracted to illegitimate alternatives will be greater (Allan and Steffensmeier, 1989; McGahey, 1986).

Variations in the Age Curve by Crime Type

The factors that help account for the sharply peaked age curves for the more common crimes also help explain the flatter age curves found for other types of crimes. The offenses that show the youngest peaks and sharpest declines are crimes that fit the low-yield, criminal mischief, "hell-raising" category: vandalism, petty theft, robbery, arson, auto theft, burglary, and liquor law and drug violations. The high risks or low yields of such crimes reduce their attraction to maturing young adults with strengthening bonds to society and fewer sources of peer reinforcement for such behavior. However, some turn to offense categories that carry lower risks (or higher yields, greater opportunities, less public censure) for adults, such as gambling, alcohol consumption, certain types of fraud, and some types of violence.

Those offenses with flatter age curves are often those for which the structure of illegiti-mate opportunities changes rather than disappears with age. For example, some opportunities for fraud, such as falsification of identification to purchase alcohol or gain entry to adult establishments, exist for young people; but being too young to obtain credit, they lack the opportunities for common frauds such as passing bad checks, defrauding an innkeeper, or credit card forgery. Similarly, young people have more opportunities than do older people for some kinds of violence (for example, playground fights or gang violence) but less opportunity for other kinds of violence that stem from primary group conflicts (for example, spousal violence).

Older people may shift to less visible criminal roles such as bookie or fence. Or as a spinoff of legitimate roles, they may commit surreptitious crimes or crimes that, if discovered, are unlikely to be reported to the authorities, such as embezzlement, stock fraud, bribery, or price-fixing. Unfortunately, we know relatively little about the age distribution of persons who commit these and related lucrative crimes, but the fragmentary evidence that does exist suggests that they are likely to be middle age or older (Shapiro, 1984; Pennsylvania Crime Commission, 1991). An analysis of the age distribution of persons identified as major gambling and loansharking racketeers in the state of Pennsylvania for the 1980–1990 period provides partial confirmation that the age curves for lucrative crimes like racketeering or business crimes not only peak much later but tend to decline more slowly with age (Steffensmeier and Allan, 1993). Most gambling and loanshark kingpins are between their mid-forties and mid-sixties, with some continuing to practice their trade well into their seventies. Evidence suggests that other lucrative rackets in the underworld are also largely populated by older persons. Fences of stolen goods, for example, are typically middle-aged or older (Steffensmeier, 1986).

Still less is known of the age distribution of "respectable" or upperworld offenders who commit lucrative business crimes such as fraud, price-fixing, and bribery. Although data on the age distribution of such crimes are not plentiful, media reports typically include information on age of offenders in business crime cases that attract public attention. An analysis of data extracted from *New York Times* articles on profitable business crimes (defined here as those involving gains of $25,000 or more) during the period 1987–1990 reveals a preponderance of middle-aged or older offenders (Steffensmeier and Allan, 1993). The modal age falls between ages 40 and 50. In contrast, recall that juveniles constitute well over half of those arrested for conventional crimes like burglary or larceny. Of course, one would not expect youths to hold the types of legitimate positions that provide access to such criminal opportunities. But that is the point: The age-stratification of illegitimate opportunities parallels that for legitimate opportunities.

Minority Differences in the Age–Crime Curve

For African-American inner-city youths, the high level of youth inequality that characterizes modern societies is compounded by problems of racial discrimination that persist in our nation. They are less able to leave behind the inequality of youth status (Wilson, 1987). As they move into young adulthood, they continue to experience limited access to the adult labor market. An inequality perspective would predict that adult offending levels among African Americans would therefore continue at higher levels than among whites, and that the proportion of total African-American crime that is committed by African-American adults will be greater than the proportion of total white crime that is committed by white adults.

This hypothesis is supported by a comparison of the adult percent of property crime arrests (controlling for differences in juvenile and adult populations) for African Americans and whites (Steffensmeier and Allan, 1993). Across all crime categories, the adult percent of arrests (APA) is greater for African Americans than for whites, in some cases strongly so. African-American APA exceeds 50 percent for nine of ten property crime categories, whereas white APA exceeds 50 percent for only four categories. Significantly, those property crime categories for which the African-American APA is closest to the white APA are precisely those categories for which African Americans might be assumed to have less access to criminal opportunity: fraud, forgery, and embezzlement.

The greater probability of criminal careers continuing into adulthood for members of minorities is substantiated by Sullivan's (1989) case study research with New York street gangs. He reports that white, African-American, and Hispanic-American youth gangs all engage in property crime during their teens. But white gang members begin to drift away from the group and from delinquent activities during their late teens as they begin to move into jobs, often secured through family contacts. With African-American and Hispanic-American youth, however, the greater dearth of job opportunities delays desistance from delinquency.

Cross-Cultural and Historical Differences in the Age–Crime Curve

The relationship between age stratification and the steep rise and fall in the age curve for ordinary property crime is also supported by cross cultural and historical differences in the age–crime curve. If age inequality is indeed a major determinant of the skewed shape of that curve in contemporary society, then a flatter shape would be predicted for societies and for historical periods in which the culture provides for a smoother transition between the periods of youth and adulthood.

For example, in small preindustrial societies, the passage to adult status is relatively simple and continuous. Formal "rites of passage" at relatively early ages avoid much of the status ambiguity and role conflict that torment American adolescents. Youths often begin to assume responsible and economically productive roles well before they reach full physical maturity. It is not surprising, therefore, to find that such societies have significantly flatter and less skewed age–crime patterns (for a review, see Steffensmeier et al., 1989).

Much the same is true for earlier periods in the history of the United States and other industrial nations. The traditional school calendar, with its long summer vacations, testifies to the integral economic roles of youths when agriculture was the dominant economic activity of the nation and the help of young people was crucial to the harvesting of many crops. Youth economic productivity continued through the early years of industrialization when wages were so low that working-class children were expected to leave school at an early age and do their part in helping to support their families (Horan and Hargis, 1991). The responsible roles assumed by many youths in earlier periods forestalled the feelings of rebellion seen among contemporary teens who are isolated from truly productive roles within their families.

Although the stresses of adolescence have been noted since ancient times, it is also widely believed that social processes associated with the coming of industrialization and the postindustrial age have aggravated those stresses, resulting in increased levels of juvenile criminality in recent decades. The structure of modern societies, therefore, encourages crime and delinquency among the young because these societies "lack institutional procedures for moving people smoothly from protected childhood to autonomous adulthood" (Nettler, 1978: 241).

Because reliable age statistics on criminal involvement are not available over extended historical periods, we are limited largely to comparisons that cover only the past fifty years or so. An examination of UCR arrest data clearly shows that changes in the shape of the age curves across the 1940–1980 period are generally significant for nearly all offenses, whereas changes for the 1940–1960 period or the 1960–1980 period are significant mainly for the more youth-oriented offenses, such as ordinary property crimes and drinking and drug violations (Steffensmeier et al., 1989). Moreover, research comparing the criminality of recent birth cohorts with earlier ones finds that juveniles are more violent now than in the past. When a cohort of juveniles born in 1945 was compared with one born in 1958, Tracy et al. (1990) discovered a 300 percent increase in violent crime in the 1958 cohort (see also Shannon, 1988).

The shift toward a greater concentration of offending among the young may be due partly to changes in law enforcement procedures and data collection. Nevertheless, the likelihood that real changes have in fact occurred is supported by the consistency of the changes from 1940 to 1960 and from 1960 to 1980 and over nearly all offense types. Support for the conclusion that real change has taken place over the past century also is found in the age breakdown of U.S. prisoner statistics covering the years 1890 to 1980 (Steffensmeier et al., 1989). As with the UCR statistics, the prison statistics show that age curves are more peaked today than a century ago and that changes in the age–crime curve are gradual and can be detected only when a sufficiently large time frame is used.

Findings showing a general decline in peak age and a greater concentration of offending among adolescents today are consistent with the view that contemporary teenagers in industrialized nations are subject to greater status anxiety than in previous periods of history and that the transition from adolescence to adulthood is more turbulent now than in the past (Friday and Hage, 1976; Greenberg, 1977; Glaser, 1978). In the post–World War II period, there have been major changes in the family, in education, in the labor force, in the military, and in adolescence more generally (Clausen, 1986). In comparison to earlier eras, youths have had less access to responsible family roles, productive economic activity, and participation in community affairs. In response to this generational isolation, they have formed adolescent subcultures oriented toward consumption and hedonistic pursuits. The weakened social bonds and the reduced access to valued adult roles, along with accentuated subcultural influences, all combine to increase situationally induced pressures to obtain valued goods; display strength, daring, or loyalty to peers; or simply to "get kicks" (Gold, 1970; Briar and Piliavin, 1965).

CRIMINAL CAREERS

The youthful peak and rapid drop-off in offending that constitutes the most common societal pattern for conventional crimes is but one of a number of patterns identified when criminal careers are tracked for individual offenders. With respect to individual lawbreakers, Jolin and Gibbons (1987) describe four different age–crime patterns:

1. Early entry into lawbreaking, followed usually (but not always) by desistance from crime at a relatively early age, the common pattern described previously

2. "Career criminality," characterized by entry into lawbreaking during the teens or early twenties but with no withdrawal from crime until middle age

3. "Career criminals," who also begin offending at an early age and continue during adulthood but who do not cease offending at middle age

4. "Old first timers," whose initial involvement in crime does not occur until middle age or later

In large cities, as many as half of all males will experience police contacts for nontraffic offenses at some time during their lives. Although this is most likely to occur during adolescence, about half of all adult arrestees have had no juvenile arrests. Most individuals, particularly those with no juvenile police contacts, have very brief criminal "careers," with only one or two police contacts over the life span. On the other hand, a small proportion have numerous police contacts over an extended period of their lives (Tracy et al., 1990).

These career delinquents and career criminals account for a large proportion of all serious crime. In reference to sex differences, the research also shows that the female chronic offender is responsible for a larger proportion of all serious crime committed by females than is the case for her male counterpart (see Chapter 22). For now, it is important to note that the research on individual career criminals (for example, the juvenile chronic offender) shows that their age patterns differ in important ways from the age distribution for criminal conduct in the population at large (Blumstein et al., 1986). Rather than a pattern of declining involvement following a high frequency of criminal acts in late adolescence and young adulthood, the career criminal has a relatively constant high rate of involvement from adolescence through adult-hood, often not terminating until the late thir-ties or early forties, or older.

Generally, after the rise in criminal involve-ment during the teenage years, there is a high termination rate and relatively little recruitment into crime after age 20. Because large numbers of offenders terminate their careers quickly during the early "break-in" period, adult crimi-nal careers are reasonably short, averaging under six years for serious offenses. Relatively few of-fenders avoid these early high termination rates and remain active in criminal careers into their thirties, but those who do are the ones with the most enduring careers. Termination rates do be-gin to rise again at older ages, but not until after age 40 (Blumstein and Cohen, 1987).

Among the factors identified by cohort re-search as predictive of adult criminal careers are labor market difficulties and severity of juvenile disposition. As we noted, most juveniles "ma-ture out" of youthful delinquency when they are faced by age-graded expectations oriented toward more "adult" behavior and as they ac-quire greater stakes in conformity in the form of work, education, marriage, family, commu-nity involvement, and other adult responsibili-ties. However, those juveniles who have been stigmatized and perhaps alienated by severe ju-venile dispositions will be handicapped in en-tering the job market, particularly if they are additionally handicapped by poor education or minority status. If jobs are available to them at all, they are likely to be low-status, low-paying jobs that will not be adequate to support a fam-ily or to develop the stakes in conformity that can offset the attractions of illegal alternatives. Those who have been confined in institutions may be able to offset their limited legitimate opportunities with expanded criminal opportu-nities in the form of skills and contacts that can

be developed in such settings. As individuals be-come more committed to a criminal lifestyle, legitimate attachments become more remote. Thus, the age–crime curves of individual career criminals are much flatter, with a fairly constant high rate of offending until much later in life.

Retiring from a Life of Crime

What accounts for the fact that, ultimately, most persistent lawbreakers "burn out," often in spite of what correctional agencies do or do not do to them? Of course, some offenders simply die, and assuming that active criminals are more prone to injury and death, at older ages the population will increasingly consist of persons who are less willing or able to be criminally involved. The available evidence, however, indicates that with-drawal from crime usually occurs well before the offenders in question have become infirm or enfeebled. Thus, exiting from crime cannot be attributed simply to physical deterioration.

Empirical research suggests that exiting from a criminal career requires the acquisition of meaningful bonds to conventional people or institutions. Thieves leave a life of crime as they form attachments to a life of conformity and develop a reluctance to give up those new bonds by risking further imprisonment. One important tie to the conventional order is a job that seems to have the potential for advance-ment and that is seen as meaningful and eco-nomically rewarding. A good job shifts a crimi-nal's attention from the present to the future and provides a solid basis for the construction of a noncriminal identity. It also alters an individ-ual's daily routine in ways that make crime less likely (Meisenhelder, 1977; Shover, 1983).

Good personal relationships with conven-tional people such as a spouse, lover, children, or friends also create bonds to the social order that an individual wants to protect. These people may be "psychologically present" if the individual faces situations that offer a temptation to engage in criminal activity. Family members and lovers also provide a place of residence, food, and help in the development of everyday skills such as paying bills and scheduling time. Other bonds that may lead people away from crime include involvement in religion, sports, hobbies, or other activities (Irwin, 1970).

The development of social bonds may be coupled with cognitive factors that are triggered by a sort of burnout or belated deterrent effect as offenders grow tired of the hassles of repeated involvement with the criminal justice system. Offenders may come to regard the frequent traveling and other features of theft as overly burdensome. They may have violated the code of the underworld and be excluded from opportunities to work with "good" thieves. They may have experienced a long prison sentence that jolts them into quitting or that entails the loss of contacts that make the continuation of a criminal career difficult, if not impossible. Or inmates may develop a fear of dying in prison, especially given that repeated convictions yield longer sentences. Still other offenders may quit or "slow down" as they experience declining abilities and efficiency with increasing age, loss of "nerve," or sustained narcotics or alcohol use (Prus and Sharper, 1977; Adler and Adler, 1983; Steffensmeier, 1986).

Older Criminals

Although crime rates among older persons are relatively low, two patterns of offending can still be found: (1) those whose first criminal involvement occurs relatively late in life and (2) those who started crime at an early age and continue their involvement beyond the forties and fifties.

Interestingly, a fair number of previously law-abiding persons become involved in crime at an older age, particularly in shoplifting, homicide, and alcohol-related offenses. What evidence is available on first-time older offenders suggests that situational stress and lack of alternative opportunities play a primary role. The unanticipated loss of one's job or other disruptions of social ties can push some individuals into their first law violation at any age (Jolin and Gibbons, 1987; Alston, 1986).

Older offenders who persist in crime are more likely to belong to the criminal underworld. These individuals are relatively successful in their criminal activities or are extensively integrated into subcultural or family criminal enterprises. They seem to receive relational and psychic rewards (for example, pride in their expertise) as well as monetary rewards from lawbreaking and, as a result, see no need to withdraw from lawbreaking (Reynolds, 1953; Klockars, 1974; Steffensmeier, 1986). These older offenders are also unlikely to see many meaningful opportunities for themselves in the conventional or law-abiding world. Consequently, "the straight life" may have little to offer successful criminals, who will be more likely to persist in their criminality for an extended period. But they, too, eventually slow down as they grow tired of the cumulative aggravations and risks of criminal involvement or as they encounter the diminishing capacities associated with the aging process.

Finally, contrary to the assertion in some articles in the popular and social science press about a "geriatric crime wave," there has not been an increase in the frequency or severity of elderly crime per capita in recent decades (Steffensmeier, 1987). The proportionate involvement of the elderly in crime is about the same now as it was twenty-five to thirty years ago. When the elderly do break the law, moreover, their lawbreaking involves minor alcohol-related or theft offenses rather than serious crimes.

Effects of Age Structure on a Nation's Crime Rate

The dramatically higher age-specific offending rates for young people suggests that shifts in the age composition of the population could produce sizeable changes in societal crime rates. In recent decades there have, in fact, been major shifts in age composition. The so-called baby-boom generation born between the end of World War II and the early 1960s brought a large, steady increase in the proportion of the population aged 12 to 25—the most crime-prone age group—during the 1960s and 1970s, a period when the nation's crime rate was also increasing steadily. Since 1980, the size of the youth cohort has fluctuated, and so has the crime rate. Criminologists have undertaken extensive investigations of the impact of age structure fluctuations on crime over the last three decades.

Ferdinand (1970) found that about 50 percent of the increase in the Index crime rate during the 1960s could be attributed to various population shifts, particularly the movement of the baby-boom generation into the crime-prone years. Similarly, Steffensmeier and Harer (1987), using statistics from both the UCR and NCVS, found that virtually all the reported decrease in the Index crime rate during the early 1980s could be attributed to the declining proportion of teenagers in the population—that is, to a baby-bust effect.

More recently, Steffensmeier and Harer (forthcoming) report that the large impact of age composition on crime rates during the 1980s has diminished during the 1990s. The across-the-board declines in both the UCR and the NCVS crime rates during the years of the Clinton presidency cannot, therefore, be explained solely by age-composition changes.

Numerous explanations have been offered for crime rate trends in recent decades. One controversial explanation of the recent downtrend has attributed the decline to dramatic increases in incarceration rates that presumably incapacitate or prevent crimes by locking up high-frequency offenders who commit a disproportionate amount of all index crimes (see review in Butterfield, 1998). However, the rise in incarceration rates extends backward to at least the late 1970s and therefore predates the 1990s drop in crime. Therefore it appears unlikely that higher imprisonment rates explain much, if any, of the recent drop in crime—just as they don't account for its rise in the late 1980s.

Alternative explanations for recent downward trends in crime rates include the robust economy of the 1990s, an abatement of the crack epidemic of the late 1980s, and the wide variety of criminal justice initiatives undertaken in the past decade, such as Operation Weed and Seed, Pulling America's Communities Together, and SafeFutures (Kelling, 1998). Steffensmeier and Harer (forthcoming) speculate that offenders may be shifting from risky, low-return offenses like burglary (also robbery) to others that are more lucrative (drug dealing) or less risky (fraud). This sort of shift is noted by one established burglar and dealer in stolen goods (Steffensmeier, 1997: 3):

> It used to be, you had a lot of run-of-the-mill thieves, a lot of in-between burglars, not bad but not good either. But you also had quite a few good burglars and guys who were decent, had a name and knew their way around. The in-between ones were wannabees. If a good burglar

needed an extra man or was looking for a partner, he'd check them out. The hangouts and grapevine it ain't like it once was. Fewer younger guys are taking it up—guys who are 18, 19, in their 20s. Main thing today is dope—now they are peddling dope, and using it too. It's a faster buck and not that much to learn. A burglar today is more like a car thief—pop a window and take what's inside or drive away with the whole car. I never done that. Take the Elton brothers, they is your average thief today. I would buy [stolen goods] from them. Peddle dope, break into cars and vans, and maybe pull off a regular burglary, say, if I gave them a tip on a place. Into a little bit of everything. It's more of that today.

However, there is at least one more way that the declining crime rates of the 1990s may be explained by ongoing changes in the age structure: The aging population may be catalyzing shifts in the nation's "collective conscience" toward greater "civility." In other words, a maturing population may be cultivating more mature values in the population at large (see Wolfe, 1998). The median age of adults has risen steadily as baby boomers enter their forties and fifties. Aging boomers now make up about 30 percent of the population, and they head nearly four in ten households. This enormous, accumulating age shift has now achieved the critical mass needed to trigger a major change in our cultural values and collective conscience away from the narcissistic, materialistic values of youth. The center or midpoint of influence on America's popular culture and moral constitution is undergoing a massive and unprecedented shift, in David Wolfe's words, "away from the young adult years to the middle years, when people's

values characteristically undergo a major realignment" (1998: 17).

Effects of Cohort Size

A related issue concerns the question of "cohort size" on a nation's crime rate. That is, are higher age-specific crime rates for large age cohorts reaching adolescence from roughly 1960 to 1975 a result of the post–World War II baby boom? A number of demographers (Easterlin, 1978; Ryder, 1965) have proposed that a nation's crime rate may fluctuate not only in response to changes in the age structure of the population but also according to the relative size of particular age cohorts. They argue that social constraints and life opportunities will differ for abnormally large or small youth cohorts. In large cohorts, too many young people compete for jobs and education, and they believe they are comparatively worse off economically than members of other cohorts, even though they have been socialized to want the same sorts of material goods. The growth of large juvenile cohorts also can complicate adult society's attempt to reorient the self-interests of youth to the adult community interests and can encourage development of youth subcultures and generational conflict.

The idea that large youth cohorts will exhibit a relatively higher crime rate than small youth cohorts is an intriguing one, and a number of studies have sought to test the hypothesis. Some studies report "significant" cohort size effects (Maxim, 1985; Smith, 1986), whereas others do not find any such effects (Steffensmeier and Harer, 1987). However, whether or not significant effects are reported, the more important finding is that all the studies are in agreement that cohort size accounts for very little of the variation in the nation's crime rate over an extended period. The levels of criminality are more similar than different between large and small youth cohorts. In some respects, this is hardly surprising, because a nation's crime rate is obviously influenced by other well-established correlates of crime (such as income inequality and access to crime opportunities), which are likely to nullify the small effects of cohort size on crime rates.

Age-by-Gender Differences in Crime

A final issue concerns the combined effects of age and gender on crime. The age–gender–crime relationship is, of course, two-sided. On the one hand, one can consider gender differences in the age distribution of offending and ask whether males and females have similar or different age–crime curves. Conversely, one can consider age differences in the sex ratio of crime and ask whether different age groups are similar in the female-to-male percentage of offending. A related issue in light of our discussion of changes in the age–crime relationship since World War II is whether the age–gender–offending relationship is constant over time and across crime categories.

If we study UCR arrest statistics to investigate the age–gender–crime relationship in each of three periods—1935, 1960, and 1985—we find, first, that the age curves of male and female offenders are very similar within any given period and across all offenses, with the exception of prostitution. To the extent that age by sex differences exist, the tendency is for somewhat lower peak ages of offending among females—apparently because of their earlier physical maturity and the likelihood that young adolescent females might date and associate with older delinquent male peers. But overall, although male levels of offending are always higher than female levels at every age and for virtually all offenses, the female-to-male ratio remains fairly constant across the life span (Steffensmeier and Streifel, 1991).

Second, the age–crime curves of both sexes have shifted since World War II toward younger and more peaked distributions. Moreover, the magnitude and direction of the shift is virtually identical for both sexes and for most offenses. This finding is consistent with the view discussed earlier that youths today are subject to greater status anxiety than in previous periods of history.

Third, the single major difference in the age curves of males and females is for prostitution (and to some extent vagrancy, often a euphemism for prostitution in the case of female arrestees), with females having a much greater concentration of arrests among the young. Although this difference may be due in part to more stringent enforcement of prostitution statutes when young females are involved (Chesney-Lind, 1986), the younger and more peaked female age curve is also a function of the extent to which opportunity structures for sexual misbehaviors differ between males and females. Clearly, sexual attractiveness and the marketability of sexual services are strongly linked to both age and gender: Older women become less able to market sexual services, whereas older men can continue to purchase sexual services from young females or from young males (Steffensmeier and Streifel, 1991).

Finally, when the age–gender–crime relationship is examined in terms of the sex ratio or the female-to-male percentage of crime at different ages, the ratio is remarkably similar across age groups for any given crime at any given period. Over time, if the female percentage of arrests for a particular crime increases, remains stable, or decreases for one age group, comparable changes are found for all age groups.

CONCLUSION

Criminologists have long recognized that both age and gender are very robust predictors of crime rates. Although it is beyond the scope of our purposes here to develop an integrated theory of age and gender differences in crime, it is important ultimately to develop fuller explanations for lower rates of offending among females (of all ages) relative to males and among older persons (both male and female) relative to younger persons. We expect such explanations to center on the data and the theoretical constructs that we have noted in this chapter. Namely, the lower rates of females and older persons can be seen as consequences of gender and age differences in goals and the means to achieve them, in social control, in socialization, and in access to criminal opportunities (including those that dovetail with biological and physiological variables). Moreover, articulating the etiology of the higher levels of criminality among males and among the young should contribute toward greater understanding of crime in general and of other behavioral differences between males and females, young and old.

DISCUSSION QUESTIONS

1. Both gender and age seem related to involvement in criminal activity. In what ways is this so, and how do gender and age interact with each other to influence criminality?

2. We often hear about the "new female" criminal. To what extent does this term have any validity? How has women's involvement in crime changed over the past forty years?

3. Part of the puzzle regarding gender and age differences in criminality involves the opportunity to commit crime. Discuss how our society is structured regarding criminal opportunity for the two sexes and for people of different ages.

4. What crimes might be called "female crimes" in this society and why? What explanations can be offered for lower rates of female involvement in violent crime?

5. Age seems to have something to do with the types of crimes people commit. Describe that connection. Indicate the link between age and "criminal career."

6. Crime rates in this country began to rise in the 1960s, about the time that baby-boom children entered high school. Explain the connection between these two phenomena.

REFERENCES

Adler, F. 1975. *Sisters in Crime*. New York: McGraw-Hill.

Adler, P. A., and P. Adler. 1983. "Shifts and Oscillations in Deviant Careers: The Case of Upper-Level Drug Dealers and Smugglers." *Social Problems* 31: 195–207.

Agnew, R. 1992. "Foundation for a General Strain Theory of Crime and Delinquency." *Criminology* 30: 47–87.

Allan, E., and D. Steffensmeier. 1989. "Youth, Unemployment, and Property Crime: Differential

Effects of Job Availability and Job Quality on Juvenile and Young Adult Arrest Rates." *American Sociological Review* 54: 107–123.

Alston, L. 1986. *Crime and Older Americans.* Springfield, IL: Thomas.

Amato, P. 1996. *More than Money? Men's Contributions to Their Children's Lives.* Paper presented at Men in Families Symposium, The Pennsylvania State University.

American Correctional Association. 1983. *Female Classification: An Examination of the Issues.* National Institute of Corrections. Washington, DC: U.S. Government Printing Office.

Anglin, D., Y. Hser, and W. McGlothin. 1987. "Sex Differences in Addict Careers." *American Journal of Drug and Alcohol Abuse* 13: 59–71.

Arnold R. 1989. "Processes of Criminalization from Girlhood to Womanhood." In *Women of Color in American Society.* Edited by M. Zinn and B. Dill. Philadelphia: Temple Univ. Press.

———. 1995. "The Processes of Criminalization of Black Women." Pp. 136–146 in *The Criminal Justice System and Women.* Edited by B. Price and N. Sokoloff. New York: McGraw-Hill.

Beattie J. 1975. "The Criminality of Women in Eighteenth Century England." In *Women and the Law: A Social Historical Perspective.* Edited by D. Weisberg. Cambridge, MA: Schenkman Publishing Co.

———. 1995. "Crime and Inequality in 18th Century London." In *Crime and Inequality.* Edited by J. Hagan and R. Peterson. Stanford, CA: Stanford University Press.

Beutel A., and M. Marini. 1995. "Gender and Values." *American Sociological Review* 60: 436–448.

Blumstein, A., and J. Cohen. 1987. "Characterizing Criminal Careers." *Science* 237 (August): 985–991.

Blumstein, A., J. Cohen, J. Roth, and C. Visher. 1986. *Criminal Careers and "Career Criminals."* Vols. 1 and 2. Washington, DC: National Academy Press.

Bottcher, J. 1995. "Gender as Social Control: A Qualitative Study of Incarcerated Youths and Their Siblings in Greater Sacramento." *Justice Quarterly* 12: 33–57.

Bowker L., H. Gross, and M. Klein. 1980. "Female Participation in Delinquent Gang Activities." Pp. 158–179 in *Women and Crime in America.* Edited by L. Bowker. New York: Macmillan.

Briar, S., and I. Piliavin. 1965. "Delinquency, Situational Inducements, and Commitment to Conformity." *Social Problems* 13: 33–45.

Broidy, L. 1985. "Gender Differences in Emotional Development: A Review of Theories and Research." *Journal of Personality Research* 53: 102–149.

Broidy, L., and R. Agnew. 1997. Gender and Crime: A General Strain Theory Perspective." *Journal of Research in Crime and Delinquency* 34: 275–306.

Butterfield, F. 1998. "Reason for Dramatic Drop in Crime Puzzles the Experts." *New York Times.* March 29: NE16.

Campbell, A. 1984. *The Girls in the Gang.* Oxford: Basil Blackwell.

———. 1990. "Female Participation in Gangs." In *Gangs in America.* Edited by C. Huff. Newbury Park, CA: Sage.

Caspi, A., D. Lynam, T. Moffitt, and P. Silva. 1993. "Unraveling Girls' Delinquency: Biological, Dispositional, and Contextual Contributions to Adolescent Misbehavior. *Developmental Psychology* 29: 19–30.

Cernkovich, S., and P. Giordano. 1987. "A Comparative Analysis of Male and Female Delinquency." *Sociological Quarterly* 20: 131–145.

Chesney-Lind, M. 1973. "Judicial Enforcement of the Female Sex Role: The Family Court and the Female Delinquent." *Issues in Criminology* 8: 51–69.

———. 1986. "Women and Crime: The Female Offender." *Signs: Journal of Women in Culture and Society* 12: 78–96.

———. 1989. "Girls' Crime and Woman's Place: Toward a Feminist Model of Female Delinquency." *Crime and Delinquency* 35: 5–29.

————. 1997. *The Female Offender.* Thousand Oaks, CA: Sage.

Chesney-Lind, M., and R. Shelden R. 1992. *Girls, Delinquency, and Juvenile Justice.* Pacific Grove, CA: Brooks/Cole.

Clausen, J. A. 1986. *The Life Course: A Sociological Perspective.* New York: Prentice-Hall.

Cloward, R., and F. Piven. 1979. "Hidden Protest: The Channeling of Female Protest and Resistance." *Signs: Journal of Women in Culture and Society* 4: 651–669.

Cohen, A. 1966. *Deviance and Social Control.* Englewood Cliffs, NJ: Prentice-Hall.

Collins, R. 1992. "Women and the Production of Status Cultures." In *Cultivating Differences.* Edited by M. Lamont and M. Fournier Chicago: University of Chicago Press.

Coltrane, S. 1995. "The Future of Fatherhood." Pp. 255–274 in *Fatherhood: Contemporary Theory, Research, and Social Policy.* Edited by W. Marsiglio. Thousand Oaks, CA: Sage.

Covington, J. 1985. "Gender Differences in Criminality Among Heroin Users." *Journal of Research in Crime and Delinquency* 22: 329–353.

Daly, K. 1989. "Gender and Varieties of White-Collar Crime." *Criminology* 27: 769–793.

————. 1994. *Gender, Crime and Punishment.* New Haven, CT: Yale University Press.

Decker, S., R. Wright, A. Redfern, and D. Smith. 1993. "A Woman's Place Is in the Home: Females and Residential Burglary." *Justice Quarterly* 10: 143–162.

Denno, D. 1994. "Gender, Crime, and the Criminal Law Defenses." *Journal of Criminal Law and Criminology* 85: 80–180.

Department of Health and Human Services. 1984. *Drug Abuse and Drug Abuse Research.* Rockville, MD: National Institute on Drug Abuse.

Dobash, R., R. Dobash, M. Wilson, and M. Daly. 1992. "The Myth of Sexual Symmetry in Marital Violence." *Social Problems* 39: 71–91.

Easterlin, R. 1978. "What Will 1984 Be Like? Socioeconomic Implications of Recent Twists in Age Structure." *Demography* 15: 397–421.

Eggebeen, D., and P. Uhlenberg. 1985. "Changes in the Organization of Men's Lives." *Family Relations* 34: 251–257.

Elliott, D. S., S. S. Ageton, D. Huizinga, B. A. Knowles, and R. J. Canter. 1983. *The Prevalence and Incidence of Delinquent Behavior: 1976–1980: National Estimates of Delinquent Behavior by Sex, Race, Social Class and Other Selected Variables.* Boulder, CO: Behavioral Research Institute.

English, K. 1993. "Self-Reported Crime Rates of Women Prisoners." *Journal of Quantitative Criminology* 9: 357–382.

Fagot, B., and M. Leinbach. 1983. "Play Styles in Early Childhood: Social Consequences for Boys and Girls." Pp. 93–116 in *Social and Cognitive Skills: Sex Roles and Children's Play.* Edited by M. Liss. New York: Academic Press.

Ferdinand, T. 1970. "Demographic Shifts and Criminality: An Inquiry." *British Journal of Criminology* 10: 169–175.

Friday, P., and J. Hage. 1976. "Youth Crime in Postindustrial Societies." *Criminology* 14: 347–368.

Gilfus, M. 1992. "From Victims to Survivors to Offenders: Women's Routes of Entry and Immersion into Street Crime." *Women & Criminal Justice* 4: 63–89.

Gilligan, C. 1982. *In a Different Voice.* Cambridge, MA: Harvard University Press.

Giordano, P., S. Cernkovich, and M. D. Pugh. 1986. "Friendships and Delinquency." *American Journal of Sociology* 91: 1170–1202.

Glaser, D. 1978. *Crime in Our Changing Society.* New York: Holt, Rinehart & Winston.

Gold, M. 1970. *Delinquent Behavior in an American City.* Pacific Grove, CA: Brooks/Cole.

Gove, W. 1985. "The Effect of Age and Gender on Deviant Behavior: A Biopsychosocial Perspective." In *Gender and the Life Course.* Edited by A. Rossi. New York: Aldine.

Greenberg, D. 1977. "Delinquency and the Age Structure of Society." *Contemporary Crises* 1: 66–86.

Greenfeld, L., and S. Minor-Harper. 1991. *Women in Prison*. Washington, DC: U.S. Department of Justice.

Hagan, J. 1989. *Structural Criminology*. New Brunswick, NJ: Rutgers University Press.

———. 1991. "Destiny and Drift: Subcultural Preferences, Status Attainments, and the Risks and Rewards of Youth." *American Sociological Review* 56 (Oct.): 567–582.

Hagan, J., A. Gillis, and J. Simpson. 1987. "Class in the Household: A Power-Control Theory of Gender and Delinquency." *American Journal of Sociology* 90: 1151–1178.

———. 1993. "The Power of Control in Sociological Theories of Delinquency." In *Advances in Criminological Theory*. Vol. 4. Edited by F. Adler and W. Laufer. New Brunswick, NJ: Transaction Books.

Hanawalt, B. 1979. *Crime and Conflict in English Communities, 1300–1348*. Cambridge, MA: Harvard University Press.

Harris, A., 1977. "Sex and Theories of Deviance: Toward a Functional Theory of Deviant Type-Scripts." *American Sociological Review* 42: 3–16.

Hartnagel, T., and M. Mizanuddin. 1986. "Modernization, Gender Role Convergence, and Female Crime: A Further Test." *International Journal of Contemporary Sociology* 27: 1–14.

Hindelang, M. 1979. "Sex Differences in Criminal Activity." *Social Problems* 27: 143–156.

———. 1981. "Variations in Sex-Race-Age-Specific Incidence Rates of Offending." *American Sociological Review* 46: 461–474.

Heimer, K. 1995. "Gender, Race, and the Pathways to Delinquency: An Interactionist Explanation." In *Crime and Inequality*. Edited by J. Hagan and R. Peterson. Stanford, CA: Stanford University Press.

Hirschi, T., and M. R. Gottfredson. 1983. "Age and the Explanation of Crime." *American Journal of Sociology* 89: 552–584.

Horan, P. M., and P. G. Hargis. 1991. "Children's Work and Schooling in the Late Nineteenth-Century Family Economy." *American Sociological Review* 56: 583–596.

Horowitz, A., and H. White. 1987. "Gender Role Orientation and Styles of Pathology Among Adolescents." *Journal of Health and Social Behavior* 28: 158–170.

Inciardi, J., D. Lockwook, and A. Pottieger. 1993. *Women and Crack-Cocaine*. New York: Macmillan.

Irwin, J. 1970. *The Felon*. Englewood Cliffs, NJ: Prentice-Hall.

Irwin, J., and D. R. Cressey. 1962. "Thieves, Convicts and the Inmate Subculture." *Social Problems* 10: 142–155.

James, J. 1977. "Prostitutes and Prostitution." In *Deviants: Voluntary Action in a Hostile World*. Edited by E. Sagarin and F. Montanino. New York: Scott, Foresman.

Jensen, G., and K. Thompson. 1990. "What's Class Got to Do with It? A Further Explanation of Power-Control Theory." *American Journal of Sociology* 95: 1009–1023.

Jolin, A., and D. Gibbons. 1987. "Age Patterns in Criminal Involvement." *International Journal of Offender Therapy and Comparative Criminology* 31: 237–260.

Kelling, G. 1988. "Police and Communities: The Quiet Revolution." *Perspectives on Policing*. Washington DC: U.S. Department of Justice.

———. 1998. *The Bureau of Justice Assistance Comprehensive Communities Program: A Preliminary Report*. Washington, DC: U.S. Department of Justice.

Klockars, C. B. 1974. *The Professional Fence*. New York: Free Press.

Kruttschnitt, C. 1994. "Gender and Interpersonal Violence." Pp. 295–378 in *Understanding and Preventing Violence: Social Influences*. Vol. 3. Edited by J. Roth and A. Reiss. Washington, DC: National Academy of Sciences.

Leuptow, L., and L. Garovich. 1992. *The Persistence of Sex Stereotypes Amid the Reconstruction of Women's Roles.* Paper presented at the annual meeting of the American Sociological Association, Pittsburgh, PA.

Maas, P. 1973. *King of the Gypsies.* New York: Bantam Books.

Maccoby, E. 1985. "Social Groupings in Childhood: Their Relationship to Prosocial and Antisocial Behavior in Boys and Girls." In *Development of Antisocial and Prosocial Behavior: Theories, Research and Issues.* Edited by D. Olwens, J. Block, and M. Radke-Yarrow. San Diego: Academic Press.

Mann, C. R. 1984. *Female Crime and Delinquency.* Tuscaloosa: University of Alabama Press.

Mawby, R. 1980. "Sex and Crime: The Results of a Self-Report Study." *British Journal of Sociology* 31: 525–543.

Maxim, P. 1985. "Cohort Size and Juvenile Delinquency: A Test of the Easterlin Hypothesis." *Social Forces* 63: 661–679.

Mazur, A. 1986. "U.S. Trends in Feminine Beauty and Overadaptation." *The Journal of Sex Research* 22: 281–303.

McCarthy, B., and J. Hagan. 1992. "Mean Streets: The Theoretical Significance of Situational Delinquency and Homeless Youths." *American Journal of Sociology* 98: 597–627.

McGahey, R. 1986. "Economic Conditions, Neighborhood Organization, and Urban Crime." In *Communities and Crime.* Edited by A. Reiss, Jr., and M. Tonry. Chicago: University of Chicago Press.

Meisenhelder, T. 1977. "An Exploratory Study of Exiting From Criminal Careers." *Criminology* 15: 319–334.

Messerschmidt, J. 1986. *Capitalism, Patriarchy, and Crime: Toward a Socialist Feminist Criminology.* Totowa, NJ: Rowman & Littlefield.

———. 1993. *Masculinities and Crime: Critique and Reconceptualization of Theory.* New Jersey: Rowman and Littlefield.

Miller, E. 1986. *Street Woman.* Philadelphia: Temple University Press.

———. 1998. "Up It Up: Gender and the Accomplishment of Street Robbery." *Criminology* 36: 37–65.

Miller, W. 1980. "The Molls." In *Women, Crime, and Justice.* Edited by S. Datesman and F. Scarpitti. New York: Oxford University Press.

Nettler, G. 1978. *Explaining Crime.* New York: McGraw-Hill.

Parmelee, M. 1918. *Criminology.* New York: Macmillan.

Pennsylvania Crime Commission. 1991. *1990 Report—Organized Crime in Pennsylvania: A Decade of Change.* Commonwealth of Pennsylvania.

Pettiway, L. 1987. "Participation in Crime Partnerships by Female Drug Users." *Criminology* 25: 741–767.

Piaget, J. 1932. *The Moral Judgement of the Child.* London: Kegan Paul.

Pollock-Byrne, J. 1990. *Women, Prison & Crime.* Belmont, CA: Wadsworth.

Prus, R., and C. Sharper. 1977. *Road Hustler.* Lexington, MA: Lexington Books.

Reckless, W. 1950. *The Crime Problem.* New York: Appleton-Century.

Reynolds, Q. 1953. *I, Willie Sutton.* New York: Farrar, Straus & Young.

Richie, B. 1995. *The Gendered Entrapment of Battered, Black Women.* London: Rutledge.

Rossi, P. 1984. "Gender and Parenthood." *American Sociological Review* 49: 1–19.

Rowe, A., and C. Tittle. 1977. "Life Cycle Changes and Criminal Propensity." *Sociological Quarterly* 18: 223–236.

Ryder, N. 1965. "The Cohort as a Concept in the Study of Social Change." *American Sociological Review* 47: 774–787.

Sampson, R. J., and J. H. Laub. 1990. "Crime and Deviance Over the Life Course: The Salience of Adult Social Bonds." *American Sociological Review* 55 (Oct.): 609–627.

Seltzer, J., and S. Bianchi. 1988. "Children's Contact with Absent Parents." *Journal of Marriage and the Family* 50: 663–677.

Shannon, L. 1988. *Criminal Career Continuity: Its Social Context.* New York: Human Sciences Press.

Shapiro, S. 1984. *Wayward Capitalists: Target of the Securities and Exchange Commission.* New Haven, CT: Yale University Press.

Shock, N. 1984. *Normal Human Aging: The Baltimore Longitudinal Study of Aging.* Washington, DC: U.S. Government Printing Office.

Shover, N. 1983. "The Later Stages of Ordinary Property Offender Careers." *Social Problems* 30: 208–218.

Shover N., S. Norland, J. James, and W. Thornton. 1979. "Gender Roles and Delinquency." *Social Forces* 58: 162–175.

Simmons, R., and D. Blyth. 1987. *Moving Into Adolescence.* New York: Aldine.

Simon, R. 1975. *The Contemporary Woman and Crime.* Washington, DC: National Institutes of Mental Health.

Simpson, S., and L. Ellis. 1995. "Doing Gender: Sorting Out the Caste and Crime Conundrum." *Criminology* 33: 47–77.

Singer, S., and M. Levine. 1988. "Power-Control Theory, Gender, and Delinquency: A Partial Replication with Additional Evidence on the Effects of Peers." *Criminology* 26: 627–647.

Smart, C. 1976. *Women, Crime and Criminology.* London: Routledge & Kegan Paul.

Smith, M. D. 1986. "The Era of Increased Violence in the United States: Age, Period, or Cohort Effect?" *Sociological Quarterly* 27: 239–251.

Steffensmeier, D. 1980. "Sex Differences in Patterns of Adult Crime, 1965–77: A Review and Assessment." *Social Forces* 58: 1080–1108.

———. 1983. "Organization Properties and Sex-Segregation in the Underworld: Building a Sociological Theory of Sex Differences in Crime." *Social Forces* 61: 1010–1132.

———. 1986. *The Fence: In the Shadow of Two Worlds.* Totowa, NJ: Rowman & Littlefield.

———. 1987. "Invention of the 'New' Senior Citizen Criminal." *Research on Aging* 9: 281–311.

———. 1993. "National Trends in Female Arrests, 1960–1990: Assessment and Recommendations for Research." *Journal of Quantitative Criminology* 9: 413–441.

———. 1997. *Interview with a Dying Thief.* Paper presented at the annual meetings of the American Society of Criminology, San Diego, CA.

Steffensmeier, D., and E. Allan. 1988. "Sex Disparities in Arrests by Residence, Race, and Age: An Assessment of the Gender Convergence/Crime Hypothesis." *Justice Quarterly* 5: 53–80.

———. 1993. "Age-Inequality and Property Crime." In *Age Stratification and Crime.* Edited by John Hagan and Ruth Peterson. University of Chicago Press.

———. 1995. "Gender, Age, and Crime." Pp. 83–113 in *Handbook of Contemporary Criminology.* 2nd ed. Edited by J. Sheley. Belmont, CA: Wadsworth.

———. 1996. "Gender and Crime: Toward a Gendered Theory of Female Offending." *Annual Review of Sociology* 22: 459–487.

———. 1998. "The Nature of Female Offending: Patterns and Explanations." In *Female Offenders: Critical Perspectives and Effective Interventions.* Edited by R. Zaplin. Gaithersburg, MD: Aspen Publishers.

Steffensmeier, D., and R. Clark. 1980. "Sociocultural vs. Biological/Sexist Explanations of Sex Differences" in "Crime: A Survey of American Criminology Textbooks, 1919–1965." *American Sociologist* 15: 246–255.

Steffensmeier, D., and M. Harer. 1987. "Is the Crime Rate Really Falling? An 'Aging' U.S. Population and Its Impact on the Nation's Crime Rate, 1980–84." *Journal of Research in Crime and Delinquency* 24: 23–48.

————. Forthcoming. "Making Sense of Recent U.S. Crime Trends, 1980–98: Age Composition Effects and Other Explanations. *Journal of Research in Crime & Delinquency.*

Steffensmeier, D., and D. Haynie. Forthcoming. "Structural Sources of Urban Female Crime: Does Gender Make a Difference?" *Criminology.*

Steffensmeier, D., and C. Streifel. 1991. "The Distribution of Crime by Age and Gender Across Three Historical Periods—1935, 1960, 1985." *Social Forces* 69: 869–894.

Steffensmeier, D., and R. Terry. 1986. "Institutional Sexism in the Underworld: A View from the Inside." *Sociological Inquiry* 56: 304–323.

Steffensmeier, D., E. Allan, and C. Streifel. 1989. "Development and Female Crime: A Cross-National Test of Alternative Explanations." *Social Forces* 68: 262–283.

Steinmetz, S., and J. Lucca. 1988. "Husband Beating." Pp. 233–246 in *Handbook of Family Violence.* Edited by R. Hasselt, A. Morrison, S. Bellack, and M. Hersen. New York: Plenum.

Stoneman, A., G. Brody, and C. MacKinnon. 1984. "Naturalistic Observations of Children's Activities and Roles While Playing with Their Siblings and Friends." *Child Development* 55: 617–627.

Straus, M., and R. Gelles. 1990. *Physical Violence in American Families.* New Brunswick, NJ: Transaction Books.

Sullivan, M. 1989. *"Getting Paid": Youth Crime and Work in the Inner City.* Ithaca: Cornell University Press.

Sutherland, E. 1937. *The Professional Thief.* Chicago: University of Chicago Press.

Swart W. 1991. "Female Gang Delinquency: A Search for 'Acceptably Deviant Behavior.'" *Mid-American Review of Sociology* 15: 43–52.

Thrasher, F. 1927. *The Gang: A Study of 1,313 Gangs in Chicago.* Chicago: University of Chicago Press.

Tittle, C. R. 1988. "Two Explanatory Regularities (maybe) in Search of an Explanation: Commentary on the Age/Crime Debate." *Criminology* 26: 75–85.

Tracy, P., M. Wolfgang, and R. Figlio. 1990. *Delinquency Careers in Two Birth Cohorts.* New York: Plenum.

Triplett, R., and L. Myers. 1995. "Evaluating Contextual Patterns of Delinquency: Gender-Based Differences." *Justice Quarterly* 12: 59–79.

U.S. Department of Justice. 1996. "Uniform Crime Reports." Federal Bureau of Investigation. Washington, DC: U.S. Department of Justice.

Walby, S. 1990. *Theorizing Patriarchy.* Cambridge, MA: Basil Blackwell.

Warr, M. 1993. "Age, Peers, and Delinquency." *Criminology* 31: 17–40.

Weiner, N. 1989. "Violent Criminal Careers and 'Violent Career Criminals.'" Pp. 35–138 in *Violent Crime, Violent Criminals.* Edited by N. Weiner and M. Wolfgang. Newbury Park, CA: Sage.

Wilson, J. Q., and R. Herrnstein. 1985. *Crime and Human Nature.* New York: Simon & Schuster.

Wilson, W. J. 1987. *The Truly Disadvantaged: The Inner City, the Underclass, and Public Policy.* Chicago: University of Chicago Press.

Wolfe, D. 1998. "The Psychological Center of Gravity." *American Demographics* 38: 16–19.

Zeitz, D. 1981. *Women Who Embezzle or Defraud: A Study of Convicted Felons.* New York: Praeger.

Chapter Outline

5

Looking for Patterns:
Race, Class, and Crime

ANTHONY R. HARRIS
University of Massachusetts, Amherst

JAMES A. W. SHAW*
University of Massachusetts, Amherst

Compared to their proportion in the general U.S. population, African Americans are consistently overrepresented in criminal justice system data. In 1996, African-American men were imprisoned at a rate six times that of white men (Donziger, 1996). In 1997, a little over 12 percent of the U.S. population was counted as African American. That same year, of all *Uniform Crime Reports* (UCR) arrests for Index crimes (see Chapter 3 in this text), those of African Americans totaled just over 34 percent.

As reported in the 1997 *Uniform Crime Reports* (Federal Bureau of Investigation, 1998), African Americans accounted for about 25 percent of the arson arrest total (13,554), 40 percent of the motor vehicle theft arrest total (112,519), 30 percent of the burglary arrest total (239,880), and 33 percent of the larceny-theft arrest total

(1,001,574). Given that only one of about eight Americans is African American, these percentages greatly exceed what would be expected by chance alone regarding arrests for serious, common law property crimes. When population size is held constant and arrest rates per 100,000 of particular population groups are calculated, the group comparison is more striking. Figure 5.1 presents such rate-adjusted data for African Americans and whites on Index crimes against property. The rate-adjusted ratio of African Americans to whites arrested is 2.2 for arson, 4.4 for motor vehicle theft, 2.8 for burglary, and 3.3 for larceny-theft.

For crimes against the person, African-American overrepresentation is even greater, by almost half. African Americans accounted for 42 percent of all Index arrests for crimes against

*We would like to thank Igor Zernitsky for his help in assembling the 1997 UCR data.

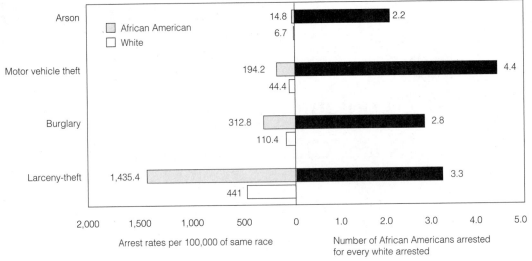

FIGURE 5.1   Index crimes against property, 1997

SOURCE: Federal Bureau of Investigation, 1998.

the person in 1997: about 57 percent of the homicide arrest total (12,539), 41 percent of the forcible rape arrest total (21,655), 58 percent of the armed robbery arrest total (92,366), and 37 percent of the aggravated assault arrest total (363,816). Once again, adjustment is made for population size. The rate-adjusted ratio of African Americans to whites arrested for homicide is 8.8, 4.4 for forcible rape, 9.0 for armed robbery, and 3.9 for aggravated assault. These rate-based comparisons are seen in Figure 5.2.

Race differences in UCR data are striking regardless of whether one looks at rates of arrest or at absolute numbers of arrests. They are so strong, in fact, that basic changes in crime rates for a geographic unit may reflect no more than changes in its racial composition. Chilton (1986), for example, argues effectively that between 1960 and 1980, 57 percent of the increase in combined arrests for twelve of the largest cities in the United States can be linked to an increase of the proportion of the African-American population in

these cities—even though the African-American arrest *rate* remained quite stable during this time.

BIAS IN THE UCR CRIME INDEX

Striking as these findings seem, several nagging questions remain. Index crimes focus primarily on what might be called blue collar, or street, crimes. Because a strong relationship still exists between race and occupation, Index crimes by their very nature focus us away from white collar and "silk collar" crimes (see Chapter 11 of this text), and thus away from white offenders.

First, if white collar and silk collar offenses are included, does the race–crime link change? That is, do Index crimes really provide a race-blind Index from the start? Second, suppose we answer yes to the first question and assume that Index crimes are a fair, representative, and race-blind subset of all possible crimes in contemporary America. If we do, it soon becomes obvious that letting an a priori set of crimes be used as a

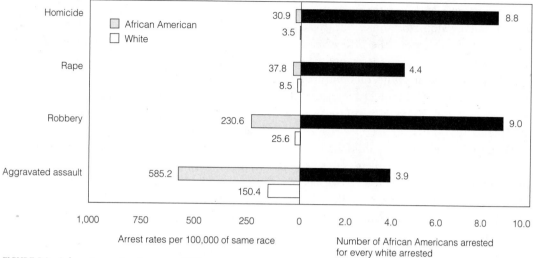

FIGURE 5.2   Index crimes against the person, 1997

SOURCE: Federal Bureau of Investigation, 1998.

fair index is one thing, but operationally measuring that Index is quite another. To begin, even if the a priori Index is fair, in real life it is given meaning only by arrests. Suppose that racial prejudice causes a victim to "see" an African-American burglar when, in fact, the burglar was white? Or suppose that the same sort of prejudice leads the police to arrest an African American for armed robbery when, in fact, the robber was white? As Wilson and Herrnstein (1985: 460) note, even under the best of circumstances,

> the racial or ethnic identity of a person is far less certain than his sex or age. The ancestors of many African Americans and Orientals include some, perhaps many, Caucasians, and vice-versa; when parentage is mixed, a decision that someone is "really" African American, Oriental, or Caucasian is a bit arbitrary. At times it is even ludicrous, as when custom dictates that a person who has only one African American grandparent

is an African American, whereas a person who has three white grandparents may not be white.

In short, suppose that however race-blind the UCR Index before the fact, it is subverted by the prejudice and bias of everyday life into a "disfavored-race" index. Are the arrests composing Index crimes race-biased?

The strong relationship between race and occupation is critical, for it involves a link between race and social class. But race in contemporary America has other important correlates besides social class, including access to employment networks, type and quality of neighborhood lived in, years of education, life expectancy, family structure, IQ scores, and historical experience.

These correlates, along with class, form a generally tight package or bundle of factors. To a large extent, this bundle of relationships reflects our nation's entire social history, including the grim decades of slavery, times of enormous wealth and freedom for some, but appalling poverty and bondage for others. To at least the same extent, this bundle reflects our nation's present social structure, with income inequality and occupational immobility for some but new levels of well-being and material success for others.

Thus, when we ask the third basic question—if there is a relation between race and crime, what causes it?—we realize that because these correlates are so tightly bundled, there is no simple answer. In the center of the often-told American tale of social advantage and disadvantage, these correlates of race form an extremely tight and, to a large extent, virtually inseparable tangle.

A Priori Race Bias

It is important to realize from the start that the UCR Index is not a priori blind to race. This view is based on an understanding of race-related opportunities in contemporary America. The present UCR Index opens a certain kind of window onto crime, a window onto "the streets." Undoubtedly, this crime window is of great importance to all Americans. However, the window is defined not just by what it allows us to see; it is at least as much defined by what it *excludes* from our sight, namely, much white collar and probably most silk collar crime.

Because African Americans are underrepresented and whites overrepresented in white and silk collar occupations, we must conclude that the set of crimes called UCR Index crimes is skewed away from criminal opportunities where whites are overrepresented. This does not imply that the UCR Index is biased against lower-class African American street crime per se but rather that it is biased away from middle class and elite whites' "suite" (white collar) crime. No matter what we do, it seems that UCR data do not adequately measure upper-level white collar and silk collar crime. This type of crime includes such crimes as stock market fraud, price-fixing and product misrepresentation, corporate tax evasion, industrial pollution, maintenance of unsafe working conditions, and illegal intervention in the political process (Sheley, 1985: 127). Because race is strongly correlated with occupation, and because the conventional UCR Index is intrinsically biased away from silk collar crime, the UCR Index is intrinsically biased away from white, silk collar criminals and toward African-American, blue collar criminals.

Empirical Race Bias

Is the UCR Index empirically race-biased because it represents arrests, not crimes? Given our answer to the first question, the reader might expect us to conclude that it is. But our answer to the second question is no: The UCR Index is not empirically race-biased because it measures arrests, not crimes. The reasoning behind this position is quite complicated. It does not have to do with a priori race biases in the choice of which crimes are included in, and excluded from, the UCR Index (that is, with issues raised in our first question). Instead, the reasoning is based on the empirical relationship between arrests for the UCR Index crimes and the "true" distribution of UCR Index crimes as estimated by data other than UCR (or arrest) data.

Self-Report Data In the 1960s, it became fashionable in many academic circles to deplore the use of UCR data as a fair measure of crime in the United States (see Kitsuse and Cicourel, 1963). To a large degree, this disdain was based on the assumption that police as a group were racially prejudiced and tended to arrest African Americans in preference to whites. As a solution, many criminologists advocated the use of the "offender source"—that is, self-report studies (see Chapter 3). These purported to bypass inherent problems in the arrest-based UCR Index by "going directly to the horse's mouth"—to offenders themselves. Typically, such studies offered respondents checklists of mostly minor crimes, such as petty larceny and vandalism. Self-report questionnaires were administered almost exclusively to juvenile populations, particularly students in high school, a limitation that has proven to be quite serious (see Conklin, 1992; Harris and Hill, 1982; Sheley, 1985).

A major conclusion from this research was that UCR ("official/arrest") data overrepresented males from disadvantaged population groups, particularly African-American and lower socioeconomic-status (SES) groups. For example, Hirschi's (1969) study found that if self-reports were used as the guide, the prevalence of African-American delinquent acts exceeded the prevalence of white delinquent acts by only 10 percent (the ratio of self-reported African-American delinquency prevalence to white delinquency prevalence was 1.1 to 1), but if official police contacts were the guide, the prevalence of African-American contact exceeded the prevalence of white contact by 100 percent (the ratio of African-American official contact to white official contact was 2.0 to 1). These findings, and others like them, implied that virtually all differences between disadvantaged and advantaged groups at point of arrest could be attributed to police bias.

Victim-Report Data For two decades, opponents of UCR data insisted that these data were mirrors of police racism, not criminal behavior.

Opponents of self-report data argued that these data generally measured not-so-serious crimes such as vandalism and status offenses such as truancy and were provided by mostly "good kids"—youths who had *not* dropped out of high school, who had *not* been shot to death, who were *not*, at present, "doing time." In the mid-1970s, a third source of crime data was tapped. It cast the deciding vote: National Crime Victimization Survey (NCVS) data strongly supported the view that the offender characteristics seen in UCR data, and not those found in self-reports, were correct.

Figure 5.3 is based on averaged annual NCVS data from 1973 to 1977. Crimes included are common law personal crimes where face-to-face contact occurs, such as armed robbery or assault. In these cases, victims are asked to report perceived demographic characteristics of offenders, including gender, race, and age. In the first and only study of its type (Hindelang, 1981), estimated offender rates are thus computed (rates = offenses reported by victims, adjusted per 100,000 potential offenders in each population group). The victim reports used in Figure 5.3 graphically corroborate UCR data on the race–street-crime relationship: African Americans, particularly African-American males, are substantially overrepresented in the reports. If male and female rates are summed within race and across age categories, the aggregated rate-adjusted race ratio for the entire data set stands at about five African-American offenses per one white offense.

The "average" year for this observation is 1975. Just two years later, for the four UCR personal crimes of assault, aggravated assault, rape, and robbery, the rate-adjusted race ratios stood at 4.6, 5.6, 7.5, and 13.6, respectively (Hill and Harris, 1982). But the offender rates in Figure 5.3 combine these UCR crimes. If UCR and

FIGURE 5.3

Crimes against the person,
based on victim-report
estimates* in 1973–1997
national crime surveys

SOURCE: Adapted from Hindelang,
1981.

*Estimated number of personal crimes
produced annually per 100,000 of
each group.

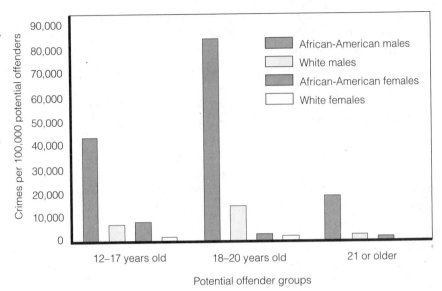

NCVS data really do correspond (see Biderman et al., 1991, on the general issue of UCR and NCVS correspondence), we would expect the NCVS aggregated race ratio (5.3) to resemble most closely the race ratio for the highest-volume offenses of the four UCR crimes, and it does. These high-volume offenses are assault and aggravated assault (where the race ratios for 1977 are 4.6 and 5.6, respectively). For rape during the same period, a similar UCR–NCVS match has been noted by Hindelang (1978). In addition, Hindelang observes a close UCR–NCVS match on race effects for armed robbery (see also Conklin, 1972; Silberman, 1978; Pruitt and Wilson, 1983).

Victims appear to be telling us that arrests are probably a reasonable indicator of real race-based differences in the commission of street crime (see McNeely and Pope, 1981, for a different view). Equally important, NCVS data suggest that the self-report findings were correct for less serious crime but that unless one were to equate petty theft with armed robbery, the findings were largely useless. One major key to rec-

onciling discrepancies between the offender and the state (UCR) estimates obviously lay in limitations in self-report sampling techniques: Self-report studies typically undersampled seriously delinquent offenses (Wilbanks, 1987) and seriously delinquent youths (Hindelang et al., 1979).

In what is still the best self-report study to date, Elliott and Ageton (1980) analyzed data from a national sample of over 1,700 juveniles regarding their delinquencies in 1976. They note a link between race and self-reported delinquency, not particularly noteworthy for less serious delinquencies, like status offenses, but significant for serious or predatory delinquencies. In a parallel and rare look at adult self-report data, the Rand Inmate Survey finds that African-American overrepresentation in arrest data really does reflect African-American overrepresentation in serious criminal activities (Petersilia, 1985).

Once revealed, these UCR and self-report discrepancies suggest that at least three major misunderstandings of crime in America occurred among criminologists in the 1960s and the 1970s. The first was the most critical because it reflected so clearly on social policy. It involved a serious underestimation of the nature of institutional racism. In truth, could not racism in America be so far-reaching that it strongly affected people's willingness to choose criminal behavior, as well as which type of criminal behavior to choose? The second misunderstanding involved the intellectually and morally vacuous equating, by some criminologists, of delinquencies like petty theft, where $2 worth of candy might be pilfered, with crimes like aggravated assault, where the injured victim might require hospitalization, endure months of lost income, and suffer years of trauma. The third misunderstanding, somewhat more technical, involved a woefully incorrect reading of the nature of police behavior: Police were incorrectly perceived as being in the business of looking for people, particularly African Americans, to arrest. A very important unasked question was, Could not racism in America be so severe that the demographically overrepresented victims of street crime were, in fact, the demographically overrepresented perpetrators of street crime and not the white middle class?

Reevaluating UCR Data: Crime Seriousness and the Reactive Police Model Surely, the UCR Index offers a narrow window through which to see certain types and patterns of crime. As we noted, the Index in this sense is biased away from white collar and silk collar crimes; in addition, the Index observes these patterns by counting arrests (see Chapter 3 of this text). However, arrests represent only one kind of data-gathering operation, and one that rests heavily on police practices. Evidence gathered over the past twenty years gives us reason to be suspicious of police attitudes toward minorities (Chevigny, 1969; Sheley and Harris, 1976). But it is equally clear that the data produced by arrests are a complex function of actual offenses,

the victim's or bystander's behavior, and police practices themselves.

In arrests for less-serious, non-Index crimes, there is ample reason to believe the police role may well be more proactive than reactive, resulting in the overarrest of African Americans compared to whites (see Harris, 1997). A good example of this is the trend that started in the 1980s and involved the increasing targeting and arrest of African-American offenders for crack cocaine use/sales and virtually no change in the targeting and arrest of white offenders for powder cocaine use/sales (Tonry, 1994; Blumstein, 1995; Donziger, 1996). On the other hand, there is ample reason to believe the role of the police in most Index crime arrests in the United States is far more reactive rather than proactive (Reiss, 1971; Conklin, 1972). That is, in most such arrests, police react to reports of serious crime called in by victims or bystanders; they do not initiate arrests based on what they see from patrol cars or on the beat. This has important implications. Under the reactive model, police "take what they get . . . what is reported to them," and as we know, victims and observers are likely to report more-, rather than less-serious, crimes (Block and Block, 1980). Consequently, the police react to and follow through on reported offenses that are quite serious and that tend to produce race-skewed arrests that reflect race differences in actual Index crimes committed (see Black, 1980; Blumstein et al., 1993). Thus, to the degree that the reactive police model accurately describes arrests for Index crimes, then victims and other observers are more likely than police to be the primary source of race bias (see the discussion in Smith et al., 1984).

Who Is the Victim? Like their liberal counterparts, conservative stereotypes die hard. The dominant image of the overrepresented victim of street crime in America—supposedly a person who is both middle class and white—is largely incorrect. NCVS data from 1997 (Rand, 1998) indicate that, with one exception, African Americans report being victimized at a higher rate than do whites. Moreover, the past decade has seen a dramatic increase in victimization reported by African Americans, thus further widening the African-American–white victimization gap. For the most serious or violent crimes, including rape, aggravated assault, and armed robbery, African-American victimization rates in 1997 were 28 percent higher than white rates. For robbery alone, the African-American victimization rate exceeds the white rate by 95 percent. For household victimizations, African-American rates are again higher. African Americans are about 48 percent more likely to be burglarized than are whites, 11 percent more likely to suffer a household larceny than whites, and about 103 percent more likely to report a motor vehicle theft. For personal theft victimization, the African-American rate exceeds the white rate by 136 percent.

Even when additional factors such as income are taken into account, the statistically overrepresented victim of serious street crime clearly resembles the statistically overrepresented offender: male, young, poor, and African American. There is thus good reason to think that, if there is race bias in the system, it occurs long before arrest occurs.

CAUSES OF THE RACE–STREET-CRIME RELATIONSHIP

There seems little doubt that in America at present, African Americans' overrepresentation in arrests is based mainly on their overrepresentation in criminal behavior "on the streets." In answering our second question, we must conclude that the behavior–arrest relation is not the major area in which to find racism. Such concerns are more wisely focused on the third, and final, question: If there is a real relation between race and street crime, why does it exist?

Judging the usefulness of theories about the causes of the race–street-crime relationship is equivalent to evaluating the explanatory power of the key contemporary correlates of race. Chief among these is social class. Other key correlates include factors in the areas of constitution, family structure, subculture, and historical caste (see Wilson and Herrnstein, 1985).

SOCIAL CLASS

The correlation between race and class in America is so strong that any relation observed between race and crime might be nothing more than a cloaked relation between class and crime. If this were true, we could say that the race–street-crime relation was "explained" by social class, a position that has been frequently argued.

The Use and Misuse of Self-Report Data

We will not attempt a rigorous definition of social class here. Various measures of social class include income, years of education, and occupational status or parents' occupational status. By whatever measure, we need data to evaluate the possibility that social class explains the race–street-crime relation. As it turns out, UCR data do not even try to include information relevant to the arrestee's social class; neither do NCVS data. With one major exception, to which we will return, this leaves us with self-reports.

We noted earlier that one of the problems with self-report data had been the tendency to undersample seriously delinquent offenses. A related problem involved the tendency to truncate delinquency. Respondents were often classified as "delinquent" if they admitted to ever having committed any one of a broad range of infractions, from truancy to burglary. At best, this procedure was not a good idea. By this standard, most American teenage males, if not females, would appear in the delinquent category as budding Jeffrey Dahmers. As clearly noted by Wilson and Herrnstein (1985: 37), this procedure "obscures differences between persons who break the law once or twice (many males have done that) and those who break it twenty, thirty, or fifty times per year."

A third problem with self-report data had been the tendency to undersample seriously delinquent youth—at the least youth who were truant from school or worse, youth who were doing time in a juvenile detention facility—on the day of the self-report survey. It should come as no surprise, then, that these problems led to some profoundly counterproductive conclusions about delinquency and crime in America. One extraordinarily senseless conclusion was that once self-reports, not arrests, were made the yardstick, there was virtually no relationship between social class and "true" delinquent behavior. A related conclusion, not limited to mere delinquency and, incredibly enough, based primarily on self-report data from high school students, went even farther: There was virtually *no* relation between class and crime in America (see Tittle et al., 1978).

Countering this claim, Hindelang et al. (1979) effectively argued that the discrepancy between self-report and arrest findings is mostly an illusion based on the measurement of different "behavioral domains"—a polite way of distinguishing between trivial delinquencies, occasionally engaged in by virtually all teenagers, and serious delinquencies, very frequently engaged in by a small number of youth, probably dropouts, who are well on their way to a career in crime. For our purposes, Hindelang et al. do not go far enough. In a review of ninety empirical studies of the class–crime link, Braithwaite (1981) fails to find support for the link in only 23 percent (twenty-one) of the studies. And Braithwaite's research omits ecological studies of crime (comparison of crime rates by geographic sector), though these studies consistently report a class–crime association (Sheley, 1985: 154).

Juveniles

Elliott and Ageton's major self-report study of a national probability sample of juveniles (1980) helps explain the race–class relation to street crime. Though this study does not allow us to see the effect of race on delinquency, holding class effects constant (or, for that matter, class, holding race effects constant), it does allow us to see, very clearly, the relative magnitude of race and class effects on delinquency in a national sample and the important interaction of these effects with type of delinquency (predatory versus nonpredatory). To measure class, Elliott and Ageton rely on the occupational status of the primary breadwinner in the juvenile's immediate family. Their results are depicted in Figure 5.4.

Figure 5.4 graphically underscores two basic points. One is that class and race differences are trivial for nonpredatory or "victimless" delinquencies, including public disorder crimes such as drunkenness, status crimes such as truancy, and drug violations such as barbiturate use. For nonpredatory crimes, the maximum class ratio observed is thus 1.05 to 1.00 (working class to

FIGURE 5.4

Delinquency by race and class, based on self-report estimates from 1976 *National Youth Survey*

SOURCE: Adapted from Elliott and Ageton, 1980.

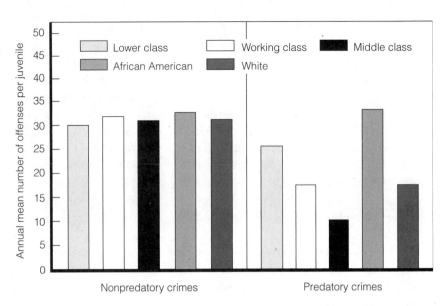

lower class), a trivial 5 percent difference at most, whereas the race ratio is 1.06 to 1.00 (African Americans to whites), a trivial 6 percent difference at most. These findings are consistent with later findings as well (Hagan and Parker, 1985; Hagan et al., 1987).

In contrast, class and race differences are unmistakable for the more serious predatory delinquencies, including crimes against persons (for example, aggravated assault and robbery) and crimes against property (for example, burglary and auto theft). For this set, annual self-reported delinquent acts vary by class from a low mean of 10.6 for middle-class youth to a high mean of 25.5 for lower-class youth, with working-class youth standing at a mean of 17.4. Mean annual delinquent acts reported by whites stand at 16.8, and by African Americans at 33.3. For predatory crimes, the maximum class ratio observed is thus 2.41 to 1.00 (lower class to middle class), a nontrivial 141 percent difference, whereas the race ratio is 1.99 to 1.00 (African Americans to whites), a nontrivial 99 percent difference.

Additional analysis by Elliott and Ageton (1980: 106), which cannot be observed from Figure 5.4, "suggests a relatively high involvement of lower-class African American youth in serious offenses against the person"—that is, in that particular subset of street crimes most likely to lead to arrest.

Elliott and Ageton's data strongly indicate that in modern America, real race and real class differences exist in serious delinquency. Like victim data, these data cross-validate the reasonable use of arrest data as a basis for race comparisons. Unfortunately, these data do not really disentangle race from class. To do this, we need to look at what is probably the best empirical study of street crime ever done in America: the Wolfgang et al. (1972) study of the criminal histories of the birth cohort of white and African-American males born in 1945 and living in Philadelphia between 1955 and 1962, that is, between their tenth and seventeenth birthdays. Some serious questions arise concerning the researchers' final measure of social class, or better,

SES, and once again, we are limited to juveniles; nevertheless, their work has withstood scrutiny extremely well.

In reviewing the findings from the 1972 study, we immediately run into the race–class tangle. If we use general prevalence (percentage having police contact for any offense) as our guide, SES has a more powerful effect than does race. If, however, we use serious incidence (police contact rate per 1,000 for serious offenses) as our guide, the reverse is true: Race has a more powerful effect than does SES. Though the effects of SES and race are in the theoretically expected direction, the findings are contradictory with respect to the relative importance of the two.

As it turns out, these contrary findings are related to the problematic correlation between race and class. Some of the observed race effect is "really" a class effect, and some of the observed class effect is "really" a race effect. In the birth cohort, are there independent effects of race, controlling for the effects of class, and class, controlling for the effects of race? And if so, which effects are stronger? The answers are clear: Both effects exist, though the independent race effect is stronger. Although the impact of class on general prevalence still exists after the effects of race have been accounted for, the independent effects of race are somewhat stronger. And on the basis of serious incidence, net class effects again exist, but independent race effects are substantially stronger (see Harris, 1989, for details).

Some additional observations may be made. First, as in the case of the Elliott and Ageton (1980) findings, race and class effects are stronger for more serious offenses. Second, in a particularly striking comparison, the serious incidence rate for upper-SES African Americans in the co-

hort is substantially *higher* than the serious incidence rate for lower-SES whites in the cohort. In itself, this finding puts enormous pressure on any simple attempt to reduce race to the economic dimensions of class. Third, it turns out that, although the factors of race and class have clear, independent effects on the chances of being a one-time offender in the study, these factors have an even greater impact on the chances of continued involvement in delinquency, that is, on being a recidivist (repeat offender). Among one-time offenders, holding race effects constant, lower-SES youth have a 41 percent higher rate of serious incidence than do upper-SES youth. Among recidivists, however, this difference increases to 119 percent. Among one-time offenders, holding class effects constant, African-American youth have a 72 percent higher rate of serious incidence than do white youth. Among recidivists, however, this difference increases dramatically to 274 percent. Independent race effects are thus far greater for juveniles who are repeatedly in trouble with the law than for juveniles who appear to be "deterred" after the first police contact.

Finally, it is worth noting that the clear "race-net-of-class" findings for this birth cohort—including the strikingly higher serious incidence rate for upper-SES African Americans than for lower-SES whites—are replicated in a second birth cohort study in Philadelphia by Tracy et al. (1990). Exactly how much of this race disproportionality in police contact is due to genuine race differences in street crime, and exactly how much of the disproportionality is due to discriminatory police practices, remains a general question (see Blumstein et al., 1993; Farrington et al., 1996). But for juveniles, at least, there seems little doubt that currently in the United States there are significant and real race differences in street crime net of class and police discrimination.

Adults

Though they allow us to help sort out net race effects from net class effects on street crime, observations from the Philadelphia birth cohort are limited to juveniles. What about adults? In a follow-up study of a subset of the first Philadelphia cohort, Thornberry and Farnworth (1982) report still greater SES differences (controlling for the effects of race) once the 1945 cohort reached adulthood. In addition, they note that this class–street-crime link is greater for African Americans than for whites. In related terms, half of the ninety studies reviewed in Braithwaite's (1981) omnibus review of the class–crime link allow arrest-based comparisons for adults; in these studies consistent, inverse relationships are found between SES and street crime, though it is not clear whether these relationships are generally net of race.

Unfortunately, at present, no data allow a direct assessment of the race–street-crime relation for adults after the effects of social class have been accounted for. But there are many good reasons to expect it is at least as strong, if not stronger, than the comparable relation for juveniles. First, for juveniles, race and class clearly make a greater difference as we move to more serious offenses and greater risk of contact with law. If race and class make the largest difference where the stakes are highest, should we not expect race and class to make a still greater difference as we move from the protected status of juveniles to the unprotected status of adults?

Second, studies that look at the relationship of any demographic factor to crime, particularly street crime, face a higher than usual risk of what sociologists call "selection bias" (see Berk and Ray, 1982; Zatz and Hagan, 1985). This bias involves the theoretical impact of lost, unseen, or dropout portions of the sample under scrutiny. The disappearance of serious offenders from any sample would result in the severe underestimation of the effects of race or class. And this problem literally would multiply in looking at groups that faced repeated arrest and incarceration. Thus, if selection bias presents a serious problem for estimates of street crime by juveniles, it presents an extraordinary problem for estimates of race differences in street crimes by adults. For example, in the early 1980s estimates indicated that whereas 14 percent of white males in large cities were arrested at least once for an Index offense, the comparable figure was 51 percent for African-American males (Blumstein and Graddy, 1982). In 1992, 56 percent of all African-American men age 18 to 35 in Baltimore were under some form of criminal justice supervision, such as jail, prison, probation, and so on; in 1997 in Washington, D.C., the comparable figure was 50 percent (Lotke, 1998). And, based on current rates of first incarceration, estimates indicate that whereas 4 percent of all white males will enter state or federal prison during their lifetime, nearly 30 percent of all African-American males will (Bonczar and Beck, 1997).

CONSTITUTIONAL DIFFERENCES

Our review has indicated that one of the strongest theoretical correlates of race—class or SES—cannot alone account for the race–street-crime link. Some of the race–crime link is explained, but a substantial amount remains unexplained. Is it possible that a major portion of the remaining net race difference can be accounted for by constitutional differences between African Americans and whites?

What is meant by the term "constitutional differences"? Clearly, we might mean inherited differences that existed prior to socialization and to the acquisition of culture. But this does not go far enough. Differences in skin color are inherited and exist prior to socialization and acculturation, but no one believes that skin color represents a constitutional difference. By "constitutional," we must mean something deeper than surface difference, something predisposing an individual to think or behave in one way as opposed to another, a racially correlated set of inherited differences in cognitive or behavioral style or content.

On this basis, one common domain of difference might involve temperament, such as the predisposition to be aggressive or to be passive. Another domain might involve general intelligence, such as the predisposition to be good at solving problems in spatial relations or to be slow in seeing the potentially negative consequences of one's own behavior. Yet another domain might include somatotype—that is, a blend of body build and temperament (Sheldon, 1949)—such as the combined predisposition to be muscular, energetic, and aggressive or to be pear-shaped, lethargic, and passive.

In contemporary America, some of these predispositions appear to be correlated with race. It is well known, for example, that race and IQ are correlated (Shuey, 1966; Osborne, 1980; Gordon, 1980; Bailey, 1989; Herrnstein and Murray, 1994). It also appears that, at least among males, race and body build are correlated (Damon et al., 1962, 1966; Malina, 1973). Can such findings make sense of the race–street-crime link? Let us look at some of the specifics.

Somatotype

Other constitutional correlates of race besides IQ have been identified. At least among young males, somatotype is one. Fifty years ago, Sheldon (1949) found that mesomorphy—that is, heavy-boned muscularity often paired with high energy and aggressiveness—was empirically linked to delinquency among young white males. Since then, according to a number of researchers (Damon et al., 1962, 1966; Malina, 1973; Malina and Rarick, 1973), young African-American males have shown higher rates of mesomorphy than comparable whites.

Like the findings on IQ, the findings on somatotype indicate a significant difference by race. Unlike the findings on IQ, however, the findings on somatotype do not show consistent variation within race: Although among juvenile white males, mesomorphy has a credibly documented relationship to delinquency, among juvenile African-American males there appears to be no relationship between mesomorphy and delinquency (McCandless et al., 1972). And somatotype theory seems stretched to the breaking point in its ability to explain the fact that the African-American female street crime rate also far exceeds that of their white female counterparts; unlike the IQ studies we will look at momentarily, the studies that produce the inconsistent somatotype findings are almost entirely restricted to the juvenile male population.

IQ

Because known empirical relationships exist between race and street crime and class and street crime, and between race and IQ and class and IQ, we might expect to find a relationship between IQ and street crime. And indeed, we can. One question is whether this relationship holds true net of race and class. A theoretically more important question is whether the race–street-crime relationship holds true net of IQ *and* class. The answer to both questions is yes, at least as far as the research, heavily skewed by juvenile samples, allows us to see.

The first Philadelphia birth cohort again proves useful. Data from this study make it clear that race, class, and delinquency are correlated with IQ, but they also reveal that IQ has very little impact on delinquency. Other research findings on the IQ–delinquency relationship show similar or somewhat stronger patterns (see Reiss and Rhodes, 1961). In England, West (1982) finds IQ differences between delinquent and nondelinquent boys of close to 6 points on average. And after reviewing a number of studies, Hirschi and Hindelang (1977) find a general difference of close to 9 points, net of class and race. To some extent, the magnitude of mean IQ differences between delinquent and non-delinquent groups varies according to how delinquency is measured. As might be expected, the difference is greater when arrests, rather than self-reports, are the guide. We see, then, no reason to dispute the empirical IQ–delinquency link per se—the link appears clear. The questions are (1) Does the link statistically account for the race–street-crime relationship? and (2) If so, how does it explain the relationship?

In answer to the first question, we note that in the first Philadelphia cohort data, net of class and race, mean IQ scores between delinquent and nondelinquent boys differ by about 3–5 points. In these same data, and by about the same quantity, IQ also varies separately by class, net of race and delinquency status. More important, net of class and delinquency status, race differences in IQ of about 8–11 points are seen. The relationship between race and IQ is, in fact, so consistent that in one very revealing compari-

son, it inverts and trivializes the IQ–delinquency relationship: Nondelinquent, upper-SES African Americans, with a 0 percent prevalence rate, show a lower mean IQ score (100.3) than the most delinquent, lower-SES, whites (101.9). Obviously, if among juveniles there is a relationship between IQ and crime, IQ does a far better job of accounting for differences within race as opposed to those across race, and even then, differences within race accounted for are small.

These studies of the IQ–delinquency relationship typically compare males only, but what happens if gender is brought into the picture? Though we know that race is a powerful correlate of crime, we know that gender is an even more powerful correlate (Harris, 1977; Hindelang, 1979). Thus, if it is to provide a forceful general explanation of street crime, IQ must be able to deal with the gender variable. But can it?

Wilson and Herrnstein (1985: 470) point out that "African American IQ scores are, on the average, about twelve to fifteen points lower than those of whites." Because gender differences in IQ are not significant, African-American female IQ must be about 12–15 points lower at the mean than white male IQ. In the first Philadelphia cohort, which only included males, differences of 3–4 points in mean IQ are associated with gaps of from 0 to 26 percent (upper-SES whites) to 0 to 53 percent (lower-SES African Americans). Imagine, then, what an impact 12–15 points would make in the comparison between African-American females and white males. If, that is, IQ represented a powerful general explanation of criminal involvement, we would expect African-American female prevalence to run four to five times the comparable white male rate. Obviously, it does not.

More recently, in their controversial study of IQ and social class, *The Bell Curve: Intelligence and Class Structure in American Life,* Herrnstein and Murray (1994) furthered the argument that criminality is caused by low IQ. The book captured the public imagination and found its place in the national discussion on social policy. Analyzing a national sample of 14- to 22-year olds, the authors showed that the connection between IQ and criminality holds up even after controlling for variables such as social class or age. Unfortunately, by dropping all the females in the sample, Herrnstein and Murray chose to preclude what we consider to be the acid test of any constitutional theory of crime—can it explain gender differences?

The book quickly came under attack from other scholars (Massey, 1995; Fraser 1995; Fischer et al., 1996; Kincheloe et al., 1996). For example, Cullen et al. (1997) argued that the book's conclusions were derived from ideology rather than "intelligent criminology." Cullen and his associates pointed out that in Herrnstein and Murray's research, IQ accounted for less than 10 percent of the observed differences between delinquent and nondelinquent youths. Furthermore, *The Bell Curve* did not consider all the available theoretically important variables (a standard approach to help ensure that a variable does not appear to have inflated effects). Charging that Herrnstein and Murray ignored such variables as area and family background, Cullen et al. included these variables in a reexamination of the data. They found that small effects of IQ remained, but were typically outweighed by sociological variables. We are left to conclude that, although IQ might help explain delinquency rates among white males and among African-American males, there are so many implicit paradoxes involved that it cannot explain the white–African-American difference in juvenile or adult street crime—let alone suite crime.

Generally, constitutional explanations of the race–street-crime relationship are, at best, not very useful, and in the wrong hands, such explanations can become ludicrous. For example, the African-American homicide rate currently is almost nine times the white homicide rate (see Figure 5.2). In the nineteenth century, however, the ratio was closer to 3 to 1 (Lane, 1979). One way of playing the constitutional difference game would be to conclude that African-American–white differences in constitutional factors have therefore changed significantly in the last hundred or so years. Alternatively, the crime *rates* of American whites historically have far exceeded those of African Americans (Nettler, 1984). Thus, another way of playing the constitutional difference game would be to conclude that the addition of white genes to African-American genes over time in America has caused the "naturally" low baseline of African-American crime to rise (see also Neapolitan, 1998). Obviously, such conclusions are foolish.

SUBCULTURE

Americans of all races share a broad variety of cultural values and beliefs. Some of these are shared with respect to the collectivity, including faith in the value of democracy and the belief that it can be realistically attained. Some of these are shared with respect to the individual, including faith in the value of personal material success and the belief that it can be realistically attained. Although African Americans and whites may share values and beliefs, however, in the margins of poverty, group differences in values and preferences may be important enough to produce group differences in behavior, including street crime. Two such potentially important areas of difference are (1) group members' stress on the value of delayed gratification and (2) their approval of the use of violence.

Delayed Gratification

Willingness to delay gratification refers to a person's general ability to behave in ways that "see" beyond the short-run pleasures and pains of everyday life, and to consider, equally, that some of today's pleasures may well lead to a great deal of tomorrow's grief. Many substance-related behaviors, from heroin use to alcohol consumption to cigarette smoking, provide good examples of the frequently seen preference for short-run "gains" over long-term costs (see Ainslie and Herrnstein's related discussion, 1981; Wilson and Herrnstein, 1985; DiIulio, 1995). Some groups have a greater ability to delay gratification than others.

As might be expected, the value of delayed gratification does seem to vary by social class (see Wells and Smith, 1970). Lower-income groups do not appear to see as much value in delaying gratification as do middle-income groups. This type of finding has played a key role in supporting the idea that there is a "culture of poverty" that keeps the poor poor (see Lewis, 1968). No research indicates that the value of delayed gratification varies by race independently of class, but let us suppose that this difference exists. The critical question is, Can the delayed gratification hypothesis really explain, as it is supposed to do, the race–street-crime relationship?

The delayed gratification hypothesis suggests that the ghetto poor genuinely value or prefer short-term over long-term pleasures, that this preference is not tied to realistic assessments of getting on in life, and that the preference lasts for life. It seems to produce impulsiveness and to get the poor into trouble generally. In these terms, the preference for short-term over long-term pleasures seems highly irrational, perhaps even somewhat immature.

One clear way of restating the delayed gratification hypothesis is in terms of what economists call a "discount rate." From this perspective, the poor have a high discount rate, meaning they generally prefer a smaller amount of money in hand today over the promise of a larger amount of money tomorrow. If, in this fashion, you preferred $95 today over the promise of $100 a year from today, you would have the very low discount rate of 5 percent ($100 minus $95, divided by $100); if, on the other hand, you preferred $50 in hand today over the promise of $100 a year from today, you would have the very high discount of 50 percent ($100 minus $50, divided by $100).

Note that, once the delayed gratification hypothesis is recast into a hypothesis of discount rates, all those who have ever been poor for even a week, such as college students, recognize that the preference for immediate gains is entirely rational and thoroughly attuned to getting on in life—that is, is quite reasonably aligned with one's present resources, capital, savings, and so on, as well as with one's immediate demands. Note also that you were offered $50 today versus the *promise* of $100 next year. As any ghetto youth knows, promises are often difficult to keep; as any ghetto adult knows, life insurance premiums in the ghetto are very high. This element of uncertainty is theoretically very important in assessing the usefulness of the delayed gratification hypothesis. To the extent that the preference for short-term over long-term gains involves an adult's realistic assessment of the chances that he or she will actually be around to receive $100 next year, the delayed gratification hypothesis states little more than that the poor are needy. If so, this means that the ghetto poor do not really have short-time horizons and are not permanently "impulsive." It also strongly suggests that if they were to experience a major situational improvement, the ghetto poor's discount rate would drop, and the appearance of the preference for short-term over long-term gains would disappear.

Approval of Violence

What of the second value-based explanation involving group differences in the approval of violence? As initially formulated by Wolfgang and Ferracuti (1967), the so-called subculture of violence hypothesis tried to explain group differences in homicide rates. This theory relied on the idea that people in groups with high rates of violence tend to grow up and live in subcultures that seem to define violence as an acceptable form of behavior. The usefulness of this value hypothesis is necessarily restricted to crimes that are exclusively violent or to those with a violent component.

Much research has been done on the subculture of violence hypothesis (see Erlanger, 1975; O'Connor and Lizzotte, 1978; Blau and Blau, 1982; Sampson, 1987; Parker, 1989). One variation recasts the subculture of violence as a "subculture of angry aggression" (Bernard, 1990). More in line with the explosion of crack cocaine in the inner cities in the past decades—a potent and violent "alternative economy" that evolved in tandem with the devastating loss of less-skilled manufacturing jobs in American cities and the growth of an urban "underclass" (see Wilson, 1987)—Rose and McClain's (1990) formulation points to the role of a "subculture of materialistic aggression" in the joint production of "big and easy money" *and* increased homicide in urban areas.

But as with the research on the role of father absence, little empirical support has yet been provided for the subculture of violence hypothesis (see Chapter 7 in this text). An important example is Cao et al.'s (1997) recent test of the thesis. Using national survey data, they find that it is actually whites who are more likely to approve of violence than African Americans, basically contradicting the subcultural hypothesis. And Hagedorn (1994) and Jankowski (1995) show that for many, crime is simply a way to make good money when faced with few practical alternatives, and these authors also point out that many criminals would prefer to find success in the safety of a white collar office. In this light, it does not seem appropriate to argue that those who would prefer legitimate jobs approve of a subculture of violence.

There are, however, good reasons to think that the hypothesis fails prior to the gathering of any data. Critical differences exist between people's motivation to commit crime and their motivation to *avoid* committing crime. Hirschi (1969), among others, has stressed that the latter issue—what stops people from committing crime?—is more important than the former. If Hirschi is right, and there is good reason to suspect he is, this means that in looking for differences between individuals who do and who do not commit crime, we should not be looking for the presence or absence of "green lights" to commit crime; instead, we should be looking for the presence or absence of "red lights" to stop people from committing crime. In terms of sociological theory—if, again, Hirschi is right—this means that in looking for differences between groups of people who commit crime at varying rates, we should not be looking for the presence or absence of values that positively prescribe the commission of crime; rather, we should be looking for the presence or absence of values that proscribe it.

The injunction to search for proscriptive norms in the case of economically motivated crime is apt. Crime is often the shortest distance between two points; in modern America, the question frequently concerns what stops people from taking the shorter route to economic gain. If this red-light question is fitting for economically motivated crimes, it is even more fitting for crimes of violence, particularly those that involve no obvious economic gain. Researchers who look for subcultures that are committed to violence (see Erlanger, 1974) are doomed to find little of interest; research in which proscription against violence is measured is far more likely to succeed. In their classic work on delinquency, Short and Strodtbeck (1965), for example, found that lower-class African-American delinquents and middle-class white nondelinquents in Chicago differed far more on proscriptions concerning what they should not do than on prescriptions concerning what they should.

Based on Hirschi's admonition, we conclude that if we were to look for race differences in the presence or absence of red lights that rule out the use of violence (that is, proscriptive norms), we might find a viable contender in the explanation of the race–violent-street-crime relationship. As we shall see shortly, there are still broader gains to be made in understanding the race–street-crime relationship if instead of searching for the presence of green lights, we search for the absence of red ones.

FAMILY STRUCTURE

The amount of drunkenness, immorality, and criminality among the parents of many boys, as brought out by local and individual studies, makes the home in many cases as unfavorable . . . as does the loss of a parent or both parents (Shideler, 1918: 725).

In looking at the impact of family structure on crime, mainstream criminology has focused almost exclusively on the impact of broken families, particularly father-absent families, on the delinquencies of juveniles. In doing so, the tendency has been to assume mistakenly (1) that juveniles in the home are always better off with any father at all, rather than with none at all, and (2) that families and family structure play a role in the production of juvenile, but not adult, crime. These assumptions have caused considerable confusion in the quest to establish the impact of family structure on crime. This conclusion becomes painfully clear in the context of the race–street-crime relationship.

Shinn's (1978) omnibus review of the effects of father absence on IQ and school achievement found that in 57 percent of the studies of African-American homes, father absence was associated either with no negative consequences or with positive consequences (such as better school performance). To some extent, these unexpected findings may reflect the fact that "paternal absence . . . is sometimes the norm rather than the exception in low-income, minority communities" (Farnworth, 1984).

In 1997 among African Americans, female-headed households made up 57 percent of African-American families with children under 18; for whites the comparable figure was 11 percent (U.S. Bureau of the Census, 1998). The still-higher rate of father-absent households among lower-income African Americans, particularly among the African-American underclass, is well documented, with estimates of female-headed households in this "underclass" ranging up to 70 percent (Wilson and Herrnstein, 1985; Urban Institute, 1988). Rather than ask about the effects of the father's absence in the ghetto, perhaps it might make more sense to ask about the effects of the father's *presence*.

In the United States today, African-American males age 25 and over who are fortunate enough to be working full time will, at the median, earn about 77¢ for every $1 earned by comparable white males (Bureau of Labor Statistics, 1998), a rather unbalanced picture in its own right. But such grim comparisons are based on weekly earnings by full-time wage earners. During the course of a year, African-American males—at a 20 percent rate—are almost twice as likely to be unemployed as white males (Bureau of Labor Statistics, 1999); this percentage is certainly far higher among underclass African-American males and, based on findings by the Urban Institute (1988), may reach as high as 60 percent. In addition, out of every 10,000 such males, far more than 30 percent have served or will serve time in jail or prison (Bonczar and Beck, 1997).

With these images in mind, we are not really surprised that findings on the impact of father absence on ghetto delinquency are mixed at best. Farnworth's excellent (1984) review of a variety of father-absent studies notes some major anomalies. Among these are Robins and Hill's (1966) finding that the father's presence is more likely than his absence to promote early delinquency among African-American males; Rosen's (1969) finding that the father's presence increased the violent delinquency of African-American males; and Austin's (1978) finding that, although the father's presence decreased the delinquency of white juveniles, especially white females, his presence did not lower the delinquency of African-American juveniles, and actually increased it for African-American females. In a related study, Montare and Boone (1980) find that, although the father's presence decreased aggressive play in young white males, for young African-American males it promoted aggressive play. To these may be added Farnworth's own 1984 study in which she, like Rosen, linked the father's presence in lower-income African-American families to the increased likelihood of violent delinquency for males, and this time, for females as well. More recently, Wells's and Rankin's (1991) "meta-analysis" of the body of research linking broken homes and delinquency finds similar anomalies and inconsistencies.

There seems reason, then, to doubt the simple assertion that "father knows best," at least as far as the modeling of delinquency goes (but see Kellam et al., 1982; Matsueda and Heimer, 1987). One way of looking at this type of finding is through the lens of social psychology. From this perspective, we recognize the key is not the quantity of parents but the quality of parenting (this is very convincingly argued by Wilson and Herrnstein, 1985). Another way of looking at it is through the lens of employability. From this perspective, one of the sorry correlates of race in America is the comparatively high rate of lower-class African-American fathers locked into a viciously self-perpetuating cycle of unemployment and street crime (see Thornberry and Christenson, 1984), particularly among the extremely poor. In a work of major importance, Sampson (1987) amply and lucidly documents the point that this cycle correlates very strongly with rates of female-headed homes, producing a situation where father's joblessness is the single most likely cause of family disruption and instability, leading to the weakened ability of families to exercise social control of their members, which, in its turn, becomes a major factor in producing African-American violence, especially among juveniles. This position is strongly supported in Phillips's (1997) finding that African-American homicide rates are more strongly affected by such weakened social controls than by levels of income inequality and poverty.

Though the theme is virtually undeveloped in mainstream criminology, there is more than ample reason to expect that family structure affects adult as well as juvenile criminality, especially in the margins of extreme poverty. The presence of a chronically unemployed or underemployed father at home produces major stresses. We know from the huge Federal Income Tax Maintenance studies of the 1970s that direct cash subsidies to poor families have a significant impact on the breakup of these families: Subsidized white families broke up 36 percent more frequently than did control groups, and subsidized African-American families 42 percent more frequently (SRI International, 1983). Apparently, in many cases, mothers with subsidies simply were "better off" without their husbands than with them.

To some extent, the current American welfare system produces family structures conducive to crime and is itself the culprit. So too, the current American criminal justice system, in league with that same welfare system, is also culpable. As some data suggest (see Liker, 1982), a prisoner's wife and children may well lead a materially better life while he is in prison than when he returns home; an ex-con, with no job and few prospects is an extra tally in the denominator of a now-reduced welfare check. Many husbands in such situations are thoroughly aware of this and of their economic marginality in the legitimate labor market. Like Crutchfield's (1995) juveniles, marginally employed in the secondary service sector of the economy, drifting back and forth between more-profitable crime and less-profitable, minimum-wage work, these adult common-law husbands and fathers are also subject to the loss of the restraining (red-light) effect that full-time employment has on one's ability to frequent bars or street corners or to hang out at pool halls with other marginally employed males.

In summary, as long as the meaning of an "intact" home is not trivialized to mean the co-appearance of *any* father and *any* mother, unstable family structure is undoubtedly a major, direct antecedent to street crime and provides a powerful explanation of the race–street-crime relationship. It is entirely plausible that the intact underclass African-American family is as prone to produce delinquency as the broken middle-class home. And it is also plausible that the intact underclass African-American family places even more pressure to commit street crime on its adult members, especially male, than on its juveniles.

INEQUALITY AND CASTE

Earlier, we noted that race differences in the commission of street crime remain after social class is accounted for. This probably is less true for middle-class communities than for lower-class communities. But because street crime is disproportionately a lower-class phenomenon, stronger race differences occur precisely where more street crime occurs. We have thus far examined four competing hypotheses to explain race difference in street crime—class, constitutional factors, subculture, and family structure—and we have found all four wanting. Although we do not really expect any one hypothesis to carry the full burden of explanation, we would still like to identify one that is particularly satisfying. Perhaps something important has been left out, or perhaps we have to look for new evidence in unusual places. Are there key correlates of race that we have missed, key correlates other than social class that make one race more advantaged overall than the other? The answer is yes. These key correlates include four concepts, the last two of which we will combine: (1) relative deprivation, (2) the highly concentrated effects of extreme poverty in a de facto segregated community, or what we will call hyper-ghettoization, (3) historical experience, and (4) caste.

Relative Deprivation

I don't feel enormously discriminated against, but I do feel penalized because while I wait [for promotion], my salary is lower and I don't get to buy some of the things I would like. So I have been doing some extra work selling drugs. . . . [spoken by a 33-year-old African-American industrial worker] (Jankowski, 1995: 88).

In themselves, absolute levels of poverty, or wealth, are not particularly useful predictors of crime. The primary yardstick citizens of different times and places use to measure their success, and their frustration, is not absolute but is, instead, *relative* to local levels of success and frustration. Though few among the billion or so adults in China in 1999 would kill, or dream of killing, because they could not afford a car, we are to the point in America where such deprivation—such relative inequality—could well be viewed as painful and unfair, an understandable, though perhaps not yet excusable, basis for crime.

In trying to understand the motivation to commit crime across time and place, it is much more useful to focus on the subjective pains of relative deprivation—including the bitter feelings of injustice and inequality—than the objective pains of absolute poverty. This means that it would be important for any powerful theory of crime to identify the major social correlates of perceived deprivation. Unfortunately, in America today, race would still need to be identified as such a correlate, quite possibly the most important. Despite a century of legal effort, racial inequality remains a prominent feature of American life, producing the most so-

cially visible form of injustice and deprivation (see Jankowski, 1995).

There can be no doubt that the experience of this deprivation, net of class, is likely to provide a strong motive for crime. However, although there can also be no doubt that the primary reference groups—the yardsticks of success and failure—of whites in America largely remain other groups of whites, there are doubts about the most likely primary reference group for African Americans, or, for that matter, any large minority group (see Balkwell, 1990). Depending on the context of comparison, the historical era, and the specific subset of the minority group in question, this reference group might vary dramatically.

Theories based on the frustrations of inequality are not new. In Henry and Short's landmark (1954) work, *Suicide and Homicide,* trends in economic inequality are used to help explain white and African-American differences in violence toward the self versus violence toward others. Since Blau and Blau's important piece on racial inequality and violence (1982), a major research effort has been underway to locate the causes of street crime, particularly violent street crime, in the matrix of social inequality (see Simpson, 1991, for a discussion of gender, caste, and violent crime). Thus, the key questions have been raised: What specific kinds of social inequalities produce crime, and what specific kinds of crimes do these inequalities produce?

Blau and Blau's major (1982) finding was that economic inequality in general, and racial inequality in particular, were clearly tied to overall criminal violence. More recent findings tend to distinguish violence both by race of offender and by type of inequality. In a study of 1980 data, Harer and Steffensmeier (1992) find that although intra-race (white versus white) inequality is a strong predictor of violent crime among whites, intra-race (African American versus African American) inequality is not associated with violent crime by African Americans. Moreover, in the same study, inter-race inequality predicted neither white nor African-American violent crime. However, in line with more recent work (particularly Sampson, 1987) that focuses on the *indirect* effects of economic deprivation on crime through family disruption, Shihadeh and Steffensmeier (1994) do find clear and strong indirect effects of intra-race inequality on rates of African-American violence. That is, inequality has an impact on crime, but only because inequality first has an impact on family disruption.

In trying to account for related, surprising findings on homicide, Smith (1992) observes that African Americans and whites "may be subject to different social forces." In truth, this may be as profound a statement on the race–street-crime relationship as has appeared in the literature in the past fifty years: Similar puzzles characterize the history of research on the relationship (see also Hill and Crawford, 1990). The important and controversial research by LaFree et al. (1992) on the determinants of African-American and white crime rates in America from 1957 to 1988 may be the best such example. Among other surprising findings, LaFree and his associates report that measures of economic well-being and opportunity have expected effects on white crime rates but very unexpected effects on African-American crime rates. For example, whereas fluctuations upward in measures of white economic well-being and opportunity over the three decades are, as expected, associated with drops in robbery and burglary rates among whites, upward fluctuations in separate measures of overall African-American well-being and opportunity are associated with *increases* in robbery and burglary rates among African Americans.

LaFree et al. are sensitive to the possibility that these findings may reflect the "swamping"

effects of a growing arrest rate of urban underclass males and do not reflect increases in crime among lower- ("working poor") and middle-class African Americans generally. This view likely is correct; the trend may be due to a growing sense of "double-deprivation" among the urban underclass. That is, during the past thirty years and accelerating during the 1980s, the expanding African-American middle class has become an increasingly problematic reference group for the African-American underclass. As the gap between these two groups has grown (see Wilson, 1987), so too has the burden of the relative deprivation experienced by the African-American underclass, in effect doubling from what was previously simply an inter-race inequality to both an inter-race *and* intra-race inequality. This double-barreled combination would seem to be deadly and, with the growth of an alternative crack-cocaine economy in the inner cities, an increasingly plausible alternative explanation of African-American–white differences in street crime among the poor. These points seem supported by Morenoff and Sampson's (1997) conclusion that most somewhat-advantaged African Americans escaping the ghetto core are only making it to peripheral inner-city neighborhoods, where, we conclude, they are increasingly becoming targets of underclass violence.

Hyper-Ghettoization

Is it possible to reproduce [find] in white communities the structural circumstances in which many blacks live? (Sampson and Wilson, 1995: 39)

Representing what criminologists refer to as the early Chicago school of thought, Shaw and McKay (1942) showed in their classic study that neighborhoods lacking social stability had higher crime rates. Over time, criminologists moved away from community-level explanations and back to more individualistic explanations, like IQ differences, or feelings of inequality, or the personal approval of violence as a means to an economic end. Recently, however, interest has revived in this ecological approach, with a focus on the special effects that concentrated poverty within neighborhoods and communities, especially those that are predominantly African American, can have on street crime (Sampson, 1987; Wilson, 1987; Massey, 1990; Massey and Denton, 1993; Sampson and Wilson, 1995). We will call this ecological amalgam of intertwined factors "hyper-ghettoization." By this we mean physically dilapidated, socially isolated, de facto segregated urban ghettos where there is uniform impoverishment and unemployment, where legitimate industry and commerce have fled through deindustrialization and by choice, and where the social institutions that influence, restrain, and control human behavior are strikingly diminished in quantity and quality. Examples of such constraining institutions include two-parent families, schools, churches, libraries, and jobs with decent wages. From this perspective, hyper-ghettoization reflects the meaning of "a place" far more than it does the dimensions of "a people" or "a race." That urban residences in the United States are still racially segregated (Massey, 1990; Massey and Denton, 1993) is no surprise. And, in itself, there is no reason segregation should increase crime rates. The question is thus, Why does racial segregation have such a dramatic effect on crime rates?

The starting point in the "concentration of poverty" argument (Wilson, 1987) lies in the key observation that predominantly African-American neighborhoods are significantly more uniformly impoverished than white neighborhoods (Sampson and Wilson, 1995; Shihadeh and Flynn, 1996; Shihadeh and Ousey, 1996, Krivo et al., 1998). The clear trend in America's

cities is for poor African Americans to live in poor neighborhoods, but for poor whites to live in non-poverty areas. For example, whereas recently less than 7 percent of poor whites lived in areas of extreme poverty nationally, 38 percent of African Americans did (Sampson and Wilson, 1995). The situation is more extreme in large metropolitan areas. Recently in New York City, 70 percent of poor African Americans lived in poverty-stricken neighborhoods, but 70 percent of poor whites lived in non-poverty neighborhoods (cited in Sampson and Wilson, 1995). As a result, the apparent national effect of race on street crime, net of class at the individual level, may well be primarily a function of the relative ghettoization of poor African Americans compared to poor whites (Sampson and Wilson, 1995; Krivo and Peterson, 1996).

Hyper-ghettoization is more than uniform poverty in a de facto segregated neighborhood. The strong connection between racial segregation and urban African-American crime is a partial consequence of African Americans' exclusion from mainstream society and politics (Shihadeh and Flynn, 1996). Economic, physical, and social conditions in African-American neighborhoods can decline with little cost to the larger society. Massey (1993, 1995), for example, argues that segregated African-American neighborhoods are more vulnerable to downturns in the economy because jobs in poor African-American neighborhoods are less stable and are often the first to be eliminated when the economy falters. Further, African Americans find it harder even in good economic times to get a well-paying job, a primary means of proving one's worth. Property values in hyper-ghettoized neighborhoods are low, making it difficult for some cities to generate the income to support social institutions such as good schools, libraries, and recreation areas, which in turn serve as means of informal social control. Because of the powerful trend toward deindustrialization in the United States in the last three decades of the twentieth century, stable industrial jobs have rapidly moved out of central cities. Some of these jobs have been lost to the inner city because they have moved overseas; jobs that moved to nearby suburbs are typically inaccessible to ghetto residents who do not own cars or have access to reliable public transportation (Sullivan, 1989; Wilson, 1987, 1996).

Over the last several decades, there has been a growing African-American middle class, but this has done little to alleviate the concentration of poverty in poor African-American neighborhoods. Middle-class African Americans have rapidly moved out of the poorest African-American ghetto neighborhoods (Wilson, 1987, 1996; Sampson and Wilson, 1995; Shihadeh and Flynn, 1996; Morenoff and Sampson, 1997). This means the increasingly uniform concentration of poor people in impoverished neighborhoods. The effect on street crime is vicious and hyperbolic (ever-increasing). Not only is ghettoization likely to cause higher crime rates, higher crime rates are likely to cause increasing de facto racial segregation of ghettoized neighborhoods, because whites living in these poor neighborhoods have been much more likely than African Americans to move out when crime rates increase (Liska et al., 1998; Liska and Bellair, 1995; South and Crowder, 1998). Thus, in looking at street crime one should not merely look at the simple negative effects of poverty and deprivation. This effect is not constant across different levels of poverty and deprivation; when poverty is genuinely concentrated in a neighborhood and when businesses are gone from it, the effects on crime increase exponentially (Wilson, 1987, 1996; Crane, 1991; Krivo and Peterson, 1996).

One wonders then *if the social structural conditions that cause increased street crime rates among African Americans were replicated for whites, would the rate of such crime among whites equal that of African Americans?* Indeed, this is an important but extremely difficult question to answer empirically because there are so few whites currently in such structural conditions. For example, in a study of race and delinquency in Pittsburgh, Peeples and Loeber (1994) could not find any poverty-stricken neighborhoods with enough whites in them to compare to poverty-stricken African-American neighborhoods. Lowering the bar for defining a neighborhood as "underclass" resulted in more whites being in their underclass sample, but, ironically, also effectively eliminated African Americans from the non-underclass group, thus creating the opposite problem.

Because this question has been difficult to address empirically does not mean it is as difficult to address theoretically. Although race is correlated with significant economic deprivation and residential segregation, unfortunately it is not limited to those consequences. The last, unexplicated feature of hyper-ghettoization lies in the concept of caste. Because we, as other peoples, are still tied so strongly to focusing on the visible features of others, and because of the racism and prejudice coupled to that tie, it is by no means realistic to imagine equal outcomes for whites and African Americans living under the same structural conditions. Consider employment. To many employers dark skin still signals inferiority and white skin signals competence. They are often reluctant to hire African Americans from impoverished neighborhoods and openly disdainful of "African-American" demeanor and speech patterns. One such employer explains why he would be reluctant to hire someone from Cabrini Green, one of Chicago's poorest neighborhoods: "If I could tell [they came from Cabrini Green], I don't think I'd want to hire them. Because it reflects on your credibility . . . I'd wonder about your credibility" (Wilson, 1996: 116).

Historical Experience and Caste

Wilson and Herrnstein (1985: 474) set the stage for introducing the second alternative pair of "old" concepts—historical experience and caste—by pointing to a very basic paradox: "The [historical] experience of the Chinese and the Japanese [in America] suggests that social isolation, substandard living conditions, and general poverty are not invariably associated with high rates of crime among racially distinct groups."

African- and Asian-Americans have, in common, faced difficult social conditions in America's past, yet, at present, show widely disparate levels of involvement in street crime. Apparently, by itself, caste cannot explain the African-American–white difference in street crime. But there is still a missing element in the equation, one involving core differences in the historical experiences of these different groups—most critically the deplorable experience of slavery. Although references to slavery are rarely drawn out in contemporary discussions of race, the practice of slavery was abolished in America only some 120 years ago, well within historical earshot of the present generation. There is good reason to expect that at a bare minimum, the emotional tone of slavery and reconstruction is still communicated in contemporary, oral family histories among African Americans.

In related terms, a number of very important differences separated early Asian- from early African-American arrivals to America. One was that the earliest Chinese arrivals were relatively well-to-do. More critical, and often overlooked, the Chinese (and Japanese) came to seek their fortune *voluntarily*. Many were abused, but were still free to negotiate their own labor rate. In contrast, most of the first African Americans, not so long ago, came to America against their will, as slaves. They were told what to do, and there was no labor rate to negotiate.

What is common to Asian- and African-Americans in U.S. history is caste and the accompanying negative experiences, including visible discrimination, imputations of differences that arrive at birth and continue to death, residential segregation, and the hostility of many whites. What is *uncommon* to Asian- and African-Americans in U.S. history is the recent experience of slavery and the meaning of caste to people who realize that their world is characterized by the expectation of their defeat.

These analyses are all too well known to most African Americans, particularly those in the underclass. For them, the history of class in America is largely the history of race, the history of social mobility little more than the history of a huge, white, backslapping fraternity. For them, in short, there is by virtue of caste a recent link to a real historical process in which they, the African-American underclass, have been cast as outsiders, as people who have been promised full membership in the fraternity but who have been functionally disqualified from it from the start. The point is sharply underscored in David Harris's (1997) article about pretextual traffic stops. In it, Harris observed that during a recent sixteen-month period, twelve Maryland State Police detained and searched over 700 motorists; six of the twelve had a higher than 80 percent rate of stopping African-American motorists, one more than 95 percent, and two stopped *only* African Americans.

Commenting on the problems faced by African-American children in hyper-ghettoized neighborhoods, Shihadeh and Flynn (1996) note that many intelligent and motivated African-American children in poor segregated low-income neighborhoods are discouraged from succeeding for fear of being labeled too "white" by their peers. If because of one's skin color one is penalized for trying to succeed in culturally conventional ways, where are the green lights pulling in the direction of nondelinquent choices and self-definition? At the same time, if one appears to have been disqualified from full membership because one is African American, and if, in addition, one is poor, the analytic question really becomes, Are there any further penalties to be paid if one is caught committing a crime? Exactly what else is there to lose? The answer is, very little. Where are the red lights? The answer is, there are very few and they are very dim.

For the underclass African-American male's white counterpart, also poor, also uneducated, in a less obvious way also residentially segregated, there is a major difference: He can regale himself with tales of Horatio Alger and Abraham Lincoln—white folks, members of the fraternity. With a little effort, the right clothes, and so on, he could even pass for a full-fledged member of the fraternity. For him, the same analytic question can be asked: Is there any further tax to be paid if he is caught committing a crime? The answer is yes—membership in the fraternity is lost. His African-American counterpart has already paid his taxes by virtue of being African American, not by virtue of being poor.

Many studies over two decades lend support to the argument that a person's caste provides a potentially very important, though rather ironic, factor in inhibiting or not inhibiting crime. Unexpectedly, these studies look mostly at the potential aftermath of committing crime: What is the impact of getting caught on one's sense of identity and self-worth? They strongly suggest that being a member of the caste-disadvantaged underclass ironically provides an "insulator" against the ego losses and stigma of being caught (Harris, 1976; Heimer, 1995; Shihadeh and Flynn, 1996). Alternatively, the studies also strongly imply that being caste-advantaged or white, even if you are poor, acts as a red light in deterring street crime. For ex-

ample, at the start of Ageton and Elliott's (1974) longitudinal study of high school youth, African Americans with *no* police contact show more strongly delinquent self-conceptions than do comparable whites (see also Short and Strodtbeck, 1965; Schwartz and Stryker, 1970; Jensen, 1972). But with increased police contact over the years, and net of class, whites' sense of themselves as delinquent increased substantially more than African Americans'; such contact appeared to lower whites' self-esteem but not that of African Americans. Similarly, among an almost exclusively lower-class sample of young adult offenders in a New Jersey correctional facility (Harris, 1976), time spent in prison appeared to affect whites far more than African Americans, with white inmates maintaining significantly stronger delinquent self-conceptions *and* significantly lower self-esteem than African-American inmates (replicated in the Rand Inmate Survey of adult prisoners in California; see Peterson et al., 1981; Harris, 1988). In short, we must conclude that the disadvantages of race are not equivalent to the disadvantages of class or of coming from a poor neighborhood, and that these disadvantages exist over and above class, in the form of historical caste—quite possibly the single most powerful single factor in the overall race–street-crime relationship.

RACE, WHITE COLLAR CRIME, AND SUITE CRIME

We have pursued in detail the question of the race–street-crime relationship, both empirically and theoretically. But what would happen if the UCR Index were to include traditional white collar arrests? Would the race–crime relationship in fact change directions, such that whites were now overrepresented? A superficial look at the data, surprisingly, suggests that the relationship does not change. African Americans accounted for about 31 percent of all UCR "white collar crime" arrests in 1997, including 32 percent of forgery arrests, 31 percent of fraud arrests, and 34 percent of embezzlement arrests. The rate-adjusted ratios of African Americans to whites arrested for these crimes thus run at about the same level as they did for Index crimes against property. Paradoxically, even if the UCR Crime Index included traditional white collar crimes, the same 3 to 1 African American–to–white weighting would be seen as that observed for 1997 Index crimes against property! This finding appears to put a great deal of pressure on theories that stress situational disadvantages in trying to explain the race–crime relationship. The finding also appears to support Hirschi and Gottfredson's theoretical attempts (1987, 1989) to search for the causes of white collar crime in the demographic correlates of such UCR white collar crimes as fraud and embezzlement.

As it turns out, such theoretical efforts are probably wasted (see Steffensmeier, 1989). It is highly unlikely that these UCR data actually represent arrests for what is commonly understood as white collar crime, that is, the phenomenon to be explained. Although the arrestees for these crimes may have worn white shirts at the time of the crime or the arrest, the criminal events involved are generally not occupationally related, that is, are neither committed by individuals in the course of work in a legitimate occupation nor committed by individuals working as legitimate employees in legitimate firms.

We need to distinguish far more carefully race differences in the offenses of isolated entrepreneurs who work "on the fly" or of relatively low-level bureaucrats who work in cubicles from race differences in the offenses of middle- and upper-level managers and executives who work in offices and suites. There are at present very few detailed data on the demographics of white collar offenders, but the few that exist (Wheeler et al., 1988; Daly, 1989) allow us to distinguish between lower- and middle-level offenders. These findings show that African Americans are overrepresented among lower-level offenders by a factor of about 2.5 to 1, that middle-level offenders are more than twice as likely to be college educated as lower-level offenders, and that whites are overrepresented among middle-level offenders by a factor of about 2.7 to 1 (Harris, 1989).

Thus, as we try to focus on higher levels of white collar crime, we begin to see traces emerging of the photographic negative of the race-street-crime relationship: an image in which whites are overrepresented by a factor approximating African Americans' overrepresentation in street crime. If this "inverted" race–crime relationship holds for middle-level white collar crime, whites are undoubtedly overrepresented in corporate, silk collar, or suite crime, to an extent equal to, if not greater than, African Americans' overrepresentation in street crime. This observation underscores our theoretical need to examine the relationship of race to crime *in general,* not just to street crime, in the United States.

In looking at street crime, one question we asked was whether race could be reduced to social class. It could not be, and we concluded that the disadvantages of race existed over and above those of class. The same question may be raised vis-à-vis suite crime: Can the association between race and suite crime be reduced to that between class and suite crime? Our answer here is a, somewhat tentative, no; the advantages of race exist over and above those of class. The opportunity to commit suite crime is still greater for a class-advantaged white than a class-advantaged African American. Paradoxically, we

FIGURE 5.5
Suggested relationships
among crime, race, and
SES

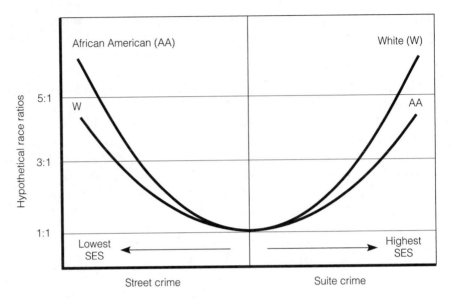

must conclude that, although caste disadvantage net of class is a cause of street crime, caste advantage net of class is a cause of suite crime.

This conclusion reflects an attempt to think about the relationship between race and crime in modern America in a unified way and to challenge the ways in which we have tended to see crime in the past—as essentially a phenomenon occurring on the streets. Perhaps a view in which white criminal figures are in the foreground and African-American criminal figures in the background is a tough picture for the public to accept, a "bad gestalt." But this need not be the case for criminology.

The schematic diagram in Figure 5.5 suggests that in fact there is only *one* basic race–crime relationship in America, and it is parabolic, not linear. Figure 5.5 also illustrates the point that race, or caste, is first and foremost aligned with social class in shaping the adult opportunity to commit one type of crime, street crime, versus the opportunity to commit another type of crime, suite crime. The parabolic relationship graphically suggests that race or caste differences net of class have the greatest impact at the extreme edges of the class spectrum. Ironically, upper-class whites and underclass African Americans may well have something rare but theoretically very important in common: a pronounced, and perhaps highly rational, lack of fear when it comes to committing crime. On the one hand, elite whites are likely to believe that their chances of being caught or severely punished for crime are very low. On the other hand, if as an underclass African American, one feels that "the joint is like the projects, except they feed you free," then one is likely to believe that, in getting caught for crime, one does not have very much left to lose.

CONCLUSION

The key criminological issues to resolve about race must reduce to other, more manageable issues: general questions involving the social pressures to commit crime, the social constraints against committing crime, the opportunities to commit crime, and the relative attractiveness of one type of crime versus another type of crime. Mostly, these are the classical questions in criminology. The issue of race's relationship to crime ought not to signal the question, Which racial group is more likely to commit crime? Rather, it ought to signal the question, Which type of crime is this disadvantaged group, or this advantaged group, more likely to commit? America's longstanding history of the caste segregation of African Americans and whites has created a parallel caste segregation in the commission of street and suite crime.

DISCUSSION QUESTIONS

1. Some criminologists have argued that there is no systematic proof that socioeconomic status is linked to serious criminality. Are they correct? What is the quality of the evidence bearing on this question?

2. Official arrest statistics point to an overrepresentation of African Americans in certain types of crime. What are those types? To what extent do other sources of information about criminality support the conclusion suggested by the official arrest statistics?

3. One hypothesis regarding overrepresentation of African Americans in arrest populations is that police bias enters into the arrest situation. To what extent does Harris's analysis support this hypothesis?

4. Turn the typical question around. What types of crime are white Americans more likely to be involved in? What does the answer suggest about the interrelationship among race, class, and criminal opportunity?

5. What are "constitutional" differences among peoples? To what extent do they explain differential involvement in crime across races?

6. We hear much today about crime resulting from the breakdown of the American family. To what extent does this phenomenon influence racial differences in criminal involvement?

REFERENCES

Ageton, S., and D. S. Elliott. 1974. "The Effects of Legal Processing on Self Concept." *Social Problems* 22: 87–100.

Ainslie, G., and R. J. Hernstein. 1981. "Preference Reversal and Delayed Reinforcement." *Animal Learning and Behavior* 9: 476–482.

Austin, R. L. 1978. "Race, Father-Absence, and Female Delinquency." *Criminology* 15: 487–504.

Bailey, J. M. 1989. "A Critique and Reinterpretation of Gordon's IQ-Commensurability Property." *International Journal of Sociology and Social Policy* 9: 64–74.

Balkwell, J. W. 1990. "Ethnic Inequality and the Rate of Homicide." *Social Forces* 69: 53–70.

Berk, R. A., S. Messinger, D. Rauma, and J. E. Berecochea. 1983. "Prisons as Self-Regulating

Systems: A Comparison of Historical Patterns in California for Male and Female Offenders." *Law & Society Review* 17: 547–586.

Berk, R. A., and S. C. Ray. 1982. "Selection Biases in Sociological Data." *Social Science Research* 11: 352–398.

Bernard, T. 1990. "Angry Aggression Among the 'Truly Disadvantaged.'" *Criminology* 28: 73–96.

Biderman, A. D., J. P. Lynch, and J. L. Peterson. 1991. *Understanding Crime Incidence Statistics: Why the UCR Diverges from the NCS.* New York: Springer-Verlag.

Black, D. J. 1980. *The Manners and Customs of the Police.* New York: Academic Press.

Blau, J. R., and P. M. Blau. 1982. "The Cost of Inequality: Metropolitan Structure and Violent Crime." *American Sociological Review* 47: 114–129.

Block, R., and C. R. Block. 1980. "Decisions and Data: The Transformation of Robbery Incidents into Official Robbery Statistics." *Journal of Criminal Law and Criminology* 71: 622–636.

Blumstein, A. 1995. "Youth Violence, Guns, and the Illicit-Drug Industry." *Journal of Criminal Law & Criminology* 86: 10–36.

Blumstein, A., and E. Graddy. 1982. "Prevalence and Recidivism in Index Arrests: A Feedback Model." *Law & Society Review* 16: 265–290.

Blumstein, A., J. Cohen, and A. M. Williams. 1993. *"The Racial Disproportionality of United States' Prison Populations."* Working draft, unpublished manuscript. Heinz School, Carnegie-Mellon University, Pittsburgh, PA.

Bonczar, T. and A. Beck. 1997. *Lifetime Likelihood of Going to State or Federal Prison.* Washington, DC: U.S. Department of Justice.

Braithwaite, J. 1981. "The Myth of Social Class and Criminality Reconsidered." *American Sociological Review* 46: 36–57.

Bureau of Justice Statistics. 1991. *Correctional Populations in the United States.* 1989. Washington, DC: Bureau of Justice Statistics.

Bureau of Labor Statistics. 1998. *Employment and Earnings.* Washington, DC: U.S. Department of Labor.

———. 1999. *Employment and Earnings.* Washington, DC: U.S. Department of Labor.

Cao, L., A. Adams, and V. Jensen. 1997. "A Test of the Black Subculture of Violence Thesis: A Research Note." *Criminology* 35: 367–379.

Chevigny, P. 1969. *Police Power.* New York: Vintage Books.

Chilton, R. 1986. "Age, Sex, Race, and Arrest Trends for Twelve of the Nation's Largest Central Cities." In *The Social Ecology of Crime: Theory, Research, and Public Policy.* Edited by J. Byrne and R. Sampson. New York: Springer-Verlag.

Conklin, J. E. 1972. *Robbery and the Criminal Justice System.* Philadelphia: Lippincott.

———. 1992. *Criminology.* 4th ed. New York: Macmillan.

Crane, J. 1991. "The Epidemic Theory of Ghettos and Neighborhood Effects on Dropping Out and Teenage Childbearing." *American Journal of Sociology* 96: 1226–1259.

Crutchfield, R. 1995. "Ethnicity, Labor Markets, and Crime." Pp. 194–211 in *Ethnicity, Race, and Crime.* Edited by D. F. Hawkins. Albany: State University of New York Press.

Cullen, F., P. Gendreau, G. Jarjoura, and J. Wright. 1997. "Crime and the Bell Curve: Lessons from Intelligent Criminology." *Crime & Delinquency* 43: 387–411.

Daly, K. 1989. "Gender and Varieties of White-Collar Crime." *Criminology* 27: 769–793.

Damon, A., H. K. Bleibtreu, O. Elliot, and E. Giles. 1962. "Predicting Somatotype from Body Measurements. *American Journal of Physical Anthropology* 20: 461–474.

Damon, A., H. W. Stoudt, and R. A. McFarland. 1966. *The Human Body in Equipment Design.* Cambridge, MA: Harvard University Press.

DiIulio, J. 1995. "Comment on Douglas S. Massey's *'Getting Away With Murder: Segregation and*

Violent Crime in Urban America.'" University of Pennsylvania Law Review 143: 1275–1284.

Donziger, S. 1996. *The Real War on Crime: The Report of the National Criminal Justice Commission.* New York: Harper Perennial.

Elliott, D., and S. Ageton. 1980. "Reconciling Race and Class Differences in Self-reported and Official Estimates of Delinquency." *American Sociological Review* 45: 95–110.

Erlanger, H. S. 1974. "The Empirical Status of the Subculture of Violence Thesis." *Social Problems* 22: 280–292.

———. 1975. "Is There a 'Subculture of Violence' in the South?" *Journal of Criminal Law and Criminology* 66: 483–490.

Farnworth, M. 1984. "Male-Female Differences in Delinquency in a Minority-Group Sample." *Journal of Research in Crime and Delinquency* 21: 191–213.

Farrington, D., R. Loeber, M. Stouthamer-Loeber, W. Van Kammen, and L. Schmidt. 1996. "Self-Reported Delinquency and a Combined Delinquency Seriousness Scale Based on Boys, Mothers, and Teachers: Concurrent and Predictive Validity for African-Americans and Caucasians." *Criminology* 34: 493–517.

Federal Bureau of Investigation. 1998. *Crime in the United States, 1997.* Washington, DC: U.S. Government Printing Office.

Fischer, C., M. Hout, M. Sanchez Jankowski, S. Lucas, A. Swidler, and K. Voss. 1996. *Inequality by Design: Cracking the Bell Curve Myth.* Princeton, NJ: Princeton.

Fraser, S. 1995. *The Bell Curve Wars: Race, Intelligence, and the Future of America.* New York: BasicBooks.

Gordon, R. A. 1980. "Research on IQ, Race and Delinquency." Pp. 37–66 in *Taboos in Criminology.* Edited by E. Sagarin. Beverly Hills, CA: Sage.

Hagan, J., and P. Parker. 1985. "White-collar Crime and Punishment: The Class Structure and Legal Sanctioning of Securities Violations." *American Sociological Review* 50: 302–317.

Hagan, J., J. Simpson, and A. R. Gillis. 1987. "Class in the Household: A Power-Control Theory of Gender and Delinquency." *American Journal of Sociology* 92: 788–816.

Hagedorn, J. 1994. "Homeboys, Dope Fiends, Legits, and New Jacks." *Criminology* 32: 197–219.

Harer, M., and D. Steffensmeier. 1992. "The Differing Effects of Economic Inequality on Black and White Rates of Violence." *Social Forces* 70: 1035–1054.

Harris, A. R. 1976. "Race, Commitment to Deviance, and Spoiled Identity." *American Sociological Review* 41: 432–442.

———. 1977. "Sex and Theories of Deviance: Toward a Functional Theory of Deviant Typescripts." *American Sociological Review* 42: 3–16.

———. 1988. *Self-esteem Among Black and White Prisoners: A Secondary Analysis of the 'Rand Inmate Survey' Data.* Unpublished report, Department of Sociology, University of Massachusetts, Amherst.

———. 1989. *Caste and Crime: Opportunity Theory Revisited.* Unpublished manuscript, Department of Sociology, University of Massachusetts, Amherst.

Harris, A. R., and G. D. Hill. 1982. "The Social Psychology of Deviance: Toward a Reconciliation with Social Structure." *Annual Review of Sociology* 8: 161–186.

Harris, D. 1997. "'Driving While Black' and All Other Traffic Offenses: The Supreme Court and Pretextual Traffic Stops." *The Journal of Criminal Law & Criminology* 87: 544–582.

Heimer, K. 1995. "Socioeconomic Status, Subcultural Definitions, and Violent Delinquency." *Social Forces* 75: 799–833.

Henry, A. F., and J. F. Short Jr. 1954. *Suicide and Homicide: Some Economic, Sociological and Psychological Aspects of Aggression.* New York: Free Press.

Herrnstein, R., and C. Murray. 1994. *The Bell Curve: Intelligence and Class Structure in American Life.* New York: Free Press.

Hill, G. D., and E. Crawford. 1990. "Women, Race, and Crime." *Criminology* 28: 601–626.

Hill, G. D., and A. R. Harris. 1982. "Changes in the Gender-Patterning of Crime, 1953–1977: Opportunity vs. Identity." *Social Science Quarterly* 62: 658–671.

Hindelang, M. J. 1978. "Race and Involvement in Common Law Personal Crimes." *American Sociological Review* 43: 93–109.

———. 1979. "Sex Differences in Criminal Activity." *Social Problems* 27: 143–156.

———. 1981. "Variations in Sex-Race-Age-Specific Incidence Rates of Offending." *American Sociological Review* 46: 461–474.

Hindelang, M. J., T. Hirschi, and J. Weis. 1979. "Correlates of Delinquency: The Illusion of Discrepancy Between Self-report and Official Measures." *American Sociological Review* 44: 995–1014.

Hirschi, T. 1969. *Causes of Delinquency.* Berkeley: University of California Press.

Hirschi, T., and M. R. Gottfredson. 1987. "Causes of White-collar Crime." *Criminology* 25: 949–974.

———. 1989. "The Significance of White-collar Crime for a General Theory of Crime." *Criminology* 27: 359–371.

Hirschi, T., and M. J. Hindelang. 1977. "Intelligence and Delinquency: A Revisionist View." *American Sociological Review* 42: 571–587.

Jankowski, M. 1995. "Ethnography, Inequality, and Crime in the Low-Income Community." Pp. 80–94 in *Crime and Inequality.* Edited by J. Hagan and R. Peterson. Stanford, CA: Stanford University Press.

Jensen, G. F. 1972. "Delinquency and Adolescent Self-conceptions: A Study of the Personal Relevance of Infraction." *Social Problems* 20: 84–102.

Kellam, S. G., R. G. Adams, C. H. Brown, and M. E. Ensminger. 1982. "The Long-term Evolution of the Family Structure of Teenage and Older Mothers." *Journal of Marriage and the Family* 44: 539–554.

Kincheloe, J., S. Steinberg, and A. Gresson. 1996. *Measured Lies: The Bell Curve Examined.* New York: St. Martin's.

Kitsuse, J. I., and A. V. Cicourel. 1963. "A Note on the Use of Official Statistics." *Social Problems* 11: 131–138.

Krivo, L., and R. Peterson. 1996. "Extremely Disadvantaged Neighborhoods and Urban Crime." *Social Forces* 75: 619–650.

Krivo, L., R. Peterson, H. Rizzo, and J. Reynolds. 1998. "Race, Segregation, and the Concentration of Disadvantage: 1980–1990." *Social Problems* 45: 61–80.

LaFree, G., K. A. Drass, and P. O'Day. 1992. "Race and Crime in Postwar America: Determinants of African-American and White Rates, 1957–1988." *Criminology* 30: 157–185.

Lane, R. 1979. *Violent Death in the City: Suicide, Accident, and Murder in 19th Century Philadelphia.* Cambridge, MA: Harvard University Press.

Lewis, O. 1968. *La Vida.* New York: Vintage Books.

Liker, J. 1982. "Wage and Status Effects of Employment on Affective Well-Being Among Ex-felons." *American Sociological Review* 47: 264–283.

Liska A., and P. Bellair. 1995. "Violent Crime Rates and Racial Composition: Convergence Over Time." *American Journal of Sociology* 101: 578–610.

Liska, A., J. Logan, and P. Bellair. 1998. "Race and Violent Crime in the Suburbs." *American Sociological Review* 63: 27–38.

Lotke, E. 1998. "Hobbling a Generation: Young African American Men in Washington, DC's Criminal Justice System—Five Years Later." *Crime & Delinquency* 44: 355–366.

Malina, R. M. 1973. "Biological Substrata." *Comparative Studies of Blacks and Whites in the United States.* Edited by K. S. Miller and R. M. Dreger. New York: Seminar Press.

Malina, R. M., and G. L. Rarick. 1973. "Growth, Physique, and Motor Performance." *Physical Activity, Human Growth and Development.* Edited by G. L. Rarick. New York: Academic Press.

Massey, D. 1990. "American Apartheid: Segregation and the Making of the Underclass." *American Journal of Sociology* 96: 329–357.

———. 1995. "Getting Away With Murder: Segregation and Violent Crime in Urban America." *University of Pennsylvania Law Review* 143: 1203–1232.

Massey, D., and N. Denton. 1993. *American Apartheid: Segregation and the Making of the Underclass.* Cambridge, MA: Harvard.

Matsueda, R. L., and K. Heimer. 1987. "Race, Family Structure, and Delinquency: A Test of Differential Association and Social Control Theories." *American Sociological Review* 52: 826–840.

McCandless, B. R., W. S. Persons III, and A. Roberts. 1972. "Perceived Opportunity, Delinquency, Race, and Body Build Among Delinquent Youth." *Journal of Consulting and Clinical Psychology* 38: 281–287.

McNeely, R. L., and C. E. Pope. 1981. *Race, Crime, and Criminal Justice.* Beverly Hills, CA: Sage.

Montare, A., and S. L. Boone. 1980. "Aggression and Paternal Absence: Racial-Ethnic Differences Among Inner-City Boys." *Journal of Genetic Psychology* 137: 223–232.

Morenoff, J., and R. Sampson. 1997. "Violent Crime and the Spatial Dynamics of Neighborhood Transition: Chicago 1970–1990." *Social Forces* 76: 31–64.

Neapolitan, J. 1998. "Cross-National Variation in Homicides: Is Race a Factor?" *Criminology* 36: 139–156.

Nettler, G. 1984. *Explaining Crime.* 3d ed. New York: McGraw-Hill.

O'Connor, J. F., and A. J. Lizotte. 1978. "The 'Southern Subculture of Violence' Thesis and Patterns of Gun Ownership." *Social Problems* 25: 420–429.

Osborne, R. T. 1980. *Twins: Black and White.* Athens, GA: Foundation for Human Understanding.

Parker, R. N. 1989. "Poverty, Subculture of Violence, and Type of Homicide." *Social Forces* 67: 983–1007.

Peeples, F., and R. Loeber. 1994. "Do Individual Factors and Neighborhood Context Explain Ethnic Differences in Juvenile Delinquency?" *Journal of Quantitative Criminology* 10: 141–157.

Petersilia, J. 1985. "Racial Disparities in the Criminal Justice System: A Summary." *Crime & Delinquency* 31: 15–34.

Peterson, M., H. Braiker, and S. Polich. 1981. *Who Commits Crimes: A Survey of Prison Inmates.* Boston: Oelgeschlager, Gunn & Hain.

Phillips, J. 1997. "Variation in the African-American Homicide Rates: An Assessment of Potential Explanations." *Criminology* 35: 527–559.

Pruitt, C. R., and J. Q. Wilson. 1983. "A Longitudinal Study of the Effect of Race on Sentencing." *Law & Society Review* 17: 613–635.

Rand, M. 1998. *Criminal Victimization 1997: Changes 1996–97 with Trends 1993–97.* Washington, DC: U.S. Department of Justice.

Reiss, A. 1971. *The Police and the Public.* New Haven, CT: Yale University Press.

Reiss, A. J., and A. L. Rhodes. 1961. "The Distribution of Juvenile Delinquency in the Social Class Structure." *American Sociological Review* 26: 720–732.

Robins, L. N., and S. Y. Hill. 1966. "Assessing the Contributions of Family Structure, Class and Peer Groups to Juvenile Delinquency." *Journal of Criminal Law, Criminology, and Police Science* 57: 325–334.

Rose, H. M., and P. D. McClain. 1990. *Race, Place, and Risk: Black Homicide in Urban America.* Albany, NY: State University of New York Press.

Rosen, L. 1969. "Matriarchy and Lower-class Negro Male Delinquency." *Social Problems* 17: 175–189.

Sampson, R., J. 1987. "Urban Black Violence: The Effect of Male Joblessness and Family Disruption." *American Journal of Sociology* 93: 348–382.

Sampson, R., and W. Wilson. 1995. "Toward a Theory of Race, Crime, and Urban Inequality." Pp. 37–54 in *Crime and Inequality.* Edited by J. Hagan and R. Peterson. Stanford, CA: Stanford University Press.

Schwartz, M., and S. Stryker. 1970. *Deviance, Selves, and Others.* Washington, DC: American Sociological Association.

Shaw, C. R., and H. D. McKay. 1942. *Juvenile Delinquency and Urban Areas.* Rev. ed. Chicago: University of Chicago Press.

Sheldon, W. H. 1949. *Varieties of Delinquent Youth: An Introduction to Constitutional Psychiatry.* New York: Harper & Brothers.

Sheley, J. F. 1985. *America's "Crime Problem."* Belmont, CA: Wadsworth.

Sheley, J. F., and A. R. Harris. 1976. "A Rejoinder to Wiley and Hudik's 'Police-Citizen Encounters.'" *Social Problems* 23: 630–631.

Shideler, E. H. 1918. "Family Disintegration and the Delinquent Boy in the United States." *Journal of Criminal Law and Criminology* 8: 709–732.

Shihadeh, E., and N. Flynn. 1996. "Segregation and Crime: The Effect of Black Social Isolation on the Rates of Black Urban Violence." *Social Forces* 74: 1325–1352.

Shihadeh, E., and G. Ousey. 1996. "Metropolitan Expansion and Black Social Dislocation: The Link Between Suburbanization and Center-City Crime." *Social Forces* 75: 649–666.

Shihadeh, E., and D. Steffensmeier. 1994. "Economic Inequality, Family Disruption, and Urban Black Violence: Cities as Units of Stratification and Social Control." *American Journal of Sociology* 103: 837–862.

Shinn, M. 1978. "Father Absence and Children's Cognitive Development." *Psychological Bulletin* 85: 295–324.

Short, J. F., and F. L. Strodtbeck. 1965. *Group Process and Gang Delinquency.* Chicago: University of Chicago Press.

Shuey, A. M. 1966. *The Testing of Negro Intelligence.* New York: Social Science Press.

Silberman, C. E. 1978. *Criminal Violence, Criminal Justice.* New York: Random House.

Simpson, S. 1991. "Caste, Class, and Violent Crime: Explaining Difference in Female Offending." *Criminology* 29: 115–135.

Smith, D. A., C. A. Visher, and L. A. Davidson. 1984. "Equity and Discretionary Justice: The Influence of Race on Police Arrest Decisions." *Journal of Criminal Law and Criminology* 75: 234–249.

Smith, M. D. 1992. "Variation in Correlates of Race-Specific Urban Homicide Rates." *Journal of Contemporary Criminal Justice* 8: 137–149.

South, S., and K. Crowder. 1998. "Leaving the 'Hood: Residential Mobility Between Black, White, and Integrated Neighborhoods." *American Sociological Review* 63: 17–26.

SRI International. 1983. *Final Report of the Seattle-Denver Income Maintenance Experiment. Vol. 1: Design and Results.* Washington, DC: U.S. Government Printing Office.

Steffensmeier, D. 1989. "On the Causes of White-collar Crime: An Assessment of Hirschi and Hindelang's Claims." *Criminology* 27: 345–358.

Sullivan, M. 1989. *"Getting Paid": Youth Crime and Work in the Inner City.* Ithaca: Cornell University Press.

Thornberry, T. P., and R. L. Christenson. 1984. "Unemployment and Criminal Involvement: An Investigation of Reciprocal Causal Structures." *American Sociological Review* 49: 398–411.

Thornberry, T. P., and M. Farnworth. 1982. "Social Correlates of Criminal Involvement: Further Evidence on the Relationship Between Social Status and Criminal Behavior." *American Sociological Review* 47: 505–518.

Tittle, C. R., W. J. Villemez, and D. A. Smith. 1978. "The Myth of Social Class and Criminality: An Empirical Assessment of the Empirical Evidence." *American Sociological Review* 43: 643–656.

Tonry, M. 1994. "Racial Politics, Racial Disparities, and the War on Crime." *Crime & Delinquency* 40: 475–494.

Tracy, P., M. Wolfgang, and R. Figlio. 1990. *Delinquency Careers in Two Birth Cohorts.* New York: Plenum.

U.S. Bureau of the Census. 1998. *Selected Characteristics of Households by Type, Region, and Race of*

Households. Washington, DC: U.S. Bureau of the Census.

Urban Institute. 1988. *Growth of the Underclass 1970–1980.* Urban Institute discussion paper, April 1988. Washington, DC: Urban Institute.

Wells, L., and J. Rankin. 1991. "Families and Delinquency: A Meta-Analysis of the Impact of Broken Homes." *Social Problems* 38: 71–93.

Wells, R. T., and T. S. Smith. 1970. "Development of Preference for Delayed Reinforcement in Disadvantaged Children." *Journal of Educational Psychology* 61: 118–123.

West, D. J. 1982. *Delinquency: Its Roots, Careers and Prospects.* Cambridge, MA: Harvard University Press.

Wheeler, S., D. Weisburd, N. Bode, and E. Waring. 1988. "White Collar Crime and Criminals." *American Criminal Law Review* 25: 331–357.

Wilbanks, W. 1987. *The Myth of a Racist Criminal Justice System.* Monterey, CA: Brooks/Cole.

Wilson, J. Q., and R. Herrnstein. 1985. *Crime and Human Nature.* New York: Simon & Schuster.

Wilson, W. 1987. *The Truly Disadvantaged: The Inner City, the Underclass, and Public Policy.* Chicago: University of Chicago Press.

———. 1996. *When Work Disappears: The World of the New Urban Poor.* New York: Knopf.

Wolfgang, M. 1958. *Patterns in Criminal Homicide.* Philadelphia: University of Pennsylvania Press.

Wolfgang, M. E., and F. Ferracuti. 1967. *The Subculture of Violence: Towards an Integrated Theory in Criminology.* Beverly Hills, CA: Sage.

Wolfgang, M., R. M. Figlio, and T. Sellin. 1972. *Delinquency in a Birth Cohort.* Chicago: University of Chicago Press.

Zatz, M. S., and J. Hagan. 1985. "Crime, Time, and Punishment: An Exploration of Selection Bias in Sentencing Research." *Journal of Quantitative Criminology* 1: 103–126.

Chapter Outline

- Rediscovering Victims and Studying Their Plight

- Exploring the Risks of Becoming a Victim
  Measuring Victimization: Sources of Data
  Informing Authorities: Reporting Rates
  Recognizing Differential Risks

- Fixing Blame: The Controversy over Shared Responsibility

- Understanding and Avoiding Victimization

- Seeking Reimbursement for Victimization
  Restitution by Offenders
  Civil Lawsuits Against Offenders and Third Parties
  Compensation from Insurance Policies and Government Funds

- Campaigning for Greater Victims' Rights
  The Criminal Justice System: Theory and Practice

- Searching for Justice Informally
  Restorative Justice
  Vigilantism

- Conclusion

6

Victims of Crime:

Issues and Patterns

ANDREW A. KARMEN
John Jay College of Criminal Justice,
City University of New York

REDISCOVERING VICTIMS
AND STUDYING THEIR PLIGHT

For centuries, the real flesh-and-blood individuals harmed bodily, mentally, and economically by criminals were largely ignored by the public as uninteresting people, whereas their pressing needs were routinely overlooked within the legal system. But in recent decades, crime victims finally have been "rediscovered" by the police, prosecutors, judges, lawmakers, political activists, journalists, authors, businesses selling products and services, and social scientists studying the crime problem.

Starting in the 1960s, several social movements began to call attention to the plight of crime victims. The emerging women's movement challenged the traditional indifference shown toward female victims of male violence by initiating self-help projects like rape crisis centers and shelters for battered women. The civil rights and civil liberties movements demanded equal protection for all under the law in order to quell police brutality against members of minority groups as well as terrorist violence (such as lynchings, bombings, assassinations) unleashed by segregationist hate groups. The law-and-order movement criticized landmark decisions handed down by the Supreme Court that changed the operations of the justice system in ways that seemed to favor criminals (including suspects, defendants, and prisoners) at the expense of the innocent people they injured. By the 1980s, a broad-based victims' rights movement coalesced to empower individuals trying to exert some influence over how officials handled their cases.

Today, the suffering of crime victims is receiving much more attention than ever before. Counselors, therapists, social workers, members of support groups and other advocates provide direct services to victims injured emotionally, physically, and financially. Considerable progress has been made, but serious problems persist. Although the news media regularly depict the experiences of street-crime victims, much of the coverage is highly sensationalized and crudely insensitive (see Chapter 1 in this volume). A whole industry marketing security products (like guns, locks, and alarms) and services (such as insurance, guards, and self-defense courses) promises it can help prevent victimization or at least minimize its aftershocks, but the sales pitches often intentionally heighten the audience's sense of vulnerability and insecurity, exploit irrational fears, and foster illusions. Highly trained professionals—such as paramedics and counselors—along with dedicated volunteers attend to the casualties of street crimes, but the depth and scope of the needs and misery they encounter usually overwhelm the limited resources set aside for victim assistance. Police chiefs, district attorneys, judges, corrections officials, and parole board members acknowledge the legitimacy of victims' demands for progress reports and input into decision making, but these criminal justice officials are reluctant to alter their own priorities and standard operating procedures.

Victims have also been "discovered" by social scientists. The first scholars in the 1940s, 1950s, and 1960s to consider themselves victimologists were criminologists. But they appeared to be more interested in stigmatizing victims for bringing about their own misfortunes than in helping them return to the condition they were in before the crime occurred. This initial bias—that victims might unwittingly or even intentionally contribute to the incidents in which they were harmed—was counteracted in the 1970s and 1980s, when the fledgling discipline attracted academics and practitioners whose primary concern was aiding

people in distress. Now, victimology has become a recognized area of specialization within criminology, with its own journals, conferences, courses, and textbooks. It is an interdisciplinary field, drawing heavily on sociology, psychology, social work, medicine, and law. Its knowledge base expands exponentially as special populations of victims with specific problems requiring innovative solutions are studied. For example, victims of sexual assaults, of domestic violence, of crashes caused by drunk drivers, and of bias crimes motivated by irrational hatred now demand and attract attention. Victimologists are systematically examining how familiar groups face threats that were previously unanalyzed, such as children sexually abused by their parents or kidnapped by strangers, tourists preyed on while on vacation, college students raped on and off campus, police officers injured or killed in the line of duty. Victimologists carry out research to gather data revealing rates, trends, and patterns of risk; investigate the way the criminal justice system handles victims; evaluate the effectiveness of programs intended to aid recovery; and analyze the social and political reactions to the threat and reality of victimization. A major issue that currently divides victimologists is whether the scope of the field should be confined to just those who are harmed by illegal acts (mostly "street crimes" of violence and thefts of property) or broadened to embrace the suffering brought about by accidents, diseases, natural disasters, and political oppression. (For an overview of the discipline, see Viano, 1976; Schafer, 1977; Parsonage, 1979; Galaway and Hudson, 1979; Schneider, 1982; Elias, 1986; and Karmen, 1996.)

Viewed through the lens of social constructionism, the rediscovery process has been fostered by a virtual "victim industry" that is guided by these ideological tenets: (1) victimization is widespread and clear-cut, yet often unrecognized despite its serious consequences; and (2) the public in a sensitized society needs to learn to respect victims' claims that they have been harmed, should not be blamed for their misfortunes, and should be supported in their campaigns to reform social institutions (Best, 1997).

This chapter highlights some of the key concerns in victimology: what categories of people are harmed by street criminals the most frequently and the least often—and why; whether some victims are partly to blame; how individuals try to avoid victimization; what methods are available for reimbursing losses; which new legal rights victims have secured and whether they truly have an impact on how cases are processed within the justice system; and what informal means victims are resorting to in order to resolve their conflicts with offenders.

EXPLORING THE RISKS OF BECOMING A VICTIM

Measuring Victimization: Sources of Data

Victimologists need accurate statistics about crimes and victims in order to estimate losses, calculate rates, test theories that explain why some people fall into high-risk groups, and evaluate prevention strategies and recovery programs. Unfortunately, many of the figures generated by official record-keeping agencies are collected in ways that undermine their credibility and usefulness. The two most widely cited sources of data are the Federal Bureau of Investigation's (FBI) *Uniform Crime Reports* (UCR) and the Department of Justice's National Crime Victimization Survey (NCVS) (refer to Chapter 3 of this volume for a more detailed comparison).

From a victimologist's point of view, the FBI's annual UCR has two very serious shortcomings: First, it does not provide any information about the characteristics of crime victims except for those who were murdered; second, the UCR is strictly a compilation of crimes known to the police. Because crimes that were not reported to the authorities cannot be included in the calculations, UCR figures unavoidably underestimate the actual (but unknown) rates of rape, robbery, aggravated assault, burglary, larceny, and motor vehicle theft.

The NCVS represents an improvement over the UCR. The questionnaire is used during interviews with about 94,000 individuals age 12 or over in roughly 45,000 households (Maltz and Zawitz, 1998) and collects data about the backgrounds of people identifying themselves as victims (their age, sex, race/ethnicity, household size, family income, marital status, and area of residence), their relationships to offenders (whether they are strangers), details about the crimes (such as where and when they occurred and what weapons were used), and the extent to which they were harmed (whether they suffered financial losses and physical injuries). Survey interviewers gather information about incidents that the police know about plus those that the police were not told about (called the "dark figure" of unreported crime) and the reasons why victims did or did not report the crimes to the authorities.

Although victimologists find the NCVS a more valuable and accurate source of data than the UCR, NCVS annual reports suffer from some shortcomings too. As noted in Chapter 3, even though the NCVS interviewers probe for information about unreported incidents, underestimates of the actual rates still can result if respondents do not want to discuss events that they never revealed to the police as well. There is also the possibility that respondents forget about or choose to ignore incidents that they already reported to the police. "Memory decay" refers to forgetfulness about (presumably minor) crimes suffered during the preceding six months, since they were last telephoned or visited by the NCVS staff. Overreporting can arise from "forward telescoping," when a respondent believes an incident occurred within the six-month interval, but it actually took place farther back in time and should not be counted. Interviewers take the victim's accounts at face value; no police investigation is initiated. But this practice can lead to over-reporting, if, for example, some people mistakenly assume that a possession actually lost through carelessness was stolen by a criminal. And finally, as in all surveys, two problems arise. The first is that respondents can deliberately exaggerate or conceal the truth of what really happened—the credibility of what people tell pollsters is always subject to doubt. The second problem is that findings from a survey based on a sample are just rough estimates, with a margin of error plus or minus x percentage points (see Maltz and Zawitz, 1998). Finally, despite the wealth of detail gathered by the NCVS, its scope is limited to street crimes of violence and theft; the survey excludes kidnapping, commercial burglaries, and robberies, as well as other harmful acts like swindles and instances of blackmail. (For more detailed methodological critiques, see Garofalo, 1981; Levine, 1976; O'Brien, 1985; Reiss, 1986; and Skogan, 1986.)

The NCVS was redesigned in 1994 to improve its accuracy by altering its format, by prompting respondents to remember more details, and by adding some categories of offenses such as sexual assaults other than rapes. But the key statistics derived from the annual surveys continue to be the rates of rape, robbery, assault, and personal larceny for every 1,000 individuals in a year; and of burglary, larceny, and vehicle theft per 1,000 households per year. (Chapters 7

and 8 of this text discuss victimization rates for acts of violence and theft.)

In 1996, projections from the NCVS indicated that about 9.1 million crimes of violence (rapes, robberies, and assaults), 27.3 million thefts of household property (including burglaries and motor vehicle thefts), and 300 thousand personal thefts (like pickpocketings and purse-snatchings) were committed across the country. The robbery rate was estimated to be 5.2 victims for every 1,000 persons 12 years old and older that year. The rape and sexual assault rate was computed to be about 1.4 per 1,000 persons 12 years old and over. For every 1,000 households, over 47 were burglarized, and nearly 14 suffered a car theft. (When interpreting all these rates, note that unsuccessful attempted crimes are combined with completed acts.) The most common kind of victimization disclosed by survey respondents was "household larceny," which was defined to include all thefts and attempted thefts of property and cash from a residence by persons invited in (such as maids, repairpeople, or party guests, as opposed to intruders) or thefts of possessions from a home's immediate vicinity (such as lawn furniture) by trespassers. About 206 out of every 1,000 households experienced losses of this kind during 1996. These victimization rates for crimes of violence and for crimes against property were the lowest since the NCVS started in 1973 (Ringel, 1997).

NCVS findings can be used not only to derive estimates of the odds of being victimized in a year but also over an entire lifetime. Annual rates yield the impression that victimization is an unusual event because only a few people out of every 1,000 are unfortunate enough to be targeted by offenders during a given year. But when the cumulative odds of becoming a victim are estimated for a time period spanning six decades or more (starting at age 12), what seems highly unlikely during any single year appears to be much more of a possibility somewhere down the road. For example, according to projections based on NCVS findings from the mid-1980s, just about all persons (99 percent) currently 12 years old will someday become victims of theft (a personal larceny with or without contact). Lifetime likelihoods are correspondingly lower for persons who are already well past the age of 12. Of course, the methodological problem surrounding estimates of lifetime likelihoods arises from the unpredictability of future conditions. If social conditions change radically over the next few decades, projected percentages of the proportion of the public that will be robbed or assaulted or raped could be significantly inaccurate (see Koppel, 1987).

Informing Authorities: Reporting Rates

Victimologists study the findings of NCVS surveys to discover what proportions of crimes are reported to the police and to find out the reasons why people do or do not inform the authorities about their personal troubles. In 1994, victims said they filed formal complaints with the police concerning only 36 percent of all the different types of incidents that they disclosed to survey interviewers. Reporting rates vary according to the type and seriousness of the crime and the characteristics of the victim (for example, age or social class). Several patterns are worth noting: Crimes are more likely to be reported if they involve violence rather than just theft, if they are completed rather than merely attempted, and if victims sustain physical injuries or suffer financial losses they consider to be substantial. Teenagers are less inclined to call for help than older people, and members of higher-income families complain to the authorities about thefts more often than those from lower-income households.

Of all the crimes asked about on the survey, completed auto thefts are reported at the highest rate (92 percent). (Failed attempts to steal vehicles are reported much less often, only 50 percent of the time.) Victims inform the police about completed vehicle thefts for several reasons: They hope their stolen cars, trucks, and vans will be recovered; their insurance policies require filing a formal complaint to receive reimbursement; and they do not want the police to assume they were behind the wheel if the vehicle is later involved in an accident or is used in a crime. The lowest reporting rates were noted for minor thefts of personal possessions (33 percent) and for household larcenies (27 percent). As for the more serious crimes, robberies and aggravated assaults were reported 55 percent and 52 percent of the time, respectively. Only 32 percent of those victims of sexual assaults and rapes who were willing to discuss the incidents with NCVS interviewers said they had also informed the authorities in 1994 (Perkins and Klaus, 1996).

Victims report crimes to the police for a variety of reasons: to recover stolen property, to become eligible for insurance reimbursement, to fulfill a sense of civic duty, to prevent the offender from striking again against someone else, and to get an offender into legal trouble. Relatively few victims tell NCVS interviewers that they failed to notify the authorities because they were intimidated and worried about reprisals (however, frightened victims might not reveal their fears to survey employees). Some say they did not want to invest the time and effort to get involved in the criminal justice process. Victims do not report crimes when they believe that the incidents are not serious enough; that the

Table 6.1   Percent of Victimizations Reported to the Police, 1973–1994

	1974	1976	1978	1980	1982	1984	1986	1988	1990	1992	1994
All crimes	33	35	33	36	36	35	37	36	38	36	36
Personal Crimes	30	32	30	33	33	33	34	34	35	42	42
Crimes of violence	47	49	44	47	48	47	50	48	48	43	42
Rape[a]	52	53	49	41	53	56	48	45	54	32	32
Robbery	54	53	51	57	56	54	58	57	50	58	55
Assault	45	48	43	45	46	45	48	46	47	41	40
Aggravated	53	58	53	54	58	55	59	54	59	*	52
Simple	39	41	37	40	40	40	41	41	42	*	36
Crimes of theft	25	27	25	27	27	26	28	27	29	*	33
Personal larceny[a]											
With contact	34	36	34	36	33	31	38	35	37	*	*
Without contact	24	26	24	27	27	26	28	27	28	*	*
Household Crimes	37	38	36	39	39	38	41	40	41	34	34
Household burglary	48	48	47	51	49	49	52	51	51	51	51
Household larceny	25	27	24	28	27	27	28	26	27	27	27
Motor vehicle theft	67	69	66	69	72	69	73	73	75	77	78

SOURCE: National Crime Victimization Data, 1974–1994, as reported in Bastion (1992); Perkins and Klaus (1996).

[a]Survey was redesigned in 1992; rape reporting rate and personal larceny rate not comparable after 1992.

*Data unavailable

conflicts are personal matters; that nothing can be done; or that the police do not want to be bothered or are inefficient, ineffective, or insensitive (Sparks et al., 1977; Harlow, 1985; Gottfredson and Gottfredson, 1988). Contrary to widespread impressions, NCVS findings consistently reveal that African-American victims are more likely, not less likely, than white victims to call the police and request assistance, especially in cases of aggravated assault, rape, and robbery.

In general, reporting rates are rather stable from year to year. Despite public relations campaigns by police officials to encourage victims to file complaints, no dramatic increases in reporting rates can be detected. The overall reporting rate for all kinds of personal and household property and violent crimes has improved from 32 percent when the first survey was carried out (1973) to approximately 36 percent during the most recent survey (1995). Yet, for specific crimes, the reporting rate may fluctuate considerably over the years. For example, the reporting rate for forcible rapes (by strangers as well as acquaintances) has dipped to as low as 41 percent and has risen to as high as 61 percent. These yearly changes in reporting rates for the crimes covered in the NCVS appear in Table 6.1.

Victimologists suspect that the most underreported crimes are offenses committed by nonstrangers, especially physical and sexual assaults by intimates like family members and lovers (Pagelow, 1989). Acts that are not well detected by either the NCVS or the UCR—because victims are as reluctant to reveal their plight to interviewers as they are to police officers—include wife-beating (Frieze and Browne, 1989), acquaintance rape (Koss, 1992) and incidents in which children are physically abused (Mash and

Wolfe, 1991) or sexually abused, especially incestuously (Garbarino, 1989). The incidence (number of victimizations occurring) and the prevalence (percent of people victimized) of underreported crimes like these must be estimated by researchers from other sources and from self-report surveys.

Recognizing Differential Risks

The victimization rates derived from the annual NCVS surveys can be used to estimate the risks faced by "typical Americans" and "average households." But NCVS findings can also be used to provide a sense of the odds of being victimized for specific groups within the population. When these national statistics are broken down into their constituent parts, distinct patterns emerge that reveal that different categories of people face widely varying risks (see Harlow, 1987). This notion of differential rates and varying risks can be illustrated by an analysis of robberies committed during 1996.

The burden of robbery victimization falls unevenly, striking certain kinds of people much more than others (see Table 6.2). For 1996, the overall robbery rate for all categories of persons was estimated to be 5.2 per 1,000 individuals. But NCVS calculations indicate that males were robbed at more than twice the rate as females. African Americans faced nearly three times the risk that white people did. Teenagers and young adults were robbed many times more often than were middle-aged and elderly people. Single persons who were never married plus those who were separated or divorced experienced far greater risks than married people. Persons from lower-income families were more likely to be robbed than were persons from higher-income families. Residents of urban areas

Table 6.2   Differential Robbery Rates, 1996

VICTIM CATEGORY	ROBBERY VICTIMIZATION RATE PER 1,000 PERSONS
All persons	5.2
Sex	
Male	7.2
Female	3.4
Race	
White	4.2
African American	11.4
Other	7.4
Ethnicity	
Hispanic American	8.4
Non–Hispanic American	4.9
Age	
12–15	10.0
16–19	12.0
20–24	10.0
25–34	7.1
35–49	3.8
50–64	1.8
65 and older	1.1
Marital status	
Married	2.0
Widowed	1.1
Divorced or separated	8.8
Never married	10.4
Family income	
Less than $7,500	9.9
$7,500–14,999	8.5
$15,000–24,999	5.4
$25,000–34,999	5.5
$35,000–49,999	4.5
$50,000–74,999	3.3
$75,000 and above	2.0
Area of residence	
Urban	10.4
Suburban	3.3
Rural	2.6

SOURCE: From C. Ringel (1997).

FIGURE 6.1

Rates of violent crimes (including murders, rapes, robberies, and assaults) per 1,000 population, by sex

SOURCE: U.S. Department of Justice (1997).

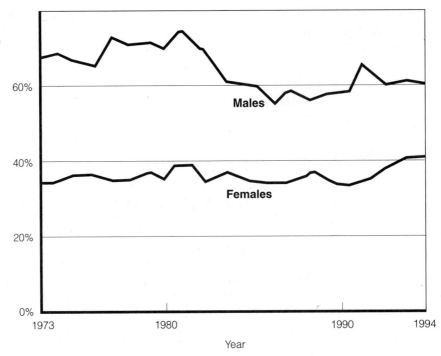

were robbed at a much higher rate than their rural and suburban counterparts. The highest robbery rates were suffered by people who fell into all the high risk groups: young, male, low income, single African Americans living in big cities.

The recognition of such differential rates can help correct widely held stereotypes derived from the news media's coverage or from the campaigns of politicians about who suffers most from street crime. For example, the data indicate that, although females and the elderly may be easier to rob, young males, especially from minority groups, are victimized much more often. It is important, however, to watch for changes in these profiles. The data presented in Figure 6.1, for example, suggest that the ratio of male to female violent crime victimization is declining.

FIXING BLAME: THE CONTROVERSY OVER SHARED RESPONSIBILITY

The suspicion that certain victims said or did something that in some manner contributed to their being harmed is what inspired criminologists to become victimologists from the 1940s through the 1960s (see Von Hentig, 1941, 1948; Ellenberger, 1955; Wolfgang, 1958; Schafer, 1968; Amir, 1967). The concepts of victim *facilitation, precipitation,* and *provocation* were formulated to specify the actions taken by victims right before and during the incidents that contributed to their losses and injuries.

Facilitation is said to occur when victims fail to take conventional precautions and thus through negligence make the criminals' task easier. Classic examples include facilitating unlawful entry burglaries (accomplished without the use of force) by leaving a window open or a door unlocked; and making auto theft easier by leaving keys dangling from a car's ignition lock. *Precipitation* suggests an even more active level of participation by the victim. In cases of murder, for example, victim precipitation is said to occur whenever the person who was slain was the first to resort to physical force (especially brandishing a deadly weapon) during a conflict. According to several studies, between 20 and 40 percent of all homicides could have been considered victim-precipitated (Wolfgang, 1958; Voss and Hepburn, 1968; National Commission on the Causes and Prevention of Violence, 1969).

Surely the most controversial application of the concept of shared responsibility was the definition of a victim-precipitated rape as an incident culminating in forced intercourse in which the female first agreed to sexual relations, or clearly encouraged the male verbally or through gestures, but then retracted the invitation (Amir, 1967; National Commission on the Causes and Prevention of Violence, 1969).

The concepts of precipitation and *provocation* have been used interchangeably, perhaps obscuring an important difference between singling oneself out for attack by attracting a motivated offender (precipitation) and instigating an otherwise law-abiding person to launch a counterattack (provocation). For example, supporters of clemency for battered women who ultimately slay their tormentors argue that the dead victims were actually offenders who provoked their otherwise law-abiding wives to resort to violence in self-defense (Browne, 1987).

Some victimologists seek to determine the proportion of murders, rapes, robberies, assaults, and car thefts that were victim-facilitated, -precipitated, or -provoked, but others reject such endeavors as encouraging an unfair tendency to blame victims for their own plights. Victim-blaming has been denounced as a form of scapegoating, in which people are held responsible for situations beyond their control. Victim-blaming shifts the burden of accountability away from offenders and away from the social conditions that generate criminal behavior. For example, finding fault with the words and deeds of battered women and rape victims diverts attention from the institutionalized sexism within a society's culture and legal system (Brownmiller, 1975; Browne, 1987). Similarly, blaming auto theft on careless motorists relieves manufacturers of any responsibility for having designed cars that are easy to steal because vehicle security was a low priority of top executives (Karmen, 1979, 1980, 1981).

Indeed, the attempt to establish the degree of shared responsibility, if any, on the victims' part raises a host of theoretical problems. Critics contend that victim-blaming arguments merely restate self-serving rationalizations originating with offenders and that such arguments are plagued by the fallacy of circular reasoning, picturing offenders as reactive, with the victims' actions as the necessary and sufficient conditions for crimes to occur (see Weis and Borges, 1973; Franklin and Franklin, 1976; Sheley, 1979; Reiff, 1979; and Karmen, 1991).

While the experts debate these theories, the issue of fixing responsibility retains great practical importance within the criminal justice system and arises routinely at every stage of case processing (McDonald, 1976; Williams, 1978). For example, in the aftermath of a barroom brawl, judgments about the degree of shared responsibility can influence the police officers' decision to arrest just the victor, or the injured party as well. Concerns about the appearance of shared responsibility for causing the brawl might convince a prosecutor to engage in plea negotiations rather than press for a conviction for assault and risk acquittal by a trial jury. The sentencing judge might consider aggressive acts by the wounded victim to be provocations that mitigate the severity of punishment deserved by the assailant.

UNDERSTANDING AND AVOIDING VICTIMIZATION

Victimologists and criminologists share a common interest in explaining why some categories of people are more likely to be preyed upon by criminals than are others (that is, they bear differential risks) and why certain individuals lead more dangerous lives (perhaps they share responsibility through facilitation, precipitation, or provocation) than others (who are crime-conscious and take precautions). According to recent research, the variables that account for differences in risk levels include lifestyles (how people spend their time and money), routine activities (how some patterned ways of behaving attract potential offenders), exposure to motivated (often dangerous) offenders and threatening situations, the availability of suitable targets (how easily goods such as electronic devices may be stolen), the presence or absence of capable guardians (police, private security, or alarm systems), and the proximity to high-crime "hot spots" (Cohen et al., 1981; Messner and Tardiff, 1985; Garofalo, 1986; Sherman et al., 1989; Miethe et al., 1990; see Chapters 7 and 8 in this text for further discussions of these factors).

Considerable attention has recently been given to issues of victimization prevention. Where once we spoke of crime prevention (mainly major governmental campaigns designed to get at the social roots of street crime by tackling problems like poverty, unemployment, racial discrimination, failing school systems, and lack of teenage recreational facilities), today we speak as often of measures taken by individuals or small groups to anticipate, recognize, and appraise risks, along with actions designed to reduce or eliminate these threats (National Crime Prevention Institute, 1978). These preemptive moves and defensive tactics have a simple intent: to deter or deflect would-be offenders from their intended targets (Cohen et al., 1981). Thus, people become more conscious of limiting their exposure to dangerous persons and potentially threatening situations. They may limit the amount of time they are out after dark. They may travel in groups rather than alone. They may seek to establish more "defensible space" through the utilization of sentries (human, animal, or mechanical) and of "target-hardening" techniques such as fences, bars, and locks (Newman, 1972; Skogan and Maxfield, 1981).

The effectiveness of victimization prevention strategies is extremely difficult to evaluate, given the problems involved in trying to measure how many potential offenders are discouraged from committing crimes. Some evidence supports the "valve theory" (National Commission on the Causes and Prevention of Violence, 1969) that if one avenue of illegal opportunities is shut off (for example, protecting bus drivers from robbery by requiring passengers to have exact change), then criminally inclined persons will shift their attention to more vulnerable targets (perhaps cab drivers). The growing proliferation of burglar alarms, for example, may not have had any appreciable impact on the overall rate of attempted or completed forcible entries, but such security hardware might cause a social redistribution of the burden of victimization. Would-be burglars might avoid homes with visible alarm systems, especially in communities with neighborhood patrols, and increasingly strike unprotected homes in unguarded areas. If so, the victimization prevention measures some people are taking are deflecting predators onto others (Rand, 1985; Barr and Pease, 1990). To the extent that purchasing security equipment is a function of income, the privileged are enhancing their safety at the expense of the underprivileged.

The tradeoff between security and risk ultimately hinges on personal decisions. In principle, more security requires greater expenditures of money, time, and effort up to a point of diminishing returns. Individuals decide—often on the basis of irrational, emotional, or vague impressionistic factors—what sacrifices to limit exposure to danger are reasonable, how safe is safe enough, and what constitutes an acceptable risk (see Lynn, 1981). Increasingly, however, sufficient victimization research results are accumulating to inform criminal justice discussions and media reports. These, in turn, are providing more structure to individuals' efforts to fashion victimization prevention strategies.

SEEKING REIMBURSEMENT
FOR VICTIMIZATION

Crimes incur costs borne by victims, the government (in the form of criminal justice system expenses) and the entire society (as in insurance coverage or anti-theft devices). The toll exacted on crime victims can be classified as tangible short-term costs (including out-of-pocket expenses such as time lost from work, medical bills, and property losses) and intangible long-term losses that undermine the quality of life (such as pain and suffering). Using findings from the NCVS in the late 1980s, researchers took the number of projected incidents of various crimes and multiplied them by the estimated average costs of each type of crime to calculate aggre-

gate figures for the whole country. The tangible short-term costs of victimizations impose an annual "crime tax" of roughly $425 on every person in the United States. Translating the long-term intangible costs of emotional trauma and disability into dollars and cents (as is done in civil lawsuits), the crime tax to repair the damage done by offenders (including murderers, robbers, rapists, drunk drivers, arsonists, burglars, child abusers, and perpetrators of domestic violence, but not counting drug law violators or white collar criminals) rises to a theoretical equivalent of $1,800 per person per year, or a symbolic grand total of $450 billion annually (see Miller et al., 1996).

Immediate victims (as opposed to secondary victims, who also suffer harm) can try to recover their financial losses in a number of ways: (1) by receiving restitution from the offender, (2) by winning a civil court judgment against the offender or some responsible third party, and (3) by collecting reimbursement from a private insurance policy or a governmental compensation fund.

Restitution by Offenders

In many states, victims are now entitled to receive restitution in the form of payments or services from the offenders who harmed them. This ancient practice can be found in the Code of Hammurabi, the laws of Moses, the law of the Roman Empire, and the original legal codes of the thirteen colonies before the American Revolution. It was revived by legislation passed by Congress and many states during the 1980s, although restitution by juvenile offenders always has been an option in family court. Today, a growing number of judges are handing down "alternative," "constructive," or "creative" sentences in order to tailor the punishment to fit the crime. In 1995, a national survey determined that about 40 percent of all adults on probation for committing felonies and 18 percent convicted of misdemeanors had been ordered by judges to pay restitution to their victims (Bonczar, 1997). The renewed interest in restitution reflects a number of pressures, including the demands of the victims' movement, the crisis of overcrowding in jails and prisons, and a growing disenchantment with traditional forms of rehabilitation and punishment.

Advocates of restitution argue that many opportunities arise for arranging reimbursement: as a settlement of a conflict in lieu of arrest; as a condition for dropping charges; as a term of a negotiated plea; or as a condition of a suspended sentence, probation, or parole. However, advocates of a greater reliance on restitution are split over priorities and goals. Some view restitution as an additional penalty and contend that offenders must first pay their debts to society by being punished through confinement before they can repay their financial debts to their actual victims. For others, the primary consideration is that restitution serve as a means of rehabilitation by developing in offenders a sense of responsibility for wrongdoing, by cultivating good work habits and marketable skills, and by building self-confidence through tangible accomplishments. Still others see restitution as a vehicle for reparation and then reconciliation, whereby the offenders make amends, repair damage, and thus restore balance and harmony (see Galaway and Hudson, 1979; Hudson and Galaway, 1977; McGillis, 1986; McDonald, 1987; Hillenbrand, 1990).

Major obstacles stand in the way of any expanded dependence on restitution as a routine sanction. First, suitable jobs for offenders are difficult to find. Second, judges remain reluctant to impose restitution unless agreements are likely to be enforced. Third, probation and parole officials resent being relegated to the status of collection agencies. Finally, many appropriate cases slip through the cracks in the system, through a process called "shrinkage" or "funneling," because of unreported crimes, unsolved cases, dropped counts, and dismissed charges.

Civil Lawsuits Against Offenders and Third Parties

Victims who do not receive court-ordered restitution can launch civil lawsuits against their offenders. If the lawsuit is successful, the victim not only can feel vindicated but also may collect judgments reflecting actual out-of-pocket expenses (for medical bills and lost earnings), compensation for the mental anguish of pain and suffering, and even punitive damages. To prevail, the plaintiff must convince a judge or a jury by a preponderance of the evidence (a somewhat easier criterion to meet than guilt beyond a reasonable doubt) that the defendant caused economic, physical, and mental harm. However, victims contemplating civil litigation confront several obstacles: the substantial contingency fees charged by lawyers (ranging up to 50 percent of a victorious victim's award); incidental expenses that must be paid, even in defeat (filing fees, expert witness fees, deposition costs); the ordeal of another round of protracted legal proceedings, including testifying, jury deliberations, or negotiations leading to an out-of-court settlement; and the difficulty of actually collecting money awarded by a civil court jury or judge (see Stark and Goldstein, 1985).

When offenders are not apprehended, or appear to be "judgment-proof"—that is, without substantial income or assets—victims might press third-party lawsuits against persons or entities who, they contend, share responsibility with the offenders for their plight. The victim must prove in court that a special relationship existed with the third party, whose gross incompetence or negligence was a proximate cause of a failure to prevent a foreseeable crime from being committed. Third parties can be private individuals, institutions, or corporations. In these cases, suits can pit students against school systems, tenants against landlords, customers against store owners, and employees against employers. Charges may involve failure to provide conventional security measures or negligently putting dangerous persons into positions of trust.

Another set of third parties can be government officials and agencies. For instance, the police can be sued for negligence, either malfeasance (improper acts) or nonfeasance (failure to act). On rare occasions, criminal justice officials can be sued for wrongful release of dangerous persons known to pose a foreseeable risk to specific potential targets. Correctional authorities can be sued for gross negligence leading to the escape of prisoners or for failure to warn intended victims about the lawful release of former prisoners or mental patients. One result of successful third-party lawsuits is that criminal justice officials who exercise professional judgment when deciding whom to let out on probation, parole, work release, educational release, or furlough now must pay more attention to the potential threat to public safety posed by the release of a prisoner in their care (see Carrington, 1977, 1978; Stark and Goldstein, 1985; Austern, 1987).

Compensation from Insurance Policies and Government Funds

Victims can be compensated for their financial losses by insurance companies or by governmental boards. Private companies sell policies that provide coverage to offset expenses arising from medical bills (health insurance), lost earnings (income maintenance insurance), loss of future support (life insurance), and stolen or damaged property (homeowner's, automobile owner's, and boat owner's insurance). By purchasing policies beforehand, victims and their dependents can be financially covered in the event of crimes like murder, robbery, assault, theft, burglary, and vandalism.

Several patterns of loss and recovery stand out. More families are better insured against medical costs than against property losses. Large losses are more likely to be the subject of claims than small ones because of deductible clauses that force victims to absorb the first $100 or more of outlays. Higher-income households are more likely to purchase protection in advance than are other families. And those who face the greatest risks and need insurance the most are the least likely to be offered policies or to be able to afford coverage. Only victims of motor vehicle theft are likely to receive significant reimbursements from private insurance; most burglary losses are not reimbursed (Harland, 1981).

As a response to the inadequacy of private insurance underwriting, the ancient practice of governmental assistance to crime victims has been revived by the federal government and by nearly all the fifty states, a trend that started in the 1960s. Advocates of government-financed and government-administered compensation funds developed several different arguments to justify the establishment of public insurance coverage: to fill a glaring hole in the existing safety net of social welfare programs; to routinize acts of compassion and charity to deserving persons suffering needlessly from unforeseen tragedies; to fulfill the social obligations incurred by governments that take responsibility for maintaining order and then fail to protect them from harm; and to provide an incentive to victims to report crimes, assist police investigations, press charges, and testify for the prosecution.

Those who were against the establishment of these state funds, or who opposed their growth and expansion into new areas of coverage, countered that the tendency to bail out people in financial distress smacked of governmental paternalism at the expense of self-reliance, that taxpayers already were burdened by the costs of running the criminal justice system, and that "welfare state tax-and-spend" social insurance programs encroached on the preserve of private enterprise (see Geis, 1976; Meiners, 1978; Carrow, 1980).

The existing state compensation programs across the country have a great deal in common. All of them restrict eligibility to innocent victims of violent crimes who were physically wounded and as a result suffered out-of-pocket expenses or to their families or dependents who incurred funeral expenses and lost support of a breadwinner. The various state boards have different rules concerning reporting procedures and filing deadlines, hiring attorneys, proving financial need, limiting the amount of awards, and excluding acts of intrafamily violence (Austern et al., 1979; McGillis and Smith, 1983).

In many states, compensation programs are now funded in part or entirely from penalty assessments levied on traffic law violators, misdemeanants, and felons, and in some places from bail forfeitures, community service work by offenders, and gun license fees. But the compensation boards do not give money away freely. Many eligible victims are never informed about the opportunity for reimbursement, and of those who do apply, many have their claims rejected because of stringent requirements. And in some states, the boards run out of money before the year is over. Of those who do receive awards, many must wait years to collect and then feel demeaned by the process. To some extent, the establishment of compensation funds was an exercise by lawmakers in "symbolic politics" intended to mollify the humanitarian concerns of the public about the plight of victims (Elias, 1983).

CAMPAIGNING FOR GREATER VICTIMS' RIGHTS

Just like other groups—most notably minorities, women, homosexuals, students, and prisoners—victims have been struggling to secure rights and guarantees of fair treatment since the late 1960s. Unlike the rights of suspects, defendants, convicts, and even crime reporters, however, victims' rights are not derived from any of the amendments to the U.S. Constitution. In the American adversarial justice system, only two parties participate in criminal proceedings: the state (representing the victim only to a degree) and the accused. Because victims lacked standing (in legal terms), their role until recently has been limited to signing the complaints that set the criminal justice process into motion and serving as walking pieces of evidence brought into courtrooms to testify for the prosecution. In 1982, Congress enacted a law setting forth standards for the fair treatment of victims and witnesses. Throughout the 1980s, many states granted victims opportunities to participate in decision making within the criminal justice process. By the late 1990s, these legislative packages, known as "Victims' Bills of Rights," had been passed in 49 states and buttressed in 22 states by amendments to state constitutions (Tomz and McGillis, 1997). What the victims' rights movement seeks is aptly summed up by a model amendment that reads, "The victim of crime or his or her rep-resentative shall have the right to be informed of, to be present at, and to be heard at all crim-inal justice proceedings at which the defendant has such rights, subject to the same rules which govern defendants' rights" (National Victim Center, 1988). In 1996, President Clinton endorsed the efforts of the victims' rights movement to amend the Constitution, and Congress considered variously worded bills as the lengthy process slowly moved along. Reforms that empower victims at the expense of criminal justice agencies and officials (including the police, prosecutors, judges, corrections administrators, and parole boards) meet resistance from those branches of government. Reforms that place defendants and convicts at a disadvantage raise the concerns of civil libertarians about changes in procedures supposedly in behalf of victims that actually enhance the power of the state (see the President's Task Force, 1982; Karmen, 1992; Elias, 1993; Mawby and Walklate, 1993).

The Criminal Justice System: Theory and Practice

Ideally, the police can serve victims in a number of crucial ways. They can respond promptly when called, administer first aid, apprehend the suspect, gather evidence sufficient for conviction in court, recover any property that was stolen, and protect the complainant as a key prosecution witness from any intimidation or reprisals for cooperating with the authorities. In practice, the police might respond slowly, deliver a "second wound" by being insensitive, fail to solve the crime or recover stolen property, and close the investigation without telling the victim (see Brandl and Horvath, 1991; Karmen, 1996). To address these problems, some states have passed statutes requiring that victims "be read their rights"—that is, be informed of all of their obligations (to cooperate and testify), their opportunities (to participate and to apply for compensation), and the services available to them (to receive counseling and protection from harassment). In some jurisdictions, victims

also have gained the right to be kept posted about any progress (arrests, bail, prosecutions, plea negotiations, convictions, sentences, parole hearings) in their cases.

In theory, the prosecutor's office is a public law firm that vigorously represents the best interests of victims at no cost to them. Prosecutors can serve victims by securing indictments and convictions and by recommending sentences that reflect the seriousness of the harm done to the victims. In reality, prosecutors' offices often are large bureaucracies that sacrifice the interests of victims to what are perceived to be the best interests of the government, the entire society, the prosecutor's reputation, or the personal careers of the attorneys working there (see Chapter 16 of this volume). In response, the victims' movement in some states has secured guarantees of fair treatment that include advance notification of changes in the dates of court appearances; secure waiting facilities in courthouses; reasonable witness fees for testifying; intercession by government attorneys on behalf of the victim with landlords, employers, and creditors who might be unaware of the victim's plight; expedited return of stolen property recovered by the police and held as evidence; and information about negotiated pleas. To regain the confidence and cooperation of the public, many district attorneys have set up victim–witness assistance programs to deliver these services (Kelly, 1990; Tomz and McGillis, 1997).

Ideally, judges are impartial arbiters who exercise professional discretion as they preside over fair trials and hand down appropriate sentences. In practice, victims might feel neglected or even endangered by the decisions and rulings of judges. To ensure equitable treatment, the victims' movement in some states has secured guarantees that judges will consider the victim's safety when setting bail, take the victim's needs into account when scheduling court appearances, and weigh seriously the victim's views as set forth in an impact statement (detailing the physical, emotional, and financial consequences of the crime) that may be written or stated in person (termed "allocution") before handing down sentences (Villmoare and Neto, 1987; Stark and Goldstein, 1985; National Organization for Victim Assistance, 1988; Elias, 1990).

SEARCHING FOR
JUSTICE INFORMALLY

Victims who don't want to turn over their cases to criminal justice officials for formal processing have two informal options: to seek peaceful resolutions of their conflicts as part of an emerging trend toward "restorative justice" or to try to inflict retaliatory violence, do-it-yourself style, in the vigilante tradition.

Restorative Justice

Restorative justice refers to a bold, new, experimental paradigm whose goal is not punishment but reconciliation between the offender and the victim, to the advantage of the entire community. Unlike the traditional "retributive model" of justice, whereby the police and prosecution respond punitively to lawbreaking as offenses against the state and threats to the social order, restorative justice treats criminally inflicted injuries and losses as social damage that must be repaired. For this nonpunitive alternative to adjudication and incarceration to work effectively, offenders have to acknowledge their responsibilities, express remorse, undergo rehabilitation, and make amends to all those they harmed through creative restitution. Restorative justice through dispute resolution started out as a way of handling misdemeanors (like acts of vandalism, minor thefts, and simple assaults), but even felonies

(such as burglaries and serious assaults) are sometimes diverted by the courts to victim–offender reconciliation programs (VORPs) (Alper and Nichols, 1981; McGillis, 1982; Wright and Galaway, 1989; Galaway and Hudson, 1990; Pepinsky and Quinney, 1991; Wright, 1991; Umbreit, 1995).

The primary method for determining appropriate ways of resolving cases is through alternative dispute resolution (ADR), a mediation-oriented process offered at "neighborhood justice centers." ADR uses an informal "moot model" of far-reaching inquiry, unfettered dialogue, and flexible negotiation as a replacement for the strictly limited testimony and evidence that can be introduced within the winner-take-all adversary model that guides formal case processing. In this method of problem-solving, a neutral third party—preferably a mediator, but if necessary an arbitrator—replaces the prosecutor, defense attorney, judge, and jury. Because the goal is to resolve an ongoing conflict before it escalates by hammering out a mutually acceptable settlement, the most appropriate kinds of cases involve quarreling parties who have a prior relationship (such as family members, neighbors, co-workers, and fellow students) that must be repaired and incidents in which both parties shared responsibility for the violations of law. (The clear-cut labels "victim" and "offender" may not fit the facts of the case.) Compromise settlements usually involve apologies, pledges to alter behavior or to stay away from each other, promises to enter treatment programs, and restitution agreements (see Umbreit, 1994).

Vigilantism

Whereas restorative justice embodies an informal approach whose aim is to achieve reconciliation between the two estranged parties, return them to a condition of well-being, and bring back harmony to their community, vigilantism embodies an informal approach in which retaliation and subjugation is the goal. Punishment of the offender directly by the victim (or family members or supporters) is considered a prerequisite for "justice." Vigilantism's roots go back to the time of the frontier and pioneers, when the total absence of a formal criminal justice system compelled upright citizens to take the law into their own hands. Today, the impulse toward vigilantism arises within those who have completely lost confidence in the ability of the police, prosecution, courts, and prisons to mete out to predatory street criminals their "just desserts."

Vigilantism occurs when victims (and their allies) intentionally use excessive force to inflict on-the-spot summary punishments upon suspects. Examples include crowds chasing and stomping accused purse-snatchers, family members beating up assailants of a youngster, rape victims ambushing and attacking rapists, retaliatory mob hits, and street gang drive-by shootings to avenge the loss of a fallen comrade. By definition, vigilante violence is illegal because those who impose street justice appoint themselves judge, jury, and even executioner. Their retaliatory violence exceeds the legal limits on the justifiable use of force in self-defense and disregards provisions in the law about proportional responses and imminent danger. Vigilantes cast aside the constitutional guarantees of due process safeguards for the accused and run the risk of physically harming innocent persons they mistakenly assume are guilty. An outbreak of vigilantism brings about a transformation of relationships: Offenders become victims and victims turn into victimizers (see Brown, 1975; Burrows, 1976; Rosenbaum and Sederberg, 1976).

CONCLUSION

Clearly, victimology helps counteract the tendency of criminology to reduce itself to "offenderology." Until criminologists developed an interest in victims, they tended to be preoccupied with lawbreakers: their characteristics, the causes of their illegal behaviors, their handling by the criminal justice system, and their potential for rehabilitation. Now, criminology is better balanced because it also studies the characteristics and situations of people harmed by criminals: how the police, prosecutors, judges, and other officials and agencies handle them and how they might be restored to the conditions they were in before criminals harmed them.

DISCUSSION QUESTIONS

1. Victimology is a relatively recent field of study. What are its roots, and why has its popularity risen in recent years?

2. The most common form of crime reported to NCVS surveyers is "household larceny." What is it and how does it differ from other types of property theft?

3. Some categories of people seem to have higher victimization rates than do others. Discuss some of these patterns and, especially, the reasons for them.

4. What percentage of crime victims actually report their victimization to the police? Do the reporting figures vary by type of crime?

5. What factors influence whether the victim of a crime will report it to the police? What have been the effects of campaigns to increase the percentage of crimes reported?

6. The notion of victim precipitation suggests that some victims do things to encourage their victimization. Are there problems with this notion? Are there better ways to conceptualize victim involvement in crime commission?

REFERENCES

Alper, B., and L. Nichols. 1981. *Beyond the Courtroom.* Lexington, MA: Lexington Books.

Amir, M. 1967. "Victim Precipitated Forcible Rape." *Journal of Criminal Law, Criminology and Police Science* 58: 439–502.

Austern, D. 1987. *The Crime Victim's Handbook.* New York: Penguin Books.

Austern, D., B. Galaway, R. Godegast, R. Gross, R. Hofrichter, J. Hudson, T. Hutchinson, and M. Young-Rifai. 1979. *Compensating Victims of Crime—Participant's Handbook: Criminal Justice Utilization Program.* Washington, DC: University Research Corporation.

Barr, R., and Pease, K. 1990. "Crime Placement, Displacement, and Deflection." Pp. 277–318 in *Crime and Justice: An Annual Review of Research.* Edited by M. Tonry and N. Morris. Chicago: University of Chicago Press.

Bastion, L. 1992. *Criminal Victimization in the United States, 1991.* Washington, DC: Bureau of Justice Statistics.

Best, J. 1997. "Victimization and the Victim Industry." *Society* 35: 9–17.

Bonczar, T. 1997. *Characteristics of Adults on Probation, 1995.* Washington, DC: U.S. Department of Justice.

Brandl, S., and F. Horvath. 1991. "Crime Victim Evaluation Of Police Investigative Performance." *Journal of Criminal Justice* 19: 2: 109–121.

Brown, R. 1975. *Strain of Violence: Historical Studies of American Violence and Vigilantism.* New York: Oxford University Press.

Browne, A. 1987. *When Battered Women Kill.* New York: Free Press.

Brownmiller, S. 1975. *Against Our Will: Men, Women, and Rape.* New York: Simon & Schuster.

Burrows, W. 1976. *Vigilante!* New York: Harcourt Brace Jovanovich.

Carrington, F. 1977. "Victim's Rights Litigation: A Wave of the Future?" *University of Richmond Law Review* 11: 447–470.

———. 1978. "Victim's Rights: A New Tort." *Trial* (June): 39–41.

Carrow, D. 1980. *Crime Victim Compensation: U.S. Department of Justice Program Model.* Washington, DC: U.S. Government Printing Office.

Cohen, L. E., J. Kluegal, and K. Land. 1981. "Social Inequality and Criminal Victimization." *American Sociological Review* 46: 505–524.

Cohn, E., L. Kidder, and J. Harvey. 1978. "Crime Prevention vs. Victimization Prevention: The Psychology of Two Different Reactions." *Victimology* 3: 285–296.

Elias, R. 1983. *Victims of the System.* New Brunswick, NJ: Transaction Books.

———. 1986. *The Politics of Victimization: Victims, Victimology, and Human Rights.* New York: Oxford University Press.

———. 1990. "Which Victim Movement? The Politics of Victim Policy." Pp. 226–250 in *victims of Crime: Problems, Policies, and Programs.* Edited by A. Lurigio, W. Skogan, and R. Davis. Newbury Park, CA: Sage.

————. 1993. *Victims Still*. Thousand Oaks, CA: Sage.

Ellenberger, H. 1955. "Psychological Relationships Between the Criminal and His Victim." *Archives of Criminal Psychodynamics* 2: 257–290.

Franklin, C., and A. Franklin. 1976. "Victimology Revisited." *Criminology* 14: 125–136.

Frieze, I., and Browne, A. 1989. "Violence in Marriage." Pp. 163–218 in *Crime and Justice: An Annual Review of Research*. Edited by M. Tonry and N. Morris. Chicago: Univ. of Chicago Press.

Galaway, B., and J. Hudson. 1979. *Victims, Offenders, and Restitutive Sanctions*. Lexington, MA: Lexington Books.

————(eds.). 1990. *Criminal Justice, Restitution, and Reconciliation*. Monsey, NY: Willow Tree Press.

Garbarino, J. 1989. "The Incidence and Prevalence of Child Maltreatment." Pp. 219–261 in *Crime and Justice: An Annual Review of Research*. Edited by M. Tonry and N. Morris. Chicago: University of Chicago Press.

Garofalo, J. 1981. "Victimization Surveys: An Overview." Pp. 98–103 in *Perspectives on Crime Victims*. Edited by B. Galaway and J. Hudson. St. Louis: Mosby.

————. 1986. "Lifestyles and Victimization: An Update." Pp. 135–155 in *From Crime Policy to Victim Policy*. Edited by E. Fattah. New York: St. Martin's Press.

Geis, G. 1976. "Compensation to Victims of Violent Crime." Pp. 90–115 in *Contemporary Issues in Criminal Justice*. Edited by R. Gerber. Port Washington, NY: Kennikat.

Gottfredson, M., and D. M. Gottfredson. 1988. *Decision Making in Criminal Justice: Toward the Rational Exercise of Discretion*. 2d ed. New York: Plenum.

Harland, A. 1981. *Restitution to Victims of Personal and Household Crimes*. Washington, DC: U.S. Department of Justice.

Harlow, C. 1985. *Reporting Crime to the Police: Bureau of Justice Statistics Special Report*. Washington, DC: U.S. Department of Justice.

————. 1987. *Robbery Victims: Bureau of Justice Statistics Special Report*. Washington, DC: U.S. Department of Justice.

Hillenbrand, S. 1990. "Restitution and Victim Rights in the 1980s." Pp. 188–204 in *Victims of Crime: Problems, Policies, and Programs*. Edited by A. Lurigio, W. Skogan, and R. Davis. Newbury Park, CA: Sage.

Hudson, J., and B. Galaway. 1977. *Restitution in Criminal Justice*. Lexington, MA: Lexington Books.

Karmen, A. 1979. "Victim Facilitation: The Case of Auto Theft." *Victimology* 4: 361–370.

————. 1980. "Auto Theft: Beyond Victim Blaming." *Victimology* 5: 161–174.

————. 1981. "Auto Theft and Corporate Irresponsibility." *Contemporary Crises* 5: 63–81.

————. 1991. "The Controversy Over Shared Responsibility: Is Victim-Blaming Ever Justified?" Pp. 395–408 in *To Be A Victim: Encounters With Crime And Injustice*. Edited by D. Sank and D. Caplan. New York: Plenum Press.

————. 1992. "Who's Against Victims' Rights? The Nature of the Opposition to Pro-Victim Initiatives in Criminal Justice." *St. John's Journal of Legal Commentary* 8: 157–176.

————. 1996. *Crime Victims: An Introduction to Victimology*. 3d ed. Belmont, CA: Wadsworth.

Kelly, D. 1990. "Victim Participation in the Criminal Justice System." Pp. 172–187 in *Victims of Crime: Problems, Policies, and Programs*. Edited by A. Lurigio, W. Skogan, and R. Davis. Newbury Park, CA: Sage.

Koppel, H. 1987. *Lifetime Likelihood of Victimization: Bureau of Justice Statistics Technical Report*. Washington, DC: U.S. Department of Justice.

Koss, M. 1992. "The Underdetection Of Rape: Methodological Choices Influence Incidence Estimates." *Journal of Social Issues* 48 (1): 61–75.

Levine, J. 1976. "The Potential for Crime Overreporting in Criminal Victimization Surveys." *Criminology* 14: 307–331.

Lynn, W. 1981. "What Scientists Really Mean by 'Acceptable Risk.'" *U.S. News & World Report* 90: 60.

Maltz, M., and M. Zawitz. 1998. *Displaying Violent Crime Trends Using Estimates From the National Crime Victimization Survey.* Washington, DC: U.S. Department of Justice.

Mash, E., and D. Wolfe. 1991. "Methodological Issues In Research On Physical Child Abuse." *Criminal Justice and Behavior* 18 (1): 8–29.

Mawby, R., and S. Walklate. 1993. *Critical Victimology.* Thousand Oaks, CA: Sage.

McDonald, W. 1976. *Criminal Justice and the Victim.* Newbury Park, CA: Sage.

———. 1987. *Restitution and Community Service: National Institute of Justice Crime File Study Guide.* Washington, DC: U.S. Department of Justice.

McGillis, D. 1982. "Minor Dispute Processing: A Review of Recent Developments." Pp. 60–76 in *Neighborhood Justice: Assessment of an Emerging Idea.* Edited by R. Tomasic and M. Freeley. New York: Longman.

———. 1986. *Crime Victim Restitution: An Analysis of Approaches.* Washington, DC: National Institute of Justice.

McGillis, D., and P. Smith. 1983. *Compensating Victims of Crime: An Analysis of American Programs.* Washington, DC: U.S. Department of Justice.

Meiners, R. 1978. *Victim Compensation: Economic, Political, and Legal Aspects.* Lexington, MA: Heath.

Messner, S. F., and K. Tardiff. 1985. "The Social Ecology of Urban Homicide: An Application of the Routine Activities Approach." *Criminology* 23: 241–267.

Miethe, T., M. Stafford, and D. Sloane. 1990. "Lifestyle Changes and Risks of Criminal Victimization." *Journal of Quantitative Criminology* 6: 357–375.

Miller, T., M. Cohen, and B. Wiersema. 1996. *The Extent and Costs of Crime Victimization: A New Look.* Washington, DC: U.S. Department of Justice.

National Commission on the Causes and Prevention of Violence (NCCPV). 1969. *The Offender and His Victim.* Washington, DC: U.S. Government Printing Office.

National Crime Prevention Institute (NCPI). 1978. *Understanding Crime Prevention.* Louisville, KY: National Crime Prevention Institute.

National Organization for Victim Assistance (NOVA). 1988. *Victim Rights and Services: A Legislative Directory.* Washington, DC: National Organization for Victim Assistance.

National Victim Center. 1988. "Constitutional Amendment." *Networks* (Spring): 6.

Newman, O. 1972. *Defensible Space.* New York: Macmillan.

O'Brien, R. 1985. *Crime and Victimization Data.* Beverly Hills, CA: Sage.

Pagelow, M. 1989. "The Incidence And Prevalence Of Criminal Abuse Of Other Family Members." Pp. 263–313 in *Crime and Justice: An Annual Review of Research.* Edited by M. Tonry and N. Morris. Chicago: University of Chicago Press.

Parsonage, W. 1979. *Perspectives on Victimology.* Beverly Hills, CA: Sage.

Pepinsky, H., and R. Quinney. 1991. *Criminology As Peacemaking.* Indianapolis: Indiana University Press.

Perkins, C., and P. Klaus. 1996. *Criminal Victimization in the United States, 1994.* Washington, DC: U.S. Department of Justice.

President's Task Force on Victims of Crime. 1982. *Final Report.* Washington, DC: U.S. Government Printing Office.

Rand, M. 1985. *Household Burglary.* Washington, DC: U.S. Department of Justice.

Reiff, R. 1979. *The Invisible Victim.* New York: Basic Books.

Reiss, A. 1986. "Official Survey Statistics." Pp. 53–79 in *From Crime Policy to Victim Policy.* Edited by E. Fattah. New York: St. Martin's Press.

Ringel, C. 1997. *Criminal Victimization, 1996: Changes 1995–1996 With Trends 1993–1996.* Washington, DC: U.S. Department of Justice.

Rosenbaum, J., and P. Sederberg. 1976. *Vigilante Politics.* Philadelphia: University of Pennsylvania Press.

Schafer, S. 1968. *The Victim and His Criminal.* New York: Random House.

————. 1977. *Victimology: The Victim and His Criminal.* Reston, VA: Reston Publishing.

Schneider, H. 1982. *The Victim in International Perspective.* New York: de Gruyter.

Sheley, J. F. 1979. *Understanding Crime: Concepts, Issues, Decisions.* Belmont, CA: Wadsworth.

Sherman, L., Gartin, P., and Buerger, M. 1989. "Hot Spots of Predatory Crime: Routine Activities and the Criminology Of Place." *Criminology* 27: 27–40.

Skogan, W. G. 1986. "Methodological Issues in the Study of Victimization." Pp. 80–116 in *From Crime Policy to Victim Policy.* Edited by E. Fattah. New York: St. Martin's Press.

Skogan, W. G., and M. G. Maxfield. 1981. *Coping with Crime: Individual and Neighborhood Reactions.* Beverly Hills, CA: Sage.

Sparks, R., H. Genn, and D. Dodd. 1977. *Surveying Victims.* New York: Wiley.

Stark, J., and H. Goldstein. 1985. *The Rights of Crime Victims.* Chicago: Southern Illinois University Press.

Tomz, J., and D. McGillis. 1997. *Serving Crime Victims and Witnesses.* 2d ed. Washington, DC: U.S. Department of Justice.

Umbreit, M. 1994. "Victim Empowerment Through Mediation: The Impact of Victim-Offender Mediation in Four Cities." *Perspectives* (of the American Probation and Parole Association) (Summer): 25–28.

————. 1995. "A Restorative Justice: Implications for Organizational Change." *Federal Probation* 59: 47–54.

U.S. Department of Justice. 1997. *Sex Differences in Violent Victimization, 1994.* Washington, DC: U.S. Department of Justice.

Viano, E. 1976. *Victims and Society.* Washington, DC: Visage.

Villmoare, E., and V. Neto. 1987. *Victim Appearances at Sentencing Under California's Victims' Bill of Rights. NIJ Research in Brief.* Washington, DC: U.S. Department of Justice.

Von Hentig, H. 1941. "Remarks on the Interaction of Perpetrator and Victim." *Journal of Criminal Law, Criminology, and Police Science* 31: 303–309.

————. 1948. *The Criminal and His Victim.* New Haven, CT: Yale University Press.

Voss, H., and J. Hepburn. 1968. "Patterns in Criminal Homicide in Chicago." *Journal of Criminal Law, Criminology, and Police Science* 59: 499–508.

Weis, K., and S. Borges. 1973. "Victimology and Rape: The Case of the Legitimate Victim." *Issues in Criminology* 8: 71–115.

Williams, K. 1978. *The Effects of Victim Characteristics on Judicial Decisions.* PROMIS Research Project Report. Washington, DC: Institute for Law and Social Research.

Wolfgang, M. 1958. *Patterns in Criminal Homicide.* Philadelphia: University of Pennsylvania Press.

Wright, M. 1991. *Justice For Victims And Offenders.* Philadelphia: Open University Press.

Wright, M. and B. Galaway. 1989. *Mediation and Criminal Justice: Victims, Offenders and Community.* Newbury Park, CA: Sage.

Types of Crime

In Part Two, we reviewed crime statistics and presented profiles of offenders and victims. In Part Three, we examine various types of crime: violent offenses, property crime, vice offenses, organized crime, and white collar crime. Our purpose again is to gain a fuller sense of the inaccuracies of most people's ideas about various forms of offense behavior and, thus, to allow readers to assess more accurately the "crime problem" and to propose solutions to it.

Robert Nash Parker and Doreen Anderson-Facile open Part Three with a detailed examination of violent crime—the offenses that bother the public most, though they occur less frequently than do the other types of crime reviewed in this section. In Chapter 7, "Violent Crime Trends," Parker and Anderson-Facile begin by outlining recent crime rate trends and noting that, by most indicators, violent crime generally is declining. They expand the usual examination of types of violent crime with a look at crimes among "intimates," persons who harm others close to them. They challenge the traditional view that the South has the highest rate of violent crime; in fact, the West now seems to lead in this category. Two related theories are explored as explanations of violent crime rates and situations. The first is the routine activities approach, which locates violent crime levels in the extent to which everyday lifestyle activities place people in varying risk situations. The second is the situational transaction model, by which we come to understand that much violent crime results from interactions whereby perceived insults are not amicably negotiated by the parties involved. The remainder of the chapter is devoted to what the research findings tell us about homicide, rape, robbery, and assault.

The routine activities approach to understanding crime patterns is carried over to Chapter 8, "Property Crime Trends," in which Robert J. Bursik Jr., examines property crime characteristics and trends using both police statistics and victimization survey results. His review suggests that rates have declined somewhat in recent years. He then turns his attention to the variable so often linked in the public's mind to property crime: unemployment. He concludes that the unemployment–crime relationship remains viable and is clearly more complex than previously has been thought. Shifting to the notion of criminal opportunity, Bursik locates property crime levels in differential exposure of property to crime risk. The primary determinant of the likelihood of a successful burglary, for example, is the behavior of the residents of the potential target home. Bursik closes with a reminder that we err too often by thinking that property crime is easily understood and, thus, controlled. This misperception underlies the many seemingly contradictory anticrime policies that confront us.

In Chapter 9, "Vice Crimes: Personal Autonomy Versus Societal Dictates," Henry Lesieur and Michael Welch explore an entirely different form of crime from the violent and property offenses just discussed. They introduce us to the thorny issue of offenses without victims—that is, behaviors that occur between consenting adults. In most senses, the outlawing of these behaviors represents the imposition of one group's definition of proper personal morality on another group. Further, as the authors note, there has been a marked tendency to view the "outlaws" as mentally, emotionally, and in some cases, physically ill; thus, the rise of what is called the medical model of deviance. This backdrop informs their discussions of prostitution, pornography, consensual sodomy and related sexual activity, gambling, and drugs. Lesieur and Welch close by discussing how vice peddlers remain in business only because of the substantial demand for their services. Indeed, much vice activity is intimately intertwined with legitimate activity.

The discussion of vice crimes leads naturally into an examination of the organized interests seemingly behind them. Jay Albanese introduces us to these interests in Chapter 10, "The Mafia Mystique: Organized Crime." His study of organized crime centers on what he considers an empirically groundless conception of the Mafia in America. He argues persuasively that our preoccupation with the Mafia has hindered any meaningful understanding of organized crime's dynamics. Recent research indicates that the notion of a national syndicate should be replaced by a sense of flexible, informal networks of associations at a local level. More importantly, Albanese ties organized crime's success or failure to prevailing market conditions. Thus, if the local configuration of suppliers, customers, regulators, and competitors is favorable, organized crime will flourish. Paradoxically, to the extent that government intrudes into private decisions—for example, those involving sexual behaviors—market conditions for organized crime are enhanced. Albanese concludes with a discussion of the effects of prosecution efforts against mob figures in recent years, noting that although these law enforcement activities have had short-term disruptive effects on organized crime, they also have caused organized crime to shift into safer, more sophisticated criminal markets.

Neal Shover and Andrew Hochstetler direct our attention to yet another aspect of crime in Chapter 11, "Crimes of Privilege," also known as white collar crime. This form of crime is probably our most costly economically, but it is also our most ignored. White collar crime refers to law violations committed by persons or groups in the course of otherwise respected and legitimate occupational or financial activities. These offenses include employee theft, drug violations by physicians, bribery and corruption of public officials, fraud and deception by legitimate businesses, monopolies and business conspiracies, governmental civil liberties violations, and maintenance of unsafe work conditions. The authors investigate legislative and prosecutorial responses to various forms of white collar crime as well as examining civil and regulatory efforts to control it. They examine the keys to most forms of such crime, opportunity and motivation, and the context in which these develop into "careers" in white collar crime. Shover and Hochstetler close with discussions of the recent global nature of white collar crime and the challenges we face in trying to prevent and control it.

Chapter Outline

◆ Violent Crime in the United States: Levels and Trends

Homicide Rates

Intimate Partner Homicides

Rape Rates

Robbery Rates

Assault Rates

◆ Regional Variation, Relationships, and Weapons

Victim–Offender Relationship

Weapons

◆ Explaining Violent Crime: Recent Developments

The Lifestyle–Routine Activity Approach

The Situational Approach

◆ Research on the Correlates of Homicide

Economic Deprivation

Subculture of Violence

Lifestyle–Routine Activities

Situational Factors

Victim–Offender Relationship

◆ Research on the Correlates of Rape, Robbery, and Assault

◆ A Research Agenda for Violent Crime

◆ Conclusion

7

Violent Crime Trends

ROBERT NASH PARKER
University of California, Riverside

DOREEN ANDERSON-FACILE
University of California, Riverside

Violent crime is probably the most problematic and anxiety-provoking of all the behaviors discussed in this book. It is more personal than any other type of crime. Victims of violent crime often are threatened or injured physically and may even lose their lives. In addition, victims of violent crimes often suffer psychological trauma that can last for months or years after their physical injuries have healed. How much violent crime is there in our society, and why does it happen? What do we know about the causes of violent crime? These will be the major topics in this chapter. This discussion will focus on four particular crimes: homicide, rape, robbery, and aggravated assault.

Our definitions of these four crimes are drawn from the *Uniform Crime Reports* (UCR) (FBI, 1997), the standard source for much of the

crime data available in this country. The UCR is an annual FBI publication that describes crime from all reporting law enforcement agencies (see Chapter 3). Homicide, as defined by the UCR, is the willful or non-negligent killing of one human being by another individual or group of individuals. Acts not included in this definition are deaths caused by negligence, attempts to kill, assaults that lead to the victim's death, and accidental deaths. Also not included is justifiable homicide, when, for example, the victim was engaged in the commission of a serious crime. Rape is defined as the carnal knowledge of a female forcibly and against her will. Included in this definition are attempted rapes and assaults directed toward rape; however, statutory rape, which usually occurs without force but involves a victim under the legal

Table 7.1   Levels and Rates of Violent Crime in the United States, 1996

TYPE OF CRIME	UNIFORM CRIME REPORTS (UCR)		NATIONAL CRIME VICTIMIZATION SURVEY (NCVS)	
	Level	*Rate**	*Level*	*Rate**
Homicide	19,650	7.4	—	—
Rape	95,770	36.1	153,000	40.0
Robbery	537,050	202.4	1,134,000	520.0
Assault	1,029,810	388.2	1,910,000	880.0

SOURCES: Data are from *Criminal Victimization in the United States—1996* (U.S. Department of Justice, 1997) and *Uniform Crime Reports 1996* (U.S. Department of Justice, 1997: 62).

*Rate per 100,000 population.

age of adult responsibility, is excluded. Robbery is defined as the taking or attempt to take anything of value from the care, custody, or control of a person or persons by force or threat of force or violence or by putting the victim in fear. Finally, aggravated assault, which will be referred to here simply as assault, is defined as an unlawful attack by one person on another for the purpose of inflicting serious bodily injury. This crime involves the use of a weapon or other means likely to produce death or great bodily harm; simple assaults, a much larger category of crimes, are excluded.

VIOLENT CRIME

IN THE UNITED STATES:

LEVELS AND TRENDS

The first two columns of Table 7.1 list the levels and rates of violent crime as reported in the UCR for the year 1996. The second two columns list levels and rates of rape, robbery, and assault based on data collected in the National Crime Victimization Survey (NCVS) for 1996 (U.S. Department of Justice, 1997). The NCVS is a survey administered randomly to roughly 50,000 households and published in collaboration with the United States Census Bureau (see Chapter 3). The initial purpose of this survey was to complement the information from the UCR by recording victimization and crime incidents not necessarily reported to the police and to provide more detailed information about the crime and its victim. Clearly, as shown in the table, the NCVS data indicate violent crime to be much greater and a more serious problem than do the data from the UCR, with the NCVS data yielding rate estimates two to three times greater for robbery and assault. (For a discussion of why people do not report crimes to the police, see Chapter 6.)

In the abstract, numbers like those in Table 7.1 are difficult to evaluate. For example, is 7.4 per 100,000 a high or low rate of homicide? Most people—criminologists, students, and the general public—want to know whether the crime rate is increasing, decreasing, or staying

FIGURE 7.1
UCR homicide rate,
1977–1996

SOURCES: Data are from Uniform
Crime Reports, 1995 (U.S.
Department of Justice, 1996: 58)
and Uniform Crime Reports,
1996 (U.S. Department of Justice,
1997: 62).

the same over time. The only way to answer such a question is to examine trends over time to help us place a particular crime rate within the context of recent experience.

Homicide Rates

Figure 7.1 presents the trend in homicide rates from the UCR over the period 1977–1996. Although the graph reveals that homicide rates fluctuated over this period, from a high of 10.2 in 1980 to a low of 7.4 in 1996, notice how the range of 7 to 10 per 100,000 forms the lower and upper bounds within which homicides rates have varied. During the late 1970s, government and law enforcement officials and concerned

citizens were disturbed over what was perceived as a great increase in homicides; during the early to mid-1980s, some of the same leaders were claiming credit for falling rates of violence. During the latter part of the 1980s and into the 1990s, concern over increasing rates of violence was once again the subject of newspaper articles and television news programs. Now as we near the end of the 1990s, we again see a decline in homicide rates, but consideration of the data shown in Figure 7.1 suggests the danger of over-interpreting each annual fluctuation. In fact, homicide rates have exhibited remarkable stability over the last decade and a half.

An important element of homicide is the relationship between the victim and the offender.

If we believe the stereotypes we see in movies and on our TV sets, then we would also believe that homicidal maniacs and serial killers are running rampant through our streets, killing unsuspecting, innocent people at random. This is not the case. In fact, when a homicide does occur, the victim and the offender frequently know each other in some capacity, whether as family members, friends, co-workers, or acquaintances.

Depending on what data one draws upon to determine the victim–offender relationship, the percentage of homicides in which the victim and the offender know each other ranges from 45 to 87 (see Ridel, 1998, for a corresponding finding). That the range is so great is due to the way in which the police report the relationship between the victim and offender. There are many categories in which the police can classify the relationship between the victim and offender (i.e., brother, mother, husband, employee, co-worker, and stranger). However, the difficulty in analyzing homicide trends occurs when the relationship is unknown to the investigator. The relationship between victim and offender may be classified as "unknown" due to many factors, such as lack of information about the victim or offender or because the details of the homicide are unclear (Avakame, 1998; Ridel, 1999). Regardless, the "unknown-relationship" category creates a problem when trying to conduct analysis of homicide data.

Intimate Partner Homicides

Family violence exemplifies the importance of the victim–offender relationship in crime. Although it is virtually impossible to determine the extent of family violence in the United States, it is not difficult to determine the prevalence of intimate partner homicide. The UCR provides not only the homicide summary data but also the gender composition and the victim/offender relationship. This allows criminologists to track the overall rate of homicide, more specifically homicide rate by gender, race, age, and marital/relationship status. By isolating these demographic variables, criminologists can identify data that measure the relative risk of intimate partner homicide.

Figure 7.2 presents the rates of intimate partner homicide by gender in the overall population for the years 1977 through 1995. The rate for intimate partner homicide in the United States is fairly low for both men and women, with men having a range of .36 to 1.13 per 100,000 and women having a range of .90 to 1.36 per 100,000. This graph also reveals that the overall intimate partner homicide rate for both men and women is declining. It is important to note, however, that the rate declines at a much greater pace for men than it does for women. In the population as a whole, the probability that a person will be a victim of intimate partner homicide is lower than the probability of being a victim of homicide in general; the risk of the latter is very low itself. Despite the low rates and the general decline, it would be incorrect to suggest that the problem of intimate partner homicide is subsiding.

In Figure 7.3 we focus on intimate partner homicides as a percentage of overall homicide rates, and a very different picture emerges. Clearly, women are murdered by their intimate partners more often than are men. Intimate female partner homicide ranges from 24.05 to 32.88 percent of all homicides. Intimate male partner homicide is dramatically lower, ranging from 2.96 to 8.17 percent of all homicides. In addition, the rate of intimate male partner homicide is decreasing over time, mirroring the trend we see in the general population.

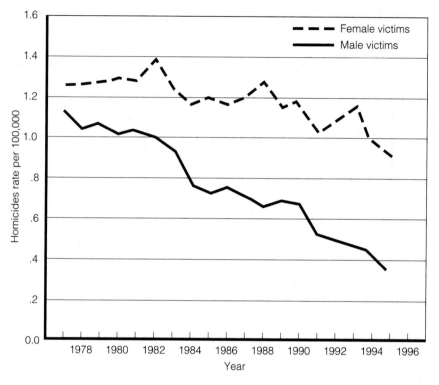

FIGURE 7.2
Intimate partner
homicide rates per
100,000 population,
1977–1995

SOURCE: Data are from Uniform
Crime Reports, 1977–1995
(U.S. Department of Justice,
1978–1996).

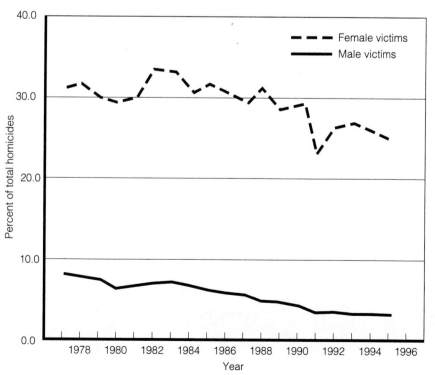

FIGURE 7.3
Percent intimate partner
homicide by gender of
victim, 1977–1995

SOURCE: Data are from Uniform
Crime Reports, 1977–1995
(U.S. Department of Justice,
1978–1996).

FIGURE 7.4
Intimate partner homicide
relative risk by gender:
ratio of female to male
victims, 1977–1995

SOURCE: Data are from Uniform
Crime Reports, 1977–1995
*(U.S. Department of Justice,
1978–1996).*

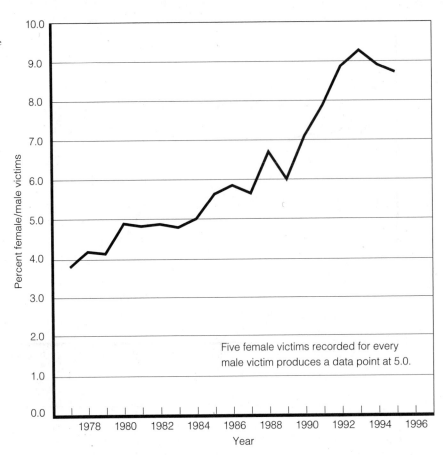

However, this is not the case for women; as seen in Figure 7.4, the relative risk of being killed by one's intimate partner is increasing at alarming rates for females.

The private nature of intimacy and family life makes it virtually impossible to get a complete picture of the extent of intimate and family violence in the United States. Victims are often reluctant to call the police when a conflict occurs within the home, and criminal justice and law enforcement officials historically have also been reluctant to address family vio-

lence because the home is considered a private domain. Consequently, the UCR does not reflect the entire scope of the problem. Although the redesign of the NCVS in 1993 resulted in more valid and reliable information regarding the extent of family violence (U.S. Department of Justice, 1995), this source also falls short of providing criminologists and social scientists with a complete statistical understanding of the frequency and nature of intimate and family violence. As a result, we have presented data on intimate partner homicide as an indicator of a

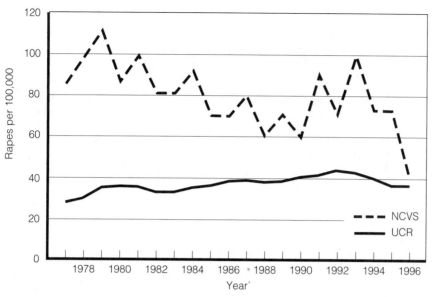

FIGURE 7.5
UCR/NCVS rape
rates, 1977–1996

SOURCES: Data are from Criminal Victimization in the United States—1977–1996 (U.S. Department of Justice, 1978–1997); Uniform Crime Reports, 1995 (U.S. Department of Justice, 1996: 58); and Uniform Crime Reports, 1996 (U.S. Department of Justice, 1997: 62).

larger more complex problem beyond the scope of this review.

Rape Rates

As noted in Table 7.1, the NCVS data revealed substantially higher rates and levels of violence than did the UCR data. Figures 7.5, 7.6, and 7.7 compare the trends over the last twenty years as reported in these two sources. Figure 7.5, in which rape rates are compared, shows that the NCVS and the UCR describe the prevalence of rape in the United States very differently. The UCR rape rates, as reported to the police, began to climb in the mid-1980s and continued to do so into the 1990s. This trend reflects the change in police and prosecutor behavior toward rape cases and rape victims, as well as legislation in many states that has made it more difficult for those defending people accused of rape to discourage reporting by casting partial blame on the victim.

Conversely, the NCVS reports that rape rates fluctuated dramatically, ranging from 40 to 110 rapes per 100,000. These data reveal a peak in 1979 of 110 rapes per 100,000, followed by a general decline throughout the 1980s. However, the rates begin to climb again in the 1990s with another peak in 1993 of 100 rapes per 100,000. Most significant is the astonishing drop in rape rates in 1996 in which the NCVS data and the UCR data almost converge. This could be due to methodological changes in the way the NCVS collects its data. The NCVS is increasingly dependent on telephone surveys to gather data (U.S. Department of Justice, 1989), and this method could create problems because respondents may be reluctant to discuss issues of sexual violence over the phone. However, we can only speculate as to why the NCVS reports such a dramatic drop in rape rates in 1996. Whether the drop represents an actual trend remains to be seen.

FIGURE 7.6
UCR/NCVS
robbery rates,
1977–1996

SOURCES: Data are from Criminal Victimization in the United
States*—1977–1996 (U.S. Department of Justice, 1978–1997);*
Uniform Crime Reports, 1995
*(U.S. Department of Justice, 1996:
58); and* Uniform Crime Reports, 1996 *(U.S. Department of
Justice, 1997: 62).*

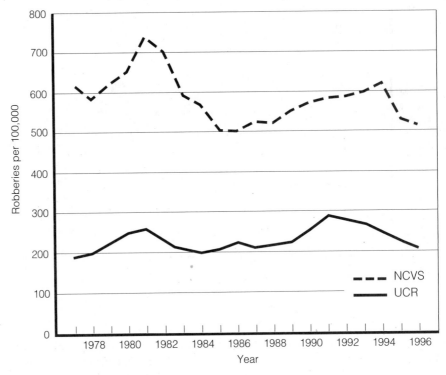

Robbery Rates

Figure 7.6, which presents trends in robbery rates, is striking for the similarity between the trends in the two sources. Both sources show that robbery rates increased sharply in the late 1970s. In addition, both sources indicate peaks in 1981, with rates of 258.7 and 740.0, respectively, for the UCR and the NCVS. In the early 1980s, robbery rates were on a general decline. Over the next few years, rates in both sources began to increase, with UCR robbery rates reaching their highest point in 1991, at 272.7 robberies per 100,000. However since 1991, both the UCR and the NCVS reveal a significant decline in robbery rates.

Assault Rates

Finally, NCVS and UCR assault rates, presented in Figure 7.7, show a trend toward convergence in which the gap between the reports to the police and the NCVS data is decreasing. The UCR assault rates show a steady increase, with some minor fluctuation, throughout the 1980s and into the 1990s. In fact, after reaching a plateau in the early 1980s, UCR assault rates began to increase, and by 1992 the rate for this violent crime reached a decade-and-a-half high of 441.80 assaults per 100,000. Conversely, the NCVS data reveal a downward trend in assault rates beginning in 1977, reaching a low in 1986 and again in 1990 of 790 assaults per 100,000.

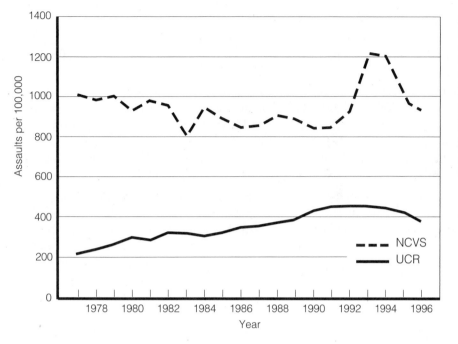

FIGURE 7.7
UCR/NCVS
assault rates,
1977–1996

SOURCES: Data are from Crim-
inal Victimization in the
United States—1977–1996
(U.S. Department of Justice,
1978–1997); Uniform Crime
Reports, 1995 *(U.S. Depart-*
ment of Justice, 1996: 58); and
Uniform Crime Reports,
1996 *(U.S. Department of Justice,*
1997: 62).

However, for a short period in 1993 and 1994, the NCVS rates were at their highest with 1,200 and 1,190 per 100,000 respectively. Since then, the assault rates have declined in both the UCR and NCVS, similar to those of the other violent crimes reviewed in this chapter.

In summary, the violent crime trends in the United States show a definite decline, but it would be reckless to propose that the current trends will continue. In fact, if we analyze the violent crime graphs presented in this chapter in five-year increments, we see that they reveal no conclusive pattern. Even though the available evidence does suggest that violence is declining, we should be very careful how we interpret these trends. It is critical to remember that the reasons for an increase or decrease in violent crime are numerous and that the only way to truly understand the causes of these changes is through rigorous scientific research. Therefore, violent crime is likely to remain an important topic on the national agenda into the twenty-first century.

REGIONAL VARIATION, RELATIONSHIPS, AND WEAPONS

Three additional important issues in assessing how much violence there is in the United States need to be addressed. Violent crime, unline hair or eye color, is not uniformly distributed across people, places, and alternative mens or methods. Indeed, if we examine the distribution of homicide, rape, robbery, and assult rates for the four U.S. Census Bureau–defined regions of the country in 1996, we find that the West has the highest rates of violent crime, followed by the Midwest, the Northeast, and the South, respectively (U.S. Department of Justice, 1997:5). The fact that the West currently has the highest rates of violence is interesting in light of the number of theoretical and research studies that have attempted to explain why the South exhibited the highest rates of violent crime from the 1950s through the mid-1970s. However, as we will discuss later in this chapter, theories have been advanced recently to explain violence that does not depend on the unique history and culture of the South. Regardless, the fact remains that rates of violence vary substantially by region of the country.

Victim–Offender Relationship

Rates of violence also vary in terms of the people involved as victim and offender and the nature of their prior relationship. In 1995, the majority of homicide victims had some prior relationship with their murderer. Of those cases in which a relationship can be determined, the clear majority occurs between those who have some kind of personal relationship, for example, friend, neighbor, or co-worker. Although family members, especially spouses and those involved in sexually intimate relationships, represent about one-fourth of the total, less-intimate relationships between the victim and the offender are more typical in the case of homicide.

Often a homicide is described as "relationship between victim and offender unknown" or "victim and offender strangers to each other." The two categories should not be confused. The distinction is important in that a homicide categorized as "stranger" means that the victim and the offender had no prior relationship. In the case of the category "unknown," the relationship between the victim and the offender is not known (perhaps strangers, perhaps not). This is important because, for a very large portion of homicides (39 percent in 1995), the police were unable to determine whether a prior relationship existed between victim and killer, either because they did not discover who the offender was or because available evidence made it impossible to determine any prior relationship. Nothing suggests that, in all or even most of these cases, the victim and the offender were strangers, but this certainly was true in some cases. Our ability to understand why homicide happens is therefore compromised.

The percentage of stranger homicides has remained fairly stable over the past twenty years, ranging from 12.4 to 17.6 percent of all homicides. Conversely, the percentage of homicides categorized as "unknown" has increased over the last twenty years and increased more steadily since the mid-1980s. The range for homicides categorized as "unknown" since 1977 is 26 to 40 percent of all homicides. Researching homicides with percentages this high in the categories of stranger and unknown make understanding the causal factors contributing to homicide difficult.

Weapons

How are violent crimes carried out? Homicides most often are committed with firearms, with the largest subcategory of weapon used being handguns. Knives and other cutting or stabbing instruments rank a distant second, followed by personal weapons such as hands and feet, blunt objects like lamps or clubs, and finally other weapons, a category that includes poison and murder by drowning, arson, or explosives. Among robberies, personal attacks without any weapon other than the human body account for about 40 percent of incidents. Firearms are used in about the same percentage of cases, and knives and other weapons in about 20 percent of robberies.

Unlike homicide or robbery, in which firearms play a major role, firearms are used in just over 20 percent of assaults. This may be explained by the fact that firearms are more deadly than are other weapons and, therefore, the use of a firearm may lead to upgrading an assault to a homicide. In fact, some researchers have argued that most homicides are gun assaults in which the victim ended up dead (Zimring, 1972; Reed, 1971; Doerner, 1983; Doerner and Speir, 1986). However, the truth may lie in the opposite direction—that is, most gun assaults are homicides in which the victim did not die. Regardless, clubs, blunt objects, tire irons, lead pipe, and the like are the most commonly used weapons in assaults. Violent crimes, therefore, differ with regard to the methods offenders use to inflict violence on their victims.

EXPLAINING VIOLENT CRIME: RECENT DEVELOPMENTS

For much of the past thirty years, economic deprivation, subculture-of-violence, and deterrence theories (see Chapters 13 and 14) framed thought and research on the causes of violent crime. However, in the previous decade, two new approaches—the lifestyle or routine activity approach and the situational approach—were developed to answer one simple question: What explains social patterns of criminal activity?

The Lifestyle–Routine Activity Approach

The lifestyle–routine activity approach was developed under each of these labels by two different groups of scholars—the former by the criminologists Hindelang, Gottfredson, and Garofalo (1978); and the latter by Cohen and Felson (1979). Although these two approaches were developed separately, they are virtually the same and have been merged in the work of most researchers and theorists (see Maxfield, 1987). For Hindelang et al., the central question was: Why are some people much more likely to be victims of violent crime? For Cohen and Felson, the question of interest was: Why have crime rates gone up to such an extent since World War II, when the social conditions that are supposed to cause violent crime (for example, poverty) have improved so dramatically during the same period? For both, the answer lay in the nature of everyday life in this country and the changes that have occurred during the past forty years.

Cohen and Felson in particular draw their inspiration from the work of Hawley (1950), whose theory of human ecology has been widely applied to other areas of social science such as demography, family studies, and geography. In particular, Cohen and Felson argue that Hawley's concepts of the rhythm, tempo, and timing of daily movements and activities of individuals and families as they go about the business of obtaining the necessities of life—food, shelter, companionship, entertainment—are the keys to understanding rates of crime in our society. They argue that certain changes in these aspects of daily life have created the conditions for increased violent crime: More couples in which both persons work outside the home, more people living by themselves in independent households, the proliferation of outside-the-home recreational activities, the extension of shopping hours into the night, more persons eating outside the home, and so on. Cohen and Felson suggest that the effect of these social trends has been to bring together more often, in time and space, suitable targets for violence and motivated offenders; at the same time, fewer capable guardians have been present. Thus, the normal everyday activities that people engage in—working, going out for a movie, shopping at a store open late—place them at higher risk of being a victim of violent crime.

For Hindelang et al., this notion of risk is of primary concern. Certain lifestyles either require or tend to lead to increased movement of peo-ple and associated goods across time and space, thereby exposing individuals to more human contact in general and to more contact with potential offenders in particular. Why are certain lifestyles so risky? Hindelang et al. argue that at least three factors help determine the level of risk of any particular lifestyle: First, certain people occupy statuses with role expectations that are more or less risky. For example, most young single people are actively involved in dating, which raises their risk of victimization by increasing their exposure to potential offenders. Dating brings people out at night to attend parties or to go to bars and clubs; it means accepting the occasional blind date, and so on. Second, one's position in the social structure places certain limits or constraints on behavior. For example, a retail sales clerk often will be required to work in the evening, when targets, offenders, and the lack of guardians converge. Finally, in-dividuals or groups make choices or adapt to the potential risks that role expectations and structural constraints place on

them, thereby lowering or raising their risk. For example, individuals may decide to avoid bars and to date only people they meet through their church or synagogue, to decline working for a retail company that stays open late, or always to be inside their homes or apartments by a certain hour. In short, lifestyles–routine activity theory suggests that violent crime rates are a consequence of the fact that people, sometimes willingly and sometimes unwillingly and unknowingly, engage in risky behavior that exposes them to the potential for violent crime. The larger the number of people who engage in such risky behavior, the higher the rates of violent crime.

The Situational Approach

One of the advantages of the lifestyle–routine activity theory is that it places the source of violent crimes, at least in part, within the scope of normal activities of individuals. The situational approach to violence further develops this idea by arguing that violence results, in Luckenbill's (1977) terms, from a "situated transaction" between the victim and the offender.

Luckenbill suggests that homicides result from a specific, six-stage set of dynamic interactions. In **stage 1,** the victim typically makes a move, usually verbal but sometimes behavioral, that is seen by the offender as an affront to his or her self-esteem, authority, or overall character. Although the intent of the victim's opening move may not necessarily have been to provoke the offender, Luckenbill argues that, in most cases, the intent was clear. In **stage 2,** the offender verifies the meaning of the victim's opening action, often by consulting bystanders or observers. (Seventy percent of the cases examined in Luckenbill's study occurred in the presence of observers. This is strong evidence of the social nature of homicide.) The offender's initial reaction constitutes **stage 3,** during which the vast majority of offenders respond with a verbal challenge to the victim, typically requesting a halt in the behavior or remarks that initiated the transaction. Often, this challenge is coupled with a threat about what will happen if the victim does not comply. In **stage 4,** the victim continues the transaction, explicitly agreeing to the escalation of the situation toward violence by refusing to comply with the offender's request in stage 3. Thus, in **stage 5,** the actual violence occurs in short order. At this point, weapons may be secured from the environment or from the usual equipment carried by each participant. (Luckenbill found that, in 36 percent of the cases he examined, offenders carried the weapon they used in the homicide as a part of their daily routine.) **Stage 6,** the final aspect of the transaction, encompasses the offender's actions after the crime: Does the offender flee or call the police, or is the offender restrained by the bystanders (as happened in 35 percent of Luckenbill's cases)?

Luckenbill's situational theory argues that violence is a dynamic, social, and interactional phenomenon that can be understood fully by examining the way in which the victim and the offender act and react at each stage in the interaction process, as well as by considering the role that others play in the transaction. Although this approach is not inconsistent with the lifestyles–routine activity approach discussed previously, notice how much more finely grained it is in explaining why violence occurred. Carrying weapons is a part of a risky lifestyle, as is seeking leisure with others in public settings. (Forty-two percent of the cases Luckenbill examined occurred in public places

like bars, taverns, and street corners.) However, this theoretical approach points out that, in order for the risk to be actuated, the victim must be an active social participant, play certain roles at certain times, and engage in concrete and direct action. The same is true for the offender; notice that at any time during the first four stages, either the offender or the victim could have decided to pursue another course. Clearly, in our society, people argue a lot and insult one another a great deal without ultimately resorting to violence.

RESEARCH ON THE CORRELATES OF HOMICIDE

Perhaps because it is the crime with the most serious consequences, homicide has dominated much of the research on violence. Further, data on homicide often are the best and most complete of all data on violent crime. Specifically, research has focused, especially at the national level, on several factors as correlates of homicide: economic deprivation, subculture of violence, lifestyle–routine activities, situational factors, and victim–offender relationships (Parker and Smith, 1979; Loftin and Parker, 1985; Williams and Flewelling, 1987, 1988; Parker, 1989; Decker, 1996; Avakame, 1998; Kovandzic et al., 1998).

Economic Deprivation

Research on economic deprivation as a correlate of homicide has utilized two major indicators of deprivation: poverty and inequality. Poverty is defined as absolute deprivation, an absence of economic resources; inequality is defined as relative deprivation, in which one has fewer economic resources than do others in society. The findings of most studies are consistent for both of these concepts, although in the opposite direction. For example, in a study of the relationship between homicide rates and poverty in America's largest cities, poverty was found to be consistently and positively related to various types of homicide rates, independent of such variables as racial composition, the region in which the city was located, and population size and density (Loftin and Parker, 1985). However, with regard to inequality, Golden and Messner (1987) found that measures of inequality of various kinds had no impact on homicide rates, again independent of such variables as racial composition, region, and population density. A more recent study (Kposowa et al., 1995) found that equality and poverty had both positive and negative effects on homicide. Kovandzic and colleagues, in a recent review of the literature on the impact of income inequality and poverty on urban homicide, state that "a general consensus on the theoretical and empirical connections among these variables has yet to be reached" (1998: 569).

Subculture of Violence

Research on the subculture of violence and homicide has also been extensive, with many studies contrasting economic deprivation explanations with those of the subculture of violence. This concept, originally advanced by Wolfgang and Ferracuti (1967), is based on the existence of a subculture in which violence is part of normative expectations governing everyday behavior. In a pioneering study, Loftin and Hill (1974) criticized earlier subculture-of-violence studies of the high rates of homicide then found in the South for ignoring the potentially important effects of poverty on homicide rates. Loftin and

Hill created an index called "structural poverty" and found that, when poverty was held independent, the South no longer differed from other regions in its homicide rate.

These findings have been replicated a number of times with different units of analysis (Bailey, 1984; Williams, 1984; Messner and Golden, 1992), and with data from different periods (Bailey, 1984; Loftin and Parker, 1985; Williams and Flewelling, 1987; Harer and Steffensmeier, 1992; Phillips, 1997; Kovandzic et al., 1998). One study at the state level, by Huff-Corzine et al. (1986), suggested that both the subculture-of-violence and economic deprivation theories might be supportable, particularly when homicide was broken down by the race of the victim. These researchers found that poverty and regional indicators affected white homicide rates but not nonwhite rates. The more recent studies, however, do not find a great deal of evidence for the Southern subculture-of-violence thesis (Williams and Flewelling, 1987; Parker, 1989; Messner and Golden, 1992; Phillips, 1997; Kovandzic et al., 1998). Recall, too, that the data concerning region mentioned previously in this chapter shed further doubt on this thesis by showing that the West, not the South, currently has the highest homicide rate in the United States. Thus, we must ask: Did the West become more "Southern"? Did the South become less "Southern"? The Southern subculture-of-violence thesis may simply have been an artifact of the time when criminologists and others began to study homicide.

With regard to a racially based subculture of violence, the picture has been less clear. Messner (1983a, 1983b) finds several important effects of the percentage of the population that is African American on homicide rates, as do Bailey (1984), Huff-Corzine et al. (1986), Williams and Flewelling (1987), and Parker (1989). However,

Sampson (1987) provides convincing evidence that the position of African Americans in the socioeconomic structure is the root cause of homicide. Once the effects of economic deprivation and its outcomes, namely, family disruption, are properly specified, Sampson finds that racial composition, the usual indicator of the African-American subculture of violence, has no impact on homicide rates. In fact, Sampson finds that similar processes explain white and African-American violence, again undermining the existence of a unique African-American cultural effect. Thus, the vast majority of the empirical evidence suggests that regional and racial subcultures of violence either do not exist or, if they do, have little impact on homicide rates (Harer and Steffensmeier, 1992; Phillips, 1997; Kovandzic et al., 1998).

Lifestyle–Routine Activities

A number of researchers have studied the relationship between homicide and lifestyle–routine activities. Cohen and Felson (1979), in analyzing the United States as a whole from 1947 through 1974, derived a measure referred to as the "household activity ratio," consisting of the number of households with married women in the labor force plus the number of households headed by a single adult with children, divided by the total number of households of all kinds. Cohen and Felson argued that these two types of households were most vulnerable to crime because their lifestyles either required or allowed increased absence from home, more time outside the home in labor force participation, and more leisure activities outside the home. The household activity ratio was found to be a positive correlate of the homicide rate.

Carroll and Jackson (1983) have attempted to gain additional understanding of the role of routine activities in producing violent crime. They argue that the household activity ratio, because of its differential impact on various types of individuals in the economy, produces greater economic inequality, which in turn leads to increased rates of violence. On the one hand, routine activities of dual-income, intact households, not surprisingly, permit more out-of-home leisure, but also increase their potential exposure to violent crime. On the other hand, the difficulties of being a single parent, often with little labor force experience, cause the socioeconomic status of women heads of households to decline and consign many of their children to a life of poverty, alienation, and victimization. In an analysis of ninety-three large, non-southern cities, Carroll and Jackson do, indeed, find that the household activities ratio has a positive impact on economic inequality, which in turn has a positive impact not only on homicide but on rape and assault as well. These results are interesting in light of the lack of importance most studies of homicide and economic deprivation have assigned to various indicators of inequality.

Finally, Messner and Tardiff (1985) present a fairly unique analysis of the impact of routine activities on homicide, in that they analyze individual homicides rather than rates of large aggregated units like cities or states. Using data gathered in New York City, Messner and Tardiff find support for several hypotheses derived from the routine activities theory: Males are more likely than females to be victims of homicide away from home; whites are more often victims than are persons of other races of homicides involving strangers; those who are employed are more likely to be victims farther away from home than are those who are unemployed. In each case, lifestyle–routine activities theory suggests that victims more likely had lifestyles that subjected them to greater exposure to potential homicide offenders. Thus, the routine activities approach has shown great promise empirically as an important correlate of homicide, although a great deal more research is necessary before its impact can be fully understood.

Situational Factors

Recent research on the situational factors involved in homicide has produced some modifications of the correlates found through tests of the other theoretical perspectives. Studies in this vein have highlighted two themes: the importance of victim action in the events leading up to a homicide and the importance of considering the victim–offender relationship when attempting to determine the correlates of homicide rates. Luckenbill (1977) and Felson and Steadman (1983) have focused on the sequence of events that terminates in the death of one of the actors involved. In both of these studies, victim actions prior to the actual killing were important in determining the outcome. For example, Felson and Steadman found that persons in disputes who were aggressive and who used weapons were more likely to be killed than were those who did not act in this manner. Luckenbill (see discussion on page 202, 203) found that most victims were unwilling to allow the offenders to "save face" in a dispute, thus making violence seem the best way for the offender to resolve the situation.

Victim–Offender Relationship

Results from studies of homicide rates suggest that the nature of the prior victim–offender relationship leads to the identification of different factors as important correlates of homicide rates. For example, Williams and Flewelling (1988), in a study of 168 large cities for the period 1980 through 1984, found that, although poverty and divorce rates affected all the types of homicide they considered, the magnitude of those effects varied widely depending on the victim–offender relationship and the circumstances. For other factors, however, the determination of the correlates of homicide rates depended on the victim–offender relationship so that southern regional indicators were important correlates for only one type of homicide: "family other" (homicides involving family members as victim and offender, but where circumstances did not directly involve family-based conflicts or arguments). Racial composition of the population was most important in predicting acquaintance homicide rates and less important for other types. Similarly, Parker (1989) found that southern regional indicators had no positive impact on any type of homicide, whereas poverty affected all types of homicide except those involving robbery. With regard to racial compo-sition, the percentage of the population that is African American is an important correlate of robbery and acquaintance-related homicide, but not familial homicide or homicides involving other crimes.

RESEARCH ON THE CORRELATES OF RAPE, ROBBERY, AND ASSAULT

Smith and Bennett (1985) published one of the few studies focusing on the correlates of rape. In their study of 250 standard metropolitan statistical areas (SMSAs) for the period 1979 through 1981, they included measures of poverty, inequality, racial composition, the southern region, and family structure. They found that the most important correlates of the rape rate were poverty, percentage African American, and percentage divorced, thus paralleling much of the research discussed previously on the correlates of homicide rates. Similarly, Golden and Messner (1987) found that various measures of inequality had little or no impact on rape rates in their sample of SMSAs.

Cohen and Felson (1979) examined the relationship between rape rates over time (1947–1974) and the household activity ratio and found that the latter was an important correlate of the former. Maxfield (1987), in a study that treated rape, assault, and robbery as a single measure of personal crime, also found that several measures derived from lifestyle–routine activity theory were important correlates of violence. These included employment status, household composition (with households made up of one adult living with children being particularly likely to report victimizations), and routine leisure activities away from home. Thus, the research reviewed here on rape suggests that the important correlates of this crime parallel those for homicide.

A number of studies have examined the relationship between economic deprivation and robbery, assumed to be the most clearly economic of the four violent crimes considered here. Using data from neighborhoods in three SMSAs, Smith and Jarjoura (1988) found that poverty and residential mobility together were important correlates of robbery and assault (combined into a single category). Sampson (1987) found that per capita income had consistently negative effects on white and African-American robbery offending rates, and Carroll and Jackson (1983) found that income inequality in ninety-three non-southern cities was an important correlate of robbery rates. However,

Golden and Messner (1987), in a broader sample of SMSAs, found that various measures in inequality were not important predictors of robbery rates, controlling for other important correlates such as racial composition and percentage divorced.

A relationship between subcultural indicators (such as racial composition or the southern region) and robbery rates seems nonexistent. Sampson (1987), for example, found no impact of these variables on robbery rates, and Smith and Jarjoura (1988) also failed to find an effect for percentage African American or the regional indicator. The picture has been significantly brighter in terms of evidence for a relationship between lifestyle–routine activity variables and robbery, however. For example, Miethe et al. (1987) found that pursuing out-of-home leisure activities more than one night per week was an important correlate of robbery and assault rates, with other important factors such as poverty and age structure controlled. In an analysis of British data, Sampson and Wooldredge (1987) also found that the number of nights spent outside the home per week was an important correlate of robbery victimization. Both Cohen and Felson (1979) and Smith and Jarjoura (1988) found that household structure (number of hours per day characterized by the presence of adults in the home exercising guardianship over persons and property) was an important correlate of robbery rates and victimization. Thus, a great deal of support has been found for routine-activities and lifestyle indicators as major correlates of robbery.

As was the case for robbery, lifestyle–routine activity measures are more successful than are subcultural measures in showing relationships with assault. Cohen and Felson (1979) and Smith and Jarjoura (1988) once again found important effects for household structure as a correlate of this type of violence. Both Miethe et al. (1987) and Maxfield (1987) found that pursuit of leisure activities outside the home is an important correlate of measures of violence that include assault.

To summarize, what do we know about the correlates of rape, robbery, and assault? Although the empirical evidence on the correlates of these crimes of violence is neither as extensive nor as definitive as that concerning homicide, the conclusions to be drawn from the research reviewed here are very similar. Economic deprivation, perhaps both inequality and poverty (rather than just the latter, as is the case with homicide), seem to be the most consistent correlates. However, even more so than for homicide, routine activities–lifestyle measures are strong and consistent correlates of these types of violence and, over time, may prove to be more important than deprivation-related measures. The case against subcultures as correlate, although not as extensive as it was for homicide, is equally negative.

A RESEARCH AGENDA
FOR VIOLENT CRIME

It would be easy to conclude from what has been presented in this chapter that the empirical knowledge base for homicide, although not perfect, is substantially more extensive than that for the other three violent crimes discussed here. Why have there been so few studies of non-lethal violence? First, homicide has a kind of mystique about it that attracts both scholarly and public attention. It is the most final of crimes in its consequences and is therefore perceived as the most serious crime; yet data presented at the beginning of this chapter suggest that the other

three crimes are much more important in their impact, based on sheer number of occurrences, on society. Perhaps because of this mystique, studies of homicide have been stimulated by the availability of substantially better data than those available for non-homicidal violence. We are not able to analyze victim–offender relationships for cities, SMSAs, and states for the crimes of robbery, assault, and rape. We have not had detailed data on weapon or circumstance. We also have not asked for better data on these other crimes, perhaps because, in the case of rape, most criminologists are male and most rape victims are female, or because, in the case of assault, we have assumed that assaults are just uncompleted homicides. Whatever the reason, more and better data and research quite likely will reveal substantial differences between the correlates of homicide and the correlates of rape, robbery, and assault.

Violence within the family was, until recently, a seeming contradiction in terms. After all, family is supposed to be a haven of love and concern in a world of strife and turmoil. However, in recent decades, the pioneering research of Straus and Gelles (1986) has revealed the family to be one of our most violent institutions. Although researchers favoring the situational approach have begun to study family relationships, among others, in the context of homicide, additional research on the correlates of violence of all types is needed; the family may be an arena in which intervention to prevent violence has some chance of success, but our knowledge base first must be substantially increased.

We must also examine the level of analysis at which research on violent crime is conducted. We read about studies done with individual cases, neighborhoods, central cities, SMSAs, states, and the United States as a whole, and a detailed examination of the findings from some of these studies shows that data from different levels of aggregation yield different evidence concerning the correlates of homicide. For example, in one study that specifically examined this problem (Parker, 1985), contradictions were found between the state and county levels of analysis concerning the impact of racial composition and poverty on homicide rates, two of the major areas of focus in the research literature. Do anomalies like this exist simply because of counting and aggregation procedures, or are they due to some more fundamental feature of the way individuals react in different contexts?

The research by Sampson and Wooldredge (1987) cited earlier in this chapter provided an example of the potential for multilevel analysis that exists in the study of crime in general and violence in particular. In addition to studying the likelihood of victimization as determined by individual lifestyle–routine activity measures such as marital status and nights spent outside the home per week, Sampson and Wooldredge were able to examine simultaneously the impact of the neighborhood context in which respondents lived: Percentage of family disruption in the geographic area around the respondent's residence, level of street activity, and degree of social cohesion extant in the area all had independent effects on victimization. We might ask as well: What is the impact on victimization if one is richer or poorer than is typical for a given neighborhood? What would homicide rates be like in a city that almost never hands out a death penalty in a state that uses such punishment frequently? These and many other interesting hypotheses and relationships await discovery if we can concentrate our efforts on obtaining multilevel data and constructing multilevel theories.

A paper by Land et al. (1990) suggests an additional direction for research that may prove to be very important in gaining increased understanding of the causes of violence. Their study examined the large body of research reviewed previously with regard to homicide and pointed out that a number of inconsistencies exist across studies about factors considered to be the most important or even significant predictors of homicide. In addition to problems of inconsistent measurement of indicators and use of different levels of aggregation (for example, cities, metropolitan areas, or states) across studies, a major unresolved issue is whether findings regarding homicide vary by decade. That is, does the reason that one study concludes that variable x predicts homicide and another study concludes that variable x does not predict homicide lie in the fact that the first study used 1960 data and the second used 1980 data? More generally, Land et al. pose the question of structural change or stability in the causes of homicide over time, and after examining data for 1950, 1960, 1970 and 1980, they find that resource deprivation, population density and size, and family structure are consistent predictors of homicide in each of the four decades they examine. Studies like this clearly expand the scope of research on violent crime.

CONCLUSION

Although following the recommendations made thus far requires direct action from scholars and citizens, a final recommendation may eventually be implemented simply because of the regular progress of scientific knowledge. Many of the studies cited here in the deprivation and subculture areas were specifically designed to compare these two theories. However, with the development of two new perspectives, the lifestyle–routine activity approach and the situational approach, as well as renewed interest in deterrence theory, a number of studies exist side by side in the literature that do not attempt to compare these perspectives. Yet, some of the most interesting results come from studies that attempt to bring together disparate perspectives for comparison; for example, Sampson's (1987) attempt to examine subculture, deprivation, and routine–lifestyles activities; Carroll and Jackson's (1983) study of inequality and lifestyles–routine activities; Parker's (1989) examination of deprivation and subculture in the context of a situational approach; Land and associates' (1990)

study of structural stability and change across four decades; the study of inequality and poverty by Kovandzic et al. (1998); Avakame's (1998) study of stranger and intimate partner homicide. Bringing additional theoretical perspectives into the research makes it more complicated and difficult, but these examples suggest that the benefits outweigh the costs. This is not to say that better studies—within these perspectives or from new perspectives that may develop—are not valuable, but simply to urge more research in which explanations and measures successful in previous research are brought face to face in a single model of the correlates of violent crime. Increased knowledge surely will result from such studies.

DISCUSSION QUESTIONS

1. Discuss recent trends in violent crime in terms of the sources of data indicating those trends. Do UCR and NCVS figures differ regarding the pictures they show over time? If so, regarding what specific types of violent crime? Why?

2. We hear much about firearms and crime in this country. In what percent of homicides are firearms used? How about in other forms of violent crime? What are the implications of these findings for anticrime policy?

3. Describe the lifestyle and routine activities approaches to the explanation of crime. What kinds of activities seem associated with violent victimization? In what ways is this issue related to the discussion of "victim precipitation" in Chapter 6?

4. What is "intimate partner homicide"? Are the targets of this form of murder more likely to be men or women? Which is likelier, that an individual will be the victim of an intimate partner homicide or of a homicide in general?

5. Overall, what factors seem most linked to homicide in this country? Poverty? Economic inequality? Population characteristics? Or is homicide simply governed by situational factors that are impossible to measure?

6. Summarize what we know about the factors seemingly tied to robbery and rape. Is economic inequality the best predictor of robbery rates?

REFERENCES

Avakame, E. 1998. "How Different is Violence in the Home? An Examination of Some Correlates of Stranger and Intimate Homicide." *Criminology* 36: 601–632.

Bailey, W. C. 1984. "Poverty, Inequality, and City Homicide Rates: Some Not So Unexpected Results." *Criminology* 22: 531–550.

Carroll, L., and P. I. Jackson. 1983. "Inequality, Opportunity, and Crime Rates in Central Cities." *Criminology* 21: 178–194.

Cohen, L. E., and M. Felson. 1979. "Social Change and Crime Rates Trends: A Routine Activities Approach." *American Sociological Review* 44: 588–608.

Decker, S. 1996. "Deviant Homicide: A New Look at the Role of Motives and Victim-Offender Relationships." *Journal of Research in Crime and Delinquency* 33: 427–449.

Doerner, W. G. 1983. "Why Does Johnny Reb Die When Shot? The Impact of Medical Resources Upon Lethality." *Sociological Inquiry* 53: 1–15.

Doerner, W. G., and J. C. Speir. 1986. "Stitch and Sew: The Impact of Medical Resources Upon Criminally Induced Lethality." *Criminology* 24: 319–330.

Federal Bureau of Investigation. 1978–1997. *Crime in the United States.* (1977–1996). Washington, DC: U.S. Department of Justice.

Felson, R. B., and H. J. Steadman. 1983. "Situational Factors in Disputes Leading to Criminal Violence." *Criminology* 21: 59–74.

Golden, R. M., and S. F. Messner. 1987. "Dimensions of Racial Inequality and Rates of Violent Crime." *Criminology* 25: 525–542.

Harer, M. D., and D. Steffensmeier. 1992. "The Differing Effects of Economic Inequality on Black and White Rates of Violence." *Social Forces* 70: 1035–1054.

Hawley, A. 1950. *Human Ecology: A Theory of Community Structure.* New York: Ronald.

Hindelang, M. J., M. R. Gottfredson, and J. Garofalo. 1978. *Victims of Personal Crime: An Empirical Foundation for a Theory of Personal Victimization.* Cambridge, MA: Ballinger.

Huff-Corzine, L., J. Corzine, and D. C. Moore. 1986. "Southern Exposure: Deciphering the South's Influence on Homicide Rates." *Social Forces* 64: 906–924.

Kovandzic, T. L. Vieraitis, and M. Yeisley. 1998. "The Structural Covariates of Urban Homicide: Reassessing the Impact of Income Inequality and Poverty in the Post-Reagan Era." *Criminology* 36: 569–599.

Kposowa, A., K. Breault, and B. Harrison. 1995. "Reassessing the Structural Covariates of Violent and Property Crimes in the USA: A County Level Analysis." *British Journal of Sociology* 46: 79–105.

Land, K. C., P. L. McCall, and L. E. Cohen. 1990. "Structural Covariates of Homicide Rates: Are There Any Invariances Across Time and Space?" *American Journal of Sociology* 95: 922–963.

Loftin, C., and R. Hill. 1974. "Regional Subculture and Homicide." *American Sociological Review* 39: 714–724.

Loftin, C., and R. N. Parker. 1985. "The Effect of Poverty on Urban Homicide Rates: An Error in Variables Approach." *Criminology* 23: 269–287.

Luckenbill, D. F. 1977. "Homicide as a Situated Transaction." *Social Problems* 25: 176–186.

Maxfield, M. G. 1987. "Lifestyles and Routine Activity Theories of Crime: Empirical Studies of Victimization, Delinquency, and Offender Decision-making." *Journal of Quantitative Criminology* 3: 275–281.

Messner, S. F. 1983a. "Regional and Racial Effects on the Urban Homicide Rate: The Subculture of Violence Revisited." *American Journal of Sociology* 88: 997–1007.

———. 1983b. "Regional Differences in the Economic Correlates of the Urban Homicide Rate: Some Evidence on the Importance of Context." *Criminology* 21: 477–488.

Messner, S., and R. Golden. 1992. "Racial Inequality and Racially Disaggregated Homicide Rates: An Assessment of Alternative Theoretical Explanations." *Criminology* 30: 421–447.

Messner, S. F., and K. Tardiff. 1985. "The Social Ecology of Urban Homicide: An Application of the Routine Activities Approach." *Criminology* 23: 241–267.

Miethe, T. D., M. C. Stafford, and J. S. Long. 1987. "Social Differentiation in Criminal Victimization: A Test of Routine Activities/Lifestyle Theories." *American Sociological Review* 52: 184–194.

Parker, R. N. 1985. "Aggregation Ratio Variables, and Measurement Problems in Criminological Research." *Journal of Quantitative Criminology* 1: 269–280.

———. 1989. "Poverty, Subculture of Violence, and Type of Homicide." *Social Forces* 67: 983–1007.

Parker, R. N., and M. D. Smith. 1979. "Deterrence, Poverty, and Type of Homicide." *American Journal of Sociology* 85: 614–624.

Phillips, J. 1997. "Variation in African-American Homicide Rates: An Assessment of Potential Explanations." *Criminology* 35: 527–559.

Reed, J. S. 1971. "To Live—and Die—in Dixie: A Contribution to the Study of Southern Violence." *Political Science Quarterly* 86: 429–443.

Ridel, M.. 1998. "Counting Stranger Homicides: A Case Study of Statistical Prestidigitation." *Homicide Studies* 2: 206–218.

———. 1999. "Sources of Homicide Data." In *Studying and Preventing Homicide*. Edited by

M. D. Smith and M. A. Zahn. Thousand Oaks, CA: Sage.

Sampson, R. J. 1987. "Urban Black Violence: The Effect of Male Joblessness and Family Disruption." *American Journal of Sociology* 93: 348–382.

Sampson, R. J., and J. D. Wooldredge. 1987. "Linking the Micro- and Macro-Level Dimensions of Lifestyle-Routine Activity and Opportunity Models of Predatory Victimization." *Journal of Quantitative Criminology* 3: 371–393.

Smith, D. A., and G. R. Jarjoura. 1988. "Social Structure and Criminal Victimization." *Journal of Research in Crime and Delinquency* 25: 27–52.

Smith, M. D., and N. Bennett. 1985. "Poverty, Inequality, and Theories of Forcible Rape." *Crime and Delinquency* 31: 295–305.

Straus, M. A., and R. J. Gelles. 1986. "Societal Change and Change in Family Violence From 1975 to 1985 as Revealed by Two National Surveys." *Journal of Marriage and the Family* 48: 465–479.

U.S. Department of Justice. 1978–1997. *Criminal Victimization in the United States.* (1977–1996). Washington, DC: U.S. Department of Justice.

———. 1978–1997. *Uniform Crime Reports.* (1977–1996). Washington, DC: U.S. Department of Justice.

———. 1989. *New Directions for the National Crime Survey.* Washington, DC: U.S. Department of Justice.

———. 1995. *Violence against Women: Estimates from the Redesigned Survey.* Washington, DC: U.S. Department of Justice.

Williams, K. R. 1984. "Economic Sources of Homicide: Reestimating the Effects of Poverty and Inequality." *American Sociological Review* 49: 283–289.

Williams, K. R., and R. L. Flewelling. 1987. "Family Acquaintance, and Stranger Homicide: Alternative Procedures for Rate Calculation." *Criminology* 25: 543–560.

————. 1988. "The Social Production of Criminal Homicide: A Comparative Study of Disaggregated Rates in American Cities." *American Sociological Review* 53: 421–431.

Wolfgang, M. E., and F. Ferracuti. 1967. *The Subculture of Violence: Towards an Integrated Theory in Criminology.* Beverly Hills, CA: Sage.

Zimring, F. E. 1972. "The Medium Is the Message: Firearm Caliber as a Determinant of Death from Assault." *Journal of Legal Studies* 1: 97–123.

Chapter Outline

8

Property Crime Trends

ROBERT J. BURSIK, JR.
University of Missouri, St. Louis

O ne of the most deceptively simple concepts in criminology is that of property
crime. Although opinions differ concerning the
particular illegal behaviors that should constitute such crimes, most widely accepted images of property crime are consistent with that
of Hepburn (1984: 73): "any criminal behavior by which property is transferred." As such,
they can be considered to represent transactions
in which a consumer acquires an economic
good without the permission of the supplier
(Van Dijk, 1994).

With the development of capitalist market
societies in the eighteenth century, the concept
of property generally became equated with guar-
anteed, legal assurances that an individual can
exclude others from the use or benefit of some
material resource (MacPherson, 1978: 9–10). As
a result, the kinds of illegal behaviors that are
most immediately identified as being property

crimes represent transgressions against private
property. Thus, a motor vehicle theft involves
the illicit use of a means of transportation by
someone to whom full access rights to that vehicle have not been granted.

In this chapter, we seek a better sense of the
notion of property crime through examination
of a number of issues. Of major importance is
the definition of property crime. We begin with
Part I *Uniform Crime Report* (UCR) offenses and
then focus on a crime that only recently has
joined the list of major offenses—arson. Next,
we examine a number of lesser property offenses
and explore recent trends in property crime. Finally, two themes that merit much criminological attention are reviewed: (1) the relationship of
unemployment to property crime and (2) the
extent to which property crime rates reflect
the opportunities for crime provided by potential victims.

CURRENT DEFINITIONS OF PROPERTY CRIME

The classification of particular behaviors as property crime is not a completely straightforward process. Consider, for example, the crime of robbery, defined in the UCR as "the taking or attempting to take anything of value from the care, custody, or control of a person or persons by force or threat of force or violence and/or by putting the victim in fear" (FBI, 1997: 395). Although such a definition makes it clear that robberies involve the violation of property rights, such behaviors are classified as personal rather than property crimes by the UCR because of the nature of the interaction between the offender and the victim. However, Hepburn (1984) convincingly argues that robbery is primarily a property offense because of the illegal transfer of a material resource from the victim to the offender. The decision to categorize robbery as a property crime might therefore affect the conclusions that can be drawn concerning the distribution and causes of property crime overall. Considerable attention should be given to the offenses that are included in overall indices of property crime before unwarranted comparisons among various studies are made.

UCR PART I OFFENSES

The index of Part I property crime provided by the UCR is computed on the basis of the following four different offenses (FBI, 1997: 395):

Burglary—breaking or entering The unlawful entry of a structure to commit a felony or a theft. Attempted forcible entry is included.

Larceny-theft (except motor vehicle theft) The unlawful taking, carrying, leading, or riding away of property from the possession or constructive possession of another. Examples are thefts of bicycles or automobile accessories, shoplifting, pickpocketing or the stealing of any property or article that is not taken by force and violence or by fraud. Attempted larcenies are included. Embezzlement, confidence games, forgery, worthless checks, and so on, are excluded.

Motor vehicle theft The theft or attempted theft of a motor vehicle. A motor vehicle is self-propelled and runs on the surface and not on rails. Specifically excluded from this category are motorboats, construction equipment, airplanes, and farming equipment.

Arson Any willful or malicious burning or attempt to burn, with or without intent to defraud, a dwelling house, public building, motor vehicle or aircraft, personal property of another, and so on.

Most studies of property crime focus only on these offenses. Although these classifications are very general, much greater detail is available from the UCR concerning the rates of particular crimes within each category. For example, the larceny-theft rates can be further broken down in terms of purse snatching, pickpocketing, shoplifting, theft from motor vehicles, bicycle theft, theft from buildings, theft from coin-operated machines, and other miscellaneous thefts.

Although the UCR statistics for Part I offenses are the most common source of data used in the study of property crime, they still are somewhat problematic in that information is available only for those crimes that come to the attention of the police (see Chapter 3). We must recognize that a large percentage of property crime is never reported to the police and, therefore, is not reflected in these data; estimates for 1996 indicate that, although 76 percent of motor vehicle thefts came to the attention of law enforcement agencies, the proportion was much lower for other property offenses: burglary, 51 percent; theft, 28 percent (U.S. Department of Justice, 1997).

The Special Case of Arson

Crimes of arson have a unique history as UCR Part I offenses. Although arson for economic profit always has been considered an extremely serious offense, the designers of the initial reporting system believed that relevant statistics could not be gathered in "a uniform manner" because the crime is so frequently and easily concealed (International Association of Chiefs of Police, 1929: 180). Therefore, arson originally was classified as a Class 21 ("all other offenses") crime, along with such activities as criminal anarchism and the desecration of graves. However, the number of arsons reported to the National Fire Protection Association increased by over *3,100 percent* between 1951 and 1977, and the Law Enforcement Assistance Administration estimated that arson losses accounted for almost 40 percent of all total fire damages in 1977 (reported in Brady, 1983). As a result, in October 1978, arson was reclassified as a Part I offense by congressional mandate. This is one of only two significant revisions that have been made to the UCR classification system in the history of the program (the other was in response to the passage of the Hate Crime Statistics Act of 1990).

However, an interpretation of the UCR arson statistics is somewhat problematic. In fact, the FBI cautions that the data made available to the agency are not "sufficient" (FBI, 1997: 62). For example, although 11,250 law enforcement agencies reported such offenses during 1996, only 8,325 of them (representing 68 percent of the U.S. population) submitted reports for all twelve months of the year (FBI, 1997: 54); this is far below the population coverage for the other Index offenses. Jackson (1988) has presented evidence suggesting that the volume of the 1985 arson figures represented only 59 percent of the reported arsons in the United States, and that the rate per 100,000 persons reported in the UCR may be less than half the actual rate. Thus, the validity and reliability of the arson figures are highly questionable. In part, this may be due to confusion concerning reporting responsibilities. Battle and Weston (1978), for example, note that many police officials believe arson is the primary responsibility of fire departments, whereas many fire departments believe the responsibility lies with the police departments. In addition to state and local agencies, at least eleven federal agencies, ranging from the FBI to the U.S. Department of Forestry, also have programs geared toward detecting and investigating arson (Incove et al., 1979: 50). Thus, unlike the other property crime recorded in the UCR, arson typically does not fall solely within a police jurisdiction (Jackson, 1988: 183). Although the UCR has attempted to create liaisons with the law enforcement, fire service, and insurance communities to upgrade the quality of reporting practices (FBI, 1980), the collection of accurate data involves a complicated coordination of the efforts of various agencies—not only public and private, but also local and national.

The arson statistics differ from those of the rest of the Part I offenses in two other important ways. A fire is recorded as arson only after an investigation has determined it to have been "willfully or maliciously set"; fires of "suspicious or unknown origin" are excluded (FBI, 1997: 395). As Jackson (1988: 123) notes, the reports of the other offense types need not be substantiated by an investigation before being reflected in the crime rate. In addition, *all* reported cases of arson are reflected in the UCR statistics. This differs from the hierarchical rule that applies to all the other Index crimes: that is, when a series of offenses occurs within a single incident, only the most serious of those crimes is reflected in the UCR. For these reasons, extreme caution must be used when evaluating trends over time in the extent of arson and when comparing such trends with those characterizing the other Index property offenses.

UCR PART II OFFENSES

Property crime also may be studied in terms of the following Part II offenses reported by the UCR (FBI, 1997: 395):

Forgery and counterfeiting Making, altering, uttering, or possessing, with intent to defraud, anything false in the semblance of that which is true. Attempts are included.

Fraud Fraudulent conversion and obtaining money or property by false pretenses. Included are confidence games and bad checks, except forgeries and counterfeiting.

Embezzlement Misappropriation or misapplication of money or property entrusted to one's care, custody, or control.

Stolen property: buying, receiving, possessing Buying, receiving, and possessing stolen property, including attempts.

Vandalism Willful or malicious destruction, injury, disfigurement, or defacement of any public or private property, real or personal, without consent of the owner or persons having custody or control.

Although the UCR contains data pertaining to the number of crimes reported to the police, as well as to the percentage of these crimes that have been cleared through an arrest for Part I offenses, only arrest statistics are available for Part II offenses. Many researchers believe that the gatekeeping processes of the criminal justice system make such arrest data fairly unrepresentative of the overall patterns of property crime. For example, in 1996, only 18.1 percent of all property crime reported to the police were cleared by an arrest; the offense-specific clearance rates range from lows of 13.8 percent for burglary and 14.0 percent for motor vehicle theft to a high of 20.3 percent for larceny-theft; similarly, only 26.9 percent of all reported robberies were cleared by an arrest (FBI, 1997: 205). Therefore, the data pertaining to Part II offenses rarely are analyzed.

CURRENT TRENDS IN PROPERTY CRIME IN THE UNITED STATES

Table 8.1 lists the UCR estimates of recent patterns of Part I property crimes reported to the police in the United States. We can note several trends in these data. For example, the rates tended to increase until the mid-1970s, when they stabilized somewhat. However, they again began to increase, reaching a peak in

Table 8.1   UCR Estimated Rate of Part I Property Offenses Known to Police, 1960–1996*

YEAR	ROBBERY	BURGLARY	LARCENY-THEFT	MOTOR VEHICLE THEFT	PROPERTY CRIME TOTAL
1960	60.1	508.6	1,034.7	183.0	1,726.3
1961	58.3	518.9	1,045.4	183.6	1,747.9
1962	59.7	535.2	1,124.8	197.4	1,857.5
1963	61.8	576.4	1,219.1	216.6	2,012.1
1964	68.2	634.7	1,315.5	247.4	2,197.5
1965	71.7	662.7	1,329.3	256.8	2,248.8
1966	80.8	721.0	1,442.9	286.9	2,450.9
1967	102.8	826.6	1,575.8	334.1	2,736.5
1968	131.8	932.3	1,746.6	393.0	3,071.8
1969	148.4	984.1	1,930.9	436.2	3,351.3
1970	172.1	1,084.9	2,079.3	456.8	3,621.0
1971	188.0	1,163.5	2,145.5	459.8	3,768.8
1972	180.7	1,140.8	1,993.6	426.1	3,560.4
1973	183.1	1,222.5	2,071.9	442.6	3,737.0
1974	209.3	1,437.7	2,489.5	462.2	4,389.3
1975	218.2	1,525.9	2,804.8	469.4	4,800.2
1976	199.3	1,448.2	2,921.3	450.0	4,819.5
1977	190.7	1,419.8	2,729.9	451.9	4,601.7
1978	195.8	1,434,6	2,747.4	460.5	4,642.5
1979	218.4	1,511.9	2,999.1	505.6	5,016.6
1980	251.1	1,684.1	3,167.0	502.2	5,353.3
1981	258.7	1,649.5	3,139.7	474.4	5,263.9
1982	238.9	1,488.8	3,084.8	458.8	5,032.5
1983	216.5	1,337.7	2,868.9	430.8	4,637.4
1984	205.4	1,263.7	2,791.3	437.1	4,492.1
1985	208.5	1,287.3	2,901.2	462.0	4,650.5
1986	225.1	1,344.6	3,010.3	507.8	4,862.7
1987	212.7	1,329.6	3,081.3	529.4	4,940.3
1988	220.9	1,309.2	3,134.9	582.9	5,027.1
1989	233.0	1,276.3	3,171.3	630.4	5,077.9
1990	257.0	1,235.9	3,194.8	657.8	5,088.5
1991	272.7	1,252.0	3,228.8	659.0	5,139.7
1992	263.6	1,168.2	3,103.0	631.5	4,902.7
1993	255.9	1,099.2	3,032.4	606.1	4,737.6
1994	237.7	1,042.0	3,026.7	591.3	4,660.0
1995	220.9	987.1	3,043.8	560.4	4,591.3
1996	202.4	943.0	2,975.9	525.9	4,444.8
Percent change, 1987–1996	−4.8	−29.1	−3.4	−0.7	−10.0

SOURCE: Maguire and Pastore, 1997: 306.

*All rates are per 100,000 U.S. residents.

Table 8.2   National Crime Victimization Survey Crime Trends, 1973–1996*

YEAR	BURGLARY	THEFT	MOTOR VEHICLE THEFT	TOTAL
1973	110.0	390.8	19.1	519.9
1974	111.8	421.0	18.8	551.5
1975	110.0	424.1	19.5	553.6
1976	106.7	421.0	16.5	544.2
1977	106.2	420.9	17.0	544.1
1978	103.1	412.0	17.5	532.6
1979	100.9	413.4	17.5	531.8
1980	101.4	378.0	16.7	496.1
1981	105.9	374.1	17.2	497.2
1982	94.1	358.0	16.2	468.3
1983	84.0	329.8	14.6	428.4
1984	76.9	307.1	15.2	399.2
1985	75.2	296.0	14.2	385.4
1986	73.8	284.0	15.0	372.7
1987	74.6	289.0	16.0	379.6
1988	74.3	286.7	17.5	378.4
1989	67.7	286.5	19.2	373.4
1990	64.5	263.8	20.6	348.9
1991	64.6	266.8	22.2	353.7
1992	58.6	248.2	18.5	325.3
1993	58.2	241.7	19.0	318.9
1994	56.3	235.1	18.8	310.2
1995	49.3	224.3	16.9	290.5
1996	47.2	205.7	13.5	266.4
Percentage change, 1987–1996	−29.7	−36.7	−28.8	−15.8

SOURCES: Rand et al., 1997; U.S. Department of Justice, 1997.

*Rates per 1,000 U.S. households. The 1973–1991 data have been adjusted to make them comparable to data collected after the redesign of the NCVS in 1992 (see Rand et al., 1997).

1980, followed by several years of general decline. Modest increases in the rates of all offenses except burglary were apparent between 1984 and 1991, followed by steadily decreasing rates for all offenses represented in the table during the years for which records are available (1987–1996).

The various alternative sources of crime data sometimes provide very different pictures of the existing patterns of criminal behavior. This is apparent when we compare Table 8.1 with Table 8.2, which lists the trends in property crime between 1973 and 1996 as reflected in the data collected by the National Crime Victimization Survey (NCVS). According to the NCVS report, there has been a general decline since 1973 in the rate of all property crimes. However, as O'Brien (see Chapter 3) has noted, extreme caution must be used in making direct comparisons between the rates provided by the UCR and the NCVS. First, the different definitions of property crime used by the two sources of data make such comparisons problematic. In addition, as Biderman et al. (1991) have pointed out, many of the activities reflected in the UCR rate are not used in the creation of the NCVS rate (and vice versa). For example, whereas the UCR rates include commercial crime, the NCVS rates do not. This has an especially large effect on estimates of property crimes such as larceny. In addition, different population estimates are used in the computation of the crime rates. Biderman et al. demonstrate that the estimates used by the UCR tend to result in increasingly inflated estimates in the years directly preceding the collection of the updated U.S. Census Bureau population estimates. In general, Biderman et al. conclude that we need to know much more concerning the behavior of these components over time before a valid comparison of such trends can be made.

Finally, generalizations concerning overall trends in property crime should be made with extreme caution given the important changes in the age structure that have characterized the United States (Steffensmeier and Harer, 1991; see also Chapter 4). Note that the rates in Table 8.1 are calculated on the basis of the entire U.S. population, whereas those in Table 8.2 are calculated on the basis of household residents who are at least 12 years old. One of the few well-established facts of criminology concerns the important differences that exist in age-specific rates of crime: After a peak in mid- to late adolescence, an offender's crime level tends to decline with age (Gottfredson and Hirschi, 1990). If the relative size of a high-risk age grouping increases over time, the crime rate would reflect this demographic shift with an increased rate of illegal behavior. However, such increases would not necessarily reflect an increase in the rate of criminal activity within any particular

age group (Sagi and Wellford, 1968; Chilton and Spielberger, 1971; Steffensmeier and Harer, 1991). Rather, it might simply imply that an increasingly greater proportion of the total population represents those in high-risk age groups.

Overall, although it is relatively easy to account for the differences in the UCR profiles over time, it remains extremely difficult to provide a definitive presentation of the actual trends in property crime (Blumstein et al., 1991; McDowall and Loftin, 1992; Menard, 1992). Therefore, although there definitely has been a decrease in the rate of crime through 1996, the magnitude of this decline is not clear.

Unemployment and Property Crime

Given the different assumptions that underlie the many causal theories of criminal behavior (see Part Four), a wide variety of factors has been examined in relation to the distribution of property crime. However, whether these theories assume that society is generally characterized by cooperation and consensus or by conflict and diversity, nearly all the dominant frameworks predict that a strong positive relationship should exist between rates of unemployment and property crime (Bursik and Grasmick, 1993; Cantor and Land, 1985; Devine et al., 1988; Hughes and Carter, 1981; Long and Witte, 1981; Sampson and Wilson, 1995; Thornberry and Christenson, 1984; Wilson, 1987).

Given this relative consensus concerning the expected form of the relationship, one would assume that the empirical relationship would be fairly strong, regardless of its interpretation. Surprisingly, three extensive reviews of existing research (Gillespie, 1978; Freeman, 1983; Long and Witte, 1981) fail to find consistent results.

Some studies present evidence of the expected relationship; some fail to document any such association; and some even find a negative association between unemployment and property crime rates (Cantor and Land, 1985: 217). There are several possible explanations for the prevalence of such contradictory evidence. Wilson and Herrnstein (1985: 315) note that both crime and unemployment may represent outcomes of some third common cause. If the effects of this common cause were taken into account, then the association between crime and unemployment should disappear. That is, despite all the predictions to the contrary, there may not actually be a relationship between these two rates. On the other hand, Devine et al. (1988) provide evidence that the failure to specify fully the processes related to property crime (such as the distribution of opportunities) may actually suppress the relationship between unemployment and property crime. In particular, specification issues can have a great effect on the conclusions that are drawn from time-series analyses (see the exchange between Hale and Sabbagh, 1991, and Cantor and Land, 1991).

In addition, Chiricos (1987) argues that the different levels of aggregation used in these studies may account for some of the inconsistencies. He notes that studies using statistics for the nation as a whole generally produced results less consistent with the hypothesized unemployment–crime rate association than have studies that analyzed data at lower levels of aggregation, such as the state, county, standard metropolitan statistical area (SMSA) or census tract. He argues that the results from these lower levels of aggregation may be the most valid because smaller aggregates tend to have much more homogeneous compositions. Analyses at this level also may provide a better sense of the noneconomic aspects of unemployment that can filter through a community (such as

widespread demoralization) and that may be related to crime.

A growing body of research suggests that the effects of unemployment on crime are conditional on certain social contexts. Allan and Steffensmeier (1989) present evidence that this relationship varies by age, the type of property crime, and the way in which unemployment has been measured (similar findings have been reported by Baron and Hartnagel, 1997; Britt, 1997). For example, although unemployment is related to the rates of property crime committed by juveniles age 14–17, this is not the case for crimes committed by those 18–24. Likewise, LaFree et al. (1992) conclude that unemployment is related to white but not African-American rates of property crime. Finally, a growing body of evidence proposes that the nature of the unemployment-crime relationship is contingent on the stage of capitalist development and the associated structures of resource accumulation (Carlson and Michalowski, 1997; Grant and Martinez, 1997).

Such considerations have two basic implications. First, many criminologists may have rejected prematurely the unemployment-crime hypothesis. Second, if it in fact exists, the relationship is much more complex than has been generally recognized. This complexity is well illustrated by Cantor and Land (1985), who argue that, although rises in the unemployment rate may increase the criminal motivation of potential property offenders, such increases in unemployment may influence property crime rates negatively; that is, the higher the unemployment rate, the lower the rate of property crime. This counterintuitive prediction reflects two different processes. First, as some individuals are removed from employment outside the home, there may be a greater concentration of activities in or near the home. This increased ability to guard one's property may decrease the number of situations in which the successful commission of a property offense may occur. Second, higher unemployment reflects a general slowdown in production and consumption activities for all persons, therefore providing less new and attractive property to be stolen.

Criminal Opportunities and Property Crime

As noted in Chapter 7 of this text, theories of criminal opportunities emphasize the processes by which potential victims and offenders converge in space and time (see Gottfredson, 1981: 715). Such orientations have a long history in criminology. In fact, Shaw (1929), who had a major impact on the development of one of the most traditional offender-based theories in American criminology (social disorganization), also noted that a prominent feature of areas with high delinquency rates was the presence of large amounts of commercial or industrial property, which provided the opportunities for property crime. Three decades later, Morris (1957: 20–21) argued that it was necessary to differentiate between the background characteristics that may predispose an individual to crime and the situations in which these potentialities become actualized.

Boggs (1965) examined the question of why potential targets of crime were exploited more in certain areas than others. She concluded that targets differ in kind and amount over space, and that the selection of a target reflected the familiarity that existed between offenders and their targets and the potential profitability of the criminal act. Several years later, Gould (1969) took a similar position, noting that in addition to the value of certain property and the ease with which it can be stolen, the abundance of particular targets was related to variation in rates of property crime.

In the late 1970s, two more-developed theoretical approaches to criminal opportunity appeared nearly simultaneously. Two reasons may be suggested for the appearance of these models. The first was the publication of two books that strongly influenced the development of the opportunity perspective. The first, *Defensible Space,* by Oscar Newman (1972), was ostensibly concerned with architectural design. However, Newman's primary emphasis was on the "real and symbolic barriers, strongly defined areas of influence and improved opportunities for surveillance . . . that combine to bring an environment under the control of its residents" (p. 3). That is, Newman's thesis is grounded in the assumption that particular architectural designs could decrease the opportunity for criminal victimization. Similarly, *Residential Crime,* by Thomas Reppetto (1974), emphasized the relationships among the ease of access, the degree of local surveillance, and rates of property crime. In addition, through his consideration of an enormous body of data, Reppetto stressed the importance of physical building design, the visibility of potential crime sites, and the travel and work patterns of potential victims. The issues initially raised by Newman and Reppetto are clearly reflected in the many contemporary "crime prevention through environmental design" programs that have been instituted throughout the United States (Felson and Clarke, 1997; National Crime Prevention Council, 1997).

The second likely reason for the historical timing of opportunity theories was the increasing attention being paid to the development of victimization research (see Chapter 6). As Gould (1969: 50) argued, an understanding of the role of victims in the etiology of property crime is essential to the development of an opportunity theory because victims are the actual targets of crime.

The growing emphasis on victimization research culminated in the publication of *Victims of Personal Crime,* by Hindelang et al. (1978), which presented a theory of victimization called the lifestyle model. This model assumes that the manner in which individuals allocate their time to vocational and leisure activities is related to the probability of being in a particular place at a particular time. These lifestyle differences are associated with differential exposure to situations in which a person (or that person's property) has a high risk of victimization (Gottfredson, 1981: 720; Hindelang et al., 1978; Garofalo, 1987). Such differences are assumed to be determined by individual and group adaptations to structural constraints and role expectations reflected in the demographic characteristics of potential victims (Hindelang et al., 1978: 243; Garofalo, 1987: 26). In turn, lifestyle differences affect one's exposure to the risks of victimization inherent in particular places and times, as well as one's potential association with others who are more or less likely to commit crime. Victimization is assumed to reflect the direct effects of such exposure and association.

As Parker pointed out in Chapter 7 of this text, a very similar perspective, called the routine activities approach, was presented by Cohen and Felson (1979). In addition to assuming that crime represents a convergence in time and space of motivated offenders and suitable targets, Cohen and Felson introduced the central dimension of the guardianship (that is, surveillance and protection) of persons and property by fellow citizens as they go about their routine activities. In a later paper, Cohen et al. (1981) provided more detail concerning the dynamics that underlie the convergence of potential victims and offenders, incorporating the dimensions of exposure (the physical visibility and accessibility of persons or objects to potential offenders at any given time or place), proximity (the physical distance between areas where potential targets of crime reside and areas where relatively large populations of potential offenders are found), and target attractiveness (the material or symbolic desirability of personal or property targets, the physical size of those targets, and the ease of transportability) into their model. Further important extensions of this orientation have incorporated a consideration of the degree to which "handlers" oversee the activities of potential offenders and the role of "managers" (e.g., security guards, bouncers) who have formal obligations to supervise people's activities, potential offenders and victims alike, in particular places (Eck and Weisburd, 1995).

The widespread interest in these two models is not solely a reflection of the desire for theoretical refinement. Rather, the lifestyle and routine activities models make certain predictions concerning victimization that have important implications for the development and implementation of crime control policies. In the broadest sense, Garofalo (1987: 40) notes that any social policy that affects the routine activities of a population may be reflected in changes in the distribution of criminal opportunities. However, the opportunity model also suggests much more immediate strategies for the control of property crime, such as reducing the physical opportunities for offending or increasing the chances that an offender will be caught. Both Newman and Reppetto, for example, noted that apartment buildings provided with door monitors or guards were less vulnerable to burglary. More recently, Felson (1994) has presented the results of an experiment that found that some relatively simple changes in the physical design of convenience stores could lead to fairly rapid and dramatic decreases in the rates at which they were victimized.

A voluminous body of research focusing on the role of the guardianship factor has been produced by Cohen and Felson and by their colleagues using the UCR statistics (see Cohen et al., 1980; Felson and Cohen, 1980; Cohen et al., 1981; Cantor and Land, 1985, is also related). A particularly interesting question that has been raised in this research concerns the relative abilities of the guardianship factor and the unemployment rate to explain recent trends in property crime. Although a large body of evidence has been presented in support of the routine activities perspective, especially in those studies analyzing the NCVS and other self-reported data (see, for example, Lynch and Cantor, 1992; Sampson, 1985; Smith and Jarjoura, 1988), some studies have concluded that the relationship with property crime is fairly weak. However, a recent series of studies of Seattle suggests that this relationship may be mediated strongly by certain features of the neighborhood in which the potential is located (Rountree, et al., 1994; Miethe and Meier, 1994). Unfortunately, the ability only to indirectly measure some of the central dynamics of the model makes such conclusions fairly tentative. Nevertheless, the perspective is an extremely promising one that should continue to generate exciting future research as more detailed data become available.

Criminal Opportunities and Potential Property Offenders

Just as potential victims of property crimes are characterized by lifestyles and routine activities that determine their movement in space and time, potential offenders also exhibit differential patterns of behavior that affect the number of criminal opportunities they encounter. Criminology has a long tradition of research that has described the background characteristics of property offenders (see, for example, Shover, 1973, 1996; Pope, 1980) as well as the relationship between police operations and the geographic distribution of such activity (see McIver, 1981). More recently, a great deal of attention has focused on the decision-making processes that lead to the commission of an illegal act (see Bennett and Wright, 1984; Brantingham and Brantingham, 1984; Cromwell et al., 1991; Cornish and Clarke, 1986; Decker and Wright, 1994; Rengert and Wasilchick, 1985; Rengert, 1989; Wright and Decker, 1997).

Unfortunately, there are no large data sets comparable to the UCR and NCVS that easily facilitate such studies; likewise, self-reports based on large samples of respondents have yet to be widely used for the study of adult criminal motivation. However, a group of studies has used alternative forms of data collection to provide some insight into these decision-making processes (Bennett and Wright, 1984; Carter, 1974; Cornish and Clarke, 1986; Cromwell et al., 1991; Rengert and Wasilchick, 1985; Tunnell, 1992; Wright et al., 1995). Because studies generally have been limited to relatively small samples of property offenders (particularly burglars), the representativeness of the ensuing findings is not entirely clear. Nevertheless, these studies suggest that the dynamics that shape the convergence of potential offenders and victims in time and space also are strongly influenced by the lifestyles and routine activities of those offenders.

This is most apparent in the processes concerning the selection of a geographic area in which to commit a property offense. Carter (1974: 126) notes that potential offenders have only a vague environmental image of the entire geographic space available for victimization. Likewise, Rengert and Wasilchick (1985: 72) argue that property offenders "are not aware of all the area around them and do not give equal consideration to all of the area they are aware of." Rather, they select potential areas of victimization on the basis of information they have gathered primarily through their noncrime-related recreational and work travel patterns (although this information may be supplemented by information supplied by other offenders). That is, such decisions are made, to a large extent, on the basis of observations made in the course of their routine activities.

Once the general target area has been determined, the particular household to be victimized must be chosen. The findings of Bennett and Wright (1984: 194–196) indicate that two primary factors underlie this decision. The first, which they call "surveillability," reflects the likelihood that the offender will be detected by others in the area. For example, offenders often prefer to victimize households located on the corners of an intersection, because the potential number of neighbors that may observe an illegal entry is minimized (Rengert and Wasilchick, 1985: 84). In addition, such considerations as the degree of cover provided by the target and the ease of access to that cover also shape the possibility of being observed.

The second factor, noted in most studies, concerns the occupancy of the household. Over 90 percent of the offenders interviewed by Bennett and Wright (1984: 196) indicate that they would never attempt a burglary in a house that they suspected was occupied. Therefore, property offenders may use a series of cues to determine the occupancy status of the targeted household, such as the presence of uncollected mail and newspapers, the absence of lights, and so forth. Some of these techniques are fairly ingenious, such as noting funeral announcements or an air conditioner that is turned off on a very hot day (Rengert and Wasilchick, 1985: 81).

However, Renger and Wasilchick also note that potential offenders attempt to maximize the probability of a successful burglary by restricting their activities to those times in which the vacancy of a household is most likely. Sometimes, the probability of a vacancy can be manipulated by the potential burglar. For example, a technique that reportedly has been used in Chicago to ensure that a household is vacant is to provide the victim with tickets to a sold-out athletic event with a note attached, apparently signed by a good friend of the victim, indicating that the owner of the tickets has to go out of town and could not use them. The potential offender can then be fairly sure that the household will be unoccupied for the course of that event. Such an approach obviously necessitates a degree of research by the potential offender concerning the tastes and personal networks of the victim. Yet, this technique and variants of it apparently have been very successful.

Nonetheless, the primary determinant of the likelihood of a successful burglary is the behavior of the residents themselves. Rengert and Wasilchick present evidence that when the typical routine of a resident, such as that of the traditional housewife, necessitates extended periods of activity in or near the household, the periods of vacancy are very unpredictable and sporadic. On the other hand, households in which all the members have schedules that necessitate long periods of absence (for example, through employment or school) have large, predictable periods of vacancy. According to Rengert and Wasilchick (pp. 21–24), these are the targets preferred by successful burglars. Other factors related to the selection of targets are also noted in these studies, such as the expected profitability of the theft, familiarity with the area, and the presence of alarm systems (Carter, 1974: 133).

CONCLUSION

Property crime has very immediate and costly consequences; it is by far the most prevalent form of illegal behavior in the United States (accounting for over 80 percent of all crimes reported to the police), and the FBI has estimated that the economic costs of such crime during 1996 exceeded $15 billion (FBI, 1997: 36). Therefore, all citizens have a vested interest in property crime.

However, the societal processes reflected in property crime are extremely complex, and the control of such behavior is very difficult for several reasons. For one thing, there is nothing inherently "natural" in the laws that define property crime. For example, Michalowski (1985) argued that the development of property rights in the nineteenth-century United States reflected the view that thefts and burglaries represented "attacks upon the very basis of the emerging capitalist order" (p. 108). On the other hand, Messner and Rosenfeld (1997) developed a very convincing argument suggesting that the core value system of our country actually encourages such illegal behavior. Therefore, the definition of property crime itself is subject to an ongoing process of reevaluation and development. In addition, the general public often assumes that criminologists know much more than we actually do concerning the causes of such crime. The most central limitation of the current state of knowledge is that all the sources of data used to examine the distribution and causes of property crime so that social control programs can be developed suffer from certain deficiencies. Therefore, programs that have been developed to combat property crime have had to assume, often incorrectly, that these deficiencies were not serious.

This chapter has attempted to introduce the reader to the basic definitional, data-related, and theoretical issues involved in the study of property crime. The emphasis on the *basic* has been intentional, for the goal here has been to provide the reader with a sufficient familiarity with the issues involved in property crime so as to make informed evaluations of the sometimes-contradictory conclusions and proposals concerning the control of property crime that appear in the popular and professional literature.

DISCUSSION QUESTIONS

1. What crimes traditionally have been counted as Index property crimes? What do these offenses have in common?

2. Arson now is on the list of such crimes, but we rarely see statistics about arson. Why?

3. As with violent crime trends, trends in property crime are calculated using both UCR and NCVS data. Do the same pictures emerge when we examine these data?

4. Bursik discusses criminal opportunities as they relate to property crime. Review the core of this discussion and identify the key elements of opportunity.

5. How do property offenders select their targets? What can be done to change the opportunity for property crime?

6. Many believe that property crime rates will rise as unemployment rates rise. Is this assumption borne out in the research that has been done on the subject? Does the picture change when we look at certain age or race categories? If so, why?

REFERENCES

Allan, E., and D. Steffensmeier. 1989. "Youth, Unemployment, and Property Crime: Differential Effects of Job Availability and Job Quality on Juvenile and Young Adult Arrest Rates." *American Sociological Review* 54: 107–123.

Baron, S., and T. Hartnagel. 1997. "Attributions, Affect and Crime: Street Youth's Reactions to Unemployment." *Criminology* 35: 409–434.

Battle, B. P., and P. B. Weston. 1978. *Arson: Detection and Investigation.* New York: Arco.

Bennett, T., and R. Wright. 1984. "Constraints to Burglary: The Offender's Perspective." Pp. 181–200 in *Coping With Burglary.* Edited by R. Clarke and T. Hope. Boston: Nijhoff.

Biderman, A. D., J. P. Lynch, and J. L. Peterson. 1991. *Understanding Crime Incidence Statistics: Why the UCR Diverges from the NCS.* New York: Springer-Verlag.

Blumstein, A., J. Cohen, and R. Rosenfeld. 1991. "Trend and Deviation in Crime Rates: A Comparison of UCR and NCS Data for Burglary and Robbery." *Criminology* 29: 237–263.

Boggs, S. L. 1965. "Urban Crime Patterns." *American Sociological Review* 30: 899–908.

Brady, J. P. 1983. "Arson, Urban Economy and Organized Crime: The Case of Boston." *Social Problems* 31: 1–27.

Brantingham, P. J., and P. L. Brantingham. 1984. *Patterns in Crime.* New York: Macmillan.

Britt, C. 1997. "Reconsidering the Unemployment and Crime Relationship: Variation by Age Group and Historical Period." *Journal of Quantitative Criminology* 11: 143–166.

Bursik, R. J., Jr., and H. G. Grasmick. 1993. "Economic Deprivation and Neighborhood Crime Rates, 1960–1980." *Law and Society Review* 27: 540–558.

Cantor, D., and K. C. Land. 1985. "Unemployment and Crime Rates in the Post–World War II U.S.: A Theoretical and Empirical Analysis." *American Sociological Review* 50: 317–332.

———. 1991. "Exploring Possible Temporal Relationships of Unemployment and Crime: A Comment on Hale and Sabbagh." *Journal of Research in Crime and Delinquency* 28: 418–425.

Carlson, S., and R. Michalowski. 1997. "Crime, Unemployment and Social Structures of Accumulation: An Inquiry into Historical Contingency." *Justice Quarterly* 14: 209–241.

Carter, R. L. 1974. *The Criminal's Image of the City.* Unpublished dissertation. University of Oklahoma, Department of Geography.

Chilton, R., and A. Spielberger. 1971. "Is Delinquency Increasing? Age Structure and the Crime Rate." *Social Forces* 49: 487–493.

Chiricos, T. G. 1987. "Rates of Crime and Unemployment: An Analysis of Aggregate Research Evidence." *Social Problems* 34: 187–212.

Cohen, L. E., and M. Felson. 1979. "Social Change and Crime Rate Trends: A Routine Activities Approach." *American Sociological Review* 44: 588–608.

Cohen, L. E., M. Felson, and K. C. Land. 1980. "Property Crime Rates in the U.S.: A Macrodynamics Analysis 1947–1977 With Ex Ante Forecasts for the Mid 1980's." *American Journal of Sociology* 86: 90–118.

Cohen, L. E., J. Kluegal, and K. Land. 1981. "Social Inequality and Criminal Victimization." *American Sociological Review* 46: 505–524.

Cornish, D. B., and R. V. Clarke. 1986. *The Reasoning Criminal: Rational Choice Perspectives on Offending.* New York: Springer-Verlag.

Cromwell, P. F., J. N. Olson, and D. W. Avary. 1991. *Breaking and Entering: An Ethnographic Analysis of Burglary.* Newbury Park, CA: Sage.

Decker, S., and R. Wright. 1994. *Burglars on the Job: Streetlife and Residential Break-ins.* Boston: Northeastern University Press.

Devine, J., J. Sheley, and M. Smith. 1988. "Macroeconomic and Social-Control Policy Influences on Crime Rate Changes, 1948–1985." *American Sociological Review* 53: 407–420.

Eck, J., and D. Weisburd. 1995. *Those Who Discourage Crime.* Monsey, NY: Criminal Justice Press.

Federal Bureau of Investigation. 1980. *Crime in the United States, 1979.* Washington, DC: U.S. Government Printing Office.

———. 1997. *Crime in the United States, 1996.* Washington, DC: U.S. Department of Justice.

Felson, M. 1994. *Crime and Everyday Life: Insights and Implications for Society.* Thousand Oaks, CA: Pine Forge Press.

Felson, M., and R. Clarke (Eds.). 1997. *Business and Crime Prevention.* Monsey, NY: Criminal Justice Press.

Felson, M., and L. E. Cohen. 1980. "Human Ecology and Crime: A Routine Activity Approach." *Human Ecology* 8: 389–406.

Freeman, R. B. 1983. "Crime and Unemployment." Pp. 89–106 in *Crime and Public Policy.* Edited by J. Q. Wilson. San Francisco: ICS Press.

Garofalo, J. 1987. "Reassessing the Lifestyle Model of Criminal Victimization.: Pp. 23–42 in *Positive Criminology.* Edited by M. R. Gottfredson and T. Hirschi. Beverly Hills, CA: Sage.

Gillespie, R. W. 1978. "Economic Factors in Crime and Delinquency: A Critical Review of the Empirical Evidence." Pp. 601–626 in *Unemployment and Crime: Hearings Before the Subcommittee on Crime of the Committee on the Judiciary.* House of Representatives. Washington, DC: U.S. Government Printing Office.

Gottfredson, M. 1981. "On the Etiology of Criminal Victimization." *Journal of Criminal Law and Criminology* 72: 714–726.

Gottfredson, M., and T. Hirschi. 1990. *A General Theory of Crime.* Stanford: Stanford University Press.

Gould, L. C. 1969. "The Changing Structure of Property Crime in an Affluent Society." *Social Forces* 48: 50–59.

Grant, D., and R. Martinez, Jr. 1997. "Crime and the Restructuring of the U.S. Economy: A Reconsideration of the Class Linkages." *Social Forces* 75: 769–799.

Hale, C., and D. Sabbagh. 1991. "Testing the Relationship Between Unemployment and Crime: A Methodological Comment and Empirical Analysis Using Time Series Data From England and Wales." *Journal of Research in Crime and Delinquency* 28: 400–417.

Hepburn, J. R. 1984. "Occasional Property Crime." Pp. 73–94 in *Major Forms of Crime.* Edited by R. F. Meier. Beverly Hills, CA: Sage.

Hindelang, M. J., M. R. Gottfredson, and J. Garofalo. 1978. *Victims of Personal Crime: An Empirical Foundation for a Theory of Personal Victimization.* Cambridge, MA: Ballinger.

Hughes, M., and T. J. Carter. 1981. "A Declining Economy and Sociological Theories of Crime: Predictions and Explications." Pp. 5–26 in *Crime and Criminal Justice in a Declining Economy.* Edited by K. N. Wright. Cambridge, MA: Oelgeschlager, Gunn and Hain.

Incove, D. J., V. B. Wherry, and J. D. Shroeder. 1979. *Combatting Arson-for-Profit.* Columbus, OH: Battelle Press.

International Association of Chiefs of Police. 1929. *Uniform Crime Reporting: A Complete Manual for Police.* New York: Little & Ives.

Jackson, P. G. 1988. "Assessing the Validity of Official Data on Arson." *Criminology* 26: 181–195.

LaFree, G., K. A. Drass, and P. O'Day. 1992. "Race and Crime in Postwar America: Determinants of African-American and White Rates, 1957–1988." *Criminology* 30: 157–185.

Long, S. K., and A. D. Witte. 1981. "Current Ecnomic Trends: Implications for Crime and Criminal Justice." Pp. 69–143 in *Crime and Criminal Justice in a Declining Economy.* Edited by K. N. Wright. Cambridge, MA: Oelgeschlager, Gunn and Hain.

Lynch, J., and D. Cantor. 1992. "Ecological and Behavioral Influences on Property Victimization at Home: Implications for Opportunity Theory." *Journal of Research in Crime and Delinquency* 29: 335–362.

MacPherson, C. B. 1978. "The Meaning of Property." Pp. 1–14 in *Property: Mainstream and Critical Positions.* Edited by C. B. MacPherson. Toronto: University of Toronto Press.

Maguire, K., and A. Pastore. 1997. *Sourcebook of Criminal Justice Statistics, 1996.* Washington, DC: U.S. Department of Justice.

McDowall, D., and C. Loftin. 1992. "Comparing the UCR and NCS Over Time." *Criminology* 30: 125–132.

McIver, J. P. 1981. "Criminal Mobility: A Review of Empirical Studies." Pp. 20–47 in *Crime Spillover.* Edited by S. Hakim and G. F. Rengert. Beverly Hills, CA: Sage.

Menard, S. 1992. "Residual Gains, Reliability, and the UCR-NCS Relationship: A Comment on Blumstein, Cohen and Rosenfeld." *Criminology* 30: 105–113.

Messner, S., and R. Rosenfeld. 1997. *Crime and the American Dream.* 2d ed. Belmont, CA: Wadsworth.

Michalowski, R. 1985. *Order, Law and Crime.* New York: Random House.

Miethe, T., and R. Meier. 1994. *Crime and Its Social Context: Toward an Integrated Theory of Offenders, Victims, and Situations.* Albany, NY: State University of New York Press.

Morris, T. 1957. *The Criminal Area: A Study in Social Ecology.* London: Routledge & Kegan Paul.

National Crime Prevention Council. 1997. *Designing Safer Communities: A Crime Prevention Through Environmental Design Handbook.* Washington, DC: U.S. Department of Justice.

Newman, O. 1972. *Defensible Space.* New York: Macmillan.

Pope, C. E. 1980. "Patterns in Burglary: An Empirical Examination of Offense and Offender Characteristics." *Journal of Criminal Justice* 8: 39–52.

Rand, M., J. Lynch, and D. Cantor. 1997. *Criminal Victimization, 1973–1995.* Washington, DC: U.S. Department of Justice.

Rengert, G. 1989. "Behavioral Geography and Criminal Behavior." Pp. 161–175 in *The Geography of Crime.* Edited by D. J. Evans and D. T. Herbert. London: Routledge.

Rengert, G., and J. Wasilchick. 1985. *Suburban Burglary: A Time and a Place for Everything.* Springfield, IL: Thomas.

Reppetto, T. J. 1974. *Residential Crime.* Cambridge, MA: Ballinger.

Rountree, P., K. Land, and T. Miethe. 1994. "Macro-Micro Integration in the Study of Victimization: A Hierarchical Logistic Model Analysis Across Seattle Neighborhoods." *Criminology* 32: 387–414.

Sagi, P. C., and C. F. Wellford. 1968. "Age Composition and Patterns of Change in Criminal Statistics." *Journal of Criminal Law, Criminology and Police Science* 59: 29–36.

Sampson, R. 1985. "Neighborhood and Crime: The Structural Determinants of Personal Victimization." *Journal of Research in Crime and Delinquency* 22: 7–40.

Sampson, R., and W. Wilson. 1995. "Toward a Theory of Race, Crime, and Urban Inequality." In *Crime and Inequality.* Edited by J. Hagan and R. Peterson. Stanford, CA: Stanford University Press.

Shaw, C. R. (with the collaboration of F. M. Zorbaugh, H. D. McKay, and L. S. Cottrell). 1929. *Delinquency Areas.* Chicago: University of Chicago Press.

Shover, N. 1973. "The Social Organization of Burglary." *Social Problems* 20: 499–513.

———. 1996. *Great Pretenders: Pursuits and Careers of Persistent Thieves.* Boulder, CO: Westview Press.

Smith, D. A., and G. R. Jarjoura. 1988. "Social Structure and Criminal Victimization." *Journal of Research in Crime and Delinquency* 25: 27–52.

Steffensmeier, D., and M. Harer. 1991. "Did Crime Rise or Fall During the Reagan Presidency? The Effects of an 'Aging' U.S. Population on the Nation's Crime Rate." *Journal of Research in Crime and Delinquency* 28: 330–359.

Thornberry, T. P., and R. L. Christenson. 1984. "Unemployment and Criminal Involvement: An Investigation of Reciprocal Causal Structures." *American Sociological Review* 49: 398–411.

Tunnell, K. D. 1992. *Choosing Crime: The Criminal Calculus of Property Offenders.* Chicago: Nelson-Hall.

U.S. Department of Justice. 1997. *National Crime Victimization Survey. Crime Victimization 1996.*

Changes 1995–96 with Trends 1993–96. Washington, DC: U.S. Department of Justice.

Van Dijk, J. 1994. "Understanding Crime Rates: On the Interactions Between the Rational Choices of Victims and Offenders." *British Journal of Criminology* 34: 105–121.

Wilson, J. Q., and R. Herrnstein. 1985. *Crime and Human Nature.* New York: Simon & Schuster.

Wilson, W. J. 1987. *The Truly Disadvantaged: The Inner City, the Underclass, and Public Policy.* Chicago: University of Chicago Press.

Wright, R., and S. Decker. 1997. *Armed Robbers in Action: Stickups and Street Culture.* Boston: Northeastern University Press.

Wright, R., R. Logie, and S. Decker. 1995. "Criminal Expertise and Offender Decision-Making: An Experimental Study of the Target Selection Process in Residential Burglary." *Journal of Research in Crime and Delinquency* 32: 39–53.

Chapter Outline

◆ The Debate over Vice Crimes

◆ The Medicalization of Vice Crime
Benefits of the Medicalization Approach
Drawbacks to the Medicalization Approach

◆ Prostitution
A Brief History
The Legal Status of Prostitution
Types of Prostitutes
The Socialization of Prostitutes
The Victimization of Prostitutes

◆ Pornography
Historical Considerations
The Politicization of Pornography
Is Pornography Harmful?

◆ Consensual Sodomy and Related Sexual Activity
A Brief History
Recent Legal and Law Enforcement Activities

◆ Gambling
A Brief History
Compulsive Gamblers

◆ Drugs
Opiates and Cocaine
Marijuana
Public Drunkenness
Drunken Driving

◆ Overlapping Social Worlds

◆ Conclusion

9

Vice Crimes:
Personal Autonomy
Versus Societal Dictates

HENRY R. LESIEUR
Institute on Problem Gambling

MICHAEL WELCH*
Rutgers University

Crimes against morality, also called vices, "are activities thought by many to be immoral and liable to bring spiritual and even bodily harm to those engaging in them" (Sheley, 1985: 115–116). These activities, including public drunkenness, possession of illegal substances like cocaine and marijuana, illegal gambling, illegal consensual sex acts (for example, oral and anal intercourse, adultery, and prostitution), and pornography, are said to offend morality. As we enter a new century, if we count related offenses like drunk driving, disorderly conduct, and vagrancy, over five million people are arrested yearly for offending morality—36 percent of all arrests in 1996 (see Table 9.1).

The many people arrested yearly for vice crimes signals the importance of these crimes for our society and its criminal justice system.

In this chapter, we examine the debate over whether vice activities should be treated as crimes. We look as well at the recent trend toward defining vice activities as illnesses and addressing them as we would any medical problem. Against this backdrop, we focus on several types of vice crimes: prostitution, pornography, illegal consensual sex, gambling, and drugs. We close by looking at the overlapping social worlds of people who, directly or indirectly, both engage in and condemn various activities labeled "vice crimes" in this society.

THE DEBATE OVER VICE CRIMES

Moralists and civil libertarians have taken different positions concerning whether private morality should be controlled through the criminal

*The authors thank Mark Evangelista and Thomas Payne for their assistance.

Table 9.1   Total Number of Arrests for Vice Crimes As a Percent of All Arrests*

VICE CRIME	1960		1970		1980	
	Number	Percent	Number	Percent	Number	Percent
Prostitution	26,482	0.67	51,700	0.64	88,900	0.85
Other sex offenses†	50,101	1.27	59,700	0.74	67,400	0.65
Drug abuse violations	27,735	0.70	415,600	5.12	580,800	5.56
Liquor laws	106,347	2.69	309,000	3.81	463,500	4.44
Driving under the influence	183,943	4.65	555,700	6.85	1,426,700	13.66
Drunkenness	1,412,167	35.66	1,825,500	22.49	1,125,800	10.78
Disorderly conduct	475,502	12.00	710,000	8.75	769,700	7.37
Vagrancy	153,201	3.87	113,400	1.40	30,700	0.29
Gambling	122,946	3.10	91,700	1.13	87,000	0.83
Total Vice Crimes	2,558,424	64.67	4,132,300	50.92	4,640,500	44.40

SOURCE: Adapted from UCR data (e.g., FBI, 1997).

*Arrests for 1960 are for reporting agencies; those for 1970, 1980, 1990, and 1996 are FBI estimates of both reported and unreported arrests.

†Sex offenses include some offenses with victims.

justice system. For example, Mill (1892), Hart (1963), Geis (1979), and others have advocated that crime and sin should not necessarily be equated; in other words, there should be a realm of activity that is "not the law's business." Countering this, Lord Devlin (1965: 23) has advocated state intervention in private morality because "society cannot ignore the morality of the individual any more than it can his loyalty; it flourishes on both and without either it dies."

Why criminalize vice? Homosexual activity and prostitution are called by some abominations that not only corrupt youth but undermine the ideals of family and morality, and both are blamed for spreading AIDS and venereal diseases. Pornography, claim its opponents, is a cause of rape and other sexual violence. Alcohol, drugs, and gambling create havoc and personal ruin for both the users and their families; drugs in particular are said to lead to more serious forms of criminal behavior. Proponents of laws outlawing alcohol consumption, drug use, and gambling argue that such "vices" create poverty and are part of the cycle of social and economic inequality. Further promotion of these behaviors, they assert, could lead to a disintegration of society.

On the other hand, the criminalization of private morality produces what Schur (1965; see also Bedeau, 1974) has termed "victimless crime." Schur refers to "the willing exchange, among adults, of strongly demanded but legally proscribed goods or services" (p. 169). One feature of victimless crimes is a lack of agreement in the general population about what laws should be passed, how those laws should be enforced, and how violators should be punished. A second feature is the element of exchange: A product (like drugs or pornography) or service (like gambling or sex) is exchanged for money, sex, and so on. The third feature, Schur suggests, is the lack of apparent harm associated with the offense—with the exception of possible harm to the offenders themselves. Schur also notes that victimless crime laws often lack enforceability because of the lack of a complainant.

Table 9.1   *(continued)*

VICE CRIME	1990		1996	
	Number	*Percent*	*Number*	*Percent*
Prostitution	111,400	0.78	99,000	0.65
Other sex offenses†	107,600	0.76	95,800	0.63
Drug abuse violations	1,087,500	7.68	1,506,200	9.93
Liquor laws	714,700	5.03	677,400	4.46
Driving under the influence	1,810,800	12.76	1,467,300	9.67
Drunkenness	910,100	6.41	718,700	4.73
Disorderly conduct	733,000	5.16	842,600	5.55
Vagrancy	38,500	0.27	27,800	0.18
Gambling	19,300	0.14	21,000	0.14
Total Vice Crimes	5,534,900	38.99	5,455,800	35.97

One associated trait of some but not all victimless crimes is the development of a deviant subculture based on peoples' need to have contact with others who are also involved in the same illegal acts. A deviant subculture exists when people come together to solve common problems surrounding their deviant status. Drug addicts, for example, share values, attitudes, rationalizations, skills, and knowledge about illicit drug use and sales. In addition, because of the illegal nature of the activity, black markets arise that drive up the price. A consequence of the resulting high price is that drug addicts resort to crimes like shoplifting, prostitution, and robbery to pay for drugs; Schur refers to this as "secondary crime" (p. 174). Aside from secondary crime, the net result of victimless crimes is to create a class of criminals whose only "crime" may be to engage in an activity that certain segments of a society have deemed deviant.

Kadish (1967), in a classic article concerning the "crisis of overcriminalization," commented on problems that arise as a result of attempts to enforce public standards of private morality. According to Kadish, the moral message of the law is contradicted by the lack of total enforcement. Only some activities are enforced; others are ignored. Some activities may not be engaged in by youths (e.g., drinking) but are permissible for adults, which tends to breed cynicism toward the law. Similarly, when laws are not enforced, widespread disrespect for the law may result, as in the case of marijuana laws (see Kaplan, 1970).

Further, when public campaigns or media activities raise the specter of unenforced laws, law enforcement agencies become more active, resulting in discriminatory enforcement of the law (see Sheley and Hanlon, 1978). Therefore, anticrime drives are launched for reasons unrelated to the purpose of the law. This "anticrime" activity is most likely to be directed toward the most vulnerable groups of society, most notably the poor. According to Kadish (1967), vice laws also waste resources because police personnel who could be used to combat street crime are instead diverted to vice squads, and then driven to excessive behavior in pursuit of violators. Civil liberties issues arise as wiretapping and bugging are used in attempts to fight offenses like gambling and narcotics trafficking. In addition, police must engage in demeaning and degrading behavior, such as undercover operations in men's rooms and the use of police decoys to arrest prostitutes. Some of this police behavior is even illegal (for example, entrapment). Finally, like Schur, Kadish notes that the illegal nature of a vice activity gives rise to black markets, which, in turn, create large-scale organized systems of crime that engage in, among other activities, bribery and corruption of officials.

Similar approaches have been taken by Packer (1968), Skolnick (1968), Kaplan (1970), and Morris and Hawkins (1970), whose critiques fueled legislative efforts in some states to decriminalize consensual sodomy, marijuana consumption (in eleven states), and public drunkenness. Weppner and Inciardi (1978), in writing about marijuana, have noted that those states that do not decriminalize such behaviors incur serious human, social, and financial costs, including a heavier burden on the criminal justice system because of increased demands on enforcement and corrections agencies. Finally, Nettler (1982: 126) notes the potential link between totalitarianism and vice laws:

> Totalitarian regimes are strengthened by an ideology that includes moral conceptions of how people should behave. Modern tyrants therefore have no hesitation about punishing activities they define as immoral, activities ranging from homosexuality and prostitution to drunkenness, absenteeism from work, the use of narcotics and the expression of "wrong" ideas. There is no free-

dom in Cuba or in the People's Republic of China to be a "drag queen," a whore, an addict, or a dissident. Moreover, there is no public debate [about these issues].

THE MEDICALIZATION OF VICE CRIME

Many (by no means all) of the customers, dealers, prostitutes, and other victimless crime offenders are classified by one authority or another as "addicts" who have a "disease." Programs like Alcoholics Anonymous, Narcotics Anonymous, and Gamblers Anonymous promote the disease conception of alcoholism, narcotics addiction, and compulsive gambling (see Sagarin, 1969). Such programs are, in turn, supported to a greater or lesser extent by the psychiatric establishment. The designation by the American Psychiatric Association of homosexuality as a mental disorder was challenged and eventually overturned in 1973 when that organization decided by vote that only "ego-dystonic" (that which creates intense internal discomfort for the individual) homosexuality should be classified as a disorder. The *Diagnostic and Statistical Manual* of the American Psychiatric Association classifies "vices" as behavioral disorders: psychoactive substance dependence (for alcohol and other drug problems) and pathological gambling (American Psychiatric Association, 1987). The primary characteristics of psychoactive substance dependence represent the paradigm or model of addiction and deserve mention. According to the American Psychiatric Association (1987: 167–168), the criteria for diagnosis include

1. Taking the substance more often or over a longer period than intended.

2. Failed attempts to cut down or stop using the substance.

3. Spending much time in activities to get the substance or recovering from its use.

4. Frequent interference with work, school, or home as a result of use or use when it is hazardous to do so (for example, driving while intoxicated).

5. Giving up important social, occupational, or recreational activities in order to use.

6. Persistent use of the substance in spite of problems.

7. Development of physical tolerance.

8. Withdrawal symptoms.

These symptoms have to last at least a month or persist over a long time. In other words, use without interference (item 4) does not qualify as dependence.

Benefits of the Medicalization Approach

The medicalization of deviant behavior has both brighter and darker sides (Conrad and Schneider, 1992). In their ideal form, medical definitions increase tolerance and compassion for human problems. The alcoholic, for example, is no longer "weak willed," but instead is "sick." Consequently, the individual cannot be blamed for what she or he did while sick. The ill person is "treated" rather than "punished" as the prestige and power of the medical profession is brought to bear on the problem. Medical controls are, by their very nature, more flexible and efficient than judicial controls because they can be easily adjusted to the needs of the individual patient and can be applied without formal proceedings. In drunk-driving programs, for example, the offender can be required to at-

tend education sessions that concentrate on the disease conception of alcoholism. Many of these programs assess each client for alcoholism and have the power to mandate further treatment where alcoholism is detected.

Drawbacks to the Medicalization Approach

The virtues of medicalization also can be viewed as drawbacks, however, because the altered label (from badness to sickness) creates confusion over issues of responsibility. For example, if compulsive gamblers are sick, how culpable are they for crimes engaged in while they gambled? Should they be provided with treatment and offered an opportunity to make restitution rather than be sentenced to prison? This issue is continually debated in the courts (Lorenz and Rose, 1988), where two systems of justice result: one for those who can hire expert witnesses to testify in court and one for those who cannot.

When medical control is applied, it is based on the assumption that it is more effective at altering (controlling) behavior than no treatment at all. However, this assumption frequently is not justified. For example, little evidence suggests that individual, group, or milieu therapy works in the prison environment (Lipton et al., 1975). In addition, the assumption that medical control is more humane than the criminal justice system is not always warranted. Although medical control can entail greater leniency, it can also lead to harsher treatment of the offender: psychosurgery, electroshock "therapy," implanted electrodes, and the like.

The dominance of a medical model also implies an individualistic approach to the offender (Conrad and Schneider, 1992). For example, drug treatment plans commonly focus on personality disorders, education about genetic inheritance of the disease, deficiencies in self-esteem, and personal traumatic experiences. However, treatment professionals rarely enter the communities their clients come from, and individual and group therapy takes place in hospitals or outpatient settings with little, if any, attention paid to the outside world.

Social science research widely acknowledges that treatment for alcohol and other drug dependencies is more effective with middle-income than with lower-income individuals (Armor et al., 1976). When treatment fails, given that individual causes are granted paramount importance, individuals are blamed for failing. Rather than reorienting rehabilitation to fit the conditions, the failures are rationalized on individualistic grounds, or the treatment center refocuses its efforts on treating those clients who can be influenced by the methods used (that is, middle-income individuals). For the most part, social conditions are overlooked because they are not amenable to medical intervention. Doctors do not treat inequality, racism, and urban blight but do participate in alcohol detoxification and methadone maintenance programs designed to return individuals to those very conditions. The medical approach fails to recognize that rates of street crime and of heroin and crack use are highest in the inner-city areas characterized by severe social problems.

Activities that we commonly call vice represent probably the clearest intersection of the worlds of crime, medicine, and religion. Illegal drugs have been and still are used for medical purposes: Heroin is prescribed for cancer patients in the United Kingdom, and THC (the psychoactive ingredient in marijuana) is dispensed to glaucoma patients in the United States. Wine is still used in religious services in the West; hallucinogens have been known as the flesh of the gods and treated with reverence among South and Central American Indian tribes (Furst, 1972). Finally, house prostitutes were once part of early Near Eastern religions.

In some instances, the intersection between crime and medicine leads to some misleading metaphors (such as the use of the word "sick") regarding vice crimes, particularly those involving sex. For example, a porn queen may be considered "sick" only in the sense that she is extremely offensive to the opponents of pornography. Such metaphors should not be taken literally, because medical techniques usually are not applied to alter these behaviors.

With the above general comments in mind, we now examine aspects of several forms of vice in the United States: prostitution, pornography, consensual sodomy and related sexual activity, gambling, and drug activity.

PROSTITUTION

Many observers argue that prostitution is not a crime; rather, it is a consensual contract between adults (Pateman, 1988; also see Rhode, 1989). In either case, its practice is widespread throughout most cultures of the world. The controversy surrounding prostitution cannot be fully understood apart from its social and historical context, especially as it relates to the regulation of women's sexuality. Generally, such regulation has two major sources. The first is puritanical. That is, women who exhibit promiscuous tendencies are often punished on grounds that their conduct is immoral; hence, a puritanical approach to prostitution leads to forms of repression. The second source involves capitalistic motives by which men profit from the prostitution. Whereas women sell their labor by engaging in prostitution, most of the profit is absorbed by men who control the enterprise (pimps). Both the puritanical and the capitalistic sources are structured within a patriarchal framework insofar as men dictate the terms of regulating women's sexuality.

A Brief History

Often regarded as the world's oldest profession, prostitution dates back to ancient societies. Bullogh (1980) points to ancient Mesopotamia as having the earliest record of prostitution. There, priests engaged in sexual activities for procreation, and women were expected to contribute by giving themselves to "temple duty." A similar system was developed in Greece, where licensed brothels financed the temple of Aphrodite in 550 B.C. (Rathus, 1983). During the Middle Ages, prostitution also was part of the economic structure insofar as the church imposed taxes on it (Hagan, 1986). A cross-cultural and historical approach to prostitution demonstrates that prostitutes have earned a respectable social status in some societies. For example, Davis (1961) notes that the Greek *hetaerae,* the Roman *lupanaria,* the Indian *devadasis,* and the Japanese *geishas* all enjoyed elevated social status and prestige.

History also shows that prostitution has not been exclusively heterosexual. During the 1700s, for example, molly houses served as places for homosexual prostitution, where the men often dressed in drag and threw parties for their customers (Karlen, 1971). Karlen points to a famous molly house in an English resort managed by Margaret Clap, whose surname became the popular term for a venereal disease.

In early American history, tight-knit communities worked against prostitution. However, as America underwent industrialization and urbanization (along with immigration), prostitution became widespread. Indeed, in most growing urban centers, prostitution was not only visible but also viewed as part of metropolitan life. Prostitutes worked in nearly every neighborhood of the city and solicited in bakeries, cigar stores, delicatessens, barber shops, hotels, saloons, theaters, and fine restaurants. Their clients were men of every ethnic group, social class, and occupation (Gilfoyle, 1992; also see Roberts, 1992). The term "hookers" derives from the label given women who provided sexual services for Union General "Fighting Joe" Hooker and his army. In the early twentieth century, "red light districts" earned their name from railroad workers who hung red lamps outside their tents during visits to prostitutes—the red light helped the dispatcher locate these men for railroad duty (Winick and Kinsie, 1971).

The contemporary history of prostitution is highlighted by some sensational portrayals of famous houses of ill repute: for example, the notorious Texas brothel that inspired the play and film *The Best Little Whorehouse in Texas,* as well as New Orleans' Storyville and Nevada's Mustang Ranch, Pink Pussycat, and Miss Kitty's. In the 1980s, the socially prominent former debutante Sydney Biddle Barrows glamorized prostitution by managing a bordello on the Upper West Side of Manhattan in New York City. Ms. Barrows, a descendant of the Mayflower settlers, became known as the Mayflower Madam, and her prostitutes earned between $125 and $400 an hour.

Taking care not to glamorize prostitution as a promising road to financial independence, we note that, as has been the case throughout much of history, women continue to turn to prostitution because of the low value of female labor in society. As George Bernard Shaw noted, "Prostitution is caused not by female depravity and male licentiousness but simply by underpaying, undervaluing, and overworking women. If, on the large scale, we get vice instead of what we call virtue, it is because we are paying more for it" (1905: preface). As we shall see in this section, prostitution also invites other forms of exploitation and victimization.

In tracking the popularity of prostitution over time, Kinsey et al. (1948, 1953) and Hunt (1974) surveyed the frequency with which men visited prostitutes. Kinsey and associates revealed that before World War II, about 50 percent of white men had sought the services of a prostitute. More recently, Hunt found that 45 percent of noncollege-educated and 35 percent of college-educated males had visited prostitutes. Whether this represents a true decline is unclear because survey methods in the two studies are not directly comparable. Nonetheless, with the wave of health concerns in the 1990s (AIDS, herpes, and so forth), observers speculate that visits to prostitutes are becoming less common or, at the very least, clients are becoming more cautious by using condoms.

Health concerns have been addressed by both opponents and advocates of legalized prostitution. Opponents argue that prostitution should remain illegal to minimize public health risks, whereas advocates assert that it is precisely through legalization that health risks can be monitored better (for example, through regular AIDS and venereal disease screening).

The Legal Status of Prostitution

The history of prostitution suggests that one may view it as an extension of social life rather than as a social problem. Yet, nations vary in their views of prostitution. For example, in the Netherlands, prostitution is legal and carefully regulated to minimize the risk of disease. On the other hand, in some Mideastern nations and third-world countries, prostitution is not tolerated. In fact, in Somalia, prostitution is punishable by death. Clearly, with respect to prostitution, the United States is neither as liberal as the Netherlands nor as draconian as Somalia. Nev-

ertheless, federal, state, and local governments traditionally have attempted to control prostitution socially through legal reform, in which prostitution is commonly defined "as the practice of having sexual relations with emotional indifference on a promiscuous and mercenary basis" (Hagan, 1986: 243).

At the federal level, prostitution is controlled by the Mann Act of 1925 (also known as the "white slave" act), which prohibits the transportation of women across state lines (or bringing them into the country) for the purposes of prostitution. The penalty is a $5,000 fine or a five-year sentence, or both. With the exception of Nevada, which has legalized brothels in some counties, states enforce their own statutes on prostitution. Prostitutes can be arrested for such violations as accosting, soliciting, or being a "common prostitute"; in addition, they may be cited for violating disorderly conduct or vagrancy statutes. Prostitutes also have been arrested and detained for health regulation violations.

Prostitution is a misdemeanor, and convicted prostitutes usually are fined or serve a sentence of less than one year. Between 1960 and 1996, prostitution arrest rates almost doubled (see Table 9.2). Whether this is a product of increased willingness by police to arrest women, the heightened extent of prostitution itself as a result of drug-related activity, or some other factors is not known precisely. We do know that police generally are tolerant of prostitution except when instructed or pressured to launch temporary enforcement campaigns. These enforcement campaigns, also known as "social sanitation," are initiated when prostitution becomes overly visible, especially in commercial or residential areas (Welch, 1994). Therefore, the street prostitute is the most common target of police activity. Most major cities informally designate a district, commonly referred to as an

Table 9.2   Arrest Rates for Vice Crimes*

VICE CRIME	YEAR				
	1960	**1970**	**1980**	**1990**	**1996**
Prostitution	24.3	32.5	41.2	47.1	42.7
Other sex offenses†	46.1	32.5	30.5	43.8	37.2
Drug abuse violations	25.5	228.5	256.0	449.2	594.3
Liquor laws	97.8	146.7	205.5	285.3	258.6
Driving under the influence	169.1	279.4	626.3	718.8	533.9
Drunkenness	1,298.2	997.8	504.2	370.3	275.3
Disorderly conduct	437.1	484.8	347.9	299.6	330.1
Vagrancy	140.8	85.1	14.1	16.1	11.4
Gambling	113.0	55.9	22.4	8.0	8.9

SOURCE: Adapted from UCR data (e.g., FBI, 1997).

*Rates per 100,000 population.

†Sex offenses include some offenses with victims.

adult entertainment district or "combat zone," where prostitutes can market their trade without much police interference.

Types of Prostitutes

Streetwalkers are the most visible prostitutes and are commonly found in the combat zones of major cities as well as those districts identified as drug areas. Consequently, streetwalkers face the worst occupational hazards: They remain vulnerable to diseases, arrests, and mistreatment by pimps and customers. The financial rewards of this form of prostitution are relatively low, and the working conditions (meeting clients in streets, alleys, stairwells, cars, or cheap hotels) are markedly inferior. Streetwalkers often are members of poverty-stricken minority groups. Moreover, many pursue prostitution to finance their chemical dependency (Inciardi et al., 1991; Inciardi, 1989).

Another type of prostitute is the bar girl ("b-girl"), who works in cooperation with the management of a tavern, ordering diluted drinks for herself and allowing the client to pick up the tab before the actual act of prostitution. Bars near military bases have traditionally served as popular settings for bar girls (see Winick and Kinsie, 1971). Yet another type of prostitute is the house girl, who works in a brothel and is directly managed by the madam. Today, most brothels have been replaced by massage parlors and escort services, from which comparable services are purchased.

Male prostitutes are similarly categorized as street hustlers, bar hustlers, and escort service employees (Luckenbill, 1986). However, unlike their female counterparts, their form of prostitution is generally homosexual in nature. Very little research attention has been paid to male prostitution, though 40 percent of the arrestees for "prostitution and commercialized vice" (which would include pimps) are male (FBI, 1997: 231).

At a higher level of professionalism is the call girl, who reportedly charges as much as $500 per client and may earn as much as $100,000 annually (Siegel, 1986). Call girls often have had middle-class upbringings and claim to provide more than just sexual services. For example, they purport to enhance the self-esteem of their clients as well as sexually satisfy them. Although call girls may also be vulnerable to abuse by their customers, they have been known to conduct "background checks" on their customers before their "date." The working conditions for the call girls are much better than those for other prostitutes insofar as they work in expensive hotels or their own apartments. Compared to other types of prostitutes, the call girl assumes high occupational status and prestige.

The Socialization of Prostitutes

The role of the prostitute is not always fully embraced by a person who is identified as a prostitute. In fact, the socialization of a prostitute is best understood by tracking the various stages that reflect the gradual transformation of a prostitute's identity. Davis (1978) describes a process known as being "turned out." During the first stage, the woman learns that it is exciting and profitable to sell sex instead of "giving it away." Then the woman enters a stage of transitional deviance: Her self-definition is conventional, yet she uses prostitution as a part-time occupation. In the final stage, she accepts the deviant identity of a prostitute. Traditionally, the socialization process involves group interaction insofar as argot, social support, and apprenticeships are generated by other prostitutes.

Occupational mobility also exists within prostitution and apparently resembles conventional occupational paths. As with conventional occupations, the following qualities enhance mobility for male and female prostitutes: race, mental acumen, personal contacts, self-presentation, and ambition (Goldstein, 1983; Luckenbill, 1986).

Recently, investigations have focused on the "pseudo-families" of streetwalkers that under-score the relationship between women prostitutes and their "men" (or pimps). Whereas the initial attraction to a pseudo-family lies in its glitter and economic opportunity, Romenesko and Miller (1989) report that, in such overwhelmingly heteropatriarchal arrangements, prostitutes soon find themselves trapped and their life chances dramatically reduced instead of enhanced. This downward mobility becomes clearer as younger, more attractive, and more obedient women join the "family," thereby marginalizing the older prostitutes.

Finally, attempts have been made to formalize prostitution as a legitimate profession. In the United States, COYOTE ("Call Off Your Old Tired Ethics") emerged as a social movement that set out to challenge traditional beliefs about prostitution. COYOTE launched several campaigns in the 1970s and 1980s to sever prostitution from its historical association with sin and crime. Organizers of COYOTE emphasized that prostitution should be viewed in light of civil and labor rights, which also include promoting freedom for women who wish to use their bodies as they see fit (Weitzer, 1991; Jenness, 1990).

The Victimization of Prostitutes

Prostitution clearly has a less-than-glamorous side. It is often interpreted as an extension of women's inferior social status (Millett, 1973). A closer look at the stereotypical "independent" working girl reveals a woman who is greatly exploited by her customers and management (Sheehy, 1973). These women are dominated by men who wish to fulfill their own sexual fantasies, and they suffer abuse from the pimps who control their income and their work lives (Conklin, 1986). Additionally, Heyl (1979) identifies other ways in which men profit from female prostitution: as landlords, as owners of massage parlors, and as politicians who base their campaigns on "cleaning up vice."

The criminal justice system also is accused of contributing to the victimization of the prostitute. For example, more women are arrested for providing illegal services than are men who also work as prostitutes. During enforcement campaigns, the prostitute, not the client, is usually arrested and prosecuted. Prostitutes often are beaten and abused, and sometimes are murdered, yet these abuses are passively viewed by the public as "occupational hazards." For example, during the 1978 "Hillside Strangler" mass murders in Los Angeles, the community initially was unconcerned because the victims were presumed to be prostitutes. Public anger was aroused only when this perception proved to be inaccurate (Balkan et al., 1980).

Another form of victimization associated with prostitution is the contraction of illnesses, especially venereal diseases and AIDS. Although rates of contraction likely are exaggerated in the public's mind—prostitutes generally are quite careful to protect themselves—increased levels of exposure surely accompany persistent impersonal sex. However, it is important to emphasize that though prostitutes (in particular, streetwalkers) have exceedingly high rates of AIDS contraction, this is due primarily to high-risk intravenous drug use (such as sharing hypodermic needles) (Cohen et al., 1988).

Of current public concern is the prevalence of the underage prostitute (under the age of 18), which remains common in large cities. For example, Hagan (1986) notes that 10,000 underaged male prostitutes (mostly homosexual prostitutes, who are also called "chicken-hawks") work in New York City alone, and half of Portland's prostitution workforce are underaged girls. Underaged prostitution has also been identified

in New Orleans, where eighteen Boy Scouts ages 8–15 operated as a sex ring.

Unlike adult prostitution, commonly viewed as a more victimless crime, child and adolescent prostitution is more closely monitored by state and federal law enforcement officials. The general view is that the youth is, indeed, the victim in underage prostitution, so additional efforts are made to rescue youths from this form of exploitation. The most common characteristic of male and female adolescent prostitutes is their status as runaways from physically or sexually abusive homes. While attempting to survive on the streets of large cities, these youth turn to substance abuse and prostitution to alleviate the burdens of transient living arrangements and homelessness (Simons and Whitbeck, 1991; Cates, 1989; Campagna and Poffenberger, 1988; Robinson, 1990; Seng, 1989).

PORNOGRAPHY

Pornography often is as controversial as prostitution largely because it shares many of the same issues: degradation, exploitation, and capitalistic patriarchy. However, at times pornography is *more* controversial than prostitution, especially when issues of censorship and potential harm are introduced. Concerns surrounding censorship and First Amendment protections of reading and pictorial materials run deep among many citizens, even if such materials are deemed offensive. But what motivates many attempts to censor pornography is the claim that such materials are potentially harmful insofar as they may inspire some men to commit acts of sexual violence.

In this section, we shall explore historical considerations, the politicization process, and issues of harm as they relate to pornography. Yet, the focus of this section will remain on adult pornography, not child pornography ("kiddie porn"). Because child pornography is routinely prosecuted as a crime (via the federal Child Protection Act of 1984), it does not meet the definition of a vice (or victimless) crime.

Historical Considerations

Pornography shares more common historical and theoretical links with prostitution than is often acknowledged. In fact, the term "pornography" is traced to the graphic sexual writings or pictures (*graphos*) of prostitutes (*pornos*). Over the course of history, the term became synonymous with sexually explicit material intended to promote sexual arousal. Recently, attempts have been made by some feminists to return to the original definition of the term. "From their perspective, it was important to distinguish between pornography, which involved scenes of degradation and dominance, and other forms of erotic material premised on equality and mutual respect" (Rhode, 1989: 263; also see Dworkin, 1981).

Pornography existed in ancient Greek and Roman societies, as well as during the rise of Christianity, but there was little attempt to suppress or censor such images. In the early years of the printing press (in the mid-sixteenth century), English law required printers to receive licenses from the church and the state. Yet, at the time, there was little interest in censoring sexual material because church and state officials were more concerned about subversive political literature (Rhode, 1989; Donnerstein et al., 1987; Barber, 1972).

In colonial America and through the early 1800s, pornography was not widespread; consequently, there was little legal interest in banning sexual materials. Eventually the same social forces that promoted prostitution (secularization, indus-

trialization, migration, and urbanization) also affected the growth of pornography. Accordingly, a legal interest in controlling the distribution of sexual materials also grew. In 1873, the federal Act for the Suppression of Trade and Circulation of Obscene Literature and Immoral Use was passed, primarily under the leadership of Anthony Comstock. The implications of this statute were far-reaching. Because it was designed to suppress materials that would corrupt minds that were open to immoral influences, such a law was broad, vague, and equipped with unlimited discretionary power. Indeed, under the forty-year reign of Postal Inspector Comstock, approximately 160 tons of material (ranging from classical art to indecent playing cards) were destroyed (Rhode, 1989; Boyer, 1968).

Although the courts after World War I began to take into account the merits of the work as a whole in determining whether material was obscene, existing definitions of pornography remained expansive. Decades later, the Supreme Court (in *Roth* v. *United States,* 1956) declared that obscene material was not within the zone of constitutionally protected speech; however, it was still not clear what constituted obscene material. Indeed, the famous phrase by Supreme Court Justice Potter Stewart best characterized the controversy over the definition of obscenity when he quipped, "I know it when I see it."

Finally, in *Miller* v. *California* (1973), the high court formulated a three-part test to determine whether material met the definition of obscene. Material that met these qualifications was subject to prohibition:

1. Whether an average person applying contemporary community standards would find that the work as a whole appealed to the "prurient interest."

2. Whether the work depicted sexual conduct in a "patently offensive way."

3. Whether the work taken as a whole lacked "serious literary, artistic, political, or scientific value."

The Politicization of Pornography

The history of pornography cannot be understood apart from its political context. Pornography is controversial not only because many people consider it morally and aesthetically offensive but also because they believe that it degrades women. Moreover, it also has been suggested that pornography (especially violent pornography) directly (or indirectly) leads to sexual assaults against women. In light of this controversy, an unusual political alliance has formed between right-wing conservatives and some left-wing feminists who favor banning pornography. Indeed, one of the most controversial ordinances enacted to curb pornography had strong support from both conservatives and some feminists.

This controversial ordinance, drafted by Andrea Dworkin and Catherine MacKinnon in 1983, was first proposed in Minneapolis and later adopted in Indianapolis (though here it ultimately was declared unconstitutional by the courts). The ordinance defined pornography as the "sexually explicit subordination of women, graphically depicted in words or pictures," which debases women in several contexts: enjoying pain, rape, or humiliation; serving as sexual objects for domination, conquest, exploitation, and possession; or appearing in positions of "servility or submission or display." The ordinance declared that "trafficking" in pornography (or coercing one to participate in the making of the material) would be a civil offense.

Consequently, "any aggrieved individual could claim injunctive relief and monetary damages under judicial or special administrative proceedings" (Rhode, 1989: 266–267).

Civil libertarians harshly criticized Dworkin and MacKinnon for drafting and advocating this antipornography legislation, arguing that it undermined individuals' rights to freedom of expression and to privacy. In fact, the American Civil Liberties Union (ACLU) selected Dworkin and MacKinnon as two of their 1992 recipients of the Arts Censors of the Year Awards. This dubious distinction is intended to recognize individuals "who have tried to impose their personal ideological, moral or religious standards on all Americans" (*Civil Liberties,* 1992–1993: 7). Dworkin and MacKinnon were selected "for drafting and advocating legislation that would allow lawsuits aimed at banning sexually oriented entertainment, and allow victims of sexual crimes to collect damages from the producers and distributors of such entertainment" (*Civil Liberties,* 1992–1993: 7).

Is Pornography Harmful?

The cornerstone of the Indianapolis ordinance is its presumption of harm stemming from pornography. Recently, the debate over the harmful effects of pornography has been renewed. Baron and Straus's (1987, 1989) research found pornography consumption to be related to rape rates. But in a similar study, Gentry (1991) failed to find support for such a conclusion. She found no relationship between the circulation of sexually oriented magazines (*Chic, Club, Gallery, Genesis, Hustler, Oui, Penthouse,* and *Playboy*) and rape rates. In sum, Gentry emphasizes: "If subsequent research confirms the findings reported here, we may conclude that efforts to control the consumption of sexually oriented magazines in an effort to reduce violence against women are misdirected" (1991: 285).

To date, three major government-sponsored commissions have found that exposure to nonviolent pornography does not cause sexual violence against women (Commission on Obscenity and Pornography, 1970; Attorney General's Commission on Pornography, 1986; and Special Committee on Pornography and Prostitution in Canada, 1985). The 1970 Commission on Obscenity and Pornography "found no evidence that explicit sexual material plays a significant role in the causation of delinquency or criminal behavior." Accordingly, the commission recommended the repeal of local, state, and federal laws against the sale, exhibition, and distribution of sexual materials to consenting adults.

Other studies reveal a cathartic effect, meaning that there is a reduction in aggression by subjects exposed to nonviolent pornography (Donnerstein, 1984; Donnerstein et al., 1987; Malamuth and Donnerstein, 1983; Nelson, 1982). In a cross-national study, Kutchinsky (1991; also see 1973) examined criminal justice statistics in Denmark, West Germany, Sweden, and the United States (1964–1984) and found support for the hypothesis that the legalization of pornography reduced sex crimes in these nations. Some studies actually identify positive aspects of pornography, especially in the form of education. Nicholson and Duncan (1991) included 388 U.S. university students in their study and found, "Men generally report gaining a greater amount of their sex knowledge from pornography than do women, but substantial numbers of women report that pornography was a source of information regarding certain topics, especially oral–anal sex and foreplay" (1991: 802).

Additional research focuses on exposure to violence rather than exposure to pornography per se as a possible cause of sexual assaults because some sex offenders have reported that violent pornography fosters erotic notions of rape (Fishbach and Malamuth, 1978). In experiments comparing violent and nonviolent pornography, Sullivan (1980) found that pornography that incorporated violence promoted aggression among male subjects. Conversely, the nonviolent erotic material failed to promote aggression toward females. These findings are consistent with other research (Malamuth and Donnerstein, 1983), and more researchers are concluding that it is exposure to violence (regardless of whether presented in a sexual context) that leads to sexual aggression (Donnerstein and Linz, 1986; Gray, 1982; Baron and Straus, 1987).

The Attorney General's Commission on Pornography (the Meese Report) (1986) also examined the relationship between pornography and violence. However, its recommendations are not consistent with its findings. Although the commission conceded the lack of a causal connection between pornography and violent sex offenses, it nevertheless recommended strict enforcement of obscenity laws and an increase in penalties for their violation. This created a controversy that was further compounded by the fact that two of the commission members refused to sign the document (Turkington, 1986; Nobile and Nadler, 1986). Nonetheless, Attorney General Meese mounted an ambitious campaign against distributors of pornography by expanding the use of the RICO (the Racketeer Influenced and Corrupt Organizations) statute (see Chapter 10) and establishing the National Obscenity Enforcement Unit (Snow, 1990; Welch, 1988). Ironically, this enforcement campaign occurred amid generally liberal sentiments toward pornography. A 1996 national survey found that only four in ten Americans would legally ban the distribution of pornography outright. Six in ten would ban only distribution to persons under 18 years of age (National Opinion Research Center, 1996).

Yet, despite the publication of empirical investigations that state that there is no conclusive evidence that pornography poses a violent threat to women, many feminists challenge such findings (see Dworkin, 1981, 1985; MacKinnon, 1984; Morgan, 1980; Ratterman, 1982; McCarthy, 1982). It is important to emphasize that adjectives such as "harmful" and "dangerous," which are common descriptors of pornographic material, are actually metaphors to describe material regarded as "offensive." Feminist scholars argue that what many consider simply offensive actually harms women as a group:

> The harm resulting from pornography is not confined to discrete acts of aggression against individual women. It also extends to women as a group, by eroticizing inequality, by linking female sexuality with female subordination, and by making that subordination a powerful source of male pleasure. Pornography that objectifies and brutalizes women in order to entertain men cannot help but affect the social construction of gender (Rhode, 1989: 269).

It is also argued that pornography degrades men as well as women. Brod (1988) notes that "pornography's image of male sexuality works to the detriment of men personally even as its image of female sexuality enhances the powers of patriarchy" (p. 265). In other words, the view of male sexuality is also distorted by pornographic scenes, and this may lead to a form of alienation among men.

In sum, feminists point to the political aspects of inequality, arguing that pornography perpetuates and eroticizes society's male-dominated hierarchy. Traditional conservatives also focus not on the political aspects of pornography, but rather as it deals with morality. Conservatives are concerned with prohibiting materials that they view as "smut" and believe that ordinances against pornography "not only protect women, but would restore them to what ladies used to be" (Rhode, 1989: 269). Considering the traditional views of women among conservatives, many feminists are understandably hesitant to form political alliances with right-wing anti-pornography crusaders.

CONSENSUAL SODOMY AND RELATED SEXUAL ACTIVITY

In many jurisdictions, oral–genital sexual and anal sexual relations—regardless of whether between consenting adults and whether accomplished behind closed doors—are outlawed. As we shall see below, application of such laws to heterosexual activity varies as does the rate of enforcement of the laws even regarding homosexual activity.

Considering the large number of adults who are gay or lesbian, it is suggested that homosexuality be regarded more as variant than as deviant. The Kinsey Institute for Sex Research reported that in the 1960s, 4 percent of the total male population were gay, and 1–2 percent were lesbian. Applying these figures to the 1990 census, the gay population may consist of 12 to 15 million individuals; however, these are considered by some to be conservative estimates. Indeed, the National Gay and Lesbian Task Force (the nation's largest gay and lesbian organization) estimates that homosexuals make up 10 percent of the general population, or approximately 25 million Americans.

Regardless of the size of the homosexual population, as well as growing social tolerance toward gays and lesbians, numerous religious, moral, medical, political, and legal sanctions remain against them. Indeed, today there is considerable public support for laws banning homosexual relations. In a 1996 Gallup poll, 47 percent of the adults surveyed believed that homosexual relations between consenting adults should *not* be legal (44 percent favored legal homosexual relations, and 9 percent had no opinion) (Gallup, 1996). In this section, a discussion of homosexuality (in the context of vice crimes) will include a brief history and overview of recent legal and law enforcement activities.

A Brief History

Homosexual activity was common among ancient Babylonians and Egyptians. Similarly, the ancient Greeks considered homosexuality (as compared with heterosexuality) to be a more genuine expression of love (Karlen, 1971). Among ancient Greeks, however, most homosexuality often took the form of pederasty—that is, sexual activity between men and boys.

The criminalization of homosexual activity actually began during the Middle Ages and the Renaissance in Europe; sodomy (both homosexual and heterosexual) became a crime punishable by death (Karlen, 1971). In 1533, Henry VIII enacted the buggery statute, which outlawed homosexual anal intercourse (Barlow, 1987). These laws remained active until 1861 in England and 1889 in Scotland, where anal intercourse was still punishable by death. Many homosexuals were burnt at the stake along with alleged witches. In fact, the pejorative term "faggot" derives from the practice of using kindling wood, known as faggots, to burn homosexuals (Katz, 1976). In early America, some colonies also imposed the death penalty on

homosexuals, though these laws were "reformed" by Thomas Jefferson in 1776 when death was replaced by castration (Katz, 1976). More recently, Hitler's armed forces persecuted and exterminated homosexuals along with Jews and other political, ethnic, and religious outcasts, and homosexuals have been persecuted by the Castro regime in Cuba.

Finally, as technology in science and medicine advanced, so did interest in applying such technology to reorient homosexuals toward becoming heterosexual through clinical experiments. Through the 1940s and 1950s, this unsuccessful practice persisted among some American psychiatrists who believed that homosexuality was a curable disease. Similar experiments continue in China and Russia. Although such "cures" do not occur in the United States as a medical practice, a religion-based movement is currently underway to "reform" the behavior of practicing homosexuals. Its premise is that, although urges cannot be disposed of completely, they can be managed to the degree that a homosexual can be reoriented toward an appreciation of heterosexual interests and, thus, bring the peace that accompanies moral correctness.

Recent Legal and Law Enforcement Activities

Modern statutes prohibiting oral–genital and anal sex are based on the notion that these acts are unnatural and, therefore, should be unlawful for heterosexuals and homosexuals alike. Although such statutes are infrequently enforced, male homosexuals are occasionally the targets of enforcement campaigns. In fact, a Supreme Court decision upheld state laws that forbid consensual sodomy. In *Bowers* v. *Hardwick* (1986), the U.S. Supreme Court ruled that the state of Georgia, as well as other states, could constitutionally prohibit sodomy as long as the state offered a rational base for such a law. In that case, the Supreme Court interpreted the Constitution as not guaranteeing any fundamental right to engage in consensual sodomy.

Attempts to decriminalize homosexual acts generally arose in the late 1960s, when homosexuals began "coming out of the closet" to fight society's repression of their sexual preference. Some homosexuals stress that they choose their lifestyle, whereas others assert that their sexuality is biologically determined. Either way, homosexuals do not want to be viewed as pathological, sinful, or criminal. One of the goals of this movement was the repeal of state statutes prohibiting sodomy (for both homosexual and heterosexual couples). Such legal reforms occurred in Illinois, Connecticut, and Nebraska, with each state adopting the American Law Institute's Model Penal Code policy (Section 207.5), which legalizes consensual sexual relationships. Today, seven states have sodomy laws prohibiting sexual acts between people of the same sex. Sixteen states and the District of Columbia have sodomy laws applying to people of the opposite sex as well as to homosexuals.

Law enforcement campaigns to control consensual homosexual activities have targeted public places such as parks, theaters, bathhouses, and men's restrooms (tearooms). In a classic sociological study, Humphreys (1970) explored these interactions while engaging in participant observation as the "watchqueen" in a tearoom. One of Humphreys's most revealing findings in this controversial research was that many of the participants were seemingly conventional men stopping at the tearoom on their way home from work. These participants did not fit the stereotype of gay men. Rather, many were married, some had children, and most followed "straight" lifestyles without a gay identity. Among the motivating forces for the tearoom

trade were invisibility, anonymity, variety, and intense excitement.

Law enforcement campaigns against gays in public places reflect homophobic hatred for what are perceived as deviant groups. Fleming (1983), who conducted a case study of raids on bawdy houses from 1979 to 1981 (before the AIDS epidemic was recognized), noted that social antipathy toward gays increased as gays were subjected to the enforcement of laws regulating sexual conduct. Fleming commented on how the regular functions and routines of police were complicated because the bawdy house raids drew police resources away from other criminal activities. As a consequence of law enforcement campaigns against homosexuals, socially harmless people were branded as criminals.

GAMBLING

Like pornography, prostitution, and homosexual activity, gambling has long been identified as a vice. Opposition to it, however, typically has been along social class lines, the assumption being that the poor were less able to control themselves and therefore required control by the law.

A Brief History

The first recorded gambling law was in ancient Egypt, where the masses were forbidden to gamble under the penalty of slavery in the mines. Such a system, Wykes (1964) notes, benefited the wealthy, who could thereby depend on having a pool of workers not sitting idly by engaging in leisurely pursuits. Lest we think such class-biased legislation was restricted to the ancient Egyptians, Wykes uncovered legislation enacted in 1190 by Richard of England and Philip of France restricting betting to the nobility, who themselves could not wager any more than 20 shillings in a twenty-four-hour period.

(The kings, of course, were exempt from the law.) Sociologists who have researched vagrancy laws also find a class bias. Vagrancy statutes, initiated in England in 1349, were modified in 1743 to include illegal betting, and offenders could be branded, enslaved, or executed with repeat offenses (Chambliss, 1964). More recently, the "Street Betting Act" in Britain made working-class wagering on the streets (off-track betting) illegal and kept it that way from 1906 until 1960, when the British approach to gambling was modified (Dixon, 1980).

Although such laws have existed for centuries, no evidence suggests that outlawing gambling has eliminated the practice. Steinmetz (1969), Wykes (1964), and others have documented the numerous failures in this respect throughout the world. Quite obviously, too, not all cultures have condemned or outlawed gambling. The cultural ambivalence of numerous societies toward gambling and the creation of gambling laws is illustrated in the checkerboard history of U.S. statutes (Commission on the Review of the National Policy Towards Gambling, 1976; Rosecrance, 1988). Most recently, of all the victimless crimes, gambling has been legalized at the most rapid pace: Forty-eight states have legalized some form of gambling; lotteries in particular have become popular (LaFleur and Hevener, 1992). The growth of gambling since the mid-1980s has been in the billions of dollars (Christiansen and McQueen, 1992). In addition, some form of gambling is available on Indian reservations in twenty-one states with casino style gambling in many (National Indian Gaming Association, 1992). The primary reason for the increase in legalized gambling has been budgetary, and this has removed much of the moral stigma from gambling (Rosecrance, 1988). Coincidentally, there has been a dramatic decline in gambling arrests,

from 122,946 in 1960 to 21,000 in 1996 (see Tables 9.1 and 9.2, pp. 234–235 and 241).

Compulsive Gamblers

Although the moral stigma has been removed from much of gambling itself, it does remain for individuals who gamble to excess. Compulsive (pathological) gamblers experience difficulties in personal, family, financial, vocational, and legal realms as a consequence of their gambling. They become outcasts as a result of neglecting their families, failing to repay loans, taking time out from work to gamble, and engaging in crimes to support an increasingly expensive addiction (Lesieur, 1984).

Studies have uncovered a wide variety of illegal behaviors among compulsive gamblers. Livingston (1974) found compulsive gamblers involved in check forgery, embezzlement, employee theft, larceny, armed robbery, bookmaking, hustling, running con games, and fencing stolen goods. Lesieur (1984) uncovered these patterns as well and found that gamblers engaged in systematic loan fraud; tax evasion; burglary; pimping; prostitution; drug dealing; and hustling at pool, golf, bowling, cards, and dice. He found that compulsive gamblers first employ legal avenues for funding. As involvement in gambling intensifies, legal options for funding dwindle, and gamblers seek money through increasingly serious illegal activity. For some, the amount of money runs into the millions of dollars. Larceny, embezzlement, forgery, and fraud are the most common offenses among pathological gamblers (Blaszczynski and McConaghy, 1992; Brown, 1987; Lesieur, 1984; Meyer and Fabian, 1992).

A study of pathological gambling among prisoners at Yardville and Clinton prisons in New Jersey found that 30 percent of the inmates showed clear signs of pathological gambling (Lesieur and Klein, 1985), and another done in Western Australia uncovered 22 percent as "probable problem gamblers" (Jones, 1990). Pathological gamblers in hospitals, Gamblers Anonymous programs, and prisons admit involvement in a wide range of illegal behaviors in order to finance their gambling activities or to pay gambling debts, but they vary in the types of crimes they committed. This difference appears to be based on socioeconomic variations among the samples. Whereas prisoners are more likely to have been unemployed, Gamblers Anonymous members and hospital inpatients are more likely to be involved in embezzlement, employee theft, tax evasion, and tax fraud—that is, white collar crimes. An exception to this pattern is the greater likelihood of forgery among female prisoners with no significant difference among other samples (Blaszczynski and McConaghy, 1992; Brown, 1987; Lesieur et al., 1985; Lesieur, 1987; Nora, 1984). By contrast, prisoners are more likely to commit commonplace crimes. With the exception of larceny, all the financially motivated commonplace crimes—including burglary, robbery, pimping, selling drugs, and fencing stolen goods—are engaged in much more frequently by prisoners. In addition, the female prisoners engage in prostitution at a greater rate than do female Gamblers Anonymous members. Selling drugs is more popular among the prisoners and hospital inpatients than among the members of Gamblers Anonymous. Virtually all pathological gamblers who sell drugs to finance their gambling habit are either drug addicts or abusers (Lesieur and Klein, 1985).

A third cluster of crimes is engaged in by compulsive gamblers—gambling-system–related crimes such as bookmaking, writing numbers, and working in an illegal gambling setting—in much the same way that drug sales are related to drug addiction (Lesieur, 1984). Compulsive gamblers are also heavily involved in gambling-related hustles and cons. Pool, bowling, and golf hustling, as well as card and dice cheating (also called hustling), are more likely to occur earlier in their careers. While engaging in these activities, compulsive gamblers become embroiled in heavy wagering and losses at other forms of gambling (most frequently, betting on athletic events and horse races). Compulsive gambling hustlers move on to other crimes like bookmaking and con games because of increasing indebtedness.

It appears that many con artists could be classified as pathological gamblers. Other categories of thieves, hustlers, and streetwise persons also have recognized that they were addicted to gambling (Joey, 1974; Theresa and Renner, 1973; Prus and Irini, 1980; Lesieur, 1984). In his study of the American confidence worker, Maurer (1974: 150–155) recognized that most are gamblers who make a lot of money illegally but spend the bulk of it gambling. Indeed, they showed signs of addiction. Maurer notes that most con artists recognize that they are hooked but feel unable to stop: "This indulgence of the gambling instincts becomes more than relaxation; their gratification is the only motive which many con men have for grifting [stealing]. . . . They win and lose, win and lose, always losing more than they win, until they come away broke and full of reasons why their *systems* didn't work that time" (p. 155).

DRUGS

What is a drug? When this question was asked in 1973, 80 percent of both juveniles and adults perceived heroin, cocaine, barbiturates, marijuana, and amphetamines as drugs (National Commission on Marijuana and Drug Abuse, 1973). In the same survey, only 39 percent of adults and 34 percent of juveniles considered alcohol to be a drug, and only 27 percent of adults and 16 percent of juveniles viewed tobacco as a drug. In another study, selling heroin and LSD were ranked as more serious than forcible rape and assassination of a public official (Rossi et al., 1974). Using heroin was perceived to be more serious than armed robbery or assault on a police officer. Public drunkenness was ranked as the least serious of 140 offenses surveyed. This public sentiment existed even though alcohol is more toxic to the body than most illegal drugs—including heroin (Goode, 1984). The average penalty in some states for possession and sale of illegal drugs is harsher than for all offenses except rape, murder, and kidnapping (Bradley, 1984).

In annual surveys between 1975 and 1996, Johnston et al. (1998) found similar results among high school students. In each of those years, regular use of cigarettes and alcohol was perceived to be less dangerous than regular use of any illegal drug, in spite of overwhelming evidence that alcohol and tobacco are correlated with more deaths than are all illegal drugs combined. Further, alcohol is associated with 40 percent of all auto accident fatalities (Haberman, 1987; National Highway Traffic Safety Administration, 1997), as well as being linked with cirrhosis of the liver, pancreatitis, gout, several forms of cancer, neurological disorders including dementia, brain abnormalities, and general tissue damage (Secretary of Health and Human Services, 1983, 1990). Tobacco, like alcohol an addictive drug, is associated with diseases of the lungs (including cancer and emphysema) and heart disease; smokers are one-and-a-half times as likely to die in any one given year as nonsmokers (Grawunder and Steinmann, 1980).

Both alcohol and tobacco are associated with low birth weight in infants (and consequent higher risk of mental retardation) (Duncan and Gold, 1982).

Ironically, in spite of their popularity and current legal status, alcohol and tobacco, as well as caffeine, have been outlawed in the past. The general public is familiar with Prohibition and the movement to ban "demon rum," but the history of attempts to control tobacco and caffeine is less well known. The American Indians brought tobacco with them when they were taken to the Spanish court by early explorers (Brecher et al., 1972). After their introduction into Europe, even though tobacco and snuff were seen by many as ungodly and unclean, people squandered away fortunes on the drug, which had to be shipped from the New World. In 1642, Pope Urban VIII issued a bull (that is, an edict) of excommunication against those who used tobacco. Some European states outlawed it, and Sultan Murad IV of the Ottoman Empire even decreed the death penalty for smoking tobacco. Nevertheless, according to Brecher et al. (1972), no country that has taken up tobacco has been successful in outlawing it, regardless of the penalty. Similar attempts at the suppression of coffee, tea, and cocoa (all containing caffeine) have failed. In sixteenth-century Egypt, for example, coffee was under controls similar to those pertaining to marijuana in the United States today. Sale was a crime, and stocks of coffee were burned. In Europe, medical opinion was used to back up opposition to the drug. Antagonism continued there even into the twentieth century as actual cases of overuse, including coffee psychosis and deliriums, were cited.

Public views of different drugs are in all probability a product of the legislation of morality (Duster, 1970). Some evidence suggests that laws themselves create a moral sentiment in opposition to the behavior being regulated. We forget that caffeine and nicotine are drugs (both have stimulant properties) because they are legal. Because of the impact on present laws of historical attempts to regulate various substances, it is important for readers to obtain a knowledge of the history of specific drug laws.

Opiates and Cocaine

Evidence that coca, a leaf with stimulant properties similar to caffeine, was used about 2,300 years ago in Peru and Ecuador comes from the discovery in graves of statues with puffed-out cheeks indicating coca leaf chewing (Grinspoon and Bakalar, 1985). At the time of the Spanish conquest, the Incas used coca leaves in divination, and the leaves were scattered by priests before religious rites. In 1551 and 1567, Catholic bishops called coca use idolatry and obtained a royal decree denouncing it. However, the Spaniards encouraged the use of coca by workers in gold and silver mines for its stimulant properties. Today, the coca leaf appears on the Peruvian coat of arms and is used as a folk medicine in Peru and Colombia and in religious ceremonies by some Colombian Indians. Cocaine, an alkaloid, was first extracted from coca in 1860 (Grinspoon and Bakalar, 1985). It is a short-acting stimulant that can be used as a local anesthetic. Consequently, it rapidly became popular for its medicinal qualities, as well as for recreational purposes. In 1863, Angelo Mariani patented Vin Mariani, a combination of coca extract and wine that was endorsed by numerous individuals, including the pope. By 1886, Coca-Cola was also being produced using coca extract. (It was later removed, and caffeine substituted.) Both Coca-Cola and Vin Mariani were seen as elixirs and stimulants. By the latter part of the nineteenth century, cocaine was recommended as a treatment for timidity and depression and as a cure for morphine addiction.

Eventually, when people began exhibiting signs of cocaine dependence and psychosis after extended use, cocaine came to be touted as a "dangerous drug," associated with "Jew peddlers," "Negro users," and crime. By 1914, when the Harrison Act taxed and prohibited its use for all but medical purposes, more states controlled cocaine sales than sales of opiates. In 1922, Congress prohibited most importation of coca leaves and cocaine and defined cocaine as a narcotic (it is not). In 1951, Congress passed the Boggs amendment, which called for mandatory prison terms for possession or failure to register for importation of cocaine; penalties were increased in 1956.

Opium has a different but interconnected history. In the nineteenth century, opium (usually in the form of morphine) was as accessible as aspirin is today (Brecher et al., 1972; Duster, 1970; Inciardi, 1986; Lindesmith, 1965). It was sold in grocery stores in various forms as an over-the-counter medication. Patent medicines like Dover's Powder, Ayer's Cherry Pectoral, Mrs. Winslow's Soothing Syrup, and Godfrey's Cordial were easily obtainable—even by mail. Like many patent medicines, morphine was promoted as a cure for a wide variety of diseases, and in the late nineteenth century, it was thought to be the lesser of two evils when compared with alcohol. It was argued that morphine was cheaper, was less likely to be associated with criminal activity, contributed to general family happiness, and entailed no physical degeneration. Most users in the nineteenth century were white women, and the average user was about 40 years old. Morphine was also used across all social classes.

The first anti-opium laws in the United States were passed in response to Chinese immigration (Brecher et al., 1972). In the 1850s and 1860s, opium smoking was introduced to the United States by thousands of Chinese who came to America to construct the Western railroads. Many of these workers stayed in West Coast cities, which produced an anti-Chinese sentiment that was vented when, in 1875, San Francisco passed an ordinance prohibiting opium smoking in smoking-houses or "dens." Other cities and states followed suit by passing progressively more stringent laws against the drug. Opium was dealt a further blow by the Food and Drug Act of 1906, which led to product labeling. By this time, the general public had become aware of the addictive qualities of the drug, and the patent medicine industry declined. Its death blow came with the passage of the Harrison Act of 1914, a law designed to provide for the registration and taxation of opium and coca leaves and their derivatives. The act, in part, read: "Nothing contained in this section shall apply . . . to the dispensing or distribution of any of the aforesaid drugs to a patient by a physician, dentist, or veterinary surgeon registered under this Act in the course of his professional practice only" (Lindesmith, 1965: 4).

Despite this wording, physicians were arrested for dispensing opiates (including morphine and heroin) to addicts. The last eight words were eventually interpreted by the Supreme Court to mean that maintenance of opiate addicts (many of whom had been addicted by these same physicians) was not "professional practice" because it was not directed toward a cure (Lindesmith, 1965). Over 25,000 physicians were arrested in the years following passage of the act, and some 3,000 went to prison (*Newsweek,* 1988; Goode, 1984). As a result of the attack on physicians, the composition of the addict population changed. By the 1920s, the vast majority of narcotics addicts were young, lower-class males, a pattern that continued into the 1990s (Goode, 1993; Kandel and Maloff, 1983).

Currently, at the federal level, drugs are regulated through the Comprehensive Drug Abuse Prevention and Control Act of 1970, which classifies drugs into five schedules according to their "abuse" potential (Drug Enforcement Administration, 1985). Trafficking in schedule I and II drugs (including heroin, benzodiazepines, hallucinogens, cocaine, marijuana, and some barbiturates and amphetamines) can be punished by up to fifteen to twenty years in prison and $125,000–$250,000 in fines, depending on the amount sold. The sale of marijuana (in amounts under one kilogram) and schedule III drugs (weak narcotic solutions like codeine and paregoric, some barbiturates, and widely prescribed amphetamines) can result in a maximum of five years in prison and up to $50,000 in fines.

Drug arrests rose dramatically between 1960 and 1996, primarily because of the widespread use of illegal drugs in the late 1960s and early 1970s and an increasingly antidrug mood in the country (see Tables 9.1 and 9.2, pp. 234–235 and 241). Periodic "epidemics," like that involving crack (a smokeable form of cocaine) in the mid- to late 1980s, increase enforcement efforts and create a class of criminals whose only offense is experimentation with drugs. In spite of sensational cases involving crack homicides (caused primarily by participation in the drug trade), the vast majority of crack users are nonviolent.

Marijuana

Between 1973 and 1978, eleven states decriminalized marijuana (Murphy, 1986). This change was primarily a product of the alteration in the population that was using the substance. From the 1930s to the 1950s, marijuana use was associated with African Americans, Mexican Americans, jazz musicians, and other low-status or culturally deviant groups (Polsky, 1969: 144–182). Penalties for possession were particularly dra-conian: "Typically, simple possession was a felony that carried penalties of two years for the first offense, five for the second, and ten for the third" (Himmelstein, 1986: 4). During the turbulent 1960s, middle-class individuals experimented with the drug, and it became popular across all social strata. Arrests for possession reached the middle class with increasing frequency, and pressure emerged from this quarter to alter the laws. All states except Nevada eventually reduced possession of small amounts of marijuana to a misdemeanor. Marijuana was decriminalized (reduced to the equivalent of a traffic offense for possession of small amounts—usually an ounce or less) in eleven states (Himmelstein, 1986; Jamieson and Flanagan, 1987: 62–65; Galliher and Cross, 1982). Indicating the drug's fluctuating legal status, Alaska has recriminalized marijuana; California's citizens have voted to legalize it for medicinal purposes.

Public Drunkenness

The drug that precipitated the decriminalization movement is alcohol. A public health rather than a criminal justice approach to the problem of drunkenness was advocated by the 1967 President's Commission on Law Enforcement and Administration of Justice in reaction to the medicalization of alcoholism and the overcrowding of the courts and jails by chronic inebriates. When the commission advocated the elimination of penalties for public drunkenness, thirty-seven states removed public drunkenness from their criminal law statutes (Whitford, 1983). Whereas in 1960, public drunkenness accounted for almost 36 percent of all arrests, by 1996, arrests dropped to less than 5 percent; arrests for other public-inebriety–related offenses

(notably disorderly conduct and vagrancy) also declined in this period. Despite this trend, however, there were 1,589,100 arrests for public drunkenness, disorderly conduct, and vagrancy combined in 1997.

Ample evidence suggests that public drunks are arrested primarily because shopkeepers and store owners in central cities pressure police to do so, claiming the presence of drunks hurts their business (Speigelman and Wittman, 1983). For these businesses, detoxification facilities serve a similar purpose—they get the inebriate off the street. However, detoxification facilities' personnel prefer to work only with voluntary patients and hence try to avoid (and may refuse entry to) the most troublesome of the skid-row types (Aarronson et al., 1978). Short-term detoxification also tends to be ineffective with chronic public inebriates (Daggett and Rolde, 1980) and represents a more expensive alternative than jail primarily because it requires medical professionals. Thus, localities continue to rely on understaffed alternatives to jail and maintain the jail as a backup.

Drunken Driving

In 1960, drunken driving arrests represented fewer than 5 percent of all arrests; by 1996, they accounted for nearly 10 percent of all arrests. In actual numbers, they increased from slightly less than 200,000 to just under 1,500,000 during those years. State legislatures have stiffened penalties for driving while intoxicated, and the risk of punishment for the inebriated driver has increased greatly. Although arrests have increased, it is important to note that the police and the courts remain reluctant to enforce these laws maximally. DUI charges are frequently reduced to reckless driving (Ball and Lilly, 1986). Where they have not been reduced, legal challenges have been mounted, courts have become backlogged with these cases, and jail overcrowding has been exacerbated (Forcier et al., 1986; Nienstedt, 1986). Nationwide, DUI offenders account for 10 percent of jail inmates (U.S. Department of Justice, 1998) and 18 percent of all individuals on probation (U.S. Department of Justice, 1997). The increasing use of criminal sanctions is occurring in spite of little evidence that jail terms reduce recidivism and accidents, whereas evidence suggests that license suspensions and revocations more likely produce reductions (Hingson and Howland, 1990).

OVERLAPPING SOCIAL WORLDS

Americans have a love–hate relationship with vice. Various forms of vice are simultaneously practiced and condemned by an overwhelming proportion of the population. As a result, there is substantial overlap between the conventional and the deviant. People fluctuate between one and the other, flirting with the deviant while maintaining respectability. Matza (1964: 63–64) uses the term "subterranean values" to denote those elements in American culture that support some deviance. This overlap and movement back and forth between the conventional and the deviant receives considerable support through conventional social institutions.

One example of the expression of subterranean values is widespread support for illegal sports gambling. Newspapers publish point spreads for gambling purposes and sports commentators help gamblers make their picks for the day. Sports bettors also rely on legal information services like the *Gold Sheet* and an estimated 600–700 telephone call-in and "sports sheet" services (Frey and Rose, 1987). Similarly, racetrack bettors consult newspapers, including the likes of the *Washington Post,* the *Miami Herald,* and the *Chicago Tribune,* to obtain betting lines on the day's races (D'Angelo, 1987).

In a study of illegal gambling occurring in connection with legal bingo games, Lesieur and Sheley (1987) introduced the concept of **illegal appended enterprise** to denote a situation in which illegal activities both depend upon and support legitimate enterprises. In this case, illegal gambling benefits charities that run bingo games because the illegal activity attracts customers; at the same time, the illegal games need to have the customers of the legal operation in order to stay in business. Other illegal appended enterprises with symbiotic relationships in the world of vice include hotel prostitution (Prus and Irini, 1980); independent bookmaking businesses run from the neighborhood bar (Perrucci, 1969); and drug sales from pizza shops, video gamerooms, and hotel lobbies (Henry, 1978; Valentine, 1978). In addition, there is at least tacit support for illegal behavior in "head shops," which sell pipes, cigarette papers, and other accoutrements of the drug world. Some businesses make it obvious that they combine both legal and illegal enterprises; others operate more secretly.

Not only do legitimate and illegitimate worlds overlap, but illegitimate worlds overlap as well. For example, in *Black Mafia,* Ianni (1974) discusses the Harlem network where prostitution, drugs, gambling houses, and boosting (professional shoplifting) intersect with boutiques and dry cleaning establishments that act as fronts for the illegal operations. In a different fashion, Prus and Irini (1980) discuss the intersecting worlds of hookers, strippers, rounders (professional thieves), the hotel and barroom staff, and desk clerks (involved in many varieties of illegal hustling in connection with their occupation), who all operate in one way or another in the hotel community.

Those who engage in illegal activity and work part-time in that world (they are far more numerous than full-time workers) straddle both the legitimate and illegitimate worlds (D'Angelo, 1984). Because the vast majority of Americans engage in one form of illegal activity or another, we are actually a nation of straddlers. Some of us rail against the immorality of others while engaging in what others would call immoral conduct. As straddlers, we conceal our own immorality and avoid self-indictment by cleverly giving our offenses another name.

CONCLUSION

We have explored a number of themes in this chapter. Clearly, vice crime is not limited to a small number of people in this society; indeed, many people engage in behaviors that, technically, violate the law, and many more engage in activities that others want to outlaw. Few people realize the extent to which the economies of their communities rely in part on the delivery of products and services deemed illegal by the same communities. The decision to outlaw vices necessitates the allocation of large amounts of criminal justice resources to enforce laws against acts that have no complaining victim. Some would argue that governments produce even more crime by the very act of legislating against vices. For example, laws against drugs produce black markets that drive up drug prices and foster property crimes by people seeking to pay for drug habits. Ultimately, the lack of a complaining victim is the crux of the vice crime issue. To what extent should governments be permitted to enter the private worlds of consenting adults, to tell them what they may or may not do as long as they do not directly interfere with the rights of others not wishing to engage in the same behaviors?

DISCUSSION QUESTIONS

1. Why criminalize the vices? To what extent can a balance be struck between personal autonomy and governmental control of behavior? What has been our experience with governmental control? With such experience in mind, what is gained and what is lost by making drug possession a crime?

2. Once a vice is criminalized, why is it so difficult to change its legal status?

3. The medical model of vice crime has become increasingly popular in recent years. Discuss the key elements and assumptions of the model. Why is it popular? What problems are associated with the model?

4. What is the process by which people enter into the occupation of prostitution? How do prostitutes move up the income ladder in their occupation? In this sense, is prostitution different from most conventional occupations?

5. The rather vocal movement to outlaw pornography rests upon the assumption that pornography influences behaviors ranging from violence toward women to the treatment of women as sex objects. What does the research literature tell us in this regard? What constitutional issues also enter the debate?

6. The authors note that, regarding vice, legal and illegal worlds often overlap. Discuss this concept and provide examples.

REFERENCES

Aarronson, D. E., C. T. Dienes, and M. C. Musheno. 1978. "Changing the Public Drunkenness Laws: The Impact of Decriminalization." *Law and Society Review* 12: 405–416.

American Psychiatric Association. 1987. *Diagnostic and Statistical Manual.* 3d ed., rev. Washington, DC: American Psychiatric Association.

Armor, D. J., J. M. Polich, and H. B. Stambul. 1976. *Alcoholism and Treatment.* Santa Monica, CA: Rand Corporation.

Attorney General's Commission on Pornography. 1986. *Final Report of the Attorney General's Commission on Pornography.* Washington, DC: U.S. Department of Justice.

Balkan, S., R. J. Berger, and J. Schmidt. 1980. *Crime and Deviance in America: A Critical Approach.* Belmont, CA: Wadsworth.

Ball, J. C., B. K. Levine, R. G. Demaree, and J. F. Neman. 1975. "Pretreatment Criminality of Male and Female Drug Abuse Patients in the United States." *Addictive Diseases* 1: 481–489.

Ball, R., and R. Lilly. 1986. "The Potential Use of Home Incarceration for Drunken Drivers." *Crime and Delinquency* 32: 224–247.

Barber, D. F. 1972. *Pornography and Society.* London: Skilton.

Barlow, H. 1987. *Introduction to Criminology.* Boston: Little, Brown.

Baron, L., and M. A. Straus. 1987. "Four Theories of Rape: A Macrosociological Analysis." *Social Problems* 34: 467–489.

————. 1989. *Four Theories of Rape in American Society: A State-Level Analysis.* New Haven: Yale University Press.

Bedeau, H. A. 1974. "Are There Really 'Crimes Without Victims'?" Pp. 66–76 in *Victimless Crimes: Two Sides of a Controversy.* Edited by E. Schur and H. A. Bedeau. Englewood Cliffs, NJ: Prentice-Hall.

Blaszczynski, A., and N. McConaghy, 1992. *Pathological Gambling and Criminal Behaviour.* Report to the Criminology Research Council. Canberra, Australia.

Boyer, Paul S. 1968. *Purity in Print: The Vice Society Movement and Book Censorship in America.* New York: Charles Scribner's Sons.

Bradley, R. J. 1984. "Trends in State Crime-Control Legislation." In Search Group, Inc. *Information Policy and Crime Control Strategies.* Washington, DC: U.S. Department of Justice.

Brecher, E. M., and the editors of *Consumer Reports.* 1972. *Licit & Illicit Drugs.* Boston: Little, Brown.

Brod, H. 1988. "Pornography and the Alienation of Male Sexuality." *Social Theory and Practice* 14: 3: 265–284.

Brown, R. I. F. 1987. "Pathological Gambling and Associated Patterns of Crime: Comparisons with Alcohol and Other Drug Addictions." *Journal of Gambling Behavior* 3: 98–114.

Bullogh, V. 1980. *Sexual Variance in Society and History.* Chicago: University of Chicago Press.

Campagna, D. S., and D. L. Poffenberger. 1988. *The Sexual Trafficking in Children.* Dover, MA: Auburn.

Cates, J. A. 1989. "Adolescent Male Prostitution by Choice." *Child and Adolescent Social Work* 6 (2) 151–156.

Chambliss, W. J. 1964. "A Sociological Analysis of the Law of Vagrancy." *Social Problems* 12: 67–77.

Christiansen, E. M., and P. A. McQueen. 1992. "The Gross Annual Wager of the United States— Part I: Handle." *Gaming and Wagering Business* 13: 22–37.

Civil Liberties. 1992–1993. 378 (Winter): 7.

Cohen, J., P. Alexander, and C. Wofsky. 1988. "Prostitution and AIDS: Public Policy Issues." *AIDS & Public Policy Journal* 3 (2) 16–22.

Commission on Obscenity and Pornography. 1970. *The Report of the Commission on Obscenity and Pornography.* New York: Bantam Books.

Commission on the Review of the National Policy Towards Gambling. 1976. *Gambling in America.*

Washington, DC: U.S. Government Printing Office.

Conklin, J. E. 1986. *Criminology.* 2d ed. New York: Macmillan.

Conrad, P., and J. W. Schneider. 1992. *Deviance and Medicalization: From Badness to Sickness.* 3rd ed. Columbus, OH: Merrill.

D'Angelo, R. 1984. *The Social Organization of Sports Gambling: A Study in Conventionality and Deviance.* Ph.D. dissertation, Bryn Mawr College.

———. 1987. "Sports Gambling and the Media." *Arena Review* 11: 1–4.

Daggett, L. R., and E. J. Rolde. 1980. "Decriminalization of Drunkenness: Effects on the Work of Suburban Police." *Journal of Studies on Alcohol* 41: 819–828.

Davis, K. 1961. "Prostitution." Pp. 275–276 in *Contemporary Social Problems.* Edited by R. K. Merton and R. A. Nisbet. New York: Harcourt, Brace & World.

Davis, N. 1978. "Prostitution: Identity, Career, and Legal Economic Enterprise." Pp. 195–222 in *The Sociology of Sex.* Edited by J. Henslin and E. Sagarin. New York: Schocken Books.

Devlin, P. 1965. *The Enforcement of Morals.* London: Oxford University Press.

Dixon, D. 1980. " 'Class Law': The Street Betting Act of 1906." *International Journal of the Sociology of Law* 8: 101–128.

Donnerstein, E. 1984. "Erotica and Human Aggression." Pp. 127–154 in *Aggression: Theoretical and Empirical Reviews.* Edited by R. E. Geen and E. I. Donnerstein. New York: Academic Press.

Donnerstein, E. I., and D. G. Linz. 1986. "The Question of Pornography: It Is Not Sex, but Violence That Is an Obscenity in Our Society." *Psychology Today,* December, 56–59.

Donnerstein, E. I., D. G. Linz, and S. Pernod. 1987. *The Question of Pornography: Research Findings and Policy Implications.* New York: Free Press.

Drug Enforcement Administration. 1985. *Drugs of Abuse.* Washington, DC: U.S. Department of Justice.

Duncan, D., and R. Gold. 1982. *Drugs and the Whole Person.* New York: Wiley.

Duster, T. 1970. *The Legislation of Morality.* New York: Free Press.

Dworkin, A. 1981. *Pornography: Men Possessing Women.* New York: Putnam.

———. 1985. "Against the Male Flood: Censorship, Pornography and Equality." *Harvard Women's Law Journal* 8: 1–29.

Federal Bureau of Investigation. 1997. *Crime in the United States—1996.* Washington, DC: U.S. Government Printing Office.

Fishbach, S., and N. Malamuth. 1978. "Sex and Aggression: Proving the Link." *Psychology Today* 12: 112–122.

Fleming, T. 1983. "Criminalizing a Marginal Community: The Bawdy House Raids." Pp. 37–60 in *Deviant Designations: Crime, Law and Deviance in Canada.* Edited by T. Fleming and L. A. Visano. Toronto: Butterworth.

Forcier, M. W., N. R. Kurtz, D. G. Parent, and M. D. Corrigan. 1986. "Deterrence of Drunk Driving in Massachusetts: Criminal Justice System Impacts." *The International Journal of the Addictions* 21: 1197–1220.

Frey, J. H., and I. N. Rose. 1987. "The Role of Sports Information Services in the World of Sports Gambling." *Arena Review* 11: 44–51.

Furst, P. 1972. *Flesh of the Gods: The Ritual Use of Hallucinogens.* New York: Praeger.

Galliher, J. F., and J. R. Cross. 1982. "Symbolic Severity in the Land of Easy Virtue: Nevada's High Marijuana Penalty." *Social Problems* 29: 380–386.

Gallup, G. 1996. *The Gallup Poll Monthly, No. 375.* Princeton, NJ: The Gallup Poll.

Geis, G. 1979. *Not the Law's Business.* New York: Schocken Books.

Gentry, C. 1991. "Pornography and Rape: An Empirical Analysis." *Deviant Behavior: An Interdisciplinary Journal* 12: 277–288.

Gilfoyle, T. J. 1992. *New York City, Prostitution, and the Commercialization of Sex, 1790–1920.* New York: W. W. Norton & Company.

Goldstein, P. J. 1983. "Occupational Mobility in the World of Prostitution: Becoming a Madam." *Deviant Behavior* 3–4: 267–279.

Goode, E. 1984. *Drugs in American Society.* 2d ed. New York: Knopf.

———. 1993. *Drugs in American Society.* New York: McGraw-Hill.

Grawunder, R., and M. Steinman. 1980. *Life and Health.* New York: Random House.

Gray, S. H. 1982. "Exposure to Pornography and Aggression Toward Women: The Case of the Angry Male." *Social Problems* 29: 387–398.

Grinspoon, L., and J. B. Bakalar. 1985. *Cocaine: A Drug and Its Social Evolution.* New York: Basic Books.

Haberman, P. W. 1987. "Alcohol Use and Alcoholism among Motor Vehicle Driver Fatalities." *The International Journal of the Addictions* 22: 1119–1128.

Hagan, F. E. 1986. *Introduction to Criminology: Theories, Methods, and Criminal Behavior.* Chicago: Nelson-Hall.

Hart, H. L. A. 1963. *Law, Liberty and Morality.* Palo Alto, CA: Stanford University Press.

Henry, S. 1978. *The Hidden Economy.* Oxford: Martin Robertson.

Heyl, B. 1979. "Prostitution: An Extreme Case of Sex Stratification." In *The Criminology of Deviant Women.* Edited by F. Adler and R. J. Simon. Boston: Houghton Mifflin.

Himmelstein, J. L. 1986. "The Continuing Career of Marijuana: Backlash . . . Within Limits." *Contemporary Drug Problems* 13: 1–21.

Hingson, R., and Howland, J. 1990. "Use of Laws to Deter Drinking and Driving." *Alcohol Health and Research World* 14: 36–43.

Humphreys, L. 1970. *Tearoom Trade: Impersonal Sex in Public Places.* Chicago: Aldine.

Hunt, M. 1974. *Sexual Behavior in the 1970's.* New York: Dell.

Ianni, F. A. J. 1974. *Black Mafia.* New York: Simon & Schuster.

Inciardi, J. A. 1986. *The War on Drugs: Heroin, Cocaine, Crime, and Public Policy.* Palo Alto, CA: Mayfield.

———. 1989. "Trading Sex for Crack Among Juvenile Drug Users: A Research Note." *Contemporary Drug Problems* 16: 689–700.

Inciardi, J. A., A. F. Potteiger, M. A. Forney, D. D. Chitwood, and D. C. McBride. 1991. "Prostitution, IV Drug Use, and Sex-For-Crack Exchanges Among Serious Delinquents: Risks For HIV Infection." *Criminology* 29(2): 221–236.

Jamieson, K. M., and T. J. Flanagan. 1987. *Sourcebook of Criminal Justice Statistics—1986.* Washington, DC: U.S. Government Printing Office.

Jenness, V. 1990. "From Sex as Sin to Sex as Work: COYOTE and the Reorganization of Prostitution as a Social Problem." *Social Problems* 37: 403–420.

Joey (with D. Fisher). 1974. *Killer.* New York: Pocket Books.

Johnston, L., P. O'Malley, and J. Bachman. 1998. *National Survey Results on Drug Use from the Monitoring of the Future Study, 1975–1997.* Washington, DC: U.S. Department of Health and Human Services, National Institute on Drug Abuse.

Jones, G. 1990. "Prison Gambling." *The National Association for Gambling Studies* 2: 5–15.

Kadish, S. H. 1967. "The Crisis of Overcriminalization." *The Annals of the American Academy of Political and Social Science* 374: 158–170.

Kandel, D. B., and D. R. Maloff. 1983. "Commonalities in Drug Use: A Sociological Perspective." Pp. 3–28 in *Commonalities in Substance Abuse and Habitual Behavior.* Edited by P. K. Levinson, D. R. Gerstein, and D. R. Maloff. Lexington, MA: Lexington Books.

Kaplan, J. 1970. *Marijuana—The New Prohibition.* New York: World.

Karlen, A. 1971. *Sexuality and Homosexuality.* New York: Norton.

Katz, J. 1976. *Gay American History: Lesbians and Gay Men in the USA*. New York: Avon Books.

Kinsey, A., W. B. Pomeroy, and C. E. Martin. 1948. *Sexual Behavior in the Human Male*. Philadelphia and London: Saunders.

———. 1953. *Sexual Behavior in the Human Female*. Philadelphia and London: Saunders.

Kutchinsky, B. 1973. "The Effect of Easy Availability of Pornography on the Incidence of Sex Crimes." *Journal of Social Issues* 29: 95–112.

———. 1991. "Pornography and Rape: Theory and Practice? Evidence from Crime Data in Four Countries where Pornography is Easily Available." (Paper presented at the 14th International Congress on Law and Mental Health, Montreal, Canada.) Published in *International Journal of Law and Psychiatry* 14 (1–2): 47–64.

LaFleur, T., and P. Hevener. 1992. "U.S. Gaming at a Glance." *Gaming and Wagering Business* 13: September 15–October 14: 34.

Lesieur, H. R. 1984. *The Chase: Career of the Compulsive Gambler*. Cambridge: Schenkman.

———. 1987. "The Female Pathological Gambler." In *Gambling Research: Proceedings of the Seventh International Conference on Gambling and Risk Taking*. Edited by W. R. Eadington. Reno, NV: Bureau of Business and Economic Research.

Lesieur, H. R., and R. Klein. 1985. *Prisoners, Gambling and Crime*. Paper presented at the annual meeting of the Academy of Criminal Justice Sciences, Las Vegas, NV. April.

Lesieur, H. R., and J. F. Sheley. 1987. "Illegal Appended Enterprises: Selling the Lines." *Social Problems* 34: 249–260.

Lesieur, H. R., S. B. Blume, and R. M. Zoppa. 1985. "Alcoholism, Drug Abuse, and Gambling." *Alcoholism: Clinical and Experimental Research* 10: 33–38.

Lindesmith, A. R. 1965. *The Addict and the Law*. New York: Vintage Books.

Lipton, D., R. Martinson, and J. Wilks. 1975. *The Effectiveness of Correctional Treatment: A Survey of Treatment Evaluation Studies*. New York: Praeger.

Livingston, J. 1974. *Compulsive Gamblers: Observations on Action and Abstinence*. New York: Harper Torchbooks.

Lorenz, V. C., and I. N. Rose. 1988. "Compulsive Gambling and the Law." Special issue of *Journal of Gambling Behavior* 5: 4.

Luckenbill, D. F. 1986. "Deviant Career Mobility: The Case of Male Prostitutes." *Social Problems* 33: 283–296.

MacKinnon, C. 1984. "Not a Moral Issue." *Yale Law and Policy Review* 2: 321–345.

Malamuth, N. M., and E. Donnerstein. 1983. "The Effects of Aggressive-Pornographic Mass Media Stimuli." Vol. 15, pp. 103–196 in *Advances in Experimental Social Psychology*. Edited by L. Berkowitz. New York: Academic Press.

Matza, D. 1964. *Delinquency and Drift*. New York: Wiley.

Maurer, D. 1974. *The American Confidence Man*. Springfield, IL: Thomas.

McCarthy, S. 1982. "Pornography, Rape, and the Cult of Macho." Pp. 218–232 in *Crisis in American Institutions*. Edited by J. H. Skolnick and E. Currie. Boston: Little, Brown.

Meyer, G., and T. Fabian. 1992. "Delinquency Among Pathological Gamblers: A Causal Approach." *Journal of Gambling Studies* 8: 61–77.

Mill, J. S. [1859] 1892. *On Liberty*. London: Longmans, Green.

Millett, K. 1973. *The Prostitution Papers*. New York: Ballantine.

Morgan, R. 1980. "Theory and Practice: Pornography and Rape." Pp. 125–132 in *Take Back the Night: Women on Pornography*. Edited by L. Lederer. New York: Morrow.

Morris, N., and G. Hawkins. 1970. *The Honest Politician's Guide to Crime Control*. Chicago: University of Chicago Press.

Murphy, S. E. 1986. *Marijuana Decriminalization: The Unfinished Reform.* Ph.D. dissertation, University of Missouri, Columbia.

National Commission on Marijuana and Drug Abuse. 1973. *Patterns and Consequences of Drug Use.* Washington, DC: U.S. Government Printing Office.

National Indian Gaming Association. 1992. *Issues and Facts.* Washington, DC: National Indian Gaming Association.

National Highway Traffic Safety Administration. 1997. *Traffic Safety Facts 1996.* Washington, DC: U.S. Department of Transportation.

National Opinion Research Center. 1996. *General Social Survey, 1996.* Storrs, CT: The Roper Center for Public Opinion Research, University of Connecticut.

Nelson, E. 1982. "Pornography and Sexual Aggression." Pp. 171–248 in *The Influence of Pornography on Behavior.* Edited by M. Yaffe and E. C. Nelson. New York: Academic Press.

Nettler, G. 1982. *Criminal Careers.* 4 vols. Cincinnati: Anderson.

Newsweek. 1988. New York Academy of Medicine. 1963. "Report on Drug Addiction." *Bulletin of the New York Academy of Medicine* 39: 417–473.

Nicholson, T., and D. F. Duncan. 1991. "Pornography as a Source of Sex Information for Students at a Southwestern State University." *Psychological Reports* 68 (3): 802.

Nienstedt, B. C. 1986. *Testing Deterrence: The Effects of a DWI Law and Publicity Campaigns.* Unpublished dissertation, Arizona State University, Tempe.

Nobile, P., and E. Nadler. 1986. *United States of America vs. Sex: How the Meese Commission Lied About Pornography.* New York: Minotaur Press.

Nora, R. 1984. *Profile Survey on Pathological Gamblers.* Paper presented at the Sixth National Conference on Gambling and Risk Taking, Atlantic City, NJ. December.

Packer, H. L. 1968. *The Limits of the Criminal Sanction.* Stanford, CA: Stanford University Press.

Pateman, C. 1988. *The Sexual Contract.* Stanford, CA: Stanford University Press.

Perrucci, R. 1969. "The Neighborhood 'Bookmaker': Entrepreneur and Mobility Model." In *Urbanism, Urbanization and Change: Comparative Perspectives.* Edited by P. Meadows and E. H. Mizruchi. Reading, MA: Addison-Wesley.

Polsky, N. 1969. *Hustlers, Beats and Others.* Garden City, NY: Doubleday Anchor.

Prus, R., and S. Irini. 1980. *Hookers, Rounders and Desk Clerks.* Toronto: Gage.

Rathus, S. 1983. *Human Sexuality.* New York: Holt, Rinehart & Winston.

Ratterman, D. 1982. "Pornography: The Spectrum of Harm." *Aegis* (Autumn): 42–52.

Report of the Special Committee on Pornography and Prostitution. 1985. *Pornography and Prostitution in Canada.* Ottawa: Canadian Government Publishing Centre.

Rhode, D. 1989. *Gender and Justice.* Cambridge, MA: Harvard University Press.

Roberts, N. 1992. *Whores in History.* New York: Harper Collins.

Robinson, M. 1990. "Social Science and the Citizen: A Third of Homeless Teenagers Survive by Prostitution." *Society* 28 (1): 2.

Romenesko, K., and E. M. Miller. 1989. "The Second Step in Double-Jeopardy: Appropriating the Labor of Female Street Hustlers." *Crime and Delinquency* 35 (1): 109–135.

Rosecrance, J. 1988. *Gambling Without Guilt: The Legitimation of an American Pastime.* Pacific Grove, CA: Brooks/Cole.

Rossi, P. H., R. A. Berk, and B. K. Eidson. 1974. *The Roots of Urban Discontent.* New York: Wiley.

Sagarin, E. 1969. *Odd Man In: Societies of Deviants in America.* Chicago: Quadrangle Books.

Schur, E. M. 1965. *Crime Without Victims.* Englewood Cliffs, NJ: Prentice-Hall.

Secretary of Health and Human Services. 1983. *Fifth Special Report to the U.S. Congress on Alcohol and Health.* Washington, DC: U.S. Government Printing Office.

————. 1990. *Seventh Special Report to the U.S. Congress on Alcohol and Health.* Rockville, MD: National Institute on Alcohol Abuse and Alcoholism.

Seng, M. J. 1989. "Child Sexual Abuse and Adolescent Prostitution: A Comparative Analysis." *Adolescence* 24: 665–675.

Shaw, G. B. 1905. *Author's Apology From Mrs. Warren's Profession.* New York: Brentano's Press.

Sheehy, G. 1973. *Hustling: Prostitution in Our Wide Open Society.* New York: Delacorte Press.

Sheley, J. F. 1985. *America's "Crime Problem."* Belmont, CA: Wadsworth.

Sheley, J. F., and J. J. Hanlon. 1978. "Unintended Effects of Police Decisions to Actively Enforce Laws: Implications for Analysis of Crime Trends." *Contemporary Crises* 2: 265–275.

Siegel, L. G. 1986. *Criminology.* 2d ed. St. Paul, MN: West.

Simons, R. L., and L. B. Whitbeck. 1991. "Sexual Abuse as a Precursor to Prostitution and Victimization Among Adolescent and Adult Homeless Women." *Journal of Family Issues* 12 (3): 361–379.

Skolnick, J. H. 1968. "Coercion to Virtue." *Southern California Law Review* 41: 3.

Snow, R. L. 1990. "Funding by Offenders." *Law and Order* 38 (4): 67–70.

Special Committee on Pornography and Prostitution in Canada. 1985. *Pornography and Prostitution in Canada.* Ottawa: Canadian Government Publishing Centre.

Speigelman, R., and F. D. Wittman. 1983. "Urban Redevelopment and Public Drunkenness in Fresno: A California Move Toward Recriminalization." *Research in Law, Deviance and Social Control* 5: 141–170.

Steinmetz, A. [1870] 1969. *The Gaming Table.* Montclair, NJ: Patterson Smith.

Sullivan, W. 1980. "Violent Pornography Elevates Aggression, Researchers Say." The *New York Times,* September 30, C1, C3.

Theresa, V., and T. C. Renner. 1973. *My Life in the Mafia.* Greenwich, CT: Fawcett.

Turkington, C. 1986. "Pornography and Violence." *American Psychological Association's Monitor* (August): 8–9.

U.S. Department of Justice. 1997. *Characteristics of Adults on Probation, 1995.* Washington, DC: U.S. Department of Justice.

U.S. Department of Justice. 1998. *Profile of Jail Inmates, 1996.* Washington, DC: U.S. Department of Justice.

Valentine, B. 1978. *Hustling and Other Hard Work: Lifestyles in the Ghetto.* New York: Free Press.

Weitzer, R. 1991. "Prostitutes' Rights in the United States: The Failure of a Movement." *Sociological Quarterly* 32 (1): 23–41.

Welch, M. 1988. *The Contradiction and Deception of the Meese Report on Pornography: Avoiding the Real Issue of Violence.* Paper presented at the annual meeting of the American Society of Criminology, Chicago.

————. 1994. "Jail Overcrowding: Social Sanitation and the Warehousing of the Urban Underclass." Pp. 251–276 in A. Roberts (Ed.), *Critical Issues in Crime and Justice.* Thousand Oaks, CA: Sage.

Weppner, R. S., and J. A. Inciardi. 1978. "Decriminalizing Marijuana." *International Journal of Offender Therapy and Comparative Criminology* 22: 115–126.

Whitford, D. 1983. "Getting Police Off the Skid Row Merry-Go-Round." *Police* 6: 12–22.

Winick, C. 1964. "Physician Narcotic Addicts." Pp. 261–279 in *The Other Side: Perspectives on Deviance.* Edited by H. S. Becker. New York: Free Press.

Winick, C., and P. M. Kinsie. 1971. *The Lively Commerce: Prostitution in the U.S.* Chicago: Quadrangle Books.

Wykes, A. 1964. *The Complete Illustrated Guide to Gambling.* Garden City, NY: Doubleday.

Chapter Outline

10

The Mafia Mystique:
Organized Crime

JAY S. ALBANESE
Virginia Commonwealth University

Organized crime always has conveyed a mystique that made it appear larger than life. This image was fostered by a widespread belief that some mysterious organization was behind certain crimes, and it was pumped up by popular fiction and by Hollywood. Today, it is difficult to distinguish where the reality ends and the fiction begins. Many people have no clear conception of what the "Mafia" actually is, what it does, and whether it is a large or small part of all organized crime. For nearly a century, the nature and origins of organized crime have been obscure, preventing a clear sense of what should be done about it.

This chapter will outline the nature and history of organized crime in North America and demonstrate how the Mafia came to dominate most discussions of organized crime. A review of important events and research, focusing on the past thirty-five years, will demonstrate how the characterization of organized crime as dominated by the Mafia is a gross oversimplification. New models, or paradigms, to explain organized crime have now emerged that challenge some historical beliefs and shed more light on how organized crime develops and carries out its illicit activities. As this chapter will suggest, a model of organized crime as an illicit business "enterprise" is superior to other existing models that portray it as an ethnically based form of deviant behavior.

THE NATURE OF
ORGANIZED CRIME

The various popular images of organized crime often make it difficult to define the phenomenon properly. Like any form of criminal behavior, however, it is best defined by the nature of the conduct involved, rather than by who commits it, because many different types of groups engage in organized crime. Historically, the government has chosen to define organized crime in terms of the ethnic derivation of those who engage in it. For example, in its final report, the President's Commission on Organized Crime (1987) defined "organized crime today" by describing known organized crime groups and distinguishing them according to their membership; included were Italian, Mexican, African American, Chinese, Canadian, Vietnamese, Japanese, Cuban, Colombian, Irish, and Russian groups, in addition to motorcycle and prison gangs. As this chapter will demonstrate, however, organized crime is explained most satisfactorily in terms of the behaviors involved rather than in terms of its continually changing participants.

Three types of activities characterize organized crime: the provision of illicit goods, the provision of illicit services, and the infiltration of legitimate business. Provision of illicit goods involves the manufacture, sale, or distribution of illegal drugs, untaxed cigarettes, stolen property, and other goods that are either illegal or sold without proper government approval. Provision of illicit services includes running gambling operations, lending money, and offering sex outside the control of the law. Illegal lotteries, lending money in excess of legal interest rates (loansharking), and prostitution are examples of illicit services. Common to the provision of both illicit goods and services is the crime of conspiracy. Conspiracy occurs when two or more people agree to commit an unlawful act or to commit a lawful act by unlawful means. The distinction between organized crime and an individual prostitute, gambler, loanshark, or drug possessor has to do with conspir-acy. Only when individuals organize (through a conspiracy) to provide illicit goods or services do the crimes of individuals become organized crime.

The third type of organized crime, the infiltration of legitimate business, occurs when a company (or government agency) is coerced through the use of force, threats, or intimidation to sell out to criminal interests, hire someone against its will, or engage in undesirable business or labor agreements. Whereas conspiracy characterizes the provision of illicit goods and services, extortion characterizes the infiltration of legitimate business. Extortion occurs when anything of value is taken and the owner is placed under duress due to threats of future force or violence. For example, legitimate businesspersons sometimes are forced to pay protection money to organized criminals in order to prevent vandalism on company property or to ensure labor peace. The nature of organized crime can be defined, therefore, as the provision of illicit goods and services (conspiracy) and the infiltration of legitimate business (extortion).

The precise extent of organized crime is unknown, as is its cost to society. Its extent is difficult to determine because most organized crime activity is never detected. Its costs to society were acknowledged by the 1967 President's Crime Commission Task Force on Organized Crime and the 1987 President's Commission on Organized Crime, but both these investigations observed that reliable estimates of the costs of organized crime were not available. It has been recognized, however, that the costs of organized crime in terms of illicit profits, unpaid taxes, disruption of legitimate business, and political and commercial corruption far exceed the costs to society incurred from street crimes (President's Commission, 1967; President's Commission on Organized Crime, 1987).

THE ORIGINS OF
THE MAFIA MYSTIQUE

Most historians have traced the alleged roots of organized crime in North America to a rather ambiguous event. The superintendent of police of New Orleans, Louisiana, David Hennessey, was shot by a group of unknown assassins in 1890. On his deathbed, the superintendent is said to have uttered either "Sicilians have done for me" or "Dagoes." This was interpreted at the time as indicating that Italians were responsible for his murder. Based on Hennessey's statement, seventeen Italian immigrants were arrested and accused of belonging to a Sicilian assassination league (Nelli, 1981; Smith, 1990). Although none of the suspects was convicted (due to a lack of evidence), an angry mob broke into the jail and killed eleven of the defendants.

Several separate historical inquiries into the Hennessey murder have since been conducted in both the United States and Canada. Each has concluded that his murder resulted from a business rivalry between two Italian families that controlled the dock area of New Orleans: the Matrangas and the Provenzanos. Hennessey supported the Provenzanos, and his partiality apparently provoked the Matrangas into having him killed (Albini, 1971; Dubro, 1986; Nelli, 1981; Smith, 1990).

Of course, no Sicilian assassination league existed. Popular belief held that more than 1,000 Italian criminals had emigrated to the area in the late 1800s. During an investigation into the murders of the Italian defendants, however, au-

thorities discovered that only about 300 Italian immigrants had criminal records (most of them for petty offenses), and this total of 300 was less than 1 percent of the Italian population of the city. The strong community hostility toward the suspects in Hennessey's murder reflected anti-immigrant sentiments associated with the large Italian immigration into North America during this period.

The anti-Italian sentiment did not die easily. The language barrier and apparent secretive nature of Sicilian immigrants (see Servadio, 1978: 3) fueled the belief in a "secret society" of Italians that engaged in criminal activity. Since the New Orleans incident, a continuous debate has raged over whether organized crime in North America evolved, was imported, or was modeled after an Italian Mafia—even though numerous historical investigations have been unable to document a central Mafia organization that existed beyond the local level in Italy (Albini, 1971; Hess, 1973; Blok, 1974; Servadio, 1978; Arlacchi, 1986).

THE KEFAUVER
HEARINGS OF THE 1950s

After Superintendent Hennessey's death in 1890, the notion of the Mafia as a fundamental source of organized crime quickly faded. In the twenty-five years from 1918 to 1943, the word "mafia" appeared in the *New York Times* only four times, with most public attention during this period focused on Chicago's gangsters. The Illinois Crime Survey of 1929 produced what may be the first objective investigation of organized crime in the United States. After the murder of a Chicago prosecutor and the subsequent grand jury investigations, authorities concluded that "an underworld system of control" existed in Chicago that "has no formal organization" but is "held together by powerful leaders" who control criminal gangs (Landesco, 1929: 278). From the early 1900s to the late 1920s, the "overlordship of the underworld" in Chicago was said to be controlled by Big Jim Colosimo, John Torrio, Scarface Al Capone, and Mont Tennes. These men engaged primarily in gambling and bootlegging activities, but there was no clear Mafia connection among them. In addition, Chicago had thirteen different chiefs of police from 1900 to 1925, only one of whom served for as long as four years. This high turnover resulted, "almost without exception," from charges of graft or incompetence (p. 278). The Illinois Crime Survey found that the "huge revenues from bootlegging have given gangsters enormous funds with which to buy political protection and immunity from prosecution" (p. 279). It was also reported that these "gangsters" had recently begun to expand their activities into the infiltration of legitimate business.

This study of organized crime in Chicago during the early 1900s was not imitated in other cities. More recent investigations of organized gambling activities and political corruption, however, have revealed that continuing criminal enterprises often maintain themselves through co-optation or coercion of law enforcement or elected officials (see Brady, 1984; Chambliss, 1971, 1988). As the Illinois Crime Survey reported in 1929, a "mutuality of services" exists between organized crime and the political system: "The politician affords protection or immunity from prosecution, the gangster rallies his friends for legal as well as fraudulent voting" (Landesco, 1929: 280). Chambliss (1988) reported a similar finding in his study of

illegal gambling in Seattle. He noted that the gambling activities were protected from prosecution by corrupt police officers who, in turn, were protected by corrupt politicians. Likewise, Brady (1984) found instances of arson in some abandoned buildings in Boston in which alleged racketeers bought properties at inflated prices with equally high mortgages and insurance coverage. Buildings were then intentionally torched and paid for by the insurance consortium, which spreads out its losses within the industry. In this way, legitimate businesses (for example, real estate companies, banks, and insurance companies) tacitly conspired with organized criminals (Brady, 1984: 216).

In 1950, organized crime and the Mafia became synonymous in the public's mind. A United States senator, Estes Kefauver, held televised hearings across the country throughout 1950 at which law enforcement officials and criminals testified. The officials claimed that a centralized criminal organization called the Mafia controlled much of organized crime in North America, but the criminals denied knowledge of the existence of such an organization. Kefauver's investigation concluded, however, that the Mafia exists: a "sinister criminal organization" that operates in several nations and is a "direct descendant" of a Mafia in Sicily.

Perhaps the most disappointing aspect of the Kefauver hearings was the fact that no actual investigation of organized crime ever took place. The televised hearings produced only *opinions* about the nature of organized crime. Police and public officials offered their opinions about organized crime, and Kefauver added his, but no one bothered to gather any evidence to substantiate these views. The most comprehensive analysis of the Kefauver hearings was conducted by the historian William

Moore. He concluded that the committee's statements were "overblown and unfounded," largely ignored "the economic, legal, and social conditions giving rise to organized crime," and implied that it "originated outside of American society" and was continued here by "immoral men, bound together by a mysterious ethnic conspiracy" (Moore, 1974: 134, 237; see also Bell, 1953; Turkus and Feder, 1951).

Despite its flawed attempt to shed light on organized crime, the Kefauver committee solidified the view that most organized crime was at least controlled, if not operated, by a Mafia comprising exclusively men of Italian origin. This apparently unshakeable belief was reinforced in 1957, when sixty-five men of Italian origin who had gathered in Apalachin, New York, were arrested. Theirs was termed a "meeting of the Mafia" because some of the men had criminal records (Smith, 1990). Several government investigations were conducted into this "Mafia meeting," and a trial was held in which those who refused to testify were charged with contempt, but no objective evidence was ever produced to connect these men with criminal activity. The U.S. Court of Appeals reversed the decisions brought against the men who had been convicted for obstructing justice by refusing to answer questions about the Apalachin incident. The court labeled the case no more than "pervasive innuendo" that "this was a gathering of bad people for an evil purpose." The judges concluded that "a prosecution framed on such a doubtful basis should never have been allowed to proceed so far" (*U.S.* v. *Buffalino*, 285 F.2d 408, 1960). Despite this conclusion, the Apalachin incident continued to be cited by many as "proof" of the existence of a Mafia that controlled most of organized crime in North America.

THE PAST THIRTY-FIVE YEARS: THE GENERATION OF THE INFORMANT

Since 1963, we have seen a barrage of information about organized crime. Some is fact, much is fiction, and the largest portion never has been examined critically to determine the difference. The bulk of this information came from government informants, most of whom were criminals who agreed to provide the government with evidence in exchange for immunity from prosecution.

The first government informant who revised public thinking about organized crime was Joseph Valachi, the first insider to claim that there was, in fact, a centralized organization of Italian criminals in North America. Valachi claimed to be a member of a crime family in New York City. He testified about a confederacy of criminal groups in North America called Cosa Nostra and alleged never to have heard of the Mafia. Interestingly, the President's Crime Commission in 1967 resolved this discrepancy by suggesting the Mafia had changed its name to Cosa Nostra even though no extrinsic evidence proved the existence either of a particular name or of a name change. Rather, the name Mafia or Cosa Nostra apparently was merely a popular way to describe organized crime in general.

According to Valachi, this federation of criminals of Italian origin arose from a 1930s gangland war called the Castellammarese War. The war resulted in the current organization of the Cosa Nostra into families that controlled organized crime in various cities in North America. In general, a single family, or group, directed activities in a given city, except for New York City, where five groups divided the territory.

Though little effort was made to corroborate much of what Valachi said, his testimony resulted in the now-familiar charts and family trees of organized crime groups, consisting of "bosses," "lieutenants," and "soldiers," that have been reproduced in various government reports on organized crime (President's Commission, 1967; President's Commission, 1987).

Valachi's claim of a national gangland war in which up to sixty people reportedly died has not found support among objective investigators. Several independent evaluations have been able to confirm only a handful of deaths during this period, and no evidence of a gangland "war" (Block, 1978; Nelli, 1981). Valachi's description of the organization of the Cosa Nostra was also accepted uncritically. He offered a description of a militaristic structure, but also spoke of a looser confederation. He agreed that the function of the family is "mutual protection," but "otherwise, everybody operates by himself. They may take partners but that is their option" (U.S. Senate, 1963: 116, 194). Thus, Valachi indicated that organized crime may not have been as "organized" as was commonly believed at the time.

In any event, no one (including police officials) could provide supporting information regarding the existence of the Cosa Nostra or of the Castellammarese War independent of Valachi (U.S. Senate, 1963). Further, objective indications of Valachi's veracity, such as convictions in criminal trials, never were presented. Hawkins (1969: 46) has observed that Valachi "contradicted himself and was contradicted by others," and that his testimony "produced nothing in the way of tangible results." Yet, Valachi's testimony gave the Senate committee what it "wanted to hear . . . , and once [Valachi] had satisfied that desire there was little need to be

skeptical or press for additional, independent information" (Smith, 1990: 234).

Valachi's version of organized crime was taken by the government to indicate that "organized crime is a society that seeks to operate outside the control of the American people and their governments." Further, "the core of organized crime consists of 24 groups" operating as "criminal cartels" in large cities—although Valachi was able to identify only sixteen organized crime groups (President's Commission, 1967: 1, 6). The cartels allegedly controlled the bulk of illegal gambling, loansharking, narcotics trafficking, and prostitution in North America.

EMPIRICAL INVESTIGATIONS OF THE 1970S

In the 1970s, for the first time, organized crime groups drew the attention of independent researchers. The result was a growing collection of empirical investigations conducted by nongovernment officials into the nature of organized criminal activity.

Local Ethnic Group Models

The pioneering study was conducted by Albini (1971), who focused his investigation in both Italy and the United States. He relied on historical data, as well as on the accounts of informants on the streets and local police officials. He found that those involved in organized crime "do not belong to an organization." Instead, organized crime is a network of patron–client relationships wherein a person's connections provide him with access to a particular illicit activity. Rather than a "criminal secret society, a criminal syndicate consists of a system of loosely structured relationships" that exists so each participant can further his own welfare (p. 288). Albini's conclusions about the nature of organized crime represented the first empirically based effort drawing conclusions that differed radically from the government's perception of organized crime as a "nationwide conspiracy."

Albini's findings received support from the anthropologists Ianni and Reuss-Ianni (1973), who conducted a study of an organized crime family in New York City. Ianni lived with the family for two years as a participant-observer and became part of its social milieu. Like Albini, the Iannis found that criminal groups "have no structure apart from their functioning" (p. 20). Based on their observations of this family and of several other criminal groups, they concluded that such groups are *not,* as criminal justice officials had indicated earlier, a "private government of organized crime" or a "cartel with national oversight" (U.S. Senate, 1965: 117; President's Commission, 1987: 42). Instead, they are loosely organized local groups, often consisting of members of the same ethnic derivation.

Another investigation that arrived at a similar conclusion was conducted by Anderson (1979). Using federal law enforcement data concerning a family suspected of being part of the Cosa Nostra, Anderson performed an economic analysis of the group's activity. Like the Iannis, she found that the use of violence was minimal and that no evidence linked the group to any national cartel. Interestingly, she also found that the family was "neither of major significance in the economy of the city where it operates nor a serious threat to its legitimate business competitors" (p. 140). Organized crime groups were less financially successful than the government had claimed they were in

amassing "huge profits" (President's Commission, 1967: 1).

In yet another investigation, Abadinsky (1981) constructed a life history of a former organized criminal (now in the witness protection program). The respondent, "Vito," described the structure of organized crime as neither complex nor bureaucratic. Abadinsky agreed with Anderson that "successful prosecution of a few leaders ('headhunting') does not have a significant impact on the organization; clients will shift to other patrons and continue their operations" (p. 126).

Clearly, though these various investigations each employed somewhat different approaches, their findings are remarkably consistent. They found organized crime to be characterized by informal networks of associations existing at the local level and often composed of individuals of similar ethnic origin.

Enterprise Models

A second group of objective investigations of organized crime was conducted from the mid-1970s into the 1980s. Once again, each researcher employed slightly different investigative techniques, making the consistency of their findings still more impressive. In his comprehensive history of organized crime in the United States, Smith (1990) found that organized crime and legitimate business engage in the same activities but do so at different ends of the "spectrum of legitimacy." He developed this notion into a "spectrum-based theory of enterprise" in subsequent publications (Smith, 1978, 1980). According to Smith, organized crime enterprises arise in the same way as do legitimate businesses. Loansharking, for example, exists for the same reason that banks do: Many potential customers wish to borrow money for various purposes; the supply of money to lend is assured through an interest rate charged on all loans; there are few enough competitors in the marketplace to assure a profit; and government regulators place certain restrictions on the market but nevertheless make it possible to survive and make a profit.

This configuration of suppliers, customers, regulators, and competitors forms the basis for both the legal and the illegal enterprise of lending. The only difference between the two (beyond their differing methods of debt collection), according to Smith, is the interest rate charged. As the legal interest rate changes, or as the legal lending market is opened up to more customers, the market for loansharking is affected proportionately. A similar analogy could be drawn for legal and illegal gambling, narcotics trafficking, and prostitution. The provision of illicit services, the source of much of the income generated by organized crime, is made possible, according to this view, by arbitrary distinctions between licit and illicit enterprise.

Block's (1979) historical investigation into the illicit cocaine market in New York during the early part of the twentieth century supported Smith's characterization of organized crime as a form of enterprise. Using archival data, Block discovered that the cocaine trade was not run by a single ethnic group or conspiracy but instead was characterized "by criminal entrepreneurs who formed, re-formed, split and came together again as the opportunity arose" (p. 94). He found, based on a review of the records of over 2,000 criminals, that these individuals "were in reality criminal justice entrepreneurs" organized through a "web of small but efficient organizations" (p. 95). Block's findings also indicated that ethnic ties

did not appear to govern the organization of these activities. He discovered evidence "of interethnic cooperation which clearly suggests that at times parochialism was overcome by New York's criminals" (p. 95). Similar interethnic operations were found by McIllwain (1997) in a study of Chinese organized crime in the United States. Likewise, an account of the Irish "Westies" gang in Manhattan's Hell's Kitchen described efforts to cooperate with Cosa Nostra groups in New York City (English, 1991: 136–178).

Additional support for the enterprise model of organized crime appeared in a study of the solid waste collection and vending machine industries by Reuter et al. (1983). Using law enforcement files and street informants, they found that racketeer infiltration in these industries "may be a problem of small and declining importance" (p. 14). Improving technology has produced "market forces which simply prevent old-time muscle tactics and coercion from being effective." As a result, the racketeer is forced to "act like any other member of the industry, making decisions based on economic factors and shaped by market demand" (p. 33). In fact, continued assertions of racketeer involvement in these industries was found to make it more difficult for legitimate entrepreneurs to survive and make a profit.

A separate investigation by Reuter (1983) into loansharking and illegal gambling in New York City reached a similar conclusion. He found these markets populated by "small and ephemeral enterprises" that survive or fail based on market factors. In addition, no centralization of the illicit markets was established because "economic forces arising from the illegality of the product tend to fragment the market" (p. 176). In 1985, Adler similarly found the illicit narcotics market in pseudonymous "Southwest

County" to be "largely competitive . . . rather than visibly structured." The smugglers themselves often referred to their activities as "one of the last arenas of free enterprise in existence" (p. 80). Individual entrepreneurs and small organizations, rather than centralized bureaucracies, characterized the market. Finally, Arlacchi (1986) ascertained through his own investigation that organized criminals in Italy have been "radi-cally transformed by [their] identification with market forces" (p. 119). Rather than pursuing honor, which Arlacchi claims was the objective years ago, organized criminals now seek wealth and power through enterprises that keep costs and competition to a minimum and maintain their access to financial resources.

Comparing the Various Models

The three different models, or paradigms, of organized crime discussed to this point can be compared. The traditional view, established through criminals turned informants and in government reports, describes organized crime as a national conspiracy controlled largely by one group. Based on this view, the logical prevention strategy has been to neutralize the leaders of the group. Once they are incarcerated or otherwise neutralized, the conspiracy will collapse.

The second model, established through several different empirical investigations, depicts organized crime as a collection of locally organized ethnic groups. This model suggests that prosecution of organized crime leaders will lead only to their being replaced by others because the culture and the patron–client relationships that permit the existence of organized crime will still exist. Control of organized crime, according to this model, will be effected only through increased awareness of its costs to the

community and through legalization of those consensual behaviors that are now in high public demand but are illegal.

Finally, the enterprise model is similar to the local ethnic-groups model in that organized crime is characterized by an informal, decentralized structure that rarely employs violence to achieve its goals. Rather than focus on the unity within ethnic groups, however, the enterprise model sees market conditions as the controlling factor in the establishment and maintenance of organized crime. If the configuration of suppliers, customers, regulators, and competitors is favorable, then organized crime will flourish (Albanese, 1987a). The control of organized crime, according to this view, will be achieved only when the market conditions that breed it are better understood. Arbitrary distinctions between legal and illegal lending, narcotics trade, gambling, and sexual services are examples of market conditions, created by government, that favor the establishment of organized crime groups (see Albanese, 1993; Haller, 1992).

RECENT PROSECUTION TOOLS

Joseph Valachi's testimony, echoed in the 1967 President's Crime Commission report, resulted in several important new laws designed to combat organized crime in the 1970s and 1980s. These laws created powerful prosecution tools for the government.

The Omnibus Crime Control and Safe Streets Act of 1968: Title III

The first law passed in response to the concern about organized crime was Title III of the Omnibus Crime Control and Safe Streets Act of 1968. The provisions of this statute permitted

Table 10.1   Court-Authorized Orders for Interception of Wire, Oral, or Electronic Communications by Most Serious Offense Under Investigation, United States, 1997

OFFENSE	TOTAL	FEDERAL	STATE
All offenses	1,186	569	617
Narcotics	870	467	403
Racketeering	93	30	63
Gambling	98	20	78
Homicide and assault	31	2	29
Kidnapping	6	5	1
Loansharking, usury, and extortion	24	16	8
Larceny and theft	22	4	18
Bribery	13	4	9
Other	29	21	8

SOURCE: Maguire and Pastore (1998: 376).

federal law enforcement officials to use wiretaps or electronic microphones to eavesdrop on the conversations of suspected organized criminals, provided they first obtained a warrant. This enabled electronic surveillance information to be admitted as evidence in federal court for the first time. Subsequent decisions by the U.S. Supreme Court have further broadened the scope of wiretap authority so that prosecutors may introduce as evidence information overheard regarding third parties not the subject of the warrant, warrantless pen register recording (that is, lists of telephone numbers dialed), and warrantless electronic beeper surveillance (use of a radio transmitter whose signal reveals the location of a vehicle or container), among other things (for a summary, see Albanese, 1996; see also Table 10.1).

The desirability of electronic surveillance as an investigative tool has been widely debated. Proponents argue that it is an efficient means of infiltration of criminal organizations. The use of undercover agents, as an alternative, is seen as time consuming, dangerous, and not always feasible in organized crime cases. Likewise, it is argued that the warrant requirements and procedural restrictions prevent unnecessary invasions of privacy. A large number of convictions also have resulted from wiretaps—from 1970 to 1992, convictions arising from electronic surveillance increased by 44 percent to 2,685.

Critics of electronic surveillance point both to its prohibitive cost and to its violation of basic rights to privacy. In 1992, wiretaps and bugs averaged $46,492 per tap, because of the intensive personnel required to monitor and analyze conversations. From 1970 to 1992, the number of wiretaps installed increased by more than 40 percent to 846, but the proportion of incriminating conversations overheard dropped from 45 to 19 percent of all intercepted conversations. This has led critics to argue that electronic surveillance is not being used scrupulously. Further, arrests have resulted in convictions only about half the time. The disputable ability of electronic surveillance to investigate criminal conspiracies effectively, its high costs, the fear of violations of privacy rights, and scandals regarding illegal electronic surveillance by police in at least twenty states since 1969 are certain to keep the debate over its desirability alive (Katz, 1983; Krajick, 1983; National Wiretap Commission, 1976; Schlegel, 1988). As a reflection of uncertainty about electronic surveillance, twenty-one states still prohibit its use.

The Organized Crime Control Act of 1970

The second legislative outcome of Valachi's testimony and the 1967 President's Crime Commission was the Organized Crime Control Act of 1970. Witness immunity, the witness protection program, investigative grand juries, and new racketeering provisions were among the significant components of the act.

Witness Immunity The witness immunity provisions allow federal prosecutors to grant reluctant witnesses immunity from prosecution in exchange for their testimony. Witnesses who fail to testify under a grant of immunity are held in contempt of court and can be jailed indefinitely until they testify. The rationale is to permit prosecution of higher-level organized crime figures using the testimony of less important offenders. The lack of objective evidence of the utility of this provision, however, has led critics to point to several significant organized crime trials in which the defendants were acquitted because of the jury's unwillingness to believe the government's immunized witness (Dershowitz, 1987). In addition, "use" immunity provided under this law allows incriminating evidence to be used against the witness if it is obtained independently of his

or her testimony. As Block and Chambliss (1981: 205) observed, "proving evidence was tainted" would be difficult. The intuitive credibility problems of immunized testimony and its potential misuses have not yet been addressed through an objective cost–benefit examination of witness immunity in organized crime cases.

Witness Protection The witness protection program, also established as part of the Organized Crime Control Act, provides a mechanism for the government to protect witnesses whose lives are in danger from persons against whom they have testified. The program, administered by the U.S. Marshal's Service, gives protected witnesses new identities and moves them to a different location to begin a new life. The U.S. General Accounting Office evaluated the program in 1984 and found that federal organized crime cases utilizing protected witnesses resulted in a high proportion of convictions (75 percent), and of those convicted, 70 percent were sentenced to two years or more in prison. This was twice the rate of federal organized crime cases not involving protected witnesses. On the other hand, protected witnesses had been arrested an average of 7.2 times prior to their admission to the program, and 21 percent were arrested again within two years of gaining entrance to the program. In addition, the program's size and cost have far exceeded projections: More than 4,400 witnesses and 8,000 family members have been relocated at an annual cost of $25 million. Clearly, therefore, the benefits of the program (high conviction rate and longer sentences) must be weighed against its costs (crimes by protected witnesses and the program's $25 million annual expenditure).

Special Grand Juries Title I of the Organized Crime Control Act established special grand juries designed to investigate more effectively organized crime activities that cross state lines. Like traditional grand juries, special grand juries hear evidence from prosecutors to determine if probable cause exists for indictment. In addition, special grand juries can issue a public report on organized crime or corruption in a specified area at the end of their term. They also can conduct continuing investigations along with police. Some states have established state-wide grand juries that perform an analogous function across county lines. Supporters of these investigative juries argue that such broad authority is needed to investigate organized crime, which often is multijurisdictional. In addition, such juries may be better insulated from local political pressures that can prevent investigations into organized crime at the local level. Critics argue that special grand juries have been used to harass individuals based on their political leanings and to "invent" cases rather than determine whether one already exists (Rhodes, 1984). As might be expected, both proponents and detractors can cite examples to support their positions, but no objective cost–benefit evaluation has yet been undertaken to determine the actual worth of such grand juries over a large number of cases.

Racketeering Provisions Perhaps the most controversial prosecution tool established as part of the Organized Crime Control Act is the section on Racketeer Influenced and Corrupt Organizations (RICO). This section prohibits acquisition, operation, or income from an enterprise through a pattern of racketeering activity. "Enterprise" has been defined as any individual or group, a "pattern" is two or more

Table 10.2   Brief History of Criminal Enterprise Statutes

Federal prosecutors have available two sets of statutes to dismantle criminal enterprises that function like businesses. The continuing criminal enterprise (CCE) statute (21 U.S.C. 848) targets only drug traffickers who are responsible for long-term and elaborate conspiracies. The antiracketeering statute (18 U.S.C. 1951–1968), which includes the Racketeer Influenced and Corrupt Organizations Act (RICO), targets offenders working at the top levels of various kinds of criminal organizations.

Continuing Criminal Enterprise Statute (21 U.S.C. 848)

1984	Enacted
1986	Effective
1987	Fines for first offenders increased from maximum of $100,000 to $2 million for individuals
1988	Mandatory minimum prison terms for first violations increased from 10 to 20 years

Federal Racketeering Statutes (18 U.S.C. 1951ff.)

1934	Interference with commerce by threats or violence (Sec. 1951)
1961	Interstate and foreign travel in aid of racketeering enterprises (Sec. 1952)
1961	Interstate transportation of gambling paraphernalia (Sec. 1953)
1962	Offenses related to employee benefit plans (Sec. 1954)
1970	Illegal gambling businesses (Sec. 1955)
1970	RICO (Secs. 1961–68; amended to clarify or broaden scope of prohibited activities, or adjust penalties in 1978, 1984, 1986, 1988, 1989, 1990)
1984	Use of interstate commerce facilities (including mails) in commission of murder-for-hire (Sec. 1958)
1984	Violent crimes in aid of racketeering activities (Sec. 1959)
1986	Money laundering (Sec. 1956)
1986	Monetary transactions in property derived from specific unlawful activity (Sec. 1957)

SOURCE: Carlson and Finn (1993: 1, 6).

offenses within a ten-year period, and "racketeering activity" is any offense punishable by a year or more in prison. Persons violating this

**Table 10.3   Racketeering Offenders Convicted
July 1, 1987–June 30, 1990, by Specific Racketeering Offense**

CONVICTION OFFENSE	RACKETEERING OFFENDERS	
	*Number**	*Percent*
Racketeering offenses	2,326	100
Interfere with commerce by threats or violence	350	15
Travel in aid of racketeering	654	28
Interfere with employee benefit plans	10	**
Illegal gambling	428	18
Money laundering	179	8
Transactions in property derived from unlawful activity	13	1
RICO	637	27
Multiple offenses	55	2

SOURCE: Carlson and Finn (1993: 4).

*Excludes 14% of racketeering offenders, 460 offenders, for whom a specific statute violation could not be determined.

**Less than 0.5%.

law are subject to extended penalties of up to twenty years imprisonment, fines up to $25,000, forfeiture of any interest in the enterprise, and treble civil damages and dissolution of the enterprise itself (see Tables 10.2 and 10.3).

Although RICO was established to fight organized crime, it has been used to prosecute illegal activities in a county sheriff's department, a state tax bureau, the Philadelphia traffic court, the Tennessee governor's office, and several corporations (Poklemba and Crusco, 1982). This broad application of RICO has made it perhaps the most controversial part of the Organized Crime Control Act.

The disagreement over the proper scope of RICO was ultimately resolved in 1985 in a U.S. Supreme Court case involving two corporations (*Sedima* v. *Imrex Co.*). The case arose from a civil suit between two companies involved in a joint venture where one company thought it was being defrauded by the other in an overbilling scheme. A RICO suit was filed against the other corporation, charging it with mail and wire fraud (to establish the pattern) and claiming $175,000 in overbilling. Treble damages and attorney's fees were sought under RICO.

The U.S. Supreme Court had to determine whether preexisting criminal convictions were required to establish a pattern under RICO and whether simple monetary loss constituted a racketeering injury sufficient for a RICO suit. In a 5–4 decision, the Court held that "no such requirement exists" for prior criminal convictions to initiate a RICO suit, as long as at least two offenses are charged in the suit to establish the pattern. The Court also held that no more harm is required under RICO "separate from the harm from the predicate acts." The RICO suit between the corporations was upheld, thereby permitting the broad application of RICO to all forms of organized crime, whether committed by professional criminals or by corporations. This broad application of the RICO provisions will undoubtedly expand the law's use in the future, and it formed the basis for many of the cases of "insider trading" among Wall Street firms during the 1980s. State RICO laws that apply to patterns of state law violations now exist in half the states.

Clearly, all five investigative tools discussed here involve tradeoffs. It is more than a simple empirical issue to determine whether the socioeconomic costs versus benefits of electronic surveillance, witness immunity, the witness protection program, special grand juries, and the RICO provisions make them desirable law enforcement tools. Value judgments must be made, inasmuch as powerful investigative and prosecution tools may be abused at one time or another. That is, such use of prosecutorial tools likely was not envisioned when they were created. Abuse has been alleged by some in independent counsel Kenneth Starr's investigation of President Clinton during 1997 and 1998, for example. Starr has been accused of "treating the presidency as an organized crime family" by using grand juries, immunity, and threats of prosecution to provide incriminating information (Stanglin, 1998). Whether sufficient safeguards are in place and the abuses are few enough, compared to the results gained in combating organized crime, remains arguable. In order to make educated judgments, however, it is necessary to gather more information regarding the effective uses, and abuses, of these tools in practice.

THE MOB TRIALS
OF THE 1980s AND 1990s

Despite the research findings of the past twenty-five years, the government's approach to organized crime has favored prosecution of alleged leaders rather than alteration of market conditions. The government experienced a great deal of success in the 1980s, however, beginning with the testimony of a number of criminals turned informant. Unlike Joseph Valachi, some of these informants, such as Jimmy Fratianno, appeared to be high-ranking members of organized crime. Although Fratianno's testimony had inconsistencies, it resulted in the conviction of a number of high-ranking organized criminals during that decade (Albanese, 1983). Other insiders were granted immunity or placed in the witness protection program. The result was an unprecedented effort to prosecute organized crime out of existence.

The alleged leaders of sixteen of the twenty-four "Mafia" groups identified by the government were indicted between 1983 and 1986. Nearly 5,000 federal organized crime indictments were issued by grand juries in 1985 alone (Powell et al., 1986). This increase in prosecutions was not due to new laws but rather to the utilization of existing laws and the application of more investigative resources to the problem. On the federal level, the Reagan administration authorized more than 700 federal wiretaps in its first four years, more than double that of the previous four years. Many of the prosecutions of the 1980s took place in New York City and relied on the investigative efforts of a reorganized New York State Organized Crime Task Force. In addition, the RICO provisions came to be utilized more frequently once the U.S. Supreme Court had upheld its broad application in both civil and criminal cases.

Significant organized crime prosecutions continued into the 1990s (Albanese, 1996). Some examples of major racketeering and conspiracy convictions of the decade include the following:

1990: Charles Porter (age 58) and Lewis Raucci (age 61). Leaders of the Pittsburgh organized crime group, they were sentenced to 28 years in prison.

1991: Nicholas Bianco (age 59). A leader of the New England organized crime group, he was sentenced to 11 years in prison.

1992: Victor Orena (age 58). Boss of the Colombo family in New York City, he was sentenced to life in prison.

1992: John Gotti (age 51). Boss of the Gambino family in New York City, he was sentenced to life in prison.

1993: Michael Tacetta (age 46) and Michael Perna (age 50). Leaders of the Lucchese group in New Jersey, they were sentenced to 30 years in prison.

1993: Johnny Eng (age 36). A leader of the Flying Dragons in New York City's Chinatown, he was sentenced to 24 years in prison.

1997: Vincent Gigante (age 69). Leader of the Genovese family in New York City, he was sentenced to 12 years in prison.

1999: Rosario Gangi (age 58). Alleged Genovese family leader in New York City, his sentence is pending.

1999: John "Junior" Gotti (age 35). Alleged boss of the Gambino family in New York City, his sentence is pending.

Many other convictions occurred during the 1990s, but they were generally of persons playing lesser roles in organized crime than were played by those noted above. Importantly, the convictions have continued throughout the 1990s and, thus, indicate the ongoing nature of the Justice Department's efforts against organized crime.

Six facts become apparent when one examines the defendants, their roles, their alleged offenses, and the sentences handed down in these cases.

First, many of the cases clearly were significant. Most involved racketeering convictions that entailed the infiltration of legitimate business through bribery or extortion. The sentences imposed on the principals, excluding the life sentences, average more than twenty-five years per offender.

Second, many of the cases involved organized crime in New York City, although many other parts of the United States were affected as well. Convictions involving organized crime operations in New England, Chicago, Las Vegas, and Philadelphia attest to the national scope of the prosecution results.

Third, the prosecution's focus remains on organized crime of Italian-Americans. The overwhelming majority of cases involved Mafia groups, although conviction of members of the United Bamboo Chinese gang and various Jamaican groups for narcotics distribution and murder conspiracy charges indicates a change in enforcement focus and perhaps a shift in the types of groups participating in organized crime activity.

Fourth, the debate over the existence of a Mafia was finally rendered moot in a 1986 trial, when the defendants (the alleged bosses of the New York City crime families) conceded that the "Mafia exists and has members." Further, the defense confirmed the existence of a "Commission"—a ruling council of leaders of several of the larger Mafia "families" (Jacobs, 1994)—that was mentioned in wiretapped conversations of the defendants. Sicilian informer Tommaso Buscetta stated that he was told by Joseph Bonanno in 1957 that "it was very advisable" to set up a Commission in Sicily "to resolve disputes" among criminal groups (Lubash, 1985). In his autobiography, Bonanno (1984: 127–188) claims to have set up such a commission in America, though he refused to testify in the Commission trial and was jailed for contempt. However, the role of the Commission, according to the defendants, was only to approve new members and to mediate conflicts among the groups. The prosecution argued, however, that four of the defendants participated in "the ruling council of La Cosa Nostra, or the 'Mafia' which directed criminal activity" (Lubash, 1986; Smothers, 1986).

The defense in the Commission trial argued that the Mafia represented a loose social and business association of individuals with similar backgrounds, but without a criminal purpose, that could be likened to a businessmen's professional association whose goal is the *avoidance* of conflict (Magnuson, 1986). Thus, the purpose of the defense's admissions was to challenge the government "to prove it has actually engaged in the crimes of which it has been accused" (Oreskes, 1986). The charges included bid-rigging of concrete prices, extortion, and in the case of one defendant, murder. The charges ultimately were proved, and each defendant was sentenced to a hundred years in prison.

Fifth, at least five significant mob trials resulted in acquittals and mistrials. Some observers have argued that the government's heavy reliance on former criminals as paid government witnesses is a questionable practice. Juries are not always willing to convict a defendant when the case is based largely on the testimony of a criminal turned informant (Dershowitz, 1987).

Finally, many of those convicted during the 1980s and 1990s were senior citizens: The average age of the principals was 62, and some were over 70. Given an average sentence of twenty-five years, even counting parole eligibility, an entirely new leadership likely will emerge among Italian-American organized crime groups.

THE FUTURE OF ORGANIZED CRIME

What impact the outcomes of the mob trials of the 1980s and 1990s will have on organized crime is not yet clear. The combination of convictions of older leaders of criminal groups, convictions for serious crimes, long prison sentences, involvement of a number of cities, and emerging organized crime groups does, however, suggest some interesting projections. Certainly, the mob trials will have some immediate impact on organized crime, although modification of public policy will be required for longer-term changes. The future of organized crime can be characterized by probable changes in the nature of its operations, in its level of violence, and in its primary activities.

The mob trials have resulted in increased violence within and among organized crime groups. John Gotti was convicted in 1992 of planning the 1985 murder of Paul Castellano, the leader of New York City's Gambino family. Gotti sought the family leadership for himself. The car-bomb killing of Frank DeCiccio, a Gotti affiliate, soon after Castellano's murder, likely occurred in retaliation by Castellano loyalists (O'Brien and Kurins, 1991). The violence likely will continue in the struggle for leadership of organized crime groups and in the effort to avoid prosecution through protection of illicit enterprises and the elimination of suspected informants (Anderson, 1979: 144).

Police in New York City and in Los Angeles, for example, have claimed that building murder and other violent crime cases against gang and organized crime offenders is made difficult because of witness intimidation (Curriden, 1994).

A second projection has organized criminals shifting to safer activities that are better insulated from street-level investigation and prosecution. Increasing organized crime involvement in credit card and airline ticket counterfeiting and in illicit toxic waste disposal are examples of this trend (Powell et al., 1986). In 1997, there were federal indictments of more than thirty stockbrokers, corporate officials, and alleged mobsters in New York and New Jersey on charges of securities fraud and racketeering. Each of these cases involved networks of brokers who purchased shares in hundreds of companies at very cheap prices and then sold them to the public at much higher prices (a practice called "chop stocks") (Weiss, 1997a, 1997b). As a result, the infiltration of legitimate business—rather than the more visible activities necessary to cater to the vices of narcotics, gambling, and prostitution—may prove to be an area of greater interest to organized crime, thus blurring the distinction between white collar crime and organized crime.

A third projection involves the sophistication of organized crime. The general success of the mob trials in prosecuting traditional organized crime may result in changes in the operation of illicit enterprises. As McIntosh (1975) suggested, the "technology" or sophistication of organized crime responds to law enforcement effectiveness. Once law enforcement strategy becomes more effective, as the mob trials indicate, "we can expect the criminal technology to reach rapidly the same level of efficiency in order to maintain acceptable levels of success"

(Albanese, 1987b: 73). This sophistication may take the form of increased interest in the *financing* of criminal activities and decreased involvement in the *operation* of criminal enterprises. Gambling and narcotics sales have been cited as the two largest sources of organized crime revenue. It is possible that traditional racketeers who wish to remain in the gambling and narcotics businesses will cease operating these higher-risk enterprises and rather be content to finance other illicit entrepreneurs for a percentage of the profits. Illegal profits can then be laundered through legally owned businesses, such as restaurants and nightclubs. In order to accomplish this, organized criminals may make a greater effort in the future to infiltrate legitimate businesses to obtain access to money for financing and to have the means to launder illicitly obtained cash (Albanese, 1995). Labor union funds and the construction industry have been favorite targets in the past.

As a result, the successful prosecution of organized crime leaders in recent years may be a mixed blessing. Although it may disrupt operations for a short period, it also will shift organized crime activities to safer, but more complex, scams and possibly encourage further organized crime infiltration into legitimate business to finance illicit enterprise and to launder illegally obtained profits.

Without more attention to the market conditions under which organized crime operations emerge and flourish, however, we must resign ourselves to the short-term satisfaction of periodically incapacitating a relatively small number of organized criminals. A longer-term remedy will result only when the economic opportunities for organized crime are better understood and the large market for illicit products is reduced.

CONCLUSION

The goal of this chapter was to challenge the reader's everyday assumptions about organized crime. Most people's notion of organized criminals relies on and perpetuates the Mafia mystique—organized crime conducted by a national band of interlocked families of Italian descent. As our review of the issue indicates, the evidence challenges this notion. Indeed, if we compare it with other models of organized crime based on serious empirical investigation, we find that organized crime is far more local than national in character, that family is of little consequence, and that members of many ethnic groups engage in organized crime. More important, organized crime is driven by local eco-

nomic and business conditions—just as any legitimate local enterprise is driven. This means, of course, that if the criminal justice system pursues only the leaders of organized criminal groups, little control can be exerted over organized crime. To the extent that the government has been successful in prosecuting leaders of local organized crime groups, these groups have been moving to other, more subtle forms of criminal activity, as market conditions would dictate, or they have been replaced by new organized criminal groups who cater to the demands of the illicit marketplace. Ultimately, control of organized crime will occur only when we fully understand and can disrupt the market conditions that shape it.

DISCUSSION QUESTIONS

1. Criminal justice professionals often caution that organized crime is a serious problem for society. Is it? If so, why?

2. Why are the extent and cost of organized crime so difficult to determine?

3. Albanese discusses three models of organized crime. What are they? How different are these models in terms of their assumptions and their implications for control?

4. Is there really a nationally linked Mafia or Cosa Nostra? Discuss the evidence for both sides of this question.

5. What strategies have federal and state governments developed to combat organized crime? Have they been successful?

6. Discuss the projections for the future of organized crime.

REFERENCES

Abadinsky, H. 1981. *The Mafia in America: An Oral History.* New York: Praeger.

Adler, P. A. 1985. *Wheeling and Dealing: An Ethnography of an Upper-Level Drug Dealing and Smuggling Community.* New York: Columbia University Press.

Albanese, J. 1983. "God & the Mafia Revisited: From Valachi to Fratianno." In *Career Criminals.* Edited by G. Waldo. Beverly Hills, CA: Sage.

———. 1987a. "Predicting the Incidence of Organized Crime." In *Organized Crime in America:*

Concepts and Controversies. Edited by T. Bynum. Monsey, NY: Willow Tree Press.

———. 1987b. *Organizational Offenders: Understanding Corporate Crime.* Niagara Falls, NY: Apocalypse.

———. 1993. "Models of Organized Crime." *Handbook of Organized Crime in the United States.* Edited by R. Kelly, K. Chin, and R. Schatzberg. Westport, CT: Greenwood Publishing.

———. 1995. *Contemporary Issues in Organized Crime.* Monsey, NY: Willow Tree Press.

———. 1996. *Organized Crime in America.* 3d ed. Cincinnati: Anderson.

Albini, J. L. 1971. *The American Mafia: Genesis of a Legend.* New York: Irvington.

Anderson, A. G. 1979. *The Business of Organized Crime.* Stanford, CA: Hoover Institution Press.

Arlacchi, P. 1986. *Mafia Business: The Mafia Ethic and the Spirit of Capitalism.* London: Verso.

Bell, D. 1953. "Crime as an American Way of Life." *The Antioch Review* 13: 131–154.

Block, A. A. 1978. "History and the Study of Organized Crime." *Urban Life* 6: 455–474.

———. 1979. "The Snowman Cometh: Coke in Progressive New York." *Criminology* 17 (May): 75–99.

Block, A. A., and W. J. Chambliss. 1981. *Organizing Crime.* New York: Elsevier North Holland.

Block, R. 1977. *Violent Crime.* Lexington, MA: Lexington Books.

Blok, A. 1974. *The Mafia of a Sicilian Village, 1860–1960.* New York: Harper & Row.

Bonanno, J. 1984. *A Man of Honor.* New York: Pocket Books.

Brady, J. P. 1984. "The Social Economy of Arson: Vandals, Gangsters, Bankers and Officials in the Making of an Urban Problem." In *Research in Law, Deviance and Social Control.* Edited by S. Spitzer and A. Scull. Greenwich, CT: JAI Press. 6: 199–242.

Carlson, K., and P. Finn. 1993. *Prosecuting Criminal Enterprises.* Washington, DC: Bureau of Justice Statistics, U.S. Department of Justice.

Chambliss, W. J. 1971. "Vice, Corruption, Bureaucracy, and Power." *Wisconsin Law Review* 4: 1150–1173.

———. 1988. *On the Take: From Petty Crooks to Presidents.* 2d ed. Bloomington: Indiana University Press.

Curriden, M. 1994. "Witness Threats a Problem." *American Bar Association Journal* 80: 18–20.

Dershowitz, A. M. 1987. "Gotti Case Shows Flaws of Buying Witnesses." *The Buffalo News,* March 20, C3.

Dubro, J. 1986. *Mob Rule: Inside the Canadian Mafia.* Toronto: Totem Books.

English, T. J. 1991. *The Westies.* New York: St. Martin's.

Haller, M. H. 1992. "Bureaucracy and the Mafia: An Alternative View." *Journal of Contemporary Criminal Justice* 8: 1–10.

Hawkins, G. 1969. "God and the Mafia." *Public Interest* 14: 24–51.

Hess, H. 1973. *Mafia and Mafiosi: The Structure of Power.* Lexington, MA: Heath.

Ianni, F. A. J., and E. Reuss-Ianni. 1973. *A Family Business: Kinship and Social Control in Organized Crime.* New York: New American Library.

Jacobs, J. 1994. *Busting the Mob: United States V. Cosa Nostra.* New York: New York University Press.

Katz, G. 1983. "Police Bugs Could Tap City for Millions." *USA Today,* April 29, 3.

Krajick, K. 1983. "Should Police Wiretap?: States Don't Agree." *Police Magazine* (May).

Landesco, J. 1929. *Organized Crime in Chicago.* Part III of the Illinois Crime Survey. Chicago: University of Chicago Press.

Lubash, A. H. 1985. "Mafia Member Testifies on Sicily 'Commission'." The *New York Times*, November 1, B3.

———. 1986. "Persico Asks Jury Not to Be Duped by Mafia Label." The *New York Times*, September 19, 1, 24.

Magnuson, E. 1986. "Hitting the Mafia." *Time*, September 29, 14–22.

Maguire, K. , and A. Pastore (eds.). 1998. *Sourcebook of Criminal Justice Statistics, 1997*. Washington, DC: U.S. Department of Justice, Bureau of Justice Statistics.

McIllwain, J. 1997. "From Tong War to Organized Crime: Revising the Historical Perception of Violence in Chinatown." *Justice Quarterly* 14: 25–50.

McIntosh, M. 1975. *The Organization of Crime*. London: Macmillan.

Moore, W. H. 1974. *The Kefauver Committee and the Politics of Crime, 1950–1952*. Columbia: University of Missouri Press.

National Wiretap Commission. 1976. *Electronic Surveillance Report*. National Commission for the Review of Federal and State Laws Relating to Wiretapping and Electronic Surveillance. Washington, DC: U.S. Government Printing Office.

Nelli, H. S. 1981. *The Business of Crime: Italians and Syndicate Crime in the United States*. Chicago: University of Chicago Press.

O'Brien, J. F., and A. Kurins. 1991. *Boss of Bosses: The FBI and Paul Castellano*. New York: Simon and Schuster.

Oreskes, M. 1986. "Commission Trial Illustrates Changes in Attitude on Mafia." The *New York Times*, September 20, B29.

Poklemba, J., and P. Crusco. 1982. "Public Enterprises and RICO: The Aftermath of *United States* v. *Turkette*." *Criminal Law Bulletin* 18: 197–203.

Powell, S., S. Enerson, O. Kelly, D. Collins, and B. Quick. 1986. "Busting the Mob." *U.S. News & World Report*, February 3, 24–31.

President's Commission on Law Enforcement and Administration of Justice. 1967. *Task Force Report: Organized Crime*. Washington, DC: U.S. Government Printing Office.

President's Commission on Organized Crime. 1987. *The Impact: Organized Crime Today*. Washington, DC: U.S. Government Printing Office.

Reuter, P. 1983. *Disorganized Crime: The Economics of the Visible Hand*. Cambridge, MA: MIT Press.

Reuter, P., J. Rubinstein, and S. Wynn. 1983. *Racketeering in Legitimate Industries: Two Case Studies*. Washington, DC: National Institute of Justice.

Rhodes, R. P. 1984. *Organized Crime: Crime Control vs. Civil Liberties*. New York: Random House.

Schlegel, K. 1988. "Life Imitating Art: Interpreting Information from Electronic Surveillances." Pp. 101–112 in *Critical Issues in Criminal Investigation*. 2d ed. Edited by M. J. Palmiotto. Cincinnati: Pilgrimage Press.

Servadio, G. 1978. *Mafioso: A History of the Mafia from Its Origins to the Present Day*. New York: Dell.

Smith, D. C. 1978. "Organized Crime and Entrepreneurship." *International Journal of Criminology and Penology* 6: 161–177.

———. 1980. "Paragons, Pariahs, and Pirates: A Spectrum-Based Theory of Enterprise." *Crime and Delinquency* 26: 358–386.

———. 1990. *The Mafia Mystique*. Rev. Ed. Lanham, MD: University Press of America.

Smothers, R. 1986. "Tapes Played at Mob Trial Focus on Money and Power." The *New York Times*, January 26, 20.

Stanglin, D. 1998. "Starr Gazing." *U.S. News & World Report*, March 2, 19.

Turkus, B. B., and S. Feder. 1951. *Murder, Inc.* New York: Manor Books.

U.S. Senate. 1963. *Organized Crime and Illicit Traffic in Narcotics: Hearings Part I*. Committee on Government Operations Permanent Subcommittee on Investigations. 88th Congress, 1st Session. Washington, DC: U.S. Government Printing Office.

———. 1965. *Report on Organized Crime and Illicit Traffic in Narcotics.* Committee on Government Operations Permanent Subcommittee on Investigations. 89th Congress, 1st Session. Washington, DC: U.S. Government Printing Office.

Weiss, G. 1997a. "The Mob on Wall Street: Why You Can't See It." *Business Week,* March 24, 186–190.

———. 1997b. "Chop Stocks Are on the Rise." *Business Week,* December 15, 112–128.

Chapter Outline

- Privileged Offenders

- Background and Controversy

- Costs and Victims
  Intangible Costs
  Reasons for Underreporting
  The Ultimate Victims

- Legal and Organizational Construction of Responsibility
  Prosecuting Organizations
  The Decision to Prosecute
  Variations in Sentencing
  Civil Prosecution and Regulation
  Other Controls

- Explaining White Collar Crime
  Opportunities
  Predisposed Offenders

- Decision Making and Criminal Careers

- Global White Collar Crime

- Conclusion: The Challenge of White Collar Crime

II

Crimes of Privilege

NEAL SHOVER
University of Tennessee, Knoxville

ANDREW L. HOCHSTETLER
University of Tennessee, Knoxville

Work in the Imperial Food Plant in Hamlet, North Carolina, was unpleasant. Employees in this poultry-processing plant deep-fried chicken parts and complained among themselves about working conditions, but they seldom filed complaints. North Carolina is a right-to-work state, and those who objected openly paid a price for doing so. Plant equipment was aged, and maintenance personnel were kept busy repairing it. On September 3, 1991, hydraulic fluid from a conveyor belt under repair sprayed over a gas-fired chicken fryer. A 30-second fireball sent flames and dense toxic smoke through the plant, which had no fire alarms or sprinkler systems. Employees rushed to escape from the inferno, but many were trapped inside the building. In violation of law, the plant owners had padlocked exit doors, ostensibly to prevent pilferage of meat by employees. By the time firefighters arrived, the plant was destroyed, 25 people were dead, and another 40 were injured (*New York Times*, 1991a). The state of North Carolina subsequently fined the company $808,150 and, the following year, plant owner Emmett Roe pleaded guilty to involuntary manslaughter and was sentenced to nearly 20 years' imprisonment. As part of the plea agreement, charges against the 56-year-old plant manager and Roe's 29-year-old son, who was plant operations manager, were dropped (Aulette and Michalowski, 1993; *Los Angeles Times*, 1992).

On December 4, 1998, the Burlington Northern and Santa Fe Railway Company pleaded guilty to charges that it dumped lead residue near a creek in the Ozark foothills and agreed to pay $19 million in criminal fines, restitution, and cleanup costs. From 1968 to 1994, the railway company had operated a rail siding in Crawford County, Missouri, where it cleaned rail cars used in lead mines, and gondolas containing lead residue concentrate also were dumped. The railroad discharged lead sulfide into a creek without a federal permit, and lead residue was moved to various parts of Crawford County and used as fill materials. The company pleaded guilty to one felony count of violating the federal Superfund law and to one misdemeanor violation of the Clean Air Act. Tests found lead in some private water supplies, but no evidence of lead in any public drinking water supply. In a public statement, the company said the settlement would not affect its fourth-quarter earnings (*St. Louis Post-Dispatch,* 1998).

On the surface, the Burlington Northern Railroad's acts of poisoning the environment and the actions that caused 25 deaths in Hamlet, North Carolina, appear dissimilar in their origins and in the harm they caused. Beyond this, however, they share one important characteristic: They are white collar crimes.

PRIVILEGED OFFENDERS

Many if not most white collar crimes are committed by offenders whose lives are distinguished by privilege to some degree. Much of this is rooted in class inequality. Material precariousness and the unrelenting need to generate income for basic needs are alien to their worlds and lives. Their automobiles start on command; their refrigerators and wine racks are adequately, if not amply, stocked; their homes are commodious, comfortable, and secure; and their children are well clothed and well fed. They are privileged, and this allows them not only options but also the leisure to evaluate their options carefully before making choices.

The privilege of class is the most important characteristic of white collar criminals, but they are also privileged by the respectable work they do. "Dirty work" consists of jobs or tasks that most people want carried out albeit the work is undesirable (Hughes, 1971). Collecting and processing household trash or any kind of manual labor are examples. In addition to their location in a wealth-and-property hierarchy, white collar criminals occupy privileged positions in the hierarchy of professions: Thus, when they confront officialdom or mid-level bureaucrats, they receive a polite and sympathetic hearing; they are rarely subjected to gratuitous, sanctimonious, and classist comments about their "inappropriate" behavior; and they stand a reasonable chance of prevailing—all in contrast to less-privileged criminals.

White collar criminals come from many backgrounds. Wealth, respectability, and privilege are not discrete variables, and any population—particularly in large and demographically heterogeneous nation states—can be arrayed on a continuum from the poorest and least reputable to the wealthiest and most respectable citizens. The expanse is extremely wide, encompassing minority single mothers with annual incomes of less than $10,000, attorneys and medical doctors with investment accounts, and presidents of *Fortune* 500 corporations whose annual compensation exceeds $2 million. The ranks of white collar criminals represent an equally expansive range and variety of backgrounds, occupations, and incomes, from bank tellers to high-level political leaders. The total variation depends on how broadly one defines white collar crime, but the presence of many non-elite offenders is one reason some investigators refer to white collar crime as "crime of the middle classes" (Weisburd et al., 1991). What distinguishes white collar criminals, however, is the privilege afforded by an assured and adequate income and by their respectable status. The poor and disreputable fodder routinely encountered in police stations and in studies of street crime seldom appear in the ranks of white collar criminals.

In their innocuous appearance, the crimes committed by white collar criminals differ conspicuously from street crimes. The latter typically are committed by confronting victims or entering their homes or businesses to steal, whereas white collar crimes generally are committed by using guile, deceit, or misrepresentation to create and exploit for illicit advantage the appearance of a routine, legitimate transaction. Fraud, which is the use of deception to secure unfair or unlawful gain, is the core component of many white collar crimes.

Other white collar crimes are committed by abusing for illicit purposes the power of organizational position or public office. This can take a variety of forms, some as subtle and unobtrusive as fraud and others as violent and disruptive of lives as assault. When employers knowingly or negligently subject their workers to an unsafe work environment, they commit white collar crime. When elected officials receive kickbacks from businesses for awarding them contracts for public work (*Pittsburgh Post-Gazette,* 1998) or coerce from their employees contributions for political campaigns, they commit white collar crime (*Cleveland Plain Dealer,* 1996). Consider the crimes of David Lanier, a judge and former mayor of Dyersburg, Tennessee (*Memphis Commercial Appeal,* 1992; *Washington Post,* 1997b). In 1992, a federal jury convicted Lanier on seven counts of sexually assaulting women who worked in his courthouse or came before him with legal matters. Evidence suggested that he had engaged in this pattern of conduct over a

period of years. One victim, a 26-year-old woman with a child custody case before Lanier, testified that she was forced to perform oral sex on him in his chambers. Prior to judicial imposition of sentence of 25 years' confinement, the prosecutor cast Lanier as a criminal for whom "power was the aphrodisiac . . . [Victims'] crying turned him on."

BACKGROUND AND CONTROVERSY

In America, interest in the criminal behavior of citizens not handicapped by poverty and disrepute dates to the early years of the twentieth century. From the outset, scholarly objectives were fused with strong elements of muckraking and moral condemnation. Among the first to turn attention to crimes of privilege was sociologist E. A. Ross (1907). Noting that changing conditions of social and economic life had created both opportunities for and new forms of crime, Ross referred to those who exploit these criminal opportunities as "criminaloids." He warned that

> [T]oday the villain most in need of curbing is the respectable, exemplary, trusted personage who, strategically placed at the focus of a spider-web of fiduciary relations, is able from his office-chair to pick a thousand pockets, poison a thousand sick, pollute a thousand minds, or imperil a thousand lives. It is the great-scale, high-voltage [criminal] that needs the shackle (pp. 29–30).

Leaving little doubt as to the moral reproach he believed they deserved, Ross likened criminaloids to "wolves" (p. 89). His analysis and call received little attention from academia, and three decades passed before another academic turned his attention to the problem of upper-world crime. Unlike Ross, his successor left an enduring legacy.

In his presidential address to the American Sociological Society in 1939, Edwin Sutherland coined the term and called for more attention to "white-collar crime." He defined it "crime committed by a person of respectability and high social status in the course of his occupation" (Sutherland, 1983: 7). This formulation gave initial direction to scholarly investigations of white collar crime and its perpetrators, but investigators since have struggled with the controversies manifest in Sutherland's definition, which highlights both the status characteristics of white collar criminals and the crimes committed in their occupational role. Sutherland considered their respectable social status to be the most important characteristic distinguishing white collar criminals from street offenders (Geis, 1992). Status-based definitions are urged by all who, like Sutherland, believe that differentials of power and influence are key to identifying, framing satisfactorily, and unraveling fundamental questions about crime and crime control (e.g., Braithwaite, 1991).

In contrast to this approach, others call for a formal, status-neutral definition that would obviate both the need for and the utility of the category white collar crime. Abuse of trust, or trust crime, is an example of this approach (Shapiro, 1990). Abuse of trust is exploitation of a fiduciary position by an agent responsible for custody, discretion, information, or property rights. It occurs when bankers make unsecured loans to friends at low interest, when accounting firms issue optimistic reports for businesses on the brink of insolvency, when managers privy to corporate secrets whisper in a broker's ear, or when service station clerks steal and sell customers' credit card numbers.

When recast as abuse of trust, the definition of white collar crime expands to include victimization by neighborhood auto repair shops and local construction companies. The odds that a given citizen will be a victim of these kinds of white collar crime are much higher than the odds of being targeted by international banking conspirators. The scope of behaviors encompassed by abuse of trust is extremely broad, and this approach makes it easy to lose sight of potentially important distinguishing characteristics of "respectable" criminals, the crimes they commit, and reactions to their crimes.

COSTS AND VICTIMS

Regardless of how one defines it, no one seriously disputes that white collar crime exacts a heavy aggregate financial and bodily toll that dwarfs losses to street crime. Some white collar crimes have hundreds or thousands of victims, and losses from only a few highly publicized incidents can surpass the total annual monetary cost of street crime. The savings and loan debacle of the 1980s, for example, is expected to cost American taxpayers more than $300 billion (Calavita et al., 1997; Zimring and Hawkins, 1993). However, it is more often true that no one can estimate with precision or confidence the sum exacted by white collar crime. There are no authoritative procedures or guidelines for doing so, and results are influenced heavily by the assumptions one starts with. Development of comprehensive, reliable estimates requires systematically collected data on the prevalence of white collar crime, the numbers of victims, and their losses. At present these data do not exist. In marked contrast to information about street crime, data on white collar offenses and offenders are not routinely collected, collated, and disseminated by centralized offices of state or federal government (Reiss and Biderman, 1980). For those interested in gaining a statistical picture of the extent and distribution of white collar crime, there is no counterpart of the Federal Bureau of Investigation's Uniform Crime Reporting program.

Although detailed statistics are not available, we know nonetheless that white collar crime exacts a serious toll. The tangible costs of white collar crime include victims' loss of money, property, and physical injuries or death, but less-tangible costs include pain, suffering, and reduced quality of life. Estimates of the harm caused by crime are influenced heavily by whether the less-tangible costs are acknowledged, measured, and priced. The less-tangible costs of white collar crime may be singularly wide-reaching and destructive (Meier and Short, 1983). The number of workplace casualties caused by criminal action or neglect, for example, cannot be determined, but few doubt it is high. Employer failure to provide a safe and healthful working environment exacts an especially heavy toll (Reiman, 1995). Damage to health generally is incremental and long term rather than catastrophic; high levels of workplace carcinogens, for example, take time off the end of lives, long after employees have been replaced or have retired.

Especially egregious and destructive crimes attract the bulk of media and scholarly attention, but a substantial proportion of white collar crimes, clearly, are not complex, have few victims, and result in modest financial losses. Still, the number of citizens victimized annually by white collar crimes is large (Titus and Gover, 1999). Nearly one-third (31 percent) of respondents in a national sample of American households reported, for example, that an attempt to defraud them by telemarketing or investment schemes had been made in the preceding 12 months. Fifteen percent of respondents were victims of a successful fraud, with an average monetary loss of $217 (Titus et al., 1995). Repeat victimization is also a serious problem (Titus and Gover, 1999).

Intangible Costs

Many white collar crimes probably leave victims more angry and inconvenienced following modest financial losses than emotionally wrecked and financially destroyed. For some, however, the impact of white collar crime matches in intensity the experiences of street-crime victims (Shover et al., 1994). One study found that nearly 30 percent of major fraud victims reported a serious depressive episode in the 20 months following their loss (Ganzini et al., 1990). The effects of victimization, moreover, can ripple far beyond immediate victims to harm others. When organizations dispose of hazardous materials in reckless and criminal fashion, the costs may include increased risk of health problems for innocent parties as well as the financial costs of cleaning up the poisonous legacies (Barnett, 1994; Pearce and Tombs, 1998).

Because it violates trust, white collar crime also has a less-tangible cost: It may breed distrust, lower social morale, and "attack the fundamental principles of [social] institutions" (Sutherland, 1983: 10). When public officials use their office for illicit enrichment, or when police and prosecutors knowingly manufacture evidence, the result may be harm to public trust in government and loss of confidence in public institutions, leaders, and processes (Meier and Short, 1983). When public officials and agencies appear to tolerate or condone white collar crime, it may complicate the task of convincing citizens they should be honest. Following the collapse of the Soviet Union, for example, the hardships caused by economic restructuring and official corruption and inefficiency led to a massive tax revolt by citizens and businesses. Interviews by a news correspondent suggested that

> people avoid taxes in Russia because they figure the state's going to get them anyway. Mother Russia wants their money, usually in the form of bribes to one or several of her employees. . . . [A]nd then there is the sense many Russians have: that their tax ruble will be squandered on some high-ranking official's Mediterranean villa (*Boston Globe,* 1998).

Rampant and highly visible white collar crime erodes public morality and commitment to conformity by suggesting that everyone is behaving selfishly.

Confidence in economic institutions may be eroded as well. In the absence of trust, "people would not delegate discretionary use of their funds to other entrepreneurs . . . [and] capitalism would break down as funds were stuffed into mattresses, savings accounts, and solo business enterprises rather than invested in the business ventures of . . . corporations" (Shapiro, 1984: 2). In 1997, when thousands of Albanian citizens lost money in collapsed pyramid schemes, it caused a run on banks, riots, and political chaos (*Washington Post,* 1997a). The potential delegitimation effects of white collar crime are extremely important, but they have been neglected by investigators (Peters and Welch, 1980; Shover et al., 1994).

Reasons for Underreporting

One of the most important reasons that statistical data on white collar crime are deficient is that a large but unknown proportion of it goes unreported; many victims are unaware they have been victimized. Unlike robbery, burglary, and other street crimes, acts of white collar crime typically do not stand out in victims' experiences; many have the look of routine, legitimate transactions. How many persons overcharged a few pennies on grocery purchases are both aware of this and have reason to believe it stems from company policy? The number is not large. How many of these would do something about it? The number is small. Victims who realize or suspect what has happened may have no idea where to report the incident; it is characteristic of white collar crimes that the appropriate places or agencies to report the incident either are unknown or unfamiliar. For these reasons, many victims do not report, as was true of 85 percent of fraud victims in a sample of American households (Titus et al., 1995). Those who do report to authorities are motivated by hopes of recovering what they lost or of protecting others from a similar experience. Victims who do not report frequently believe the incident either was not worth the trouble of doing so or that no real harm was done. Others elect to handle the matter privately. These attitudes are appreciably different from what is known about the reporting decisions of street-crime victims. Another important reason victims of white collar crimes do not report is that, often, they reserve a measure of blame for themselves. Believing they should have been more careful in the first place, victims often feel a sense of embarrassment and prefer that others not learn what happened (Levi, 1992; Shover et al., 1994). The uncertainties and problems of white collar crime victims give offenders a substantial advantage over their less-privileged criminal cousins.

Victims who find their way to the police, prosecutors, or regulatory officials generally meet with experiences remarkably similar to and no less frustrating than the experiences of street-crime victims. Often they must negotiate a maze of agencies and institutions, most of uncertain jurisdiction and commitment; criminal-justice agents generally receive little training on how to recognize and respond to white collar crimes. A study of fraud in California that victimized many elderly citizens notes the "callous indifference that the system demonstrates toward those whom it is particularly charged with assisting." The investigators commented further that many victims

> feel their needs have extremely low priority and that, at best, they are tolerated and then often with ill humor. Their role, they say, seems much like that of the expectant father in the hospital at delivery time: necessary for things to have gotten underway in the past but at the moment rather superfluous and mildly bothersome. . . . [T]he offender, at least, is regarded by criminal justice functionaries as a doer, an antagonist, someone to be wary of, . . . The victim, on the other hand, is part of the background scenery (Geis, 1976: 14–15).

Although research on victims of white collar crime typically begins with and does not extend beyond individuals, organizations also are harmed by it. Remarkably little is known about them and their reactions to the experience, but harmful effects are easy to imagine. Small businesses, for example, may be forced into bankruptcy and their employees onto unemployment rolls. Many organizational victims of white collar crime perhaps have an interest in keeping quiet about their experience. Knowledge of their apparent vulnerability or incompetence, particularly if it reaches investors, creditors, or potential customers, could erode confidence in managers' acumen. For charitable organizations, public trust is a powerful determinant of financial contributions, effectiveness, and stability. In 1995, a federal jury in New York City found William Aramony, former president of United Way of America, guilty of fraudulently diverting for his own use large sums of the charity's money. The stolen funds were used to pay for chauffeurs, luxury apartments, and exotic vacations for the defendant and his teenage girlfriend. Other monies were given to a friend who operated a charitable company, and large sums were funneled into Aramony's personal accounts (*New York Times,* 1995a). His attorney unsuccessfully argued that Aramony's crimes were caused by shrinkage in the area of the brain that controls impulses and inhibitions. He also argued in mitigation that Aramony had "given more to this country than any man I have ever known. . . . [H]e has fed the hungry, clothed the naked [and] given homes to the homeless" (*New York Times,* 1995a). Convicted of multiple charges, the 67-year-old Aramony was sentenced to seven years in prison. For several years thereafter, United Way funding drives suffered from public knowledge that funds had been shepherded incompetently.

The Ultimate Victims

When public bureaucracies are victimized by white collar crime, the larger community of taxpaying citizens may be the ultimate victim. They must pay the fare, for example, when local school districts are charged artificially high prices for products because of price-fixing by ostensibly competitive suppliers. For more than a decade, for example, major American fluid milk producers rigged bids for milk sold in school lunch programs, costing taxpayers millions of dollars (*Knoxville News-Sentinel,* 1993; *Washington Post,* 1991). The bid-rigging involved some of the nation's largest dairies and extended into 20 states. As of 1993, $91.4 million in criminal fines and civil damages had been levied, and 48 individuals and 43 companies had been convicted of or had pleaded guilty to federal criminal charges.

LEGAL AND ORGANIZATIONAL CONSTRUCTION OF RESPONSIBILITY

Because a form of conduct is demonstrably and seriously injurious does not ensure it will be the focus of public or private controls. The state can turn a blind eye toward harmful behaviors or choose to make them the focus of attention. It can take the lead in identifying and crafting controls, or it can wait until pressed to do so through action by citizens and organized groups. If it does elect to take action, the state can fashion responses and remedies ranging from revocation of professional license to civil penalties and, ultimately, to criminal sanctions.

The outcome of campaigns for new or tougher controls on a form of conduct is never assured, and nowhere is this more true than of efforts to impose new restrictions on business interests. The state of the economy and the level of corporate profits are critical contextual determinants of the reception afforded reformers; the likelihood that they will be successful increases during economic good times and decreases dramatically during recessionary periods (Shover et al., 1986). In addition, many harmful practices and behaviors do not win the kind of popular condemnation needed for successful criminalization, and this may be particularly true of campaigns to impose new or more effective controls on powerful interests. These efforts invariably meet with opposition from trade and professional organizations who typically charge that harmful practices are attributable to a few bad apples and that most individuals or firms are exemplary citizens. They claim, therefore, that proposed legislation either is unnecessary and heavy handed or that it would harm legitimate economic interests.

Would-be burglars and robbers are neither consulted nor listened to when officials shape burglary statutes and penalties, but it is very different for more-privileged offenders; they and their representatives play an active part in crafting the laws and regulatory standards that circumscribe their conduct. Through monetary contributions and social contacts, they gain access to legislators to ensure their views are made known and taken seriously (Lofquist, 1993). The actions of privileged interests are motivated by the wish to avoid restrictions on their discretionary behaviors and, where loss or concession is unavoidable, to accept the obligation to do only what is "practicable." In this way, even criminalization movements that appear successful may yield statutes that are little more than symbolic threats to injurious conduct (Calavita, 1983).

Successful criminalization is the exception. The bulk of the state's effort and output instead is rules that carry minimal civil penalties for most forms of white collar rule-breaking; the body of statute law that organizations and citizens in their occupational roles are expected to meet is small when compared with the volume of regulatory rules that confronts them. Their success at defeating, stalling, or converting to their own purposes legislation meant to criminalize their harmful behaviors is the first step in a process of accumulating advantages afforded to white collar criminals by the state (Yeager, 1992).

Prosecuting Organizations

Legislative provision of criminal penalties for injurious conduct does not ensure that they will be used frequently or that their full force will be felt by offenders. State agencies and functionaries are given substantial discretion in these matters; officials have at their disposal an array of options for responding to white collar crime. In spite of this, the overwhelming majority of white collar offenders avoid prosecution and severe sanctions because investigating and responding to their crimes can be an expensive and resource-depleting enterprise. One reason is that many of their crimes are organizational in nature.

In the industrialized and post-industrialized world, most individuals are employed by and in organizations. In local labor union offices, in state agencies, or in business firms ranging in size from three-employee painting contractors to the General Motors Corporation, they labor on behalf of their organizational employer. Many white collar crimes are committed by the self-employed in their occupational role, and others are committed for exclusively personal goals or enrichment by employees, managers, or owners of organizations. Motivated by desire to contribute to or accomplish organizational goals, individuals or groups employed by and in legitimate organizations commit a variety of crimes (Ermann and Lundman, 1978). Organizational white collar crime occurs, for example, when corporations negligently conduct and report the results of medical tests (*Wall Street Journal,* 1995b). The fact that organizational crime is distinguished by the subsidiary importance of individual reward in favor of organizational benefit (Clinard and Quinney, 1973) does not deny that participants may benefit personally in some ways. Medical doctors employed part-time by kidney dialysis firms, for example,

sometimes receive financial bonuses, cars, and other perks for drumming up referrals from their private practices (*New York Times,* 1995b).

Organizational characteristics and dynamics generally play some part in the onset and the course of organizational white collar crimes (e.g., Needleman and Needleman, 1979; Jamieson, 1994)—including indoctrination and incentive programs, differential authority, specialized expertise, and formalized channels of communication—not only provide opportunities for crime but also facilitate individual willingness to participate. Organizations serve criminals by diffusing responsibility and by providing confidence in organizational opacity to external scrutiny (Katz, 1980).

Local-level officials may have difficulty investigating organizational-level crime. They have finite budgets and personnel resources and must use them judiciously. When they investigate suspected crimes, officials routinely encounter behaviors that can range from straightforward and easily understood acts to complex behaviors of many individuals that are difficult to comprehend and reconstruct. The problems of investigating and prosecuting unsophisticated white collar crimes committed by individuals are marginally greater than problems associated with street crimes, but more-complex crimes frequently present the challenge of confronting large and powerful organizations. The organizational veil obstructs and can make virtually impossible the task of determining how crimes occurred, who was responsible for them, and who participated (Wheeler and Rothman, 1982). By the time prosecutors pinpoint the origins of illegal decisions in an organization, time has passed, cover stories have been constructed, and a defense has been mounted.

Effective investigation and prosecution of white collar crimes require that reactive law enforcement be dispensed with in favor of techniques commonly employed against syndicated crime: undercover investigators, informants, and sting operations. Threats and inducements are used to elicit information from knowledgeable insiders about how crimes occurred and the identities of participants. This is one reason why guilty but key participants in white collar crimes may avoid harsh sanctions: Their centrality and the information they can provide give them bargaining power with regulators and prosecutors. The words of a street criminal could not be more accurate:

> [Dealing] is the backbone of American justice. It doesn't matter if you've killed your kindly old parents, robbed the orphans' fund, or criminally molested an entire Sunday school class; if you have something to deal with, you can disentangle yourself from the law without earning a single gray hair behind bars. . . . The whole thing is marvelously flexible (MacIsaac, 1968: 204–205).

Evidence of forthcoming prosecution can set off a "mad rush to the courthouse" by suspects willing to trade information for immunity or lenient penalties (Ross, 1980).

The Decision to Prosecute

What factors do local prosecutors take into account in screening cases of possible organizational crime? (Benson and Cullen, 1998). Data collected from 419 urban American prosecutors and case studies of four jurisdictions show that they pay particular attention to the number and the extent of physical injuries to victims, whether there was evidence of multiple offenses, and the extent of economic harm caused by offenders. Their decisions also are heavily influenced by the availability of resources and occasionally by concern for local economic interests. Prosecutors indicated that they sometimes do not aggressively pursue crimes committed by local businesses for fear of harming employment and the local economy.

When guilty individuals cannot be identified or clear-cut evidence of criminal intent cannot be put together, prosecutors may decide to charge or pursue settlement with the offending organization instead of with individual employees. At the University of Tennessee, a 1998 investigation, for example, discovered that for eight years, employees of Follett Campus Resources, a company responsible for buying used books at contractually established prices and reselling them to the campus bookstore, had been underpaying students and overcharging the bookstore. All purchases were transacted in cash and no receipts were issued, but the investigation indicated that students typically were underpaid between 50¢ and $3 per book. Investigators were unable to determine how much money was taken, but the volume of books traded suggested it was substantial. When they were unable to identify responsible individuals, prosecutors declined criminal prosecution, and Follett instead paid a settlement of $330,000. (*Knoxville News-Sentinel,* 1998).

Success at identifying culpable individuals does not ensure successful prosecution; compared with street offenders, white collar offenders are more likely to retain private defense counsel who can contest charges and offer exculpatory interpretations of the offending behaviors. This increases the costs of prosecution and makes prosecutors and regulatory officials more receptive to settlements that provide lenient punishment and settlement terms in exchange for reducing moral condemnation (Weisburd et al., 1991). In 1991, for example, Stanford University came under scrutiny by the U.S. Navy for improper expenditure of research funds. The Navy charged that university officials had used federal funds to pay for a variety of activities of dubious relationship to funded research grants, including wedding expenses for Stanford's president, silverware, silk sheets, and upkeep of a yacht donated to the university's athletic department. Due in part to the controversy surrounding the case, Stanford's president resigned in 1992, and in 1993 the university "quietly repaid $1.2 million, a far cry from the $200 million Naval investigators claimed [Stanford had] overbilled the government" (*Baltimore Sun,* 1994). The Navy in turn asserted in a written statement that "it does not have a claim that Stanford engaged in fraud, misrepresentation, or other wrongdoing."

Variations in Sentencing

For defendants whose crimes are disposed of in criminal court, matters usually are not as bleak as the institutional setting would suggest. Judges commonly justify not imposing prison time by citing defendants' suffering and damaged reputations caused by their arrest and prosecution. When sentencing Medicaid fraudsters, for example,

> [J]udges recognize that damage to a physician's reputation is a form of punishment in itself. As one Medicaid official noted, "You put [a doctor's] name on the front page of the paper as a thief, you've destroyed him." . . . In this peculiar bit of folk wisdom, falls from high places are the stuff of tragedy, but the tumbles of those who had not climbed so high are assumed to be less

painful—the latter are supposed to suffer less because they are accustomed to having so little. Nonetheless, judges typically refer to the loss of standing already experienced by a white-collar criminal as a basis for a light sentence (Jesilow et al., 1992: 99).

Table 11.1, which compares statutory penalties for selected federal white collar crimes with those for street crimes, shows a substantial differential in presumptive sentences. Presumptive sentences are the range of months from which judges must choose to sentence unless aggravating or mitigating factors are present; aggravating factors permit higher sentences, whereas mitigating factors permit lower ones. Columns 3 and 6 list several aggravating factors and the presumptive sentences they require when no previous criminal convictions and no other factors are present. Although Table 11.1 does not take sufficient account of the immense discretion available to prosecutors and the myriad considerations that influence sentencing, it does show that more stringent penalties are reserved for offenders whose booty is extracted using the methods of the street. Offenders whose criminal transactions do not take place in the street and do not require physical confrontations with victims are not punished as severely. Sentencing enhancements can add significantly to the penalties imposed on white collar criminals, but sentences as lengthy as those routinely handed out to street offenders are judicial options for only the most gluttonous or destructive white collar defendants.

Research has shown that the nature and extent of defendants' prior criminal record, the seriousness of their crimes, and whether criminal intent is clearly evident are among the strongest determinants of sentencing outcome.

Table 11.1   Presumptive Sentences and Selected Aggravating Factors for White Collar and Street Crimes

WHITE COLLAR CRIME	PRESUMPTIVE SENTENCE (months)	SELECTED AGGRAVATING FACTORS	PRESUMPTIVE SENTENCE (months)
Commercial bribery and kickback/$ gain:		Jeopardized soundness of financial institution	51–63
$2,000	0–6		
$250,000	24–30		
$1.5 million	33–41		
Conflict of interest by federal officers and employees	0–6	Planned harm to government	6–12
Insider trading/$ gain:		Abuse of position of trust or special skill at $120,000	24–30
$120,000	18–24		
$1.5 million	33–41		
$20 million	51–63		
Mishandling of hazardous toxic substances or pesticides	0–6	Substantial likelihood of death or serious injury	24–30
Extortion under color of official right:		More than one incident; pervasive corruption of government	May warrant upward departure
$2,000	6–12		
$250,000	27–33		
$1.5 million	33–41		
Bid-rigging, price-fixing, or market allocation agreements among competitors ($/volume of affected commerce):		Organizer or leader of a conspiracy involving four or more people	15–21
$1–4,000	6–12		
$1.5 million	10–16		
$20 million	21–27		
$200 million	24–30		

SOURCE: U.S. Sentencing Commission (1995).

Table 11.1 *(continued)*

STREET CRIME	PRESUMPTIVE SENTENCE (months)	SELECTED AGGRAVATING FACTORS	PRESUMPTIVE SENTENCE (months)
Residential burglary:		More than minimal planning	30–37
$2,500	24–30		
$250,000	37–46	Theft or use of firearm	27–33
$1.5 million	46–57		
Business burglary:		More than minimal planning	15–21
$2,500	10–16		
$250,000	21–27		
$1.5 million	27–33	Theft or use of firearm	15–21
Cocaine trafficking:		Dangerous weapon possessed	33–41
25–50 grams	27–33		
300–400 grams	41–51	Use of special skill	33–41
2–3.5 kilograms	78–97		
		Unusually high quantity	May warrant upward departure
Aggravated assault	18–24	More than minimal planning;	24–30
		dangerous weapon brandished;	27–33
		life-threatening injury	37–46
Extortion by force or threat of injury:		Firearm was brandished	41–51
		Preparation to carry out a threat of injury	37–46
$2,000	27–33		
$250,000	37–46		
$1.5 million	46–57		
Larceny:		Jeopardized the soundness of a financial institution;	51–63
$1,000	0–6		
$10,000	4–10		Enhancement based on amount of material stolen
$70,000	10–16	firearms or drugs stolen	
$1.5 million	27–33		

Prosecutors and judges use as indicators of seriousness the financial or social harm caused by defendants, the number and types of their victims, and the legally prescribed range of penalties for their crimes (Wheeler et al., 1988). Offenders who victimize many people drawn disproportionately or exclusively from unusually vulnerable groups and who give indisputable evidence of sustained criminal intent receive the heaviest penalties. (These case characteristics are strong predictors of sentences for street-level offenders as well.) Beyond this, however, it is difficult to capture or describe the conflicting results from individual-level research on the sentencing of white collar criminals. Not only is it difficult in these studies to determine whether sentencing disparity is caused by sociodemographic characteristics of the offender or by the offense, but there may also be contextual variation in sentencing; statistical relationships may not work the same in all jurisdictions.

The extent and the source of inter-class variation in official punishment is one of the most important problems in criminology. Research on the sentencing of white collar offenders has little to say about it, because most research in this area is limited to examination of intra-class variation. Put differently, because the samples used in sentencing studies generally do not include appreciable numbers of the very wealthy and privileged, the capacity to examine sentences across the full range of wealth and status is absent.

It is worth keeping in mind, moreover, that at several points of the criminal process, defendants can be diverted from the path that ends in judicial sentencing. Their success at earlier stages may be so great that, by sentencing time where official decisions are most visible, few elite criminals remain and evidence of leniency is least apparent. Analysis of sentencing decisions erroneously creates the appearance of equal justice and severity, but criminal court sentencing of white collar criminals is not representative of the overall treatment afforded them and their crimes by the state apparatus (Mann, 1985). More than 60 percent of fines and civil penalties levied against corporations under criminal statutes are less than $10,000 (Etzioni, 1993). Owing to the efforts of the U.S. Sentencing Commission, some modest increases are evident in recent years, but penalties imposed on white collar criminals and their organizations generally are less severe than sentences meted out to street offenders.

When responding to white collar crimes and illegalities, officials generally opt for conciliatory and restorative interventions rather than criminal penalties; use of harsh sanctions is extremely infrequent (Shover et al., 1986; Weisburd et al., 1991; Jesilow et al., 1992). Typical are findings from an analysis of 499 investigations undertaken by the U.S. Securities and Exchange Commission between 1948 and 1972 (Shapiro, 1985). Of every 100 suspects investigated, 93 had committed securities violations that carry criminal penalties, and legal action was taken against one-half of these; 11 were selected for criminal action, 6 were indicted, 5 were convicted, and 3 were sentenced to prison. In other words, civil, administrative, and diversionary actions were the norm. Analysis of all actions taken against 477 of the largest U.S. manufacturing firms in 1975 and 1976 produced similar findings: 75.8 percent received no sanctions, 21 percent received civil fines, and only 2.4 percent received criminal fines (Clinard and Yeager, 1980).

Civil Prosecution and Regulation

In light of the fiscal and investigatory barriers to the use of criminal sanctions for white collar offenders, prosecutors frequently pursue civil or administrative remedies instead when crime is apparent. Uncertain of their ability to convict specific individuals and lacking the resources needed to investigate more extensively, they opt for the less-onerous standard of proof these responses require. A 1991 case provides an example: Federal worker safety regulations require mines to keep coal dust levels in mines below 2 milligrams per cubic meter of air. To monitor the level of coal dust, air samples are taken by filters encased in collection devices at various locations in the mine. The filters must be changed periodically, and used ones sent to the appropriate mine safety agency. Discovery of high levels of coal dust can lead to the mine's shutdown. According to agency reports, mine operators were vacuuming the filters or spraying them before use with a household dust-reducing product to keep them from accumulating dense layers of coal dust. The regulatory agency received 4,710 faked samples from 847 coal mines across the United States, or 40 percent of the mines it is charged with sampling. In response, the U.S. Department of Labor imposed on 500 mining companies a total of $5 million in civil penalties for tampering with safety testing equipment. Despite what could be seen as lenient treatment, many of the companies appealed the imposition of these penalties (*New York Times,* 1991b).

In addition to the proscriptions and standards of criminal and civil law, administrative controls monitor the practices of organizations and the occupational conduct of citizens. At all levels of government, from local to national, a host of regulatory agencies and personnel are empowered by legislative bodies to monitor and enforce standards of fair and reasonable behavior. Established before the turn of the twentieth century, the Interstate Commerce Commission was one of the first and has since been

joined by a host of others, from the familiar Securities and Exchange Commission and the Environmental Protection Agency to the not-so-familiar Office of Surface Mining Reclamation and Enforcement. The first line of responsibility for controlling many forms of white collar crime is lodged in these regulatory bureaucracies.

However, more than five decades of research raise persistent questions about the effectiveness of these agencies. Fronted by a phalanx of attorneys, publicists, and hired technical experts, the most powerful groups and firms subjected to oversight press upon regulatory agencies their self-interested notions of what are fair and reasonable rules and responses to violations. Unlike reformers, the companies are in the battle for the long haul, they press the fight on many fronts, and their advance, if largely imperceptible, is relentless. Their efforts are helped by the fact that many reformers eventually relax their guard or abandon the field for other causes, assuming that once put in place, regulation will rectify old problems. This is one reason that critics have pointed to the apparent capture of regulatory agencies by the industries they ostensibly regulate. Overall, most agencies seem unable or unwilling to mount serious efforts against white collar criminals.

With this in mind, some academics, policymakers, and business leaders have suggested that regulatory enforcement is best accomplished when the enforcers and those subject to regulation work cooperatively to promote and achieve compliance (Braithwaite, 1983; Reiss, 1984). Labeled the "compliance approach" or cooperative regulation, this movement has been strong and pervasive at all levels of government. The potential shortcomings of compliance strategies, however, are worrisome: Companies may take advantage of cooperative and lenient regulators (Pearce and Tombs, 1990; Snider, 1993).

Regulators with a mandate to cooperate with business are easily controlled or captured. Using punitive sanctions only as a last resort undermines their efficacy; as advocates of crime-control policies grounded in the notion of crime as choice point out, permissiveness breeds further crime. Some companies will get by with whatever violations and crimes they can, secure in the knowledge that they can redress those for which they are caught before costly punishments are imposed.

Other Controls

Besides the web of state organizations and personnel engaged in detecting, investigating, and responding to white collar misconduct and crime, a variety of private organizations do the same. The American Medical Association and similar professional societies, for example, promulgate and enforce codes of ethics and generally accepted practices. Most such societies also have procedures for hearing complaints of improper conduct and imposing sanctions. The New York Stock Exchange and the Chicago Board of Trade are examples of organizations that employ private membership requirements, rule-making machinery, and enforcement procedures as controls on the conduct of members. Private parties may file civil complaints against individuals or organizations charging them with harmful conduct, and courts can impose substantial awards for charges found to have merit. Civil complaints may be filed in addition to or in lieu of criminal charges.

Several states and the federal government have enacted legislation providing employment protection and, in some cases, monetary rewards for so-called "whistleblowers." Under the terms of these statutes, insiders with knowledge of wrongdoing are encouraged to come forward and report to authorities without fear of reprisals. Nearly two decades of experience with this mechanism for promoting white collar accountability has raised doubts about its efficacy for improving compliance with the law. Whistleblowers almost invariably are targets of retaliatory actions by their employers or professional peers; these commonly include demotion or termination of employment; transfer to monotonous, unpleasant, or dangerous work assignments; and threats of physical harm (Glazer and Glazer, 1989). Companies generally combat whistleblowers' allegations by calling into question their motives and character. Faced with what, in most cases, is unwelcome notoriety and the financial costs of securing legal representation to resist these actions, whistleblowers often find the experience extremely disruptive of life, work, and career routines. For many whistleblowers, the toll on physical and emotional health is devastating.

It is not only threat of punishment and fear of being found out that constrain the behavior of individuals and organizations. Commitment to norms of morality and ethics, a concern for self-respect, community standing, and a determination not to let down those who look to one as moral exemplar are other reasons for obeying the law (Paternoster and Simpson, 1993). Some individuals and organizations value their good reputation and emphasize to managers and employees the overriding importance of operating ethically and in compliance with law. Persuasive evidence suggests that the upper echelons of organizations set the moral tone of the workplace, and that other employees play by the rules thus established (Clinard, 1983; Hambrick and Mason, 1984). Many corporations, for example, promulgate codes of ethics as a sign of commitment to ethical conduct, and fear of adverse publicity is believed by many to restrain the behavior of potential white collar offenders (Fisse and Braithwaite, 1984). Large sums of money invested by some companies in advertising and charitable contributions to cultivate an ethical public image is strong evidence that an upstanding reputation, whether earned or manufactured, is a valuable asset.

Very little is known about the effectiveness of non-public strategies and responses to white collar crime, but professional oversight bodies rarely impose the harshest penalties in their arsenal on those guilty of serious ethical violations; the great majority of offenders get off with comparatively mild sanctions. In addition to this and lessons from the fate of whistleblowers, what has been learned about the nature of organizational codes of ethics also gives reason for doubt. Corporate codes of ethics generally emphasize the importance of employee fidelity to organizational policies and norms and say remarkably little about the importance of compliance with legal norms. There also appears to be little relationship between the presence of these codes and firm-level regulatory compliance (Mathews, 1987).

Whatever potential civil suits, whistleblowing, and codes of ethics may have for controlling white collar crime, there is little reason to believe that control efforts are uniform for all types of offenders. Prospects are discouraging particularly where such efforts are directed at large corporate actors who increasingly respond to attacks (*Wall Street Journal,* 1995a). Large corporations have the resources not only to fight these efforts but also to retaliate against critics. In 1998, for example, Beverly Enterprises, one of America's largest nursing home operators, filed a defamation suit against Kate Bronfenbrenner,

a Cornell University labor researcher (Cornell University, 1998), for remarks she made in a speech. At the request of several members of congress, Dr. Bronfenbrenner had spoken at a town hall meeting in Pittsburgh, Pennsylvania, on unfair labor practices by employers to curb organizing efforts by employees. She called Beverly Enterprises "one of the nation's most notorious labor law violators." In May 1998, Beverly's suit was dismissed by a U.S. District Court judge who ruled that Bronfenbrenner's statements were protected by legislative immunity under Pennsylvania state law. Although the targets of retaliatory actions generally prevail, the financial and emotional costs of fighting them can be staggering. Civil suits against critics also serve as lessons to others to think carefully before targeting the privileged and powerful.

EXPLAINING
WHITE COLLAR CRIME

Aggregate-level rates of white collar crime vary substantially both temporally and spatially. Research on federal enforcement actions taken against 477 large manufacturing firms by 25 federal agencies during 1975 and 1976 found that rates of violation were highest in the oil, pharmaceutical, and motor vehicle industries and lowest in the apparel and beverages industries (Clinard and Yeager, 1980). Analysis of data from different branches of Swedish industry found that regulatory compliance is lowest in non-manufacturing and considerably higher in manufacturing (Barnett, 1986). In the United States, there is evidence of substantial temporal variation in corporate antitrust offending (Simpson, 1987; Geis and Salinger, 1998).

The theory of crime as choice has gained unrivaled dominance as a general explanation for variation in criminal behavior and as justification for crime prevention programs and state initiatives aimed at street criminals. The notion of crime as choice has been applied to white collar crime as well (Shover and Bryant, 1993). In this theoretical construction, crime is purposeful, chosen behavior. Criminal acts are products of cognition and calculation in which decision makers examine and assess available options and their potential net payoffs, paying particular attention to the chances of being caught and punished. Many substantively narrow criminological theories are compatible logically with the crime-as-choice theory, including those that interpret crime as a product of weak self-control (Gottfredson and Hirschi, 1990; Hirschi, 1986).

Prevailing estimates of the formal risk of crime occupy a prominent place in crime-as-choice theory. The level of commitment to and resources invested in rule enforcement is an important determinant of the rate of white collar crime because it shapes collectively held notions about the legitimacy and credibility of state control. When it is widely believed that the law is little more than technical rules devoid of moral content, when the law and its agents are rejected as unnecessary or arbitrary extensions of state power, when the likelihood of detection and sanctioning is thought to be minimal, or when penalties threatened by the law or by others are dismissed as inconsequential, the pool of individuals and organizations predisposed to offend grows. There is consistent, though weak, support for this proposition from research on street-level property crime, but its applicability to the situation of variable sanctions and the rate of white collar crime has received little attention from investigators.

Opportunities

In addition to variations of risk, the theory of crime as choice posits that variation in crime rates in large measure is produced by variation in opportunities and in motivation. Criminal opportunities are arrangements or situations that offer attractive potential for criminal reward to individuals and groups with little apparent risk of detection or penalty (Coleman, 1987). Inviting opportunities for crime are available wherever offenders believe either that no one of consequence is monitoring them or that anyone who uncovers evidence of their crimes probably would not trigger punitive responses. For street criminals, opportunities are homes filled with electronic equipment that are left unoccupied much of the day; for white collar criminals, opportunities are impersonal trust relationships and positions of organizational power.

The supply of white collar criminal opportunities seems large and diverse, as suggested clearly by the rapid growth of opportunities to defraud, to harm, or to injure. Changes in record-keeping technology and in the growth of electronic commerce have occasioned an explosion of white collar criminal opportunities. Today, funds can be transferred around the world instantaneously over telephone lines and satellite networks. "Finance capitalism" has emerged, a productive enterprise distinguished not by manufacture of goods or services but instead by production of paper profits through manipulation of financial accounts (Calavita et al., 1997).

Finance capitalism is production at the computer keyboard, increasingly from the privacy of the home. A glimpse of the criminal consequences of this process is provided by an offender whose illicit and poorly supervised transactions contributed significantly to the collapse of one of England's oldest banking institutions (Leeson, 1996). Despite mounting losses, he continued making high-risk investment decisions in the impersonal and remote contexts characteristic of finance capitalism:

> All the money we dealt with was unreal: abstract numbers which flashed across screens or jumped across the trading pit with a flurry of hands. Our clients made or lost thousands of pounds, we just made a commission. . . . We just arbitraged back to back with no risk or filled other people's orders. The real money was our salaries and our bonuses, but even that was a bit artificial: it was all paid by telephonic transfer (Leeson, 1996: 56).

New communications technologies are one way that macrolevel changes in economic and social arrangements influence the ways individuals relate to one another and to organizations. This in turn influences the supply of white collar criminal opportunities. Transaction systems have become more impersonal and difficult to monitor easily as commercial exchanges based on face-to-face communication yield to impersonal exchanges within and between organizations (Vaughan, 1982). Manipulation of financial records, embezzlement, and other crimes can now be accomplished despite thousands of miles between the offender and the manipulated records. Use of computers, access codes, and passwords now link remote parties. Trade flows through middle agents who are as anonymous to customers as the producer of the products or services they purchase. Offenders and their victims may know one another outside of their business transactions, but increasingly they do not. Nor is the process simply of verifying credentials the easy matter it was when parties interacted personally or within geographically circumscribed and culturally shared worlds. White collar criminals are quick to exploit the growth of impersonal transactions and trust.

The state is another important source of increasing criminal opportunities. In the United States, for example, fundamental shifts following World War II in public welfare functions expanded government largesse for citizens across the income spectrum and made accessible public monies for those inclined to exploit them criminally. Schemes by doctors and pharmacists to defraud Medicaid/Medicare show that profit can be substantial, the risk of detection minimal, and the temptation, therefore, great (Jesilow et al., 1992). The risk of detection, apprehension, and prosecution for fraud in state welfare programs is low for rich and poor alike.

The state also affects the supply of white collar criminal opportunities when it adopts measures to promote or to regulate business activities. Presidential decisions and congressional legislation during the 1980s, for example, helped transform and increase criminal opportunities, most visibly in the U.S. savings and loan industry—in part because regulatory overseers simultaneously relaxed their monitoring and enforcement (Calavita et al, 1997; Zey, 1998).

Predisposed Offenders

The supply of opportunities explains part of the variation in the rate of white collar crime, but there also must be individuals and organizations willing to take criminal chances. Sources of variation in the supply of predisposed individuals and organizations are matters of theoretical conjecture but little research. Fluctuation in the business cycle often has been linked theoretically to changes in the rate of white collar crime, chiefly because of its presumed influence on the supply of offenders (Simpson, 1986). Economic downturns stimulate crime by depressing income and pushing increasing numbers of citizens and organizations closer to insolvency, desperation, and crime (Clinard and Yeager, 1980; Simpson, 1986; Baucus and Near, 1991).

Temporal and spatial cultural variations also play a part in determining the supply of predisposed offenders. Criminogenic cultures stimulate crime by providing potential offenders with perspectives and rationalizations that either conflict with or call into question ethical and legal norms (Reichman, 1993). Despite broad consensus on cultural contributions to white collar crime, empirical support for this explanation is weak (Barnett, 1986; Baucus and Near, 1991). As yet there are no studies "that develop systematic and independent measures of both business illealities and corporate or industry cultures" (Yeager, 1986: 100).

The relative strength of a culture of competition that elevates and rewards success above all else contributes to characteristic motivations and justifications for crime (Coleman, 1987). Individuals in competitive cultures are driven to strive for success, usually but not exclusively financial. They worry ceaselessly about conditions that stand in their way. Competitive cultures stimulate excess and crime amid widespread belief that "everyone is getting rich [or ahead]." In competitive cultures, people evaluate personal success in terms of wealth and material possessions. Maintaining and improving financial well-being and its trappings are priorities, and progress is assessed by comparison with associates and peers. Money is spent ostentatiously on houses, cars, jewelry, vacations, and other displays of wealth. Pervasive insecurity can be a powerful motivation for crime for rich and poor alike;

even the well-heeled may not feel secure in what they have acquired. In these circumstances, many come to believe that to pass up any opportunity, legal or otherwise, is folly.

Within competitive cultures, the motivations of highly privileged offenders and less-privileged ones differ considerably. The latter characteristically commit crime to meet immediate financial needs, to prevent financial collapse, to support drug addictions and gambling problems, or to sustain self-indulgent lifestyles beyond their financial reach (Cressey, 1953). Crises frequently precipitate their crimes, and they imagine the footsteps of auditors and law enforcement bearing down on them (Weisburd and Waring, 1998). Their desperate need for money leads them to select crimes that provide short-term relief at sometimes great risk. These offenders exist in a tumultuous and precarious psychological state not unlike the street-level thief. In moments of clarity, they realize that, try as they might, they will have no one to blame or accept responsibility for their actions when called into account, but their problems and the need for easy and quick money overshadow fear of arrest. Usually, less-privileged offenders operate alone or in small groups, and their crimes sometimes make use of underworld ties (Levi, 1981; Henry, 1978).

In contrast, financial demands on many elite offenders are not so burdensome, and they are able to pick and choose from criminal opportunities. They can sacrifice immediate payoff for safety and long-term returns. Security is an added prerequisite of their financial and organizational position. Elite offenders do not jump desperately into crimes that provide a quick dollar; they can afford to bide their time and wait for criminal opportunities. They are not driven toward crimes by secret crises so much as lured into them by the discovery of enticing opportunities. They operate with little apparent fear of being arrested, branded as a criminal, and compelled to negotiate with state officials over the terms of plea agreements or deals.

Opportunities to engage in many forms of street crime are widely distributed throughout the general population, but white collar crime requires access to social networks, information, and positions of authority. One of the most important differences between white collar criminals and their street-offending cousins is the former's access to an array of low-risk criminal opportunities; for this reason, they can commit crimes beyond the reach of the poor and less-privileged.

DECISION MAKING
AND CRIMINAL CAREERS

The prevalence of white-collar crime, like that of individual-level and organization-level criminal participation, varies substantially. Regardless of whether the rate of white collar crime is high or low, some individuals and organizations maintain exemplary records of compliance with the law even as others violate habitually. In addition to his pioneering conceptual examination of white collar crime, Sutherland examined the magnitude of individual-level and firm-level criminal intensity. He did so by tabulating the decisions of courts and administrative commissions against 70 of the largest U.S. manufacturing, mining, and mercantile corporations over the life of the company, an average span of 45 years (Sutherland, 1983). His analysis showed that each of the 70 corporations had at least one administrative decision against it, with an average of 14.0 per firm. The number of such

decisions per firm ranged from 1 to 50. Sixty percent of the firms had criminal court convictions, with an average of four convictions per company.

Other investigators report similar findings. Clinard and Yeager (1980) tallied 1,529 cases of penalties imposed on 477 of the largest manufacturing firms in the U.S. in 1975 and 1976. Their analysis showed that, whereas a small proportion of firms apparently commit a disproportionate share of violations, an even larger proportion had no record of infractions. Another study of the 1,043 largest industrial and non-industrial companies in the years 1980–1990 found that 11 percent were convicted of criminal charges or signed consent decrees for one or more of five serious offenses (corrupt practices/bribery; criminal fraud; illegal political contributions; tax evasion; price-fixing; and bid-rigging) (Ross, 1980). As in previous studies, some companies were found to be repeat offenders: There was substantial variation in compliance with regulatory rules. Kagan and Scholz (1984: 89) note "[t]here are major petroleum refineries in the same county in California each inspected for air pollution violations virtually every day [that] have sharply different [compliance records] according to enforcement officials." Similarly, analysis of data on 3,800 violations of the British Factory Act by 200 firms over a five-year period showed great variation in firm-level compliance (Carson, 1970). Some individuals and firms are model citizens and others are career criminals. What explains variation in the individual intensity of white collar offending, whether it be illegalities or felonies?

Threatened aversive consequences are a fundamental explanatory variable in the theory of crime as choice; predisposed offenders presumably weigh the potential costs and benefits before choosing crime (Paternoster and Simpson,1993). Because white collar criminals are thought to be more rational than street offenders, the impact on their decisions of legal threats and other controls should be substantial (Weisburd and Waring, 1998). Street offenders routinely choose to offend in hedonistic contexts of street culture where drug consumption clouds both judgment and the ability to calculate beforehand (Shover, 1996; Wright and Decker, 1997). Conversely, many white collar workers live and work in worlds structured to promote, monitor, and reward prudent and deliberate decision making. Whether the threat of sanctions is a more effective deterrent to crime for them as compared with street criminals is disputed (Vaughan, 1998). The impact of threat almost certainly varies with severity; notices of violation for regulatory offenses are one thing, imprisonment or large fines are another.

The social stigma and economic losses sustained by convicted white collar criminals probably vary by type of offense and offender. Self-employed professionals often recover rather quickly from the experience of arrest and conviction, but public-sector employees sometimes pay a much stiffer price in terms of restricted employability. Arrests of white collar offenders (relative to those of street offenders) are infrequent but, seen through their own eyes, shocking and unjust (Benson, 1985).

Interviews with convicted white collar offenders show them generally to be an unrepentant lot who are remarkably slow to accept responsibility for their crimes. Whereas convicted street offenders characteristically acknowledge their guilt to all who inquire once proceedings have ended, white collar offenders often protest their innocence long past this point, insisting, for example, that what they did caused no harm and hardly merited prosecutors' attention (Benson,

1985; Jesilow et al., 1992). Failure to apply the notion of intentional choice to their lawbreaking—wherein criminality was knowingly contemplated and carried out—is one of the most important distinguishing characteristics of white-collar criminals; they make "mistakes" and "mislead," but they do not steal or lie. Such strong denial blunts standard social controls.

No one denies that the cost of prosecution and conviction for white collar crimes can devastate offenders and their families. Few clear-headed offenders with anything appreciable to lose would commit crime if they thought criminal prosecution or long-term imprisonment were likely consequences. The possibility that some convicted white collar offenders see crime as a good bet is suggested by the high rate of recidivism (30 percent) observed among some (Weisburd et al., 1995). Evidence on this point is extremely limited, however. Recidivism may be concentrated among the most economically marginal and least privileged in their ranks.

Analysis of arrest records shows that white collar offenders typically offend less frequently than do many street offenders, but many are not strangers to the criminal justice system (Benson and Moore, 1992). White collar criminal careers generally are unremarkable. This is apparent from analysis of information included in presentence investigation reports on 1,094 individuals tried for white collar crimes in seven federal districts during 1976–1978 (Weisburd et al., 1991). Defendants were designated white collar offenders based on their conviction for one or more of eight statutory offenses: securities fraud, antitrust violations, bribery, bank embezzlement, postal and wire fraud, false claims and statements, credit and lending institution fraud, and tax fraud. Analysis showed that most of the crimes committed were not complex, had few victims, and resulted in modest financial losses. Most were the crimes of only modestly privileged, unsophisticated white collar offenders, and few approximated the popular depiction of white collar criminals as elite or "fat-cat" businesspeople. Males were overrepresented, and their crimes ranged from petty to sophisticated. Nearly all women's crimes by contrast were small-time, less organized, and less profitable than crimes committed by males (Daly, 1989). Whereas more than half of the males were managerial or professional workers, employed female offenders worked disproportionately in clerical positions. Generally, the higher the proportion of women committing a type of offense, the higher the proportion of non-whites and less educated committing it. Women's modest take from white collar crime reflects both the limited criminal opportunities available to clerical personnel and the absence of women from the top ranks of large organizations (Zeitz, 1981).

White collar offenders are older, wealthier, and better educated than street criminals. They are less likely to have serious problems with alcohol or other drugs (Benson and Moore, 1992). Some do not differ appreciably from street offenders, particularly when a broad definition of white collar crime is used (Croall, 1989, 1992). A substantial proportion of those committing crimes of deception, for example, are unemployed when their crimes are committed (Daly, 1989; Weisburd et al., 1991). White collar offenders are more specialized than street criminals, but it is not unusual for repeat offenders to have arrest records that include street crimes.

The criminal careers of highly privileged white collar offenders differ in notable respects. Most white collar crimes are short-lived and involve few offenders. Criminal conspiracies, however, may persist for decades; upon their retirement, offenders sometimes hand over criminal operations to their successors (Baker and Faulkner, 1993). Whereas many street offenders desist from serious crime by age 30, some of the most lucrative white collar criminal opportunities are inaccessible until potential offenders near middle-age, when their professional careers are established. In one study, the typical white collar offender was 40 years of age (Benson and Moore, 1992). Frequently their crimes are organizational. Criminal career onset generally is not motivated by devastating personal financial problems, but crime may be more likely to occur in faltering enterprises (Jenkins and Braithwaite, 1993). Case studies of elite crimes show that criminal careers typically begin gradually with the discovery of illicit shortcuts that improve the perceived performance of companies and thereby indirectly line the pockets of those responsible (Yeager and Reed, 1998). Improvement in organizational profit margin—not impending financial collapse—is the likelier motivation for elite crime. As Sutherland (1983) noted, white collar offenders frequently are introduced to criminal opportunity and techniques by acquaintances. Friends or others eager to please in the business realm may realize, for example, that it is in their interest to include powerful people in their crimes. Officers of failed savings and loans often traded illegal loans and fraudulent investments with friends or contacts at other firms (Calavita et al., 1997). Elites may be introduced to crime also by the realization that they are accountable to few and that others are slow to question suspicious activities of the boss or star employee.

Organizational crime often begins when owners or management place demands for improved or higher performance on subordinates, which causes innovative and unimaginative employees alike to become less concerned with legalities (Needleman and Needleman, 1979). A reluctant engineer told to write a misleading test report on a faulty aircraft brake reported that eventually his superior advised, "Write the goddamn thing and shut up about it" (Vandivier, 1992: 132). Research on compliance with regulatory standards by Australian nursing homes showed that pressure from senior management to show larger profits was a significant source of noncompliance (Jenkins and Braithwaite, 1993). At other times, management can turn their heads so as not to see lawbreaking.

In 1961, managers of some of the nations' largest manufacturers of heavy electrical equipment were convicted of price-fixing. Evidence showed how top managers can encourage illegal activity by subordinates without directing them to violate the law (Geis, 1967). Bid-rigging in the heavy electrical equipment industry was an established business practice and did not require specific directives from above; unreasonable performance expectations, introduction to colleagues familiar with the business, and rewards for pricing co-conspirators were sufficient. This suggests that once the wheels of elite white collar crimes are set in motion, they may require remarkably little oversight. Unlike the embezzler who impulsively taps the till, elite organizational white collar criminals employ a hands-off approach. This helps explain why high-ranking corporate executives or state officials accused of crimes are less likely than subordinates to be brought to trial or sentenced (Hagan and Parker, 1985; Calavita et al., 1997).

GLOBAL WHITE COLLAR CRIME

The faces of white collar crime and the control challenge that it poses have both altered fundamentally with the emergence of a global economy. White collar crime, in response, is ever-changing as well. Criminals adapt constantly to exploit opportunities and avoid external controls made possible by technological, political, and economic change. Growth of the world economic system has opened up new opportunities for crime. Simple confidence games and business frauds can now span national borders by putting to use widely available communication technologies. Police and prosecutors in most local jurisdictions and third-world nations do not have the budget, expertise, or other resources to pursue these cases. Even wealthy nations must pick and choose cases worth investigating.

Whereas offenders whose crimes cross the U.S.–Canadian border may have a good chance of being apprehended, there is little hope of apprehending fraudsters operating out of Nigeria or headquartered in disfavored nations. There is even less chance of recovering monies that are channeled unimpeded through multiple third-world banks before settling in the accounts of white collar criminals. The war on drugs has improved prosecutors' ability to pursue cases and money trails across international borders, but small prosecutorial teams find it especially difficult to match the international networks and money-moving expertise acquired by investors, bankers, accountants, and corrupt officials during international business careers. Increasingly, the challenge of white collar crime must be met with coordinated interagency responses representing multiple state and national governments.

Trade agreements among nations have created new economic production and trading entities, the increasingly free flow of goods and services, and new criminal opportunities.

Agricultural subsidies in the European Community, for example, are designed to ensure quality, sufficient production, and stable incomes for farmers. Existence of these subsidies ensures, however, that misrepresentation of the quality, the origins, or the destination of goods can be a profitable venture. In the simplest schemes, some growers have exploited subsidies paid for withholding surplus wine from the market: They buy cheap wine abroad, label it as their own product, and collect the subsidy on both (Clarke, 1993; Passas and Nelken, 1993). Criminal opportunities are made available to meat shippers as well when they are charged less tax to export their product than to sell it locally. With the stroke of a pen on a packing slip, meat that is produced and sold domestically appears to have crossed a border, and illicit profit is made.

The signatories to international trade agreements typically pledge to adopt and enforce elementary regulations for worker and product safety. All nations are not equally prepared or committed to monitor these conditions, however. The result is reproduction on a grander scale around the world of the same exploitation that is common, if largely invisible, within America. Transnational corporations (TNCs) are major actors in these trends. In 1984, the Union Carbide Corporation, one of the largest companies headquartered in the United States, released methyl isocyanate and hydrogen cyanide gas into the atmosphere from their plant in Bhopal, India. According to the Indian government's count, the incident killed 3,329 people and seriously injured some 20,000 (Pearce and Tombs, 1998). Immediately following the disaster, the chairman of the company indicated that the chemical plant had not complied with standard safety protocols and had used procedures that were not permitted in the United States.

His statement soon was retracted, however, and the company then blamed unidentified saboteurs and inadequate Indian regulations. In 1987, Indian prosecutors filed criminal charges against Union Carbide, its CEO, and eight officers of its Indian subsidiary (*Los Angeles Times,* 1989).

Union Carbide, however, won a judgment in U.S. courts establishing that Indian courts had sole jurisdiction over all civil litigation resulting from the disaster. Observers speculated that company lawyers believed they would receive favorable treatment and less costly judgments from Indian courts. The case was settled for $470 million in 1989, a sum that included payments of approximately $1,000 per claimant. It was also agreed in the settlement that Union Carbide would be immune from all pending litigation and that criminal charges against officers of the company would be dropped. The Indian Supreme Court subsequently ruled that criminal charges would stand, but it is unlikely that any of those charged will be extradited from their first-world homes to face manslaughter charges.

The Bhopal case shows that an urgent problem brought on by the development of the global economy may determine which laws and regulatory rules will be used as standards for individual and organizational behavior (Michalowski and Kramer, 1987). Should crime be defined so as to include violations of international agreements that may not violate criminal statutes of all nations or states? When business is conducted in countries with inconsistent laws and rules, which is the standard for determining criminal conduct? Should regulations be aimed at producers or importers? The difficulties of controlling white collar criminals were enormous even in a world of national economies and corporate actors, but the ability of corporations to move funds almost instanta-neously and to shield their operations behind the laws of friendly nations complicates matters substantially. Corporate owners and managers can threaten to relocate their company to coun-tries with less restrictive regulatory regimes and thus deprive their current host country of jobs and tax revenue. Third-world countries may be incapable of resisting or controlling large corpo-rations' relocation, self-interested interpretations of rules, and harmful conduct. Desire to attract industry is a powerful incentive for potential host countries to develop physical and legal infrastructures beneficial to corporations. The most attractive resources many countries can offer are cheap labor and weak regulation.

A transnational managerial class has emerged to operate the increasingly powerful transna-tional corporations. Prepared for international business careers by education and corporate grooming, they occupy upper echelons of global firms. They move easily between the sometimes far-flung countries in which their employers do business, and their primary allegiance is to the profitability of transnational corporations. They consider themselves citizens of the world and are not reluctant to move production and jobs from north to south to circumvent national regulatory rules and regimes. That products are manufactured under conditions considered criminal in developed nations usually does not stop their import there. The transnational man-agerial class has an increasing say in the shape of the business environment in most nation-states and, subsequently, in the world.

Technological change and the emergence of TNCs have produced an unprecedented widen-ing of the population at risk of victimization by white collar crime. Reeling under their burden of indebtedness, third-world countries produce for distant markets where consumers are un-aware of the locations and the conditions under which their purchases are manufactured. Across the globe, the willingness of states to confront white collar crime has waned substantially under the exigencies of competition and reassurances from business that oversight is heavy-handed, unnecessary, and costly. It is clear that states have moved significantly in the direction of coopera-tive regulation. This is reflected in international regulations and accords with a stated primary objective of protecting the transnational free market. The question raised by this move and the growing dominance of large organizations is whether they now are "beyond the law" (Tonry and Reiss, 1993).

CONCLUSION:
THE CHALLENGE OF
WHITE COLLAR CRIME

We conclude by noting that the privileges af-forded those who commit white collar crimes are pivotal to their crimes' commission. The of-fenders' relatively privileged position permits them to choose crimes that pay and to protect themselves from the criminal justice system and from the public's scorn. Although some are cer-tainly more privileged than others, white collar criminals are allowed to mitigate their deliber-ate criminal decisions using excuses unavailable to their street-crime counterparts. Their stories resonate with those familiar with finance, office politics, business competition, and regulation, whereas street-criminals' explanations often fall on deaf ears. Academic understanding and pub-lic policy are inevitably influenced by empathy for criminals of privilege.

Where advances have been made in combating white collar crime, they have originated in movements against it. The demands of these movements counteract influence on state policy from anti-regulation constituencies and constrain the ability of state representatives to cozy up to privileged interests and white collar criminals. Consumer groups, for example, have been successful in improving regulatory standards for the pharmaceutical industry (Braithwaite, 1993). Use of boycotts and adverse publicity can raise the risks to business of trading with countries where illegal labor practices predominate.

The movement against white collar crime, to the extent that one exists, is largely reactive. Business is allowed to proceed freely until some tragic offense reminds people and the government that oversight is needed. When life-threatening or blatant white collar crimes come to light, regulations are enforced and preventive measures are taken until media and public attention subside. When videotapes of children slaving in brick factories abroad make it to U.S. television, when people die painful deaths by fire, or when the president is caught in an illegal act, the movement against white collar crime is injected with short bursts of energy.

Public opinion surveys show that some white collar offenses are judged to be as serious as violent street crimes, particularly ones that result in physical harm to innocent parties (Schrager and Short, 1980; Wolfgang et al., 1985). Those who expect that the public will be incensed to discover, for example, that they have paid three cents extra for orange juice because of fixed prices, therefore, inevitably are disappointed (Box, 1983). Mundane crimes like price-fixing in the folding box industry and insider trading do not hold the media's attention. When damage from white collar crime is imperceptible and diffuse, offenders easily escape detection and condemnation. Despite the perception in some quarters of a social movement against crime in the suites, it is unclear that the public generally has an abiding concern about white collar criminals. Assessed against the accomplishments of the larger victims' rights movement, the movement against white collar crime thus far has seen little success in raising public consciousness or in changing public policy significantly.

DISCUSSION QUESTIONS

1. Though many people use the term "white collar crime," the concept is not well defined. What is white collar crime generally, and what kinds of offenses are encompassed by the term?

2. Do we receive different pictures of white collar criminals when we focus on the class and status of offenders instead of the characteristics of offenses themselves?

3. In what ways does white collar crime harm people? Discuss both direct and indirect forms of victimization.

4. How successfully has our government combated white collar crime? What factors have influenced that success rate? Will we ever view crimes of privilege in the same manner that we now view street crime?

5. Shover and Hochstetler frame white collar criminal activity as a product of individual calculation and choice interacting with opportunity. Discuss this notion and provide examples.

6. Can we speak of white collar "career" criminals in the same sense that we talk of "career" street crime offenders?

REFERENCES

Aulette, J. R., and R. J. Michalowski. 1993. "Fire in Hamlet: A Case Study of a State-Corporate Crime." Pp. 171–206 in *Political Crime in Contemporary America: A Critical Approach*. Edited by K. D. Tunnell. New York: Garland.

Baker, W. E., and R. R. Faulkner. 1993. "The Social Organization of Conspiracy: Illegal Networks in the Heavy Electrical Equipment Industry." *American Sociological Review* 58: 837–860.

Baltimore Sun. 1994. "What Happened to Stanford's Expense Scandal?" November 20, 4F.

Barnett, H. C. 1986. "Industry Culture and Industry Economy: Correlates of Tax Noncompliance in Sweden." *Criminology* 24: 553–574.

———. 1994. *Toxic Debts and the Superfund Dilemma*. Chapel Hill: University of North Carolina Press.

Baucus, M. S., and T. M. Dworkin. 1991. "What Is Corporate Crime? It Is Not Illegal Corporate Behavior." *Law & Policy* 13: 231–244.

Baucus, M. S., and J. P. Near. 1991. "Can Illegal Corporate Behavior Be Predicted? An Event History Analysis." *Academy of Management Journal* 34: 9–36.

Benson, M. L. 1985. "Denying the Guilty Mind: Accounting for Involvement in a White-Collar Crime." *Criminology* 23: 589–599.

Benson, M. L., and F. T. Cullen. 1998. *Combating Corporate Crime: Local Prosecutors at Work*. Boston: Northeastern University Press.

Benson, M. L., and E. Moore. 1992. "Are White-Collar and Common Criminals the Same?" *Journal of Research in Crime and Delinquency* 29: 251–272.

Boston Globe. 1998. "People's Play: Hide-and-Seek with Tax Ruble." October 5, A2.

Box, S. 1983. *Power, Crime and Mystification*. London: Tavistock.

Braithwaite, J. 1983. "Enforced Self-Regulation: A New Strategy for Corporate Crime Control." *Michigan Law Review* 80: 1466–1507.

———. 1991. "Poverty, Power, and White-Collar Crime: Sutherland and the Paradoxes of Criminological Theory." *Australia-New Zealand Journal of Criminology* 24: 40–58.

———. 1993. "Transnational Regulation of the Pharmaceutical Industry." *Annals of the American Academy of Political and Social Science* 525: 12–30.

Calavita, K. 1983. "The Demise of the Occupational Safety and Health Administration: A Case Study in Symbolic Politics." *Social Problems* 30: 437–448.

Calavita, K., H. N. Pontell, and R. H. Tillman. 1997. *Big Money Crime: Fraud and Politics in the Savings and Loan Crisis*. Berkeley: University of California Press.

Carson, W. G. 1970. "White-Collar Crime and the Enforcement of Factory Legislation." *British Journal of Criminology* 10: 383–398.

Clarke, M. 1993. "EEC Fraud: A Suitable Case for Treatment." Pp. 162–186 in *Global Crime Connections: Dynamics and Control*. Edited by F. Pearce and M. Woodiwiss. London: Macmillan.

Cleveland Plain Dealer. 1996. "Bonanno Gets Year in Jail for Misuse of Court Post." February 3, 1A.

Clinard, M. B. 1983. *Corporate Ethics and Crime: The Role of Middle Management*. Beverly Hills, CA: Sage.

Clinard, M. B., and R. Quinney. 1973. *Criminal Behavior Systems: A Typology*. 2d ed. Holt, Rinehart & Winston.

Clinard, M. B., and P. C. Yeager. 1980. *Corporate Crime*. New York: Free Press.

Coleman, J. W. 1987. "Toward an Integrated Theory of White-Collar Crime." *American Journal of Sociology* 93: 406–439.

———. 1989. *The Criminal Elite: The Sociology of White-Collar Crime*. 3rd ed. New York: St. Martin's Press.

Cornell University. 1998. "Defamation Lawsuit Against Cornell Labor Researcher Is Dismissed." News Release, May 27.

Cressey, D. R. 1953. *Other People's Money*. Glencoe, IL: Free Press.

———. 1995. "Poverty of Theory in Corporate Crime Research." Pp. 413–431 in *White-Collar Crime: Classic and Contemporary Views*. Edited by G. Geis, R. F. Meier, and L. M. Salinger. New York: Free Press.

Croall, H. 1989. "Who Is the White-Collar Criminal?" *British Journal of Criminology* 29: 157–174.

———. 1992. *White-Collar Crime*. Buckingham, U.K.: Open University Press.

Daly, K. 1989. "Gender and Varieties of White-Collar Crime." *Criminology* 27: 769–793.

Ermann, M. D., and R. J. Lundman. 1978. "Deviant Acts by Complex Organizations: Deviance and Social Control at the Organizational Level of Analysis." *Sociological Quarterly* 19: 55–67.

Etzioni, A. 1993. "The U.S. Sentencing Commission on Corporate Crime: A Critique." *Annals of the American Academy of Political and Social Science* 525: 147–156.

Fisse, B., and J. Braithwaite. 1984. *The Impact of Publicity on Corporate Offenders*. Albany: State University of New York Press.

Ganzini, L., B. McFarland, and J. Bloom. 1990. "Victims of Fraud: Comparing Victims of White-Collar and Violent Crime." *Bulletin of the American Academy of Psychiatry and Law* 18: 55–63.

Geis, G. 1967. "The Heavy Electrical Equipment Antitrust Cases of 1961." Pp. 139–150 in *Criminal Behavior Systems*. Edited by M. B. Clinard and R. Quinney. New York: Holt, Rinehart & Winston.

———. 1976. "Defrauding the Elderly." Pp. 7–19 in *Crime and the Elderly*. Edited by J. Goldsmith and S. Goldsmith. Lexington, MA: D.C. Heath.

———. 1992. "White-Collar Crime: What Is It?" Pp. 31–52 in *White-Collar Crime Reconsidered*. Edited by K. Schlegel and D. Weisburd. Boston: Northeastern University Press.

Geis, G., and L. S. Salinger. 1998. "Antitrust and Organizational Deviance." Pp. 71–110 in *The Sociology of Organizations: Deviance in and of Organizations*. Vol. 15. Edited by P. A. Bamberger and W. J. Sonnenstuhl. Stamford, CT: JAI.

Glazer, M. P., and P. M. Glazer. 1989. *The Whistleblowers: Exposing Corruption in Government and Industry*. New York: Basic Books.

Gottfredson, M. R., and T. Hirschi. 1990. *A General Theory of Crime*. Palo Alto, CA: Stanford University Press.

Hagan, J., and P. Parker. 1985. "White-Collar Crime and Punishment." *American Sociological Review* 50: 302–316.

Hambrick, D. C., and P. A. Mason. 1984. "Upper Echelons: The Organization As a Reflection of Its Top Managers." *Academy of Management Review* 9: 193–206.

Henry, S. 1978. *The Hidden Economy*. Oxford, U.K.: Martin Robertson.

Hirschi, T. 1986. "On the Compatibility of Rational Choice and Social Control Theories of Crime." Pp. 105–121 in *The Reasoning Criminal*. Edited by D. B. Cornish and R. V. Clarke. New York: Springer-Verlag.

Hughes, E. C. 1971. "Good People and Dirty Work." Pp. 87–97 in *The Sociological Eye*. Vol. 1. Edited by E. C. Hughes. Chicago: Aldine Atherton.

Jamieson, K. M. 1994. *Organization of Corporate Crime: Dynamics of Antitrust Violation*. Thousand Oaks, CA: Sage.

Jenkins, A., and J. Braithwaite. 1993. "Profits, Pressure and Corporate Lawbreaking." *Crime, Law and Social Change* 20: 221–232.

Jesilow, P., H. N. Pontell, and G. Geis. 1992. *Prescriptions for Profit—How Doctors Defraud Medicaid*. Berkeley: University of California Press.

Kagan, R. A., and J. T. Scholz. 1984. "The Criminology of the Corporation and Regulatory Enforcement Strategies." Pp. 67–96 in *Enforcing Regulation*. Edited by K. Hawkins and J. M. Thomas. Boston: Kluwer-Nijhoff.

Katz, J. 1980. "Concerted Ignorance: The Social Psychology of Cover-Up." Pp. 149–170 in *Management Fraud: Detection and Deterrence*. Edited by R. K. Elliot and J. J. Willingham. New York: Petercelli.

Knoxville News-Sentinel. 1993. "Milk Industry Bid-Rigging Found in 20 States." May 23, A8.

———. 1998. "UT Picks a New Firm to Handle Used-Book Purchases." December 14, A1.

Leeson, N. (with E. Whitley). 1996. *Rogue Trader*. Boston: Little, Brown.

Levi, M. 1981. *Phantom Capitalists: The Organization and Control of Long-Firm Fraud*. London: Heinemann.

———. 1992. "White-Collar Crime Victimization." Pp. 169–194 in *White-Collar Crime Reconsidered*. Edited by K. Schlegel and D. Weisburd. Boston: Northeastern University Press.

Lofquist, W. S. 1993. "Legislating Organizational Probation: State Capacity, Business Power, and Corporate Crime Control." *Law & Society Review* 27: 741–784.

Los Angeles Times. 1989. "Did He Do the Right Thing? Chairman's Role in Bhopal Disaster Remains Ambiguous." February 15, D3.

———. 1992. "Chicken Plant Owner Gets Jail for Fatal Blaze." September 15, A16.

MacIsaac, J. 1968. *Half the Fun Was Getting There*. Englewood Cliffs, NJ: Prentice-Hall.

Mann, K. 1985. *Defending White-Collar Crime: A Portrait of Attorneys at Work*. New Haven, CT: Yale University Press.

Mathews, M. C. 1987. "Codes of Ethics: Organizational Behavior and Misbehavior." Pp. 107–130 in *Research in Corporate Social Performance and Policy: Empirical Studies of Business Ethics and Values*. Vol. 9. Edited by W. C. Frederick. Greenwich, CT: JAI.

Meier, R. F., and J. F. Short, Jr. 1983. "The Consequences of White-Collar Crime." Pp. 23–50 in *White-Collar Crime: An Agenda for Research*. Edited by H. Edelhertz. Lexington, MA: Lexington.

Memphis Commercial Appeal. 1992. "Jury Convicts Lanier of Abusing Power for Sex." December 19, A1.

Michalowski, R. J., and R. C. Kramer. 1987. "The Space Between Laws: The Problem of Corporate Crime in a Transnational Context." *Social Problems* 34: 34–53.

Needleman, M. L., and C. Needleman. 1979. "Organizational Crime: Two Models of Criminogenesis." *Sociological Quarterly* 20: 517–528.

New York Times. 1991a. "25 Are Killed and 40 Are Hurt in Blaze at Carolina Plant." September 4, A1.

———. 1991b. "U.S. Fines 500 Mine Companies for False Air Tests." April 5, A12.

———. 1995a. "Former United Way Chief Guilty in Theft of More than $600,000." April 4, A1.

———. 1995b. "At Big Kidney Chain, Deals for Doctors, Ruin for Rivals." December 5, A1.

Passas, N., and D. Nelken. 1993. "The Thin Line Between Legitimate and Criminal Enterprises: Subsidy Frauds in the European Community." *Crime, Law and Social Change* 19: 223–243.

Paternoster, R., and S. Simpson. 1993. "A Rational Choice Theory of Corporate Crime." Pp. 37–58 in *Routine Activity and Rational Choice.* Edited by R. V. Clarke and M. Felson. New Brunswick, NJ: Transaction.

Pearce, F., and S. Tombs. 1990. "Ideology, Hegemony, and Empiricism: Compliance Theories of Regulation." *British Journal of Criminology* 30: 423–443.

————. 1998. *Toxic Capitalism: Corporate Crime and the Chemical Industry.* Brookfield, CT: Dartmouth.

Peters, J. G., and S. Welch. 1980. "The Effects of Charges of Corruption on Voting Behavior in Congressional Elections." *American Political Science Review* 74: 697–708.

Pittsburgh Post-Gazette. 1998. "Board Member Could Face Criminal Charges over Garbage Contract." November 8, W13.

Reichman, N. 1993. "Insider Trading." Pp. 55–96 in *Beyond the Law: Crime in Complex Organizations.* Edited by M. Tonry and A. J. Reiss, Jr. Chicago: University of Chicago Press.

Reiman, J. H. 1995. *The Rich Get Richer and the Poor Get Prison.* 2d ed. Englewood Cliffs, NJ: Prentice-Hall.

Reiss, A. J., Jr. 1984. "Selecting Strategies of Social Control over Organizational Life." Pp. 23–36 in *Enforcing Regulation.* Edited by K. Hawkins and J. M. Thomas. Boston: Kluwer-Nijhoff.

Reiss, A. J., Jr., and A. D. Biderman. 1980. *Data Sources on White-Collar Law-Breaking.* Washington, DC: U.S. Department of Justice, National Institute of Justice.

Reiss, A. J., Jr., and M. Tonry. 1993. "Organizational Crime." Pp. 1–11 in *Beyond the Law: Crime in Complex Organizations.* Edited by M. Tonry and A. J. Reiss, Jr. Chicago: University of Chicago Press.

Ross, E. A. 1907. *Sin and Society: An Analysis of Latter-Day Iniquity.* Boston: Houghton Mifflin.

Ross, I. 1980. "How Lawless Are Big Companies?" *Fortune.* December 1, 57–64.

St. Louis Post-Dispatch. 1998. "Railroad Will Pay $19 Million for Dumping Lead by a Siding in the Ozarks." December 5, 19.

Schrager, L. S., and J. F. Short, Jr. 1980. "How Serious a Crime? Perceptions of Organizational and Common Crimes." Pp. 14–31 in *White-Collar Crime: Theory and Research.* Edited by G. Geis and E. Stotland. Beverly Hills, CA: Sage.

Shapiro, S. P. 1984. *Wayward Capitalists: Targets of the Securities and Exchange Commission.* New Haven, CT: Yale University Press.

————. 1985. "The Road Not Taken: The Elusive Path to Criminal Prosecution for White-Collar Offenders." *Law & Society Review* 19: 179–217.

————. 1990. "Collaring the Crime, not the Criminal: Reconsidering 'White-Collar Crime.'" *American Sociological Review* 55: 346–365.

Shover, N. 1996. *Great Pretenders: Pursuits and Careers of Persistent Thieves.* Boulder, CO: Westview.

————. 1998. "White-Collar Crime." Pp. 133–158 in *Handbook of Crime and Punishment.* Edited by M. Tonry. New York: Oxford University Press.

Shover, N., and K. M. Bryant. 1993. "Theoretical Explanations of Corporate Crime." Pp. 141–176 in *Understanding Corporate Criminality.* Edited by M. B. Blankenship. New York: Garland.

Shover, N., D. A. Clelland, and J. P. Lynxwiler. 1986. *Enforcement or Negotiation? Constructing a Regulatory Bureaucracy.* Albany: State University of New York Press.

Shover, N., G. L. Fox, and M. Mills. 1994. "Long-Term Consequences of Victimization by White-Collar Crime." *Justice Quarterly* 11: 301–324.

Simpson, S. S. 1986. "The Decomposition of Antitrust: Testing a Multi-Level, Longitudinal Model of Profit-Squeeze." *American Sociological Review* 51: 859–875.

————. 1987. "Cycles of Illegality: Antitrust Violations in Corporate America." *Social Forces* 65: 943–963.

Simpson, S. S., R. Paternoster, and N. L. Piquero. 1998. "Exploring the Micro-Macro Link in Corporate Crime Research." Pp. 35–70 in *The Sociology of Organizations: Deviance in and of*

Organizations. Vol. 15. Edited by P. A. Bamberger and W. J. Sonnenstuhl. Stamford, CT: JAI.

Snider, L. 1993. "Regulating Corporate Behavior." Pp. 177–210 in *Understanding Corporate Criminality.* Edited by M. B. Blankenship. New York: Garland.

Sutherland, E. H. 1940. "White-Collar Criminality." *American Sociological Review* 5: 1–11.

———. 1945. "Is 'White-Collar Crime' Crime?" *American Sociological Review* 10: 132–139.

———. [1949] 1983. *White-Collar Crime: The Uncut Version,* with an introduction by G. Geis and C. Goff. Reprint. New Haven, CT: Yale University Press.

Titus, R. M., and A. R. Gover. 1999. "Personal Fraud: The Victims and the Scams." In *Crime Prevention Studies.* Edited by R. Clarke, G. Farrell, and K. Pease. Monsey, NY: Criminal Justice Press.

Titus, R. M., F. Heinzelmann, and J. M. Boyle. 1995. "Victimization of Persons by Fraud." *Crime and Delinquency* 41: 54–72.

Tonry, M., and D. P. Farrington (eds.). 1995. *Building a Safer Society—Strategic Approaches to Crime Prevention.* Chicago: University of Chicago Press.

Tonry, M., and A. J. Reiss, Jr. (eds.). 1993. *Beyond the Law: Crime in Complex Organizations.* Chicago: University of Chicago Press.

U.S. Sentencing Commission. 1995. *Federal Sentencing Guidelines Manual.* St. Paul, MN: West.

Vandivier, K. 1992. "Why Should My Conscience Bother Me?" Pp. 205–228 in *Corporate and Governmental Deviance: Problems of Organizational Behavior.* Edited by M. D. Ermann and R. J. Lundman. New York: Oxford University Press.

Vaughan, D. 1982. "Transaction Systems and Unlawful Organizational Behavior." *Social Problems* 29: 373–379.

———. 1998. "Rational Choice, Situated Action, and the Social Control of Organizations." *Law & Society Review* 32: 23–61.

Wall Street Journal. 1995a. "Firms Find New Ways to Target Bad Press." November 10, B8.

———. 1995b. "A No Contest Plea by Chem-Bio Averts Trial over Pap Smear." December 5, B6.

Washington Post. 1991. "Virginia Dairy Charged with Price Fixing." July 31, D6.

———. 1997a. "Months of Anarchy in Albania Yield Financial Ruin, Public Fear: Lawlessness and Tattered Institutions Impede Return to Normality." August 4, A13.

———. 1997b. "Ex-Judge Sent Back to Jail in Sex-Abuse Case Appeal." August 16, A14.

Weisburd, D., and E. Waring. 1998. *White-Collar Crime and Criminal Careers.* New York: Cambridge University Press.

Weisburd, D., E. Waring, and E. Chayet. 1995. "Specific Deterrence in a Sample of Offenders Convicted of White-Collar Crimes." *Criminology* 33: 587–607.

Weisburd, D., S. Wheeler, E. Waring, and N. Bode. 1991. *Crimes of the Middle Classes.* New Haven, CT: Yale University Press.

Wheeler, S., and M. L. Rothman. 1982. "The Organization As Weapon in White-Collar Crime." *Michigan Law Review* 80: 1403–1426.

Wheeler, S., K. Mann, and A. Sarat. 1988. *Sitting in Judgment: The Sentencing of White-Collar Criminals.* New Haven, CT: Yale University Press.

Wolfgang, M. E., R. M. Figlio, P. E. Tracy, and S. I. Singer. 1985. *The National Survey of Crime Severity.* Washington, DC: U.S. Department of Justice, Bureau of Justice Statistics.

Wright, R., and S. Decker. 1997. *Armed Robbers in Action: Stick-Up and Street Culture.* Boston: Northeastern University Press.

Yeager, P. C. 1986. "Analyzing Corporate Offenses: Progress and Prospects." Pp. 93–120 in *Research in Corporate Social Performance and Policy.* Vol. 8. Edited by J. E. Post. Greenwich, CT: JAI.

———. 1992. *The Limits of Law: Public Regulation of Private Pollution.* New York: Cambridge University Press.

Yeager, P. C., and G. E. Reed. 1998. "Of Corporate Persons and Straw Men: A Reply to Herbert, Green, and Larragoite." *Criminology* 36: 885–897.

Zey, M. 1998. "Embeddedness of Interorganizational Corporate Crime in the 1980s: Securities Fraud of Banks and Investment Banks." Pp. 71–110 in *The Sociology of Organizations: Deviance in and of Organizations.* Vol. 15. Edited by P. A. Bamberger and W. J. Sonnenstuhl. Stamford, CT: JAI.

Zeitz, D. 1981. *Women Who Embezzle or Defraud: A Study of Convicted Felons.* New York: Praeger.

Zimring, F. E., and G. Hawkins. 1993. "Crime, Justice and the Savings and Loan Crisis." Pp. 247–292 in *Beyond the Law: Crime in Complex Organizations.* Edited by M. Tonry and A. J. Reiss, Jr. Chicago: University of Chicago Press.

PART FOUR

Explaining

Criminal Behavior

Attempting to explain criminal behavior is probably the most complex of criminological endeavors. The search for the causes of crime traditionally has taken two forms. In the first, criminal behavior is viewed as an inherent or acquired individual trait with genetic, biological, or psychological roots. In the second, criminality is explained mainly by sociological variables; crime is believed to originate in problems inherent in the structural or cultural makeup of society. Some sociological explanations treat the individual criminal passively. That is, they do not attempt to explain how societal factors induce the individual to commit crimes. Instead, they deal simply with the relationship between variations in societal crime levels and variations in other societal conditions. Others try to account more directly for criminal behavior by establishing a link between societal conditions and the individual: How does the societal condition actually produce effects within society's members?

Despite considerable scientific debate historically concerning biogenetic causal explanations of criminal activity, such explanations remain popular, especially in attempts to account for violent crime. In Chapter 12, "Nature, Nurture, and the Development of Criminality," Kristen C. Jacobson and David C. Rowe make the case that we should indeed be considering the potential effects of biological and genetic factors on aggression and criminality. They argue persuasively that considerable evidence points to correlations among these variables. More importantly, they point out that we need not be pulled into a false "nature versus nurture" debate. By seeking explanations of the ways in which biological and genetic phenomena might influence social behavior, we continue to recognize the importance of the social environment. It is possible that, to the extent that biology and genetics are at work, their effects may be altered or mediated by social factors. Similarly, perhaps biological or genetic factors will operate in the crime arena only when they interact with social variables. Finally, admitting the possibility of biological or genetic influences on crime does not negate the possibility of wholly independent social causes of criminality. The point, the authors argue, is that we should not close our minds to these multiple possibilities.

Robert Agnew reviews more traditionally sociological explanations of criminal behavior in Chapter 13, "Sources of Criminality: Strain and Subcultural Theories." Strain theory essentially locates crime in the individual's inability to achieve socially promoted goals through legitimate means. Blocked from conventional channels of goal achievement, individuals turn to property offenses to compensate. Frustrated and angry, some engage in violent crime. Agnew examines both classic and revised renditions of this approach and then offers his own general revision of both. He turns next to an evaluation of subcultural crime theory. This brand of explanation links criminal behavior to individuals' interaction with groups that possess values conducive to crime. He examines the evidence, first, for the existence of social subgroups who hold criminal values and, second, for whether individuals exposed to such groups are more criminal. In each instance, Agnew offers a qualified yes.

In Chapter 14, "Sources of Criminality: Control and Deterrence Theories," by Marvin Krohn, the focus shifts from the basic question informing the previous two chapters. Rather than try to understand why people violate the law, control theorists study the factors that constrain people from violating the law. They assume at base that most people are motivated toward crime and ask, Why don't they do it? Why do people obey the law? Krohn locates the answer in the amount of freedom individuals possess and the extent to which they perceive themselves at risk of losing what they value: relationships, investments, possessions. Krohn also examines the deterrence doctrine, with roots traced to the same assumptions as control models generally. Deterrence research investigates the inhibitory power of threatened legal punishments on offense behavior. He concludes that the findings of such research are weak and ambiguous and that we should resist the temptation to build anticrime policy around the deterrence doctrine.

Chapter Outline

12

Nature, Nurture, and the Development of Criminality

KRISTEN C. JACOBSON
*Virginia Institute for Psychiatric
and Behavioral Genetics*

DAVID C. ROWE
The University of Arizona

Biological predictors of criminal and antisocial behavior have fascinated behavioral scientists for over 100 years. The categorization of criminals by their physical characteristics can be found in Egyptian hieroglyphics over 4,000 years old. Physiognomy, the "reading of faces," was an accepted practice in medieval times, and allusions to the physical attributes of criminals can be found in works by Homer, Shakespeare, and in the Bible (Wilson and Herrnstein, 1985: 70–71). The earliest scientific study of the physical attributes of criminals is attributed to Cesare Lombroso during the post-Darwinian climate of the late nineteenth century. According to Lombroso's 1876 book, *The Criminal Man,* many criminals were "born criminals," throwbacks to an earlier evolutionary period who could be identified by certain physical characteristics. Lombroso compared the physical characteristics of Italian prisoners with those of Italian soldiers.

He discovered that criminals were more likely than soldiers to have asymmetrical faces or heads, large ears and lips, receding chins, long arms, short legs, and flat feet. Likewise, although disputing Lombroso's claims, Charles Goring ([1913] 1972) also believed that criminals differed from non-criminals in certain physical characteristics. In Goring's study, criminals were found to be shorter and thinner than non-criminals. Finally, Hooten (1939), although disputing Goring's specific claims, concluded that, on the basis of physical characteristics, criminals were "organically inferior" organisms.

During the post–World War II era, however, interest in the biological underpinnings of criminal and antisocial behavior waned. This change was due, in part, to three primary reasons: First, the earlier "biological" theories of physical attributes proposed by Lombroso, Goring, and Hooten were proven to be without scientific merit. Second, the eugenics movement during the turn of the century had its roots in the belief that, by limiting the reproduction of "genetically inferior" individuals, society could produce an improvement in the human species. Unfortunately, this movement culminated with the atrocities perpetrated during World War II, causing many behavioral scientists to view biological and genetic explanations for behavior with distaste. Third, mainstream interest in the biological influences on behavior waned with the increasing popularity of social class theory in sociology, behaviorism, and psychoanalysis—theories that placed the roots of criminal behavior squarely in the environment. These three theories of criminal behavior were embraced by the political ideology of the day, because they suggested that interventions targeted toward changing the community or family environment could "cure" people of crime. The political implications of these theories may have been largely responsible for their popularity over the course of nearly five decades, even as evidence against them continued to accrue (Wright, 1998).

The problem with social class, psychoanalytic, and behaviorist explanations for aggressive and criminal behavior is that they all completely ignore genetic factors. Specifically, although sociology placed the cause of crime in the social structure, focusing particularly on the association between social class and crime, an individual's genetically influenced characteristics may be causally related both to social class and to aggressive behavior. Thus, the often-observed correlation between lower-class status and crime may not indicate that poverty or neighborhood disorganization causes criminal behavior, but rather that other characteristics of individuals contribute to *both* criminal behavior and lower social class. Likewise, the social modeling expla-

nation that suggested that individuals "learned" criminal behavior from their parents ignores the fact that family members share genes as well as environments. Therefore, any resemblance in aggressive and criminal behavior among family members may be due to common genetic factors and/or their common environment.

This chapter will review the growing body of evidence that suggests that antisocial behavior has at least some biological component (Rowe and Osgood, 1984). We focus not only on criminal behavior, but also on antisocial behavior, broadly defined. This includes aggression and certain psychiatric disorders, such as antisocial personality disorder, conduct disorder, and attention-deficit disorder. It has been recognized that factors such as violence and psychiatric disorders often co-occur with and/or predate criminal activity. Hence, from a developmental perspective, we feel the inclusion of these other kinds of antisocial behavior is relevant for understanding the etiology of criminal behavior.

We open the chapter by challenging some of the criticisms of biological and genetic research on aggression and criminality that have been made by ardent environmentalists. We feel that the "nature *or* nurture" debate on the origins of criminal behavior is sadly outdated. Behavioral genetic research, in particular, has provided considerable evidence that individual differences in many phenotypes is a product of both nature *and* nurture. It is our contention that both factors are important; researchers who wholly disregard one or the other do so at their own peril.

We then present a short review of some of the potential biological bases of aggressive and antisocial behavior. Next, we briefly describe the most common behavioral genetic methods used to identify genetic and environmental influences on aggressive and antisocial behavior and follow by presenting some of the most recent evidence from behavioral genetic studies. The next section comments on the development of criminality and antisocial behavior. Finally, we end with a discussion of how genes and environment may interact to produce aggressive and criminal behavior, of how environmental conditions may moderate the expression of genetic potential for aggressive and criminal behavior, and of promising directions for future research.

CRITICISM OF THE CRITICS

Currently, most criminologists receive little training in behavioral genetics. Although this may change in the near future, criminologists today are often exposed to behavioral genetics only through the writings of the ideological critics of the field (e.g., Lewontin et al., 1984) without having completed any independent study of behavioral genetics. Although detailing all the specific concerns raised by these ideological critics is beyond the focus of this chapter, these criticisms are often methodologically focused. Twin studies that suggest genetic effects, in particular, receive criticisms such as "because identical twins are treated more alike than fraternal twins, they are more alike in behavior."

Such concerns do capture the attention of behavioral geneticists. Indeed, many studies have been conducted by behavioral geneticists, using different methodologies, to address both these concerns, as well as to test other assumptions of behavioral genetic research designs (Plomin et al., 1997; Rowe, 1994). The "look-alike" theory is easily seen to be flawed: It demands that physical appearance correlate with criminality. Yet we know that criminologists have already rejected the Lombrosian view that physical appearance predestinates crime. If appearance does not influence a trait, how can "alike in appear-

ance" make twins "alike in the trait"? Behavioral genetic studies have nonetheless examined the quantitative contribution of appearance similarity to behavioral trait similarity in identical twins (Rowe, 1994); it has been found to be negligible.

The equal-environments assumption of the twin method states that identical twins do not receive more equal trait-relevant treatments than do fraternal twins. Although it is clear that identical (monozygotic; MZ) twins are more likely, on average, to be treated similarly than fraternal (dizygotic; DZ) twins (e.g., to be dressed alike as children), it is unclear whether similarity in treatment is related to greater twin similarity in traits. There are many ways to test this assumption. One used in an early study by Loehlin and Nichols (1976) was to examine the effect of similar treatments within a sample of identical twins. Intensity of treatment similarity varies among identical twin pairs; some parents make more of an effort to treat them alike than do other parents. Loehlin and Nichols discovered, however, that those identical twin pairs receiving the more intense similarity of treatment were *not* more alike than other identical twins in traits such as personality and cognitive ability. Using both identical and fraternal twins, other studies have tested the equal-environments assumption for adult psychiatric and substance dependence disorders and found that neither similarity of physical appearance (Hettema et al., 1995), similarity of parental treatment, nor frequency of socialization (Kendler and Gardner, 1998) predict twin similarity for most psychiatric and substance dependence disorders. The exceptions pertain to bulimia and smoking initiation (but not nicotine dependence; see Kendler and Gardner, 1998).

We encourage criminologists to delve directly into behavioral genetic texts (e.g., Plomin et al., 1997) for a survey of the literature on twin studies and other research designs used in genetic research. The summaries of the research literature presented by the ideological critics of behavioral genetics are not always trustworthy or fair to researchers who have tried to identify and test problematic aspects of genetic theories (Wright, 1998).

If criminologists continue to ignore the increasing evidence that antisocial and criminal behavior have at least some genetic component, then a true understanding of how nature interacts with nurture in the development of antisocial and criminal behavior will not be achieved. However, an acceptance of this position has been slow in coming. For example, over ten years ago, Mednick (1987) discussed four reasons why criminologists should consider genetic influences in their theories. Of the four points he listed, three are of particular importance. First, he pointed out that the treatment of offenders under current environmental assumptions has been largely unsuccessful. Second, he argued that understanding how biology and environment may interact to produce criminal behavior could only serve to improve the effectiveness of treatment and prevention strategies. Third, he pointed out that acknowledging that a trait or behavior has a genetic or biological component does not mean that the trait or behavior would be unyielding to intervention.

Moreover, simply because behaviors may have some underlying genetic or biological component does not necessarily mean that strategies for treatment and prevention need to involve radical medical interventions. Modifying the environments of individuals at genetic or biological risk for criminality may be all that is necessary to prevent them from becoming criminals. Moreover, we argue that understanding how biological and genetic factors influence criminal behavior may be an effective means of identifying more precisely those individuals who may be at risk for the development of criminal behavior. Thus, the purpose of this chapter is to review the more promising aspects of research on the biological and genetic contributions to crime and to antisocial behavior in the hopes that more criminologists will begin to consider biological and genetic factors in their theories of the development of criminal behavior.

BIOLOGICAL INFLUENCES ON BEHAVIOR

In the latter half of the chapter, we present evidence from behavioral genetic studies that demonstrates that genetic factors do account for some of the variation in aggressive and criminal behavior. However, the demonstration that aggressive and criminal behavior is genetically influenced does not generally illuminate the features of human biology through which this genetic influence occurs. Thus, the present section reviews some of the most promising evidence for specific biological determinants and correlates of aggressive and criminal behavior: heart rate, serotonin, and hormones.

Heart Rate and Aggressive and Criminal Behavior

Perhaps the most replicated finding has been that criminal behavior is associated with a below-average resting heart rate. For example, the Cambridge Study in Delinquent Behavior is a longitudinal study (i.e., one that studies the same subjects at multiple points in time) that assessed multiple measures of aggressive and criminal behavior among 411 British males, including reports of official convictions from ages 10 to 40,

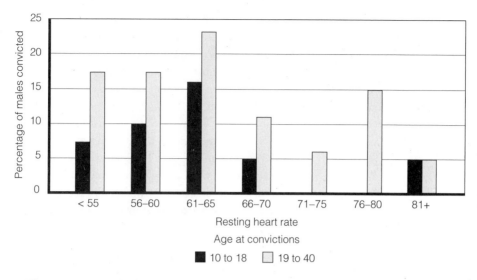

FIGURE 12.1 Percentage of violence convictions by resting heart rate

SOURCE: Data from D. P. Farrington, 1997.

parent and teacher reports of delinquent behavior between the ages of 8 and 15, and self-reported delinquency at ages 8 to 13. Measures of autonomic arousal (involuntary nervous responses), including resting heart rate, were obtained when subjects were 18. Some of the results from this study have been summarized by Farrington (1997). Figure 12.1 shows the proportions of males convicted of violent crimes at ages 10–18 and ages 19–40 by their resting heart rate, based on the results presented by Farrington (1997). The average resting heart rate among all males at age 18 was approximately 68 beats per minute. As can be seen in Figure 12.1, males with resting heart rates below 66 beats per minutes had rates of official convictions for violence that were higher than males with heart rates greater than or equal to 66 beats per minute. This was particularly true for official conviction rates when males were ages 10 to 18. The proportion of males convicted for violent crimes at any point between ages 10 and 40 was .25 for males with resting heart beats below 66, com-

pared to .11 for males with higher resting heart rates. Moreover, the resting heart rate measure remained a significant predictor of violence (including measurement via official convictions, self-report, and teacher reports) even after controlling for individual and social factors such as smoking, parent convictions, poor parent-child relations, low IQ, and lack of concentration (Farrington, 1997).

Likewise, investigators using the British National Survey of Health and Development, a longitudinal survey of over 5,300 children born in England, Scotland, or Wales during March 1946, found that resting heart rate at age 11 predicted convictions for violent crimes and sexual offenses up to age 21 (Wadsworth, 1976). Specifically, low heart rates were found for 81 percent of violent offenders and 67 percent of sexual offenders, compared to 54.3 percent of nondelinquents (Wadsworth, 1976). Likewise, in their nine-year prospective, longitudinal study, Raine and colleagues reported that low resting heart rate among an unselected sample of schoolboys at age 15 predicted crime at age 24 (Raine et al., 1990).

Overall, there is considerable evidence for a link between a low resting heart rate and higher rates of antisocial behavior, especially violence. One review of fourteen studies of non-institutionalized children and adolescents found that a low resting heart rate was significantly associated with antisocial behavior in all fourteen studies (Raine, 1993). Likewise, a more recent meta-analysis found significant effect sizes in the expected direction for 22 out of 25 independent samples (reported in Raine et al., 1997). Moreover, the average effect size was approximately 0.53, indicating a moderate relationship between low resting heart rate and antisocial and criminal behavior. It has been suggested that the low resting heart rate is indicative of under-arousal of the autonomic nervous system (ANS). This has been further supported by the finding that other measures of ANS arousal—such as the level of upset or excitement indicated by changes in the skin surface (termed "skin conductance orientation," this measurement is also used in lie detector tests)—are also associated with violence and crime (Raine et al., 1990; for effects of autonomic processing between heart rate and respiration, see Mezzacappa et al., 1997).

Serotonin and Aggressive Behavior

Results from a variety of animal and human studies have indicated that brain serotonergic systems may regulate aggressive behavior. The serotonin system is thought to be related to the ability to constrain or inhibit behavior. Thus, lower than desirable serotonergic functioning is thought to ease constraints on aggressive behavior (Spoont, 1992). In clinical studies of humans, low levels of the primary serotonin metabolite

(CSF 5-HIAA) have discriminated between aggressive patients and matched controls (e.g., Coccaro, 1989; Virkkunen et al., 1994) and have predicted later aggressive behavior among children (Kruesi et al., 1992) and adults (Virkkunen et al., 1989).

Likewise, a recent epidemiological study has demonstrated a link between whole blood serotonin and aggressive and criminal behavior among a non-clinical sample of humans (Moffitt et al., 1997, 1998). Specifically, Moffitt and colleagues obtained rates of lifetime official convictions and self-reports of delinquency and aggression during the past year from a sample of 781 21-year-olds from a single birth cohort in New Zealand. Using blood samples, investigators also calculated whole-blood serotonin levels for each individual. Higher levels of whole-blood serotonin are thought to be indicative of lower serotonergic functioning; thus, the hypothesis was that higher levels of blood serotonin would be associated with higher rates of aggressive and criminal behavior. Their study found partial support for their hypothesis; namely, the expected relationship was observed among males, but not females. Specifically, investigators created two groups of men based on both self-reports and official convictions: violent men versus nonviolent men (including some who had committed nonviolent offenses). As expected, whole-blood serotonin levels were significantly higher among the violent men (effect size = .56). This effect remained even after investigators controlled (independently) for factors such as drug use, platelet count, body mass, psychiatric disorder, socioeconomic status (SES), nonviolent crime, and family relations. Similarly, whole-blood serotonin levels were correlated with aggression among a sample of 43 adolescent males incarcerated in a residential treatment facility for juvenile offenders (Unis et al., 1997). Levels of blood serotonin were not related to violence among females. Overall, the evidence suggests that less than desirable serotonergic functioning may be partially responsible for criminal behavior, especially for violent or aggressive crimes perpetrated by males.

Hormones and Aggressive Behavior

Animal studies, particularly castration studies, have pointed to the role of hormones in the expression of aggressive and violent behavior (e.g., Albert et al., 1990; Simon et al., 1984; Wagner et al., 1979). Differences in sex-specific hormones have been posited to be partly responsible for the higher levels of aggressive and criminal behavior among males. One of the most consistently studied hormones is testosterone. Although some evidence suggests that higher levels of testosterone are related to increased aggressive behavior, the demonstration of a causal relation between any specific sex hormone, including testosterone, and behavior has been somewhat inconsistent (see Archer, 1991, for an excellent, albeit somewhat dated, review of research on testosterone and aggression).

On the one hand, there is considerable evidence from studies of non-human animals, both naturalistic and experimental, that higher levels of testosterone are associated with increases in aggressive behavior. Moreover, a relatively large body of research on humans demonstrates an association between higher levels of testosterone and more aggressive behavior among older adolescent and adult males. For example, Brooks and Reddon (1996) reported that higher levels of serum testosterone differentiated violent offenders from nonviolent and sexual offenders in their selected sample of 15–17-year-old males. Virkkunen et al. (1994) also found that mean levels of CSF-free testosterone differentiated

alcoholic, impulsive offenders from a sample of healthy volunteers. Likewise, testosterone levels were correlated at .36 and .38 with self-reports of physical and verbal aggression, respectively, in an unselected sample of 58 16-year-old Swedish males, even after controlling for pubertal status (Olweus et al., 1980). Further analysis of their data revealed that higher testosterone levels were correlated with greater reports of provoked, but not unprovoked, aggressive behavior (Olweus et al., 1980). In a causal analysis using data from the same sample, Olweus et al. (1988) reported that, although other variables also had an effect on provoked aggressive behavior in ninth grade, the level of testosterone in ninth grade had a direct effect on provoked aggressive behavior, even after controlling for variables assessed in sixth grade, including previous aggressive behaviors. For unprovoked aggressive behavior, higher testosterone levels had an indirect effect on behavior through lower frustration tolerance, but no direct effect (Olweus et al., 1988). Finally, results from a large sample of military veterans indicated that multiple measures of aggression and psychopathology, including retrospective reports of childhood deviance, adult delinquency, and adult substance abuse, were correlated with higher levels of serum testosterone (Dabbs and Morris, 1990; however, testosterone levels also interacted with socioeconomic status; see discussion on p. 340).

On the other hand, the evidence that testosterone levels are related to levels of aggressive behavior among children and younger adolescent males is less consistent. For example, Constantino et al. (1993) reported that serum testosterone levels failed to differentiate between eighteen highly aggressive, 4–10-year-old boys and a group of eighteen carefully matched controls. Schaal and colleagues (1996) found that boys who were more aggressive from the ages of 6 to

12 had *lower* levels of testosterone at age 13 years. At age 13, boys are undergoing puberty, and consequently hormonal levels are changing rapidly. Perhaps this factor explains the anomalous direction of this result.

In one of the few studies of testosterone to include female children and adolescents, Inoff-Germain and colleagues (1988) found that hormone levels, including sex steroids (e.g., testosterone and estradiol), gonadotropins, and adrenal androgens, were better predictors of observed aggressive behavior among 9–14-year-old females than among 10–14-year-old males. Although a few of the gonadotropins and adrenal androgens were associated with some manifestations of observed aggressive behavior among males, testosterone itself was not related to any of the aggressive behaviors (although testosterone was related to the expression of modulated anger once testosterone-estradiol binding globulin was removed from the analyses; consult Inoff-Germain et al., 1988, for more details). Among females, the sex steroid estradiol was significantly related to most measures of observed aggressive behavior.

The unexpected direction of the gender difference reported in Inoff-Germain et al. (1988) is somewhat puzzling, considering that earlier reports using the same data set suggested that the association between hormones and aggressive behavior was stronger among males than among females. For example, Susman et al. (1987) reported that nine different indicators of hormones, entered into a multiple regression, explained a significant amount of variance in maternal ratings of delinquency and rebellious behaviors among boys (although hormones failed to predict maternal ratings of aggression). Among girls, none of the multiple regressions was significant once age and pubertal status were controlled for, indicating that hormones

have little direct influence on antisocial behavior among females. Likewise, Nottelmann et al. (1987) reported that hormones were more consistently associated with both self-reports of adjustment and maternal ratings of behavioral problems among males than among females. Again, however, hormone levels failed to predict aggressive behavior. In all three of these studies, testosterone, in and of itself, was not related to any type of antisocial behavior among either boys and girls. In fact, a lower testosterone-to-estradiol ratio among males (indicating lower relative levels of testosterone) was actually associated with *higher* levels of adjustment and behavioral problems among males (Nottlemann et al., 1987). Hence, research on younger children and adolescents has failed to find a consistent relationship between testosterone and aggression, even among males.

One possible reason for the discrepancy between results is that studies vary widely in the way testosterone is measured (e.g., plasma-free testosterone is hypothesized to have a stronger association with aggressive behavior than plasma-total testosterone levels; see Archer, 1991) and in the way antisocial and aggressive behavior is defined and measured (that is, illegal behavior versus problematic behavior in school). A second possibility is that the failure to find a consistent relationship between testosterone and aggression among younger children and adolescents (or among adolescents spanning a wide range of pubertal statuses) simply reflects reality. Specifically, it is possible that the biological changes that occur during puberty trigger the influence of testosterone on aggressive behavior. Nevertheless, if serum testosterone levels are only related to aggression after puberty, then they cannot explain the gender differences in aggression that are found even among young (i.e., 3–6-year-old) children (Maccoby and Jacklin, 1980). The explanation could lie, however, in the prenatal organizing effect of testosterone on brain development, which is a source of sex differences in many mammalian species (Ellis and Ames, 1987).

A final problem with the research on the relationship between testosterone and aggression concerns the nature of causality. Experimental studies with animals have demonstrated that removing sex-linked hormones reduces aggressive behavior, and replacing the hormones increases aggressive behavior (e.g., Wagner et al., 1979). However, parallel studies with humans are sparse. Moreover, a number of studies have shown that hormone levels are extremely responsive to environmental conditions (see Booth and Osgood, 1993; Mazur and Booth, 1998). For example, in a longitudinal study of university tennis players, Booth and colleagues (1989) found that levels of testosterone rose prior to a competitive tennis match. Moreover, levels of testosterone declined more rapidly during and after the match among the losers of the match than among the winners. Based on studies such as these, it is possible that the correlation between testosterone and aggressive and criminal behavior may not indicate that higher levels of testosterone cause aggressive behavior, but rather that aggressive behavior changes levels of testosterone. Further support for this hypothesis comes from the longitudinal study by Olweus and colleagues (1988) discussed above. Although their causal analysis indicated that levels of testosterone at age 16 were directly related to age 16 (provoked) aggressive behaviors, aggressive behaviors three years prior also predicted level of testosterone, although the effect was rather weak.

A slightly different hypothesis is that increases in testosterone simply augment already-existing levels of aggressive behavior. For example, in a study of captive adult male Talapoin

monkeys, Dixson and Herbert (1977) found that injecting gonadectomized (i.e., castrated) male monkeys with testosterone significantly increased their aggressive behavior toward subordinate male monkeys, but not toward dominant male or female monkeys. Thus, the authors concluded that the effect of testosterone on aggressive behavior may depend upon both physical condition and previous social experiences.

In conclusion, opinion is still divided among experts concerning the causal influence of higher testosterone levels with increased aggressive behavior. The only way to either prove or disprove this hypothesis is through more research. In particular, longitudinal studies and/or studies that can experimentally manipulate levels of hormones are needed. Also needed is greater attention to the link between hormones and aggressive and antisocial behavior among females.

BEHAVIORAL GENETICS AND ANALYSIS OF AGGRESSION AND CRIMINAL BEHAVIOR

The preceding sections reviewed research on some specific biological predictors and correlates of aggressive and criminal behavior. However, one advantage to using behavioral genetic designs is that the precise genetic (and environmental) influences do not have to be specified. The following sections briefly describe behavioral genetic terminology and methods and present the evidence for genetic and environmental influences on variation in antisocial behavior.

Terms Used in Behavioral Genetics

In behavioral genetic analyses, variation in any given phenotype is decomposed into variation from three sources: shared environmental factors, nonshared environmental factors, and genetic factors.

Shared environmental factors include those environmental factors that serve to make individuals in a family similar to one another; common examples are socioeconomic status, family structure, and shared peer influences. To be considered a shared environmental influence, three conditions must hold: First, the environmental influence must be shared by both individuals. Second, the shared environmental influence must be related to the phenotype under study. For example, exposure to radon gas may be a shared environmental influence for the development of cancer, but it is less likely to be a shared environmental influence for personality development. Third, the shared environmental influence must have the *same* influence on behavior for both individuals. For example, the experience of parental divorce is an environmental factor that is shared by two siblings in the same family. However, if one sibling responds to the parental divorce by throwing himself into his studies, and the other sibling responds by acting out and skipping school, then parental divorce is not likely to be a shared environmental influence for the cognitive development of these two siblings. If divorce typically had dissimilar effects on siblings, it would count mostly as a nonshared environmental influence.

Nonshared environmental influences are any environmental influences that serve to make individuals dissimilar. Nonshared environmental influences can occur if exposure to the environment is not shared by siblings. For example, birth order, accidents, and different peer groups are nonshared environmental influences. Likewise, as stated above, "shared" environmental factors that have different influences on behavior of individuals in the same family are also considered to be nonshared environmental factors.

Behavioral Genetic Methods

Two primary designs are used in behavioral genetic research. The first method involves obtaining data from an adopted individual and both his or her adoptive and biological parents. Barring effects of selective placement, any behavioral and attitudinal resemblance between an adopted individual and his or her adopted parents is due to shared environmental influences, because adopted parents and children generally do not share genes. If individuals resemble their biological parents more than their adopted parents, then genetic factors are indicated. Genetic factors can also be calculated by comparing the level of behavioral and attitudinal patterns of adoptive siblings with that obtained from full siblings. To the extent that the level of patterning among biological (i.e., full) siblings is greater than patterning among adoptive siblings, then genetic factors are implicated.

The second method commonly used in behavioral genetic research compares correlations among siblings who differ in degree of genetic relatedness, that is, monozygotic (MZ, or identical) and dizygotic (DZ, or fraternal) twins, full siblings, half siblings, and unrelated siblings. MZ twins share 100 percent of their genes; DZ twins and full siblings, on average, share 50 percent of their genes; half siblings, on average, share 25 percent of their genes; and unrelated siblings have no genes in common. If levels of patterning regarding a measured behavior or trait (a phenotype, in behavioral genetic terminology) increase with the level of genetic relatedness, genetic influences are indicated. In other words, genetic influences on a behavior or trait are implied if the pattern for the MZ twins is more apparent than that for the DZ twins and full siblings, and the pattern for the DZ twins and full siblings is more apparent than that for the half siblings, which, in turn, is more apparent than that for the unrelated siblings.

Scientists have designed sophisticated analytic statistical methods to sort out the effects of shared and nonshared environmental influences from genetic influences. That is, they have developed methods by which to attribute a percentage of a given behavior or trait to environmental factors (such as family culture and school situation) and the remaining percentage to genetic factors. The percentage attributed to genetic factors is called heritability.

Behavioral Genetic Study Results

Results from both twin and adoption studies support the hypothesis that aggressive and criminal behavior have some genetic component (see Brennan and Mednick, 1993; and DiLalla and Gottesman, 1989, for reviews). Results from two meta-analyses indicate that the average heritability estimate for aggressive and antisocial behavior is approximately .50 (Mason and Frick, 1994; Miles and Carey, 1997).

Perhaps the most famous adoption study of criminal and antisocial behavior used data from the comprehensive Danish Adoption Register. Using court conviction records from 14,427 adoptees, their biological mothers and fathers, and their adopted mothers and fathers, Mednick and colleagues (Brennan and Mednick, 1993; Mednick et al., 1984) reported that rates of criminal convictions among males increased with biological parent convictions, but not adoptive parent convictions. For example, the rate of criminal convictions among male adoptees with neither

biological or adoptive parent convictions was 13.5 percent. When adoptive parents, but not biological parents, had criminal convictions, the rate of criminality among adoptees increased only to 14.7 percent. In contrast, the rate of criminal convictions when biological parents, but not adoptive parents, had criminal convictions increased to 20 percent. Although the highest rate of criminal convictions (24.5 percent) occurred among adoptees whose biological and adoptive parents both had criminal convictions, the influence of the adoptive parents' criminal convictions was not significant, nor was the interaction between adoptive and biological parents' criminal convictions (Mednick et al., 1984). Recidivism of the biological parent (i.e., the number of biological parent convictions) was also associated with adoptees' offending rates, but only for property offenses. As Figure 12.2 demonstrates, the percentage of adoptees who committed property offenses increased dramatically with the number of biological parent convictions. In contrast, the relationship between number of biological convictions and rate of violent offenses was not significant.

In *A General Theory of Crime*, Gottfredson and Hirschi (1990) criticized the findings from Mednick's adoption study. They noted that the findings were stronger in Mednick's original urban sample than in the more rural sample later added from the rest of Denmark. Although Mednick's attempt to replicate his urban study was viewed as a failure, the effect holds in the sample taken as a whole and may be weaker in non-urban areas for many reasons. Fortunately, other adoption studies also implicate genetic influences on crime and antisocial behavior, so Mednick's findings do not stand in isolation.

For example, similar findings were reported in Cadoret's (1978) study of antisocial behavior

FIGURE 12.2

Percentage of male adoptees convicted,

by number of convictions of biological parents

SOURCE: Reprinted with permission from S. A. Mednick, W. F. Gabrielli, and B. Hutchings (1984). "Genetic Influences in Criminal Convictions: Evidence from an Adoption Cohort." Science, 224, 891–894. Copyright 1984 American Association for the Advancement of Science.

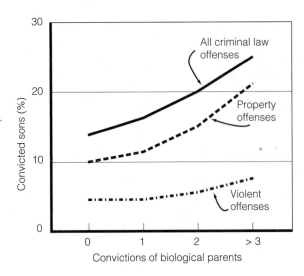

and psychopathology among a sample of 246 adopted children and adults in Iowa. Among the adults, psychiatric disorder was found for 78 percent of individuals with an antisocial biological background (83 percent if both biological parents had a psychiatric disorder and 51 percent if only one biological parent had a psychiatric disorder), compared to a 28 percent incidence of psychopathology among controls. Moreover, 22 percent of adults with an antisocial biological background were themselves diagnosed with antisocial personality, compared to 0 percent in both the control group and other diagnosis groups. However, among the children in the study, virtually identical rates of psychiatric disorders were found among children with an antisocial biological background (25 percent) and controls (27 percent). Thus, results from the Iowa Adoption Study indicate that genetic factors may play a critical role in the development of adult, but not childhood, antisocial personality disorder. However, it should be noted that among the child sample, many individuals were

preadolescents. Hence, some of these individuals may later receive a diagnosis of antisocial personality. In a separate study of adult adoptees, Cadoret and colleagues (1995) found evidence of biological influences on retrospective reports of both conduct disorder and adolescent aggressivity (but not child aggressivity).

Twin and sibling studies of children, adolescents, and adults also support the notion of genetic influences on antisocial and aggressive and delinquent behavior. For example, the average weighted MZ twin concordance rate for adult criminality was .51, compared to a weighted average of .22 among adult DZ twins (see DiLalla and Gottesman, 1989: Table 2), signifying genetic influence. Likewise, a population-based study of Danish adults revealed a heritability estimate of .54 for adult criminality using correlations calculated from concordance rates among MZ and DZ twins (Cloninger and Gottesman, 1987).

Even more compelling evidence exists for genetic influences on child and adolescent antisocial behavior, delinquency, and aggression. For example, Ghodsian-Carpey and Baker (1987) reported heritabilities of .24–.94 for maternal ratings of multiple indicators on aggressive behavior among 4- to 7-year-old twins. Aggressive behavior in adolescence also appears to have a genetic component. Results from large-scale twin studies in four different countries indicate that genetic factors account for a significant portion of the variation in adolescent delinquent and aggressive behavior. Specifically, Eley and colleagues (1999) found that the heritability of aggressive behavior as measured by mothers' reports on the Child Behavior Checklist (CBCL) ranged from .69–.70 among samples of over 1,000 Swedish 9–10-year-old twin pairs and over 500 British 8–16-year-old twin pairs. Also using mother reports on the CBCL, Gjone and Stevenson (1997) calculated the heritability of aggressive behavior to be .85 among 7–17-year-old same-sex twins from five Norwegian birth cohorts. An additional study of 181 7–15-year-old same-sex twins from the Western Reserve Twin Project in the United States reported that the heritability of aggression (measured by parent reports on the CBCL) was .60 (Edelbrock et al., 1995). In addition, all of these studies reported that shared environmental factors did not significantly influence twin similarity for aggressive behavior.

In contrast, there is some evidence that genetic influences are weaker, and shared environmental influences are stronger, for adolescent delinquent behavior. Using adolescent self-reports of antisocial behavior (including minor delinquency, theft, and aggression) from approximately 265 same-sex American twin pairs, Rowe (1983, 1986) reported that models without genetic factors fit significantly more poorly than models with genetic influences. However, a model that also included shared environmental factors did not fit significantly more poorly than the model without shared environmental factors, suggesting that both genetic and shared environmental factors contribute to adolescent delinquency. Rowe and Gulley (1992) argued from sibling similarity data that the source of the shared environmental influence was siblings' exposure to peer groups that either encouraged or discouraged antisocial behavior.

Gjone and Stevenson (1997) also reported a lower heritability for the Delinquency scale of the CBCL, compared to the heritability they obtained for the Aggression scale (.59 versus .89, respectively). Likewise, using the same measure on twin pairs from Sweden and Britain, Eley et al. (1999) found that the heritability of delinquency was lower than the heritability of aggression. Moreover, whereas shared environmental factors did not contribute to the variation in adolescent aggressive behavior, they explained between 27 and 64 percent of the variation in delinquent behavior. Finally, two smaller twin studies found that genetic factors contributed only marginally to variation in adolescent antisocial delinquent behavior. Thapar and McGuffin (1996), using a sample of 198 same-sex child and adolescent twins from the Cardiff (Wales) Twin Register found that genetic factors explained only 28 percent of the variation in maternal reports of antisocial behavior (five items assessing primarily delinquent, non-aggressive behaviors), compared to 40 percent explained by shared environment. In addition, the genetic factors just missed statistical significance at conventional levels. Similar results were reported in Edelbrock et al. (1995): Genetic factors and shared environmental factors each explained approximately 35 percent of the variation in adolescent delinquency, although, again, the genetic influence just missed statistical significance.

THE DEVELOPMENT OF ANTISOCIAL BEHAVIOR

The Continuity of Antisocial Behavior

Psychiatrists and psychologists have recognized that criminal behavior may be closely related to other disorders, such as attention deficit disorder and conduct disorder in childhood, and antisocial personality disorder (ASP) in adulthood. For example, the majority of adult criminals are also thought to suffer from antisocial personality disorder, although this is partly due to the fact that committing illegal activities is one of the diagnostic criterion for ASP. When different manifestations of antisocial behavior across developmental periods are considered, criminologists are mainly in agreement that there is remarkable stability to antisocial behavior. Using data from four longitudinal studies of males, Robins (1978) concluded that, although most children with antisocial behavior problems do not become antisocial adults, virtually all adults diagnosed with antisocial behavior disorder were antisocial children. What is particularly remarkable about this result is that it was replicated in four independent samples, even though the samples represented males from different racial and social backgrounds and from different historical eras (Robins, 1978). Childhood behaviors were more predictive of adult antisocial behavior than family variables, including parental antisocial behavior, family structure, and social class.

In a prospective follow-up of 103 male children diagnosed with attention deficit disorder with hyperactivity (ADHD) between the ages of 6 and 12 and 100 matched controls, Mannuzza and colleagues (1989) reported that rates of official arrests and convictions at ages 16–23 were higher among the ADHD sample than controls. These patterns were particularly pronounced for repeat offenders (arrest rate = 26 percent among ADHD sample, compared to 8 percent among controls), felony arrests (25 percent versus 7 percent), and arrests for aggressive offenses (18 percent versus 7 percent). Similar results have been reported by others (e.g., Satterfield et al., 1982), and other studies have also demonstrated that attention problems, impulsivity, and activity are all precursors to later antisocial behavior (Loeber and Hay, 1997).

Aggressive behavior in childhood has also been found to predict delinquent and criminal behavior during adolescence and young adulthood. For instance, in a follow-up study of over 1,000 subjects from a cohort of 10-year-olds in Sweden, Stattin and Magnusson (1989) reported that teacher ratings of aggression at age 13 predicted conviction by age 26, particularly multiple convictions. As an example, almost half (45.4 percent) of males with the highest aggression score at age 13 had been convicted of four or more offenses, compared to none of the males who scored lowest on aggression at age 13. A similar pattern was seen among girls, although the overall frequency of convictions was much lower. Teacher ratings of aggression at age 10 were also predicted of later criminality, although this was true only for boys. Finally, aggressive behavior predicted convictions for both violent offenses and property offenses, but was less strongly associated with crimes for drug offenses, traffic offenses, and crimes for personal gain.

The studies summarized above show a strong phenotypic continuity of antisocial behavior, but cannot reveal why behavior remains stable or why it changes. Developmental behavioral genetic studies are a means of investigating developmental stability and change in behavior. In this type of study, genetically informative kin are interviewed or observed on more than one occasion. Van den Oord and Rowe (1997) examined the developmental stability of problem behavior, including antisocial behavior, in a study of full siblings, half siblings, and cousins. The data set came from a study that started as a household probability sample of adolescents in the United States. The children of the original participants were later enrolled in the study. Some of them were born as full or half siblings. The measure of problem behavior was maternal (or head-of-household) ratings of their 4- to 10-year-old children on the Problem Behavior Index. The longitudinal data spanned three age periods: wave 1, 4–6 years old; wave 2, 6–8 years old; and wave 3, 8–10 years old.

Inspection of the data revealed several patterns that were more formally investigated through sophisticated statistical testing. Behavioral stability over four years was nearly as great as it was over two years, indicating that influences were not simply transmitted culturally but were trait dispositions. Genetic influences on problem behavior were also indicated because genetically more-alike siblings resembled one another more than did genetically more-distant ones; for example, for total problem behaviors at wave 2, the patterning for full siblings was greater than that for half siblings, which in turn was greater than that for cousins. Finally, patterns persisted over waves of subjects, suggesting genetic influences on the maintenance of similarity of siblings' problem behavior over time.

Statistical analysis also yielded estimates of heritability, shared environmental effects, and nonshared environmental effects on the development of problem behavior. For example, when estimates were averaged across all three waves, 29.9 percent of the variation in problem behavior was attributed to genetic influences, 16.8 percent to shared environmental influences, and 53.3 percent to nonshared environmental influences. Further, nonshared environmental influences made no contribution to stability of problem behavior, although they did explain individual differences in problem behavior at any one given time. Identifying the genetic and shared environmental factors that contribute to stability of problem behavior should enable better prediction of who will become long-term criminals.

Who Becomes a Criminal?

Although virtually all adult criminals were delinquent during adolescence, many adolescents who participate in delinquent activities desist from crime as adults. Likewise, although age of onset of antisocial behavior is the single best predictor of adult criminal outcomes (Farrington et al., 1990) and early arrest is predictive of greater recidivism (Loeber, 1982), by the time an individual is arrested for his or her antisocial activities, it may be difficult, if not impossible, to alter that developmental trajectory. Of great importance for prevention and intervention, then, is a means of identifying those individuals who are at greatest risk of becoming adult criminals.

Moffitt (1993) proposed a developmental taxonomy of adolescent delinquency that distinguished adolescents who participate in deviant activities primarily during adolescence (the Adolescent Limited Delinquent [ALD]) from adolescents whose patterns of antisocial behavior are consistent across the life course (the Life-Course Persistent delinquent [LCP]). Moffitt proposes that a relatively small percentage of adolescents are LCP delinquents, but that these individuals will continue their deviant activities throughout their lifespan. This is consistent with the finding that a relatively small proportion of people who are chronic offenders (15 percent in Philadelphia) were responsible for a disproportionate share of all arrests, especially serious ones

(74 percent of all arrests and 82 percent of Index-crime arrests; Wolfgang et al., 1987: 79). In addition to making differential predictions about the continuation of deviant activities in adulthood, Moffitt's theory also proposes that LCP individuals can be distinguished from ALD individuals on the basis of behavioral and temperamental characteristics in childhood.

Moffitt and colleagues (1996) have presented data in support of the distinction between LCP and ALD individuals. In their longitudinal study of a single birth cohort in a large New Zealand city, they reported that LCP adolescents were more likely than ALD adolescents to be rated as having a "difficult" temperament at age 3 (defined by factors such as restlessness, short attention spans, and negativism). Moreover, the distinguishing characteristics of ALD and LCP adolescents may appear even earlier. Indeed, Tremblay et al. (in press) investigated the onset and frequency of physical aggression in 17-month-old children and suggested that Moffitt's distinction between life-course persistent versus limited delinquency was already present, with a minority of children unable to inhibit aggression upon their entry into kindergarten. Tremblay (personal communication to the authors, November 12, 1998) also found that the predictors of toddler aggression, such as criminality in a biological parent and poor parenting styles, were like those studied in much older children.

Because characteristics such as temperament and aggression in childhood are influenced by genetic characteristics (Plomin et al., 1997), it is possible that behavioral genetic designs might also aid in understanding the distinction between ALD and LCP delinquents. For example, although Moffitt states that it is almost impossible to distinguish LCP and ALD delinquents using cross-sectional studies of adolescents, she also proposes that LCP individuals are more

likely than ALD individuals to engage in more serious and more violent activities (Moffitt, 1993). She supports this assertion with the result that LCP adolescents were more likely than ALD adolescents to display psychopathic traits in adolescence and to participate in violent activities (Moffitt et al., 1996). In twin studies of adolescent delinquency and aggression, aggressive behavior has been found to be more heritable than is delinquent behavior (e.g., Edelbrock et al., 1995; Eley et al., 1999; Gjone and Stevenson, 1997), reinforcing the notion that adolescents who engage in more serious delinquent activities may differ from those who do not on the basis of specific genetically influenced characteristics. As research in molecular genetics continues to identify the specific genes associated with precursors of LCP delinquency, such as ADHD and conduct disorder, it might be possible to identify individuals at risk on the basis of their genotypes. Such information would be of tremendous importance for the development of prevention programs.

THE JOINT INFLUENCE OF NATURE AND NURTURE

Thus far, we have considered the role of biological and genetic factors in the etiology of delinquent, antisocial, aggressive, and criminal behavior. Although occasionally inconsistent, results from the majority of studies are overwhelmingly in support of some kind of biological and/or genetic influence on antisocial behavior. However, we do not mean to imply that the environment had no role in the etiology of antisocial behavior. To begin with, theoretical frameworks such as that presented by Moffitt (1993) or the life-course perspective advocated by Simons et al. (1998) suggest that although genetic factors may

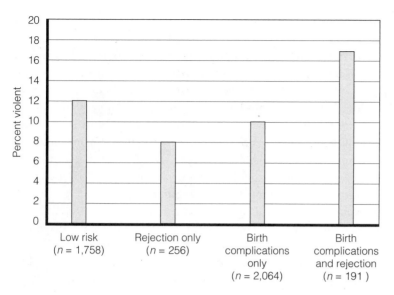

FIGURE 12.3

Interaction of birth complications with early maternal rejection in predisposing individuals to criminal violence at age 34

SOURCE: A. Raine, P. Brennan, and S. A. Mednick (1997). "Interactions Between Birth Complications and Early Maternal Rejection in Predisposing Individuals to Adult Violence." American Journal of Psychiatry, 154, 1269. Copyright 1997, the American Psychiatric Association. Reprinted by permission.

be partly responsible for the initial occurrence of antisocial behavior, environmental factors play a large role in the maintenance and escalation of antisocial behavior. Moreover, behavioral genetic studies point to the importance of the environment to explain variation in antisocial behavior. For delinquent behavior among adolescents, shared environmental factors are strongly implicated. Environmental factors are also implied in the etiology of aggressive behavior, but the nature of these influences appear to be nonshared by siblings in the same family.

Nevertheless, there is a growing consensus that genetic and environmental influences on variation in antisocial behavior may not operate in an additive fashion; that is, studies that attempt to identify the *independent* effects of biological factors and environmental factors may mask the true complexity of organism–environment interaction. Promising directions for research on aggressive and criminal behavior can be found in models that emphasize the joint influences of environment and biology. Examples of such models are the biosocial perspective (e.g., Raine,

Brennan, and Farrington, 1997) and the different gene-environment interaction models currently used in behavioral genetic research on psychopathology (e.g., Cadoret et al., 1995; Kendler and Eaves, 1986). What is particularly novel about these approaches is that, in addition to acknowledging that both biology and environment may contribute independently to development of criminality, both models emphasize that biology and environments may also interact to influence behavior. In particular, it is thought that a genetic tendency toward aggressive and criminal behavior might be expressed only in given circumstances—most often, a harsh rearing environment.

For example, Raine, Brennan, and Mednick (1997) reported that birth complications interacted with early maternal rejection to predict adult violence. Specifically, adult violent offenders were more likely to have experienced both birth complications and early maternal rejection than just one of these risk factors (see Figure 12.3). The interactive effect of birth complications and early maternal rejection was especially strong in predicting the onset of violence before age 18. Interestingly, Raine, Brennan, and Mednick found that this interaction effect did not generalize to non-violent criminal offenses.

Using data from male American veterans, Dabbs and Morris (1990) reported that higher levels of testosterone predicted adult deviance and retrospective reports of childhood delinquency only among males from a low socioeconomic background. Among adolescents from higher SES backgrounds, testosterone was not related to childhood or adult deviance. Likewise, a different study using the same sample found an interaction effect between testosterone levels and a measure of social integration (defined by factors such as educational attainment, organizational ties, job stability, and marriage) for adult deviance (Booth and Osgood, 1993). Specifically, the difference in adult deviance associated with low, medium, and high levels of testosterone was greatest when participants reported low levels of social integration. When social integration was high, there was virtually no relationship between level of testosterone and adult deviance. These two studies suggest that biological risk factors might contribute to antisocial behavior only when environmental conditions are poor.

There is also evidence from behavioral genetic studies for interaction between genes and environment in the development of antisocial behavior. For example, Cadoret and colleagues (1995, 1997) found evidence for an "environmental trigger" in their Iowa adoption study of aggressivity and conduct disorders. In their research, biological risk, defined as having a biological parent with antisocial personality disorder (ASP), interacted with adverse adoptive home environments (defined by factors such as psychopathology, drug abuse, and divorce or separation in the adoptive family) to predict diagnosis of child and adolescent aggressivity and conduct disorder. For example, Figure 12.4 shows the relationship between number of adverse home environmental factors and number of adolescent aggressivity symptoms for adoptees with and without a biological parent with ASP. As can be seen in this figure, adoptees without a biological parent with ASP exhibited no relationship between the number of adverse adoptive home environment factors and the number of aggressivity symptoms. In contrast, among adoptees with a biological parent diagnosed with ASP, the number of aggressivity symptoms increased with the number of adverse adoptive home environmental factors. Cadoret et al. (1997) also reported that specific environmental conditions, such as conflict with the adoptive mother and father, interacted with biological predisposition to predict adolescent aggressive behavior.

Finally, data from the National Longitudinal Study of Adolescent Health suggest that certain environmental contexts may enhance or suppress genetic influences on aggressive behavior (i.e., the heritability of aggression). Specifically, Rowe et al. (1999) found that the heritability of aggression was higher among adolescents in schools characterized by higher average levels of family warmth. This result is somewhat different from Cadoret's adoption finding, because in his study adverse adoptive environments seemed to promote a genetic potential for antisocial behavior. However, identifying specific environmental characteristics that interact with specific environmental risk is not the same as identifying environments where the genetic expression of antisocial behavior is enhanced. Rowe and associates' (1999) interpretation was that aggression required a greater genetic bias to be expressed in the "good" environments of the emotionally warmer and more accepting families.

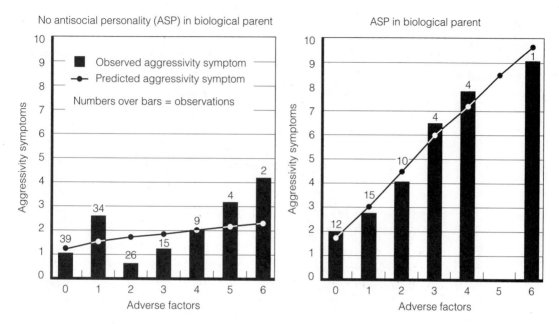

FIGURE 12.4 Interaction between biological risk and adverse adoptive home environment

SOURCE: R. J. Cadoret, L. D. Leve, and E. Devor (1997). "Genetics of Aggressive and Violent Behavior." The Psychiatric Clinics of North America 20: 310. Copyright 1997, W. B. Saunders Publishing Company. Reprinted by permission.

CONCLUSIONS AND FUTURE DIRECTIONS

We have reviewed the evidence that genetic factors influence the development of criminal behavior. The heritability of aggression and nonviolent offending is substantial, with as much as 50 percent of the variation in these behaviors attributable to genetic differences among people. Yet we also found evidence for more complex influences in the genetically informative studies, including genotype–environment interactions between those genotypes that are susceptible to antisocial behavior and adverse family environments. The amount of shared environmental influence on delinquency is also greater than for most behavioral traits, with these influences apparently especially strong in adolescence. The developmental stability of antisocial behaviors also has a genetic basis, although shared environmental influences may make a smaller contribution. The current behavioral genetic work, however, leaves other research questions unanswered. First, the vast majority of studies of aggression and criminal behavior have focused exclusively on males. There is evidence, however, that the genetic influences on aggression and property crime overlap in males and females (see Cloninger et al., 1976; Eley et al., 1999; and Rowe et al., 1995, for discussions of sex differences). In addition, most studies focus on violent crime or on nonviolent crimes such as property offenses. White collar crimes have not received much investigation by behavioral geneticists. There is little attention in criminology to theoretical explanations for the strong assortative mating for criminality—i.e., the observation that individuals with criminal tendencies are likely to select as spouses individuals who also have criminal tendencies—(Rowe and Farrington, 1997). Mating patterns may have genetic as well as social consequences. In conclusion, we hope that by presenting the evidence for biological and genetic influences on antisocial behavior we will encourage more criminologists to both consider these types of influences in their theories and also to incorporate aspects of biology and genes into their research designs.

DISCUSSION QUESTIONS

1. What is the "nature versus nurture" debate? How has it been used historically in discussions of the sources of criminal behavior?

2. According to the authors, is it possible to characterize explanations of criminal behavior as "nature and nurture"? How might this be possible?

3. Briefly discuss the evidence for at least a partial influence of biological factors, such as heart rate and serotonin levels, upon antisocial and criminal behavior.

4. Many people have argued for years that hormone levels, especially testosterone levels, are associated with aggressive behavior. What does the research evidence suggest about such an association?

5. Scientists for a long time have been trying to determine how much of criminal behavior is genetically based or heritable. How have they explored the issue through sibling studies? What have researchers found about the relative impact of genetic versus shared environmental influences on adolescent delinquent behavior?

6. The authors suggest that criminal behavior may not be a matter of genetic and environmental influences acting independently or ever added together. Instead, criminal behavior might occur when nature and nurture interact. What is the evidence for this view?

REFERENCES

Albert, D. J., R. H. Jonik, N. V. Watson, B. B. Gorzalka, and M. L. Walsh. 1990. "Hormone-Dependent Aggression in Male Rats Is Proportional to Serum Testosterone Concentration but Sexual Behavior Is Not." *Physiology and Behavior* 48: 409–416.

Archer, J. 1991. "The Influence of Testosterone on Human Aggression." *British Journal of Psychology* 82: 1–28.

Booth, A., G. Shelley, A. Mazur, G. Tharp, and R. Kittok. 1989. "Testosterone, and Winning and Losing in Human Competition." *Hormones and Behavior* 23: 556–571.

Booth, A., and D. W. Osgood. 1993. "The Influence of Testosterone on Deviance in Adulthood: Assessing and Explaining the Relationship." *Criminology* 31: 93–117.

Brennan, P. A., and S. P. Mednick. 1993. "Genetic Perspectives on Crime." *Acta Psychiatrica Scandinavica,* Suppl. 370: 19–26.

Brooks J. H., and J. R. Reddon. 1996. "Serum Testosterone in Violent and Nonviolent Young Offenders." *Journal of Clinical Psychology* 52: 475–483.

Cadoret, R. J. 1978. "Psychopathology in Adopted-Away Offspring of Biologic Parents with Antisocial Behavior." *Archives of General Psychiatry* 35: 176–184.

Cadoret, R. J., L. D. Leve, and E. Devor. 1997. "Genetics of Aggressive and Violent Behavior." *The Psychiatric Clinics of North America* 20: 301–322.

Cadoret, R. J., W. R. Yates, E. Troughton, G. Woodworth, and M. A. Stewart. 1995. "Genetic-Environmental Interaction in the Genesis of Aggressivity and Conduct Disorders." *Archives of General Psychiatry* 52: 916–924.

Cloninger, C. R., K. O. Christiansen, T. Reich, and I. Gottesman. 1976. "Implications of Sex Differences in the Prevalences of Antisocial Personality, Alcoholism, and Criminality for Familial Transmission." *Archives of General Psychiatry* 35: 941–951.

Cloninger, C. R., and I. Gottesman. 1987. "Genetic and Environmental Factors in Antisocial Behavior Disorder." Pp. 92–109 in *The Causes of Crime: New Biological Approaches.* Edited by S. A. Mednick, T. E. Moffitt, and S. A. Stack. Cambridge: Cambridge University Press.

Coccaro, E. F. 1989. "Central Serotonin and Impulsive Aggression." *British Journal of Psychiatry* 155 (Suppl. 8): 52–62.

Constantino, J. N., D. Grosz, P. Saenger, D. W. Chandler, R. Nandi, and F. J. Earls. 1993. "Testosterone and Aggression in Children." *Journal of the American Academy of Child and Adolescent Psychiatry* 32: 1217–1222.

Dabbs, J. M., and R. Morris. 1990. "Testosterone, Social Class, and Antisocial Behavior in a Sample of 4,462 Men." *Psychological Science* 1: 209–211.

DiLalla, L. F., and I. Gottesman. 1989. "Heterogeneity of Causes for Delinquency and Criminality: Lifespan Perspectives." *Development and Psychopathology* 1: 339–349.

Dixson, A. F., and J. Herbert. 1977. "Testosterone, Aggressive Behavior and Dominance Rank in Captive Adult Male Talapoin Monkeys." *Physiology and Behavior* 18: 539–543.

Edelbrock, C., R. Rende, R. Plomin, and L. A. Thompson. 1995. "A Twin Study of Competence and Problem Behavior in Childhood and Early Adolescence." *Journal of Child Psychology and Psychiatry* 56: 775–785.

Eley, T. C., P. Lichtenstein, and J. Stevenson. 1999. "Sex Differences in the Etiology of Aggressive and Non-Aggressive Antisocial Behavior: Results from Two Twin Studies." *Child Development* 70: 155–168.

Ellis, L., and M. A. Ames. 1987. "Neurohormonal Functioning and Sexual Orientation: A Theory of Homosexuality-Heterosexuality." *Psychological Bulletin* 101: 233–258.

Farrington, D. P. 1997. "The Relationship Between Low Resting Heart Rate and Violence." Pp. 158–183 in *Biosocial Bases of Violence.* Edited by A. Raine, P. A. Brennan, D. P. Farrington, and S. A. Mednoff. New York: Plenum Press.

Farrington, D. P., R. Loeber, D. S. Elliott, D. J. Hawkins, D. B. Kandel, M. W. Klein, J. McCord, D. Rowe, and R. Tremblay. 1990. "Advancing Knowledge about the Onset of Delinquency and Crime." Pp. 283–342 in *Advances in Child Psychology.* Edited by B. Lahey and A. Kazdin. New York: Plenum Press.

Ghodsian-Carpey, J., and L. A. Baker. 1987. "Genetic and Environmental Influences on Aggression in 4- to 7-Year-Old Twins." *Aggressive Behavior* 13: 173–186.

Gjone, H., and J. Stevenson. 1997. "A Longitudinal Study of Temperament and Behavior Problems: Common Genetic or Environmental Influences?" *Journal of the American*

Academy of Child and Adolescent Psychiatry 36: 1448–1456.

Goring, C. [1913] 1972. *The English Convict: A Statistical Study.* Patterson Smith reprint. Montclair, NJ: Patterson Smith.

Gottfredson, M. R., and T. Hirschi. 1990. *A General Theory of Crime.* Stanford, CA: Stanford University Press.

Hettema, J. M., M. C. Neale, and K. S. Kendler. 1995. "Physical Similarity and the Equal-Environments Assumption in Twin Studies of Psychiatric Disorders." *Behavior Genetics* 25: 327–335.

Hooten, E. A. (1939). *Crime and the Man.* Cambridge: Harvard University Press.

Inoff-Germain, G., G. S. Arnold, E. D. Nottelmann, E. J. Susman, G. B. Cutler, and G. P. Chrousos. 1988. "Relations Between Hormone Levels and Observational Measures of Aggressive Behavior of Young Adolescents in Family Interactions." *Developmental Psychology* 24: 129–139.

Kendler, K. S., and L. J. Eaves. 1986. "Models for Joint Effect of Genotype and Environment on Liability to Psychiatric Illness." *American Journal of Psychiatry* 143: 279–289.

Kendler, K. S., and C. O. Gardner. 1998. "Twin Studies of Adult Psychiatric and Substance Dependence Disorders: Are They Biased by Differences in the Environmental Experiences on Monozygotic and Dizygotic Twins in Childhood and Adolescence?" *Psychological Medicine* 28: 625–633.

Kruesi, M. J. P., E. D. Hibbs, T. P. Zahn, C. S. Keysor, S. D. Hamburger, J. J. Bartko, and J. L. Rapoport. 1992. "A Two-Year Prospective Follow-up Study of Children and Adolescents with Disruptive Behavior Disorders." *Archives of General Psychiatry* 49: 429–435.

Lewontin, R. C., S. P. R. Rose, and L. J. Kamin. 1984. *Not in Our Genes.* New York: Pantheon.

Loeber, R. 1982. "The Stability of Antisocial and Delinquent Child Behavior: A Review." *Child Development* 53: 1431–1446.

Loeber, R., and D. Hay. 1997. "Key Issues in the Development of Aggression and Violence from Childhood to Early Adulthood." *Annual Review of Psychology* 48: 371–410.

Loehlin, J. C., and R. C. Nichols. (1976). *Heredity, Environment, and Personality: A Study of 850 Sets of Twins.* Austin, TX: University of Texas Press.

Lombroso, C. 1876. *The Criminal Man (L'uomo Delinquente).* Milan: Hoepli.

Maccoby, E. E., and C. N. Jacklin. 1980. "Sex Differences in Aggression: A Rejoinder and Reprise." *Child Development* 51: 964–980.

Mannuzza, S., R. G. Klein, P. H. Konig, and T. L. Giampino. 1989. "Hyperactive Boys Almost Grown Up." *Archives of General Psychiatry* 46: 1073–1079.

Mason, D. A., and P. J. Frick. 1994. "The Heritability of Antisocial Behavior: A Meta-Analysis of Twin and Adoption Studies." *Journal of Psychopathology and Behavioral Assessment* 16: 301–323.

Mazur, A., and A. Booth. 1998. "Testosterone and Dominance in Men." *Behavioral and Brain Sciences* 21: 353–397.

Mednick, S. A. 1987. Introduction: "Biological Factors in Crime Causation: The Reactions of Social Scientists." Pp. 1–6 in *The Causes of Crime: New Biological Approaches.* Edited by S. A. Mednick, T. E. Moffitt, and S. A. Stack. Cambridge: Cambridge University Press.

Mednick, S. A., W. F. Gabrielli, and B. Hutchings. 1984. "Genetic Influences in Criminal Convictions: Evidence from an Adoption Cohort." *Science* 25: 891–894.

Mezzacappa, E., R. E. Tremblay, D. Kindlon, J. P. Saul, L. Arseneault, J. Seguin, J., R. O. Pihl, and F. Earls. 1997. "Anxiety, Antisocial Behavior, and Heart Rate Regulation in Adolescent Males." *Journal of Child Psychology and Psychiatry* 38: 457–469.

Miles, D. R., and G. Carey. 1997. "Genetic and Environmental Architecture of Human Aggression."

Journal of Personality and Social Psychology 72: 207–217.

Moffitt, T. E. 1993. "'Life-Course-Persistent' and 'Adolescent-Limited' Antisocial Behavior: A Developmental Taxonomy." *Psychological Review* 100: 674–701.

Moffitt, T. E., A. Caspi, N. Dickson, P. Silva, and W. Stanton. 1996. "Childhood-Onset Versus Adolescent-Onset Antisocial Conduct Problems in Males: Natural History From Ages 3 to 18 Years." *Development and Psychopathology* 8: 399–324.

Moffitt T. E., G. L. Brammer, A. Caspi, J. P. Fawcett, M. Raleigh, A. Yuwiler, and P. Silva. 1998. "Whole Blood Serotonin Relates to Violence in an Epidemiological Study." *Biological Psychiatry* 43: 446–457.

Moffitt, T., A. Caspi, P. Fawcett, G. L. Brammer, M. Raleigh, A. Yuwiler, and P. Silva. 1997. "Whole Blood Serotonin and Family Background Relate to Male Violence." Pp. 231–249 in *Biosocial Bases of Violence*. Edited by A. Raine, P. A. Brennan, D. P. Farrington, and S. A. Mednoff. New York: Plenum Press.

Nottelmann, E. D., E. J. Susman, G. Inoff-Germain, G. B. Cutler, D. L. Loriaux, and G. P. Chrousos. 1987. "Developmental Processes in Early Adolescence: Relationships Between Adolescent Adjustment Problems and Chronologic Age, Pubertal Status, and Puberty-Related Serum Hormone Levels." *Journal of Pediatrics* 110: 473–480.

Olweus, D., Å. Mattson, D. Schalling, and H. Löw. 1980. "Testosterone, Aggression, Physical, and Personality Dimensions in Normal Adolescent Males." *Psychosomatic Medicine* 42: 253–269.

———. 1988. "Circulating Testosterone Levels and Aggression in Adolescent Males: A Causal Analysis." *Psychosomatic Medicine* 50: 261–272.

Plomin, R., J. C. DeFries, G. E. McClearn, and M. Rutter. 1997. *Behavioral Genetics*. New York: W. H. Freeman.

Raine, A. 1993. *The Psychopathology of Crime: Criminal Behavior as a Clinical Disorder*. San Diego, CA: Academic Press.

Raine, A., P. Brennan, and D. P. Farrington. 1997. "Biosocial Bases of Violence: Conceptual and Theoretical Issues." Pp. 1–20 in *Biosocial Bases of Violence*. Edited by A. Raine, P. A. Brennan, D. P. Farrington, and S. A. Mednoff. New York: Plenum Press.

Raine A., P. Brennan, and S. A. Mednick. 1997. "Interaction Between Birth Complications and Early Maternal Rejection in Predisposing Individuals to Adult Violence: Specificity to Serious, Early-Onset Violence." *American Journal of Psychiatry* 154: 1265–1271.

Raine, A., C. Reynolds, P. H. Venables, and S. A. Mednick. 1997. "Biosocial Bases of Aggressive Behavior in Childhood: Resting Heart Rate, Skin Conductance Orienting, and Physique." Pp. 107–126 in *Biosocial Bases of Violence*. Edited by A. Raine, P. A. Brennan, D. P. Farrington, and S. A. Mednoff. New York: Plenum Press.

Raine, A., P. H. Venables, and M. Williams. 1990. "Relationships Between CNS and ANS Measures of Arousal at Age 15 and Criminality at Age 24." *Archives of General Psychiatry* 47: 1003–1007.

Robins, L. N. 1978. "Sturdy Childhood Predictors of Adult Antisocial Behaviour: Replications from Longitudinal Studies." *Psychological Medicine* 8: 611–622.

Rowe, D. C. 1983. "Biometrical Genetic Models of Self-Reported Delinquent Behavior: A Twin Study." *Behavior Genetics* 13: 473–489.

———. 1986. "Genetic and Environmental Components of Antisocial Behavior: A Study of 265 Twin Pairs." *Criminology* 24: 513–532.

———. 1994. *The Limits of Family Influence*. New York: The Guilford Press.

Rowe, D. C., D. M. Almeida, and K. C. Jacobson. 1999. "Genetic and School Context Influences on Aggression in Adolescence." *Psychological Science* 10: 277–280.

Rowe, D. C., and D. P. Farrington. 1997. "The Familial Transmission of Criminal Convictions." *Criminology* 35: 177–201.

Rowe, D. C., and B. Gulley. 1992. "Sibling Effects on Substance Use and Delinquency." *Criminology* 30: 217–233.

Rowe, D. C., and D. W. Osgood. 1984. "Heredity and Sociological Theories of Delinquency: A Reconsideration." *American Sociological Review* 49: 526–540.

Rowe, D. C., A. T. Vazsonyi, and D. J. Flannery. 1995. "Sex Differences in Crime: Do Means and Within-Sex Variation Have Similar Causes?" *Journal of Research in Crime and Delinquency* 32: 84–100.

Satterfield, J. H., C. M. Hoppe, and A. M. Schell. 1982. "A Prospective Study of Delinquency in 110 Adolescent Boys with Attention Deficit Disorder and 88 Normal Adolescent Boys." *American Journal of Psychiatry* 139: 795–798.

Schaal, B., R. E. Tremblay, R. Soussignan, and E. J. Susman. 1996. "Male Testosterone Linked to High Social Dominance but Low Physical Aggression in Early Adolescence." *Journal of the American Academy of Child and Adolescent Psychiatry* 34: 1322–1330.

Simon, N. G., R. Gandelman, and J. L. Gray. 1984. "Endocrine Induction of Intermale Aggression in Mice: A Comparison of Hormonal Regimens and Their Relationship to Naturally Occurring Behavior." *Physiology and Behavior* 33: 379–383.

Simons, R., C. Johnson, R. Conger, and G. Elder. 1998. "A Test of Latent Trait Versus Life-Course Perspectives on the Stability of Adolescent Antisocial Behavior." *Criminology* 36: 217–243.

Spoont, M. R. 1992. "Modulatory Role of Serotonin in Neural Information Processing: Implications for Human Psychopathology." *Psychological Bulletin* 112: 330–350.

Stattin, H., and D. Magnusson. 1989. "The Role of Early Aggressive Behavior in the Frequency, Seriousness, and Types of Later Crimes." *Journal of Consulting and Clinical Psychology* 57: 710–718.

Susman, E. J., G. Inoff-Germain, E. D. Nottelmann, D. L. Loriauz, G. B. Cutler, and G. P. Chrousos. 1987. "Hormones, Emotional Dispositions, and Aggressive Attributes in Young Adolescents." *Child Development* 58: 1114–1134.

Thapar, A., and P. McGuffin. 1996. "A Twin Study of Antisocial and Neurotic Symptoms in Childhood." *Psychological Medicine* 26: 1111–1118.

Tremblay, R. E., C. Japel, D. Perusse, M. Boivin, M. Zoccolillo, J. Montplaisir, and P. McDuff. (In press.) "The Search for the Age of 'Onset' of Physical Aggression: Rousseau and Bandura Revisited." *Criminal Behavior & Mental Health*.

Unis, A. S., E. H. Cook, J. G. Vincent, D. K. Gjerde, B. D. Perry, C. Mason, and J. Mitchell. 1997. "Platelet Serotonin Measures in Adolescents with Conduct Disorder." *Biological Psychiatry* 42: 553–559.

Van den Oord, E. J., and D. C. Rowe. 1997. "Continuity and Change in Children's Social Maladjustment: A Developmental Behavior Genetic Study." *Developmental Psychology* 33: 319–322.

Virkkunen, M., J. DeJong, J. Bartjo, F. K. Goodwin, and M. Linnoila. 1989. "Relationship of Psychobiological Variables to Recidivism in Violent Offenders and Impulsive Fire Setters." *Archives of General Psychiatry* 46: 600–603.

Virkkunen, M., R. Rawlings, R. Tokola, R. E. Poland, A. Guidotti, C. Nemeroff, G. Bissette, K. Kalogeras, S. L. Karonen, and M. Linnoila. 1994. "CSF Biochemistries, Glucose Metabolism, and Diurnal Activity Rhythms in Alcoholic, Violent Offenders, Fire Setters, and Healthy Volunteers." *Archives of General Psychiatry* 51: 20–27.

Wadsworth, M. E. 1976. "Delinquency, Pulse Rate and Early Emotional Deprivation." *British Journal of Criminology* 16: 245–256.

Wagner, G. C., L. J. Beuving, and R. R. Hutchinson. 1979. "Androgen-Dependency of Aggressive Target-Biting and Paired Fighting in Male Mice." *Physiology & Behavior* 22: 43–46.

Wolfgang, M. E., T. P. Thornberry, and R. M. Figlio. 1987. *From Boy to Man, from Delinquency to Crime*. Chicago: University of Chicago Press.

Wilson, J. Q., and R. J. Herrnstein. 1985. *Crime and Human Nature*. New York: Simon and Schuster.

Wright, W. 1998. *Born That Way: Genes, Behavior, Personality*. New York: Knopf.

Chapter Outline

- Strain Theory

  Classic Strain Theory

  Revisions in Classic Strain Theory

  Contemporary General Strain Theory

- Subcultural Crime Theory

  Criminal Groups and Criminal Values

  The Origins of Criminal Subcultures

  The Impact of Criminal Subcultures on the Individual

  Empirical Evidence Regarding Subcultural Crime Theory

- Conclusion

13

Sources of Criminality:

Strain and

Subcultural Theories

ROBERT AGNEW
Emory University

This chapter examines two major sociological theories of criminal behavior: strain theory and subcultural crime theory. Although these theories are conceptually distinct from each other and thus are treated separately, there is good reason for placing them both in the same chapter: Strain and subcultural theories often have been combined into more comprehensive theories (Elliott et al., 1979; Sheley, 1983). Certain of the theorists we will discuss, in fact, can be classified both as strain and subcultural theorists.

Numerous versions of both strain and subcultural theory have been advanced, and it is not possible to describe all these versions in their full complexity. The focus, rather, will be on describing the essential features of strain and subcultural crime theories and the major variations in these theories. Both theories have been used to explain juvenile delinquency and virtually every type of adult crime. In particular, they

have been applied to explanations of why some *groups* have higher crime and delinquency rates than do other groups, and why some *individuals* are more likely to engage in crime and delinquency than are other individuals (see Cressey, 1960; Agnew, 1987b). These theories differ from the biologically oriented theories described in Chapter 12 in that they explain crime fully in terms of the individual's social environment rather than biogenetic characteristics.

STRAIN THEORY

Strain theory argues that crime results when individuals are unable to get what they want through legitimate channels. In such cases, individuals become frustrated, and they may try to satisfy their wants through illegitimate channels or strike out at others in their anger. The several versions of strain theory differ from one another in specifying (1) the wants that individuals in our society pursue, (2) the factors that prevent individuals from satisfying their wants, and (3) the factors that influence whether the ensuing frustration results in crime. (All strain theories acknowledge that only some strained individuals turn to crime.)

We will focus on three major versions of strain theory. First, we will review the classic strain theories of Merton (1938), Cohen (1955), and Cloward and Ohlin (1960). Second, we will review a set of revisions in these classic strain theories, represented most prominently in the work of Elliott et al. (see Elliott and Voss, 1974; Elliott et al., 1979, 1985). And third, we will review Agnew's (1992) General Strain Theory.

Classic Strain Theory

Merton's (1938) was the first major strain theory of crime. It has inspired much research, and most revisions in strain theory trace their origins to it (Clinard, 1964; Cole, 1975). Merton's theory seeks to explain a wide range of deviance in both adults and juveniles. The strain theories of Cohen (1955) and Cloward and Ohlin (1960), however, focus on the explanation of juvenile delinquency—particularly, the gang delinquency of lower-class urban males. All three theories are treated together, although relevant differences between the theories are noted.

The Wants that Individuals Pursue Classic strain theory argues that everyone in the United States, poor as well as rich, is encouraged to strive for success. This encouragement comes from parents, school and government officials, religious figures, and the mass media. Merton argues that the primary success goal in the United States is money, whereas Cohen asserts that individuals are encouraged to pursue the somewhat broader goal of middle-class sta-

tus. That is, individuals are urged to seek the financial success, reputation, and lifestyle associated with the middle class. Cloward and Ohlin present something of a compromise, suggesting that success goals vary somewhat within and between social classes. Some people seek to become a part of the middle class, whereas others simply desire monetary success. Most lower-class individuals, however, are said to desire only monetary success. These theories recognize that not all individuals adopt this cultural emphasis on success but argue that a "substantial" or "significant" number of people in all social classes develop high success goals (Merton, 1968).

The Barriers to the Satisfaction of These Wants Although everyone is encouraged to strive for success, large segments of the population are prevented from achieving such success through legitimate channels. In the United States, one is supposed to achieve success through hard work, careful planning, self-denial, and honesty. Through these means, one first obtains a good education and then a good job. Classic strain theory, however, argues that large segments of the population—especially lower-class individuals—are prevented from achieving success through these channels. In particular, strain theorists posit, lower-class individuals are socialized in families that do not place a high value on such qualities as hard work, careful planning, and self-denial, as well as other traits necessary for successful goal achievement. Lower-class families do not provide the adolescent with the instruction and support necessary to do well in school. Lower-class individuals often encounter discrimination in the school system and other middle-class environments. Lower-class families lack the money to finance an advanced education for their children. And lower-class families lack the finances and connections to set up their children in business or a profession. As a result, lower-class individuals often are unable to achieve success through legitimate channels. And this creates much strain or frustration in them.

The Links Between Strain and Crime The frustration engendered by goal blockage does not necessarily lead to crime. In fact, Merton states that most strained individuals remain conformists, continuing to accept the cultural emphasis on monetary success and trying to achieve such success through legitimate channels. Other individuals, however, try to reduce their frustration by employing one of four possible adaptations to strain (goal blockage)— several of which may involve crime. According to Merton, individuals may adapt to strain by rejecting either the cultural emphasis on success or the legitimate means by which success is supposed to be achieved. In some cases, new goals and means may be substituted for the old ones.

Innovation According to Merton and to Cloward and Ohlin, the adaptation most closely linked to crime is innovation. Here, the individual continues to accept the cultural goal of monetary success but rejects the legitimate means to obtain such success. Rather, the individual resorts to such illegitimate means as theft, prostitution, and drug selling. Crime in this view is utilitarian—it is a means to achieve a goal.

Cohen, however, does not employ this adaptation in his explanation of delinquency. According to Cohen (1955: 36), the adaptation of innovation may explain "adult professional crime and the property delinquency of some older and semi-professional juvenile thieves," but it does not explain most juvenile delinquency. Most juvenile delinquency, Cohen states, is nonutilitarian in nature. Delinquents, for example, do not steal because they need the money; rather, they steal for "the hell of it." Stolen items

often are "discarded, destroyed, or casually given away" (p. 26). Even though Cohen's description of most delinquency as nonutilitarian appears to be exaggerated (see Cloward and Ohlin, 1960, especially Chapter 7), the point that at least some delinquency is nonutilitarian is well taken. At best, the adaptation of innovation explains only some delinquency.

Ritualism A second adaptation to strain is ritualism. Here, the individual continues to accept institutional means (for example, hard work and honesty) but lowers success goals to the point at which they can be satisfied or abandons the goal of success altogether. The behavior associated with ritualism may be viewed as deviant but is seldom criminal. This adaptation, according to Merton, is expressed in such cultural clichés as "I'm not sticking my neck out," "I'm playing it safe," "I'm satisfied with what I got," and "Don't aim high and you won't be disappointed."

Retreatism A third adaptation to strain is retreatism, in which the individual rejects both institutional means and the cultural emphasis on monetary success and middle-class status. Merton argues that the individual withdraws or retreats from society, becoming, for example, an alcoholic, a drug addict, or a vagrant. Cloward and Ohlin provide an example of this adaptation in their description of a retreatist subculture made up of adolescents who have oriented their lives around drug use.

Rebellion A final adaptation, rebellion, involves (1) the rejection of both goals and legitimate means and (2) the substitution of new goals and means in their place. Rebellion often manifests itself in political action. Cohen, however, uses the adaptation of rebellion to explain the origins of lower-class juvenile gangs. He argues that lower-class adolescents often are unable to achieve middle-class status through legitimate channels. One solution to this problem involves setting up an alternative status system in which they can compete successfully. In particular, Cohen suggests that they set up a status system that values everything the middle-class condemns. The middle class, for example, opposes physical violence and the theft and destruction of property. The delinquent subculture set up by lower-class boys, however, accords high status to individuals who engage in violence, theft, and vandalism. The oppositional nature of the delinquent subculture is partly explained by the fact that lower-class boys feel hostile toward the middle-class world that so often frustrates and humiliates them. The delinquent subculture legitimizes the expression of such hostility by placing a positive value on violence and property crime.

Factors Determining the Reaction to Strain Individuals may thus adapt to strain in a number of ways, only some of which involve crime. A major question, then, is what factors determine how one adapts to strain. Why, for example, does one strained individual become a ritualist whereas another becomes an innovator?

Commitment to Legitimate Means According to Merton and to Cloward and Ohlin, strain or goal blockage is more likely to result in crime when the individual is not strongly committed to legitimate means. Merton goes on to argue that there are class-related differences in the commitment to means. Lower-class individuals are imperfectly socialized and do not place a high value on means such as honesty and hard work. As a result, these individuals are more likely to turn to crime when faced with goal blockage. Cloward and Ohlin argue that even individuals who are committed to legitimate means may come to reject them. In particular, individuals who fail to

achieve success by following legitimate means may come to reject these means, especially if they blame the social system (rather than themselves) for their failure.

Interaction with Other Strained or Delinquent Individuals Cohen and Cloward and Ohlin also argue that the likelihood of delinquency is strongly influenced by whether the individual interacts with other strained or delinquent individuals, who may provide the adolescent with social support for delinquency. Because delinquency may be sanctioned by others and yet may arouse some guilt in the adolescent, the support of other adolescents is quite important in overcoming these barriers. Further, other adolescents may foster delinquency by (1) teaching the adolescent how to engage in delinquency and (2) providing opportunities to engage in delinquency.

Cohen and Cloward and Ohlin go on to discuss certain of the factors that influence whether strained individuals will interact with other strained or delinquent individuals. The adolescent's family plays an important role in this area. If adolescents are closely supervised by parents and feel a strong attachment to them, they are less likely to come under the influence of delinquent peers (see Elliott et al., 1985, for an expanded discussion of this point). Also important is the nature of the adolescent's neighborhood. In particular, Cloward and Ohlin argue that different types of neighborhoods provide different opportunities for delinquency.

Evaluation of Classic Strain Theory Classic strain theory, in sum, argues that everyone in the United States is encouraged to pursue success, but many lower-class and some middle-class people are unable to achieve such success through legitimate channels. This creates much frustration, which may, in turn, lead to crime.

The individuals who engage in such crime are not biologically or psychologically disturbed, nor are they evil individuals. Rather, they are simply "responding normally to the social situation in which they find themselves" (Merton, 1968: 186).

The first proposition of classic strain theory—that the universal emphasis on success is internalized by significant numbers of people in all social classes—has been challenged by a number of researchers claiming that lower-class individuals have low aspirations for success and therefore are not under any strain. Hyman (1953) was the first to raise this argument, and most subsequent research has shown that lower-class individuals have lower absolute levels of aspiration than do middle-class individuals (see Agnew and Jones, 1988, for a review). That is, lower-class individuals on average desire less education, less money, and less-prestigious occupations than do middle-class individuals. However, a large number of lower-class individuals—a majority in some studies—have absolute levels of aspiration as high as the middle class (Agnew and Jones, 1988). Further, limited evidence suggests that, relative to what they have, lower-class individuals desire success as much as, if not more than, do middle-class individuals (see Empey, 1956; Cloward and Ohlin, 1960; Agnew et al., 1996).

The second proposition of classic strain theory—that, relative to middle-class individuals, lower-class individuals are less able to achieve their goals through legitimate channels—has limited support. Lower-class individuals are somewhat more likely to report that they do *not* expect to achieve their success goals and that they are dissatisfied with their monetary situation (Agnew, 1987a; Agnew et al., 1996). It is important to note, however, that many middle-class individuals also report that they do not expect to achieve their goals and are dissatisfied with their monetary situation. Strain is therefore more

likely in the lower class, but it is not confined to the lower class. The existence of middle-class strain may partly explain the existence of middle-class crime (see Chapter 5 of this text).

The final proposition of classic strain theory—that strained individuals are more likely to engage in crime—also has limited support. Surprisingly, only a few studies have examined the relationship between monetary strain and crime, and most of these studies suffer from serious problems (see Bernard, 1984; Burton and Cullen, 1992; Agnew, 1994a, 1997a; Agnew et al., 1996; Passas and Agnew, 1997). Nevertheless, there is some evidence that crime is more common among people who are dissatisfied with their monetary situation (Agnew, 1994a: 423–426; Burton and Dunaway, 1994; Agnew et al., 1996). Further, criminals often report that they engage in income-generating crime because they want money but cannot easily get it any other way (e.g., MacLeod, 1987; Sullivan, 1989; Anderson, 1990; Padilla, 1992; Jankowski, 1995).

Indirect support for this proposition is also provided by studies that suggest that crime rates are higher where high levels of economic deprivation and economic inequality exist. Such studies have compared neighborhoods, cities, metropolitan regions, and countries to each other. Economic deprivation is measured in terms of such things as income levels, poverty rates, unemployment rates, and employment rates in the "secondary labor market"—where jobs have low pay and poor benefits. Areas with high levels of economic inequality are those in which a few people or certain groups receive a very disproportionate share of the income (e.g., a few people receive most of the income, or whites earn much more than African Americans). Many individuals argue that economic deprivation and inequality are associated with crime for reasons related to classic strain theory. Economic deprivation, at least in the United

States, is said to lead to strain. And inequality is also said to lead to strain, because poor individuals and groups become frustrated by their inability to obtain the wealth that surrounds them. Importantly, not all studies find a relationship among economic deprivation, inequality, and crime; and there is some dispute over why deprivation and inequality might be associated with crime (see Agnew, 1997b, for an overview). The data in this area provide tentative support for classic strain theory.

Revisions in Classic Strain Theory

Classic strain theory has limited support. Although more research on the theory is needed, data suggest that the failure to achieve success may be one of the factors leading to crime. Certain theorists, however, have sought to expand the power of classic strain theory by arguing that individuals may pursue goals other than monetary success/middle-class status and that goal achievement is a function of more than social class.

The Goals that Individuals Pursue Classic strain theory argues that the dominant goals in our society are monetary success and middle-class status. Some theorists, however, assert that individuals and groups pursue a variety of different goals (Elliott and Voss, 1974; Greenberg, 1977; Elliott et al., 1979; Agnew, 1984a; Elliott et al.,1985). Certain of these alternative goals are said to be especially relevant to the explanation of crime and delinquency.

Some theorists claim that adolescents are more concerned with the achievement of immediate goals than of long-range goals such as monetary success or middle-class status (Quicker, 1974; Elliott and Voss, 1974; Greenberg, 1977; Empey and Stafford, 1991; Agnew, 1984a; Elliott et al., 1985). In particular, they point to research

suggesting that most adolescents are not overly concerned about their future educational or occupational status. Rather, they are more concerned with the present—with achieving such immediate goals as popularity with peers and potential romantic partners, good grades, athletic success, owning a car, and getting along well with parents (Agnew, 1984a, 1987a). The failure to achieve such goals is said to generate much strain and delinquency. This idea has not been well tested, although the few studies that have examined it have not been very supportive (see Elliott and Voss, 1974; Agnew, 1984a; Elliott et al., 1985).

Other theorists argue that adolescents have an especially strong desire for autonomy from adults (Agnew, 1984b, 1997b; Greenberg, 1977; Moffitt, 1993, 1997; also see Tittle, 1995). Autonomy may be defined as power over oneself: the ability to resist the demands of others and engage in action without the permission of others. Adolescents are often encouraged to be autonomous, and they may come to desire autonomy as they physically and socially mature. At the same time, adolescents are often denied the autonomy they desire from adults. This denial of autonomy may lead to delinquency for several reasons: Delinquency may be a means of asserting autonomy (e.g., sexual intercourse or disorderly behavior), achieving autonomy (e.g., running away from home or stealing to gain financial independence from parents), or venting frustration against those who deny autonomy. Limited data provide some support for these arguments (Agnew, 1984b).

Still other theorists argue that much crime stems from the failure to achieve status and respect, with the desire for *masculine* status being especially relevant to crime (see Greenberg, 1977; Majors and Billson, 1992; Messerschmidt, 1993; Anderson, 1994). There are class and race differences in definitions of what it means to be a "man," although most such views emphasize traits like independence, dominance, toughness, competitiveness, and heterosexuality (see Messerschmidt, 1993). Certain people, however, may find that they have trouble living up to such masculine images, especially juveniles, lower-class people, and minority group members. Such people may attempt to "accomplish masculinity" through crime. They may engage in crime to demonstrate that they possess traits like toughness, dominance, and independence. As well, they may attempt to coerce others into giving them the respect they believe they deserve as "real men." In this connection, they may adopt a tough demeanor, respond to even minor shows of disrespect with violence, and occasionally assault and rob others to establish a tough reputation. There have been no large-scale tests of this idea, although several observational studies provide support for it (Anderson, 1994; Majors and Billson, 1992; Messerschmidt, 1993).

The Barriers to Goal Achievement Some theorists also argue that goal achievement is a function of several factors in addition to social class. Goal achievement, for example, may be influenced by one's intelligence, creativity, physical attractiveness, athletic ability, personality characteristics, and other factors. Popularity with potential romantic partners, for example, may be just as much (if not more) a function of appearance and personality as it is of social class. Recognizing these additional determinants of goal achievement helps strain theory better explain middle-class crime and delinquency. Although many of these additional factors are related to social class, the relationship often is far from perfect. Middle-class individuals, as well as their lower-class counterparts, may lack the skills or traits necessary to achieve their goals through legitimate channels.

Contemporary General Strain Theory

Several additional revisions in strain theory have been suggested (see, for example, Merton, 1964; Mizruchi, 1964; Bernard, 1990; Adler and Laufer, 1995; Passas and Agnew, 1997). One revision that appears to have some potential for explaining criminal behavior is the author's own General Strain Theory (Agnew, 1992, 1995a, 1997b; Broidy and Agnew, 1997).

Classic and revised strain theories assume that strain results from one's inability to achieve positively valued goals. These goals may be monetary success, middle-class status, popularity with peers, autonomy, and so forth. The General Strain Theory (GST) argues that there are several types of strain, which are caused by negative relations with others, that is, relations whereby individuals are not treated as they want to be treated. Three major types of strain, or negative relations with others, occur when others (1) prevent or threaten to prevent one from achieving positively valued goals, (2) remove or threaten to remove positively valued stimuli that one possesses, or (3) present or threaten to present one with noxious or negatively valued stimuli.

The classic and revised strain theories consider only the first type of strain—the failure to achieve positively valued goals. GST incorporates and extends the arguments of the classic and revised theories in this area. For example, GST points to a new goal that may be relevant to crime—the desire to be treated in a just or fair manner. Individuals who are not treated fairly or who do not get their just rewards experience strain. The second type of strain, involving the loss of positive stimuli, includes such things as the loss of a boyfriend or girlfriend, moving from one's neighborhood, or the death of a parent. The individual loses something that is valued. The third type of strain, involving the presentation of noxious or negative stimuli, includes criminal victimization of various types, a wide assortment of stressful life events, and negative relations—marked by insults, verbal threats, and the like—with parents, peers, teachers, and others.

These types of strain increase the likelihood that individuals will experience such negative emotions as disappointment, depression, and fear; anger and frustration, however, are especially important in the GST. These negative emotions create pressure for corrective action, and crime is one possible response. Crime may be a method for reducing strain, that is, for achieving positively valued goals, for protecting or retrieving positive stimuli, or for terminating or escaping from negative stimuli. Crime may be used to seek revenge against those who have mistreated us. And crime may occur as individuals try to manage their negative emotions through illicit drug use. Whether individuals respond to strain with delinquency is said to depend on a number of factors, including the individual's temperament, problem-solving skills, level of conventional social support, level of social control, and association with delinquent peers.

At heart, the GST is very simple. It argues that if we treat people badly, they may get mad and engage in crime. The theory has not yet been tested in its entirety, but preliminary tests are encouraging (Agnew, 1985, 1989; Paternoster and Mazerolle, 1994; Brezina, 1996, 1998; Agnew and Brezina, 1998; Hoffman and Su, 1997; Mazerolle and Piquero, 1997; Hoffman and Miller, 1998; see also Hagan and McCarthy, 1997). Agnew and White (1992), for example, constructed a measure of strain that focused on the loss of positive stimuli and the presentation of negative stimuli. Adolescents who scored high on this measure reported that they had lost a close friend through death, that their parents had divorced, that they did not get along with their classmates, that their parents and teachers mistreated them in a variety of ways, that their neighborhood had numerous problems, and so forth. These adolescents were more likely to engage in delinquency. More generally, studies indicate that delinquency is associated with such strains as negative relations with parents and teachers, child abuse, conflict with peers, criminal victimization, neighborhood problems, and a range of stressful life events—like parental divorce, family financial problems, and changing schools. Further, certain studies indicate that these strains increase the likelihood of delinquency by increasing the individual's level of anger and frustration.

At the same time, it is important to note that only some of the individuals who experience these strains turn to delinquency. GST seeks to identify which types of individuals are most likely to respond to strain with delinquency— such as individuals who are low in social control or who associate with delinquent peers. Research has produced mixed results. For example, some studies find that those with delinquent peers are more likely to respond to strain with delinquency, whereas other studies do not. The reasons for these results are not yet clear.

Overall, however, studies are generally supportive of the main themes of GST. And strain theory, in both its classic and contemporary forms, is one of the dominant theories of crime and delinquency. The next theory we will consider, subcultural crime theory, is perhaps *the* dominant theory of crime and delinquency.

SUBCULTURAL CRIME THEORY

Subcultural crime theory argues that certain groups or subcultures in our society approve of crime or hold values conducive to crime. Individuals who interact with the members of these groups may eventually adopt the criminal values of the group and engage in crime. Individuals who engage in theft, for example, may do so because they learned from others that theft is good or at least permissible. Such individuals are not necessarily strained (although strain theory is often used to explain the origin of criminal groups or subcultures). Subcultural theory, then, states that criminal behavior is learned in interaction with others who approve of crime or hold values conducive to crime. Sutherland provides the leading statement of this position (Sutherland and Cressey, 1978; also see Matsueda, 1988).

Numerous versions of subcultural theory exist, and these versions differ from one another in specifying (1) the groups that have criminal values and the nature of these values, (2) the origins of these groups, and (3) the ways in which these groups affect the individual.

Criminal Groups and Criminal Values

Subcultural theorists have argued that there are four types of criminal groups or subcultures: (1) groups that unconditionally approve of all or most crime and condemn all conventional behavior, (2) groups that unconditionally approve of select forms of crime (usually minor crimes) but otherwise are committed to conventional behavior, (3) groups that justify or approve of crime under certain conditions but otherwise have some commitment to conventional behavior, and (4) groups that do not explicitly approve of crime but have values that are conducive to crime.

Unconditional Approval of Crime This position represents the most extreme form of subcultural deviance theory and is best expressed in the work of Cohen (1955). As we noted in the previous section, Cohen uses strain theory to explain the origin of delinquent gangs among lower-class urban males. He argues that such males are unable to achieve middle-class status through legitimate channels, so they adapt by setting up an alternative status system in which they can compete successfully. Their hostility toward the middle class, among other things, leads them to create an oppositional subculture; that is, they come to value everything the middle class condemns. In particular, they come to value the property and violent crimes so strongly opposed by the middle class. They also come to condemn everything the middle class values, including conventional forms of behavior such as studying and hard work. The delinquent subculture is initially made up of the strained males described earlier, but after it comes into existence, it may recruit nonstrained individuals.

Cohen is careful to note that members of the delinquent subculture continue to have a lingering attachment to the conventional values they violate. This attachment, however, is repressed, and if anything, is dealt with by overreacting against these conventional values or, in Cohen's terms, through "reaction formation."

Unconditional Approval of Select Forms of Crime Most subcultural crime theorists are less extreme than Cohen. They do not believe that certain groups unconditionally approve of all crime and condemn all conventional behavior. Many subcultural crime theorists claim that certain groups have some commitment to conventional values but unconditionally approve of select forms of crime, usually minor crimes. Various theorists have argued, for example, that all young people, or at least certain segments of the youth population, approve of such activities as underage drinking, underage driving, sexual intercourse, gambling, truancy, and curfew violations (Matza, 1964; Vaz, 1967). A similar argument has been made with respect to the lower class. And finally, it has been argued that white collar executives in certain corporations approve of certain forms of corporate crime, such as restriction of competition and consumer fraud (see Conklin, 1977).

Approval of Crime Under Certain Conditions Perhaps the most common argument made by subcultural crime theorists is that some groups generally approve of conventional behavior but believe that criminal behavior is justified, even required, under certain conditions. For example, the youths about whom Cloward and Ohlin (1960) write cannot achieve monetary success through conventional channels. Rather than set up an alternative status system, they try to achieve monetary success through illegitimate channels, such as theft. They soon come to justify their theft by arguing that the social system has unfairly prevented them from achieving success through legitimate channels. They do not generally approve of theft, but view their theft as necessary and justified given their situation. Further, they continue to engage in conventional behavior in other areas of their lives (Cloward and Ohlin, 1960: 19).

Wolfgang and Ferracuti (1967) developed a similar theory in order to explain the high rate of homicide among young males in urban slums, particularly among African-American males. They point out, for example, that the homicide rate among nonwhite males age 20–24 in their Philadelphia study is 92 per 100,000. This compares to a rate of 3.4 for white males of the same ages. According to Wolfgang and Ferracuti, this difference is explained by the value system of the young African-American males. Although they accept many conventional values, they differ from the larger society in that they believe violence is justified in certain situations. "A male is

usually expected to defend the name and honor of his mother, the virtue of womanhood . . . and to accept no derogation about his race (even from a member of his own race), his age, or his masculinity" (1967: 153). So individuals in this group believe that one should retaliate with violence in response to certain types of insults and threats. They develop what Wolfgang and Ferracuti refer to as a "subculture of violence." A similar argument has been used to explain the higher rate of homicide in the South (see Hawley and Messner, 1989; Messner, 1988; Parker, 1989). Anderson (1994) also presents a contemporary version of this argument in his description of the "code of the streets." The code is said to be most common among young African-American males living in poor, inner-city communities. The code centers around the issue of "respect" and encourages young males to respond to shows of disrespect with violence.

Finally, Sykes and Matza (1957) have attempted to categorize the justifications that delinquents employ for their behavior. According to Sykes and Matza, most delinquents believe that crime is bad and conventional behavior is good. These delinquents, however, are taught that crime is justifiable in certain situations. In particular, they learn certain "techniques of neutralization"—justifications or rationalizations that specify the situations in which crime is justified or at least excusable. These techniques are used before the commission of a delinquent act, and they make the act possible by neutralizing one's belief that crime is bad (for an alternative view, see Sheley, 1980). Sykes and Matza list five techniques of neutralization:

1. Denial of responsibility. Delinquents using this technique claim that their acts are due to forces beyond their control, such as unloving parents or drug use.

2. Denial of injury. Here delinquents claim that their acts are harmless, that their shoplifting, for example, does not hurt stores because insurance will cover the loss.

3. Denial of the victim. Delinquents claim that their victims got what they deserved. They claim, for example, that they stole from a dishonest store owner or they beat someone up in self-defense.

4. Condemnation of the condemners. Here delinquents claim that those who condemn them also engage in questionable behavior. Adolescents who use marijuana, for example, may point to the drinking behavior of their parents, or thieves may point to the corruption among police and politicians.

5. Appeal to higher loyalties. Delinquents state that loyalty to friends and others may sometimes necessitate delinquent behavior. Delinquents may steal, for example, to help their family.

Sykes and Matza capture the sentiments underlying these techniques, in order, with the following phrases: "I didn't mean it," "I didn't really hurt anybody," "They had it coming," "Everybody's picking on me," and "I didn't do it for myself." Sykes and Matza, then, go beyond Cloward and Ohlin and Wolfgang and Ferracuti in stating that there are a wide range of justifications for criminal behavior. Still other justifications, thought to be common among delinquents and others, have been listed by additional theorists (see Minor, 1981; Bandura, 1990; Conklin, 1992).

Values Conducive to Crime A number of theorists have argued that certain groups have values that are conducive to crime but do not explicitly approve of or justify crime. That is, they hold values that make crime appear a more attractive alternative than might otherwise be the case. Matza and Sykes (1961) provide the most explicit description of these values in their paper on subterranean values (see also Curtis, 1975). They state that delinquents in all social classes tend to pursue certain values that are conducive to delinquency.

First, Matza and Sykes (1961: 713) state that delinquents are "deeply immersed in a restless search for excitement, 'thrills,' or 'kicks.'" Many other theorists have made the same argument. Miller (1958), for example, states that lower-class individuals in general and lower-class gang members in particular place great value on "excitement" and "thrills." The same desire for excitement and thrills has been said to characterize middle-class delinquents (Vaz, 1967). This search for excitement can, of course, be satisfied through legitimate as well as illegitimate means. Criminal activities, however, hold a special appeal because they have the added element of danger—of "experimenting with the forbidden." Individuals who value excitement, then, are likely to view crime as a more attractive alternative in a given situation than are others.

Second, delinquents are said to have a disdain for hard work and a desire for quick, easy success. Again, this theme is emphasized by several researchers. In his theory of middle-class delinquency, for example, England (1960) states that delinquents reject such values as "hard work, thrift, study, and self-denial." Miller (1958) makes the same point in his discussion of lower-class culture. At the same time, however, delinquents have "grandiose dreams of quick success." They desire much money and all the luxuries money can buy. Crime, of course, would have an obvious appeal to someone who places a low value on hard work and a high value on money and pleasure.

Third, delinquents are said to place much value on toughness—on being "macho." In particular, much emphasis is placed on being physically strong, on being able to defend oneself, on not letting others "push you around," and on showing bravery in the face of physical threat. According to Miller, the hero for the delinquent is the "tough guy," represented "by the movie gangster of the thirties, the private eye, and the movie cowboy." Clearly, individuals who place a high value on toughness will view delinquent acts like fighting as more attractive than do others.

The Origins of Criminal Subcultures

Subcultural crime theorists explain the origin of criminal subcultures primarily in terms of strain theory and, to a lesser extent, in terms of the tendency of some groups to focus on and distort certain values in the dominant culture. Strain theory is used to explain the origins of criminal subcultures in two ways, both of which have already been illustrated. The first way involves that adaptation to strain known as innovation. When individuals cannot achieve their goals through legitimate channels, they may try to achieve their goals through illegitimate channels like theft. And in doing so, they may come to justify their illegal behavior (see Minor, 1984). Cloward and Ohlin (1960) provide the best illustration of this approach: Such individuals justify their crime by claiming that the social system unfairly prevents them from achieving monetary success through legal channels.

This argument also has been used to explain why adolescents (1) value excitement, pleasure-seeking, and toughness and (2) approve of such minor misdeeds as drinking, sexual intercourse, and truancy. Several theorists have pointed out that adolescents occupy a very special position in our society. On the one hand, they are physically

adults and often are told to "behave like adults." On the other hand, they often are treated like children and denied many of the privileges of adulthood—like the right to drink, vote, and marry. Adolescents find this situation frustrating, and they often respond by engaging in the "symbolic equivalents of the adult behavior denied them" (Bloch and Neiderhoffer, 1958: 29). According to Bloch and Neiderhoffer, they engage in such behaviors as "drinking, sexual escapades, wild automobile rides, immature assertiveness, violent reactions to parental restraints, protests against authority, and other forms of intransigence" (p. 30). They soon come to approve of such behaviors, as well as the more general values associated with these behaviors.

The second way in which strain may lead to the development of criminal subcultures involves that adaptation to strain known as rebellion. When individuals are unable to achieve status through legitimate channels, they may create an alternative status system in which they can successfully compete. Cohen (1955) provides the best illustration of this argument in his discussion of the origin of delinquent gangs: Unable to achieve middle-class status through legitimate means, lower-class adolescents rebel and set up a status system in which they can compete. For reasons discussed previously, this status system values criminal behavior and condemns conventional behavior.

Finally, several theorists have argued that deviant subcultures derive not so much from strain but from the tendency of some individuals and groups to focus on and distort certain values that are part of the dominant culture. The leading proponents of this position are Matza and Sykes (1961). In their article on subterranean values, they claim that values such as toughness, excitement, and pleasure-seeking are emphasized in the larger culture although they are not as overtly stressed as are other values. The larger culture, for example, does place some value on toughness and violence—a fact quickly confirmed by an examination of any of the mass media. Delinquents, however, come to place more emphasis on this value than do other individuals. Matza (1964) makes a similar argument with respect to the techniques of neutralization. The justifications delinquents employ for their behavior are not invented anew; rather, they are derived from the criminal law and larger culture. To illustrate, the law recognizes that certain conditions excuse or justify violence. Under certain conditions, for example, the law allows individuals to use physical force to defend themselves. Delinquents, according to Matza (1964: 61), distort and extend these conditions. For example, they come to believe that physical force is justified in a much wider variety of situations than the law allows—not only when one is physically threatened but also in response to a wide range of threats and insults.

According to this argument, then, criminal subcultures do not necessarily have their origins in strain. Rather, they reflect the tendency of some groups to focus on and distort certain values in the dominant culture. Matza and Sykes, however, do not clearly indicate why some groups and individuals display this tendency and others do not.

The Impact of Criminal Subcultures on the Individual

Why do the individuals in criminal subcultures turn to crime? Most versions of subcultural crime theory give the same answer: The individuals in these subcultures interact with others who hold criminal values, and eventually they come to adopt these values themselves. That is, they come to approve of crime or hold values conducive to crime. They then act in conformity with their values.

Of course, not everyone who interacts with the members of a criminal subculture becomes a criminal. Individuals are likely to adopt criminal values and turn to crime to the extent that (1) they are isolated from conventional groups, (2) they interact frequently and over a long period with the members of a criminal subculture, and (3) they like and respect the members of the criminal subculture. So individuals who associate primarily with conventional groups and only occasionally come into contact with criminal subcultures are unlikely to develop criminal values (Sutherland and Cressey, 1978).

Recently, certain theorists have expanded subcultural crime theory and argued that criminal subcultures may also lead individuals to engage in crime without affecting their values. The social learning theory of Akers (1985, 1998), in particular, specifies two additional ways in which criminal subcultures may cause individuals to engage in crime.

First, the members of criminal subcultures may reinforce criminal behavior when it occurs, either positively or negatively. In positive reinforcement, the individual is rewarded for his or her criminal behavior. The gang member who wins a fight, for example, may receive much praise from fellow gang members (much of the reinforcement for crime comes in the form of social approval from one's friends and associates). Rewarding a criminal act increases the probability that the act will be repeated in the future. In negative reinforcement, the criminal act results in the removal of something negative—some painful or aversive stimulus. Gang members, for example, may stop accusing an individual of being a coward after the person engages in a fight. The removal of this negative or aversive stimulus also increases the likelihood that the criminal act will be repeated in the future. In general, individuals tend to repeat those acts that result in reinforcement.

It is important to note, however, that social learning theorists argue that the reinforcement for crime does not always come from the members of criminal subcultures. For example, conventional parents often inadvertently reinforce aggressive behavior. To illustrate, imagine a parent and young child in the checkout line at a supermarket. The child asks for a candy bar and the parent refuses. The child starts screaming and kicking, and everyone is soon staring at the parent. Eventually, the embarrassed parent lets the child have the candy bar. The child then stops screaming and kicking. Without realizing it, the parent has just reinforced the child's aggressive behavior (and the child has reinforced the parent for "giving in"). Patterson (1982) provides an excellent discussion of the ways in which parents often inadvertently reinforce aggressive behavior.

Second, the members of criminal subcultures may provide models for criminal behavior. Individuals, in particular, may come to imitate the criminal behavior they see other members of the subculture displaying. As Akers points out, such behavior is most likely to be imitated if the observer (1) likes or respects the model, (2) sees the model receive reinforcement or show pleasure, and (3) is in an environment in which imitating the model's behavior is reinforced.

Empirical Evidence Regarding Subcultural Crime Theory

Research on subcultural crime theory has focused on several questions. First, are there in fact groups and individuals who approve of crime or hold values conducive to crime? Second, are the individuals in such groups more likely to engage in crime? And third, if such individuals are more likely to engage in crime, is it because they have adopted criminal values? Research, then, has focused on establishing the existence of criminal

subcultures and exploring their impact on the individual. Little research has focused on the origins of criminal subcultures, although certain case studies suggest that strain may play a central role in the development of criminal subcultures (e.g., Blazak, 1995; see also Cernkovich, 1978; Matsueda et al., 1992).

Who Approves of Crime? A number of studies have tried to determine if certain groups are more likely to approve of crime or hold values conducive to crime than are other groups. Somewhat more common, however, are studies that simply ask whether *any* individuals approve of crime or hold values conducive to crime.

First, these studies suggest that no groups unconditionally approve of all crime and condemn conventional behavior. All major groups, and the overwhelming majority of individuals, tend to believe that criminal behavior generally is bad and conventional behavior generally is good (Buffalo and Rogers, 1971; Siegel et al., 1973; Kornhauser, 1978; Dorn, 1969; Matsueda et al., 1992). In one of the best studies in this area, Short and Strodtbeck (1965) interviewed a sample of adolescent boys in Chicago. Included were gang and nongang boys, white and African-American boys, and lower-class and middle-class boys. Each boy was asked to evaluate a number of conventional and deviant images. For example, each boy was asked how he would evaluate "someone who works for good grades at school" and "someone who gets his kicks by using drugs." All groups evaluated the conventional images equally highly—African American the same as white, lower class the same as middle class, and gang the same as nongang. Further, most of the deviant images were negatively evaluated.

However, although crime generally is condemned and conventional behavior generally is approved, there are differences in the extent to which crime is condemned and conventional behavior is approved. Some groups and individuals condemn crime less strongly than do others, with a number of individuals being close to amoral in their view of crime (that is, they neither approve nor disapprove of crime). In Short and Strodtbeck's study, for example, gang members and lower-class boys rated the deviant images less negatively than did the middle-class boys (see also Hirschi, 1969; Sheley, 1980). Likewise, certain studies suggest that some individuals approve of conventional behavior less strongly than do others (Hirschi, 1969). The extent to which one approves of conventional behavior or condemns criminal behavior does have a relationship to crime. It is unclear, however, to what extent these results can be explained in terms of subcultural crime theory—they are probably better explained in terms of social control theory (Hirschi, 1969; Kornhauser, 1978; see also Chapter 14 in this text). In particular, social control theory would argue that some individuals are close to amoral because of a breakdown in the socialization process. That is, these individuals were not effectively socialized by parents and others and so lack a strong commitment to any system of values.

Second, certain studies indicate that many individuals unconditionally approve of specific types of crime—particularly minor forms of crime. For example, significant numbers of individuals favor the legalization of such minor forms of crime as marijuana use and gambling (Conklin, 1971; Johnston, 1973; Eve, 1975). A 1996 survey of high school seniors found that 31.2 percent felt that using marijuana should be "entirely legal" (Maguire and Pastore, 1997). Some evidence also suggests that executives in certain corporations approve of various types of white collar crime (see Conklin, 1977). Only a small number of people unconditionally approve of more serious types of crime (Rossi et al.,

1974; Kornhauser, 1978; Minor, 1981; Wolfgang et al., 1985; Agnew, 1994a). This is true even if we focus on criminals and delinquents themselves. Matza (1964), for example, found that, of the institutionalized delinquents in his sample, only 3 percent generally approved of theft, 2 percent approved of auto theft, 1 percent approved of vandalism, and 1 percent approved of fighting with a weapon. Group differences in the approval of minor crime do emerge in certain of the studies that have been done in this area, although such differences tend to be slight (see, for example, Conklin, 1971; Eve, 1975).

Third, research suggests that many individuals do approve of or believe that crime is justified under certain conditions. A number of studies in this area have focused on Wolfgang and Ferracuti's subculture of violence theory and Sykes and Matza's techniques of neutralization (Minor, 1981; Agnew and Peters, 1985; Agnew, 1994b; Cao et al., 1997; Heimer, 1997; Markowitz and Felson, 1998). These studies, in particular, have measured the extent to which individuals approve of or justify crime/violence in certain conditions. Agnew (1994b), for example, found that 16 percent of the adolescents in a national sample agreed with the following statement: "If people do something to make you really mad, they deserve to be beaten up." In a study by Sheley and Wright (1995), 61 percent of the juvenile inmates in six correctional facilities and 28 percent of the students in ten inner-city high schools agreed that it is "okay to shoot someone who hurts or insults you."

Although the research tells us that a significant percentage of people believe that crime is justified under certain conditions, we have less information on whether some groups are more likely than other groups to feel this way. The most recent data, however, suggest that young people, males, urban residents, and possibly lower-class people are more likely to hold beliefs that justify crime/violence under certain conditions. Data on race and Southern residence are somewhat mixed, although they suggest that these variables are not strongly related to beliefs regarding the justifiability of crime/violence (see Blumenthal et al., 1972; Rogers and Buffalo, 1974; Agnew and Peters, 1985; Messner, 1988; Hawley and Messner, 1989; Luckenbill and Doyle, 1989; Parker, 1989; Bernard, 1990; Matsueda et al., 1992; Cao et al., 1997; Heimer, 1997; Markowitz and Felson, 1998).

Finally, a number of studies indicate that individuals hold values that are conducive to crime (Silverman and Dinitz, 1974; Agnew, 1984b, 1984c). Lerman (1968), for example, presented a sample of youths from Manhattan's Lower East Side in New York City with a list of eight traits having to do with toughness ("ability to be hard and tough"), excitement ("ability to find kicks"), pleasure ("ability to make a fast buck"), and conventional behaviors ("ability to get good grades"). When the youths were asked to pick the trait they admired most, 15 percent of the males and 7 percent of the females picked one of the deviant traits. Cernkovich (1978) likewise found that a significant percentage of adolescents valued such things as toughness, excitement, and pleasure. It is difficult to make firm statements about which groups are more likely to hold values conducive to crime. Additional research is needed in this area.

The data suggest, then, that many individuals and possibly groups in our society unconditionally approve of minor crimes, conditionally approve of crime, and hold values conducive to crime. Are people who associate with these individuals and groups more likely to be criminals?

How Are Criminal Subcultures and Crime Related? Most research on this question has tried to determine whether individuals with delinquent associates or friends are more likely to be delinquent themselves. (It is usually assumed that these delinquent friends have delinquent values.) The data indicate that a strong relationship exists between having delinquent friends and delinquency (Short and Nye, 1957; Jensen, 1972; Johnson, 1979). Hirschi (1969), for example, found that among those boys who had four or more friends picked up by the police, 75 percent had committed delinquent acts; among those boys without any friends picked up by the police, only 27 percent had committed delinquent acts.

Some researchers have raised questions about this relationship. They argue that the association between delinquent friends and delinquency is not necessarily because delinquent friends cause one to engage in delinquency. In fact, it may be the other way around—individuals who engage in delinquency may seek out delinquent friends. There is some evidence for this view, but longitudinal studies also indicate that adolescents who associate with delinquent friends at one point in time are more likely to be delinquent at a later point in time—in other words, that associating with delinquent friends does have a causal effect on delinquency (Elliott et al., 1985; Krohn et al., 1985; Massey and Krohn, 1986; Burkett and Warren, 1987; Paternoster and Triplett, 1988; Agnew, 1991; Thornberry et al., 1994; Elliott and Menard, 1996; Thornberry, 1996).

Why Do Criminal Subcultures Cause Crime? Finally, researchers have asked why individuals with delinquent associates are more likely to be delinquent themselves. The leading argument in this area is that individuals who interact with delinquent friends develop delinquent values and turn to crime for that reason. Delinquent values, in other words, mediate the relationship between delinquent friends and crime. There is some indirect support for this position. Associating with delinquent friends increases the likelihood that one will adopt delinquent values (although data indicate that engaging in delinquency also increases the likelihood one will adopt delinquent values—probably because individuals seek to justify or rationalize their behavior). Further, data indicate that delinquent values increase the likelihood that one will engage in delinquency. That is, there is a positive relationship between delinquency and (1) values that justify or approve of crime under certain conditions; (2) values that are conducive to crime, such as excitement, pleasure-seeking, and toughness; and (3) the approval of select forms of crime, such as marijuana use. (For selected studies in these areas, see Lerman, 1968; Jensen, 1972; Cernkovich, 1978; Johnson, 1979; Minor, 1984; Agnew and Peters, 1985; Matsueda and Heimer, 1987; Warr and Stafford, 1991; Matsueda et al., 1992; Agnew, 1994a; Thornberry et al., 1994; Elliott and Menard, 1996; Heimer, 1997; Zhang et al., 1997.)

Several studies have focused directly on the relationship between delinquent friends, delinquent values, and delinquency. These studies suggest that, although delinquent values may explain part of the effect of delinquent friends on crime, they do not necessarily explain all the effect. In particular, most studies find that, when we hold delinquent values constant, delinquent friends still have an effect on crime (Jensen, 1972; Johnson, 1979; Jaquith, 1981; Matsueda, 1988; Johnson et al., 1987; Agnew, 1994a; Heimer, 1997; Zhang et al., 1997). These studies should be interpreted cautiously because researchers have examined only a limited range of delinquent values. Nevertheless, researchers have begun to explore additional ways in which delinquent friends may cause delinquency.

The work of Akers (1985, 1998) and his associates is prominent in this area. As indicated, he suggests that other individuals may cause delinquency not only by affecting values but also by reinforcing delinquency and providing models for delinquency. Limited support has been provided for this argument (Krohn et al., 1985; Akers, 1998). And still other mechanisms by which delinquent friends might cause delinquency have been suggested (see Short and Strodtbeck, 1965; Johnson et al., 1987).

CONCLUSION

Two major theories of crime have been reviewed: strain and subcultural crime theory. Although distinct, these theories often have been joined into more comprehensive theories. Strain theory frequently is used to explain the origin of criminal subcultures, and subcultural crime theory frequently is used to explain why only some strained individuals turn to crime.

Three major versions of strain theory were presented. Classic strain theory dominated criminology during the 1950s and 1960s (Cole, 1975; Bernard, 1984) and had a large impact on public policy as well. Among other things, classic strain theory was one of the inspirations behind the War on Poverty, which tried to reduce crime and other social maladies by providing poor people with the opportunity to succeed through legitimate channels (Empey and Stafford, 1991). Empirical studies have produced limited support for classic strain theory, with data suggesting that monetary strain may be one of the causes of crime. More recent revisions in classic strain theory suggest that crime also results from the inability to achieve other goals, such as autonomy and masculine status. Limited data indicate that these revisions hold some promise for explaining crime. Agnew's General Strain Theory argues that the failure to achieve one's goals is only one of three major types of strain. Strain also results from the loss of positively valued stimuli and the presentation of negatively valued stimuli. Several studies provide support for the central propositions of GST: These types of strain increase the likelihood of crime and they affect crime partly by increasing the individual's level of anger and frustration. GST also has important policy implications, suggesting that we implement programs that reduce the individual's level of strain and increase the ability of individuals to respond to strain in a noncriminal manner. Such programs include family training and instruction in anger management (see Agnew, 1995b, for a fuller discussion).

Subcultural crime theory argues that individuals engage in crime because they are socialized in groups that approve of crime or at least hold values conducive to crime. The data are generally supportive of this theory. Like strain theory, subcultural crime theory has had an im-

pact on public policy. Several major programs have tried to reform criminals by removing them from their criminal subcultures and placing them in conventional groups where they are resocialized. The early years of the Synanon program provide an example. Drug addicts in this program were isolated from their old drug-using friends and associates and instead interacted primarily with a group of reformed addicts, who attempted to convince them that drug use and the drug lifestyle were bad (Volkman and Cressey, 1963). Organizations like Alcoholics Anonymous and Narcotics Anonymous employ similar procedures. Other programs try to change the values of delinquent peer groups, match delinquents or at-risk juveniles with conventional adults, and teach juveniles the skills to resist negative peer influences (see Empey and Stafford, 1991; Elliott et al., 1985, Chapter 8; Barlow, 1995). Although these programs have not been uniformly successful, they show some promise. In short, subcultural crime theory appears to have some potential for dealing with the crime problem.

DISCUSSION QUESTIONS

1. Discuss the ways in which sociological theories of criminality differ from biologically oriented theories. Are they competing theories?

2. In the eyes of strain and subcultural theorists, is criminal behavior "abnormal"?

3. What are the major sources of strain in your life (that is, what goals or wants have you been unable to satisfy and what types of negative treatment have you experienced)? Have you responded to this strain with crime? If not, why not?

4. Give examples of the four major types of criminal values. How has strain theory been used to explain the origin of these values?

5. Data suggest that violence in the media has a small-to-moderate effect on violent behavior. Drawing on subcultural crime theory, explain why media violence might cause violent behavior.

6. Strain and subcultural crime theories are often tested by asking samples of adolescents about the extent of their

delinquency. They are also asked a set of questions designed to measure the key elements of strain and subcultural crime theories. What questions would you ask to measure the key elements of strain and subcultural crime theories?

REFERENCES

Adler, F., and W. Laufer. 1995. *Advances in Criminological Theory, Volume 6: The Legacy of Anomie Theory.* New Brunswick, NJ: Transaction Books.

Agnew, R. 1984a. "Goal Achievement and Delinquency." *Sociology and Social Research* 68: 435–451.

———. 1984b. "Autonomy and Delinquency." *Sociological Perspectives* 27: 219–240.

———. 1984c. "The Work Ethic and Delinquency." *Sociological Focus* 17: 337–346.

———. 1985. "A Revised Strain Theory of Delinquency." *Social Forces* 64: 151–167.

———. 1987a. *Challenging Strain Theory: An Examination of Goals and Goal-Blockage in an Adolescent Sample.* Paper presented at the 1987 meeting of the American Society of Criminology, Montreal.

———. 1987b. "On 'Testing Structural Strain Theories.'" *Journal of Research in Crime and Delinquency* 24: 281–286.

———. 1989. "A Longitudinal Test of the Revised Strain Theory." *Journal of Quantitative Criminology* 5: 373–387.

———. 1991. "A Longitudinal Test of Social Control Theory and Delinquency." *Journal of Research in Crime and Delinquency* 28: 126–156.

———. 1992. "Foundation for a General Strain Theory of Crime and Delinquency." *Criminology* 30: 47–87.

———. 1994a. "Delinquency and the Desire for Money." *Justice Quarterly* 11: 411–427.

———. 1994b. "The Techniques of Neutralization and Violence." *Criminology* 32: 555–580.

———. 1995a. "The Contribution of Social-Psychological Strain Theory to the Explanation of Crime and Delinquency." In *Advances in Criminological Theory, Volume 6: The Legacy of Anomie Theory.* Edited by F. Adler and W. Laufer. New Brunswick, NJ: Transaction Books.

———. 1995b. "Controlling Delinquency: Recommendations from General Strain Theory." In *Crime and Public Policy.* Edited by H. D. Barlow. Boulder, CO: Westview.

———. 1997a. "The Nature and Determinants of Strain: Another Look at Durkheim and Merton." In *The Future of Anomie Theory.* Edited by N. Passas and R. Agnew. Boston: Northeastern University Press.

———. 1997b. *A Macro-Strain Theory of Community Differences in Crime Rates.* Paper presented at the 1997 meeting of the American Society of Criminology, San Diego.

———. 1997c. "Stability and Change in Crime Over the Life Course: A Strain Theory Explanation." In *Advances in Criminological Theory, Volume 7: Developmental Theories of Crime and Delinquency.* Edited by T. Thornberry. New Brunswick, NJ: Transaction Books.

Agnew, R., and T. Brezina. 1998. "Relational Problems with Peers, Gender, and Delinquency." *Youth and Society* 29: 84–111.

Agnew, R., F. Cullen, V. Burton Jr., T. Evans, and R. Dunaway. 1996. "A New Test of Classic Strain Theory." *Justice Quarterly* 13: 681–704.

Agnew, R., and D. Jones. 1988. "Adapting to Deprivation: An Examination of Inflated Educational Expectations." *Sociological Quarterly* 29: 315–337.

Agnew, R., and A. Peters. 1985. "The Techniques of Neutralization: An Analysis of Predisposing and Situational Factors." *Criminal Justice and Behavior* 12: 221–239.

Agnew, R., and H. R. White. 1992. "An Empirical Test of General Strain Theory." *Criminology* 30: 475–499.

Akers, R. 1985. *Deviant Behavior: A Social Learning Approach*. Belmont, CA: Wadsworth.

———. 1998. *Social Learning and Social Structure: A General Theory of Crime and Deviance*. Boston: Northeastern University Press.

Anderson, E. 1990. *Streetwise: Race, Class and Change in an Urban Community*. Chicago: University of Chicago Press.

———. 1994. "The Code of the Streets." *Atlantic Monthly* 273 (3): 81–94.

Bandura, A. 1990. "Selective Activation and Disengagement of Moral Control." *Journal of Social Issues* 46: 27–46.

Barlow, H. D. 1995. *Crime and Public Policy*. Boulder, CO: Westview.

Bernard, T. 1984. "Control Criticisms of Strain Theories: An Assessment of Theoretical and Empirical Adequacy." *Journal of Research in Crime and Delinquency* 21: 353–372.

———. 1990. "Angry Aggression Among the 'Truly Disadvantaged.'" *Criminology* 28: 73–96.

Blazak, R. 1995. *The Suburbization of Hate: An Ethnographic Study of the Skinhead Subculture*. Ph.D. dissertation, Emory University.

Bloch, H., and A. Niederhoffer. 1958. *The Gang*. New York: Philosophical Library.

Blumenthal, M. D., R. L. Kahn, F. M. Andrews, and K. B. Head. 1972. *Justifying Violence: Attitudes of American Men*. Ann Arbor, MI: Institute for Social Research.

Brezina, T. 1996. "Adapting to Strain: An Examination of Delinquent Coping Responses." *Criminology* 34: 39–60.

———. 1998. "Adolescent Maltreatment and Delinquency: The Question of Intervening Processes." *Journal of Research in Crime and Delinquency* 35: 71–99.

Broidy, L., and R. Agnew. 1997. "Gender and Crime: A General Strain Theory Perspective." *Journal of Research in Crime and Delinquency* 34: 275–306.

Buffalo, M. D., and J. W. Rogers. 1971. "Behavioral Norms, Moral Norms, and Attachment: Problems of Deviance and Conformity." *Social Problems* 19: 101–113.

Burkett, S. R., and B. O. Warren. 1987. "Religiosity, Peer Associations, and Adolescent Marijuana Use: A Panel Study of Underlying Causal Structures." *Criminology* 25: 109–131.

Burton, V., Jr., and F. Cullen. 1992. "The Empirical Status of Strain Theory." *Journal of Crime and Justice* 15: 1–30.

Burton, V., Jr., and R. Dunaway. 1994. "Strain, Relative Deprivation, and Middle-Class Delinquency." In *Varieties of Criminology*. Edited by Greg Barak. New York: Praeger.

Cao, L., A. Adams, and V. Jensen. 1997. "A Test of the Black Subculture of Violence Thesis: A Research Note." *Criminology* 35: 367–379.

Cernkovich, S. A. 1978. "Value Orientation and Delinquency Involvement." *Criminology* 15: 443–458.

Clinard, M. B. 1964. *Anomie and Deviant Behavior*. New York: Free Press.

Cloward, R. A., and L. E. Ohlin. 1960. *Delinquency and Opportunity*. New York: Free Press.

Cohen, A. 1955. *Delinquent Boys*. New York: Free Press.

Cole, S. 1975. "The Growth of Scientific Knowledge: Theories of Deviance as a Case Study." Pp. 175–220 in *The Idea of Social Structure: Papers in Honor of Robert K. Merton*. Edited by L. A. Coser. New York: Harcourt Brace Jovanovich.

Conklin, J. E. 1971. "Criminal Environment and Support for the Law." *Law & Society Review* 6: 247–259.

———. 1977. *Illegal But Not Criminal: Business Crime in America*. Englewood Cliffs, NJ: Prentice-Hall.

———. 1992. *Criminology*. 4th ed. New York: Macmillan.

Cressey, D. R. 1960. "Epidemiology and Individual Conduct: A Case from Criminology." *Pacific Sociological Review* 3: 47–58.

Curtis, L. A. 1975. *Violence, Race, and Culture.* Lexington, MA: Lexington.

Dorn, D. S. 1969. "A Partial Test of the Delinquency Continuum Typology: Contracultures and Subcultures." *Social Forces* 47: 305–314.

Elliott, D., and H. Voss. 1974. *Delinquency and Dropout.* Lexington, MA: Lexington Books.

Elliott, D., and S. Menard. 1996. "Delinquent Friends and Delinquent Behavior: Temporal and Developmental Patterns." In *Delinquency and Crime: Current Theories.* Edited by J. Hawkins. Cambridge: Cambridge University Press.

Elliott, D., D. Huizinga, and S. S. Ageton. 1985. *Explaining Delinquency and Drug Use.* Beverly Hills, CA: Sage.

Elliott, D., S. Ageton, and R. Canter. 1979. "An Integrated Theoretical Perspective on Delinquent Behavior." *Journal of Research in Crime and Delinquency* 16: 3–27.

Empey, L. 1956. "Social Class and Occupational Aspirations: A Comparison of Absolute and Relative Measurement." *American Sociological Review* 45: 95–110.

Empey, L. T., and M. C. Stafford. 1991. *American Delinquency: Its Meaning and Construction.* Belmont, CA: Wadsworth.

England, R. W. 1960. "A Theory of Middle Class Juvenile Delinquency." *Journal of Criminal Law, Criminology and Police Science* 50: 535–540.

Eve, R. 1975. " 'Adolescent Culture,' Convenient Myth or Reality? A Comparison of Students and Their Teachers." *Sociology of Education* 48: 152–167.

Greenberg, D. 1977. "Delinquency and the Age Structure of Society." *Contemporary Crises* 1: 66–86.

Hagan, J., and B. McCarthy. 1997. *Mean Streets.* Cambridge: Cambridge University Press.

Hawley, F. F., and S. F. Messner. 1989. "The Southern Violence Construct: A Review of Arguments, Evidence, and the Normative Context." *Justice Quarterly* 6: 481–511.

Heimer, K. 1997. "Socioeconomic Status, Subcultural Definitions, and Violent Delinquency." *Social Forces* 75: 799–833.

Hirschi, T. 1969. *Causes of Delinquency.* Berkeley: University of California Press.

Hoffman, J., and A. Miller. 1998. "A Latent Variable Analysis of General Strain Theory." *Journal of Quantitative Criminology* 14: 83–110.

Hoffman, J., and S. Su. 1997. "The Conditional Effects of Stress on Delinquency and Drug Use: A Strain Theory Assessment of Sex Differences." *Journal of Research in Crime and Delinquency* 34: 46–78.

Hyman, H. 1953. "The Value Systems of the Different Classes: A Social-Psychological Contribution to the Analysis of Stratification." Pp. 488–499 in *Class, Status, and Power.* Edited by R. Bendix and S. M. Lipset. New York: Free Press.

Jankowski, M. 1995. "Ethnography, Inequality, and Crime in the Low-Income Community." In *Crime and Inequality.* Edited by J. Hagan and R. Peterson. Stanford, CA: Stanford University Press.

Jaquith, S. M. 1981. "Adolescent Marijuana and Alcohol Use: An Empirical Test of Differential Association Theory." *Criminology* 19: 271–280.

Jensen, G. F. 1972. "Parents, Peers, and Delinquent Action: A Test of the Differential Association Perspective." *American Journal of Sociology* 78: 562–575.

Johnson, R. E. 1979. *Juvenile Delinquency and Its Origins.* Cambridge, MA: Harvard University Press.

Johnson, R. E., A. C. Marcos, and S. J. Bahr. 1987. "The Role of Peers in the Complex Etiology of Adolescent Drug Use." *Criminology* 25: 323–340.

Johnston, L. 1973. *Drugs and American Youth.* Ann Arbor, MI: Institute for Social Research.

Kornhauser, R. R. 1978. *Social Sources of Delinquency.* Chicago: University of Chicago Press.

Krohn, M., W. F. Skinner, J. L. Massey, and R. Akers. 1985. "Social Learning Theory and Adolescent Cigarette Smoking: A Longitudinal Study." *Social Problems* 32: 455–471.

Lerman, P. 1968. "Individual Values, Peer Values, and Subcultural Delinquency." *American Sociological Review* 33: 219–235.

Luckenbill, D. F., and D. P. Doyle. 1989. "Structural Position and Violence: Developing a Cultural Explanation." *Criminology* 27: 419–436.

MacLeod, J. 1987. *Ain't No Makin' It.* Boulder, CO: Westview.

Maguire, K., and A. Pastore (eds.). 1997. *Sourcebook of Criminal Justice Statistics, 1996.* Washington, DC: U.S. Department of Justice.

Majors, R., and J. Billson. 1992. *Cool Pose.* New York: Lexington Books.

Markowitz, F., and R. Felson. 1998. "Socio-Demographic Differences in Attitudes and Violence." *Criminology* 36: 117–138.

Massey, J. L., and M. D. Krohn. 1986. "A Longitudinal Examination of an Integrated Social Process Model of Deviant Behavior." *Social Forces* 65: 106–134.

Matsueda, R. L. 1988. "The Current State of Differential Association Theory." *Crime and Delinquency* 34: 277–306.

Matsueda, R. L., and K. Heimer. 1987. "Race, Family Structure, and Delinquency: A Test of Differential Association and Social Control Theories." *American Sociological Review* 52: 826–840.

Matsueda, R. L., R. Gartner, I. Piliavin, and M. Polakowski. 1992. "The Prestige of Criminal and Conventional Occupations: A Subcultural Model of Criminal Activity." *American Sociological Review* 57: 752–770.

Matza, D. 1964. *Delinquency and Drift.* New York: Wiley.

Matza, D., and G. M. Sykes. 1961. "Juvenile Delinquency and Subterranean Values." *American Sociological Review* 26: 712–720.

Mazerolle, P., and A. Piquero. 1997. "Violent Responses to Strain: An Examination of Conditioning Influences." *Violence and Victims* 12: 3–27.

Merton, R. 1938. "Social Structure and Anomie." *American Sociological Review* 3: 672–682.

———. 1964. "Anomie, Anomia, and Social Interaction: Contexts of Deviant Behavior." Pp. 213–242 in *Anomie and Deviant Behavior.* Edited by M. B. Clinard. New York: Free Press.

———. 1968. *Social Theory and Social Structure.* New York: Free Press.

Messerschmidt, J. W. 1993. *Masculinities and Crime.* Lanham, MD: Rowan and Littlefield.

Messner, S. F. 1988. "Research on Cultural and Socioeconomic Factors in Criminal Violence." *The Psychiatric Clinics of North America* 11: 511–525.

Miller, W. 1958. "Lower Class Culture as a Generating Milieu of Gang Delinquency." *Journal of Social Issues* 14: 5–19.

Minor, W. W. 1981. "Techniques of Neutralization: A Reconceptualization and Empirical Examination." *Journal of Research in Crime and Delinquency* 18: 295–318.

———. 1984. "Neutralization as a Hardening Process: Considerations in the Modeling of Change." *Social Forces* 62: 995–1019.

Mizruchi, E. 1964. *Success and Opportunity.* New York: Free Press.

Moffitt, T. 1993. "Adolescence-limited and life-course-persistent antisocial behavior: A developmental taxonomy." *Psychological Review* 100: 674–701.

———. 1997. "Adolescence-limited and life-course-persistent offending: A complementary pair of developmental theories." In T. P. Thornberry (ed.), *Advances in Criminological Theory: Developmental Theories of Crime and Delinquency.* New Brunswick, NJ: Transaction Books.

Padilla, F. 1992. *The Gang as an American Enterprise.* New Brunswick, NJ: Rutgers University Press.

Parker, R. N. 1989. "Poverty, Subculture of Violence, and Type of Homicide." *Social Forces* 67: 983–1007.

Passas, N., and R. Agnew. 1997. *The Future of Anomie Theory*. Boston: Northeastern University Press.

Paternoster, R., and P. Mazerolle. 1994. "General Strain Theory and Delinquency: A Replication and Extension." *Journal of Research in Crime and Delinquency* 31: 235–263.

Paternoster, R., and R. Triplett. 1988. "Disaggregating Self-Reported Delinquency and Its Implication for Theory." *Criminology* 26: 591–625.

Patterson, G. R. 1982. *Coercive Family Processes*. Eugene, OR: Castalia.

Quicker, J. 1974. "The Effect of Goal Discrepancy on Delinquency." *Social Problems* 22: 76–86.

Rogers, J. W., and M. D. Buffalo. 1974. "Neutralization Techniques: Toward a Simplified Measurement Scale." *Pacific Sociological Review* 17: 313–331.

Rossi, P. H., E. Waite, C. E. Bose, and R. Berk. 1974. "The Seriousness of Crimes: Normative Structure and Individual Differences." *American Sociological Review* 39: 224–237.

Sheley, J. F. 1980. "Is Neutralization Necessary for Criminal Behavior?" *Deviant Behavior* 2: 49–72.

———. 1983. "Critical Elements of Criminal Behavior." *Sociological Quarterly* 24: 509–525.

Sheley, J. F., and J. D. Wright. 1995. *In the Line of Fire*. New York: Aldine De Gruyter.

Short, J. F., and F. I. Nye. 1957. "Reported Behavior as a Criterion of Deviant Behavior." *Social Problems* 5: 207–213.

Short, J. F., and F. L. Strodtbeck. 1965. *Group Process and Gang Delinquency*. Chicago: University of Chicago Press.

Siegel, L. J., S. A. Rathus, and C. A. Ruppert. 1973. "Values and Delinquent Youth: An Empirical Re-examination of Theories of Delinquency." *British Journal of Criminology* 13: 237–244.

Silverman, I. J., and S. Dinitz. 1974. "Compulsive Masculinity and Delinquency." *Criminology* 11: 498–515.

Sullivan, M. 1989. *"Getting Paid": Youth Crime and Work in the Inner City*. Ithaca: Cornell University Press.

Sutherland, E. H., and D. R. Cressey. 1978. *Criminology*. Philadelphia: Lippincott.

Sykes, G., and D. Matza. 1957. "Techniques of Neutralization: A Theory of Delinquency." *American Sociological Review* 22: 664–670.

Thornberry, T. 1996. "Empirical Support for Interactional Theory: A Review of the Literature." In *Delinquency and Crime: Current Theories*. Edited by J. Hawkins. Cambridge: Cambridge University Press.

Thornberry, T., A. Lizotte, M. Krohn, M. Farnworth, and S. Jang. 1994. "Delinquent Peers, Beliefs, and Delinquent Behavior: A Longitudinal Test of Interactional Theory." *Criminology* 32: 47–83.

Tittle, C. 1995. *Control Balance: Toward a General Theory of Deviance*. Boulder, CO: Westview.

Vaz, E. W. 1967. "Juvenile Delinquency in the Middle-Class Youth Culture." Pp. 131–147 in *Middle-Class Juvenile Delinquency*. Edited by E. Vaz. New York: Harper & Row.

Volkman, R., and D. R. Cressey. 1963. "Differential Association and the Rehabilitation of Drug Addicts." *American Journal of Sociology* 29: 129–142.

Warr, M., and M. Stafford. 1991. "The Influence of Delinquent Peers: What They Think or What They Do?" *Criminology* 29: 851–866.

Wolfgang, M. E., and F. Ferracuti. 1967. *The Subculture of Violence: Towards an Integrated Theory in Criminology*. Beverly Hills, CA: Sage.

Wolfgang, M., R. M. Figlio, P. E. Tracy, and S. I. Singer. 1985. *The National Survey of Crime Severity*. Washington, DC: U.S. Department of Justice, Bureau of Justice Statistics.

Zhang, L., W. Wieczorek, and J. Welte. 1997. "Developmental Trends of Delinquent Attitudes and Behaviors: Replications and Synthesis Across Domains, Time, and Samples." *Journal of Quantitative Criminology* 13: 181–215.

Chapter Outline

- ◆ Social Disorganization Theory

- ◆ The Legacy of the Social Disorganization Perspective: The Ecology of Crime
  Social Structural Characteristics
  Community Dynamics
  Routine Activities

- ◆ Social Bonding Theories
  Origins of Social Bonding Theories
  Elements of the Social Bond
  Research on Social Bonding
  Evaluation of Social Bonding Theory

- ◆ Self-Control Theory
  Research on Self-Control Theory
  Evaluation of Self-Control Theory

- ◆ Individually Oriented Theories
  Self-Concept Theory
  Self-Esteem Approaches

- ◆ The Deterrence Doctrine
  Basic Principles of Deterrence
  Research on Deterrence
  Evaluation of the Deterrence Doctrine

- ◆ Conclusion

14

Sources of Criminality: Control and Deterrence Theories

MARVIN KROHN
State University of New York at Albany

Social control theories and their subset, deterrence theories, reflect diverse notions of the specific social or social/psychological factors that constrain criminal behavior. However, they all seek an answer to a common question and share common assumptions that distinguish them from other theoretical perspectives on crime. Simply stated, the question addressed by all social control theories relates to why and how people conform to the rules of society. The question implies that the critical issue in explaining criminal or delinquent behavior is finding what constrains people from committing such behavior and also that it is less important to find why people are motivated to commit criminal behavior. Control theorists assume that deviant behavior is either naturally attractive, situationally induced, or rationally chosen; they strive instead to provide an explanation for conforming behavior: Why do people obey the rules?

The question posed by social control theorists focuses on social integration and social regulation. In his book *Suicide*, Emile Durkheim ([1897] 1951) examined the societal conditions that constrain or prevent people from taking their own lives. He looked first at the concept of social integration. Although Durkheim never explicitly defined social integration, he clearly had in mind the degree to which individuals and groups are attracted to and attached to society and social institutions. For example, Durkheim observed that married people, especially those with children, have lower rates of suicide than do unmarried people. Attachment to these significant others allows individuals to find meaning in social institutions and, as a consequence, to be less likely to pursue purely individual interests. Durkheim stated that "the bond that unites them with the common cause attaches them to life and the lofty goal they envisage prevents their feeling personal troubles so deeply" (p. 210). As integration decreases, people will be less constrained from responding to their personal troubles in a nonconforming manner (for example, suicide).

In addition to integrating individuals into its institutions, society provides norms by which people's behaviors are regulated. Durkheim assumed that people have potentially insatiable desires; thus, cultural norms are necessary to limit those desires and to define the proper means to achieve them. Without clearly defined and effective norms, individual behavior variations in pursuit of desires would increase. For example, norms define appropriate and inappropriate responses to failure and frustration. To the extent that such regulation of behavior sees suicide as an inappropriate response to personal crisis, suicide rates are held down.

The concepts of social integration and social regulation are intertwined. Social integration is fostered by rules of conduct, making groups and institutions (for example, church and the family) more of a presence in peoples' lives. Durkheim also recognized that social regulation could be effective only where there was a degree of social integration. That is, people would have to feel attached to a community to adhere willingly to its rules. Although a community could still enforce its will on individual members, this would be an ineffective form of control in the long run. Social integration, then, refers to the attraction of people to society, whereas social regulation refers specifically to the power society has to coerce certain forms of behavior. The interplay of these two factors is seen throughout diverse social control theories. Some of these perspectives fail to distinguish clearly between the two; others emphasize the role of either integration or regulation. What characterizes all, however, is a concern about what social and social/psychological factors constrain criminal behavior.

Against this backdrop, this chapter will examine social disorganization theory and its emphasis on the ecology of crime. We will explore two major types of control theory: social bonding theories and individually oriented theories. Finally, we will discuss the classic deterrence doctrine and its present-day forms.

SOCIAL DISORGANIZATION THEORY

Sociology as a recognized discipline in the United States emerged around the turn of the twentieth century, inspired by the upheavals that had taken place in European society throughout the previous century. In the United States, as in Europe, the ongoing dramatic changes in the production system significantly disrupted social life. The dominant form of economic production was shifting from agriculture to industry. Urbanization in the United States was fueled by a continuing supply of immigrants as well as by the migration of rural workers to the city to seek employment in the growing number of factories.

Perhaps nowhere was this social disruption more evident than in the city of Chicago from the early to the mid-1900s. With its population rapidly expanding because of the influx of immigrants and the general westward movement of the U.S. population, Chicago became a natural laboratory for sociologists at the University of Chicago to examine an eclectic array of theoretical ideas borrowed from their primarily European mentors. Perhaps because of the "Chicago School's" willingness to draw on a diverse set of ideas, their social disorganization theory contains elements of several theoretical perspectives. It has been characterized as a social control theory, a strain theory, and a cultural deviance theory (Firestone, 1976). At its heart, however, it is a social control model (Kornhauser, 1978); therefore, it is treated as such in this chapter.

Park et al. (1925) set the research agenda for a continuing investigation of modern urban life. They likened the growth of the city to ecological processes among plant life, emphasizing competition over land use as the population grows and areas of the city expand. The process of competition led to adaptations resulting in eventual cooperation in a continuing dynamic equilibrium. However, in this process, areas of the city would experience changes that would render social institutions ineffective, a condition they labeled "social disorganization" (Burgess, 1925).

Specifically, Burgess suggested that Chicago was growing in a series of concentric circles from the center of the city out to the residential suburbs. These concentric zones were characterized by the dominant activities taking place within them. For example, the central business zone was used primarily for commerce and industry. The second zone, the zone of transition, most clearly illustrated the process of expansion whereby commerce and industry were encroaching on what previously had been residential property. Because the transition was not complete, however, people still lived in this zone. And because the housing was not particularly desirable, it was here that the poor and the people who had recently arrived in the city (immigrants and migrants) lived. From this second zone, the city grew by establishing ever-more desirable residence areas as one moved farther away from the central zone.

By examining behavior patterns within these zones, Park and Burgess (1925) and, later, Shaw and McKay (1931, 1942) established that the second zone, the zone in transition, contained the highest rates of deviant behavior, ranging from mental illness to crime. Based on the nature of this area, several explanations for the observed pattern were advanced. Because the available residences were typically the cheapest housing within a reasonable distance from the factories, a disproportionate number of poor people lived in this zone. Immigrants and migrants coming to Chicago also needed cheap housing and thus located in disproportionate numbers in this area. As residents became financially established, they would move to better housing outside this zone, and new immigrants and migrants would replace them. Hence, the population of the zone of transition was, itself, ever changing.

Among the likely candidates to explain these high rates of crime were poverty, cultural conflict, and mobility. Instead of focusing on any one of these conditions, however, the Chicago sociologists introduced the term "social disorganization" to describe the intervening mechanism between the social conditions described and the rates of crime. The combined effects of a lack of resources, cultural ambiguity, and a highly transitory population resulted in these areas having inadequate and unstable social institutions, which meant residents were not being socially integrated into these institutions or with one another. Social institutions were therefore unable to control the behavior of the residents through either social integration or normative regulation.

Shaw and McKay were able to discount the possibility that the values of a particular ethnic or racial group resulted in a high rate of crime. By examining patterns of crime and population distribution over time, they observed that, even though the dominant ethnic and racial composition of an area was constantly shifting, the high crime rates persisted. In their study of changes over time, they also observed that high rates of crime persisted even when the growth rate was stable. To explain the persistence of crime, Shaw and McKay developed what Kornhauser (1978) has characterized as a mixed model of delinquency. In this model, they emphasized the lack of opportunities (strain) that people living in these areas experienced and the subcultural traditions (cultural deviance) that were being transmitted from one generation to another.

THE LEGACY OF THE SOCIAL DISORGANIZATION PERSPECTIVE: THE ECOLOGY OF CRIME

The influence of the social disorganization perspective has continued in what has come to be known as the ecological tradition, which focuses on the relationships between social structural characteristics of urban areas and crime or delinquency rates. Although some aspects of the theoretical arguments and methodology of the University of Chicago sociologists have been abandoned or modified, much of the ecological tradition centers on variables identified in their early work.

Social Structural Characteristics

One of the first studies to use more sophisticated statistical techniques to explore implications of the social disorganization perspective was Lander's (1954) investigation of delinquency rates among 155 Baltimore census tracts. Lander found social structural variables grouped into two types: (1) the social class composition of an area, in terms of overcrowding, substandard

housing, rental costs, and level of education, and (2) the level of social disorganization, in terms of percentage of nonwhites and owner-occupied homes. Comparing the contribution of these variables to the explanation of the variance in delinquency rates across the census tracts, Lander concluded that social disorganization variables were more important than the social class characteristics. Interestingly, the percentage of nonwhites was curvilinearly related to delinquency rates: That is, as the number of nonwhites increased from 0 to 50 percent, the rate of delinquency increased, but as the number of nonwhites increased from 50 to 100 percent, the rate of delinquency decreased. Lander interpreted these findings as suggesting that increasing numbers of nonwhites at first reflect a community that is in transition and subject to social disorganization. At some point, the percentage of nonwhites reaches a sufficient level to allow the community to stabilize and, therefore, be better able to regulate its residents.

Two subsequent studies attempted to replicate Lander's findings. Although neither duplicated his results regarding the percentage of nonwhites, both reaffirmed the importance of home ownership (Bordua, 1958; Chilton, 1964). Chilton concluded that there was no clear support for the social disorganization perspective.

One of the difficulties with the Lander, Bordua, and Chilton studies is deciding how to interpret the findings. For example, Gordon (1967) correctly observed that all the indicators included in the studies could be interpreted to measure aspects of socioeconomic status (SES). Hence, the results could be interpreted as supporting a strain argument instead of a social disorganization perspective. Kornhauser (1978) countered that assertion by noting that in other studies, SES has not consistently been related to delinquent behavior or rates of delinquency, whereas more pure social disorganization variables (mobility, heterogeneity) have been.

The analysis of aggregate neighborhood characteristics is continuing with the use of better measures of structural characteristics and alternative measures of crime or victimization. For example, Warner and Pierce (1993) examined the effects of poverty, racial heterogeneity, mobility, family disruption, and structural density on calls to the police. They argued that calls to the police may be better measures of crime than are official reports given that the latter may be inflated because poor nonwhites are especially vulnerable to arrest. They find that poverty is related to all types of crimes, whereas heterogeneity is related to burglary only. Smith and Jarjoura (1988), using victimization data, found that poverty and heterogeneity were significant predictors of violent crime only when other variables (such as family structure) were not included in the equation. Heterogeneity and mobility were related to burglary rates even after other predictors were included in the equation.

Community Dynamics

Although research on social structural characteristics identified by the early social disorganization perspective continued, the perspective itself fell out of favor for much of the 1960s and 1970s. It was criticized for failing to appreciate the diversity of values that exists within urban areas (Matza, 1969); for not recognizing that communities in urban areas indeed may be organized, but around unconventional values; and for failing to define clearly its main concept—social disorganization—thereby making the identification and operationalization of variables difficult (Bursik, 1988; Bursik and Grasmick, 1993; Liska, 1987; Gibbons and Jones, 1975). Recently, however, the ecological approach has been re-

vived with the publication of two important edited collections (Byrne and Sampson, 1984; Reiss and Tonry, 1986).

Perhaps the most important contribution of the articles contained in the 1984 and 1986 volumes is the recognition that the dynamics of communities change over time and are affected by social and political events that occur around them. This recognition has led researchers to analyze *community* careers of crime (Schuerman and Kobrin, 1986; Reiss, 1986), much like one might analyze individual crime careers. Schuerman and Kobrin investigated the twenty-year histories of the highest crime-rate areas in Los Angeles County using a developmental model. They suggested that these histories could be categorized into three distinct stages, reflecting periods (1) when changes in community crime rates are emerging, (2) when crime rates undergo significant transitions, and (3) when crime rates apparently are enduring. The correlates of high crime-rate areas varied depending on the stage of the communities' crime career. For example, changes in land use from single-family to multiple-dwelling houses were important precursors of changes in the amounts and types of crime in those neighborhoods categorized as emerging. However, in transitional or enduring crime communities, land use was less strongly related to crime level, and socioeconomic status factors were more strongly related to it.

The most recent development in social disorganization theory has been to characterize social organization variables (such as sense of "community spirit") as mediating between social structural characteristics (such as poverty, mobility, and heterogeneity) and rates of crime (Sampson and Groves, 1989; Elliott et al., 1996; Bursik and Grasmick, 1993; Krohn, 1986). If aggregate characteristics of communities such as poverty, mobility, and heterogeneity have an effect on crime rates, it is because people in those communities have difficulty generating the type of social organization that allows for effective social control. For example, Sampson and Groves (1989) suggest that such communities will contain fewer local friendship networks, less supervision of peer groups, and reduced organizational participation by residents. They examine a model that suggests these variables intervene between social structural characteristics and victimization rates. Their findings support the overall framework of the theory. Elliott et al. (1996) examine a similar model with data from two research sites (Chicago and Denver) and report weak support for some of the hypothesized links.

Bursik and Grasmick (1993), in their systemic theory of social disorganization, recognize that there are different dimensions of social control. They distinguish between primary relationships, secondary relationships, and public sources of social control; and they suggest that different sources of social control operate as intervening variables between a community's social structural characteristics and crime. Rose and Clear (1998) modify the model by suggesting an inverse relationship between informal social control (primary and secondary relations) and formal social control (public sources). The systemic approach provides a clear specification of the relationship between social structural characteristics of communities and the way in which they affect social control. This approach suggests a number of interesting avenues of research as data on different types of social control have become available on the neighborhood or community level.

Routine Activities

The routine activities approach has its roots in the ecological tradition and shares social dis-

organization theory's focus on factors that control the occurrence of crime. Although assuming the existence of motivated offenders (and, therefore, not including a measure of this variable in analyses), the approach emphasizes the roles of guardianship and the suitability of targets in generating crime (Cohen and Felson, 1979). Guardianship refers to how well the potential target of a crime (for example, a household) is protected. Such protection could be provided by neighbors looking after the home when residents are not there, the use of locks and other security devices, or merely the presence of someone in the household. Guardianship, combined with whether the target is appealing (target suitability), determines the probability of crime.

Research has supported the main implications of the theory (see Chapters 7 and 8 in this text). For example, Cohen and Felson (1979) found that crime rates are related to the proportion of households that are female-headed or in which both husband and wife are employed. This finding represents a measure of the absence of guardianship because it assumes that those households would be less likely to have someone at home during the day. Bennett (1991) has applied a similar approach to an assessment of crime in fifty-two nations over a twenty-five-year period. He finds that aggregate indicators of target suitability, guardianship, and proximity to a pool of motivated offenders are directly related to property crime rates.

The reliance on such indirect measures of routine activities requires assumptions about why these measures have an effect on the probability of crime (Mustaine and Tewksbury, 1998). Some studies have relied on more direct measures of routine activities (Miethe et al., 1987; Sampson and Wooldredge, 1987; Massey et al., 1989; Mustaine and Tewksbury, 1998). What individuals did at night, as well as their primary activity during the day, have both been found to be related to the probability of being victimized (Miethe et al., 1987; Sampson and Wooldredge, 1987). Massey et al. (1989) have also found that the number of friends one has in the neighborhood decreases the probability of household victimization—presumably because of increased guardianship. Although these direct measures of routine activities provide more assurance that the results are consistent with routine activities theory, Mustaine and Tewksbury (1998) argue for even more refinement in measures of routine activities. They have found that knowing whether people leave the home is not as important in predicting larceny victimization as knowing where they are going and what they are doing.

The new directions pursued in the ecological tradition have revitalized it. Currently, researchers are working to integrate the social control (bonding), social disorganization, and routine activities approaches to explaining crime (Felson, 1986; Hirschi, 1986; Miethe and Meier, 1994; Thompson and Fischer, 1996). Such an integration is justified on the basis of theoretical assumptions common to the approaches and may well lead to new directions for ecological research. For example, Miethe and Meier (1994: 64) present a causal model in which persons with weak social bonds are hypothesized to be more likely to encounter situations in which attractive potential targets are poorly guarded. Poorly controlled potential offenders and poorly protected targets (including persons who are more likely to put themselves at risk) are hypothesized to be related to larger social contexts, such as quality of physical setting, closeness of interpersonal relationships within that setting, and so forth. The combination of these factors is said to increase the likelihood of criminal events.

SOCIAL BONDING THEORIES

Social disorganization theorists were well aware of the importance of social institutions (such as the church) and social groups (such as the family) in integrating and regulating individuals. However, they conceptualized the problem at the community level, viewing the overall social disorganization of an area as reflecting the ineffectiveness of specific institutions. Theoretical perspectives that we will refer to as social bonding theories (in order to distinguish them from the broader categorization of social control) narrow the focus of attention to those specific institutions and groups.

Origins of Social Bonding Theories

Nye (1958) published an early version of social bonding theory. Though he recognized that delinquency could be produced 'by learning, Nye also stated that it could result from the absence of control. For Nye, social control resulted from the socialization process wherein individuals developed their sense of right and wrong (conscience), which Nye saw as a form of internalized control. Behavior is also indirectly controlled through one's affectional ties to significant others (for example, parents) and through the availability of opportunities to satisfy needs. That is, if such opportunities were available, people would conform in their behavior. Nye also recognized the importance of direct control through restricting people's behavior and punishing them if they fail to conform.

Following Nye's, the most prominent social bonding theory is the version presented by Hirschi (1969). Hirschi's answer to the question of why juveniles conform most of the time revolves around his concept of the social bond; that is, the ties that people have with the conventional social order. The stronger the tie to the social order, the more constrained individuals will be from behaving in ways that may jeopardize their position in that order. Hence, the stronger the social bond, the lower the probability of delinquent behavior. If those ties are weakened or severed, individuals are free to deviate. Note that a weakening of the social bond does not necessarily mean that a person will deviate; rather, it simply puts that person in a position where it is possible. Hirschi assumes that deviation is likely because such behavior is attractive.

Elements of the Social Bond

Hirschi identified four elements of the social bond—attachment, commitment, involvement, and belief—which are similar to the types of social control identified by Nye: **Attachment** refers to the affective or emotional ties one has with other people. Individuals with good relationships with other people will not want to do anything to threaten those relationships. For example, if parents and their child have a good relationship, the child will not want to do anything to disappoint the parents.

Commitment refers to the degree to which people want to pursue conformist lines of conduct. Those people who want to participate in some activity that may entail adherence to rules of conduct (such as an athletic team) or who have aspirations to achieve some conformist goal (such as a college education) will be more likely to conform to avoid jeopardizing such participation or goals.

Involvement refers to the time spent in conventional activities, which can have another kind of constraining effect. According to Hirschi, the more time someone spends in conventional lines of action, the less time available for deviant behavior. One of the difficulties with involvement as a separate element of the social

bond is that it is often difficult to distinguish empirically from commitment. If one wants to participate in a current activity (commitment), one probably will spend quite a bit of time doing so (involvement). Hence, the two variables are often so highly intercorrelated that they cannot be applied separately (Krohn and Massey, 1980).

Belief refers to the strength of peoples' attitudes toward conformity. Hirschi is interested in the varying extent to which individuals believe they should obey the rules of society. Beliefs that require or justify crime are not as important as the weakening of beliefs in the moral validity of conventional standards of conduct. Although the element of belief generally has been found to be a good predictor of delinquent behavior (Krohn and Massey, 1980; Sheley, 1980, 1983), the fact that it has been measured in a variety of ways has made it problematic. Some researchers have conceptualized belief primarily in terms of general standards of behavior (as Hirschi suggests), whereas others have interpreted the concept in terms of specific attitudes that neutralize or justify deviant behavior. Although most of these different measurements have been shown to be related to criminal behavior, the strength of the relationship and the meaning of the findings vary.

The four elements of the social bond may operate in a variety of social arenas. Hence, one could be attached to a member of the family as well as to a teacher or religious leader. However, for adolescents, the most critical social arenas are the family, peer group, school, and religion. For adults, they are family, religion, and work. Though Hirschi implies that attachment should be considered causally prior to the other elements (Massey and Krohn, 1986), he does not specify a causal order among any of the four elements of the social bond. Yet, he does indicate that all four should be interrelated. For example, stronger ties to one's family may make people more likely to be committed and involved in conventional pursuits and to believe in conventional values. Of course, a weakening of commitment or belief might also adversely affect relationships with the family. As we will note in reviewing the research on social bonding theory, the causal order question is a difficult but important one.

Research on Social Bonding

An extensive research literature is devoted to the relationship between variables relevant to social bonding theory and delinquent and drug-using behavior. We will briefly review studies that have examined the elements of the social bond in a multivariate analysis rather than those that focused on only one element.

Hirschi provided research evidence when he first presented his theory in 1969. He surveyed a large sample of adolescents from Richmond, California, asking them about their relationships with parents, peers, and teachers; their participation and success in school; their educational aspirations; and their attitudes toward the law and their parents' values. He correlated these measures with self-reported delinquent behavior to determine whether hypotheses concerning attachment, commitment, involvement, and belief were supported. The results supported most of his hypotheses, though at a weak to moderate level. Importantly, however, the study questioned the assumption that attachment to conventional others is always a barrier to delinquency. Hirschi found that having friends who were delinquent did increase the probability of delinquent behavior by his respondents. Yet, subsequent research has also found a positive, rather than the predicted negative, relationship between attachment to peers (conventional or delinquent) and delinquent behavior (Empey and Lubeck, 1971;

Hindelang, 1973; Krohn and Massey, 1980). Peer relationships in general tend to pull youths away from parents and other adults, making youths more vulnerable to delinquent influences. Truly delinquent peer relationships directly encourage delinquency.

Two more recent studies examined the viability of Hirschi's theory. Krohn and Massey (1980), using a sample of 3,065 boys and girls in grades seven to twelve in six communities (ranging from rural to urban), not only examined this issue but did so for delinquent behaviors of varying degrees of seriousness. They found that some indicators of commitment, attachment, and belief were negatively related to four scales measuring self-reported alcohol and marijuana use, minor delinquent behavior, use of hard drugs, and serious delinquency. Measures that tapped the commitment element were most strongly related to involvement in delinquency. The theory did a better job of explaining less-serious forms of delinquent behavior than more-serious forms and did slightly better in explaining female delinquency than male delinquency.

Wiatrowski et al. (1981) extended the examination of the elements of the social bond by testing a causal model of Hirschi's theory. Adding a measure of SES and academic ability to Hirschi's basic model, they found that parental attachment was indirectly related to self-reported delinquent behavior through school-related variables (such as attachment to teachers) and belief (such as the notion that theft is immoral). School-related variables and belief were directly related to delinquent behavior. Approximately one-third of the variance in delinquent behavior was explained by the social bonding variables. These findings appear to be similar across ethnic groups (Junger and Marshall, 1997; Cernkovich and Giordano, 1992).

An important limitation to the studies by Krohn and Massey and by Wiatrowski et al. is that they both use cross-sectional data (data collected at a single point in time). The logic of Hirschi's theory suggests that an erosion in the social bond precedes delinquent behavior, and both the aforementioned studies assumed this to be the case. However, with data collected at only one point in time, it was not possible to determine if this progression actually occurs. When Agnew (1985, 1991) examined the effect of elements of the social bond as measured at one point in time on delinquency reported at a subsequent time, he concluded that the bonding measures are not effective predictors of delinquency.

A partial investigation of the causal structure of social bonding theory was done by Liska and Reed (1985). They used data on 1,886 tenth-grade boys who were then resurveyed at the end of their eleventh-grade year. They focused on the causal order among parental attachment, school attachment, and self-reported delinquent behavior. Using sophisticated models, they found that, instead of the simple causal structure suggested by Hirschi, more complicated relationships were observed. That is, stronger parental attachment appeared to reduce delinquency, but delinquency also was found to reduce school attachment. Thus, the assumption that a decrease in school attachment precedes delinquent behavior was called into question. One difficulty with the study was that the boys were already in high school when they were first surveyed; the causal order suggested by Hirschi might exist for younger schoolchildren. Nevertheless, the Liska and Reed study has forced us to reconsider what appeared to be commonsense assumptions of the social bonding perspective.

Thornberry et al. (1991) have also examined the causal order of social bonding theory.

They used three waves of data (i.e., information collected from the same persons at three points in time) to examine the interrelationships among attachment to parents, commitment to school, and delinquency. They found that commitment to school and delinquency are involved in a mutually reinforcing relationship over time. Increased commitment to school reduces delinquency, and increased participation in delinquency reduces commitment to school. Attachment to parents and delinquent behavior are reciprocally related from wave 1 to wave 2, but attachment to parents measured at wave 2 has no causal effect on wave 3 delinquent behavior. Delinquent behavior at wave 2 does reduce attachment to parents at wave 3, however. It is important to note that respondents surveyed in this study were younger than those in the Liska and Reed study, which may account for the differences in the findings.

The elements of the social bond have more recently been employed to explain the discontinuity in crime over the life course (Sampson and Laub, 1990, 1993, 1997; Thornberry and Krohn, forthcoming). Most people who commit delinquent behavior do not go on to become adult criminals. As adolescents pass into young adulthood, many acquire more stakes in conformity (Karacki and Toby, 1962) by making investments (time, money, emotions) in a course of action (Becker, 1960). Sampson and Laub (1990: 611) hypothesize that "social bonds to adult institutions of informal social control (e.g., family, education, neighborhood, work) influence criminal behavior over the life course. . . . "

Some evidence supporting this position can be found in the literature on drug use (Brown et al., 1974; Henley and Adams, 1973). Henley and Adams, for example, in assessing what factors led to the cessation of marijuana use among a sample of young adults, found that the best predictor of cessation was getting married (attachment). Marital attachment and stability both appear to reduce both drug use and criminal behavior (Sampson and Laub, 1990; Quinton et al., 1993; Pickles and Rutter, 1991; Horney et al., 1995). Job stability has also been shown to lead to desistance from crime and drug use (Sampson and Laub, 1990; Donovan et al., 1983; Kandel and Raveis, 1989; Horney et al., 1995).

Evaluation of Social Bonding Theory

Social bonding theory is intuitively appealing because it focuses on the relationships between the individual and social institutions that should help constrain criminal behavior. It is a flexible theoretical perspective in that it is not class-based, as are some other theories (for example, strain). The theory should be as applicable to middle-class crime as it is to lower-class crime. Indeed, Hirschi and Gottfredson (1987) suggested that it could be used to account for white collar criminality. Another advantage to the perspective is that it may, in part, explain why we mature out of crime.

On the other hand, the research evidence presents a more ambiguous picture of social bonding theory. Although cross-sectional studies (looking at juveniles at a single point in time) have clearly established a relationship between elements of the social bond and delinquent behavior, when combined in multivariate analysis they are able to explain only a moderate-to-small amount of the variance. Longitudinal studies (looking at the same juveniles at several points in time) have offered even less support for social bonding theory. The relationships examined are not as strong. Longitudinal research also has raised the possibility that the attenuation in the elements of the social bond may be a consequence rather than (or as well as) a cause of delinquent behavior.

A more serious problem also must be addressed. Social control theorists typically do not concern themselves with what motivates a person to commit a delinquent or criminal act, only with what stands in the way of committing such an act (Hirschi, 1969). Others have argued that the assumption that everyone is motivated to deviate at one time or another limits the potential of social control theory because, whether or not the assumption is correct, it fails to account for the various factors that may influence one form of deviance rather than another (Sheley, 1983). Do we assume, for example, that everyone is motivated to rob banks but that we all face differing levels of constraint on such acts? A number of scholars have suggested that we construct mixed models that account for both motivation and constraint (Elliott et al., 1985; Johnson, 1979; LaGrange and White, 1985; Massey and Krohn, 1986). Hirschi (1979) counters that such "integrative" attempts change the very nature of control theory and ultimately confuse the concepts of motivation and constraint. The debate has yet to be fully resolved.

SELF-CONTROL THEORY

Social bonding theory focuses on the ties that individuals have with social groups and institutions throughout their lives. Gottfredson and Hirschi's (1990) self-control theory, on the other hand, focuses on one of the important consequences of the socialization process that is developed very early in a child's life. Self-control is conceived as the difference in the extent to which people are vulnerable to temptations, "the barrier that stands between the actor and the obvious momentary benefits crime provides" (Hirschi and Gottfredson, 1993: 53). It is not the motivating force for crime. Individuals who are low in self-control tend to be "impulsive, insensitive, physical, risk-taking, short-sighted and non-verbal" (Gottfredson and Hirschi, 1990: 90). They will also be more likely to engage in criminal acts and, prior to the age of responsibility, to engage in analogous behaviors such as problematic school comportment.

Low self-control develops primarily as a result of ineffective child-rearing. Parents who do not adequately monitor their child's behavior, who are unable to recognize deviant behavior when it occurs, and who do not punish such behavior effectively are likely to have children who have difficulty resisting temptations (Gottfredson and Hirschi, 1990: 97). Self-control can be affected by other experiences such as school, but the difference among individuals in their likelihood to commit crime appears early in their lives and remains stable over the life course.

Gottfredson and Hirschi (1990) suggest that their theory is particularly useful in explaining both the versatility in criminal behavior and its stability over time. They assert that research overwhelmingly demonstrates that offenders are very versatile in the criminal behaviors that they commit rather than specializing in any one type of behavior. They explain this versatility by suggesting that criminal behavior is a manifestation of "an underlying tendency to pursue short-term, immediate pleasure" (Gottfredson and Hirschi, 1990: 93). Because there are many possible consequences of the pursuit of immediate pleasure, it is not surprising that individuals with low self-control commit criminal acts.

It is also not surprising that the best predictor of future criminal behavior is past criminal behavior. If criminal behavior reflects low self-control that is a more or less stable trait, then those who develop low self-control early in their lives will be more likely to continue to pursue immediate pleasure later in life than those who develop high self-control. Gottfredson and Hirschi (1990: 108) recognize that other social-control factors in the life course may intervene, but argue that "the low self-control group continues over time to exhibit low self-control."

Research on Self-Control Theory

Research on self-control theory has generated a debate over how to measure self-control. Hirschi and Gottfredson (1993: 49) advocate the use of direct behavioral measures of self-control, stating that "the best indicators of self-control are the acts we use self-control to explain: criminal, delinquent, and reckless acts." To counter the circularity of such measurements, they suggest the use of behaviors such as whining, pushing, and shoving among young children and smoking, drinking, and excessive television watching among teenagers. For example, in a survey of drivers who had been pulled over by the police, Keane et al. (1993) measured risk-taking behavior by whether drivers used their seat belts and by impaired drivers' perception of how likely it would be for them to be stopped by the police. They measured impulsiveness by responses to the question "Did anyone try to discourage you from driving tonight?" They tried to assess the driver's lifestyle by asking respondents to report the number of alcoholic drinks they had consumed in the previous seven days. Keane et al. found that these measures were positively associated with blood alcohol concentration in respondents.

Grasmick et al. (1993) took a very different approach to the measurement of self-control. They did not measure self-control with behavioral measures such as drinking or smoking as suggested by Hirschi and Gottfredson (1993) because they saw these behaviors as consequences of low self-control rather than as personality traits. Rather, they measured self-control by asking respondents to agree or disagree with statements such as "I would do almost anything on a dare" (risk-taking) and "Sometimes I feel like smashing things" (temper). They developed a twenty-three-item scale measuring low self-control and found the scale score to be positively related to both self-reported fraud and the use of force. However, Grasmick et al. suggested that their findings were not as strong as what Gottfredson and Hirschi would expect and, therefore, that additional variables were needed to account for crime.

Evans et al. (1997) used both a self-characterization measure of low self-control and a behavioral measure using self-reported items such as smoking, alcohol and drug use, and speeding to predict crime among a sample of adult respondents. They found that both measures of low self-control were significantly related to crime, with the behavioral measure being more strongly related than the self-characterization measure. They also included variables drawn from other theories, such as bonding measures, to determine if these measures were spuriously related to crime and would drop out once self-control measures are included. Evans et al. concluded that self-control did not explain criminality to the exclusion of the other theoretical approaches.

Evaluation of Self-Control Theory

Self-control theory is another intuitively appealing explanation of crime that has already had an important impact. The theory, however, is not without its critics. One of the more cogent criticisms of self-control theory centers on the basic tautology that forms the core of the theory. Gottfredson and Hirschi use the concept of self-control to describe the barrier between the actor and the benefits of committing a crime. Although they reject the notion that low self-control is the propensity to commit crime, the way that the notion of social control is used in the theory and the way that Hirschi and Gottfredson advocate measuring the concept both lead to such an interpretation (Akers, 1991; Barlow, 1991; Sampson, 1992). The hypothesis that low self-control increases the probability of crime can be restated: The propensity to commit crime increases the probability that crime will be committed. Akers suggests that an operational indicator of social control independent of criminal behavior needs to be identified.

Hirschi and Gottfredson (1993) recognize the need for such independent indicators and recommend using either predelinquent indicators of problem behavior among children (whining, pushing, or shoving) or behaviors that are not criminal (using alcohol). However, it can be argued that such measures do not resolve the issue. Both the behavior that is being used as the independent variable (e.g., drinking) and criminal behavior may be a reflection of low self-control, or both behaviors could be caused by some other factor. Without a measure of low self-control that does not incorporate problem behaviors, there is no way to resolve the issue.

Sampson (1992) is critical of self-control theory because it suggests that low self-control, once formed early in childhood, is rather stable. Sampson suggests that this approach denies the importance of later life events such as marriage, having children, and employment, in the development or at least moderation of self-control.

Self-control theory will continue to generate a great deal of attention. Yet, the lasting contribution that it makes will be contingent on its further development. The concept of low self-control will need to be clarified. Moreover, a more systematic statement of the theory incorporating a set of testable hypotheses will need to be developed.

INDIVIDUALLY ORIENTED THEORIES

Thus far, the critical question posed by all social control theories has been answered by emphasizing the capacity of communities to integrate and regulate their residents (social organization) and by focusing on people's relationships with conventional social institutions and groups (social bonding). The theories reviewed in this section—self-concept theory and self-rejection theory—locate the source of constraint or containment primarily within the individual. They suggest that the critical factor in constraining people is what they think of themselves.

Self-Concept Theory

Reckless (1961, 1973) has been the chief advocate of self-concept or containment theory. When viewed in its entirety, his theoretical statement includes not only inner containments but also outer containments (for example, supervision and opportunity for acceptance), internal pushes (for example, rebellion and hostility), external pressures (for example, poverty and group conflict), and external pulls (for example, deviant companions and criminal subculture). However, for Reckless, inner containment in the form of a positive self-concept is the critical factor that insulates people from the various pushes, pulls, and pressures that may lead them to delinquent behavior. His concept of inner containment reflects a grab bag of poorly defined variables such as self-concept, self-control, goal orientation, and normative commitment. The key problem with these concepts is that they are related to

delinquency by definition. For example, if a lack of self-control is defined as the inability to control impulses toward deviant behavior (as Reckless defined it), then a relationship must inevitably exist between a lack of self-control and delinquency.

Self-concept is the variable on which Reckless et al. focus their research. Reckless was perplexed by how some boys living in areas of high delinquency managed to remain nondelinquent. He hypothesized that a favorable self-concept was the reason that some boys were able to resist criminogenic influences. In a series of research articles (see, for example, Reckless et al., 1956, 1957a, 1957b; Reckless and Dinitz, 1972), Reckless and colleagues examined this hypothesis. They first requested teachers to identify "good" boys who were unlikely to get in trouble with the law and "bad" boys who were likely to do so. They found that items measuring what they labeled as self-concept differentiated the "good" from the "bad" boys. Following these boys over the next four years, they found that those with a more positive self-concept were less likely to acquire official records.

The research on self-concept theory has been criticized for a number of methodological problems (Orcutt, 1970; Schrag, 1972; Schwartz and Tangri, 1965; Tangri and Schwartz, 1967). Most important, Reckless and associates' method of measuring self-concept contained items that probably reflected the boys' prior troublesome behavior rather than being a measure of self-concept itself. For example, their self-concept scale included the following items:

Have you ever been told that you were headed for trouble?

Have most of your friends been in trouble with the law?

Subsequent research using better measures of self-concept has failed to support Reckless's argument (Jensen, 1973; McCarthy and Hoge, 1984). Jensen correlated measures of self-esteem, self-control, and acceptance of moral beliefs with self-reported delinquent behavior. The weak relationships he found led him to conclude that elements of inner containment may not be as important for delinquency as are variables reflecting the social environment (such as family, class, and neighborhood).

Schrag (1972) has observed that Reckless's formulation contains few testable statements. Further, he concluded that its "logical and empirical defects call for a fundamental reconstruction" (p. 89). Although Schrag was correct in his criticism of the perspective, a reformulation of Reckless's theory would probably not be an efficient means of salvaging any insights one might derive from his work. Rather, it might be more profitable to begin anew in focusing on individual sources of constraint.

Self-Esteem Approaches

In some respects, the work of Kaplan and his associates can be seen as just such a new beginning. Kaplan's (1980) self-rejection or self-derogation theory begins with the assumption that people will behave so as to minimize negative self-attitudes and maximize positive ones. Devaluing experiences ("put downs") may occur in the course of social interaction in membership groups. If they do, and if the individual is unable to cope with them, he or she will develop attitudes of self-rejection or self-derogation. These attitudes will, in turn, result in a loss of motivation to conform to the normative patterns represented by the membership group. Up to this point, Kaplan's argument falls well within the assumptive parameters of the social control perspective. However, he then suggests that the individual also will be motivated to deviate from those normative patterns. Hence, Kaplan does not present a pure social control argument; nevertheless, the thrust of the theory suggests that it be reviewed as one.

Self-rejection theory is a much more carefully constructed and researched perspective than self-concept theory (Kaplan, 1972; Kaplan et al., 1982, 1986). The hypotheses are identified clearly, and the arguments are presented logically and do not suffer from the same form of circular reasoning evident in Reckless's work. The key concerns about self-rejection theory that remain to be clarified are how well measures of self-rejection help explain deviant behavior and, more important, the causal order of the variables in the model. In terms of the latter issue, self-rejection and measures of family and school involvement and deviant behavior have been found to be related in a more complex way than originally suggested by Kaplan (Kaplan et al., 1986).

Rosenberg et al. (1989), using a measure that also taps self-acceptance, find that low self-esteem is positively related to delinquent behavior. They also observe a relationship that suggests that participating in delinquency leads to an improvement in self-esteem, although the relationship is not statistically significant. The relationship between self-esteem and delinquent behavior is different for lower and higher social classes. Among lower-class boys, low self-esteem has a larger positive effect on delinquency than it does for higher-class boys. However, delinquency is more effective in boosting self-esteem among higher-class boys than it is for lower-class boys.

Jang and Thornberry (1998) summarize previous literature on self-esteem into two basic lines of argument. The first ties delinquency to low self-esteem, and the second links the two variables through what the authors term "self-enhancement." That is, youths with low self-esteem are thought to assert their independence from convention through delinquent acts and thus to gain the respect of peers who are supportive of such acts. In the less-conventional arena, then, self-esteem is increased. In their test of the hypothesis, Jang and Thornberry do not find that low self-esteem causes delinquency (though they are careful to suggest that their measurement of self-esteem may have produced this finding). However, their findings do indicate that, independent of delinquent behavior, associating with delinquent friends increases self-esteem.

Recent research on self-esteem has used better measures and examined more-complex models. Although studies have found that some measure of self-esteem plays a role in leading to delinquent behavior, the relationships are, at best, weak. The predicted self-enhancing effect of delinquency on self-esteem has not been supported. Although more research needs to be conducted to compare the various measures of self-esteem (see Rosenberg et al., 1995), it appears that self-esteem is not an important factor in explaining delinquent behavior.

THE DETERRENCE DOCTRINE

The perspectives discussed thus far have been theoretical statements that have implicit or explicit social policy implications. The deterrence doctrine, on the other hand, is essentially a policy orientation that has theoretical implications. Labeling the perspective a doctrine rather than a theory, Gibbs (1975: 5) characterizes it as "a congery of vague ideas with no unifying factor other than their being legacies of two major figures of moral philosophy, Cesare Beccaria and

Jeremy Bentham." Nevertheless, the deterrence doctrine has generated hypotheses, and scholars continue the process of incorporating research findings into interrelated statements. Unfortunately, that process has proved more difficult than the early statements concerning deterrence would have suggested.

Basic Principles of Deterrence

The deterrence doctrine is similar to other social control perspectives in that it focuses on reasons that people do *not* commit crimes. However, the other social control perspectives emphasize the role of social integration in constraining people and in allowing for effective regulation, whereas the emphasis in the deterrence doctrine is clearly on the social regulative role of the legal apparatus.

As Gibbs indicates, the deterrence doctrine was first stated systematically by Beccaria (1764) and Bentham (1892) in reaction to a harsh, inequitable, and often-capricious criminal justice system. They sought to establish policy guidelines to reform the system based on utilitarian principles and hedonistic psychology. They assumed that social policy should operate to generate the greatest good for the greatest number of people. Further, they argued that people behaved rationally so as to maximize the rewards for their behavior and minimize the potential costs. Thus, the objective of the criminal justice system should be to deter people from committing crime by having the cost of punishment outweigh the potential reward from the criminal act. Punishment should be severe enough *only* to offset the potential reward.

Formally defined, deterrence is "the omission of an act as a response to the perceived risk and fear of punishment for contrary behavior" (Gibbs, 1975: 2). Deterrence can be further subdivided into two types defined by the intended target. Specific deterrence occurs when a person is punished with the intention of preventing that person from committing future crimes. General deterrence occurs when the intention is to prevent people other than (or in addition to) the criminal actor from committing crimes by setting an example. Clearly, in practice, the two are not mutually exclusive, and typically we try to accomplish both goals. The distinction is necessary, however, to assess the effectiveness of punishment.

Most of the work on the deterrence doctrine has focused on two of the three variables originally identified by Beccaria and Bentham: They suggested that the effectiveness of punishment varies in terms of its certainty (the likelihood that you will be punished), severity, and celerity (the swiftness with which punishment is meted out). Celerity of punishment is difficult to assess and has not been included in most studies of deterrence.

Research on Deterrence

The research on deterrence has been concerned primarily with the general deterrent effect of punishment. Specific deterrence often is confounded by other factors involved in punishing individuals, such as rehabilitative efforts, incapacitation, or simply the passage of time.

Research on general deterrence has been done at the aggregate (or ecological) level as well as at the individual (or perceptual) level. The review of research that follows will exclude the work on the deterrent effect of capital punishment that is covered in Chapter 23 of this text.

The Aggregate Level Aggregate-level research takes an ecological unit, most frequently a state, and examines the correlation between rates of crime and computed measures of certainty and

severity of punishment. Certainty is computed as the ratio of the number of arrests, convictions, or prison admissions to the number of crimes reported. Severity is computed as the average length of sentence for a particular crime. Tittle (1969) examined the relationship among these variables for all Index (*Uniform Crime Index;* see Chapter 3 in this text) offenses. He found that states with a higher probability of punishment (certainty) had lower overall crime rates. However, severity of punishment was significantly related only to homicide rates. Subsequent studies have confirmed the low-to-moderate inverse relationship between certainty and overall crime rates (Logan, 1972; Bailey et al., 1974; Geerken and Gove, 1977). A possible explanation for failing to establish a relationship between severity and most types of crime is that an inverse correlation exists between certainty and severity. That is, in states that have harsh penalties, people are less likely to be convicted (Logan, 1972). When Logan statistically controlled for certainty, a slight inverse relationship was found between severity and crime rates.

Tittle and Rowe (1974), further examining the relationship between certainty and crime rates, found evidence for what they called a "tipping effect." For cities and counties in the state of Florida, certainty made a difference in crime rates only after a 30 percent certainty rate was reached. This suggests that some threshold of certainty must be reached before it is likely to have a deterrent impact (see also Chamlin, 1991).

Bursik et al. (1990) argue that prior studies of deterrence have used too large a unit of aggregation (cities, counties, states) when exploring the deterrence argument. They suggest that the neighborhood is the appropriate level of aggregation and examine neighborhood arrest data and subsequent illegal behavior. Their analysis does not find support for hypotheses derived from deterrence theory.

Although the research evidence consistently finds a relationship between aggregate measures of certainty and crime rates, the meaning of such findings is ambiguous. For example, the observed inverse relationship could be due to system overload. If crime rates exceed the capacity of the system to locate and arrest offenders, then a negative relationship between certainty and crime rates would occur. However, the cause and effect would be reversed and not support a deterrence argument. By using data from ninety-eight cities over a six-year period, Greenberg et al. (1979) were able to examine the past effect of certainty on present crime rates and the past effect of crime rates on certainty. Their results supported neither the deterrence nor the overload hypothesis. Rather, they concluded that the relationship between certainty and crime rates is due to some unknown social conditions that affect both crime and certainty.

A few studies have investigated the possibility of social factors that would explain the observed relationship between certainty and crime rates. When the effect of variables such as poverty, urbanization, and socioeconomic status are controlled, the relationship between certainty and crime rates has been found to be reduced substantially (Pogue, 1986; Parker and Smith, 1979; Tittle and Rowe, 1974).

Based on extensive reviews of aggregate-level deterrence research, Nagin (1978; see also Blumstein et al., 1978) has argued that, although the majority of studies found a negative relationship between the probability of sanctions and crime rates, the evidence in support of deterrent effects upon criminal behavior actually is rather weak. He based his finding on the observation that most studies of deterrent effects utilized much the same sources (such as National Prisoner Statistics and UCR data) and, thus, could have been expected to support each other. Further, Nagin asserted that these types of data are problematic in that extraneous factors—such as poverty level, region of the country, and unemployment rates—could account for both the levels of crime reported and the probability of punishment. The single study examined by Nagin that did not find the expected inverse correlation (Forst, 1976) was the more thorough in that it incorporated variables of this type. Importantly, in a recent update of empirical studies of the issue of deterrence, Nagin (1998) suggests that the quality of research has improved significantly. He asserts now that "our law enforcement apparatus exerts a substantial deterrent effect" (p. 36).

The most problematic feature of aggregate studies on deterrence is the assumption that people are aware of the certainty and severity of punishment and that these perceptions affect the probability that these people will commit crime. However, Erickson and Gibbs (1978) found that juveniles are ignorant of the penalties for crimes and the probabilities of getting caught. Rather, their perceptions of certainty are related to how they ranked the seriousness of the offense (Erickson et al., 1977). Apparently, their perceptions of certainty were related to how they believed the legal system should operate rather than how it does operate (Empey, 1982).

The Individual Level An alternative method of examining the deterrence doctrine is to ask individuals directly what they perceive the likelihood of arrest and the severity of punishment to be for specific offenses and to acquire self-reported data on whether they had committed any of those offenses. One of the first such studies was done by Waldo and Chiricos (1972) using a sample of male first-year college students. They found an inverse relationship between perceived certainty of punishment and criminal behavior, but not between perceived severity and crime. A number of subsequent studies on adolescents and college students have provided support for that same general conclusion (Grasmick and Bryjak, 1980; Silberman, 1976; Jensen et al., 1978; Anderson et al., 1977).

More recently, studies on diverse populations have appeared. Hollinger and Clark (1983) examined whether employee theft was deterred by perceptions of certainty and severity of sanction. They found both dimensions of deterrence were significantly related to theft but that certainty was more strongly related. These results held across different types of corporations, but age did condition the relationships; that is, older employees, with more to lose, were more affected by their perceptions of certainty and severity. This suggests that commitment may interact with certainty of punishment to deter employee theft.

Piliavin et al. (1986) questioned the applicability of the deterrence doctrine to a sample of serious offenders. When they surveyed 3,300 adult offenders and adolescents who had dropped out of school, they found that perception of personal risk was not related to subsequent crime. Although the cost side of the rational choice model was not related to criminal behavior, the reward side was. That is, a measure of whether people perceived greater opportunities to earn money illegally was significantly and substantially related to criminal behavior.

As in the case of aggregate-level research, the possibility exists that the relationship between certainty and self-reported criminal behavior is spurious because of a third variable that is related to and causally prior to both certainty and criminal behavior. For example, Meier and

Johnson (1977) found that having criminal associates minimizes the deterrent effect, whereas Erickson et al. (1977) concluded that moral condemnation of behaviors explains the relationship between certainty and criminal behavior. Burkett and Ward (1993) suggest that moral condemnation conditions the deterrent relationship. When people do consider the act sinful or very wrong, they refrain from committing it regardless of the threat of legal sanction.

Specifying the appropriate causal order is also of paramount importance in individually based research on deterrence. Saltzman et al. (1982) raised the possibility that the observed inverse correlation between certainty and delinquent behavior may be due to what they called an "experiential effect." This term refers to the possibility that individuals who had already committed delinquent behavior without being caught or punished would have lower levels of perceived certainty based on that experience. By acquiring data at two points in time, Saltzman et al. were able to compare the experiential hypothesis to the deterrence hypothesis. They found that the experiential effect was stronger than the deterrent effect, suggesting that if people commit criminal behavior without negative consequences, they will think that they are not likely to get caught for doing so in the future. Unfortunately, even their own research has not consistently supported the experiential effect in favor of the deterrent effect (Paternoster et al., 1985). Therefore, they concluded rather pessimistically that "even after a decade of intensified perceptual deterrence research, very little is known about the relationship between perceptions and behavior" (p. 430).

Nagin and Paternoster (1991) suggest that part of the problem with prior research is that it has too narrowly conceived of the deterrence process. Consistent with the perspective offered by Williams and Hawkins (1986), they suggest that preventive mechanisms that are triggered by formal sanctions should be included in a deterrence explanation of crime. Thus, they suggest that commitment costs (effect on past accomplishments), attachment costs (loss of valued relationships), and the stigma of arrest be included in deterrence models. They find that both sanction threats and perceived commitment costs have independent crime-inhibiting effects. However, they do not find that the perception of high commitment costs increases the effect of perceived certainty on crime.

Evaluation of the Deterrence Doctrine

As suggested at the outset of the discussion of deterrence, the perspective was not generated as a theory of behavior but rather as a doctrine concerning the proper role of punishment. To date, a formal theory of deterrence has yet to be achieved. Indeed, Gibbs (1975) has suggested that because of the difficulties in identifying a unique effect of deterrence, we might be better served by generating a theory about the general preventive consequences of punishment. This type of theory, incorporating such outcomes as incapacitation, would be more inclusive than deterrence.

The research on deterrence has illustrated quite well the problems with the perspective. The aggregate-level research requires assumptions about a citizen's knowledge of sanctions, assumptions that appear to be incorrect. Results at both the aggregate and individual level have suggested that the observed relationship between certainty of punishment and crime may be spurious. Finally, there remains the problem of determining whether punishment is affecting crime or crime is affecting the level of real or perceived punishment. Although the research results clearly indicate a relationship between certainty of punishment and crime, until these issues are resolved, it will not be possible to determine whether even this most basic assumption of the deterrence perspective is viable. Gibbs (1975: 1) noted that his book represented "a continuous denial of immediate prospects for satisfactory answers to questions about crime, punishment and deterrence." Over two decades later, we find that statement still summarizes the state of the deterrence doctrine.

Research aside, the deterrence doctrine developed as a recommendation of appropriate objectives for the criminal justice system. Therefore, not surprisingly, one of its appeals is its clear policy implications (Wilson, 1975); clear, that is, if one does not take into account the weak or ambiguous research results described here.

The doctrine suggests that the most appropriate strategy to deter crime would be to increase the probability of punishment. To do so, however, would be very difficult and might engender other social and economic costs that may not make the effort worthwhile. For example, increasing the probability of arrest would require more police and possibly a greater infringement on civil liberties. More court and correctional personnel would be needed if the strategy included increasing the probability of conviction and incarceration. The economic costs of such a strategy would be great. Given the unclear message from deterrence research, it may not be prudent to invest in such policies if their only purpose is to deter crime.

CONCLUSION

The social control perspectives reviewed in this chapter all share an emphasis on identifying those social or social psychological factors that constrain people from committing delinquent or criminal behavior. They differ in the level (community to individual) of their analysis and, to some extent, in their relative emphasis on social integration and social regulation.

Clearly, the social control perspectives have served to reorient criminologists to the study of factors that inhibit crime. Hirschi (1987) has suggested that this emphasis can be seen as a revitalization of the classical image of man as a rational actor who is constrained from deviating only by those social forces that make coexistence possible. This emphasis has highlighted the role of primary social institutions such as the family, schools, church, and legal system. By focusing research efforts on these institutions, we have learned much about how and why they generate conformity.

The research effort also has raised a number of questions about the viability of some of the assumptions contained in these perspectives and about their ability to explain criminal behavior. Two problems appear to be generic to social control perspectives: First, the assumption that everyone possesses the motivation for criminal behavior—and that this universal motivation, a constant, therefore does not need to be included in social control theory—limits the ability of the social-control perspective to explain many forms of criminal behavior (Sheley, 1983). At some point, theories of motivation (e.g., strain theories) will have to be integrated, at least to a degree, with theories about the freedom to violate the law (social-control theories) (Elliott et al., 1985; Massey and Krohn, 1986). As Hirschi (1979) has noted, however, such a unified theory of criminality is not easy to achieve. Most theories are based on fairly intricate assumptions, making it highly difficult to paste theories together.

The second generic problem for social control perspectives is to determine the appropriate causal order among the variables in the respective models. For example, does a weak commitment to school lead to delinquency, or does engaging in delinquent behavior result in juveniles becoming less committed to school and to getting an education? Does more effective enforcement lead to lower crime rates, or do higher crime rates result in law enforcement being less effective? These types of questions are critical not only for evaluating the theoretical perspectives but also for using them to generate any policy recommendations.

It is in the area of policy that social control perspectives are most appealing. They identify arenas that can be manipulated to some extent (the law, schools). Moreover, the logic of the arguments would suggest preventive approaches rather than dealing with crime after people are already engaging in it or interacting with others who are doing so. Also important is that the perspective is consistent with the current political ideology regarding the need to return to more traditional methods of socialization and control.

Gibbons (1975) suggested that social control theory apparently will be an enduring contribution to the discipline. He was correct. What is not yet known is just what the nature of that enduring contribution will be. These perspectives may simply have served to reemphasize arenas of social integration and regulation within integrated models of criminal behavior. Or more elaborate social control models incorporating both social structural and social psychological factors may be developed. How social control theorists and researchers deal with some of the concerns raised here will determine just what its contribution will be.

DISCUSSION QUESTIONS

1. Discuss the essential manner in which social control theory differs from strain and subcultural theories of criminality. State the basic question that each theory asks.

2. What is social disorganization theory and to what degree does it explain the criminal behavior of individuals?

3. In what ways is social disorganization theory linked to research on crime and routine activities? Discuss how social disorganization theory might be applied to our crime situation today.

4. Discuss Hirschi's notion of social bonding as it relates to juvenile delinquency. How much support exists in the research literature for the social bonding approach?

5. In what ways does social bonding theory differ from self-concept and self-rejection approaches?

6. Discuss the deterrence doctrine and distinguish between general and specific deterrence. What variables are necessary to understand the doctrine? How well has the doctrine fared when subjected to empirical testing?

REFERENCES

Agnew, R. 1985. "Social Control Theory and Delinquency: A Longitudinal Test." *Criminology* 23: 47–61.

———. 1991. "A Longitudinal Test of Social Control Theory and Delinquency." *Journal of Research in Crime and Delinquency* 28: 126–156.

Akers, R. L. 1991. "Self Control as a General Theory of Crime." *Journal of Quantitative Criminology* 7: 201–211.

Anderson, L. S., T. G. Chiricos, and G. P. Waldo. 1977. "Formal and Informal Sanctions: A Comparison of Deterrent Effects." *Social Problems* 25: 103–114.

Bailey, W., J. D. Martin, and L. Gray. 1974. "Crime and Deterrence: A Correlational Analysis." *Journal of Research in Crime and Delinquency* 11: 124–143.

Barlow, H. D. 1991. "Gottfredson and Hirschi: Explaining Crimes and Analogous Acts, or the Unrestrained Will Grab at Pleasure Whenever They Can: A General Theory of Crime." Book essay, *The Journal of Criminal Law and Criminology* 82: 229–242.

Beccaria, C. 1764. *An Essay on Crimes and Punishments.* Philadelphia: Nicklin.

Becker, H. 1960. "Notes on the Concept of Commitment." *American Journal of Sociology* 66: 32–40.

Bennett, R. R. 1991. "Routine Activities: A Cross-National Assessment of a Criminological Perspective." *Social Forces* 70: 147–163.

Bentham, J. 1892. *Introduction to the Principles of Morals and Legislation.* Oxford: Clarendon Press.

Blumstein, A., J. Cohen, and D. Nagin. 1978. *Deterrence and Incapacitation: Estimating the Effects of Criminal Sanctions on Crime Rates.* Washington, DC: National Academy of Sciences.

Bordua, D. 1958. "Juvenile Delinquency and 'Anomie': An Attempt at Replication." *Social Problems* 6 (Winter): 230–238.

Brown, J. W., D. Glaser, E. Waxer, and G. Geis. 1974. "Turning Off: Cessation of Marijuana Use After College." *Social Problems* 21 (April): 527–538.

Burgess, E. W. 1925. "The Growth of the City." Pp. 47–62 in *The City.* Edited by R. E. Park and E. W. Burgess. Chicago: University of Chicago Press.

Burkett, S. R., and D. A. Ward. 1993. "A Note on Perceptual Deterrence, Religiously Based Moral

Condemnation, and Social Control." *Criminology* 31: 119–134.

Bursik, R. J. 1988. "Social Disorganization and Theories of Crime and Delinquency: Problems and Prospects." *Criminology* 26: 519–552.

Bursik, R. J., and H. G. Grasmick. 1993. *Neighborhoods and Crime: The Dimensions of Effective Community Control.* New York: Lexington.

Bursik, R. J., H. G. Grasmick, and M. B. Chamlin. 1990. "The Effect of Longitudinal Arrest Patterns on the Development of Robbery Trends at the Neighborhood Level." *Criminology* 28: 431–450.

Byrne, J., and R. Sampson. 1984. *The Social Ecology of Crime: Theory, Research and Public Policy.* Chicago: University of Chicago Press.

Cernkovich, S. A., and P. C. Giordano. 1992. "School Bonding, Race and Delinquency." *Criminology* 30: 261–291.

Chamlin, M. B. 1991. "A Longitudinal Analysis of the Arrest-Crime Relationship: A Further Examination of the Tipping Effect." *Justice Quarterly* 8: 187–200.

Chilton, R. 1964. "Continuity in Delinquency Area Research: A Comparison for Baltimore, Detroit and Indianapolis." *American Sociological Review* 24 (February): 71–83.

Cohen, L. E., and M. Felson. 1979. "Social Change and Crime Rate Trends: A Routine Activities Approach." *American Sociological Review* 44: 588–608.

Donovan, J. E., R. Jessor, and L. Jessor. 1983. "Problem Drinking in Adolescence and Young Adulthood: A Follow-Up Study." *Journal of Studies on Alcohol* 44: 109–137.

Durkheim, E. [1897] 1951. *Suicide.* Translated by G. Simpson. New York: Free Press.

Elliott, D., D. Huizinga, and S. S. Ageton. 1985. *Explaining Delinquency and Drug Use.* Beverly Hills, CA: Sage.

Elliott, D. S., W. J. Wilson, D. Huizinga, R. J. Sampson, A. Elliott, and B. Rankin. 1996. "The Effects of Neighborhood Disadvantage on Adolescent Development." *Journal of Research in Crime and Delinquency* 33: 389–426.

Empey, L. 1982. *American Delinquency: Its Meaning and Construction.* Homewood, IL: Dorsey.

Empey, L., and S. G. Lubeck. 1971. *Explaining Delinquency.* Lexington, MA: Heath.

Erickson, M. L., and J. P. Gibbs. 1978. "Objective and Perceptual Properties of Legal Punishment and the Deterrence Doctrine." *Social Problems* 25: 253–264.

Erickson, M. L., J. P. Gibbs, and G. F. Jensen. 1977. "The Deterrence Doctrine and Perceived Certainty of Legal Punishments." *American Sociological Review* 42: 305–317.

Evans, T. D., F. T. Cullen, V. S. Burton Jr., R. G. Dunaway, and M. L. Benson. 1997. "The Social Consequences of Self-Control: Testing the General Theory of Crime." *Criminology* 35: 475–504.

Felson, M. 1986. "Linking Criminal Choices, Routine Activities, Informal Control and Criminal Outcomes." Pp. 119–128 in *The Reasoning Criminal.* Edited by D. Cornish and R. Clarke. New York: Springer-Verlag.

———. 1994. *Crime and Everyday Life: Insights and Implications for Society.* Thousand Oaks, CA: Pine Forge Press.

Firestone, H. 1976. *Victims of Change.* Westport, CT: Greenwood Press.

Forst, B. 1976. "Participation in Illegitimate Activities: Further Empirical Findings." *Policy Analysis* 2: 477–492.

Geerken, M. R., and W. R. Gove. 1977. "Deterrence, Overload and Incapacitation: An Empirical Evaluation." *Social Forces* 56: 424–447.

Gibbons, D. C. 1975. *The Criminological Enterprise.* Englewood Cliffs, NJ: Prentice-Hall.

Gibbons, D. C., and J. F. Jones. 1975. *The Study of Deviance: Perspectives and Problems.* Englewood Cliffs, NJ: Prentice-Hall.

Gibbs, J. P. 1975. *Crime, Punishment and Deterrence.* New York: Elsevier.

Gordon, R. A. 1967. "Issues in the Ecological Study of Delinquency." *American Sociological Review* 32: 927–944.

Gottfredson, M. R., and T. Hirschi. 1990. *A General Theory of Crime.* Stanford, CA: Stanford University Press.

Grasmick, H. G., and G. J. Bryjak. 1980. "The Deterrent Effect of Perceived Severity of Punishment." *Social Forces* 59: 471–491.

Grasmick, H. G., C. R. Tittle, R. J. Bursik Jr., and B. J. Arneklev. 1993. "Testing the Core Empirical Implications of Gottfredson and Hirschi's General Theory of Crime." *Journal of Research in Crime and Delinquency* 30: 5–19.

Greenberg, D., R. Kessler, and C. Logan. 1979. "A Panel Model of Crime Rates and Arrest Rates." *American Sociological Review* 44: 843–850.

Henley, J. R., and L. D. Adams. 1973. "Marijuana Use in Postcollegiate Cohorts: Correlates of Use, Prevalence Patterns and Factors Associated with Cessation." *Social Problems* 20: 514–520.

Hindelang, M. J. 1973. "Causes of Delinquency: A Partial Replication and Extension." *Social Problems* 20: 471–487.

Hirschi, T. 1969. *Causes of Delinquency.* Berkeley: University of California Press.

———. 1979. "Separate and Unequal Is Better." *Journal of Research in Crime and Delinquency* 16: 34–38.

———. 1986. "On the Compatibility of Rational Choice and Social Control Theories of Crime." Pp. 105–118 in *The Reasoning Criminal.* Edited by D. Cornish and R. Clarke. New York: Springer-Verlag.

———. 1987. *Exploring Alternatives to Integrated Theory.* Paper presented at the Albany Conference on Theoretical Integration in the Study of Deviance and Crime, Albany, New York.

Hirschi, T., and M. R. Gottfredson. 1987. "Causes of White-collar Crime." *Criminology* 25: 949–974.

———. 1993. "Commentary: Testing the General Theory of Crime." *Journal of Research in Crime and Delinquency* 30: 47–54.

Hollinger, R., and J. Clark. 1983. "Deterrence in the Workplace: Perceived Certainty, Perceived Severity and Employee Theft." *Social Forces* 62: 398–419.

Horney, J. D., W. Osgood, and I. H. Marshall. 1995. "Criminal Careers in the Short-Term: Intra-Individual Variability in Crime and Its Relation to Local Life Circumstances." *American Sociological Review* 60: 655–673.

Jang, S. J., and T. P. Thornberry. 1998. "Self-Esteem, Delinquent Peers, and Delinquency: A Test of the Self-Enhancement Thesis." *American Sociological Review* 63: 586–598.

Jensen, G. F. 1973. "Inner Containment and Delinquency." *Journal of Criminal Law and Criminology* 64: 46–70.

Jensen, G. F., M. Erickson, and J. Gibbs. 1978. "Perceived Risk of Punishment and Self-Reported Delinquency." *Social Forces* 57: 57–78.

Johnson, R. E. 1979. *Juvenile Delinquency and Its Origins.* Cambridge, MA: Harvard University Press.

Junger, M., and I. H. Marshall. 1997. "The Interethnic Generalizability of Social Control Theory: An Empirical Test." *Journal of Research in Crime and Delinquency* 34: 79–112.

Kandel, D. B., and V. H. Raveis. 1989. "Cessation of Illicit Drug Use in Young Adulthood." *Archives of General Psychiatry* 46: 109–116.

Kaplan, H. B. 1972. "Toward a General Theory of Psychosocial Deviance: The Case of Aggressive Behavior." *Social Science and Medicine* 6: 593–617.

———. 1980. *Deviant Behavior in Defense of Self.* New York: Academic Press.

Kaplan, H. B., S. S. Martin, and C. Rubbins. 1982. "Application of a General Theory of Deviant Behavior: Self-Derogation and Adolescent Drug Use." *Journal of Health and Social Behavior* 23: 274–294.

Kaplan, H. B., S. S. Martin, and R. J. Johnson. 1986. "Self-Rejection and the Explanation of Deviance: Specification of the Structure Among Latent Constructs." *American Journal of Sociology* 92: 384–411.

Karacki, L., and J. Toby. 1962. "The Uncommitted Adolescent: Candidate for Gang Socialization." *Sociological Inquiry* 32: 203–215.

Keane, C., P. S. Maxim, and J. T. Teevan. 1993. "Drinking and Driving, Self-Control and Gender: Testing a General Theory of Crime." *Journal of Research in Crime and Delinquency* 30: 30–46.

Kornhauser, R. R. 1978. *Social Sources of Delinquency.* Chicago: University of Chicago Press.

Krohn, M. 1986. "The Web of Conformity: A Network Approach to the Explanation of Delinquent Behavior." *Social Problems* 33: 81–93.

Krohn, M., and J. Massey. 1980. "Social Control and Delinquent Behavior: An Examination of the Elements of the Social Bond." *Sociological Quarterly* 21: 529–543.

LaGrange, R. L., and H. R. White. 1985. "Age Differences in Delinquency: A Test of Theory." *Criminology* 23: 19–45.

Lander, B. 1954. *Toward an Understanding of Juvenile Delinquency.* New York: Columbia University Press.

Liska, A. 1987. *Perspectives on Deviance.* 2d ed. Englewood Cliffs, NJ: Prentice-Hall.

Liska, A., and M. D. Reed. 1985. "Ties to Conventional Institutions and Delinquency: Estimating Reciprocal Effects." *American Sociological Review* 50: 547–560.

Logan, C. H. 1972. "General Deterrence Effects of Imprisonment." *Social Forces* 51: 63–72.

Massey, J. L., and M. D. Krohn. 1986. "A Longitudinal Examination of an Integrated Social Process Model of Deviant Behavior." *Social Forces* 65: 106–134.

Massey, J. L., M. D. Krohn, and L. Bonati. 1989. "Property Crime and the Routine Activities of Individuals." *Journal of Research in Crime and Delinquency* 26: 378–400.

Matza, D. 1969. *Becoming Deviant.* Englewood Cliffs, NJ: Prentice-Hall.

McCarthy, J. D., and D. R. Hoge. 1984. "The Dynamics of Self-Esteem and Delinquency." *American Journal of Sociology* 90: 396–410.

Meier, R. F., and W. T. Johnson. 1977. "Deterrence as Social Control: The Legal and Extralegal Production of Conformity." *American Sociological Review* 42: 292–304.

Miethe, T. D., and R. E. Meier. 1994. *Crime and Its Social Context: Toward an Integrated Theory of Offenders, Victims and Situations.* Albany, NY: State University of New York Press.

Miethe, T. D., M. C. Stafford, and J. S. Long. 1987. "Social Differentiation in Criminal Victimization: A Test of Routine Activities/Lifestyle Theories." *American Sociological Review* 52: 184–194.

Mustaine, E. E., and R. Tewksbury. 1998. "Specifying the Role of Alcohol in Predatory Victimization." *Deviant Behavior* 19: 173–200.

Nagin, D. 1978. "General Deterrence: A Review of the Empirical Evidence." Pp. 95–139 in *Deterrence and Incapacitation: Estimating the Effects of Criminal Sanctions on Crime Rates.* Edited by A. Blumstein, J. Cohen, and D. Nagin. Washington, DC: National Academy of Sciences.

———. 1998. "Criminal Deterrence Research at the Outset of the Twenty-First Century." *Crime and Justice* 23: 1–42.

Nagin, D. S., and R. Paternoster. 1991. "The Preventive Effects of the Perceived Risk of Arrest: Testing an Expanded Conception of Deterrence." *Criminology* 29: 561–587.

Nye, F. I. 1958. *Family Relationships and Delinquent Behavior.* New York: Wiley.

Orcutt, J. D. 1970. "Self-concept and Insulation Against Delinquency: Some Critical Notes." *Sociological Quarterly* 2: 381–390.

Park, R. E., E. W. Burgess, and R. D. McKenzie. 1925. *The City.* Chicago: University of Chicago Press.

Parker, R. N., and M. D. Smith. 1979. "Deterrence, Poverty, and Type of Homicide." *American Journal of Sociology* 85: 614–624.

Paternoster, R., L. E. Saltzman, G. P. Waldo, and T. G. Chiricos. 1985. "Assessments of Risk and Behavioral Experience: An Exploratory Study of Change." *Criminology* 23: 417–436.

Pickles, A., and M. Rutter. 1991. "Statistical and Conceptual Models of 'Turning Points' in Developmental Processes." Pp. 133–165 in *Problems and Methods in Longitudinal Research: Stability and Change.* Edited by D. Magnusson, L. Bergman, G. Rudinger, and B. Torestad. New York: Cambridge University Press.

Piliavin, I., R. Gartner, C. Thorton, and R. L. Matsueda. 1986. "Crime, Deterrence and Rational Choice." *American Sociological Review* 51: 101–119.

Pogue, T. F. 1986. "Offender Expectations and Identification of Crime Supply Functions." *Evaluation Review* 10: 455–482.

Quinton, D., A. Pickles, B. Maughn, and M. Rutter. 1993. "Partners, Peers, and Pathways: Assortative Pairing and Continuities in Conduct Disorder." *Development and Psychopathology* 5: 763–783.

Reckless, W. 1957. "The 'Good Boy' in a High Delinquency Area." *Journal of Criminal Law, Criminology and Police Science* 68: 18–25.

———. 1961. "A New Theory of Delinquency and Crime." *Federal Probation* 25: 42–46.

———. 1973. *The Crime Problem.* 5th ed. Santa Monica, CA: Goodyear.

Reckless, W. C., and S. Dinitz. 1972. *The Prevention of Juvenile Delinquency: An Experiment.* Columbus: Ohio University Press.

Reckless, W. C., S. Dinitz, and B. Kay. 1957a. "The Self-component in Potential Delinquency and Potential Nondelinquency." *American Sociological Review* 21: 744–756.

———. 1957b. "The 'Good Boy' in a High Delinquency Area." *Journal of Criminal Law, Criminology and Police Science* 68: 18–25.

Reckless, W. C., S. Dinitz, and E. Murray. 1956. "Self Concept as an Insulator Against Delinquency." *American Sociological Review* 21: 744–746.

Reiss, A. 1986. "Official Survey Statistics." Pp. 53–79 in *From Crime Policy to Victim Policy.* Edited by E. Fattah. New York: St. Martin's Press.

Reiss, A. J., Jr., and M. Tonry. 1986. *Communities and Crime.* Chicago: University of Chicago Press.

Rose, D. R., and T. R. Clear. 1998. "Incarceration, Social Capital, and Crime: Implications for Social Disorganization Theory." *Criminology* 36: 441–479.

Rosenberg, M., C. Schooler, and C. Schoenbach. 1989. "Self-Esteem and Adolescent Problems: Modeling Reciprocal Effects." *American Sociological Review* 54: 1004–1018.

Rosenberg, M., C. Schooler, C. Schoenbach, and F. Rosenberg. 1995. "Global Self-Esteem and Specific Self-Esteem: Different Concepts, Different Outcomes." *American Sociological Review* 60: 141–156.

Saltzman, L., R. Paternoster, G. P. Waldo, and T. G. Chiricos. 1982. "Deterrent and Experiential Effects: The Problem of Causal Order in Perceptual Deterrence Research." *Journal of Research in Crime and Delinquency* 19: 172–189.

Sampson, R. J. 1992. *A General Theory of Crime.* Book review, *Social Forces* 71: 545–546.

———. 1997. "The Embeddedness of Child and Adolescent Development: A Community-Level Perspective on Urban Violence." Pp. 31–77 in *Violence and Childhood in the Inner City.* Edited by J. McCord. New York: Cambridge University Press.

Sampson, R. J., and W. B. Groves. 1989. "Community Structure and Crime: Testing Social-Disorganization Theory." *American Journal of Sociology* 94: 774–802.

Sampson, R. J., and J. H. Laub. 1990. "Crime and Deviance Over the Life Course: The Salience of Adult Social Bonds." *American Sociological Review* 55 (October): 609–627.

———. 1993. *Crime in the Making: Pathways and Turning Points Through Life.* Cambridge, MA: Harvard University Press.

———. 1997. "A Life-Course Theory of Cumulative Disadvantage and the Stability of Delinquency." Pp. 133–161 in *Developmental Theories of Crime and Delinquency.* Edited by T. P. Thornberry. New Brunswick, NJ: Transaction.

Sampson, R. J., and J. D. Wooldredge. 1987. "Linking the Micro- and Macro-Level Dimensions of Lifestyle-Routine Activity and Opportunity Models of Predatory Victimization." *Journal of Quantitative Criminology* 3: 371–393.

Schrag, C. 1972. *Crime and Justice: American Style.* Washington, DC: U.S. Government Printing Office.

Schuerman, L., and S. Kobrin. 1986. "Community Careers in Crime." Pp. 67–100 in *Communities and Crime.* Edited by A. J. Reiss Jr., and M. Tonry. Chicago: University of Chicago Press.

Schwartz, M., and S. S. Tangri. 1965. "A Note on Self-concept as an Insulator Against Delinquency." *American Sociological Review* 30: 922–926.

Shaw, C. R., and H. D. McKay. 1931. *Social Factors in Juvenile Delinquency.* Vol. 2 of *Report of the Causes of Crime.* National Commission of Law Observance and Enforcement. Washington, DC: U.S. Government Printing Office.

———. 1942. *Juvenile Delinquency and Urban Areas.* Rev. ed. Chicago: University of Chicago Press.

Sheley, J. F. 1980. "Is Neutralization Necessary for Criminal Behavior?" *Deviant Behavior* 2: 49–72.

———. 1983. "Critical Elements of Criminal Behavior." *Sociological Quarterly* 24: 509–525.

Silberman, M. 1976. "Toward a Theory of Criminal Deterrence." *American Sociological Review* 41: 442–461.

Smith, D. A., and G. R. Jarjoura. 1988. "Social Structure and Criminal Victimization." *Journal of Research in Crime and Delinquency* 25: 27–52.

Tangri, S. S., and M. Schwartz. 1967. "Delinquency Research and the Self-concept Variable." *Journal of Criminal Law, Criminology and Police Science* 58: 182–190.

Thompson, C. Y., and B. Fischer. 1996. "Predicting Household Victimization Utilizing a Multi-Level Routine Activity Approach." *Journal of Crime and Justice* 19: 49–66.

Thornberry, T. 1987. "Toward an Interactional Theory of Delinquency." *Criminology* 25: 863–892.

Thornberry, T. P., and M. D. Krohn. Forthcoming. "The Development of Delinquency: An Interactional Perspective." In *Handbook of Law and Social Science: Youth and Justice.* Edited by S. O. White. New York: Plenum.

Thornberry, T. P., A. J. Lizotte, M. D. Krohn, M. Farnworth, and S. J. Jang. 1991. "Testing Interactional Theory: An Examination of Reciprocal Causal Relationships Among Family, School, and Delinquency." *The Journal of Criminal Law and Criminology* 82: 3–35.

Tittle, C. R. 1969. "Crime Rates and Legal Sanctions." *Social Problems* 16: 408–423.

Tittle, C. R., and A. R. Rowe. 1974. "Certainty of Arrest and Crime Rates: A Further Test of the Deterrence Hypothesis." *Social Forces* 52: 455–462.

Waldo, G. P., and T. G. Chiricos. 1972. "Perceived Penal Sanction and Self-reported Criminology: A Neglected Approach to Deterrence Research." *Social Problems* 19: 522–540.

Warner, B. D., and G. L. Pierce. 1993. "Reexamining Social Disorganization Theory Using Calls to the Police as a Measure of Crime." *Criminology* 31: 493–517.

Wiatrowski, M. D., D. B. Griswold, and G. Elder. 1981. "Social Control Theory and Delinquency." *American Sociological Review* 46: 525–541.

Williams, K. R., and R. Hawkins. 1986. "Perceptual Research on General Deterrence: A Critical Overview." *Law and Society Review* 20: 515–572.

Wilson, J. Q. 1975. *Thinking About Crime.* New York: Basic Books.

PART FIVE

Criminal Justice

When a society creates rules, it also creates the need for rule enforcers. In larger societies, legal systems generally are complex, and legislative, enforcement, and judicial duties are relatively distinct from one another. Indeed, the public's notion that criminal justice agencies constitute one large, integrated system is misguided. In fact, the criminal justice system in the United States is a collection of somewhat interrelated, semiautonomous bureaucracies. Criminal justice agencies possess considerable discretion, often bounded only by other agencies' abilities to embarrass them in the political arena. At root, however, all agencies face the same dilemma: They have developed missions for themselves that they may not be able to complete. In one fashion or another, they are charged with reducing crime and dissuading current and potential offenders from violating the law. Their record in this regard is problematic.

Stephen Mastrofski examines policing in America in precisely this manner in Chapter 15, "The Police in America." In the first of the chapters concerning criminal justice agencies, Mastrofski lends a historical perspective to the issue of policing in America. Though the concept of police as we know them originated in England, our concept differs in that U.S. officers traditionally have been given more personal freedom to accomplish order. This situation has provoked a seemingly perpetual process of police reform designed to eradicate police corruption, define the role that police are to play in this society, and establish the outer limits of police discretion. Mastrofski closes with a discussion of the exceptional difficulty of the crime control mission for contemporary police and cautions that, to maintain social legitimacy, the police must develop new mechanisms by which to engage in social control.

In Chapter 16, "The Social World of America's Courts," Martha Myers examines the decision-making behavior of the two most powerful figures in the courthouse, the district attorney and the judge. She notes that although these actors have a considerable amount of autonomy in the exercise of their duties, their great discretion is not unbridled. Instead, it is structured in large part by the types of cases before the court, by decisions made in earlier reviews of the cases, and by largely indirect community pressures. What is clear from the author's careful analysis is that the court represents the operations of people who are concerned with more than the simple processing of offenders, the accomplishment of justice, and the punishment of crime. Courtroom decisions occur in a political arena. Yet, blatant discrimination in sentencing seems to have decreased in American courtrooms. Extralegal factors do influence decisions, but they seem to do so in a subtler way—through reliance by decisionmakers on previous bureaucratic process outcomes and recommendations, for example.

Chapter 17, Francis Cullen and Jody Sundt's "Imprisonment in the United States," and Chapter 18, Todd Clear and Karen Terry's "Correction Beyond Prison Walls," investigate the correction of offenders in America. Cullen and Sundt trace the history of confinement in this country, including reform movements that eventually produced the individualized treatment model. Within this approach, inmates were viewed as persons in need of therapy and counseling by which they could be rehabilitated. This model has given way in recent years to a custody model whereby prisoners are viewed as requiring incapacitation. The result of this shift has been a serious crowding problem in jails and prisons and a burst of prison construction. The authors describe the inmate culture that has developed over the years in America's changing prisons. They detail as well the amounts, types, and causes of violence within prisons. The prison experience of women is contrasted with that of men. Finally, Cullen and Sundt offer a sketch of working in the correction field and close with a discussion of the future of correction in America.

Clear and Terry use the notion of prison overcrowding as the springboard to a discussion of nonincarcerative correction. This is correction by which convicted persons are supervised while remaining in the community. As the authors note, this is the more common means of dealing with offenders; to abolish it would be to swell the ranks of prisons many times over. Nonincarcerative correction includes probation, work release, treatment programs, parole, and so forth. Some forms seek to change offenders, whereas others wish to control them. Are such programs effective? Clear and Terry suggest that, overall, incarceration and nonincarceration seem to produce much the same results when types of prisoners compared are equal. They close by pointing out how little we still know about the various forms of correction they discuss, including how well or how poorly different types of programs fare relative to one another.

Chapter Outline

- Origins and Development of Modern Policing

- The Role of the Police

- The Distribution of Police

- Who the Police Are

- How Police Are Organized

- How Officers Spend Their Time

- Police Discretion and Its Control

- Explaining Police Behavior
  Situational Explanations
  Psychological Explanations
  Organizational Explanations

- Controlling Discretion
  The Rule of Law
  Rule-Making by Police Administrators
  Professional Governance
  Trends in Discretion Control

- In Search of Police Legitimacy and Support
  Support for Police Agencies: How Are They Doing?
  Police Legitimacy and the Crime Control Mission
  The Myth and Evidence of Police Crime Control

- Conclusion

15

The Police in America

STEPHEN D. MASTROFSKI
George Mason University

ORIGINS AND DEVELOPMENT
OF MODERN POLICING

America's modern police were modeled after the London Metropolitan Police, which
were formed in 1829 in response to large-scale
public disorders, violent crimes, political riots,
and common property crimes in a city undergoing industrialization and urbanization. English society had experienced crime waves for
over a century, and by the 1820s old methods of crime and disorder control (the watch,
constables, and sheriffs) were clearly ineffective
(Bittner, 1970; Lane, 1992). Yet there was widespread concern that the formation of an institution with adequate powers to deal with crime
and disorder would concentrate too much power
in the hands of the executive, leading to tyrannical suppression of precious civil liberties. In
this context, the Metropolitan Police emerged

and developed. Several features were intended
to legitimize the police: They were (1) a public,
not private, enterprise; (2) staffed by full-time,
paid employees; (3) focused on crime prevention via a more-or-less constant presence on patrol beats; (4) uniformed, and therefore clearly
identifiable; (5) organized in military fashion;
and (6) unarmed, except for a small truncheon
(Klockars, 1985).

By making police work a public responsibility, Parliament strengthened the likelihood that a
respected social institution, the national government, would control those who did the work
and thus minimize the rampant corruption of
the private entrepreneur "thief takers," who were
despised in English society for entrapping citizens or making false accusations (Klockars, 1985:
34). By making the new police full-time employees, the government gave them something
to lose (their jobs) should they perform badly,

thereby providing a means of control not available to private and part-time policing.

By restricting the police mission to crime prevention and their principal deployment to patrol, the founders of the Metropolitan Police restricted the scope of police intervention mostly to occasions when citizens summoned them for help or the constable observed from the street something deserving his attention. Patrolling on beats also made it easier for supervisors to locate constables to ensure that they were on the job. The uniform increased the constable's visibility to the public, provided a ready symbol of authority, and made it impossible for the officer to assume the *agent provocateur* role (an early form of entrapment) that had been a frequent resort of private thief takers. By forbidding constables to carry firearms, the founders limited an officer's capacity to resort to the most powerful coercive tool available, forcing him instead to rely on and nurture other bases for securing the compliance of sometimes-reluctant, and even rebellious, members of the public: the authority of his office, his power to ensure compliance through personal acts or summoning other constables, his persuasive abilities, and his skill in negotiation. The assumption of a military-style organization was intended to establish internal accountability through recruitment and assignment practices (that severed ties between the police and policed), a chain of command, and strictly enforced discipline. Finally, London's police commissioners stressed impersonal administration of the law, attention to procedural regularity, and civil liberties. Administrators emphasized that officers should secure the public's voluntary compliance with police and support for their actions by minimizing use of coercion and relying as much as possible on the impersonal authority they could derive from their image as *legal* actors. The clear purpose of constituting such a police force was to ensure that the public viewed them as there to police and serve a broad spectrum of the public according to legal standards, as opposed to those emanating from social class or the desire to further private interests.

American communities were much influenced by London's new police, but during the mid- to late 1800s, they made several important adaptations to suit the peculiarities of American society, many of which endure to this day (Miller, 1977). American police were creatures of local, not national government, thus fostering a fragmented, decentralized system of urban policing across the nation. Their staffing, organization, and activities were therefore heavily influenced by the ebb and flow of local politics and the inclinations of the elected politicians to whom they were accountable. Rather than create a police force that might transcend political and social strife (or at least give the appearance of doing so), American cities placed their police very much in the center of those conflicts (often between different ethnic groups and sometimes between social classes), making little effort to link officers' authority to higher, impersonal sources (Monkkonen, 1981). Further, the founders of early American police forces shunned some aspects of the London police that were viewed as authoritarian and antidemocratic: Military organization and uniforms were unpopular in the late 1800s because they were widely associated with the still-recent tyranny of royal governance in colonial times.

The new American police were expected to maintain order without much interference from such institutional restraints as a highly developed procedural law and were therefore inevitably forced to rely on their personal power, such as might derive from physical strength, street savvy, cunning, and contacts. Wielding personal power required considerable freedom to interpret the law (that is, decide what constituted trespassing or assault, for example) or ignore it entirely without fear of being countermanded. Not surprisingly, then, American police were freer to use force against citizens, and although initially forbidden to carry firearms, they quickly moved to reinforce their personal authority with such weapons—in no small part because the population they policed was far more likely than Londoners to be armed as well. American police departments were far less willing or able to impose discipline on how officers exercised their personal authority. To the extent that discipline was imposed, it came largely from loyalty to the local political party in power and in turn involved such things as the ability of an officer to deliver votes and enforce the law as it pleased those in power (Fogelson, 1977; Walker, 1977).

It was not until the late nineteenth and early twentieth centuries that reform movements in America began to make inroads into the power of the political machines into which the police had become thoroughly integrated. In attempting to break the hold of the machines on the police (and sometimes vice-versa), the reformers of the next half century relied at various times on the images of the police as law enforcers, soldiers in a war against crime, and professionals selected for their skill, honesty, and devotion to service—not to politicians (Klockars, 1988: 241–247). Reform efforts were stoked by scandals of corruption and brutality and by images of police as ineffective and inefficient in the face of growing crime and disorder in urban America, as waves of immigrants moved into and through cities that were expanding rapidly (Monkkonen, 1981). By the mid-twentieth century, the power of the political machines was broken in most cities. The Federal Bureau of Investigation and the Los Angeles Police Department became for many the models of what police agencies at their best could be: legalistic, militaristic, corruption-free, immune from outside political influence, and dedicated to the eradication of crime (Fogelson, 1977).

However, in all practical senses, adherence of these and other model police agencies to these ideals was largely illusionary. Although police departments were more autonomous from political parties, corruption and brutality had not been eliminated. Day-to-day police work was still filled with a wide range of minor disorders; law enforcement and crime fighting were only a small part of a police officer's job. The law and bureaucratic structures still played a peripheral role in shaping the highly discretionary decisions of the individual police officer on his beat. And despite the war-on-crime rhetoric that justified substantial growth in America's police force in the 1960s, crime rates continued to rise. Studies suggested that crime-control tactics held in high esteem by police (preventive patrol, rapid response to calls for service, and specialist criminal investigators) demonstrated no substantial impact on the capacity of police to apprehend criminals and reduce crime (Kelling, 1978). At the same time, large-scale urban riots and unrest projected an image of police who were unable to maintain order and who had alienated the poor, the racial minorities, and the nation's youths (President's Commission on Law Enforcement and Administration of Justice, 1967).

Once again calls were made to reform the police—to make them more accessible and more effective against crime and a host of other, related problems plaguing urban areas (Wilson, 1975). By the 1980s, a different vision of what policing could accomplish and how it could be done had emerged and rapidly gained popularity among some of the nation's most visible police leaders and reformers. Going by the name "community policing," it called for a reformulation of the role of the police, going beyond mere enforcement and crime-fighting to solving a broad array of urban problems (Greene and Mastrofski, 1988). It emphasized various tactics and strategies thought to bring the police and the policed into closer partnerships to solve these problems. And it advocated new indicators of police performance to replace the crime, arrest, and clearance statistics that had previously served to legitimate police budgets: citizen satisfaction with police, public fear of crime, and numbers of calls for service.

This thumbnail history of American policing suggests three recurring themes that frame the issues central to an understanding of what policing is and how it is done. The first theme is the *role* of police: what their function is and should be. The second is the *control* of police: how much discretion police have and how it is governed. The third is *legitimacy:* how police are made acceptable to society and receive its support. These themes are at the core of the most important efforts to define and transform American police, and they serve to organize this chapter.

THE ROLE OF THE POLICE

To understand the police, we must first be able to define them, a conceptually difficult task (Manning, 1993). The most widely cited contemporary definition of modern police is Bittner's (1970: 39, 46), who wrote that the police role "is best understood as a mechanism for the distribution of non-negotiable coercive force employed in accordance with the dictates of an intuitive grasp of situational exigencies." In another essay he described this function as doing something about situations in which "something-ought-not-to-be-happening-and-about-which-something-ought-to-be-done-NOW!" (1974: 30).

From Bittner's perspective, the essence of the police role is to handle situations that appear to require decisive intervention to prevent or correct something that is or might be amiss. The two key elements of this role are the capacity to use violent methods ("coercive force") and to do it on short notice—within a time frame that usually precludes the kind of careful investigation, diagnosis, tests, and mulling of evidence available to decision makers in courts of law or doctors' offices (Klockars, 1985: 16–17). Bittner presented police work as keeping or restoring the peace. He noted that, even though police are uniquely endowed with a general authority to use violence within their jurisdiction, they actually exercise their authority in its more extreme forms quite infrequently.

As Muir (1977) notes, the police typically use methods falling far short of physical coercion: asking questions; making commands, requests, suggestions, threats, and warnings; negotiating; persuading; various forms of "controlling assistance" (for example, taking a public drunk to a detoxification center); and simply being physically present. Nonetheless, the police capacity and authority to use violence suffuses their work and makes possible their capacity to use nonviolent forms of intervention and control effectively, including their authority to arrest. Finally, in attempting to restore or maintain peace, the police produce only provisional solutions to problems—not permanent solutions that alter the forces underlying those problems. Thus, for Bittner, the law and legal institutions have very little influence on the actual exercise of police coercive powers because the police were granted authority to coerce, and those institutions responsible for making the laws (legislatures) and monitoring police compliance (the courts) cannot stipulate with much precision when and how those powers should be used.

In contrast, Reiss (1971, 1992, 1993) argues that Bittner's perspective is too restrictive and lacks grounding in broader theories of social organization, formal organizations, and interorganizational relations. In attempting to set forth what is unique about police, Reiss contends that Bittner overlooks the many ways in which police and police organizations are like other occupations and organizations. Further, the coercive powers of police (up to and including lethal force) are not sovereign to police. Others have been granted coercive authority in restricted circumstances or for restricted populations (for example, prison guards, mental health workers, bailiffs, private security agents, and the National Guard). Additionally, Reiss takes issue with the notion that the order maintenance function of police is purely situational, meaning that it occurs exclusively in small-scale encounters between one or a few officers and a few members of the public. Various forms of traffic regulation, crowd management, and regulation of businesses through license revocation are examples wherein the context of order maintenance is strikingly different. Reiss argues as well that the domain of police discretion to coerce, enforce the law, or otherwise intrude into the public's freedom is not fixed but rather responsive to changes in the environment of policing. For example, changes in constitutional law since the 1960s have placed severe restrictions on the use of a wide range of police powers (including interrogation, arrest, lethal force, and search and seizure). Whether or not police abide by these strictures, there is *some* degree of accountability; police coercive powers are not, at least presently, absolute or "non-negotiable." Reiss also suggests that environmental change, by affecting who is recruited into police work and the values they hold, has

implications for the nature of police discretion and how it is exercised.

Finally, Reiss, along with others, has noted that the core technology of policing is the "production and processing of information" (Reiss, 1992: 82; Muir, 1977; Manning, 1992a, 1992b). That is, the police decide what to do about their clients by collecting, analyzing, coding, and communicating information about them. This is part of the process of determining their fate. In this regard, they are not unlike other street-level bureaucrats and professionals, such as educators, administrators, social workers, and health care deliverers, who perform key intake functions of diagnosing and categorizing types of complainants, victims, and offenders so that others in the system have some idea of what to do with them (Lipsky, 1980; Prottas, 1978). The patrol officer who responds to a domestic fight will be expected to determine whether a crime has occurred, who has criminal liability and of what sort, whether further police investigation is required, whether medical and other forms of assistance are warranted, and whether any of a host of other potential forms of intervention may be needed. If, as is often the case, the officer decides not to use any formal intervention options, he or she must still decide whether and how to handle the situation informally and how to characterize the incident to the hierarchy that monitors performance. The police domain may be broader than those of other street-level bureaucrats, but police share with bureaucrats the function of achieving some authoritative disposition of problems and, sometimes, persons.

Recently, Ericson and Haggerty (1997) have argued that the role of information broker actually defines the core function of public policing in post-modern society. They maintain that the police are one of many institutions that attempt to gather and use information to assess, respond to, and control risks of danger, whether they are health risks, financial risks, risks of loss or damage to other property, moral risks, and so on. Dealing with these risks is a dominant feature of contemporary society, a risk society. The police are part of a loose network of other organizations, such as other criminal justice agencies, insurance companies, banks, credit bureaus, transportation agencies, educational institutions, health and social welfare organizations, and so on, all of which enjoy symbiotic relationships through the sharing of information. The principal means by which risks are managed is the gathering and sharing of information by these organizations. The police are, of course, users of other agencies' information to control risks (such as when officers check stopped motorists' license and registration information, which is provided by the Department of Transportation), but they are also key providers of information to the host of other institutions involved in risk management. The data police generate on individual offenders, and the risks of crime and mishap in geographic areas, for example, are essential to the hiring decisions of organizations, decisions about the location of businesses, establishing automobile insurance rates, and so on.

For Ericson and Haggerty, the defining capacity of post-modern police forces in developed nations is not the capacity to coerce, but the capacity to know. Although they do not deny the coercive powers of police, Ericson and Haggerty maintain that the risk management potential of police is more profoundly experienced through their gathering and brokering of information. They hold that this function is reshaping American police forces, which spend increasing time and resources on information gathering and brokering with a variety of surveillance technologies—some simple and some high-tech to meet the demands both within

their organization and from external users. Although Ericson and Haggerty's empirical research is based on observations and interviews with a relatively small number of Canadian police, their groundbreaking theoretical contribution opens many intriguing future pathways for understanding public policing's role in a much broader social context.

THE DISTRIBUTION OF POLICE

In 1996, there were about 922,000 sworn officers and civilians employed in America full- or part-time in police protection activities at the federal, state, and local levels (Reaves and Goldberg, 1998: 1). Of these, approximately 664,000 were full-time sworn state and local officers. An additional 48,000 were part-time sworn state and local officers. The national average number of full-time sworn officers per 1,000 inhabitants in 1996 was 2.4 for all law enforcement agencies and 2.3 for law enforcement agencies serving cities (FBI, 1997). The number of police employees in the United States continues to grow in the wake of the 1994 Crime Act, which authorized the Justice Department to provide funding to state and local governments for an additional 100,000 law enforcement officers throughout the nation. The number of state and local full-time personnel grew 10 percent between 1992 and 1996 (Reaves and Goldberg, 1998: 1)

In general, American police are concentrated where Americans concentrate: in large urban areas (Reaves and Goldberg, 1998: 3). Further, the police tend to concentrate where crime and other problems are concentrated, which is also in large cities (see Table 15.1). However, small cities, suburban counties, and rural areas enjoy much higher ratios of officers to reported crime

Table 15.1 Fifty Largest Local Police Departments, by Number of Full-time Sworn Personnel, June 1996

CITY OR COUNTY	FULL-TIME OFFICERS, 1996	PERCENT CHANGE, 1992–1996	CITY OR COUNTY	FULL-TIME OFFICERS, 1996	PERCENT CHANGE, 1992–1996
New York (NY)[a]	36,813	27.8	Denver (CO)	1,427	5.9
Chicago (IL)	13,237	5.0	Memphis (TN)	1,420	1.3
Los Angeles (CA)	8,998	13.9	Jacksonville-Duval Co. (FL)	1,394	12.0
Philadelphia (PA)	6,398	.8	New Orleans (LA)	1,342	−12.7
Houston (TX)	5,298	24.3	Charlotte-Mecklenberg (NC)[b]	1,286	21.3
Detroit (MI)	3,904	1.3	San Jose (CA)	1,281	5.4
Washington (DC)	3,587	−26.6	Seattle (WA)	1,237	.2
Nassau Co. (NY)	3,009	10.7	Prince George's Co. (MD)	1,230	8.3
Baltimore (MD)	2,933	3.9	Newark (NJ)	1,222	10.0
Dallas (TX)	2,864	−.5	Kansas City (MO)	1,173	2.5
Dade Co. (FL)	2,825	12.5	Fort Worth (TX)	1,172	21.2
Suffolk Co. (NY)	2,744	17.9	Pittsburgh (PA)	1,154	5.4
Phoenix (AZ)	2,433	22.1	Nashville (TN)	1,129	7.1
Milwaukee (WI)	2,105	2.0	Fairfax Co. (VA)	1,067	6.9
Boston (MA)	2,100	6.7	Miami (FL)	1,012	−1.9
San Francisco (CA)	2,000	14.0	Oklahoma City (OK)	1,009	5.2
San Diego (CA)	1,986	3.4	Indianapolis (IN)	991	2.3
Honolulu (HI)	1,981	3.4	Portland (OR)	983	12.1
San Antonio (TX)	1,872	16.7	El Paso (TX)	979	24.4
Columbus (OH)	1,730	18.9	Cincinnati (OH)	958	.6
Cleveland (OH)	1,729	3.1	Austin (TX)	946	14.0
Las Vegas-Clark Co. (NV)	1,696	18.7	Montgomery Co. (MD)	939	13.5
St. Louis (MO)	1,631	6.0	Buffalo (NY)	898	−6.7
Baltimore Co. (MD)	1,535	−2.8	Tampa (FL)	889	8.7
Atlanta (GA)	1,474	−2.8	Minneapolis (MN)	886	5.7

SOURCE: From Reaves and Goldberg (1998: 6).

[a]The New York City transit and housing police agencies, which employed a combined total of 6,890 full-time officers in 1992, were consolidated into the New York City Police Department on April 30, 1995.

[b]Charlotte Police and Mecklenberg County Police merged on October 1, 1993.

than do larger cities. Although some police specialists work out of headquarters and routinely serve the entire jurisdiction, patrol officers, who are the most numerous, are geographically dispersed throughout most of their workday. That is because patrol officers are "first responders," expected to handle reported problems quickly and otherwise spend their free time watchful

for problems. They tend to be concentrated at places and times where the workload (in terms of calls for service) is concentrated (Bieck et al., 1991: 88). Even within the geographic areas or beats to which they are assigned, patrol officers tend to focus on the people and places believed most likely to cause and experience problems. A study of Minneapolis found that half of all dispatched calls went to about 3 percent of all addresses and intersections (Sherman et al., 1989: 37). Although it is widely accepted that municipal services, including police, were distributed according to political favoritism during the time of urban political machines, most studies of the distribution of police services suggest that police operate now by a bureaucratic standard, concentrating services where the quantity and severity of crime and calls for service are greatest. The racial and socioeconomic characteristics of neighborhoods are generally unrelated to levels of service delivery (Worden, 1984) although it may influence the *nature* of the service rendered (Smith, 1986).

WHO THE POLICE ARE

Reformers have long held that an important way to influence how policing is done is through the recruitment and selection of officers (Berman, 1987; Fogelson, 1977; Walker, 1977). For most of its brief history, American policing has been dominated by white males who have modest (at least by professional standards) amounts of formal education and training. Policing traditionally served as a source of employment for immigrants to America, whose involvement in machine politics yielded patronage jobs in the nineteenth century for waves of Irish, German, Italian, Polish, and other immigrant groups (Monkkonen, 1981; Fogelson, 1977). Certain ethnic and racial groups have not been as well represented relative to their presence in the population: Africans, Asians, and Hispanics. Recently, however, some of these groups have become a growing presence in American police departments, because of the implementation of affirmative action standards, employment discrimination litigation, growing minority-group political power in large cities, and supportive administrative leadership within government and police (Potts, 1983; Walker, 1985). The proportion of police who are African American rose from less than 4 percent in the mid-1960s to about 13 percent by the late 1980s (Walker, 1989: 246). A 1993 national sample survey of local police departments with 100 or more officers shows that 11 percent of the force was African American, 6 percent Hispanic American, and 2 percent other minority group. Nearly as large a proportion of county sheriffs were also minority (Maguire and Pastore, 1997: 39). Although African Americans are underrepresented in many jurisdictions, on a national level they are approaching parity with their representation in the population.

Women are quite underrepresented in America's police forces, although their number is growing. In 1976, the FBI reported that 2.4 percent of sworn officers were female; by 1996, this fraction had grown to 10 percent (FBI, 1977, 1997). Policewomen were traditionally assigned to specialist and administrative duties, but by 1979 they were almost as likely as policemen to receive a general patrol assignment, a trend that appears to be continuing (Martin, 1989).

Very few local police departments require a college education to enter the force or advance (Reaves and Smith, 1995), but most recognize college education as an important element in promotion decisions (Carter et al., 1989). One survey of police departments shows that the average educational level of police has increased from 12.4 years in 1967 to 13.6 years in 1988 (Carter et al., 1988). Some college education is now common to a large majority of officers, although relatively few have acquired four-year degrees (Carter and Sapp, 1991: 8–11).

Training in police work has been a growth industry in recent decades. Since 1967, most states have mandated minimum entry-level training standards, and many departments require much higher levels (Ostrom et al., 1978). The amount of entry-level training varies considerably. A survey of the nation's larger state and local agencies showed that entry-level training requirements varied from 16 to 3,096 hours (including both classroom and field training) (Reaves and Smith, 1995). Some 14 percent of the departments required less than 600 hours, and 29 percent required 1,200 or more hours of recruit training. The median municipal department required 640 hours of classroom training and 480 hours of field training for recruits. The amount of specialized training required of police is, of course, substantially less than that required for physicians, lawyers, or teachers, but the current trend toward more formal training and education is clear. This aspect of professionalization has long been a key element of police reform and promises to continue enhancing the professional status of the occupation (Berman, 1987; Carter et al., 1988; Fogelson, 1977; Walker, 1977).

Despite the clear progress in formal training, policing in America remains an occupation whose members enter untrained and then advance solely through the organization (Reiss, 1992: 55). Unlike other professions, access to higher ranks within the occupation is not awarded for special education and training outside the job (for example, the military officer corps and physicians). Lateral transfers from one police organization to another are still relatively infrequent. Policing is done mostly by people who enter a given force and remain on that force for all or most of their career.

HOW POLICE ARE ORGANIZED

Today, American police remain predominantly creatures of local government. According to one study, of the estimated 18,769 state and local law enforcement agencies operating in the United States in 1996, approximately 13,578 were general-purpose local police departments, 49 were state organizations, 3,088 were sheriffs' departments, and 1,316 were state or local agencies with specialized jurisdiction (for instance, transit or harbor police) (Reaves and Goldberg, 1998: 1). Although America's state and local police are disproportionately concentrated in large departments serving large urban areas (about 63 percent serve in the 5 percent of agencies with 100 or more sworn), small departments serving small populations account for the vast majority of agencies (78 percent of the agencies have fewer than 25 full-time sworn officers and account for only 15 percent of the nation's municipal sworn force) (Reaves and Goldberg, 1998: 3). The structure of American policing thus remains localized, decentralized, and fragmented (Geller and Morris, 1992; Reiss, 1992: 61–68). However, this arrangement may not be as inefficient as many claim because of interagency coordination, both formal and informal (Ostrom et al., 1978).

Police agencies today, especially those that employ the vast majority of officers, are organized bureaucratically. Since the late nineteenth century, American police forces have engaged in bureaucratization (Reiss, 1992: 69). Some of the key bureaucratic features of police organizations include hierarchical differentiation (a multilevel, formal rank structure from police officer to chief), functional differentiation (job specialties, such as community policing, criminal investigations, narcotics and vice, communications, training), routinization of procedures and practices that are formalized (written), and centralization of command (ultimate authority rests at the top of the police hierarchy, and decision making within the hierarchy is accountable up the chain of command yet protected from outside influences).

An example of command centralization is found in the contemporary police communications system, which uses the telephone (to communicate with the public), two-way radio (to communicate with officers), and computer (to enter and retrieve information about the work demands and availability of officers to receive work assignments and to record what the officers did) (Manning, 1992b; Reiss, 1992). Police administrators can structure how officers are deployed and mobilized by establishing dispatch policies carried out by communications personnel. These policies state which kinds of citizen requests for assistance receive priority and outline procedures for assigning officers to respond. Further, the system controls radio communications among officers and enables management to monitor their location and activities. There are, of course, many ways in which the administrator's capacity for command and control through this system can be subverted (Manning, 1992a), but it has undeniably enabled a degree of centralized control that would be otherwise unavailable to a workforce that is so highly dispersed and invisible to supervisors (Reiss, 1993). Other organizational structures that emphasize top-down command and control include personnel systems (hiring, promotion, and discipline of employees), training, and records systems that document police activities.

Numerous forces circumscribe the effects of the bureaucratization of police forces (Manning, 1997; Reiss, 1992: 73–91). Perhaps most important is the desire of police to control, or at least manage, their work environment. Because so much police work requires quickly determining whether there is a problem and what it is, most police work is infused with a high degree of uncertainty. This uncertainty requires that the officer on scene be granted considerable leeway to determine what the problem is and what to do

about it. Rules and formal procedures to control police discretion, though important, are often cumbersome and counterproductive. Further, given the high dispersion and unpredictability of occasions for police intervention with the public, most police–citizen encounters occur with a low degree of visibility to the rest of the organization, and the officer himself or herself is the principal source of information on what occurred during that encounter. Police supervisors are present at the scene in only about 3 to 7 percent of encounters with the public, according to recent observational studies (Parks et al., 1997, 1998).

In addition to the task environment of everyday police work, a number of institutions, both formal and informal, are intended to influence police practice, and these limit the capacity of the department hierarchy to shape police work (Reiss, 1992: 75–91). Some of these institutions were created specifically to make American police accountable to external authority: mayors and city managers, civil service boards, civilian review boards, police unions, prosecutors, the judiciary, labor relations boards, and a host of other state and federal regulatory agencies. Also included are groups that lobby or pressure police and others in government to shape what police do, for example, victim advocate groups, civil liberties groups, business associations, and neighborhood and civic associations. Although police departments have varied in their ability to withstand pressure from such forces, none has been completely buffered from them.

The creation of specialist job functions is one of the ways that organizations attempt to become, or appear, more efficient, and police agencies have followed this path. In general, the larger the department, the larger the proportion of the force that is given to specialist functions, such as criminal investigations, juvenile, communications, and forensics. However, even the largest police departments, which have the highest proportion of their force devoted to specialist functions, still rely on the generalist patrol officer as the "backbone of policing," typically devoting more officers to this than any other division (Ostrom et al., 1978: 319). These generalists constitute the largest group of police practitioners, composing 70 percent of the sworn staffing of local agencies (Reaves and Goldberg 1998: 6). And their work greatly influences the work performed by most police specialists, having important implications for success or failure of those specialist units. Specialist crime investigators rely heavily on the information reported by the patrol officer who first responded to the scene of a crime, and the capacity to apprehend a suspect and successfully prosecute is determined largely by the patrol officer's ability to find and interview witnesses on the scene and collect other evidence (Chaiken et al., 1977; Eck, 1983). The enduring commitment of most personnel to the generalist patrol assignment is particularly remarkable when compared to the marked decline in reliance on generalists in other occupations, such as medicine, the military, and education. This is undoubtedly due to the need of police to be flexible in dealing with a more unpredictable, or turbulent, environment (for example, the threat of riots and other disasters, large and small) (Reiss, 1993).

Despite the generalist orientation of police work, increased specialization is a clear trend in the twentieth century. This is especially so in the use of civilians in the organization. In just the period between 1971 and 1991, full-time city police employees who were civilians increased from 13 to 22 percent (FBI, 1972, 1992). In municipal departments with 100 or more officers, civilians are heavily concentrated in technical support functions (communications, crime

analysis, maintenance), whereas sworn personnel are overwhelmingly concentrated in field operations (patrol, criminal investigations, juvenile, narcotics) (Reaves and Smith, 1995). Further, "civilianization" has become a hallmark of progressive police reform and is associated with a variety of other contemporary trends, such as increased use of technology (especially information management), research, and planning (Reiss, 1992).

HOW OFFICERS SPEND THEIR TIME

One enduring research finding about police over the last quarter century is that most of the workload is made up of minor disorders and requests for miscellaneous services; relatively little of their work focuses on criminal offenses, and very little of that focuses on felonies and offenses that capture newspaper headlines and television time (Mastrofski, 1983; Whitaker et al., 1982). However, a recent observational study of general patrol officers found that they spent nearly half of their time on problems that were classified as crimes (Parks et al., 1998: 2–16). More importantly, the common interpretation of time–budget studies may be misleading (Greene and Klockars, 1991). Officers may conduct a variety of activities during a given incident that make it difficult to characterize that incident accurately as "crime" or "non-crime." Responding to a domestic dispute may involve not only crime-related actions, such as investigation and arrest, but also non-crime actions, such as offering comfort and other services to disputants.

It is clear from time–budget studies of patrol behavior that officers undertake actions that visibly demonstrate their coercive powers much less frequently than entertainment media and news accounts imply. Very large portions of their workday are given to general patrol, administrative tasks, meals, and breaks (Greene and Klockars, 1991: 281). A recent observational study of patrol officers in one medium and one large municipal department showed that typically less than one-fourth of an officer's time is spent in interactions with the public involving police business (Parks et al., 1997, 1998). And relatively little time (typically about 10 percent) is spent on surveillance and other specific problem-directed activities that do not involve direct contact with the public. As much or more of a patrol officer's time is spent just en route to destinations. Even studies of police who specialize in criminal investigation reveal that large portions of detectives' workdays are committed to administrative and legal-processing tasks, not the kind of detective work characterized in popular fiction. The most common forms of activity when police do engage citizens are inquiry (in the form of questioning or searching), making a written report, lecturing, and rendering some form of assistance (most often, just providing information) (Bayley, 1986; Whitaker et al., 1982: 71).

Arrest or issuing a citation is the exception, not the rule. A study from the mid-1960s found that an arrest was made in only 8 percent of the recorded incidents where there was some indication of a criminal offense (Reiss, 1971: 74). A study of police in the mid-1990s found that, in one department, patrol officers averaged an arrest about once every two eight-hour shifts (Parks et al., 1998: 2–37). Citations, by far the most frequent method of formally entering offenders into the legal process, occurred in only 35 percent of the traffic stops observed in another study (Whitaker et al., 1982: 71), and in many large departments, traffic enforcement is done mostly by patrol officers who specialize in it. Police physical force is very rare, and verbal threats to use force, though more frequent, are still uncommon (Mastrofski, 1983: 43; Parks et al., 1997, 1998). One must be careful not to overinterpret these data, because studies of attorneys and physicians would probably reveal similar sorts of diffuse activity, only a small portion of which is clearly identified with their core function (appearing in court, meeting with patients). That police exercise the more dramatic aspects of their authority with relative infrequency does not diminish the importance of that authority.

POLICE DISCRETION
AND ITS CONTROL

Until the 1960s, there was little scholarly interest in the exercise of police discretion, because of a widely held belief that police rarely exercised it, being governed by the requirements of law and departmental regulations. However, some legal scholars then argued that the law itself often gave officers substantial leeway to decide whether certain actions, such as arrest or search and seizure, were required or justified (Goldstein, 1960; LaFave, 1965; Davis, 1975). They noted that the occasions for invoking the law were typically low visibility to the public at large and even to most other police, thus providing a protective environment to foster discretion. Further, they noted many competing motivations that might incline an officer *not* to follow the requirements of the law, such as trading leniency for information after finding illicit narcotics on a suspect.

Several researchers also noted that police decision making occurred within a subculture distinctly attributable to the occupation and that the effect of this subculture was to deflect officers from the rule of law and make them resistant to governance by police administrators, as well as by institutions outside the department (Brown, 1981; Manning, 1997, 1980; Reuss-Ianni, 1983; Rubinstein, 1973; Skolnick, 1966; Van Maanen, 1974; Westley, 1970). In his review of this body of research, Manning (1989) notes several recurring themes interwoven in the attitudes and beliefs that officers use to manage the pressures of their work. One of these is that police work is infused with *uncertainty;* the events they are asked to manage are often not what they appear to be, and the consequences of their actions and those of others involved in these events are also unpredictable, laden with the potential for danger or disorder. Second, and understandable in light of uncertainty, is the theme of *mutual dependency* among officers—to help deal with physical, emotional, and career threats from the department hierarchy, the public, and watchdog groups. A third theme is *autonomy* from the very sources of threat within and outside the department that make dependency so valued. That is, officers treasure independence in exercising judgment about when and how their authority is to be used. Finally, the theme of *authority* permeates the police perspective. Maintaining authority or control of events is seen as essential in the face of uncertainty. Others have noted that these and other elements of the police subculture are not unique to it (Herbert, 1997).

Research on the police subculture has tended to look for commonalities among police to explain widespread patterns of behavior. For example, the subcultural explanation was used to understand why police tended *not* to enforce the law or why citizens who showed insufficient deference to police authority were more likely to be sanctioned by police, regardless of the legal evidence. Another line of research, however, has focused on the diversity of behavior patterns among police. This was stimulated by Wilson's oft-cited research that distinguished styles of policing among agencies: watchman, legalistic, and service (1968). Several years later, a number of scholars began to differentiate styles of policing exhibited by individual officers (Broderick, 1987; Muir, 1977; White, 1972).

EXPLAINING POLICE BEHAVIOR

Noting that the practice of policing varies among officers, and even from situation to situation, scholars have attempted to account for variance in police behavior. Most studies have concentrated on the use of arrest; a few have looked at the use of physical force; and very few have looked at other aspects of police discretion, such as more subtle forms of control, information gathering, or rendering assistance to victims (Riksheim and Chermak, 1993).

Situational Explanations

Situational explanations rely on the features of the specific incident that drew police attention. Such features include the characteristics and behaviors of the citizens involved (for example, their age, race, and sex), what they asked police to do, how the citizens were related to each other, their degree of deference to police, other indicators of their governability (for example, sobriety), the nature of the presenting offense or problem, and the quality of available evidence. According to this perspective, officers use these situational considerations to decide whether to arrest someone (Black, 1980).

Among the most consistent finding is that a suspect's failure to show deference to police substantially increases the likelihood of arrest, constituting, in the officer's eyes, contempt for his or her authority. Some recent research suggests that when the *illegality* of (some) contemptuous behavior (for example, assault on an officer) is taken into account, the effects of citizen demeanor toward the officer are greatly diminished (Klinger, 1994; Mastrofski et al., 1995; see also Lundman, 1996; Klinger, 1996; and Fyfe, 1996). However, research that distinguishes disrespectful (but legal) citizen actions toward police from those that are illegal shows that disrespect remains a significant predictor of the police arrest decision (Parks et al., 1998: 2–45). Ultimately, when citizens affront police in an illegal fashion, it is impossible to know without asking whether the officer's subsequent actions are conditioned by the lack of respect, the illegality, or both (Worden et al., 1996: 327).

Other situational influences that show some consistent effects are the preference of the victim, the seriousness of the offense, and the strength of the evidence. When a victim expresses a preference for arrest, the probability of an arrest increases substantially. Generally, the more serious the problem (for example, felony versus misdemeanor), the greater the likelihood of an arrest, although some research finds the effects conditional on the sex of the suspect (Visher, 1983) or the organizational culture of the police department (Smith and Klein, 1983). The presence of injuries has little effect on arrest likelihood, and weapon use increases the risk of arrest in some cases, but not in others (Riksheim and Chermak, 1993). Finally, evidence quality, a basic indicator of the extent to which officer decision making is governed by legal considerations, generally shows a positive influence on the probability of arrest. The victim's ability to identify a suspect, the rapidity of the crime report, whether the officer directly observed evidence of a crime, the availability of witnesses, corroborating evidence, the availability of a warrant, and other considerations have been shown to be relevant (Black, 1980; Riksheim and Chermak,

1993). In recent studies of patrol officers, the strength of the evidence has been among the most powerful predictors of arrest (Mastrofski et al., 1995; Parks et al., 1998: 2–45).

Findings are inconsistent across studies with regard to the characteristics of citizen–police encounters (see Figure 15.1). The age, race, and sex of the suspect show significant effects in some analyses but little or none in others. For example, the suspect's race, one of the most frequently estimated effects, often fails to show significant influence once other situational factors are controlled (Riksheim and Chermak, 1993). Some studies have found a significant effect for suspect race (Smith and Visher, 1981), although it is conditional on the victim's presence and on the suspect being both African American and female (Smith, 1984). Other recent studies find no race effects (Mastrofski et al., 1995; Parks et al., 1998: 2–45).

Without more research, it is hazardous to accept generalizations about the influence of most of the situational factors that capture greatest public interest, such as the suspect's race. Not only is it difficult to find a coherent pattern in the results of these studies, most of them fail to take into account the race of the victim or complainant, which arguably does more to shape the officer's perception of the need for arrest than does the race of the suspect (Black, 1980) and has been found to be an important factor in other aspects of the criminal process, such as sentencing and imposition of the death penalty.

Psychological Explanations

Psychological explanations are of two sorts: the kind that assumes that individual officers develop predispositions to exercise their discretion in certain ways that pattern their behavior, and the kind that assumes that police react to the

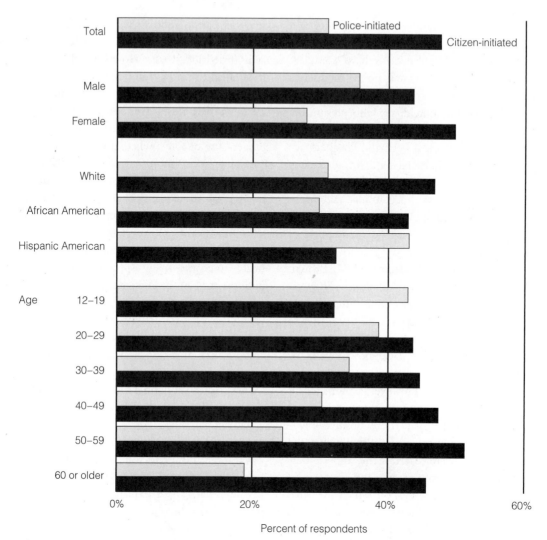

Other types of contacts—such as having a casual encounter with police, attending a community meeting with police, or contacts wherein the initiator cannot be determined—are not included in these statistics.

FIGURE 15.1 Percentage of face-to-face contacts that were police- or citizen-initiated in 1996, by race, age, and sex of respondents

SOURCE: Greenfeld et al. (1997).

behavior of the citizens with whom they must deal in an encounter.

Predisposition explanations assume a variety of factors that shape an individual's behavioral tendencies: the officer's personal background, formative experiences that shape personality, and

the formal and informal socialization acquired as a police officer (including training and the nature and extent of exposure to the police subculture). These predispositions are variously measured as attitudes, beliefs, and perceptions, or as personal characteristics (sex, race, years of experience) hypothesized to embody certain attitudes and proclivities.

Predisposition explanations have considerable appeal to reformers and police themselves because they place responsibility for corrective action on specific individuals, who presumably can be identified by their personalities and orientations as well as their behavior. This perspective makes relevant several kinds of correctives that currently enjoy favor among policymakers and reformers: altering recruitment and selection standards, training, counseling, and dismissal. Despite the theoretical elegance and appeal of several treatises that develop psychological typologies of police (Broderick, 1987; Brown, 1981; Muir, 1977; White, 1972), there is little systematic support for the proposition that officers possess workstyle predispositions that generate predictable behavior patterns. Officer attitudes, beliefs, and perceptions have shown weak-to-nonexistent effects on arrest behavior (Riksheim and Chermak, 1993). However, a more recent analysis of officers' attitudes toward community policing shows that, the more positively oriented officers were to community policing, the less likely they were to arrest the suspects they encountered (Mastrofski et al., 1995).

Personal characteristics, on which there has been more research, have demonstrated mixed effects. Studies of officer education indicate no influence on arrest behavior. A few studies indicate that male officers are more proactive and arrest-prone than female officers, although most studies find differences between the sexes to be inconsequential. However, most of these studies are not designed to detect sex-related differences of greatest theoretical and practical interest (Mastrofski, 1990). Only a few studies rigorously explore behavioral differences that might be attributable to the officer's race. One study found that African-American officers are more aggres-sive on patrol, more arrest-prone, and more likely to adopt a neutral demeanor toward citizens (Friedrich, 1977). However, other studies have failed to find a significant officer-race impact on the resort to arrest (Smith and Klein, 1983; Worden, 1989). This absence of individual officer effects has also been found in analyses of officers' use of force, whether officially deemed "reasonable" or "improper" (Worden, 1992).

Predisposition models have not yet shown much power to explain police behavior, particularly when their effects are compared to those of situational factors. However, most of these studies employed psychological measures that were unable to capture many aspects of officer predisposition that are theoretically most relevant to the behavior in question. A study of drunk-driving arrest productivity attempts to rectify this problem by drawing on a set of personal and organization-based motivational factors bearing direct relevance to drunk-driving enforcement. It finds substantial individual-level influence on officer arrest productivity (Mastrofski et al., 1994).

A second kind of psychological approach is called interactionist, focusing on how each party to a police–citizen contact reacts to the actions of the other. These explanations break down police–citizen encounters into specific, discrete actions, or "utterances," and note how each party responds to the most recent utterance or string of utterances by the other party (Sykes and Brent, 1983). Friendly or cooperative acts by one party tend to elicit a similar response from the other. Police often respond to resistance by persisting in their requests or demands rather than escalating tensions. Although a large general literature in social psychology takes an interactionist approach (Tedeschi and Felson, 1994), there is relatively little research on the microprocesses of police–citizen interaction. This is remarkable, given that police training and informal socialization both emphasize the importance of reading and responding effectively to the behavior of the citizens with whom the officer is engaged, especially when violence, aggression, and coercion seem to be an above-ordinary probability.

Organizational Explanations

Some studies concentrate on the characteristics of police organizations and their environments to account for variation in the exercise of officer discretion. Most research of this sort focuses on those features of the organization that ostensibly serve to control discretion: policies, rules, and structures. Wilson's (1968) study of eight police departments is the most influential. Wilson argued that the degree of bureaucratization (for example, formality of rules and records, differentiation of job assignments, and centralization of rule-making authority) and professionalism (for example, education and training) in a department shapes the patterns of arrest practice. The police leadership plays the central role in shaping these organizational characteristics over time so that the choice of that leadership is critical in determining the style of policing practiced in a community. Wilson presented data in support of the thesis that the type of chief selected is influenced by the type of selection process employed, which is itself a product of local politics and the political culture, that set of widely held expectations within a community as to "how issues will be raised, governmental objectives determined, and power for their attainment assembled" (p. 233). For example, reformed, "good government" cities were predicted to select chiefs who would develop bureaucratic and professional structures, leading to a legalistic style of policing (characterized by high arrest rates for a wide range of offenses), whereas old-style, "un-reformed" cities would be inclined to select chiefs who were less bureaucratic and professionally minded, thus producing a watchman pattern of arrests (fewer for many minor offenses and more dependent on the offender's race).

Wilson and a number of others have confirmed organizational effects by looking at variations in arrest and use of force patterns aggregated to the department level (Crank, 1990; Gardiner, 1969; Langworthy, 1986; Mastrofski, 1981; Slovak, 1986; Wilson and Boland, 1978). These studies find weak-to-moderate relationships between a variety of organizational characteristics (department size, bureaucratization, political and demographic environment) and arrest rates. Generally, larger, more bureaucratized agencies have higher arrest rates (but see Mastrofski et al., 1987). Other studies have focused on specific department policies and, especially in the area of use of lethal force, have found that restrictive policies and intensive review practices have been associated with lower rates of police discharge of firearms at citizens (Fyfe, 1988).

In contrast, relatively few studies have explored the impact of organizational characteristics on the behavior of individual officers, especially on an encounter-by-encounter basis. Such studies are particularly valuable, for they permit a comparison of the effects of organizational factors with situational and individual-level variables. These studies tend to confirm that situational characteristics account for most of the explanatory power of the statistical models. However, many also find significant organizational effects. For example, Friedrich (1980) found that whether a department's organizational ethos is traditional, professional, or transitional has an effect on the proclivity of officers to use force. Smith (1984) found that the propensity to arrest in domestic disputes was significantly greater for officers in departments that scored high on both bureaucratization and professionalism. Smith also found that the impact of some situational factors depended on these two organizational factors, implying that different types of organizations do in fact propagate different decision algorithms for street-level officers (Smith and Klein, 1983). A study of drunk-driving enforcement in six communities found that the effects of training on DUI arrests depended upon the level of organizational reinforcement for making DUI arrests (Mastrofski and Ritti, 1996). Training had little or no effect on arrest productivity where reinforcement was lacking.

Despite the widespread finding of police ethnographers that the informal police subculture dominates the everyday perspective of the officer, few studies of discretion have explored the unofficial, or informal, aspects of the police organization. In his review of the literature, Worden (1992) observes that many scholars have emphasized the importance of the informal peer socialization process, but very few have attempted to distinguish how this process can vary within and between police departments. Some studies have suggested that the size of the department influences the nature and strength of the effects of peer pressure to conform street-level practice to informal expectations (Brown, 1981; Mastrofski et al., 1987), but the results are not entirely consistent. One case study of a large urban department indicates that informal pressures from the rank and file can subvert top management's efforts to control the drunk-driving arrest rate (Mastrofski and Ritti, 1992). Different perspectives on drunk-driving enforcement seem to flourish among various cliques, even within the same agency, and these produce distinctly different arrest patterns between the high-arrest "ratebusters" and the typical officers (Mastrofski et al., 1994).

CONTROLLING DISCRETION

Research over the last thirty years has emphasized the considerable discretion enjoyed by low-ranking police officers, a discretion most powerfully shaped by the informal rules of the police subculture. Most police scholars believe that formal systems of discretion control that enjoy external legitimacy are marginalized by the powerful effects of the occupational subculture, relegating the formal control systems largely to the management of outward appearances (Goldstein, 1990; Manning, 1997; Van Maanen 1983). Administrators and reformers have explored a wide range of strategies to control how officers exercise their discretion. Most fall into one or more of three categories: (1) external legal institutions, (2) administrative rule-making and other means available to administrators, and (3) professional governance.

The Rule of Law

In America, much homage is paid to the notion of a government of laws, not of men and women. Indeed, one of the fundamental features of American government is the check-and-balance system among the various branches: the executive (of which the police are a part), the legislative (which at the state level determines the criminal code and at the local level sets the budget), and the judiciary (which considers the facts, interprets the law, and reviews police actions). In the late nineteenth and much of the twentieth century, many reformers fervently hoped that the police could be more closely and effectively governed by laws passed by legislatures and later by procedural standards set by appellate courts and enforced by lower courts. The "due process" revolution of the Warren Court created tremendous interest among jurists, prosecutors, defense attorneys, and legal scholars about what standards should apply to police, resulting in a large increase in appellate cases on matters such as the appropriate basis for making an arrest or stopping and searching a citizen, methods of interrogation, and use of deceptive investigation methods. In the 1980s, as political sentiment shifted, greater interest was shown in shaping police discretion by making changes to the criminal code. Some offenses (such as public intoxication or mental illness) were decriminalized, removing arrest as a legitimate option (Aaronsen et al., 1984; Murphy, 1986; Teplin, 1986). New offenses were created or made more serious (including a variety of actions associated with drugs, spousal rape, and various forms of child abuse), and in some cases, the legal basis for police discretion was eliminated (in instances of drunk driving or domestic violence).

How effectively have the courts, legislatures, and other legal institutions controlled the police? The answer depends largely on one's expectations. If one adheres to the unrealistic but still-common supposition that police will be absolutely governed by these legal institutions, then a great deal of social science clearly indicates that the institutions have failed (Klockars, 1985: Chapter 5). First, most laws, even so-called mandatory arrest laws, still leave considerable leeway to officers. For example, new laws mandate that police must make an arrest when evidence is available indicating that a misdemeanor domestic assault has occurred, but the officer must still make judgments about whether the facts of the case meet the legal standards, and there is still room for debate about where to draw the lines (Sherman, 1992b). Most offenses observed by and reported to police are misdemeanors, and in many of these cases, the statutes themselves do not require an arrest but simply empower the officer to make an arrest.

Second, and more important, the law fails even to recognize most of the discretionary choices open to police and therefore provides no guidance on what to do when an arrest cannot be made. For example, suppose an officer is dispatched to a domestic dispute and makes a careful determination that, although the parties are engaged in heated disagreement, no law has been violated. Therefore, the officer is legally obliged not to make an arrest. But what is the officer to do as an alternative? Warn or threaten one or both parties that they could be arrested if things get out of hand in the future? Order or encourage one of the parties to leave the premises? Try to arbitrate, mediate, or otherwise conciliate the disputants? Encourage the parties to seek family counseling or legal advice? Ask other family members or neighbors to intercede in the matter? Or should the officer just inform all parties that there has been no violation of the law and then depart, risking that the dispute will escalate sometime in the future to more severe consequences? The laws of most states are silent regarding which of these responses is appropriate under what circumstances. Further, whether the officer's actions satisfied legal criteria is seldom the most appropriate question to ask if one seeks a standard that goes beyond legal minimalism. The standards of the craft of policing are often considerably higher than those imposed by the law (Bittner, 1983).

As previously noted, patrol officers make arrests in only a small percentage of the cases where a suspect is present, but the law is virtually mute about what to do with the many cases that simply do not meet the legal standards for an arrest. Some contemporary reformers suggest that criminal laws might be adjusted to cover a wider range of police options or that police could become more involved in using and adapting civil laws to deal with certain kinds of disorderly behavior (Goldstein, 1990), but even these enlargements of the legal penumbra could not conceivably cover the range of police discretionary options in a way that would make most police officers and citizens comfortable that the path to fair and effective policing could be specified a priori by lawmakers (Klockars, 1985: 113).

It is particularly important to note how limited are the legal mechanisms for overseeing police compliance with even the narrow range of substantive and procedural criminal law that some believe constitutes the bulwarks of discretion control. The courts are thought to serve a central function in this regard, yet they can review the actions of police only when the actions are brought into court. With the exception of the rare internal affairs investigation or special blue-ribbon study, the street-level police officers themselves play the most important role in determining which of their actions come to the court's attention. Officers who conduct an illegal search or drug seizure run a very low risk that their actions will be reviewed by the courts, unless one officer files charges against another. And if an officer does file charges, the closest review the case will receive will be by the supervisor on duty, who often has a vested interest in protecting subordinates from censure or other discipline, which supervisors often view as arbitrary and out of proportion to the seriousness of the officer's error or offense (Van Maanen, 1983). Further, cases with major police procedural errors that make it past the supervisor are usually screened out in the prosecutor's office or reduced in severity via plea bargaining. They rarely become an issue before the judge, and when they do, it is even rarer that they cause the case to be lost (Davies, 1983; National Institute of Justice, 1982; Oaks, 1970), and rarer still that

those in the chain of command down to the street officer suffer any discipline or corrective action because "constable blundered."

Institutions charged with the responsibility for seeing that police follow the law may be quite limited in their capacity to impose their influence on police decision making, but we must take care not to conclude that the law exerts little influence on police. The law and legal institutions convey and reinforce social norms that over time may be internalized by police. Early studies of officers' reactions to changes in procedural law about interrogation indicated that Supreme Court rulings appeared to have little impact on how officers behaved (Medalie et al., 1968; Milner, 1971). This may have been due in part to ignorance of the new rulings or misperception of what the Court required, but there is also reason to think that, over the subsequent decades, police interrogation practices changed at least in part because police recruitment, training, and supervision changed in response to Court rulings (Orfield, 1987), thus altering subcultural norms about what is and is not acceptable interrogation practice. Some have suggested that this has resulted only in a switch from routine application of the highly coercive third degree to more subtle, but still nefarious, psychological techniques that rely on deception and isolation of the defendant (Leo, 1992). Nonetheless, the courts have played an important role in encouraging even this shift, giving far more latitude for these methods in criminal investigations than for the application of force (Klockars, 1984). The residue of legal influence may also be found in studies of the arrest decision that compare the relative influence of legal and extralegal factors. As earlier noted, legal considerations appear to outweigh extralegal ones.

Legislative changes to the criminal code also show evidence of influencing police street-level practices. For example, the decriminalization of public drunkenness in the late 1960s and early 1970s produced a marked decline in arrests (Aaronsen et al., 1984), and conversely, the get-tough-on-drunk-drivers reform wave in the early 1980s that mandated arresting offenders was followed by a substantial increase in the rate of DUI arrests (Greenfield, 1988). And although it is harder to obtain reliable figures, it is estimated that the widespread shift to mandatory arrest for misdemeanor domestic violence also precipitated a substantial increase in the arrest rate for these cases (Sherman, 1992b: 109). Detailed studies of street-level officers repeatedly show, however, that police discretion may be affected, but not eliminated, by legislative mandate (Aaronsen et al., 1984; Buzawa, 1982; Mastrofski and Ritti, 1992; Mastrofski et al., 1994; Teplin, 1986).

Another avenue of legal influence is filing civil suits for monetary damages and injunctions against the police officer and his or her department. Since the 1970s, changes in case law (especially in the area of federal civil rights) have increased the potential for plaintiffs to receive substantial awards from state and local governments for wrongful and negligent performance by police (McCoy, 1984). It does appear that more civil suits are being filed (Mastrofski, 1990: 47), and a few awards against municipalities that exceeded a million dollars received great attention (Skolnick and Fyfe, 1993: 202). Little systematic analysis is available, but one study based on insurance records does suggest that the risks of paying awards over $10,000 are quite small (McCoy, 1987). Ironically, police apprehension about these risks, generally based on sensational news stories, may far exceed the reality. The nature and extent of this trend's impact on street-level practices may be profound but remains empirically unexplored.

Another legal mechanism designed to deal with abuse of police powers is the civilian review board, a special agency fully or partially composed of nonpolice who have oversight responsibility for reviewing complaints against police officers. Civilian review boards vary in their structure and power to investigate complaints and make recommendations about their disposition (Kerstetter, 1985; Muir and Perez, 1992). In many cases, nonlawyers and laypersons serve on the board. However, all boards are governed by rules that set forth criteria for reviewing cases and stipulate procedural rights of officers who are accused of wrongdoing. Although these boards are often characterized as "community" rather than legal institutions, they are clearly expected to apply laws and rules and to be bound by them in their deliberations. The impact of civilian review on police practice—as opposed to reviews performed entirely within the police department—has not been submitted to rigorous empirical inquiry. However, one impressionistic, comparative analysis of several types of review systems concluded that purely internal review systems are more effective in shaping street-level police behavior than those involving external civilian review (Muir and Perez, 1992).

Rule-Making by Police Administrators

Recognizing the limits of legal institutions for governing police discretion, many reformers since the 1960s have advocated administrative rule-making (Walker, 1986: 365). The police executive is expected to see that rules and guidelines are issued that regulate, as well as define, the limits of police discretion. Because criminal laws typically employ broad, general terms, advocates of administrative rule-making argue that police executives need to create written departmental guidelines to channel discretion in ways that further the law's intent and that are practicable from the officer's point of view. For example, a department might issue a series of guidelines about when to issue a citation when dealing with a noise disturbance—a type of situation that is very ambiguous. Such a guideline might indicate that the officer should take into account the amount of noise, the time of day, the ambient noise typical for that location at that time, the number of people disturbed by the noise, and the prior record of the offender. Or, in the case of a more serious offense, the department might specify in some detail the circumstances under which an officer is and is not permitted to use lethal force and then set forth a detailed process for reviewing officers' decisions to resort to such force. Administrative rule-making such as this is the central feature of the national police agency accreditation movement begun in the late 1970s (Mastrofski, 1986) and has since been advocated by a variety of scholars and blue-ribbon commissions (Goldstein, 1977; Schmidt, 1974; Walker, 1986).

Despite the popularity of administrative rule-making among contemporary progressive reformers, skepticism and caution have also been expressed about this process (Aaronsen et al., 1984; Klockars, 1985: 112; Mastrofski, forthcoming; Walker, 1992: 215). Skeptics suggest that being more forthright about the nature and extent of police discretion and more explicit about their own policies will make it more difficult for police executives to take refuge in the law on controversial issues. It may be impossible to write rules that are sufficiently precise to cover the particulars of a given situation and sufficiently numerous to cover the variety of situations—and still be comprehensible and useful to an officer in the field attempting to make decisions with limited time and information. Rules and guidelines also are easily dodged and reports distorted; it is difficult to verify the nature of the circumstances and the particulars of police action without relying heavily on the very people whose actions are under review.

Finally, rules and guidelines, as with laws, serve to provide a moral lamp unto the officer's feet, but if they are to be effective, they must also be linked to consequences that the officer cares about. This requires an effective system of internal accountability, which in American police departments tends to rely heavily on supervision and record-keeping (Reiss, 1993). Routine supervision is the responsibility of the line supervisor, but as previously noted, observational studies show that those who have supervisory responsibilities have or take limited opportunities to observe the work of their subordinates directly, and they are often more sympathetic to the concerns of the street-level officer than to those of the administrators whose rules they are supposed to apply (Van Maanen, 1983, 1984). Consequently, much of the capacity to hold officers accountable for their behavior relies on records of that behavior that they themselves create and can manipulate to serve their ends (Chatterton, 1983).

Independent verification of those records (through follow-up interviews with citizen-participants, for example) is quite rare (Reiss, 1993). When independent follow-up does occur, it is usually through the department's internal affairs unit. These units do engage in proactive investigations of police misbehavior, but the most common investigation is a reaction to a citizen's complaint (Reiss, 1971). There is little evidence on the impact of internal affairs units on police behavior. Some have argued that they are most effective when the police chief ensures that investigations are rigorous and that substantiated allegations of misconduct result in meaningful discipline (Goldstein, 1977). However, even with the special resources available to internal affairs units, establishing the facts is often problematic, boiling down to contradictory testimony between the complaining citizen and the accused officer. Many cases are dismissed because there is no independent corroborating evidence, and other officers, who make the most compelling witnesses, are unwilling or unable to offer it. Finally, internal affairs units concentrate exclusively on identifying misbehavior and bad performance; their punitiveness epitomizes much of the entire internal system of police accountability in concentrating on punishable actions, virtually ignoring competent or exemplary performance. Police organizations are by no means unique in this regard, but their focus on the negative makes it difficult to use positive incentives to structure police behavior.

In addition to an effective compliance-monitoring system, effective governance by administrative rule-making requires a system of incentives and disincentives that can be offered or withheld with some degree of certainty. This kind of power is rarely available to contemporary police administrators. Indeed, substantial fragmentation of policymaking power among a number of formal and informal governing bodies inside and outside the department is far more characteristic (Reiss, 1992: 87). Unions, civil service boards, courts, regulatory agencies, local elected and appointed officials, civilian review and advisory boards—all these and others make illusory the notion of a hierarchical, rule-bound

infrastructure with the police chief in command at the top (Mastrofski, 1997).

Relatively few studies of the impact of administrative rule-making on police discretion have been conducted. Some researchers have found that restrictive-use deadly force policies have been followed by substantial reductions in the frequency of use of deadly force (Fyfe, 1979, 1988; Sherman, 1983). Research on rule-making in handling public drunks and making pornography arrests appears to have produced mixed results (Aaronsen et al., 1984: 408–436), and case studies of the implementation of domestic violence arrest policies at three sites suggest that effects of rule-making can be quite variable (Sherman, 1992b: 112). Finally, rule-making about criminal investigations procedures had little impact on police compliance with evidence-gathering standards (Krantz et al., 1979).

Although the evidence is impressionistic, it has been suggested that rule-making is most likely to be effective for behaviors that have high visibility or are easily monitored (Walker, 1992: 216) and when police leaders can use external pressure generated by crises to alter old practices (Sherman, 1983; Skolnick and Fyfe, 1993: 185). It has also been suggested that rule compliance is greater when citizens know what the rules require of police and are therefore in a position to point out to the officer when he or she is not conforming (Walker, 1993: 49). The threat of a report to higher authority, particularly when the citizen knows how to file such a grievance—with the prospect that it will be taken seriously—is thought to provide additional reasons for compliance. The extent to which these conditions can be met, especially for the disadvantaged segments of society, remains to be demonstrated. Finally, it might be observed that rules are most likely to be obeyed when they meet the personal needs of the officers, such as when they reduce ambiguity about how the department will react to a given action (Brown, 1981), when they involve less "hassle" for officers (Mastrofski et al., 1994), and when they are seen to produce results desired by officers (Bayley and Bittner, 1984).

Professional Governance

A third system for governing police discretion is police professionalism, which requires that

1. Officers pursue broad societal or client-based interests, not their own;

2. They identify standards of performance based on a special, technically sophisticated body of knowledge that is empirically validated and documented;

3. They be thoroughly educated in achieving these standards;

4. They be given the leeway to exercise their judgment as their professional knowledge and skills dictate; and that

5. Other police professionals serve as the principal reviewers of their performance.

These features—the classic characteristics of what some call the "true" professions: medicine, law, education (Klockars, 1985: 108; Walker, 1992: 209)—stand in sharp contrast to the precepts of the police subculture, which stress secrecy, loyalty to one's peers over external accountability, the unsuitability of general principles to guide action, and the desirability of work experience over formal training and education.

Of all the systems of discretion control, professionalism is the least developed for police. Of the five criteria listed, the police have a secure grasp only on point 1 above, something that was acquired as much by the pursuit of bureaucratic and legalistic objectives as professional ones. Rather than operating from a documented knowledge base (point 2), policing as practiced daily is most accurately characterized as craft-based (Wilson, 1968: 283). That is, its practitioners obtain their most critical skills on the job—either from others more experienced or by trial and error. Very little of what police learn in their formal education and special training is used on the street. Despite the profusion of criminological research in the last three decades, the term "police science" is more wish than fact, and this limits the capacity of police to become true professionals. Most of the research on police effectiveness has, if anything, demolished long-held views about once-cherished police tactics and strategies that presumably deterred crime, apprehended offenders, and solved cases. Although the amount of research that can document what works and what does not is increasing, research remains painstakingly slow, even in so narrow a domain as the benefits of arrest in domestic disputes, where more resources have been committed to rigorous, experimental evaluation than any other (Sherman, 1992b: 267).

The amount of education and training (point 3) that police receive has been growing considerably in recent decades, due in no small part to professionalization efforts. The quality of this training is also undoubtedly improving, and its relevance to and impact on everyday practice may be increasing, although there is not sufficient evidence to know at this point (Mastrofski, 1990: 15). At present, it may be doing more to bolster the image of police as professional than to affect the reality. However, the true test of its impact is the extent to which the training is accepted by the trainees. There is some evidence from the field that police even today are highly selective about the training they accept as relevant and useful, especially when the training is supposed to transform their practice in fundamental ways. Officers are still more persuaded by craft-based than scientific knowledge. They are inclined to place greater faith in the lessons they and their colleagues learn personally and share informally (Bayley and Bittner, 1984).

Police professionalism has made the least progress in the fourth and fifth requirements. The rhetoric that has long suffused police professionalization movements in America belies the real nature of that movement's thrust: bureaucratization (Klockars, 1988; Reiss, 1992). Indeed, what the legalistic and militaristic reformers most valued and what they called professionalism was officer adherence to the law and to the edicts that wended their way down the department hierarchy. This is precisely the opposite of what true professionalism demands, which is the freedom to exercise one's judgment as the circumstances and one's knowledge dictate (point 4). Police officers enjoy considerable discretionary leeway in reality, but it is neither embraced nor supported by professional standards; it simply exists and is quietly ignored until an officer does something that draws publicity. Finally, there are very few mechanisms for police practitioners to govern discretion by reviewing each other's performance (point 5), such as boards of physicians, educators, attorneys, accountants, and engineers use either to certify competence or review malpractice complaints. To the extent that such reviews take place, they occur either within the department hierarchy (a bureaucratic phenomenon), the courts, or on rare occasion, a civilian review board with authority to review evidence.

Although true professional status seems beyond the reach of most police in the foreseeable future, it has, if anything, become an even more important—almost a defining—part of the con-

temporary police progressive's agenda. Bittner (1970) articulated a vision of professionalism, and others have subsequently offered blueprints on how it might be achieved (Bayley and Bittner, 1984; Goldstein, 1977, 1990; Sparrow et al., 1990). At least one state has introduced a peer-review process to revoke or suspend a police officer's license to practice policing (Skolnick and Fyfe, 1993: 197). Finally, police themselves seem to be warming to the idea of a professionalism based on systematic scientific research (Klockars and Harver, 1993).

Trends in Discretion Control

Presently, police officers are subjected to all or most of these professional governance systems of control to some degree. It is often difficult to assess the separate impact of these forces on officer discretion because—in addition to the external, readily observable processes by which they might influence police—other forces may be internalized, changing officers' values, premises, and ways of perceiving problems. Further, they will not necessarily present police with conflicting objectives; they may, in fact, reinforce each other. For example, administrative rule-making is often presented as a way to *extend* the influence of the law, and professional education and training curricula are heavily laden with legal topics. Finally, all of these systems of control are themselves products of larger, diffuse social forces that influence a society's cultural orientations and ways of defining and solving problems. It is difficult to know how much a new law changes the habits of society generally and how much the law itself is a symptom of broader social changes. Walker (1993) argues that the idea of legal control of police (especially through the courts) reached its apogee in the 1960s and that, within a decade, reformers had achieved a new consensus that administrative rule-making was the preferred mechanism of discretion control. He also suggests that professionalism has failed to play a strong part in everyday policing because broader social currents in America continue to run in the direction of increased rule-making and bureaucratization, even for the profession with the highest status, medicine. And periodic scandals and critical incidents, such as the Rodney King affair, make it difficult for professionalism's advocates to rely more heavily on the standard professional nostrums (recruit screening, training, and peer review) for control of the worst abuses. Administrative rule-making, the dominant control paradigm today, more accurately reflects the intentions of reformers; it is not at all clear that this form of rational administration has actually permeated police practice to a great extent (Manning, 1997; Mastrofski et al., 1987).

One trend that may influence the development and interplay of formal control systems is the rapid growth of communications and computerized information technology. Just as the telephone and radio increased the department hierarchy's capacity for centralized monitoring of street-level officers in the second quarter of the twentieth century, developing technologies may further enhance or complicate management's ability to review, and even intervene in, officer decision making on the street (Reiss, 1992: 82). Videotaping traffic stops has been advocated as a way to determine after the fact whether an officer's actions met legal standards (Skolnick and Fyfe, 1993). It takes little imagination to go a step further and suppose that police will soon be able to transmit video and audio information live from the scene to headquarters via portable instruments worn by the officers. Probably more consequential is the growing capacity of police administrators to use information technology to process the tremendous amounts of data about police decisions and their consequences that are archived in police agencies (Bratton, 1998). However, the extent to which such technological innovations enhance administrators' discretion control remains to be seen (Manning, 1992a).

IN SEARCH OF POLICE LEGITIMACY AND SUPPORT

The previous section focused on the individual officer. However, because it is also important to understand policing at a broader, more abstract level, this section looks at the organization rather than the individual. It focuses on the structures and practices American police organizations use to sustain legitimacy and thus accrue support for their continued existence and authority.

Support for Police Agencies: How Are They Doing?

Like all public agencies, police departments are not self-sustaining, but rely heavily on their environment to continue and flourish. The support that police departments seek can take a variety of forms. The most obvious is financial: the resources derived from taxes, fines, seizures, fees, grants, and other revenues that pay for the people and material of the department. Support can also be expressed in other, political ways: votes for policies and programs important to the organization, such as the effort by some departments to get voters and their elected leaders to pass gun control legislation. Or support for police can be expressed in terms of trust and autonomy granted. For example, to the extent that police departments are able to review and discipline allegations of police misconduct without interference from courts and civilian review boards, they enjoy a substantial degree of autonomy for self-governance. Support for police departments can also take the mundane form of participation or at least acquiescence in some police-sponsored activity. This could be citizens participating in a crime watch group, placing a call to the police to report a crime, or testifying in court. It could even take the form of doing as police command, such as complying with a curfew or ensuring that one's children do.

By most convenient indicators, local police departments have done remarkably well in obtaining support in the last half century. Between 1938 and 1982, police per capita expenditures in America's larger cities quadrupled, adjusting for inflation. Much of this increase, especially in the 1960s and early 1970s, was due to substantial gains in officers' pay and benefits, reflecting in part the growing power of unions and also the enhanced status of the occupation (Fogelson, 1977). The number of sworn officers per capita in these departments increased considerably after World War II until 1973 and has remained fairly stable since then, whereas civilian employment has continued to grow. In 1994 Congress passed the Clinton administration's "100,000 cops on the street" bill, which authorized nearly $9 billion for hiring additional police officers over the next few years. The popularity of adding more police, even in a time when serious crime rates are declining, speaks powerfully to the considerable support granted to this institution, which now employs nearly one million people full-time.

In recent decades, public opinion surveyors have monitored support for police. The pattern of responses shows remarkable stability; positive assessments of the job local police are doing have fluctuated within a few points of the 60 percent level since 1967 (Flanagan et al., 1982: 196; Flanagan and Maguire, 1992: 178), although African-American respondents are consistently less likely to offer positive assessments than white respondents (Albrecht and Green, 1977). When the question is asked somewhat differently, the level of support is even higher. In 1965, 70 percent of a national sample said they had "a great deal of respect" for their police; it rose to 77 percent in 1967, but dropped to 60 percent in the immediate aftermath of the Rodney King incident in 1991 (Flanagan and Maguire, 1992: 179).

What one can infer about public support for police from surveys is hard to say. Even when public opinion takes a precipitous dive, it is exceedingly rare for the department to be disbanded. When Americans are unhappy with their police department, they tend to blame it on the top leadership, forcing out the old regime and bringing in a new chief. This accounts for the fairly short tenure of most police executives, especially in larger departments. The forced retirement of former Los Angeles police chief Daryl Gates in the aftermath of the Rodney King incident and the subsequent riot is a dramatic example of what has been termed a ritual of "moral degradation" (Crank and Langworthy, 1992). The commission that criticized Gates's handling of the riot also recommended that more resources be committed to prevent and respond to future civil unrest (Webster and Williams, 1992). The department endures but is exorcised of the leader who is blamed for the crisis.

Short of being replaced, police administrators under fire face the prospect of having their department reorganized or losing significant control over their departments. Even during the height of negative publicity about American police in the late 1960s and early 1970s, the most drastic political movements opposed to existing arrangements called, not for abolition of the police, but merely for reorganizing them by various methods of "community control" (Skolnick, 1971; Wilson, 1975). Much of the impetus for the current community policing movement is best understood as a response to or anticipation of negativity from the public that was perceived as widespread in the 1960s and early 1970s (Kelling and Moore, 1988; Manning, 1988).

People's opinion about police may be related to the nature of their direct contact with police or exposure to news stories. However, research does not provide a clear indication that these relationships are strong, and it is not entirely clear what the direction of influence is (Surette, 1992; Brandl et al., 1994). A person's general predisposition about police may have more influence on his or her assessment of police performance in a specific incident than the reverse. Regardless of fluctuations over time in what people think of their police, it appears that the public's actual demand for their services is unabated and, if anything, growing continuously. If calls for service are any indication, American police are desired now more than ever, even in the nation's largest cities, where populations are in decline. Some have argued, however, that the "market share" of police work has declined because private police have grown substantially, indicating a dilution of faith in police to provide for public and private security in the face of heightened concern about crime and disorder (Sparrow et al., 1990: 48).

Another indicator of support for police organizations is the degree of autonomy their administrators are granted in running the department. Police are and always have been among the most penetrated public service organizations in America. Even when the popularity of good government autonomy reforms was highest, systems for governing police—both formal and informal—

provided ample opportunities for outside control and influence (Manning, 1993; Mastrofski, 1988; Reiss, 1993). Nonetheless, some chiefs have been more successful than others in securing autonomy in their running of the department, some of the more widely known cases being Harold Brier in Milwaukee, Daryl Gates in Los Angeles, and Frank Rizzo in Philadelphia (Skolnick and Fyfe, 1993: 134–136). However, the capacity to sustain a high degree of autonomy seems ephemeral and often overstated, because maintaining administrative autonomy is accomplished in large part by anticipating what powerful external political forces want or will accept from their police (Wilson, 1968). If one attempts to discern broad patterns of autonomy or lack thereof across the wide range of police departments in America, one is likely to see bigger differences in the manner by which external control is exerted rather than the total amount of autonomy from it. For example, reformers during the heyday of the political machines bemoaned the lack of bureaucratic autonomy of police agencies and were especially aggrieved that chiefs exerted so little control over departmental hiring, promotion, firing, and operational matters (Fogelson, 1977; Walker, 1977). But not too long after the power of the machines was broken, scholars and police administrators lamented the many ways in which the chief's capacity to govern had been meted out to other external agencies: courts and affirmative action regulatory agencies, unions, and most recently civilian review boards. External governance of police may be more fragmented today than it was when political machines were powerful, but it cannot be said with confidence that police are generally more autonomous. Indeed, the current movement toward working in partnership with community groups—as embodied in community policing—is testimony to the continuing dependence of police organizations on currying favor with constituencies by being open and responsive to them.

Police Legitimacy and the Crime Control Mission

Being perceived as legitimate means being perceived as conforming to what people see as "right" or "appropriate" (Scott, 1992: 305). Organizations can also seek support by brute force or threats, or they can secure support by making deals, but as the sociologist Max Weber noted, it takes a lot of effort to sustain an organization for long periods by these methods, and the result is often a high degree of instability both inside and outside the organization. Not surprisingly, then, most major American institutions try to justify themselves by getting society to accept them as legitimate. This affords such institutions a range of discretion in which they can exercise their authority without having to justify it each time or expend precious resources in coercion or negotiation. The importance of maintaining legitimacy is paramount to police because of American society's ambivalence about the core element of police authority: the capacity to coerce.

From their very beginnings, American police have been concerned with establishing their legitimacy. The various waves of reform can be interpreted as attempting to establish new bases of police legitimacy (Fogelson, 1977). Efforts to legalize, militarize, and professionalize police each appeal to somewhat different sets of values about what police should be and do, and these movements responded to values that were growing in popularity in American society at the time. The present reform movements to make police community- and problem-oriented may

also be interpreted as attempting to establish new bases of legitimacy in a changing political climate (Bayley, 1988; Kelling and Moore, 1988; Klockars, 1988; Manning, 1984; Mastrofski, 1988).

Attaching such missions or mandates to the police has been the dominant means by which police departments sustain themselves over their history, altering their vision of their mission to fit the times (Manning, 1997). What is expected or hoped for from police at any given time may not be what they can actually deliver, but police organizations nonetheless adapt their structures and operations to conform—or at least appear to conform—to those expectations. Because it is difficult to define and measure precisely how well police meet those expectations, police adopt structures and practices that are widely accepted as constituting such performance, whether or not they in fact do.

There are many ways in which police organizations attempt to enhance their legitimacy (Crank and Langworthy, 1992). The creation of specialist units to deal with new, emerging problems is a convenient way to signify that a department is doing something about those problems. As targets in the "war against crime" change, so do the police specialists. The proliferation of narcotics enforcement units in the last decade is an example of a widespread effort to signify that something is being done about drug crime, although all indications suggest that neither illicit drug consumption nor drug-related crimes have abated (Reuter and Kleiman, 1986). Legitimacy is also derived from such things as the uniforms and appearance police assume, the civil service systems (signifying that jobs are obtained by merit, not political influence), the training (signifying that officers are professionals), participation in professional organizations, accreditation of the department by a state or national law enforcement accrediting agency (signifying organizational efficiency), an internal affairs unit (signifying internal control), and the conspicuous use of technological gadgetry (signifying up-to-date methods in the use of computers, weapons, and forensics).

Among the most important sources of police legitimacy in the years following World War II were several strategies thought to be essential to the police mission of crime control: random preventive patrol, rapid response to reports of crime, and follow-up investigations by detectives. When departments engaged in these activities, they were regarded as adhering to the popular vision of an effective police department, even though there was no rigorous evidence about the effectiveness of these strategies. When research was eventually conducted, it suggested that these strategies contributed little to the deterrence of crime and the apprehension of criminals (Kelling, 1978; Walker, 1989). These crime control strategies served to enhance police legitimacy—even though they had no demonstrated relationship to actual accomplishment of police objectives. They had thus become institutionalized, and they endure even today, decades after the best available evidence suggested that they have no bearing on crime rates. These and other structures persist as important features of police work because they incorporate certain myths about crime and policing that remain powerful in American society and useful to police departments (for example, that government can quickly solve large, complex social and economic problems). These structures help police reassure the public that they are doing something about crime and justify budget requests to sustain or enlarge the police resource domain. This view of how police secure legitimacy is referred to in

organizational theory as the "institutional perspective" (Crank and Langworthy, 1992).

Championing the crime-fighting mission has been a much-used approach to seek police legitimacy since the Great Depression. Most recently, politicians, pundits, and police leaders have been eager to give the lion's share of the credit for declining crime rates to the police, and especially, to their own favorite policing programs and strategies (Witkin, 1998). Yet, it is not entirely clear that the general public holds police accountable for the level of crime. When asked to volunteer ways to reduce crime, adding more police is mentioned by very few survey respondents (Flanagan and Maguire, 1992: 207); the association between respondents' fear of crime and their evaluations of police performance is very weak (Garofalo, 1977: 30); and only one-fourth or less feel that "our system of law enforcement works to really discourage people from committing crimes" (Flanagan et al., 1982: 201). Yet the public seems to have lenient standards when asked to assess how good a crime-control job police are doing. It may be that, despite the best efforts of advocates of the police crime control mission, the public's support for police derives from something more amorphous: the desire for police presence (Walker, 1989: 129; Whitaker et al., 1982: 44).

The Myth and Evidence of Police Crime Control

If the crime control capacity of police is mythical, it is nonetheless important to note that the term as used here refers to beliefs that are unverified or unverifiable, not necessarily proven false. Popular beliefs about the police's crime control capacity are mythical because they endure independent of any evidence about the police contribution to the control of crime. In the three decades following World War II, police themselves promoted the mythical view that they constituted "the thin blue line" between social chaos and legal order, a view without much hard evidence one way or the other. Rigorous scientific efforts to validate the extent of the police's crime control capacity began to emerge in the 1970s. Even so, the amount of research in this area is minuscule compared to that in medicine, education, and engineering, for example. Not surprisingly, researchers hold differing views about whether police efforts can decrease crime. In general terms, these views fall into two groups (Sherman, 1992a). One group argues that police have little or no impact on the level of crime because they have no control over the powerful forces (unemployment, age demographics, poverty, family dysfunctions, culture clashes, the value placed on personal liberty, the availability of guns and drugs, biological factors, community dynamics) that determine how much crime there will be. The second group, though often acknowledging that police can do little to affect the root causes of crime, nonetheless argues that police can and do influence crime rates by supplementing or shoring up social institutions that have a lot to do with crime control (e.g., families and schools). The question is "How much and under what circumstances?"

The most comprehensive review of the research on this issue was conducted by Lawrence Sherman and colleagues (1997). They argue that the crime control capacity of police is closely intertwined with the control capacity of other social institutions—communities, families, schools, the labor market, "places," and other criminal justice agencies—that operate in a variety of settings. No single institution is sufficiently powerful to ensure public order and safety, but where

there is enough reinforcement from several institutions, the police may have a substantial crime prevention impact. One might extend the logic of this argument: Under conditions where institutions of social control are either very weak or very strong, the contribution of the police to crime control is marginal, but where other social institutions operate at a middle level of effectiveness, that is where police may have the greatest impact. This theory implies the need for a triage approach to the application of police resources. However, most American jurisdictions concentrate police resources in precisely those areas where other mechanisms of social control are either very strong (because those parts of society can afford it) or where police are used to compensate for the breakdown of those other social institutions. Thus, society concentrates police precisely in the kinds of places where they are unlikely to demonstrate much effect on crime— unless other social institutions are strengthened as well.

Unfortunately, very little research evaluating the crime control effectiveness of the police takes into account the strength of other social institutions that might contribute to crime prevention. Therefore, Sherman and colleagues' (1997) review of empirical research on policing for crime prevention does not control for the broader social institution context, but rather makes judgments about the implications of research on the rigor of the research design used. He examines evidence on eight hypotheses about policing and crime:

- The more police a city employs, the less crime it will have.

- The shorter the police travel time from assignment to arrival at a crime scene, the less crime there will be.

- The more random patrol a city receives, the more a perceived omnipresence of the police will deter crime in public places.

- The more precisely patrol presence is concentrated at the "hot spots" and "hot times" of criminal activity, the less crime there will be in those places and times.

- The more arrests police make in response to reported or observed offenses of any kind, the less crime there will be.

- The higher the police-initiated arrest rate for high-risk offenders and offenses, the lower the rates of serious violent crime.

- The more quantity and better quality of contacts between police and citizens, the less crime there will be.

- The more police can identify and minimize proximate causes of specific patterns of crime, the less crime there will be.

Taking the rigor of the reviewed studies into account, Sherman et al. (1997) concluded that there is strong evidence of a crime control effect for increased directed patrols on street-corner hot spots, proactive arrests of serious repeat offenders, proactive drunk driving arrests, and arrests of employed suspects of domestic violence. Strategies for which there is strong evidence of ineffectiveness include neighborhood block watch, arresting some juveniles for minor offenses, arresting unemployed suspects of domestic assault, drug market arrests, and community policing with no clear crime-risk focus. A number of strategies are rated "promising": traffic enforcement patrols against illegal handguns, certain forms of community participation (public meetings and door-to-door visits), community policing strategies that enhance police legitimacy, aggressive enforcement of quality-of-life violations in public spaces, adding extra police to

the force, and warrants for arresting suspects who were absent when the police responded to a domestic violence complaint. These conclusions are offered provisionally, based on the best evidence in a field that has relatively little rigorous evidence available.

A major lesson drawn from the review by Sherman et al. is that, to achieve maximum effectiveness, police resources must be targeted strategically in those places where effectiveness is most likely. If this is so, the implications for police legitimacy are profound. The public police of most developed nations have sustained a high degree of legitimacy in their relatively short history precisely because their benefits have been viewed as more or less equally distributed throughout communities. Because citizens assess the benefits of policing in the most tangible terms—the visible presence of the police—different groups within society clamor and compete for this police presence and evaluate those responsible for public policing in terms of how their own group fares in the competition for visible police presence. Success in American politics—be it local, state, or federal—relies heavily on seeing that all major groups get a piece of the pie. This strategy is effectively demonstrated in the terms of the highly popular Crime Control Act of 1994, which stipulated that half of all federal funds for hiring additional police must go to police agencies serving under 150,000 people—even though these departments deal with substantially less than half of the recorded serious crime in the United States and typically already enjoy higher ratios of full-time sworn personnel per serious crime. Switching to a strategic allocation of police resources based on maximizing crime control effectiveness would require a fundamental change in the way that the public and political leaders evaluate outcomes in the politics of crime control. Such shifts are not without precedent (as in certain aspects of public health), but nonetheless require profound changes in the structure and patterns of decision making about who does what, when, and where in public policing.

It remains to be seen whether a substantial crime control capacity for police can be established on a foundation of solid scientific evidence. Crime control, nonetheless, would appear to have enduring appeal as a basis for legitimacy to those who make policy and administer police agencies. Much of the impetus for community policing, for example, arose from criticism of the failures and excesses of earlier efforts to fit police departments into the crime-fighting mold popular among police leaders since the Depression. Scholars criticized police agencies for unrealistically defining their mission strictly in terms of law enforcement (Goldstein, 1979). Support grew for the notion that police priorities should not come from criminal statutes and court decisions, not even from city hall, but from the very neighborhoods in which the officers worked. When the denizens of these neighborhoods were asked what problems they felt needed police attention, the top priorities were indeed the mundane aspects of police work—noisy neighbors, barking dogs, abandoned autos, traffic, street people, and rowdy juveniles (Skogan, 1990). Indeed, the common thread that ties together the diverse tactics and strategies gathered under the tent of community policing is linking the police and their community in closer partnership. Foot patrols, mini-stations, neighborhood crime prevention, advisory boards, and a host of other programs are all justified by this objective. At the same time, however, the community policing movement has been pulled into the war against drugs and violent crime. Highly publicized examples are federally sponsored programs, such as the Bush administration's

"Weed and Seed" program and the Clinton administration's program to make community policing a centerpiece of its initiative against violent crime. Less visible, but perhaps more telling, is the manner in which local community policing programs have been evaluated. Nearly all evaluations focus on the extent to which crime was reduced or citizens' fears and perceptions of crime were diminished (Sherman, 1986; Skogan, 1990). Whether or not these concerns are uppermost in the minds of the public (as opposed to the more mundane concerns just mentioned), and whether or not they pervade the everyday practices of police, crime control is likely to remain a central concern of those who devise, criticize, and administer public policies pertaining to police.

CONCLUSION

This chapter has highlighted three enduring themes: the role, control, and legitimacy of American police. Debate, ambiguity, and unresolved empirical issues swirl about each of these. Much of the debate about the police role derives from differing values about what police should be, although there are many unresolved questions about what they could be. The realization that police exercise discretion in the practice of their authority to intervene in citizens' private lives has spawned increasing concern about how to control that discretion. How and how much to control the state's power have always been central issues in America; they will undoubtedly continue to be matters of central importance in the twenty-first century, even should policing continue the trend of relying on less-obtrusive means of surveillance and deception instead of the more obvious forms of coercion. Finally, the bases of police legitimacy shift with the prevailing political and cultural winds.

Despite the dubiousness and outright resistance with which Americans greeted the new police organizations that emerged in the nineteenth century, they have long since become "sacred" (Manning, 1991: 357), enduring even in the face of repeated reminders of their limited ability to control crime, disorder, corruption, and brutality. The existence of public police seems more secure today than ever, even in the face of tight local budgets and various crises of legitimacy arising from allegations of brutality, corruption, and illegal discrimination.

What seems more mutable are the structures and practices of public policing, which are the objects of transformation by many groups external to police (Mastrofski and Uchida, 1993). Although it is difficult to say what impact the current efforts to transform police, such as community policing, will have, it does appear that the police leadership itself is taking an increasingly consequential role in the process. The emergence of a growing national market for top police executives in the most desirable police jobs, instead of the long-time practice of hiring from within the department, is one indication that changes are afoot. America's police leaders are moving away from traditional roles in other ways as well, by participating in progressive associations, obtaining graduate degrees, and using social science research (Klockars and Harver, 1993). The nationalization of crime and disorder as perpetually potent political issues since the 1960s has meant that presidents, Congress, and federal funding agencies have helped frame and shape local policing issues. To the extent that the selection of local police leadership is more responsive to issues raised in the broader national arena, and to the extent that police administrators themselves take a more active role in shaping that national agenda, the prospects of greater administrative homogeneity across local departments are enhanced.

The implications of these administrative trends for street-level police work are not obvious, but other systemic trends suggest dramatic consequences for everyday policing. Perhaps none is more compelling today than the resource limits placed on police in using the criminal process for handling problems. The rest of the criminal justice process is already overtaxed in most metropolitan areas: Jails are full, court dockets are overflowing, prisons are over capacity, and community corrections programs cannot keep up with demand. The get-tough, enforcement approach to crime that dominated the criminal justice system in the 1980s has produced more people and paper than the system can handle in the 1990s, and there are no reasonable prospects that sufficient court and correctional resources will be available in the future to keep pace.

Faced with the reality of an overloaded criminal justice system, the police must find ways to engage in social control by other means—or simply give up on some problems, people, or geographic areas. That means that police must become even more selective about using criminal sanctions—whether by default or through a managed process. But it is not at all clear that alternative systems of social control are sufficiently developed either (Aaronsen et al., 1984; Black, 1980). These conditions provide compelling reasons for students of police to refocus their attention on how police respond in the areas of their discretion that thus far have remained darkly shrouded under the "informal" or "no arrest" categories. Whether and how police mobilize other government agencies and the private sector on these occasions, and how effective and efficient these responses are, are yet to be demonstrated. Determining who gets what from police, and the consequences therefrom, remains a challenge for future research.

DISCUSSION QUESTIONS

1. Though our notion of modern policing originated in England, it differs from the English version. In what ways?

2. Discuss the role of the police in our society and the problems linked to that role.

3. Discuss the notion of police discretion and provide examples.

4. How easy is it to monitor and control police behavior in the field? What can communities do to constrain discretion? What can departments themselves do?

5. What does it mean to have a "professional" police department? Discuss the aspects of policing that make professionalization difficult.

6. Does the public support its local police? Discuss trends in support for the police. What happens when the public loses confidence in the police?

REFERENCES

Aaronsen, D., C. Dienes, and M. Musheno. 1984. *Public Policy and Police Discretion.* New York: Clark Boardmen.

Albrecht, S., and M. Green. 1977. "Attitudes Toward Police and the Larger Attitude Complex." *Criminology* 15: 485–494.

Bayley, D. 1986. "The Tactical Choices of Police Patrol Officers." *Journal of Criminal Justice* 14: 329–348.

———. 1988. "Community Policing: A Report from the Devil's Advocate." In *Community Policing: Rhetoric or Reality.* Edited by J. R. Greene and S. Mastrofski. New York: Praeger.

Bayley, D., and E. Bittner. 1984. "Learning the Skills of Policing." *Law and Contemporary Problems* 47: 35–59.

Berman, J. 1987. *Police Administration and Progressive Reform.* New York: Greenwood.

Bieck, W., W. Spelmen, and T. Sweeney. 1991. "The Police Function." Pp. 59–95 in *Local Government Police Management.* Edited by W. Geller. Washington, DC: International City Management Association.

Bittner, E. 1970. *The Functions of Police in Modern Society.* Bethesda, MD: U.S. National Institute of Mental Health.

———. 1974. "A Theory of Police: Florence Nightingale in Pursuit of Willie Sutton." Pp. 17–44 in *The Potential for Reform of Criminal Justice.* Edited by H. Jacob. Newbury Park, CA: Sage.

———. 1983. "Legality and Workmanship." In *Control in the Police Organization.* Edited by M. Punch. Cambridge, MA: MIT Press.

Black, D. J. 1980. *The Manners and Customs of the Police.* New York: Academic Press.

Brandl, S., J. Frank, R. Worden, and T. Bynum. 1994. "Global and Specific Attitudes Toward the Police: Disentangling the Relationship." *Justice Quarterly* 11: 119–134.

Bratton, W. 1998. *Turnaround: How America's Top Cop Reversed the Crime Epidemic.* New York: Random House.

Broderick, J. 1987. *Police in a Time of Change.* 2d ed. Prospect Heights, IL: Waveland Press.

Brown, M. 1981. *Working the Streets.* New York: Russell Sage Foundation.

Buzawa, E. 1982. "Police Officer Response to Domestic Legislation in Michigan." *Journal of Police Science and Administration* 10: 415–424.

Carter, D., and A. Sapp. 1991. *Police Education and Minority Recruitment.* Washington, DC: Police Executive Research Forum.

Carter, D., A. Sapp, and D. Stephens. 1988. "Higher Education as a Bona Fide Occupational Qualification for Police." *American Journal of Police* 7: 1–27.

———. 1989. *The State of Police Education.* Washington, DC: Police Executive Research Forum.

Chaiken, J., P. Greenwood, and J. Petersilia. 1977. "The Criminal Investigation Process." *Policy Analysis* 3: 187–217.

Chatterton, M. 1983. "Police Work and Assault Charges." Pp. 194–222 in *Control in the Police Organization.* Edited by M. Punch. Cambridge, MA: MIT Press.

Crank, J. 1990. "The Influence of Environmental and Organizational Factors on Police Style." *Journal of Research in Crime and Delinquency* 27: 166–189.

Crank, J., and R. Langworthy. 1992. "An Institutional Perspective on Policing." *Journal of Criminal Law and Criminology* 83: 338–363.

Davies, T. 1983. "A Hard Look at What We Know (and Still Need to Learn) About the 'Costs' of the Exclusionary Rule: The NIJ Study and Other Studies of 'Lost' Arrests." *American Bar Foundation Research Journal* 1983: 611–690.

Davis, K. C. 1975. *Police Discretion.* St. Paul: West.

Eck, J. 1983. *Solving Crimes.* Washington, DC: Police Executive Research Forum.

Ericson, R., and K. Haggerty. 1997. *Policing the Risk Society.* Toronto: University of Toronto Press.

Federal Bureau of Investigation. 1972. *Crime in the United States—1971.* Washington, DC: U.S. Government Printing Office.

———. 1977. *Crime in the United States—1976.* Washington, DC: U.S. Government Printing Office.

———. 1992. *Crime in the United States—1991.* Washington, DC: U.S. Government Printing Office.

———. 1997. *Crime in the United States—1996.* Washington, DC: U.S. Government Printing Office.

Flanagan, T. J., and Maguire, K. 1992. *Sourcebook of Criminal Justice Statistics, 1991.* Washington, DC: U.S. Department of Justice, Bureau of Justice Statistics.

Flanagan, T. J., D. van Alstyne, and M. Gottfredson. 1982. *Sourcebook of Criminal Justice Statistics, 1981.* Washington, DC: U.S. Department of Justice.

Fogelson, R. 1977. *Big-City Police.* Cambridge, MA: Harvard University Press.

Friedrich, R. 1977. *The Impact of Organizational, Individual, and Situational Factors on Police Behavior.* Unpublished Ph.D. dissertation, University of Michigan.

———. 1980. "Police Use of Force: Individuals, Situations, and Organizations." *Annals of the American Academy of Political and Social Science* 452: 82–97.

Fyfe, J. 1979. "Administrative Interventions on Police Shooting Discretion." *Journal of Criminal Justice* 7: 309–323.

———. 1988. "Police Use of Deadly Force: Research and Reform." *Justice Quarterly* 5: 165–205.

———. 1996. "Methodology, Substance, and Demeanor in Police Observational Research: A Response to Lundman and Others." *Journal of Research in Crime and Delinquency* 33: 337–348.

Gardiner, J. 1969. *Traffic and the Police.* Cambridge, MA: Harvard University Press.

Garofalo, J. 1977. *Public Opinion About Crime.* Washington, DC: U.S. Government Printing Office.

Geller, W., and N. Morris. 1992. "Relations Between Federal and Local Police." Pp. 231–348 in *Modern Policing.* Edited by M. Tonry and N. Morris. Chicago: University of Chicago Press.

Goldstein, H. 1977. *Policing a Free Society.* Cambridge, MA: Ballinger.

———. 1979. "Improving Policing: A Problem-oriented Approach." *Journal of Crime and Delinquency* 25: 236–258.

———. 1990. *Problem-Oriented Policing.* New York: McGraw-Hill.

Goldstein, J. 1960. "Police Discretion Not To Invoke the Criminal Process." *Yale Law Journal* 69: 543–588.

Greene, J., and C. Klockars. 1991. "What Police Do." Pp. 273–284 in *Thinking About Police: Contemporary Readings.* Edited by C. Klockars and S. Mastrofski. New York: McGraw-Hill.

Greene, J., and S. Mastrofski. 1988. *Community Policing: Rhetoric or Reality.* New York: Praeger.

Greenfeld L., P. Langan, and S. Smith. 1997. *Police Use of Force: Collection of National Data.* Washington, DC: Bureau of Justice Statistics, U.S. Department of Justice.

Greenfield, L. 1988. "Drunk Driving." *Bureau of Justice Statistics Special Report.* Washington, DC: U.S. Department of Justice.

Herbert, S. 1997. *Policing Space: Territoriality and the Los Angeles Police Department.* Minneapolis: University of Minnesota Press.

Kelling, G. 1978. "Police Patrol Services: The Presumed Effect of a Capacity." *Crime and Delinquency* 54: 173–184.

Kelling, G., and M. Moore. 1988. "From Political to Reform to Community: The Evolving Strategy of Police." Pp. 3–25 in *Community Policing: Rhetoric or Reality.* Edited by J. R. Greene and S. D. Mastrofski. New York: Praeger.

Kerstetter, W. 1985. "Who Disciplines the Police?" In *Police Leadership: Crisis and Opportunity.* Edited by W. Geller. New York: Praeger.

Klinger, D. 1994. "Demeanor or Crime? Why 'Hostile' Citizens Are More Likely to Be Arrested." *Criminology* 32: 475–493.

———. 1996. "Bringing Crime Back In: Toward a Better Understanding of Police Arrest Decisions." *Journal of Research in Crime and Delinquency* 33: 333–336.

Klockars, C. B. 1972. "A Theory of Probation Supervision." *Journal of Criminal Law, Criminology and Police Science* 63: 550.

———. 1984. "Blue Lies and Police Placebos: The Moralities of Police Lying." *American Behavioral Scientist* 27: 529–544.

———. 1985. *The Idea of Police.* Newbury Park, CA: Sage.

———. 1988. "The Rhetoric of Community Policing." In *Community Policing: Rhetoric or Reality.* Edited by J. R. Greene and S. D. Mastrofski. New York: Praeger.

Klockars, C. B., and W. E. Harver. 1993. *The Production and Consumption of Research in Police Agencies in the United States.* Report to the National Institute of Justice. University of Delaware.

Krantz, S., B. Gilman, and C. Benda. 1979. *Police Policymaking.* Lexington, MA: Lexington Books.

LaFave, W. 1965. *Arrest.* Boston: Little, Brown.

Lane, R. 1992. "Urban Police and Crime in Nineteenth-Century America." In *Modern Policing.* Edited by M. Tonry and N. Morris. Chicago: University of Chicago Press.

Langworthy, D. 1986. *The Structure of Police Organizations.* New York: Praeger.

Leo, R. 1992. "From Coercion to Deception." *Crime, Law, and Social Change* 18: 35–59.

Lipsky, M. 1980. *Street-Level Bureaucracies.* New York: Russell Sage Foundation.

Lundman, R. 1996. "Demeanor and Arrest: Additional Evidence From Previously Unpublished Data." *Journal of Research in Crime and Delinquency* 33: 306–323.

Maguire, K., and A. Pastore. 1997. *Sourcebook of Criminal Justice Statistics, 1996.* Washington, DC: U.S. Department of Justice.

Manning, P. 1977. *Police Work.* Cambridge, MA: MIT Press.

———. 1980. *Narcs' Game.* Cambridge, MA: MIT Press.

———. 1984. "Community Policing." *American Journal of Police* 3: 205–227.

———. 1988. "Community Policing as a Drama of Control." In *Community Policing: Rhetoric or Reality.* Edited by J. R. Greene and S. D. Mastrofski. New York: Praeger.

———. 1989. "The Occupational Culture of the Police." In *The Encyclopedia of Police Science.* Edited by L. Hoover et al. Dallas: Garland Press.

———. 1991. "The Police." In *Criminology: A Contemporary Handbook.* Edited by J. F. Sheley. Belmont, CA: Wadsworth.

———. 1992a. "Technological Dramas and the Police: Statement and Counterstatement in Organizational Analysis." *Criminology* 30: 327–346.

———. 1992b. "Information Technologies and the Police." In *Modern Policing.* Edited by M. Tonry and N. Morris. Chicago: University of Chicago Press.

———. 1993. *Toward a Theory of Police Organization Polarities and Change.* Paper delivered at the International Conference on Social Change in Policing. Central Police University of R.O.C., Taipei (August).

———. 1997. *Police Work: The Social Organization of Policing.* 2d ed. Prospect Heights, IL: Waveland Press.

Martin, S. 1989. *Women on the Move?: A Report on the Status of Women in Policing.* Washington, DC: The Police Foundation.

Mastrofski, S. 1981. "Policing the Beat: The Impact of Organizational Scale on Patrol Officer Behavior in Urban Residential Neighborhoods." *Journal of Criminal Justice* 9: 343–358.

———. 1983. "The Police and Non-Crime Services." Pp. 33–61 in *Evaluating the Performance of Criminal Justice Agencies.* Edited by G. P. Whitaker and C. D. Phillips. Newbury Park, CA: Sage.

———. 1986. "Police Agency Accreditation: The Prospects of Reform." *American Journal of Police* 5: 45–81.

———. 1988. "Community Policing as Reform: A Cautionary Tale." In *Community Policing: Rhetoric or Reality.* Edited by J. R. Greene and S. D. Mastrofski. New York: Praeger.

———. 1990. "The Prospects of Change in Police Patrol: A Decade in Review." *American Journal of Police* 9: 1–79.

———. 1997. *The Romance of Police Leadership.* Paper delivered at the Conference on Crime and Social Organization in honor of Albert J. Reiss Jr. Rutgers University, New Brunswick, NJ.

———. Forthcoming. "Police Agency Accreditation: A Skeptical View." *Policing: An International Journal of Police Strategies & Management.*

Mastrofski, S. D., and R. Ritti. 1992. "You Can Lead a Horse to Water . . . : A Case Study of a Police Department's Response to Stricter Drunk Driving Laws." *Justice Quarterly* 9: 465–491.

———. 1996. "Police Training and the Effects of Organization on Drunk Driving Enforcement." *Justice Quarterly* 13: 291–320.

Mastrofski, S. D., R. Ritti, and D. Hoffmaster. 1987. "Organizational Determinants of Police Discretion: The Case of Drinking and Driving." *Journal of Criminal Justice* 15: 387–402.

Mastrofski, S. D., R. Ritti, and J. Snipes. 1994. "Expectancy Theory and Police Productivity in DUI Enforcement." *Law and Society Review* 28: 113–148.

Mastrofski, S., R. Worden, and J. Snipes. 1995. "Law Enforcement in a Time of Community Policing." *Criminology* 33: 539–563.

Mastrofski, S. D., and C. Uchida. 1993. "Transforming the Police." *Journal of Research in Crime and Delinquency* 30: 330–358.

McCoy, C. 1984. "Lawsuits Against the Police." *Criminal Law Bulletin* 20: 49–56.

———. 1987. *Constitutional Tort Litigation.* Paper delivered at the annual meeting of the American Political Science Association, Chicago.

Medalie, R., L. Zeitz, and P. Alexander. 1968. "Custodial Police Interrogation in our Nation's Capitol." *Michigan Law Review* 66: 1347–1422.

Miller, W. R. 1977. *Cops and Bobbies.* Chicago: University of Chicago Press.

Milner, N. 1971. *The Court and Local Law Enforcement.* Beverly Hills, CA: Sage.

Monkkonen, E. 1981. *Police in Urban America: 1860–1920*. Cambridge: Cambridge University Press.

Muir, W. K., Jr. 1977. *The Police: Street Corner Politicians*. Chicago: University of Chicago Press.

Muir, W. K., and D. Perez. 1992. "Administrative Review of Alleged Police Brutality." In *And Justice for All*. Edited by W. Geller and H. Toch. Washington, DC: Police Executive Research Forum.

Murphy, S. E. 1986. *Marijuana Decriminalization: The Unfinished Reform*. Ph.D. dissertation, University of Missouri, Columbia.

National Institute of Justice. 1982. *The Effects of the Exclusionary Rule*. Washington, DC: U.S. Government Printing Office.

Oaks, D. 1970. "Studying the Exclusionary Rule in Search and Seizure." *University of Chicago Law Review* 37: 665–757.

Orfield, M. 1987. "The Exclusionary Rule and Deterrence: An Empirical Study of Chicago Narcotics Officers." *University of Chicago Law Review* 54: 1016–1069.

Ostrom, E., R. Parks, and G. Whitaker. 1978. *Patterns of Metropolitan Policing*. Cambridge, MA: Ballinger.

Parks, R., S. Mastrofski, A. Reiss Jr., R. Worden, W. Terrill, C. DeJong, and J. Snipes. 1997. *Indianapolis Project on Policing Neighborhoods: A Study of the Police and the Community*. Report to the National Institute of Justice. Bloomington, IN: Indiana University.

Parks, R., S. Mastrofski, A. Reiss Jr., R. Worden, W. Terrill, C. DeJong, M. Stroshine, and R. Shepard. 1998. *St. Petersburg Project on Policing Neighborhoods: A Study of the Police and the Community*. Report to the National Institute of Justice. Bloomington, IN: Indiana University.

Potts, L. 1983. *Responsible Police Administration: Issues and Approaches*. University, AL: University of Alabama Press.

President's Commission on Law Enforcement and Administration of Justice. 1967. *The Challenge of Crime in a Free Society*. Washington, DC: U.S. Government Printing Office.

Prottas, J. 1978. "The Power of the Street-Level Bureaucrat in Public Service Bureaucracies." *Urban Affairs Quarterly* 13: 285–312.

Reaves, B., and A. Goldberg. 1998. *Census of State and Local Law Enforcement Agencies, 1996*. Washington, DC: U.S. Department of Justice.

Reaves, B., and P. Smith. 1995. *Law Enforcement Management and Administrative Statistics, 1993: Data for Individual State and Local Agencies with 100 or More Sworn Officers*. Washington, DC: U.S. Department of Justice.

Reiss, A. 1971. *The Police and the Public*. New Haven, CT: Yale University Press.

———. 1992. "Police Organization in the Twentieth Century." In *Modern Policing*. Edited by M. Tonry and N. Morris. Chicago: University of Chicago Press.

———. 1993. *Towards a Theoretical Perspective on Enforcing Law and Maintaining Domestic Order*. Paper delivered at the annual meeting of the American Society of Criminology, Phoenix.

Reuss-Ianni, E. 1983. *The Two Cultures of Policing*. New Brunswick, NJ: Transaction Books.

Reuter, P., and M. Kleiman. 1986. "Risks and Prices: An Economic Analysis of Drug Enforcement." In *Crime and Justice*. Edited by M. Tonry and N. Morris. Chicago: University of Chicago Press.

Riksheim, E., and S. Chermak. 1993. "Causes of Police Behavior Revisited." *Journal of Criminal Justice* 21: 353–382.

Rubinstein, J. 1973. *City Police*. New York: Farrar, Straus & Giroux.

Schmidt, W. 1974. "A Proposal for a Statewide Law Enforcement Administrative Law Council." *Journal of Police Science and Administration* 2: 330–338.

Scott, W. R. 1992. *Organizations*. Englewood Cliffs, NJ: Prentice-Hall.

Sherman, L. W. 1983. "Reducing Gun Use: Critical Events, Administrative Policy, and Organizational

Change." In *Control in the Police Organization*. Edited by M. Punch. Cambridge, MA: MIT Press.

———. 1986. "Policing Communities: What Works?" In *Communities and Crime*. Edited by A. J. Reiss Jr., and M. Tonry. Chicago: University of Chicago Press.

———. 1992a. "Attacking Crime: Policing and Crime Control." In *Modern Policing*. Edited by M. Tonry and N. Morris. Chicago: University of Chicago Press.

———. 1992b. *Policing Domestic Violence: Experiments and Dilemmas*. New York: Free Press.

Sherman, L., P. Gartin, and M. Buerger. 1989. "Hot Spots of Predatory Crime: Routine Activities and the Criminology Of Place." *Criminology* 27: 27–40.

Sherman, L., D. Gottfredson, D. MacKenzie, J. Eck, P. Reuter, and S. Bushway. 1997. *Preventing Crime: What Works, What Doesn't, What's Promising?* Washington, DC: U.S. Department of Justice.

Skogan, W. G. 1990. *Disorder and Decline*. New York: Free Press.

Skolnick, J. 1966. *Justice Without Trial*. New York: Wiley.

———. 1971. "Neighborhood Police." *The Nation* (March 22): 372–373.

Skolnick, J., and J. Fyfe. 1993. *Above the Law: Police and the Excessive Use of Force*. New York: Free Press.

Slovak, J. 1986. *Styles of Urban Policing*. New York: New York University Press.

Smith, D. 1984. "Police Control of Interpersonal Disputes." *Social Problems* 31: 468–481.

Smith, D. A., and C. Visher. 1980. "Gender and Crime: An Empirical Assessment of Research Findings." *American Sociological Review* 48: 509–514.

———. 1981. "Street Level Justice: Situational Determinants of Police Arrest Decisions." *Social Problems* 29: 167–177.

Smith, D. A., and J. Klein. 1983. "Police Agency and Characteristics and Arrest Decisions." In *Evaluat-*

ing Performance of Criminal Justice Agencies. Edited by G. Whitaker and C. Phillips. Beverly Hills, CA: Sage.

Smith, D. A., C. A. Visher, and L. A. Davidson. 1984. "Equity and Discretionary Justice: The Influence of Race on Police Arrest Decisions." *Journal of Criminal Law and Criminology* 75: 234–249.

Smith, M. D. 1986. "The Era of Increased Violence in the United States: Age, Period, or Cohort Effect?" *Sociological Quarterly* 27: 239–251.

Sparrow, M., M. Moore, and D. Kennedy. 1990. *Beyond 911: A New Era for Policing*. New York: Basic Books.

Surette, R. 1992. *Media, Crime, and Justice*. Pacific Grove, CA: Brooks/Cole.

Sykes, R. E., and E. E. Brent. 1983. *Policing: A Social Behaviorist Perspective*. New Brunswick, NJ: Rutgers University Press.

Tedeschi, J., and R. Felson. 1994. *Violence, Aggression, and Coercive Actions*. Washington, DC: American Psychological Association.

Teplin, L. 1986. *Keeping the Peace*. Washington, DC: U.S. Government Printing Office.

Van Maanen, J. 1974. "Working the Street." Pp. 83–130 in *Prospects for Reform in Criminal Justice*. Edited by H. Jacob. Beverly Hills, CA: Sage.

———. 1983. "The Boss: A Portrait of the American Police Sergeant." In *The Control of the Police*. Edited by M. Punch. Cambridge, MA: MIT Press.

———. 1984. "Making Rank: Becoming an American Police Sergeant." *Urban Life* 13: 155–176.

Visher, C. A. 1983. "Gender, Police, Arrest Decisions, and Notions of Chivalry." *Criminology* 21: 5–28.

Walker, S. 1977. *A Critical History of Police Reform*. Lexington, MA: Lexington Books.

———. 1985. "Racial Minority and Female Employment in Policing: The Implications of 'Glacial' Change." *Crime and Delinquency* 31: 555–572.

———. 1986. "Controlling the Cops: A Legislative Approach to Police Rulemaking." *University of Detroit Law Review* (Spring): 361–391.

————. 1989. *Sense and Nonsense About Crime: A Policy Guide.* 2d ed. Pacific Grove, CA: Brooks/Cole.

————. 1992. *The Police in America: An Introduction.* New York: McGraw-Hill.

————. 1993. "Historical Roots of the Legal Control of Police Behavior." In *Police Innovation and Control of the Police: Problems of Law, Order and Community.* Edited by D. Weisburd and C. Uchida. New York: Springer-Verlag.

Webster, W., and H. Williams. 1992. *The City in Crisis.* Report by the Special Advisor to the Police Commissioners on the Civil Disorder in Los Angeles. Los Angeles, CA.

Westley, W. 1970. *Violence and the Police.* Cambridge, MA: MIT Press.

Whitaker. P., S. Mastrofski, E. Ostrom, R. Parks, and S. Percy. 1982. *Basic Issues in Police Performance.* Washington, DC: U.S. Department of Justice, National Institute of Justice.

White, S. 1972. "A Perspective on Police Professionalism." *Law and Society Review* 7: 61–85.

Wilson, J. Q. 1968. *Varieties of Police Behavior.* Cambridge, MA: Harvard University Press.

————. 1975. *Thinking About Crime.* New York: Basic Books.

Wilson, J. Q., and B. Boland. 1978. "The Effect of the Police on Crime." *Law and Society Review* 12: 267–390.

Witkin, G. 1998. "The Crime Bust." *U.S. News and World Report.* May 25: 28–37.

Worden, R. 1984. "Patrol Officer Attitudes and the Distribution of Police Services: A Preliminary Analysis." In *Understanding Police Agency Performance.* Edited by G. P. Whitaker. Washington, DC: National Institute of Justice.

————. 1989. "Situational and Attitudinal Explanations of Police Behavior: A Theoretical Reapprasial and Empirical Assessment." *Law and Society Review* 23: 667–671.

————. 1992. "The 'Causes' of Police Brutality." In *And Justice for All: A National Agenda for Understanding and Controlling Police Abuse of Force.* Edited by W. A. Geller and H. Toch. Unpublished manuscript. Washington, DC: Police Executive Research Forum.

Worden, R., R. Shepard, and S. Mastrofski. 1996. "On the Meaning and Measurement of Suspects' Demeanor Toward the Police: A Comment on 'Demeanor and Arrest.'" *Journal of Research in Crime and Delinquency* 33: 324–332.

Chapter Outline

16

The Social World of
America's Courts

MARTHA A. MYERS
University of Georgia

In the heart of every county and major city, the courthouse stands as a daily reminder of justice in America. Now, more than ever before, its doors are open to public view. Most states allow cameras to document their criminal trials and, for the first time, we can glimpse the inner workings of America's courts. It is a tantalizing glimpse when exceptional cases involve celebrities, bizarre crimes or, in some cases, both. The everyday reality of our courts, however—where millions of criminal cases are prosecuted each year—is quite different. On a typical day, there are no celebrities, no bizarre crimes, and few, if any, jury trials. No television cameras illuminate the everyday lives of courthouse workers or the powerful ties that bind them together as a community. The social world of our courts, then, is largely invisible to the public it serves. The empirical research summarized in this chapter helps bring this social world to light.

COURT STRUCTURE

AND ORGANIZATION

By their very nature, America's courts are difficult to understand and study because the United States has not one, but two, court systems (see Figure 16.1). Federal courts overlap state courts geographically, but have sole jurisdiction over cases involving violations of federal statutes. Each of the ninety-four federal district courts is headed by a judge who is appointed by the president and confirmed by the Senate. To initiate criminal prosecutions, each federal district has an office of the U.S. Attorney, who also is appointed by the president and confirmed by the Senate. Criminal prosecutions, mostly of white collar and drug offenses, comprise just a small part of federal court caseloads. At the same time, they consume a disproportionate share of court resources (Mecham, 1998). In 1997, for

FIGURE 16.1
The Dual Court System
of the United States

SOURCE: Adapted from Neubauer, 1988.

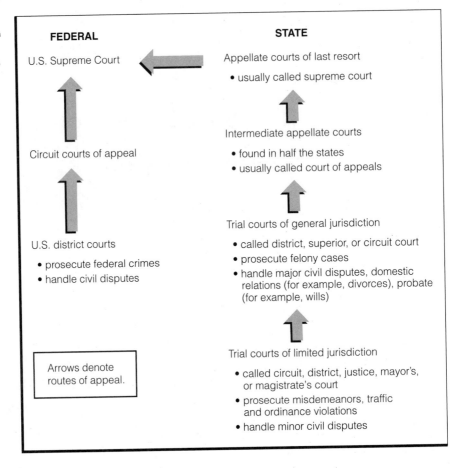

example, only 16 percent of all cases filed in federal court were criminal cases, whereas 40 percent of all federal cases that resulted in a trial involved criminal charges.

Each state has its own court system, which has jurisdiction over violations of state criminal statutes. These courts are more diverse and autonomous than federal courts because state constitutions and statutes have developed over time, often on an ad hoc basis. More than 2,600 courts of general jurisdiction are responsible for the prosecution of felonies; they handle more

than four million cases per year. Nearly 14,000 courts of limited jurisdiction are responsible for misdemeanors and ordinance violations; they handle more than nine million cases per year (Ostrom and Kauder, 1996). Lower courts are more decentralized and specialized than courts of general jurisdiction. A single urban area, for example, may be served by several lower courts, some of which handle only certain types of cases (for example, prostitution or traffic violations). Prosecutors in these jurisdictions manage a large bureaucracy and leave decisions in specific cases to a staff of assistant district attorneys. Smaller jurisdictions may have a single court to handle all criminal cases and a prosecutor who only works part-time (DeFrances et al., 1996). Regardless of the size of their jurisdiction, most prosecutors and judges are elected locally and must respond to the concerns of their local constituencies.

The decentralized and complicated organization of our court system poses a challenge to researchers who seek a global understanding of the behavior of prosecutors, judges, and defense counsel. State courts of general jurisdiction, where felony prosecution occurs, have garnered the most research attention. Comparative research across jurisdictions is essential for a complete understanding of these courts, but it is severely hampered by diversity in state criminal statutes, sentencing law, and court organization (Nardulli et al., 1988; Ulmer, 1997b).

State courts of limited jurisdiction have received less scholarly attention. This neglect is anomalous because lower courts not only handle the majority of all offenders, but also make pretrial release decisions for felony defendants. A breed apart from their felony court counterparts, many lower courts are grossly underfinanced and informally administered (Neubauer, 1996). The process of being convicted, which involves being detained in jail, may be even more punishing than the actual sanction the judge imposes (Flemming, 1982). For defendants accused of felonies, the pretrial release decision reached by lower courts is pivotal. Those who fail to obtain release are more likely to be convicted and, upon conviction, tend to be punished more severely than comparable defendants who secure release prior to the disposition of their case (Blumstein et al., 1983; Holmes et al., 1987).

Finally, federal courts have interested researchers only since the early 1980s. More formal and less hurried than are state courts, they handle fewer cases. In 1994, for example, more than 2.5 million cases were filed in state felony courts, whereas federal district courts handled only 45,473 criminal cases (Court Statistics Project Staff, 1995; Mecham, 1995). Because a single code governs all federal courts, researchers are able to explore in some detail the role that the surrounding community plays during prosecution. Also, because the federal code prohibits both common-law crime (for example, drug use and robbery) and white collar offenses (for example, mail fraud and draft evasion), researchers can better assess whether social class has any impact on sentencing.

Because empirical knowledge of our state and federal courts is uneven, our understanding of the social world that exists inside America's courthouses remains incomplete. Nonetheless, two members of the court clearly share the center stage in any criminal prosecution. This review therefore begins with the prosecutor, who initiates a defendant's contact with the court, and concludes with the judge, who determines whether the offender will have contact with the court in the future.

THE PROSECUTOR

In the past, private citizens, the judiciary, and (later) the police were the central characters in the prosecution of crime (Steinberg, 1984). Few of these traditional practices persist today. In some jurisdictions, the police still file charges directly with the court (Mellon et al., 1981). In others, prosecutors ratify police screening decisions (Feeley and Lazerson, 1983) or negotiate the appropriate charge with officers (Stanko, 1981; Emerson and Paley, 1992). In most jurisdictions, though, prosecutors stand at the courthouse door alone, deciding which defendants will be overlooked and which will be required to enter (Albonetti, 1987). Within the courthouse, the prosecutor's power over the defendant continues virtually undiminished. District attorneys determine precisely which charges—whether felonies, misdemeanors, or some combination—are filed against defendants. To prosecute, they must show probable cause in a preliminary hearing before a judge. Often ceremonial in nature, these hearings may even be waived (Neubauer, 1996). Federal courts and nineteen states also require a grand jury indictment before criminal prosecution can begin. Indictments, or "true bills," are formal written documents accusing a person or persons of committing a specific offense. Grand juries return indictments if they find enough evidence to warrant convening a jury trial to establish the defendant's guilt beyond a reasonable doubt. Prosecutors are in a powerful position during this process because they choose which witnesses and evidence grand juries consider. The defendant and defense counsel may not even be allowed to present their version of the facts, much less to confront and cross-examine witnesses. Not surprisingly, deliberations are brief. As one appellate court judge colorfully put it, most grand juries would "indict a ham sandwich" if the prosecutor asked them to do so (Carroll, 1985).

In many other states, indictments are optional, and prosecutors can begin formal prosecution after filing an "information" with the court (Emerson, 1983). Like an indictment, an information formally accuses an individual of a specific offense, citing the time, date, and location of the offense, as well as the identity of the victim, if any. After formal charges have been filed, prosecutors may decide at any point to cease prosecution entirely, often by submitting to the court a motion to nolle prosequi (or "nol-prossing"). Together with the initial screening decision, dismissals account for the "loss" of nearly half of all cases brought to the prosecutor (Boland et al., 1992; DeFrances et al., 1996). Insufficient evidence and problems with witnesses are the most often-cited reasons for declining further prosecution. If, however, prosecution proceeds, once the case against the defendant is prepared, prosecutors decide whether to accept a guilty plea or to proceed to trial. In states with capital punishment, they also decide whether to seek the death penalty.

Prosecutors exercise a discretion that has few limits, formal or informal. Appellate courts prohibit discriminatory and vindictive prosecution, but otherwise are reluctant to violate the separation of powers doctrine by regulating prosecutorial decisions. Since colonial times, grand juries have served to protect the accused against unfounded charges and oppressive government. Today, grand juries are "sleeping watchdogs," who serve little meaningful screening or supervisory function. Calls for their reform or outright abolition are often heard (Emerson, 1983). More generally, the public may constrain and limit prosecutor behavior, but seldom does it affect the daily operation of the prosecutor's office (Nardulli et al., 1988).

In short, there are few effective limits on prosecutorial discretion, and fears of potential abuse are widespread. In large part, these fears are unwarranted. Prosecutors are powerful, but they do not, indeed cannot, act alone. They are members of courtroom workgroups that interact over time and share common backgrounds, interests, and decision-making responsibilities (Nardulli et al., 1988; Jacob, 1991; Flemming et al., 1992; Ulmer, 1997a). The group includes defense counsel and judges who, in collaboration with prosecutors, develop strategies that enable the group to dispose of cases with maximum speed and minimal conflict.

In theory, defense counsels may refuse to cooperate with prosecutors, but for a variety of reasons seldom do so. Because the majority of all defendants are unable to retain private counsel, they are represented either by assigned counsel or by a public defender (Neubauer, 1996). Assigned counsel may lack the ability or motivation to provide a vigorous defense for a client. Their compensation is minimal when compared to the fees charged in private practice, their criminal trial experience is often limited, and the court seldom provides the funds needed to conduct investigations or obtain the services of expert witnesses. In contrast, public defenders are attorneys who receive a salary from the jurisdiction for their services (DeFrances et al., 1996). Sustained experience with criminal cases enables them to prepare a more adequate defense than assigned counsel can muster.

Whether as assigned counsel or public defender, membership in the courtroom workgroup generates a strong interest in cooperating with the prosecution. Although relationships vary across jurisdictions (Nardulli et al., 1988; Flemming, 1990; Flemming et al., 1992), defense counsel and district attorneys seldom are full adversaries, except in serious cases where punishment rather than the defendant's guilt is at issue (Mather, 1979). Not surprisingly, then, the defense often is considered a co-opted double agent who has few bargaining chips when negotiating with the prosecutor (Neubauer,

1996). If the defendant agrees, counsel can press for a trial until the prosecutor tenders a better plea-bargaining offer (Frohmann, 1997). Yet this strategy can be costly, because defendants who exercise their right to a trial and are subsequently convicted usually receive a more severe sentence than those who pleaded guilty to the same offense (Blumstein et al., 1983; Ulmer, 1997b).

The prosecutor's relationships with judges vary considerably as well (Ulmer, 1997b). In some jurisdictions, judges dominate the charging and plea-bargaining decisions (McIntyre and Lippman, 1970; Flemming, 1990). More typically, though, judges exercise little control over prosecutors. Judges have no authority during plea negotiations if the concessions offered are solely under the prosecutor's purview, such as the reduction or dropping of charges. As members of the same community, however, judges and prosecutors share similar notions about the worth of the case before them. As a result, judges supervise plea bargains, ratify bargains previously negotiated between counsel and prosecution, or participate in the negotiations in varying degrees during pretrial conferences (Ryan and Alfini, 1979; McCoy, 1993; Ulmer, 1997b).

Given the extent of their discretion and their membership in courtroom workgroups, how do prosecutors actually exercise their discretionary power? To what extent, if any, do they act arbitrarily? To answer these questions, researchers have used many techniques, from observations and interviews to quantitative analyses of actual decisions. They have successfully studied only a few dozen of the more than 2,300 state prosecutors' offices, and most of the studies were conducted in urban areas. Thus, the generalizations that follow provide only an initial understanding of prosecutors' decision-making behavior.

Case Screening

When deciding whether to accept or fully prosecute a case, prosecutors compare the case against an ideal that will ensure conviction should the case go to trial before a jury (Frohmann, 1997). This ideal is variously labeled the "good" (Rauma, 1984), "strong" (Myers and Hagan, 1979), or "solid" (Stanko, 1982) case. The first, and probably most crucial, element of the strong case is a serious offense. Not surprisingly, prosecutors are more likely to file charges and prosecute fully if the offense is statutorily serious (Jacoby et al., 1982; Albonetti, 1987) or if the victim was injured (Myers, 1982; Rauma, 1984).

Clear evidence of the defendant's guilt is the second element of the strong case and is especially critical at the initial charging stage (Jacoby et al., 1982; Feeney et al., 1983). District attorneys are likely to prosecute fully if eyewitnesses identified the defendant, the police recovered weapons or stolen property, the defendant or accomplice(s) made statements, or numerous witnesses are willing to testify (Myers and Hagan, 1979; Myers and LaFree, 1982). Researchers have yet to establish the relative importance of evidence in comparison with other elements of the strong case. Some contend that it has the strongest influence on prosecutor decisions, whereas others argue that the victim's credibility and the seriousness of the offense are more important considerations (Myers and Hagan, 1979; Jacoby et al., 1982; Feeney et al., 1983). Clearly, the specific kinds of evidence that prosecutors consider crucial depend on which decision is at issue (for example, initial

screening or full prosecution), as well as on whether the offense is a felony or misdemeanor (Myers, 1982; Albonetti, 1986, 1987).

The third element of the strong case is a defendant who is both dangerous and culpable. Prosecutors tend to file charges against and prosecute fully defendants who have a serious prior record or who allegedly used a weapon to commit the crime (Albonetti, 1986, 1987; Schmidt and Steury, 1989). As we will see, prosecutors assess the defendant's culpability in conjunction with the culpability and credibility of the victim. At issue here is whether prosecutors take into account defendant attributes that have little or no direct bearing on their culpability or dangerousness. Apparently, some do. For example, some prosecutors pursue cases against African-American, male, and unemployed defendants more rigorously than comparable cases involving whites, women, or employed defendants (Blumstein et al., 1983; Nagel and Hagan, 1983; Albonetti, 1987; Spohn et al., 1987). In yet other jurisdictions, prosecutors consider the defendant's race in conjunction with other attributes such as age and prior record (Albonetti and Hepburn, 1996).

The final element of the strong case is a "stand-up" victim, one whom the jury would believe and would consider undeserving of victimization (Stanko, 1981–1982, 1982). From the prosecutor's point of view, believable victims are articulate and consistent when giving testimony; "innocent" victims did nothing to precipitate or provoke their own victimization. Accurate assessments of the credibility and culpability of crime victims are difficult to make. To develop them, prosecutors rely on stereotypic notions about certain locales in their jurisdiction, the people who live within these areas, or those who have occasion to venture into them (Frohmann, 1997). For example, prosecutors presume that white jurors from more affluent locales will fail to understand or believe victims who had been acquainted with the defendant, reside in disreputable areas of the city, were engaged in deviant or criminal behavior at the time of their victimization, or had entered a crime-ridden area (Albonetti, 1987; Spohn and Spears, 1996; Frohmann, 1997). To assess the credibility of female victims, prosecutors invoke gender stereotypes about how women should act when victimized and how cooperative they are likely to be as witnesses (Stanko, 1982; Frohmann, 1991). Failure to conform to these stereotypes could account for the reluctance of prosecutors in some jurisdictions to accept and prosecute fully cases involving female victims (Myers and Hagan, 1979; Foley and Powell, 1982). Clearly, however, female victims are not perceived universally as less credible, because elsewhere their cases are treated no differently from those involving male victims (Albonetti, 1987).

In general, then, stereotypes transform the social background and behavior of victims, witnesses, and defendants into the legally relevant factors of credibility and culpability that become essential when determining whether and how the case should be pursued. Prosecutors also focus on race and pursue cases more vigorously if the defendant is African American and the victim is white (Spohn and Spears, 1996). Where homicide is alleged, prosecutors are more likely to upgrade police charges and seek the death penalty in cases where an African American allegedly murdered a white (Paternoster, 1991). Prosecutors are also more likely to initiate prosecution, to file serious charges, and to prosecute fully if an African-American man allegedly raped a white woman (LaFree, 1989). These trends do not necessarily constitute evidence of discrimination against African-American defendants or victims, because not all studies controlled adequately for legally relevant factors, such as evidence with which race might be confounded. Nevertheless, findings like these raise the disturbing possibility that some prosecutors define the victimization of whites, especially when African Americans are perpetrators, as more serious criminal events than the comparable victimization of African Americans.

Plea Bargaining

No court practice arouses public anger more than the offering of concessions to defendants who plead guilty. Plea bargaining has a long if not venerable tradition in American courts (Monkkonen, 1991). Even at the turn of the century, jury trials were the exception rather than the rule in rural and urban courts (see Table 16.1). In the public mind, though, neither justice nor the victim's interests are served by secret negotiations that leave defendants with lesser charges or more lenient sentences than they would have received had a jury found them guilty. Knowledge of the social world of our courts allows us to understand this often-maligned process. Clearly, plea bargaining allows some defendants to receive less than the maximum charge or penalty possible. This occurs because all parties involved—prosecutor, defense, and defendant—have identified factors that demonstrate the defendant simply does not deserve the maximum. It is possible, for example, that not all elements of the crimes charged (e.g., possession of a weapon) can be proven beyond a reasonable doubt. Thus, prosecutors do not engage in plea bargaining for the purely self-interested motive of saving their understaffed offices time and money, but rather to produce punishments that are certain and proportionate. To arrive at such punishments, they and defense counsel jointly determine the facts of the case and the relevant law that applies to the facts (McCoy, 1993; Emmelman, 1996; Frohmann, 1997). The strength of the evidence and seriousness of the offense are cornerstones of that determination. As we will see, defendants who gain the most during plea bargaining are less-serious, marginal offenders; serious offenders with prior records gain little (Smith, 1986).

Light Cases Most plea bargains are straightforward and implicit because the case is light (minor) and evidence of the defendant's guilt is clear (Mather, 1979). In these situations, standardized but unstated "recipes" are available, and explicit bargaining is unnecessary (Sudnow, 1965; Maynard, 1988). For example, to determine whether the serious charge of burglary can be reduced to the less serious offense of petty theft, public defenders examine the case to see if it resembles the routinely encountered or typical burglary: Who was involved? Where did the offense occur? How much property was taken? Answers to these and other questions determine whether the case is a typical burglary. If it is, the public defender, on the client's behalf, will withdraw the original plea of not guilty and enter a plea of guilty to petty theft, a change the prosecutor usually accepts readily.

Serious Cases Serious cases are different because the nature of the offense and the existence of a prior record make lengthy incarceration a distinct possibility. In these situations, bargaining is more explicit, and the prosecutor and defense counsel may reach a compromise only after lengthy negotiations (Emmelman, 1996; Frohmann, 1997). Attributes of defendants, victims, and the offense are selectively brought into play in an effort to provide what both prosecutor and defense counsel agree is a just or deserved outcome. Numerous concessions may be offered. The prosecutor may recommend to the judge a lenient sentence, reduce the severity of the charge, dismiss additional charges, or dismiss other cases pending against the defendant. More concessions are offered if the evidence is weak or complex, both of which would consume too many of the court's limited resources (Jacoby et al., 1982; McDonald, 1985). In contrast, fewer concessions are offered if the offense is particularly serious or if the defendant used a weapon or had a long serious prior record (McDonald, 1985; Holmes et al., 1987). Not surprisingly, then, defendants with lengthy prior records are more likely to insist on trial (Myers and LaFree, 1982), especially if they have been charged with a serious offense (Myers, 1982). In these situations, defendants may feel that they have little to lose if the jury convicts, but much to gain if it acquits. The "Perry Mason" case, with a serious crime and reasonable doubt about the defendant's guilt, rarely is encountered but presents the most difficult situations for defense counsel and prosecutors to resolve (Mather, 1979).

Other Factors Apart from evidence of the defendant's dangerousness and culpability, prosecutors consider other factors when offering concessions and assessing the feasibility of trial. The defendant's gender and race affect the terms of the plea, but not as strongly or consistently as do the defendant's offense and prior record. In some jurisdictions, male defendants obtain more favorable charge and sentence reductions

Table 16.1   Offenses of Felons Convicted in State Courts, by Type of Conviction, 1994

MOST SERIOUS CONVICTION OFFENCE	PERCENT OF FELONS CONVICTED BY				
		Trial			
	Total	Total	Jury	Bench	Guilty plea
	%	%	%	%	%
All offenses	100	11	6	5	89
Violent offenses	100	20	14	6	80
Murder[a]	100	42	35	7	58
Rape	100	25	19	6	75
Robbery	100	15	10	5	85
Aggravated assault	100	18	11	7	82
Other violent[b]	100	22	15	7	78
Property offenses	100	10	5	5	90
Burglary	100	11	6	5	89
Larceny[c]	100	10	4	6	90
Fraud[d]	100	9	5	4	91
Drug offenses	100	8	3	5	92
Possession	100	6	1	5	94
Trafficking	100	10	4	6	90
Weapons offenses	100	10	5	5	90
Other offenses[e]	100	10	5	5	90

SOURCE: Adapted from Largan and Brown, 1997: 9.

Note: Data on conviction type were available for 676,809 cases.

[a]Includes non-negligent manslaughter.

[b]Includes offenses such as negligent manslaughter, sexual assault, and kidnapping.

[c]Includes motor vehicle theft.

[d]Includes forgery and embezzlement.

[e]Composed of nonviolent offenses such as receiving stolen property and vandalism.

than do females (Figueira-McDonough, 1985). In New York, charge reductions do not vary by race if the case is disposed of early in the process. But if African-American defendants do not plead guilty at their first presentation, they receive less-favorable reductions than comparable whites (Bernstein et al., 1977). Elsewhere, African Americans and Hispanic Americans receive more favorable charge reductions than do whites (Holmes et al., 1987). Similarly, research suggests that some types of defendants are more likely than are others to go to trial. These include African Americans charged with felonies, with property crimes, or with victimizing whites (Myers, 1980, 1982; Myers and LaFree, 1982). Prosecutors also prefer going to trial if the victim appears especially credible and blameless. For example, trial is more likely if the victim is white, employed, a stranger to the defendant, better educated than the defendant, and untainted with allegations of misconduct before the offense (Myers and Hagan, 1979; LaFree, 1980; Myers, 1980; Bienen et al., 1988).

Prosecutorial Approaches

Throughout the United States, prosecutors may make the same set of decisions, but they do not make them in precisely the same manner. The weight given to evidence differs (Jacoby et al., 1982; Feeney et al., 1983), as do plea-bargaining strategies (McDonald, 1985; Nardulli et al., 1988; Flemming, 1990; McCoy, 1993) and use of the death penalty (Paternoster, 1991). Screening and plea-bargaining policies vary in part because the communities that prosecutors serve differ, often dramatically (Jacoby et al., 1982; Nardulli et al., 1988; Flemming, 1990; Ulmer, 1997b). In some of the largest urban offices, for example, prosecutors use a legal sufficiency policy: They accept cases only if the evidence supports the charge; other considerations are irrelevant. Because initial screening in these jurisdictions is not stringent, prosecutors use various dispositions, including charge bargaining and dismissals at preliminary hearings and trials. In overloaded courts with scarce resources, prosecutors pursue a system efficiency policy: Screening is more stringent, and the emphasis is on early and speedy dispositions by whatever means available. Dismissals are infrequent, and plea bargains to reduce charges are common. Yet another policy, defendant rehabilitation, emphasizes diversion from the criminal justice system. Decisions are based more on attributes of the defendant than on the offense

per se. Fewer cases are accepted but, once filed, they are pursued vigorously. Screening and plea-bargaining strategies are also dictated by the prosecutor's position within the courtroom workgroup (Flemming, 1990). Some prosecutors are courthouse insurgents, who radically alter office policies in a conscientious attempt to change a tradition that placed their office in a subservient position to judges and defense counsel. They may direct assistant district attorneys to screen cases loosely but to follow strict guidelines for accepting guilty pleas. In sum, then, prosecutors' decisions are shaped not simply by the case before them, but by the broader court and community contexts that surround them.

Assessing Plea-Bargaining Reform

As noted earlier, plea bargaining is a longstanding tradition in America's courts. Its unpopularity with the public has led several jurisdictions to ban or limit the practice. Their success is mixed (McCoy, 1993). In 1985, for example, Alaska's attorney general ordered prosecutors to desist from reducing or dismissing charges as inducements to a guilty plea. To minimize sentence bargaining, prosecutors were not permitted to recommend sentences to the judge. Despite some circumvention in the form of judicial negotiation with defense counsel, the ban appears to have been successful. Needless to say, the state of Alaska is hardly typical. Its state attorney sets prosecution policy for the entire state, felony caseloads are small, and oil revenues allowed courts to absorb the costly jury trials that resulted from the plea-bargaining ban.

Elsewhere, efforts to restrict or eliminate charge bargaining have simply shifted discretion to judges, who engage in implicit or explicit bargaining over the sentence. For example,

California's ban on plea bargaining in cases involving twenty-five serious felonies shifted negotiations to the lower courts, where negotiation occurred over what charges to file (McCoy, 1993). As a result, prosecutors screened cases more stringently, filed only those that met the convictability standard, and obtained and reviewed evidence on these cases earlier in the process. Lower court judges became more powerful because they could control plea negotiations and set the sentence, subject to higher court ratification. This shift in the balance of power between prosecutors and lower court judges created few problems. As members of the courtroom workgroup, judges and prosecutors had usually agreed on the "going rate," the range of acceptable sentences for a given offense, long before the reform was instituted.

Thus, plea bargaining appears destined to remain the disposition the public loves to hate. Attempts to eliminate it are short-lived and ineffective, in large part because the alternative—a jury trial—is simply too uncertain, too expensive, and often unwarranted. We now turn our attention to the second major court figure, the judge, who must face not only the convicted offender and defense attorney but also the public, the prosecutor, and the probation department, all of whom may have strong opinions about the kind of punishment the offender deserves.

THE SENTENCING JUDGE

As never before, the public, politicians, and legislators are keeping a watchful eye on the behavior of judges responsible for punishing offenders. For decades, the most common criticism was that judges had entirely too much discretion. Their broad freedom to impose sen-

tences left too much room for lenience that was undeserved, for discrimination against minorities, and for the disparate treatment of similar offenders. To curtail judicial discretion, legislatures across the United States have increased penalties, mandated minimum sentences, and required judges to sentence within specific guidelines. As a result, today's judges face a quite different environment than they did twenty-five years ago.

Empirical research cannot assess the claim that judges are too lenient, because allegations of lenience are based on value judgments about the punishment offenders should receive. Research can, nevertheless, assess precisely *how* judges sentence. It can determine whether judges base decisions on inappropriate considerations and whether they are inconsistent in their application of sentences. As will become clear, sentencing behavior is most strongly determined by factors commonly regarded or required by law as legally relevant. Chief among these are the nature of the offense and the offender's prior record. Factors of doubtful legitimacy (for example, gender and age) or of clear illegitimacy (for example, race) play smaller and intermittent roles during sentencing. As alluded to previously, judges also consider previous outcomes and decisions—such as recommendations from prosecutors and probation officers, the offender's pretrial release status, and whether the defendant pleaded guilty or was convicted at trial. These previous decisions are especially crucial because they are major conduits through which factors of questionable legitimacy enter the sentencing process. Finally, most judges are elected officials and, as creatures of their environment, attach different significance to the offender's identity and behavior. Judicial and community attributes affect sentencing indirectly, then, by determining the criteria judges consider appropriate when sentencing and the weight that they attach to these criteria. The following sections consider each of these generalizations in greater detail.

The Role of the Offense and Prior Record

The most striking and consistent finding of empirical research is that the offense and the offender's prior criminal record are pivotal considerations during sentencing (Blumstein et al., 1983). This is true both in courts of general jurisdiction and in courts with jurisdiction over misdemeanors (Neubauer, 1996). It is true in highly bureaucratized courts as well as those that are less bureaucratized (Dixon, 1995). Finally, offense and prior record are dominant considerations in states without guidelines as well as in states whose laws curtail judicial discretion during sentencing (Myers and Talarico, 1987; Kramer and Steffensmeier, 1993).

Even though judges invariably consider the offense and the offender's prior record, they do not attach precisely the same weight to them. Though not in a consistent pattern, judges do attach greater weight to a prior criminal record if the offender is African American and lesser weight if the offender is white (Welch et al., 1984; Miethe and Moore, 1986; Nelson, 1994). Even in a state with sentencing guidelines (Pennsylvania), the seriousness of the offense matters more during the sentencing of male offenders than it does during the sentencing of female offenders (Ulmer, 1997b). In federal courts, the opposite appears to be the case. Judges weight the offense and prior record more heavily for female offenders than for comparable male offenders (Albonetti, 1998).

The precise significance of the offense also depends on where and when sentencing occurs (Myers and Talarico, 1987). In Georgia, for example, violent and drug offenders are more likely than the average offender to be sentenced to prison. Both groups of offenders are at an even greater disadvantage in counties facing serious crime problems. Judges in these counties are much more likely than judges in counties with less-serious crime problems to sentence violent and drug offenders to prison. Serious offenders also tend to receive longer prison terms than less-serious offenders. Nevertheless, they are at a particular disadvantage in communities experiencing high rates of unemployment. In these communities, judges punish serious offenders more severely than do judges in communities where unemployment is not a problem.

In short, then, judges base sentencing decisions on two major factors of legal relevance: offense and prior record. Each factor is likely to become even more important as states increasingly adopt guidelines that require judges to consider these factors. Guidelines vary, however, in how finely the distinction between offenses is drawn (Tonry, 1996). Some collapse crimes into ten to twelve categories, whereas federal guidelines have forty offense levels. Guidelines also differ in how prior record is measured. Most consider prior convictions, but some guidelines give greater weight to convictions for felonies rather than for misdemeanors, violence rather than theft, and more-recent rather than less-recent crimes. Regardless of how they are measured, both the offense and the defendant's prior criminal record are outcomes of past decisions made by police officers, prosecutors, and the courts. To the extent that any of these decisions were based on inappropriate considerations, they incorporate previous discrimination. Despite their legal relevance, then, offense and prior record can operate as conduits through which legally suspect factors, such as race and social class, indirectly affect sentences. Thus, the line that demarcates the legally relevant from the legally irrelevant or inappropriate is neither a hard nor a fast one.

The Role of Social Status

In states with sentencing guidelines, the law is clear: The offender's social or economic position in society has no place in the calculus judges may use during sentencing. In states without guidelines, the law offers judges little or no guidance. Although judges may agree among themselves that race is a morally objectionable criterion on which to base sentences, they may disagree about the acceptability of using other social background information (e.g., social class) to determine which specific punishment will serve to deter or rehabilitate. The issue of central importance, then, is the extent to which judges actually do take into account factors whose relevance is clearly illegitimate or of doubtful legitimacy. Of interest in the following sections are the offender's race, ethnicity, sex, and socioeconomic status and attributes of the victim.

Race For over half a century, research has sought to estimate the amount of race discrimination in sentencing (Ulmer, 1997b). Only recently has analysis become sophisticated enough to disentangle the effect of race from those legally relevant factors with which it is often confounded. Overall, race now is not consistently important. Rather, it plays a role during sentencing only under certain conditions (Spohn, 1995). Put differently, the extent to which race matters depends on the offense, other offender attributes, the victim, and the nature of the court and surrounding community.

Race appears to matter more for offenders convicted of less-serious crimes. In these cases

judges have greater freedom to exercise discretion, which often places African Americans at a disadvantage compared to whites. Where the offense is serious, though, judges are heavily constrained by the law (Spohn and Cederblom, 1991). Race differences often, but not always, subside. The nature of the offense matters as well. Zatz (1984), for example, found no race differences in the punishment of property offenders. Yet among violent offenders, significant race differences did exist. Surprisingly, African Americans did not always receive harsher punishment than comparable non-African-Americans. African-American men convicted of rape received longer sentences than did white rapists; African Americans convicted of homicide received significantly *shorter* sentences than did comparable whites or Hispanic Americans. Peterson and Hagan (1984) document parallel differences in the sentences imposed on drug offenders in federal courts. During the antidrug crusades of the 1970s, African-American drug users were sentenced more leniently than were whites because they were perceived as victims of traffickers. Sharp race differences emerged only for African-American traffickers, whom judges considered doubly villainous for victimizing fellow African Americans, who were already disadvantaged socially and economically.

Other studies indicate that the effect of race depends on whom the offender chooses to victimize. Miethe (1987) found no significant race differences in sentences among offenders who victimized someone they knew. Yet among offenders who victimized a stranger, African Americans were more likely than whites to be incarcerated. In general, African Americans who victimize whites seem to receive harsher penalties (Myers and LaFree, 1982; Walsh, 1987). Indeed, in capital homicide cases, the race of the victim is often more significant than the race of the offender (Paternoster, 1991) and may reflect not only the devalued status of African-American victims but also the presumably greater threat to society posed by the victimization of members of a socially advantaged group (Hawkins, 1987). The race of both the offender and the victim is also a key consideration in rape cases, where it determines whether judges search for further evidence that the offender committed a "genuine" rape and therefore deserves severe punishment (Spohn and Spears, 1996). In cases involving white offenders and victims, for example, judges appear to be uninterested in the victim's relationship with the offender or in the riskiness of her behavior prior to the rape. In cases involving African-American offenders and victims, though, judges consider the victim's relationship with the offender. African-American men who raped African-American women they did not know are punished more harshly than those who victimized an acquaintance. In cases involving African-American offenders and white victims, judges carefully scrutinize the victim's behavior before the rape. African Americans who raped white women who were taking risks (e.g., drinking in a bar alone) receive shorter sentences than African Americans who raped white women who engaged in no risk-taking behavior.

Race differences during sentencing also depend on the court and the broader community (Myers and Talarico, 1987). Southern Baptist and fundamentalist judges, for example, are more likely than their colleagues to incarcerate African Americans; but they also impose significantly shorter sentences on them (Myers, 1988). At this point, it is unclear whether African-American judges treat African-American offenders more leniently than do their white colleagues. Spohn (1990) found that African-American and white judges do not sentence differently. Other researchers discovered that African-American judges ignored race until they set prison terms. For this decision, African-American judges showed lenience toward African-American offenders. The sentences they imposed were shorter than the sentences their white colleagues imposed on comparable African Americans.

Judges in rural communities also sentence African-American and white offenders differently than do urban judges. The original expectation was that discrimination would occur more frequently in rural areas, whereas the bureaucratization and impersonality of urban courts would not permit race considerations to intrude. Some evidence supports this expectation, but it is by no means conclusive. The anonymity of some urban and suburban courts appears to allow personal preferences to intrude. Race differences are more pronounced in other communities as well, in particular those that are racially unequal and predominantly African-American. Interestingly, however, in these contexts, white rather than African-American offenders are at a disadvantage (Myers and Talarico, 1986a, 1986b; Myers, 1987).

In sum, the significance attached to race varies, and African Americans are often but not always punished more severely than whites. The precise role played by race may be even more elusive, however. African-American defendants are significantly less likely than comparable whites to be released prior to trial and to secure the services of a private attorney (Holmes et al., 1996). Although their inability to hire private counsel reflects a comparative lack of economic resources, the difficulty African-American defendants have in achieving release could be due in part to the different way they are treated by lower court judges when setting bail. For the most part, bail decisions depend on the defendant's dangerousness, which is inferred from the seriousness of the offense and the defendant's prior record (Neubauer, 1996). In assessing dangerousness, judges give more weight to the prior record of African-American defendants and less weight to the prior record of comparable white defendants (Albonetti et al., 1989). Bail decisions also depend on the risk of flight to avoid trial, which is inferred from the defendant's ties to the community. In assessing ties, judges give more weight to the education and income of white defendants and less weight to the same accomplishments of African-American defendants. The overweighting of indicators of dangerousness and the underweighting of community ties could explain the difficulty African-American defendants have in obtaining release pending resolution of their case. Whatever its source, the inability of African Americans to achieve release and to secure private counsel ultimately places them at a disadvantage during sentencing: Judges impose more severe sentences on offenders currently in jail and those represented by public counsel.

Have guidelines eliminated the last vestiges of racial differences in sentencing? Apparently not. Race clearly diminishes in importance with the use of guidelines (McDonald and Carlson, 1993; Tonry, 1996; Ulmer, 1997b), but wherever discretion remains, race differences emerge. African Americans are still more likely to be incarcerated and to receive longer sentences than comparable whites (Tonry, 1996; Albonetti, 1997; Ulmer, 1997b; Albonetti, 1998). Where guidelines allow departures from the stipulated disposition or sentence, race operates indirectly. African Americans are at a comparative disadvantage because judges depart from guidelines more often when sentencing whites than when sentencing comparable African

Americans (Kramer and Steffensmeier 1993; Albonetti, 1997).

Ethnicity Only recently have researchers begun to consider whether the offender's ethnic background matters during sentencing (see Wooldredge, 1998, for a review). In some jurisdictions, Hispanic Americans are punished no differently than comparable whites, whereas in others, even under sentencing guidelines, Hispanic Americans receive harsher punishment (Holmes et al., 1996; Albonetti, 1997). Like race, ethnicity determines the weight judges attach to other factors such as the offense, prior record, and background of the offender. For example, Hispanic-American drug offenders are punished more harshly than their white counterparts. In contrast, Hispanic Americans convicted of an assault or homicide are punished less harshly than comparable whites (Unnever, 1982; Bienen et al., 1988; Unnever and Hembroff, 1988). A record of prior incarcerations puts all offenders at a disadvantage, but Hispanic Americans pay a higher price: Their prison sentences are longer than the sentences judges impose on whites with comparable records (Wooldredge, 1998). Similarly, lower-income Hispanic Americans receive longer terms of incarceration than lower-income whites. Finally, ethnic background influences sentences indirectly (Holmes et al., 1996). Hispanic Americans are less likely than comparable whites to secure private counsel. In two ways, this inability works to their disadvantage during sentencing. First, offenders with privately retained counsel are sentenced more leniently than offenders with assigned counsel. Second, private counsel enhances a defendant's ability to secure release prior to trial. Upon conviction, offenders who achieved release before trial or plea bargaining are sentenced more leniently than comparable offenders who remained in jail. Directly, indirectly, or in combination with other factors, then, the offender's ethnicity is sometimes, though not always, a significant consideration during sentencing.

Gender In state and federal courts, women are sentenced more leniently than are comparable men, particularly for the initial incarceration decision (Daly and Bordt, 1995; Ulmer, 1997b). This continues to be the case even in jurisdictions that have instituted guidelines to reduce gender disparities (Steffensmeier et al., 1993; Ulmer 1997b; Albonetti, 1998). Lenience toward female offenders is both a recent (Feeley and Little, 1991; Boritch, 1992) and contingent phenomenon (Albonetti, 1998). It depends, for example, on whether the female offender has dependent children. "Familial paternalism" is the term for the judge's assessment of the greater social and financial costs of replacing women's labor in the family. Familial paternalism also could help account for other trends noted in the literature: the greater importance judges place on the marital status of female rather than male offenders (Bernstein et al., 1979) and the lenience some judges extend only to African-American women (Gruhl et al., 1984).

The significance of gender also varies as a function of the court and the surrounding community. Of particular interest is research that examines whether gender differences depend in sentencing on the sex of the judge. In a northeastern jurisdiction, male but not female judges sentenced female offenders more leniently than comparable male offenders (Gruhl et al., 1981). Yet, in a southeastern state, male judges were more punitive than female judges toward female offenders (Myers and Talarico, 1987). Female offenders are also more likely to receive lenience in communities that cannot or do not wish to bear the costs of incarcerating large numbers of women with families. These include urban areas and communities with high income inequality and serious unemployment (Myers and Talarico, 1986b, 1987; Myers, 1987; Daly and Bordt, 1995).

Finally, gender plays a more diffuse and cumulative role because it influences the prior outcomes on which judges rely during sentencing. In particular, female offenders are more likely than comparable males to receive probation-officer recommendations for lenience (Myers, 1979), to secure private attorneys (Holmes et al., 1996), and to be released prior to trial (Holmes et al., 1996). Each outcome ultimately works to their advantage later in the process, because judges impose more lenient sentences on offenders with private counsel, those who secured pretrial release, and those for whom lenience was recommended.

Socioeconomic Status Researchers have only recently turned their attention to the impact that the offender's socioeconomic status has on sentences (D'Alessio and Stolzenberg, 1993). Lower-status offenders tend to receive more severe sentences than comparable higher-status offenders, but this relationship is neither consistent nor strong. Status is important for some types of offenders (e.g., narcotics) and not for others. Of greater significance is its adverse effect on several previous decisions that judges consider important during sentencing. Among these are whether the offender retained private counsel or pretrial release (Holmes et al., 1996), the seriousness of the conviction charge (Hagan and Parker, 1985), and the probation officer's recommendation (Unnever et al., 1980; Drass and Spencer, 1987).

Most of the research cited above was conducted in state courts, where white collar offenders are rarely encountered. It is possible, then, that the social class standing of offenders varies too little to affect sentences consistently. Federal courts prosecute a wider variety of offenders, thus allowing us to estimate better the role of status during sentencing. Even here, though, there is no consistent evidence of lenience toward higher-status offenders. Instead, the role that status plays depends on several factors. Among these are political events, the U.S. attorney's stance toward white collar offenders, and the nature of the offense itself. After Watergate, for example, white collar offenders in prestigious occupations were punished more severely than offenders whose occupations were less prestigious (Wheeler et al., 1982). At the same time, offenders with irreproachable backgrounds (for example, stable marriages and religious involvement) were treated more leniently. These findings applied to large urban districts that prosecuted a variety of white collar offenders. In a district that more closely approximates the average in size and caseload, the offender's status had no effect on sentencing (Benson and Walker, 1988).

The Victim During Sentencing

Though once central to criminal prosecution, the crime victim has often been neglected by both judges and prosecutors. Since the 1970s, state and federal governments have begun to redress this neglect by providing victims with assistance during prosecution and giving them the opportunity to affect sentencing upon conviction (Schmalleger, 1997). The majority of states have passed victims' rights amendments, and all states and federal courts allow or mandate victim-impact statements during sentencing. These written documents describe the losses, suffering, and trauma experienced by the victim or the victim's survivors; they are submitted directly to the judge or to probation officers in charge of developing pre-sentence investigation reports. As yet, their precise impact on sentences is unknown. Preliminary indications suggest that these statements have little effect because judges and prosecutors already have established ways of sentencing (Davis and Smith, 1994).

Although judges seldom consider the crime's impact on the victim during sentencing, they do nevertheless attend to other attributes of the victim. As noted earlier, the race of the victim becomes important during the sentencing of homicide and rape offenders. In general, offenders who victimize women are punished more severely than offenders who victimized men (Myers, 1979; Hagan, 1982). So, too, are those who victimize strangers (Spohn and Spears, 1996). It merits emphasis that the role that victim characteristics play during sentencing is neither constant nor simple. It is more prominent in jurisdictions where probation officers recommend sentences to the judge and in cases in which the judge has had contact with the victim during a trial (Myers, 1979, 1981). Recall also that judges faced with sentencing a rape offender attend not only to the race of the victim, but also to the victim's behavior and relationship with the offender before the rape (Spohn and Spears, 1996).

The Community and Sentencing

Although generally aware that the social and political environment affects judicial behavior, researchers have yet to establish the extent of its impact with any precision. The choice of sanctions for misdemeanants appears to be affected by economic resources in the community (Ragona and Ryan, 1984). Not surprisingly, fines are preferred in counties with limited economic resources and jail space. Judges in federal courts also are sensitive to community influences (for example, antidrug crusades) and events (for example, abortion clinic bombings). Events such as war foster more punitive sentences for draft offenders (*Columbia Journal of Law and Social Problems,* 1969), and they influence the relevance of race and religion as well. Hagan and Bernstein (1979) characterize the period between 1963 and 1968 as one of uncompromisingly coercive control of draft resisters. Antidraft demonstrations occurred frequently, and editorials advocated strict enforcement of Selective Service laws. During this period, African-American draft resisters were more likely than white draft resisters to be incarcerated, as were conscientious objectors such as Jehovah's Witnesses. Between 1969 and 1976, demonstrations became less frequent, and editorials urged draft law reform, noting the wastefulness of imprisoning draft resisters. During this period, judges exercised selective co-optive control, reserving harsh punishment for offenders who objected to the draft more publicly and demonstratively.

Not all judges respond equally to community pressures. Gibson (1980), for example, found that only certain judges incorporate information about the community crime rate into their sentencing decisions, in particular, those who have greater contact with their constituency, who have experienced electoral defeat, or who have assumed a delegate role orientation (which considers it appropriate to be influenced by the environment). Similarly, public preferences for certain sanctions become more important if the judge is elected (Ryan, 1980). Finally, community factors tend to affect

judicial sentencing behavior only where sentencing law leaves judges with some discretion (Miethe and Moore, 1986; Ulmer, 1997b).

Sentencing Reform and Its Impact

No reform has generated more controversy than the sentencing guidelines that went into effect in federal courts in 1987. For many critics, federal guidelines place judges in a straitjacket, rendering them unable to consider factors that lie outside the sentencing grid but nonetheless are essential for an assessment of the offender's blameworthiness (Tonry, 1996). In contrast, state-level guidelines enjoy widespread support and have achieved some, but not all, of their goals. In curbing judicial discretion, sentences and even plea-bargaining practices often become more uniform and consistent (Tonry, 1996; Ulmer, 1997b). The offense and offender's prior record are clearly the most salient considerations during sentencing; the offender's race, ethnicity, sex, and social status recede into the background (Tonry, 1996). Although much evaluation remains to be done, it has already become clear that no guidelines, however strict, can eliminate unwarranted disparity or possible discrimination entirely or permanently (Ulmer, 1997b). Guidelines must be applied by court officials in specific cases, and their application depends on the workgroup's relationships with each other and with the outside world. As long as guidelines provide a menu of options (e.g., sentencing ranges or departures from guidelines), judges can use them in various ways: to reward defendants who plead guilty, to punish defendants who insist on a jury trial and are convicted, or to offset prosecutor demands for punishment that is harsher than the judge considers warranted (Ulmer and Kramer, 1998).

Even in states with guidelines, judges exercise broad discretion over unregulated sanctions (e.g., those that fall short of incarceration) and over unregulated offenders (i.e., misdemeanants). Most offenders, then, continue to face the twin prospects of disparity and discrimination.

What of other attempts to alter the sentencing process? Recall that many states stiffened penalties by introducing mandatory minimums or longer sentences for repeat offenders. Among the most publicized reforms is "three strikes and you're out" legislation, which in some states mandates a life sentence without parole for offenders convicted of a third felony. Two rationales underlie the imposition of tougher penalties: deterrence and the selective incapacitation of the small number of repeat offenders who presumably are disproportionately responsible for higher crime rates. In general, efforts to make punishment more certain and harsh have fared poorly (Tonry, 1996). Though three-strikes legislation has not overwhelmed the court system as some had predicted (Clark et al., 1998), a recent assessment of three-strikes legislation in California, which has the highest number of offenders prosecuted under the law, concluded that serious crime rates have not fallen significantly (Stolzenberg and D'Alessio, 1997).

CONCLUSION

It is relatively easy to criticize America's prosecutors and judges and to fear that they abuse their broad discretionary powers. But as this review indicates, it is exceedingly difficult to substantiate criticisms and fears with reliable data about how judges and prosecutors actually behave. Vindictive prosecutors and discriminatory judges surely exist, but the sheer diversity of the American court system makes it extremely difficult to document the precise extent of abuses or to identify exactly where such officials are likely to be found. We do know that they are unlikely to be common. But disparities and discrimination may well be masked behind a legitimate reliance on decisions reached by others, whether it be a prior record of convictions, the defendant's pretrial release status, the prosecution charge itself, or the recommendations of other court officials. A reliance on past decisions both cloaks and legitimates early discrimination, thus eliminating the need for it later in the process.

Although the lot of the researcher is not an easy one, the public and its elected representatives face an even more difficult task, for it is their responsibility to develop and monitor policies that prevent or eliminate abuses of discretionary power. Reforms are likely to be unnecessary or unrealistic unless they are grounded in a clear understanding of how prosecutors and judges work. As this chapter has shown, we have only begun to provide that understanding.

DISCUSSION QUESTIONS

1. What is the prosecutor's role in the court system? What is the role of the defense attorney in the court system? Discuss the relationship between the two attorneys and the judge in the administration of justice. How adversarial is our court system?

2. What is the purpose of the grand jury? To what extent do prosecutors influence the work of the grand jury?

3. Myers describes four elements that influence a prosecutor's decision to go forward with a case. Discuss these elements and comment on the role that characteristics of the victim play in prosecutorial decisions.

4. What is plea bargaining and what influences it?

5. Does plea bargaining provide just outcomes? Discuss the various attempts that have been made to reform plea bargaining. Can it be eliminated?

6. Judges are criticized often for their sentencing decisions. Discuss the factors that enter into the sentencing process. How important are the guilty party's sociodemographic attributes—gender, race, social class—in influencing the sentence?

REFERENCES

Albonetti, C. A. 1986. "Criminality, Prosecutorial Screening, and Uncertainty: Toward a Theory of Discretionary Decision-Making in Felony Cases." *Criminology* 24: 623–644.

———. 1987. "Prosecutorial Discretion: The Effects of Uncertainty." *Law & Society Review* 21: 291–313.

———. 1997. "Sentencing under the Federal Sentencing Guidelines: Effects of Defendant Characteristics, Guilty Pleas, and Departures on Sentence Outcomes for Drug Offenses, 1991–1992." *Law & Society Review* 31: 789–822.

———. 1998. "The Role of Gender and Departures in the Sentencing of Defendants Convicted of a White-Collar Offense Under the Sentencing Guidelines." Pp. 3–48 in *Sociology of Crime, Law and Deviance, Vol. 1.* Edited by J. Ulmer. Stamford, CT: JAI Press.

Albonetti, C., R. Hauser, J. Hagan, and I. Nagel. 1989. "Criminal Justice Decision-Making as a Stratification Process: The Role of Race and Stratification Resources in Pretrial Release." *Journal of Quantitative Criminology* 5: 57–82.

Albonetti, C., and J. Hepburn. 1996. "Prosecutorial Discretion to Defer Criminalization: The Effects of Defendant's Ascribed and Achieved Status Characteristics." *Journal of Quantitative Criminology* 12: 63–81.

Benson, M. L., and E. Walker. 1988. "Sentencing the White-Collar Offender." *American Sociological Review* 53: 294–302.

Bernstein, I., J. Cardascia, and C. Ross. 1979. "Defendant's Sex and Criminal Court Decisions." Pp. 329–354 in *Discrimination in Organizations.* Edited by R. Alvarez, K. Lutterman, and Associates. San Francisco: Jossey-Bass.

Bienen, L., N. Weiner, D. Denno, P. Allison, and D. Mills. 1988. "The Reimposition of Capital Punishment in New Jersey: The Role of Prosecutorial Discretion." *Rutgers Law Review* 41: 27–37.

Blumstein, A., J. Cohen, S. E. Martin, and M. Tonry. 1983. *Research on Sentencing: The Search for Reform.* Vol. 1. Washington, DC: National Academy Press.

Boland, B., P. Mahanna, and R. Sones. 1992. *The Prosecution of Felony Arrests, 1988.* Washington, DC: U.S. Department of Justice, Bureau of Justice Statistics.

Boritch, H. 1992. "Gender and Criminal Court Outcomes: An Historical Analysis." *Criminology* 30: 293–325.

Carroll, M. 1985. "Wachtler Urges Legislators to Approve Court Changes." *New York Times,* April 23, B2.

Clark, J., J. Austin, and D. Henry. 1998. " 'Three Strikes and You're Out': Are Repeat Offender Laws Having Their Anticipated Effect?" *Judicature* 81: 144–149.

Columbia Journal of Law and Social Problems. 1969. "Sentencing Selective Service Violators: A Judicial Wheel of Fortune." 5: 164–196.

Court Statistics Project Staff. 1995. *State Court Caseload Statistics, 1994.* Williamsburg, VA: National Center for State Courts.

D'Alessio, S., and L. Stolzenberg. 1993. "Socioeconomic Status and the Sentencing of the Traditional Offender." *Journal of Criminal Justice* 21: 61–77.

Daly, K., and R. Bordt. 1995. "Sex Effects and Sentencing: An Analysis of the Statistical Literature." *Justice Quarterly* 12: 141–175.

Davis, R., and B. Smith. 1994. "The Effects of Victim Impact Statements on Sentencing Decisions: A Test in an Urban Setting." *Justice Quarterly* 11: 453–469.

DeFrances, C., S. Smith, and L. van der Does. 1996. *Prosecutors in State Courts, 1994.* Washington, DC: U.S. Department of Justice, Bureau of Justice Statistics.

Dixon, J. 1995. "The Organizational Context of Criminal Sentencing." *American Journal of Sociology* 100: 1157–1198.

Drass, K. A., and J. W. Spencer. 1987. "Accounting for Pre-sentencing Recommendations: Typologies and Probation Officers' Theory of Office." *Social Problems* 34: 277–293.

Emerson, D. D. 1983. *Grand Jury Reform: A Review of Key Issues.* Washington, DC: U.S. Department of Justice, National Institute of Justice.

Emerson, R., and B. Paley. 1992. "Organizational Horizons and Complaint-Filing." Pp. 231–247 in *The Uses of Discretion.* Edited by K. Hawkins. Oxford: Clarendon.

Emmelman, D. 1996. "Trial by Plea Bargain: Case Settlement as a Product of Recursive Decision-making." *Law & Society Review* 30: 335–360.

Feeley, M. M., and M. H. Lazerson. 1983. "Police-Prosecutor Relationships: An Interorganizational Perspective." Pp. 216–243 in *Empirical Theories about Courts.* Edited by K. O. Boyum and L. Mather. New York: Longman.

Feeley, M. M., and D. L. Little. 1991. "The Vanishing Female: The Decline of Women in the Criminal Process, 1687–1912." *Law & Society Review* 25: 719–757.

Feeney, F., F. Dill, and A. Weir. 1983. *Arrests Without Conviction: How Often They Occur and Why.* Washington, DC: Department of Justice, National Institute of Justice.

Figueira-McDonough, J. 1985. "Gender Differences in Informal Processing: A Look at Charge Bargaining and Sentence Reduction in Washington, DC." *Journal of Research in Crime and Delinquency* 22: 101–133.

Flemming, R. 1982. *Punishment Before Trial: An Organizational Perspective on Felony Bail Processes.* New York: Longman.

———. 1990. "The Political Styles and Organizational Strategies of American Prosecutors: Examples from Nine Courthouse Communities." *Law and Policy* 12: 25–50.

Flemming, R., P. Nardulli, and J. Eisenstein. 1992. *The Craft of Justice: Politics and Work in Criminal Court Communities.* Philadelphia: University of Pennsylvania Press.

Foley, L. A., and R. S. Powell. 1982. "The Discretion of Prosecutors, Judges, and Juries in Capital Cases." *Criminal Justice Review* 7: 16–22.

Frohmann, L. 1991. "Discrediting Victims' Allegations of Sexual Assault: Prosecutorial Accounts of Case Rejections." *Social Problems* 38: 213–226.

———. 1997. "Convictability and Discordant Locales: Reproducing Race, Class, and Gender Ideologies in Prosecutorial Decisionmaking." *Law & Society Review* 31: 531–555.

Gibson, J. L. 1980. "Environmental Constraints on the Behavior of Judges: A Representational Model of Judicial Decision Making." *Law & Society Review* 14: 343–370.

Gruhl, J., C. Spohn, and S. Welch. 1981. "Women as Policymakers: The Case of Trial Judges." *American Journal of Political Science* 25: 308–322.

———. 1984. "Women as Criminal Defendants: A Test for Paternalism." *Western Political Quarterly* 37: 456–467.

Hagan, J. 1982. "The Corporate Advantage: A Study of the Involvement of Corporate and Individual Victims in a Criminal Justice System." *Social Forces* 60: 993–1022.

Hagan, J., and I. N. Bernstein. 1979. "Conflict in Context: The Sanctioning of Draft Resisters, 1963–1976." *Social Problems* 29: 109–122.

Hagan, J., and P. Parker. 1985. "White-collar Crime and Punishment: The Class Structure and Legal Sanctioning of Securities Violations." *American Sociological Review* 50: 302–317.

Hawkins, D. 1987. "Beyond Anomalies: Rethinking the Conflict Perspective on Race and Criminal Punishment." *Social Forces* 65: 719–745.

Holmes, M. D., H. C. Daudistel, and R. A. Farrell. 1987. "Determinants of Charge Reductions and Final Dispositions in Cases of Burglary and Robbery." *Journal of Research in Crime and Delinquency* 24: 233–254.

Holmes, M., H. Hosch, H. Daudistel, D. Perez, and J. Graves. 1996. "Ethnicity, Legal Resources, and Felony Dispositions in Two Southwestern Jurisdictions." *Justice Quarterly* 13: 11–30.

Jacob, H. 1991. "Decision Making in Trial Courts." Pp. 211–233 in *The American Courts: A Critical Assessment.* Edited by J. Gates and C. Johnson. Washington, DC: CQ Press.

Jacoby, J. E., L. Mellon, E. Ratledge, and S. Turner. 1982. *Prosecutorial Decisionmaking: A National Study.* Washington, DC: U.S. Department of Justice, National Institute of Justice.

Kramer, J., and D. Steffensmeier. 1993. "Race and Imprisonment Decisions." *Sociological Quarterly* 34: 357–376.

LaFree, G. D. 1980. "Variables Affecting Guilty Pleas and Convictions in Rape Cases: Toward a Social Theory of Rape Processing." *Social Forces* 58: 833–850.

———. 1989. *Rape and Criminal Justice: The Social Construction of Sexual Assault.* Belmont, CA: Wadsworth.

Largan, P., and J. Brown. 1997. *Felony Sentences in State Courts, 1994.* Washington, DC: U.S. Department of Justice, Bureau of Justice Statistics.

Mather, L. M. 1979. *Plea Bargaining or Trial?* Lexington, MA: Heath.

Maynard, D. 1988. "Narratives and Narrative Structure in Plea Bargaining." *Law & Society Review* 22: 449–481.

McCoy, C. 1993. *Politics and Plea Bargaining: Victims' Rights in California.* Philadelphia: University of Pennsylvania Press.

McDonald, D., and K. Carlson. 1993. *Sentencing in the Federal Courts: Does Race Matter? The Transition to Sentencing Guidelines, 1986–1990. Summary.* Washington, DC: U.S. Department of Justice, Bureau of Justice Statistics.

McDonald, W. F. 1985. *Plea Bargaining: Critical Issues and Common Practices.* Washington, DC: U.S. Department of Justice, National Institute of Justice.

McIntyre, D., and D. Lippman. 1970. "Prosecutors and Disposition of Felony Cases." *American Bar Association Journal* 56: 1156.

Mecham, L. 1995. *Judicial Business of the United States Courts: 1994 Report of the Director.* Washington, DC: Administrative Office of the U.S. Courts.

Mecham, L. 1998. *Judicial Business of the United States Courts: 1997 Report of the Director.* Washington, DC: Administrative Office of the U.S. Courts.

Mellon, L. R., J. E. Jacoby, and M. A. Brewer. 1981. "The Prosecutor Constrained by His Environment: A New Look at Discretionary Justice in the United States." *Journal of Criminal Law and Criminology* 72: 52–81.

Miethe, T. D. 1987. "Stereotypical Conceptions and Criminal Processing: The Case of the Victim-Offender Relationship." *Justice Quarterly* 4: 571–593.

Miethe, T. D., and C. A. Moore. 1986. "Racial Differences in Criminal Processing: The Consequences of Model Selection on Conclusions about Differential Treatment." *Sociological Quarterly* 27: 217–237.

Monkkonen, E. (Ed.) 1991. *Crime and Justice in American History*. Vol. 2: *Courts and Criminal Procedure*. Westport, CT: Meckler.

Myers, M. A. 1979. "Offended Parties and Official Reactions: Victims and the Sentencing of Criminal Defendants." *Sociological Quarterly* 20: 529–540.

———. 1980. "Predicting the Behavior of Law: A Test of Two Models." *Law & Society Review* 14: 835–857.

———. 1981. "Judges, Juries and the Decision to Convict." *Journal of Criminal Justice* 9: 289–303.

———. 1982. "Common Law in Action: The Prosecution of Felonies and Misdemeanors." *Sociological Inquiry* 52: 1–15.

———. 1987. "Economic Inequality and Discrimination in Sentencing." *Social Forces* 65: 746–766.

———. 1988. "Social Background and the Sentencing Behavior of Judges." *Criminology* 26: 649–675.

Myers, M. A., and J. Hagan. 1979. "Private and Public Trouble: Prosecutors and the Allocation of Court Resources." *Social Problems* 26: 439–451.

Myers, M. A., and G. D. LaFree. 1982. "Sexual Assault and Its Prosecution: A Comparison with Other Crimes." *Journal of Criminal Law and Criminology* 73: 1282–1305.

Myers, M. A., and S. M. Talarico. 1986a. "The Social Contexts of Racial Discrimination in Sentencing." *Social Problems* 33: 236–251.

———. 1986b. "Urban Justice, Rural Justice? Urbanization and Its Effect on Sentencing." *Criminology* 24: 367–391.

———. 1987. *The Social Contexts of Criminal Sentencing*. New York: Springer-Verlag.

Nagel, I. H., and J. Hagan. 1983. "Gender and Crime: Offense Patterns and Criminal Court Sanctions." Pp. 91–144 in *Crime and Justice: An Annual Review of Research*. Vol. 4. Edited by M. Tonry and N. Morris. Chicago: University of Chicago Press.

Nardulli, P., J. Eisenstein, and R. Flemming. 1988. *The Tenor of Justice: Criminal Courts and the Guilty Plea Process*. Urbana: University of Illinois Press.

Nelson, J. 1994. "A Dollar or a Day: Sentencing Misdemeanants in New York State." *Journal of Research in Crime and Delinquency* 31: 183–201.

Neubauer, D. 1996. *America's Courts and the Criminal Justice System*. 5th ed. Belmont, CA: Wadsworth.

Neubauer, D. W. 1988. *America's Courts and the Criminal Justice System*. 3d ed. Pacific Grove, CA: Brooks/Cole.

Ostrom, B., and N. Kauder. 1996. *Examining the Work of State Courts, 1995: A National Perspective from the Court Statistics Project*. Williamsburg, VA: National Center for State Courts.

Paternoster, R. 1991. *Capital Punishment in America*. New York: Lexington Books.

Peterson, R. D., and J. Hagan. 1984. "Changing Conceptions of Race: Towards an Account of Anomalous Findings of Sentencing Research." *American Sociological Review* 49: 56–70.

Ragona, A. J., and J. P. Ryan. 1984. *Beyond the Courtroom: A Comparative Analysis of Misdemeanor Sentencing*. Washington, DC: U.S. Department of Justice, National Institute of Justice.

Rauma, D. 1984. "Going for the Gold: Prosecutorial Decision Making in Cases of Wife Assault." *Social Science Research* 13: 321–351.

Ryan, J. P. 1980. "Adjudication and Sentencing in a Misdemeanor Court: The Outcome Is the Punishment." *Law & Society Review* 15: 79–108.

Ryan, J. P., and J. J. Alfini. 1979. "Trial Judges' Participation in Plea Bargaining: An Empirical Perspective." *Law & Society Review* 13: 479–507.

Schmalleger, F. 1997. *Criminal Justice Today.* 4th ed. Upper Saddle River, NJ: Prentice Hall.

Schmidt, J., and E. H. Steury. 1989. "Prosecutorial Discretion in Filing Charges in Domestic Violence Cases." *Criminology* 27: 487–510.

Smith, D. 1986. "The Plea Bargaining Controversy." *Journal of Criminal Law and Criminology* 77: 949–957.

Smith, D. A. 1986. "The Neighborhood Context of Police Behavior." In *Communities and Crime.* Edited by A. Reiss and M. Tonry. Chicago: University of Chicago Press.

Spohn, C. 1995. "Courts, Sentencing, and Prisons." *Daedalus* 124: 119–143.

Spohn, C., and J. Cederblom. 1991. "Race and Disparities in Sentencing: A Test of the Liberation Hypothesis." *Justice Quarterly* 8: 305–327.

Spohn, C., and J. Spears. 1996. "The Effect of Offender and Victim Characteristics on Sexual Assault Case Processing Decisions." *Justice Quarterly* 13: 649–679.

Spohn, C., J. Gruhl, and S. Welch. 1987. "The Impact of the Ethnicity and Gender of Defendants on the Decision to Reject or Dismiss Felony Charges." *Criminology* 25: 175–191.

Stanko, E. A. 1981. "The Arrest Versus the Case: Some Observations on Police/District Attorney Interaction." *Urban Life* 9: 395–414.

———. 1981–1982. "The Impact of Victim Assessment on Prosecutors' Screening Decisions: The Case of the New York County District Attorney's Office." *Law & Society Review* 16: 225–239.

———. 1982. "Would You Believe This Woman? Prosecutorial Screening for 'Credible' Witnesses and a Problem of Justice." Pp. 63–82 in *Judge, Lawyer, Victim, Thief: Women, Gender Roles, and Criminal Justice.* Edited by N. Rafter and E. Stanko. Boston: Northeastern University Press.

Steffensmeier, D., J. Kramer, and C. Streifel. 1993. "Gender and Imprisonment Decisions." *Criminology* 31: 411–438.

Steinberg, A. 1984. "From Private Prosecution to Plea Bargaining: Criminal Prosecution, The District Attorney, and American Legal History." *Crime and Delinquency* 30: 568–592.

Stolzenberg, L., and S. D'Alessio. 1997. "'Three Strikes and You're Out': The Impact of California's New Mandatory Sentencing Law on Serious Crime Rates." *Crime and Delinquency* 43: 457–469.

Sudnow, D. 1965. "Normal Crimes: Sociological Features of the Penal Code in a Public Defender Office." *Social Problems* 12: 255–276.

Tonry, M. 1996. *Sentencing Matters.* New York: Oxford University Press.

Ulmer, J. 1997a. "The Organization and Consequences of Social Pasts in Criminal Courts." *Sociological Quarterly* 36: 587–605.

———. 1997b. *Social Worlds of Sentencing: Court Communities under Sentencing Guidelines.* Albany: State University of New York Press.

Ulmer, J., and J. Kramer. 1998. "The Use and Transformation of Formal Decision-Making Criteria: Sentencing Guidelines, Organizational Contexts, and Case Processing Strategies." *Social Problems* 45: 248–267.

Unnever, J. D. 1982. "Direct and Organizational Discrimination in the Sentencing of Drug Offenders." *Social Problems* 30: 212–225.

Unnever, J. D., and L. A. Hembroff. 1988. "The Prediction of Racial/Ethnic Sentencing Disparities: An Expectation States Approach." *Journal of Research in Crime and Delinquency* 25: 53–82.

Unnever, J. D., C. E. Frazier, and J. C. Henretta. 1980. "Race Differences in Criminal Sentencing." *Sociological Quarterly* 21: 197–205.

Walsh, A. 1987. "The Sexual Stratification Hypothesis and Sexual Assault in Light of the Changing Conceptions of Race." *Criminology* 25: 153–173.

Welch, S., J. Gruhl, and C. Spohn. 1984. "Sentencing: The Influence of Alternative Measures of Prior Record." *Criminology* 22: 215–227.

Wheeler, S., D. Weisburd, and N. Bode. 1982. "Sentencing the White-collar Offender: Rhetoric and Reality." *American Sociology Review* 47: 641–659.

Wooldredge, J. 1998. "Analytical Rigor in Studies of Disparities in Criminal Case Processing." *Journal of Quantitative Criminology* 14: 155–79.

Zatz, M. S. 1984. "Race, Ethnicity, and Determinate Sentencing." *Criminology* 22: 147–171.

Chapter Outline

17

Imprisonment
in the United States

FRANCIS T. CULLEN
University of Cincinnati

JODY L. SUNDT
Southern Illinois University at Carbondale

Prisons are a continuing source of curiosity and controversy. For most Americans, prisons remain much like a distant foreign land—exotic enough to excite our voyeuristic impulses but sufficiently unfamiliar to inspire trepidation, if not fear. We learn about prisons from television shows and movies, which often dramatize the chaos and dangerousness of these institutions, and from documentaries and exposés, which often emphasize the suffering and inhumanity that inmates endure. Some of us, like sightseers, are given "tours" of correctional facilities—usually with the warning not to interact with the "local" population. For most of us, however, in-person contact with prisons is limited to the images we gain peering through the windows of our vehicles as we drive by buildings surrounded by high fences topped by circles of razor-sharp wire. It is perhaps understandable that, as these sights slip from view, we are prompted to wonder, "What's it really like inside there?"

Prisons are more than secure fences or high walls and are more complex than can be captured from watching shows, which typically caricature inmate life, or even documentaries, which have only a short time to portray a multi-faceted reality. As Gresham Sykes (1958) demonstrated four decades ago, prisons are best seen as an ongoing "society of captives." Like other social settings, this society is marked by mundane daily routines, by conflict and cooperation, by continuity and change, and by human relationships—among inmates and between the kept and their keepers. But prisons are also distinctive communities whose fabric is affected by the inherent nature of confining people twenty-four hours a day within a limited space and by the characteristics of those who are forced to reside in close company. Various scholars have thus endeavored to describe and explain the nature of life in this unique, but still very human, community.

Since their inception, prisons have sparked enormous controversy. Americans have long looked to prisons to play a major role in reducing crime—whether this is by transforming law breakers into the law-abiding, scaring offenders straight, or caging the wicked so that they cannot victimize the community. But many Americans have the sneaking suspicion that prisons fall short of these lofty, if not unreasonable, expectations—that they may be the kind of social environments that make inmates more, rather than less, criminogenic (Cullen et al., forthcoming). If prisons are indeed imperfect, if not counterproductive, places, then we might question whether they should be the linchpin of the nation's strategy to fight crime. At present, this issue is particularly significant precisely because, year in and year out, the United States sets a new record high for the number of its citizens it places behind bars. For better or for worse, this "imprisonment binge," as Irwin and Austin (1994) call it, is the stubborn reality that must be confronted and debated in virtually every policy discussion about the contemporary American prison. Do we lock up too many or too few offenders? Should we allocate public monies to build more prisons or invest our funds in programs that attack the root causes of crime? These and similar considerations will surface throughout this chapter.

In the pages to follow, we will focus on seven main topics. We begin by tracing the origins of the American penitentiary and then, in the second section, we discuss some of the major forces that have shaped life within correctional institutions. The third section reports on the amazing growth of imprisonment in the United States and on the characteristics of the people who make up the nation's bulging prison population. The fourth section examines the nature of life in prisons' society of captives, including a discussion of inmate victimization. In the fifth part, we turn our attention to an often-omitted group—female inmates and the institutions in which they reside. In the sixth section, we shift direction and concentrate not on the kept but on their keepers—correctional officers. We end the chapter by considering the future of imprisonment in the United States.

PRISONS OVER TIME AND IN CONTEXT

The Birth of the Penitentiary

There is a natural tendency to assume that what we find in our world today has always, at least in some form, been with us. Existing social realities are often taken for granted. In the case of the prison system, however, this assumption would be erroneous. When the first settlers from Europe came to North America, they did not quickly build jail cells in which to house those who would inevitably flaunt the law. Of course, they lacked the resources to construct prisons and then to feed, clothe, and guard offenders—all expensive propositions. But the major barrier to using prisons was not financial; it was conceptual. To the colonists, it would not have made sense to place offenders in a building with bars and locks for the purpose of punishment or reform.

Instead, they used types of punishments that conformed to the nature of their community and to how they understood their world. In colonial America, law breakers with property and means were usually penalized with fines. Less affluent offenders were placed in the stocks or pillory, whipped, and/or branded with a letter that signified their crime (e.g., a "t" for a thief). Repeat offenders were likely to be banished into the wilderness or sent to the gallows. All punishments were carried out in public (Earle, 1969; Rothman, 1995).

This societal reaction to offenders made sense for two reasons. First, because the colonists lived in small, self-contained communities, offenders shamed by being punished in public were unable to escape the watchful, if not scornful, eyes of their neighbors. Second, the colonists equated crime with sin. In their religious worldview, they had the righteous duty to punish wayward souls and condemn sinful conduct. They hoped that, faced with harsh treatment and public embarrassment, offenders would be scared enough to resist future untoward temptations. But on this count, they were not overly optimistic. People were sinners, and criminal sanctions could not magically change this fact. For those who proved intractably deviant, the gallows was the ultimate solution (Rothman, 1971, 1995).

As colonial America developed, local town jails became more commonplace. Unlike contemporary institutions, these had no special prison architectural design but resembled regular households, with the keeper and his family typically living on the premises. This structure did not seem ill-suited because locking up offenders was not employed as a form of punishment. Instead, jails were used to detain people only until they could be tried and then, if convicted, sanctioned or punished shortly thereafter (Barnes, 1972; Rothman, 1971).

A key shift in the function of jails, however, occurred after the Revolutionary War. With anti-British fervor running high, the legitimacy of many things originally imported from England, including severe penalties and, in particular, capital punishment for a wide range of offenses, were called into question. In the new nation, the legal system should be enlightened. Building on the ideas of classical school thinkers such as Cesare Beccaria, leaders argued that criminal sanctions should be made less harsh and should be imposed equitably and with certainty. This legal system, they claimed, not only would be more just but also would reduce crime. Embracing the view that citizens were not merely sinners but rational decisionmakers, they argued that an appropriately administered legal system would deter crime by teaching people that punishment was certain and, although not excessive, was severe enough to make illegal conduct unprofitable. But "as they enacted these reforms," observes Rothman (1995: 114), "the states immediately confronted the question of what punishment should substitute for execution. If they were not to hang the convicted criminal, what penalty should they impose?" The answer was to imprison repeat and serious offenders for lengthy periods of time. In this way, the function of imprisonment was fundamentally changed from detention to punishment.

By the 1820s, faith in this legal experiment was difficult to sustain. Crime showed no signs of declining, and the prisons themselves "had become the scene of rampant disorder, with escapes and riots commonplace" (Rothman, 1995: 115). This failure might have led Americans to disband prisons and to search for alternative solutions to lawlessness, but precisely the opposite occurred. They sought to imbue prisons with a new, optimistic purpose. In this view, the prison was no longer merely to punish offenders but to serve as a "penitentiary." This language is significant, because it shows the emergent belief that an institutional environment, if only designed correctly, could have the power to move inmates to do penance for their misdeeds—indeed, could *reform* the very nature of offenders, turning them from criminals into morally upright citizens. Prisons thus could serve the dual goals of making society safer and of improving the lives of offenders. Perhaps not surprisingly, visitors from around the world—including Alexis de Tocqueville, who subsequently authored the famous *Democracy in America*—traveled to the United States to study this bold initiative in correctional thinking and practice (see de Beaumont and de Tocqueville, [1833] 1964).

How could criminals be reformed? Advocates of the penitentiary asserted that the key to such moral transformation was to place offenders within a freshly created, orderly, moral society that would reflect the principles that had existed in earlier colonial days—a time before American communities had grown in size, experienced an influx of different peoples, and become less organized. These principles were clear: religious exhortation and belief, discipline, hard work, and no exposure to criminal influences. Sealed off from the larger society by high and thick walls, the prison offered a ready setting in which to construct this community, which reformers were convinced would purify offenders of their wayward tendencies (Rothman, 1971). The words of Gustave de Beaumont and Alexis de Tocqueville ([1833] 1964: 90) capture this perspective:

> We have no doubt, but that the habits of order to which the prisoner is subjected for several years, influence very considerably his moral conduct after his return to society. The necessity of labor, which overcomes his disposition to idleness; the obligation of silence which makes him reflect; the isolation which places him alone in the presence of his crime and his suffering; the religious instruction which enlightens and

comforts him; the obedience of every moment to inflexible rules; the regularity of a uniform life; in a word, all the circumstances belonging to this severe system, are calculated to produce a deep impression upon his mind.

A great debate ensued over how precisely to design and administer the penitentiary community. Reformers in Pennsylvania, many of them Quakers, offered the "solitary" system, which they implemented in prisons in Cherry Hill, Philadelphia, and Pittsburgh. Inmates were isolated in a single cell, which they left for only one hour each day to exercise in an adjoining yard. They spent their day alone, working (e.g., weaving, shoemaking, tailoring), reading the Bible, and contemplating their fate. They were not allowed to associate with other inmates or to correspond with friends or family; human contact was limited largely to visits from the prison superintendent and the prison chaplain. Reformers in New York, who initially tried their ideas at a prison located in Auburn, advocated the "congregate" or "silent" system. Inmates slept alone, but they ate, worked, and attended church services together (thus the term "congregate"). The risk of offenders passing bad influences to one another was stifled by the requirement, backed up by the threat of the whip, that inmates not talk but remain silent (Barnes, 1972; de Beaumont and de Tocqueville, [1833] 1964; Rothman, 1971, 1995).

In building their penitentiaries, most states emulated New York's Auburn prison. The congregate system's major advantage was financial: It was more expensive to house inmates in solitary confinement, as the Pennsylvanians proposed, and more profitable to allow inmates to work and make products together. Yet, by the middle of the nineteenth century and especially after the Civil War, many prisons experienced overcrowding that made silence and isolation of inmates unenforceable. Thus, the effectiveness and feasibility of the "silent" congregate model was widely questioned and generally abandoned. At the same time, prisons came no longer to be viewed as places merely to house or punish offenders but as places in which to do good works. The purpose of corrections thus was broadened to include the possibility that inmates, arguably among the least attractive societal members, should not be forsaken or warehoused but should remain an object of concern and be reformed.

Explaining the Origins and Use of the Penitentiary

For many years, it was common to view the transition to the penitentiary from the public whipping post, stocks, and the gallows as evidence of increasing enlightenment and civilization (Ignatieff, 1981). Although good intentions were not always realized, each step in the development of the American prison, from the penitentiary to the modern correctional institution, was seen as a matter of progress, though slow and incremental. Influenced by the social turmoil and political scandals of the 1960s, however, a new group of revisionist scholars challenged this accepted historical account of the prison. Cynical about the government and wary of its immense power, which they believed was exercised coercively and virtually without restraint in prisons, they argued that correctional institutions were not a sign of inevitable progress but rather were social products that served underlying, hidden interests. Much like psychoanalysts searching the unconscious for the real but unstated motives behind human conduct, these scholars urged that we probe beneath accepted explanations of the penitentiary's origins to find what its "real" causes might have been (Colvin, 1997; Garland, 1995; Ignatieff, 1981).

David Rothman's (1971) *Discovery of the Asylum* offered a fascinating account of the penitentiary's appeal to Jacksonian Americans by linking together social context, theories of crime, and policy. By the 1820s, U.S. society was in the throes of considerable upheaval, as communities grew in size, the economy was changing, and people in unprecedented numbers moved about the still-new nation. In this context, Americans experienced their society as disorderly and, equally important, attributed the cause of crime to this disorder. Rothman argued that this theory of crime created the rationale for the penitentiary: If exposure to disorder causes crime, then placing offenders in an orderly environment will reverse the criminogenic process. As noted, the prison offered the setting in which to create this reformative environment. Advocates of the competing Auburn and Pennsylvania models, which in retrospect seem to have much in common, fought so vehemently because they believed that each detail of the internal design of the penitentiary was crucial to building the precise kind of order that could inculcate moral character in inmates. Equipped with this belief, these reformers worked diligently to make the penitentiary, in all its exquisite details, an enduring reality.

Rothman's insights alert us to a more general point: Prisons—their origins, alterations to them, how much they are used—reflect broader changes in society and how these changes are experienced and interpreted by Americans. Employing prisons to control crime is not an inevitable, rational policy decision but a choice that is shaped by our social experiences and our understandings of why crime takes place. This insight, as we will see, rings true today.

Although innovative and valuable, Rothman's perspective has been subjected to an important criticism: He does not pay much attention to the fact that the vast majority of people locked up in prison, regardless of the historical period, have been poor. "Critical" or Marxist scholars, however, believe that this is *the* fundamental consideration in understanding the nature of imprisonment in the United States. For them, the prison is not a progressive, well-intentioned invention but an instrument or strategy of power used by the rich to control the poor (Ignatieff, 1981). As one commentator observed, "the rich get richer and the poor get prison" (Reiman, 1984).

Critical criminologists thus argue that the prison was created and has since been used to serve the interests of the capitalist class who owns the factories and otherwise runs the economy. The prison ingeniously helped the capitalists with two problems, one continuing and one episodic, but both of which were tied to the increased use of wage laborers in the U.S. economy. Fundamental to a capitalist economy is that people who do not own the means of production, such as the factories, work for those who do and receive wages for their efforts. Capitalists have a stake in keeping wages as low as possible to increase their profits. A continuing problem, however, is what to do with the poor who do not accept this low-wages-for-hard-work deal but instead drift into idleness, vice activities, and/or petty crime. The penitentiary helped to solve this problem in two ways. First, it sought not to punish the body and risk making the wayward less productive, but to discipline the spirit and transform the person into a more useful worker (see Foucault, 1977). In Ignatieff's (1981: 170) words, "the disobedient poor were drawn into a circle of asceticism, industriousness, and obedience. They would return to society convinced of the moral legitimacy of their

rulers." Second, the penitentiary would stand as a concrete reminder to the working poor that their fate could be worse. The uncooperative members of the lower class were stigmatized as criminals and subjected to harsh living conditions, making employment, even for low wages, seemingly a preferable option. According to critical scholars, this is the chief reason for the "principle of less eligibility"—the idea that prison inmates should have a lower standard of living than free citizens in the community (e.g., why should inmates have a free college education when poor people do not?).

The episodic problem for the capitalists is that the economy is unstable and in bad times produces a large population of surplus labor. Unemployed, if not woefully impoverished, this population poses a potential threat to rise up and challenge the existing order. Prisons thus serve as a tool for controlling this threat. As rates of unemployment rise, prison populations rise accordingly; as unemployment declines and the poor are needed to labor in the factories, prison populations shrink. Scholars have argued that this link between unemployment and imprisonment holds, regardless of the actual levels of crime in society. There is some evidence to support this contention (Chiricos and Delone, 1992; Colvin, 1997).

The critical perspective is a useful corrective to the view that American corrections is not affected at all by class relations and inequalities in power. The weakness of a critical view, however, is that it seeks to explain the origins and operation of prisons entirely by class conflict. Such a unidimensional view, however, is open to several criticisms (Colvin, 1997; Ignatieff, 1981). First, it assumes that the motives expressed by prison reformers were disingenuous. Is it really true that they were trying to suppress, rather than help, poor offenders? Second, the critical explanation assumes, in effect, a conspiracy between society's economic elites and those who administer the correctional system. But it is unclear that the interests of these groups are the same or that they meet to plot the subjugation of the surplus population. Third, a critical perspective fails to explain why the use of prisons is supported not just by the rich but also by the disadvantaged (Jacoby and Cullen, 1998). In fact, it can be argued that, to the extent that the poor criminals mainly victimized poor citizens, the disadvantaged derive the most benefit from predatory offenders being locked up (DiIulio, 1994a). Finally, critical scholars do not explain why capitalists constructed an institution that is so ineffective in disciplining and controlling poor offenders. Research has long shown that inmates are not powerless, but play an intimate role in negotiating what goes on inside institutions (Sykes, 1958). Similarly, there is little evidence that incarcerating offenders curbs their appetite for crime.

THE CHANGING NATURE OF PRISONS

It would take a lengthy roster of books to describe in detail the many changes imprisonment in the United States has experienced in the past two centuries (see, e.g., Colvin, 1997; Irwin, 1980; Jacobs, 1977; McKelvey, 1977; Morris and Rothman, 1995). Our goal here thus must be more modest. Out of the many considerations that could be surveyed, we discuss six major changes that continue to affect contemporary American corrections.

Federal Prisons

American corrections, like criminal justice in general, is highly decentralized, with individual communities largely running their own justice systems. The first U.S. jails were local. Penitentiaries, however, represented a marked departure from this locus of control. They were built, paid for, and administered by state governments. Today, municipalities and counties still run jails, which, in addition to detaining those awaiting trial, confine convicted offenders who are sentenced to less than one year behind bars. State prisons are reserved for more serious, repeat offenders, who are penalized with at least a year's incarceration.

But there is another correctional system, this one administered by the Federal Bureau of Prisons. It supervises well in excess of 100,000 inmates, housed in over 80 facilities (Camp and Camp, 1997; Gilliard and Beck, 1998). It was not until 1891 that the U.S. Congress authorized the construction of three federal prisons. Before this time, people who broke federal laws were incarcerated in state prisons. This arrangement was scuttled when, in 1887, the Congress, under pressure from unions and manufacturers fearing competition from goods made by cheap inmate labor, barred federal convicts from being leased as workers to private contractors. In response, states increasingly refused to accept federal offenders, thus necessitating the new federal prison system. The Federal Bureau of Prisons was formally started in 1929 (Keve, 1991; Rotman, 1995).

Ideally, the federal system would prosecute criminal acts or conspiracies that crossed state boundaries or that threatened national security. In practice, the federal legal code, with over 3,000 offenses on the books, often duplicates state laws (Meese, 1999). This "federalization of crime," as it has been called (Meese, 1999), clouds the distinctiveness of the federal criminal justice system; it also means that this system can be used, for better or worse, to prosecute virtually any form of crime, regardless of state jurisdiction. In recent years, federal law enforcement has been deeply involved in the "war on drugs." The result is that approximately 60 percent of federal inmates are serving time for drug-related offenses. In 1980, this figure stood at but a quarter of the inmate population (Bureau of Justice Statistics, 1992; Gilliard and Beck, 1998).

The Rise of Scientific Rehabilitation

The founders of the penitentiary believed that, if designed properly, the internal workings of the prison would create law-abiding citizens. Inmates were largely an undifferentiated mass, all of whom needed moral reform and should be subjected to the same institutional regimen. As noted above, this model lost credibility as prisons became crowded and crime did not diminish. However, in the latter part of the 1800s and especially in the first two decades of the 1900s, often called the Progressive Era, a "new penology" emerged that attempted to revitalize the idea that inmates could be reformed. At the core of this paradigm was the belief that the treatment of offenders should be scientific and individualized (Rothman, 1980).

Informed by the emerging social sciences, Progressives argued that people broke the law because of a variety of psychological and sociological factors. Two robbers, for example, might well commit their crime for vastly different reasons, one perhaps out of poverty and the other because of mental illness. Using the latest scientific knowledge, each offender thus had to be studied individually to determine the unique set of factors that was causing his or her criminality. In turn, transforming offenders into nonoffenders was not simply a matter of moral exhortation or of putting them in solitary confinement as was done in the penitentiary; the factors causing the crime, once identified, had to be changed. To accomplish this task, experts

schooled in treatment—for example, psychiatrists and social workers—would rehabilitate offenders. Importantly, the Progressives favored indeterminate sentences in which offenders would be released from prison only when parole boards, on the advice of these treatment experts, determined that they had been "cured."

This ideal of individualized treatment was rarely achieved in reality. Scientific knowledge on crime was in short supply; prisons rarely hired experts or trained their staff; treatment programs were too often ineptly run or lacking altogether; and the treatment needs of offenders were rarely placed above the custodial needs of their keepers (Rothman, 1980; Rotman, 1995). Still, the Progressives' reform movement had three important consequences. First, it helped to bring into the prison, albeit in less than needed numbers, a variety of people whose job it was to rehabilitate offenders (e.g., counselors, teachers). Second, it succeeded in solidifying the view that prisons should be instruments of rehabilitation and not merely punishment. Third, it laid the foundation for the creation, following World War II, of correctional institutions, prisons whose very name carried the mandate to reform its charges (Irwin, 1980; Rotman, 1995). In the best of these institutions, efforts were made to classify offenders and to create a therapeutic milieu in which offenders received counseling, education, and vocational development.

In the late 1960s and early 1970s, however, rehabilitation came under attack as being ineffective and as the source of many ills in the correctional system. Believing prisons to be inherently inhumane and brutalizing, liberals blamed rehabilitation for giving corrections officials (guards, wardens, treatment staff, parole boards) unfettered discretion to keep inmates locked up under the pretense of rehabilitating them. In fact, liberals argued, rehabilitation was mainly a tool for control: If inmates protested or rebelled, they would not be released. Conservatives also opposed rehabilitation, but for the opposite reason. They contended that correctional treatment was a source not of coercion but of excessive leniency. In this view, savvy but predatory offenders "conned" treatment staff and parole boards into releasing them early from prison, teaching the offenders in the process that punishment was not certain or harsh enough for crime not to pay (Cullen and Gilbert, 1982).

This bipartisan attack robbed rehabilitation of its status as the dominant correctional philosophy—a status it had held for much of the century. As the treatment ideal was tarnished, an ideological vacuum emerged as to what the purpose of prisons should be. The liberal message that prisons were inhumane places that should be used sparingly did not prove persuasive. Instead, over the past three decades, conservatives have been more successful than liberals in filling this ideological vacuum, suggesting that prisons should be used to "get tough with offenders"—a topic we return to on p. 485. The decline of rehabilitation, however, did not mean that treatment programs disappeared. Prisons continued to provide education, vocational training, individual and group counseling, drug treatment, and so on.

Further, in recent years, a revisionist perspective has emerged that argues that rehabilitation should be "reaffirmed" (Cullen and Applegate, 1997; Cullen and Gilbert, 1982). Two considerations buttress this position. First, even though the American public is punitive toward criminals, it continues to define rehabilitation as an important goal of imprisonment (Cullen et al., forthcoming). Thus, in a statewide survey in Ohio, more than 8 out of 10 respondents agreed that "it is important to try to rehabilitate adults who have committed crimes and are now in the correctional system" and that "it is a good idea to provide treatment for offenders who are in prison" (Applegate et al., 1997: 247).

Second, in the attack on rehabilitation, many critics readily accepted evaluation research results purportedly showing that treatment programs have little effect on recidivism rates (Martinson, 1974). This view became known as the "nothing works" doctrine and seemingly sealed rehabilitation's fate; after all, how could treatment programs be defended if they "did not work"? Recently, however, an impressive body of research has shown that, in fact, many interventions with offenders are effective in lowering future criminal participation. Moreover, programs that target for change the known predictors of recidivism (e.g., the antisocial values offenders hold) and follow certain "principles of effective treatment" (e.g., use cognitive-behavioral programs) achieve substantial reductions in recidivism (see Andrews and Bonta, 1998; Cullen and Applegate, 1997; MacKenzie, 1998). The challenge remains, however, to use this knowledge on "what works" to develop new interventions and/or to reshape current prison-based programs so that treatment services will be delivered more effectively to inmates. The public's stake in reforming offenders is clear, for the average prison inmate will be returning to the community thirty months after being placed behind bars (Bureau of Justice Statistics, 1999).

The Prisoners' Rights Movement

In the 1950s and 1960s, oppressed groups in the United States increasingly turned to the federal courts to guard their constitutionally protected civil rights. Within criminal justice, the pursuit of civil rights created the movement to extend due process protections to offenders from arrest through incarceration. The desire to provide legal protections to inmates, however, was especially challenging because they had traditionally been viewed as "slaves of the state," people who, by their conviction, had forfeited their right to citizenship and the protections this status afforded. Accordingly, until the 1960s, the courts had largely taken a hands-off position regarding the handling of offenders in prisons. Bad as this treatment might be, it was none of the courts' business (Jacobs, 1983; Rotman, 1995).

A 1964 U.S. Supreme Court case reversed the hands-off doctrine when the court ruled that African-American Muslim prisoners could not be denied the Koran to read and their right to worship. Although a narrow ruling, this case showed that "prisoners have constitutional rights" and that "prison officials were not free to do with prisoners as they pleased" (Jacobs, 1983: 37). Over the next two decades, numerous other cases were brought that eventually moved beyond the rights of religious worship and freedom of speech to examine whether awful living conditions in prisons, including overcrowding and inadequate medical services, violated the constitutional prohibition against cruel and unusual punishment (Feeley and Hanson, 1990). The U.S. Supreme Court stopped short of mandating the right to a comfortable life in prison, such as the right to an inmate residing in a single cell (Jacobs, 1983). Still, the vast majority of state correctional systems experienced "major prison litigation and judicial intervention," in some cases leading to the entire system being placed under the control of the courts (DiIulio, 1990: 288; see also Morris, 1995). As DiIulio (1994b: A21) notes, "in 1970, not a single prison system was operating under sweeping court orders"; two decades later, "508 municipalities and more than 1,200 state prisons were operating under conditions of confinement or consent decrees." Today, 35 states are under an order by a federal court to improve prison conditions

(Lacayo, 1995). These legal interventions are credited with producing noticeable changes in the lives of inmates. As Jacobs (1983: 59) observes:

> Inmates who previously were not permitted to have the Koran, religious medallions, political and sociological monographs, and law books now possess them. Inmates once afraid to complain to relatives and public officials about their treatment are now less afraid. Censorship of outgoing mail has been all but eliminated. Censorship of incoming mail is less thorough and intrusive, increasing the privacy of written communication. Prisoners in isolation, segregation, and other disciplinary confinement suffer less from brutal punishments, cold, hunger, infested and filthy cells, and boredom. In some cases, Arkansas, for example, unspeakable tortures have been stopped. In some jails and penitentiaries, prisoners are spared the misery of greater overcrowding than already exists because court decrees limit the number of inmates. In numerous institutions major advances in the quality and delivery of medical services can be directly attributed to court decisions.

It is not clear, however, that the effects of prison litigation have always been uniformly positive and uncomplicated (Feeley and Hanson, 1990). For better or for worse, legal rulings and consent decrees meant that states had to devote increasing amounts of money to corrections (e.g., build more prisons to lessen crowding)— money that could have been spent in other areas, such as education (DiIulio, 1994b; Feeley and Hanson, 1990). Further, the prisoners' rights movement not only tried to improve inmates' lives but to shift the balance of power between the kept and their keepers. At least in the short run, judicial rulings risk destabilizing prison order and making prisoners more vulnerable to inmate-on-inmate violence. Few commentators would suggest that such rulings always or inevitably lead to disorder (Feeley and Hanson, 1990). However, when court interventions are resisted and inappropriately managed by prison authorities, are resented by correctional officers who feel the courts are on the side of criminals, prompt rapid staff turnover, sweep away old (albeit repressive) systems of control, and perhaps embolden inmates, the possibility increases for disorder and violence to occur (DiIulio, 1987; Eckland-Olson and Martin, 1990).

At least to a degree, contemporary prisons reflect the reality that administrators and correctional officers must operate within the broad boundaries of constitutional principles. Officials have responded by changing institutions from informal organizations where discretionary decisions prevailed into more formalized bureaucracies in which staff are mandated to adhere to rules and regulations in their interactions with inmates (Jacobs, 1983; Crouch and Marquart, 1990). Regulations may constrain, but they do not wipe away, all informal relations and decision making. They also do not ensure that the custodians will follow the spirit rather than merely the letter of the law (Crouch and Marquart, 1990). Still, the prison environment has been unalterably affected by the prisoners' rights movement, giving inmates redress against the truly inhumane and brutal treatment that once existed unnoticed behind the high walls of the prison.

The Changing Racial Composition of Prisoners

Despite advances in civil rights, African Americans and whites in the United States typically live apart from one another in segregated neighborhoods (Massey and Denton, 1993). A notable exception is the American prison—a setting in which members of different racial and ethnic groups are forced into close contact. Further, unlike the larger society where over 7 in 10 residents in the U.S. are non-Hispanic whites (U.S. Bureau of the Census, 1998: 34), a majority of the nation's prison population are members of minority groups (Gilliard, 1999; Gilliard and Beck, 1998). At mid-year 1998, 41.3 percent of the inmates in state and federal prisons were white. Despite composing only approximately 12.7 percent of the nation's residents (U.S. Bureau of the Census, 1998: 34), African Americans make up 41.2 percent of the prison population. Hispanics composed 15.5 percent of the prison population; the other 2 percent of inmates were Native Americans, Alaska Natives, Asians, and Pacific Islanders (Gilliard, 1999; see also Camp and Camp, 1997; Gilliard and Beck, 1998).

The overrepresentation of African Americans in U.S. prisons is disquieting. For African Americans, the incarceration rate for state and federal prisons per 100,000 people, 1,571, is more than 2 times that of Hispanics (688) and 8 times that of whites (193). For an African-American male age 25 to 29, the incarceration rate per 100,000 is an extraordinary 8,317; the comparable figure for Hispanics and whites is, respectively, 2,609 and 829 (Gilliard and Beck, 1998). An African-American male born today has a 1 in 4 chance of going to prison during his lifetime. For Hispanic males, the odds are 1 in 6; for white males the figure is 1 in 23 (Bonczar and Beck, 1997; see also Mauer, 1997).

The current tendency for prisons to be increasingly populated by African Americans is related to the "war on drugs" that began in the mid-1980s (Egan, 1999a; Mauer, 1997). Between 1985 and 1989, African Americans' proportion of all drug arrests jumped from 30 percent to 42 percent, even though African Americans' use of drugs is generally lower than that of white Americans (Tonry, 1995). On the federal level, draconian punishments for possession with the intent to distribute crack cocaine (9 in 10 defendants are African American) versus relatively lenient punishments for possession of powder cocaine (only 1 in 5 defendants are African American) has resulted in a large jump in African Americans in federal institutions (Gilliard and Beck, 1998; Kennedy, 1997; Tonry, 1995). The disproportionate concentration of minorities in the nation's correctional facilities, however, also represents a longer-term process. The percentage of whites among admissions to state and federal prisons has been declining over the past 75 years. In 1926, the figure stood at 79 percent; in 1950, at 69 percent; and in 1960, at 66 percent. By the 1980s, a majority of new admissions to state and federal prisons were African American (Miller, 1996: 55).

Historically, African-American and white prisoners were segregated, sometimes in separate institutions, sometimes in separate cellblocks. African-American inmates experienced prejudice and discrimination. Virtually all wardens and correctional officers were white. By the 1970s, however, the court rulings ended de jure segregation and many formal discriminatory practices in prison (Henderson et al., 1998). Buoyed by these rulings and by political activism outside prisons, minority inmates increasingly embraced African-American militancy and protested against prison conditions and authorities. At the same time, the number of African-American inmates continued to rise. Many of these offenders were drawn from inner-city neighborhoods, had a penchant for violence, and came into prison sporting membership in a gang (Irwin, 1980; Jacobs, 1977, 1983).

Taken together, these changes reshaped race relations. "By 1970," notes Jacobs (1983: 67), "racial avoidance and conflict had become the most salient aspect of the prisoner subculture." As Irwin (1980: 182) observes, "in prison . . . races, particularly African American and white, are divided and hate each other." In informal relations, the members of racial and ethnic groups continued to eat, recreate, and live in the same cells together; de facto segregation persisted (Carroll, 1988). Most noteworthy, African-American inmates transformed their position of power in the prison from subjugation to dominance. Their increasing numbers were only part of the reason for this shift in power. Their power also was enhanced by their greater group solidarity—based on racial identity and, in some states, on gang membership—and by their "ability to intimidate whites" (Jacobs, 1983: 73). In contrast, "white cliques are too weak to offer individuals any protection in the predatory prison subculture" (Jacobs, 1983: 73). As Nathan McCall (1994: 156) notes in *Makes Me Wanna Holler: A Young Black Man in America*:

> Whites in general caught hell in jail, especially in my new cellblock. . . . White junkies, whose drug dealings had often taken them to inner-city spots, did well because they'd grown comfortable around African Americans. But that was less the case with those sheltered, smug whites, such as that businessman we'd put through hell. They wore their racial fears and prejudices on their sleeves. At night, when the lights went out, those whites who couldn't hold their own were harassed, sexually and otherwise, by the wolves.

The Penal Harm Movement

After the rehabilitative ideal lost its status as the preeminent correctional philosophy in the mid-1970s, the question remained as to what doctrine would guide crime control policies. As numerous commentators have shown (see Currie, 1998), elected officials have chosen to fight crime chiefly by "getting tough." Todd Clear (1994) has called this approach, which now is three decades old, the "penal harm movement." Whereas rehabilitation, whatever its faults, held open the hope of helping offenders, penal harm forfeits this hope in favor of a conscious, unapologetic intention to inflict as much pain as possible on inmates. The penal harm approach is not hegemonic—many citizens and workers in corrections do not support it in totality (Cullen et al., forthcoming; Lacayo, 1995)—but it has had an enormous impact on correctional policies.

The penal harm movement's most dramatic influence has been in the array of laws passed that have attempted to place more people in prison for longer periods of time (e.g., three-strikes-and-you're-out laws, truth in sentencing laws, mandatory minimum prison sentences). But there also has been a push to lower living standards in prison—to inflict an asceticism on inmates that shows that "better and more humane penal environments are no longer what are desired" (Sparks, 1996: 89). Writing in 1995, Lacayo noted that the "hottest development in criminal justice is a fast-spreading impulse to eliminate anything that might make it easier to endure a sentence behind bars" (p. 31). Reflecting this impulse, legislators have publicized their efforts to intensify the pains of imprisonment by reducing such inmate amenities as grants for college education, television privileges, computers in cells, and exercise through weightlifting. This endorsement of penal harm is usually justified on the basis of deterrence and desert: A harsh life in prison will make offenders think twice about breaking the law again and, in any case, the state should spend as little money as possible to house those who have hurt their

fellow citizens. There is no evidence that such harshness will reduce recidivism or save much money. What is also unknown, but feared by prison officials, is that needlessly depriving inmates of education, television, and computers may increase their idleness and, in turn, make the prison staff's task of keeping inmates in order more difficult to achieve.

Privatization of Prisons

Many services in prisons are contracted to private vendors (e.g., food service, medical services) (see, more generally, Lilly and Deflem, 1996). The more controversial issue, however, is whether correctional institutions should be constructed and operated by private vendors (Logan, 1990; Ryan and Ward, 1989). Part of this debate is philosophical: Should the state surrender its obligation to legally sanction offenders to a third party? And part of the debate is whether, in the pursuit of profit, private companies will inevitably cut corners and exploit inmates. Historically, the leasing of inmates to labor on behalf of companies had bleak results, as offenders were often treated inhumanely by their private overseers (Colvin, 1997; McKelvey, 1977). Advocates of privatization counter that, under the constraint of contracts that hold companies accountable, private prisons can be run humanely and effectively, especially in light of the poor conditions in many existing, publicly administered institutions.

The push for privatizing prisons began with much publicity in the 1980s as states confronted a practical problem: the need to create space, as cheaply as possible, for housing their growing prison populations. The first modern-day private prison opened in 1984; as of 1995, 91 facilities were in operation (Pratt and Maahs, 1999). Most of these institutions are minimum or medium

Table 17.1   Ten States with Largest Prison Populations and Highest Incarceration Rates Per 100,000 Residents, June 30, 1998

STATES	NUMBER OF INMATES	STATES	INCARCERATION RATE
1. California	158,742	1. Louisiana	709
2. Texas	143,299	2. Texas	700
3. New York	70,723	3. Oklahoma	628
4. Florida	65,280	4. Mississippi	547
5. Ohio	49,289	5. South Carolina	543
6. Michigan	44,501	6. Nevada	529
7. Illinois	42,140	7. Arizona	504
8. Georgia	38,194	8. Alabama	501
9. Pennsylvania	35,644	9. Georgia	492
10. North Carolina	32,407	10. California	477

SOURCE: Data from Gilliard, 1999.

security and are relatively small in size, with an average population of 447 inmates. They also compose only a fraction of the adult correctional facilities in the United States, which number over 1,500 (Camp and Camp, 1997: 57, 78–79). Although private prisons are unlikely to fade away, their future growth likely depends on their ability to demonstrate continued cost efficiency. Are they really cheaper to run? On this count, however, the data are not overly promising. In a meta-analysis of 24 studies, Pratt and Maahs (1999) found that, at least with regard to adult institutions, private prisons were not less costly to administer than public prisons.

THE NATION'S PRISON POPULATION

The Numerical Count

On June 30, 1998, more than 1.2 million Americans were incarcerated in state and federal prisons, 1,102,653 in state facilities and 107,381 in the federal system. When the number of jail inmates—592,462—is added into this count,

more than 1.8 million people were behind bars at mid-year 1998 (Gilliard, 1999; see also Gilliard and Beck, 1998). The nation's incarceration rate stood at 668 per 100,000 residents (Gilliard, 1999; see also Walmsley, 1998).

It can be misleading, however, to focus on the "nation's" overall prison population. As Table 17.1 shows, there is considerable diversity in the scale of imprisonment across states. For example, one-third of the U.S. state prison inmates are incarcerated in just three states: California with 158,742 inmates; Texas with 143,299 inmates; and New York with 70,723 inmates. Over 55 percent of the nation's prison population is confined in just 10 state systems. Further, the rate of incarceration per 100,000 residents differs dramatically among states, ranging from a low of 117 in Minnesota to a high of 709 in Louisiana. Note that states with high incarceration rates tend to be concentrated in the South and West, whereas states with low incarceration rates tend to be located in the North.

Unless placed in some context, it is difficult to say whether locking up over 1.8 million Americans is unusual or merely a reflection of what nations worldwide tend to do. In short, is the United States a punitive society? Cross-national comparisons are revealing but also complicated. The best method for making such comparisons is to juxtapose incarceration rates per 100,000 people. Examining the number of residents in prison would be misleading, because large countries would naturally tend to have more people behind bars. By using the incarceration rate, we are able to see—regardless of a nation's size and based on a standard method of comparison—whether a nation is more or less likely to imprison its members.

As Figure 17.1 shows, the United States has a very high incarceration rate (see also Mauer, 1994). It is exceeded only by Russia's figure of 685 per 100,000 residents. Compared to other advanced industrial nations, it is inordinately elevated. For example, the U.S. rate of 668 is more than 5 times higher than England's and about 6 times higher than those of our neighbors to the north, Canada, and to the south, Mexico. It is also 6 to 7 times higher than those of most western European nations. And it is more than 16 times higher than our major economic rival, Japan (Walmsley, 1998).

Although these figures make a prima facie case that the United States is punitive compared with other nations, an alternative hypothesis may explain why America incarcerates so many of its citizens: The United States has many more criminals than other nations. James Lynch (1995) provides perhaps the more informative analysis of these competing views in his study of incarceration rates in the United States, Australia, Canada, England and Wales, and West Germany. Lynch reports that drug and property offenders serve more time in the United States than in other nations. For homicide and serious violent offenses, however, prison stays seem similar across nations. Thus, although partially because

of greater punitiveness, America's high incarceration rate also reflects the nation's "high levels of lethal violence" (Lynch, 1995: 37). We should note, however, that since Lynch's study was published, time spent in U.S. prisons has been rising for violent offenders. Between 1993 and 1997, the average time served by violent offenders released from prison jumped from 43 months to 49 months (Bureau of Justice Statistics, 1999).

The Growth of Imprisonment

In examining trends in prison populations from 1925 to the present, two unmistakable facts emerge: the amazing *stability* of the incarceration rate from the early part of the century until the early 1970s, and the amazing *growth* of the incarceration rate in the century's last three decades (Blumstein, 1995). Between 1925 and 1975, the nation's incarceration rate for state and federal prisons averaged 108.5 per 100,000 residents. This rate fluctuated somewhat, but it stayed within the range of 79 to 134 (Blumstein, 1995: 260; Blumstein and Cohen, 1973). The prison population grew in size, but this was mostly a reflection of the nation's increasing population. Between 1961 and 1972, the rate actually decreased from 119 to 93.

Between 1925 and 1970, the state and federal prison population's numerical count rose from 91,669 to 196,441 (Langan et al., 1988). This increase, however, was due mainly to the enlarging size of the U.S. population generally. Thereafter, the era of stability ended. By 1980, the prison population broke the 300,000 barrier; the 400,000 barrier fell just three years later in 1983; and by 1986, the 500,000 mark was topped. By 1990, more than three-quarters of a million U.S. residents were behind bars. By the mid-1990s, the prison population exceeded 1 million. In 1998, the figure stood at over

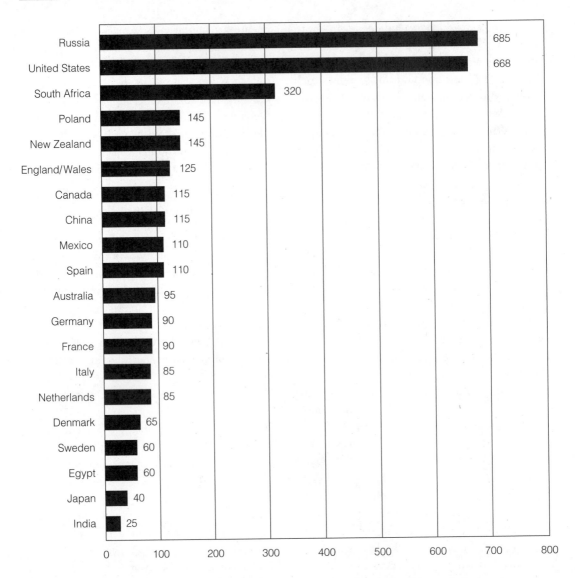

FIGURE 17.1 Incarceration rates for selected nations

SOURCE: Data from Walmsley, 1998; and Gilliard, 1999.

1.2 million (see Figure 17.2). Again, the incarceration rate for state and federal prisoners, which until the early 1970s had averaged about 108 per 100,000 people, now is 4 times higher.

What caused this steady, dramatic rise in prison populations? Arguably, it was set in motion by a large jump in the crime rate in the decade beginning in the mid-1960s. But the

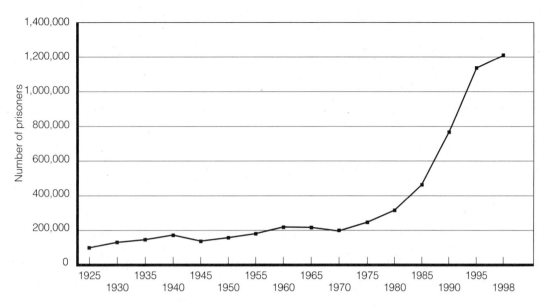

FIGURE 17.2 State and federal prison population, 1925–1998

SOURCE: Data from Langan et al., 1988; Gilliard, 1999; and Gilliard and Beck, 1998.

link between the size of the crime rate and the size of the prison population, although present, is not ironclad (Clear, 1994; Currie, 1998; Petersilia, 1992; Zimring and Hawkins, 1995). Take, for example, the states of Oregon and Utah that in 1997 ranked, respectively, fifth and ninth nationally in crime rates but only forty-first and forty-third in incarceration rates. Or the states of Texas and Mississippi that in 1997 ranked sixteenth and twenty-seventh in crime rates but first and fifth in incarceration rates (Federal Bureau of Investigation, 1998; Gilliard and Beck, 1998). Most instructive, between 1990 and 1997, the number of Index Crimes reported to the FBI fell by over 1.3 million offenses, including a decrease of over 185,000 violent offenses (Federal Bureau of Investigation, 1998: 66). By contrast, during the same period, the prison population rose by more than 470,000 inmates (see Figure 17.2) (Gilliard and

Beck, 1998; see also Butterfield, 1997; Egan, 1999b).

If not merely crime rates, what factors have spurred the recent "imprisonment binge" (Irwin and Austin, 1994)? Langan (1991) shows that between 1974 and 1986, less than 10 percent of the rise in the prison population was due to increases in reported crimes or arrests. Instead, the most important factor—accounting for half of the jump in population—was the increasing likelihood that courts would convict and sentence offenders to prison. More recently, it appears that toughening punishments for violent offenders and for drug offenders have helped to sustain the growth in prison populations. Most criminologists doubt whether locking up more and more offenders for longer and longer periods is an effective long-term strategy for controlling crime (Coughlin, 1996; Clear, 1994; Currie, 1998; Bennett et al., 1996). But this view is not shared by many elected officials. For the size of the prison population is not simply a result of more crime but of a decision, made increasingly often by countless U.S. policymakers and judges, to "get tough" with the nation's lawbreakers.

Characteristics of the Inmate Population

The inmate population does not mirror the nation's general sociodemographic makeup but rather is socially patterned. As we have seen, prisons are disproportionately populated by members of minority groups. More than nine in ten inmates are male, and the average age of inmates is about 28. Less than 4 percent of the nation's inmates are not citizens of the United States. In state prisons, almost half the offenders are imprisoned for violent crimes, and about a quarter each for property and drug crimes. In the federal system, three in five inmates are incarcerated for drug offenses, and the proportion of inmates for violent and property offenses are 12.4 percent and 8.4 percent respectively. Most inmates are incarcerated in medium- and minimum-security prisons. About 6 percent of inmates are isolated in protective custody or disciplinary segregation. In terms of health issues, 2.3 percent of the prison population have been identified as being HIV positive; this figure is six times the average for the general U.S. population. AIDS-related diseases cause about 1,000 deaths yearly in state prisons, which is about one-third of all inmate deaths. The leading cause of mortality among inmates is other diseases or natural causes. Suicides are responsible for about 5 percent of deaths in prison, with homicides accounting for little more than half that figure (Camp and Camp, 1997; Gilliard and Beck, 1998; Maruschak, 1997).

THE SOCIETY OF CAPTIVES

With close to 2 million people incarcerated in the United States, we have a virtual city of convicts. Inmates, for the most part, do not experience their incarceration alone, but rather as members of prison communities. Indeed, in many ways prisons are societies analogous to the towns and communities found in free society. Each prison, for instance, develops its own economy, social and political structures, system of values, traditions, and even languages. Further, prisons are composed of members with varying backgrounds, preferences, and needs who shape the climate and flavor of the prison community.

Prisons, of course, also differ from other communities in important ways. Most apparent is the fact that the people who compose this "society of captives" are just that—captives, involuntarily held apart from the law-abiding. As a result, the prison community is constrained in ways that other communities are not. Prisoners are not free to determine their activities, their resources are limited, and their relationships are limited. Furthermore, members of the prison community are incarcerated as a punishment. The goals of the punishment shape the way in which prisons are structured and inmates react to incarceration. Similarly, administrative styles and objectives can affect significantly the nature of the prison community. Sentencing practices and the priorities of the criminal justice system also determine who is incarcerated, for what, and for how long.

Our interest in examining the "society of captives" and in understanding how inmates adapt to prison is multifaceted. On one level, the prison community is a dramatic and unique setting in which to observe a number of social processes. In short, prisons are intriguing places, and it is fascinating to learn how people adapt to this extreme environment. On another level, there are pragmatic reasons for studying the nature of prison life. First, by examining the prison experience of inmates, we gain insight into how people adjust to and are affected by incarceration. This knowledge can help us to organize prisons that are safer, more humane, and more efficient. Second, from the opening of the first penitentiary, Americans have held the belief that the prison experience will, or should, bring about a lasting effect on those who are incarcerated, whether through discipline, rehabilitation, or deterrence. Consequently, it is important to explore how adjustment in prison is related to adjustment in society following release.

Living in Prison

Donald Clemmer (1940) was the first to systematically examine the social world of the prison. In his classic study of the maximum security prison, he argued that when people enter prison, their traditional beliefs, attitudes, and values are replaced by the cultural values of the prison and a criminal lifestyle. Further, he maintained that inmates experience a process of socialization, which he termed "prisonization," while incarcerated. In this way, inmates learn the norms of the prison and how to function within the inmate social system. Importantly, he also posited that the longer they are behind bars, the more removed prisoners become from conventional values and accepted ways of doing things. Thus, Clemmer saw incarceration and the process of prisonization as destructive.

Although Clemmer's specific hypotheses about prisonization and the inmate social system have been criticized as overly vague and only mixed support has been found for his predictions about the effect of incarceration on future behavior (Goodstein and Wright, 1989),

his observations nevertheless established a lively research agenda. In particular, penologists have focused attention on exploring the attitudes and values of inmates, how inmates adapt to incarceration, and what effect these attitudes and adaptations have on inmate behavior inside and outside of the prison. Furthermore, as we will discuss below, considerable attention has been devoted to understanding the determinants of these attitudes and behaviors.

Norms and Values Like other communities and organizations, prisons possess their own set of norms and values. These norms and values, termed the "inmate code," form a script for governing inmate conduct and help to define appropriate and inappropriate behavior. Robert Johnson (1996: 113) notes that "the public culture of the prison has norms that dictate behavior 'on the yard' and in other public areas of the prison such as the mess halls, gyms, and the larger program and work sites." In general, the inmate code emphasizes and values toughness, hostility, and manipulation and derides friendly, caring, and responsible behavior, especially toward prison staff. The two primary rules of the inmate code are "do your own time" and "don't inform on another convict" (Sykes, 1958).

In many regards, the inmate code serves to differentiate inmates from the prison staff and promotes the "rejection of the rejectors." Goodstein (1979) has found, for instance, that most inmates think of themselves as tough and rebellious in their dealings with staff, and that a third of inmates report that the use of deception in their relationships with guards is legitimate and even mandatory in order to gain early release. Although a few inmates publicly accept the authority of the prison, these "square johns" are often ridiculed in prison. Inmates who adhere to the inmate code, in contrast, are rewarded and may be admired. As these observations suggest, the inmate code is decidedly pro-criminal and antisocial.

A number of recent changes in the prison and its population have undermined the authority of the inmate code. Indeed, it is unlikely that a single, dominant inmate code exists to the extent that it once did. As the prison has become more permeable to the outside community, the inmate code has lost some of its dominance. In addition, a more racially and ethnically diverse inmate population has introduced competing norms into the prison. Finally, there are now a greater number of inmates serving short sentences, which has created more inmate turnover and instability in the prison social system. As a result, inmates have less stake in committing to the inmate code. Thus, it is perhaps best to think of the inmate code as a general set of beliefs and attitudes rather than as a rigid code of conduct.

Adaptive Social Roles and Niches One of the primary challenges that inmates face is learning how to "do their time." Some inmates experience difficulty adjusting to prison; most inmates, however, settle into a routine, adopt a lifestyle or social role, and develop a niche in which they feel comfortable. The environment of the prison (its climate, resources, and goals) shapes the way that inmates adapt to prison, as do the preferences and needs of individual prisoners (as will be discussed in greater detail directly). Forces in the community can also affect the way that inmates experience prison. For example, the expansion of inmate rights and, more generally, the Civil Rights movement had a tremendous impact on the way that inmates viewed their incarceration and their status as a prisoner (see Jacobs, 1977). For all of these reasons, the social world of the prison is dynamic;

prison social systems differ over time and from one prison to the next as prison environments, inmates, and the larger social context change.

Scholars of the prison have a long-standing fascination with the social world of the prison. The first systematic studies of the prison were concerned with documenting and understanding the inmate subculture. Researchers such as Donald Clemmer (1940) and Gresham Sykes (1958) identified a number of social roles that inmates adopt while incarcerated. The most frequently identified social roles are the "right guy" or "real man" (a convict who lives by the inmate code and has a pro-criminal orientation), the "square john" (an inmate who identifies with non-criminal values) the "punk" (a passive homosexual inmate), and the "rat" (a prisoner who informs on other inmates and squeals to the authorities).

In a subsequent study, Irwin (1980) observed that inmates tend to adapt one of four lifestyles: "doing time," "gleaning," "jailing," and functioning as a "disorganized criminal." The doing time lifestyle is adopted by inmates who view prison as a temporary break from their criminal careers; for these individuals, prison is a cost of doing business. The inmates who embrace this lifestyle try to do their time in the greatest comfort possible, avoid trouble by adhering to the inmate code, and try to get out of prison as quickly as possible. Other inmates may pass their time by gleaning, i.e., taking full advantage of rehabilitation programs and other activities to change their lives and acquire skills. Jailing is a lifestyle that is manifested by those inmates who strongly identify with the inmate code and have few commitments to the outside social world. These inmates are familiar with the workings of institutions and are likely to have spent a good deal of their life incarcerated or in other institutions.

Inmates who are jailing make prison their home, take on leadership roles or positions of power in inmate society, and participate in the underground economy. The disorganized criminal lifestyle describes those inmates who have difficulty adapting or are unable to adapt to prison. These individuals may have developmental or physical disabilities, mental illnesses, or emotional disorders. The disorganized criminal is easily manipulated by other inmates and may experience significant adjustment problems (e.g., they may become emotionally disturbed, attempt suicide, or engage in self-mutilation).

Johnson (1996) notes that these social roles and the inmate code form the public culture of the prison. Whereas some inmates behave according to stereotypes and social roles, adhering to the inmate code of toughness and hostility, there is also a private culture in prison. "Most prisoners," observes Johnson (1996: 120), "attempt to carve out a private prison world composed of niches or sanctuaries, offering sheltered settings and benign activities that insulate them from the mainline prison." Although inmates may publicly support the inmate code, privately they seek out settings, or niches, in the prison that meet their personal needs (Johnson, 1996; Toch, 1977). Inmates differ in terms of their environmental needs and preferences and, likewise, prisons vary in the extent to which they are able to accommodate these needs and preferences. In particular, inmates differ with regard to their need for activity, privacy, safety, emotional feedback, support, structure, and freedom; prison environments similarly vary along these ecological dimensions. Thus, inmates who have a high need for activity might spend their time in the gym where they can interact with other people and remain active. Inmates who have a need for privacy may seek out a job in the prison library or simply spend time alone in their cell. Inmates who are fearful and feel a need for safety may remain close to guards or friends or seek protective custody (see Johnson, 1996: 173–174).

Johnson (1996) argues that prisons should do more to facilitate the development of appropriate niches for inmates to ease adjustment problems. Currently, prisons do little to promote mature coping—they do not encourage inmates to adapt to prison in ways that are productive, responsible, and pro-social. Instead, the inmate code and adaptive roles and lifestyles such as jailing promote immature coping, the resolution of conflict with violence, and antisocial beliefs and lifestyles. Indeed, prison social systems tend to reward antisocial behavior and discourage behavior that is responsible and caring. As an alternative, Johnson (1996: 256–257) suggests that we organize prison communities to promote "mature coping" and ensure that inmates develop niches in prison where they can learn to solve their problems productively and are held responsible for doing so.

The Deprivation Model

Aside from describing *how* inmates adapt to prison, considerable effort has been devoted to exploring *why* inmates adjust to incarceration in certain ways. How, for example, can we account for the development of adaptive social roles in the prison community? Gresham Sykes (1958), in his classic study *The Society of Captives,* offered significant insight into these questions. He observed that prisons are essentially depriving places. Specifically, Sykes identified five "pains of imprisonment" that are inherent to the prison experience: the deprivations of freedom, goods and services, heterosexual relations, autonomy, and security. Sykes argued that these deprivations are frustrating to inmates and that prisoners respond to these frustrations by making certain adaptations. Inmates, he argued, tend to adjust to prison by becoming highly individualistic or by turning to one another and joining forces in opposition to the prison's authority. These adaptations, according to Sykes, were a direct and functional response to the pains of imprisonment. By taking on social roles (which Sykes called "argot roles"), inmates are able to mitigate the pains of imprisonment. In short, Sykes contended that the nature of the prison environment shaped significantly the way in which inmates behaved in prison. Inmate behavior can be understood as a response to the deprivations that inmates experience in prison.

Probably the most dramatic illustration of the deprivation model was provided by a group of Stanford psychologists who were interested in exploring the extent to which inmate and guard behavior were determined by individual personality and disposition or by the prison environment and adherence to social roles (Haney et al., 1973). In a classic experiment, a group of college students were randomly assigned to be either "inmates" or "guards" and were placed in a mock prison. The participants were given few instructions about how to carry out their respective roles. An effort was made, however, to empower the guards by providing them with uniforms, nightsticks, and other symbols of authority. Inmates, in contrast, were placed in degrading uniforms and an effort was made to depersonalize them and emphasize their reduced status.

The results of the experiment were dramatic. Within just six days, the experiment, which was planned to last two weeks, was discontinued because the behavior of the guards and inmates had become "pathological." Several of the inmates experienced breakdowns, extreme emotional depression, crying, rage, and acute anxiety. Among the guards, the experimenters observed high levels of aggression and negativity; one-third of the guards exhibited behaviors that were labeled "tyrannical" and a number of the guards reported that they found the use of power exhilarating. Further, the researchers observed that even the "good" guards tolerated the dehumanizing, brutal behavior of their fellow officers. These findings led the researchers to conclude that the behaviors of the participants were the result of the roles that they had been assigned and the "inherent pathological characteristics of the prison situation itself" (Haney et al., 1973: 90). Thus, like Sykes (1958), they maintained that inmates' (and guards') behavior and attitudes can be understood as reactions to the nature of the prison environment itself.

The Importation Model

As just discussed, the prison underwent several significant changes during the 1960s and 1970s. Notably, during this period the prison became less autonomous as societal forces exerted more influence on the daily workings of the prison. In addition, important changes were occurring among inmates. In this context, the deprivation model lost some of its intuitive appeal. Questions arose about whether one dominant prison subculture or inmate code existed and whether these orientations were in fact unique and indigenous to the prison. Moreover, it was becoming clear that personal characteristics, most notably race and ethnicity, were extremely important in shaping how people reacted to and behaved in prison.

As an alternative to the deprivation model, Irwin and Cressey (1962) proposed the importation model. According to the importation model, the critical determinants of how inmates react to prison are their experiences and attitudes prior to incarceration—experiences and orientations that are imported into prison. Although the importation model does not deny the importance of the pains of imprisonment or the process of prisonization, this perspective maintains that how prisoners adjust to these features of the prison experience is a function of adaptive patterns learned outside of prison.

Consistent with this model, Irwin and Cressey (1962) suggest that the inmate subculture is, in fact, three subcultures: the thief subculture, convict subculture, and legitimate subculture. The thief subculture is common to thieves everywhere and emphasizes group loyalty, coolheadedness, and reliability. The convict subculture is more closely tied to the prison. The individuals who belong to this subculture have extensive experience in prisons and jails and have spent much of their life institutionalized. This subculture emphasizes utilitarianism and the manipulation of the prison system for personal gain. The values of the convict subculture are argued to have originated on the city streets and are held by the hard-core members of the lower class. The legitimate subculture, unlike the thief and convict subcultures, is composed of inmates who identify with conventional norms and values. These inmates follow the official rules of the prison, do not become involved in the inmate social system, and try to do their time with as little trouble as possible.

Our understanding of the prison experience of inmates continues to be informed by both the deprivation and importation models. These models have proven helpful in explaining a range of phenomena including prison violence, social roles, and inmates' attitudes. Still, neither model alone is complete, and both are limited in their explanatory ability. As a result, penologists have recently turned to other theoretical explanations to help account for the ways in which inmates react to and experience incarceration (Adams, 1992). For example, researchers have begun to draw on the general literature on stress and coping to explain prison adaptations. In addition, increased attention has been given to the ways in which individual characteristics, such as personality, interact with environmental characteristics, such as predictability and safety. According to the interactionist perspective, adjustment problems are greatest when individuals and environments are mismatched (Wright and Goodstein, 1989). Further, adjustment problems in prison can be prevented or remedied by placing inmates in correctional environments that are consistent with their needs and personality.

The Effects of Imprisonment

Discussions about prisonization and the pains of imprisonment leave the impression that prisons are detrimental, even damaging places. Indeed, it is often assumed that prisons wreak psychological havoc on its inhabitants. Relatedly, discussions about the prison subculture suggest that the prison experience may do little to bring about positive change and may in fact reinforce criminal attitudes and lifestyles. In short, it is common to think of inmates as coming out worse than when they went in. Although there is some truth to each of these positions, the effect of imprisonment on inmates is more complex than either of these views suggests.

A voluminous body of research has been done on the effect of incarceration on inmates' adjustment to prison and their psychological well-being (see Adams, 1992; Bonta and Gendreau, 1987; Bukstel and Kilmann, 1980). In general, it has been found that the effect of prison is not uniform; rather, prisons seem to make some people worse, have no effect on others, and make some better. However, notable patterns exist among these findings: for instance, important individual differences. African-American inmates experience fewer problems adjusting to prison—such as emotional distress, suicide, and self-mutilation—than do whites. Younger inmates tend to experience fewer emotional and psychological problems but are more disruptive and violent than older inmates. For inmates who have mental illness or psychological disorders, prison can aggravate existing problems or create extreme challenges to already-limited or stressed coping abilities. Environmental characteristics of the prison also influence the effect of incarceration. Each prison has its own unique atmosphere, and inmates respond to and are influenced by these environments. Overcrowding, for example, can contribute to inmates' adjustment problems. Other features of the prison such as the level of security, internal freedoms, and the availability of resources can affect the way that inmates react to incarceration. In general, however, prison adjustment is influenced by a complex interaction between individual and environmental factors.

The relationship between incarceration and recidivism is also complex and beyond the scope of this chapter to explore in detail (see Andrews and Bonta, 1998: 262–265). Evidence suggests, however, that incarceration increases the likelihood of recidivism (Sampson and Laub, 1993). A recent meta-analysis by Gendreau et al. (1999) is also instructive in this regard: This research reveals that the longer people spend in prison, the more likely they are to commit crime. Importantly, this result was found among both high- and low-risk offenders. Still, it is not clear that prisons are invariably "schools of crime." Although incarceration appears to increase the likelihood of recidivism in general, evidence also suggests that prison can be beneficial in reducing recidivism under certain conditions (Palmer, 1974).

Inmate Violence and Victimization

Are prisons dangerous places or, under the watchful eye of custodians, are they largely free from crime despite being populated by criminals? Clearly, levels of victimization and general disorder vary across correctional institutions (DiIulio, 1987). Still, as Wooldredge (1998: 493) concludes, there is evidence that "inmate crime is very prevalent" (see also Carroll, 1988; Irwin, 1980). For example, a survey of three Ohio prisons found that in the previous six months alone, 48 percent of the inmate respondents reported experiencing a criminal victimization; 1 in 10 inmates had suffered a physical assault (Wooldredge, 1998). Similarly, a study of offenders incarcerated in New Mexico discovered that in just a three-month period, 14 percent had been a victim of a personal crime and 20 percent had been a victim of a property crime (Wooldredge, 1994). Also relevant is a study that analyzed, over a three-year period, the official disciplinary records of offenders in thirty-six New York facilities to discern how much crime they had committed. Notably, almost 1 in 10 inmates had assaulted another inmate; over one-third had been involved in an altercation with a fellow inmate; 13 percent had engaged in theft; and about 12 percent had destroyed property (Wooldredge and Carboneau, 1998).

Not every offender is equally likely to victimize others or to be victimized while incarcerated. Research indicates, for example, that the inmates likelier to commit crimes in prison are young, have a prior history of violent crime, are mentally or emotionally unstable, are from urban rather than rural areas, have fewer family ties, are concerned for their physical safety, and are housed in crowded institutions (Wooldredge, 1991; Wooldredge and Carboneau, 1998). Inmates who are victimized share characteristics with their victimizers, such as being young, having fewer family ties, and having a violent past. These findings suggest that inmates who are alike socially and personally may associate with one another, which in turn creates opportunities for interpersonal conflict and victimization to occur. Other inmates, such as those with higher socioeconomic status, are also more victimized; in these instances, the victims may be selected and preyed upon due to their perceived vulner-ability. It also appears that certain lifestyles in prison either protect against victimization (e.g., participation in education programs) or increase the risk of victimization (e.g., spending leisure time around other inmates watching television) (Wooldredge, 1994, 1998).

Inmate victimization can also take place in the course of prison riots. Collective disturbances are not daily occurrences in correctional institutions, although inmate revolts may have totaled as many as 300 between 1970 and 1990 (Useem and Kimball, 1991: 3). The two bloodiest riots occurred about a decade apart at Attica (New York) Correctional Facility in 1971, where forty-three people died, and at the Penitentiary of New Mexico in 1980, where thirty-three people died. These riots, however, differed in an important respect. At Attica, most of the casualties (twenty-nine inmates and ten guards held captive) died when state troopers stormed the prison and fired, seemingly without restraint, on inmates and hostages alike. This assault reinforced for many observers the belief that the government was excessively coercive and that prisons were a failed social institution. Attica

thus helped to spur calls for prison reform. At New Mexico, however, all inmate deaths were at the hands of other inmates, with many murders involving torture and mutilation. The extent and brutality of this riot—the inmates' "descent into madness" as one survivor of the uprising termed it (Rolland, 1997)—seemed to confirm the view that offenders were hopelessly violent and should be kept caged for as long as possible.

The New Mexico insurgency might suggest that the reason for prison riots, especially those involving injury and deaths, can be traced to the kinds of people who are in a given prison. This conclusion, however, is overly simplistic, because it does not explain why a riot at a given prison occurs at a particular time but not at another or why, more generally, prisons that house similar kinds of inmates do, or do not, experience a disturbance (Colvin, 1992). Useem and Kimball (1991) contend that the chief cause of riots is not the kind of inmates in an institution but what correctional administrators do. Based on their analysis of prison disturbances, they argue that the breakdown in the administration of the prison leads to a toxic combination of factors: The living conditions for inmates become more depriving; inmates lose confidence in the custodial staff and question their legitimacy; and grave security lapses emerge and are not fixed. In this situation, inmates, deprived and angry, have the motivation to revolt and, once an insurgency starts, the existing security defects allow it to spiral out of control. Useem and Kimball thus suggest that prison riots flow from a complex set of conditions but also that, through more effective correctional management, most can be prevented either from arising initially or from developing into a widespread and bloody insurrection.

The "Supermax" Prison

The need to manage violent inmates has recently led to the increased popularity of a new type of living environment: the super-maximum security facility—also known as a "supermax" or "maxi-max" prison. Modeled after the federal penitentiaries at Alcatraz and Marion (Immarigeon, 1992; Ward, 1994), the contemporary supermax prison is a high-security facility or housing unit that segregates inmates, restricts their movement, and limits their direct access to other inmates and prison staff (National Institute of Corrections, 1997). The supermax prison in Ohio, for example, requires inmates to spend twenty-three hours a day in an eight-by-ten-foot cell. "Inmates will be taken from their cells, one at a time, for one hour a day to take a shower and exercise in a bare-bones cell. The only exceptions will be to meet visitors and go to the doctor, dentist or barber. They will watch educational TV and eat meals in their small cells" (Ludlow, 1995). Sophisticated electronic surveillance and security features and high guard-to-inmate ratios are other common features of supermax prisons.

At the present, fifty-seven supermax facilities or units are in use in the United States; sixteen of these units are operated in Texas alone (National Institute of Corrections, 1997). When surveyed as to why they developed supermax prisons, correctional departments commonly cited the need to manage violent and seriously disruptive inmates and the need to control gang activity (National Institute of Corrections, 1997). Thus, the existence of these facilities is based on the premise that prison violence can be curbed by isolating dangerous and disruptive inmates. It also is thought that supermax prisons will both dissuade their own inhabitants and deter other inmates from engaging in violence in the future

(Hallinan, 1995; Toch, 1998: 10–11). However, whether supermax prisons are more effective than other strategies in fostering safety and in preventing disorder—especially given their high financial cost—remains to be demonstrated. They have also been criticized as being needlessly harmful to inmates and as an unconstitutional form of cruel and unusual punishment (Bronstein, 1991; Irwin and Austin, 1994; Wachtler, 1997; more generally, see Johnson, 1996). In 1995, for example, a federal court ruled that California's supermax prison at Pelican Bay violated "the Eighth Amendment's restraint on the excessive use of force" (Hentoff, 1995: A17). In fact, the chief judge in the case concluded that the use of force at Pelican Bay was "gratuitous, intended to maliciously inflict injury rather than to restore order" (quoted in Hentoff, 1995: A17).

WOMEN IN PRISON

Although a significant number of women are incarcerated in American prisons and jails, policymakers, researchers, and the public often overlook, or neglect, female inmates. This oversight obscures and biases our understanding of the prison and raises questions about the treatment of female inmates. As we will discuss, women's prisons evolved in a unique direction and continue to differ from prisons for men in significant ways. Furthermore, women experience prison differently than do men and face unique problems associated with their incarceration and criminality.

Trends in the Incarceration of Women

The incarceration rate of women has grown faster than the rate for men since 1981 (Kline, 1993; Pollock-Byrne, 1990) and have more than tripled in the last ten years (Maguire and Pastore, 1998). The number of female inmates has also increased substantially. At the end of 1997, 79,624 women were incarcerated in state and federal prisons. Since 1990, the female inmate population has escalated by an average of 8.9 percent annually, whereas the growth rate of males has been 6.9 percent. Further, since 1990, the female prison population has increased by close to 83 percent, although the male prison population rose "only" 61 percent. In addition, women now make up a larger percentage of the total prison population than they ever have before. In 1997, 6.4 percent of all prisoners were female, compared to a low of 2.9 percent in 1970 (Gilliard and Beck, 1998; Maguire and Pastore, 1998).

Although these trends are remarkable, some caution should be applied in their interpretation. The U.S. prison population remains overwhelmingly male. Although females constitute a higher proportion of the inmate population, the numerical gender gap in imprisonment is actually widening. In 1980, there were 291,312 more men in prison than women; by the end of 1997, this figure had grown to over 1 million more men incarcerated than female offenders (Gilliard and Beck, 1998; Langan et al., 1988).

Historical Differences

Feminist scholars argue that traditional accounts of the history of the prison are incomplete, if not faulty, when they ignore the ways in which women have been punished (Feinman, 1984; Fox, 1984; Rafter, 1985). For example, if historians like David Rothman had recognized that women were also held in the early penitentiaries but were not subject to the same routine and discipline that men were, maintains Nicole Hahn Rafter (1985: 234), they "might have concluded that the discipline of male convicts was shaped by notions of masculinity, concepts of manhood and beliefs about what men (though not women) could endure." Although views about gender (like class) are unlikely the sole influence on the development of prisons, feminist scholars have sensitized us to the importance of considering how gender roles affect the punishment of men and women. This relationship is particularly stark when the history of women's prisons is examined.

During the colonial period, male and female offenders were punished similarly (Feinman, 1984). Female offenders were subject to fines, corporal punishment, public shaming, and death. As views about gender began to change and women's role in society become more circumscribed, however, women were subject to a different standard of morality and, as a result, to a different standard of punishment.

Following the American Revolution, the cult of "true womanhood" determined the proper roles of women, especially white, middle- and upper-class women: wife and mother. In these roles, women were placed on a pedestal and viewed as the keepers and sources of morality and social stability (Feinman, 1984: 3). Because women were thought to determine the moral boundaries of society, those who committed crimes or violated their "natural" role were viewed as especially depraved; they had not only sinned but had threatened the moral order (Feinman, 1984; Freedman, 1974). Given the belief that female deviants experienced a greater fall to sin, it was thought that women were incapable of reform. As a result, female criminals were subject to greater social stigma, stricter punishments, and more neglect (Feinman, 1984). While the prison reformers of the time were hotly debating the merits of the separate and silent systems for the punishment of men, women were placed in separate wings or rooms within men's prisons where they continued to be housed together in overcrowded cells without consideration for classification, industrious work, or isolation from corrupting influences.

Freedman (1974) explains that, during the later half of the nineteenth century, and especially following the Civil War, female criminality began to be reinterpreted and the punishment of women reevaluated. A general movement to investigate the social sources of deviance was extended to females, and the image of the fallen women underwent a social change. Specifically, greater emphasis was placed on the social forces, such as poverty, intemperance, and poor parenting, that led women to criminality. Most importantly, however, women began to be viewed as innocent victims of men's exploitation and corrupting influences. The argument was made that every fallen woman was once an innocent girl who needed only to be shown the path to true womanhood.

Female prison reformers were influential in drawing attention to the plight of the female offender. They pointed to the abuses that women had suffered in prison, often at the hands of male prison guards. In addition, they began to argue that if the female criminal was removed to separate prisons run by and for women, their virtue might be restored. What better way was there to reform female criminals than to prevent their sexual abuse by male guards and to provide them with a virtuous example of true womanhood? Moreover, what better place to bring about the reform of the female criminal than in an institution that mirrored the domestic ideal? Hence, female prison reformers proposed that woman be placed in reformatories built to resemble cottages in which women would be taught the virtues of domesticity (see Feinman, 1984; Fox, 1984; Freedman, 1974; Rafter, 1985).

The pressure exerted by female prison reformers was successful, and in the late 1800s prisons run by women for the separate confinement of female offenders began to open. Two types of prisons were established for female offenders: reformatories and custodial institutions (Rafter, 1985). The women's reformatories were designed to hold young, less-serious offenders, including many misdemeanants, and to socialize women to be good mothers and wives. The reformatories appeared to be concerned primarily with addressing women's morality, arguably punishing women for deviating from their social role. The training in the reformatories consisted of household work, including sewing, knitting, washing and ironing clothes, cooking, gardening, and farming (Freedman, 1974). The custodial institutions, in contrast, housed more serious offenders, older women, and minorities—in short, women who did not fit the ideal of middle-class womanhood (Rafter, 1985). These institutions also offered domestic training but were similar to men's prisons in architecture, discipline, and programming (e.g., factory work).

Contemporary women's prisons continue to differ from men's prisons in a number of significant ways. Women's prisons are typically smaller, fewer in number, more isolated, and less secure than men's prisons (Belknap, 1996; Morash et al., 1994; Pollock-Byrne, 1990). Significantly, female inmates have access to fewer and less diverse vocational, educational, and treatment programs (Fox, 1984; Morash et al., 1994). Furthermore, programming and training in women's prisons continue to emphasize traditionally "feminine" occupations (e.g., sewing), domesticity, and service jobs. Female inmates also receive less medical treatment, despite the fact that they have more medical problems than male inmates do—although they seem to receive more treatment for mental health problems (Morash et al., 1994).

In brief, women's prisons receive less funding than men's prisons and as a result have fewer resources (Morash et al., 1994). Not surprisingly, research reveals that the needs of incarcerated women go unmet or are not sufficiently met. In particular, Morash et al. (1998) report that women lack sufficient access to family-related services, substance abuse treatment, mental and physical health programming, and vocational training.

Many of the characteristics of women's prisons have historical origins. For example, the isolated locations of many women's prisons stem from the desire of early prison reformers to keep women away from the "evil" influences of the city (Freedman, 1974). "Economy of scale" has also been cited as a reason why women are treated differently from men and tend to receive fewer resources (Morash et al., 1994; Rafter, 1989): It is less expensive per inmate to provide programming to a large number of male inmates than to a small number of female inmates. Belknap (1996: 97–98; see also Fox, 1984) has argued, however, that the treatment of women in prison is due to institutionalized sexism. Similarly, others maintain that gender stereotypes and sexism continue to influence how women are treated in prison and the types of programs that are available to them (Rafter, 1989).

Gender and the Social World of Imprisonment

Early research that examined the prison experiences of women focused on whether the women identified with the inmate code and adapted to prison by taking on social roles similar to those found in male prisons. This research revealed that women tend to have different reactions to incarceration and to adapt to prison in ways that are unique to their prior experiences (particularly gender socialization) and unique to the environment of women's prisons. For example, although female inmates appear to hold values consistent with the inmate code found in male prisons, they seem to be less committed to the code (Giallombardo, 1966; Ward and Kassebaum, 1965). Similarly, research has revealed that women adopt argot roles like those found in men's prisons, but that these roles reflect the different needs and priorities of women (Giallombardo, 1966; Heffernan, 1972; Mahan, 1984).

Most of the research on the experiences of female inmates has focused on the social organization of women's prisons. This research reveals that women's prisons are characterized by less racial conflict and fewer political concerns; similarly, female inmates are thought to be more cooperative than men are (Pollock-Byrne, 1990). Whereas men's prisons are inclined to be organized around gangs, women tend to adapt to prison by forming close relationships with other inmates and forming "pseudo families" (see Carter, 1981; Fox, 1984; Giallombardo, 1966). These families may comprise only a couple, or may include "children," "aunts," "uncles," and "grandparents" (Mann, 1984). The relationships are not necessarily sexual (but may be) and are frequently formed to provide intimacy, companionship, and affection. More recent research suggests, however, that this form of adaptation may have been exaggerated in the past or no longer exists in women's prisons to the extent that it once did (Bowker, 1981; Mahan, 1984; Mawby, 1982).

The prison experience of women also differs significantly from that of men with regard to violence. Women's prisons are not characterized by the same level of violence as is found in men's prisons. This is not to say that female inmates do not engage in violence or intimidation.

Pollock-Byrne (1990) reports that female inmates have been raped by other inmates, are the subjects of violent intimidation, and are the victims of theft. Still, less violence is found in women's prisons, women are less likely to carry and manufacture weapons, and women are less likely to join gangs for protection (Pollock-Byrne, 1990; see also Tischler and Marquart, 1989).

The distinct social organization of women's prisons has been attributed to both the importation model and the deprivation model. For example, it has been argued that women's prison experiences are shaped most significantly by their prior gender socialization to feminine roles (Giallombardo, 1966). In contrast, it has been noted that the characteristics of women's prisons (their less-oppressive architecture, more maternalistic and paternalistic care, fewer resources, and greater isolation) may constitute a unique set of deprivations. In other words, women may adapt to prison differently because women's prisons are different. In general, however, most researchers have concluded that issues related to gender (an importation factor) seem to be the most significant determinant of women's prison experiences (Pollock-Byrne, 1990: 138–143).

Special Issues

Feminist criminologists and others concerned with the treatment of female offenders have criticized departments of corrections, policymakers, and social scientists for failing to recognize adequately the singular experiences and needs of female inmates. For instance, simply advocating for the equal treatment of male and female inmates does not begin to address the unique problems that women face in prison. Some of the issues that are particularly pressing for female inmates are parenting and children,

prior sexual and physical abuse, and chemical dependency.

One of the most painful and distressing aspects of incarceration for women is being separated from their families (Pollock-Byrne, 1990). Three-fourths of women in prison have children, and the vast majority of these children are under the age of 18 (Snell, 1994). Importantly, women are far more likely than men to have been the primary emotional and financial supporters of their children prior to incarceration (Koban, 1983). As a result, female prisoners are faced with difficult choices about the care of their children while they are imprisoned. Among inmates with young children, only 25 percent of women, but nearly 90 percent of men, report that their children were living with the other parent while they were incarcerated (Snell, 1994). The majority of children of incarcerated women live with their grandparents or other relative (Snell, 1994). Other women face losing custody of their children, and some must place their children in a foster home or more institutionalized setting.

Women's prisons vary with regard to their policies on the placement of infants born to female inmates and the visitation of children. The Bedford Hills Correctional Facility in New York, for example, provides a nursery for inmates' children up to age 1. In addition to providing child care, the nursery promotes parenting skills and emotional support for inmates. Programs are also offered for older children such as a summer camp, overnight weekend visits, and structured activity programs (Morash et al., 1998: 8). Some women's prisons also make special arrangements for women to visit their children. For example, special visiting rooms with toys, brightly colored furniture, and friendly pictures can help to make young children feel more comfortable visiting their mothers (Pollock-Byrne, 1990: 67–70). Still, these types of programs are more the exception than the rule; only two out of five prisons allow extended visits between mothers and children and fewer provide nurseries for infants born to women in prison (Belknap, 1996).

The challenge for corrections, and society generally, is to determine whether our interests lie in protecting children and doing what is best for them or in punishing the criminal in prison. Toch (1998: 4) has commented, for instance, that "it is an inconsistent policy to incarcerate women on a large scale," but to then "make gargantuan efforts to find placements for their children, to open cooperative nurseries in prisons, and to worry about reunion and visiting." One possible alternative is to make greater use of community-based sanctions that provide for the punishment and control of female inmates (e.g., house arrest) but that also allow women to maintain close relationships with their children.

Another issue that is ostensibly unique to women's prison is the high incidence of prior sexual and physical abuse experienced by female inmates. More than 4 out of 10 women in prison report being a victim of physical or sexual abuse. Compared to men in prison, women are three times more likely to report any prior abuse and are six times more likely to report being a victim of sexual abuse since the age of 18. In addition, among female inmates who report prior abuse, half of these women said that the abuser was a spouse, ex-spouse, or intimate partner. It is also interesting to note that women who have experienced physical or sexual abuse are more likely to have committed a violent crime. Moreover, a significant minority of women in prison for homicide killed a spouse, ex-spouse, or other person with whom they were intimate (Snell, 1994).

Female inmates have specific needs associated with their histories of abuse that are germane to their ability to adjust to prison and avoid re-offending upon their release. Recent research points to the importance of providing programming for female offenders that addresses issues related to victimization. Morash et al. (1998) report, for instance, that programs for women that focus on gender-specific issues, including victimization and domestic violence, are more successful than those that do not.

Finally, a significant number of women in prison have histories of substance abuse. For example, close to 54 percent of women in prison used drugs in the month prior to their arrest. In addition, women in prison tend to use drugs more frequently than do men (Snell, 1994). Further, a larger number of female inmates have been incarcerated for drug-related crimes. As these numbers and trends suggest, many women in prison tend to have a greater need for drug treatment, although they are slightly less likely than men to receive such treatment (Morash et al., 1994).

GUARDING INMATES

Within the last two decades, increasing attention has been devoted to understanding the work role of the correctional officer (see, e.g., Jacobs and Retsky, 1975; Lombardo, 1981; Philliber, 1987). This attention stems in part from the realization that correctional offices are the linchpins of prison and jail management. No other member of the correctional work group has more direct contact with prisoners or is more intimately involved with their social control than the prison guard (Jacobs and Retsky, 1975). Consequently, our understanding of the nature of incarceration would be incomplete without considering the work of the correctional officer.

Who Are Correctional Officers?

Stereotypes abound about the nature of prison work and those engaged in it. Correctional officers have been variously described as "hacks" and "screws" who suffer from a range of psychological defects. There is a tendency to assume that those who work in prisons are either inherently sadistic or are soon transformed into inhumane keepers as they are socialized to their role and dehumanized by the nature of prison work. Although these views are not without some foundation (Crouch and Marquart, 1980; Haney et al., 1973; Johnson, 1996; Kauffman, 1988), in contemporary prisons the brutal, authoritarian guard is now an exception. Who, then, are correctional officers and what type of professional orientation do they adopt?

Traditionally, correctional officers were white males who were drawn primarily from the rural communities in which most prisons are found. This pattern has begun to change, however, as departments of corrections have made an effort to recruit a more diverse group of officers. In 1996, for example, 68 percent of the correctional officers employed in adult corrections were white, 23 percent were African American, 7 percent were of Hispanic origin, and 2 percent were of another race (Maguire and Pastore, 1997). Interest in developing a more racially diverse correctional officer force stems in part from the desire to employ officers who share similar socioeconomic and cultural backgrounds with the inmates whom they supervise. It has been argued that minority correctional officers lend an additional degree of legitimacy to the prison and that they may be more likely to adopt a positive orientation toward inmates (Jacobs

and Kraft, 1978). Although the correctional officer force continues to differ significantly from the inmate population in terms of racial composition, prisons now employ a greater proportion of minorities than is found in the U.S. population as a whole.

Efforts have also been made to open the correctional officer force to women. Although women have worked in prisons for female inmates since the opening of the first women's prison, it was only in the late 1970s that women began to gain access to work in men's prisons (Pollock-Byrne, 1990). The addition of female guards to male prisons has generally been heralded as a positive influence. For example, it has been argued that the mere presence of women in men's prisons may have a calming effect on inmates and may help to normalize the prison environment (Van Voorhis et al., 1991).

Currently, 81 percent of employees in state and federal correctional facilities who occupy custody positions are male, and 19 percent are female (Maguire and Pastore, 1997). Despite the increased involvement of women in prison work, however, many barriers to the full acceptance of female correctional officers still exist. For example, female officers report that there are barriers to their full integration into the work force, including hostility from their male co-workers, differential access to job assignments, and sexual harassment (Jurik, 1985; Pollock-Byrne, 1990; Zimmer, 1986). Moreover, the correctional officer force remains the most sexually segregated of all of the criminal justice occupations (National Institute of Justice, 1998).

Another trend that has influenced the character of the correctional officer force is professionalization. In response to allegations of racism, brutality, and ineffectiveness during the 1960s and 1970s, many departments of corrections responded by attempting to professionalize the correctional officer force. The main thrust of the professionalization movement in corrections has been to increase the level of education held by prison guards (Jurik et al., 1987). Some effort has also been made, however, to raise standards of selection, training, and institutional performance (Poole and Regoli, 1980).

Research on the attitudes of correctional officers also challenges the portrayal of the guard as an exclusively control-oriented disciplinarian. Studies that have examined the extent to which guards hold attitudes that are punitive and custodial as opposed to rehabilitative and oriented to the delivery of human services to inmates are markedly consistent in showing that officers are supportive of both treatment and control (Arthur, 1994; Cullen et al., 1989; Harris, 1968; Jacobs, 1978; Jacobs and Kraft, 1978; Toch and Klofas, 1982; Whitehead and Lindquist, 1989; more generally, see Johnson, 1996: Philliber, 1987). Thus, Cullen et al. (1989: 40) have noted that "although they [correctional officers] see maintaining order as a core feature of their role and harbor some negative attitudes towards inmates, they also appear to define themselves more as 'correctional officers' than as 'guards' and to believe in the potential of prison treatment programs to reform inmates."

Maintaining Order and Providing Services

One of the primary roles of the correctional officer is to maintain security and control over the inmate population. Historically, officers have been provided with a great deal of power to accomplish this objective. Prior to the 1960s, for example, guards had almost total discretion over how to discipline and reward the inmates under their supervision. Reforms, court interventions, and changes in the organization and

management of prisons, however, have altered the traditional power base of correctional officers and changed the way that they maintain order. As a result, correctional work has become more formal, legalistic, and rational (Jacobs, 1977; Johnson, 1996).

Consequently, an intriguing issue is how guards maintain control over an inmate population that may not be cooperative and is at times openly hostile to guards and prison administrators. Hepburn (1985) has demonstrated that correctional officers draw on a number of different sources of power to maintain order, including legitimate power, reward power, coercive power, expert power, and referent power. Legitimate power is the power that officers have by virtue of their formal position of authority in the prison. Reward power is power that officers exert by providing inmates with various privileges in exchange for their cooperation. In contrast, the basis of coercive power resides in officers' ability to punish inmates for disobedience. Expert power is rooted in the officers' special skills, knowledge, or expertise. Finally, guards who are respected and admired by inmates possess referent power. Depending on their skills, experience, and resources, officers may exert different types of power in order to maintain security.

Whereas these formal sources of power are important to understanding how correctional officers perform their work, guards also rely on various forms of informal social control to keep the prison running smoothly. For example, some guards resort to repressive measures to keep inmates in line (Hepburn, 1989; Lombardo, 1981; Marquart, 1986). The use of verbal threats, obscenities, and insults (backed by the threat or use of physical coercion) may be used to intimidate inmates and assert the authority of the officer. Other officers may adopt a detached, formal relationship with inmates and emphasize

their punitive and custodial role. Another informal approach to maintaining order is to enter
into a relationship with inmates based on mutual accommodation. As Hepburn (1989: 199)
explains, "in a relationship of accommodation,
guards maintain stability and order among prisoners by granting special favors and permitting
minor violations, in exchange for which prison
leaders are expected to maintain control over
other prisoners." Thus, guards may selectively
enforce rules, overlook violations (e.g., gambling
or sex), and provide privileges to obtain inmate
cooperation (Marquart and Crouch, 1984).

It should also be noted that correctional officers perform a diverse and sometimes divergent range of tasks. Correctional work not only
involves "guarding" but also has expanded to
include counseling, protecting, and processing
the inmates under the care of the officer. Today, correctional officers are increasingly called
on to engage in human service and problem-
solving (Johnson and Price, 1981; Hepburn
and Knepper, 1993). Johnson (1996: 229–241)
has noted, for example, that concerned guards
may undertake a variety of activities on the behalf of inmates such as providing inmates with
goods and services (e.g., food or a new cell assignment), acting as referral agents or advocates,
and helping inmates with institutional adjustment problems.

Occupational Reactions

Much has been made of the detrimental effects of working in prison. In fact, prison work
has frequently been likened to incarceration.
Philliber (1987: 9) has observed, for example,
that a review of the research on correctional officers "yields the distinct impression that COs
are alienated, cynical, burned out, stressed out but
unable to admit it, suffering from role conflict of
every kind, and frustrated beyond imagining."

Although there is some truth to this characterization, the work experiences of correctional
employees are more complex than these generalizations imply. As discussed below, correctional work has the potential, in varying degrees, to be both stressful and rewarding.

In one of the first studies of correctional
officers, Cheek and Miller (1983) found that,
compared to police officers, prison guards reported higher levels of hypertension, ulcers, and
heart disease. Further, it was discovered that correctional officers experienced rates of divorce
twice as high as those reported for other blue
collar and white collar employees. These findings led Cheek and Miller to conclude that correctional officers experienced high levels of
stress. Similar conclusions have been reached
in a number of related studies, which indicate
that correctional officers experience more stress
than other prison employees and police officers
(Gernstein et al., 1987; Long et al., 1986;
Patterson, 1992; Robinson et al., 1996; Saylor
and Wright, 1992; but see Blau et al., 1986).

Research that has examined the level of
job satisfaction reported by correctional officers
also paints a somewhat discouraging portrait of
prison work. Toch and Klofas (1982) found, for
example, that 75 percent of their sample of New
York correctional officers felt that "the average
guard would change jobs if he had a chance."
Similarly, Cullen et al. (1990) observed that
correctional officers report lower levels of job
satisfaction than those found for other occupational categories (see also Blau et al., 1986;
Cullen et al., 1993; Robinson et al., 1996; Saylor
and Wright, 1992). Further, although three-
fourths of the correctional officers in their sample reported that they were either "very satisfied" or "somewhat satisfied" with their work,
close to 60 percent also said that they would
"prefer some other job." Findings such as these
have led some to conclude that the prison guard

may in fact be the "classic example of an alienated worker" (Lombardo, 1981: 104).

Although correctional work seems to be
more stressful and unrewarding than other types
of work, the quality of correctional employment
is not uniform but differs among individuals and
from one institution to the next. For instance,
working in maximum security prisons tends
to be more stressful than working in other security levels (Britton, 1997; Cullen et al., 1985; Van
Voorhis et al., 1991). Similarly, those officers
who feel that their work is dangerous are more
likely to find their job stressful and unrewarding
(Cullen et al., 1985; Grossi and Berg, 1991;
Grossi et al., 1996). Feelings of role conflict or
role ambiguity have also been associated with
feelings of stress and job dissatisfaction (Cullen
et al., 1985; Grossi and Berg, 1991; Hepburn and
Albonetti, 1980; Hepburn and Knepper, 1993;
Lindquist and Whitehead, 1986; Triplett et al.,
1996). In contrast, the opportunity to participate in decision making and human service delivery has been found to increase officers' feelings of job satisfaction (Hepburn and Knepper,
1993; Lindquist and Whitehead, 1986). Relatedly, those officers who feel supported by their
supervisors find their work more rewarding and
less stressful (Britton, 1997; Cullen et al., 1985;
Grossi et al., 1996; Van Voorhis et al., 1991).
These findings, along with others, suggest that
prison work is not uniform across institutions
but differs according to certain characteristics of
the work environment.

CONCLUSION:
CHOOSING THE FUTURE

Although the clock ticks at a steady pace, the
beginning of a new century is imbued with special significance. It is a juncture that prompts us
to pause and take stock, to contemplate the wisdom of current policies and arrangements, and
to consider whether fresh approaches are called
for. With regard to imprisonment in America,
two issues are likely to dominate discourse: How
many people should we lock up in the nation's
prisons? And what purpose should prisons
serve? (Cullen et al., 1996)

In prognosticating the future, the safest bet is
to predict continuity; we should anticipate "more
of the same." In this scenario, America's prison
population would continue to grow, pushing
past the 2 million mark and rising steadily into
the foreseeable future. We would also expect that
the penal harm movement (Clear, 1994) would
not lose steam but would fuel the passage of
ever-harsher laws and trigger policies to make
prisons a meaner environment in which to live.
Inmates would strive to carve out niches and
many would avail themselves of treatment programs, but they would do so in institutions that
are increasingly crowded and depriving.

The risk in predicting continuity, however, is
that history teaches us that prisons are dynamic
institutions. From our perspective in the present
era, the future appears fully determined, and exploring the possibility of reform strikes us as a
foolhardy dance with idealism. Within certain
constraints, however, the future is not ineluctable;
different futures can be chosen. Fresh ideas can
be put forward and new policies implemented
(Cullen and Wright, 1996).

Within corrections, therefore, we must consider whether we are in the midst, or close to
the end, of the penal harm movement, a period that has persisted for three decades. If this
movement is losing strength, and some commentators suggest that a progressive era in social
policy is on the horizon (see Dionne, 1996),
then opportunities for new ways of thinking
and for reform might be upon us. Given the
high cost of incarceration, it is not implausible
that citizens and policymakers might question

whether the endless expansion of prison populations is prudent. Neither is it implausible that there will be a push to consider whether prisons should be more than instruments of harm—whether they should serve, as the founders of the penitentiary had hoped, the larger social purpose of transforming law breakers into the law-abiding. There is, then, a choice to be made about the future of imprisonment in the United States. And in smaller and larger ways, it is a choice in which we are all implicated.

DISCUSSION QUESTIONS

1. Prisons have not always been a feature of U.S. society. Describe the pre-prison environment and explain when and why prisons emerged.

2. The concept of prisons and correction have undergone change over time. Describe the changes and discuss the factors that have shaped correction as we currently know it.

3. Compared to that of other nations, is the incarceration rate in the United States high or low? Have prison populations in the United States been rising or falling? Why?

4. In what ways are prisons societies within walls? How do the social worlds of male and female inmates differ and in what ways are they similar?

5. Who guards our prisoners and to what extent are correctional officers as a group professional in their approach to their occupation?

6. Looking into the future, to what extent can we expect change in the manner in which we "correct" offenders? Will we continue to build more and more prisons and to lock up offenders for long periods of time? In your view, what should be the future of imprisonment in the United States?

REFERENCES

Adams, K. 1992. "Adjusting to Life in Prison." Pp. 275–359 in *Crime and Justice: A Review of Research,* Vol. 16. Edited by M. Tonry. Chicago: University of Chicago Press.

Andrews, D., and J. Bonta. 1998. *The Psychology of Criminal Conduct,* 2d ed. Cincinnati: Anderson.

Applegate, B., F. Cullen, and B. Fisher. 1997. "Public Support for Correctional Treatment: The Continuing Appeal of the Rehabilitative Ideal." *The Prison Journal* 77: 237–258.

Arthur, J. 1994. "Correctional Ideology of Black Correctional Officers." *Federal Probation* 58: 57–66.

Barnes, H. 1972. *The Story of Punishment,* 2d ed. Montclair, NJ: Patterson Smith.

Belknap, J. 1996. *The Invisible Women: Gender, Crime, and Justice.* Belmont, CA: Wadsworth.

Bennett, W., J. DiIulio, and J. Walters. 1996. *Body Count: Moral Poverty . . . and How to Win America's War Against Crime and Drugs.* New York: Simon & Schuster.

Blau, J., S. Light, and M. Chamlin. 1986. "Individual and Contextual Effects on Stress and Job Satisfaction: A Study of Prison Staff." *Work and Occupations* 13: 131–156.

Blumstein, A. 1995. "Stability of Punishment: What Happened and What Next?" Pp. 259–274 in *Punishment and Social Control*. Edited by T. G. Blomberg and S. Cohen. New York: Aldine de Gruyter.

Blumstein, A., and J. Cohen. 1973. "A Theory of the Stability of Punishment." *Journal of Criminal Law and Criminology* 64: 198–207.

Bonczar, T., and A. Beck. 1997. *Lifetime Likelihood of Going to State or Federal Prison*. Washington, DC: U.S. Department of Justice.

Bonta, J., and P. Gendreau. 1987. "Reexamining the Cruel and Unusual Punishment of Prison Life." *Law and Human Behavior* 14: 347–372.

Bowker, L. 1981. "Gender Differences in Prisoner Subcultures." Pp. 409–419 in *Women and Crime in America*. Edited by L. Bowker. New York: Macmillan.

Britton, D. 1997. "Perceptions of the Work Environment among Correctional Officers: Do Race and Sex Matter?" *Criminology* 35: 85–106.

Bronstein, A. 1991. "U.S. Policies Create Human Rights Violations." *National Prison Project Journal* 61: 4–5, 13–14.

Bukstel, L., and P. Kilmann. 1980. "Psychological Effects of Imprisonment on Confined Individuals." *Psychological Bulletin* 88: 469–493.

Bureau of Justice Statistics. 1992. *Drugs, Crime, and the Justice System: A National Report*. Washington, DC: U.S. Department of Justice.

———. 1999. "Press Release: State Sentencing Law Changes Linked to Increasing Time Served in State Prisons." Washington, DC: U.S. Department of Justice, Bureau of Justice Statistics (Internet site: www.ojp.gov/bjs/pub).

Butterfield, F. 1997. "Punitive Damages: Crime Keeps on Falling, But Prisons Keep on Filling." *New York Times*, September 28, Section 4, 1, 4.

Camp, C., and G. Camp. 1997. *The Corrections Yearbook—1997*. South Salem, NY: Criminal Justice Institute.

Carroll, L. 1988. *Hacks, Blacks, and Cons: Race Relations in a Maximum Security Prison*. Updated ed. Prospect Heights, IL: Waveland.

Carter, B. 1981. "Reform School Families." Pp. 419–431 in *Women and Crime in America*. Edited by L. Bowker. New York: Macmillan.

Cheek, F., and M. Miller. 1983. "The Experience of Stress for Correction Officers: A Double-Bind Theory of Correctional Stress." *Journal of Criminal Justice* 11: 105–120.

Chiricos, T., and M. Delone. 1992. "Labor Surplus and Punishment: A Review and Assessment of Theory and Evidence." *Social Problems* 39: 421–446.

Clear, T. 1994. *Harm in American Penology: Offenders, Victims, and Their Communities*. Albany: State University of New York Press.

Clemmer, D. 1940. *The Prison Community*. Boston: Christopher.

Colvin, M. 1992. *The Penitentiary in Crisis: From Accommodation to Riot in New Mexico*. Albany: State University of New York Press.

———. 1997. *Penitentiaries, Reformatories, and Chain Gangs: Social Theory and the History of Punishment in Nineteenth-Century America*. New York: St. Martin's Press.

Coughlin, E. 1996. "Throwing Away the Key: Many Criminologists Doubt the Wisdom of the Push to Imprison More People." *The Chronicle of Higher Education*, April 26, A9, A17.

Crouch, B., and J. Marquart. 1980. "On Becoming a Prison Guard." Pp. 63–105 in *The Keepers: Prison Guards and Contemporary Corrections*. Edited by B. Crouch. Springfield, IL: Charles C. Thomas.

———. 1990. "*Ruiz:* Intervention and Emergent Order in Texas Prisons." Pp. 94–114 in *Courts, Corrections, and the Constitution: The Impact of Judicial Intervention on Prisons and Jails*. Edited by J. DiIulio Jr. New York: Oxford University Press.

Cullen, F., and B. Applegate. 1997. *Offender Rehabilitation: Effective Correctional Intervention.* Aldershot, UK: Ashgate.

Cullen, F., B. Fisher, and B. Applegate. Forthcoming. "Public Opinion About Punishment and Corrections." In *Crime and Justice: A Review of Research.* Edited by M. Tonry. Chicago: University of Chicago Press.

Cullen, F., and K. Gilbert. 1982. *Reaffirming Rehabilitation.* Cincinnati: Anderson.

Cullen, F., E. Latessa, R. Kopache, L. Lombardo, and V. Burton Jr. 1993. "Prison Warden's Job Satisfaction." *The Prison Journal* 73: 141–161.

Cullen, F., B. Link, J. Cullen, and N. Wolfe. 1990. "How Satisfying Is Prison Work? A Comparative Occupational Approach." *Journal of Offender Counseling, Services and Rehabilitation* 14: 89–108.

Cullen, F., B. Link, N. Wolfe, and J. Frank. 1985. "The Social Dimensions of Correctional Officer Stress." *Justice Quarterly* 2: 505–533.

Cullen, F., F. Lutze, B. Link, and N. Wolfe. 1989. "The Correctional Orientation of Prison Guards: Do Officers Support Rehabilitation?" *Federal Probation* 53: 33–42.

Cullen, F., P. Van Voorhis, and J. Sundt. 1996. "Prisons in Crisis: The American Experience." Pp. 21–52 in *Prisons 2000: An International Perspective on the Current State and Future of Imprisonment.* Edited by R. Matthews and P. Francis. New York: Macmillan.

Cullen, F., and J. Wright. 1996. "Two Futures for American Corrections." Pp. 198–219 in *The Past, Present, and Future of American Criminal Justice.* Edited by B. Maguire and P. Radosh. New York: General Hall.

Currie, E. 1998. *Crime and Punishment in America.* New York: Metropolitan Books.

de Beaumont, G., and A. de Tocqueville. [1833] 1964. *On the Penitentiary System in the United States and Its Application in France.* Carbondale: Southern Illinois University Press.

DiIulio, J. 1987. *Governing Prisons: A Comparative Study of Correctional Management.* New York: The Free Press.

———. 1990. "Conclusion: What Judges Can Do to Improve Prisons and Jails." Pp. 287–322 in *Courts, Corrections, and the Constitution: The Impact of Judicial Intervention on Prisons and Jails.* Edited by J. J. DiIulio Jr. New York: Oxford University Press.

———. 1994a. "The Question of Black Crime." *The Public Interest* 117 (Fall): 3–32.

———. 1994b. "A Philadelphia Crime Story." *Wall Street Journal,* October 26, A21.

Dionne, E. 1996. *They Only Look Dead: Why Progressives Will Dominate the Next Political Era.* New York: Simon & Schuster.

Earle, A. [1896] 1969. *Curious Punishments of Bygone Days.* Montclair, NJ: Patterson Smith.

Eckland-Olson, S., and S. Martin. 1990. "*Ruiz:* A Struggle over Legitimacy." Pp. 73–93 in *Courts, Corrections, and the Constitution: The Impact of Judicial Intervention on Prisons and Jails.* Edited by J. J. DiIulio Jr. New York: Oxford University Press.

Egan, T. 1999a. "The War on Crack Retreats, Still Taking Prisoners." *New York Times,* February 28, 1, 20–21.

———. 1999b. "Less Crime, More Criminals." *New York Times,* March 7, Section 4, 1, 16.

Federal Bureau of Investigation. 1998. *Crime in the United States, 1997: Uniform Crime Reports.* Washington, DC: U.S. Department of Justice.

Feeley, M., and R. Hanson. 1990. "The Impact of Judicial Intervention on Prisons and Jails: A Framework for Analysis and a Review of the Literature." Pp. 12–46 in *Courts, Corrections, and the Constitution: The Impact of Judicial Intervention on Prisons and Jails.* Edited by J. J. DiIulio Jr. New York: Oxford University Press.

Feinman, C. 1984. "An Historical Overview of the Treatment of Incarcerated Women: Myths and Realities of Rehabilitation." *The Prison Journal* 63: 12–26.

Foucault, M. 1977. *Discipline and Punish: The Birth of the Prison.* New York: Pantheon.

Fox, J. 1984. "Women's Prison Policy, Prisoner Activism, and the Impact of the Contemporary Feminist Movement: A Case Study." *The Prison Journal* 64: 15–36.

Freedman, E. 1974. "Their Sister's Keepers: A Historical Perspective of Female Correctional Institutions in the U.S." *Feminist Studies* 2: 77–95.

Garland, D. 1995. "Penal Modernism and Postmodernism." Pp. 181–209 in *Punishment and Social Control.* Edited by T. G. Blomberg and S. Cohen. New York: Aldine de Gruyter.

Gendreau, P., C. Goggin, F. Cullen, and D. Andrews. 1999. *The Effects of Incarceration and Community Sanctions on Recidivism.* Unpublished paper, University of New Brunswick at Saint John.

Gernstein, L., C. Topp, and G. Correll. 1987. "The Role of the Environment and Person When Predicting Burnout Among Correctional Personnel." *Criminal Justice and Behavior* 14: 352–369.

Giallombardo, R. 1966. "Social Roles in a Prison for Women." *Social Problems* 13: 268–288.

Gilliard, D. 1999. *Prison and Jail Inmates at Midyear 1998.* Washington, DC: U.S. Department of Justice.

Gilliard, D., and A. Beck. 1998. *Prisoners in 1997.* Washington, DC: U.S. Department of Justice.

Goodstein, L. 1979. "Inmate Adjustment to Prison and the Transition to Community Life." *Journal of Research in Crime and Delinquency* 16: 246–272.

Goodstein, L., and K. Wright. 1989. "Inmate Adjustment to Prison." Pp. 229–251 in *The American Prison: Issues in Research and Policy.* Edited by L. Goodstein and D. L. MacKenzie. New York: Plenum.

Grossi, E., and B. Berg. 1991. "Stress and Job Dissatisfaction Among Correctional Officers: An Unexpected Finding." *International Journal of Offender Therapy and Comparative Criminology* 35: 73–81.

Grossi, E., T. Keil, and G. Vito. 1996. "Surviving 'The Joint': Mitigating Factors of Correctional Officer Stress." *Journal of Crime and Justice* 19(2): 103–120.

Hallinan, J. 1995. "Supermax Prisons: They're Supertough, Superexpensive and Supergood for Poor Communities." *The Sunday Patriot-News,* December 10, G1.

Haney, C., C. Banks, and P. Zimbardo. 1973. "Interpersonal Dynamics in a Simulated Prison." *International Journal of Criminology and Penology* 1: 69–97.

Harris, L. 1968. *Corrections 1968: A Climate for Change.* Washington, DC: Joint Commission on Correctional Manpower and Training.

Heffernan, E. 1972. *Making It in Prison: The Square, the Cool and the Life.* New York: Wiley.

Henderson, M., F. Cullen, L. Carroll, and W. Feinberg. 1998. *Racial Integration of Prison Cells: A National Survey of Wardens.* Paper presented at the annual meeting of the Academy of Criminal Justice Sciences, Albuquerque, NM (April).

Hentoff, N. 1995. "Supermaximum Pelican Bay." *The Washington Post,* February 25, A7.

Hepburn, J. 1985. "The Exercise of Power in Coercive Organizations: A Study of Prison Guards." *Criminology* 23: 146–164.

————. 1989. "Prison Guards as Agents of Social Control." Pp. 191–206 in *The American Prison: Issues in Research and Policy.* Edited by L. Goodstein and D. MacKenzie. New York: Plenum.

Hepburn, J., and C. Albonetti. 1980. "Role Conflict in Correctional Institutions: An Empirical Examination of the Treatment-Custody Dilemma Among Correctional Staff." *Criminology* 17: 445–459.

Hepburn, J., and P. Knepper. 1993. "Correctional Officers as Human Service Workers: The Effect on Job Satisfaction." *Justice Quarterly* 10: 315–335.

Ignatieff, M. 1981. "State, Civil Society, and Total Institutions: A Critique of Recent Social Histories of Punishment." Pp. 153–192 in *Crime and Justice:*

An Annual Review of Research, Vol. 3. Edited by M. Tonry and N. Morris. Chicago: University of Chicago Press.

Immarigeon, R. 1992. "The Marionization of American Prisons." *National Prison Project Journal* 7: 1–5.

Irwin, J. 1980. *Prisons in Turmoil.* Boston: Little, Brown.

Irwin, J., and J. Austin. 1994. *It's About Time: America's Imprisonment Binge.* Belmont, CA: Wadsworth.

Irwin, J., and D. Cressey. 1962. "Thieves, Convicts, and The Inmate Culture." *Social Problems* 10: 142–155.

Jacobs, J. 1977. *Stateville: The Penitentiary in Mass Society.* Chicago: University of Chicago Press.

————. 1978. "What Prison Guards Think: A Profile of the Illinois Force." *Crime and Delinquency* 24: 185–196.

————. 1983. *New Perspectives on Prisons and Imprisonment.* Ithaca, NY: Cornell University Press.

Jacobs, J., and L. Kraft. 1978. "Integrating the Keepers: A Comparison of Black and White Prison Guards in Illinois." *Social Problems* 25: 304–318.

Jacobs, J., and H. Retsky. 1975. "Prison Guard." *Urban Life* 4: 5–29.

Jacoby, J., and F. Cullen. 1998. "The Structure of Punishment Norms: Applying the Berk-Rossi Model." *Journal of Criminal Law and Criminology* 89: 245–312.

Johnson, R. 1996. *Hard Time: Understanding and Reforming the Prison,* 2d ed. Belmont, CA: Wadsworth.

Johnson, R., and S. Price. 1981. "The Complete Correctional Officer: Human Service and the Human Environment of Prison." *Criminal Justice and Behavior* 8: 523–539.

Jurik, N. 1985. "An Officer and a Lady: Organizational Barriers to Women Working as Correctional Officers in Men's Prisons." *Social Problems* 32: 375–388.

Jurik, N., G. Halemba, M. Musheno, and B. Boyle. 1987. "Educational Attainment, Job Satisfaction, and the Professionalization of Correctional Officers." *Work and Occupations* 14: 106–125.

Kauffman, K. 1988. *Prison Officers and Their World.* Cambridge, MA: Harvard University Press.

Kennedy, R. 1997. *Race, Crime, and the Law.* New York: Vintage Books.

Keve, P. 1991. *Prisons and the American Conscience: A History of U.S. Federal Corrections.* Carbondale: Southern Illinois University Press.

Kline, S. 1993. "A Profile of Female Offenders in State and Federal Prisons." Pp. 1–6 in *Female Offenders: Meeting the Needs of a Neglected Population.* Laurel, MD: American Correctional Association.

Koban, L. 1983. "Parent in Prison: A Comparative Analysis of the Effects of Incarceration on the Families of Men and Women." *Research in Law, Deviance and Social Control* 5: 171–183.

Lacayo, R. 1995. "The Real Hard Cell: Lawmakers Are Stripping Inmates of Their Perks." *Time,* September 4, 31–32.

Langan, P. 1991. "America's Soaring Prison Population." *Science* 251 (March 29): 1568–1573.

Langan, P., J. Fundis, L. Greenfeld, and V. Schneider. 1988. *Historical Statistics on Prisoners in State and Federal Institutions, Year-end 1925–86.* Washington, DC: U.S. Department of Justice.

Lilly, J., and M. Deflem. 1996. "Profit and Penality: An Analysis of the Corrections-Commercial Complex." *Crime and Delinquency* 42: 3–20.

Lindquist, C., and J. Whitehead. 1986. "Burnout, Job Stress and Job Satisfaction Among Southern Correctional Officers: Perceptions and Causal Factors." *Journal of Offender Counseling, Services and Rehabilitation* 10: 5–26.

Logan, C. 1990. *Private Prisons: Cons and Pros.* New York: Oxford University Press.

Lombardo, L. 1981. *Guards Imprisoned: Correctional Officers at Work.* 2d ed. Cincinnati: Anderson.

Long, N., G. Shouksmith, K. Voges, and S. Roache. 1986. "Stress in Prison Staff: An Occupational Study." *Criminology* 24: 331–345.

Ludlow, R. 1995. "'Supermax' Prison for Worst of Worst Inmates." *The Cleveland Plain Dealer,* September 5, B6.

Lynch, J. 1995. "Crime in International Perspective." Pp. 11–38 in *Crime*. Edited by J. Q. Wilson and J. Petersilia. San Francisco: ICS Press.

MacKenzie, D. 1998. "Criminal Justice and Crime Prevention." Chapter 9 in *What Works, What Doesn't, What's Promising: A Report for the National Institute of Justice*. Edited by W. Sherman, D. Gottfredson, D. MacKenzie, J. Eck, P. Reuter, and S. Bushway. Washington, DC: U.S. Department of Justice, National Institute of Justice.

Maguire, K., and A. L. Pastore. 1997. *Sourcebook of Criminal Justice Statistics 1996*. Washington, DC: U.S. Department of Justice.

———. 1998. *Sourcebook of Criminal Justice Statistics 1997*. Washington, DC: U.S. Department of Justice.

Mahan, S. 1984. "Imposition of Despair: An Ethnography of Women in Prison." *Justice Quarterly* 1: 357–385.

Mann, C. 1984. *Female Crime and Delinquency*. Montgomery: University of Alabama Press.

Marquart, J. 1986. "Prison Guards and the Use of Physical Coercion as a Mechanism of Prisoner Control." *Criminology* 24: 347–366.

Marquart, J., and B. Crouch. 1984. "Co-opting the Kept: Using Inmates for Social Control in a Southern Prison." *Justice Quarterly* 1: 491–509.

Martinson, R. 1974. "What Works? Questions and Answers About Prison Reform." *The Public Interest* 35 (Spring): 22–54.

Maruschak, L. 1997. *HIV in Prisons and Jail, 1995*. Washington, DC: U.S. Department of Justice.

Massey, D., and N. Denton. 1993. *American Apartheid: Segregation and the Making of the Underclass*. Cambridge, MA: Harvard University Press.

Mauer, M. 1994. *Americans Behind Bars: The International Use of Incarceration, 1992–1993*. Washington, DC: The Sentencing Project.

———. 1997. "Racial Disparities in Prison Getting Worse in the 1990s." *Overcrowded Times* 8 (February): 1, 8–13.

Mawby, R. 1982. "Women in Prison: A British Study." *Crime and Delinquency* 28: 24–39.

McCall, N. 1994. *Makes Me Wanna Holler: A Young Black Man in America*. New York: Random House.

McKelvey, B. 1977. *American Prisons: A History of Good Intentions*. Montclair, NJ: Patterson Smith.

Meese, III, E. 1999. "The Dangerous Federalization of Crime." *Wall Street Journal,* February 22, A19.

Miller, J. 1996. *Search and Destroy: African-American Males in the Criminal Justice System*. New York: Cambridge University Press.

Morash, M., T. Bynum, and B. Koons. 1998. *Women Offenders: Programming Needs and Promising Approaches*. Washington, DC: U.S. Department of Justice, National Institute of Justice.

Morash, M., R. Haarr, and L. Rucker. 1994. "A Comparison of Programming for Women and Men in U.S. Prisons in the 1980s." *Crime and Delinquency* 40: 197–221.

Morris, N. 1995. "The Contemporary Prison: 1965–Present." Pp. 227–259 in *The Oxford History of the Prison: The Practice of Punishment in Western Society*. Edited by N. Morris and D. Rothman. New York: Oxford University Press.

Morris, N., and D. J. Rothman. 1995. *The Oxford History of the Prison: The Practice of Punishment in Western Society*. New York: Oxford University Press.

National Institute of Corrections. 1997. *Supermax Housing: A Survey of Current Practice*. Washington, DC: U.S. Department of Justice, National Institute of Corrections.

National Institute of Justice. 1998. *Women in Criminal Justice: A Twenty-Year Update*. Washington, DC: U.S. Department of Justice, National Institute of Justice.

Palmer, T. 1974. "The Youth Authority's Community Treatment Project." *Federal Probation* 38: 3–14.

Patterson, B. 1992. "Job Experience and Perceived Job Stress Among Police, Correctional, and Probation/Parole Officers." *Criminal Justice and Behavior* 19: 260–285.

Petersilia, J. 1992. "California's Prison Policy: Causes, Costs, and Consequences." *The Prison Journal* 72: 8–36.

Philliber, S. 1987. "Thy Brother's Keeper: A Review of the Literature on Correctional Officers." *Justice Quarterly* 4: 9–37.

Pollock-Byrne, J. 1990. *Women, Prison, and Crime.* Belmont, CA: Wadsworth.

Poole, E., and R. Regoli. 1980. "Examining the Impact of Professionalism on Cynicism, Role Conflict, and Work Alienation Among Prison Guards." *Criminal Justice Review* 5: 57–65.

Pratt, T., and J. Maahs. 1999. "Are Private Prisons More Cost-Effective Than Public Prisons? A Meta-Analysis of Evaluation Research Studies." *Crime and Delinquency* 45: 358–371.

Rafter, N. 1985. "Gender, Prisons, and Prison History." *Social Science History* 9: 233–247.

———. 1989. "Gender and Justice: The Equal Protection Issue." Pp. 89–109 in *The American Prison: Issues in Research and Policy.* Edited by L. Goodstein and D. L. MacKenzie. New York: Plenum.

Reiman, J. 1984. *The Rich Get Richer and the Poor Get Prison: Ideology, Class, and Criminal Justice,* 2d ed. New York: John Wiley and Sons.

Robinson, D., F. Porporino, and L. Simourd. 1996. "Do Different Occupational Groups Vary on Attitudes and Work Adjustment in Corrections?" *Federal Probation* 60: 45–53.

Rolland, M. 1997. *Descent Into Madness: An Inmate's Experience of the New Mexico State Prison Riot.* Cincinnati: Anderson.

Rothman, D. 1971. *The Discovery of the Asylum: Social Order and Disorder in the New Republic.* Boston: Little, Brown.

———. 1980. *Conscience and Convenience: The Asylum and Its Alternatives in Progressive America.* Boston: Little, Brown.

———. 1995. "Perfecting the Prison: United States, 1789–1865." Pp. 111–129 in *The Oxford History of Prison: The Practice of Punishment in Western Society.* Edited by N. Morris and D. Rothman. New York: Oxford University Press.

Rotman, E. 1995. "The Failure of Reform: United States, 1865–1965." Pp. 169–197 in *The Oxford History of Prison: The Practice of Punishment in Western Society.* Edited by N. Morris and D. Rothman. New York: Oxford University Press.

Ryan, M., and T. Ward. 1989. *Privatization and the Penal System: The American Experience and the Debate in Britain.* Milton Keynes, UK: Open University Press.

Sampson, R., and J. Laub. 1993. *Crime in the Making: Pathways and Turning Points Through Life.* Cambridge, MA: Harvard University Press.

Saylor, W., and K. Wright. 1992. "Status, Longevity, and Perceptions of the Work Environment Among Federal Employees." *Journal of Offender Rehabilitation* 17: 133–160.

Snell, T. 1994. *Women in Prison.* Washington, DC: U.S. Department of Justice.

Sparks, R. 1996. "Penal 'Austerity': The Doctrine of Less Eligibility Reborn?" Pp. 74–93 in *Prisons 2000: An International Perspective on the Current State and Future of Imprisonment.* Edited by R. Matthews and P. Hampshire. UK: Macmillan.

Sykes, G. 1958. *Society of Captives: A Study of a Maximum Security Prison.* Princeton, NJ: Princeton University Press.

Tischler, C., and J. Marquart. 1989. "Analysis of Disciplinary Infraction Rates Among Female and Male Inmates." *Journal of Criminal Justice* 17: 507–513.

Toch, H. 1977. *Living in Prison: The Ecology of Survival.* New York: Macmillan.

———. 1998. *Corrections: A Humanistic Approach.* Guilderland, NY: Harrow and Heston.

Toch, H., and J. Klofas. 1982. "Alienation and Desire for Job Enrichment Among Correction Officers." *Federal Probation* 46: 35–44.

Tonry, M. 1995. *Malign Neglect: Race, Crime, and Punishment in America.* New York: Oxford University Press.

Triplett, R., J. L. Mullings, and K. Scarborough. 1996. "Work Related Stress and Coping Among Correctional Officers: Implications from Organizational Literature." *Journal of Criminal Justice* 24: 291–308.

U.S. Bureau of the Census. 1998. *Statistical Abstract of the United States, 1998*. Washington, DC: U.S. Department of Commerce.

Useem, B., and P. Kimball. 1991. *States of Siege: U.S. Prison Riots, 1971–1986*. New York: Oxford University Press.

Van Voorhis, P., F. Cullen, B. Link, and N. Wolfe. 1991. "The Impact of Race and Gender on Correctional Officers' Orientation to the Integrated Environment." *Journal of Research in Crime and Delinquency* 28: 472–500.

Wachtler, S. 1997. "A Rage to Punish." *Tikkun* 12: 28–30.

Walmsley, R. 1998. *World Prison Populations: An Attempt at a Complete List*. Unpublished manuscript (November). London, UK.

Ward, D. A. 1994. "Alcatraz and Marion: Confinement in Super Maximum Custody." Pp. 81–94 in *Escaping Prison Myths: Selected Topics in the History of Federal Corrections*. Edited by J. W. Roberts and N. Morris. Washington, DC: The American University Press.

Ward, D., and G. Kassebaum. 1965. "Homosexuality: A Mode of Adaptation in a Prison for Women." *Social Problems* 12: 159–177.

Whitehead, J., and C. Lindquist. 1989. "Determinates of Correctional Officers' Professional Orientation." *Justice Quarterly* 6: 69–87.

Wooldredge, J. 1991. "Correlates of Deviant Behavior Among Inmates of U.S. Correctional Facilities." *Journal of Crime and Justice* 14: 1–25.

———. 1994. "Inmate Crime and Victimization in a Southwestern Correctional Facility." *Journal of Criminal Justice* 22: 367–381.

———. 1998. "Inmate Lifestyles and Opportunities for Victimization." *Journal of Research in Crime and Delinquency* 35: 480–502.

Wooldredge, J., and T. Carboneau. 1998. *A Multilevel Analysis of Inmate Crime*. Paper presented at the annual meeting of the American Society of Criminology, Washington, DC (November).

Wright, K., and L. Goodstein. 1989. "Correctional Environments." Pp. 253–270 in *The American Prison: Issues in Research and Policy*. Edited by L. Goodstein and D. MacKenzie. New York: Plenum.

Wright, K., and W. Saylor. 1992. "A Comparison of Perceptions of the Work Environment Between Minority and Non-Minority Employees of the Federal Prison System." *Journal of Criminal Justice* 20: 63–71.

Zimmer, L. 1986. *Women Guarding Men*. Chicago: University of Chicago Press.

Zimring, F., and G. Hawkins. 1995. *Incapacitation: Penal Confinement and the Restraint of Crime*. New York: Oxford University Press.

Chapter Outline

- The Question of Philosophy
  Types of Programs
  Program Orientation: Control Versus Change

- The Question of Diversion
  Conceptual Issues
  Substantive Issues
  Effectiveness Issues

- Traditional Field Services Programs
  Probation
  Parole

- Issues in Traditional Supervision
  The Relationship
  Supervision Roles
  Classification
  Caseload Size
  Conditions of Supervision
  Revocation
  Effectiveness

- Nontraditional Field Services
  Intensive Supervision
  Electronic House Arrest
  Release Programs

- The Cost Effectiveness of Subincarceration

- Conclusion

18

Correction

Beyond Prison Walls

TODD CLEAR
John Jay College of Criminal Justice, New York

KAREN TERRY
John Jay College of Criminal Justice, New York

Prison crowding in the United States has been and remains a chronic problem of a general penal policy that equates punishment with incarceration (Sherman and Hawkins, 1981). Any account of nonincarcerative forms of punishment in the United States must begin with a frank realization that this country has a firmly established history of apprehending and processing far more offenders than its cell space allows.

The existence of nonincarcerative correction is much like the 80 percent of the iceberg that floats below the surface of the water—its vast presence remains hidden beneath the tip that is perceived by the casual observer as "the iceberg." The figures are somewhat startling: Of all offenders under correctional care on any given day, nearly three-fourths are under some form of community supervision (Bureau of Justice Statistics, 1999a). To expect prison or jail space for

these individuals in a system already suffering overcrowding is simply to fantasize; to create new space for them would require public funds of unprecedented proportions. Nonincarcerative correction is much more than the most common (and most frequently experienced) form of correctional intervention; it is the very foundation on which our postadjudication system of social control rests. This chapter examines the major issues surrounding nonincarcerative correction.

THE QUESTION OF PHILOSOPHY

Scholars may debate the finer points of the philosophy of imprisonment, but one glaring fact remains central: Prison fundamentally represents a loss of freedom. What, by contrast, is the philosophy of the nonincarcerative alternative? Is the intention to provide a type of correction without loss of freedom?

The very phrasing of the question exposes the analytical problem: Nonincarcerative methods are described as alternatives to incarceration. In practice, however, nonincarcerative methods operate as the correctional method of choice, and incarceration is actually the alternative. That is why authors recently have begun referring to nonincarcerative correction as "intermediate punishments" (Champion, 1996) or "intermediate sanctions" (McCarthy, 1987; Morris and Tonry, 1990) rather than as "alternatives to incarceration." By intermediate sanctions, they mean the many correctional approaches falling between traditional prison and traditional probation.

Types of Programs

In this chapter, the term "subincarcerative correction" will be used to denote all the forms of correction that exist short of full-scale sentences to prison or jail. Many types of programs, in addition to traditional probation and parole, fit this definition. The most common are:

Intensive Supervision Operating in either probation or parole settings, intensive supervision programs provide increased scrutiny of the offender's behavior by maintaining enhanced levels of contact. Usually, correction workers have at least weekly contact and sometimes as much as daily personal contact under these programs.

House Arrest Some offenders are sentenced to loss of freedom via being restricted to their own homes. There are several versions of this type of sanction; some call for curfews at night and weekend lockup (to allow for employment),

whereas others call for continual, twenty-four-hour home detention.

Electronic Monitoring Usually used in conjunction with a house arrest or intensive supervision program, electronic monitoring mandates that an offender be fitted with a bracelet-like device that indicates when the offender has strayed from a designated location, normally the home.

Urine Screening By testing urine samples, correctional authorities are able to determine if an offender has been using drugs or alcohol.

Fines Used to punish the offender with a monetary penalty, these are traditionally issued in flat sums. Some communities have recently introduced a system of "day fines," which impose monetary punishments more equitably among those of different economic statuses. Fines are seldom used, particularly as a sole sanction. Instead, they are normally assessed in conjunction with another type of punishment, such as probation.

Community Service Often used as a companion sanction to probation, community service orders require the offender to work a specified number of hours without compensation on some project providing general benefit to the community.

Halfway Houses and Work/Study Release Centers (Furloughs) Usually, these types of semi-incarcerative programs allow a person to be free during working hours in order to obtain or keep a job but require a return to the facility overnight. Often used when the offender is released from a custodial setting, these programs help the offender adjust more successfully into the community.

Boot Camps Offenders are placed in a quasi-military program for a brief term (usually 90–180 days). This provides a highly structured regime that aims to instill discipline and obedience to orders through physical training and work.

Shock Probation Also called "split sentences," these programs provide a brief incarcerative term (usually 30–120 days) followed by a brief period of probation. The aim of this sentence is to deter future criminal activity by demonstrating the seriousness of the criminal law and the hardships of confinement.

Treatment Programs Often, offenders with special types of problems (for example, sexual adjustment, substance abuse, or emotional adjustment problems) will be sentenced to enter special treatment programs designed to help them overcome their difficulties. Inpatient programs provide treatment to offenders while they are residents in the program; outpatient programs provide treatment while the offender continues to reside at home.

To this limited selection of special approaches can be added the traditional forms of probation and parole supervision. This array of programs is so varied that it is difficult even to find a name that encompasses them all. They are primarily nonincarcerative, but many rely on intermittent or short-term stays in secure facilities. They all involve community supervision, but some include residential supervision as well. For that same reason, the commonly used term "field services" often is misleading.

Program Orientation: Control Versus Change

In terms of overall philosophy, these programs can be divided into two general classes of orientation. Some programs seek primarily to change offenders by helping them overcome some problem or attitude that contributes to criminal behavior. Others seek to establish effective control over the offender's predilections toward criminality by reducing the opportunity for criminal behavior. The programs in both classes are utilitarian in that they seek to reduce the instance of crime. In fact, all subincarcerative programs engage in both control and change strategies; the difference is that some programs are more compatible with one philosophical approach than the other. For example, intensive supervision and electronic monitoring programs emphasize the use of surveillance to reduce or eliminate opportunities for crime. By contrast, treatment and semi-incarcerative programs help the offender develop and strengthen a crime-free lifestyle.

It should be obvious that the claims of control and change made by these programs are no different from similar claims made on behalf of the incarcerative sanction. Years ago, subincarcerative programs could be distinguished by the fact that they were less punitive than was confinement, and this was often their stated intention. However, recent experience with the programs finds that, because of the surveillance and treatment requirements, they have grown sufficiently onerous that a significant number of offenders prefer regular incarceration to a community alternative (Clear et al., 1988). Therefore, subincarcerative programs may be thought of rightfully as at least potentially punitive.

Just as the dual aims of control and change mix poorly in the context of the coercive environment of the prison, so it is also commonly the case for subincarcerative programs. One example illustrates the problem: How should an offender be handled who drinks to the point of intoxication and then drives? Obviously, such an offender represents a risk to the community, and it is incumbent on the correctional authorities to control the risk. This would suggest such measures as coercive antabuse (a drug that makes the user ill when alcohol is ingested), loss of driving privileges, or even house arrest to prevent driving at night. On the other hand, the problem of alcohol abuse will never be overcome fully until the person makes a change in personal lifestyle, and this approach would connote treatment such as Alcoholics Anonymous or other counseling. Although it may be logical to try both approaches in the short run, at some point the ability to change must be tested through relaxation of the requirements of control. Indeed, this competition between control and change characterizes the process of influencing behavior in any setting (Kelman, 1961).

Perhaps the main distinction of these programs is that they uniformly claim to be cheaper than confinement. Incarceration is without question an expensive government program. By comparison, all subincarcerative programs require a considerably smaller investment of tax dollars to operate, at least on the face of it, than does prison. A second claim these programs make is that their presence helps obviate incarceration. This latter claim reflects a concept often referred to as "diversion" and deserves greater discussion.

THE QUESTION OF DIVERSION

The dictionary defines the word *divert* as "to turn aside from a course or direction." When correctional authorities say they are "diverting"

an offender, they mean they are altering a course of action that ordinarily would lead to prison or jail. Yet, because the vast majority of offenders can never really be candidates for extended incarceration of any kind, simply because that resource is so scarce, it stretches the meaning of the term to call all these programs "diversionary." For most offenders, the existence of subincarcerative programs means correctional authorities may adopt some form of change or control in the face of limited institutional resources.

The question of diversion in the subincarcerative arena can be divided into three areas of inquiry: conceptual (diversion from what?), substantive (how does diversion work?), and effectual (how many are diverted?).

Conceptual Issues

In its original usage, the idea of diversion meant to avoid involving the offender in the formal criminal justice system, mostly by avoiding prosecution. However, many of the early diversion programs failed to demonstrate a significant potential for this approach (Zimring, 1974), although nearly every major jurisdiction in the United States now has a diversionary program allowing certain defendants to take steps that will result in charges being dropped.

More recently, the concept of diversion has come to include the intentional avoidance of any more serious consequence. For example, a man who has been convicted of a serious crime would be eligible for prison, but authorities might seek to divert him to some less onerous sanction. This more general meaning of diversion therefore can apply to any stage in the criminal justice system, even the postadjudication stage. Some convicted offenders might be diverted from any correctional intervention (through a fine, court costs, or some reduced type of community service). More serious offenders might be diverted from jail through treatment programs. The most serious offenders might be diverted from prison through intensive supervision or work release programs. For all these offenders bound for some form of correctional control, the system intervenes to divert them to a lesser level of control.

Substantive Issues

Two questions arise: (1) How is it known where an offender is bound? and (2) How does the system reroute the offender to less onerous subinstitutional correction?

The first question is not as simple as it sounds, for it is a what-if question: What would have happened if the diversion program had not been in existence? The approach of many of the subincarcerative programs is to set up a new diversionary program (such as house arrest) and to extend eligibility to those offenders whose crimes qualify them for a prison or jail term (normally excluding violent, predatory, or repetitive offenders). This is an intuitively attractive approach: Excluding the violent offender maintains public confidence, and diversion presumably is achieved by accepting only prison eligibles.

Unfortunately, research has shown this approach to be seriously flawed. Most penal codes establish eligibility for incarceration very broadly—few felons actually are ineligible for prison. Yet, in nearly every jurisdiction, a large proportion—even a majority—of ordinary felons never end up in custody for any length of time (Morris and Tonry, 1990). One study in Oregon (Clear et al., 1986) found that only those who posed the highest risk (that is, violent repeaters) and those convicted of the most serious criminal conduct (such as forcible rape, arson, and homi-

cide) had high rates of imprisonment. The low-risk, low-seriousness offenders—those ordinarily eligible for subincarcerative programs—were already being placed on probation 85 percent of the time. In fact, offenders who fell in the group between the two extremes—sometimes excluded from consideration for special diversion programs—already received probation 55 percent of the time. Studies of probation caseloads in California (Petersilia, 1985), New York (New York City Department of Probation, 1973), Tennessee (Fox et al., 1987), and Georgia (Erwin, 1987) have found large numbers of serious, high-risk offenders already on probation.

This poses a serious challenge to the diversion movement. To divert offenders who ordinarily would receive probation would be to give them a sanction less than probation, and no serious current diversion proposal seeks to do that. Instead of diverting, these programs run the risk of doing what often is called "widening the net of social control"—that is, increasing the level of control for offenders beyond the probation they ordinarily would have received. Often, in order to target a group of offenders that is truly confinement-bound, the eligibility criteria have to include offenders whose crimes are so serious as to call into question the wisdom of diversion.

Some critics of the diversion movement argue that too much attention is given to the problem of net widening. Instead, they argue, the institutions of social control have broken down in some areas of the country to the point that "net repairing" is needed (Petersilia, 1987). These critics believe that true diversion is unwise, and that the system should expand its current methods to make them more control-oriented. Whatever the merits of this argument, the point remains that in order truly to divert, subincarcerative programs face serious problems in framing the description of eligible offenders.

If the criteria are drawn too restrictively, the program risks diverting people from probation rather than prison. If the program taps a highly concentrated group of confinement-bound offenders, there is a real risk of loss of public and political support.

Public support is essential if a community corrections program is going to be effective. Unfortunately, public sentiment supports the incarceration of offenders regardless of cost (Shilton, 1995) or seriousness of offense (Bennett, 1995). According to one study, individuals consider jail to be the most effective and safest sentencing option available for judges to administer to offenders, though they acknowledge the cost-effectiveness of community corrections programs (Sigler and Lamb, 1995). As a result of this societal perspective, public officials are reluctant to appear "soft on crime" by backing traditional community-based corrections. They tend to support the more punitive of the subincarcerative sanctions (Gendreau et al., 1994), which may increase the level of social control over individuals who would have otherwise received less-punitive sanctions.

Many programs have approached the problem by focusing on how the offender gets admitted to the program as much as on who is eligible. The usual technique is to develop elaborate admission criteria. One of the steps is to establish, often through the court or the plea bargaining process, that the person is truly bound for confinement. In Georgia, for example, judges sign a statement that they would have placed the person in prison without the diversion program (Erwin, 1987). In New Jersey, judges actually sentence offenders to prison and then later modify their sentence order (Pearson, 1988). Such careful screening helps guarantee high true diversion rates. A second step is to assess the offender and determine whether he or she is likely to be successful in the program. Diversion programs that do careful offender assessments often have high rates of rejection of potential participants (Erwin, 1987; Clear et al., 1988; Pearson, 1988).

Effectiveness Issues

The problem of the target group has been a difficult one for correction leaders to solve and has limited the effectiveness of the diversion movement. An overview evaluation of numerous diversion efforts by Krisberg and Austin (1980) concluded that on the whole, little evidence supports the belief that they have not merely widened the net. This is true mainly because most programs have not been able to target offenders correctly; instead, they serve as alternatives to lesser sanctions.

This finding has ominous implications for program costs. Most advocates of subincarceration point out that these programs are cheaper to run than the confinement alternative, with the implication that their use saves tax dollars. Although the programs are indeed cheaper than incarceration, they do not actually save money unless they are truly used as alternatives to confinement. The fact that so many programs have not been used this way must be viewed as a major failure of the subincarcerative movement. Their addition to the correctional arsenal actually adds to the correctional costs, because they almost always are more expensive than the less severe sanction they are replacing for most offenders.

This does not mean these programs have been total failures, however. Saving public funds is merely one of several goals often attributed to them. They also can be evaluated in terms of achieving the dual aims of control and change. In the sections that follow, specific types of subincarcerative programs are assessed. A fair summary of all these evaluations taken together would be that the difference in long-term rates of criminality between offenders sentenced to average periods of confinement and those diverted to most types of subincarceration is negligible or even favors the latter programs. This suggests that, viewed in the long range, the subincarcerative methods fare about as well or better than prison in changing and controlling offenders. Yet, this general summary also reflects a web of evaluation problems and issues.

TRADITIONAL FIELD SERVICES PROGRAMS

The two traditional field services programs are probation and parole supervision. The issues in each program are similar, although they have different administrative patterns and programmatic histories.

Probation

Probation, which is the most common correctional sanction in the United States, has two main purposes: to punish the offender through incapacitation in the community and to rehabilitate the offender (Pearce and Olderman, 1995). Probation began in the United States in 1841, when John Augustus, the famous Boston shoemaker and philanthropist, first "stood bail" for inebriates in order to avoid what he considered worthless jail sentences (National Probation Association, 1939). Formal probation was first instituted in the Commonwealth of Massachusetts in 1869. By 1925, when the U.S. Congress

established adult probation, nearly all states had formal adult and juvenile probation systems. In 1956, Mississippi became the last state to enact a juvenile probation system (Hussey and Duffee, 1980).

Because the organization of probation in the United States is a hodgepodge of arrangements (U.S. Department of Justice, 1978), the probation system has been slow to change and has represented a weak political link in the correction process. In days when tax dollars are difficult to find, underorganized probation departments often find it difficult to compete with other government services for support. In the last two decades, probation caseloads have grown considerably faster than have probation resources. Additionally, probation has had to begin responding to the challenge of increasingly serious cases (Harlow and Nelson, 1984).

Parole

The harshness of English criminal law was responsible for the development of the parole system. By the late 1700s, the English penal system was characterized mainly by overcrowding, disease, and brutality—and at a high cost to the government. A policy of transportation of criminals was undertaken to rid Great Britain of the thousands of English poor who literally had been stuffed into old jails and "hulks"—unserviceable ships anchored in London harbor. The English courts sentenced offenders to extremely lengthy terms of confinement to be served under cruel conditions, but even these sentences were less feared by the poor than was the imposition of "transportation."

During most of the 1700s, 40,000 convicts were sent to the American colonies and the Caribbean, a practice that was abandoned after the American Revolution. From the 1780s until 1868, nearly 150,000 convicts were sent to Australia and its environs (Hughes, 1987). These offenders were subjected to penal servitude and to whippings, starvation, and other forms of privation. In reaction to the brutish penal systems of the day, a remarkable reformer, Alexander Maconochie, advocated leading convicts to a better life through example and teaching instead of corporal punishment. In 1840, he established the "mark" system in Australia's dreaded Norfolk Prison, which allowed convicts to earn their way out of prison through good behavior. This was followed by Sir Walter Crofton's similar "ticket of leave" system in Ireland in 1854 (Barnes and Teeters, 1959). These systems were the predecessors of modern parole.

In the United States, indeterminate sentencing first was established in New York in 1869, and formal parole administered in Elmira Reformatory in 1876 (Barnes and Teeters, 1959). The idea of the indeterminate sentence was that the duration of the prisoner's punishment would be determined by his or her behavior after sentencing as much as by the crime itself. Those offenders showing initiative and reformation would be released earliest; those who resisted authority would pay the price in longer time served. By 1944, every state in the United States had a parole law.

The U.S. parole system differed in several respects from the programs of Maconochie and Crofton, but one difference was critical. Under the earlier systems, convicts earned release by following a published set of rules and earning marks according to an established formula. In contrast, the U.S. system required the convict to apply to prison authorities for release and to demonstrate reformation. The difference was momentous. The earlier system left control of the release decision in the inmate's hands, whereas the Ameri-

can innovation placed it in the hands of correctional administrators. The difference was to play a major role in the sentencing reform movements of the 1970s (Hussey and Duffee, 1980).

Organizationally, parole in the United States is always operated at the state level of government under the executive branch. In the majority of jurisdictions, parole supervision is distinguished from release, with the former operated by a parole board and the latter by the department of correction. In other jurisdictions, parole supervision is administered by the releasing authority. The advent of the determinate sentencing movement of the 1970s challenged the idea of parole release in many states, but the supervision of released offenders was a concept that survived challenge nearly everywhere.

ISSUES IN
TRADITIONAL SUPERVISION

The basic transaction of traditional correctional field services is "field supervision"—the maintenance of contact between the offender and the probation or parole worker as a means of service and surveillance (Studt, 1978). Considerable research has investigated the supervision relationship in field services and has identified a number of controversies in field supervision.

The Relationship

Probation and parole officers often emphasize the importance of the relationship they are able to establish with their clients. Through this relationship, they are able to influence the attitudes and behaviors of the clients assigned to them. Studies of the relationship show its dynamics to be a complicated process. McCleary (1978) spent six months observing a parole office in

1974 and found that, based on their experiences, the caseworkers formed general stereotypes of clients early in the supervision relationship. Some of the types were pejorative ("criminals"); others were related to the goals of control ("dangerous man") and change ("sincere client"). The parole officer selected a supervision approach that fit the client type and established a relationship designed to pursue supervision goals.

Observers agree that the relationship between the caseworker and the client does not always develop the way the officer believes it should, however, because the organization's bureaucracy also has an impact on the supervision effort. McCleary found that the bureaucracy operated as a constraint on the flexibility of the relationship. Similarly, Takagi (1976) evaluated a sample of parole failures to find that "organizational variables" such as office policy and bureaucratic pressures for consistency resulted in cases being unnecessarily classified as failures. Klockars (1972) has theorized that the bureaucracy and its requirements are so important that they constitute a third element in the supervision relationship. He proposes that the supervision relationship actually is a process in which the attachment gradually strengthens between the officer and the client, while the bond between officer and bureaucracy grows weaker by contrast. Therefore, in successful relationships, the caseworker–client bond becomes stronger and more important than the caseworker–organization bond. This allows the caseworker to use authority to influence the client and still justify ignoring minor misbehavior.

Supervision Roles

The relationship also is constrained by officer attitudes. Studt (1978) observed parole work in California and found that officers had personalized approaches to conducting the work. These individualized supervision rationales resulted in wide differences in supervision strategies, to the point that, in effect, each parole officer constituted his or her own agency.

Several researchers have classified officers in terms of the roles they undertake, based on their philosophies. One of the first such studies was conducted by Glaser (1964), who identified two dimensions of supervision philosophy: (1) concern for assistance (analogous to "change") and (2) concern for control based on four stereotypic "officer types." Subsequent research (Clear and O'Leary, 1982) found that these types of officers tended to develop different supervision plans for offenders.

Most researchers have treated the concerns for control and change as though they are in conflict—a caseworker must choose between one or the other because they are incompatible (Stanley, 1976). Based on this idea, Georgia recently experimented with a team caseload approach in which a surveillance officer was paired with a probation officer, with the former responsible for control and the latter for assistance. Authorities believed such a system would help avoid confusion by separating the roles. In practice, however, the teams reported that their roles tended to meld, and studies of their casework practices showed little distinction among the officers in the manner in which they carried out the assignments (Erwin and Clear, 1987). The researchers concluded that, even though officers differ in their role philosophies, the roles of control and change may be mutually supportive and not as contradictory as is ordinarily believed.

Classification

Because of differences in officer attitudes, the typing process is unreliable. Studies of officers' attempts to classify offenders find that substantial disagreement often arises over the client's risk to the community and responsiveness to supervision (Clear and O'Leary, 1982). When officer classifications are unreliable, it is difficult to establish officer accountability for judgments made about cases without simply second-guessing. In order to achieve greater reliability and to enhance accountability, it has become common practice to develop classification instruments that provide a set of variables with weights that will be used to "score" the supervision class of the offender. The use of quantitatively established classification instruments has helped increase greatly the reliability of classification decisions (Baird, 1981).

Most classification systems in use today are multidimensional. Often, they combine two instruments—"risk" assessment (the predicting of the likelihood of a new offense) and "needs" assessment (a summary measure of the overall degree of problems in an offender's life)—to determine the amount of supervision a case will require.

The two main methods of assessing offenders are through clinical and actuarial models of assessment. Both models are used to predict future offending behavior through assessing offender risk. Their aim is to match the highest-risk offenders with the most intensive supervisory or treatment programs. Though clinical models—those in which an "expert" uses his or her judgment to assess future risk level—are the most common form of assessment, it is the actuarial models—those that use empirically tested correlations between objective risk measure and recidivism—that are most accurate (Gendreau et al., 1996: 65). This holds true particularly for special populations of offenders, such as sexual offenders and those who are mentally disordered. Despite the benefits, the use of objective risk and needs devices is not without problems (Clear and Gallagher, 1985; Clear, 1988).

Caseload Size

One of the most controversial areas of study is "the search for the magic number" (Carter and Wilkins, 1976), or the attempt to determine the optimal caseload size for field supervision. Despite the frequency of numbers cited in the literature as standards for caseload size, such as sixty or thirty-five, there is no empirical basis for any prescribed caseload size being optimal. Field supervisors can monitor up to 200 cases at one time (Barajas, 1993), which causes frustration in officers and would seem to make effective supervision nearly impossible. However, studies of caseload size have found consistently that simply reducing the size of the caseload does not increase the effectiveness of supervision (Albanese et al., 1985; Morris and Tonry, 1990). Although such findings are difficult to understand or explain, the uniformity of the evidence is persuasive: Smaller caseloads do not result in greater success.

The most plausible explanation for this phenomenon is that there is an "interaction effect"—that the same supervision technique will help some offenders, hurt others, and when applied across the board, have no overall effect. Summary reviews of field supervision strategies find much support for the existence of the interaction effect (Warren, 1973; Palmer, 1975; Gendreau and Ross, 1981). If the interaction hypothesis is correct, the solution is to specialize supervision, taking different approaches for different types of cases, and not merely do the same thing, although more intensively, with everybody.

This approach, often called "differential supervision," has been found consistently to produce results superior to the traditional approach of equal supervision for all clients (Baird et al., 1986; Andrews, 1987). The success of the differential supervision approach has led researchers to abandon the search for the magic number of cases in favor of a workload model that measures the time a case requires under differential supervision (National Institute of Corrections, 1981). Workload systems have been more differentially effective in determining the best staffing level for supervision (Harlow and Nelson, 1984).

Another emerging system of supervision is that of group reporting, where one supervisor meets with several offenders at scheduled times. The frequency of meetings depends upon the risk level of the offender. One study on group reporting (Soma, 1994) explained how field supervisors with high caseloads often lose contact with the offenders, particularly those convicted of minor offenses. Group reporting increases the level of communication between the field supervisor and offenders and helps maintain face-to-face contact on a regular basis. This approach is not without problems; however, it allows the supervisor to focus on high-risk offenders in need of individual attention without losing contact with lower-risk offenders.

Conditions of Supervision

The formal conditions of supervision are established by the requisite sentencing authority (the court or the parole board) and define binding requirements placed on the offender. In fact, because case law consistently has held that the supervision officer does not have the discretion to alter the conditions of supervision, they may also be thought of as binding on the supervision officer.

Despite the centrality of conditions to the supervision process, there have been few studies of them. Given the dearth of research on conditions, several writers have attempted to define the policy that should apply to conditions. The generally accepted standard for setting conditions is that they should be reasonably related to the circumstances that produced the original criminal behavior. Unfortunately, this is such a narrow standard that many experts question its usefulness. In addressing the narrowness problem, attention should be given to three general types of conditions (O'Leary and Clear, 1982):

1. Punitive conditions, such as community service and restitution, are designed to demonstrate to the offender community disapproval of the criminal conduct.

2. Risk conditions, such as drug treatment, are designed to reduce the probability of future conduct by ameliorating specific problems in the offender's situation.

3. Management conditions, such as reporting address changes, are designed to provide basic support for the supervision process.

Under this logic, only the minimum number of conditions needed to carry out these three functions should be imposed: Punitive conditions should be commensurate with the crime's seriousness, and risk conditions should be the least drastic needed to control the risk.

Revocation

The offender's status as a supervised offender in the community is ended through revocation. Despite much controversy about whether the freedom granted an offender under probation or parole is a legal entitlement (Newman, 1985), the courts have held that federal probation is a privilege and not a right (*U.S.* v. *Birnbaum,* 1970). Once granted, however, parole (*Morrissey* v. *Brewer,* 1972) and probation (*Gagnon* v. *Scarpelli,* 1973) can be removed only with just cause and due process.

There are two general types of revocation. When an offender is convicted of a new crime, this constitutes a violation of the requirement to remain law-abiding and serves as a prima facie (at first view) basis for revocation. When an offender fails to abide by the conditions of supervision, even if the misbehavior does not constitute a violation of the law, the person's status may be revoked. This is called a "technical" revocation.

In practice, a great deal of discretion may be exercised in making the revocation decision. When offenders under supervision for traditional felonies commit minor offenses (such as shoplifting), a revocation may not result. Technical violations often are followed by a warning or by lesser sanctions such as forty-eight hours in jail, with a revision in conditions. By the same token, if a condition is considered central to supervision, especially if it relates to risk (such as required therapy for a sex offender), violation often will result in removal from the community and confinement.

One study of revocations compared patterns of client misbehavior and response in five jurisdictions (Baird et al., 1986). The major finding was that practices vary widely, both within and among jurisdictions. This disparity in response to violations was further complicated by the fact that virtually no relationship seemed to exist between the type of violation, the type of response, and subsequent misbehavior, including criminal behavior. In other words, there was no

support for the idea that rules violations are flags for impending criminal behavior.

Crowded institutions since the 1980s have placed a premium on dealing with violations short of full revocation and confinement. At the same time, revoked offenders make up a significant proportion of all prison and jail intakes. So long as discretion attaches to the decisions to impose conditions and enforce them, this area will remain controversial.

Effectiveness

The effectiveness of traditional supervision methods remains a controversial subject. Many experts find little basis for confidence that supervision accomplishes much, and a few would agree with Martinson's (1976) classic assessment that probation supervision in some areas is "a kind of a standing joke." Langan (1992) showed that within three years of sentencing, nearly two-thirds of felony probationers were rearrested for either a new felony or a technical violation.

But the real question about the effectiveness of supervision is, Compared to what? Only a few studies have tried to compare supervision to other alternatives. Saks and Logan (1984) matched a sample of Connecticut mandatory releases (without supervision) with a similar sample of parolees released during the same period. There was an initial advantage in favor of the parolees, but within three years, the records of criminal activity looked nearly identical. They concluded that parole did not prevent criminal activity but instead retarded it; their study played a significant role in the parole abolition movement in Connecticut.

By contrast, Petersilia (1987) measured a sample of serious California felons sentenced to prison against a matched sample of offenders (with similar characteristics) sentenced to probation. Here, the prison group showed an initial advantage, but after four years, there was no difference in criminal activity between the groups. Using similar methodologies, comparisons of prison to probation have shown little difference in rates of arrest or numbers of arrests across time (Barry and Clear, 1984; Clear et al., 1988). Other studies have shown that persons who receive supervision after brief periods of incarceration appear to fare no differently than those who receive only supervision (Vaughan, 1980). The only comparative study to show a major difference in performance (Murray and Cox, 1979) indicated that young serious offenders placed on probation performed slightly worse than a similar sample of offenders placed in training schools. This study has been criticized, however, for overestimating the criminal behavior rates of the training school sample before training school (McCleary, 1981).

Based on studies such as these, it would be easy to conclude that traditional supervision makes little or no difference. That would be stretching the interpretation of these studies, however, because none represents a tightly controlled experiment, and all have been criticized for their methodological flaws. The more significant point is this: If supervision appears not to be markedly superior to nonsupervision, it also appears to be little different from confinement. Based on this conclusion, the best approach would seem to be to do nothing to offenders because supervision is not more effective than doing nothing, and incarceration is not more effective than supervision. Obviously, this is an exceedingly unlikely policy, and the research results are simply not convincing enough to justify eradication of either supervision or confinement.

NONTRADITIONAL FIELD SERVICES

Since the middle of the 1980s, nontraditional methods of supervision have proliferated. The main impetus for this has been the tremendous crowding found in virtually all traditional correctional realms. Numerous programs have been developed to help address this problem, but three primary types can be identified: intensive supervision, house arrest with electronic monitoring, and partial release. Each type of program raises particular issues about its use.

Intensive Supervision

Intensive supervision programs (ISPs) have become perhaps the most common response to institutional crowding across the country. The claims of the intensive supervision programs are ambitious, if not spectacular: Protect the community, reduce crowding, save tax dollars, demonstrate probation effectiveness, and rehabilitate clients. ISPs differ from standard probation in three distinct ways: caseload size, level of supervisory contact, and offender eligibility. The caseload of ISPs is usually no more than twenty-five offenders per supervisor, resulting in an increased level of supervision for each offender (Pearce and Olderman, 1995). In some communities, only non-violent offenders are eligible for ISP, mirroring the eligibility requirements of regular probation (Petersilia and Turner, 1993; Erwin, 1986; Pearson, 1988). In most areas, however, a wide variety of offenders—including violent, high-risk offenders—are eligible (Byrne, 1986).

The two major studies on the ISPs, in Georgia (Erwin, 1986) and in New Jersey (Pearson, 1988), have produced some significant findings. Offenders placed in the program did as well as or better than those with other sentences on several performance criteria, including new arrests. The results suggest that ISPs can perform a useful role in overcoming the crowded conditions that plague most prison and jail systems. A more recent survey of fourteen jurisdictions nationwide replicated the findings in Georgia; namely, those sentenced to an ISP had approximately the same rate of rearrest as those sentenced to regular probation.

The picture for ISPs is not completely rosy, however. One problem, related to diversion, was discussed previously. The Georgia and New Jersey programs appear to have been successful in achieving high rates of diversion, and this is their main reason for existence. But this is by no means the uniform experience of other ISPs around the country. In fact, in the experiments mentioned previously, it proved difficult to identify appropriate diversion cases for ISP.

In New Jersey and Georgia, the diversion emphasis has meant that these programs have been exceedingly careful in the kind of offenders admitted to supervision. The result has been that both programs have provided intensified supervision to "the best of the bad"—low-risk offenders who were in prison or prison-bound. Although this has helped ensure high rates of program success, it also has resulted in an ironic reversal of appropriation of correctional resources. The ISPs in these states represent the toughest level of supervision the states can provide. Undoubtedly, the quality of supervision provided by these programs is far superior to traditional supervision programs, as a result of greater resources, more effective staff, and better management. Because of the careful selection of offenders for diversion, this heightened supervision practice is applied to a clientele that in Georgia is nearly 40 percent low-risk, and in New Jersey around 50 percent. In other words, the toughest supervision in the

subincarcerative arsenal is used to control a population of offenders that is not markedly different in risk to the community than a caseload of regular probationers.

How can this be? The reason is that the prisons in New Jersey and Georgia contain large numbers of low- and moderate-risk offenders—enough to fill their ISPs. The ISP provides the rationale for their release from incarceration. Yet, because probation has such a mediocre reputation, it seems that from a public viewpoint, something more than regular probation is needed, if release is to be feasible. So the ISP is made to be tough and serious even though the cases it supervises are, for the most part, not much different from typical community supervision cases. The fact that far more-serious offenders come out of prison each day onto regular parole caseloads three to five times as large is an irony the system has not yet addressed.

The placement of better risks in an ISP is not entirely benign, however. The requirements of the ISPs are more strict than those of regular probation and are much more strictly enforced. As a result, even though ISP clients commit fewer crimes than their probation counterparts, they have a considerably higher failure rate (Erwin, 1986; Pearson, 1988; Petersilia and Turner, 1993). They may not commit crimes, but they certainly fail to meet the enhanced program requirements and often go to prison as a result. Some critics have asked whether the ISP movement creates failures by selecting the best cases and then holding them accountable for extreme performance requirements. This is not an idle question. The typical ISP requires twice-weekly contacts (one a surprise home visit), periodic urine screening for drugs or alcohol, community service, payment of fines and program fees, and attendance at treatment programs—as well as full-time employment. In the jurisdictions they evaluated, Petersilia and Turner (1993) showed that offenders in ISPs had significantly higher re-arrest rates for technical evaluations (65 percent) than those on regular probation (35 percent). To survive the stringent requirements of an ISP without incident for six to nine months poses a great difficulty to the offenders sentenced to an ISP.

The final issue is historical. The ISP movement of the 1980s follows an earlier version in the 1960s, one based on treatment and assistance. Once its conceptual rationale fell out of favor, the older ISP movement disintegrated. The ISP of the 1990s follows a more punitive philosophy, with rehabilitation receding in importance (Gendreau et al., 1994). It remains an interesting question whether the current movement will survive its ironies and achieve its apparent potential. If prison crowding ended tomorrow, would ISP survive?

Electronic House Arrest

Another response to institutional crowding has been the sentencing of offenders to serve time in their own homes instead of in institutions. The use of the home as a sanction has considerable appeal—it is cheaper than prison or jail, it keeps families intact, and it ensures a loss of freedom without the brutalizing aspects of the custodial facility. The main problem is ensuring offender compliance.

For years, court-ordered home detention was a legal possibility with little practical support because of problems in enforcement. Technological advances in surveillance devices made home detention a practical reality, and by 1987, electronic house arrest (EHA) was an operating aspect of correctional processes in nearly two dozen jurisdictions (Petersilia, 1987).

Several versions of electronic monitoring now are available on the market. They work on the basis of a three-way communication between a stable device that sends and receives signals, a bodily device (worn by the offender on the wrist or the ankle) that sends signals to the stable device, and a centralized computer that records the communication between the other two. In order for the device to record an answer, the offender wearing the bracelet must be nearby. All monitoring systems have a single intention: to indicate whether an offender is in a particular spot at a particular time. Some monitors work only intermittently, checking for the offender's presence at preprogrammed intervals. Other, more costly versions provide constant monitoring of the location of the person wearing the monitor.

The problems with electronic monitoring systems are not so much technical as programmatic. First, electronic monitoring requires a heavy investment of staff resources. Whenever the machine indicates the offender is AWOL, authorities must respond immediately if the electronic supervision approach is to have any credibility. Second, there is the problem of what to do in response to violations. Given the serious prison crowding that gives electronic monitoring systems their impetus, it seems incredible that mere absence from the house would result in any significant confinement without additional evidence that some criminal behavior was involved. Yet, if the monitor is to deter, disobeying a home arrest order must be punished somehow. Third, EHA does not account for crimes that occur within the offender's home. In order to ensure offender compliance, there must be additional monitoring systems such as random house calls, verification through neighbors, or urine screening—all of which require the additional allocation of funds. Finally, and more fundamentally, what is the appropriate target group for monitors? The use of the equipment is helpful only when the offender is unlikely to obey the order without it or when there is a substantial risk of criminal activity to be avoided through home detention (Clear, 1988). In other words, electronic monitoring makes sense only when the offender is at risk of some harmful behavior; otherwise, the monitor is superfluous. Yet, the equipment is so new that most programs have extensive eligibility exclusions. These result in a pool of offenders for monitoring who represent low-risk, reasonably compliant clients. Whether these offenders would seriously violate home detention orders without monitoring devices—indeed, whether they would receive custodial sentences in the first place—remains an unanswered question.

Release Programs

Numerous types of release programs have been developed to counteract prison crowding, including work/study release programs, halfway houses, treatment facilities, and restitution centers. Nearly all these programs have two characteristics in common: (1) They incarcerate the offender only during limited hours of the day, usually when he or she is not working, and (2) they provide special treatment programs to help the offender deal with adjustment problems prior to release to the community.

Unfortunately, few substantial evaluations of these programs have been done. Evaluations of halfway houses find that offenders do at least as well after release from them as they do after release from traditional prisons (Sullivan et al., 1974; Pearce and Olderman, 1995). Additionally, they appear to increase the level of social adjustment by helping offenders integrate back into the community (Pearce and Olderman, 1995). Whether residential programs really represent an

improvement over regular supervision has not been tested effectively. Perhaps their most valuable contribution to the system is to provide an enforcement sanction for field services violators short of complete confinement.

THE COST EFFECTIVENESS OF SUBINCARCERATION

Many observers are impressed with the comparative humaneness of subincarcerative approaches to correction. The original rationale for the development of these correctional approaches, to mitigate the abusive harshness of imprisonment, remains important today. But it is probably true that subincarceration receives most of its support because it is cheaper than confinement—the public dollar talks loudest when public values and priorities are confused.

The argument for the relative cheapness of these programs is persuasive. Housing an offender in prison costs over $20,000 per year, or, if including the cost of health care, approximately $24,000. Additionally, building a prison costs an average of $50,000 per bed (Buddress, 1997). By contrast, regular probation costs about $500 per year; intensive probation $3,000–$5,000 per year; a community supervision worker, with the capacity to handle 20 to 100 offenders a year, costs $20,000–$40,000 a year; and a work release facility costs $20,000–$40,000 per bed to build and $10,000–$20,000 per bed to operate. Without question, when choosing on the basis of cost alone, subincarcerative methods are far preferable (Funke and Wayson, 1975).

These figures do not mean that growth in the subincarcerative apparatus has resulted in cost savings. First, in order for these programs to be cost savers, they must be used instead of confinement. America's jails and prisons are full to the brim. It is difficult to imagine that many more bodies could be stuffed into existing facilities, and this suggests that the growth of subincarcerative systems has enabled the corrections process to continue operating despite overcrowding, rather than reducing crowding. If so, the new correctional approaches actually are more expensive because their programs have not reduced appreciably the costs of running prisons (Clear et al., 1982).

Advocates of the efficiency of subincarceration argue that these systems have helped avoid expensive prison and jail expansion. Perhaps so, but this argument loses some of its persuasiveness in the face of two facts: Even as the United States is in a period of unprecedented expansion of subincarcerative programs, the percentage of inmates has increased at an average of 7.3 percent per year since 1985 (Bureau of Justice Statistics, 1999b). Moreover, under the tighter fiscal policies of the early 1970s, wholesale increases in imprisonment rates and community supervision rates were accomplished while there was a relative reduction in dollars spent on traditional probation and parole services in most areas. If there is a relationship between the growth of subincarceration and the reduction in the costs of social control, it is a complex one.

There is also a problem of secondary costs. The new subincarcerative approaches make a point of advertising their toughness (Petersilia, 1987). For this to be credible, there must be follow-up that includes enforcement of the "tough" requirements. Anything else makes a mockery of the new program's touted toughness. This often can mean an expensive imposition of confinement for rules violations that fall far short of new criminal activity. It is ironic indeed that after careful consideration by au-

thorities, the original criminal behavior does not result in incarceration, but subsequent misbehaviors that are not illegal force the offender into confinement. An illustration is provided by a diversion program in Oregon, in which a burglar was placed on probation in lieu of 180 days in jail. When he failed to attend drug treatment, he was given five years in prison (Clear et al., 1986). Whatever savings were created by the original decision were totally voided by the tough enforcement.

In sum, the costs of correction are very difficult to calculate, and new programs designed to save money may not always do so, regardless of their advantages in per offender costs (McDonald, 1980). No one can argue with the desirability of saving money on correction, but simply expanding the use of subincarcerative methods will not necessarily save dollars.

CONCLUSION

The discussion in this chapter has highlighted several areas of controversy for which improved policy information is needed. However, four broad areas of inquiry suggest themselves as particularly necessary for those interested in developing useful knowledge.

First, much better information is needed about how and how well traditional programs work. This is particularly true of the semi-incarcerative methods such as work release programs and treatment centers. These programs are widely used simply because they seem to make sense in the face of the overwhelming presence of the prison as an alternative. But compared to the prison, little is known about them and their consequences. Does the use of the residential method reduce the rate of return to crime? For whom and under what circumstances?

Second, the same types of questions apply to traditional supervision, but they have a greater research base on which to build. The models need to specify types of offenders, types of interventions, and types of intervenors: What kinds of supervision methods work best for which types of offenders? What types of supervision worker attitudes are associated with success? Researchers have made a great deal of headway on this topic, but much more remains to be done.

Third, information comparing the relative success of different correctional approaches needs to be generated. Carefully established experimental programs need to compare the effectiveness of probation to prison, probation to intensive probation, and so forth, not only in terms of the costs but also in terms of the impacts of these programs.

Fourth, the public policy context of correction must be better understood. Most policymakers infer public values, but the few public surveys that have been done show the public to be far less punitive than is ordinarily believed. Why, then, is it so difficult to implement reasoned policies through the political process? Do policymakers influence the public, or vice versa?

Underlying any research agenda must be one central fact: There has always been an interplay between the harshness of the formal correction system and the need to mitigate that harshness through less onerous methods. It is as though we design a penal system in the abstract for the image we have of offenders—depraved and dangerous, unknown predators—and then implement a system that takes into account the neighbors, family members, and friends we actually process in it.

DISCUSSION QUESTIONS

1. Discuss the concept of subincarcerative correction. What does it mean, and what are the most common types of subincarcerative programs?

2. What is the basic orientation of subincarcerative programs—control of the offender or change in the offender's behavior? Are these aims mutually exclusive? Are there times when one must be sacrificed for the other?

3. We often hear about diversionary programs operating in place of incarceration. What is diversion? Does it seem to work? How many and what kinds of offenders are diverted?

4. Discuss the concept of parole, including its history. Many people think of parole as the careless return of dangerous persons to society. Among the more common complaints is that paroled offenders are poorly supervised in the communities to which they are returned. What does the evidence actually suggest?

5. Review the evidence regarding the effectiveness of traditional methods of probation and parole supervision and of more-recent, less-traditional methods of field supervision. What are the advantages and disadvantages of each?

6. Is subincarcerative correction *cost* effective? Discuss the problems encountered in trying to measure cost effectiveness in this context.

REFERENCES

Albanese, J. S., B. A. Fiore, J. H. Porwell, and J. R. Storit. 1985. *Is Probation Working? A Guide for Managers and Methodologists*. Lanham, MD: University Press of America.

Andrews, D. M. 1987. *Differential Supervision of Offenders*. Paper presented at the annual meeting of the American Probation and Parole Association, Salt Lake City (August).

Baird, C. S. 1981. "Probation and Parole Classification: The Wisconsin Model." *Corrections Today* 43: 36.

Baird, C. S., T. R. Clear, and P. M. Harris. 1986. *The Behavior Control Tools of Probation Officers*. Report to the National Institute of Justice (April.)

Barajas, E. 1993. "Defining the Role of Community Corrections." *Corrections Today* 55: 28–32.

Barnes, H. E., and N. D. Teeters. 1959. *New Horizons in Criminology*. Englewood Cliffs, NJ: Prentice-Hall.

Barry, D., and T. R. Clear. 1984. *The Effects of Criminal Sanctions*. Report to the National Institute of Justice (April).

Bennett, L. 1995. "Current Findings on Intermediate Sanctions and Community Corrections." *Corrections Today* 57: 86–89.

Buddress, L. 1997. "A Cost-Effective and Successful Community Corrections System." *Federal Probation* 61: 5–12.

Bureau of Justice Statistics. 1999a. *Correctional Populations in the United States, 1996*. Washington, DC: U.S. Department of Justice.

———. 1999b. *Prison and Jail Inmates at Midyear, 1998*. Washington, DC: U.S. Department of Justice.

Byrne, J. 1986. "The Control Controversy: A Preliminary Examination of Intensive Probation Supervision in the United States." *Federal Probation* 2: 4–16.

Carter, R. M., and L. T. Wilkins. 1976. "Caseloads: Some Conceptual Models." In *Probation, Parole and Community Corrections*. Edited by R. M. Carter and L. T. Wilkins. New York: Wiley.

Champion, D. 1996. *Probation, Parole, and Community Corrections*. 2d ed. Englewood Cliffs, NJ: Prentice-Hall

Clear, T. R. 1988. *Statistical Prediction in Corrections*. Santa Monica, CA: Rand Corporation.

Clear, T. R., and V. O'Leary. 1982. *Controlling the Offender in the Community*. Lexington, MA: Lexington Books.

Clear, T. R., and K. W. Gallagher. 1985. "Probation and Parole Supervision: A Review of Current Classification Practices." *Crime and Delinquency* 31: 423.

Clear, T. R., P. Harris, and A. Record. 1982. "Managing the Costs of Incarceration." *The Prison Journal* 62: 1.

Clear, T. R., C. A. Shapiro, and S. Flynn. 1986. "Identifying High-Risk Offenders for Intensive Supervision." *Federal Probation* 40: 24.

Clear, T. R., C. A. Shapiro, S. Flynn, and E. Chayet. 1988. *Final Report of the Probation Development Project*. New Brunswick, NJ: Rutgers University Program Resources Center.

Erwin, B. S. 1986. *An Evaluation of Georgia's Intensive Probation Supervision Program*. Atlanta: Georgia Department of Corrections.

———. 1987. *Evaluation of Intensive Probation Supervision in Georgia*. Atlanta: Georgia Department of Corrections.

Erwin, B. S., and T. R. Clear. 1987. "Rethinking Role Conflict in Community Supervision." *Perspectives* 11: 21.

Fox, J., et al. 1987. *Final Report on the Tennessee Intensive Supervision Project*. Richmond, KY: Eastern Kentucky State Press.

Funke, G. S., and B. L. Wayson. 1975. *Comparative Costs of State and Local Facilities*. Washington, DC: Correctional Economics Center.

Gendreau, P., and B. Ross. 1981. *Effective Corrections*. Toronto: Butterworth.

Gendreau, P., F. Cullen, and J. Bonta. 1994. "Intensive Rehabilitation Supervision: The Next Generation in Community Corrections?" *Federal Probation* 58: 72–78.

Gendreau, P., C. Goggin, and M. Paparozzi. 1996. "Principles of Effective Assessment for Community Corrections." *Federal Probation* 60: 64–70.

Glaser, D. 1964. *Effectiveness of a Prison and Parole System.* Indianapolis, IN: Bobbs-Merrill.

Harlow, M., and K. Nelson. 1984. *Managing Probation and Parole Services in an Era of Fiscal Restraint.* Washington, DC: National Institute of Corrections.

Hughes, R. 1987. *Fatal Shore.* New York: Knopf.

Hussey, F. A., and D. E. Duffee. 1980. *Probation, Parole and Community Field Services: Policy Structure and Practice.* New York: Harper & Row.

Kelman, H. 1961. "Processes of Opinion Change." *Public Opinion Quarterly* 25: 57–69.

Klockars, C. B. 1972. "A Theory of Probation Supervision." *Journal of Criminal Law, Criminology and Police Science* 63: 550–572.

Krisberg, B. 1975. *Crime and Privilege.* Englewood Cliffs, NJ: Prentice-Hall.

Krisberg, B., and J. Austin. 1980. *The Unmet Promise of Alternatives to Incarceration.* San Francisco: National Council on Crime and Delinquency.

Langan, P. 1992. *Recidivism of Felons on Probation.* Washington, DC: U.S. Department of Justice.

Martinson, R. 1976. "California Research at the Crossroads." *Crime and Delinquency* 22:180.

McCarthy, B. R. 1987. *Intermediate Punishments.* Monsey, NY: Willow Tree.

McCleary, R. 1978. *Dangerous Men: The Sociology of Parole.* Beverly Hills, CA: Sage.

———. 1981. *Time Series Analysis for the Social Sciences.* Beverly Hills, CA: Sage.

McDonald, D. 1980. *The Price of Punishment.* Boulder, CO: Westview Press.

Morris, N., and M. Tonry. 1990. *Between Prison and Probation: Intermediate Punishment in a Rational Sentencing System.* New York: Oxford University Press.

Murray, C. A., and L. A. Cox. 1979. *Beyond Probation: Juvenile Corrections and Chronic Delinquents.* Beverly Hills, CA: Sage.

National Institute of Corrections. 1981. *Model Probation and Parole Management Project.* Washington, DC: National Institute of Corrections.

National Probation Association. 1939. *John Augustus: First Probation Officer.* New York: National Probation Association.

New York City Department of Probation. 1973. *Differential Supervision of Offenders.* New York: New York City Department of Probation.

Newman, D. J. 1985. *Introduction to Criminal Justice.* New York: Random House.

O'Leary, V., and T. R. Clear. 1982. *Controlling the Offender in the Community.* Lexington, MA: Lexington Books.

Palmer, T. 1975. "Martinson Revisited." *Journal of Research in Crime and Delinquency* 12: 133–152.

Pearce, S., and J. Olderman. 1995. *Community Corrections in the United States: A Summary of Research Findings.* Raleigh: North Carolina Sentencing and Policy Commission.

Pearson, F. S. 1988. *Final Findings of Research on New Jersey's Intensive Supervision Program.* New Brunswick, NJ: Rutgers University Institute of Criminology.

Petersilia, J. 1985. "Racial Disparities in the Criminal Justice System: A Summary." *Crime & Delinquency* 31: 15–34.

———. 1987. *Extending Options for Criminal Sentencing.* Santa Monica, CA: Rand Corporation.

Petersilia, J., and S. Turner. 1993. *Evaluating Intensive Supervision Probation/Parole: Results of a Nationwide Experiment.* Washington, DC: National Institute of Justice.

Saks, H. R., and C. H. Logan. 1984. "Does Parole Make a Lasting Difference?" In *Criminal Justice: Law and Politics.* 4th ed. Edited by G. F. Cole. Pacific Grove, CA: Brooks/Cole.

Sherman, M., and G. Hawkins. 1981. *Imprisonment in America: Choosing the Future.* Chicago: University of Chicago Press.

Shilton, M. 1995. "Community Corrections Acts May Be Rx Systems Need." *Corrections Today* 57: 32–36, 66.

Sigler, R., and D. Lamb. 1995. "Community-Based Alternatives to Prison: How the Public and Court Personnel View Them." *Federal Probation* 59: 3–9.

Soma, J. 1994. "Group Reporting—A Sensible Way to Manage High Caseloads." *Federal Probation* 58: 26–28.

Stanley, D. T. 1976. *Prisoners Among Us.* Washington, DC: Brodangs.

Studt, E. 1978. *Surveillance and Service in Parole.* Washington, DC: National Institute of Corrections.

Sullivan, D. C., L. J. Seigel, and T. R. Clear. 1974. "The Halfway House, Ten Years Later." *Canadian Journal of Corrections* 16: 3.

Takagi, P. 1976. "The Parole Violators Organizational Reject." In *Probation, Parole, and Community Corrections.* Edited by R. M. Carter and L. T. Wilkins. New York: Wiley.

U.S. Department of Justice. 1978. *State and Local Probation and Parole Systems.* Washington, DC: U.S. Government Printing Office.

Vaughan, D. 1980. "Shock Probation and Shock Parole: The Impact of Changing Correctional Ideology." In *Corrections: Problems and Prospects.* Edited by D. M. Peterson and C. W. Thomas. Englewood Cliffs, NJ: Prentice-Hall.

Warren, M. Q. 1973. "All Things Not Being Equal . . ." *Criminal Law Bulletin* 9 (4): 483.

Zimring, F. E. 1974. "Measuring the Impact of Pre-Trial Diversion from the Criminal Justice System." *University of Chicago Law Review* 31: 241.

PART SIX

Crime Control Issues

Much of the public has its mind made up about the "causes" of crime in America today: drugs, gangs, and guns. Politicians and editorialists argue that these factors are behind a majority of contemporary property crime and a significant amount of contemporary violent crime. In Chapter 19, "Same Old, Same Old: American Drug Policy in the 1990s," Samuel Staley describes patterns in federal spending on the "war on drugs" during the past several years. Budgeting for efforts to halt drug production overseas and to stop the movement of drugs into this country has remained steady while money spent on domestic law enforcement and on prevention and treatment programs has increased significantly. Yet, there is little evidence that greater spending has had a serious impact on drug use patterns in this country. Further, the globalization of the drug trade has made it more complex and more difficult to address. Staley offers little hope for greater antidrug gains through greater federal spending. He argues that attempts to address the drug problem are more effective at the local level and best accomplished when aimed at demand reduction.

The contemporary public also believes that we would eliminate a major portion of crime were we able to rid ourselves of gangs. This theme is not new, of course. A considerable amount of legislation, law enforcement, and court activity has been directed at the "gang problem" for decades. Scott Decker and G. David

Curry offer insight into these efforts in Chapter 20, "Responding to Gangs: Does the Dose Match the Problem?" They note that gang membership grew during the 1990s and now affects geographic areas once thought safe from such problems. They outline the elements of what might constitute productive gang-intervention strategies and, using these guidelines, examine state legislative and federal policy efforts to combat gangs. Finally, Decker and Curry argue that, although suppression of gangs by law enforcement agencies seems a necessary response to gang activity, suppression alone will not address the problem of gangs.

Many people also attribute much of our crime problem to the availability of guns in this society. They respond with calls for gun control, and those who oppose gun control counter that it penalizes the noncriminal owner for the abuse of guns by criminals. James Wright and Teri Vail review the pertinent research evidence bearing on the conventional wisdom of gun control in Chapter 21, "The Guns–Crime Connection." They begin by noting the variety of definitions of gun control, ranging from registration to prohibition of ownership. Some seem reasonable and pose few problems for persons on either side of the debate. Others are quite restrictive and, gun control opponents argue, represent major infringements on individual liberty without offering gains in the area of crime control. Wright and Vail focus on this last claim and ultimately agree that proponents of gun control are on the weaker ground. Felons will not be deterred from carrying guns even in the face of severe penalties—especially when the supply of guns in America currently is immense. Deaths due to crimes of passion likely will decrease little with gun control in a society that has not yet addressed the issue of why we have so much dispute-oriented violence. Wright and Vail warn against the deceptively simple notion that the crime rate will fall if we outlaw the cheap handgun (the "Saturday night special"). Criminals, especially more serious ones, have little use for such guns, nor would they be likely to give up on guns were cheap ones less available. In the final analysis, the authors conclude, those looking to control crime through controlling guns will have to look elsewhere for a solution to the crime problem.

Given the difficulties of linking our crime problem to our drug, gang, and gun problems, one contemporary school of thought regarding crime control suggests that if solutions depend on identifying the causes of crime, we shall be waiting forever for them. But if by "solution" we mean addressing the fact that crime is an inexplicable given for which the only remedy is "getting tough" with criminals, then perhaps something can be done: Criminals who are caught will be given no more chances to violate the law, and those not caught will be deterred from further crime by the fate of their unsuccessful peers.

This rather simplistic approach has focused its attention particularly on career felons. Considerable evidence indicates that a significant proportion of serious crimes are committed by a relatively small number of particularly dangerous individuals. Proponents of selective incapacitation policies advocate a greater concentration on repeat offenders by police and prosecutors, longer prison terms for convicted persons, and a reduction in probations and paroles given to offenders. Christy Visher examines this issue in considerable depth in Chapter 22, "Career Criminals and Crime Control." She describes the career offender as commonly in his (most are male) twenties, violating the law weekly if not daily, having a long record of juvenile and adult crimes, committing multiple types of offenses, and consuming large quantities of illicit drugs. However, Visher also notes that knowledge of this profile in no sense makes selective incapacitation of people who fit it easy. Predictive scales to this point have been fairly inaccurate. The information on which those scales often are based does not serve well, and information that may serve well is available less often. Visher concludes that we are far from able to put selective incapacitation policy to work.

Finally, in discussions of "getting tough" with criminals, no more passionate crime control issue exists than that of capital punishment. For some, the death penalty is a simple matter of justice: To take another's life is to lose one's own life. In purer crime control terms, however, the major death penalty issue is whether capital punishment deters criminal behavior in others. Can convicted murderers be prevented from future criminal behavior by other means? Are potential murderers swayed from such crimes by the fact that convicted murderers are put to death? In Chapter 23, "Capital Punishment in America," M. Dwayne Smith addresses these issues with available empirical evidence and finds little support for the deterrence doctrine. He also raises an important issue that should be confronted by all who debate capital punishment's worth: racial discrimination in assignment of the death penalty. This matter once was of such significance that it brought executions to a standstill in this country. States have rewritten their laws to eliminate discriminatory and arbitrary death sentences, and many people believe the issue is no longer pertinent. Smith suggests that we have been less than successful in eliminating race as a variable in death sentences; it is simply more subtly embedded in the assignment of capital punishment. He presents evidence for this position, raises other provocative questions about capital punishment, and speculates about the death penalty in the future.

Chapter Outline

◆ Federal Spending Trends

◆ Drug Use Trends

◆ Drugs and Crime

◆ Drug Availability and Trafficking

◆ Cities and Gangs

◆ Conclusion: Drug Control Principles and Policy

19

Same Old, Same Old: American Drug Policy in the 1990s

SAMUEL R. STALEY
Urban Futures Program
Reason Public Policy Institute

Seven. That was how many times Eduardo Bonilla and Jose Lopez thought Mark "Corky" Miller needed to be shot to punish him for reneging on a drug debt. The two Los Angeles residents had traveled to a normally quiet suburb in southwestern Ohio to mete out the punishment. They, and at least two other accomplices, purchased guns and knives from a local department store, shot Miller, and fled to Chicago, one of their members seriously wounded. The murder shocked the Ohio community of thirty-five thousand more accustomed to fighting urban sprawl and shopping malls than drug gangs (Kissell, 1998).

Eleven hundred miles south, police were tracking down Anthony "Little Bo" Fail in connection with a dozen killings in inner-city Miami (Fields, 1998). The deaths were the result of a gang war between Fail and the John Does

gang, sparked by the arrest of the Does gang's leader. "There's a kind of corporate takeover happening," said a local police lieutenant. The local police established a 25-person task force to spearhead and coordinate efforts to track down Smith, who was arrested several months later (James, 1999).

Both these events are headline-grabbing reminders that, although overall crime and murder rates are heading toward record lows, drug abuse and the drug trade are still frustratingly persistent components of life in America. More than one-third of all persons admitted to state or federal prison for the first time were incarcerated for drug offenses (Bonczar and Beck, 1997: 5). The most frequent offense (21.4 percent) among first-time admissions for all offenses—violent, property, drug, and public-order offenses—was drug trafficking. A 1997 report on homicide rates in eight U.S. cities found that participation in the crack market, rather than crack use, drove drug-related violence (National Institute of Justice, 1997: 6).

The newest episode of America's drug war is in full swing. This chapter assesses recent trends in drug-control policy through an analysis of spending patterns, evidence on drug-control strategies, trends in drug use and public attitudes, and data on drug-related crime. The analysis concentrates primarily on the federal effort because national crime policy still provides the framework within which America's war on drugs is fought. Local law-enforcement agencies provide the foot soldiers in the war, but sentencing, incarceration, international policy, and supply reduction remain largely federal responsibilities. In the conclusion, policy implications are discussed.

FEDERAL SPENDING TRENDS

One of the more important aspects of modern drug-control policy is the degree to which funding and drug-fighting elements have been centralized. The Office of National Drug Control Policy (ONDCP) coordinates federal resources to leverage local efforts. All federal agencies whose mission may be affected by drug use or abuse are required to build a drug-control component into their budget process. The ONDCP is charged with monitoring, evaluating, and coordinating these resources.

The overall budget for drug control has grown steadily, but not every program has received the same level of increased support. Funds for international drug-control efforts and interdiction have remained relatively stable while resources for demand reduction and domestic law enforcement have increased several times

over. According to ONDCP sources (1998), federal resources spent through the drug-control budget have climbed to $17 billion since the new phase of the war on drugs began in 1982. The ONDCP expects funding to hover around this level through 2003, but the total current national budget still dwarfs the amount spent in the late 1980s (see Figure 19.1). In 1990, total federal spending on the war on drugs was just $9.8 billion, 57 percent of the requested 1999 funding level. Since 1986, total federal spending on drug-control programs has increased nearly six fold. The most significant increases have been for domestic law enforcement, with expected resources to increase to almost $9 billion by 1999, a 690 percent increase over 1986 levels. Domestic law enforcement continues to be the focus of national drug policy efforts, capturing 52 percent of the total 1999 budget.

ONDCP (1998) budget figures show that the second fastest-growing category of spending is demand reduction, which includes research, drug treatment, and drug abuse prevention. Whereas research funding hovers near $240 million, authorized funding for treatment increased to $2.9 billion in 1997. Prevention programs received almost $2 billion in funding. Combined, demand reduction programs increased by 469 percent from 1986 to 1997. If fiscal year (FY) 1999 funding requests are included, funding for these programs will increase to $5.9 billion, or 576 percent, over 1986 levels. In contrast, funding for international drug control efforts (assisting other countries in reducing drug production) and interdiction (seizing drugs at the U.S. border) has remained stable.

In terms of budgetary authority, national policy has continued to escalate the war on drugs initiated during the Reagan Administration. Although the greatest percentage increases in federal resources occurred in 1987 (a 66.3

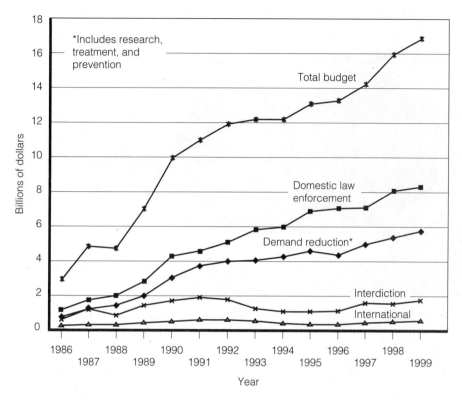

FIGURE 19.1 Changes in national drug control spending, 1986 to 1999 (requested)

SOURCE: *Office of National Drug Control Policy, 1998.*

percent increase), 1990 (a 46.4 percent increase), and 1989 (a 41.5 percent increase), federal drug control budgets received billion-dollar increases in 1991, 1992, 1995, 1997, and 1998. Federal agencies have asked for a $1.1 billion increase in FY 1999 (ONDCP, 1998).

Federal drug control efforts also have shifted in emphasis. Requested funding for FY 1999 allocates 52 percent of total federal resources to domestic law enforcement (see Figure 19.2). Another 34 percent is allocated to demand reduction, and only one-tenth of the budget is specified for interdiction. This is a substantial change from funding in the early years of the contemporary drug war: In 1987, 28.2 percent of federal resources were directed toward stop-

ping drug supplies at the border (see Figure 19.3). By 1999, interdiction's share of the total (requested) drug control budget had fallen to 10.6 percent. Despite rhetoric favoring an increased emphasis on treatment and prevention, the share of resources devoted to demand reduction strategies remained virtually constant during the 1990s, rising from 29.6 percent in 1987 to 33.7 percent in 1991 and 34.4 percent in 1999. The share of resources devoted to domestic law enforcement, on the other hand, ballooned from under 38.9 percent in 1987 to more than 51.84 percent of all federal expenditures in 1999.

These priorities are consistent with the ONDCP's five funding goals: (1) reduce youth

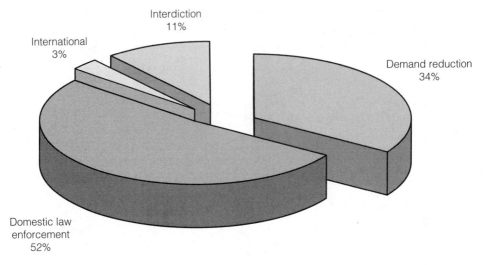

FIGURE 19.2 Distribution of national drug control spending, FY 1999 (requested)

SOURCE: *Office of National Drug Control Policy, 1998.*

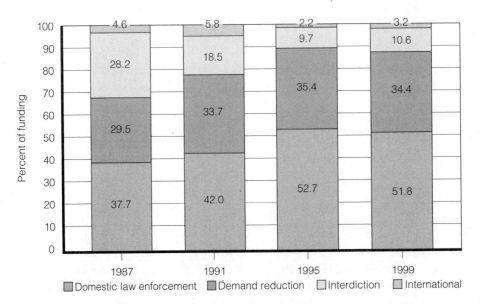

FIGURE 19.3 Change in funding priorities for federal drug strategy, 1987–1999 (requested)

SOURCE: *Office of National Drug Control Policy, 1998.*

drug use; (2) make treatment available to chronic users; (3) significantly reduce the flow of drugs at the border; (4) reduce drug-related crime; and (5) reduce the supply of drugs on the streets. According to ONDCP's budget summary (1998), supply-side drug strategies are expected to consume 56.6 percent of the federal drug control budget over the five-year period for fiscal years 1998 through 2003.

These data may, in fact, understate total federal spending on antidrug efforts. More than 20 organizations collect and produce information on antidrug efforts, but a single source for this information does not exist. Most organizations do not have separate line items in their budgets for antidrug activities, and personnel often perform multiple tasks (U.S. General Accounting Office, 1998a).

These data also ignore state and local efforts. Currently, of overall justice system expenditures, the federal government contributes just 14.8 percent of the total. State governments contribute another 31.5 percent, most (about 60 percent) targeted toward state prisons and corrections. Local law enforcement agencies spend 53.7 percent of all funds committed to the criminal justice system, 60 percent of which is dedicated to police protection (Maguire and Pastore, 1998: Tables 1.2 and 1.4). The key issue, however, is whether the increased funding for the antidrug efforts (on federal or local levels) has had a perceptible impact on drug use and illegal drug trafficking. The next two sections assess these issues in more detail.

DRUG USE TRENDS

Research into trends in drug use provide little evidence that federal drug policy has had a significant impact (Johnston et al., 1998). Take the case of marijuana, the most widely used of the major illegal drugs. Johnson et al. report that in 1986, 38.8 percent of surveyed high school seniors said they had used marijuana within the last year. In 1997, 38.5 percent reported using marijuana in the previous year, a decline of just 0.8 percent over the period (see Figure 19.4). The twelve-year trend, however, masks a seven-year decline from 1985 to 1992—from 40.6 percent to 21.9 percent—then a steady increase through 1997. Alcohol use exhibits a similar long-term pattern. Previous-year use of alcohol dropped 12.6 percent from 1985 to 1997. After bottoming out in 1993, when 72.7 percent of high school seniors reported using alcohol in the previous year, use rebounded to 74.8 percent in 1997.

Cocaine use appears to have moderated more significantly during this period. In 1986, 12.7 percent of high school seniors reported using cocaine within the last twelve months. By 1997, reported cocaine use had dropped to 5.5 percent, a 56.7 percent drop. Once again, however, this eleven-year trend masks a trend reversal beginning in the early 1990s: Cocaine use by high school seniors dropped to just 3.1 percent in 1992 and then steadily increased through 1997.

Reported heroin use, on the other hand, has shown an increase, climbing from less than 1 percent of high school seniors reporting use within the previous year in 1986 to 1.2 percent in 1997. Although the percentage increase is large (140 percent), heroin remains far less popular among teenagers. The drug of choice among this group continues to be alcohol followed by marijuana and cocaine.

More dramatic reductions in drug use were found among young adults (those aged 17 to 22) (Johnston et al., 1998). Between 1986 and 1997,

FIGURE 19.4 Drug use within the "last twelve months" by high school seniors, 1985–1997

SOURCE: Johnston et al., 1998.

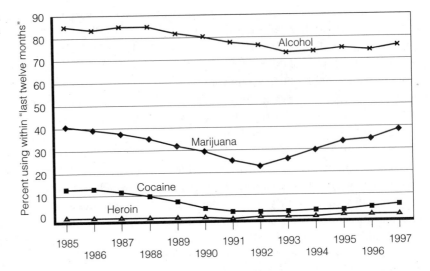

FIGURE 19.5 Drug use within last year by young adults, 1986–1997

SOURCE: Johnston et al., 1998.

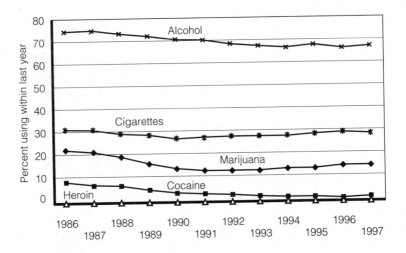

marijuana use declined by 31.8 percent, cocaine use by 78.0 percent, and alcohol use by 10.1 percent (see Figure 19.5). Nevertheless, the data continue to indicate the general pattern found among high school seniors: general declines in use until 1992 followed by increases in drug use throughout the mid- and late 1990s.

Overall, with the exception of cocaine, late-1990s drug use patterns are not significantly dif-ferent from those of the mid-1980s. The most significant difference is the trend. Drug use de-clined steadily until the early 1990s. Then both high school students and young adults began us-ing drugs more frequently.

These trends support the belief that drug use follows waves that are resistant to public policy solutions. Despite antidrug rhetoric and public-education campaigns such as "Just Say No," drug use is a chronic element of American culture. Although national data on drug use levels and trends before the 1970s are not available, widespread use (and abuse) triggered public policy action at numerous times throughout history. The first restrictions on heroin were prompted by concerns about mixing of the sexes between whites and Chinese in opium dens (Musto, 1987). Restrictions on cocaine emerged around the turn of the century to prevent its unrestricted use in unregulated medicines, and marijuana was effectively criminalized in the wake of increased use during alcohol prohibition (Staley, 1992: 185–189; Thornton, 1991). The law enforcement effects of prohibition were also short term. The immediate effect of prohibition was to reduce alcohol consumption by two-thirds, but alcohol consumption increased by 60 to 70 percent during the early 1920s (Myron and Zwiebel, 1991). Drug law enforcement varies depending on the general public's belief in the danger drugs pose to society (Musto, 1987: 260). Thus, as drug use increases, fear of its social impact increases and tends to drive drug policy.

Perceptions of risk and drug use may be particularly relevant to understanding these trends. Drugs associated with the highest levels of risk are the least used. Johnston and colleagues (1998), for example, found that high school seniors attribute high degrees of risk to heroin and cocaine; three-quarters believed that occasional use of these drugs put themselves at "great risk." Not surprisingly, these drugs are the least frequently used. Just 5.5 percent of seniors said they had used cocaine within the last thirty days and less than 2 percent said they had used heroin. Concerns about drug-use risks were different for alcohol and marijuana, where only one-quarter of the high school seniors surveyed believed occasional use of either substance put them at great risk. Despite these relatively low

levels of risk, 38.5 percent of the seniors surveyed said they had used marijuana within the last thirty days, and 74.8 percent reported they had used alcohol, suggesting a greater cultural constraint on marijuana use than on alcohol. (Part of the discrepancy may be attributed to the level of use associated with "great risk." The survey asked if respondents believed one or two drinks per day would put them at great risk; the question about marijuana was more generally defined as "occasional use.")

Marijuana use provides an illustrative case. Use within the last thirty days among high school seniors exceeded 40 percent in 1985, when about one-quarter believed occasional use would put them at great risk. As the perception of risk increased, peaking in 1991, marijuana use declined and bottomed out in 1992 (suggesting a one-year lag between risk perception and use). Then perceptions of risk softened, and marijuana use increased again. In this case, the relationship is symmetrical: Use levels and perceptions of risk in 1997 end up at almost the same point as they were in 1985 (see Figure 19.6).

Although the case of marijuana use illustrates the point, the relationship is not as direct for other drugs such as cocaine and heroin. In part, the weaker correlation may be due to the relatively low frequency of use for these drugs. Because less than 2 percent of respondents use heroin and high levels of risk are associated with heroin use, a small change in the perceptions of risk among a large non-using population may not produce detectable changes in use patterns among a small number of users. Similarly, a relatively small group of users who perceive lower risks with heroin could significantly affect use figures (e.g., a change of 1 percent to 1.5 percent is a 50 percent increase in use), but may not be reflected in attitudes toward the drug among the general population.

FIGURE 19.6 High school
seniors' perceptions of risk
versus use of marijuana,
1985–1997

SOURCE: Johnston et al., 1998.

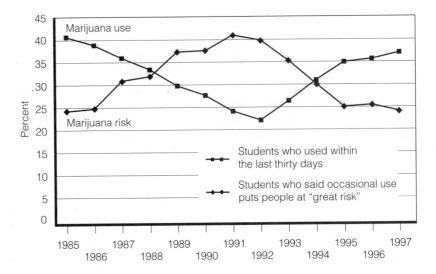

Drug-use trends suggest that informal and non-policy factors influence drug use significantly. Culture may play a particularly important role. The broader culture accepts alcohol use, despite its widely known association with violent behavior and potential for addiction. The broader society is less supportive of drugs such as cocaine, heroin, amphetamines, or barbiturates. These cultural constraints may place effective social limits on drug use in the general population and appear to reflect broader norms and values with connection to public policy (see Staley, 1992: Chapter 4).

Similarly, peer group and family remain the most important predictors of drug use (Staley, 1992). These influences are most important for hard-core users and addicts (Inciardi et al., 1993). Drug education efforts, particularly those targeted toward youth, will need to be oriented in two directions: one toward those who resist the temptations of using drugs in the first place, and the second toward those more susceptible to peer pressure and their immediate environment. General messages such as "Just Say No" may

help reinforce a young adult's level of resistance to using illegal drugs, but will probably have little impact on a heavy user or that person's peer group. Hard-core users also tend be less educated and from low-income segments of society (Inciardi et al., 1993), suggesting that traditional, middle-class–oriented approaches to public education may not be effective when targeting this group. Given the personalized nature of drug use, local education and treatment responses tailored to the needs of specific families, individuals, and groups are likely to be more effective drug policy approaches.

Decisions about whether individuals use drugs (legal or illegal) will depend on a complex set of factors, most of them not directly affected by public policy. When researchers at Columbia University's National Center on Addiction and Substance Abuse asked teenagers (12 to 17 years old) why their peers used drugs, 29 percent believed kids used drugs because they thought it was "cool." Another 23 percent believed their peers used drugs because they were doing what their friends did, and 20 percent felt other teenagers used because drugs made them feel good (Maguire and Pastore, 1998:Table 2.41).

When asked why teenagers did not use drugs, 23 percent said they were afraid of permanent damage. Another 19 percent said they were afraid their parents or school officials would find out. Only 11 percent said that it was morally wrong, and just 7 percent said that they did not use drugs because it was against the law (Maguire and Pastore, 1998: Table 2.42). Given these attitudes, the fact that drug policy has been relatively ineffective should not be a surprise.

DRUGS AND CRIME

Research has been generally unsuccessful in finding a direct link between criminality and drug use per se (Chaiken and Chaiken, 1990). The pharmacological effects of the most abused drugs do not "cause" criminal behavior so much as they reduce inhibitions regarding such behavior. Moreover, criminal behavior more often is a result of participation in the market for illegal drugs, either as a buyer or a seller.

Gentry (1995) has surveyed the literature concerning the relationship between drugs and crime. She reports that most studies have focused on heroin or cocaine users and found that heavy drug users and addicts had criminal histories prior to their drug use. Involvement in drug abuse and drug dealing exacerbates and intensifies criminal activity, but does not establish the pattern. By implication, criminal activity would diminish if users and dealers were no longer active in the drug market. The link between criminal behavior and drug use weakens further when nonpoor users are considered. Middle-income users and addicts rarely become criminals, suggesting that correlations between drug use and criminality may evidence more

a lifestyle than a directly causal relationship. Similarly, Sheley (1994) found that gun activity among juveniles was significantly related to drug selling, but not necessarily to drug use. Drug sellers, he speculated, were more likely to carry guns because of the nature of the drug trade.

In a study of homicide rates in eight U.S. cities, drugs were cited as a significant problem by local law enforcement agencies (National Institute of Justice, 1997: 5). Yet, with the exception of cocaine use rates, rates of drug use were not associated with higher or lower homicide rates, suggesting that the association between cocaine use and violence may be due to aspects of users' participation in the crack market. Crack sales, the study noted, typically occur outdoors, increasing the exposure of both buyer and seller to external intervention (e.g., rival dealers). Crack sales also are characterized by less stable relationships between buyers and sellers than is the case for other forms of drug market transactions.

DRUG AVAILABILITY
AND TRAFFICKING

When high school seniors were asked about the availability of drugs, the patterns revealed by their answers were surprisingly consistent with previous years, although some limited progress seems apparent (Johnston et al., 1998). The reported availability of cocaine fell slightly from 1985 to 1997, from 48.9 percent of seniors saying the drug was easy to get to 48.5 percent. The decline was even more significant from 1989 (when perceived availability peaked at 58.7 percent) to 1997. The availability of both marijuana and heroin appeared to increase, whereas the availability of cocaine decreased. In fact, by 1997, almost nine out of ten seniors said that

FIGURE 19.7 High school seniors' perceptions of drug availability, 1985–1997

SOURCE: Johnston et al., 1998.

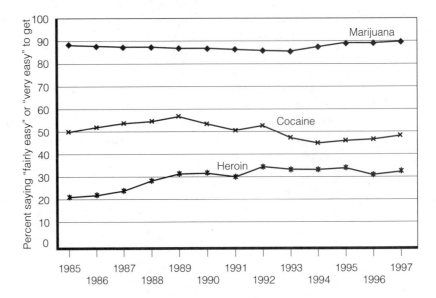

marijuana was "fairly easy" or "very easy" to get, an increase over 1985, when 85.5 percent reported similar levels of availability (see Figure 19.7). Exposure to heroin increased more dramatically, rising from 21 percent in 1985 to 33.8 percent in 1997.

When the cocaine data are broken down by type, the impact of drug control efforts seems less impressive. Whereas the availability of cocaine appeared to decline by about 10 percent, the availability of crack—its more addictive and volatile sister—remained virtually constant (see Figure 19.8). Crack cocaine availability seemed to peak in 1989, when 47 percent of high school seniors thought it was easy to get. Availability in 1997 was only slightly higher than 1985 levels and higher than reported availability in 1991 and 1994.

The impact of law enforcement efforts on availability appears to be small. A 1997 joint report published by the National Institute of Justice and ONDCP analyzed drug use and drug buying behavior among more than two thousand persons arrested for drug violations in Chicago, Manhattan, Portland, San Antonio, San Diego, and Washington, D.C. (Riley, 1997: 18–19). Among the questions was whether drug users had failed to purchase drugs in the previous year, even though they wanted to buy drugs and had the money to make the buy. Only respondents in Manhattan reported police activity as a significant reason they could not buy drugs. In Manhattan, about 40 percent of powder-cocaine purchases, 63.6 percent of crack purchases, and 55.3 percent of heroin purchases were foiled by police activity. The next highest reported rate was found in Chicago, where 18.8 percent of heroin users and 16.7 percent of crack users indicated police activity was the primary reason they couldn't buy drugs. Moreover, the police activity was not specifically drug-trade related. Local police were enforcing "quality-of-life statutes against panhandling, drug dealing, fare beating, and other crimes" (Riley, 1997: 18).

Despite the higher reported impact of law enforcement efforts on failed transactions, drug

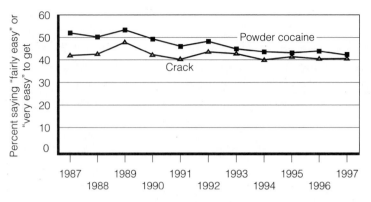

FIGURE 19.8 High school seniors' perception of cocaine availability, 1987–1997

SOURCE: *Johnston et al., 1998.*

users did not indicate that the general failure rate was significantly different in Manhattan from where it was in other cities. In fact, the highest reported failure rate for powder-cocaine transactions was Chicago (50 percent). San Antonio had the highest reported failure rates for crack (56.3 percent) and heroin (42.9 percent) (Riley, 1997: 18). In most cases, users reported that the failure occurred because the dealer was not available or was out of supply, not because of the presence of local law enforcement.

On a larger, global scale, law enforcement efforts have had little impact on the production of key drugs. World production of cocaine continues at about 700 million metric tons annually. Worldwide interdiction efforts net about 200 million metric tons annually, or about 30 percent, half of which was seized by U.S. law enforcement agencies. Annual domestic consumption is relatively stable near 100 million metric tons (Staley, 1992; U.S. Drug Enforcement Administration, 1996). Thus, world production continues at levels far exceeding domestic U.S. demand. In addition, cocaine prices remain stable.

In fact, the trafficking industry is becoming more settled. The effective limit on the expansion of the drug trade appears to be the size of the illegal drug market; note that, whereas half of

high school seniors said cocaine was easy to get, only 5.5 percent reported using it within the last thirty days. Many analysts consider urban drug markets saturated. This is implied in the responses to the National Household Survey of Drug Abuse (see pp. 547–551), which found little change in either use patterns or availability. "While cocaine use in the United States has declined over the past decade," notes the U.S. Drug Enforcement Agency (1996), "the rate of use in recent years has stabilized at high levels. These rates were driven largely by crack cocaine, the use of which has reached the saturation point in large urban areas throughout the country." Meanwhile, the heroin and amphetamine markets, although relatively small in scale, have proliferated.

The drug trade has become even more complex and sophisticated as cartels and gangs have grown relatively unchecked. Southeast Asian heroin is smuggled in by West African couriers. Colombian cocaine cartels use Mexican gangs to move shipments across U.S. borders. Major entry points for the cocaine trade now include New York City, southern Texas, southern California, and southern Florida. The number and types of ethnic street gangs have expanded to include African-American, Cuban, Dominican,

Haitian, Jamaican, Mexican, and Puerto Rican criminal groups. Heroin distributors include Chinese, Greeks, Israelis, Pakistanis, Turks, and ethnic groups from southwest and southeast Asia. Many gangs have become increasingly sophisticated, keeping detailed accounting records and using high-technology information systems to run their operations (U.S. Drug Enforcement Administration, 1996).

Disruptions in producer organizations seem to have little impact on the global drug trade. Arrests of high-level cartel officials fail to curb international production. Cartel leaders simply run their organizations from jails or devolve power and decision making to trusted lieutenants. When the Burmese Army shut down the Shan United Army in Asia, heroin production shifted to Laos, Cambodia, and Vietnam (U.S. Drug Enforcement Administration, 1996). Increased efforts by U.S. law enforcement agencies targeted at outdoor marijuana producers pushed growers indoors, allowing them to cultivate plants with even higher potency. The THC content of commercial-grade marijuana has doubled from the 1970s and 1980s (U.S. Drug Enforcement Administration, 1996). Similar shifts in trafficking patterns are a hallmark of the drug industry (Staley, 1992).

CITIES AND GANGS

Cities continue to play a pivotal role in drug trafficking and use (Staley, 1992). Larger cities, particularly traditional central cities, are located near major airports and interstate highways and serve as natural wholesale and retail distribution centers for illicit activity. Gangs have also found larger cities hospitable places for organizing networks and expanding their influence.

The role of gangs in the distribution of drugs may be exaggerated, however (Sheley

and Wright, 1995). Most dealers arrested for drug trafficking are nongang members. Maxson (1995), for example, found that 25 percent of arrests for cocaine sales in Los Angeles involved gang members. Her analysis of drug trafficking in the suburban cities of Pasadena and Pomona in Southern California indicated that gang members made up 30 percent and 21 percent of arrests respectively. Moreover, gangs fill a variety of niches and functions for urban youth, not just drug trafficking (Huff, 1990). Nevertheless, some gangs have established themselves as key drug trafficking organizations, and cities continue to provide the home base for their activities.

The urban focus of drug trafficking has larger social implications. Drug dealing is an important supplemental source of income for many urban residents. In Riley's (1997) study of drug purchasing and use patterns in eight U.S. cities, most arrestees reported that their main source of income was full- or part-time work. The exceptions appeared to be arrestees who used multiple drugs. In Manhattan, drug dealing was the primary source of income for those arrested for offenses involving both heroin and crack cocaine. In Portland, Oregon, drug dealing was the primary source of income for arrests involving both heroin and crack cocaine as well as heroin and powder cocaine. In San Diego, buyers of heroin and powder cocaine indicated that their primary source of income was drug dealing. For all other cities and categories, the primary source of income was either full- or part-time work or public assistance.

The urban focus on drug dealing and use also has racial implications. As a group, African Americans are at the highest risk for being sent to prison. The lifetime expectancy of serving in prison for African Americans is 28.5 percent (Bonczar and Beck, 1997), significantly higher than for any other racial group. The lifetime expectancy for white imprisonment, in contrast, is 4.4 percent.

Drug arrests contribute significantly to this discrepancy because the prosecution of the war on drugs impacts inner-city, low-income, and minority communities, particularly African Americans, more heavily than middle-income and non-minority communities. Law enforcement efforts on the local level have focused on the crack market because it is visible and because local police believe it is associated with a higher level of violence (Riley, 1997). Drug trafficking arrests make up 21.4 percent of new admissions into prison, the single largest cohort. New incarcerations for drug possession contribute another 11.3 percent of new admissions. Thus, one-third of all new admissions to prison are on drug-related charges. Moreover, African-American involvement in gangs increases this group's exposure to illicit activity and violence. Crack use is more highly concentrated among African Americans than other minority groups (Fagan, 1990).

Urban decline also provides fertile territory for drug sales and a large labor pool of relatively unskilled workers. Persistent poverty and poor economic performance in many inner-city neighborhoods provides a large number of potential workers, particularly among the young. Many of these workers lack the skills and education necessary to achieve middle-income earnings in a high-tech, information-based economy.

Changes in technology are unlikely to change the logic of the drug economy. The illegal nature of drug trafficking places a premium on interpersonal contact. To minimize the potential for fraud—to enforce contracts—buyers and sellers will meet face-to-face to ensure the transaction is completed. The use of technology such as the Internet and other forms of electronic transfer, distribution, and communication can only be effective when transactions are visible and trust exists on both ends of the exchange. Thus, although computers and electronic forms of sales may work within trafficking organizations, they are less likely to emerge as important features of the broader drug market or of inter-organizational sales.

CONCLUSION: DRUG CONTROL PRINCIPLES AND POLICY

Given recent trends, federal drug policy seems to have had only a marginal impact on drug use and trafficking. Presumably, an increase in drug control spending should lead to a reduction in use if, in fact, the spending is effective. From 1986 to 1997, the total drug control budget increased 411.4 percent, spending for demand reduction increased by 469.2 percent, and spending on supply reduction increased by 482.5 percent. During the same period, marijuana use by high school seniors fell by less than 1 percent, cocaine use fell by 56.7 percent, alcohol use fell by 11.5 percent, and heroin use increased by 140 percent.

What would happen if federal spending was increased further? Based on recent experience, a 10 percent increase in federal spending on all drug control programs—about $1.5 billion—would reduce cocaine use by high school seniors by less than two-tenths of one percent (0.152 percent). Cocaine use would fall for college students by 0.214 percent and by 0.209 percent for young adults. If current spending were doubled, cocaine use would fall by 0.276 percent for high school seniors, 0.389 percent for college students, and 0.379 percent for young adults.

Based on this experience, skepticism is warranted about attempts to increase funding for existing programs and strategies. The resilience and flexibility of drug suppliers continues to frustrate law enforcement efforts on all levels. Despite increasing emphasis on supply reduction and allocating billions more dollars to the effort, drug availability remains widespread. Drug trafficking organizations continue to find innovative ways to sidestep law enforcement efforts abroad and at home. The critical step for drug control policy is to shift emphasis and narrow its focus.

The following principles should be considered as a way of framing drug policy reform:

1. **Public policy impacts on drug use are small and indirect.** The war on drugs has had little perceptible impact on drug use trends. The impact of public policy appears to be indirect at best, influencing only perceptions of risk. Little evidence suggests that federal or local drug control efforts have significantly reduced the supply of drugs.

2. **Solutions to drug abuse problems will be local.** Different cities and localities face different problems with respect to drug use and abuse. As a result, the strategies used will need to reflect the specifics of the local drug problem. A 1994 survey of successful antidrug programs by the National Institute of Justice found that the most successful programs did not focus exclusively on drug problems (Weingart et al., 1994). Broad-based programs targeted at stabilizing or revitalizing neighborhoods or blocks were more successful and more permanent than programs that focused exclusively on drug control.

3. **Demand-reduction strategies are likely to have the largest impact.** Sig-

nificant supply reduction may be impossible given the institutional context of the United States. The nation's long border, diverse cities, and numerous ports-of-entry (via air, land, or sea) make interdiction efforts futile. Drug trafficking organizations are nimble and flexible, shifting production technologies and distribution modes quickly and efficiently to respond to the newest supply-reduction efforts. As a constitutional democracy limited by protections for civil liberties, U.S. federal and local law enforcement officials will be limited in their ability to pursue draconian antidrug policies such as those found in Singapore and other nations. As a result, strategies that focus on lowering demand are likely to have more impact.

4. **Realism should be a cornerstone of drug policy.** Although programs such as "Just Say No" may be popular politically, they have little impact practically. Drug policy should recognize the cultural constraints on drug use and the evolutionary nature of experimentation and use. Drug control strategies should be grounded in these larger, culturally constraining patterns.

5. **Policymakers should be cognizant of unintended consequences.** Although gangs were not created by drug policy, the lucrative drug market gave many gangs willing to engage in drug dealing unprecedented wealth and opportunity to expand their influence. As a result, gang-related violence has escalated, becoming the fastest-growing component of national homicide rates. Similarly, although asset forfeiture was initially introduced as a way to reduce the profitability of drug dealing, state laws increasingly

expand its use to include lesser forms of criminal behavior and broaden its application to indirect participants (Benson and Rasmussen, 1996). Policymakers must also contend with the fact that law enforcement resources are finite, and prosecuting the drug war may siphon funds away from other types of crimes, such as robbery, burglary, or assault. Economists have found evidence that local jurisdictions that emphasize drug-related law enforcement tend to experience increases in nondrug-related crimes (Benson et al., 1992; Brumm and Cloninger, 1995).

A more salient issue is whether the criminal justice system is the appropriate institutional mechanism for addressing drug abuse issues. Many of the social ills and harms associated with drug abuse are artifacts of public policy. By making drug use and trafficking illegal, public policy creates an environment prone to violence and antisocial behavior. The violence associated with drug dealing, including the crack market, are not endemic to drug sales. Drug dealers arm themselves because they operate outside the law—a consequence of policy—and do not have recourse to the judicial system to redress grievances or other tangible economic harms resulting from fraud or quality control. Just as the violence surrounding alcohol distribution dissipated in the aftermath of prohibition, the violence associated with illicit drug dealing would likely fall once currently illegal transactions were subjected to a legally binding and enforceable civil justice system (Benjamin and Miller, 1991: 89–112, 174; Staley, 1992: 145–177; Thornton, 1991: 111–126).

Drug treatment appears to provide a more promising avenue for addressing issues of addiction. Although the evidence on the effectiveness of programs is mixed at best, programs targeted toward specific types of addictions and using varied approaches are achieving limited success (U.S. Government Accounting Office, 1998b). The effectiveness of treatment programs, however, is still limited by the willingness of drug users to participate and their commitment to ending their addiction.

To be effective, drug control efforts in the long run will need to focus on reducing the size of the market by limiting demand. This approach suggests a focus on treatment, education, and prevention rather than on supply reduction. Ultimately, a demand-oriented strategy also suggests a targeted local approach rather than a federal one.

DISCUSSION QUESTIONS

1. Describe trends concerning federal spending on the war on drugs. To what form of antidrug activity does most of the budgeted money go? Have we stepped up our efforts to stop drugs before they reach the United States?

2. List the five funding priorities of the Office of National Drug Control Policy. What percent of the federal dollars spent to fight the war on drugs is devoted to each priority?

3. What do we know about trends in drug use? What drugs seem to be the most popular among users? What changes have we seen in these trends? Compare the data on use of drugs with that on spending on the war on drugs. What is your conclusion?

4. The popular assumption is that drug use is linked to criminality. To what extent does this seem to be true? In what ways is the sale of drugs linked to criminality?

5. Discuss trends in the use of heroin and cocaine (including crack). Are we now experiencing epidemics in the use of these drugs?

6. Link the drug trade to characteristics of cities in the United States. To what extent do our antidrug efforts seem to address the relationship between drugs and the city?

REFERENCES

Benson, B., I. Kim, D. Rasmussen, and T. Zuehkle. 1992. "Is Property Crime Caused by Drug Use or by Drug Enforcement Policy?" *Applied Economics* 24: 679–692.

Benson, B., and D. Rasmussen. 1996. "Predatory Public Finance and the Origins of the War on Drugs: 1984–1989." *Independent Review* 1: 163–189.

Bonczar, T., and A. Beck. 1997. *Lifetime Likelihood of Going to State or Federal Prison.* Washington, DC: U.S. Department of Justice, Bureau of Justice Statistics.

Brumm, H., and D. Cloninger. 1995. "The Drug War and the Homicide Rate: A Direct Correlation?" *Cato Journal* 14: 509–517.

Chaiken, J., and M. Chaiken. 1990. "Drugs and Predatory Crimes." Pp. 203–239 in *Drugs and Crime.* Edited by M. Tonry and J. Wilson. Chicago: University of Chicago Press.

Fagan, J. 1990. "Social Processes of Delinquency and Drug Use Among Urban Gangs." Pp. 189–219 in *Gangs in America.* Edited by C. Huff. Newbury Park, CA: Sage.

Fields, T. 1998. "Miami Police Target Gang Leader." *Associated Press* [On-line]. December 30. Available at www.ap.com.

Gentry, C. 1995. "Crime Control Through Drug Control." Pp. 477–494 in *Criminology: A Contemporary Handbook* 2d ed. Edited by J. Sheley. Belmont, CA: Wadsworth.

Huff, C. 1990. *Gangs in America.* Newbury Park, CA: Sage.

Inciardi, J., R. Horowitz, and A. Pottieger. 1993. *Street Kids, Street Drugs, Street Crime: An Examination of Drug Use and Serious Delinquency in Miami.* Belmont, CA: Wadsworth.

James, I. 1999. "Reputed Miami Drug Lord Captured." *Associated Press* [On-line]. January 5. Available at www.ap.com.

Johnston, L., P. O'Malley, and J. Bachman. 1998. *National Survey Results on Drug Use from Monitoring the Future Study, 1975–1997.* Vol. 1, Secondary School Students. Washington, DC: U.S. Department of Health and Human Services, National Institute on Drug Abuse.

Kissell, M. 1998. "Girl Guilty in Deaths." *Dayton Daily News* [On-line]. December 24. Available at www.daytonnews.com.

Maguire, K., and A. Pastore. 1998. *Sourcebook of Criminal Justice Statistics.* Washington, DC: Bureau of Justice Statistics, U.S. Department of Justice.

Maxson, C. 1995. *Street Gangs and Drug Sales in Two Suburban Cities.* Washington, DC: U.S. Department of Justice, National Institute of Justice.

Musto, D. 1987. *The American Disease: Origins of Narcotics Control.* New York: Oxford University Press.

Myron, J., and J. Zwiebel. 1991. "Alcohol Consumption During Prohibition." *American Economic Review* 81: 242–247.

National Institute of Justice. 1997. *A Study on Homicide in Eight U.S. Cities: An NIJ Intramural Research Project.* Washington, DC: U.S. Department of Justice.

Office of National Drug Control Policy (ONDCP). 1998. *National Drug Control Strategy, 1998: Budget Summary.* Washington, DC: Executive Office of the President.

Riley, K. 1997. *Crack, Powder Cocaine, and Heroin: Drug Purchase and Use Patterns in Six Cities.* Washington, DC: National Institute of Justice and Office of National Drug Control Policy.

Sheley, J. 1994. "Drug Activity and Firearms Possession and Use by Juveniles." *Journal of Drug Issues* 24: 363–382.

Sheley, J., and J. Wright. 1995. *In The Line of Fire: Youth, Guns, and Violence in Urban America.* Hawthorne, NY: Aldine de Gruyter.

Staley, S. 1992. *Drug Policy and the Decline of American Cities.* New Brunswick, NJ: Transaction.

Thornton, M. 1991. *The Economics of Prohibition.* Salt Lake City: University of Utah Press.

U.S. Drug Enforcement Administration. 1996. *National Narcotics Intelligence Consumers Committee (NNIC) Report 1996.* Washington, DC: U.S. Department of Justice.

U.S. General Accounting Office. 1998a. *Drug Control: An Overview of U.S. Counterdrug Intelligence Activities.* Washington, DC: U.S. General Accounting Office.

———. 1998b. *Drug Abuse: Research Shows Treatment Is Effective, But Benefits May Be Overstated.* Washington, DC: U.S. General Accounting Office.

Weingart, S., R. Hartmann, and D. Osborne. 1994. *Case Studies of Community Anti-Drug Efforts.* Washington, DC: U.S. Department of Justice, National Institute of Justice.

Chapter Outline

- Youth Firearm Violence

- The Prevalence of Gangs

- Responding to Gang-Related Crime and Delinquency

- Contemporary Responses to Gangs
  Gang Legislation
  Federal Policy and Gangs

- Conclusion

20

Responding to Gangs:
Does the Dose
Match the Problem?

SCOTT H. DECKER
University of Missouri, St. Louis

G. DAVID CURRY
University of Missouri, St. Louis

The challenge of responding to gangs is substantial and is made more difficult by our inability to define and measure gangs and gang activity easily. What is a gang? To the extent that statutes apply, it is "an ongoing, organized association of three or more persons, whether formal or informal, who have a common name or common signs, colors, or symbols, *and* members or associates who individually or collectively engage in or have engaged in criminal activity" (Conly, 1993: 6). At minimum, then, three people with prior criminal records who, even informally, display common colors or other symbols might be called a gang. Their current behavior would be immaterial.

Beginning with behavior rather than organization or membership, we find gang activity has been defined as "law-violating behavior committed by juveniles or adults in or related to groups that are complexly organized al-

though sometimes diffuse, sometimes cohesive with established leadership and rules. The gang also engages in a range of crime but significantly more violence [than mere delinquent groups] within a framework of communal values in respect to mutual support, conflict relations with other gangs, and a tradition often of turf, colors, signs, and symbols" (Curry and Spergel, 1988: 382).

The very complexity, scope, and even tortuousness of these definitions indicates that we have had to create fairly elastic descriptions in order to cover all of the phenomena that we have come to call gang-related. Nonetheless, there is fair unanimity that a problem exists involving something more than individual youths breaking the law, even when they do so en masse. There is a thread that binds together law violations in a patterned and organized way to which we have come to apply the term "gang" even though we find it difficult to point precisely to what we refer. "Gang," therefore, signifies more than the nominal congregation of youth for protective and social purposes (Sheley et al., 1995).

People who study gangs seem to agree that gang members tend to be more seriously criminal than are non-gang members (Fagan, 1990; Tracy, 1987). Gangs also seem to promote criminality rather than simply happen into it (Thornberry et al., 1993). The traditionally best-known gang offense, fighting, is common to most gangs but appears relatively sporadic, less a goal than a response to threat (Spergel, 1990; Vigil, 1990). Versatility rather than specialization seems the more common characteristic of a gang (see Sheley et al., 1995, for a counterview), and planned, collective violence also is less an end than a means of expanding territory or markets (Jankowski, 1991; Padilla, 1992). Degree of structure (formal organization) varies across gangs; not all are highly militarily organized, for example. Although gangs exist in most settings, including suburban and rural areas, they are most prevalent in urban areas (Klein, 1995).

However slippery the definitions of gangs, most experts also believe that gang membership and activity has been growing in this country during the past decade. According to Justice Department estimates (Curry et al., 1996), there are more than 16,000 gangs and over half a million gang members in the United States. Compared with previous cycles of gang activity in the 1920s and 1960s, the current cycle of gang activity is spread across more cities, is more violent, and is more deeply entrenched (Klein, 1995). Gangs in the 1990s have greater access to automobiles and high-powered firearms than did their predecessors. And the conditions of urban areas, particularly the growth of the urban underclass (Jackson, 1991; Vigil, 1988; Klein, 1995), portend greater

difficulties in ending the conditions that spawn gangs.

The speed with which the gang problem has grown and the many forms that it has taken make responding to gangs a more difficult task than ever before. One of the crucial factors that shapes our ability to respond to gangs is the extent to which the public understands the true dimensions of the gang problem. Unfortunately, public perceptions of gangs are shaped more by media images, such as the evening news or movies, than by solid evidence of what gangs are. In addition, most knowledge of gangs that comes from within the criminal justice system is the product of studying only the most criminal or delinquent members of gangs. For example, Decker and Leonard (1991) found that members of an Anti-Gang Task Force based their knowledge of gangs on media portrayals, among the least reliable of sources. The popular perception sees gangs as well-organized groups of young men who are committed to a common set of goals. In addition, from this perspective, gangs are seen as profit-making enterprises, intent on franchising themselves across the country. Fortunately, there is little or no evidence to support these views.

The past decade has seen a remarkable growth in research on gangs. Ethnographic, survey, and theoretical scholarship has focused on the causes of gangs as well as on the nature of gang membership and gang activities. Such broad study contributes to our ability to formulate effective intervention strategies designed to turn gang members away from gangs and reduce the impact of gangs on communities. In addition, a number of gang intervention projects have been or are being subjected to serious evaluation. However, missing from the current inventory of knowledge about gangs is a review of the match between our understanding of the problem and the responses to that problem. In this chapter, we explore that fit.

YOUTH FIREARM VIOLENCE

In 1992 a record number of violent crimes were committed with handguns (Bureau of Justice Statistics, 1993). Evidence is mounting that firearms play an especially prominent role in violence among certain population subgroups, particularly males, juveniles, and non-whites. From 1987 through 1991, the percentage of juvenile homicides committed with guns increased from 64 to 78, and in 1991 juveniles accounted for one out of every five persons arrested on weapons charges (Allen-Hagen and Sickmund, 1993). The violent crime arrest rate for African-American youths is five times higher than that for whites; African Americans are exposed to firearms violence at much higher rates than are their white counterparts (Allen-Hagen and Sickmund, 1993). Moreover, the gap between males aged 15 to 19 and their white counterparts in the same age group is greater than for any other age category (Fingerhut et al., 1991; Blumstein, 1995). Harries and Powell (1994) report a strong spatial relationship between "stressed" census tracts (disproportionately composed of African-American residents) and juvenile gun crime, further underscoring the importance of understanding patterns of gun use for this group.

Guns appear widely available to inner-city youth, and this has important consequences for intervention designs. Based upon the results of a study of incarcerated and inner-city male juveniles, Sheley and Wright (1995) report that gun possession among their respondents was quite common and that involvement in drug sales increased gun carrying. Blumstein and Rosenfeld (1998) have observed that rates of homicide among individuals between ages 15 and 24 more than doubled between 1985 and 1993. They argue that the crack cocaine epidemic in inner cities created the need for guns to protect profits and the drug. As this occurred, guns became more widely available to youth and led to an unprecedented escalation in the youth homicide rate. Taken together, these reports suggest the importance of monitoring gun acquisition by those at risk for involvement in gun violence either as victims or offenders.

THE PREVALENCE OF GANGS

Gangs are not new, and youth gangs have been present in the United States at least since the nineteenth century. Interestingly, gangs of the late nineteenth century died out without large-scale interventions by criminal justice or social service agencies. The next generation of American gangs emerged in the 1920s. Most of the youth gang members of that era were in disorganized groups composed of recent immigrants. These gangs also faded from the scene, apparently without substantial involvement on the part of the criminal justice system or social service agencies. The next incarnation of gangs occurred during the 1960s, and again, significant numbers of racial and ethnic minorities were involved in gang activities. Intergenerational gangs emerged for the first time in large numbers in the 1960s.

The first study of the nation's gang problem was published in 1975 (Miller, 1975). Six of the twelve cities in the study were classified as "gang problem cities," and it was estimated that there were 760 to 2,700 gangs and 28,500 to 81,500 gang members in those cities. The largest concentration of gangs was in California; indeed more than 30 percent of all U.S. gangs were located in that state. In 1988, the National Youth Gang Suppression and Intervention Program

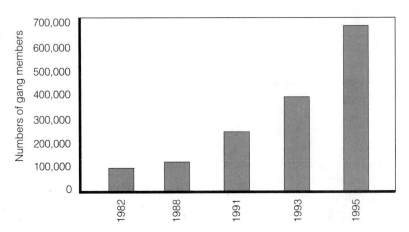

(Spergel and Curry, 1993) conducted a national survey. Of the 98 cities or localities studied, 76 percent had organized gangs or gang activities. Chronic "gang problem cities" often had a long history of serious gang problems, and emerging "gang problem cities" were often smaller cities that had recognized and begun to deal with a less serious but often acute gang problem since 1980. For 35 of the jurisdictions for which estimates were available, the researchers reported 1,439 gangs and 120,636 gang members.

In 1991, Curry et al. (1994) attempted to develop national estimates of the magnitude of the gang problem. Ninety-five percent of police departments in cities over 200,000 population reported the officially recognized presence of organizations engaged in criminal activity and involving youths within their jurisdictions. The estimate of the U.S. gang problem for 1991 was 4,881 gangs, 249,324 gang members, and 46,359 gang incidents. Curry and his colleagues conducted yet another national survey in 1993. This survey included all U.S. cities ranging in population from 150,000 to 200,000 and a random sample of smaller cities. Eighty-seven percent of these cities reported gang-related crime problems, resulting in a conservative estimate of 8,625 gangs, 378,807 gang members, and

437,066 gang crimes for the United States in 1993 (Curry et al., 1996).

By 1995, Klein (1995) also had concluded that there were between 800 and 1,100 U.S. cities with gang crime problems, including more than 9,000 gangs and at least 400,000 gang members in any given year. That same year, the National Youth Gang Center conducted its own first assessment of the national gang problem. The numbers produced by that assessment were larger than those of any prior one-year survey, finding a total of 23,388 youth gangs. In all, 1,499 agencies reported a total of 664,906 gang members (National Youth Gang Center, 1997). With national increases in violence by juveniles, these numbers are suggestive of the role that gang organization may play in such increases and the associated costs in young lives. A sense of the growth of gang membership since 1982 is provided in Figure 20.1.

RESPONDING TO GANG-RELATED CRIME AND DELINQUENCY

An effective response to gang problems will involve both proximate and fundamental interventions. Proximate causes of gangs include the threats that gangs generate, the values that reinforce violence, and the lack of legitimate activities where gang members live. Fundamental causes include racism, unemployment, and the relative disappearance of the family in American society. These problems have become more concentrated in urban areas. Neither proximate nor fundamental causes of gangs have easy solutions. The only way to address the problem is through institutional and community actions that affect the values that are the foundation of the gang.

Spergel and Curry (1993) have identified five basic gang-intervention strategies, based on survey responses from 254 law enforcement and social service agencies nationwide that were part of the National Youth Gang Suppression and Intervention Program. These strategies, reviewed below, include suppression, social intervention, organizational change, community mobilization, and social opportunities provision. Importantly, Spergel and Curry report that cities with chronic gang problems least often employ social-opportunity and community-mobilization strategies, though these were the strategies assessed as most effective among participating cities (see Figure 20.2).

Suppression strategies respond to the proximate causes of gangs. Suppression includes law enforcement and criminal justice interventions like arrest, imprisonment, and surveillance. Forty-four percent of the responding agencies reported that suppression was their primary strategy in responding to gangs. To be effective, suppression strategies must be part of a broader set of responses to the illegal actions of gang members. By itself, suppression is not likely to affect the growth of gangs or the crimes committed by gang members. Klein (1995) has argued that suppression efforts should not be implemented in ways that increase the status of gang members. Specialized police units may contribute, in latent ways, to the growth of gangs, by creating a larger gang problem through over-identification and attention. In addition, law enforcement strategies may exacerbate the racial disproportionality of arrest. Prison gangs may grow as a result of suppression efforts. Cities that follow suppression policies exclusively are likely to be frustrated in their efforts to reduce gang problems.

Social intervention approaches focus on emergency interventions, particularly in response to acts of violence or personal crisis. Thirty-two percent of the cities studied reported that they used social intervention strategies such as crisis intervention, treatment for youths and their families, and social service referrals. Such strategies are proximate, designed to address the needs of a more immediate nature. For example, gang members frequently are victims of violence or witnesses to a friend's victimization. The use of crisis intervention services in such instances is especially promising, though such intervention should occur immediately following a violent event. Crisis responses should be available at emergency rooms and should be mobilized by law enforcement, health care, or community groups. The goals for these interventions should be the separation of gang members from at-risk individuals and the provision of mentoring and other social services that extend beyond emergency rooms.

Families are an important part of social intervention strategies. Many gang members attempt to deceive their parents about their membership. Most gang members and their families face a number of challenges and have few resources upon which to draw in meeting those challenges. Interventions targeted at families are important because of their broad impact. In addition, most gang members have siblings or other relatives whose well-being may be adversely affected by the gang member. This magnifies the impact of family interventions.

FIGURE 20.2

Five strategies for local government response to gangs: reported use as primary strategy and perceived effectiveness ratings

SOURCE: Spergel and Curry (1993).

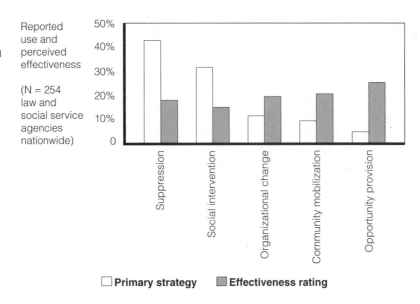

Reported use and perceived effectiveness

(N = 254 law and social service agencies nationwide)

☐ **Primary strategy**   ■ **Effectiveness rating**

Strategies that concentrate on **organizational change** require the creation of a broad consensus about gang problems. This approach was utilized by 11 percent of the cities studied. It targets the proximate causes of gangs and typically includes the development of task forces to address gang problems. In general, organizational change will lead to an awareness of the gang problem in a community and produce a new set of relations among agencies and groups who respond to such problems. Organizational change will succeed only if it has the support of the community and groups in those neighborhoods where gangs operate, optimally including local politicians and the private sector. This strategy typically occurs early in the cycle of responses to gangs, especially in cities that have experienced a number of failed attempts to develop consensus about the nature of the gang problem and appropriate interventions.

Community mobilization is a strategy designed to address the fundamental causes of gangs and gang membership. Only 9 percent of cities studied selected community mobilization

as their modal response to gangs. This strategy coordinates and targets services so that the needs of gang members may be met more effectively. It focuses on cooperation across agencies and is designed to produce better coordination of existing services. Most cities have a number of institutions and programs in place to respond to gangs and gang members. Services are seldom offered or merged in ways that are effective in meeting the needs of gang members, who often have little contact with these social institutions and programs. Effective community mobilization must include both immediate social institutions such as the family and schools, community agencies and groups, churches, public health agencies, and criminal and the juvenile justice systems.

The expansion of job prospects and educational placements is the primary focus of **social opportunities** approaches. More than any other strategy, this response confronts the fundamental causes of gang formation and gang membership. Despite this, the smallest number of cities studied, 5 percent, reported that the provision of social opportunities was their primary response to their gang problem. This approach stresses education and job-related interventions. As this approach addresses factors responsible for the creation of an urban underclass and the resultant dislocation of a large group of urban residents, it may hold the greatest prospects for success. These gang-intervention efforts incorporate job creation, training, and residential placements designed to reshape values, peer commitments, and institutional participation by gang members and those at risk for membership. The underlying value of such an approach is that it seeks to expand social capital and create new values among gang members by integrating them into legitimate social institutions. As such, social-opportunity interventions address a primary need of adolescents, the need to affiliate with a set of peers in age-graded activities.

CONTEMPORARY RESPONSES TO GANGS

As noted earlier, suppression has been the most common response to gang problems, though most observers regard it as the least effective. Spergel and Curry (1993) argue that no single response can be effective in responding to gangs. Only a balanced approach of suppression and other interventions, especially social opportunities provision, can provide a successful intervention. Next, we review a number of major policy initiatives directed at gangs in the 1990s and assess the extent to which they employ multiple intervention strategies.

Gang Legislation

By 1993, fourteen of the fifty states had enacted statutes specifically directed at criminal gang activity. A review conducted by the Institute for Law and Justice (1993) groups gang legislation into two major categories: (1) legislation that provides criminal sanctions for the justice system against offenders in gang-related crimes and (2) legislation that provides civil remedies for the victims of gang crime. Criminal sanction legislation most often enhances sentences for those found guilty of committing a gang-related crime or makes provisions for segregating incarcerated gang members. Civil remedy approaches have most often attempted to empower citizens to file civil suits against gang members collectively or individually.

Gang legislation constitutes a unique kind of organizational development and response to gang-related crime. Many law enforcement agencies engage in efforts to initiate or modify legislation related to gangs or the gang problem or try to influence legislation pertaining to gangs. Perhaps the best known gang legislation, serving as a model for other jurisdictions, was California's 1988 STEP (Street Terrorism Enforcement and Prevention) Act. STEP has created civil penalties against gang members. The police can obtain a civil injunction against named gang members that prohibits those gang members from congregating, carrying beepers, and drinking in public. The civil authority granted by STEP legislation allows the police to circumvent many of the procedural demands of the criminal law.

In their review of gang legislation in California over a ten-year period, Jackson and Rudman (1993) argue that most gang legislation, including STEP, represented a form of moral panic that was overwhelmingly devoted to gang suppression and influenced by law enforcement. Maxson (1997) provides the only direct evaluation of the impact of the STEP Act in California through a review of the process and outcome of the implementation of this act in the city of Inglewood (in the Los Angeles area). She notes that the gang members who were "stepped" seemed confused and unaware of what was happening during their court appearance and when they were civilly served with the injunction on the street. In addition, she notes that the long-term impact of this judicial act would be difficult to calculate, even under the best of circumstances. Finally, Maxson observes that the cost of implementing the act in Inglewood was difficult to justify in light of the impact of other aspects of the interventions in that jurisdiction.

Federal Policy and Gangs

DHHS's Youth Gang Drug Prevention Program In 1988, the Youth Gang Drug Prevention Program was established in the Administration on Children, Youth, and Families (ACYF), part of the U.S. Department of Health and Human Services. Applications for the first round of funding focused on single-purpose demonstration projects and innovative support programs for at-risk youths and their families. Sixteen projects were funded for 3 years. In design, these programs constituted a federally initiated, coordinated, and monitored commitment to community-organization responses to gang-crime problems. This commitment was on a scale that was historically without precedent. Nine more consortium projects were funded in 1992.

The ACYF program included a number of projects employing social-intervention strategies. Over the five years of the program, projects provided peer counseling, family education, youth empowerment, mentoring, crisis intervention, community restitution, and recreational programs. Priority funding areas for the delivery of services also targeted intergenerational gang families, adolescent females, and new immigrant and refugee youth gangs. Nonetheless, a national evaluation of the Youth Gang Drug Prevention Program (Cohen et al., 1995) concluded that, although local programs were generally effective in reducing delinquency and drug use among youth participants, the programs were *not* successful at preventing or reducing gang involvement. In 1995, the gang component of the program came to an end.

OJJDP's Comprehensive Response to America's Gang Problem The national assessments of the U.S. gang problem in the 1980s and the establishment in 1988 of the National Youth Gang Suppression and Intervention Program by the Office of Juvenile Justice and Delinquency Prevention (OJJDP) were important parts of the federal response to gangs. The goals of this program were (1) to identify and assess promising approaches and strategies for dealing with the youth gang problem, (2) to develop prototypes or models from the information thereby gained, and (3) to produce technical assistance manuals for those who would implement the models. The major outcome of the project was OJJDP's resolution that community-wide responses were required for dealing with local-level gang problems (Bryant, 1989; Spergel and Curry, 1993).

The Spergel Model (Spergel, 1994), a direct outgrowth of the earlier work of Spergel and Curry (1993), has become the driving force in the OJJDP response to gangs. It is a flexible format for responding to gang problems at the community level. Separate, required components focus on community mobilization and employment programs, with one agency acting as the lead or mobilizing agency. Key agencies that must be involved include the police, grassroots neighborhood organizations, and some form of job program. The flexibility of the Spergel Model encourages local program planners to assess the special features of local gang problems and take advantage of local agency strengths. Guidelines for community mobilization are intended to facilitate interagency cooperation and minimize interagency conflict.

With support from OJJDP, five demonstration sites received funding to implement and test the Spergel Model in a variety of urban settings with coordinated technical assistance and a systematic evaluation. In the Chicago community of Little Village, Spergel (1994; Spergel and Grossman, 1994) has been working with a network of police, outreach youth workers, probation officers, court service workers, and former gang members to reduce violence between two warring coalitions of Latino street gangs. Preliminary results of an evaluation of this project indicate a reduction in gang-related homicides, increased community organization and mobilization, and the channeling of gang-involved youths into educational programs and jobs.

As the first few years of the 1990s brought record increases in levels of juvenile violence, OJJDP became convinced that the problems of serious, violent, and chronic offending and gang-related crime were related. The agency decided that a major effort needed to be undertaken to test both the utility of the comprehensive strategy and the Spergel Model in specifically targeted geographic settings. The policy result was the Safe Futures Program. With funding from OJJDP, the Safe Futures Program has been established in four urban sites (Boston, Seattle, Contra Costa County [California], and St. Louis), one rural site (Imperial Valley, California), and one Native American reservation (Fort Belknap, Montana). Funding for Safe Futures projects is larger ($1.4 million per year) and extended over a longer period of time (a

five-year commitment) than funding for previous comparable efforts. All sites were funded initially in the fall of 1996.

The Safe Futures Program incorporates specific suppression, opportunities-provision, and neighborhood-focused services. As such, it is consistent with the Spergel Model and likely to provide a fuller test of the effectiveness of this model. One key characteristic of Safe Futures is very close monitoring by OJJDP. Often it is difficult to determine the impact of a program; implementation may differ substantially from what was planned initially. The technical assistance and close oversight is designed to overcome these difficulties. A local evaluation is mandated for each site, and all sites are participating in a national evaluation. It is too early to discern the effect of the interventions. However, one thing is clear: Mounting large-scale interventions designed to change the delivery of services to youths is very difficult. A few sites have struggled with the Spergel Model as well as local issues in moving toward implementation. For example, in St. Louis, the Safe Futures site has had difficulty integrating law enforcement—a key component of the model—into service delivery and client identification.

Community-Oriented Policing Services

Anti-Gang Initiative Community-oriented policing represents an even broader federal effort to respond to crime in a way that integrates law enforcement into a cooperative community problem-solving framework. In 1996, the Community Oriented Policing Services (COPS) office in the Justice Department launched a fifteen-city Anti-Gang Initiative (AGI) emphasizing community policing efforts, improved data collection, integration of law enforcement agencies into community-wide responses to gangs, and provision of a safer setting in which less suppressive response programs can be given a chance to develop. The sites included Austin, Boston, Chicago, Dallas, Detroit, Indianapolis, Jersey City, Kansas City, Los Angeles, Miami, Oakland, Orange County, Phoenix, Salt Lake City, and St. Louis.

The three specific goals of the program were to (1) develop strategies to reduce gang-related problems, (2) develop strategies to reduce gang-related drug trafficking problems, and (3) reduce the fear instilled by gang-related activities. Each jurisdiction was required to develop a formal written characterization of its local gang problem to include the number of gangs, members, age ranges, reasons for joining a gang, source and location of recruitment, location of activities, and incidents of gang-related crime. These characterizations called for considerable detail, detail in most cities that was simply not available through traditional law enforcement data gathering.

Eight specific strategies were identified. Three of the departments (Detroit, Jersey City, and St. Louis) chose to use special curfew enforcement strategies to target juveniles out after curfew hours. Six jurisdictions (Boston, Indianapolis, Miami, Oakland, Phoenix, and St. Louis) emphasized the need to coordinate their funded activities with ongoing efforts to combat drugs and gangs that were already in place. In Boston, this meant that the AGI effort was specifically linked to the Safe Futures funding received from OJJDP. In Phoenix, a tie was developed between G.R.E.A.T. (Gang Resistance Education and Training), a school-based gang prevention program targeted at junior high students and AGI efforts.

The most popular strategy was Organizational Development and Change. Spergel and Curry (1993) have identified this as a core response strategy of law enforcement to gang problems. Not surprisingly, eleven of the fifteen departments used some form of this strategy. Typically, this approach attempts to enhance existing interventions by changing an overall organization or strategic response by bringing new partners to the table. This often meant that police departments not only sought out the assistance of other law enforcement partners, but also turned to the schools or social service agencies for help. Six cities saw information sharing as a key strategy to be funded by AGI monies. Often this meant the use of enhanced technology to provide presentations, transfer data, or conduct analyses. For example, many cities utilized the opportunity to employ Geographic Information System technology to map gang, drug, and youth crime activities.

Eight of the jurisdictions chose to track gang members through the use of an enhanced or expanded database. In this way, they sought better to understand the number and nature of membership and use that information for developing additional strategies and tactics of suppression. Nine of the jurisdictions specifically included schools as a partner in their COPS-funded Anti-Gang Initiative. Finally, eight of the jurisdictions mounted a community organization strategy, seeking to engage citizens and neighborhoods in crime prevention and control, typically through public meetings.

Each jurisdiction was required to conduct an evaluation of its strategies. Unfortunately, to date there has been no effort to make the evaluations available in a form that could shed light on the feasibility, impact, or future of such interventions. What is clear from those sites with completed evaluations is that those areas of intervention which the police controlled (i.e., suppression) generally worked according to plan. However, partnership ventures were considerably more difficult to accomplish. Given the

Spergel Model's insistence on linking suppression and opportunities provision, the likely impact of intervention efforts will be temporary or relatively insignificant.

Youth Firearms Violence Initiative The Youth Firearms Violence Initiative (YFVI) was yet another COPS response to increased levels of firearm violence among youth. Ten cities were selected to receive $1 million dollars each for a one-year period to reduce violent firearm-related crime by youths. Police departments were to develop innovative programs that enhanced proactive crime control efforts and prevention programs targeted at young persons. Specifically, COPS wanted evidence that the number of violent firearm crimes (including gang- and drug-related activity) committed by youth had declined. Additionally, the agency expected that the number of firearms-related gang offenses and the number of firearms-related drug offenses would decline. Each participating department was required to develop new initiatives in three areas: (1) innovative strategies or tactics, (2) community policing orientation, and (3) new information systems. The ten cities included Birmingham, Bridgeport (Connecticut), Milwaukee, Richmond (Virginia), Seattle, Baltimore, Cleveland, Inglewood (California), Salinas (California), and San Antonio. Local evaluations and a national evaluation were completed examining the efforts of each site.

There was considerable variation across participating sites regarding the strategies and tactics employed to achieve these objectives. Not surprisingly, most strategies emphasized enforcement, though some combined enforcement with prevention. The tactics included such elements as focusing on specific targets (gangs), neighborhoods, firearm-related crimes, and using dedicated units to address these issues specif-

ically. Inglewood, a medium-sized city in the Los Angeles area with predominantly African-American and Hispanic residents, employed among the most innovative strategies. It chose to target a single neighborhood of relatively small size. A full-time prosecutor and probation officer worked with the police department. The prosecutor worked to develop a STEP injunction. The probation officer was responsible for seizing hundreds of firearms from youth on probation, employing his powers to search the residences of probationers. These efforts serve as an example of the kind of innovative work that can be forged between different agencies of the criminal justice system. Unfortunately, these partnerships—seen as critical to the success of the prevention and suppression of crime—vanished when grant funding ended, raising the important issue of sustainability, the extent to which expensive innovations and partnerships can persist over time.

A national evaluation of YFVI demonstrated the plausibility of the hypothesis that the interventions in most cities were accompanied by reductions in gun offenses. A specific geographic area matched to the program area was chosen for comparison purposes and gun offenses were tracked by week for the two-year period prior to YFVI efforts and the one-year period after the program. In each of the five impact evaluation sites, the decline in gun offenses per week was greater than for the comparison area. Although this is not conclusive proof that YFVI was solely responsible for the observed declines, it is consistent with that hypothesis. In almost every case, YFVI was strictly a suppression program; only rarely did it effectively integrate the activities of social service or prevention activities. However, in those cities where such activities were integrated (especially Milwaukee, Inglewood, and Seattle), those activities and relationships remained well after the close of the program.

The Boston Gun Suppression Project

Perhaps no single intervention in the 1990s has received as much public attention as the Boston Gun Suppression Project (Kennedy et al., 1996). Also known as Ceasefire, this project has been replicated in a number of cities across the country, including Minneapolis, where it has been carefully evaluated (Kennedy and Braga, 1998). At its heart, Ceasefire employs a problem-solving model known as SARA (Scanning, Analysis, Response, and Assessment) to assess youth violence. The SARA model requires that local jurisdictions gather data to determine the nature of local problems, analyze those data and, based on those processes, design a response to solve problems. The final step of the SARA model requires that the response be carefully assessed and re-calibrated. The apparent success of this intervention largely rests on two features: (1) careful background work conducted to understand the nature of youth-firearms markets, and (2) partnerships among participating groups. Kennedy and his colleagues have determined that the youth-firearms market differs from that of adults, is composed of a relatively small group of serious offenders, and is largely based on fear of attack by rival youth who often were gang members. Theft is the primary means of acquiring guns by youths.

The Boston Gun Project involves a large interagency working group that consists of representatives from the local police department; the Bureau of Alcohol, Tobacco, and Firearms (ATF); the U.S. Attorney; the local prosecutor; the departments of probation and parole; city youth outreach workers; the school district; and Kennedy's research team. The working group met regularly to review research and operational findings, and it was from these meetings that a response plan was developed. Two complementary strategies were developed, one that attempted to disrupt the illegal firearms market on the supply side, and the other targeted at the demand side. On the supply side, ATF worked with local police, prosecutors, and the U.S. Attorney to step up gun-tracing and prosecution efforts. It is the demand side on which the most interesting interventions were developed, however. Probation and parole officers engaged in night visits to their clients to enforce routine conditions of sentence that heretofore had not been regularly enforced. Curfews and room searches were conducted as part of this effort. This was coupled with a series of dramatic meetings with local gang members attended by key law enforcement officials to announce and demonstrate the effects of a zero-tolerance policy for the use of guns by youth in a number of Boston neighborhoods.

Initial evaluations of the Boston Gun Project have demonstrated that the program has been quite successful. Youth gun crime, particularly homicide, has dramatically declined in Boston. Kennedy and colleagues (1996) also have conducted both process and outcome evaluations that demonstrated key components of the project. Kennedy and Braga (1998) replicated the Ceasefire project in Minneapolis with similar results. What key features of this effort to reduce gang firearm violence made it successful? First, the intervention was based on data that came from local law enforcement and are presented in a way that leads naturally to policy interventions. Second, the use of data to guide the project did not end once the intervention began. Rather, the researchers continued to collect data and use them to refine the intervention on an ongoing basis. Third, the intervention combined the efforts of a variety of committed groups and individuals. As Spergel and Curry (1993) remind us, no program based on a single form of intervention is likely to achieve success. By combining suppression at a number of levels (federal, state, and local) with social opportunities provision and broader based enforcement (probation and parole), Boston appears to have found ways to get a handle on its gang problem.

CONCLUSION

Our review of policy responses to the problem of gangs makes clear that, conceptually and programmatically, we still have far to travel. Gangs, as we know them today, are a relatively new phenomenon posing new challenges. The last decade has produced an unprecedented increase in gangs, gun assaults, and youth homicide. These increases have spurred federal and local governments to action. In the search for appropriate responses to these problems, suppression has been the strategy most likely to be adopted. This makes sense for a variety of political and pragmatic reasons; after all, the police are a visible and generally popular resource in the effort to combat crime. However, such responses are not likely to be successful on their own. When suppression occurs in a vacuum, when it is not accompanied by other more supportive actions, the chances of making lasting changes in gang crime are diminished.

A number of federal initiatives that emphasize suppression or social opportunities provision have been undertaken in the last decade. The COPS office's Anti-Gang Initiative is a good example of programs that were based almost exclusively on suppression. This is counterbalanced by the Department of Health and Human Service's Youth Gang Drug Prevention program, which focused exclusively on opportunities provision. Although the evaluation data do not enable a definitive conclusion about the effectiveness of these interventions, it is clear that they have not made substantial inroads into the gang problem in the communities where they were funded because of their failure to implement a balanced response. If there is a single message in this chapter, it is that law enforcement and social opportunities provision must work hand-in-hand if successful interventions are to be implemented.

The success of any initiative, as demonstrated by the Boston Gun Project, hinges largely on its ability to integrate a number of approaches. Gangs are not a monolith, as the recent work of Maxson and Klein (1998) has demonstrated. Maxson and Klein produced a typology of gang structures, based on the size of the gang, its age, involvement in crime, and other salient characteristics. Their typology reinforces the diversity of gangs, and consequently the need for a variety of responses. The key to a successful response to gangs is the recognition that they vary by type within and between cities, and that successful responses must be built on a solid knowledge base. Many experts are critical of the police, who often characterize gangs and gang members as overly organized, more seriously criminal, and more dedicated to the gang than is actually the case. Researchers argue that this conception of gangs and gang members dominates the public and criminal justice understanding of this phenomenon, thereby distorting the fact that most gang members are loosely committed to their gang, that they are involved in a wide range of mostly minor criminal and delinquent acts, and that gangs are not effective vehicles for social organization. Without multiple sources of information and a coordinated response that involves both suppression and social opportunities provision, little progress will be made in responding to gangs.

DISCUSSION QUESTIONS

1. Review the definitions of gangs that were presented on page pp. 561, 562 and imagine the forms of gangs with which you are familiar. Do the definitions describe what you imagine gangs to be? Would they fit other behaviors and persons that you do not consider gang-related?

2. How many gangs do experts believe exist in the United States? How do they determine how many there are?

3. What are the five basic gang intervention strategies encouraged by the authors of this chapter? Which seem the most common in cities' attempts to deal with gangs? Which seem the most effective?

4. What is STEP and what basic strategies does it use to address the gang problem? How successful has it been?

5. Many anti-gang initiatives have revolved around decreasing the availability of firearms to juveniles. Discuss these initiatives as they are described in the chapter.

6. How optimistic are the authors regarding attempts to address the gang problem in America? In their view, what is the key to developing strategies that might decrease gang-related problems?

REFERENCES

Allen-Hagen, B., and M. Sickmund. 1993. *Juveniles and Violence: Juvenile Offending and Victimization*. Office of Juvenile Justice and Delinquency Prevention, Washington, DC: U.S. Department of Justice.

Blumstein, A. 1995. "Youth Violence, Guns, and the Illicit-Drug Industry." *Journal of Criminal Law and Criminology* 86: 10–36.

Blumstein, A., and R. Rosenfeld. 1998. "Explaining Recent Trends in U.S. Homicide Rates." *Journal of Criminal Law and Criminology* 88: 1–32.

Bryant, D. 1989. *Community-Wide Responses Crucial for Dealing with Youth Gangs*. Office of Juvenile Justice and Delinquency Prevention, Washington, DC: U.S. Department of Justice.

Bureau of Justice Statistics. 1993. *Guns and Crime*. Washington, DC: U.S. Department of Justice.

Cohen, M., K. Williams, A. Beckman, and S. Crosse. 1995. "Evaluation of the National Youth Gang Drug Prevention Program." Pp. 266–275 in *The Modern Gang Reader*. Edited by M. Klein,

C. Maxson, and J. Miller. Los Angeles: Roxbury Press.

Conly, C. 1993. *Street Gangs: Current Knowledge and Strategies*. Washington, DC: National Institute of Justice.

Curry, G. D., R. Ball, and S. Decker. 1996. *Estimating the Scope of Gang Crime from Law Enforcement Data*. Washington, DC: National Institute of Justice.

Curry, G. D., R. Ball, and R. J. Fox. 1994. *Gang Crime and Law Enforcement Recordkeeping*. Washington, DC: National Institute of Justice.

Curry, G., and I. Spergel. 1988. "Gang Homicide, Delinquency, and Community." *Criminology* 26: 381–405.

Decker, S. H., and K. L. Leonard. 1991. "Constructing Gangs: The Social Construction of Youth Activities." *Criminal Justice Policy Review* 4: 271–291.

Fagan, J. 1990. "Social Processes of Delinquency and Drug Use Among Urban Gangs." Pp. 183–219 in *Gangs in America*. Edited by C. Huff. Newbury Park, CA: Sage.

Fingerhut, L., J. Kleinman, E. Godfrey, and H. Rosenberg. 1991. *Firearm Mortality Among Children, Youth, and Young Adults 1–34 Years of Age, Trends and Current Status: United States, 1979–88*. Atlanta, GA: U.S. Public Health Service.

Harries, K., and A. Powell. 1994. "Juvenile Gun Crime and Social Stress: Baltimore, 1980–1990." *Urban Geography* 15: 45–63.

Institute for Law and Justice. 1993. *Gang Prosecution Legislative Review*. Washington, DC: U.S. Department of Justice.

Jackson, P. I. 1991. "Crime, Youth Gangs, and Urban Transition: The Social Dislocations of Postindustrial Development." *Justice Quarterly* 8: 379–398.

Jackson, P. J., and C. Rudman. 1993. "Moral Panic and the Response to Gangs in California." Pp. 257–275 in *Gangs: The Origins and Impact of Contemporary Youth Gangs in the United States*. Edited by S. Cummins and D. Monti. Albany, NY: SUNY Press.

Jankowski, M. 1991. *Islands in the Street: Gangs and American Urban Society*. Berkeley, CA: University of California Press.

Kennedy, D., and A. Braga. 1998. "Homicide in Minneapolis." *Homicide Studies* 2: 263–290.

Kennedy, D., A. Piehl, and A. Braga. 1996. "Youth Violence in Boston: Gun Markets, Serious Youth Offenders, and a Use-Reduction Strategy." *Law and Contemporary Problems* 59: 147–196.

Klein, M. 1995. *The American Street Gang*. New York: Oxford.

Maxson, C. 1997. *An Evaluation of the Youth Firearms Violence Initiative in Inglewood, California*. Unpublished manuscript, Los Angeles, CA: University of Southern California.

Maxson, C., and M. Klein. 1998. "Investigating Gang Structures." *Journal of Gang Research* 3: 33–40.

Miller, J. 1975. *Violence by Street Gangs and Youth Groups as a Crime Problem in Major American Cities*. Washington, DC: U.S. Department of Justice.

National Youth Gang Center. 1997. *1995 National Youth Gang Survey*. Washington, DC: Office of Juvenile Justice and Delinquency Prevention.

Padilla, F. 1992. *The Gang as an American Enterprise*. New Brunswick, NJ: Rutgers University Press.

Sheley, J., and J. Wright. 1995. *In the Line of Fire: Youth, Guns, and Violence in Urban America*. Hawthorne, NY: Aldine de Gruyter.

Sheley, J., J. Zhang, C. Brody, and J. Wright. 1995. "Gang Organization, Gang Criminal Activity, and Individual Gang Members' Criminal Behavior." *Social Science Quarterly* 76: 53–68.

Spergel, I. 1990. "Youth Gangs: Continuity and Change." Pp. 171–276 in *Crime and Justice: A Review of Research*, vol. 12. Edited by M. Tonry and N. Morris. Chicago: University of Chicago Press.

———. 1994. *Gang Suppression and Intervention: Problem and Response*. Washington, DC: Office of Juvenile Justice and Delinquency Prevention.

Spergel, I., and G. D. Curry. 1993. "The National Youth Gang Survey: A Research and Development Process." Pp. 359–400 in *Gang Intervention Handbook*. Edited by A. P. Goldstein and C. R. Huff. Champaign, IL: Research Press.

Spergel, I., and S. Grossman. 1994. *Gang Violence and Crime Theory: Gang Violence Reduction Project*. Paper presented at the American Society of Criminology Annual Meeting. Miami, FL.

Thornberry, T., M. Krohn, A. Lizzotte, and D. Wierschem. 1993. "The Role of Juvenile Gangs in Facilitating Delinquent Behavior." *Journal of Research in Crime and Delinquency* 30: 355–387.

Tracy, P. 1987. *Subcultural Delinquency: A Comparison of the Incidence and Severity of Gang and Nongang Member Offenses*. Boston: Northeastern University, College of Criminal Justice.

Vigil, J. D. 1988. *Barrio Gangs*. Austin, TX: University of Texas Press.

———. 1990. "Cholos and Gangs: Culture Change and Street Youth in Los Angeles." Pp. 116–128 in *Gangs in America*. Edited by C. Huff. Newbury Park, CA: Sage.

Chapter Outline

- Gun Control

- Effects of Gun Laws

- Guns, Crimes, and Numbers

- Is Strict Gun Control a Plausible Policy?
  Suicides and Accidents
  Felons and Guns
  Youth and Guns

- Crimes of Passion
  Characteristics of Crimes of Passion
  Guns As Catalysts to Violence

- Geographic Comparisons

- Public Opinion

- Gun Ownership and Self-Defense
  Motivations for Owning a Gun
  Defensive Gun Uses
  The Extent of Crime Deterrence

- The Saturday Night Special
  Serious Criminals and the SNS
  Noncriminals and the SNS
  Assault Weapons

- Conclusion

21

The Guns-Crime
Connection

JAMES D. WRIGHT
Tulane University

TERI E. VAIL
Tulane University

The conventional wisdom about gun control in the United States is very familiar and resurfaces in nearly every public policy debate about the topic. The essentials are these: Guns are plentiful and easy to obtain in this country, and they are involved in an enormous number of crimes and other acts of violence. In other countries with stricter gun laws and fewer guns in circulation, gun-related crime and violence are rare. Most of the firearms involved in crime, it is said, are of the sort for which no legitimate use or need exists—small, cheap handguns (as the argument once went) or military-style automatic and semiautomatic weapons (the argument heard more frequently today). Thus, firearms of the sort preferred by criminals could be banned without seriously infringing on the rights or prerogatives of legitimate gun owners. Many families buy guns because they feel the need to protect themselves; instead, they end up shooting one another. If there were fewer guns around, there also would be less crime and less violence.

Most of the public understands this and has supported stricter gun control for as long as pollsters have been asking the question. And yet, Congress has largely refused to act in meaningful ways, owing mainly to the powerful gun lobby. Were the power of this lobby somehow effectively countered—for example, by mobilizing public opinion—stricter gun laws would follow quickly (witness the Brady Law and the Assault Weapons Ban), and we would have embarked, at long last, on the road to a safer, more civilized society (Anderson, 1985; National Coalition to Ban Handguns, 1988; Zimring and Hawkins, 1987).

This chapter reviews the pertinent research evidence bearing on the various particulars of the conventional wisdom about gun control. Many of the key points seem self-evident but are in fact not supported by research; there is, indeed, at least some reason to question nearly every element of the conventional wisdom. A careful review of the research literature suggests that a compelling case for stricter gun controls is difficult to make on empirical grounds and that solutions to the problems of crime and violence in this nation will probably have to be found elsewhere.

GUN CONTROL

Gun control is itself a very nebulous concept. To say that one favors, or opposes, gun control is to speak in ambiguities. In the present-day American political context, "stricter gun control" can mean anything from federal registration of private firearms; to mandatory sentences for gun use when committing crime; to outright bans on the manufacture, sale, or possession of certain types of firearms. One can control the manufacturers, the importers, the wholesalers, the retailers, or the purchasers of firearms. One can control firearms themselves, or the ammunition they require, or the uses to which they are put. And one can likewise control their purchase, their carrying, or their mere possession. Gun control thus covers a very wide range of specific policy interventions, each focused on a different aspect of the problem.

There are probably more than 20,000 gun laws of various sorts already on the books in the United States (Wright et al., 1983: Chapter 12; Kates and Kleck, 1997: Chapter 4). A few of these are federal laws, such as the Gun Control Act (GCA) of 1968, the Firearms Owners' Protection Act of 1986, or the Violent Crime Control and Law Enforcement Act of 1994, but most are state and local regulations. It is erroneous to say, as gun control advocates sometimes do, that the United States has no meaningful gun control legislation. The problem, rather, is that the

gun regulations in force vary enormously from one jurisdiction to the next (such that one state's laws can be circumvented by driving to a neighboring state), or in many cases, that the regulations being carried on the books are not or cannot be enforced (Zimring, 1975; Leff and Leff, 1981; Kleck, 1997: 392–394).

Much of the gun control now in force, whether enacted by federal, state, or local statute, falls into the category of reasonable precaution and is neither more nor less stringent than measures taken to safeguard against abuses of other potentially life-threatening products, such as automobiles. Included within the category of reasonable precaution are such measures as requiring permits to carry concealed weapons (which many states have recently liberalized); bans on the ownership of automatic weapons without special permits; and bans on gun acquisition by felons, drug addicts, and alcoholics. Mandatory registration of new handgun purchases and police screening of new gun buyers are other widely adopted precautionary measures. Twenty years ago, Cook (1979; see also Cook and Blose, 1981) estimated that about two-thirds of the American population live in jurisdictions where some sort of handgun registration or permit is required by either state or local ordinances; the number is probably higher today. Many jurisdictions also have enacted "waiting" or "cooling off" periods that go beyond the five-day waiting period mandated in the Brady Law. These, too, seem reasonable at first glance, because few legitimate purposes to which a firearm might be put would seemingly be thwarted if the user had to wait a few days, or even a few weeks, between filing the application and actually acquiring the weapon.

Thus, to state that a compelling case for stricter gun controls cannot be made on empirical grounds is not meant to rule out obvious, reasonable precautions of the general sort just discussed. Most of these precautionary measures are noncontroversial (waiting periods are certainly an exception) and widely supported, even by most gun owners. The reference, rather, is to measures distinctly more restrictive than those presently on the books throughout most of the nation and, even more particularly, to measures that would deny or seriously restrict the right of the population at large to own firearms or that would ban the sale or possession of certain kinds of firearms, such as handguns, the restricted class of handguns known as Saturday night specials, or the so-called military-style firearms.

EFFECTS OF GUN LAWS

None of the 20,000 firearms regulations so far enacted has reduced the incidence of criminal violence by any appreciable amount, and most were not even intended to. One of the strictest gun regulations to be found anywhere in the country is New York's Sullivan Law, which makes it illegal to own a handgun without a difficult-to-obtain permit. That law has been on the books for more than sixty years. And yet in some years, New York City alone will contribute as much as 20 percent of all the armed robberies that occur *anywhere* in the nation and account for more than a tenth of all the nation's violent crimes. The New York City police also speculate that there may be as many as 2 million illegally owned handguns in the city (although this is probably an exaggeration). Another exceptionally stringent local handgun law is the Washington, D.C., law that, in effect, outlaws the civilian possession of handguns by D.C. residents. And yet in several recent years, Washington has been cursed with the highest homicide rate of any city in the nation. It is obviously one thing to enact legislation and quite another thereby to influence people's behavior.

Regarding the crime-reductive effects of various gun laws (Wright et al., 1983: Chapter 13; Kleck, 1997: Chapter 11), studies have been done of the Bartley-Fox law in Massachusetts (Pierce and Bowers, 1981), the District of Columbia's gun law, sometimes said to be "the toughest in the nation" (Jones, 1981; Britt et al., 1996), Detroit's "one with a gun gets you two" law (Loftin and McDowall, 1981; Loftin et al., 1983), the 1980 New York gun law (Margarita, 1985), and many other laws in other jurisdictions. None of these studies provides compelling evidence that gun laws, in whatever form, have had anything more than very marginal effects on the rates of violent crime. One of the most recent and sophisticated analyses of the issue is published in Kleck (1997: 360–367). Based on multivariate analyses of applicable gun laws in 170 cities with populations greater than 100,000, Kleck concludes that none of the laws examined consistently reduced levels of gun ownership and that "gun restrictions appear to exert no significant negative effect on total violence rates" (1997: 361). Consistent with many previous studies, these results generally do not support the idea that existing gun controls reduce gun ownership rates or violence rates.

Most of the research literature focuses on the effects of *more restrictive* firearms regulations. Ironically, there is now some evidence to suggest that *less restrictive* firearms regulations are actually of some use in bringing down levels of violence. The reference is to the emerging literature on the effects of liberalized ("nondiscretionary") concealed carrying laws (i.e., laws that make it easier for ordinary citizens to carry concealed firearms). Much of this work has been done by John Lott (1998; Lott and Mustard, 1997). As of 1998, thirty-one states had adopted such nondiscretionary concealed-handgun laws. Using crime data from 3,054 counties over eighteen years, this research represents the largest and most inclusive study on gun control to date. Lott concludes that concealed-handgun laws currently represent "the most cost-effective method available for reducing violent crime" (1998: 159).

Importantly, Lott's research has been harshly criticized. Black and Nagin (1998) re-analyzed the data used by Lott and Mustard and concluded that there was no basis for their conclusions regarding the effects of nondiscretionary laws. They argue that Lott and Mustard's reported results were sensitive to minor changes in the model and sample. If Florida were excluded from the sample, for instance, the results would change dramatically.

Ludwig (1996) also points to numerous problems with Lott and Mustard's research. He argues that the analysis suffered from a lack of adequate controls for serial correlation and for other factors that may have affected crime. In general, Ludwig argues that Lott and Mustard's models are misspecified and that there is no evidence that nondiscretionary laws have a significant deterrent effect on violent crime. It is noteworthy, however, that Lott (1998) has addressed each of these criticisms. The dialogue thus continues.

Both sides of the gun control debate now more or less grant the point that existing laws have little or no effect on rates of crime and violence, but have very different interpretations of the reasons. The pro-gun position is that gun laws do not work because they *cannot* work. They are often unenforceable or unenforced, widely ignored (especially by criminals), and go about the problem in the wrong way. For this reason, many pro-gun organizations, such as the NRA, have long supported mandatory sentences for the use of firearms in felonies, just as they have long opposed stricter regulations on the legitimate ownership and use of guns. (As a matter of fact, several studies of mandatory sentence enhancements for gun use in crime have failed to show significant crime-reductive ef-

fects; the NRA's support for such measures is largely rhetorical.)

The pro-control argument is that gun laws do not work because there are too many of them, because they are indifferently enforced, and because the laws that are in effect vary wildly from one jurisdiction to the next. States with very restrictive firearms laws often are bordered by states with very lax laws, and so existing laws in any jurisdiction are readily circumvented. To illustrate, the District of Columbia's Firearms Control Regulations Act of 1975 essentially prohibits the purchase, sale, transfer, and possession of handguns by D.C. residents; across the city boundaries, in Virginia, however, handguns can be obtained easily. Massachusetts has relatively strict laws governing the ownership of handguns and is bordered by New Hampshire and Vermont, which have some of the least restrictive handgun laws in the nation. What we need, gun control advocates argue, are strict *federal* firearms regulations that are uniform across all state and local jurisdictions. Lacking an aggressive national firearms policy, it is no wonder that the morass of state and local regulations has had no notable effect. In this sense, they argue (not without justification) that we have never given gun control a fair test.

Has gun control reduced crime and violence in the United States? The answer, clearly, is no. Would stronger controls, enacted on a national level, do so? This has to be considered an open empirical question. As we shall see, however, many of the arguments that purport that stricter national controls would work to reduce crime and violence fare poorly in the light of current research.

GUNS, CRIMES, AND NUMBERS

From the onset of the twentieth century through about 1978, some 180–200 million firearms were manufactured in or imported into the

United States. Domestic manufacture has averaged about 4.5 million units annually since 1978 (Howe, 1987: 102; Kleck, 1997: 114–115), which brings the total for the century to well over 250 million weapons. Of these, the number now remaining in private hands is not very accurately known—approximately 200 million is a reasonable guess. Survey evidence shows that about 50 percent of all U.S. households possess at least one firearm, with the average number owned (among those owning at least one) currently being around five guns (Kleck, 1997). As the data in Table 21.1 indicate, gun ownership crosses many sociodemographic lines.

Of the total firearms, roughly one-third are handguns; in other words, there are some 60–70 million handguns now in private possession in the United States. The remainder are rifles and shotguns. The most commonly owned handgun is a .38 caliber revolver, a powerful piece of weaponry; next to the .38, the .22 is the most popular. Based on recent manufacturing patterns, the 9 mm may soon replace the .22 as the second most popular handgun. Among shoulder weapons, rifles are preferred over shotguns by a thin margin.

What is the annual firearms toll in this country? How many people are killed, injured, victimized, or intimidated by firearms in the average year? Some components of the annual toll—particularly the deaths—are known precisely, others considerably less so. In recent years, the total number of homicides in the United States has been right around 25,000 annually. Expressed as a rate, this is about 10 homicides per 100,000 population. Of the 25,000 annual homicides, approximately 60 percent are committed with firearms, and of those committed with firearms, some half to three-quarters are committed with handguns.

There are also about 30,000 suicides committed in an average recent year, of which more

Table 21.1 Who Owns Guns: By Demographic Characteristics, United States, 1996

Answered "Yes" to the question "Do you own a handgun, rifle, shotgun or any other type of firearm?"

	PERCENT
National	37
Sex	
Male	55
Female	21
Race	
White	43
African American	20
Age	
18 to 29 years	32
30 to 44 years	34
45 to 64 years	47
65 years and older	42
Education	
College graduate	29
Some college	37
High school graduate	36
Less than high school graduate	47
Income	
More than $60,000	36
$40,000 to $60,000	45
$20,000 to $39,999	37
Less than $20,000	32
Community	
City	25
Suburb	34
Small town	42
Rural	51
Region	
East	33
Midwest	35
South	49
West	28
Politics	
Republican	45
Democrat	31
Independent	41

SOURCE: Data from Maguire and Pastore, 1998: 146.

NOTE: These data are from a nationwide telephone survey of 1,333 adults age 18 and older, including 1,265 registered voters, conducted by the *Los Angeles Times* Poll Sept. 7–10, 1996.

than 60 percent involve a firearm. Of these, the proportion involving a handgun is unknown. Death from firearms accidents has for some time represented about 2 percent of the total accidental death toll in the nation. In absolute numbers, fatal firearms accidents contribute approximately 1,000 deaths per year, of which about 40 percent are hunting accidents; fewer than half of the total accidental deaths involve handguns (Morrow and Hudson, 1986).

If we add it all up, we find that the number of deaths from firearms in our society in an average recent year is right around 34,000: about 15,000 gun homicides, 18,000 gun suicides, and 1,000 or so fatal accidents. Keeping things in perspective, this would amount, in an average year, to some 1.5 percent of all deaths from any cause.

The affection of all sides in the gun control debate for rhetorical formulations is legendary. In the case of gun deaths, the pro-gun forces will often stress that the total deaths from firearms in any year are no more than the total deaths due to, say, automobile accidents (about 40,000)—but nobody wants to ban cars. To counter, the pro-control forces often will express the gun toll as a number of deaths per unit of time. The resulting figure is dramatic, to be sure: On the average, someone in the United States is killed by a firearm about every fourteen minutes.

Death, of course, is an incomplete indicator of the overall firearms toll. One must also include nonfatal but injurious firearms accidents, crimes other than homicide or suicide committed with guns, unsuccessful suicide attempts with firearms, armed encounters between citizens and criminals, and so on. Although precise figures for these types of incidents are not available, rough estimates can be made.

The number of nonfatal firearms accidents is much higher than the number of fatal ones, but the actual number is known only very imprecisely. Kleck (1997: Chapter 9; 1986c) has reviewed a variety of data on the topic and concludes that the number of nonfatal but injurious firearms accidents is around 100,000 per annum.

Concerning gun crimes other than homicide and suicide, the numbers again are highly uncertain. The FBI's *Uniform Crime Reports* provide data only on crimes known to the police, and dozens of criminal victimization surveys have made it plain that this represents but a fraction of all crimes; at the same time, the victimization surveys are not entirely reliable either. The rough consensus is that there are perhaps 600,000 chargeable gun crimes committed in the United States each year (see Kleck, 1997; also Wright, 1995), not including "victimless" gun crimes such as illegal carrying of firearms (Wright, 1995).

The total firearms toll would also have to factor in many additional components, none of them known to any useful degree of precision. Taking the (roughly) 600,000 annual chargeable gun crimes and adding plausible guesses about nonfatal firearms accidents and the other sorts of incidents, we would arrive at a final tally of about one million total "gun incidents" each year—that is, incidents where a firearm of some sort was involved in some way in some kind of violent or criminal act (whether intentional or accidental, serious or trivial, fatal or nonfatal).

IS STRICT GUN CONTROL A PLAUSIBLE POLICY?

Thirty-seven thousand annual deaths add up, without doubt, to a serious toll, and it is very much in society's best interests to reduce that number. The question is whether stricter gun control would do so. Let us consider the various types of gun-related deaths.

Suicides and Accidents

The argument that stricter gun controls would reduce death by suicide stems from the well-known fact that many suicide attempts are not "attempts in earnest" but rather cries for help or attention from emotionally disturbed or depressed individuals. Firearms, it is argued, are extremely lethal. Many of these attempts to "cry for help" result in self-destruction not because that was the actual intent but because of the extreme lethality of the chosen method. If firearms were not available, people would "cry out" with different means, and because these other means are generally less lethal, fewer of them would be successful; the number of suicide attempts might remain the same, but the number of successful suicides would decline dramatically.

This argument assumes, however, that the intentionality of a suicide attempt is not correlated with the method chosen. Certainly, many people who swallow a bottle of pills are not really trying to kill themselves; they are, rather, trying to get somebody's attention. But people who kill themselves with guns can be assumed to be quite serious about it, and it is not unreasonable to assume that they would find a way to accomplish the task regardless of whether firearms were at hand. As a matter of fact, the apparent lethalities (relative "success rates") of several methods of suicide—among them hanging, carbon monoxide poisoning, and drowning—are nearly as high as for suicide attempts with firearms (see Kleck, 1997: Chapter 8, for an extensive analysis of the many complex issues involved).

The rate of accidental gun death may be more amenable to policy intervention, but this is the least important source of gun death, by far, and its rate of occurrence is already falling. About 40 percent of gun-related fatal accidents are hunting accidents (Kleck, 1997), and there is little to be done about them as long as hunters have the right to their sport. If, in other words, people are allowed to hunt, then *some* accidental deaths will be the result, just as *some* accidental death is the inevitable result of people being allowed to pursue other recreational activities: boating, swimming, racing cars, hang-gliding, sky-diving, skiing, football, and so on.

For these more or less obvious reasons, much of the gun control debate has focused on gun homicides, especially those that occur in the heat of the moment (about which we have more to say later). To be sure, if there were no guns at all, then no crimes or other acts of violence could ever be committed with them. A very practical question, however, remains to be asked: Can a "no-guns" condition ever be achieved in a nation that already possesses perhaps 200 million guns? If we take a plausible value for the number of gun incidents in a year—say, one million—and a reasonable guess about the number of guns presently owned—say, 200 million—we see that the guns now owned exceed the annual incident count by a factor of 200. In other words, the existing stock is adequate to supply all conceivable nefarious purposes for at least the next two centuries.

These numbers can be considered in another way. Suppose that, as a society, we did embark on a program of firearms confiscation, with the aim of achieving the no-guns condition. We would have to confiscate some 200 guns to get just 1 that, in any typical year, would be involved in any kind of gun incident; maybe 300–400 to get just 1 that would otherwise be involved in a chargeable gun crime; and several thousand to get just 1 that would otherwise be used to bring about someone's death. Whatever else might be said about such a policy, it is certainly not a very efficient way to reduce the level of crime and violence in the country.

Felons and Guns

It is not unreasonable, incidentally, to assume that the existing stock of privately owned firearms constitutes a potential source of guns for illicit or criminal use—not because anyone who owns a gun is potentially a criminal but because the gun can be stolen by someone who is. Several hundred thousand firearms are stolen from private residences alone each year (Wright et al., 1983: Chapter 9); to that figure one would have to add an unknown but possibly very large number stolen from retail or wholesale outlets, or from shippers and importers, or from manufacturers themselves. A survey of nearly 2,000 men doing felony time in ten state prisons all around the country found that half had stolen at least one gun at some time in their criminal careers; somewhere between 40 and 70 percent of the most recent handguns these men possessed were stolen weapons—the 30-point gap representing many inmates' own uncertainties about the ultimate source of their guns (Wright and Rossi, 1986: Chapter 10).

Results from the felon survey indicated that, to the average criminal, a gun was both a means of survival in a hostile environment and an income-producing tool. In both cases, the consequent value of the gun to a felon is many times greater than its purchase price. The average "take" in a robbery is just over $900, and previous analysis of victimization data (Cook, 1976) suggests that firearm robberies yield about three times that of a robbery committed with any other weapon. (One major reason for the difference is that criminals armed with a firearm rob more lucrative targets.) This being the case, the average

robber apparently could afford to spend many hundreds of dollars, perhaps even a few thousand, on a handgun and still recover his investment in the first week of "business." Consider, too, that results from the felon survey showed clearly that many criminals carry guns because they dread the prospect of life on the streets without one. In this light, price would be of less concern.

Demand, it is said, creates its own supply. Just as cocaine will always be available so long as there are people willing to pay $200 a gram for it, so too will guns always be available to anyone willing to spend, let us say, $1,000 to obtain one, especially when, failing all else, one need only walk into any one of every two homes and steal one. Given the economics of crime in this country, the perceived and rather urgent need felt by many felons to be armed with a gun, and the immense supply of guns already in private hands, the possibility of somehow disarming the criminal population of this country seems remote.

Youth and Guns

The issue of youth and guns is of great importance today. A number of studies have been conducted that analyze the relationship between juveniles and firearms. Regarding victimization, a Bureau of Justice Statistics report (Rand, 1990) indicates that youths between 16 and 19 are at particularly high risk of being the victim of a crime with a handgun. Twenty percent of firearm homicide victims are under 20, and another 20 percent between 20 and 24 (Zawitz, 1996). Turning to weapon ownership and carrying, several studies focus primarily on high school-aged youths and their gun patterns. A 1990 study found that 4 percent of the nationally representative sample of 11,631 students in grades nine through twelve reported carrying a gun during the previous month (U.S. Department of Health and Human Services, 1991).

Table 21.2   Firearm Possession Among Incarcerated and Inner-City Youth

Answered "Yes" to the question "Have you ever owned a gun?"

FIREARM TYPE	INMATE POSSESSION		STUDENT POSSESSION	
	%	N	%	N
Any type of gun	86	811	30	733
Target or hunting rifle	38	804	13	731
Military-style automatic or semiautomatic rifle	46	808	14	729
Regular shotgun	60	807	14	730
Sawed-off shotgun	63	811	14	728
Revolver	72	809	29	734
Automatic or semiautomatic handgun	66	816	27	732
Derringer or single-shot handgun	32	779	9	728
Homemade (zip) handgun	11	774	11	725
Owned 3 or more types of guns	73	744	13	718

SOURCE: Sheley and Wright, 1995: 40, 42.

Recent research by Sheley and Wright (1998) constitutes the broadest and most extensive survey of high school youth. Looking at the average American juvenile, they found gun possession and carrying to be relatively low. Fewer than one in ten respondents reported possessing a revolver, and only one in twenty-five possessed an automatic or semiautomatic handgun. Six percent had carried a gun outside the home within the past twelve months. Few respondents reported carrying a gun frequently. Research focusing on inner-city high school students and incarcerated youth provides insight into gun patterns of more at-risk groups (see Table 21.2). One study found that 55 percent of juvenile inmates carried a gun routinely before becoming incarcerated, and 12 percent of inner-city high school students routinely carried (Sheley and Wright, 1995). It is apparent that guns are a problem among youths. More of a problem, however, are the structural and cultural conditions that currently promote gun-related activity among youths (Sheley and Wright, 1998).

CRIMES OF PASSION

These days, no one seriously expects stricter gun controls to solve the problem of hard-core criminal violence or even make much of a dent in it. Much of the argument thus has shifted away from hard-core criminal violence and toward violence perpetrated, not for economic gain or for any other preconceived reason, but rather in the heat of the moment. These are the so-called crimes of passion, crimes that turn injurious or lethal not so much because anyone intended them to but because someone, in a moment of rage, had a firearm at hand. And perhaps, if there were fewer firearms at hand, fewer crimes of passion would occur.

Characteristics of Crimes of Passion

Crimes of passion or rage certainly happen; it is also certain that, in at least some cases, their consequences are strongly exacerbated because of an available firearm. But just how common are they? The fact is that nobody knows. The pro-control assumption that they are very common (see, for example, Zimring, 1968) is usually inferred from the well-known fact that most homicides involve persons known to one another before the event—typically, family members, friends, or other acquaintances. But it does not follow that these homicides are, ipso facto, crimes of passion committed in the heat of the moment. Prior acquaintance does *not* rule out willful, murderous intent.

Possibly the strongest case for the crime of passion scenario is the killing of family members by one another, the so-called family homicides. Unfortunately, this is another topic about which we know much less than we should. One pertinent study, conducted in Kansas City, looked into every family homicide that occurred in a single year. In 85 percent of the cases examined, the police had been called to the family residence within the previous five years to break up a domestic quarrel; in half the cases, the police had been there five or more times. Generalizing from this pattern, it would be seriously misleading to view these homicides as isolated and unfortunate outbursts occurring among normally placid and loving individuals. They are, rather, the culminating episodes in a long history of interpersonal violence and abuse between the parties, a history whose causes and precipitants are far more complex than the mere presence or absence of a gun.

Interesting differences exist between men who kill women and women who kill men. Women who kill men tend disproportionately to use a firearm for the purpose; men who kill women seem to prefer other, more brutalizing means, such as stabbing. The reason for the difference seems reasonably obvious: Women typically do not command the physical strength necessary to get the job done with any weapon other than a gun. Further, many of the women who kill men presumably do so because they

have suffered repeated episodes of physical and mental abuse (Howard, 1986). The resulting killings are tragic, certainly, but no more tragic than the history of abuse that leads up to them. Thus, in the extreme, one could argue that firearms equalize the differences between men and women; gun control puts women at an even greater disadvantage relative to men, so far as interpersonal violence is concerned (Silver and Kates, 1978; see also Lott, 1998).

The number of homicides involving family members has been exaggerated in many presentations. Evidence on victim–offender relationships in homicide is published annually by the FBI in its *Uniform Crime Reports*. These data make it plain that homicides by outright strangers (as for example, in a robbery-motivated homicide) compose only a small fraction of the total, approximately one in every eight. But this assuredly does *not* imply that the remaining seven in every eight involve loved ones slaying one another. In many cases—nearly one-third of the total—the relationship between victim and offender is simply unknown (as would be the case for unsolved homicides). Next to "unknown," the largest category is "acquaintance," accounting for approximately one additional third of the murders. Absent additional details, one might think that acquaintance refers to friends, neighbors, and other reasonably close associates, but in fact neighbors, friends, boyfriends, girlfriends, and all categories of relatives are tallied in their own separate categories. Thus, almost any degree of intimacy or closeness between "acquaintances" would cause the homicide to be tallied elsewhere in the FBI reports. *All* categories of family and relatives combined account for only about one murder in every six. Contrary to a common depiction, then, it is definitely not the case that most murders involve persons who share some degree of intimacy or closeness. Most murders, some three-quarters of them, are committed by casual acquaintances (about 30 percent), perfect strangers (about 15 percent), or persons unknown (30 percent) (see Wright, 1990, for further discussion).

Guns As Catalysts to Violence

Another facet of the crime of passion argument deserves comment: the argument that guns give people the psychic strength to do things of which they otherwise would not be capable. With a gun, harm can be inflicted at a comfortable distance, and this, it is said, is easier than assaulting somebody "up close and personal"—with a knife, for example. In the same vein, it is also sometimes argued that even the casual sight of a gun can "catalyze violence" (Berkowitz, 1968; see discussion in Kleck, 1997: 222–224).

These arguments are not consistent with several research findings. First, studies by Cook (1981b, 1983) and Kleck and Patterson (1993) found no significant differences in the rates of armed robbery between cities where guns were widely available and cities where they were not; in cities with a low "gun density," armed robbers simply robbed with other weapons. (To be sure, robbery-connected murder was somewhat less frequent in the low gun-density cities, but armed robbery itself was not.) Armed robbers, at least, apparently do not need firearms to work up the requisite courage. Also, the hypothesis that guns somehow catalyze violence has spawned a fairly extensive experimental literature, the principle findings of which are mixed and inconclusive (Kleck and Bordua, 1984).

Many crimes of passion are exactly that, but many are crimes of hatred whose outcomes depend less on the available equipment than on lethal, murderous intent. In some cases, the outcomes of these crimes would be less devastating if guns were less available; in other cases, the outcomes would be just the same. In any case,

the problem goes far deeper than the presence or absence of firearms; it is a problem rooted in a culture that glorifies, or at least condones, physical violence as a means of resolving disputes. Until this more basic cultural problem is addressed, it is not clear that stricter gun controls would make much, if any, difference.

GEOGRAPHIC COMPARISONS

A common theme in the gun control literature, one frequently offered as a rejoinder to many of the points expressed here, is the comparison of the United States with other industrialized Western nations. There are, in the United States, no strict federal controls over civilian arms, vast numbers of firearms in private hands, and an enormous amount of gun crime and gun violence. By contrast, other nations have very strict national controls, very few guns, and little or no gun crime. Is this not compelling evidence that strong laws reduce the number of guns and that a reduced number of guns means less crime and violence?

In the absence of more detailed analyses, such comparisons are highly problematic. Any two nations will differ along many dimensions—history, culture, social structure, and legal precedent, for example—and any of these differences (no less than the difference in gun laws or in the number of guns available) might well be the "real" cause of the difference in violent crime rates. Without some examination of these other potentially relevant factors, attributing the crime difference to the gun law or gun availability difference is gratuitous.

The English case is among the more commonly cited in this connection. However, it is well established that the rates of firearms ownership and of violent crime were both extremely low in England for decades before that nation's strict gun laws were passed (Greenwood, 1972).

England's gun control laws also have not prevented a very sharp increase in armed crime in that nation over the past three decades (Kopel, 1992). The Japanese case also is commonly cited. In fact, the rate of non-gun homicide in the United States is many times higher than the total homicide rate of Japan. So there is obviously more to the U.S.–Japan difference than first meets the eye.

In at least a few nations, such as Norway and Switzerland, the proportional presence of guns among the civilian population at least rivals that of the United States, but gun crime and violence are exceptionally rare. (In both cases, the degree of armament is a result of the nation's policy with respect to a standing reserve militia.) It may well be that guns are a necessary condition for high rates of violent crime, but these nations make it plain that they are not a sufficient condition.

The most detailed comparison yet published of gun laws and crime rates across nations is Kopel (1992), which provides in-depth analyses of the applicable gun laws and other social circumstances in Japan, Great Britain, Canada, Australia, New Zealand, Jamaica, Switzerland, and the United States. Kopel's conclusion is that gun control is irrelevant in peaceful nations and ineffective in violent nations, and that any effort to model U.S. gun laws on those of other advanced industrialized societies would probably prove fruitless. "Broader cultural forces, of which gun policy is only one element, are more important" than gun control per se (1992: 406).

What is true of comparisons among nations is equally true of comparisons among other geographic aggregates, for example, among regions of the country, or states, or counties. Any two states or regions, like any two countries, will differ in a number of ways, and all those ways must somehow be held constant in an analysis of differences in gun laws, gun availability, and crime rates. One seemingly obvious way to examine the effects of gun laws is to compare states or cities that have very restrictive gun laws to states or cities whose laws are less restrictive; several studies of that sort have been done (see, for example, Geisel et al., 1969; Murray, 1975; DeZee, 1983; Kleck, 1991). The results are predictably contradictory: Some find that gun laws reduce crime; others find that they do not. The relatively cruder analyses tend to fall in the former category; more sophisticated analyses tend to fall in the latter. The problem in drawing inferences from such studies is exactly that of knowing what to hold constant in the analysis so that one can be confident that the crime difference results from the difference in gun laws and not from some other unexamined factor (see Kleck, 1984, 1997, for additional discussion).

To illustrate, it has been known for some time that rates of firearms ownership are higher in the South than elsewhere in the country (Erskine, 1972; Wright and Marston, 1975). It is also well known that the homicide rate is higher in the South than elsewhere (Harries, 1974). Some cite these facts as proof that guns cause crime. It is arguable, however, whether the high homicide rates in the South result mostly from gun ownership factors, cultural factors (Nisbet and Cohen, 1996) or the generally lower socioeconomic conditions that prevail in that region (see Loftin and Hill, 1974; Erlanger, 1975; O'Connor and Lizotte, 1978; Bankston et al., 1986; see also Chapter 7). This issue continues to be debated.

Just as there are regional differences in gun ownership, so too are there differences by city size. Gun ownership is highest in small-town and rural areas and falls off sharply as city size increases (Wright et al., 1983: Chapter 6). The violent crime problem, in contrast, shows just the opposite pattern, being highest in the major urban centers and dropping off sharply in the more rural areas. We should not conclude, from this evidence alone, that guns are *not* the cause of crime or that guns somehow reduce crime. Rather, we need something more from the analysis. Without that something more, nothing of value can be inferred, just as with crude comparisons between the United States and other nations.

PUBLIC OPINION

Public opinion always has figured prominently in the gun control debate. "An important part of the gun control lobby's political construct is the idea that the public 'wants' gun control and is prevented from getting it by the 'gun lobby'" (Bordua, 1984: 54; see also Schuman and Presser, 1981). If the effectiveness of stricter gun control in reducing crime is in some doubt, at least little apparent harm would be done by such controls, and the public, it is said, is long since on the record as favoring them.

So far as can be told, the first gun control question in a national poll was asked in the 1930s. Even at that early date, large majorities said they were in favor. In 1959, Gallup instituted what is now the standard gun control question: whether one would favor or oppose a law that required a person to acquire a police permit before purchasing a gun. In the original study, and in many subsequent iterations, the proportions favoring such a law seldom have been less than 70 percent (Young et al., 1996).

These large majorities are interpreted by many as evidence of widespread popular demand for stricter gun controls. This may well be a misinterpretation; as noted previously, Cook has shown that about three-quarters of the U.S. population now reside in political jurisdictions where something very similar to the Gallup police permit mechanism is already in force. The strong majorities registered on this item, in other words, may represent more an endorsement of the status quo than a demand for new and stricter regulations.

Most questions in most polls asking about registration and permit mechanisms receive substantial majority support. It is, as suggested, a plausible guess that much of this majority comes from persons residing in jurisdictions where such measures are presently in force. Other gun control measures that sometimes are asked about, those substantially more stringent than registration or permit requirements, do not, in general, curry much popular favor. Bans on the manufacture, sale, or ownership of handguns, for example, are rejected by good-sized majorities; having the government use public funds to buy back and destroy guns is rejected by an even larger majority. Apparently, a small majority favors a ban on cheap, low-quality handguns. Mandatory sentencing for the use of a firearm in committing a crime is very popular; mandatory sentencing for the illegal carrying or possession of a firearm is less so. In general, the available evidence suggests that most people support most of the reasonable social precautions discussed at the outset of this chapter but are not anxious to see government go much further. Not incidentally, very large majorities of the population, approaching 90 percent, believe (rightly or wrongly) that the Constitution guarantees them the right to own a gun—a topic beyond the scope of this chapter (Wright, 1981). The most recent review of poll evidence on public opinion and gun control is by Kleck (1997: Chapter 10), which also concludes that majorities support a wide range of weak-to-moderate controls but that "this support does not, however, extend to stronger controls" (1997: 337).

GUN OWNERSHIP
AND SELF-DEFENSE

The ownership of guns for self-defense also figures prominently in the gun control debate. The pro-gun forces routinely invoke the specter of an unarmed population defenseless against the ravages of crime and violence. The pro-control theme also is well known: Crime is on the rise, and to cope with their fear, people buy guns. In fact, their odds of deterring any crime with a gun are essentially nil; the odds are far better that they will end up shooting one another, either by accident or in the heat of some lamentable moment. To quote briefly from one pro-control pamphlet, "Ownership of handguns by private citizens for self-protection against crime appears to provide more a psychological belief in safety than actual deterrence to criminal behavior" (Yeager et al., 1976: 35).

Motivations for Owning a Gun

To begin, it is not at all clear that fear of crime is an important motivation to buy a gun. Many studies have examined the question, but most fail to show any significant correlation between fear of crime and gun ownership (Wright and Marston, 1975; Williams and McGrath, 1976; DeFronzo, 1979; Northwood et al., 1978; Stinchcombe et al., 1980; Young, 1985; Sheley et al., 1994); a few studies show small but significant effects (see, for example, Lizotte and Bordua, 1980; McDowall and Loftin, 1983; Smith and Uchida, 1988; Ellison, 1991). The research is highly ambiguous and supports, at best, the conclusion of a weak relationship between fear and gun possession.

Despite an apparently widespread impression to the contrary, owning a firearm primarily for self-defense is itself relatively uncommon (Wright, 1984). Approximately three firearms in four (conceivably, four in five) are owned mainly for other reasons, sport and recreational reasons being the most common. Even among handgun owners, sport and recreational reasons are mentioned about as often as defense or self-protection. Thus, guns owned primarily for self-defense are outnumbered by sport and recreational guns by roughly three or four to one. And because only about half the households in the nation own any gun for any reason, the proportion of U.S. households owning a weapon primarily for self-defense is about 10 to 15 percent. (To be sure, the proportions citing "defense" as a secondary or tertiary reason are higher but still below 50 percent.)

Defensive Gun Uses

In 1995, Kleck and Gertz published findings from their 1993 National Self-Defense Survey, the first specifically designed to estimate the number of actual defensive gun uses. It excluded gun uses against animals as well as guns used in conjunction with occupational duties. The survey established whether the respondents had actually confronted a person and, if so, had done so in defense of what they perceived as the commission of a crime against them. Their findings indicated that roughly 2.5 million defensive gun uses occurred per year during the 1988–1993 period. They concluded that defensive uses of guns are three to four times more common than are known criminal uses (e.g., derived from the *UCR*). Another national survey, although of a smaller scale than the National Defense Survey, was conducted in 1994 by the Police Foundation. The findings from this research confirmed the estimated frequency of defensive gun uses reported by Kleck and Gertz.

The Extent of Crime Deterrence

The issue of defensive gun use frequency is particularly controversial. In arguing against the proposition that owning guns may promote safety through their potential for defensive use, gun-control supporters tend to ignore most other survey results and to rely nearly exclusively upon estimates drawn from the National Crime Victimization Survey (NCVS; see Chapter 3 in this volume). Kleck believes that the NCVS is unsuitable for estimating the total number of defensive gun uses. He argues that, not only are NCVS results highly inconsistent with those of at least fifteen other independent estimates of defensive gun use frequency, but the NCVS is also grossly negligent in its survey inquiries regarding defensive gun use (Kleck, 1997: 152–159).

Researchers in this field, Kellermann (Kellermann et al., 1992, 1993) perhaps the most prominent, recently have attempted to redefine violence as a public health (as opposed to criminal justice) problem. They look upon violence and factors related to violence as a source of serious amounts of needless morbidity and premature mortality in the American population. Thus, we have seen considerable growth in the amount of research on violence—particularly firearms violence—in the public health journals. Kleck (1997; Kates and Kleck, 1997) has reviewed the recent public health literature and concludes that many of the most widely cited studies tend to ignore prior research; rely on small, unrepresentative, and non-probability samples; use primitive data methods; report findings selectively; and falsely cite previous research to make it appear supportive of their conclusions (Kleck, 1997: 56–62).

It is frequently claimed that a private firearm is six times more likely to be involved in a fire-arms accident than to be used in deterring a crime. The "six-to-one" finding originates with a study in Cleveland by Rushford et al. (1975; see also Kellermann and Reay, 1986), a study that has been severely and rightly criticized (Silver and Kates, 1978). As we have just seen, data reviewed or generated by Kleck (1986a, 1988, 1997) suggest that civilians use guns to defend themselves against criminals hundreds of thousands to millions of times each year. In addition, Kleck (1988) finds that civilian weapons use is effective as a deterrent to crime: There appear to be some 1,500–2,800 felons killed in the act of committing a crime annually by gun-using civilians, far more than are killed by the police (see also Green, 1986). In contrast, a best guess about the annual number of firearms accidents, fatal and nonfatal, would be around 100,000. So it is not conceivable that serious gun accidents are "six times" more frequent than self-defense uses.

Given the total number of firearms out there, the percentage of firearms involved in an accident in a typical year has to be on the order of one-tenth of 1 percent. The average gun-owning household possesses five, but even if we therefore multiply by five, the annual risk per gun-owning household is still around 0.5 percent per year. The idea that there are many times more firearms accidents than incidents where firearms are used in self-defense is not consistent with any available evidence of which we are aware.

It is clear, however, that much crime occurs in circumstances where the victim's ownership of a gun would be irrelevant: for example, the burglary of an unoccupied residence, or the crime on the street (which presumably would catch most gun owners far away from their weapons). But evidence from the criminal victimization surveys also suggests that, when having a gun is not irrelevant, it can sometimes be an effective crime deterrent. Indeed, the probability of a successful victimization appears to go down—although, to stress a critical point, the probability of injury or death to the victim goes up (Cook, 1986)—if resistance of any sort is offered, and of the various means of resistance available, if resisting with a gun appears to be the most effective (Kleck and Bordua, 1984: 34–39).

In general, the arguments against gun ownership for self-defense fare poorly. It is not at all clear that crime or fear of crime is responsible for much gun ownership in the first place; most guns are owned for reasons having little to do with self-defense. It is also by no means clear that the actual uses of guns in self-defense are vastly outnumbered by their accidental or even intentional misuse (in fact, the precise opposite may be true) or that using a gun to deter crime is somehow ineffective. What has become increasingly clear is that there is some self-protective efficacy that needs to be taken into account when discussing gun ownership.

THE SATURDAY NIGHT SPECIAL

The small, cheap handgun known as the Saturday night special (SNS) was once singled out for much special attention. The term is used very loosely. Variously, it refers to low price, or inferior quality, or a small caliber, or a short barrel length, or some combination thereof. One problem, as Cook (1981a; see also McClain, 1984) pointed out long ago, is that the Saturday night special has not been defined with enough precision to allow special policies to be enacted for its regulation.

The special attention that was at one time given to the SNS typically was justified on two grounds: (1) that these guns have no legitimate sport or recreational use and (2) that they are the preferred firearm in crime. Thus, if we could just ban their manufacture or importation altogether, we would reduce directly the number of crime guns available and not infringe on anyone's legitimate ownership rights.

Serious Criminals and the SNS

Until recently, the only systematic evidence available on the firearms used in crime was that derived from analyses of the firearms confiscated by police in the course of criminal investigations. The confiscation studies did not present a very clear picture. One of the largest and most systematic of them (Brill, 1977) reports, based on probable cost, that the proportion of SNSs among confiscated crime handguns is less than 50 percent. Contrary to the common claim, these data do not establish the SNS as the preferred crime gun.

More recent and perhaps more telling data, based on direct surveys of imprisoned felons, are reported in Wright and Rossi (1986: Chapter 8). The conclusion was that "felons neither preferred to own, nor did they actually own, small, cheap, low-quality handguns. The strong preference, rather, was for large, well-made guns" (p. 180). Only about 14 percent of the most recent handguns owned by this sample would qualify as SNSs, and most of these were owned by men who had not used guns to commit crimes; the more serious the criminal history, the stronger the preference for large, well-made handguns. Felons in this survey were given a list of desirable handgun traits and asked to rate their importance; the top three choices, in order, were that the handgun be accurate, untraceable, and well made. Similar results have also been reported for samples of incarcerated juvenile offenders (Sheley and Wright, 1995).

The conclusion is that criminals, especially serious criminals, have relatively little use for the SNS; indeed, it seems obvious that they prefer to be at least as well armed as their most likely adversary, namely, the police; data on the handguns felons actually own suggest that most of them are successful to this end. Moreover, even if they did have some preference for the smaller, cheaper handguns, the absence of those guns would not cause them to go unarmed, but to move up to bigger, more lethal equipment— to bigger and better handguns in the absence of small, cheap ones, and to sawed-off rifles and shotguns in the complete absence of handguns of all sorts. Given what is known about the comparative lethality of big-caliber versus small-caliber guns (Zimring, 1972), not to mention the lethality of sawed-off shotguns, an SNS ban seemingly has virtually nothing to recommend it (see also Kleck, 1985, 1986b).

Noncriminals and the SNS

What about the other side of the argument, that these small, cheap guns have no legitimate use and should therefore be banned on those grounds alone, irrespective of the possible criminal response? It is obviously doubtful whether many SNSs are purchased for sporting purposes; most, in all likelihood, are purchased for self-defense by households of modest means. Whether "self-protection" from crime is a legitimate reason to own a handgun also can be disputed. But surely, all would agree that people at the highest risk from crime have the best reasons to protect themselves against it. Those at highest risk in the United States are the poor, African Americans, and central-city residents— exactly those segments of society that can least afford large, well-made, expensive handguns. The often-urged SNS ban might well deny the means of self-protection to those most evidently in need of it, or in the words of the

Congress of Racial Equality, "deny the law-abiding poor, including the law-abiding black poor, access to weapons for the defense of their families. That effect is doubly discriminatory because the poor, and especially the black poor, are the primary victims of crime and in many areas lack the political power to command as much police protection as better neighborhoods" (Innis, 1987).

Assault Weapons

The concern expressed a decade ago about small, cheap handguns has been replaced more recently by a concern with so-called military-style assault weapons, and a complete national ban on the sale, manufacture, and ownership of these weapons is now in place. The Assault Weapons Ban was enacted through the Violent Crime Control and Law Enforcement Act of 1994. (See Table 21.3 for a list of banned weapons.) The attention now being given to assault weapons illustrates what Kleck (1997: Chapter 4) calls "searching for 'bad' guns," the persistent hope among gun control advocates that if we can just find a way to ban "bad guns" and leave "good guns" alone, then we will reduce the level of crime and violence but not infringe on the rights of legitimate gun owners. Because the goodness or badness of a gun inheres entirely in the motivations and intentions of its user, and certainly not in the gun itself, this approach, although commonly urged, is bound to be unproductive.

Assault weapons are presented by the press and gun control advocates as being particularly dangerous and useful in criminal activity. This is due to their alleged greater lethality, rapid rate of fire, and large ammunition capacity (Kates and Kleck, 1997). Kleck (1997) points out, however, that all of these claims are either false or true only to a limited degree. The media commonly imply that assault weapons either fire like machine guns or can be easily converted to do so. In fact, assault weapons fire exclusively in semi-automatic mode, just as a revolver. And though it is possible to convert such a weapon to fully automatic fire, police data on seized weapons suggest that criminals very rarely have the resources to perform such procedures (Kleck, 1997: 122). Also, an assault weapon can accept a large capacity magazine, but that is an attribute of the magazine, not the weapon itself. This point is of limited relevance, however, as few violent crimes involve a large number of shots fired (Kleck, 1997: 123). Regarding the argument that assault weapons are particularly useful in criminal activity, it is important to note that any weapon that can be used for offense is just as useful for defensive purposes. As Philip Cook argued, "It seems doubtful that there are any guns that are 'useless' to legitimate owners, yet useful to criminals. Any gun that can be used in self-defense has a legitimate purpose, and therefore is not 'useless.' Similarly, any gun that can be used in crime can also be used in self-defense" (Cook, 1981: 1737).

Just as SNS handguns were once said to be the weapon of choice for criminals (but turned out not to be), assault weapons are now commonly said to be the weapons of choice, especially for drug dealers and youth gangs. There is practically no systematic evidence to support such an assertion. The fraction of guns confiscated from criminals by police that could be called assault weapons, even using liberal definitions, is not more than 1 or 2 percent (Kleck, 1997: 112). Large-caliber handguns, not assault rifles or other military-style weapons, remain the overwhelming weapon of choice among both adult and juvenile criminals (Sheley and Wright, 1993).

CONCLUSION

Attempts to control crime by regulating the ownership or use of firearms are attempts to regulate the artifacts and activities of a culture that, in its own way, is as unique as any of the myriad other cultures that compose the American ethnic mosaic. This is the American gun culture, about which Hofstadter (1970), Sherrill (1973), Tonso (1982), and others have written, and it remains among the least understood of any of the various subcultural strands that make up modern American society.

There is no question that a gun culture exists, one that amply fulfills any definition of a culture. The best evidence we have on its status as a culture is that the most important predictor of whether a person owns a gun is whether his or her father owned one, which means that gun owning is a tradition transmitted across generations (Wright et al., 1983). Most gun owners report that there were firearms in their homes when they were growing up; this is true even of criminal gun users (Wright and Rossi, 1986: Chapter 5; Sheley and Wright, 1995).

The existence and characteristics of a gun culture have implications that rarely are appreciated. For one, gun control deals with matters that people feel strongly about, that are integral to their upbringing and their worldview. Gun control advocates frequently are taken aback by the stridency with which their proposals are attacked, but from the gun culture's viewpoint, restrictions on the right to keep and bear arms amount to the systematic destruction of a valued way of life.

The gun evokes powerful, emotive imagery that often stands in the way of intelligent debate. To the pro-control point of view, the gun is a symbol of much that is wrong in American culture. It symbolizes violence, aggression, and male

Table 21.3   Legal Definition of Assault Weapons

TITLE XI—FIREARMS
Subtitle A—Assault Weapons

(b) DEFINITION OF A SEMIAUTOMATIC ASSAULT WEAPON—Section 921(a) of title 18, United States Code, is amended by adding at the end the following new paragraph:

(30) The term 'semiautomatic assault weapon' means—

(A) any of the firearms, or copies or duplicates of the firearms in any caliber,
Known as—

(i) Norinco, Mitchell, and Poly Technologies Avtomat Kalashnikovs (all models);

(ii) Action Arms Israeli Military Industries UZI and Galil;

(iii) Beretta Ar70 (SC-70);

(iv) Colt AR-15;

(v) Fabrique National FN/FAL, FN/LAR, and FNC;

(vi) SWD M-10, M-11, M-11/9, and M-12;

(vii) Steyr AUG;

(viii) INTRATEC TEC-9, TEC-DC9, and TEC-22; and

(ix) revolving cylinder shotguns, such as (or similar to) the Street Sweeper and Striker 12;

(B) a semiautomatic rifle that has an ability to accept a detachable magazine and has at least 2 of—

(i) a folding or telescoping stock;

(ii) a pistol grip that protrudes conspicuously beneath the action of the weapon;

(iii) a bayonet mount;

(iv) a flash suppressor or threaded barrel designed to accommodate a flash suppressor; and

(v) a grenade launcher;

(C) a semiautomatic pistol that has an ability to accept a detachable magazine and has at least 2 of—

(i) an ammunition magazine that attaches to the pistol outside of the pistol grip;

(ii) a threaded barrel capable of accepting a barrel extender, flash suppressor, forward handgrip, or silencer;

(iii) a shroud that is attached to, or partially or completely encircles, the barrel and that permits the shooter to hold the firearm with the nontrigger hand without being burned;

(iv) a manufactured weight of 50 ounces or more when the pistol is unloaded; and

(v) a semiautomatic version of an automatic firearm; and

(D) a semiautomatic shotgun that has at least 2 of—

(i) a folding or telescoping stock;

(ii) a pistol grip that protrudes conspicuously beneath the action of the weapon;

(iii) a fixed magazine capacity in excess of 5 rounds; and

(iv) an ability to accept a detachable magazine.

SOURCE: *Violent Crime Control Act,* U.S. Public Law 103-322, 1994.

---

dominance, and its use is seen as an acting out of our most regressive and infantile fantasies. To the gun culture's way of thinking, the same gun symbolizes much that is right in America. It symbolizes self-sufficiency and independence, and its use is an affirmation of our relationship to nature and to history. The "Great American Gun War," as Bruce-Briggs (1976) has described it, is far more than a contentious debate over crime and the equipment with which it is committed. It is a battle over fundamental values. Scholars and criminologists who study the problem of guns and crime would do well to conceptualize the problem in terms of this battle between cultures.

DISCUSSION QUESTIONS

1. Describe the various positions regarding gun control taken by interested parties.

2. To what extent have past efforts at gun control succeeded in decreasing criminal violence? What problems make such an assessment difficult?

3. Who kills whom with guns in America? Is most gun-related crime the work of felons, or are most firearm incidents crimes of passion?

4. Is the argument that guns promote violence supported by research findings?

5. Is fear of crime the reason so many people possess guns in this society? Do guns figure in many acts of self-defense?

6. Discuss the proposition that proposes that increased gun ownership would deter crime in America.

7. What is a Saturday night special? Is this type of gun at the heart of the relationship between guns and crime in this society? Are military-style assault weapons that we hear so much about lately at the heart of the gun-crime problem? Are they driving up the crime rate?

REFERENCES

Anderson, J. 1985. *Guns in American Life*. New York: Random House.

Bankston, W., C. Thompson, Q. Jenkins, and C. Forsyth. 1986. *Carrying Firearms: The Influence of Southern Culture and Fear of Crime*. Paper presented at the 1986 meeting of the American Society of Criminology, Atlanta.

Berkowitz, L. 1968. "Impulse, Aggression, and the Gun." *Psychology Today* 2: 19–24.

Black, D., and D. Nagin. 1998. "Do Right-to-Carry Laws Deter Violent Crime?" *Journal of Legal Studies* 43: 209–219.

Bordua, D. 1984. "Gun Control and Opinion Measurement: Adversary Polling and Construction of Meaning." Pp. 51–70 in *Firearms and Violence: Issues of Public Policy*. Edited by D. B. Kates. Cambridge, MA: Ballinger.

Brill, S. 1977. *Firearms Abuse: A Research and Policy Report*. Washington, DC: The Police Foundation.

Britt, C., G. Kleck, and D. Bordua. 1996. "A Reassessment of the DC Gun Law: Some Cautionary Notes on the Use of Interrupted Time Series Designs for Policy Impact Assessment." *Law and Society* 30: 361–380.

Bruce-Briggs, B. 1976. "The Great American Gun War." *The Public Interest* 45: 37–62.

Cook, P. J. 1976. "A Strategic Choice Analysis of Robbery." Pp. 173–187 in *Sample Surveys of the Victims of Crime*. Edited by W. Skogan. Cambridge, MA: Ballinger.

———. 1979. *An Overview of Federal, State, and Local Firearms Regulations*. Unpublished manuscript, Institute of Policy Sciences, Duke University.

———. 1981a. "The Saturday Night Special: An Assessment of Alternative Definitions from a Policy Perspective." *Journal of Criminal Law and Criminology* 72: 1735–1745.

———. 1981b. "The Effect of Gun Availability on Violent Crime Patterns." *The Annals of the American Academy of Political and Social Science* 455: 63–79.

———. 1983. "The Influence of Gun Availability on Violent Crime Patterns." Pp. 49–89 in *Crime and Justice: An Annual Review of Research*. Edited by M. Tonry and N. Morris. Chicago: University of Chicago Press.

———. 1986. "The Relationship Between Victim Resistance and Injury in Noncommercial Robbery." *Journal of Legal Studies* 15: 405–416.

Cook, P. J., and J. Blose. 1981. "State Programs for Screening Handgun Buyers." *The Annals of the American Academy of Political and Social Science* 455: 80–91.

DeFronzo, J. 1979. "Fear of Crime and Handgun Ownership." *Criminology* 17: 331–339.

DeZee, M. 1983. "Gun Control Legislation: Im-pact and Ideology." *Law and Policy Quarterly* 5: 367–379.

Ellison, C. 1991. "Southern Cultures and Firearms Ownership." *Social Science Quarterly* 72: 267–283.

Erlanger, H. S. 1975. "Is There a 'Subculture of Violence' in the South?" *Journal of Criminal Law and Criminology* 66: 483–490.

Erskine, H. 1972. "The Polls: Gun Control." *Public Opinion Quarterly* 36: 455–469.

Geisel, M. S., R. Roll, and R. S. Wettick. 1969. "The Effectiveness of State and Local Regulation of Handguns: A Statistical Analysis." *Duke Law Review* 4: 647–676.

Green, G. S. 1986. *Reflections on Citizen Gun Ownership and Criminal Deterrence: Theory, Research and Policy.* Paper presented at the annual meeting of the American Society of Criminology, Atlanta.

Greenwood, C. 1972. *Firearms Control: A Study of Armed Crime and Firearms in England and Wales.* London: Routledge & Kegan Paul.

Harries, K. D. 1974. *The Geography of Crime and Justice.* New York: McGraw-Hill.

Hofstadter, R. 1970. "America as a Gun Culture." *American Heritage* 21: 4ff.

Howard, M. 1986. "Husband-Wife Homicide: An Essay from a Family Law Perspective." *Law and Contemporary Problems* 49: 63–88.

Howe, W. J. 1987. "Firearms Production by U.S. Manufacturers, 1973–1985." *Shooting Industry:* 101–112.

Innis, R. 1987. "Memorandum of Law of Roy Innis and the Congress of Racial Equality." Amici Curia Brief, Brooklyn, New York.

Jones, A. 1981. *Women Who Kill.* New York: Fawcett Books.

Kates, D., and Kleck, G. 1997. *The Great American Gun Debate.* San Francisco: Pacific Research Institute for Public Policy.

Kellermann, A. L., and D. T. Reay. 1986. "Protection or Peril? An Analysis of Firearms-Related Deaths in the Home." *New England Journal of Medicine* 314: 1557–1560.

Kellermann, A., F. Rivara, N. Rushforth, J. Banton, D. Reay, J. Francisco, A. Locci, J. Prodzinski, B. Hackman, and G. Somes. 1993. "Gun Ownership as a Risk Factor for Homicide in the Home." *New England Journal of Medicine* 329: 1084–1091.

Kellermann, A., F. Rivara, G. Somes, D. Reay, J. Francisco, J. Banton, J. Prodzinski, C. Fligner, and B. Hackman. 1992. "Suicide in the Home in Relation to Gun Ownership." *New England Journal of Medicine* 327: 467–472.

Kleck, G. 1984. "The Relationship Between Gun Ownership Levels and Rates of Violence in the United States." Pp. 99–132 in *Firearms and Violence: Issues of Public Policy.* Edited by D. B. Kates. Cambridge, MA: Ballinger.

———. 1985. "Handguns and Violence: Is the 'Saturday Night Special' the Problem?" Unpublished manuscript.

———. 1986a. "Policy Lessons From Recent Gun Control Research." *Law and Contemporary Problems* 49: 35–62.

———. 1986b. "Evidence That 'Saturday Night Specials' Not Very Important for Crime." *Sociology and Social Research* 70: 303–307.

———. 1986c. "Firearms Accidents." Unpublished manuscript.

———. 1988. "Crime Control through the Private Use of Armed Force." *Social Problems* 35: 1–21.

———. 1991. *Point Blank: Guns and Violence in America.* Hawthorne, NY: Aldine de Gruyter.

———. 1997. *Targeting Guns: Firearms and Their Control.* Hawthorne, NY: Aldine de Gruyter.

Kleck, G., and D. Bordua. 1984. "The Assumptions of Gun Control." Pp. 23–44 in *Firearms and Violence: Issues of Public Policy.* Edited by D. Kates. Cambridge, MA: Ballinger.

Kleck, G., and M. Gertz. 1995. "Armed Resistance to Crime: The Prevalence and Nature of Self

Defense with a Gun." *Journal of Criminal Law and Criminology* 85: 150–187.

Kleck, G., and E. Patterson. 1993. "The Impact of Gun Control and Gun Ownership on Violence Rates." *Journal of Quantitative Criminology* 9: 249–288.

Kopel, D. B. 1992. *The Samurai, the Mountie, and the Cowboy: Should America Adopt the Gun Controls of Other Democracies?* Buffalo, NY: Prometheus.

Leff, C., and M. Leff. 1981. "The Politics of In-effectiveness: Federal Firearms Legislation, 1919–1938." *The Annals of the American Academy of Political and Social Science* 455: 48–62.

Lizotte, A., and D. Bordua. 1980. "Firearms Owner-ship for Sport and Protection: Two Divergent Models." *American Sociological Review* 45: 229–244.

Loftin, C., M. Heumann, and D. McDowall. 1983. "Mandatory Sentencing and Firearms Violence: Evaluating an Alternative to Gun Control." *Law & Society Review* 17: 287–318.

Loftin, C., and R. Hill. 1974. "Regional Subculture and Homicide." *American Sociological Review* 39: 714–724.

Loftin, C., and D. McDowall. 1981. " 'One With a Gun Gets You Two': Mandatory Sentencing and Firearms Violence in Detroit." *The Annals of the American Academy of Political and Social Science* 455: 150–168.

Lott, J. 1998. *More Guns, Less Crime: Understanding Crime and Gun Control Laws.* Chicago: University of Chicago Press.

Lott, J., and D. Mustard. 1997. "Crime Deterrence and Right-to-Carry Concealed Handguns. *Journal of Legal Studies* 26: 1–68.

Ludwig, J. 1996. *Do Permissive Concealed-Carry Laws Reduce Violent Crime?* (Unpublished Manuscript) Washington, DC: Georgetown University.

Maguire, K., and A. Pastore. 1998. *Sourcebook of Criminal Justice Statistics, 1997.* Washington, DC: U.S. Department of Justice.

Margarita, M. 1985. *The 1980 New York Gun Law: An Evaluation of Its Implementation and Impact.* Washington, DC: National Institute of Justice.

McClain, P. 1984. "Prohibiting the 'Saturday Night Special': A Feasible Policy Option?" Pp. 201–217 in *Firearms and Violence: Issues of Public Policy.* Edited by D. B. Kates. Cambridge, MA: Ballinger.

McDowall, D., and C. Loftin. 1983. "Collective Security and the Demand for Legal Handguns." *American Journal of Sociology* 88: 1146–1161.

Morrow, P., and P. Hudson. 1986. "Accidental Fire-arm Fatalities in North Carolina, 1976–1980." *American Journal of Public Health* 76: 1120–1123.

Murray, D. 1975. "Handguns, Gun Control Laws, and Firearms Violence." *Social Problems* 23: 81–93.

National Coalition to Ban Handguns. 1988. *Member-ship solicitation letter.* No date.

Nisbet, R., and D. Cohen. 1996. *Culture of Honor: The Psychology of Violence in the South.* Boulder, CO: Westview Press.

Northwood, L. K., R. Westgard, and C. Barb. 1978. "Law Abiding One Man Armies." *Society* 16: 69–74.

O'Connor, J. F., and A. J. Lizotte. 1978. "The 'South-ern Subculture of Violence' Thesis and Patterns of Gun Ownership." *Social Problems* 25: 420–429.

Pierce, G. L., and W. J. Bowers. 1981. "The Bartley-Fox Gun Law's Impact on Crime in Boston." *The Annals of the American Academy of Political and Social Science* 455: 40–47.

Rand, M. 1990. *Handgun Crime Victims.* Washington, DC: U.S. Department of Justice.

Rushford, N. C., A. F. Hirsch, and L. Adelson. 1975. "Accidental Firearms Fatalities in a Metropoli-tan County (1958–1973)." *American Journal of Epidemiology* 100: 499–505.

Schuman, H., and S. Presser. 1981. "The Attitude-Action Connection and the Issue of Gun Con-trol." *The Annals of the American Academy of Politi-cal and Social Science* 455: 40–47.

Sheley, J., C. Brody, J. Wright, and M. Williams. 1994. "Women and Handguns: Evidence from National Surveys, 1973–1991." *Social Science Research* 23: 219–235.

Sheley, J. F., and J. D. Wright. 1993. "Gun Acquisition and Possession in Selected Juvenile Samples."

Research in Brief (December). Washington, DC: National Institute of Justice.

———. 1995. *In the Line of Fire: Youth, Guns, and Violence in Urban America.* Hawthorne, NY: Aldine de Gruyter.

———. 1998. *High School Youth, Weapons, and Violence: A National Survey of Weapon-Related Behavior, Crime, and Victimization. Final Report.* Washington, DC: National Institute of Justice.

Sherrill, R. 1973. *The Saturday Night Special.* New York: Charterhouse.

Silver, C. R., and D. B. Kates. 1978. "Self-Defense, Handgun Ownership, and the Independence of Women in a Violent, Sexist Society." Pp. 139–196 in *Restricting Handguns: The Liberal Skeptics Speak Out.* Edited by D. B. Kates. Croton-on-Hudson, NY: North River Press.

Smith, D. A., and C. D. Uchida. 1988. "The Social Organization of Self-Help." *American Sociological Review* 53: 94–102.

Stinchcombe, A., R. Adams, C. A. Heimer, K. L. Scheppelle, T. W. Smith, and D. G. Taylor. 1980. *Crime and Punishment—Changing Attitudes in America.* San Francisco: Jossey-Bass.

Tonso, W. R. 1982. *Guns and Society: The Social and Existential Roots of the American Attachment to Firearms.* Washington, DC: University Press of America.

U.S. Department of Health and Human Services. 1991. *Morbidity and Mortality Weekly Report: Weapon-Carrying Among High School Students—United States, 1990.* Washington, DC: U.S. Department of Health and Human Services, Public Health Service.

Williams, J. S., and J. H. McGrath. 1976. "Why People Own Guns." *Journal of Communication* 26: 22–30.

Wright, J. D. 1981. "Public Opinion and Gun Con-trol: A Comparison of Results from Two Recent National Surveys." *The Annals of the American Academy of Political and Social Science* 455: 24–39.

———. 1984. "The Ownership of Firearms for Reasons of Self-Defense." Pp. 301–328 in *Firearms and Violence: Issues of Public Policy.* Edited by D. B. Kates. Cambridge, MA: Ballinger.

———. 1990. "In the Heat of the Moment." *Reason* 22 (4): 44–45.

———. 1995. "Ten Essential Observations on Guns in America." *Society* 32: 63–68.

Wright, J. D., and L. L. Marston. 1975. "The Ownership of the Means of Destruction: Weapons in the United States." *Social Problems* 23: 93–107.

Wright, J. D., and P. Rossi. 1986. *Armed and Considered Dangerous: A Survey of Felons and Their Firearms.* Hawthorne, NY: Aldine.

Wright, J. D., P. Rossi, and K. Daly. 1983. *Under the Gun: Weapons, Crime, and Violence in America.* Hawthorne, NY: Aldine.

Yeager, M. G., J. D. Alviani, and N. Loving. 1976. *How Well Does the Handgun Protect You and Your Family?* Washington, DC: U.S. Conference of Mayors.

Young, J., D. Hemingway, R. Blendon, and J. Benson. 1996. "Trends: Guns." *Public Opinion Quarterly* 60: 634–649.

Young, R. L. 1985. "Perceptions of Crime, Racial Attitudes, and Firearms Ownership." *Social Forces* 64: 473–486.

Zawitz, M. 1996. *Firearm Injury From Crime: Firearms, Crime and Criminal Justice.* Washington, DC: U.S. Department of Justice.

Zimring, F. E. 1968. "Is Gun Control Likely to Reduce Violent Killings?" *University of Chicago Law Review* 35: 721–737.

———. 1972. "The Medium Is the Message: Firearm Caliber as a Determinant of Death from Assault." *Journal of Legal Studies* 1: 97–123.

———. 1975. "Firearms and Federal Law: The Gun Control Act of 1968." *Journal of Legal Studies* 4 (1) (January): 133–198.

———. 1977. "Determinants of the Death Rate from Robbery: A Detroit Time Study." *Journal of Legal Studies* 6 (June): 317–332.

Zimring, F. E., and G. Hawkins. 1987. *The Citizen's Guide to Gun Control.* New York: Macmillan.

Chapter Outline

- Understanding Differences Among Offenders

- Dimensions of Criminal Careers
  Juvenile Patterns
  Offender Types
  Specialization
  Seriousness
  Career Length
  Drug Use

- Incapacitation As a Crime Control Strategy
  Incapacitation, Crime Rates, and Prison Populations
  Greenwood's Selective Incapacitation Study
  Identifying Serious, Frequent Offenders
  Offender Characteristics

- Conclusion

22

Career Criminals and Crime Control

CHRISTY A. VISHER

National Institute of Justice, Washington, D.C.

Faced with rising crime rates in the 1980s and early 1990s, the U.S. Congress passed the most ambitious crime bill in our nation's history, the Violent Crime Control and Law Enforcement Act of 1994 (the "Crime Act"). The Crime Act provided for 100,000 new police officers, called for $9.7 billion in funding for prisons, added many new federal crimes, and extended the reach of the federal death penalty. Many of the act's provisions were in response to victims' groups and policymakers who called for stiffer prison sentences that would remove criminals from our communities for longer periods. The act accomplished this objective by linking funds for new state prisons to passage of new state truth-in-sentencing statutes, which required offenders, particularly those convicted of violent offenses, to serve the majority of their sentences. However, this crime control strategy, often referred to as "incapacitation," assumes that most crime is committed by career offenders, those serious, persistent criminals who are likely to continue to commit serious crimes frequently.

At about the same time as the Congress debated the Crime Act, many states were enacting mandatory sentences for some types of offenders, particularly drug offenders and those with previous convictions. The most widely reported of these statutes were referred to as "three strikes and you're out" laws, which require mandatory life imprisonment on a third felony conviction. The nation's first such law was passed in the state of Washington in 1993, and twenty-three states had passed similar laws by 1995 (Clark et al., 1997). These laws vary substantially across the states; all states define violent felonies as "strikes," but some states include drug offenses and other nonviolent crimes.

The momentum for these notions derives from research (described below) indicating that not all offenders are equally active and that a small group of criminals is responsible for a majority of serious crime, particularly robbery, burglary, theft, and assault. The direct implication of this knowledge for crime control is that crime may be reduced substantially if these career offenders could be identified. Encouraging the criminal justice system to distinguish serious offenders from less serious ones is also an outgrowth of research attention during the 1980s on different types of criminal careers (Blumstein et al., 1986). This research has permitted more systematic attention to the characteristics of the most serious group of criminals—career offenders.

Increasing penalties for violent and other crimes has led to dramatic increases in prison, jail, and probation populations. At midyear 1997, an estimated 1.7 million persons were incarcerated in the nation's prisons and jails (Gilliard and Beck, 1998). Another approximately 4 million persons were on probation or parole (U.S. Department of Justice, 1998a). Many of those under criminal justice supervision were sentenced according to new mandatory minimum laws for drug offenders or otherwise were given increased penalties for violent crimes or prior convictions.

Do these enhanced penalties reduce crime? Is there a small group of career offenders or "superfelons"? Can they be identified? Does removing them from the community eliminate their crimes? This chapter describes what is known about career offenders and their characteristics. We will examine common perceptions of career offenders held by the public, by the criminal justice system, and by the researchers who study them. We will also discuss how they differ from other offenders. These perceptions generally overlap, but they often diverge in important respects. The chapter will also consider advantages and limitations of incapacitation strategies to reduce crime and practical problems in identifying career offenders.

UNDERSTANDING DIFFERENCES AMONG OFFENDERS

It is now widely accepted that a small group of criminals commits the majority of all serious crime. In a study of 9,945 males born in 1945 in Philadelphia, 627 (or 6.3 percent) had at least five contacts with the police before age 18. This group of 627 accounted for 18 percent of the delinquents in the sample, but they committed 52 percent of all officially recorded crimes in the juvenile years, including 70 percent of all robberies (Wolfgang et al., 1972). The same pattern was observed in a cohort of males and females born in 1958 (Tracy et al., 1990). In a similar study of 1,369 males born in 1955 in Racine, Wisconsin, the 6.5 percent of the cohort who had at least four police contacts involving a felony accounted for 70 percent of all felony crimes (Shannon, 1988: Chapter 9).

Some observers claimed that these patterns reflect only repeated police attention to some offenders and do not depict a unique group of very active, serious offenders. However, data gathered through a survey of 624 California inmates in 1977 disputed this view (Peterson and Braiker, 1980). The inmates were asked to report the frequency with which they had committed ten types of crimes in the three years prior to being incarcerated. Twenty-five percent of these offenders reported committing about 60 percent of the total armed robberies, burglaries, and auto thefts reported by the inmates, and about 50 percent of the assaults and drug deals.

A larger study carried out by the Rand Corporation questioned over 2,000 inmates in California, Michigan, and Texas prisons and jails about seven types of crimes they had committed prior to incarceration (Chaiken and Chaiken, 1982; Chaiken, 1987). Analysis of these self-report data revealed wide variation among offenders in the number of crimes they committed annually. Fifty percent of the inmates in the Rand survey reported committing fewer than five crimes per year for each crime type. Considering all crimes included in the survey (except drug deals), the typical offender reported committing less than fifteen crimes per year.

However, there was another, smaller group of offenders in the survey who reported committing crimes much more frequently. For example, the most active 10 percent of the sample inmates who had committed robbery reported committing at least 58 robberies per year, and the most active 10 percent of the burglars reported committing 187 or more burglaries per year. Overall, the most active 10 percent of the inmates reported committing about 600 of the seven survey crimes in the two-year period prior to their incarceration—more than 10 crimes per week. (Rape, kidnapping, and arson were not included in the survey.)

Taken together, many studies of delinquents and surveys of inmates indicate that most juvenile and adult offenders actually commit few crimes. Very active offenders represent a small portion of the criminal population, but they appear to commit the majority of the crimes. These findings have surprised both researchers and law enforcement officials and have fostered the need for profiles of frequent offenders so that the criminal justice system can identify them.

DIMENSIONS OF CRIMINAL CAREERS

As we have seen in the preceding discussion, clear distinctions among offenders are evident when examining the annual number of crimes they commit. Individual crime frequencies, however, are just one dimension of an offender's criminal career—that is, the longitudinal sequence of offenses committed by an individual offender. In an exhaustive review of research on criminal careers, the notion of a criminal career is further clarified: "Criminal careers may vary substantially among offenders. At one extreme are offenders whose careers consist of only one offense. At the other extreme are 'career criminals' . . . who commit serious offenses with high frequency over extended periods of time" (Blumstein et al., 1986: 13–14).

In descriptions of the criminal careers of active offenders, three characteristics have become particularly instructive: (1) the individual frequency rate, (2) the seriousness of crimes committed and the combination of offense types, and (3) the length of the criminal career (see Farrington, 1997). We have already seen how individual frequency rates vary among active offenders. Other important issues in studying criminal careers include the age of initiation into criminal activity (often called "age at onset") and the relationship between juvenile delinquency and adult crime. In the next section, these characteristics will be used to distinguish career offenders from other types of criminals.

Juvenile Patterns

A common image gleaned from news reports and television is that juvenile delinquents mature into adult professional criminals and pursue crime as a preferred occupation, becoming more specialized and sophisticated in their criminal activities. To what extent is this image accurate?

Most juvenile delinquents do not become adult criminals. According to one review of many studies of juvenile participation in crime, at least one-third of all U.S. males are detained by the police or arrested before age 18 (Visher and Roth, 1986). However, the majority of these delinquents (perhaps two-thirds) are arrested only once or twice and do not have adult arrest records. A small group of chronic juvenile offenders is much more likely to persist in criminal activity. In the Philadelphia study, half of these chronic offenders (those with five or more arrests) were arrested at least four times between ages 18 and 30 (Wolfgang et al., 1972, 1987).

Most criminal careers, especially those of persistent, career offenders, begin before age 15. And juveniles who engage in serious crime at an early age are likely to become serious adult offenders. In studies of juvenile offenders followed into adulthood, the most serious adult offenders typically began committing crimes or experienced their first arrest when they were between ages 11 and 14. These early starters accumulate more crimes during their criminal careers and are less likely to terminate their criminal activity than are offenders who began criminal activity at a later age (Petersilia, 1980; Wolfgang et al., 1972: Chapter 8; Wolfgang et al., 1987: Chapter 5; Tracy and Kempf-Leonard, 1996).

Studies of adult inmates who were asked to recall their juvenile activity also show that age at onset is an important predictor of serious, persistent criminal activity as an adult (Chaiken and Chaiken, 1982). Other juvenile patterns also characterize adult career offenders: (1) a history of committing violent crimes, particularly rob-

bery, weapons, and injury offenses; (2) frequent serious property offenses; (3) convictions before age 16; and (4) multiple sentences to juvenile institutions.

Offender Types

One influential study of inmates used self-reports of crimes committed prior to incarceration to classify inmates into one of ten offender types, depending on the specific combination of crimes they reported: (1) violent predators (those who committed robbery, assault, *and* drug deals), (2) robber-assaulters, (3) robber-dealers, (4) low-level robbers, (5) "mere assaulters," (6) burglar-dealers, (7) low-level burglars, (8) property and drug offenders, (9) low-level property offenders, and (10) drug dealers (Chaiken and Chaiken, 1982).

The offender types are listed in order of severity, with those at the top of the list generally more serious than those at the bottom. The least serious offender types, primarily those who committed only property and drug offenses, committed crimes less often. The most serious category of offenders, those called violent predators, committed both robbery and assault *and* sold drugs at very high frequencies. Violent predators made up only 15 percent of the inmates who reported committing these types of crimes.

The different levels of seriousness implied by the ten offender categories are supported by self-reported information about the annual number of robberies, burglaries, and thefts committed (see Table 22.1). Offenders classified as violent predators committed an average of 70 robberies, 144 burglaries, and 229 thefts in one year. They also committed more burglaries than the burglar-dealers or the low-level burglars.

Table 22.1 Average Annual Number of Robberies, Burglaries, and Thefts Committed by Six Offender Types

OFFENDER TYPE	ROBBERY	BURGLARY	THEFT*
Violent predators**	70	144	229
Robber-assaulters	50	48	127
Robber-dealers	32	93	132
Low-level robbers	10	31	54
Burglar-dealers	–	42	140
Low-level burglars	–	36	25
Low-level property offenders	–	–	369

SOURCE: Chaiken and Chaiken, 1982: 219–221.

*Includes larceny, auto theft, bad checks and credit cards, and fraud.

**Defined as offenders concurrently committing robbery, assault, and drug deals.

This relatively small group of serious, high-rate offenders accounted for the majority of all robberies, assaults, burglaries, and drug deals committed by the entire inmate sample.

Specialization

The findings on offender types are also important to the question of whether offenders specialize in the types of crimes they commit. Contrary to popular beliefs held by the public and by law enforcement officials, the Rand study found that offenders—at least, incarcerated offenders—are much more often generalists than specialists. Among inmates in the Rand study, only 20 percent reported committing just one of the seven types of crime in the two years preceding their incarceration. Although the ten offender types can be thought of as specialities, offenders within each type committed many different types of crimes. For example, most robbers also committed burglary, and most inmates who reported committing burglary or robbery also engaged in some form of theft, forgery, or fraud (Chaiken and Chaiken, 1982:

55–63; see also Petersilia et al., 1978; Peterson and Braiker, 1980).

Analysis of juvenile and adult official arrest histories provides a slightly different picture of offense specialization (see Cohen, 1986, for a discussion of problems with arrest data in studies of offense specialization). Among all juveniles, the type of prior offense in the arrest record is not very helpful in predicting the next arrest charge, although some evidence of specialization exists for runaway and theft. However, persistent juvenile offenders—those with numerous arrests—tend to become more specialized with each additional offense, particularly within the broad categories of violence and theft, and of robbery, drugs, and liquor offenses. Specialization among juveniles is weakest for offenses involving injury (Cohen, 1986: 366–406; Farrington et al., 1988).

Among adult offenders, some specialization is evident for all offense types when arrest records are analyzed carefully, but it is stronger for drugs, fraud, and auto theft. Specialization may occur more frequently for these offenses because they are often committed in conjunction with an organized criminal network. Violent and property offenses form distinct clusters, and adult offenders are more likely to commit offenses within a cluster than to switch to offenses outside a cluster. Offenders committing robbery are somewhat more likely to switch to other violent offenses than to property offenses. Drug offenders, however, do not consistently switch to either violent or property offenses (Cohen, 1986: 366–406; Blumstein et al., 1988).

Both types of studies—inmate surveys and analyses of arrest histories—indicate that adult offenders specialize in clusters of offenses rather than in specific offense types, although the clusters are defined somewhat differently depending on the source of the data. Juveniles are less likely to specialize. Finally, higher levels of specialization for adult offenders suggest that offenders who remain criminally active until older ages are also more specialized in their offending patterns.

Seriousness

Another dimension of criminal careers is the seriousness of offenses, particularly the extent to which offenders commit crimes of increasing seriousness over the course of their careers. Most of the research on offense seriousness and escalation is based on analyses of arrest histories. During the juvenile years, the seriousness of arrests does not steadily increase over successive arrests. However, for juveniles who remain active, some escalation occurs after a large number of arrests, particularly regarding robbery and injury offenses, and these juveniles are more likely to become adult offenders (Tracy and Kempf-Leonard, 1996).

For most adult offenders, offense seriousness generally is stable over successive arrests or decreases slightly. A different picture emerges if the analysis takes into account the length of the arrest record and excludes minor offenses such as public drunkenness. Comparing offenders with few arrests to those with many arrests confounds the experiences of less serious offenders with the experiences of more serious offenders. In one comprehensive study of offenders' criminal careers in Michigan, average seriousness is stable over the career among African-American offenders with ten arrests for serious crimes, whereas similar white offenders show increases in seriousness over successive arrests (Blumstein et al., 1988). The dominant pattern, however, is one of little change in seriousness over the adult career. Only a small group of offenders are likely to engage in increasingly serious criminal behavior.

These juvenile and adult patterns are compatible with those found in one study that examined offense seriousness for a sample of juveniles followed into adulthood using official arrest records (Rand, 1987). Figure 22.1 displays the mean offense seriousness score (based on methods discussed in Sellin and Wolfgang, 1978) from ages 9 to 26 for 106 offenders in the Philadelphia study mentioned on p. 604 who committed serious crimes. A total of 315 offenses are represented. The average seriousness score (243, indicating that the offender is committing low-seriousness crimes) is relatively stable during the juvenile years. Then, during the juvenile-adult transition period between ages 16 and 18, a marked increase in offense seriousness occurs. In the adult period, the mean seriousness score (444) is again relatively stable, although seriousness scores are about 200 points higher for adults than juveniles.

The dramatic jump in offense seriousness in the late teen years is puzzling. Although strictly juvenile offenses (for example, runaway and underage drinking) and other minor offenses are excluded, the change in offense seriousness

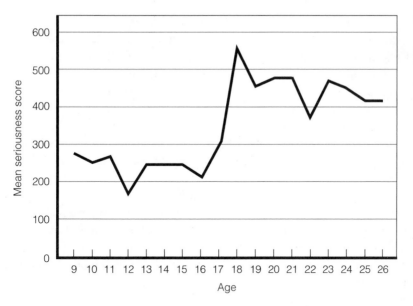

FIGURE 22.1

Seriousness score by age of offender

SOURCE: Rand, 1987: Figure 12.1.

might reflect differences in the official arrest charges for juveniles and adults. For example, a juvenile offender may be arrested for breaking and entering, whereas an adult offender may be charged with burglary. Alternatively, it may reflect a shift into organized criminal activities as former juvenile delinquents become more committed to a deviant lifestyle.

Career Length

An important dimension of criminal careers is their length. Research on career length is scarce, in part because it is difficult to determine exactly when an offender's criminal activity ends. The popular belief is that, certainly by age 30, offenders terminate their criminal careers. As a consequence, prosecutors and judges hesitate to sentence offenders near age 30 to long prison terms because they are thought to be near the end of their life of crime anyway.

Estimates of the average length of adult criminal careers involving UCR Index offenses

range from five to fifteen years (see Blumstein et al., 1986: 91–94). However, these career length estimates include only adult careers, so overall career length may be longer if the offender started criminal activity as a juvenile. This average length is derived from a sample that included offenders who drop out quickly and those who remain criminally active for much longer periods. In one study of English males followed up to age 39, the average duration of criminal careers was 9.7 years (Farrington, 1997).

Another way to study career length is to ask how many years are left in a criminal career, given the time that has already been spent committing crimes, or the residual career length. The pattern of residual career lengths in one study of males in Washington, D.C., displayed three segments: (1) a "break-in" period, in which many offenders in their twenties drop out of crime and the remaining years in crime for non-dropouts increase from five to ten years on average; (2) a "stable" period—beginning around age 30 and extending to age 39 or 40—after which time remaining in a career is about ten years; and (3) a "burnout" period beginning about age 41 (or after twenty-three years in active adult careers), in which careers terminate rapidly (Blumstein et al., 1986; Blumstein and Cohen, 1987). Thus, persistent offenders who begin their adult careers at age 18 (or before) and who are still active in their thirties are likely to continue to commit crimes for another ten years.

Different patterns emerge for property and violent offenses. Offenders who are arrested for the violent offenses of murder, aggravated assault, and rape are less likely than are property offenders (including robbers) to drop out during the early years of their careers. In this context, robbery was more similar to property crimes than to violent crimes. Thus, persistent career offenders less often are simply property offenders and more often have criminal histories that include arrests for violent offenses. However, older property offenders with long careers likely will continue committing crimes at least into their forties.

Drug Use

The consumption of illicit drugs is linked closely by the public and by law enforcement officials to the commission of property and violent crimes, but the nature of those links is the subject of extensive study in the research community. Some drug users never begin committing crimes; some criminals never begin using drugs; and among those who engage in both behaviors, drug use typically begins at the same time or shortly after criminal activity. The drug–crime relationship may also differ depending on the extent of drug use and criminal activity (see Chaiken and Chaiken, 1990).

Most adult drug-involved offenders are not violent and commit crimes infrequently (see

Chapter 19). However, we do know that the persistent career offender who commits hundreds of crimes a year usually is also a drug user. Offenders who use multiple types of illicit drugs in large amounts commit at least twice, and perhaps ten times, as many crimes per year as do other offenders. The regularity of drug use is related to the frequency of offending—daily drug users commit more crimes than do occasional users. Offenders who reduce their consumption of illicit drugs often show a sharp reduction in their frequency of criminal activity, particularly robbery, burglary, and drug dealing. But drug-involved offenders who committed crimes frequently before developing heavy drug habits show smaller reductions in criminal activity when they are not using drugs. (For a review of several relevant studies, see Chaiken and Chaiken, 1990; Cohen, 1986: 349–352). The chronic use of alcohol has also been linked to repeated involvement in violent crimes (Reiss and Roth, 1993).

Career offenders are likely to have used multiple types of illicit drugs as juveniles and exhibit especially frequent use of serious drugs such as heroin, cocaine, and barbiturates (Chaiken and Chaiken, 1982). In fact, among multiple-drug users, girls are as likely as boys, whites as likely as African Americans, and middle-class suburban youths as likely as lower-class youths raised in the city to become serious, frequent drug-involved offenders (Chaiken and Johnson, 1988). But experimentation with hard drugs or use of marijuana only does not appear to lead to serious adult criminal activity (Chaiken and Chaiken, 1982; Wish and Johnson, 1986). Thus, it is not drug use per se, but the frequency and intensity of drug use that is strongly related to serious, persistent, and frequent criminal behavior.

Many cities have begun urinalysis tests to detect recent use of illicit drugs by persons who are arrested. Although criminal justice officials suspected that a substantial proportion of those arrested were drug users, few realized the extent of drug use among arrested persons. In 1997, for example, at least half of a sample of males arrested in twenty-three large urban areas tested positive for illegal drugs, primarily cocaine (U.S. Department of Justice, 1998b). However, a single positive urine test detects only the presence of a specific drug; it does not indicate intensity of use and hence cannot be used to distinguish career offenders from less serious criminals.

INCAPACITATION AS A CRIME CONTROL STRATEGY

Incapacitation is one of the principle methods employed by the criminal justice system to control crime. Simply stated, putting offenders in prison—incapacitating them—physically prevents them from committing crimes in the community.

Two incapacitation strategies have been the focus of research and policy discussions. The common approach, known as collective incapacitation, incarcerates offenders on the basis of the crime they have committed. Occasionally, the judge also considers the offender's prior criminal record in setting a sentence. For example, under a collective incapacitation strategy, most convicted robbers receive the same sentence. A second approach, proposed in the 1980s, is called selective incapacitation. This strategy was designed to reduce crime by sentencing offenders according to predictions about whether they are likely to commit serious crimes frequently in the future. For example, under a selective incapacitation strategy, convicted robbers who were predicted to be very active offenders in the future would be sentenced to longer terms in

prison; convicted robbers who were predicted to be less active would receive more lenient sentences. Not surprisingly, this proposed strategy generated much debate in the research and policy communities. The remainder of this chapter discusses the impact of incapacitation strategies, including selective incapacitation, on crime and operational concerns involved in improving our ability to achieve crime reduction.

Incapacitation, Crime Rates, and Prison Populations

Interest in incapacitation is motivated by high crime rates, public fear of crime, and the perceived inadequacy of rehabilitation and deterrence strategies. However, the greater use of incarceration in general during the 1970s and 1980s led to dramatic increases in prison populations, but it did not bring about any significant reduction in serious crime. In fact, the evidence indicates that general incarceration strategies are not as effective as one might think.

Several studies have estimated the amount of crime that is prevented by different sentencing practices (for reviews see Cohen, 1983; Visher, 1987). One particularly interesting study of how collective incapacitation has worked took advantage of the fact that the U.S. prison population nearly doubled in the period between 1973 and 1982, from 204,211 to 396,072 inmates (Blumstein et al., 1986: 123–128). This study attempted to answer the question of how much crime was prevented by incarcerating inmates between 1973 and 1982. The conclusions were that doubling prison populations prevented only an additional 6 percent each of all robberies and burglaries that would have been committed if the inmates had been free in the community—about 9,160 robberies and 51,000 burglaries in this ten-year period.

Furthermore, a recent examination of the effects of incarceration on violent crime shows that increasing prison populations had little effect on levels of violent crime between 1975 and 1989 (Cohen and Canela-Cacho, 1993). Although average prison time served per violent crime tripled during this period, primarily because of statutes mandating minimum sentences, there was no appreciable decline in the 1975–1989 rate of violent crime. Clearly, incapacitation prevented some violent crimes, but this crime control effect was overwhelmed by other factors (e.g., urban economic problems) that increased the number of criminals still on the street (Reiss and Roth, 1993; see also Donohue and Siegelman, 1998). Moreover, there is no evidence that the early 1990s' sharp decline in violent crime rates was caused by increases in incarceration (Lynch and Sabol, 1997), although some argue that the sustained increase in incarceration during the 1980s partly explains the gradual downward trend in crime since the mid-1970s (Donohue and Siegelman, 1998).

An increasingly popular collective sentencing strategy in the 1980s and 1990s was the use of mandatory minimum sentences, which required that offenders be incarcerated for a minimum period with no sentence reduction for good behavior. Proponents believe that such sentences reduce crime significantly because they guarantee a longer period of incarceration. The likely impact on crime rates of imposing mandatory minimum sentences, however, also is much smaller than expected. Five-year mandatory prison terms for convicted offenders with at least one prior felony conviction would prevent between 5 and 15 percent of all UCR Index offenses, but prisons would need to expand still more to accommodate the additional offenders serving longer prison terms. Moreover, mandatory minimum sentencing policies are regularly circumvented by prosecutors and judges, reduce defendant's incentives to plead guilty, and increase case processing time, all of which reduce the policies' potential effectiveness in controlling crime (Tonry, 1992).

Targeting these collective incapacitation strategies at a new group of offenders in the 1980s—persons convicted of selling and possessing illicit drugs—led to large increases in our prison populations. State and federal prison populations have risen dramatically since the 1970s and show no evidence of slowing down.

Thus, during the height of increasing prison populations, an innovative control strategy—selective incapacitation—that purported to reduce crime without increasing the prison population by reserving lengthy prison sentences for the most serious, active offenders, received considerable attention. The next section discusses an influential study that claimed a selective incapacitation strategy could reduce robbery by one-fifth with no increase in incarcerated populations.

Greenwood's Selective Incapacitation Study

In 1982, Peter Greenwood, one of the researchers involved in the Rand survey of prison and jail inmates, presented some provocative findings in a report that explored whether greater reductions in crime would occur if prison sentences were based, in part, on predictions of the offender's future criminal activity. Building on the initial findings of the Rand inmate survey—that a small minority of offenders, by their own admission, committed most of the crimes—Greenwood created a prediction scale that he thought would identify these offenders (Greenwood and Abrahamse, 1982).

Seven characteristics emerged that were strongly related to high annual frequencies of robbery and burglary: (1) prior conviction for robbery or burglary, (2) incarceration for more than half of the preceding two years, (3) juvenile conviction prior to age 16, (4) commitment to a state or federal juvenile institution, (5) heroin or barbiturate use in the preceding two years, (6) heroin or barbiturate use as a juvenile, and (7) employment for less than half of the preceding two years.

To estimate offenders' potential for future crime, each of the seven characteristics merits 1 point, and thus each inmate could be given a score ranging from 0 to 7. Using a statistical model that estimated the amount of crime prevented by incarceration, Greenwood calculated that if predicted high-rate robbers (those with scores of 4–7) in California served prison terms of eight years and all other robbers served one-year jail terms, the robbery rate could be reduced by 20 percent without increasing the prison population.

Greenwood's study received considerable attention from the research community (Cohen, 1983; von Hirsch and Gottfredson, 1984; Visher, 1986). Technical reviews of his work generally agree that Greenwood's claim of a potential 20 percent reduction in robbery with no prison population increase overstates the likely effects of selective incapacitation for several reasons. First, Greenwood's analysis implicitly assumes that the length of a criminal career is longer than the prison sentence imposed, even though evidence indicates that the total criminal career averages five to ten years. Many offenders sentenced to long prison terms under a selective incapacitation policy would likely have ended their careers within a few years anyway, so part of the time spent incarcerated would not prevent any crimes. Second, the predicted reduction in crime resulting from selective incapacitation was limited to only one state in the study,

California, and was for robbery only, not for burglary. Thus, the impact of sentencing policies will vary depending on the characteristics of the offender population and aspects of the state criminal justice system.

Greenwood's study of the likely impact of selective incapacitation forced researchers and policymakers to take a more realistic look at crime control strategies targeted at career offenders. The next section addresses some specific problems associated with targeting career offenders, including criminal justice decisions such as sentencing that explicitly takes into account predictions of future criminal activity.

Identifying Serious, Frequent Offenders

An analysis of potential legal and constitutional impediments to prediction-based crime control strategies (which include selective incapacitation) reveals that state statutes and the U.S. Constitution have virtually nothing to say about limits on uses of predictions in criminal justice decisions (Tonry, 1987). Predictions or classifications based on race, ethnicity, religion, or gender are of course prohibited. But predictions based on other factors are nearly always permitted, even if they result in different impacts on racial groups, so long as that effect is unintentional. Moreover, in several criminal cases, the U.S. Supreme Court has upheld the use of predictions of dangerousness to set sentences or to detain suspects before trial (Tonry, 1987).

Indeed, other segments of the criminal justice system have implemented special procedures designed to enhance the apprehension and conviction of career offenders. For example, many large cities have career criminal prosecution units or repeat offender policing divisions that target offenders thought to be engaging in frequent, serious criminal activity. During prosecution, cases involving this type of offender generally receive more attention, often using vertical prosecution methods, which require a single prosecutor to handle the case from arraignment to trial (see Blumstein et al., 1986: Chapter 6; Chaiken and Chaiken, 1990).

Although selective incapacitation strategies were never explicitly adopted, other sentencing reforms of the 1980s attempted to accomplish the same goals. Sentencing guidelines, mandatory minimum sentences, and other sentence enhancements were aimed at increasing the severity of sentences for dangerous offenders. Unfortunately, as this section will show, "dangerousness" is not commensurate with "career offender," and hence the sentencing reforms largely did not have the intended effect (see Lynch and Sabol, 1997).

Predictions about an offender's future criminal activity cannot be perfectly accurate. Errors will be made in deciding which offenders are likely to be serious offenders in the future. In fact, research shows that accurate prediction of criminal behavior is very difficult. Predictions commonly are made about the likelihood of violent behavior among released mental patients or criminal behavior by prisoners out on parole. But as many as one-half to two-thirds of these predictions have been shown to be wrong in research on prediction (Blumstein et al., 1986; Chaiken et al., 1993; Farrington, 1987).

The following four possible results of a prediction decision about the likelihood of recidivism must be considered:

1. **True positives** The offender is predicted to recidivate, and the offender commits a new crime.

2. **True negatives** The offender is not predicted to recidivate, and no new crime is committed.

3. **False positives** The offender is predicted to recidivate, but no new crime is committed.

4. **False negatives** The offender is not predicted to recidivate, but the offender commits a new crime.

Prediction errors—false negatives and false positives—affect the community in different ways. Criminal justice officials and the public are most worried, for example, about the rapist out on bail who commits a new crime or the robber on parole who shoots a convenience store clerk during another robbery. These are false negative prediction errors—they cause emotional harm and personal loss to victims of crime and increase the public's dissatisfaction with the criminal justice system.

But false positive errors also are costly. These erroneous predictions unfairly extend the incarceration of offenders who actually are good risks. Not only do the offenders and their families suffer needlessly, society suffers because of the high cost of the wasted incarceration. Most criminal justice officials would rather err on the side of caution than risk releasing potential robbers or rapists, but this overprediction has resulted in many unnecessary incarcerations. Thus, crowding in America's prisons may be due partly to the incarceration of offenders who are unlikely to reoffend (Clear, 1988).

Using Greenwood's seven-item scale, two studies have assessed the extent to which persons predicted to be high-rate offenders were in fact frequent, serious offenders after their release from prison. Criminal history information was gathered on the California inmates from Greenwood's 1982 study (Greenwood and Abrahamse, 1982) who had been out of prison for two years (Greenwood and Turner, 1987; Klein and Caggiano, 1986). Unfortunately, the scale was unable to predict very accurately which inmates

Table 22.2   Accuracy of Greenwood Scale for Predicting Future Criminal Activity

	PREDICTED TO BE LOW TO MODERATE OFFENDER	PREDICTED TO BE FREQUENT OFFENDER
Percent arrested within twenty-four months	65–70	80–83
Percent with "safety" arrest within twenty-four months*	47	55
Percent reincarcerated within twenty-four months	32	55
Percent "failed" during entire follow-up**	75	86

SOURCE: Visher, 1987: Table 5.

*Murder, aggravated assault, rape, robbery, and burglary are referred to as "safety" crimes.

**A failure is either an arrest, a jail term, or a prison term. Offenders could be returned to prison without an arrest.

would commit new crimes, much less which ones would become career offenders. Table 22.2 provides the results of these studies. Of the inmates predicted by the scale to be low or moderate offenders, 65 to 70 percent were arrested within twenty-four months, compared to 80 to 83 percent of the predicted high-rate offenders.

Even focusing on the most serious offenses—the "safety" crimes of murder, aggravated assault, rape, robbery, and burglary—the predicted high-rate offenders were only slightly more likely to be arrested than were the predicted low- or moderate-rate offenders (55 percent for high-rate, 47 percent for others). Over half (55 percent) of the inmates thought to be the highest risks were reincarcerated, but 32 percent of the lower risks also were sent back to prison or jail.

The ability of the criminal justice system to accurately identify frequent offenders rests on the information available to criminal justice officials who make decisions. The next section discusses some issues about the types of information that are acceptable and useful.

Offender Characteristics

Many critics of Greenwood's study objected to the choice of some offender characteristics in the prediction formula, specifically employment information and aspects of juvenile criminal history. Some believe that this information should not influence sentencing because it is irrelevant to the seriousness of the offense and the offender's legal culpability for that offense. Employment and other factors, such as education and length of residence, are inappropriate because they may discriminate against poor offenders. Information related to social class may result in more severe punishment for African- and Hispanic-American offenders.

Indicators of past behavior—for example, youthful criminal activities—are objectionable to others because these behaviors are beyond the offender's current control. For this reason, many states allow juvenile records to be sealed permanently or destroyed so as not to stigmatize forever those who had a few encounters with the law during their youth. In addressing the issue of juvenile records, an influential report on career offenders suggested that these records be available to criminal justice officials only if a person continues to commit crimes as an adult (Blumstein et al., 1986: Chapter 6). In that situation, the juvenile official record can provide useful information about the nature and extent of prior criminal activity, especially for young adult offenders who may appear to have no prior record.

Research discussed previously in this chapter on the characteristics of career offenders is based largely on studies of offenders who are known to be career offenders. However, prosecutors and judges must make decisions on the basis of information available to the criminal justice system at the time of sentencing. Some studies show that some information used by police, prosecutors, and judges to identify career offenders is a weak predictor of future offending. For example, the seriousness of the current offense is not a good indicator of future criminal activity (Clear, 1988; Gottfredson and Gottfredson, 1986). Those who commit the most vicious crimes are not necessarily the most frequent offenders with the longest careers in crime. Of course, brutal murderers and rapists usually are given long prison sentences because of the nature of the crime and the desire for appropriate punishment.

The number of prior arrests, convictions, or prison terms is also not a good predictor of serious, frequent offending. This information is misleading because two types of offenders generally are involved with the criminal justice system: (1) offenders whose high rates of criminal activity result in frequent apprehensions and convictions and (2) infrequent offenders who are basically inept, unsophisticated criminals.

States that have enacted some version of a "three strikes" statute permit the judge to add twenty or thirty years to an offender's sentence if he or she has a certain number of previous convictions, usually at least two felonies. But these habitual offenders may not be the serious, frequent, drug-involved offenders that are responsible for large numbers of crimes. They are more likely to be inept criminals or low-level drug offenders, and their long incarceration may limit available prison space for more serious offenders. Similarly, mandatory minimum sentences for drug offenses (enacted in at least thirty states)

did not capture high-profile, violent drug dealers (Lynch and Sabol, 1997).

If the overall length of an offender's criminal record is not a good indicator of the frequency of criminal activity, what other characteristics predict serious frequent offending? Given two offenders with equal numbers of arrests, the one who has accumulated those arrests more rapidly is more likely the career offender. Further, in addition to information about drug use patterns, specific information about previous offenses, juvenile criminal history, and so on often included in arrest and presentence reports (but rarely in official criminal history records) is the most useful.

In a more detailed study based on the inmate survey, three broad types of offenders emerged: (1) "low-rate losers," who reported low crime frequencies and high arrest rates; (2) "high-rate losers," who reported high crime frequencies and high arrest rates; and (3) "high-rate winners," who reported high crime frequencies and low arrest rates (Chaiken and Chaiken, 1985; Chaiken and Johnson, 1988). Both types of high-rate criminals may be career offenders, but the "winners" apparently are evading detection by the criminal justice system. Closer study reveals that the winners are younger, have a history of committing crime since adolescence, use illicit drugs, are more careful about planning their crimes, often work with partners, have never been married, and hold jobs longer.

Unfortunately, much of this information is not readily available to police or prosecutors via official criminal records. When relying on official records to distinguish between career offenders and inept criminals, the following criteria may be particularly useful: (1) a prior conviction for robbery, burglary, arson, forcible rape, sex crime involving a child, kidnapping, or murder; (2) an escape from prison or failure to complete parole successfully; (3) currently on bail or free awaiting trial for another crime when arrested; (4) convictions for robbery as a juvenile; and (5) indications of persistent and frequent use of drugs (Chaiken and Johnson, 1988; Chaiken and Chaiken, 1990). The last two items of information are less readily available.

In summary, the criminal justice system's ability to identify career offenders is limited by a lack of relevant information in existing official records. First, these offenders usually are young, and their adult criminal records do not reveal the extent of their criminal activity. Second, juvenile records, when available, often are inadequate because court records may not reflect the extent of culpability or the nature of the crimes committed. The inmates in the Rand survey actually reported more juvenile arrests and incarcerations than appeared in their official records. Third, some frequent offenders successfully evade arrest and conviction for the crimes they commit for many years; hence, their criminal record gives an inaccurate picture of their criminal activity. Finally, official records rarely contain detailed information about drug involvement.

Other sources, such as arrest and presentence investigation reports, might contain predictive information about current probation or parole status, the number of offenders involved in specific crimes, employment history, specific drug use (types of drug use, drug combinations, and frequency of use), and juvenile criminal activity. These materials could be an important source of information for identifying career offenders.

CONCLUSION

Researchers' attention to identifying career offenders and Greenwood's controversial selective incapacitation strategy during the 1980s led the criminal justice system to experiment with new strategies for reducing crime. Armed with the knowledge that not all offenders commit crimes frequently and that a small number of criminals— career offenders—may account for the majority of serious crimes, the criminal justice system has developed a system of intermediate sanctions that can be tailored to specific offenders (see Clear, Chapter 18, in this text). Boot camps, drug courts, intensive supervision probation, electronic monitoring, and house arrest are some of the innovative programs being implemented around the country for less serious offenders.

Meanwhile, the notion of career offenders has crept into media reports, political speeches, and everyday conversation. Criminal justice officials are becoming more knowledgeable about how to identify career offenders. Sentencing guidelines now incorporate research findings about career offenders into legislation. A striking example is the implementation of Federal Sentencing Guidelines in 1990, which are the basis for judges' sentencing decisions for all offenders convicted of federal crimes. In developing these guidelines, the United States Sentencing Commission explicitly incorporated a defendant's criminal record into the determination of the sentence. The term of imprisonment is increased depending on prior sentences of imprisonment, the recency of those sentences, and whether the offender was under criminal justice supervision at the time of the offense (probation, parole, work release, and so on).

But attempts at crime reduction based on targeting career offenders (including incapacitation strategies) may be hampered for a number of reasons. The problems involved in identifying high-rate offenders using existing information in criminal justice records discussed earlier limits the impact of these strategies on reducing crime. Moreover, crimes will not be prevented if the incarcerated career offender simply is replaced by another offender recruited to take his or her place, especially if the offender is a drug dealer or part of an organized burglary or auto theft network. Further, if the incarcerated offender is a member of a gang or other offending group, the group may continue committing the same number of crimes without the incarcerated member.

Also, the continued emphasis in the United States on "lock'em up" strategies has not been without serious adverse consequences, including the concentration of high incarceration rates in some African-American communities, increases in out-of-wedlock births and female-headed households, weakening of ties between children and their parents, and decreases in employment among released offenders (Lynch and Sabol, 1997). One study has estimated that, if current incarceration levels continue, 29 percent of African-American males in the United States will enter prison during their lifetime (Bonczar and Beck, 1997).

In conclusion, aggressively targeting career offenders for prosecution, conviction, and incarceration may have some effect on the volume of crime in some states. However, the success of this strategy depends on the ability of the criminal justice system to identify career offenders accurately and early in their criminal careers. Better information needs to be gathered and made available to the criminal justice officials who arrest, prosecute, and sentence these offenders. Targeting career offenders will not likely provide the magic bullet for substantial reductions in crime that politicians, the public, and the criminal justice system seek. A multifaceted approach to crime control that reserves incapacitation for career offenders or for those offenders convicted of truly heinous crimes and uses crime prevention and intermediate sanctions is likely to be the most effective crime control strategy for 2000 and beyond.

The points of view expressed in this chapter are solely those of the author and do not represent the official position of either the National Institute of Justice or the U.S. Department of Justice.

DISCUSSION QUESTIONS

1. Construct a profile of the average criminal offender. Is the offender a juvenile or an adult? If an adult, will that offender likely have been a serious offender as a juvenile?

2. Do offenders usually specialize in certain types of crime, or are they more generalistic?

3. Discuss the concept of criminal career. Describe career in terms of the three segments of residual career length. Are there differences in career patterns between violent and property offenders?

4. To what extent does drug use influence career patterns?

5. Discuss the notion of incapacitation as a crime control strategy. Why have most uses of this strategy centered on selective instead of collective incapacitation?

6. What problems face selective incapacitation efforts, and how effective do they seem to have been? Selective incapacitation depends on our ability to identify offenders who will engage in criminal behavior in the future. Why is that so difficult?

REFERENCES

Blumstein, A., and J. Cohen. 1987. "Characterizing Criminal Careers." *Science* 237: 985–991.

Blumstein, A., J. Cohen, S. Das, and S. Moitra. 1988. "Specialization and Seriousness During Adult Criminal Careers." *Journal of Quantitative Criminology* 4: 303–345.

Blumstein, A., J. Cohen, J. Roth, and C. Visher. 1986. *Criminal Careers and "Career Criminals."* Vols. 1 and 2. Washington, DC: National Academy Press.

Bonczar, T., and A. Beck. 1997. *Lifetime Likelihood of Going to State or Federal Prison.* Washington, DC: Bureau of Justice Statistics.

Chaiken, J. 1987. "Tabulations of Adjusted Crime Commission Rates." Appendix A in *Identifying High-Rate Serious Criminals from Official Records.* By J. Rolph and J. Chaiken. Rand Report R-3433-NIJ. Santa Monica, CA: Rand Corporation.

Chaiken, J., and M. Chaiken. 1982. *Varieties of Criminal Behavior.* Rand Report R-2814-NIJ. Santa Monica, CA: Rand Corporation.

————. 1990. "Drugs and Predatory Crime." In *Drugs and Crime.* Edited by M. Tonry and J. Wilson. Chicago: University of Chicago Press. 203–240.

Chaiken, J., M. Chaiken, and W. Rhodes. 1993. "Predicting Violent Behavior and Classifying Violent Offenders." In *Understanding and Preventing Violence,* Vol. 4. Edited by A. J. Reiss and J. A. Roth. Washington, DC: National Academy Press.

Chaiken, M., and J. Chaiken. 1985. *Who Gets Caught Doing Crime?* Final Report to the Bureau of Justice Statistics, Grant No. 84-BJ-CX-0003. Los Angeles: Hamilton, Rabinovitz, Szanton, and Alschuler.

Chaiken, M., and B. Johnson. 1988. *Characteristics of Different Types of Drug-Involved Offenders.* Washington, DC: National Institute of Justice.

Clark, J., J. Austin, and D. Henry. 1997. *"Three Strikes and You're Out": A Review of State Legislation.* Washington, DC: National Institute of Justice.

Clear, T. R. 1988. *Statistical Prediction in Corrections.* Santa Monica, CA: Rand Corporation.

Cohen, J. 1983. "Incapacitation as a Strategy for Crime Control: Possibilities and Pitfalls." Pp. 1–84 in *Crime and Justice: An Annual Review of Research.* Vol. 5. Edited by M. Tonry and N. Morris. Chicago: University of Chicago Press.

Cohen, J. 1986. "Research on Criminal Careers: Individual Frequency Rates and Offense Seriousness." Appendix B in *Criminal Careers and "Career Criminals."* Vol. 1. Edited by A. Blumstein, J. Cohen, J. Roth, and C. Visher. Washington, DC: National Academy Press.

Cohen, Jacqueline, and J. Canela-Cacho. 1993. "Incarceration and Violent Crime: 1965–88" In *Understanding and Preventing Violence.* Vol. 4. Edited by A. J. Reiss, and J. A. Roth. Washington, DC: National Academy Press.

Donohue, J., and P. Siegelman. 1998. "Allocating Resources among Prisons and Social Programs in the Battle against Crime." *Journal of Legal Studies* 27: 1–43.

Farrington, D. 1987. "Predicting Individual Crime Rates." Pp. 53–101 in *Prediction and Classification: Criminal Justice Decision Making.* Edited by D. Gottfredson and M. Tonry. Chicago: University of Chicago Press.

————. 1997. "Human Development and Criminal Careers." In *The Oxford Handbook of Criminology.* 2d ed. Oxford: Clarendon.

Farrington, D., H. Synder, and T. Finnegan. 1988. "Specialization in Juvenile Court Careers." *Criminology* 26: 461–488.

Gilliard, D., and A. Beck. 1998. *Prison and Jail Inmates at Midyear 1997.* Washington, DC: U.S. Department of Justice.

Gottfredson, S., and D. Gottfredson. 1986. "Accuracy of Prediction Models." Pp. 212–290 in *Criminal Careers and "Career Criminals."* Vol. 2. Edited by A. Blumstein, J. Cohen, J. Roth, and C. Visher. Washington, DC: National Academy Press.

Greenwood, P., and A. Abrahamse. 1982. *Selective Incapacitation.* Rand Report R–2815-NIJ. Santa Monica, CA: Rand Corporation.

Greenwood, P., and S. Turner. 1987. *Selective Incapacitation Revisited: Why the High-Rate Offenders Are Hard to Predict.* Rand Report R–3397-NIJ. Santa Monica, CA: Rand Corporation.

Klein, S., and M. Caggiano. 1986. *The Prevalence, Predictability, and Policy Implications of Recidivism.* Rand Report R–3413-BJS. Santa Monica, CA: Rand Corporation.

Lynch, J., and W. Sabol. 1997. *Did Getting Tough on Crime Pay?* Washington, DC: Urban Institute.

Petersilia, J. 1980. "Criminal Career Research: A Review of Recent Evidence." Pp. 321–379 in *Crime and Justice: An Annual Review of Research.* Vol. 2. Edited by N. Morris and M. Tonry. Chicago: University of Chicago Press.

Petersilia, J., P. Greenwood, and M. Lavin. 1978. *Criminal Careers of Habitual Felons.* Santa Monica, CA: Rand Corporation.

Peterson, M., and H. Braiker. 1980. *Doing Crime: A Survey of California Prison Inmates.* Rand Report R–2200-DOJ. Santa Monica, CA: Rand Corporation.

Rand, A. 1987. "Transitional Life Events and Desistance from Delinquency and Crime." Pp. 134–162 in *From Boy to Man, from Delinquency to Crime.* Edited by M. Wolfgang, T. Thornberry, and R. Figlio. Chicago: University of Chicago Press.

Reiss, A. J., Jr., and J. A. Roth, eds. 1993. *Understanding and Preventing Violence.* Panel on the Understanding and Control of Violent Behavior, National Research Council. Washington, DC: National Academy Press.

Sellin, T., and M. Wolfgang. 1978. *The Measurement of Delinquency.* Montclair, NJ: Patterson Smith.

Shannon, L. 1988. *Criminal Career Continuity: Its Social Context.* New York: Human Sciences Press.

Tonry, M. 1987. "Prediction and Classification: Legal and Ethical Issues." Pp. 367–413 in *Prediction and Classification: Criminal Justice Decision Making.* Edited by D. Gottfredson and M. Tonry. Chicago: University of Chicago Press.

———. 1992. "Mandatory Penalties." Pp. 243–274 in *Crime and Justice: A Review of Research.* Vol. 16. Edited by M. Tonry. Chicago: University of Chicago Press.

Tracy, P., and K. Kempf-Leonard. 1996. *Continuity and Discontinuity in Criminal Careers.* New York: Plenum.

Tracy, P., M. Wolfgang, and R. Figlio. 1990. *Delinquency Careers in Two Birth Cohorts.* New York: Plenum.

U.S. Department of Justice. 1998a. *Probation and Parole Populations 1997.* Washington, DC: U.S. Department of Justice.

U.S. Department of Justice. 1998b. *1997 Drug Use Forecasting Annual Report on Adult and Juvenile Arrestees.* Washington, DC: U.S. Department of Justice.

Visher, C. A. 1986. "The Rand Second Inmate Survey: A Reanalysis." Pp. 161–211 in *Criminal Careers and "Career Criminals."* Vol. 2. Edited by A. Blumstein, J. Cohen, J. Roth, and C. Visher. Washington, DC: National Academy Press.

———. 1987. "Incapacitation and Crime Control: Does a 'Lock 'em Up' Strategy Reduce Crime?" *Justice Quarterly* 4: 513–543.

Visher, C. A., and J. Roth. 1986. "Participation in Criminal Careers." Appendix A in *Criminal Careers and "Career Criminals."* Vol. 1. Edited by A. Blumstein, J. Cohen, J. Roth, and C. Visher. Washington, DC: National Academy Press.

von Hirsch, A., and D. Gottfredson. 1984. "Selective Incapacitation: Some Queries on Research Design and Equity." *New York University Review of Law and Social Change* 12: 11–51.

Wish, E., and B. Johnson. 1986. "The Impact of Substance Abuse on Criminal Careers."

Pp. 52–88 in *Criminal Careers and "Career Criminals."* Vol. 2. Edited by A. Blumstein, J. Cohen, J. Roth, and C. Visher. Washington, DC: National Academy Press.

Wolfgang, M., R. M. Figlio, and T. Sellin. 1972. *Delinquency in a Birth Cohort.* Chicago: University of Chicago Press.

Wolfgang, M., T. Thornberry, and R. Figlio. 1987. *From Boy to Man, From Delinquency to Crime.* Chicago: University of Chicago Press.

Chapter Outline

- ◆ Capital Punishment in the United States

- ◆ Capital Punishment in the Post-*Gregg* Era

- ◆ Public Opinion Concerning the Death Penalty

- ◆ Debating the Major Issues
  Capital Punishment As a Deterrent to Crime
  Discrimination and Capital Punishment
  The Cost of Life Imprisonment
  Wrongful Executions
  Capital Punishment As a Moral and Symbolic Issue

- ◆ Conclusion

23

Capital Punishment
in America

M. DWAYNE SMITH
University of North Carolina at Charlotte

Capital punishment has been the focus of an exceptionally large volume of literature that is controversial, complex, often confusing, and sometimes simply wrong. Because of the often-shockingly horrible crimes committed by offenders, and because of perceived injustices in the administration of capital punishment, debate surrounding use of the death penalty is understandably emotional. This chapter attempts to go beyond the emotional positions found on both sides of the debate by exploring specific issues through an evaluation of the empirical evidence concerning capital punishment. As an aid to readers, an attempt has been made to provide current references that summarize and interpret aspects of the vast literature concerning the death penalty. We begin with an examination of the history and current status of capital punishment in the United States.

CAPITAL PUNISHMENT
IN THE UNITED STATES

For much of our history, capital punishment has been seen by a majority of Americans as an appropriate and justifiable response to crime. The English settlers of this country imported a criminal justice system wherein death sentences were imposed for a variety of offenses; consequently, executions were regular events in the early colonial settlements (Bedeau, 1982). In prohibiting "cruel and unusual punishment" through the inclusion of the Eighth Amendment in the Bill of Rights, it is unlikely that the framers of the Constitution intended to ban capital punishment, but only to limit the methods by which it might be administered (Inciardi, 1987). As a result, individual states had considerable latitude in structuring their capital punishment statutes. Although murder was the most commonly cited offense, crimes such as rape, kidnapping, treason, robbery, and even train wrecking were punishable by the death penalty in some states (Bedeau, 1982).

Since 1930, when the federal government began collecting data on state-sanctioned executions, over 4,300 executions have been recorded. The 1930s appear to have been the most active period of capital punishment in contemporary U.S. history; 1,520 executions were chronicled during that decade. With 199 executions, 1935 remains the year in which the largest number of death sentences were carried out (Maguire and Pastore, 1997: Table 6.73).

Executions decreased following the 1930s, a trend accelerated by the Civil Rights Movement of the late 1950s and early 1960s. During this period, perhaps for the first time in mainstream American politics, serious concerns regarding the constitutionality of the death penalty were raised (White, 1984). Ultimately, this led to an unofficial moratorium on capital punishment beginning in 1968. This moratorium became official four years later when a bitterly divided U.S. Supreme Court ruled, by a 5–4 vote in *Furman* v. *Georgia,* that the existing practice of capital punishment violated the Eighth and Fourteenth Amendments of the Constitution by being applied in an unacceptable manner. However, as will be discussed later in the chapter, the Court did leave open the possibility that the death penalty could be reinstated by states that instituted safeguards against such constitutional violations.

Seizing upon this opportunity, a number of states quickly rewrote their capital punishment statutes. These efforts succeeded in 1976 when the Supreme Court, in *Gregg* v. *Georgia* and two related cases, approved a revamped set of death penalty laws, thus establishing a model for states that wished to utilize the death penalty (this model will be discussed later in this chapter). Because of refinements based on several subsequent Court decisions, states were required to limit the death penalty to cases involving murder and to spell out clearly under what circumstances it could be imposed. However, considerable variation in state laws has been allowed, and the laws differ considerably in the number of circumstances for which capital punishment can be administered, the age at which one becomes legally eligible for execution, the methods used for execution, and whether juries or judges have the final authority for determining a sentence (Acker and Lanier, 1998).

In resuming the practice of capital punishment, the United States has assumed an unusual position among nations of similar social and cultural composition. Although the death penalty is a common feature throughout the world, virtually all Western industrial nations have abandoned its use (Schabas, 1997). In recent years, a formerly avid practitioner, South Africa, has abolished the death penalty; another, Russia, has severely curtailed its use. Those major nations that continue to regularly utilize capital punishment—the People's Republic of China and most countries of the Mideast, especially Iraq and Iran—tend to be culturally and politically dissimilar to the United States. Further, Zimring and Hawkins (1986) point to a general relationship between a nation's utilization of capital punishment and its disregard for human rights. This position was adopted by Amnesty International, the worldwide organization dedicated to the protection of human rights. Primarily because of the United States' use of the death penalty, Amnesty International now lists it as a nation with governmental policies violating human rights (Amnesty International, 1989).

CAPITAL PUNISHMENT IN THE POST-*GREGG* ERA

On January 17, 1977, in a widely publicized event, Gary Mark Gilmore was executed by a firing squad in Utah. Thus the moratorium on capital punishment ended, and what has become known as the "post-*Gregg*" era began (White, 1984).

Opponents of capital punishment feared that Gilmore's execution would lead to a rush of executions unparalleled in the twentieth century. Yet the rush did not occur, and the first few persons to be executed thereafter represented atypical cases (Jolly and Sagarin, 1984; Streib, 1984). In part, this can be attributed to the abnormally large number of reversals of death sentences by federal courts in the years following *Gregg,* many of which were due to ambiguities in state laws that required U.S. Supreme Court interpretation. However, by 1983, a discernible shift in attitude toward capital punishment was evident among a majority of the Court's justices. Deliberations on individual cases became less measured, and a greater tolerance for "imperfection" in states' efforts to execute emerged (White, 1987). Consequently, the pace of executions quickened, and after Gilmore's execution to the end of 1998, nearly 500 persons had been put to death. However, this number pales in comparison to the many people sentenced to death and awaiting execution. At present, this ever-increasing figure has surpassed 3,500, representing the largest death row population in U.S. history. Within this population, 47 percent are white, 42 percent are African American, and 11 percent are from other racial or ethnic backgrounds; 99 percent are male, and about 2 percent were under age 18 at the time of their offense (NAACP Legal Defense and Educational Fund, 1998).

Table 23.1 provides a list of states' death penalty status and methods of execution, as well as the number of persons awaiting execution and already put to death since 1976. Forty jurisdictions (thirty-eight states, the U.S. military, and the U.S. government) have capital punishment statutes, and thirteen (twelve states and the District of Columbia) do not. Those states with the largest death row populations (also those most likely to execute) are concentrated in the southern and western regions of the country. Two states, Texas and California, account for over a quarter of the nation's death row population, and more than half of all executions since 1976 have occurred in Texas, Virginia, and Florida.

The current picture of capital punishment suggested by Table 23.1 resembles the one existing prior to *Furman*. That is, those states previously prohibiting capital punishment continue to do so, whereas those few, mostly southern, states who avidly utilize capital punishment have resumed doing so. The remainder—a substantial group of states, including some with relatively large death row populations—have the death penalty but have carried out few executions.

Although the early years following *Gregg* suggested that the use of capital punishment would be closely monitored by U.S. courts, more recent years have seen continual setbacks for death penalty foes (see Table 23.2 for a selected list of U.S. Supreme Court decisions that have shaped current use of the death penalty, taking note of the more recent ones). The U.S. Supreme Court has increasingly withdrawn from regulating states' use of the death penalty.

Table 23.1   Inmates on Death Row, Number of Executions Since 1976, and Method of Execution, by State*

STATE	DEATH ROW POPULATION	NUMBER OF EXECUTIONS	METHOD OF EXECUTION†
Alabama	167	17	Electrocution
Alaska	No death penalty	—	
Arizona	121	12	Lethal injection or gas chamber
Arkansas	41	17	Lethal injection or electrocution
California	513	5	Lethal injection
Colorado	3	1	Lethal injection
Connecticut	5	0	Electrocution
Delaware	17	8	Lethal injection or hanging
District of Columbia	No death penalty	—	
Florida	387	43	Electrocution
Georgia	123	23	Electrocution
Hawaii	No death penalty	—	
Idaho	22	1	Lethal injection or firing squad
Illinois	161	11	Lethal injection
Indiana	45	6	Lethal injection
Iowa	No death penalty	—	
Kansas	2	0	Lethal injection
Kentucky	38	1	Electrocution
Louisiana	82	24	Lethal injection
Maine	No death penalty	—	
Maryland	17	3	Lethal injection or gas chamber
Massachusetts	No death penalty	—	
Michigan	No death penalty	—	
Minnesota	No death penalty	—	
Mississippi	63	4	Lethal injection or gas chamber
Missouri	87	32	Lethal injection
Montana	6	2	Lethal injection or hanging
Nebraska	11	3	Electrocution
Nevada	89	7	Lethal injection
New Hampshire	0	0	Lethal injection or hanging
New Jersey	15	0	Lethal injection

At the same time, state supreme courts in the most active death penalty states, mindful of political concerns, have widened considerably the legal doctrine of "harmless error"—holding that even constitutional errors in capital trials and sentencing are not serious enough to bar executions in certain situations (Acker and Lanier, 1998; Steiker and Steiker, 1998). Further,

the U.S. Congress has gone beyond *Gregg* to expand the death penalty to cover some sixty federal crimes; several of these, such as espionage, treason, and trafficking in large amounts of drugs, do not involve loss of life (Acker and Lanier, 1998). In perhaps the most sweeping legislation affecting use of the death penalty in the United States, the Antiterrorism and Effective

Table 23.1   *(continued)*

STATE	DEATH ROW POPULATION	NUMBER OF EXECUTIONS	METHOD OF EXECUTION†
New Mexico	4	0	Lethal injection
New York	1	0	Lethal injection
North Carolina	207	10	Lethal injection or gas chamber
North Dakota	No death penalty	—	—
Ohio	189	0	Lethal injection or electrocution
Oklahoma	149	11	Lethal injection
Oregon	24	2	Lethal injection
Pennsylvania	222	2	Lethal injection
Rhode Island	No death penalty	—	—
South Carolina	71	16	Lethal injection
South Dakota	2	0	Lethal injection
Tennessee	100	0	Electrocution
Texas	436	160	Lethal injection
Utah	11	5	Lethal injection or firing squad
Vermont	No death penalty	—	—
Virginia	40	57	Lethal injection or electrocution
Washington	17	3	Lethal injection or hanging
West Virginia	No death penalty	—	—
Wisconsin	No death penalty	—	—
Wyoming	1	1	Lethal injection
U.S. Government	20	0	Lethal injection or method used by state in which the conviction took place
U.S. Military	8	0	Lethal injection
Totals	3,517	487	

SOURCE: NAACP Legal Defense and Educational Fund, Inc. (1998). For the most current information, see the Death Penalty Information Center's Website at http://www.essential.org/dpic.

*Through October 1, 1998

†Method currently in use. In some states, convicted persons have a choice of methods. Also, in some states, persons convicted before a specified date are subject to one method, and those convicted after that date are subject to the current method.

Death Penalty Act, passed in April, 1996, seriously restricts the appeals that persons sentenced to death can file in federal courts and, among other things, imposes severe time limits on those appeals (the term "appeals" here is used to mean all reviews of capital trials, including *habeas corpus* hearings). The result of these recent developments has been to extend considerable discretion to states and the federal government in practicing capital punishment. This represents a marked departure from the ideology, implicit in *Gregg,* that a fair and just means of administering the death penalty was a compelling national concern (for discussions of this shift in attitude, see Acker and Lanier, 1998; Freedman, 1998; Steiker and Steiker, 1998).

Table 23.2   Supreme Court Cases Shaping Current Use of Capital Punishment

CASE	IMPLICATION OF RULING
Furman v. *Georgia* (1972)	Capital punishment ruled to be capricious and arbitrary in application, thereby violating Eighth and Fourteenth Amendments of the U.S. Constitution. All persons on death rows have sentences commuted to life imprisonment. Further executions not allowed until states address issues raised in case.
Gregg v. *Georgia* (1976) *Proffitt* v. *Florida* (1976) *Jurek* v. *Texas* (1976)	Capital punishment is held to be not inherently unconstitutional. Death penalty statutes are approved that define the circumstances under which murder becomes eligible for death penalty; bifurcated trial system is established.
Woodson v. *North Carolina* (1976)	Mandatory death penalty for all first-degree murders is unconstitutional; mitigating factors must be considered in determining sentence.
Roberts v. *Louisiana* (1976)	Mandatory death penalty for killing a law enforcement officer on duty is unconstitutional; penalty phase must have some degree of discretion.
Coker v. *Georgia* (1977)	Death penalty for rape ruled unconstitutional.
Spanzio v. *Florida* (1984)	Upheld right of state to allow presiding judge to override jury's decision in penalty phase of trial.
Ford v. *Wainwright* (1986)	Execution of persons found to be insane is unconstitutional.
Lockhart v. *McCree* (1986)	Upheld right of prosecution to exclude from a jury those who say they could never vote for a death sentence; rejected evidence that this created a conviction-prone jury at the trial phase (see Bersoff, 1987).
Tison v. *Arizona* (1987)	States may execute persons involved in a crime that included first-degree murder, even if they were not the actual murderer (note: some limitations exist as per *Enmund* v. *Florida* [1982]).
McClesky v. *Kemp* (1987)	Rejected arguments that disproportionate imposition of death penalty for cases involving white victims was unconstitutional application of capital punishment; held that social science data were insufficient evidence to demonstrate unconstitutional patterns of discrimination.
Thompson v. *Oklahoma* (1988) *Stanford* v. *Kentucky* (1989) *Wilkins* v. *Missouri* (1989)	Limits the execution of juveniles to those who were at least 16 years old at the time of their offense.
Penry v. *Lynbaugh* (1989)	Execution of persons found to be mildly to moderately mentally retarded is not unconstitutional.
Felkner v. *Turpin* (1996)	Upheld constitutionality of key restrictions placed by the Antiterrorism and Effective Death

NOTE: For detailed descriptions of these and other important U.S. Supreme Court rulings concerning use of the death penalty, see Vila and Morris (1997) and Latzer (1998).

PUBLIC OPINION CONCERNING THE DEATH PENALTY

Following *Furman,* many state legislators sought to reinstate capital punishment because they firmly believed that their constituents supported, and even demanded, such action. Erskine (1970),

in an analysis of three decades of public opinion polls, concluded that a general decrease in support for capital punishment began in 1936 and lasted until 1966, a year in which less than 50 percent of the population favored this sanction. However, an upswing in support began in the late 1960s, escalated following the *Furman* decision, and has continued until it leveled off in recent years. By the late 1990s, opinion polls routinely showed the proportion of respondents who support use of the death penalty to be above 70 percent (Maguire and Pastore, 1997: Tables 2.65, 2.66). Although some gender and racial differences remain, support extends across virtually all sociodemographic categories of the U.S. public (Smith and Wright, 1992). Only the execution of the mentally retarded seems to lack the general approval of the American public (Ellsworth and Gross, 1997).

Much of the research concerning public opinion has been directed toward *why* support (or nonsupport) for capital punishment exists, a question that has proven to be much more complex than might be assumed. In two extensive reviews, Ellsworth and Ross (1983) and Ellsworth and Gross (1997) conclude that support for or opposition to capital punishment is not strongly correlated with any set of reasoned beliefs. Instead, these opinions are heavily grounded in emotion. Bohm (1998a) affirms this position by noting that most respondents are ill-informed about the death penalty and frequently express contradictory positions; however, having relevant information presented to them seems to have little lasting impact on their stated beliefs.

Complicating the public opinion issue is the finding that support for the *principle* of capital punishment does not necessarily translate into support for the actual administration of death sentences. Several researchers (Williams et al., 1988; Smith, 1987) have conducted studies where a majority of their respondents supported capital punishment but, when probed further, expressed disagreement with a number of actual cases in which the death penalty was assessed. Conversely, several respondents who opposed the death penalty reversed themselves when presented with details of some cases in which individuals escaped the sentence. As well,

other studies have shown that support for capital punishment drops considerably when respondents are presented with the alternative of a life without parole sentence, especially if that sentence is coupled with some type of restitution to the victims' families. However, respondents have also shown skepticism that convicted persons would actually serve true life sentences and tend to underestimate substantially the prison time actually served by persons convicted of murder (Bohm, 1998).

In sum, a substantial majority of the American public currently supports capital punishment, but they do so with little understanding of the complexities or legal issues involved. Ellsworth and Gross (1997: 107) summarize the situation thusly: "Most people care a great deal about the death penalty but know little about it, and have no particular desire to know." This apparent contradiction has led researchers such as Bohm (1998a) to question the advisability of allowing public opinion to serve as a basis for public policy on this issue. Nevertheless, there is little question that a perception of strong public support currently influences much of the public policy that shapes this country's use of the death penalty. In this environment, it is difficult for those in political offices to question, much less oppose, use of the death penalty (Bright, 1998; Bedeau, 1997).

DEBATING THE MAJOR ISSUES

The debate over capital punishment in the United States dates well back into its history (Carrington, 1978). However, this exchange was largely academic until the 1960s, when serious legal challenges were mounted against the practice of capital punishment. It was not until this time that a substantial body of social science research, much of it controversial in itself, emerged to supplement the debate. Although any list of the issues framing this debate may omit concerns that some believe to be important, at least four areas addressed by recent research—and at least one crucial area beyond empirical investigation—merit discussion.

Capital Punishment As a Deterrent to Crime

Perhaps the most hotly contested issue involving capital punishment is whether it serves to restrain people from committing murder, thereby sparing the lives of countless potential victims. Many people strongly believe this to be the case, adopting the classical view that individuals rationally weigh the consequences of their actions before engaging in crime. Conceding that this model may not be appropriate for "crimes of passion" (murders resulting from heated disputes with loved ones or acquaintances), proponents contend that capital punishment now is reserved only for the most heinous of homicides, especially those committed in the course of another felony such as rape or robbery. Quite rightly, they point out that murders under these conditions are frequently committed cold-bloodedly and, often, with a viciousness that defies explanation. They argue that executing those who engage in such violations may cause other potential offenders to "think twice" about engaging in such behavior.

Although this reasoning may appear logical, does the empirical evidence support this argument? Some notable studies have purported to show a pronounced deterrent effect (see especially Ehrlich, 1975), whereas a number of others dispute this finding. In perhaps the most comprehensive reviews to date of the deterrence literature, Peterson and Bailey (1998) and Bailey and Peterson (1999) conclude that the overwhelming weight of the evidence suggests that the death penalty cannot be shown to deter criminal homicide. At the same time, they find that current evidence does not convincingly support the idea of a *brutalization effect,* whereby, as some capital punishment opponents have claimed, executions are related to an increase in homicide.

For now, we can state that those imputing a general deterrence effect to capital punishment have insufficient empirical support for their case. In response, death penalty advocates argue that, at the very least, capital punishment ensures that individual offenders will not escape from prison and murder again (van den Haag, 1998). Death penalty opponents acknowledge the possibility of a repeat offense, but also stress its relatively infrequent occurrence (see Marquart and Sorensen, 1997), and are therefore unmoved by this argument as a justification for continuing to assess death sentences.

Assuming for a moment that a deterrent effect, though empirically elusive, somehow does dampen people's propensity for murder, some difficult and potentially discomforting questions remain. For instance, historically, those states (especially southern states) that have been the most avid practitioners of capital punishment have consistently posted the nation's highest homicide rates. In contrast, many of the states without a death penalty are among those with the lowest homicide rates. At first glance, this may suggest simply that some states "need" capital punishment and thus have it. But if not the threat of death, then what controls the populations of states with low homicide rates and no death penalty? And what are the characteristics of some states that cause them to "need" capital punishment as a deterrent, especially those that already have bulging death row populations? On an even larger scale, why does the United States continue to have substantially higher rates of murder than do western European nations that, in mass, have abandoned the practice of capital punishment? (See LaFree, 1999, for a cross-national comparison of murder rates.) Answers to these kinds of questions come no more easily than do those to the daunting ones that have been addressed so far. But, at least posing such questions may take discussions of deterrence and the death penalty in different directions than are now being pursued. On the other hand, such answers would provide information that, as some public opinion research has shown (Ellsworth and Gross, 1997; Bohm, 1998a), does little to change people's minds on the issue.

Discrimination and Capital Punishment

Critics of capital punishment in the United States long have contended that it is practiced in a discriminatory fashion. Specifically, they charge that minorities (especially African Americans) and the poor are at greater risk of receiving a death sentence than are their white, more affluent counterparts. This contention has been the source of an intense and often bitter debate among supporters and opponents of the death penalty. Like other aspects of capital punishment, the evidence suggests a picture more complex than either side seems willing to acknowledge.

Capriciousness and Arbitrariness As discussed previously, at the heart of the *Furman* decision was a strong belief by several justices that capital punishment, as then practiced, violated the Eighth Amendment protection against "cruel and unusual punishment" because it was administered in a manner that was both *capricious* and *arbitrary*. That is, there seemed to be very few features distinguishing those persons

assessed the death penalty from those granted prison terms (the capricious component), giving it what some justices termed a "freakish" or "lottery-like" quality (Bowers, 1984). Further, among the few factors that distinguished those receiving a death sentence, several, most especially race, were "extralegal" ones (the arbitrary component) that, constitutionally, should not be influencing the outcome of cases.

Only two of the justices (Brennan and Marshall) in *Furman* believed that capital punishment, in itself, was cruel and unusual and should be prohibited. The remainder of the majority, though particularly concerned with the discrimination issue, left the door open for a return to capital punishment. Using the *Gregg* decision as a framework, and aided by a number of subsequent Court decisions (see Table 23.2) that defined the parameters of what would be allowed, most states have developed a bifurcated (two-part) trial system for charges of "capital murder"—those homicides that meet specific criteria (have "aggravating circumstances") and thus are subject to the death penalty. In the *trial phase,* guilt or innocence of the defendant is determined by a jury that has been "death qualified"—that is, its members all say they could impose the death penalty (see Hans, 1988, and Sandys, 1998, for discussions of the implications of death qualification). If a guilty verdict is returned, a *penalty phase* begins, in which the jury has the option of assessing a life term in prison or the death penalty. (In some states, the jury has the option of finding the defendant guilty of a lesser charge whereby a death sentence would not be applicable.) During this phase, counsel for the defense can present any mitigating circumstances that might argue against the imposition of the death penalty (Haney, 1998). In rebuttal, prosecuting attorneys can present arguments, including evidence not admissible during the trial phase (such as the defendant's prior convictions and victim-impact statements), to buttress their appeal for the death penalty. In most states, the jury's decision determines the penalty; in a few states, it is considered advisory, and final authority for sentencing rests with the presiding judge. For example, in Florida, one of the leading death penalty states, it is not unusual for judges to override jury decisions that call for prison terms and instead impose death sentences (Radelet, 1989). (See Costanzo [1997] for a more detailed description of procedures involved in capital murder trials.)

The resulting system is complex; as one body of research has shown, it is particularly confusing to many jurors who must make the decision between life or death. This is a key finding of the Capital Jury Project, a program of research begun in 1990 to better understand the dynamics affecting decision making among jurors in capital murder trials. Extensive interviews were conducted with over 900 persons who had served on capital murder juries in eleven states. The research is continuing, but the early results have been illuminating as to why trial outcomes are often less predictable than might be assumed. Essentially, a number of the ex-jurors reported being very confused—and remain so even after the trial—about the guidelines on how to make their decisions. For instance, a number of the respondents still thought that a death penalty was mandatory when, in fact, it was not. As a group, the jurors substantially underestimated the time that a person would have had to serve if sentenced to life imprisonment. And many were frank in saying that they changed their vote to a death sentence, even though they disagreed with the decision, simply to avoid a hung jury. These are but a sample of the results that lead Bowers and Steiner (1998: 345) to conclude that "con-

spicuously absent in the CJP research, so far, is evidence that aggravating and mitigating considerations are a guiding force in jurors' decision-making, at least as the U.S. Supreme Court intended them to be." Absent a firmly rational decision-making process, other factors enter in. We now turn our attention to the influence of one of the most controversial of those factors.

The Influence of Race In the *Gregg* decision that established a model for capital murder trials, a majority of the justices seemingly felt that revisions in the sentencing process could either eliminate or, at least, significantly reduce the influence of arbitrary (discriminatory) factors in the capital punishment process. Once death sentences began to be assessed in accordance with this approved model, researchers sought to measure the extent to which these expectations were being met. In 1990, responding to a request from the U.S. Senate, the U.S. General Accounting Office (GAO) prepared a report that summarized the findings of 28 of these studies. The GAO report concluded that the studies found a rather uniform pattern of discrimination based on the *race of the victim,* despite differences in methodologies, time frames, and a number of different states covered. Although the strength of the effect varied across states, offenders who killed whites were more likely to be assessed the death penalty than those killing African Americans, even when a host of circumstances that might properly account for this relationship were controlled. Since release of the GAO report, several studies conducted in more states have reported a similar race-of-victim effect (Shepard, 1998; Bienen, 1996; Kiel and Vito, 1992; Baldus, 1990).

In contrast, the GAO report found evidence for discrimination by *race of offender,* a focus of the *Furman* decision, to be quite mixed, suggesting that it is not a significant factor in most states. Notably, the results indicate that the disproportionate representation of African Americans on death rows, in and of itself, cannot be taken as evidence of discrimination. Again noting some variation among states, the studies found that African Americans are sentenced in reasonable proportion to their participation in capital murder cases. However, to reiterate, it is the killing of whites under "aggravating" circumstances that puts offenders at risk of receiving a death penalty, regardless of their race.

Why does race, albeit by race of victim, continue to play a part in death penalty decisions? Some writers suggest that the criminal justice system is still very much dominated by whites—from prosecutors to judges to juries—who tend to show greater concern over the murder of other whites, regardless of who kills them (Gross and Mauro, 1984; Baldus and Woodworth, 1998). It is noteworthy that the race-of-victim effect is due in part to the relative infrequency of death sentences for African Americans who kill other African Americans, although that category of murder tends to be rather large (Lempert, 1983). This has led to charges that the lives of African-American victims simply have less value in the crimi-nal justice system than do those of whites. Lending support to this view are several studies (Paternoster and Kazyaka, 1988; Nakell and Hardy, 1987; Radelet and Pierce, 1985; Paternoster, 1983, 1984) that find the race-of-victim effect to emanate mostly from prosecutors' discretion in seeking the death penalty. Quite simply, seeking the death penalty for the killers of whites appears to have more political value for prosecutors. Because many prosecutors hold elected positions, successful death penalty cases, especially those involving white victims,

represent political as well as legal victories in many jurisdictions. Therefore, other things being equal, prosecutors are more likely to seek the death penalty in cases involving white victims. Further, as Mello (1984) suggests, the more "aggravating circumstances" provided prosecutors by a state's death penalty laws, the more capriciousness and arbitrariness may creep into their decisions. In particular, a number of states prescribe death sentences for murders that are "unusually cruel or heinous." Such a designation is sufficiently ambiguous to allow considerable latitude in pressing for capital murder charges.

As studies emerged indicating that the race-related concerns raised in *Furman* may not have been addressed sufficiently, new challenges to death penalty practices developed. This culminated in 1987 with *McClesky* v. *Kemp,* in which the Supreme Court heard arguments that Georgia, despite reforms in its capital punishment statutes, continued to display patterns of arbitrariness. A central focus of the case was a complex, sophisticated study by Baldus et al. (1983, 1985, 1990) that demonstrated a pronounced race-of-victim effect in Georgia's death sentencing patterns. *McClesky* was particularly important because, given the Court's increasing reluctance to curtail states' use of the death penalty, the case represented the last major systemic attack that opponents could mount against the nation's capital punishment practices. By a 5–4 vote, the Court rejected *McClesky's* racial argument, reaffirming the practice of capital punishment. In so doing, the majority opinion, although noting the Baldus team's effort and even acknowledging the probable validity of its findings, seemed to view as inadequate studies utilizing such aggregate statistics to demonstrate effects on individual cases. Consequently, an entire body of social scientific literature used to reveal patterns of discrimination was all but dismissed from further consideration. (See Dorin, 1994; Bynam, 1988; Ellsworth, 1988; and Acker, 1987, for discussions of controversies associated with this case as well as its implications for the future use of social scientific evidence.)

Some later studies (for example, Heilbrun et al., 1989, and Barnett, 1985) have critiqued the Baldus et al. findings used in *McClesky* by suggesting that the race-of-victim effect could be accounted for through a more careful consideration of the total circumstances, especially the heinousness of the crime, surrounding each murder case used in the analysis. Baldus (1990) and Kiel and Vito (1989, 1992) dispute this contention. However, it has been acknowledged that the race-of-victim effect is most pronounced in cases displaying "mid-range" numbers of aggravating circumstances; it is less likely to be a factor in cases involving high levels of aggravation (Baldus and Woodworth, 1998).

Results from the GAO report and related literature have been brought to the attention of the U.S. Congress. Two pieces of proposed legislation, the Racial Justice Act and the Fairness in Death Sentencing Act, attempted to restore the ability of defendants to use statistical evidence to support claims of racial discrimination in states' death sentencing practices, though the evidence would have to meet the standard of controlling for aggravating circumstances. Both proposals encountered strong opposition from state attorneys general, especially those in southern states. The Fairness in Death Sentencing Act managed to gain approval by the U.S. House of Representatives in 1990 and 1994 but was defeated both times in the U.S. Senate. It has not been proposed since, leaving the *McCleskey* ruling the current law of the land regarding racial discrimination and the death penalty (Baldus and Woodworth, 1998).

Social Class Although the majority of research concerning discrimination in death sentences focuses on race, an even more influential, though less easily studied, source of discrimination may be operative: the social class of the defendant. A number of observers have noted that a substantial majority of those sentenced to death are financially poor at the time of their arrest. Consequently, as they move through the criminal justice system, they have limited resources with which to mount an adequate defense. Unable to hire attorneys, indigent defendants are assigned either a public defender (employed by the state) or a court-appointed attorney drawn from a pool of private attorneys who agree or are assigned to work for limited compensation from the state. Though many indigent defendants receive admirable representation (public defenders in large metropolitan jurisdictions, for instance, may be quite skilled), cases abound of capital murder defendants represented by overworked, inexperienced, and sometimes simply incompetent counsel, many of whom are unfamiliar with the unique and complex nature of capital murder trials (Mello and Perkins, 1998; Bright, 1997). The Supreme Court has expressed sympathy but has issued several rulings (especially *Strickland* v. *Washington,* 1984, and *Burger* v. *Kemp,* 1987) that make it extremely difficult to overturn a case on the basis of inadequate representation, even if defendants had no choice in the lawyer assigned to them.

A further impact of social class lies in the appellate process. If convicted, defendants are automatically entitled to a set of appeals; however, there is no obligation to provide an attorney for these appeals beyond the state level. If appeals for indigent offenders are carried forward to the federal level, it is usually by volunteer attorneys who are willing to take a case as a matter of conscience or as a public service (Dayan, 1986). Such appeals can become time-consuming and costly for these attorneys, leaving the pool of willing attorneys in short supply. In the South, especially, such service is sorely needed but frequently is discouraged by public opinion and even fellow attorneys (Wallace, 1987; Stout, 1988). For a time, a number of death penalty litigation centers were funded to aid in the appeals of indigent defendants who had received a death sentence. However, public criticism of the appeals process has spurred decreased funding of these centers, making adequate representation even less available at a time when the period during which federal appeals must be filed has been seriously curtailed (Bright, 1998).

By way of an overview of the effects of social class, it can be said that having money is no guarantee that one will escape the death penalty. However, both empirical and anecdotal evidence suggests that *not* having financial resources leaves one in an especially vulnerable and precarious position when faced with a charge of capital murder.

Capital Punishment and Discrimination: The Current Situation Does discrimination still exist in the practice of capital punishment in this country? On the basis of available evidence, the answer is a qualified yes. Race remains a factor, though apparently not so grievously as in the pre-*Furman* years. And, though its impact remains difficult to assess apart from other factors, being economically disadvantaged appears to increase the likelihood that defendants will

be assessed a death sentence. Addressing these aspects of capital punishment, the American Bar Association recently voted to call for a national moratorium on carrying out the death penalty until these issues are addressed by appropriate legislation (Carelli, 1997). So far, that call has been roundly rejected.

Is it reasonable to think that discrimination in assessing death penalties can be reduced further through judicial measures? The answer here is possibly. By holding to a minimum their aggravating circumstances, states can reduce potential sources of arbitrariness. To the extent that states conduct regular studies of capital murder sentences to identify problematic patterns of arbitrariness and send observers to jurisdictions disproportionately contributing to any objectionable patterns, judges and prosecutors would likely be more conscious of suspicious patterns in their death penalty decisions (this mirrors the essence of the Fairness in Death Sentencing Act). And by creating pools of specially prepared private attorneys or public defenders to handle capital murder trials involving indigent defendants, assurances of adequate representation would be more likely (Steiker and Steiker, 1998). Importantly, state supreme courts could do much to monitor the arbitrariness of sentences in their states. Yet, state appeals courts have become increasingly reluctant to do so. There is little doubt that the fear of political consequence for close scrutiny of death sentences, especially among justices who are elected, plays a role in this shift (Bright, 1998; Bright and Keenan, 1995).

At present, the most fundamental question is whether states are under any legal or social pressure to be particularly concerned about discrimination in their systems of capital punishment, except perhaps in its most overt forms.

Realistically, given recent state and federal court decisions as well as the weight of public opinion, the answer is no (Bright, 1998).

The Cost of Life Imprisonment

The cost of maintaining convicted murderers for the duration of their lives frequently is cited as a factor in support of capital punishment. Advocates of the death penalty maintain that, faced with an already overcrowded penal system, the lifetime care of thousands of convicted persons, many of them guilty of heinous murders, is an unnecessary and, in some ways, tauntingly cruel burden on taxpayers. Further, they suggest that the expenditures made on behalf of these individuals could be used more productively.

Traditionally, those opposed to the death penalty have responded that the principles involved in the issue do not lend themselves to financial considerations. More recently, however, studies have emerged that challenge the assumption that capital punishment is necessarily a fiscally conservative crime measure. The thrust of this literature is that a criminal justice system that employs capital punishment is significantly more expensive than one restricting its maximum sentence to life imprisonment (Bohm, 1998b). In short, the capital punishment process simply costs more than life imprisonment.

Given the expense of housing prisoners, such a claim flies in the face of conventional wisdom. Yet, as several writers have made clear, the imposition of capital punishment requires a legal system whose safeguards far exceed those of conventional trials (Bedeau, 1987). Capital murder cases involve a disproportionate number of legal maneuvers, from pretrial motions to appeals on behalf of the defendant. Such extraordinary efforts are rare in noncapital cases,

especially because many of the appeals in capital cases emanate from the penalty phase of the trial (Garey, 1985). Estimates vary concerning actual cost of appeals, but a conservative figure places the cost at two to three times greater for capital than for non-capital cases (Gradess, 1988).

When confronted with such statistics, supporters of the death penalty point to the seemingly endless number of appeals available to death row inmates and suggest that a reduction in these would reduce considerably the cost associated with executing persons (van den Haag, 1998). This sentiment was among the forces driving passage of the Antiterrorism and Effective Death Penalty Act. Although some cost reduction might be realized, the significance of the reduction is debatable. As Garey (1985) has shown, appeals are only a part of the overall cost of capital punishment, one that varies considerably across defendants. As mentioned previously, the bulk of the appeals process is handled by *volunteer* attorneys or is funded by organizations aiding indigent defendants (such as the American Civil Liberties Union, NAACP Legal Defense Fund, or Southern Poverty Law Center), thereby effectively subsidizing states' expenditures. One seemingly fair response to reducing available appeals would be to ensure adequate representation, a policy that would require additional funding (Greenhouse, 1989). Because appeals have been limited but there has been no corresponding move to improve legal representation, future research will have to determine if a lowered cost of assessing death sentences has resulted.

The available research indicates that the only realistic method of equalizing the cost of capital punishment versus life sentences would be to mandate substantially less-aggressive defenses for those accused of capital murder. In essence, this approach calls for minimizing constitutional safeguards designed to ensure a fair trial and careful review of a verdict. As the next section reveals, such outcomes can lead to serious problems.

Wrongful Executions

Opponents of the death penalty have long warned that a person may be executed for a crime he or she did not commit. Thus, in an ironic twist, the state would wrongfully kill someone, an offense for which there are no specified sanctions. Supporters of capital punishment acknowledge such a possibility but, using a strategy employed by the opposition regarding additional murders by escaped "lifers," stress the improbability of this occurrence. Though begrudging the appeals process available to convicted persons, supporters see this as a safeguard that makes the "innocent man theory" a contrived argument. In the past, it was frequently pointed out that there are virtually no verified cases in which such a miscarriage of justice actually happened (Carrington, 1978).

Responding to that challenge, Bedeau and Radelet (1987), using narrowly defined criteria for "innocence," were able to assemble 350 cases in which defendants were wrongfully convicted and for which the death penalty was assessed. Of these persons, 139 actually were sentenced to die; 23 ultimately were executed. An additional 22 persons came within seventy-two hours of being executed; 2, in fact, were already strapped in the electric chair before news of their vindication stopped their executions.

Bedeau and Radelet stressed that their figures should be considered very conservative estimates because of their stringent criteria for inclusion of cases and because it becomes extremely difficult to prove innocence after an individual has been executed. Further, they found that the "system"—that is, the appeals process—was rarely the source of correction of the judicial error. At best, the appeals process, frequently criticized as too extensive by death penalty supporters, bought time for information to surface that exonerated the wrongfully convicted person.

In a later, expanded version of this work, Radelet et al. (1992) reported a number of additional cases of wrongful convictions (though not executions), including a number during the post-*Gregg* era. Since this later work, a number of accounts have appeared in the news media of other death row inmates released following evidence of their wrongful conviction. Consequently, it would be erroneous to assume that the possibility of wrongful executions has been eliminated under contemporary death sentencing laws. (A recent article by Radelet and Bedeau [1998] describes the harsh criticism that they have encountered from federal and state officials, as well as the public, because of their work in this area.)

Responding to these findings, van den Haag (1998), reflecting the views of many supporters of capital punishment, asserts that these cases simply represent an unfortunate price that must be paid in order to enjoy the advantages that capital punishment offers a society. In short, a few wrongful executions are seen as regrettable but worth it. This position brings us to perhaps the crucial issue in the capital punishment debate, the morality of government-sanctioned killing.

Capital Punishment As a Moral and Symbolic Issue

Although empirical evidence, however controversial, can be brought to bear on the assertions of either side of the capital punishment debate, it is, as discussed earlier, rarely the basis for people's intense feelings on the issue. Instead, positions more often reflect deeply held convictions regarding the morality of taking the lives of other people, except in the extreme conditions of self-defense and war (Ellsworth and Gross, 1997). Ironically, major religious organizations profoundly disagree on this issue (Costanzo, 1997), a disagreement that has resulted in conflicting testimony from religious figures in any number of capital murder trials.

Ultimately, the moral debate about capital punishment centers on the appropriate role of retribution—or, as some would argue, vengeance—in a modern criminal justice system (Reiman, 1988; Dolinko, 1986). There was considerable discussion in both *Furman* and *Gregg* about whether "evolving standards of decency" in the United States continue to stress the retributive aspect of capital punishment. In justifying a return to capital punishment, the majority opinion in *Gregg* noted the popularity of capital punishment in opinion polls as well as the continued willingness of legislatures and juries to impose death sentences. Thus, they concluded that retribution was among the appropriate functions that capital punishment could serve, one falling well within the boundaries of current "standards of decency" in the United States.

Supporters of the death penalty heartily agree with this sentiment and argue that the death penalty is crucially symbolic in expressing, in the strongest terms possible, the collective moral outrage over the vicious, unlawful taking of human life (van den Haag, 1997, 1998; Berns, 1979). In their view, anything less than responding with the most extreme penalty available suggests a tolerance for those activities, a threat to the fundamental trust that binds members of a society. From this perspective, it is

virtually *immoral* to oppose such a sanction, especially in deference to concerns for offenders over those for victims.

Opponents of capital punishment agree that it is symbolic of society's outrage but maintain that its abolition would also be symbolic. The abolition of capital punishment, they argue, would represent society's affirmation of the sanctity of human life, a sanctity that even the state should not violate. Ideally, in their opinion, as a society progresses in its moral as well as cultural development, it abandons the hypocritical practice of engaging in precisely those activities it seeks to condemn (Gorecki, 1983). Life imprisonment, opponents claim, inflicting as it does a kind of "civil" death, represents an adequate, appropriate, and symbolic response to those who take the lives of others (Bedeau, 1987; van den Haag and Conrad, 1983).

In discussing patterns of abolition in European countries, Zimring and Hawkins (1986) report that the United States showed similar patterns, especially in the public's outcry for the death penalty's return once it was halted. What distinguishes the United States, they argue, was the lack of highly placed "moral leadership" that stood firm against its return. In other countries, resistance by key politicians and judicial figures to the immediate demands for the restoration of capital punishment ultimately led to a shift in public opinion to an abolitionist position. In contrast, no such leadership emerged in the United States after *Furman*. Ideally, the U.S. Supreme Court, insulated from the political pressures of election, would have served this function. Instead, the Court was bitterly divided in *Furman,* leaving open the possibility of a return to capital punishment. Ultimately, according to Zimring and Hawkins, the Court abandoned an opportunity for moral leadership in

Gregg, bowing, as they see it, to the politics of public opinion.

What Zimring and Hawkins do not discuss is the wildly popular notion of revenge as an artifact of American culture. Indeed, the U.S. popular media are dominated by scenarios where violent retaliation is the only logical means of addressing wrongdoing. In this popular culture arena, appeals to a higher morality or religious sentiment regarding forgiveness are in short supply and are actually subject to ridicule as signs of weakness. For this reason, the death penalty has an appeal that blends in nicely with the American view of justice, especially in an era marked by high levels of fear of crime (Walker, 1998). This context perhaps helps us understand, however minimally, why persons holding vigils that protest the death penalty are frequently ridiculed, harassed, and, in perhaps the ultimate irony, threatened with violence by crowds that gather to cheer the execution (for example, see Blaustein, 1997).

For all practical purposes, the moral debate regarding capital punishment is unresolvable, with both sides holding passionately to their beliefs. At present, the views of capital punishment supporters dominate, both politically and in terms of public sentiment. Barring unforeseen events that would dramatically alter public opinion, this situation is not likely to change in the near future.

CONCLUSION

Given recent developments, it is safe to say that the death penalty will be a part of the American criminal justice system for some time to come. Capital punishment currently enjoys strong political support that extends across political party lines. Although the composition of the U.S. Supreme Court is substantially different from that deciding *Gregg* or *McCleskey,* a decided shift in that body's rulings on capital punishment is unlikely to occur in the near future. Most federal courts are now heavily staffed by judges whose records before appointment were decidedly pro-death penalty. In states with elected supreme court justices, engaging in careful scrutiny of capital punishment cases may well invite defeat in the next election. A notable result of this strong support and its impact on the court system is a retreat from the view that death penalty cases require stringent due process. Consequently, as discussed in several sections of this chapter, those accused or convicted of capital murder now have a considerably reduced set of judicial safeguards compared with the early years immediately following *Gregg* (Denno, 1992).

Faced with these prospects, abolitionists probably will be forced to shift their reform efforts from the courts to the legislatures of death penalty states. However, given current public sentiment, success at this level, particularly in the most active states, is unlikely. Despite the dogged persistence of the anti-death penalty movement over the past three decades (Haines, 1996), it will be interesting to see if its efforts can be sustained in the face of continued setbacks at all levels of concern.

However, the relative success of capital punishment supporters in recent years may have created some unique problems. A pending crisis ironically stems from the fact that, since *Gregg,* executions have been outpaced greatly by admissions to death rows around the country. Simultaneously, the judicial appeals of death row inmates are being denied in a more rapid fashion than previously (Levinson, 1993). This has created an unprecedented death row population awaiting execution, though over half of that population is located in five states (see Table 23.1).

Harries and Cheatwood (1997) suggest several possible remedies to restore some type of stability to these states' penal systems. The most obvious solution is to accelerate the rate of executions substantially. However, this will require an increased rate of execution not seen in this country in the twentieth century. Harries and Cheatwood project the need for at least one execution six days a week for a period of approximately six to seven years; thereafter, the number of executions should approximate the death sentences assessed per year (currently about 300). As simple as this sounds, such a rate would be unheard of in the current Western world; in fact, for the past 15 years, an average of only three countries *in the world* have executed more than 100 persons in a given year (Schabas, 1997). If the United States embarks on an execution rate of this nature, its international standing could suffer considerable damage. Even advocates of capital punishment are reluctant to rapidly escalate the number of executions to the required level, fearing a backlash that might revive abolitionist sentiments, especially should some well-publicized "innocent man" executions occur (Haines, 1992).

Other possibilities mentioned by Harries and Cheatwood are for states to begin to restrict the circumstances under which the death penalty will be sought, saving it perhaps for extreme cases like serial or mass murderers. The political consequence of doing so could perhaps be softened by introducing strict life-without-parole sentencing options. Presumably, though, juries would be even more willing to impose this sentence than they would a death sentence. Realistically, some prisons could see their fragile social balance altered considerably by the introduction of large numbers of life-without-parole inmates into their populations. Another option is simply to conduct "business as usual," coping with the numbers by expanding death row facilities (usually at considerable cost) or by finding ways to increase the rate of releases.

It should be obvious that all of these strategies have practical and political drawbacks. Thus, coping with increasing death row populations will sorely test policymakers and may well affect the feasibility of capital punishment as a pragmatic sanction for coping with the crime of murder.

For now, it is extraordinarily difficult to predict the future of capital punishment. It remains to be seen whether evidence of the kind discussed in this chapter, rather than the rhetoric that so dominates this topic, will be used to guide public policy regarding the place of capital punishment in the American system of criminal justice. Be it short term or longer into the future, the debate is, assuredly, far from over.

DISCUSSION QUESTIONS

1. To what extent does the United States reflect the average situation of developed nations in its use of the death penalty?

2. Discuss capital punishment's history in this country. To what extent has public opinion about capital punishment changed in recent years? What accounts for such changes?

3. Many supporters of the death penalty argue that it deters crime. What does the research evidence have to say concerning this position?

4. Have we succeeded in eliminating discrimination from the application of the death sentence in this country? Discuss the ways in which the death penalty may still be assigned unfairly.

5. What have the courts ruled regarding current evidence of discrimination in capital punishment?

6. Both sides of the capital punishment debate see great symbolism in the use of such punishment. Discuss the symbolic effects of the death penalty. Why do Americans not perceive the same symbolism in the assignment of a life sentence in place of death?

REFERENCES

Acker, J., and C. Lanier. 1998. "Beyond Human Dignity? The Rise and Fall of Death Penalty Legislation." Pp. 77–115 in *America's Experiment with Capital Punishment*. Edited by J. Acker, R. Bohm, and C. Lanier. Durham, NC: Carolina Academic Press.

Acker, J. R. 1987. "Capital Punishment by the Numbers—An Analysis of *McClesky* v. *Kemp*." *Criminal Law Bulletin* 23: 454–482.

Amnesty International. 1989. *When the State Kills: The Death Penalty vs. Human Rights*. London: Amnesty International.

Bailey, W., and R. Peterson. 1999. "Capital Punishment, Homicide, and Deterrence: An Assessment of the Evidence and Extension to Female Offenders." In *Homicide: A Sourcebook of Social Research*. Edited by M. D. Smith and M. Zahn. Thousand Oaks, CA: Sage.

Baldus, D. C. 1990. *Equal Justice and the Death Penalty: A Legal and Empirical Analysis*. Boston: Northeastern University Press.

Baldus, D., and G. Woodworth. 1998. "Race Discrimination and the Death Penalty." Pp. 385–415 in *America's Experiment with Capital Punishment*. Edited by J. Acker, R. Bohm, and C. Lanier. Durham, NC: Carolina Academic Press.

Barnett, A. 1985. "Some Distribution Patterns for the Georgia Death Sentence." *U.C. Davis Law Review* 18: 1327–1374.

Bedeau, H. 1982. "Background and Development." In *The Death Penalty in America*. 3d ed. Edited by H. A. Bedeau. New York: Oxford University Press.

———. 1987. *Death Is Different: Studies in the Morality, Law, and Politics of Capital Punishment*. Boston: Northeastern University Press.

———. 1997. "Background and Developments." Pp. 3–32 in *The Death Penalty in America: Current Controversies*. Edited by H. Bedeau. New York: Oxford University Press.

Bedeau, H. A., and M. L. Radelet. 1987. "Miscarriages of Justice in Potentially Capital Cases." *Stanford Law Review* 40: 21–179.

Berns, W. 1979. *For Capital Punishment: Crime and the Morality of the Death Penalty*. New York: Basic Books.

Bienen, L. 1996. "The Proportionality Review of Capital Cases by State High Courts After *Gregg*: Only 'The Appearance of Justice.'" *Journal of Criminal Law and Criminology* 87: 130–314.

Blaustein, S. 1997. "Witness to Another Execution." Pp. 387–400 in *The Death Penalty in America: Current Controversies*. Edited by H. Bedeau. New York: Oxford University Press.

Bohm, R. 1998a. "American Death Penalty Opinion: Past, Present, and Future." Pp. 25–46 in *America's Experiment with Capital Punishment*. Edited by J. Acker, R. Bohm, and C. Lanier. Durham, NC: Carolina Academic Press.

————. 1998b. "The Economic Costs of Capital Punishment: Past, Present, and Future." In *America's Experiment with Capital Punishment*. Edited by J. Acker, R. Bohm, and C. Lanier. Durham, NC: Carolina Academic Press.

Bowers, W. 1984. *Legal Homicide: Death as Punishment in America, 1864–1982*. Boston: Northeastern University Press.

Bowers, W., and B. Steiner. 1998. "Choosing Life or Death: Sentencing Dynamics in Capital Cases. Pp. 309–349 in *America's Experiment with Capital Punishment*. Edited by J. Acker, R. Bohm, and C. Lanier. Durham, NC: Carolina Academic Press.

Bright. S. 1997. "Counsel for the Poor: The Death Sentence Is Not for the Worst Crime but for the Worst Lawyer." Pp. 275–318 in *The Death Penalty in America: Current Controversies*. Edited by H. Bedeau. New York: Oxford University Press.

————. 1998. "The Politics of Capital Punishment: The Sacrifice of Fairness for Executions." Pp. 117–135 in *America's Experiment with Capital Punishment*. Edited by J. Acker, R. Bohm, and C. Lanier. Durham, NC: Carolina Academic Press.

Bright, S., and P. Keenan. 1995. "Judges and the Politics of Death: Deciding Between the Bill of Rights and the Next Election in Capital Cases." *Boston University Law Review* 75: 759–835.

Bynam, A. E. 1988. "Eighth and Fourteenth Amendments—The Death Penalty Survives." *Journal of Criminal Law and Criminology* 78: 1080–1118.

Carelli, R. 1997. "Lawyer Group Seeks to Halt Executions." *Charlotte Observer* (February 4), 4A.

Carrington, F. 1978. *Neither Cruel Nor Unusual*. New Rochelle, NY: Arlington Press.

Costanzo, M. 1997. *Just Revenge: Costs and Consequences of the Death Penalty*. New York: St. Martin's Press.

Dayan, M. 1986. "Payment of Costs in Death Penalty Cases." *Criminal Law Bulletin* 22: 18–28.

Denno, D. W. 1992. " 'Death Is Different' and Other Twists of Fate." *Journal of Criminal Law and Criminology* 83: 437–467.

Dolinko, D. 1986. "Supreme Court Review—Forward: How to Criticize the Death Penalty." *Journal of Criminal Law and Criminology* 77: 546–601.

Dorin, D. 1994. "Far Right of the Mainstream: Racism, Rights, and Remedies from the Perspective of Justice Antonin Scalia's *McClesky* Memorandum." *Mercer Law Review* 45: 1035–1088.

Ehrlich, I. 1975. "The Deterrent Effect of Capital Punishment: A Question of Life and Death." *American Economic Review* 65: 397–417.

Ellsworth, P. 1988. "Unpleasant Facts: The Supreme Court's Response to Empirical Research on Capital Punishment." In *Challenging Capital Punishment: Legal and Social Science Approaches*. Edited by K. C. Haas and J. A. Inciardi. Newbury Park, CA: Sage.

Ellsworth, P., and S. Gross. 1997. "Hardening of the Attitudes: Americans' Views on the Death Penalty." Pp. 90–115 in *The Death Penalty in America: Current Controversies*. Edited by H. Bedeau. New York: Oxford University Press.

Ellsworth, P., and L. Ross. 1983. "Public Opinion and Capital Punishment: A Close Examination of the Views of Abolitionists and Retentionists." *Crime and Delinquency* 29: 116–169.

Erskine, H. 1970. "The Polls: Capital Punishment." *Public Opinion Quarterly* 34: 290–307.

Freedman, E. 1998. "Federal Habeas Corpus in Capital Cases." Pp. 417–436 in *America's Experiment with Capital Punishment*. Edited by J. Acker, R. Bohm, and C. Lanier. Durham, NC: Carolina Academic Press.

Garey, M. 1985. "The Cost of Taking a Life: Dollars and Sense of the Death Penalty." *U.C. Davis Law Review* 18: 1221–1273.

Gorecki, J. 1983. *Capital Punishment: Criminal Law and Social Evolution*. New York: Columbia University Press.

Gradess, J. 1988. "Which Is More Expensive? Execution or a Life Sentence?" *Washington Post National Weekly Edition*, May 2–8, 23.

Greenhouse, L. 1989. "Judicial Panel Urges Limit on Death Row Appeals." *New York Times,* September 22, 13.

Gross, S. R. 1985. "Race and Death: The Judicial Evaluation of Discrimination in Capital Sentencing." *U.C. Davis Law Review* 18: 1275–1325.

Gross, S. R., and R. Mauro. 1984. "Patterns of Death: An Analysis of Racial Disparities in Capital Sentencing and Homicide Victimization." *Stanford Law Review* 37: 27–153.

Haines, H. 1992. "Flawed Executions, the Anti-Death Penalty Movement, and the Politics of Capital Punishment." *Social Problems* 39: 125–138.

———. 1996. *Against Capital Punishment: The Anti-Death Penalty Movement in America, 1972–1994.* New York: Oxford University Press.

Haney, C. 1998. "Mitigation and the Study of Lives: On the Roots of Violent Criminality and the Nature of Capital Justice." Pp. 351–384 in *America's Experiment with Capital Punishment.* Edited by J. Acker, R. Bohm, and C. Lanier. Durham, NC: Carolina Academic Press.

Hans, V. P. 1988. "Death by Jury." In *Challenging Capital Punishment: Legal and Social Science Approaches.* Edited by K. C. Haas and J. A. Inciardi. Newbury Park, CA: Sage.

Harries, K., and D. Cheatwood. 1997. *The Geography of Executions.* Lanham, MD: Rowman and Littlefield.

Heilbrun, A. B. Jr., A. Foster, and J. Golden. 1989. "The Death Sentence in Georgia, 1974–84." *Criminal Justice and Behavior* 16: 139–154.

Inciardi, J. A. 1987. *Criminal Justice.* 2d ed. San Diego: Harcourt.

Jolly, R. W., Jr., and E. Sagarin. 1984. "The First Eight Executed after *Furman:* Who Was Executed with the Return of the Death Penalty?" *Crime and Delinquency* 30: 610–623.

Kiel, T. J., and F. G. Vito. 1989. "Race, Homicide Severity, and Application of the Death Penalty: A Consideration of the Barnett Scale." *Criminology* 27: 511–531.

———. 1992. "The Effects of the *Furman* and *Gregg* Decisions on Black-White Execution Ratios in the South." *Journal of Criminal Justice* 20: 217–226.

LaFree, G. 1999. "A Review and Summary of Cross-National Comparative Studies of Homicide." In *Homicide: A Sourcebook of Social Research.* Edited by M. D. Smith and M. Zahn. Thousand Oaks, CA: Sage.

Latzer, B. 1998. *Death Penalty Cases: Leading U.S. Supreme Court Cases on Capital Punishment.* Boston: Butterworth-Heinemann.

Lempert, R. 1983. "Capital Punishment in the 80's: Reflection on the Symposium." *Journal of Criminal Law and Criminology* 74: 1101–1114.

Levinson, A. 1993. "Pace of Executions Quickens Since 1977." *Houston Post,* May 9, A-14.

Maguire, K., and A. Pastore. 1997. *Sourcebook of Criminal Justice Statistics 1996.* Washington, DC: U.S. Government Printing Office.

Marquart, J., and J. Sorensen. 1997. Pp. 162–175 in *The Death Penalty in America:* Current Controversies. Edited by H. A. Bedeau. New York: Oxford University Press.

Mello, M. 1984. "Florida's 'Heinous, Atrocious, or Cruel' Aggravating Circumstance: Narrowing the Class of Death-Eligible Cases Without Making It Smaller." *Stetson Law Review* 13: 523–554.

Mello, M., and Perkins, P. 1998. "Closing the Circle: The Illusion of Lawyers for People Litigating for Their Lives at the *Fin de Siecle.*" Pp. 245–284 in *America's Experiment with Capital Punishment.* Edited by J. Acker, R. Bohm, and C. Lanier. Durham, NC: Carolina Academic Press.

NAACP Legal and Educational Defense Fund. 1998. *Death Row, USA.* Summer. New York: NAACP Legal and Educational Defense Fund.

Nakell, B., and K. A. Hardy. 1987. *The Arbitrariness of the Death Penalty.* Philadelphia: Temple University Press.

Paternoster, R. 1983. "Race of Victim and Location of Crime: The Decision to Seek the Death Penalty in South Carolina." *Journal of Criminal Law and Criminology* 74: 754–785.

———. 1984. "Prosecutorial Discretion in Requesting the Death Penalty: A Case of Victim-Based Racial Discrimination." *Law & Society Review* 18: 437–478.

Paternoster, R., and A. Kazyaka. 1988. "Racial Considerations in Capital Punishment: The Failure of Evenhanded Justice." In *Challenging Capital Punishment: Legal and Social Science Approaches.* Edited by K. C. Haas and J. A. Inciardi. Newbury Park, CA: Sage.

Peterson, R., and W. Bailey. 1998. "Is Capital Punishment an Effective Deterrent for Murder? An Examination of Social Science Research." Pp. 157–182 in *America's Experiment with Capital Punishment.* Edited by J. Acker, R. Bohm, and C. Lanier. Durham, NC: Carolina Academic Press.

Radelet, M. L. 1989. "Introduction and Overview." In *Facing the Death Penalty: Essays on a Cruel and Unusual Punishment.* Edited by M. L. Radelet. Philadelphia: Temple University Press.

Radelet, M., and H. Bedeau. 1998. "The Execution of the Innocent." In *America's Experiment with Capital Punishment.* Edited by J. Acker, R. Bohm, and C. Lanier. Durham, NC: Carolina Academic Press.

Radelet, M., H. Bedeau, and C. Putnam. 1992. *In Spite of Innocence.* Boston: Northeastern University Press.

Radelet, M. L., and G. L. Pierce. 1985. "Race and Prosecutorial Discretion in Homicide Cases." *Law and Society Review* 19: 587–621.

Reiman, J. 1988. "The Justice of the Death Penalty in an Unjust World." In *Challenging Capital Punishment: Legal and Social Science Approaches.* Edited by K. C. Haas and J. A. Inciardi. Newbury Park, CA: Sage.

Sandys, M. 1998. "Stacking the Deck for Guilt and Death: The Failure of Death Qualification to Ensure Impartiality." Pp. 285–307 in *America's Experiment with Capital Punishment.* Edited by J. Acker, R. Bohm, and C. Lanier. Durham, NC: Carolina Academic Press.

Schabas, W. 1997. *The International Sourcebook on Capital Punishment.* Boston: Northeastern University Press.

Shepard, P. 1998. "Study Examines Death Row and Race." *Charlotte Observer,* June 5, 5A.

Smith, M. D. 1987. "General Versus Specific Support for Capital Punishment." *Journal of Crime and Justice* 15: 279–286.

Smith, M. D., and J. D. Wright. 1992. "Capital Punishment and Public Opinion in the Post-*Furman* Era: Trends and Analyses." *Sociological Spectrum* 12: 127–144.

Steiker, C., and J. Steiker. 1998. "Judicial Developments in Capital Punishment Law." Pp. 47–75 in *America's Experiment with Capital Punishment.* Edited by J. Acker, R. Bohm, and C. Lanier. Durham, NC: Carolina Academic Press.

Stout, D. G. 1988. "The Lawyers of Death Row." *New York Times Magazine,* February 14, 46–54.

Streib, V. L. 1984. "Executions Under the Post-*Furman* Capital Punishment Statutes: The Halting Progression from 'Let's Do It' to 'Hey, There Ain't No Point in Pulling So Tight.'" *Rutgers Law Journal* 15: 443–487.

United States General Accounting Office. 1990. *Death Penalty Sentencing: Resource Indicates Pattern of Racial Disparities.* Washington, DC: U.S. General Accounting Office.

van den Haag, E. 1997. "The Death Penalty Once More." Pp. 445–456 in *The Death Penalty in America: Current Controversies.* Edited by H. Bedeau. New York: Oxford University Press.

———. 1998. "Justice, Deterrence, and the Death Penalty." Pp. 139–156 in *America's Experiment with Capital Punishment.* Edited by J. Acker, R. Bohm, and C. Lanier. Durham, NC: Carolina Academic Press.

van den Haag, E., and J. P. Conrad. 1983. *The Death Penalty: A Debate.* New York: Plenum Press.

Vila, B., and C. Morris. 1997. *Capital Punishment in the United States: A Documentary History.* Westport, CT: Greenwood Press.

Walker, D. 1998. *Popular Justice: A History of American Criminal Justice.* 2d ed. New York: Oxford University Press.

Wallace, A. 1987. "Wanted: Attorneys for Death-Row Inmates." *Atlanta Journal-Constitution,* October 11, B1, B10.

White, W. S. 1984. *Life in the Balance: Procedural Safeguards in Capital Cases.* Ann Arbor: University of Michigan Press.

———. 1987. *The Death Penalty in the Eighties.* Ann Arbor: University of Michigan Press.

Williams, F. P., D. R. Longmire, and D. B. Gulick. 1988. "The Public and the Death Penalty: Opinion as an Artifact of Question Type." *Criminal Justice Research Bulletin* 3: 1–5.

Zimring, F. 1992. "Inheriting the Wind: The Supreme Court and Capital Punishment in the 1990s." *Florida State University Law Review* 20: 7–19.

Zimring, F. E., and G. Hawkins. 1986. *Capital Punishment and the American Agenda.* Cambridge: Cambridge University Press.

Name Index

Subject Index